Dictionary of German Military Terms, Abbreviations and Map Symbols

With best wishes on our meeting 14 May 2024

by W. Victor Madeja

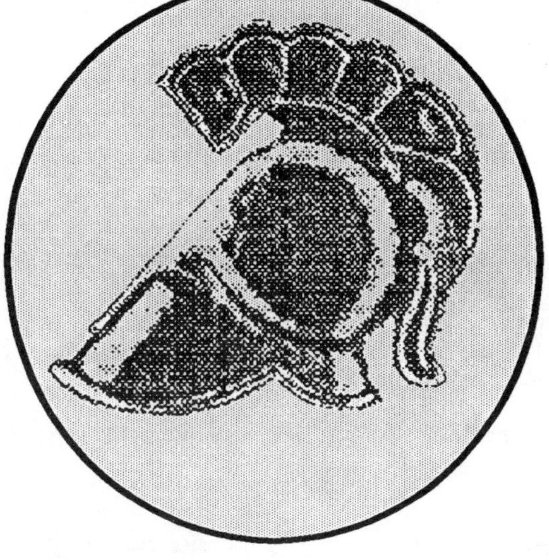

Valor Publishing Company
Allentown, Pennsylvania 18106-0385

This book directly reproduces portions of the *German Military Dictionary* that was published by the U.S. War Department in May 1944 as TM 30-506. Most of the abbreviations and map symbols were compiled from *German Military Abbreviations* (Special series No. 12) and *German Military Symbols,* that were both issued by the U.S. Military Intelligence Service of the War Department in April 1943. Some words and phrases came from the *German Phrase Book* that was issued November 1943 (again 1953) as TM-30-606. For Definitions of many of the English terms used, see TM 20-205, *Dictionary of United States Army Terms*, 18 January 1944 and U.S ranks were often given according to function as listed in TM-E-30-451.

The editor gratefully acknowledges his indebtedness to the original authors of this material.

This edition printed in Valor Textbook Format

1992

Dictionary of German Military Terms, Abbreviations and Map Symbols, Revised

First Edition 1988.

Published in United States by

Valor Publishing Company
P.O. Box 3385
Allentown, Pensylvania

Printed in U.S.A. by
Rhoads Press of Allentown

Library of Congress Cataloging in Publication Data
Madeja, W. Victor, 1948-
1. German language - Dictionaries - English
2. English language - Dictionaries - German
3. Armed Forces - Units
I. Title   Title. 83-81815

ISBN: 0-941052-75-3

Introduction

This Dictionary is directed towards students of military history and to those seeking to understand technical terms and symbols. It lists most of the common military terms and their German abbreviations. Since much of the terminology to be translated is encountered in the form of text, a few of the many differences between German and English are mentioned in the following paragraphs.

To reduce the intimidation often encountered with a new tongue and ease in recognizing similarities while translating. It might be mentioned that German, next to Dutch, is the language closest to English. This underlying similarity in the three languages can be traced to ancient Germanic, Indo-European roots. The British, Anglo-Saxon, nationality was based on primitive Germanic Saxons. The Norman conquest of England added some French twists to the British tongue but the basic structure retains Germanic roots. There is an interesting background on the language in Gordon Craig's *The Germans* in his appendix "The Awful German Language." He traces historical roots from Martin Luther and Goethe to the present. It also provides a good discussion of the militarization of the civilian language during past wars.

☐ Usage in Translation

The common German definite and indefinite **articles** "the" and "a" or "an" cause difficulty for Americans because in German these must agree with the noun in case, gender and number. For example *der*, *die*, or *des*, are all equivalent to "the". The plural form is easier since only *die* is required. This article can also be found as a demonstrative pronoun ("that"). Germans grow up memorizing *der* and *des* with the appropriate nouns. Similarly, the indefinite articles also agree with nouns in gender and case and appear as *ein* and *eine*. Both types of articles can vary in the adjective and accusative cases.

German personal **pronouns**, *er* or *es*, are equivalent to "he" or "it", and *sie* is the proper form of *"you"*. The intimate form of this is *du* and the use of that term therefore connotates an unusual degree of familiarity on the part of the user. Both "I" and "me" can be *ich, mich* or *mir* depending on case.

Most **adjectives** have endings according to case when preceded by "the" and usually end in ***e*** (in the nominative and accusative cases) or ***en*** (adjective case). It is less common to encounter adjectives after *ein* or independently. In these cases the noun modified and implied definite articles governed usage and an *es* ending sometimes occurs.

Prepositions take different cases but the adjective case is most common, which results in *der* and *das* changing to ***dem***, and *die* becomes ***der***. Often these definite articles also combine with prepositions, for example *zu dem* becomes ***zum***. Such combinations do not occur with indefinite articles although the *em* and *er* endings are the same.

German **verbs** are more difficult then in English. Simple forms can have several meanings, translatable into present, progressive, future or present perfect tenses. Verb endings agree in person with the noun or pronoun used, but may be "irregular" in the third person mainly by changing stem vowels. "Have" and "be" verb forms are similarly more difficult than in English. In compound forms, verbs can be separated so that its prefix might be at the end of the sentence or clause. If used with modal verbs ("want, must, can," etc.) then the entire action (wanted, desired, etc.) goes at the end of a clause and then the compound verbs are together. Often the meaning of a long sentence is unclear until the ending verb is understood.

Questions and **commands** are often worded in the same manner. A question mark makes this clear when written but in spoken German the inflection of the speaker determines meaning.

Large German words may cause confusion or concern those unaccustomed to basic terminology. It should be noted that these long words are often made by various **combinations** of smaller ones so that seemingly complicated terms are no more than constructions of the simple forms here provided. The familiarity with basic shorter words, prefixes, and suffixes will make it easier to recognize the longer form when it is encountered. Experience develops with practice. Carefully read a few dozen pages of the German phrases for help in this regard.

☐ Purpose

As can be seen from the above examples, using this dictionary will not be always help in speaking "proper" German, nor is a serious effort made to convey pronunciation. The main purpose of this dictionary is to facilitate a minimum working knowledge; especially when a single phrase, symbol, or abbreviation is the key between frustration and understanding. Such words often help to communicate complex technical ideas and thus facilitate comprehension of unfamiliar concepts.

Understanding is the first step in acquiring knowledge. The effective control of a language requires years of study and this small dictionary can serve as one tool toward that goal. The American user of German will feel less intimidated by the language if he can efficiently use dictionary to begin understanding the written word and symbol.

After the first few thousand errors, a written understanding will develop into ability to speak the language at a working level. Speech is more efficiently developed by studying recordings or listening to native speakers. The Berlitz® *For Travellers* series are excellent for this, especially if a tape player is readily available (on long car trips).

☐ Abbreviations

Perhaps to a greater extent than any other Armed Forces the Germans employed military abbreviations on their maps and charts, on task force tables of organization, on direction and location sign posts in combat zones, on field orders, and in every case where abbreviations may possibly be used. These abbreviations were also often used in connection with military symbols. A thorough knowledge of both abbreviations and symbols is therefore essential for those engaged in an interpretation of German documents. For that reason a second dictionary, of abbreviations, has been included alongside the first.

There is no "easy road to knowledge" in regard to these military abbreviations. Many words were abbreviated in more than one manner, sometimes in the course of a single document. Individual commanders frequently improvised abbreviations. These were often understandable from context to the officer was reading them, but could cause considerable difficulty for non-Germans. Sometimes this was intentional, so that third parties (who might encounter a document) could not be sure of the exact meaning but that was the exception.

A thorough foundation in the German language may be useful, in determining the meaning of a particular abbreviation but this was not infallible. Guessing in this may result in frustration if a key term is

Table of Contents

Authorized Abbreviations Used in Dictionary.

AA Antiaircraft	H-Dr Horse-drawn	PX Post Exchange
AAF Army Air Forces	HE High Explosive	QMC Quartermaster Corps
Adrm Airdrome	Hq Headquarters	R Rifle
Adv Gd Advance Guard	Inf Infantry	Rad Radio
Am Ammunition	Inst Instrument	Rcn Reconnaissance
Ap Airplane	LM Land Mine	Regt Regiment
Ash Airship	Maj Major	RR Railroad
AT Antitank	Math Mathematics	SA Small Arms
Avn Aviation	Mech Mechanics, Mechanical	Sgt Sergeant
AWS Aircraft Warning Service	Mecz Mechanized	Sig Signal
BC Battery Commander	Med Medical	Sig C Signal Corps
Bdg Bridge	Met Meteorological	SL Searchlight
Bln Balloon	MG Machine Gun	SR Sound Ranging
CA Coast Artillery	Mil Military	Surv Surveying
Cal Caliber	Mort Mortar	Tac Tactical, Tactics
Cam Camouflage	MP Military Police	Tech Technical
Clo Clothing	MT Motor Transport	Tg Telegraph
Cml Chemical	Mtcl Motorcycle	Tk Tank
Comd Command	Mtr Motor	Tng Training
Com Z Communications Zone	Mtz Motorized	T of Opns Theater of Operations
CP Command Post	Nav Naval	Top Topographical
FA Field Artillery	Obsn Observation	Trans Transportation
FR Flash Ranging	Ord Ordnance	Tp Telephone
Ft Fortification	Pers Personnel, Person	Trac Tractor
G Gun	Photo Photography	Trk Truck
GHQ General Headquarters	Pon Ponton	Vet Veterinary
H Cav Horse Cavalry	Prcht Parachute	Z of I Zone of the Interior
	Pvt Private	
	PW Prisoner of War	

not checked. For this reason the dictionary of abbreviations may be essential even for German users, unfamiliar with technical terminology.

Because of the extent of the field, it is unlikely that any dictionary of German military abbreviations can be complete. New abbreviations, resulted from developments in military equipment and tactics, or as the temporary shortcuts of an individual commander writing orders. A good working knowledge of the abbreviations commonly used helps in interpreting variants and meaning can frequently be inferred from the context. This list aims at completeness, within the following limits:

- ¤ Military terms borrowed from other languages in use during the First World War and earlier were frequently replaced by German equivalents so a considerable number of such terms were not retained in this list.
- ¤ The dictionary includes many common words and expressions that were found in military documents. In deciding which nonmilitary abbreviations to include, frequency of usage was a criterion.
- ¤ In a few cases German abbreviations were identical with those used in the U. S. Army. Examples are Apr. for April and mm for millimeter. Abbreviations of this type were not included except to avoid confusion (*Dez* for December; mm^2 for square millimeter).
- ¤ This dictionary includes many naval and aviation terms, but it should be noted that Germany was mainly a Continental power and most of its manpower was in its ground components (VALOR Book #5 provides an extensive supplement of both Naval and Air Force terms and symbols.

The following principles of sequence should be kept in mind. Abbreviations are arranged alphabetically, first according to the abbreviation itself, then according to the word or expression abbreviated:

- ¤ Thus *A.* for *Abteilung* precedes *A.* for *Ausbildung*, and both these abbreviations precede *Abt*.
- ¤ The *umlaut* is equivalent to the addition of e after the vowel; consequently *ä* follows *ad* and precedes *af*.
- ¤ The German capital *I* will be found under *I* although in German practice it was often written as the letter *J*.

In terms of convention, the periods are usually not given in the list although German practice varied in this regard. Also German abbreviations frequently can stand for either the singular or plural forms of the word abbreviated. The abbreviation list provides meanings only in the singular form. Despite such absence of consistent procedure in abbreviation, the following tendencies could be observed:

- ¤ A skeleton of the original words maintained to represent the entire term. Often the Germans kept enough of the original word structure to make the abbreviation a recognizable skeleton of the word for which it stood. Examples are *abkdrt.* for *abkommandiert*, *Kfz.* for *Kraftfahrzeug*. In the case of compound words, the Germans also made abbreviations by taking elements or initial letters from each of the component parts.
- ¤ A common tendency was to lop off syllables of words being abbreviated, where the user attempted to leave enough of the distinctive structure of the word to give the reader a clue. The word *Befehlshaber*, for instance, could be abbreviated *Befhb*, *Befh.*, or *B.* A writer's haste or amount of comprehension needed, often determined the degree to which this was carried.
- ¤ Words formed by combining letters of the original term to result in a pronounceable combination of letters, with the abbreviations gaining currency as a known word; examples are: ***Flak*** for *Flakzeugabwehrkanone*, ***Gestapo*** for *Geheime Staatspolizei*, and ***Stuka*** for *Sturzkampfflugzeug*.
- ¤ Since combinations of single abbreviations were common, this dictionary includes some of frequent combinations, but component parts are usually listed separately. For instance, a word like *Divisionaufklrüngsabteilung* will be under *Div.Aufkl.Abt.*, *Aufkl.*, and *Abt.* But for *Eisb.Pi.Rgt.*, it would be necessary to look under *Eisb.* and *Pi.Rgt.* separately.

The German dictionary for abbreviations is provided as a separate section alongside the standard dictionary. The definitions in the Abbreviation Dictionary often do not duplicate those in main list or may augment the definition. Sometimes two abbreviations are listed on one line. This common listing of German terms and abbreviations provides a good way to reduce duplication while also giving benefits of an accessible alphabetical sequence. The list of authorized abbreviations on the left is used in the body of the dictionary for the origin of many scientific and technical terms, especially as they pertain to the Signal Corps and other technical branches. It is based on U.S. World War 2 regulations and contemporary field manuals:

☐ Map and Tactical Symbols

The German Armed Forces used military symbols extensively on maps, in tables of organization (war establishments), and on direction and location signposts in combat zones. Military symbols were also seen on vehicles and equipment, with or without the divisional emblem. As an added bonus to the conventional dictionaries, this volume contains the Basic Army Map Symbols and describes the logic of their composition, including their revisions used after 1943.

This third "dictionary" of military map symbols is mainly oriented to providing an interpretation of the special signs that were unique to German situation maps. Since most of the German Armed Forces consisted of ground units (even most of the Air Force consisted mainly of ground troops in the form of Flak artillery and parachute combat divisions) this last section mainly depict symbols used by the Army, with some exceptions noted for the Air Force. This system consisted of basic and supplementary symbols which were combined to indicate various units and equipment. The system was elaborate in 1940, but with growth of the Armed Forces it was often found too cumbersome for field use. Major amendments were issued and adopted in early 1943. Many charts, maps, and other documents were produced during the war so there was overlap in usage and for that reason it was useful to know both the older and mid-1944 "current" symbols.

Symbols of most headquarters have been provided but symbols for some specific Army units and their organization can be found in VALOR Book #2, *Hitler's Dying Ground*. Depending on their nature, many symbols for installations have been included in this volume, including various communication systems. Although the object was to simplify understanding, the fact that two systems existed shifts emphasis from symbol recognition to organizational philosophy. Because the Navy was never more than 9% of the Armed Forces in size and due to the specialized nature of its operations (by a separate U-Boat fleet) it will be included in a new volume #6 on the German Navy.

It should be noted that the general Army principles shown also applied to the other two branches, which often used similar symbols. Much material on the Air Force (Parachutists, Infantry, Flak) or Navy ground forces (Coast Artillery) has been excluded to avoid duplication and confusion. The symbol information on the Air Force branches, along with pertinent abbreviations, will be found in Valor Book #5, *Hitler's Elite Guard* with some exceptions noted here.

There existence of alternate military symbols for the same subject and was in no way a deviation from a consistent pattern. It was rather a testimony to the logic and flexibility of the overall system. A German soldier who did not know the precise tactical symbol could construct another from well known basic symbols. The result might be fully as comprehensible as the official one. As listed here, symbols are grouped according to logical structure usually coinciding with German methods of unit classification, according to arm (*Waffengattung*);

In the translation of German terms, an attempt is made to approximate equivalent terms in the U.S. Army. In most instances where the apparent equivalents would be misleading or where none existed, then a literal translation might be provided. With the exception of the term Hq, abbreviations are rare in the U.S. translation.

Generally if the symbol pertained to reading a map, rather than understanding structural concepts, it has been included in section IV. In some cases non-English terms for place names have been included for clarity in section V. The Germans often renamed cities or used 19th Century designations for occupied territories. This was especially true in Poland which was dismembered by Austria, Prussia, and Russia after the Napoleonic wars and again in 1939.

Finally it should be noted that not all English translations are alike. A special section on British terminology is included and reflects an organization that was more common on the continent than in the United States. Some of these differences also applied to Canada..

Chapter I: German - English Terms and Abbreviations

A	Abschnitt	sector; section; zone
A	Abschusspunkt	present position (*antiaircraft artillery*)
A	Abteilung	section; detachment; department; battalion
A	Abwehr	defense
A	Alarm	alarm
a	allgemein	general (*adjective*)
A	Alt	prefix *Alt* (old)—in names of towns
a	am	at the; on the
A	Amt	office
a	an	at; on; to
A	Anhänger	trailer; supporter; follower
A	Anhalt	Anhalt (*German province*)
A	Anhang	appendix; supplement
A	Anleitung	instructions; directions
A	Anmerkung	footnote; remark; annotation
A	Ar	are (*measure; 119.6 square yards*)
A	Arbeits-	labor
A	Arbeitszug	work train
A	Armee	army (*formation above ar. corps*)
A	Artillerie	artillery
A	Artillerieführer	artillery commander (*in division*)
A	Artillerieschule	artillery school
A	Arzt	physician
A	Assistenz	assistance; assistant
a	auf	on
A	Aufklärung	reconnaissance
A	Aufschlag	impact
a	auftragsweise	in accordance with instructions
A	Ausbildung	training
A	Ausgabestelle	distributing point
A	Ausschuss	commission; committee
a/A	alter Art	old type
A.A	Aufklärungsabteilung	reconnaissance battalion
A.A	Auswärtiges Amt	Foreign Office
A.Abt	Artillerieabteilung	artillery battalion
A.Abt	Aufklärungsabteilung	reconnaissance battalion
A.A.Div.	Divisionsaufklärungsabteilung	divisional reconnaissance battalion
a.a.O	am angeführten Ort	in the passage quoted
a.a.O	an anderem Ort	in another place
ab	abgegangen	dispatched
A.B	Arbeitsbataillon	labor battalion
A.B	Armeebefehl	Army order
A.B	Artilleriebeobachtung	artillery observation
a.B	auf Befehl	by order of (*used with signa-*
A.B	Ausführungsbestimmungen	executory regulations
Abb	Abbildung	figure; illustration
abbl	abblasen	to break off combat; to finish
abbl	abblenden	to screen; to dim lights
Abdr	Abdruck	copy; impression
abds	abends	in the evening; p.m.
A.Bekl.	Armee-Bekleidungsamt	Army clothing depot
abf	abfahren; Abfahrt	to depart; departure
abf	abfertigen; Abfertigung	to dispatch; act of dispatch
abf	abführen	to lead away
abfr	abfragen	to test the line (*communica*
AbG	Abänderungsgesetz	amending law
Abg	Abgang	departure
abg	abgeändert	amended
abg	abgekürzt	abbreviated
Abg	Abgeordneter	deputy
abg	abgestürzt	crashed (*aircraft*)
abgebl.	abgeblendet	dimmed (*lights*)
abgeg.	abgegangen	dispatched; departed
abgezw.	abgezweigt	detached; branched off
Abg.H.	Abgangshafen	port of embarkation
Abg.St.	Abgangsstation	station of departure
abh	abhängig	dependent
Abk	Abkürzung	abbreviation
abkdrt.	abkommandiert	detached or detailed on special service
Abl	Ablage	depot; dump (*on maps*)
abl	abladen	to unload a pack animal
Abl	Ableitung	leakage; lead; short circuit
ABl	Amtsblatt	official journal or register
Abl.F	Ablieferungsfrist	time limit for delivery
abpr	abprallen	to ricochet
Abpr	Abpraller	ricochet; ricochet burst
abr	abrüsten	demobilize; disarm
Abr	Abrüstung	demobilization; disarmament
Abr.Int.	Abrechnungsintendant	chief accountant
Abr.Int.	Abrechnungsintendantur	chief accountant's office
Abs	Absatz	paragraph
Abs	Abschnitt	sector; section; zone
Abs	Absender	sender
Abs	Absendestelle	dispatching point; office of origin; sending point

A

Abbau *m* dismantling (*a structure, etc.*); mining (*ore*).
abbauen to dismantle (*a structure, etc.*); to mine (*ore*).
abbefördern evacuate (*PW, wounded, etc.*).
Abbildung *f* illustration, figure, diagram.
abbinden to tie, lash (*Tp wire*).
abblasen to release gas (*CWS*).
abblenden dim (*a light*).
"Abblenden!" "Out of action!" (*AA SL*).
Abblendlicht *n* dim light (*on auto headlight*).
abbrechen break off; cease; withdraw.
das Lager abbrechen to break camp.
das Gefecht abbrechen to withdraw from action.
Abbrechen des Gefechts withdrawal from action.
abbremsen to brake.
Abbremsvorrichtung *f* arresting gear (*aircraft carrier*).
abbrücken dismantle (*a bridge*).
Abdachung *f* slope (*Top*).
Abdeckplatte *f* cover plate (*G*).
abdichten to seal, calk, pack.
Abdichtung gegen Kampfgas gas-proofing (*CWS*).
Abdichtungsring *m* sealing ring, washer.
abdienen complete a period of service.
Abdrift *f* drift (*Avn, Nav*).
Abdriftmesser *m* driftmeter (*Ap*). landing area, jump area (*Prcht troops*).
Abdriftvisier *n* driftmeter (*Ap*).
abdrosseln to throttle (*an engine*).
abdrücken to fire, *i.e.* pull (*a trigger*); press (*a button*).
Abdrückvorrichtung *f* release mechanism (*G*).
Abendgesellschaftsanzug *m* special evening dress uniform.
Abfahrt *f* departure, start; downhill run (*skiing*).
Abfahrtzeit *f* time of departure, time of starting; time of descent (*skiing*).
Abfall *m* waste; drop (*Elec*).
abfallen to slope (*Top*).
abfallendes Gelände sloping terrain.
abfangen pull out, level off, flatten out (*Avn*); intercept (*Tac*).
Abfangradius *m* pull-out radius (*in dive bombing*).
Abfangwalze *f* front roller, roller bumper (*MT, Tk*).
Abfederung *f* spring system, suspension (*MT*).
abfertigen to dispatch (*messages, vehicles, trains, etc.*); to process for further disposition.
Abfertigungsgebäude *n* control tower (*Adrm*).
abfeuern to fire.
Abfeuerungseinrichtung *f* release mechanism (*Mort*).
Abfeuerungshebel *m* firing lever (*G*).
Abfeuerungsverbindung *f* firing circuit for machine gun or gun (*Tk*).
Abfeuerungsvorrichtung *f* firing mechanism.
Abfindung *f* pay and/or reimbursement, financial settlement.
Abflug *m* take-off (*Avn*); going flight, departing flight, receding flight (*AAA*).
Abfluggeschwindigkeit *f* take-off speed.
Abflugleistung *f* take-off rating.
Abfrageapparat *m* operator's telephone.
Abfrageklinke *f* operator's answering jack.
abfragen inquire as to party or line desired (*Tp*).
abfüttern to feed (*an animal*).
Abgangsfehler *m* jump, vertical jump (*Arty*).
Abgangsfehlerwinkel *m* angle of jump, jump, vertical jump (*Arty*).
Abgangsrichtung *f* line of departure (*Ballistics*).
Abgangswinkel *m* quadrant angle of departure (*Ballistics*).
Abgase *npl* exhaust gases, waste gases.
Abgasturbine *f* exhaust turbine (*Ap*).
abgeflacht flattened, flat.
abgeflachter Teil der Patrone méplat (*SA Am*).
abgekämpft battle-weary.
abgejagt winded, worn out.
abgenutzt worn, worn out, worn away; eroded (*G barrel*).
Abgeschobener *m* evacuee.
abgesessen dismounted (*Pers*).
abgesondert detached (*unit, etc.*).
abgestellt parked.
abgetragen worn (*Clo*).
abgießen to spray chemical warfare agents (*Avn*).
Abgleitschienen *fpl* bullet-deflection rails (*Tk*).
abgreifen to transfer map distances with compass or dividers, to plot (*in this sense*).
Abgreifen der Entfernung measuring map range with dividers or compass.
Abgrenzung *f* demarcation, delimitation.
abhängen take off (*a pack*); unhook (*a trailer*); hang up (*Tp*); overtake and leave behind (*slang*).
abhauen to cut down; to "beat it" (*slang*).
abheben lift up; pull up, take off (*Avn*).
Abholkommando *n* party detailed to fetch anything; aircraft ferrying detachment.
abhören intercept, listen in, monitor (*Rad, Tp*).
Abhörgefahr *f* danger of interception (*Tp, Rad*).
Abhörstelle *f* intercept station (*Sig C*); monitoring station (*Rad*).
abkippen wing over (*Avn*); withdraw from action (*slang*).
abklemmen disconnect from binding post (*Elec*).
abkommandieren to detach, to detail.
Abkommen *n* deviation; agreement, convention; point of aim (*at instant of firing*).
das Abkommen melden to call the shot.
abkommen deviate.
Abkommpunkt *m* point of called shot, point of aim.
Abkommrohr *n* subcaliber tube (*G*).
Abkommschießen *n* subcaliber firing, subcaliber practice.
Abkrümmen *n* trigger squeeze.
abkrümmen to squeeze (*a trigger*).
Abladekommando *n* unloading detail.
abladen unload, detruck, detrain.
Ablage *f* dump.
Ablagerungszaun *m* drift fence (*a type of snow fence for winter operations*).
Ablaßschraube *f* drain plug.
Ablauf *m* completion, termination; launching, starting.
Ablaufbahn *f* runway (*Adrm*); landing ramp (*for seaplanes*).
Ablaufberg *m* hump, incline (*RR*).
Ablaufposten *m* bridge-traffic control post.
Ablaufventil *n* relief valve (*Hydraulics*).
ablauschen listen in, intercept (*Rad*).
abläuten to ring off (*Tp*).
ableiten divert (*a stream, etc.*).
Ableitung *f* derivation; derivative (*Math*); leakage (*Elec*).
Ablenkung *f* diversion (*Tac*); deflection, refraction.
Ablenkungsangriff *m* diversion, feint attack (*Tac*).
Ablesemarke *f* index line, index mark.
ablesen to read (*instruments, etc.*).
Ablesfehler *m* index error.
Ablesung *f* setting, reading.
abliefern deliver.
Ablösung *f* relief (*Tac*).
ablösen relieve, take over.
Abmarsch *m* half-squad (*Cav*); departure, start.
abmarschbereit ready to start.
Abmarschführer *m* half-squad leader (*Cav*).
abmarschieren depart, start the march.
abnehmen remove, take off; decrease; accept, take.
Abnutzung *f* erosion, wear; wear and tear; attrition.
Abnutzung des Rohres erosion of the bore.
Abnutzungskampf *m* battle of attrition.
Abort *m* toilet, latrine.
abprallen to ricochet.
Abpraller *m* ricochet.
Abprallerschießen *n* ricochet fire.
Abprallwinkel *m* angle of ricochet.
abprotzen uncouple, unlimber (*Arty*).
Abregnen *n* aerial spraying (*CWS*).
abreißen to rip, tear off.
Abreißknopf *m* fuze-cord button (*hand grenade*).
Abreißschnur *f* rip cord (*Prcht*); fuze cord (*hand grenade*).
Abreißzünder *m* friction igniter, rip-cord igniter.
abriebbeständig wear-resistant.
abriegeln to block, interdict, box in, seal off (*Tac*); to bolt (*a door, etc.*).
Abriegelungsfeuer *n* box barrage (*Arty*).
Abrücken *n* departure.
abrufen to ring off (*Tp*).
abrüsten disarm.
Abrüstung *f* disarmament.
abrutschen to slip (*Avn*).
sich seitlich abrutschen lassen to fall off (*Avn*).
absacken to drop, pancake (*Avn*); to founder, sink (*slang*).
Absatteltrupp *m* unsaddling detail (*Cav*).
Absatz *m* berm (*Ft*); heel (*of shoe*); paragraph.
abschätzen to estimate (*distance, etc.*).
Abscheren *n* shear (*Mech*).
abschieben evacuate; expel, deport.
Abschied *m* departure; discharge; resignation.
ehrenvoller Abschied honorable discharge.
abschießen to down, to shoot down (*an Ap*); to disable, put out of action (*a Tk or vehicle*); to shoot (*a person*).
abschirmen to blanket, screen, cover, protect, shield.
Abschirmung *f* shielding, screening (*Rad*).
abschlachten to massacre, slaughter.
abschlagen repel; reject.
Abschleppdienst *m* recovery service, towing service (*MT*).
Abschleppen *n* towing.
Abschleppgerät *n* towing equipment.
Abschleppkommando *n* recovery party, wrecking section.
Abschleppkraftwagen *m* wrecking truck.
Abschleppzug *m* wrecker platoon, maintenance platoon (*MT*).
Abschlußplättchen *n* base cover (*Am*).
abschmieren lubricate.
abschneiden to cut off, isolate (*Tac*); to cut (*wire, etc.*).
Abschnitt *m* sector, phase (*Tac*); area, section.
Abschnittsgrenze *f* sector boundary.
Abschnittsreserve *f* sector reserve.
abschnittsweise by sectors; in phases.
abschraubbar unscrewable, detachable.
abschreiten pace off (*a distance*).
Abschrift *f* copy.
Abschub *m* evacuation (*of PW, wounded, etc.*); transportation to the rear (*of salvage, supplies, etc.*).
Abschubstelle *f* evacuation station.
Abschuß *m* discharge (*of a gun*); downed enemy airplane; disabled tank or vehicle.
Abschußentfernung *f* slant range to present position (*at instant of firing*) (*AAA*).
abschüssig steep (*Top*).
Abschußpunkt *m* present position (*at instant of firing*) (*AAA*).
Abschußrohr *n* projector (*CWS, Sig*).
abschwächen reduce (*Photo*); weaken.
Absetzbewegung *f* withdrawal, disengagement.
absetzen, sich disengage, withdraw (*Tac*); increase distance between aircraft in flight.
Absetzer *m* jumpmaster (*Prcht troops*).
Absetzgelände *n* landing area (*Prcht troops*).
Absicht *f* intent, intention.
absitzen dismount (*from H or vehicle*); do time, serve a sentence.
absondern isolate (*Med*); divide, separate; segregate (*PW*).
Absonderung *f* isolation (*Med*); division, separation; segregation (*PW*).
Absonderungsabteilung *f* isolation quarters (*Med*).
abspannen relieve strain on wire by tying (*Tp*); relieve tension, unharness, uncock, relax.
absperren close or block (*a road, etc.*); lock (*a door, etc.*); cut off, isolate (*Tac*).
abspreizen to brace.
abspringen bail out, jump (*Avn*).
Absprung *m* jump (*Prcht*).
Absprunghafen *m* jump-off base (*Avn*).
Absprung mit verzögerter Öffnung delayed jump (*Prcht*).
abspulen unreel, unwind.
abspülen rinse out, wash out.
Abspuler *m* paying-out reel, axle of hand reel (*Tp*).
Abspüren *n* gas detection (*CWS*).
Abstand *m* distance (*from front to rear*). *See also* **Zeitabstand**.
Abstandslicht *n* marker light (*MT*).
Abstandwerfen *n* pattern bombing.
abstecken stake off (*Engr, Surv*); plot (*a course, etc.*); trace, tape off (*a mine field, etc.*).
Absteckpfahl *m* stake (*Surv*).
absteifen to brace, stiffen.
absteigender Ast descending branch (*of trajectory*).
Abstellbahnhof *m* railroad yard.
abstellen to park, stop; to turn off (*an engine or motor*).
Abstellgleis *n* classification track, siding (*RR*).

Abstellplatz *m* parking place, parking area, dispersal area *(Adrm)*.
abstimmen to tune *(Rad)*.
Abstimmkondensator *m* tuning condenser *(Rad)*.
Abstimmschärfe *f* selectivity, sharpness of resonance *(Rad)*.
Abstimmskala *f* tuning dial *(Rad)*.
Abstimmspule *f* tuning coil *(Rad)*.
abstreifen to patrol *(a road, area, etc.)*.
abstufen graduate *(into degrees)*.
Absturz *m* crash, plunge *(Avn)*.
zum Absturz bringen to down *(an Ap)*.
absuchen to search, sweep.
Abszisse *f* abscissa, X-coordinate.
Abtastdose *f* pick-up unit *(record player)*.
Abteilung *f* battalion *(Cav, Arty, Armd Comd)*; detachment, unit *(Tac)*; department, section *(Adm)*.
"Abteilung, Halt!" "Squad *(company, detail, etc.)*, halt!"
Abteilungsadjutant *m* battalion adjutant.
Abteilungskommandeur *m* battalion commander.
Abteilungsnachrichtenstaffel *f* battalion communication section.
Abteilungsstab *m* battalion headquarters.
Abtransport *m* evacuation.
abtransportieren evacuate.
abtrennen cut off, separate, isolate, disconnect.
"Abtreten!" "Dismissed!" *(formal style, to an individual). Compare* **"Weggetreten!"**
abtreten lassen dismiss *(an individual)*.
Abtrift *f* drift *(Avn)*.
Abtriftmesser *m* driftmeter *(Avn)*.
Abtriftvisier *n* *See* **Abdriftvisier**.
Abtriftwinkel *m* drift angle *(Avn)*.
abtrudeln go into a spin *(Avn)*.
Abwälzstößel *m* tappet rod *(eccentric-cam type)*.
abwärts downward, downhill.
abwässern to drain *(water)*.
Abwehr *f* defense, active defense; military security.
Abwehrangelegenheiten *fpl* security matters.
Abwehrdienst *m* counterintelligence.
Abwehrerfolg *m* defensive success.
Abwehrgeschütz *n* antiaircraft gun.
Abwehrkampf *m* defensive combat.
Abwehrmaßnahme *f* defensive measure; security measure.
Abwehroffizier *m* security officer.
Abwehrvorbereitung *f* defensive preparation, preparation of defensive measures.
Abwehrwaffe *f* defensive arm; defensive weapon.
abwehrweise defensively.
Abwehrzone *f* defensive zone.
abweichen deviate.
abweichende Anfangsgeschwindigkeit velocity error.
Abweichung *f* deviation, deflection, error.
abweisen repel.
Abweiser *m* fender; recoil guard *(G mount)*.
abwerfen to drop, jettison *(Avn)*.
abwesend absent.
Abwind *m* descending air current *(Met)*.
Abwurf *m* release *(bombing). See also* Wurf.
Abwurfbehälter *m* slip tank, belly tank *(Ap)*; aerial delivery unit *(airborne operations)*.
Abwurfgerät *n* bomb-release mechanism *(Ap)*.
Abwurfgondel *f* *See* **Abwurfkiste**.
Abwurfhöhe *f* bombing altitude, bomb-release altitude *(Avn)*.
Abwurfkiste *f* aerial delivery container *(airborne operations)*.
Abwurfmeldung *f* drop message.
Abwurfpatrone *f* message container *(for drop message) (Avn)*.
Abwurfschacht *m* bomb rack *(Ap)*.
Abwurfstelle *f* message-dropping ground; drop point *(airborne supply)*.
Abwurfvorrichtung *f* bomb-release mechanism *(Ap)*.
Abwurfzielgerät *n* bomb sight *(Ap)*.
abwürgen to stall *(an engine)*.
"Abzählen!" "Count off!"
Abzeichen *n* badge, device, emblem, insignia; marking *(Ap, Tk)*.
abziehen pull *(a trigger)*; withdraw *(Tac)*; hone, whet, sharpen; make a print *(Photo)*; subtract, deduct, draw off.
Abzug *m* trigger *(SA)*; withdrawal *(Tac)*; contact print *(Photo)*; deduction *(of pay, etc.)*.
Abzugsbügel *m* trigger guard *(R)*.
Abzugsfeder *f* sear spring *(R)*.
Abzugsgabel *f* trigger-sear fork *(R)*.
Abzugsgewicht *n* trigger pull *(SA)*.
Abzugsgriff *m* lanyard handle *(G)*.
Abzugshebel *m* trigger lever *(MG)*; firing lever *(G)*.
Abzugsschiene *f* trigger bar *(AA gun)*.
Abzugsschnur *f* lanyard *(Ord)*.
Abzugsstange *f* sear *(pistol)*.
Abzugsstift *m* trigger pin *(R)*.
Abzugsstollen *m* sear, sear nose *(R)*.
Abzugsstück *n* trigger piece, firing lever *(G)*.
Abzugsvorrichtung *f* trigger mechanism *(SA)*; firing mechanism *(Ord)*.
Abzugswelle *f* firing rod *(AA gun)*.
Abzweigung *f* branch; junction line *(RR)*.
Achsantrieb *m* axle drive *(MT)*.
Achsdruck *m* axle load *(MT)*.
Achse *f* axis; ordinate; axle; shaft.
Achsel *f* shoulder. *See also* Schulter.
Achsenverschränkbarkeit *f* angle of axle swing *(MT)*.
Achsfeder *f* axle spring.
Achsfederung *f* axle suspension.
Achslager *n* axle bearing.
Achsmutter *f* axle nut.
Achsschenkel *m* wheel spindle *(MT)*.
Achsschenkellenkung *f* steering-knuckle type of steering, Ackerman steering *(MT)*.
Achsschwingschenkel *m* wheel spindle *(G)*.
Achssitze *mpl* axle seats *(for gunners)*.
Achssturz *m* pivot inclination, kingpin inclination *(MT)*.
Achszapfen *m* kingpin, steering knuckle pivot *(MT)*.
Achszapfensturz *m* pivot inclination, kingpin inclination *(MT)*.
Achterzelt *n* eight-man tent.
Achtganggetriebe *n* eight-speed transmission *(MT)*.
"Achtung!" "Attention!", "Caution!", "Danger!", "Look out!"
"Achtung! Präsentiert das, Gewehr!" "Present, Arms!"
Adamsit *m* adamsite *(CWS)*.
Aderpresse *f* tourniquet.
Adjutant *m* adjutant, aide, aide-de-camp, executive officer.
Adjutantur *f* Adjutant's Office *(department of the* Oberkommando des Heeres *serving as central clearing office for routine matters; in no sense equivalent to US Adjutant General's Department)*; personnel group of general staff sections *(in army, corps, and Div)*.
Adler *m* eagle.
Admiral *m* admiral.
Afrikakämpfer *m* veteran of the African Campaign.
Aggregat *n* unit, set; charging unit *(Elec)*.
Ago name of an aircraft manufacturing company.
Akja *m* boat-type runner *(placed under gun wheels for operations in deep snow; also used as a swamp conveyance for wounded, etc.)*.
Akten *fpl* documents, records, papers, file.
Aktenmaterial *n* official documents.
Aktenschrank *m* filing cabinet.
Aktionsbereich *m* *See* **Fahrbereich, Flugbereich,** *etc.*
Aktionsradius *m* *See* **Wirkungsbereich.**
aktiv active; regular.
aktive Truppe line troops, combat troops.
akustische Ortung sound location, acoustic orientation *(AAA)*.
Alarm *m* alarm; air-raid warning.
"Alarm aus!" "All clear!"
alarmbereit on the alert.
Alarmbereitschaft *f* alert, stand-by.
Alarmplatz *m* alarm station.
Alarmschußgerät *n* trip-wire alarm.
Alkalipatrone *f* alkali cartridge *(oxygen breathing apparatus)*.
Alleinflug *m* solo flight.
allgemeines Aufgebot levée en masse.
Allgemeines Heeresamt General Army Office *(central section in rear echelon of* Oberkommando des Heeres) *(abbr. AHA)*.
Allgemeines Luftamt General Air Office *(section of Ger Air Ministry)*.
Allgemeines Wehrmachtamt General Office of the Armed Forces *(central section in rear echelon of* Oberkommando der Wehrmacht).
allgemeingültige Anordnungen general orders.
Allradantrieb *m* all-wheel drive *(MT)*.
Alp *f* mountain pasturage.
Alter *n* age.
Altersgrenze *f* age limit.
Alterungsbeständigkeit *f* resistance to aging.
alte Wache old guard.
Altgummi *n-m* scrap rubber.
Altmaterial *n* junk, scrap, waste.
Altmetall *n* scrap metal.
Alulegierung *f* *See* **Aluminiumlegierung.**
Aluminiumlegierung *f* aluminum alloy.
Amatol *n* amatol *(Am)*.
Amboß *m* anvil *(Am)*.
amboßförmiger Kumulo-Nimbus incus *(Met)*.
Amboßschraube *f* threaded anvil *(Am)*.
Ammoniumpikrat *n* ammonium picrate *(Am)*.
Ammonpulver *n* ammonal *(Am)*.
Ammonsalpeter-Sprengmittel *n* ammonium nitrate explosive.
Amperemeter *n* ammeter.
Amperezahl *f* amperage.
Amphibienflugzeug *n* amphibian airplane.
Amphibienkampfwagen *m* amphibian tank.
Amt *n* office, bureau; administrative function; telephone central.
amtlich official.
Amtsanschließer *m* telephone-exchange connecting device *(connects field Tp with country-wide network)*.
Amtswalter *m* administrator *(Reich Labor Service)*.
Amtszusatz *m* telephone-exchange auxiliary set *(connects field central with country-wide network)*.
Anaglypt *n* anaglyph *(Surv)*.
Analphabet *m* illiterate.
Anblasrichtung *f* direction of air flow *(Avn)*.
Anderthalbdecker *m* sesquiplane.
Änderungsgeschwindigkeit *f* remaining velocity *(Ballistics)*.
andrehen to crank, to turn over *(an engine)*.
Andrehkurbel *f* crank *(MT)*.
Anerkennung *f* recognition, acknowledgment.
Anerkennungsschreiben *n* commendation.
Anfahrtsgang *m* low gear *(MT, Tk)*.
Anfall *m* surprise attack, raid.
Anfangsbuchstabe *m* initial, first letter.
Anfangsdrall *m* initial twist *(Ord)*.
Anfangsgeschwindigkeit *f* initial velocity, muzzle velocity *(Ballistics)*.
Anfangsladung *f* initial charge.
Anfangsstellung *f* initial position.
Anfeuerung *f* combustible composition *(in a flare cartridge)*.
Anfeuerungssatz *m* booster charge *(Am)*.
anfliegen to approach *(a target) (Avn)*.
Anflug *m* coming flight *(AAA)*; approach run *(bombing)*; approach flight *(Avn)*.
Anfluggrundlinie *f* principal course of approach *(Inst landing)*.
Anflugkurs *m* approaching course *(Avn)*.
Anflugrichtung *f* direction of approach *(Avn)*.
Anflugsektor *m* on-course zone *(Inst landing)*; approach zone *(Adrm)*.
Anflugwinkel *m* approach angle, angle of approach *(Avn)*.
anfordern to requisition *(Adm)*.
Anforderung *f* requisition.
Anforderungszeichen *n* requisition number.
Anführer *m* file leader.
Angaben *fpl* data, statements.
Angehöriger *m* member; relative.
die nächsten Angehörigen next of kin.
angelehnt supported by, in contact with, covered by *(Tac)*.
angelehnter Flügel supported flank.
"Angetreten!" "Fall in!" *(at attention)*.
angliedern to attach.
angreifen to attack.
Angreifer *m* attacker, aggressor.
angrenzend adjacent.
Angriff *m* attack *(Tac)*; charge *(Cav)*.
Angriff auf Stellungen attack of organized positions.
Angriff aus der Bewegung attack from march column.
Angriff mit begrenztem Ziel limited attack, attack with limited objective.
Angriffsabschnitt *m* attack sector, zone of action in attack.
Angriffsart *f* form of attack, form of offensive action.
Angriffsbefehl *m* attack order.
Angriffsbeginn *m* time of attack.
Angriffsbereitstellung *f* assembly (area) for attack.
Angriffsbreite *f* frontage in attack, attack frontage *(Tac)*.
Angriffsflug *m* air-attack flight, raid *(Avn)*.
Angriffsflügel *m* attacking wing.
Angriffsform *f* form of attack; attack formation.
angriffsfreudig aggressive.
Angriffsgefecht *n* offensive combat.
Angriffsgelände *n* terrain of attack, attack zone.
Angriffsgraben *m* assault trench.
Angriffsgruppe *f* attack group, attack echelon.
Angriffshandlung *f* offensive action.
Angriffshöhe *f* air-attack altitude, bombing altitude *(Avn)*.
angriffslustig aggressive.
Angriffsplan *m* plan of attack.
Angriffsrichtung *f* direction of attack.
Angriffsstreifen *m* attack sector.
Angriffstruppen *fpl* attack units, attack troops.
Angriffsverlauf *m* progress of an attack.

abs	absondern; Absonderung	to separate; separation
Absch.bew	Abschied bewilligt	discharge approved
Absch.Ger	Abschussgerät	grenade launcher
Abschn	Abschnitt	sector; section; zone
Abst	Abstand	distance *(tactics)*; interval
Abt	Abteilung	section; detachment; department; battalion
Abt.Chef	Abteilungschef	section chief
Abt.Dir	Abteilungsdirektor	departmental director
Abt.Gef.St	Abteilungsgefechtsstand	battalion command post
Abt.L	Abteilungsleiter	section chief
A.Btl	Ausbildungsbataillon	training battalion
Abtlg	Abteilung	section; detachment; depart-
abtr	abtreten	to withdraw; to retire from
Abtr	Abtretung	withdrawal; cession; surrender
Abt.Vorst	Abteilungsvorsteher	section manager; section
Abw	Abwehr	defense
Abw	Abwicklung	demobilization; unfolding
Abw.Min	Abwehrmine	defensive mine
Abw.Schl	Abwehrschlacht	defensive battle
Abz	Abzeichen	insignia; marking
Abz	Abzug	trigger; retreat; outlet
Abz.Vorr	Abzugsvorrichtung	firing mechanism; trigger mechanism
a.c.	anni currentis	of the current year
Achs.B	Achselband	aiguillette *(large)*
Achskl	Achselklappe	shoulder strap
Achsst	Achselstück	shoulder strap *(officer's)*
a.d	an der	on the; at the
a.D	ausser Dienst	retired
a.d,D	auf dem Dienstwege	through official channels
Adj	Adjutant	adjutant
Adj Obd H	Adjutantur des Oberbefehlshabers des Heeres	Adjutant's Office of the Commander in Chief of the Army
Adm	Admiral	admiral
ADO	allgemeine Dienstordnung	general service regulations
ADP	Arbeitsdienstpflicht	labor service duty
Adr	Adresse	address
Adw	Arbeitsdienstwilliger	labor service volunteer
ä	ärztlich	medical
A.E	Antitoxineinheiten	anti-toxin units
a.E	am Ende	at the end; in the end
A.E.G	Allgemeine-Elektrizitätsgesellschaft	electrical manufacturing firm
Ält	Ältester	oldest; senior
A.E.R	Artillerieersatzregiment	artillery replacement training regiment
A.f.B	Anleitung für die Ausführung von Behelfsbefestigungen	direction for the construction of secondary field fortifications
A.f.G	Ausbildungsvorschrift für Gebirgstruppen	training manual for mountain troops
A.Fhr	Artillerieführer	artillery commander *(in a division)*
Afl	Artillerieflieger	artillery spotting pilot
A.(F)M.K	Artilleriemunitionskolonne	artillery munitions transport column
A.Fü	Artillerieführer	artillery commander *(in a division)*
A.G	Abwehrgruppe	defense group
A.G	Aktien-Gesellschaft	limited company
AgEH	Amtsgruppe Ersatz- und Heerwesen	Section for Replacement Training and Army Matters
A.G.I	Artilleriegerätinspizient	general officer in charge of artillery equipment inspection
A.Gr	Armeegruppe	task force of varying strength
A.Gr	Artilleriegruppe	artillery task force; artillery group
A.H	Allgemeines Heeresgerät	general army equipment
AHA	Allgemeines Heeresamt	General Army Office
A.H.Q	Armeehauptquartier	army headquarters
A.Ing	Artillerieingenieur	artillery engineer
A.I.W	Artillerieinstandsetzungswerkstatt	artillery repair shop
Aj	Persönlicher Adjutant des Führers	personal adjutant of the Führer
A.K	Abschnittskommandeur	sector commander
A.K	Armeekorps	army corps
A.K	Artilleriekolonne	artillery column
A.K	Artilleriekommandeur	artillery commander from general headquarters pool
a.K	auf Kommando	detailed *(for military service)*
a.K	auf Kriegsdauer	for the duration of the war
Aka	Artillerie-Kampfartillerie	counterbattery artillery
A.Kdr	Artilleriekommandeur	artillery commander from general headquarters pool
Akk	Akkumulator	storage battery
A.K.K	Armeekraftwagenkolonne	army motor transport column
A.K.N	Artilleriekommandeur Nord	Artillery Commander, North
A.K.O	Artilleriekommandeur Ost	Artillery Commander, East
A.Kom	Artilleriekommandeur	artillery comander from general headquarters pool
A.Korps	Armeekorps	army corps
A.K.P	Armee-Kraftfahrpark	army motor park
A.K.S	Artilleriekommandeur Süd	Artillery Commander, South
akt	aktiv	active; on duty
Akt.Dpfl	aktive Dienstpflicht	active duty

Akt.R	Aktionsradius	radius of action
A.K.W	Artilleriekommandeur West	Artillery Commander, West
Akz	Aktenzeichen	file index number
A.L	Anfangsladung	initial charge (*blasting*)
A.L	Anschlussleitung	connecting circuit
allg	allgemein	general
All.Gab	Gasabwehrdienst aller Waffen	gas protection for all arms
Allg.Gr	Allgemeine Gruppe	general group
allj	alljährlich	every year; annually
All.Pi.D	allgemeiner Pionierdienst für alle Waffen	general combat engineer service for all arms
A.L.R	Allgemeines Landrecht	general civil law
A.L.R	Artillerielehrregiment	artillery instruction regiment
Am	Amerika	America
Am	amerikanisch; Amerikaner	American; an American
a.M	am Main	on the Main (*river*)
Am	Auswanderungsmesser	range corrector (*naval and antiaircraft*)
amb	ambulant	ambulatory; able to walk
Amb	Ambulanz	ambulance
amb.Beh	ambulante Behandlung	treatment of ambulatory cases (*medical service*)
A.M.K	Artilleriemunitionskolonne	artillery munitions transport column
Amn	Amnestie	amnesty
Amp	Ampulle	ampoule
Amp	Amputation	amputation
Amph	Amphibienflugzeug	amphibian plane
amtl	amtlich	official
A.M.Tr	Artilleriemesstrupp	sound and flash ranging section (*artillery*)
an	angekommen	arrived
An	Anisol	trinitroanisole
A.Nachr.Pk	Armee-Nachrichtenpark	army signal equipment park
Anf	Anfang	beginning
anf	anfangen	to begin; to commence
A.N.F	Armee-Nachschubführer	army supply commander
Anf.Geschw	Anfangsgeschwindigkeit	initial velocity or speed
Anf.Zeich	Anführungszeichen	quotation marks
ang	angestellt	employed
ang	angewandt	applied
angek	angekommen	arrived
Angr.Z	Angriffsziel	attack objective
Anh	Anhänger	trailer; supporter; follower
Anh	Anhang	appendix, supplement
Anh.W	Anhängewagen	trailer
Ank	Ankunft	arrival
Anl	Anlage	plant; establishment; enclosure; park; construction; design; outline; foundation
Anl	Anleitung	instructions; directions
Anltg	Anleitung	instructions; directions
Anltg.A.M.W	Anleitung für die Ausbildung der Minenwerferkompanien	instructions for the training of trench motor companies
Anm	Anmerkung	remark; annotation; footnote
Anmerk	Anmerkung	remark; annotation; footnote
Ann	Annahme	acceptance; receipt; assumption; supposition
anp	anpassen	to suit; to adapt
Anp	Anpassung	adaptation
A.N.R	Armee-Nachrichtenregiment	army signal regiment
ansch	anschaffen	to provide; to obtain
Ansch	Anschaffung	acquisition
ansch	anschiessen	to hit by shooting
Ansch	Anschuss	shot
Anschl.Bttr	Anschlussbatterie	adjoining battery
Anschl.Div	Anschlussdivision	adjoining division
Anschl.Tr	Anschlusstruppen	adjoining troops
Ans.Sk	Ansichtsskizze	graphic sketch
Anst	Anstalt	institution; establishment
anst	anstauen	to dam up
anst	ansteckend	contagious
anst	anstellen	to employ
Anst	Anstellung	employment
Ant	Antenne	antenna
Ant.fein	Antennenfeinabstimmung	antenna tuning
Anw	Anwärter	aspirant; candidate
Anw	Anweisung	direction; instruction
Anz	Anzeige	announcement; notice; report
Anz	Anzeiger	indicator; informer
Anz.D	Anzeigerdeckung	pit (*range*)
Anz.O	Anzugsordnung	regulations for uniforms
A.O	Ablaufoffizier	bridge traffic control officer
A.O	Anzugsordnung	regulations for uniforms
A.O	Arbeitsordnung	work plan
A.O	Artillerieoffizier	artillery officer
Ao.Ges	ausserordentlicher Gesandter	envoy extraordinary
AoGubM	ausserordentlicher Gesandter und bevollmächtigter Minister	envoy extraordinary and minister plenipotentiary

Angriffsversuch *m* attempted attack.
Angriffswelle *f* attack wave, attacking echelon.
Angriffsziel *n* objective *(of attack)*.
erstes Angriffsziel immediate objective.
Angriffszwischenziel *n* intermediate objective.
Anhalt *m* guide, general principle.
Anhaltspunkt *m* check point *(Gunnery, Air Navigation, Surv)*; item in a check list *(combat orders)*.
Anhang *m* appendix *(to a manual, etc.)*.
Anhängelast *f* trailer load *(MT)*.
Anhängen *n* See **Vermessung durch Anhängen.**
Anhänger *m* trailer *(MT)*; tender *(RR)*; tie-on tag.
Anhängezettel *m* tie-on tag.
Anhäufung *f* accumulation, concentration, piling up.
Anhöhe *f* height, hill, rise.
Anker *m* armature, rotor *(Elec)*; anchor *(Nav)*.
Ankerachse *f* armature shaft *(field Tp)*.
Ankerbalken *m* anchor stock.
Ankerflunken *m* anchor fluke.
Ankergrund *m* anchorage *(Nav)*.
Ankerlicht *n* anchor light.
Ankerlichten *n* weighing anchor.
Ankerlinie *f* line of anchors *(Bdg)*.
Ankermine *f* anchored mine, moored mine.
Ankermast *m* mooring mast.
Ankerpfahl *m* anchor stake *(for a guy line)*.
Ankerplatte *f* anchor plate *(part of a clockwork fuze)*.
Ankerplatz *m* anchorage *(Nav)*.
Ankerrödel *m* anchor rack stick *(Bdg)*.
Ankerrute *f* anchor shank.
Ankerseil *n* guy line.
Ankerstelle *f* anchorage *(Nav)*.
Ankerstich *m* anchor hitch.
Ankersucher *m* grapnel.
Ankertau *n* anchor cable.
Ankerturm *m* mooring tower.
Ankerwelle *f* armature shaft *(Elec)*.
Ankerwicklung *f* armature winding.
Ankerwinde *f* capstan.

Anklage *f* charge, complaint.
anklammern to cling tenaciously, to hold fast.
ankleben to paste, adhere, stick, fasten with adhesive.
Ankündigung *f* announcement, bulletin, notice.
Ankündigungskommando *n* preparatory command.
Ankündigungssignal *n* warning signal.
Ankunft *f* arrival.
ankurbeln to crank.
Anlage *f* installation; annex, inclosure *(in a manual)*.
anlassen to start *(an engine)*; to temper *(steel)*.
Anlasser *m* starter *(Mtr)*.
Anlaßknopf *m* starter button *(Mtr)*.
Anlaßmotor *m* starter motor *(Mtr)*.
Anlaßpatrone *f* cartridge for cartridge starter *(Mtr)*.
Anlaßpistole *f* cartridge starter *(Mtr)*.
Anlaßschalter *m* starter switch *(Mtr)*.
Anlauf *m* take-off run *(Avn)*.
Anlaufstrecke *f* take-off distance *(Avn)*.
anläuten to ring *(Tp)*.
anlegen to aim *(R)*; to dock; to put ashore; to construct.
Anlegepunkt *m* aiming point.
Anlegestelle *f* pier, wharf.
anleuchten illuminate.
Anmarsch *m* approach, approach march, advance *(Tac)*.
Anmarschweg *m* approach, approach route.
annähernd approximate.
Annäherung *f* approach.
Annäherungsformation *f* approach march formation.
Annäherungsmarsch *m* approach march *(Tac)*.
Annahme *f* assumption; acceptance, reception.
Annahmestelle *f* recruiting office; receiving office *(letters, etc.)*.
Anode *f* plate, anode *(Elec)*.
Anodenbatterie *f* plate battery, "B" battery *(Rad)*.
Anodengleichspannung *f* direct plate voltage *(Rad)*.
Anodenkreis *m* plate circuit *(Rad)*.
Anodenrückkopplung *f* plate feedback coupling *(Rad)*.
Anodenverlustleistung *f* plate dissipation *(Rad)*.
Anorak *m* parka *(Clo)*.
Anordnung *f* order.
anpassen adapt, blend *(Cam)*.
Anpeilen *n* taking of bearings, radio direction finding *(Avn)*.
anpirschen to creep up, to stalk.
Anrecht *n* claim.
Anregungsmittel *n* stimulant.
anrichten to sight, sight in, align; to cause *(damage, etc.)*.
anrollen to roll along runway *(on take-off run)*.

Anruf *m* call, call-up *(Rad, Tp)*; challenge.
Anrufantwort *f* answer to call-up *(Rad)*.
Anrufklappe *f* switchboard drop *(Tp)*.
Anrufsschauzeichen *n* incoming-call signal light *(Tp)*.
Anrufzeichen *n* call signal *(Tp)*.
Ansammlung *f* concentration *(Tac)*.
Ansatzflügel *m* stub wing *(Ap)*.
Ansaugetakt *m* intake stroke, suction stroke *(Mtr)*.
Ansaughub *m* intake stroke *(Mtr)*.
Ansaugkrümmer *m* air-intake horn *(carburetor)*.
Ansaugleitung *f* intake duct *(Mtr, Ft)*.
Ansaugrohr *n* intake pipe *(Mtr)*.
Ansaugung *f* suction.
anschaffen procure.
anschalten connect, switch on; tap *(a wire)*.
Anreicherung *f* concentration *(CWS)*.
Anschauungsmittel *npl* illustrative material, demonstration material *(Tng aids)*.
Anschießen *n* harmonization *(Ord)*.
anschießen to sight in.
Anschlag *m* aiming or firing position with rifle or machine gun; stop *(Ord)*.
anschlagen to post *(a notice, etc.)*.
Anschlagsart *f* firing position *(of the soldier)*.
Anschlagtafel *f* bulletin board.
Anschlagwinkel *m* try square.
anschließen join, close up, connect.
Anschluß *m* liaison, support, contact *(Tac)*; connection, junction, coupling.
Anschlußbahnhof *m* junction *(RR)*.
Anschlußklemme *f* binding post *(Elec)*.
Anschlußklinke *f* line jack, station-line jack *(Tp)*.
Anschlußmann *m* connecting file.
Anschlußpunkt *m* connecting point *(in axes of Sig Com)*.
Anschlußschnur *f* connecting cord *(Elec)*.
Anschlußstecker *m* plug, connecting plug *(Elec, Tp)*.
Anschlußstück *n* connecting piece, joint, coupling, union.
Anschlußteil der Garbe margin of the sheaf of fire.
Anschnallgurt *m* safety belt *(Avn)*.
Anschneidelinie *f* line of intersection.
Anschneiden *n* intersection *(Surv)*.
anschneiden to intersect; determine a fix *(air navigation)*; obtain a bearing *(Rad, FR)*.
Anschnitte *mpl* cross bearings.
Anschuß *m* sighting shot.
ansetzen launch, commit *(Tac)*; ram *(G)*.
Ansetzer *m* rammer *(G)*.
Ansichtsskizze *f* panoramic sketch *(Top)*.
Ansprache *f* designation *(of a target)*.
Anspruch *m* claim.
Anstalt *f* institution, establishment, station.
anstauen to dam up, flood.
Anstauung *f* damming, flooding; flooded area.
anstechen to tie, fasten, hitch.
Ansteckblech *n* float plate *(on a trail spade)*.
anstecken to attach, fasten, hitch; to infect.
ansteckende Krankheit communicable disease, contagious disease.
Ansteckung *f* infection.
Anstellwinkel *m* angle of pitch, blade angle *(propeller)*; angle of attack *(Avn)*.
Ansteuerungsfeuer *n* directional beacon *(Avn)*.
anstreichen run weapon up and down side of tree, etc., *(to find firing support)*; to paint.
Anstrich *m* paint.
Anströmrichtung *f* direction of air flow *(Avn)*.
anstürmen to assault, attack, charge.
ansuchen to request.
Ansumpfung *f* inundation, inundated area.
Antenne *f* antenna, aerial.
Antenne mit Rundwirkung omnidirectional antenna.
Antennenanschluß *m* antenna binding post.
Antennen-Anschlußbuchse *f* See **Antennenbuchse.**
Antennenbuchse *f* antenna jack.
Antennengebilde *n* antenna array, antenna structure, antenna system.
Antennengerät *n* antenna outfit, antenna equipment.
Antennenhaspel *f* antenna reel *(Ap)*.
Antennenkapazität *f* antenna capacitance.
Antennenkondensator *m* antenna condenser.
Antennenkopplung *f* antenna coupling.
Antennenkreis *m* antenna circuit.
Antennenleistung *f* antenna power.
Antennenmast *m* antenna mast.
Antennenspule *f* antenna tuning coil.

Antennenstab *m* antenna rod.
Antennenstellung *f* directional position of the antenna.
Antennenstromanzeiger *m* antenna ammeter.
Antennenwiderstand *m* antenna resistance.
Antiflatterbock *m* antishimmy shackle *(MT)*.
Antrag *m* request; recommendation, suggestion, proposal.
antreiben to drive, impel, propel.
antreten to fall in; begin *(an assignment)*; assume *(duties, etc.)*.
"Antreten!" "Fall in!" *(not at attention)*.
Antrieb *m* drive *(Mech)*.
Antriebsachse *f* driving axle *(MT)*.
Antriebsart *f* type of drive *(MT)*.
Antriebskegelrad *n* bevel drive pinion *(differential gear)*.
Antriebsrad *n* drive wheel *(MT)*.
Antriebsritzel *m* starter pinion *(on armature shaft of starter)*.
Antriebswelle *f* drive shaft.
Antriebszahnrad *n* drive gear *(MT)*.
A.N.-Verfahren *n* A.N. method *(of instrument landing)*.
anvisieren to sight at.
Anwärmeschuß *m* warming-up shot.
Anwärter *m* candidate; cadet.
anweisen to direct, instruct, allot.
Anweisung *f* directive; instructions;
anwerfen to crank *(an engine)*.
Anzapfleitung *f* power lead-in *(Rad)*.
Anzeiger *m* indicator, marker.
Anzeigerschiene *f* indicator slide *(MG)*.
Anziehungskraft *f* force of attraction.
anzielen to sight, to aim.
Anzug *m* uniform; suit of clothes.
anzünden to ignite, light.
Aphongetriebe *n* constant-mesh transmission *(MT)*.
Apotheker *m* pharmacist.
Apparattornister *m* instrument case *(portable Rad)*.
Apparatur *f* chassis *(Rad)*; fixtures *(Tech)*.
Appell *m* roll call; muster; inspection.
Aquadag *m* aquadag *(lubricant)*.
Arado name of an aircraft manufacturing company.
Aräometer *m* hydrometer.
Arbeiten *fpl* works *(Ft)*.
Arbeitsanzug *m* fatigue uniform, work uniform.
Arbeitsdienst *m* See **Reichsarbeitsdienst.**
Arbeitsdienstpflicht *f* liability to labor service.
Arbeitsführer *m* captain *(Reich Labor Service)*.
Arbeitsgeschütz *n* roving gun *(Arty)*.
Arbeitshub *m* power stroke *(Mtr)*.
Arbeitskommando *n* fatigue detail.
Arbeitslager *n* labor camp.
Arbeitsmann *m* workman *(Reich Labor Service)*.
Arbeitsspiel *n* functioning, action *(Mech)*.
Arbeitstakt *m* power stroke *(Mtr)*.
Arbeitsurlaub *m* leave for purposes of war work.
arbeitsverwendungsfähig fit for labor duty only *(abbr.* a.v.).
a.v. Heimat fit for labor duty in zone of interior only.
Arktik *f* smoke acid for use in extremely cold weather *(CWS)*.
arktische Kaltluft polar air *(Met)*.
Armaturenbrett *n* instrument board, instrument panel.
Armauflage *f* elbow rest *(trench or firing pit)*.
Armband *n* See **Armbinde.**
Armbanduhr *f* wrist watch.
Armbinde *f* arm band, brassard.
Armee *f* army *(a tactical unit, distinguished from* Heer, *the Army)*.
Armeebefehl *m* army field order.
Armeebekleidungsamt *n* army clothing depot.
Armeebriefstelle *f* army postal station.
Armeefeldlazarett *n* army surgical hospital.
Armeegebiet *n* army area.
Armeegruppe *f* task force usually comprising one army and miscellaneous units.
Armeeintendant *m* army intendant *(Adm official at army Hq in charge of rations, clothing, equipment, pay, etc.)*.
Armeekartenlager *n* army map depot.
Armeekorps *n* army corps.
Armeekraftfahrpark *m* army motor transport park.
Armeemunitionslager *n* army ammunition depot.
Armeenachrichtenabteilung *f* army signal battalion.
Armeenachrichtenregiment *n* army signal regiment.
Armeenachschubführer *m* commander of army services of supply *(also known as* Kommandeur der Armeenachschubtruppen).
Armeeoberkommando *n* high command of an army, army headquarters *(abbr.* OAK).

Armeesanitätsabteilung *f* army medical battalion.
Armeeverpflegungsamt *n* office of army ration supply.
Armeeverpflegungslager *n* army ration-supply depot.
Ärmel *m* sleeve *(Clo).*
Ärmelaufschlag *m* cuff *(Clo).*
Ärmelabzeichen *n* sleeve badge.
Ärmelpatte *f* cuff patch.
Armschiene *f* splint *(for arm fracture).*
Armzeichen *n* arm and hand signal, arm signal.
Arrestant *m* person under arrest.
Arrestanstalt *f* military prison.
Arrestlokal *n* detention room, guardhouse cell, guardhouse.
Arreststrafe *f* confinement, sentence of confinement.
Arrestraum im Lazarett detention ward.
Arsin *n* arsine *(CWS).*
Art *f* kind, manner, method, type.
Art. B.-Stelle *f* *See* **Artilleriebeobachtungsstelle.**
Artillerie *f* artillery.
leichte Artillerie light artillery.
schwere Artillerie medium artillery.
schwerste Artillerie heavy artillery.
Artillerieabteilung *f* artillery battalion.
Artillerieaufmarsch *m* moving up to positions *(Arty).*
Artilleriebekämpfung *f* counterbattery fire.
Artilleriebeobachter *m* artillery observer, spotter.
Artilleriebeobachtungsabteilung *f* observation battalion *(Arty).*
Artilleriebeobachtungsstelle *f* artillery observation post.
Artilleriebeschuß *m* artillery fire.
Artillerieeinschlag *m* shell hit, shell burst, point of impact *(Arty).*
Artillerieflieger *mpl* artillery reconnaissance aviation.
Artillerieflug *m* artillery mission *(Avn).*
Artillerieflugzeug *n* artillery observation airplane.
Artillerieführer *m* division artillery commander *(special staff Arty officer and Arty commander at Div Hq).*
Artilleriegliederung *f* organization of artillery.
Artilleriegruppe *f* artillery group, artillery groupment.
Artilleriekolonne *f* ammunition supply column *(Arty).*
Artilleriekommandeur *m* corps artillery commander *(in GHQ pool)*; division artillery commander *(when GHQ artillery is attached).*
Höherer Artilleriekommandeur special staff artillery officer *(at army Hq).*
Artillerienachrichtenstelle *f* artillery intelligence center.
Artillerienachrichtentrupp *m* artillery intelligence section.
Artilleriepark *m* artillery equipment park.
Artilleriepunkttafel *f* point-designation grid.
Artillerierechenschieber *m* graphical firing table.
Artilleriespähtrupp *m* artillery reconnaissance detail.
Artilleriesperrfeuer *n* artillery barrage.
Artilleriestaffel *f* artillery train.
Artillerieunterstützung *f* artillery support.
Artillerieverbindungskommando *n* artillery liaison command post, artillery liaison detachment.
Artillerieverbindungsoffizier *m* artillery liaison officer.
Artillerievermessung *f* artillery survey.
Artillerievermessungstrupp *m* artillery survey section.
Artillerievorbereitung *f* artillery preparation.
Artilleriezugmaschine *f* artillery prime mover.
Artillerist *m* artilleryman.
artilleristische Aufklärung artillery reconnaissance.
artilleristische Punkte *mpl* artillery reference points.
Arznei *f* drug, medicine, medicament.
Arzneikasten *m* medicine chest.
Arzneikiste *f* *See* **Arzneikasten.**
Arzneimittel *n* medicine, medicament.
Arzt *m* doctor, medical officer.
Ärztliche Akademie der Luftwaffe school of aviation medicine.
ärztliche Behandlung medical treatment, medical attendance.
ärztliche Untersuchung *f* medical examination, physical examination.
Asbest *m* asbestos.
Äskulapstab *m* caduceus.
Assistenzarzt *m* second lieutenant *(Med).*
Ast *m* branch; knot *(in wood).*
Astro *m* celestial navigator *(Avn slang).*
astronomische Navigation celestial navigation *(Avn).*
astronomischer Meßzug *m* astronomical survey platoon.
Astverhau *m* dead abatis made of tree branches.
Atemeinsatz *m* filter element *(gas mask).*
Atemgerät *n* oxygen apparatus *(Avn).*
Atemmaske *f* oxygen mask *(Avn).*
Atemmundstück *n* mouthpiece *(oxygen breathing apparatus).*
Atemsack *m* respirator bag *(oxygen breathing apparatus).*
Atemschlauch *m* hose *(gas mask, oxygen breathing apparatus).*
Äthylarsindichlorid *n* ethyldichlorarsine, ED *(CWS).*
Äthyldichlorarsin *n* ethyldichlorarsine, ED *(CWS). (Ger abbr.* Dick).
Attacke *f* charge *(Cav).*
Attrappe *f* dummy *(target, vehicle, etc.).*
ätzender Kampfstoff vesicant, vesicant agent, blister agent, blister gas.
Ätzmittel *n* caustic.
Ätznatron *n* lye, caustic soda, sodium hydroxide.
Aubo-Fähre *f* outboard-motor ferry *(Aubo = Außenbord).*
Aubomotor *m* outboard motor *(Aubo = Außenbord).*
Audion *n* grid-leak detector, detector, 2nd detector *(Rad).*
Aufbau *m* body *(MT)*; superstructure, *i.e.* sponson and turret *(Tk).*
Aufbaulüfter *m* ventilator *(in Tk sponson or turret).*
Aufbewahrung *f* storage.
aufbieten mobilize.
aufblasen inflate, blow up.
Aufblitzen *n* flash *(Arty fire).*
aufbrauchen to exhaust, use up.
aufbrechen to depart, start.
Aufbruchsort *m* departure point, starting point.
Aufbruchszeit *f* departure time, starting time.
aufbumsen collide, strike *(slang).*
Aufenthaltspunkt *m* stop *(RR, MT).*
auffangen to detect *(Rad)*; intercept, catch; to absorb *(recoil, etc.).*
Auffangstellung *f* prepared position in rear, rear position *(in defense).*
Auffangvorrichtung *f* buffer *(G).*
auffinden to locate *(a target).*
Aufführender *m* corporal of the guard.
Aufgabe *f* mission, task, problem.
aufgeben abandon, give up; register *(baggage, etc.)*; send *(a telegram, etc.).*
Aufgebot *m* *See* **allgemeines Aufgebot.**
aufgesessen mounted *(Pers).*
Aufgleitfront *f* warm front *(Met).*
Aufhaken *n* message pick-up *(Avn).*
Aufhängeöse *f* suspension lug *(bomb).*
Aufhängung *f* suspension *(of bombs, etc.).*
aufhetzen incite.
aufklären reconnoiter, scout, observe, patrol.
Aufklärer *m* scout, observer; reconnaissance airplane.
Aufklärertätigkeit *f* reconnaissance activity, patrol activity.
Aufklärung *f* reconnaissance *(Tac).*
Aufklärungsabteilung *f* reconnaissance battalion.
Aufklärungsbreite *f* width of reconnaissance sector *(in which Obsn Bn locates targets).*
Aufklärungsergebnis *n* results of reconnaissance.
Aufklärungsflieger *m* aircraft observer; reconnaissance aircraft.
Aufklärungsflug *m* reconnaissance mission, reconnaissance flight *(Avn).*
Aufklärungsflugzeug *m* reconnaissance airplane.
Aufklärungsgebiet *n* reconnaissance area.
Aufklärungskörper *mpl* reconnaissance elements.
Aufklärungsmaterial *n* reconnaissance information.
Aufklärungsraum *m* reconnaissance area.
Aufklärungsschwadron *f* reconnaissance troop *(Cav).*
Aufklärungsspähtrupp *m* reconnaissance patrol.
Aufklärungsstaffel *f* reconnaissance squadron *(Avn).*
Aufklärungsstreifen *m* reconnaissance sector.
Aufklärungstiefe *f* reconnaissance depth *(in which Obsn Bn locates targets).*
Aufklärungstrupp *m* reconnaissance patrol.
Aufklärungszug *m* scout car platoon; reconnaissance platoon.
Aufladekommando *n* loading detail.
Auflademotor *m* supercharged engine *(Avn).*
aufladen to boost, supercharge; to load.
Aufladung *f* detonating charge *(blasting cap)*
Auflagefläche *f* bearing surface, contact surface.
Auflagepunkt *m* center of tire impact *(MT)*; point of support *(Tech).*
Auflager *n* pedestal, support *(Bdg)*; hanger bar *(harness).*
Auflaufstück *n* knuckle lug *(G).*
auflösen disintegrate, disband, dissolve, scatter, demobilize.
Aufmarsch *m* concentration or assembly of troops for action; strategic concentration; moving up to positions *(Arty).*
Aufmarschgebiet *n* concentration area *(Tac).*
Aufmarschplan *m* plan for strategic concentration.
Aufnahme *f* covering force *(reserve force covering withdrawal from action)*; reception; photograph; taking up, establishment *(of contact, etc.).*
Aufnahmefähigkeit *f* capacity *(of roads, structures, etc.).*
Aufnahmehaken *m* pick-up hook *(for message pick-up) (Ap).*
Aufnahmering *m* receiving ring *(AA gun).*
Aufnahmestellung *f* covering position *(covering withdrawal from action).*
Aufnahmestreifen *m* tape *(Tg printer).*
aufnehmen to record *(sound, etc.)*; to receive, take up; to photograph; to survey; to establish *(contact, etc.).*
aufpflanzen to fix bayonets.
aufprotzen to couple, limber, place a gun in traveling position *(Arty).*
Aufrauhbürste *f* rotary sweeper *(road construction).*
aufräumen to clear away, mop up.
aufrecht erect, upright.
aufreißen to rip, tear up.
Aufriß *m* design, sketch, vertical section.
aufrollen to roll up *(Tac)*; to coil *(wire).*
aufrücken to move up, advance.
Aufruhr *m* riot.
Aufrüstung *f* plank scaffolding *(on a Pon).*
Aufsatz *m* sight mount, telescope mount *(in a loose sense, either the optical sight alone or the entire sight assembly)*; essay, composition.
Aufsatzeinteilung *f* elevation graduations *(sight mount).*
Aufsatzentfernung *f* corrected range *(Arty).*
Aufsatzerhöhung *f* corrected elevation *(Arty).*
Aufsatzgehäuse *n* sight-mount housing *(G).*
Aufsatzstange *f* sight adjustment rod *(G).*
Aufsatzträger *m* sight bracket, sight support *(G).*
Aufsatztrieb *m* elevation mechanism *(G).*
Aufsatztrommel *f* angle-of-elevation dial *(G).*
Aufsatzwinkel *m* angle of elevation *(Gunnery)*; superelevation *(AAA).*
Aufsatzwinkeltrieb *m* angle-of-elevation mechanism *(G).*
Aufsatzzeiger *m* telescope mount reference pointer *(matches with* Rohrzeiger *when gun is laid for elevation).*
aufschablonieren to stencil on.
aufschirren to harness.
Aufschlag *m* impact, percussion; cuff *(Clo).*
Aufschlaggelände *n* impact area.
Aufschlaggeschwindigkeit *f* striking velocity.
Aufschlagpunkt *m* point of impact, objective point.
Aufschlagweite *f* burst interval.
Aufschlagwinkel *m* angle of impact.
Aufschlagzünder *m* impact fuze, percussion fuze.
Aufschlagzünder mit Verzögerung delay fuze.
Aufschlagzünder ohne Verzögerung nondelay fuze.
Aufschreiber *m* recorder *(Arty).*
Aufschrumpfen *n* heat shrinking *(Ord).*
Aufschub *m* delay.
Aufschüttung *f* fill *(Engr, Top).*
Aufsichtsturm *m* control tower *(Adrm).*
aufsitzen to mount *(a horse or vehicle).*
das Ziel aufsitzen lassen to hold below the target in aiming.
Aufspuler *m* reel *(Tp).*
Aufsteckschlüssel *m* socket wrench.
aufsteigen to ascend, mount, rise.
aufsteigender Ast ascending branch *(of trajectory).*
Aufstellbahnhof *m* make-up yard *(RR).*
aufstellen to post *(a sentry)*; to activate or constitute *(a unit)*; to emplace *(a gun)*; to install *(an engine, etc.)*; to mount *(a gun)*; to place, to distribute *(troops, etc.)*; to establish *(an agency)*; to park *(vehicles).*
Aufstellgleis *n* make-up track *(RR).*
Aufstellung *f* formation *(of troops)*; initial organization *(of a unit)*; establishment *(of an agency)*; disposition *(Tac).*

AOK	Armeeoberkommando	army command
Ap	Abpraller	ricochet
A.P.	Artilleriepunkt; Artilleristischer Punkt	artillery reference point *(gunnery)*
a.p.	ausserplanmässig	not according to plan or schedule
A. Pf.Laz	Armee-Pferdelazarett	army veterinary hospital
A.Pf.Pk	Armee-Pferdepark	army horse park
apl	ausserplanmässig	not according to plan or schedule ment
ar	arisch	Aryan
A.R.	Artillerieregiment	artillery regiment
Arb. Abt	Arbeitsabteilung	labor detachment
Arb. Flgz	Arbeitsflugzeug	work plane
Arb. Kp	Arbeitskompanie	labor company
Ar. D	Arbeitsdienst	labor service
Arfü	Artillerieführer	divisional artillery commander
a.Rh.	am Rhein	on the Rhine
Ark	Arktikmunition	arctic ammunition
Arko	Artilleriekommandeur	artillery commander from general headquarters pool
Arm	Armee	army *(formation above army corps)*
arm	armiert	armed
Arm. Pf. Laz	Armeepferdelazarett	army horse hospital
Arm. Pf. P	Armeepferdepark	army horse park
Arm. Res	Armeereserve	army reserve
Arm.San.P	Armeesanitätspark	army medical park
Arm.VOBL	Armeeverordnungsblatt	journal of decrees of an army
Arr	Arrest	detention
Arr	Arrestant	man under detention
Ars	Arsenal	arsenal
Art	Artillerie	artillery
Art.Abt	Artillerieabteilung	artillery battalion
Art.Beob.Abt	Artilleriebeobachtungsabteilung	artillery observation detachment
Art-Besch	Artilleriebeschiessung	artillery bombardment
Art.Ers.Abt	Artillerieersatzabteilung	artillery replacement training battalion
Art.Ers.Rgt	Artillerieersatzregiment	artillery replacement training regiment
Art.F	Artillerieführer	divisional artillery commander
Art.Fl	Artillerieflieger	artillery spotting pilot
Art.Kdr	Artilleriekommandeur	artillery commander from general headquarters pool
Art.Kol	Artilleriekolonne	artillery transport column
Art.Kr.Zgm	Artilleriekraftzugmaschine	artillery prime mover
Artl	Artillerie	artillery
Artl.Res	Artilleriereserve	artillery reserve
Artl.Rgt	Artillerieregiment	artillery regiment
Art.Mun.Kol	Artilleriemunitionskolonne	artillery munitions transport column
Art.Pk	Artilleriepark	artillery equipment park
Art.Rgt	Artillerieregiment	artillery regiment
Art. Sch	Artillerieschule	artillery school
Art.St.F	Artilleriestörungsfeuer	artillery harassing fire
Art. Str. F	Artilleriestreufeuer	artillery dispersion fire
Art.Verm.Tr	Artillerievermessungstrupp	artillery survey detachment
Art. Workst	Artilleriewerkstatt	artillery repair shop
Art.Zg	Artilleriezug	artillery platoon
As	Arsenik	arsenic
AS	Artillerieschule	artillery school
A.San.Abt	Armee-Sanitätsabteilung	army medical battalion
A.San.Pk	Armee-Sanitätspark	army medical park
A.Sch.Pl	Artillerieschiessplatz	artillery firing range
Ass.Arzt	Assistenzarzt	2d lieutenant, medical corps
A.St	Auswertestelle	computing station *(sound and flash ranging gunnery)*
Asta	Ausbildungsstab der Artillerie	artillery training staff
Asti	Ausbildungsstab der Infanterie	infantry training staff
Astr.Messzug	Astronomischer Messzug	astronomical survey platoon
At	Atmosphäre	atmosphere
A.T	Aussichtsturm	observation tower *(on maps)*
A.T.B	Armeetagesbefehl	army order of the day
Atm	Atmosphäre	atmosphere
Att	Attaché	attaché
Att	Attest	certificate
attach	attachiert	attached
Attr	Attrappe	dummy
Aubo	Aussenbordmotor	outboard motor
aufh	aufheben	to raise; to cancel
Aufkl	Aufklärung	reconnaissance
Aufkl.Abt	Aufklärungsabteilung	reconnaissance battalion
Aufkl.Ers.Abt	Aufklärungsersatzabteilung	reconnaissance replacement training battalion
Aufkl.Str	Aufklärungsstreitkräfte	combat reconnaissance forces
Aufl	Auflage	edition
Aufm	Aufmarsch	initial assembly for operations
Aufn	Aufnahme	reception; photograph; delaying action
Aufn.Stg	Aufnahmestellung	delaying position; rallying position
Aufn.Tr	Aufnahmetruppen	delaying troops

Auftr.	Auftrag	order; task; mission
Auftr.	Auftreff	impact (*gunnery*)
auftrw.	auftragsweise	in accordance with instructions
Ausb.	Ausbildung	training
Ausb. Offz.	Ausbildungsoffizier	training officer
Ausb. Pers.	Ausbildungspersonal	training personnel
Ausbr.	Ausbrennung	erosion (*of a barrel*)
Ausf.	Ausfall	sortie; loss
Ausf.	Ausführung	execution; completion
Ausf. Best.	Ausführungsbestimmungen	executory regulations
Ausf.V.	Ausführungsvorschrift	executory regulations
Ausg.	Ausgabe	issue; issuance
ausg.	ausgemustert	discharged
ausgen.	ausgenommen	excepted
Ausgp.	Ausgangspunkt	point of departure
Ausg. Stg.	Ausgangstellung	position of departure
aush.	ausheben	to draft
Aush.	Aushebung	conscription; draft
Ausl.	Ausland	foreign country
Ausl.Vertr.	Auslieferungsvertrag	extradition treaty
Ausr.	Ausrüstung	arms and equipment
Ausr. S.	Ausrückstärke	initial strength; marching-out strength
ausrück.	ausrückend	evacuating; marching out; decamping
Aussch.	Ausschuss	committee; commission
Auss.T.	Aussichtsturm	observation tower (*on maps*)
Auss.W.	Aussenwerk	outworks
autom.	automatisch	automatic
Autom. Gew.	Automatisches Gewehr	automatic rifle
A.V.	Armeeverpflegungslager	army supply depot
A.V.A.	Ausbildungsvorschrift für die Artillerie	artillery training regulations
AVBl.	Armeeverordnungsblatt	journal of decrees of an army
AVf.	Allgemeine Verfügung	general order
A.V.F.	Ausbildungsvorschrift für die Fahrtruppen	training regulations for service troops for animal-drawn trains
A.V.Flak	Ausbildungsvorschrift für Flak	antiaircraft training regulations
A.V.I.	Ausbildungsvorschrift für die Infanterie	infantry training regulations
A.V.K.	Ausbildungsvorschrift für die Kavallerie	cavalry training regulations
A.V.Kdo.	Artillerieverbindungskommando	artillery liaison detachment
A.V.KfK.	Ausbildungsvorschrift für die Kraftfahrkampftruppen	training regulations for motorized combat troops
A.V.Ko.	Artillerieverbindungskommando	artillery liaison detachment
A.V.Kraft.	Ausbildungsvorschrift für die Kraftfahrtruppen	training regulations for motor transport service troops
A.V.Lb.	Ausbildungsvorschrift für Leibesübungen	physical training regulations
A.V.N.	Ausbildungsvorschrift für die Nachrichtentruppen	training regulations for signal troops
A.V.O.	Artillerieverbindungsoffizier	artillery liaison officer
A.V.P.	Ausbildungsvorschrift für die Pioniere	training regulations for engineers
A.Vpfl.	Armee-Verpflegungsausgabestelle	army rations distribution point
A.V.S.	Ausbildungsvorschrift für die Scheinwerfertruppen	training regulations for searchlight troops
A.V.T.	Artillerievermessungstrupp	instrument section (*artillery*)
A.V.W.	Arbeitsverwendungsfähigkeit für die Wehrmacht	fitness for labor employment for the army
A.V.Z.	Arbeitsverwendungsfähigkeit, Zivil	fitness for labor employment for civil service
Aw.	Artilleriewerkstatt	artillery repair shop
A.W.	Atemwiderstand	breathing resistance (*gas mask*)
AW.	Aussenwache	outer guard
AWA.	Amtsgruppe Allgemeine Wehrmachtangelegenheiten	Section for General Armed Forces Matters
Az.	Aktenzeichen	file index number
A.Z.	Alarm zu Ende	all clear signal
A.Z.	Anforderungszeichen	requisition mark
AZ.	Aufschlagzünder	percussion fuze
a.Z.	auf Zeit	temporary
Az.	Auszeichnung	decoration; distinction
Az-Mun.	Aufschlagzündermunition	percussion fuze ammunition
Az.m.V.	Aufschlagzünder mit Verzögerung	percussion fuze with delay-action
A.Z.V.	Artilleriezielbauvorschrift	artillery target construction regulations

Aufstellungsbefehl *m* initial organization order (*to activate a unit*).
Aufstromvergaser *m* updraft carburetor.
Auftakt *m* initial phase (*of an operation*).
auftanken refuel.
Auftrag *m* mission, task (*Tac*).
"Auftrag erledigt!" "Mission accomplished!"
Auftragserteilung *f* assignment of missions, assignment of tasks.
Auftragskarte *f* flight diagram (*aerial Photo*).
Auftreffen *n* impact.
Auftreffgeschwindigkeit *f* striking velocity (*of projectile*).
Auftreffpunkt *m* point of impact.
Auftreffwinkel *m* angle of impact.
Auftrieb *m* buoyancy, lift (*Avn*).
Auftriebsmittelpunkt *m* center of lift (*Avn*).
Auftritt *m* fire step.
Aufwind *m* anabatic wind, up-slope wind.
Aufzeichnung *f* record, notation, sketch.
Aufziehachse *f* winding stem (*on blasting machine, watch, etc.*)
aufziehen to mount (*Photo*); pull up, lift, hoist; to mount (*guard*); to wind (*a watch, etc.*).
Aufziehen der Wache guard mount.
Aufziehleine *f* static line (*Prcht*).
Aufzug *m* elevator, hoist.
Augenabstand *m* interpupillary distance (*Optics*).
Augenaufklärung *f* visual reconnaissance.
Augenblicksziel *n* fleeting target, transient target, fleeting objective.
Augenblickszünder *m* instantaneous fuze, nondelay fuze, quick fuze.
Augenfenster *n* eyepiece (*gas mask*).
"Augen gerade, aus!" "Ready, front!"
"Augen, links!" "Eyes, left!" (*strictly*, "Die Augen, links!" *to distinguish preparatory command from that in* "Augen, rechts!").
Augenmuschel *f* eyeguard (*Optics*).
'Augen, rechts!" "Eyes, right!"
Augenreizstoff *m* lacrimator (*CWS*).
Augenring *m* eyepiece frame of goggles (*gas mask*).
Augenschlitz *m* viewing slit (*telescopic sight*).
Augenverbindung *f* visual communication.
Ausatemventil *n* outlet valve (*gas mask*).
Ausbau *m* construction; improvement (*of a position*); dismantling, removing, dismounting (*of a gun, etc.*)
ausbauen dismount (*Ord*); improve (*Ft*); remove, dismantle.
Ausbilder *m* instructor.
Ausbildung *f* training, drill.
Ausbildungsanweisungen *fpl* training order.
Ausbildungsgerät *n* training equipment, training instrument.
Ausbildungslager *n* training camp.
Ausbildungsplan *m* training schedule.
Ausbildungsrichtlinien *fpl* training outlines, training regulations.
Ausbildungsstab *m* training staff.
Ausbildungsstufe *f* training phase.
Ausbildungsvorschrift *f* training manual, drill regulations.
Ausblick *m* objective lens (*Optics*); prospect, view.
Ausblickprismengehäuse *n* objective-prism housing (*BC telescope*).
Ausblickstutzen *m* objective-lens socket (*Optics*).
Ausbootung *f* debarkation.
Ausbrennung *f* barrel erosion, erosion of the bore (*Ord*).
Ausbruch der Feindseligkeiten outbreak of hostilities.
Ausbuchtung *f* salient.
Ausdauer *f* endurance.
Ausdehnung *f* frontage (*Tac*); expansion, extension, spreading.
auseinandergehen diverge, separate.
auseinandernehmen to strip, disassemble, dismantle, take apart.
auseinanderziehen deploy, extend, spread out (*Tac*).
ausfahren to extend, to lower (*Ap landing gear, etc.*); to ride out, drive out.
Ausfahrgleis *n* outgoing track (*RR*).
Ausfall *m* sortie (*Tac*); long lunge, long thrust (*bayonet thrust*); casualty; failure, breakdown (*of an engine, etc.*); gun out of battery (*Arty*).
Ausfertigung *f* drawing up, writing out (*a report, etc.*).
in dreifacher Ausfertigung in triplicate.
ausfragen interrogate, question.
ausführen accomplish, carry out, execute.
Ausführung *f* execution, carrying out; design, model (*Tech*).
in zweifacher Ausführung in duplicate.
Ausführungskommando *n* command of execution (*drill*).
Ausgabe *f* issue; edition.
Ausgabestelle *f* point of issue, distributing point.

Ausgang *m* departure, outcome, exit, outlet, start.
Ausgangslage *f* assault position (*Tac*); starting position, original position.
Ausgangslinie *f* line of departure, jump-off line.
Ausgangsort *m* point of departure (*air navigation*).
Ausgangspunkt *m* initial point, origin, point of departure.
Ausgangsspannung *f* output voltage.
Ausgangsstellung *f* line of departure, jump-off position (*Tac*).
Ausgangstransformator *m* output transformer (*Rad*).
ausgeben to issue, distribute.
ausgeglichen balanced, equalized, equilibrated.
Ausgehanzug *m* dress uniform.
ausgehoben drafted; silenced (*slang*).
Ausgehobener *m* draftee.
Ausgehverbot *n* curfew (*Mil Govt*).
ausgemustert rejected as unfit. *See* **Musterung, Ausmusterungsschein.**
Ausgießgerät *n* *See* **Aus- und Abgießgerät.**
Ausgleich *m* equalization, compensation, equilibration, balancing.
Ausgleichdüse *f* compensating jet (*Mtr*).
ausgleichen to balance, compensate, equalize.
Ausgleicher *m* compensator (*Ord, Mech*); equilibrator (*G*).
Ausgleicherarm *m* equilibrator anchor (*G*).
Ausgleichfläche *f* balance tab, trim tab (*Ap*).
Ausgleichgetriebe *n* differential gear.
Ausgleichsperre *f* differential lock (*MT*).
ausglühen anneal.
ausheben to conscript, draft.
Aushebung *f* draft, conscription.
Aushilfe *f* expedient, substitute, auxiliary.
ausholen to lunge.
ausklinken to release (*bombs, etc.*).
Auskolkung *f* scour (*in a river bed*).
Auskreuzung *f* bracing, cross bracing (*Ap*).
auskundschaften to spy, to scout.
Auskunft *f* information.
Auskunftsstelle *f* information center, information office; control point.
auskuppeln disengage the clutch.
Ausladebahnhof *m* detraining point, railhead.
Ausladeeinheit *f* unloading unit.
Ausladegebiet *n* detrucking area.
Ausladekommando *n* unloading detail.
ausladen to unload, detruck, detrain, etc.
Ausladeplatz *m* detrucking point.
Auslader *m* stevedore.
Ausladespitze *f* railhead, truckhead.
Ausladestelle *f* detrucking point.
Ausladeübersicht *f* detraining or unloading table.
Ausland *n* foreign country.
im Ausland abroad.
Ausländer *m* alien, foreigner.
feindlicher Ausländer enemy alien.
Auslaßrohr *n* eduction tube (*Cml cylinder*).
Auslaßventil *n* exhaust valve (*Mtr*).
Auslaßventilkammer *f* exhaust port.
Auslauf *m* outlet (*for liquids, etc.*).
auslaufen to run out; to complete a run after landing; to put to sea.
auslegen to pay out (*rope, wire, etc.*); to explain, interpret; to expose, extend; to lay out (*money*).
Ausleger *m* pack rest (*harness*); outrigger (*boats and floats*) (*AA gun*); boom (*of a crane or derrick*).
Auslegerbrücke *f* cantilever bridge.
Auslegezeichen *n* ground panel (*Sig C*).
Ausleseknopf *m* selector switch (*Ap armament control*).
Auslieferung *f* delivery; exposure (*to danger, the elements, etc.*).
auslöschen extinguish, put out (*a fire*).
Auslöseeinrichtung *f* release mechanism (*bombing*).
Auslöseknopf *m* release button.
Auslösepunkt *m* bomb release point, release point.
Auslösung *f* release (*of bombs, etc.*).
Ausmaß *n* dimension.
ausmerzen eliminate, eradicate.
Ausmusterungsschein *m* certificate of rejection (*for those unfit for Mil service*).
Ausnahmegespräch *n* urgent call (*Tp*).
Ausnahmezustand *m* state of emergency.
ausnutzen to exploit, to utilize fully.
Auspuff *m* exhaust, exhaust system (*Mtr*).
Auspuffgeräusch *n* exhaust noise.
Auspuffhub *m* exhaust stroke (*Mtr*).
Auspuffkanal *m* exhaust duct (*Mtr*).
Auspuffklappe *f* cutout (*Mtr*).
Auspuffkrümmer *m* exhaust manifold (*Mtr*).
Auspuffleitung *f* exhaust duct (*Mtr*).
Auspufftakt *m* exhaust stroke (*Mtr*).
Auspufftopf *m* muffler (*Mtr*).

Auspuffwolke *f* exhaust smoke (*Mtr*).
ausräuchern to smoke out; to fumigate.
ausrichten to dress (*drill*); to perform; to level, straighten.
sich nach links ausrichten to dress left.
Ausrichtung *f* orientation; straightening, leveling.
Ausrollen *n* landing run (*Avn*).
ausrotten wipe out, crush, annihilate.
ausrücken disengage (*gears, etc.*); depart, move up.
Ausrüstung *f* equipment, outfit, accessories, accouterments.
Ausrüstungsgegenstand *m* item of equipment.
Ausrüstungsnachweisung *f* table of equipment.
Ausrüstungsstück *n* accessory, piece of equipment.
Aussage *f* statement.
Ausschalen *n* stripping the forms (*concrete construction*).
Ausschaltehebel *m* throwout lever (*aiming circle*).
ausschalten disconnect, detach, cut out, eliminate, switch off, throw out; compensate for, correct (*an error, etc.*) (*Gunnery*).
Ausschalten der besonderen und Witterungseinflüsse ballistic correction, *i.e.* correction for interior and exterior ballistic factors.
Ausschalten der Grundstufe calibration correction, correction for velocity error (*Gunnery*). *See also* **Grundstufe.**
Ausschalten der Schnittbildversetzung halving adjustment (*coincidence range finder*).
Ausschalten der Temperatureinflüsse elasticity correction (*Gunnery*).
Ausschalten des Schallverzuges acoustic correction (*sound locator*).
Ausschalten des Windes wind correction (*Gunnery*).
Ausschalter *m* switch; throwout (*lever*).
ausscheiden to detach, to detail; to eliminate (*impurities, etc.*); to drop out, leave, separate.
ausscheren to fall out of formation (*Avn*); to fall out of line (*Nav*).
ausschiffen debark, disembark.
Ausschiffung *f* debarkation, disembarkation.
ausschirren unharness.
Ausschlag *m* decisive factor; rash (*Med*).
ausschlaggebend decisive.
ausschließen interdict; exclude.
Ausschließungsschein *m* certificate of exclusion from military service (*for criminals, subversive elements, etc.*).
Ausschuß *m* board, committee, commission.
ausschwärmen deploy (*Tac*).
ausschweben hold off (*in landing*) (*Avn*).
ausschwingen die out, die down (*oscillations*).
Außenantenne *f* outside antenna.
Außenaufhängung *f* external suspension (*of bombs*).
Außenbackenbremse *f* external contracting brake (*MT*).
Außenbefestigungen *fpl* (*Ft*) outworks
Außenbordmotor *m* outboard motor.
Außengrenzlehre *f* snap gage.
Außenhafen *m* outer harbor.
Außenhaut *f* skin, skin cover, covering (*Ap*).
Außenlandung *f* off-field landing (*Avn*).
Außenluftdruck *m* barometric pressure (*Avn*).
Außenluft-Thermometer *n* free-air thermometer (*Ap*).
Außenschieber *m* outer sleeve (*sleeve-type engine*).
Außenstelle *f* outlying station or post.
Außenverspannung *f* external bracing (*Ap*).
Außenwache *f* exterior guard.
Außenwerke *npl* outworks (*Ft*).
außerballistisch pertaining to exterior ballistics.
außer Betrieb out of order, not working.
außer Dienst retired (*abbr.* a.D.).
außer Gefecht gesetzt put out of action.
äußere Ballistik exterior ballistics.
außerplanmäßig exceeding authorized basic allowance or strength; not in accordance with plans; extraordinary.
aussenden to dispatch, send out, transmit.
Aussetzen *n* posting (*of guards*); cessation (*of rain, fire, etc.*).
Aussichtsturm *m* observation tower.
aussondern to sort.
ausspähen to spy, reconnoiter.
Ausspähung *f* espionage, reconnaissance, spying.
aussparen to leave untouched, to bypass.
ausspringender Winkel salient.
ausstatten equip.

auswechselbares Seelenrohr removable liner *(G)*.
Ausweichbewegung *f* evading movement, withdrawing movement to new position *(Tac)*.
aussteigen bail out *(Avn slang)*.
Ausstoßbüchse *f* smoke canister ejected from projectile on burst.
Ausstoßen *n* exhaust stroke *(Mtr)*; expulsion.
ausstoßen to expel, eliminate, cashier.
Ausstrahlung *f* radiation.
Austausch *m* exchange *(PW, etc.)*.
austauschbar interchangeable.
Austauschschiff *n* exchange ship, cartel ship *(Nav)*.
Austauschstoff *m* substitute material.
austreten relieve oneself, attend to one's needs.
Aus- und Abgießgerät *n* gas-spraying apparatus *(Ap, CWS)*.
Auswanderungsmesser *m* lead computer *(AA)*.
Auswanderungsstrecke *f* linear travel of target, leg between present and future positions *(AAA)*.
auswärtig foreign.
auswechselbar interchangeable, removable.
ausweichen evade, give way, withdraw, fall back *(Tac)*.
Ausweichflugplatz *m* dispersal landing field.
Ausweichgleis *n* siding *(RR)*.
Ausweichhafen *m* alternate airport.
Ausweichstelle *f* bypass *(Road)*; siding *(RR)*.
Ausweichstellung *f* alternate position.
Ausweichvermittlung *f* alternate routing *(emergency Tp Com)*.
Ausweichziel *n* alternate target, secondary target *(bombing)*.
Ausweis *m* identification *(card, document, etc.)*; pass, permit.
Ausweiskarte *f* identification card, pass, permit.
Ausweispapier *n* identification papers.
Auswerfer *m* ejector *(Ord)*.
Auswerfervorrichtung *f* ejector mechanism *(Ord)*.
Auswertelineal *n* computing slide rule *(FR)*.
auswerten evaluate, interpret, compute, plot *(maps)*.
Auswertestelle *f* computing station *(SR)*.
Auswertung *f* evaluation, interpretation.
Auszeichnung *f* decoration, medal.
ausziehen extract, draw out, pull out.
Auszieher *m* extractor *(Ord)*.
Ausziehgleis *n* lead track *(RR)*.
Auszug *m* extract, summary, departure; extension *(Tech)*.
Autobahn *f* automobile express highway.
Autofrettage *f* cold-drawing, autofrettage *(Ord)*.
Autokartograph *m* stereoscopic plotting machine.
Autokolonne *f* motor vehicle column, motor march column.
automatische Kurssteuerung automatic pilot, mechanical pilot *(Ap)*.
Autoschleppstart *m* auto-tow take-off
Axt *f* ax.
Azetylen *n* acetylene.
Azetylensauerstoffbrenner *m* oxyacetylene torch.
Azimut *n* azimuth.
Azimutalprojektion *f* azimuthal projection.
Azimutentfernungsmesser *m* depression position finder.

B

Bach *m* stream, brook, rivulet.
Bachübergang *m* stream crossing.
Backbord *n* port side.
Backbordmotor *m* port engine.
Backe *f* cheek.
Backenbremse *f* shoe brake *(MT)*.
Backenschiene *f* stock rail *(RR)*.
Backenstück *n* cheek strap *(harness)*.
Bäckerei *f* bakery.
Bäckereikompanie *f* bakery company.
Badewagen *m* shower-bath truck.
Bagger *m* excavator, dredge, power shovel.
Bahn *f* path, road; runway; railroad; orbit; course; trajectory.
Bahnanlage *f* railroad installation.
Bahndamm *m* railroad embankment.
Bahnhof *m* railroad station; trolley or bus station.
Bahnhofsleistung *f* station capacity *(number of trains loaded or unloaded per day)*.
Bahnhofsoffizier *m* railroad station traffic officer.
Bahnhofswachabteilung *f* railroad station guard detachment.
Bahnkörper *m* roadbed *(RR)*.
Bahnkrone *f* crown of roadbed *(RR)*.
Bahnplanum *n* subgrade *(RR)*.
Bahnsteig *m* platform *(RR)*.
Bahnsteigunterführung *f* platform underpass *(RR)*.
Bahntransport *m* railroad transportation.
Bahnüberführung *f* overpass *(RR)*.
Bahnübergang *m* railroad crossing.
Bahnunterführung *f* underpass *(RR)*.
Bahnverbindung *f* railroad line, railroad communication.
Bajonett *n* bayonet. *See also* **Seitengewehr.**
Bajonettangriff *m* bayonet charge.
Bajonettfechten *n* bayonet fighting.
Bajonettgriff *m* bayonet grip.
Bajonettkupplung *f* bayonet joint.
Bajonettstoß *m* bayonet thrust.
Bajonettverschluß *m* bayonet lock, bayonet joint.
Bake *f* beacon; navigation guide, channel marker, landmark *(Nav)*.
Bakenempfang *m* radio-beacon reception.
Bakterienkrieg *m* bacteriological warfare.
Baldachin *m* canopy *(center section of upper wing of biplane)*.
Balken *m* balk, beam; girder; log.
Balkenbahn *f* timber road.
Balkenfloß *n* timber raft.
Balkensperre *f* timber road block.
schwimmende Balkensperre floating boom.
Balkenstapel *m* log crib, timber crib *(Bdg)*.
Balkenverhau *m* timber obstacle.
Ballen *m* bulb *(horse)*; heel *(harness)*; bale.
Ballistik *f* ballistics.
ballistische Tageseinflüsse ballistic density and wind factors.
Ballistit *n* ballistite *(Am)*.
Ballon *m* balloon.
Ballonabweiser *m* anti-balloon device *(Ap)*.
Ballonamme *f* supply balloon, nurse balloon.
Ballonaufstiegplatz *m* balloon site.
Ballonbatterie *f* observation balloon section *(Arty)*.
Ballonbeobachter *m* balloon observer.
Ballonbeobachtung *f* balloon observation.
Ballonführer *m* balloon pilot.
Ballongurt *m* rigging band *(captive Bln)*.
Ballonhülle *f* envelope, gas bag, outer cover, balloon cover.
Ballonkorb *m* balloon basket.
Ballonmannschaft *f* balloon crew.
Ballonnetz *n* balloon net.
Ballonreifen *m* balloon tire.
Ballonsperre *f* balloon barrage.
Ballonstoff *m* balloon fabric.
Ballonvariometer *n* balloon statoscope.
Ballonventil *n* gas valve *(Bln)*.
Ballonwinde *f* balloon winch.
Balta *See* **ballistische Tageseinflüsse.**
Baltasekunden *fpl* ballistic density and wind factors in time-of-flight seconds.
Baltasekunden-Verfahren *n* procedure in correcting for ballistic density and wind.
Bananenstecker *m* banana plug.
Band *n* band, cord, tape, strip, ribbon.
Bandbreite *f* band width *(Rad)*.
Bandbremse *f* band brake *(MT)*.
Bändchenmikrophon *n* *See* **Bandmikrophon.**
Bandfeder *f* flat coil spring *(fuze)*.
Bandgestell *n* harness *(gas mask)*.
Bandmikrophon *n* ribbon microphone.
Bandsäge *f* band saw.
Bandspreizung *f* bandspread *(Rad)*.
Bank *f* bench; lathe; bank; parapet, barbette.
Bannware *f* contraband of war.
Baracke *f* temporary barracks, semipermanent cantonment building.
Barackenlager *n* cantonment, camp having semipermanent buildings.
Barbarabehelfsmeldung *f* hasty meteorological message *(Arty)*.
Barbarameldung *f* meteorological message *(Arty)* *(from* Barbara, *patron saint of Arty)*.
Barbarist *m* artilleryman *(slang)*. *See also* **Barbarameldung.**
Barbarasondermeldung *f* special meteorological message *(Arty)*.
Barbette *f* barbette.
Barbettelafette *f* barbette carriage, barbette mount *(G)*.
Bargeld *n* cash.
barometrische Reglerdose control aneroid *(Ap engine)*.
barometrisches Gefälle pressure gradient *(Met)*.
Basis *f* base; horizontal base *(Btry Surv)*.
Basislineal *n* base-line arm *(plotting protractor)*.
Bataillon *n* battalion.
Bataillonsabschnitt *m* battalion sector.
Bataillons-Adjutant *m* battalion executive officer, aide to battalion commander.
Bataillonsführer *m* battalion commander; acting battalion commander.
Bataillonsgefechtsstand *m* battalion command post.
Bataillonshornist *m* drum major *(formerly called* Tambourmajor).
Bataillonskolonne *f* battalion train.
Bataillons-Kommandeur *m* battalion commander.
Bataillonsnachrichtenstaffel *f* battalion communication section.
Bataillonsstab *m* battalion staff, battalion headquarters.
Bataillonstambourstock *m* baton.
Bataillonstroß *m* battalion train.
Bataillonsverbandplatz *m* battalion aid station.
Batterie *f* battery *(Arty, Elec)*.
Batteriebild *n* battery-location plot *(SR)*.
Batteriechef *m* battery commander.
Batteriefront *f* battery front.
Batterieführer *m* battery commander; acting battery commander.
Batteriekasten *m* battery box *(Elec)*.
Batteriekran *m* gun hoist, loading crane *(Arty)*.
Batterieoffizier *m* executive *(firing Btry)*.
Batterieplan *m* firing chart *(Arty)*.
Batteriestand *m* *See* **Batteriestellung.**
Batteriestellung *f* battery position *(Arty)*.
Batterietafel *f* battery manning table *(Arty)*.
Batterietrupp *m* battery detail, battery headquarters detail, battery commander's detail *(Arty)*.
Batteriezündung *f* battery ignition *(Mtr)*.
Bau *m* construction, structure, type of construction.
Bauart *f* type of construction.
Bauausführung *f* construction, structural design.
Baubataillon *n* construction battalion.
Bauch *m* abdomen, belly.
Bauchfreiheit *f* chassis clearance *(MT)*.
Bauchgurt *m* front cinch *(pack saddle)*.
Bauchlandung *f* belly landing *(Avn)*.
Bauchtreffer *m* sidewise-striking projectile.
Bauglied *n* structural unit, section of a structure, structure element.
Bauholz *n* lumber.
Baukompanie *f* construction company *(Mil)*.
Baumaß *n* structural dimensions.
Baumbeobachtungsstand *m* observation post in a tree.
Baumschütze *m* sniper in a tree.
Baumsperre *f* abatis, dead abatis.
Baumstamm *m* tree trunk.
Baumstammkufe *f* log runner *(log sled)*.
Baumstumpf *m* tree stump.
Baumuster *n* model, type *(Ap, MT)*.
Baumverhau *m* live abatis.
Baumwollabfall *m* cotton waste, cotton linters.
Baumwolle *f* cotton.
Bausoldat *m* engineer soldier in construction unit.
Baustab *m* construction staff.
Baustange *f* lance pole *(Tp)*.
Bautrupp *m* construction detail, construction squad.
Bautruppen *fpl* construction troops.
Bauunternehmer *m* contractor, builder.
Bauweise *f* type of construction or structure, method of construction.
Beamter *m* official, civil servant. *See also* **Wehrmachtbeamter.**
Beanspruchung *f* load, stress, strain.
beaufsichtigen supervise.
Beauftragter *m* representative.
bebaute Felder cultivated fields.
bebautes Gelände built-up area.
Bedarf *m* requirements.
bedeckt covered, overgrown; overcast *(Met)*.
fast bedeckt broken *(Met)*.
Bedeckung *f* coverage *(Met)*; escort, convoy, cover *(Tac)*.
Bedeckungsabteilung *f* covering party, escort detachment.
Bedeckungsmannschaft *f* escort personnel.
Bediener *m* controller *(AA SL)*.
Bedienung *f* gun squad; service of the piece.
Bedienungsanweisung *f* operating directions.
Bedienungseinrichtung *f* control device, operating device.
Bedienungsentlastung *f* relief of strain on pilot *(Avn)*.
Bedienungsmannschaft *f* gun crew, gun squad.
Bedienungsplatte *f* operating panel *(Rad)*.
Bedienungsschalter *m* operating switch *(Elec)*.
Bedienungsvorschrift *f* operating instructions.
bedingungslose Übergabe unconditional surrender.
Bedrohung *f* threat.
Beendigung der Luftgefahr "all clear."

B

B	Bach	brook *(on maps)*
B	Bäckerei	bakery
B	Ballon	balloon
B	Bataillon	battalion
B	Batterie	battery
B	Bau	construction
B	Bedienungsmann	member of gun crew
B	Befehl	order; command officer
b	bei	by; near; close to
B	Belagerung	siege
B	Beobachtung	observation
B	Beobachtungsstelle	observation post
B	Bereitschaft	readiness; preparedness
B	Berg	mountain *(on maps)*
B	Betriebs-	operating; working; traffic
B	Bettungsgeschütz	outrigger-base gun; gun on platform mounting
b	bewegliches	movable
B	Bombenwurf	bombing *(airplane)*
B	Brief	letter
B	Brieftaubenmeister	carrier pigeon sergeant
B	Brücke	bridge *(on maps)*
B	Brunnen	well; spring; fountain *(on ma*
B	Bucht	bay; inlet *(on maps)*
B	Büchse	rifle names)
B	Feldbäckereikolonne	field bakery column office
B.A	Bekleidungsamt	clothing depot ports
BA	Beschaffungsamt	procurement office
BA	Bespannungsabteilung	horse-drawn detachment
BA	Betriebsamt	operations office *(railway)*
B.Abt	Bauabteilung	building and construction department; construction unit
B.Abt	Beobachtungsabteilung	artillery observation or survey battalion *(sound and fl*
Bäck	Bäckerei	bakery
Bäck.K	Bäckereikompanie	bakery company
Bäck.Kol	Bäckereikolonne	bakery column
Baj	Bajonett	bayonet
baj	bajonettieren	to bayonet
Baj.Gew	Bajonettiergewehr	dummy rifle for bayonet practice
B.A.K	Ballonabwehrkanone	antiballoon gun
BAK	Bekleidungsamt Kiel	Kiel clothing depot
Ball	Ballistik	ballistics
Ball	Ballon	balloon
Ball.Bttr	Ballonbatterie	observation balloon battery
Balta	Ballistiche Tageseinflüsse	error of the moment *(ballistics)*
Balta-sekunden	Ballistische Tageseinflüsse, gestaffelt nach Flugzeitsekunden	error of the moment, distributed along time of flight curve *(ballistics)*
Bar	Baracke	barracks
Bark	Barkasse	motor launch
Barom	Barometer	barometer
Barrik	Barrikade	barricade
B.Art	Beobachtungsstelle der Artillerie	artillery observation post
Batl	Bataillon	battalion
Batls.Nachr. Zug	Bataillonsnachrichtenzug	battalion signal platoon
Batt	Batterie	battery
Battr	Batterie	battery
Battr.Tr	Batterietrupp	battery headquarters detachment
Bau.Btl	Baubataillon	construction battalion
Bauv.O.(Heer)	Bauverwaltungsordnung für das Heer	building and construction administration regulations for the Army
BAW	Bekleidungsamt Wilhelmshaven	Wilhelmshaven clothing depot
Bb	Beobachtungsbatterie	observation battery
BB	Gruppe Berlin-Brandenburg (SA)	Berlin-Brandenburg group *(Storm Troopers)*
Bb	Stab einer Beobachtungsabteilung	staff of an observation or survey battalion *(artillery)*
B.Btl	Baubataillon	construction battalion
Bbv	Bahnbevollmächtigter für Militär-Angelegenheiten	authorized railroad agent for military matters
B.d.A	Befehlshaber der Aufklärungsschiffe	commander of cruisers
B.d.A	Befehlshaber der Aufklärungsstreitkräfte	commander of reconnaissance cruiser forces
B.D.A	Besoldungsdienstalter	longevity *(pay)*; increment
B.d.A.d.O	Befehlshaber der Aufklärungsschiffe in der Ostsee	commander of cruisers in the Baltic Sea
B.d.E	Befehlshaber des Ersatzheeres	Commander of the Replacement Training Army
B.d.E	Befehlshaber des Ersatzwesens	chief of recruitment service
Bdfu	Bordfunker	board radio operator *(aviation; navy)*
B.d.G	Befehlshaber der Gendarmerie	commander of the local police
Bd.G	Brandgeschoss	incendiary shell

B.d.L.	Befehlshaber der Linienschiffe	commander of battleship force
B.d.L.	Befehlshaber der Luftstreitkräfte	Commander of the Air Forces
Bd.-MG.-T.	Boden-Maschinengewehrturm	bottom machine-gun turret (*airplane*)
B.d.O.	Befehlshaber der Ordnungspolizei	Chief of the Regular Police
B.d.S.d.N.	Befehlshaber der Sicherungsstreitkräfte der Nordsee	commander of the security forces of the North Sea
B.d.S.d.O.	Befehlshaber der Sicherungsstreitkräfte der Ostsee	commander of the security forces of the Baltic Sea
B.d.Sipo u.d.SD	Befehlshaber der Sicherheitspolizei und des Sicherheitsdienstes	Chief of Security Police and of the SS Security Service
bd.taug.	bedingt tauglich	conditionally fit
b.d.Tr.	bei der Truppe	with the troops
Bd.Z.	Bodenzünder	base percussion fuze; base detonator fuze
B.E.	besondere Einflüsse	special factors (*ballistics*)
Bed.	Bedarf	requirement
bed.	bedeutet	means
Bed.	Bedeutung	meaning
bed.	Bedienen	to serve; to operate
Bed.	Bedienung	gun crew; service
Bef.	Befähigung	qualification
Bef.	Befehl	order; command
Bef.	Befeuerung	firing; lighthouse service
Bef.	Beförderung	promotion; transport
Bef. A.	Befehlsausgabe	issuance of orders; distribution of orders
Bef.E.	Befehlsempfänger	message orderly; runner
Bef.E.	Befehlsempfang	receipt of order
Befest.	Befestigung	fortification; fastening
Bef.Gr.	Befestigungsgruppe	group of fortifications
Befh.	Befehlshaber	commander; commanding officer
Befhb.	Befehlshaber	commander; commanding officer
Befh.d.P.	Befehlshaber der Polizei	commander of police
Beg.Gef.	Begegnungsgefecht	meeting engagement
Begl.	Begleit-	accompanying
Begl.Zg.	Begleitzug	accompanying platoon (*of machine-gun company*)
beh.	behelfsmässig	emergency; hasty; makeshift
behelfsm.	behelfsmässig	emergency; hasty; makeshift
behelfsm.Bef.	behelfsmässige Befestigung	hasty fortification
Beh San. A.	Behandlung der Sanitätsausrüstung	care of medical supplies
Beil.	Beilage	annex; enclosure; appendix
beil.	beiliegend	enclosed
Beitr.O.	Beitreibungsordnung	procedure of requisition
Beiwg.	Beiwagen	sidecar
Bekl.	Bekleidung	clothing; uniform
Bekl.A.	Bekleidungsamt	clothing depot
Bekl.Fw.	Bekleidungsfeldwebel	clothing sergeant
Bekl.N.	Bekleidungs- und Ausrüstungsnachweisung	clothing and equipment tables
Bekl.Uffz.	Bekleidungsunteroffizier	clothing noncommissioned officer
Bekl.Ufw.	Bekleidungsunterfeldwebel	clothing sergeant
Bekl.V.	Bekleidungsvorschrift	clothing regulations
Bel.	Belag	overlay (*harness*); planking (*bridge*); covering; plank flooring; surface (*road*)
Bel.	Belagerung	siege
Bel.	Belastung	load; charge; burden; stress
bel.	belegen	to shell; to occupy; to cover
bel.	belegt	shelled; occupied; covered
bel.	beleuchten	to illuminate
Belag.	Belagerung	siege
Belast.	Belastung	load; charge; burden; stress
Belehr.Mp.	Belehrungsmappe	instructional map
Beleucht.Ger.	Beleuchtungsgerät	illumination equipment
Bel.Zust.	Belagerungszustand	state of siege
Beob.	Beobachter; Beobachtung	observer; observation
Beob.Abt.	Beobachtungsabteilung	artillery observation or survey battalion (*sound and flash*)
Beob.Battr.	Beobachtungsbatterie	observation battery
Beob.Ger.	Beobachtungsgerät	observation instruments
Beob.P.	Beobachtungspunkt	observation point
Beob.Pkt.	Beobachtungspunkt	observation point
Beob.Sch.	Beobachterschule	observers' school (*aviation*)
Beob.T.	Beobachtungsturm	observation tower (*on maps*)
Beob.W.	Beobachtungswagen	reconnaissance car (*for battery observation*)
Ber.	Bereitschaft	readiness; preparedness
ber.	beritten	mounted
Ber. Büchse	Bereitschaftsbüchse	canister (*gas mask*)
Bereitsch. K.	Bereitschafts-Kompanie	company in readiness
Ber. F.	Berittführer	section corporal (*cavalry*)
Berghsr.	Berghäuser	mountain houses (*on maps*)
Ber. Inf. Kp.	berittene Infanteriekompanie	mounted infantry company

Beerdigung *f* burial.
Befehl *m* order, command.
"Zu Befehl!" "Yes, sir!" *(in acknowledgment of an order).*
Befehlsausgabe *f* briefing, issuance of orders.
Befehlsbefugnis *f* authority *(Mil).*
Befehlsbereich *m* extent of command.
Befehlsbestätigung *f* confirmatory order.
Befehlserteilung *f* issuance of orders.
Befehlsgebäude *n* control tower *(Adrm).*
Befehlsgebung *f* giving of commands.
befehlsgemäß according to instructions, as ordered.
Befehlsgewalt *f* command, authority of command.
Befehlsgruppe *f* command group.
Befehlshaber *m* commander.
Befehlshaber des Ersatzheeres *See* **Chef der Heeresrüstung und Befehlshaber des Ersatzheeres.**
Befehlsnetz *n* command net.
Befehlspanzer *m* command tank.
Befehlssprache *f* terminology of orders.
Befehlsstand *m* command post, headquarters.
Befehlsstelle *f* control tower *(Adrm)*; command post, headquarters.
Befehlsübermittlung *f* transmission of orders.
Befehlsverhältnisse *npl* chain of command.
Befehlswagen *m* command car, command truck, commander's car, staff car.
Befehlsweg *m* chain of command, command channel.
befestigt fortified; secured, tied, fastened.
Befestigung *f* fortification.
Befestigungsanlage *f* fortified defense system.
Befestigungsarbeiten *fpl* fortifications, works.
Befestigungswerk *n* permanent fortification, work.
befeuern to mark or light with beacon lights *(an airway or Adrm).*
befördern to forward *(supplies, etc.)*; promote; transmit.
Beförderung *f* advancement, promotion; transmission, forwarding, transportation.
Beförderungsliste *f* promotion list.
Beförderungsmittel *n* carrier, vehicle; means of transportation; means of transmission.
Befragung *f* questioning *(of PW, etc.).*
Befugnis *f* authority, powers.
begasen to gas *(CWS).*
Begasung *f* laying of gas obstacles, gassing *(CWS).*
Begegnungsgefecht *n* meeting engagement.
beglaubigen certify, authenticate, verify, confirm.
beglaubigt authenticated, certified, notarized, verified, confirmed.
Beglaubigung *f* authentication, certification, confirmation, verification.
Begleitartillerie *f* accompanying artillery.
Begleitbatterie *f* accompanying battery.
Begleiter *m* escort; assistant driver.
Begleitfeuer *n* accompanying fire.
Begleitgeschütz *n* accompanying gun.
Begleitkommando *n* escort party, escort detachment, covering party.
Begleitpanzer *m* accompanying tank.
Begleitschiff *n* escort vessel.
Begleitschutz *m* escort, fighter escort *(Avn).*
Begleitzettel *m* emergency medical tag.
Begleitzug *m* convoy.
Begräbnis *n* burial.
begrenztes Ziel limited objective.
Begrenzungshebel *m* clamping lever *(MG).*
Begrenzungsstift *m* traversing stop *(MG).*
Behälter *m* gasoline tank; container.
Behandlung *f* treatment.
Beharrungsvermögen *n* inertia.
Behelf *m* expedient, makeshift.
Behelfsantenne *f* emergency antenna.
Behelfsbrücke *f* emergency bridge, hasty bridge.
Behelfsflоßsack *m* emergency pneumatic boat.
Behelfsgasschutz *m* emergency gas protection.
Behelfslandebrücke *f* hasty landing stage.
behelfsmäßig improvised, hasty, emergency, temporary, auxiliary, makeshift.
Behelfsmaterial *n* emergency construction material.
beherrschend commanding, dominating.
Behinderungsschießen *n* interdiction fire.
Behmlot *n* fathometer, echo depth sounder *(Nav)*; Behm sound-ranging altimeter, sonic altimeter *(Ap).*

Behörde *f* authority *(Adm, Law).*
behördlich zugelassen authorized, officially sanctioned.
beibringen inflict *(losses, etc.).*
Beiende *n* warp *(of a rope).*
Beifahrer *m* rear rider, sidecar rider *(Mtcl)*; assistant driver *(MT).*
beifügen add; attach, enclose.
beiklappbar folding.
Beil *n* ax.
Beiladung *f* igniting charge, igniter, booster charge *(Am).*
Beilage *f* enclosure, supplement *(in a manual, etc.).*
Beilpicke *f* pickax.
Beinleder *npl* leather puttees, leather leggins.
Beisitzer *m* law member.
Beißzange *f* nippers.
beitragen contribute to, cooperate.
beitreiben to requisition *(from civilians)*; to commandeer.
Beitreibung *f* requisitioning *(from civilians).*
Beitreibungsschein *m* requisition receipt *(for civilian property).*
Beiwagen *m* sidecar *(Mtcl).*
Beiwagenkrad *n* sidecar motorcycle.
Beiwert *m* coefficient.
Bekanntgabe *f* announcement.
bekleiden to revet *(Ft)*; to clothe; to hold *(office).*
Bekleidung *f* revetment *(Ft)*; clothing.
Bekleidungsentgiftung *f* clothing decontamination.
Bekleidungsnachweis *m* clothing account.
Bekleidungssack *m* duffle bag, barrack(s) bag.
Bekleidungsstück *n* article of clothing.
Beköstigungsgeld *n* garrison ration.
Beköstigungsmittel *npl* ration supplies, subsistence supplies.
Beladeplan *m* stowage chart *(for vehicle).*
Belag *m* planking *(Bdg)*; reinforcing strap *(harness).*
belagern besiege.
Belagerung *f* siege.
Belagerungszustand *m* state of siege.
belästigen to annoy, harass *(Tac).*
Belastung *f* load, maximum load *(Engr)*; inductance *(Rad).*
bleibende Belastung basic load *(Ap).*
Belastungsfaktor *m* load coefficient.
Belastungsprobe *f* load test.
Beleg *m* voucher, proof, evidence, document.
belegen to cover *(with fire)*, to fire on, to shell; to billet.
Belegung *f* coverage; shelling; billeting, quartering; condenser plate *(Rad).*
Belegungsstärke *f* density of gas coverage *(CWS).*
Belehrungsschießen *n* instruction firing.
Belehrungs- und Versuchsschießen *n* special service practice *(Arty).*
beleuchten illuminate, light.
Beleuchtung *f* illumination.
Beleuchtungsfenster *n* illuminating window *(panoramic sight).*
Belichtung *f* exposure *(Photo).*
beliefern to deliver, to supply.
Belüftung *f* ventilation.
Belüftungsanlage *f* ventilation system.
Bemannung *f* complement, crew.
benachrichtigen inform.
Benennung *f* nomenclature.
Benzin *n* gasoline.
Benzinbehälter *m* gasoline tank.
Benzinkanister *m* gasoline container.
Benzinmanometer *n* gasoline pressure gage.
Benzinstandmesser *m* fuel gage.
Benzol *n* benzol.
Beobachter *m* observer; air observer, navigator-observer.
Beobachterabzeichen *n* observer badge *(decoration).*
Beobachterfernrohr *n* observer telescope.
Beobachtersitz *m* observer's seat *(Ap).*
beobachtetes Schießen observed fire.
Beobachtung *f* observation; spotting *(Arty).*
Beobachtung der Längenabweichung vertical spotting *(Arty).*
Beobachtungsabteilung *f* observation battalion *(Arty).*
Beobachtungsbereich *m* observation area *(Arty).*
Beobachtungsfehler *m* personnel error.
Beobachtungsfernrohr *n* observation telescope *(BC telescope).*
Beobachtungskorb *m* observer's basket *(captive Bln).*
Beobachtungskuppel *f* cupola *(Tk).*
Beobachtungsmine *f* controlled mine, observation mine *(Nav).*
Beobachtungsnetz *n* observation post system *(Arty).*
Beobachtungsoffizier *m* observation post officer *(Arty).*
Beobachtungspatrone *f* explosive smoke-producing observation cartridge.

Beobachtungsraum *m* searching sector *(AAA)*: observation area.
Beobachtungsrohr *n* trench periscope.
Beobachtungsstand *m* *See* **Beobachtungsstelle.**
Beobachtungsstelle *f* observation post.
Beobachtungsturm *m* cupola *(Tk).*
Beobachtungs- und Wirkungsstreifen *m* sector of fire *(SA firing).*
Beobachtungswagen *m* observer's car.
Beobachtungswinkel *m* aiming point offset *(Arty).*
Beobachtung von seitlicher Beobachtungsstelle flank spotting *(Arty).*
Berater *m* adviser.
berechnen calculate.
Berechtigung *f* authorization; justification.
Bereich *m* area, district, zone; range, scope.
Bereifung *f* tires, set of tires.
bereit ready.
Bereitschaft *f* alert, preparedness, readiness.
Bereitschaften *fpl* alerted reserve troops or police.
Bereitschaftsbaracke *f* cantonment building for troops on the alert, alert hut.
Bereitschaftsbataillon *n* reserve battalion.
Bereitschaftslazarett *n* mobile surgical unit.
Bereitschaftsmunition *f* ammunition at the gun, ammunition kept in readiness *(Arty).*
Bereitstellung *f* moving into assembly area or position; assembly position, position of readiness *(Tac)*; making ready, preparation.
Bereitstellungsbefehl *m* assembly order.
Bereitstellungsplatz *m* assembly position, assembly point *(Tac).*
Bereitstellungsraum *m* assembly area *(Tac).*
Berg *m* hill, mountain *(collective: Gebirge n).*
bergab downhill.
bergauf uphill.
Bergedienst *m* recovery service, salvage collecting service.
Bergegerät *n* recovery equipment, salvage collecting equipment.
Bergekolonne *f* recovery column, salvage column.
Bergekommando *n* collecting unit, salvage party, recovery party.
Bergen *n* recovery, salvage.
Bergenge *f* defile.
Berger-Mischung *f* Berger-type smoke agent *(mixture composed of two parts of zinc dust to three parts of hexachlorethane).*
Berghang *m* mountain slope, hillside.
Bergjoch *n* saddle *(Top).*
Bergkamm *m* crest *(Top).*
Bergmütze *f* mountain cap, alpine cap.
Bergrücken *m* ridge *(Top).*
Bergschuhe *mpl* mountain boots, ski boots.
Bergstriche *mpl* hachures.
Bergung *f* rescue, salvage, recovery.
Bergungskolonne *f* *See* **Bergekolonne.**
Bergungsschiff *n* rescue vessel, salvage vessel.
Bericht *m* report; communiqué, news dispatch.
Berichter *m* correspondent, reporter.
berichtigen collimate *(Surv)*; correct, rectify, adjust.
Berichtigung *f* collimation *(Surv)*; adjustment, correction, rectification.
Berichtigungswalze *f* adjustment drum *(range finder).*
beritten mounted *(on horse).*
berittene Artillerie horse artillery.
Berme *f* berm *(Ft).*
bersten to burst, explode.
berücksichtigen to consider, to allow for, take into consideration.
Berücksichtigung *f* consideration, allowance for, correction for.
Berührung *f* touch, contact.
Berührungslinie *f* tangent.
Berührungspunkt *m* point of contact.
Berührungswarngerät *n* high-voltage warning device.
Berührungszeichen *n* touch signal *(Tk).*
Berührungszündung *f* contact fire *(Nav).*
Besatzung *f* garrison, crew.
Besatzungsheer *n* army of occupation.
Beschädigung *f* damage, injury.
beschaffen procure.
Beschaffung *f* procurement.
bescheinigen certify, authenticate, receipt for.
Bescheinigung *f* authentication, certificate, receipt, voucher.
beschießen to shell, to fire at.
der Länge nach beschießen to enfilade.
Beschlag *m* ferrule.
beschlagen to shoe.
Beschlagmeister *m* horseshoer *(with rank of Tech Sgt).*
Beschlagnahme *f* confiscation, seizure.

Beschlagschmied *m* horseshoer.

Beschlagschmiedobergefreiter *m* horseshoer *(with rank of Cpl).*

beschleunigen accelerate.

Beschleuniger *m* accelerator.

Beschleunigung *f* acceleration.

Beschleunigungsmesser *m* accelerometer *(Ap).*

Beschuß *m* fire, shooting.

Beschußfestigkeit *f* resistance to fire, resistance to penetration *(armor).*

beschußsicher bulletproof.

beschützen protect.

Beschwerde *f* complaint.

Beschwerungsrohr *n* counterpoise, counterweight *(G).*

Beschwerungsstück *n* *See* **Beschwerungsrohr.**

beseitigen reduce *(a stoppage) (Ord);* remove *(an obstacle).*

Beselersteg *m* hasty trestle footbridge *(named after General H. H. von Beseler: 1850-1921).*

besetzt busy *(Tp);* occupied, invaded.

Besetztschauzeichen *n* "busy" signal light *(Tp).*

Besetztzeichen *n* busy signal *(Tp).*

Besetzung *f* occupation.

Besetzungsarmee *f* army of occupation.

besichtigen inspect, review.

Besichtigung *f* inspection, review.

besiegen to defeat.

Besitz *m* property.

Besoldung *f* payment, pay, wages.

Besoldungsdienstalter *n* seniority for computation of pay.

Besoldungseinbehaltung *f* detention of pay.

Besoldungswesen *n* pay and allowance administration.

Besoldungszulage *f* additional pay.

Besoldungszulage nach dem Dienstalter longevity pay.

besonder special.

besondere Anordnungen administrative details in combat orders.

besondere Dienstzweige special services.

besondere Einflüsse interior ballistic factors.

besondere und Witterungseinflüsse interior and exterior ballistic factors.

besorgen procure.

Besorgung *f* procurement.

bespannt animal-drawn; covered with stressed skin *(Ap).*

Bespannung *f* covering *(Ap skin or fabric);* team of horses.

Besprechung *f* consultation, critique, discussion, conference.

Bestallungsurkunde *f* certificate of appointment.

Bestand *m* stock *(supplies, equipment, etc.);* inventory, supply, strength, balance, cash on hand.

Bestandsbuch *n* stock book.

Bestandsliste *f* inventory of supplies, equipment, etc.; property book.

Bestandsnachweisung *f* stock inventory, stock report.

Bestandteil *m* component.

bestätigen confirm.

Bestattung *f* burial.

Bestattungskommando *n* burial detail.

bestechen to bribe.

Bestechung *f* bribery.

Besteck *n* ship's position; set of instruments or utensils; knife, fork and spoon *(considered as unit of mess kit).*

Bestellnummer *f* requisition number.

Bestellschein *m* requisition ticket *(Adm).*

Bestellung *f* · requisition *(Adm).*

Bestimmung *f* regulation; decision; destination; determination.

Bestrafung *f* punishment.

bestreichen to graze, sweep *(with fire);* to spread, cover, coat.

bestreichendes Feuer grazing fire *(Arty).*

bestrichener Raum beaten zone *(firing).*

bestrichener Raum der Kerngarbe effective beaten zone, 85% zone *(MG fire).*

Bestückung *f* armament *(Ap, Tk).*

betätigen actuate, bring into play, set going, put into operation.

Betäubungsmittel *n* anesthetic.

Beton *m* concrete.

Betonbau *m* concrete construction.

Betonbombe *f* concrete bomb.

Betonbrücke *f* concrete bridge.

Betonbunker *m* concrete bunker, concrete pillbox.

betoniert concrete, built of or reinforced with concrete.

Betonmischmaschine *f* concrete mixer.

Betonschicht *f* layer of concrete, concrete burster course.

Betonsperre *f* concrete obstacle.

Betonstärke *f* thickness of concrete.

Betonturm *m* concrete turret *(Ft).*

Betonunterstand *m* concrete shelter, concrete dugout.

Betrag *m* amount, sum.

Betrauung *f* charge, trust.

Betrieb *m* operation *(Tp, Rad);* traffic; action; factory.

außer Betrieb not in use, out of order, not running.

Betriebsbuch *n* station log *(Rad).*

Betriebsfunkspruch *m* routine radio message.

Betriebskompanie *f* operating company *(Adrm, RR, Tp).*

Betriebsschalter *m* operating switch *(Tp).*

Betriebssicherheit *f* reliability of operation, safety of operation.

Betriebsstoff *m* fuel, gasoline, Diesel fuel.

Betriebsstoffausgabestelle *f* gasoline and lubricants distributing point.

Betriebsstoffkesselkraftwagen *m* gasoline tank truck.

Betriebsstoffkolonne *f* gasoline and lubricants supply column.

Betriebsstoffversorgung *f* gasoline and lubricants supply.

Betriebsstoffverwaltungskompanie *f* gasoline and lubricants administration company.

Betriebsstoffzusatzmittel *n* dope *(for Avn gasoline).*

Betriebsstrom *m* operating current.

Betriebsstunde *f* hour of operation.

Betriebsunterlagen *fpl* consolidated plan of telephone communication.

Bettung *f* roadbed *(RR);* ground platform *(RR gun);* base *(fixed G);* foundation *(G emplacement).*

Bettungsloch *n* gun platform excavation *(RR gun).*

Beugung *f* diffraction.

beunruhigen to disturb, harass, cause uneasiness.

Beunruhigung *f* harassment, uneasiness, disturbance, alarm.

Beunruhigungsfeuer *n* harassing fire.

beurlaubt on leave.

Beurlaubtenstand *m* reserve status.

Offizier des Beurlaubtenstandes officer commissioned for the duration *(abbr.* d.B.).

beurteilen estimate, judge, evaluate, interpret.

Beurteilung *f* estimate, appreciation, judgment.

Beute *f* booty, captured matériel, prize, pillage, loot.

Beutebergungsabteilung *f* salvage detachment for captured matériel.

Beutegeschütz *n* captured gun.

Beute-Kraftfahrzeug *n* captured motor vehicle.

Beutel *m* bag, pouch.

Beutesammelstelle *f* *See* **Beutestelle.**

Beutestab *m* salvage staff for captured enemy matériel.

Beutestelle *f* salvage depot, salvage dump *(for enemy matériel).*

Bevölkerung *f* population.

bevollmächtigen to authorize, empower.

bevollmächtigter Transportoffizier chief transportation officer *(on an army staff).*

bewachen to guard.

Bewachungsfahrzeug *n* patrol vessel, escort vessel *(Nav).*

bewaffnet armed.

Bewaffnung *f* armament.

Bewährung *f* proving of fitness, competence or durability.

beweglich mobile, movable, moving, flexible, portable.

bewegliches Geschütz flexible gun.

bewegliches Hindernis portable obstacle.

bewegliches Maschinengewehr flexible machine gun.

bewegliches Ziel moving target.

Beweglichkeit *f* mobility, maneuverability.

Bewegung *f* movement.

Bewegungsbuch *n* record of transactions.

Bewegungskontrolle *f* flight control *(Avn).*

Bewegungskrieg *m* war of movement, mobile warfare.

Bewegungsgröße *f* momentum.

bewegungsunfähig incapable of moving, immobilized; stuck, stalled *(MT).*

Bewehrung *f* cable armor *(Tp);* iron reinforcement *(concrete construction).*

Beweismaterial *n* written evidence.

Bewetterung *f* mine ventilation.

bewirken to cause, bring about, effect.

bezeugen to certify, witness.

beziehen to mount *(guard);* occupy *(a position);* collect *(pay).*

Bezirk *m* district.

Bezug *m* datum, reference, relation.

Bezugsebene *f* datum level, datum plane *(Surv).*

Bezugsfläche *f* *See* **Bezugsebene.**

Bezugslinie *f* datum line, reference line *(Surv).*

Bezugspunkt *m* check point, datum point.

Bezugsschein *m* ration card; requisition ticket.

bezwingen to reduce, overcome *(Tac).*

Biberwehr *n* beaver dam.

Biegemaschine *f* bending machine.

Biegung *f* bend, turn, flexure.

Bild *n* picture, photograph.

Bildaufklärung *f* photographic reconnaissance.

Bildauswertung *f* interpretation of photographs.

Bildberichter *m* war photographer *(in Ger propaganda company).*

Bilderkundung *f* photographic reconnaissance.

Bildflieger *m* aerial photographer.

Bildfunk *m* radiophotography, radiophoto transmission.

Bildmeßwesen *n* photogrammetry.

Bildoffizier *m* photographer *(officer).*

Bildplan *m* controlled mosaic *(aerial Photo).*

Bildplanskizze *f* partially controlled mosaic *(aerial Photo).*

Bildpunkt *m* picture point *(aerial Photo).*

Bildreihe *f* strip mosaic *(aerial Photo).*

Bildskizze *f* uncontrolled mosaic *(aerial Photo).*

Bildwerfer *m* still projector *(Photo).*

Binauralverfahren *n* binaural method *(sound locator).*

Binde *f* bandage.

binden contain *(Tac);* bind, tie.

Binder *m* necktie *(Clo).*

Bindereifen *m* rim *(G-carriage wheel).*

Binnenwasserstraße *f* inland waterway.

Bittschrift *f* petition.

Biwak *n* bivouac.

Biwakskommandant *m* bivouac commander *(ranking officer at bivouac).*

Biwaksplatz *m* bivouac (site).

blanker Draht bare wire *(Tp).*

blanke Waffe "cold steel."

blanke Waffen armes blanches, hand weapons.

Blasangriff *m* cloud attack, cloud gas attack, gas-cylinder attack.

Blase *f* blister.

blasenziehend blistering, vesicant.

blasenziehender Kampfstoff vesicant agent *(CWS).*

Blasflasche *f* gas cylinder *(CWS).*

Blaspistole *f* air gun, compressed-air cleaner *(MT).*

Blasverfahren *n* gas-cylinder method *(of gas release) (CWS).*

Blatt *n* leaf; blade; sheet; propeller blade.

Blättchenpulver *n* flake powder *(Am).*

Blattern *fpl* smallpox.

Blattfeder *f* leaf spring *(MT).*

Blaukreuz *n* sternutators *(Ger. marking "Blue Cross") (CWS).*

Blaupause *f* blueprint.

Blausäure *f* hydrocyanic acid, prussic acid *(CWS).*

Blech *n* sheet metal; nonsense *(slang).*

Blechbehälter *m* metal container.

Blechbeplankung *f* metal skin *(Ap).*

Blechbüchse *f* can; sheet-metal box or container.

Blechgehäuse *n* sheet-metal case, sheet-metal housing.

Blechkanister *m* metal container *(for water, gasoline, etc.).*

Blechschmied *m* tinsmith.

Blechtrommel *f* metal drum.

Blei *n* lead *(metal).*

Bleichmittel *n* bleach.

Bleimantel *m* lead jacket *(Am);* lead sheath *(armored cable).*

Bleiplombe *f* lead seal.

Bleisammler *m* lead-plate storage battery.

Bleispritzer *m* lead spatter, bullet spatter.

Bleitetraäthyl *n* tetraethyl lead.

Blendabdeckung *f* shutter cover *(Tk).*

Blende *f* gun mantlet, gun shield, shielded port *(Tk);* diaphragm *(Photo);* occulter *(SL);* shutter.

blenden to blind, to dazzle; to cover or shield; to lay a smoke screen.

Blendenhebel *m* shutter lever *(SL).*

Blendkörper *m* frangible glass smoke grenade.

Blendschutz-Scheibe *f* anti-glare windshield.

Blendungsschießen *n* smoke-screening fire *(Arty).*

Blickfeld *n* field of view *(Optics).*

Blindabwurf *m* emergency release *(bombing).*

Blindflug *m* blind flying, instrument flying.

Blindgänger *m* dud.

blindgeladen blank, with inert filling.

blindgeladene Granate blank shell.

Blindkurbeln *n* blindfold operation of crankwheels *(gun-laying exercise).*

Blindlandung *f* instrument landing.

Blindwiderstand *m* reactance *(Elec).*

Blinken *n* signal-lamp transmission.

Blinkfeuer *n* flashing light, blinker light *(Avn).*

Blinkgerät *n* signal lamp, signal-lamp apparatus.

Blinklampe *f* signal lamp.

Blinkspruch *m* signal-lamp message.

Blinkstelle *f* signal-lamp station.

Blinksuchtrupp *m* signal-lamp spotting squad.

Beritt-V	Vorschrift für die Berittenmachung der Offiziere, Sanitätsoffiziere, Veterinäroffiziere und oberen Beamten des Heeres	regulations for the requiring of officers, medical officers, veterinary officers, and higher officials of the army to be mounted
Berl	Berlin	Berlin
Ber.Lftsp	berittener Luftspäher	mounted air scout
Ber.Offz	berittener Offizier	mounted officer
Ber.Offz	Berufsoffizier	career officer
Ber.Pol	berittene Polizei	mounted police
Bes	Besatzung	garrison; crew
Bes	Besoldung	pay
bes.A	besondere Anordnungen	special orders
besch	beschiessen	to shell; to bombard; to fire upon
Besch	Beschiessung	shelling; bombardment; test firing
Beschl	Beschlag	metal fittings; horseshoeing
Beschl.Sch.Uffz	Beschlagschmiedunteroffizier	stable sergeant
Besch.Nachw	Beschäftigungsnachweis	proof of employment
beschr.taug	beschränkt tauglich	partially fit
Bes.G	Besoldungsgesetz	pay law
Bes.Gr	Besoldungsgruppe	pay group
Besold	Besoldung	pay
Besold.Gr	Besoldungsgruppe	pay group
Besold.Ordn	Besoldungsordnung	pay regulations
besp	bespannt	horse-drawn
Besp	Bespannung	fabric; covering (*aviation*); draft horses
Besp.Abt	Bespannungsabteilung	horse-drawn detachment
Bespr	Besprechung	conference; discussion; critique
Bes.Sch.Kl	besondere Schiessklasse	special marksmanship class
Best	Bestand	strength; stock
Best	Bestimmung	destination; regulation
Best.A	Bestandaufnahme	inventory
Best.H	Bestimmungshafen	port of destination
Bestr	Bestrafung	punishment; sweeping (*fire*)
Bestr	Bestreichung	raking (*fire*); enfilade
BestrR	bestrichener Raum	danger zone (*machine gun, rifle*)
Bet	Betriebs-	operational
Bet	Bettung	base; outrigger base; bedplate; foundation; roadbed
Bet.Gesch	Bettungsgeschütz	outrigger base gun (*antiaircraft*); gun on platform mounting
Bet.K	Betonkonstruktion	concrete construction
Betr	Betrag	amount
betr	betreffend	concerning; with reference to; regarding
Betr	Betriebs-	operational
Betr.Abt	Betriebsabteilung	operations section; management
Betr.Ass	Betriebs-Assistent	operations clerk
Betr.Fr	Betriebsfrequenz	operation frequency (*radio*)
Betr.O	Betriebsordnung	operating regulations
Betr.St	Betriebsstoff	fuel
Betr.St.Kol	Betriebsstoffkolonne	fuel column
Betr.St.Zug	Betriebsstoffzug	fuel train
Bett	Bettung	base; outrigger base; bedplate; foundation; roadbed
Bett.Gesch	Bettungsgeschütz	outrigger-base gun; gun on platform mounting
Beurl	Beurlaubter	man on leave
Beurl	Beurlaubung	leave of absence
Bev	Bevollmächtigter	authorized agent; plenipotentiary
Bew	Bewachung	guarding; watching; supervision
Bew	Bewässerung	irrigation
Bew	Bewaffnung	arms
bew	beweglich	mobile
Bew	Beweis	proof; evidence
Bewegl.Tankst	bewegliche Tankstelle	mobile filling station
Bew.M	Bewässerungs-Mühle	irrigation mill (*on maps*)
bez	bezahlt	paid
Bez	Bezirk	district
bez	bezüglich	relative to; with reference to
Bez.Kom	Bezirkskommando	district command
bezl	bezüglich	with reference to
Bez.Offz	Bezirksoffizier	district officer
bezüg	bezüglich	with reference to
bezw	beziehungsweise	and/or; respectively
Bf	Bahnhof	railroad station
Bf	Batterieführer	battery commander
B.F	Beobachtungsfernrohr	observation telescope
Bf	Brief	letter
Bfh	Befehlshaber	commander; commanding officer
Bfh. rückw. Heer. Geb.	Befehlshaber des rückwärtigen Heeresgebiets	Commander Army Group Rear Area
Bf.Offz	Bahnhofsoffizier	railroad station provost
Bfst	Befehlsstand	command post
Bfst	Befehlsstelle	command post; command authority

Bg	Berg	mountain (*on maps*)
Bg	Brigade	brigade
Bg	Brigadier	brigadier general
Bge	Berge	mountains (*on maps*)
B.G.O	Bataillons-Gasschutzoffizier	battalion chemical warfare officer
Bgr.Pl	Begräbnisplatz	cemetery (*on maps*)
Bg.St	Brigadestab	brigade staff; brigade headquarters
Bgw	Bergwerk	mine
Bh	behelfsmässig	emergency; hasty; makeshift
Bh	Beiheft	supplement
Bhf	Bahnhof	railroad station
Bhr.Ptr	Bohrpatrone	blasting cartridge; explosive cartridge
Biw	Biwak	bivouac
B.K	Bäckereikolonne	bakery column
B.K	Bekanntmachung	announcement; public notice
Bkl	Bekleidung	clothing; revetment
Bkl.(AHA)	Heeresbekleidungsabteilung	Army clothing section of General Army Office
Bkl.O	Bekleidungsordnung	clothing regulation
Bktm	Bekanntmachung	announcement; public notice
Bkw	Beobachtungskraftwagen	reconnaissance car (*for battery observation*)
Bl	Blatt	sheet; page; breast strap (*harness*)
Bl	Blaukreuz	blue cross (*gas*)
Bl	Blesse	wound
bl	blessiert	wounded
bl	blind	blind; blank
Bl	Blindgänger	dud
Bl	Blitz	lightning
Bl	Blockade	blockade
bl	blockieren	to blockade
Blasangr	Blasangriff	gas attack
Bl. Fl	Blindflug	blind flight; instrument flying
Blk	Blinkfeuer	intermittent light; revolving beacon
Blst	Blockstelle	block station (*railway*)
Bl. Vbdg	Blinkverbindung	blinker signal communication
Bl. Waff	blanke Waffen	*armes blanches (bayonet and other cutting weapons)*
B.M	Spannweite eines Flugzeugs in Metern	wingspread of an airplane in meters
B.mm	Bohrung eines Flugzeugmotors in Millimetern	bore of an airplane motor in millimeters
B-Mun	Beobachtungsmunition	tracer ammunition
B.O	Beobachtungsoffizier	observation officer
B.O	Beschwerdeordnung für die Angehörigen der Wehrmacht	complaint regulations for the members of the armed forces
B.O	Betriebsordnung	operating regulations
BO	Blutorden (NSDAP)	Order of Blood (*National Socialist Party*)
Bo	Bordstation	airplane or ship radio station
BO	Gruppe Ostmark (SA)	Austrian Section (*Storm Troopers*)
Bod.Pers	Bodenpersonal	ground personnel; ground crew
Bog.Sch	Bogenschuss	high-angle fire
BohrPatr	Bohrpatrone	blasting cartridge
Bomb	Bombardement	bombardment; shelling
Bootshs	Bootshaus	boathouse (*on maps*)
Bootskan	Bootskanone	assault-boat gun
Bootsm	Bootsmann	boatswain
Bootsm.Mt	Bootsmannsmaat	boatswain's mate
Bordger	Bordgeräte	flight instruments; flight equipment
Bordk	Bordkanone	gun mounted on airplane
Br	Brief	letter
Br	Brigade	brigade
Br	Bruch	crack-up (*aviation*); break; breech; rupture; fraction; infraction
Br	Brücke	bridge (*on maps*)
Br	Brunnen	well; spring; fountain (*on maps*)
Br.Abt	Brücken-Abteilung	bridge detachment (*combat engineers*)
BrandGr	Brandgranate	incendiary shell
Brb	Brückenbau	bridge construction
Br.Baubtl	Brückenbaubataillon	bridge construction battalion
Br.Bomb	Brandbombe	incendiary bomb
Brennst.V	Brennstoffverbrauch	fuel consumption
Brennst.V	Brennstoffvorrat	fuel supply
Brft.Zug	Brieftaubenzug	carrier pigeon platoon
Br.Gr	Brückengerät	bridge equipment
Brig	Brigade	brigade
Brig	Brigadier	brigadier general
Brigdef	Brigadeführer	brigade leader (*Storm Troops*) (*equivalent rank of U. S. major general*)

Blinktornister *m* portable signal-lamp case.
Blinktrupp *m* signal-lamp team.
Blinkverbindung *f* signal-lamp communication.
Blinkverfahren *n* lamp-signaling method.
Blinkzeichen *n* flash signal (*Sig lamp*).
Blitz *m* lightning, lightning flash.
Blitzableiter *m* lightning arrester.
Blitzbündel *n* lightning-flash cluster (*badge worn by Sig Pers*).
Blitzkrieg *m* lightning war, blitzkrieg.
Blitzlichtbombe *f* photo flashbomb.
Blitzschutzsicherung *f* lightning arrester.
Blitzstrahl *m* lightning flash.
Block *m* block; writing pad.
Blockwart *m* block warden.
Blumenkohl *m* cauliflower; Oak Leaf Cluster (*slang*).
Bluse *f* service coat, blouse.
Blut *n* blood.
Blutgruppe *f* blood group, blood type.
Blutopfer *n* heavy losses, heavy casualties.
Blutorden *m* medal awarded to participants in Munich riots of 1923.
Blutspender *m* blood donor.
blutstillend styptic.
Blutvergiftung *f* blood-poisoning.
Bö *f* squall, gust.
Bock *m* trestle, bent (*Bdg*); wagon-driver's seat.
Bockbein *n* trestle leg (*Bdg*).
Bockbrücke *f* trestle bridge.
Bockschnellsteg *m* hasty trestle bridge.
Bockschnürbund *m* square lashing (*Bdg*).
Bocksprengwerk *n* lock-spar support (*Bdg*).
Bockwagen *m* trestle carrier (*MT*).
Boden *m* ground (*Top*); base (*Am*); floor; earth; bottom.
Bodenabstandszünder *m* base delay-action fuze (*Am*).
Bodenabwehr *f* antiaircraft defense, antiaircraft artillery, ground defense.
Bodenanlage *f* ground installation.
Bodenanlage der Luftwaffe air-base service area.
Bodenantenne *f* surface antenna.
Bodenaushub *m* spoil (*Engr, Ft*).
Bodenbedienung *f* ground crew (*Avn*).
Bodenbewachsung *f* vegetation (*Top*).
Boden-Bord air-ground (*Sig Com*).
Bodenbrett *n* floor board (*MT*).
Bodendienst *m* base services (*Avn*).
Bodendruck *m* ground pressure.
spezifischer Bodendruck ground pressure per unit area (*MT, Tk*).
Bodenerhebung *f* elevation, rise (*Top*).
Bodenfalte *f* furrow, gully (*Top*).
Bodenfreiheit *f* road clearance (*MT*).
Bodenfunkdienst *m* ground radio service (*Avn*).
Bodenfunkstelle *f* ground radio station.
Bodengestaltung *f* configuration of ground, terrain features.
Bodenhaftung *f* road traction (*MT*).
Bodenkammerladung *f* base charge (*Am*).
Bodenkanzel *f* ball turret, belly turret, ventral turret (*Ap*).
Bodenkrepierer *m* dud.
Bodenlader *m* supercharger with low blower ratio (*Ap*).
Bodenlafette *f* ventral gun mount (*Ap*).
Bodenleitung *f* surface line (*Tp*).
Bodenluke *f* escape hatch in belly or floor (*Ap, Tk*).
Bodennavigation *f* pilotage (*Avn*).
Bodennebel *m* ground fog.
Bodenorganisation *f* ground personnel (*Avn*).
Bodenpeilfunkstelle *f* radio direction-finder station (*Avn*).
Bodenpeilstelle *f* See **Bodenpeilfunkstelle.**
Bodenpersonal *n* air base troops; ground crew, ground personnel, maintenance personnel, service personnel (*Avn*).
Bodenplatte *f* base plate (*Mort*).
Bodenpunkt *m* place mark (*Surv*).
Bodenschwanz *m* tail (*of a bomb*).
Bodensicht *f* ground visibility (*Avn*).
auf Bodensicht in sight of the ground.
Bodenstelle *f* ground station (*Rad*).
Bodenstrahlung *f* ground radiation (*Rad*).
Bodenstück *n* floor plate, butt assembly (*MG*); breech, breech ring (*G*).
Bodenstücksperre *f* floor-plate lock (*MG*).
Bodentreffbild *n* dispersion pattern, horizontal shot group.
Bodentreffer *m* overended shot.
Bodenverdichter *m* road grader and tamper.
Bodenwanne *f* bottom gondola (*Ap*).
Bodenwelle *f* ground wave (*Rad*).
Bodenwellenempfangszone *f* ground-wave reception zone (*Rad*).

Bodenwind *m* surface wind.
Bodenziel *n* ground target.
Bodenzünder *m* base detonating fuze.
Böenkragen *m* arcus, scud roll (*Met*).
Bogen *m* arc, arch; bend, curve; sheet (*of paper*).
Bogenbrücke *f* arched bridge.
Bogenlampe *f* arc lamp.
Bogenspitze *f* ogive (*Am*).
Bohle *f* plank.
Bohlenbahn *f* plank road.
bohren to drill, bore.
Bohrer *m* bit, drill, auger.
Bohrladung *f* borehole blasting charge.
Bohrloch *n* borehole.
Bohrpatrone *f* blasting cartridge.
Bohrung *f* bore (*Mech*).
Bohrwinde *f* brace (*a tool*).
Böigkeit *f* turbulence (*Met*).
Boje *f* buoy.
Bola *f* See **Bodenlafette.**
Bölinie *f* squall line.
Bolzen *m* bolt, pin.
Bombardierung *f* bombing, bombardment.
Bombe *f* bomb.
Bombe mit Verzugszeit time bomb.
Bombenabwurf *m* bomb release.
Bombenabwurf auf Flächenziel area bombing.
Bombenabwurfgerät *n* bomb release controls.
Bombenabwurfkurve *f* bomb trajectory.
Bombenabwurfvorrichtung *f* bomb control mechanism, bomb release mechanism (*Ap*).
Bombenabwurfwinkel *m* dropping angle (*bombing*).
Bombenabwurfzielgerät *n* See **Bombenzielgerät.**
Bombenabzughebel *m* bomb control, bomb rack control (*Ap*).
Bombenangriff *m* bombing attack, bombing raid (*Avn*).
Bombenauslösung *f* bomb release.
Bombenauslösungsvorrichtung *f* bomb control mechanism, bomb release mechanism (*Ap*).
Bombeneinschlag *m* bomb hit.
Bombenfallkurve *f* bomb trajectory.
Bombenfallzeit *f* time of fall (*bombing*).
Bombenfernrohr *n* telescopic bomb sight (*Ap*).
bombenfest bomb-resistant, bombproof.
Bombenflieger *mpl* bombardment aviation.
Bombenflugbahn *f* bomb trajectory.
Bombenflugzeug *n* bombardment airplane, bomber.
Bombengeschwader *n* bomber wing. *See also* **Geschwader.**
Bombenhebel *m* bomb release handle.
Bombenhülle *f* bomb case.
Bombenjäger *m* "bomber destroyer" (*airplane employed to combat bombers by dropping bombs on them*).
Bombenkammer *f* bomb bay (*Ap*).
Bombenklappe *f* bomb-bay doors, bomb doors (*Ap*).
Bombenkopf *m* bomb nose.
Bombenlast *f* bomb load.
Bombenloch *n* bomb crater.
Bombenmagazin *n* bomb bay (*Ap*).
Bombenreihe *f* train of bombs, bomb train.
Bombenrichtgerät *n* bomb sight.
Bombenschacht *m* bomb rack (*Ap*).
Bombenschütze *m* bombardier.
Bombenschützenstand *m* bombardier's position, bombardier's compartment.
bombensicher bomb-resistant, bombproof, heavy shellproof.
bombensichere Deckung bombproof shelter.
Bombenteppich *m* practice-bombing panel.
Bombentiefangriff *m* low-level bombing attack (*Avn*).
Bombentreffer *m* bomb hit.
Bombenvisier *n* bomb sight (*Ap*).
Bombenvolltreffer *m* direct bomb hit.
Bombenwurf *m* bomb release, bombing.
gezielter Bombenwurf precision bombing.
Bombenwurfplatz *m* target area (*bombing*).
Bombenzielapparat *m* See **Bombenzielgerät.**
Bombenzielgerät *n* bomb sight.
Bomben-Zubringewagen *m* bomb trailer.
Bombenzünder *m* bomb fuze.
Boot *n* boat; hull (*of flying boat*).
Bootshaken *m* boathook.
Bootsmann *m* boatswain (*Nav*).
Bordaufklärer *m* shipboard reconnaissance airplane.
Bordbatterie *f* aircraft radio battery.
Bordbesatzung *f* air crew.
Bordbuch *n* log book (*Ap*).
Borderkunder *m* shipboard reconnaissance airplane.
Bordflak *f* shipboard antiaircraft artillery.
Bordfliegerstaffel *f* squadron of carrier-based airplanes.
Bordflugzeug *n* shipboard airplane.
Bordfunker *m* radio operator (*Avn*).

Bordgerät *n* intercommunication telephone (*Ap, Tk*).
Bordgeräte *npl* aircraft equipment; aircraft instruments.
Bordlafette *f* gun mount on ship or airplane.
Bordlandefackel *f* landing flare (*Avn*).
Bordmannschaft *f* air crew.
Bord-Maschinengewehr *n* aircraft machine gun.
Bordmechaniker *m* flight engineer.
Bordmonteur *m* aircraft mechanic; flight engineer (*Avn*).
Bordmunition *f* aircraft ammunition.
Bordnetz *n* aircraft wiring system (*Elec*).
Bordpeiler *m* radio compass, direction finder, direction-finder operator (*Ap*).
Bordschütze *m* aerial gunner, gunner (*Avn*).
Bordsprechanlage *f* intercommunication system, interphone system (*Ap, Tk*).
Bordsprechgerät *n* intercommunication telephone, interphone (*Ap, Tk*).
Bordtelephon *n* interphone (*Ap, Tk*).
Bordverpflegung *f* flight ration (*Avn*).
Bordverständigung *f* interphone communication.
Bordverständigungsanlage *f* intercommunication system (*Ap, Tk*).
Bordwaffen *fpl* aircraft armament; tank armament.
Bordwaffenbeschuß *m* fire from aircraft weapons.
Bordwandwagen *m* gondola car (*RR*).
Bordwart *m* flight mechanic, flight engineer (*Avn*).
Bord zu Boden air-ground (*Sig Com*).
Borsalbe *f* boric acid ointment.
Borsäure *f* boric acid.
Borte *f* braid (*Clo*).
Böschung *f* escarpment, scarp, slope.
Böschung im Abtrag downward slope.
Böschung in Auftrag upward slope.
Böschungsanlage *f* batter (*Ft*).
Böschungskante *f* military crest (*Top*).
Böschungsfuß *m* foot of slope (*Top*).
Böschungskrone *f* See **Böschungskante.**
Böschungswinkel *m* angle of slope, gradient angle, gradient (*Top*).
Botschaft *f* embassy; message.
Bowdenzug *m* bowden control cable (*control cable in flexible steel conduit*).
Boxe *f* submarine pen; aircraft revetment (*colloquial*).
Boxermotor *m* opposed-piston engine.
B.-Patrone *f* See **Beobachtungspatrone.**
Brakenstange *f* side rail (limber).
Bramo *f* name of a type of aircraft engine (*abbr. of* **Brandenburgische Motorenwerke**).
Brand *m* fire; gangrene.
Brandbinde *f* absorbent gauze treated with bismuth for burns.
Brandbombe *f* incendiary bomb.
Brandbombenbündel *n* cluster of incendiary bombs.
Brander *m* fire raft.
Brandflasche *f* frangible grenade, incendiary bottle, "Molotov cocktail."
Brandgeschoß *n* incendiary bullet, incendiary projectile.
Brandgranate *f* incendiary shell.
Brandhahn *m* distributor cock (*of Ap fire extinguisher*).
Brandmasse *f* incendiary composition.
Brandmeister *m* fire marshal.
Brandmittel *n* incendiary agent.
Brandmunition *f* incendiary ammunition.

Bodenstelle *f* ground station (*Rad*).
Bodenstrahlung *f* ground radiation (*Rad*).
Bodenstück *n* floor plate, butt assembly (*MG*); breech, breech ring (*G*).
Bodenstücksperre *f* floor-plate lock (*MG*).
Bodentreffbild *n* dispersion pattern, horizontal shot group.
Bodentreffer *m* overended shot.
Bodenverdichter *m* road grader and tamper.
Bodenwanne *f* bottom gondola (*Ap*).
Bodenwelle *f* ground wave (*Rad*).
Bodenwellenempfangszone *f* ground-wave reception zone (*Rad*).
Bodenwind *m* surface wind.
Bodenziel *n* ground target.
Bodenzünder *m* base detonating fuze.
Böenkragen *m* arcus, scud roll (*Met*)
Bogen *m* arc, arch; bend, curve; sheet (*of paper*).
Bogenbrücke *f* arched bridge.
Bogenlampe *f* arc lamp.
Bogenspitze *f* ogive (*Am*).
Bohle *f* plank.
Bohlenbahn *f* plank road.
bohren to drill, bore.
Bohrer *m* bit, drill, auger.
Bohrladung *f* borehole blasting charge.
Bohrloch *n* borehole.
Bohrpatrone *f* blasting cartridge.
Bohrung *f* bore (*Mech*).

Bohrwinde *f* brace *(a tool)*.
Böigkeit *f* turbulence *(Met)*.
Boje *f* buoy.
Bola *f* *See* **Bodenlafette.**
Bölinie *f* squall line.
Bolzen *m* bolt, pin.
Bombardierung *f* bombing, bombardment.
Bombe *f* bomb.
Bombe mit Verzugszeit time bomb.
Bombenabwurf *m* bomb release.
Bombenabwurf auf Flächenziel area bombing.
Bombenabwurfgerät *n* bomb release controls.
Bombenabwurfkurve *f* bomb trajectory.
Bombenabwurfvorrichtung *f* bomb control mechanism, bomb release mechanism *(Ap)*.
Bombenabwurfwinkel *m* dropping angle *(bombing)*.
Bombenabwurfzielgerät *n* *See* **Bon benzielgerät.**
Bombenabzughebel *m* bomb contr bomb rack control *(Ap)*.
Bombenangriff *m* bombing attac bombing raid *(Avn)*.
Bombenauslösung *f* bomb release.
Bombenauslösungsvorrichtung *f* bon control mechanism, bomb relea mechanism *(Ap)*.
Bombeneinschlag *m* bomb hit.
Bombenfallkurve *f* bomb trajector
Bombenfallzeit *f* time of fall *(bom ing)*.
Bombenfernrohr *n* telescopic bon sight *(Ap)*.
bombenfest bomb-resistant, bom proof.
Bombenflieger *mpl* bombardment av ation.
Bombenflugbahn *f* bomb trajectory
Bombenflugzeug *n* bombardment ai plane, bomber.
Bombengeschwader *n* bomber win; *See also* **Geschwader.**
Bombenhebel *m* bomb release handl
Bombenhülle *f* bomb case.
Bombenjäger *m* "bomber destroyer *(airplane employed to combat bomb ers by dropping bombs on them).*
Bombenkammer *f* bomb bay *(Ap)*.
Bombenklappe *f* bomb-bay door bomb doors *(Ap)*.
Bombenkopf *m* bomb nose.
Bombenlast *f* bomb load.
Bombenloch *n* bomb crater.
Bombenmagazin *n* bomb bay *(Ap)*.
Bombenreihe *f* train of bombs, bom train.
Bombenrichtgerät *n* bomb sigh
Bombenschacht *m* bomb rack *(Ap)*.
Bombenschütze *m* bombardier.
Bombenschützenstand *m* bombardier position, bombardier's compartment
bombensicher bomb-resistant, bomb proof, heavy shellproof.
bombensichere Deckung bombproo shelter.
Bombenteppich *m* practice-bombin panel.
Bombentiefangriff *m* low-level bomb ing attack *(Avn)*.
Bombentreffer *m* bomb hit.
Bombenvisier *n* bomb sight *(Ap)*.
Bombenvolltreffer *m* direct bomb hit
Bombenwurf *m* bomb release, bomb ing.
gezielter Bombenwurf precision bombing.
Bombenwurfplatz *m* target area *(bombing)*.
Bombenzielapparat *m* *See* **Bombenzielgerät.**
Bombenzielgerät *n* bomb sight.
Bomben-Zubringewagen *m* bomb trailer.
Bombenzünder *m* bomb fuze.
Boot *n* boat; hull *(of flying boat)*.
Bootshaken *m* boathook.
Bootsmann *m* boatswain *(Nav)*.
Bordaufklärer *m* shipboard reconnaissance airplane.
Bordbatterie *f* aircraft radio battery.
Bordbesatzung *f* air crew.
Bordbuch *n* log book *(Ap)*.
Borderkunder *m* shipboard reconnaissance airplane.
Bordflak *f* shipboard antiaircraft artillery.
Bordfliegerstaffel *f* squadron of carrier-based airplanes.
Bordflugzeug *n* shipboard airplane.
Bordfunker *m* radio operator *(Avn)*.
Bordgerät *n* intercommunication telephone *(Ap, Tk)*.
Bordgeräte *npl* aircraft equipment; aircraft instruments.
Bordlafette *f* gun mount on ship or airplane.
Bordlandefackel *f* landing flare *(Avn)*.
Bordmannschaft *f* air crew.
Bord-Maschinengewehr *n* aircraft machine gun.
Bordmechaniker *m* flight engineer.
Bordmonteur *m* aircraft mechanic; flight engineer *(Avn)*.
Bordmunition *f* aircraft ammunition.
Bordnetz *n* aircraft wiring system *(Elec)*.
Bordpeiler *m* radio compass, direction finder, direction-finder operator *(Ap)*.
Bordschütze *m* aerial gunner, gunner *(Avn)*.
Bordsprechanlage *f* intercommunication system, interphone system *(Ap, Tk)*.
Bordsprechgerät *n* intercommunication telephone, interphone *(Ap, Tk)*.
Bordtelephon *n* interphone *(Ap, Tk)*.
Bordverpflegung *f* flight ration *(Avn)*.
Bordverständigung *f* interphone communication.
Bordverständigungsanlage *f* intercommunication system *(Ap, Tk)*.
Bordwaffen *fpl* aircraft armament; tank armament.
Bordwaffenbeschuß *m* fire from aircraft weapons.
Bordwandwagen *m* gondola car *(RR)*.
Bordwart *m* flight mechanic, flight engineer *(Avn)*.
Bord zu Boden air-ground *(Sig Com)*.
Borsalbe *f* boric acid ointment.
Borsäure *f* boric acid.
Borte *f* braid *(Clo)*.
Böschung *f* escarpment, scarp, slope.
Böschung im Abtrag downward slope.
Böschung in Auftrag upward slope.
Böschungsanlage *f* batter *(Ft)*.
Böschungskante *f* military crest *(Top)*.
Böschungsfuß *m* foot of slope *(Top)*.
Böschungskrone *f* *See* **Böschungskante.**
Böschungswinkel *m* angle of slope, gradient angle, gradient *(Top)*.
Botschaft *f* embassy; message.
Bowdenzug *m* bowden control cable *(control cable in flexible steel conduit)*.
Boxe *f* submarine pen; aircraft revetment *(colloquial)*.
Boxermotor *m* opposed-piston engine.
B.-Patrone *f* *See* **Beobachtungspatrone.**
Brakenstange *f* side rail (limber).
Bramo *f* name of a type of aircraft engine *(abbr. of* **Brandenburgische Motorenwerke***)*.
Brand *m* fire; gangrene.
Brandbinde *f* absorbent gauze treated with bismuth for burns.
Brandbombe *f* incendiary bomb.
Brandbombenbündel *n* cluster of incendiary bombs.
Brander *m* fire raft.
Brandflasche *f* frangible grenade, incendiary bottle, "Molotov cocktail."
Brandgeschoß *n* incendiary bullet, incendiary projectile.
Brandgranate *f* incendiary shell.
Brandhahn *m* distributor cock *(of Ap fire extinguisher)*.
Brandmasse *f* incendiary composition.
Brandmeister *m* fire marshal.
Brandmittel *n* incendiary agent.
Brandmunition *f* incendiary ammunition.
Brandsatz *m* incendiary composition, incendiary filling *(Am)*.
Brandschott *n* fire wall *(Ap)*.
Brandschutz *m* fire prevention, fire protection.
Brandspant *m* *See* **Brandschott.**
Brandstoff *m* incendiary agent.
Brand- und Asche-Taktik *f* scorched earth tactics.
Brandwirkung *f* incendiary effect.
Brandwunde *f* burn.
Bratling *m* soya-bean meat substitute.
Bratlingspulver *n* soya-bean flour.
brauchbar serviceable, usable; practicable.
Braunkohle *f* lignite.
Braunsche Röhre cathode-ray tube.
Braunstein *m* manganese dioxide.
Braunsteinbeutel *m* manganese dioxide compartment *(of Elec cell)*.
Brecheisen *n* *See* **Brechstange.**
Brechreiz *m* nausea.
Brechstange *f* crowbar, pinch-bar.
Breite *f* width.
Breitenausdehnung *f* extension in width *(Tac)*.
Breitenfeuer *n* distributed fire *(R, MG)*; sweeping fire, traversing fire *(MG)*.
Breitenfeuer mit Tiefenfeuer traversing and searching fire *(MG)*.
Breitengliederung *f* distribution, formation, or organization in width *(Tac)*.
Breitengrad *m* degree of latitude.
Breitenhöhe *f* meridian altitude *(celestial navigation)*.
Breitenkreis *m* parallel of latitude.
Breitenstreuung *f* direction dispersion, deflection dispersion *(Ballistics)*.
Breiten- und Tiefenfeuer *n* traversing and searching fire *(MG)*.
Breitenziel *n* linear target.
Breitkeil *m* inverted wedge formation *(Tac)*.
Breitseite *f* flank *(Tac)*; broadside *(Nav)*.
Breitspur *f* wide gage *(RR)*.
Bremsarm *m* brake arm *(G-carriage wheel brake)*.
Bremsausgleich *m* brake equalization; brake equalizer.
Bremsbacke *f* brake shoe.
Bremsband *n* brake band.
Bremsbelag *m* brake lining.
Bremsbock *m* brake carrier *(G carriage)*.
Bremsbuchse *f* brake bushing *(recoil mechanism)*.
Bremse *f* brake, buffer.
Bremsfeder *f* brake release spring *(MT)*.
Bremsflüssigkeit *f* recoil oil *(G)*; brake fluid *(MT)*.
Bremsfußhebel *m* brake pedal *(MT)*.
Bremsgestänge *n* brake rod *(MT)*.
Bremsgitter *n* suppressor grid *(Rad tube)*.
Bremshebel *m* brake level *(G, MT)*; locking lever *(panoramic telescope)*.
Bremsklappe *f* landing flap, wing flap *(Ap)*.
Bremsklaue *f* brake shoe *(G-carriage wheel)*.
Bremsklotz *m* brake shoe; chock wheel block.
Bremskolben *m* recoil piston *(G)*.
Bremsleistung *f* brake horsepower.
Bremslicht *n* stop light *(MT)*.
Bremsscheibe *f* brake drum.
Bremsspur *f* skid mark *(MT)*.
Bremsstrecke *f* stopping distance *(MT)*; braking section *(Ap catapult)*.
Bremsträger *m* anchor pin *(of brake shoes)*.
Bremstritt *m* brake pedal.
Bremstrommel *f* brake drum.
Bremsvorrichtung *f* recoil mechanism *(G)*; brake mechanism *(MT)*.
Bremsweg *m* stopping distance *(MT)*
Bremswirkung *f* braking effect.
Bremszylinder *m* recoil cylinder *(G)*, brake cylinder *(MT)*.
Brenndauer *f* burning rate, burning time *(fuze)*.
Brennebene *f* focal plane *(Optics)*.
Brennermotor *m* internal combustion engine.
Brenngemisch *n* gasoline mixture.
Brenngeschwindigkeit *f* burning rate, rate of burning *(fuze)*.
Brennlängenschieber *m* corrector *(fuze)*.
Brennpunkt *m* focus *(Optics)*.
Brennstoff *m* gasoline, fuel, Diesel fuel.
Brennstofflager *n* gasoline dump fuel dump.
Brennstofftankwagen *m* gasoline tank truck.
Brennstoffverbrauch *m* gasoline consumption, fuel consumption.
Brennstoffvorrat *m* gasoline supply, fuel supply.
Brennweite *f* focal distance *(Optics)*.
Brennzünder *m* powder-train fuze *(shell)*; igniting fuze, time fuze *(hand grenade)*.
Brennzünderschuß *m* time fire *(Arty)*.
Bresche *f* breach.
Brett *n* board, panel.
Bretterbahn *f* boardwalk, duckboard *(trench)*.
Bretterbock *m* plank trestle.
Bretterstapel *m* plank crib *(Bdg)*.
Brettertafel *f* plank floor *(Bdg)*.
Bretterteppich *m* plank flooring *(rope Bdg)*.
Brettstückmine *f* duckboard mine, pressure-board mine.
Briefmarke *f* postage stamp.
Brieftaube *f* carrier pigeon, homing pigeon, messenger pigeon.
Brieftaubenmeister *m* pigeoneer *(Tech Sgt)*.
Brieftaubenpfleger *m* pigeoneer.
Brieftaubenschlag *m* pigeon loft.
Brieftaubenstelle *f* *See* **Brieftaubenschlag.**
Brigade *f* brigade.
Brigadeführer *m* brigade commander. *See also* **SS-Brigadeführer.**
Brigadekommando *n* brigade headquarters.
Brillenglassalbe *f* antidim compound *(for gas mask)*.
brisant high-explosive.
Brisanz *f* brisance, explosive effect.
Brisanzgranate *f* high-explosive shell.
Brisanzschrapnell *n* high-explosive shrapnel.
Brisanzsprengstoff *m* detonating explosive.
Brombenzylzyanid *n* brombenzylcyanide *(CWS)*.
Bromzyan *n* cyanogen bromide *(CWS)*.
Brotbeutel *m* field bag, musette bag.
Brotsatz *m* bread ration.
Bruch *m* crack-up, crash *(Avn)*; fraction *(Math)*; fracture, rupture.
Bruchfestigkeit *f* breaking strength.
Bruchgrenze *f* point of rupture *(Mech)*.
Bruchlandung *f* crash landing *(Avn)*.
bruchsicher breakproof, shatterproof.
Bruchstück *n* fragment.
Brücke *f* bridge.
Brücke mit festen Stützen fixed bridge.
Brücke mit schwimmenden Stützen floating bridge.
Brückenachse *f* bridge center line.
Brückenbahn *f* bridge roadway.

Brig.St	Brigadestab	brigade headquarters
Bris	Brisanz	high explosive
Brk	Brücke	bridge *(on maps)*
Br.Kpf	Brückenkopf	bridgehead
Brlg	Brennlänge	time of burning; fuze setting
Brn	Brennerei	distillery *(on maps)*
Br.Nachr.-Zug	Brigadenachrichtenzug	signal platoon of a brigade
Br.T	Brieftaube	carrier pigeon
Brtb.Mstr	Brieftaubenmeister	carrier pigeon sergeant
Brtb.Uffz	Brieftaubenunteroffizier	carrier pigeon noncommissioned officer
Br.Tr	Brustwehrtreffer	parapet hit
Brü.B	Brückenbau	bridge construction
Brüko	Brückenkolonne	bridge train
B.S.m.O	Befehlshaber der Sicherungsstreitkräfte der mittleren Ostsee	commander of the security forces of the central Baltic Sea
B.S.N	Befehlshaber der Seestreitkräfte der Nordsee	commander of the naval forces of the North Sea
B.S.O	Befehlshaber der Seestreitkräfte der Ostsee	commander of the naval forces of the Baltic Sea
B.St	Bahnstation	railroad station
BSt	Bataillonstab	battalion staff; battalion headquarters
b.St	beim Stabe	with the staff; attached to regimental headquarters
B.St	Beobachtungsstelle	observation post
B.Stelle	Beobachtungsstelle	observation post
B.T	Beobachtungsturm	observation tower *(on maps)*
Bt	Boot	boat
BT	Brieftaube	carrier pigeon
BTaub	Brieftaub...e	carrier pigeon
BTb	Brieftaube	carrier pigeon
Btl	Bataillon	battalion
Btl. Gef. St	Bataillonsgefechtsstand	battalion command post
Btl.Kam	Bataillonskammer	battalion clothing depot
Btl.Res	Bataillonsreserve	battalion reserve
Btls	Bataillons-	battalion
Btl.St.Qu	Bataillonsstabsquartier	battalion headquarters
Btm.Maat	Bootmannsmaat	boatswain's mate
Btn	Bataillon	battalion
Btr	Betriebs-	operational
Btsm	Bootsmann	boatswain
Btsm.Mt	Bootsmannsmaat	boatswain's mate
Btsmt	Bootsmannsmaat	boatswain's mate
Bttr	Batterie	battery
B.u.E	Berichtigungen und Ergänzungen	corrections and additions
bü	bündig eingelassen	completely countersunk; sunk flush with surface
Bug-MG	Bug-Maschinengewehr	front machine-gun *(combat car)*
Bus	Kraftomnibus	motor bus
b.u.v	beschlossene und verkündet	resolved and proclaimed
BV	Besoldungsvorschrift	pay regulation
Bv.T.O	Bevollmächtigter Transportoffizier	chief transportation officer on an army staff
B.W	Bahnwärter	signalman *(railroad)* *(on maps)*
B.W	Beobachtungswagen	reconnaissance car *(for battery observation)*
B.W	Bettungswagen	vehicle with gun-emplacement material
B.W.E	Besondere- und Witterungs-Einflüsse	special and weather factors *(ballistics)*
B.W.E.-Tab	Tabelle für die Besondere- und Witterungs-Einflüsse	table for special and weather factors *(ballistics)*
B.Wg	Beobachtungswagen	reconnaissance car *(for battery observation)*
BZ	Begleitzug	accompanying platoon *(of the machine-gun company)*
BZ	bezahlt	paid
Bz	Bezirk	district
Bz	Brennzünder	time fuse
bzgl	bezüglich	relative to; with reference to
B-Zug	Begleitzug	accompanying platoon *(of the machine-gun company)*
bzw	beziehungsweise	and/or; respectively

C

C	Centrum	center (*of a city*)
c	circa	about
C	Colonie	colony (*on maps*)
C	Kanal	canal (*on maps*)
ca	circa	about
Cal	Kaliber	caliber; gauge
Cand	Kandidat	candidate
Cap	Kapelle	chapel (*on maps*)
Cath	Katholik	Catholic
cbcm	Kubikzentimeter	cubic centimeter
cbm	Kubikmeter	cubic meter
cbmm	Kubikmillimeter	cubic millimeter
ccm	Kubikzentimeter	cubic centimeter
cdm	Kubikdezimeter	cubic decimeter
Centr	Centrum	center (*of a city*)
cg	Zentigramm	centigram
C-Gesch	C-Geschoss	"C" shell (*streamlined*)
CGS-Mass Sys	Zentimeter-Gramm-Sekunden-Messordnung	centimeter-gram-second system of measurement
ch	charakterisiert	holding honorary rank
Ch	Chaussée	highway (*on maps*)
Ch	Chef	chief
Ch	Chiffre	cipher; password; code
char	charakterisiert	holding honorary rank
Charg.Pf	Chargenpferd	officer's charger; troop horse; service horse
Ch-Arzt	Chefarzt	chief physician; senior medical officer
Chef H L	Chef der Heeresleitung	Chief of the Army High Command
Chef M L	Chef der Marineleitung	Chief of the Navy High Command
chem	chemisch	chemical
Ch.H.L	Chef der Heeresleitung	Chief of the Army High Command
Ch.H.Rü	Chef der Heeresrüstung	Chief of Army Equipment
Chir	Chirurg	surgeon
Ch.M.L	Chef der Marineleitung	Chief of the Navy High Command
Ch.-Vet	Chef-Veterinär	chief veterinary; senior veterinary officer
Ch.W	Chausseewärter	highway attendant (*on maps*)
Cit	Citadelle	citadel; fort; fortress
cm³	Kubikzentimeter	cubic centimeter
C-Mine	Gasmine für Grünkreuz	gas shell marked with green cross (*asphyxiating gas*)
cmm	Kubikmillimeter	cubic millimeter
CN-Stoff	Chloracetophenon	chloracetophenone
CO-Büchse	Schutzgerät gegen Kohlenoxydvergasung	equipment against carbon monoxide contamination
Col	Kolonie	colony (*on maps*)
Col	Kolonne	column; service train
Comm	Kommissar	inspector; commissioner
Cons	Konsul, Konsulat	consul; consulate
Creed-Geber	Gebemaschine für Hörprüfungen	automatic transmitter (*for testing audibility*)
Ctr	Zentner	hundredweight; 50 kilograms
C-Zug	Zugmaschine für schwerste Artillerie	prime mover for heavy artillery

D

D	Dampfer	steamer
D	Dauerfeuer	continuous fire; sustained fire
D	Deckblatt	supplementary sheet; amendment (*to regulations*)
D	Deckflugzeug auf Kriegsschiff	airplane carried on board warship
d	der, die, das, den	the
d	deutsch	German
D	Dichte	density
D	Dienst	duty; service
D	Dieselmotor	Diesel engine
D	Division	division
D	Domäne	domain; government land (*on maps*)
D	Donarit	donarite (*explosive*)
D	Doppeldecker	biplane
d	-dorf	final syllable "-dorf" (*village*)
D	Druckschraube	pusher type propeller (*airplane*)
D	Druckvorschrift	printed service regulation
D	Dural	duraluminum (*airplane construction material*)
d	durch	through; by
D	Durchmesser	diameter
D.A	Dampferanlagestelle	steamship dock (*on maps*)
D.A	Dienstanweisung	service instruction; service regulation
D.A	Dienstaufsicht	official supervision
DA	Dienstauszeichnung	service decoration
DA	Divisionsarzt	divisional medical officer

Brückenbau *m* bridge construction; bridge structure; bridging.
Brückenbaubataillon *n* bridge construction battalion.
Brückenbaugerät *n* bridge-building equipment.
Brückenbelag *m* chess, planking *(Bdg)*.
Brückenbock *m* bridge trestle.
Brückenbogen *m* arch, span *(Bdg)*.
Brückendamm *m* approach embankment *(Bdg)*.
Brückenendwiderlager *n* abutment *(Bdg)*.
Brückenfahrbahn *f* *See* **Brückenbahn.**
Brückenfahrzeug *n* bridge-carrying vehicle.
Brückengeländer *n* bridge railing.
Brückengerät *n* bridge equipage, bridge equipment.
Brückenglied *n* bay, section *(Bdg)*.
Brückenkolonne *f* bridge column, ponton train, bridge train.
Brückenkommandant *m* bridge commander.
Brückenkopf *m* bridgehead.
Brückenkopflinie *f* bridgehead line.
Brückenkopfstellung *f* bridgehead position.
Brückenlinie *f* bridge center line.
Brückenoberbau *m* superstructure *(Bdg)*.
Brückenpanzerkampfwagen *m* bridge-carrying tank.
Brückenpfeiler *m* pile *(Bdg)*.
Brückenschlag *m* bridge construction, bridging.
Brückenskizze *f* bridge diagram.
Brückenspitze *f* open end of bridge under construction.
Brückenstelle *f* bridge site.
Brückenstrecke *f* bay *(Bdg)*.
Brückenstützweite *f* span of bridge.
Brückentrupp *m* bridge-construction party.
Brückenüberbau *m* *See* **Brückenoberbau.**
Brückenunterbau *m* foundation, substructure *(Bdg)*.
Brückenwiderlager *n* abutment *(Bdg)*
Brünierung *f* browning *(anti-rust treatment or coating on R or G barrel)*.
Brunnen *m* well.
Brustblatt *n* breast-collar body *(pack saddle)*.
Brustbohrer *m* hand drill.
Brustfallschirm *m* chest pack parachute.
Brustfernsprecher *m* head and chest set *(Tp)*.
Brustschild *m* shield *(G)*.
Brustwehr *f* breastwork, parapet.
Brustwehrkrone *f* fire crest *(trench)*.
Bruttotonnengehalt *m* gross tonnage *(Nav)*.
B.-Stelle *f* *See* **Beobachtungsstelle.**
B-Stoff *m* bromaceton *(CWS)*.
Buchse *f* jack, socket *(Rad)*; bushing.
Büchse *f* box, can, canister; case; gas-mask carrier; filter canister.
Büchsenfilter *m* canister filter *(gas mask)*.
Büchsenfleisch *n* canned meat.
Büchsenkonserven *fpl* canned food, canned ration.
Buchsring *m* bushing *(G)*.
Buchstabengruppe *f* code group *(Sig C)*.
Buchstabiertafel *f* phonetic alphabet *(Sig C)*.
Bucht *f* inlet, creek, bay.
Buchung *f* accounting.
Bug *m* bow, front, nose *(Ap, Nav, Tk)*.
Bügel *m* trigger guard; stirrup.
Buggeschütz *n* bow gun, front gun *(Tk)*.
Bugkanzel *f* forward gunner's compartment, nose turret, nose compartment *(Ap)*.
Bugpanzer *m* front armor *(Tk)*.
Bugradfahrgestell *n* tricycle landing gear *(Ap)*.
Bugschütze *m* nose gunner, bow gunner, front gunner *(Ap, Tk)*.
Bugstand *m* nose-gun station *(Ap)*.
Buhne *f* diversion dam *(Engr)*.
Bullauge *n* porthole.
Bumslandung *f* pancake landing, rough landing *(slang)*.
Buna *n* buna *(rubber)*.
Bunareifen *m* buna tire *(MT)*.
Bund *m* tie, lashing *(Engr, Tp)*; league, alliance; bunch *(of keys, etc.)*.
Bündel *n* bundle; cluster; package.
Bundesgenosse *m* ally.
Bunde und Knoten knots and ties.
Bunker *m* concrete emplacement, concrete shelter, pillbox, bunker, submarine pen.
Bunkeranlagen *fpl* group of bunkers *(Ft)*.
Bunkerlinie *f* line of concrete emplacements and pillboxes.
Bunkerstand *m* concrete emplacement.
Bunkerstellung *f* position fortified with concrete emplacements and shelters.
bunt varicolored, bright, dazzling; mixed, confused.
bunt bemalt dazzle-painted *(Cam)*.
bunte Lappen colored cloth garnish, garlands *(Cam)*.
Buntfarbenanstrich *m* camouflage painting, dazzle painting.
Buntkreuze *npl* colored cross markings *(to identify CWS munitions)*.
Buntschießen *n* simultaneous or alternate shelling with HE and Cml shells of different type.
Bürger *m* citizen.
Bürgerkrieg *m* civil war.
Bursche *m* orderly.
Bürste *f* brush.
Bussole *f* compass; declinator *(aiming circle)*.
Bussolengehäuse *n* compass case.
Bussolenring *m* compass azimuth circle.
Bussolenzug *m* compass traverse *(Arty, Surv)*.
Bz.-Schuß *m* *See* **Brennzünderschuß.**

C

Calypsol *n* a cold-resistant grease.
Ce-Stoff *m* cyanogen bromide *(CWS)*.
Celsius centigrade.
Cetenzahl *f* cetane rating *(Diesel fuel)*.
Charakter *m* honorary rank carrying specific seniority but not the pay; character, quality, peculiarity; qualification *(Law)*.
Charakterisierung *f* conferment of honorary rank as defined under *Charakter*.
Chausseewalze *f* road roller.
Chef *m* chief.
Chef der Heeresrüstung und Befehlshaber des Ersatzheeres Chief of Army Equipment and Commander of Replacement Training Army *(Commander of rear echelon of* Oberkommando des Heeres, *in charge of all non-operational branches and whole basic Army structure) (abbr. Ch Rü u B d E)*.
Chef der Luftwehr chief of administrative and supply services of German Air Ministry.
Chef der Schnellen Truppen Chief of Mobile Troops *(branch of* Oberkommando des Heeres*)*. *See also* **Schnelle Truppen.**
Chef der Zivilverwaltung chief of civil affairs section at an army headquarters.
Chef des Generalstab(e)s Chief of Staff.
Chef des Heeres-Waffenamtes Chief of Ordnance.
Chef des Transportwesens Chief of Transportation *(Tac, RR)*.
Chefveterinär *m* Chief of Veterinary Service.
chemische Kampfstoffe chemical warfare agents.
chemischer Krieg chemical warfare.
Chiffre *f* cipher.
chiffrieren encipher.
Chiffriermaschine *f* cipher device, converter *(Sig C)*.
Chiffrierung *f* encipherment.
Chinin *n* quinine.
Chirurg *m* surgeon.
Chlor *n* chlorine *(CWS)*.
Chloramin *n* chloramine-T *(CWS)*.
Chlorarsinkampfstoff *m* diphenylchlorarsine *(CWS, abbr.* Clark*)*.
Chlorat-Sprengmittel *n* chlorate explosive.
Chlorazetophenon *n* CN, chloracetophenone *(CWS)*.
Chlorazetophenon-Chlorpikrin-Lösung *f* chloracetophenone solution, CNS *(CWS)*.
Chlorcyan *n* cyanogen chloride *(CWS)*.
Chlorgas *n* chlorine *(CWS)*.
Chlorkalk *m* calcium chloride, chloride of lime, chlorinated lime, calcium bleach *(CWS)*.
Chlorkohlenoxyd *n* carbonylchloride, phosgene *(CWS)*.
Chlornatron *n* sodium hypochlorite.
Chlorpikrin *n* chlorpicrin *(CWS)*.
Chlorsulfonsäure *f* chlorsulfonic acid *(CWS)*.
Chlorvinyldichlorarsin *n* lewisite *(CWS)*.
Cholmschild *m* shield-shaped insignia awarded to troops besieged at *Kholm-on-Lovat*.
Christie-Panzerkraftwagen *m* Christie tank.
Chrom *n* chrome, chromium.
Chronograph *m* chronograph.
Chronometer *n* chronometer.
Cirruswolke *f* cirrus cloud.
Clark I diphenylchlorarsine *(CWS)*.
Clark II diphenylcyanarsine *(CWS)*.
Cletrac-Lenkgetriebe *n* Cleveland-tractor type of steering mechanism.
Cyan-Chlorarsinkampfstoff *m* diphenylcyanarsine *(CWS)*.
Cyan Clark *See* **Cyan-Chlorarsinkampfstoff.**

D

Dach *n* roof.
Dachluke *f* turret hatch *(Tk)*.
Dachpappe *f* roofing paper.
daktyloskopieren to fingerprint.
Dammkörper *m* dam embankment.
Dämpfer *m* stabilizer *(Ap)*; silencer, flash hider *(Ord)*; damper *(Tech)*.
Dampfmaschine *f* steam engine.
Dampfrohr *n* steam tube *(MG)*.
Dämpfung *f* damping *(Elec, Rad)*.
Dämpfungsfläche *f* stabilizing surface *(Ap)*.
Dämpfungsflosse *f* tail turface *(Ap)*.
Dampfwalze *f* steam roller.
Daten *npl* data.
Daube *f* stave.
Dauer *f* duration.
Dauerabzug *m* trigger for full-automatic fire *(MG)*.
Dauerbefehl *m* standing order.
Dauerfährbetrieb *m* permanent ferrying operations.
Dauerfestigkeit *f* fatigue strength, endurance limit *(Mech)*.
Dauerfeuer *n* full-automatic fire, automatic fire *(MG, R)*; continuous fire, sustained fire.
Dauerfleisch *n* preserved meat.
Dauerleistung *f* normal rating, continuous output *(Mtr)*; feat of endurance.
Dauerleitung *f* permanent line *(Tp)*.
Dauermarsch *m* forced march.
Dauerstörung *f* continuous interference *(Rad)*.
Dauerstrich *m* long dash *(Tg)*.
Dauerton *m* continuous note *(Rad)*.
Dauerunterkünfte *fpl* permanent billets.
Dauerwirkung *f* lasting effect, permanent effect.
Daumen *m* cam; thumb.
Daumenbreite *f* thumb width *(range estimation)*.
Daumensprung *m* thumb jump *(method of range estimation)*.
Daumenwelle *f* camshaft.
Dazwischensprechen *n* break-in procedure *(Rad)*.
dechiffrieren decipher.
Deckanruf *m* code call *(Tp)*.
Deckblatt *n* change sheet *(to be inserted in a manual)*.
Decke *f* casing, shoe *(of a tire)*; ceiling *(of a room)*; blanket, cover, tarpaulin.
Deckel *m* cover.
Deckelriegel *m* cover-plate latch *(MG)*.
Deckelsperre *f* cover-plate lock *(MG)*.
decken to cover, support *(Tac)*.
Deckengurt *m* surcingle *(harness)*.
Deckenlicht *n* dome light, tonneau light *(MT)*.
Deckenventilator *m* ceiling ventilator *(MT)*.
Decklandeflugzeug *n* deck-landing airplane.
Deckname *m* code name.
Deckplatte *f* casing, cover plate.
Deckung *f* cover, shelter *(Ft)*; mask *(Gunnery)*; concealment *(Tac)*.
Deckungsfeuer *n* covering fire.
Deckungsgraben *m* cover trench, slit trench, shelter trench.
Deckungshöhe *f* height of mask *(Arty)*.
Deckungsloch *n* foxhole.
Deckungsspiegel *m* trench periscope.
Deckungsstärke *f* strength of cover *(Ft)*.
Deckungstrupp *m* support party, covering party, covering detachment.
Deckungstruppe *f* covering force.
Deckungswinkel *m* angle of site to mask *(Ballistics)*.
Deckungswinkelmesser *m* site-to-mask clinometer.
Deckvermögen *n* effective coverage *(of smoke screen)*.
Deckwort *n* code word.
Deckzeichen *n* code sign, code signal.
defilieren to pass in review.
Degen *m* sword.
Degradation *f* demotion.
degradieren to break, reduce in rank.
Dehnung *f* lengthening, elongation; strain *(Mech)*.
Deich *m* dike.
Deichsel *f* limber pole, wagon shaft.
Deichselbolzen *m* pole pin *(limber)*.
Deichselstütze *f* pole prop *(limber)*.
dejustiert out of alinement.
Dekade *f* 10-day pay period.
demobilmachen demobilize.
Demobilmachung *f* demobilization.
Demolierung *f* demolition.
Denkmal *n* monument.
Desinfektionskammer *f* disinfecting chamber *(Med)*.
Desinfektionsmittel *n* disinfectant.
Detektor *m* detector *(Rad and Radar)*.
Detonationsdruck *m* blast pressure.

deuten interpret, explain, indicate.
Deutpatrone f indicator cartridge *(for Ger grenade pistol)*.
Deutsche Industrie-Norm German Industrial Standard *(abbr. DIN)*.
Deutscher Gruß Nazi salute.
Deutsches Kreuz German Cross *(decoration)*.
Dezimetergerät n microwave radio set.
Diatomitschicht f diatomite layer *(gas filter) (CWS)*.
dicht compact, dense, leakproof,
Dichte f density; concentration *(CWS)*.
Dichtemesser m densimeter, aerometer.
dichten to calk, pack, seal.
Dichtigkeit f density; impermeability.
Dichtigkeitsmesser m densimeter, aerometer; viscometer.
Dichtlinie f sealing band *(gas mask)*.
Dichtrahmen m sealing frame *(gas mask)*.
Dichtring m binder ring *(gas mask)*.
Dichtung f gasket; washer; insulation; packing.
Dichtungsring m sealing ring, washer.
Dick *See* **Äthyldichlorarsin.**
Dienst m duty, service, detail.
außer Dienst retired *(abbr.* a.D.*)*.
Dienstalter n seniority.
Dienstaltersgrenze f age limit.
Dienstältester m senior officer.
Dienstanweisung f service regulations, list of instructions.
Dienstanzug m service uniform.
Dienstausrüstung f service equipment.
Dienstbefehl m routine order.
Dienst bei der Truppe service with troops, field duty.
Dienstbeschädigung f damage or injury occurring while in service.
Dienstbescheinigung f certificate of service.
Diensteid m oath of enlistment; oath of office.
Diensteinteilung f duty roster.
Dienstentlassung f discharge without honor, dismissal.
dienstfähig fit for duty, fit for active service.
dienstfrei off duty.
Dienstgebrauch m service use, service tradition.
nur für den Dienstgebrauch restricted *(manuals, etc.)*.
Dienstgipfelhöhe f service ceiling *(Avn)*.
Dienstgrad m grade; rating *(Nav)*.
Dienstgradabzeichen n grade chevron.
Dienstgradherabsetzung f demotion.
Dienstgrad mit Patent permanent rank.
dienstlich authorized, official.
Dienstpflicht f liability for service, obligation to serve.
Dienstpflichtiger m one who is subject to military service.
Dienstplan m duty roster.
Dienststelle f duty station, command headquarters, administrative center or office.
Dienststellung f appointment.
Dienststempel m official stamp.
Dienstumschlag m official envelope.
Dienstunfähiger m noneffective, one who is unfit for service.
Dienstvorschrift f service regulation; service manual.
Dienstweg m military channel *(Adm)*.
auf dem Dienstweg through channels.
Dienstzweig m branch of the service.
Dieselkraftstoff m Diesel fuel.
Diesel-Lastwagen m Diesel truck.
Dieselmotor m Diesel engine.
Dieselschlepper m Diesel tractor.
diesig hazy *(Met)*.
Diglykolnitrat-Blättchenpulver n diglycolnitrate flake powder *(abbr.* Digl. Bl. P.*)*.
DIN *See* **Deutsche Industrie-Norm.**
Dina f *See* **Divisionsnachrichtenabteilung.**
Dinafü m *See* **Divisionsnachrichtenführer.**
Diopter m diopter, alidade.
Diopterfaden m diopter hair *(Optics)*.
Diopterlineal n alidade ruler *(aiming circle)*.
Diopterschlitz m diopter slit *(Optics)*.
Diphenylaminchlorarsin n adamsite.
Diphenylchlorarsin n diphenylchlorarsine *(CWS)*.
Dipolantenne f dipole antenna.
Disziplin f discipline.
Disziplinarstrafe f punishment for breach of discipline.
Disziplinarverfahren n disciplinary action.
Division f division.
Divisionsarzt m division surgeon *(generally with rank of* Oberstarzt, *colonel)*.
Divisionsbataillon n divisional battalion *(provisional unit whose primary mission is counterattack)*.
Divisionsbefehl m division order, division combat order.
Divisionsbegleitkompanie f division escort company *(for protection of Div Hq)*.
Divisionsfeldlazarett n division surgical hospital.
Divisionsgefechtsstand m division command post.
Divisionsintendant m *See* **Intendant.**
Divisionskommando z.b.V. special administrative division *(consists of* Landesschützen *Bns and GHQ troops in a* Wehrkreis*)*.
Divisionsnachrichtenabteilung f division signal battalion.
Divisionsnachschubführer m chief of division supply services.
Divisionsnachschubkolonne f division supply column.
Divisionspanzerabwehrabteilung f division antitank battalion.
Divisionspferdelazarett n division veterinary clearing station.
Divisionspferdepark m division remount depot.
Divisionsstab m division headquarters or headquarters personnel.
Divisionsstammleitung f division trunk line *(axis of Sig Com)*.
Dixol n an antifreeze solution.
Docht m wick.
Dockanlagen fpl dock installations.
Dolch m dagger.
Dollbord n gunwale *(rowboat)*.
Dolmetscher m interpreter, translator.
Doppelanschnitt m two-station pilot-balloon spotting *(Met)*.
Doppelbereifung f double tires, dual tires *(MT)*.
Doppelbetriebsschaltung f composite connection *(Tp)*.
Doppeldecker m biplane.
Doppelfernglas n field glass, binocular.
Doppelfernrohr n *See* **Doppelfernglas.**
Doppelflügel m "double wing" *(wing with double ailerons and flaps)*.
Doppelglas n *See* **Doppelfernglas.**
Doppellafette f two-barreled mount.
doppelläufig double-barreled.
Doppelleitung f metallic circuit *(Tp)*.
Doppelposten m double sentry.
Doppelpropeller m coaxial contra-rotating propellers *(Ap)*.
Doppelreihe f column of twos, double file.
"In Doppelreihe, angetreten!" "In column of twos, fall in!"
Doppelringtrensengebiß n double-ring snaffle bit.
Doppelringvisier n double ring sight.
Doppelschieber m double slide *(plotting protractor)*.
Doppelschraubenrichtmaschine f twin-screw elevating mechanism *(G)*.
Doppelschritt m stride *(2 paces)*.
Doppelseitensteuer n twin rudders *(Ap)*.
Doppelsprechen n phantoming *(Tp)*.
Doppelsprechschaltung f phantom circuit *(Tp)*.
Doppelsprengkabel n two-conductor firing wire *(demolitions)*.
Doppelstecker m two-way plug *(Tp, Rad)*.
Doppelsternmotor m double-row radial engine.
Doppelsteuerung f dual controls *(Ap)*.
Doppelumfassung f double envelopment *(Tac)*.
Doppelverkehr m two-way communication, two-way traffic.
Doppelzünder m combination fuze.
Dörrfleisch n dehydrated meat.
Dörrgemüse n dehydrated vegetables.
Dose f box, can.
Dosenbarometer n aneroid barometer.
Dosenlibelle f box level.
Drache(n) m kite.
Drachenballon m kite balloon.
Dragge f grapnel.
Draht m wire.
Drahtbund n wire-cable lashing.
Drahteinzäunung f wire inclosure.
Drahtgabel f wire pike *(Tp construction)*.
Drahtgeflecht n wire netting.
Drahthindernis n protective wire, wire entanglement.
Drahtigel m gooseberry *(obstacle)*.
Drahtleitung f wire line *(Tp)*.
Drahtmatte f wire mesh mat.
Drahtnachrichtenmittel n means of wire communication.
Drahtnachrichtennetz n wire net, wire system *(Sig C)*.
Drahtnetz n wire net, wire mesh.
Drahtnetz zum Tarnen chicken wire *(Cam)*.
Drahtrohr n wire-wound gun barrel.
Drahtrolle f wire roll, concertina, wire-roll entanglement.
Drahtschere f wire cutters.
Drahtschleife f wire winding, wire turn, wire loop *(Elec)*.
Drahtschlinge f wire snare, trip wire.
Drahtseil n wire cable.
Drahtseilhindernis n cable block, wire-cable obstacle.
Drahtspirale f spiral wire, helical wire.
Drahtstraße f metal mesh road, wire mesh road.
Drahttelegraphie f wire telegraphy.
Drahttelephonie f wire telephony.
Drahtverbindung f wire circuit, wire communication, connecting wire, wire connection *(Tg, Tp)*.
Drahtverhau m wire entanglement.
Drahtwalze f reinforced concertina roll.
Drahtzange f pliers *(for handling wire)*.
Drahtzaun m double-apron entanglement, double-apron fence, wire fence.
Drahtzug m flexible steel cable *(Ap)*.
Drall m rifling, twist *(Ord)*; spin *(of a projectile)*.
Drallabweichung f drift *(due to spin of projectile)*.
Drallänge f length of rifling *(Ord)*.
Drallwinkel m angle of twist *(rifling)*.
Drallwirkung f twist effect of slipstream *(Avn)*.
Drallzüge mpl grooves *(rifling)*.
Draufgängertum n audacity, daring.
Drauflosfahrt f headlong movement *(MT, Tk)*.
Drehbank f lathe.
Drehbewegung f rotation *(of projectile)*.
Drehbolzen m pivot pin.
Dreher m lathe operator.
Drehflügelflugzeug n rotor airplane.
Drehgestell n truck *(RR car)*; turntable.
Drehgriff m control grip *(Mtcl)*.
Drehkolbenpumpe f port-control fuel-injection pump *(Diesel engine)*.
Drehkondensator m variable capacitor, variable condenser.
Drehkranz m circular track *(MG mount)*.
Drehkuppel f revolving turret.
Drehlichtscheinwerfer m revolving searchlight, revolving beacon light.
Drehlichtsignal n revolving beacon.
Drehmoment n torque.
Drehpunkt m pivot, fulcrum.
Drehrahmenantenne f rotating loop antenna.
Drehring m racer *(AA gun)*.
Drehscheibenlafette f turntable gun carriage.
Drehschemellenkung f fifth-wheel steering.
Drehschieber m rotor-type valve *(Mtr)*.
Drehschwingung f torsional vibration.
Drehsinn m direction of rotation.
Drehspule f moving coil *(Elec)*.
Drehspulinstrument n moving coil instrument *(Elec)*.
Drehstabfeder f torsion-rod spring *(MT)*.
Drehstrom m three-phase alternating current.
Drehturm m revolving turret.
Drehzahl f number of revolutions, rpm.
Drehzahlmesser m tachometer.
Drehzahlregler m governor *(Mtr)*.
Drehzahlschwankung f rpm fluctuations *(Mtr)*.
Drehzapfen m pivot.
Dreiachser m six-wheel vehicle.
Dreibein n tripod.
Dreibeinlafette f tripod mount.
Dreibeinmast m tripod mast.
Dreiblattverstellschraube f three-blade controllable propeller *(Ap)*.
Dreibock m tripod cable support.
Dreieck n triangle.
Dreieckbalkensperre f triangular timber obstacle.
Dreieckrechner m computer *(circular slide rule for air navigation)*.
Dreiecksaufnahme f triangulation *(Surv)*.
Dreieckschaltung f delta connection *(Elec)*.
Dreieckzielen n sighting-triangle aiming exercise *(Gunnery)*; triangle exercise *(R practice)*.
Dreielektrodenröhre f triode tube.
Dreiergemisch n triple mixture *(gasoline 50%, benzol 40%, alcohol 10%)*.
Dreifachzünder m combination fuze *(superquick, delay and time)*.
Dreiflügelschraube f three-bladed propeller *(Ap)*.
Dreifuß m tripod.
Dreifußaufsatzstück n tripod extension piece *(MG)*.
Dreiganggetriebe n three-speed transmission *(MT)*.
dreigliedrige Division triangular division.
Dreipolröhre f triode tube *(Rad)*.
Dreipunktlandung f normal landing, three-point landing *(Avn)*.
Dreipunktschaltung f Hartley oscillator *(Rad)*.
Dreiradfahrgestell n tricycle landing gear *(Ap)*.

D.A.A	Divisionsaufklärungsabteilung	divisional reconnaissance battalion
DAD	Deutscher Arbeitsdienst	German Labor Service
DAE	Dienstaufwandsentschädigung	expense allowance
DAF	Deutsche Arbeitsfront	German Labor Front
DAI	Deutsches Auslandsinstitut	German Foreign Institute
D.A.K	Deutsche Afrika Korps	German Africa Corps
DAL	Dienstaltersliste	seniority list
D.-Am	Deutsch-Amerikaner	German-American
DAnw	Dienstanweisung	service instruction; service regulation
Dap	Dapolin	dapolin (*trademark of motor f*
Dat	Datum	date
d.a.Z	dicht am Ziel	(hit) close to the target
Da.Zahl	Dienstanweisung für Zahlstellen	service regulation for pay offices
d.B	des Beurlaubtenstandes	on the reserve list
DB	Dienstbeschädigung	injury sustained in line of dut
d.B	durch Boten	by messenger
D.B	Durchführungsbestimmungen	executory regulations
DBest	Durchführungsbestimmungen	executory regulations
DBG	Deutsches Beamtengesetz	German Civil Service Law
Dbl	Deckblatt	supplementary sheet; amend
dbr	dunkelbraun	dark brown
D.D	Doppeldecker	biplane
DD-Gesch	Dumdumgeschoss	dumdum bullet
DE	Diensteinkommen	service pay
d.E	durch Eilboten	by express messenger
Dechiff.B	Dechiffrierbüro	decoding office
Deckbl	Deckblatt	supplementary sheet; amendment (*to regulations*)
def	defensiv	defensive
Def	Defilee	defile
def	defilieren	to pass in review; to deploy out of a defile
Def.Kr	Defensiv-Krieg	defensive war
Degr	Degradation	demotion in rank
Dekr	Dekret	decree
Del	Delegierter	delegate; deputy
Dem	Demarkation	demarcation
Dem. Kom	Demobilmachungskommission	demobilization commission
Dem.Krav	Deutsche Militärkraftfahrer-Vereinigung	association of German military drivers
Dem.L	Demarkationslinie	line of demarcation
Demob	Demobilmachung	demobilization
Demol	Demolierung	demolition
Demoral	Demoralisation	demoralization
Denkm	Denkmal	monument (*on maps*)
Denkst	Denkstein	memorial stone (*on maps*)
Dep	Depesche	telegram
dep	depeschieren	to telegraph
Dep	Deplacement	displacement (*tonnage*)
Dep	Depot	depot; dump; warehouse
Dep.Bt	Depeschenboot	dispatch boat
Depesch. Bt	Depeschenboot	dispatch boat
Desarm	Desarmierung	disarmament
Desert	Deserteur	deserter
desert	desertieren	to desert
Desinf.Abt	Desinfektionsabteilung	disinfection detachment
Des.Wg	Desinfektionswagen	disinfection car (*railroad*)
Det.W	detachiertes Werk	outer fortification
Devast	Devastation	devastation
Dezentr	Dezentralisation	decentralization
Dez.Syst	Dezimalsystem	decimal system
D.F	Doppelfernrohr	battery commander's telescope; binoculars
dfg	dienstfähig	fit for active duty
D.f.Rem	Dienstanweisung für die Remontedepotadministrationen	service regulation for remount depot administrations
D.fr.K	Dienstvorschrift für die freiwillige Krankenpflege	service regulations for voluntary nursing
DFS	Deutsches Forschungsinstitut für Segelflug	German Research Institute for Gliding
DG	Drehgestell	pivot mounting
D.G.S.O	Diensttuender Gasschutzoffizier	chemical warfare officer on duty
d.h	das heisst	that is; i. e.
D.H.B	Deutsche Heeresbücherei	German Army Library
D.H.L	Deutsche Hochschule für Leibesübungen	German Physical Training College
DHR	Deutscher Hochseerundfunk	German high-seas radio
Dikt	Diktat, Diktator, Diktatur	dictation; dictated treaty; dictator; dictatorship
Dim	Dimension	dimension; extent
Din	Deutsche Industrienorm	German manufacturing standard (*size*)
Dinafü	Divisionsnachschubführer	commander of division supply services

Dipl.Ing	Diplomierter Ingenieur	graduate engineer
Dir	Direktion	administration; management
Dir	Direktor	director
Dist	Distanz	distance
Dist.R	Distanzritt	long-distance ride
Distr.Kom	Distriktskommissar	district commissar
Disz	Disziplin	discipline
Disz.Ges	Disziplinargesetz	disciplinary law
Disz.Mssn	Disziplinramassnahme	disciplinary measure
Disz.Str	Disziplinarstrafe	disciplinary punishment
Disz.Vorg	Disziplinarvorgesetzter	disciplinary superior
Div	Division	division
Div.Arzt	Divisionsarzt	divisional medical officer
Div.Aufkl.Abt	Divisionsaufklärungsabteilung	divisional reconnaissance battalion
Div.Beob.St	Divisionsbeobachtungsstelle	divisional observation post
Div.Grz	Divisionsgrenze	divisional boundary
Div.Kdeur	Divisionskommandeur	divisional commander
Div.Kdo	Divisionskommando	division staff
Div.K.K	Divisionskraftwagenkolonne	division transport motor train
Div.St	Divisionsstab	division staff
Div.St.Qu	Divisonsstabsquartier	division headquarters
Div.Verm	Divisions-Fernsprech-Vermittlung	divisional telephone exchange (*signal service*)
Div.Vet	Divisionsveterinär	divisional veterinary officer
d.J	des Jahres	of the year
DJ	Deutsches Jungvolk	German Young People's League
D.K	Deutsche Kriegsnachrichten	German war communiqués
D.K	Deutches Konsulat	German Consulate
D.K	Divisionskavallerie	divisional cavalry
Dkm	Denkmal	monument (*on maps*)
DKN	Deutsche Kriegsnachrichten	German war communiqués
D.K.V	Dienstkleidungsvorschrift	uniform regulation
d.L	der Landwehr	of the Landwehr; of the reserve
Dl	Druckluft	compressed air
D-Lager	Durchgangslager für Kriegsgefangene	collecting station (clearing station) for prisoners of war
DLH	Deutsche Lufthansa	German Lufthansa
D.L.T	drahtlose Telegraphie	wireless telegraphy
DLW	Deutsche Luftwacht	German Air Protection
D.M	Dampfmühle	steam-powered mill
Dm	Denkmal	monument
d.M	deutsche Meile	German mile
dm	Dezimeter	decimeter (*1/10 meter*)
d.M	dieses Monats	of this month
Dm	Domäne	domain; government land (*on*
Dm	Durchmesser	diameter
dm^2	Quadratdezimeter	square decimeter
dm^3	Kubikdezimeter	cubic decimeter
DmäsZ	Deutsche militärärztliche Zeitschrift	German Military Medical Journal
Dm U min	mittlere Drehzahl (Umdrehungen in Minuten)	average revolutions per minute (*automobile and air-*
DmW	Durchgangszug mit Wehrmachtteil	civilian train with section for troops
dnat	deutschnational	German-nationalistic
DNB	Deutsches Nachrichtenbüro	official German news agency
D-Nr	Dienstnummer	service number
d.O	der Obige	the above
D.O	Dienstordnung	service regulations
d.O	durch Ordonnanz	by orderly
DOB	Deutscher Offizierbund	German Officers' League
D.O.B	Deutsches Offizierblatt	German Officers' Journal
DOffBl	Deutsches Offizierblatt	German Officers' Journal
Dok	Dokument	document
Dolm	Dolmetscher	interpreter
Dom	Domäne	domain; government land
dopp	doppelt	double; twofold; twice
Dopp.Z	Doppelzünder	combination fuze; double-
Dopp.Z.S.33	Doppelzünder (33 Sekunden Brennlänge)	combination fuze (33 seconds burning time)
Do.X	Dornierflugboot	Dornier flying boat
Dpf	Dampf	steam
Dpf	Dampfer	steamer
Dpfm	Dampfmaschine	steam engine
Dpf.T	Dampfturbine	steam turbine
dpp	doppelt	double
d.R	der Reserve	of the Reserve
DR	Deutsches Reich	German Reich
DR	Dragoner-Regiment	dragoon regiment
Dr	Drall	rifling
Dr	Dreidecker	triplane
Drag	Dragoman	dragoman; interpreter, and
Drag	Dragoner	dragoon
Drawa	Drachenwarte	kite-balloon station
DRB	Deutsche Reichsbahn	German Railways
Drch-Br	Drehbrücke	swing bridge
Drehkr	Drehkranz für Flugzeugmaschinengewehr	rotating track for airplane machine gun
d.Res	der Reserve	of the reserve

Dreireihenstandmotor *m* three-bank upright engine.
Dreiwegehahn *m* three-way selector cock.
Drillich *m* denim (*also spelled* Drilch).
Drillichanzug *m* fatigue uniform, work uniform.
Drillstab *m* torsion rod (*MT*).
dringend urgent.
Dringlichkeitsliste *f* priority list.
Dringlichkeitszeichen *n* urgent signal (*Sig Com*).
DRK-Helfer *m* German Red Cross attendant.
DRK-Helferin *f* German Red Cross nurse apprentice.
DRK-Schwester *f* German Red Cross nurse.
DRK-Schwesternhelferin *f* German Red Cross junior nurse, nurse's aid.
Drohung *f* threat.
Drossel *f* throttle (*Mtr*).
Drosselgriff *m* throttle grip.
Drosselhebel *m* throttle lever.
Drosselklappe *f* throttle valve.
Drosselklappenwelle *f* throttle shaft.
Drosselrinne *f* jugular groove (*horse*).
Drosselspule *f* choke coil (*Elec*).
Drosselung *f* choking, throttling.
Druck *m* pressure.
Druckänderung *f* pressure change (*Met*).
Druckausgleicher *m* pressure equalizer.
Druckbohlenmine *f* pressure-plank mine.
Druckbrettmine *f* pressure-board mine.
drucken to print.
drücken to press, push; to push control stick or wheel forward (*Ap*).
Drücker *n* thumb nut (*sight*); trigger.
Druckgurt *m* compression chord (*truss*).
Druckkabine *f* pressure cabin (*Ap*).
Druckknopf *m* pushbutton; snap, snap fastener.
Druckleitung *f* pressure line.
Druckluft *f* compressed air.
Druckluftbremse *f* air brake.
Drucklufterzeuger *m* air compressor.
Drucklufthammer *m* pneumatic hammer.
Druckluft-Niethammer *m* pneumatic riveter.
Druckluftramme *f* pneumatic pile driver.
Druckmesser *m* pressure gage.
Drucknase *f* trigger cam (*R*).
Druckplatte *f* pressure plate (*clutch*).
Druckpunkt *m* pressure point.
Druckpunkt nehmen to take up the slack (*of the trigger*).
Druckraum *m* surge chamber.
Druckregler *m* pressure regulator.
Druckschmierung *f* pressure lubrication.
Druckschraube *f* pusher propeller (*Ap*).
Druckschrauber *m* pusher airplane.
Druckseite *f* pressure side, pressure surface (*Ap wing*).
Druckstelle *f* pressure point.
Druckstempel *m* pressure plug (*Arty*).
Druckstück *n* contact piece on trigger (*R*).
Drucktaster *m* sending key.
Druckumlaufschmierung *f* See **Druckschmierung**.
Druckvorschrift *f* Field Regulations, Field Manual (*abbr.* Dv.).
Druckzerstäuber *m* pressure spray gun (*CWS*).
Druckzünder *m* pressure firing device, pressure igniter, push igniter (*LM*).
Druckzylinder *m* master cylinder (*hydraulic brake*).
Dschungel *f* jungle.
D-Stoff *m* dimethylsulfate (*CWS*).
Dübel *m* lug (*G*).
Ducht *f* crosspiece, thwart (*boat or Pon*).
Dücker *m* sluice pipe.
Dulag See **Durchgangslager**.
Dulagluft See **Durchgangslager Luftwaffe**.
Dumdum-Geschoß *n* dumdum bullet.
Dunkelheit *f* darkness.
Dunkelkammer *f* darkroom.
Dunnit *n* dunnite (*Am*).
Dunst *m* haze, vapor.
Durchbiegung *f* deflection (*of a beam or girder*).
durchbrechen to break through, pierce.
durchbrennen to burn out (*Elec fuse*).
Durchbruch *m* break-through (*Tac*).
"Durchdecken!" "Dress and Cover!"
durchdrehen to pull (*a propeller*) through.
Durchführung *f* gland (*Bln*); carrying out, execution.
Durchgabe *f* transmission (*of Rad messages, etc.*).
Durchgangsbahnhof *m* through station (*RR*).
Durchgangsfernspruch *m* long-distance telephone call.
Durchgangslager *n* PW transit camp (*abbr.* **Dulag**).
Durchgangslager Luftwaffe PW transit camp for Air Forces personnel (*abbr.* Dulagluft).
durchgeben to transmit (*Sig C*).
Durchgriff *m* reciprocal of amplification factor in percent (*Rad*).
Durchhang *m* sag.
Durchhängen *n* droop (*Mech*).
durchkrümmen to squeeze (*the trigger*).
Durchlaß *m* culvert, passage, conduit, opening.
durchladen to load (*a magazine or belt*).
Durchlaufgleis *n* through track (*RR*).
durchlöchern pierce.
Durchmesser *m* diameter.
durchpausen to trace (*a map, etc.*).
Durchpunkt *m* point at which trajectory intersects plane of aerial target perpendicular to line of sighting.
durchsacken to drop, to do a power stall, to sink, to pancake (*Avn*).
Durchsackgeschwindigkeit *f* critical speed, stalling speed (*Avn*).
durchsagen to pass the word along.
Durchschlag *m* carbon copy (*typed*); drift pin.
Durchschläger *m* punch, drift (*tool*).
Durchschlagskraft *f* penetration, force of penetration (*Am*).
durchschmelzen to burn out (*Elec fuse*).
Durchschnitt *m* average, mean; cross section.
Durchschnittsleistung *f* average performance.
Durchschnittspanzerstärke *f* average thickness of armor (*Tk*).
Durchschreibeblock *m* carbon-copy pad.
Durchschrift *f* carbon copy (*written*).
durchsichtig transparent.
Durchstich *n* cut (*Engr, RR*).
Durchstoß *m* penetration by assault.
durchstoßen pierce, penetrate; fly through (*a layer of clouds*).
durchsuchen to search.
Durchtrittsöffnung *f* cutaway (*for ejected cartridge cases*).
durchwaten to ford.
durchziehen to pull out (*dive bombing*).
Dusche *f* shower bath.
Düse *f* injector, jet, nozzle; vent (*rocket*).
Düsenkorrektor *m* mixture control.
Dynamomaschine *f* dynamo, generator.
Dynastart *m* starter-generator.

E

Echolot *n* sonic altimeter, sound-ranging altimeter (*Avn*); fathometer, echo depth sounder (*Nav*).
Eckplatte *f* gusset.
Edelgas *n* rare gas.
Edisonsammler *m* Edison storage battery.
Edler *m* knight, noble.
Ehre *f* honor.
Ehrenbezeigungen bei Beerdigung graveside service (*Mil funeral*).
Ehrenbezeugung *f* salute.
Ehrengeleit *n* escort of honor.
Ehrenparade *f* dress parade.
Ehrenposten *m* guard of honor.
Ehrenrang *m* honorary rank.
Ehrenrat *m* court of honor.
Ehrensalve *f* volley (*at burials*).
Ehrensold *m* award.
Ehrenwache *f* guard of honor, honor guard.
Ehrenwort *n* parole, word of honor.
Ehrenzeichen *n* decoration.
eichen calibrate.
Eichenlaub *n* oak leaf cluster.
Eichstrich *m* measuring line, graduation.
Eichung *f* calibration, adjustment.
Eierhandgranate *f* egg-shaped hand grenade, "pineapple" hand grenade.
Eigenfrequenz *f* natural frequency (*Rad*).
Eigengeschwindigkeit *f* indicated air speed (*Avn*).
Eigengewicht *n* empty weight.
eigenmächtig on one's own authority, unauthorized.
eigenmächtige Entfernung absence without leave.
Eigenpeilung *f* direction finding by taking bearings from an aircraft on two or more radio stations.
Eigenschaft *f* quality, characteristic, property.
Eigenschatten *m* shadow on object (*as distinguished from shadow cast by the object*) (*Cam*).
Eigenschwingung *f* natural oscillation (*Rad*).
Eigentum *n* property.
Eigenverständigung *f* interphone (*Ap*); intravehicular communication (*Tk*).
Eignungsprüfung *f* aptitude test.
Eihandgranate *f* See **Eierhandgranate**.
Eimer *m* bucket.
"Ein!" "Contact!" (*Avn*).
Einankerumformer *m* dynamotor.
Einatemventil *n* inlet valve (*gas mask, oxygen breathing apparatus*).
Einbahnstraße *f* one-way road or street.
Einbahnverkehr *m* one-way traffic (*MT*).
Einbaufähre *f* construction float (*Bdg*).
Einbehaltung *f* detention (*of pay, etc.*).
Einbeinfahrgestell *n* landing gear with individual cantilever legs (*Ap*).
einberufen to induct into the armed forces, to call to the colors, to order to report for active duty. *See* **Einberufung**.
Einberufung *f* call to the colors (*corresponds roughly to US induction, and is followed by* Einstellung, *assignment to a unit*).
Einberufungsbefehl *m* order to report for active duty.
Einberufungskarte *f* notice of induction.
Einberufungsort *m* induction station.
Einblick *m* view into (*enemy positions, etc.*); insight; eyepiece (*Optics*).
Einblicklinse *f* eyepiece lens (*Optics*).
Einblickrohr *n* eyepiece tube.
Einblickstutzen *m* eyepiece mount.
Einbruch *m* penetration (*Tac*).
Einbruchsfeuer *n* assault fire.
Einbruchsfront *f* frontage of penetration (*Tac*); cold front (*Met*).
Einbruchstelle *f* breach, point of penetration, point chosen for penetration (*Tac*).
Einbuchtung *f* dent in the enemy's line, salient (*Tac*).
Eindecker *m* monoplane.
Eindeckung *f* cover (*Ft*).
eindringen infiltrate, penetrate.
Eindringungstiefe *f* depth of penetration or infiltration (*Tac*).
Eineinhalbdecker *m* sesquiplane.
Einerzelt *n* one-man shelter tent, pup tent.
Einfachanschnitt *m* single-station pilot-balloon spotting (*Met*).
Einfachleitung *f* ground-return circuit (*Tp*).
einfädeln to thread (*a needle*); to join a march column, to get into line.
einfahren to float bridge-sections into place; to break in (*a horse, etc.*); to harness; to drive in.
Einfahrgleis *n* incoming track (*RR*).
Einfallwinkel *m* angle of incidence.
einfetten to grease, lubricate.
einfliegen to penetrate (*air attack tactics*); make a test flight.
Einflieger *m* test pilot.
Einfliegerei *f* aircraft-testing department.
Einfluchten *n* marking out (*in fixing the azimuth*) (*Surv*).
Einflug *m* penetration (*air attack tactics*); approach flight (*Avn*); approach of a target (*AWS*).
Einfluggenehmigung *f* traffic-control clearance (*Avn*).
Einflugsmeldung *f* report of approaching target (*AWS*).
Einflugzeichen *n* "come in" signal (*Inst landing*).
Einflüsse *mpl* See **besondere und Witterungseinflüsse**.
einführen introduce, initiate, lead in.
Einfuhrhafen *m* port of entry.
Einführungsdraht *m* lead-in (*Rad*).
Einfüllstutzen *m* oil-filling plug (*recoil mechanism*); filler neck (*of gasoline or oil tank*).
eingabeln to bracket (*Arty*).
Eingabelung *f* bracket, bracketing.
Eingang *m* entrance.
Eingangswerte *mpl* initial data (*AAA*).
Eingangszündung *f* priming charge.
eingesehen exposed to observation (*emplacement, trench, etc.*).
Eingitterröhre *f* single-grid tube, triode (*Rad*).
eingleisig single-track.
eingliedern assign; incorporate, make an organic part of; classify.
Eingliederung *f* assignment; incorporation, organic arrangement; classification.
eingraben dig in, entrench; bury.
Eingreifdivision *f* reserve division.
eingreifen intervene, come to the aid of, take a hand in; to catch, mesh, engage.
einhängen suspend (*a bomb*).
Einheit *f* unit, element (*Tac*).
kleinste taktische Einheit basic tactical unit.
Einheitsführer *m* commander of a unit.

Einheitsgeschütz *m* dual-purpose gun.
Einheitsgewicht *n* specific gravity.
Einheitsgranate *f* combination high-explosive and shrapnel shell.
Einheitskanister *m* standard gasoline container, unit container.
Einheitsmaß *n* unit of measurement.
Einheitsmunition *f* fixed ammunition.
Einheitsmunitionszug *m* ammunition train carrying only one type and caliber of ammunition *(RR)*.
Einheitsmütze *f* regulation field cap *(replaces the* Feldmütze*)*.
Einheitsprinzip *n* unit principle *(Ger Mil doctrine providing maximum independence and self-sufficiency for each unit)*.
Einheitswaffe *f* dual-purpose weapon.
Einheitszeit *f* standard time.
Einheitszünder *m* combination fuze, standard fuze *(Am)*.
einholen overtake, collect, bring in; haul down.
einigeln take up a position of all-around defense.
einkesseln to encircle, trap, pocket.
Einkesselung *f* encirclement.
Einkipptrieb *m* leveling mechanism *(Mort)*.
Einkleidungsbeihilfe *f* clothing money allowance.
Einkreisempfänger *m* receiver with one resonant circuit *(Rad)*.
Einkreisung *f* encirclement.
Einkreisungsmanöver *n* encircling maneuver.
Einkreisungsschlacht *f* battle of encirclement *(Tac)*.
Einkreisungsversuch *m* attempted encirclement.
einkuppeln engage, thrown in *(the clutch)*.
einladen to load, entrain, entruck, etc.
Einladeübersicht *f* entraining table, entrucking table.
Einlaß *m* inlet, intake.
Einlaßkanal *m* intake line *(Mtr)*.
Einlaßventil *n* intake valve *(Mtr)*.
Einlaßventilkammer *f* intake-valve chamber *(Mtr)*.
einläufig single-barreled.
Einlegerohr *n* liner, subcaliber tube *(Ord)*.
einleiten begin, introduce, initiate, commence.
einleitendes Gefecht preliminary action or engagement.
einmessen to survey *(Arty)*.
Einnahme *f* capture, occupation, seizure *(of a locality)*; reception, acceptance *(of equipment, Ord, etc.)*; receipts *(money, etc.)*.
Einnahmeschein *m* receipt.
einnebeln to blanket, to lay a smoke screen.
einölen to oil, lubricate.
einpeilen take a radio bearing.
Einpolluftleiter *m* Marconi antenna, quarter-wave vertical antenna.
einrasten engage; lock; ram home; snap shut; catch.
einrichten adjust *(fire, etc.)*; orient *(a map)*; prepare, improve *(a position)*; install; furnish, equip.
Einrichten einer Karte orientation of a map.
Einrichten einer Stellung preparation or improvement of a position.
Einrichtung *f* installation; organization, establishment; adjustment; arrangement; device; orientation.
Einrumpfflugzeug *n* single-fuselage airplane.
Einsatz *m* commitment, employment; mission; operation, action; effort; insertion; duty; sortie *(Avn)*.
bei besonderem Einsatz on active duty; during special commitment *(in time of war or national emergency)*.
Einsatzbereitschaft *f* aggressiveness, initiative, readiness for action.
Einsatzbesprechung *f* orders conference, "briefing" *(Avn)*.
einsatzfähig available for assignment, commitment or employment.
Einsatz fliegen to fly a sortie *(Avn)*.
Einsatzhafen *m* home field *(Avn)*.
Einsatzhafenkommandantur *f* operational airdrome command *(sub-division of* Lufthafenbereichkommandantur*)*.
Einsatzort *m* locality to be occupied, area where units are to be sent into action.
Einsatzraum *m* operational area.
Einsatztopf *m* filter-element container *(gas mask)*.
Einschaltung *f* switching on, throwing into gear.
einschanzen dig in, entrench.
Einscheibenkupplung *f* single-plate clutch *(MT)*.
Einschießen *n* adjustment fire, trial fire *(Arty)*.
Einschießen mit hohen Sprengpunkten high-burst ranging.
Einschießen nach der Länge range adjustment.
Einschießpunkt *m* adjusting point *(adjustment fire)*.
Einschießziel *n* adjustment target *(Arty)*.
Einschiffung *f* embarkation.
Einschlag *m* impact, strike *(Arty)*; toe in *(MT)*.
Einschlagsgarbe *f* sheaf of fire at point of impact, shot group, shot pattern *(Arty)*.
Einschlagsgruppe *f* shot group, shot pattern *(of a volley)*.
Einschleifen einer Leitung connecting a line into a telephone circuit.
einschneiden to intersect, to take cross bearings.
Einschneiden auf Richtungslinie point determination along an orienting line *(Surv)*.
Einschneiden nach drei Punkten three-point resection *(Surv)*.
Einschnitt *m* cut *(Engr, RR)*.
Einschuß *m* hit.
einschwenken to pivot *(Tac, drill)*.
seitlich einschwenken to pivot to the left or right, to fan out *(Tac)*.
einsetzen to commit, employ, insert.
einsickern infiltrate *(Tac)*.
Einsitzer *m* single-seater airplane.
einspielen bring into play, throw in, engage, actuate.
Einspielen der Libellen leveling, cross-leveling *(Arty)*.
Einsprache *f* mouthpiece *(Tp)*.
einspringender Winkel reentrant.
Einspritzdüse *f* fuel injector, injection nozzle *(Mtr)*.
Einspritzpumpe *f* injection pump.
Einspruch *m* challenge.
Einstecklauf *m* subcaliber tube.
Einsteigluke *f* entrance hatch *(Tk)*.
Einsteigöffnung *f* manhole.
einstellbare Luftschraube adjustable propeller *(Ap)*.
einstellen tune in *(Rad)*; to dial *(Tp)*; adjust, set *(a fuze, etc.)*; cease *(fire, etc.)*.
Einstellhülse *f* adjustable holder *(panoramic telescope)*.
Einstellmarke *f* index; adjustable marker.
Einstellmutter *f* adjustment nut, regulating nut.
Einstellring *m* adjusting ring *(fuze)*.
Einstellung *f* adjustment, setting; cessation. *See also* **Einberufung**.
Einstellvorrichtung *f* adjustment device, setting device.
Einstellwinkel *m* angle of wing setting, angle of incidence.
Einstiegklappe *f* hatch cover *(Ap)*.
Einstiegluke *f* hatch *(Ap)*.
einstöpseln plug in *(Rad, Tp)*.
einstürzen to cave in.
einteilen graduate *(into degrees, etc.)*; to divide, classify, separate into groups.
Einteilung *f* classification; scale; graduation, division *(into degrees or units)*.
eintreffen arrive.
Eintreffzeit *f* arrival time.
Einweiser *m* guide.
Einweisungskommando *m* party of guides.
Einwohnerschaft *f* population, inhabitants.
Einzäunung *f* enclosure, stockade, compound *(PW)*.
Einzelabfederung *f* independent suspension *(of wheels)*.
Einzelabwurf *m* individual release, single release *(Bombing)*.
Einzelaufhängung *f* independent suspension *(of wheels)*.
Einzelausbildung *f* individual training.
Einzelbefehl *m* fragmentary order, extract order *(Tac)*.
Einzelfeuer *n* single-shot fire, semiautomatic fire *(MG)*.
Einzelhaft *f* solitary confinement.
Einzelkrad *n* solo motorcycle.
Einzellader *m* single loader, single-shot weapon.
Einzelschnittverfahren *n* single-intersection method *(target location in FR)*.
Einzelschuß *m* single shot, single round.
Einzelschutz *m* individual protection.
Einzelsprünge *mpl* bounds *(method of advancing)*.
Einzelwurf *m* individual release, single release *(Bombing)*.
Einzelziel *n* point target *(Bombing)*.
einziehbar retractable *(landing gear, etc.)*.
einziehen draw in, retract; withdraw *(a sentry)*; conscript, draft *(recruits)*; confiscate.
Einziehfahrgestell *n* retractable landing gear *(Ap)*.
Eisansatz *m* accumulation of ice.
Eisbrecher *m* ice apron *(Bdg)*.
Eisenbahn *f* railroad, railway.
Eisenbahnanlage *f* railroad installation.
Eisenbahnaufmarsch *m* strategic concentration by rail.
Eisenbahnbatterie *f* railway artillery battery.
Eisenbahnbaubataillon *n* railway construction battalion.
Eisenbahnbeförderung *f* transportation by rail.
Eisenbahnbetrieb *m* railway traffic; railway operation.
Eisenbahnbetriebskompanie *f* railway operating company.
Eisenbahnendpunkt *m* railway terminal, railhead.
Eisenbahnflak *f* railway antiaircraft gun; railway antiaircraft artillery.
Eisenbahngeleise *n* railroad track.
Eisenbahngeschütz *n* railway gun.
Eisenbahnhaubitze *f* railway howitzer.
Eisenbahnkesselwagen *m* tank car *(RR)*.
Eisenbahnklaue *f* spur track.
Eisenbahnknotenpunkt *m* railway center, railway junction.
Eisenbahnküchenwagen *m* kitchen car *(RR)*.
Eisenbahnnachschublinie *f* railway supply line.
Eisenbahnpanzerzug *m* armored train *(RR)*.
Eisenbahn-Pfeilerbaukompanie *f* railway pile-driving or pier-building company *(Mil)*.
Eisenbahnpioniere *mpl* railway engineer troops.
Eisenbahnstellwerk *n* railway signal tower, switch control room.
Eisenbahntankstelle *f* gasoline and lubricant railhead, bulk reduction point.
Eisenbahntransportfolge *f* railway transportation timetable.
Eisenbahntruppen *fpl* railway operating troops.
Eisenbahnwagen *m* railway car.
Eisenbeton *m* reinforced concrete, ferro-concrete.
Eisenblech *n* sheet iron.
Eiseneinlage *f* iron reinforcement *(in ferro-concrete)*.
Eisenkern *m* iron core *(Elec)*.
Eisenwalze *f* iron roller *(mine clearance)*.
eiserne Portion emergency ration *(for Pers)*.
eiserne Ration emergency ration *(for animals)*.
Eisernes Kreuz Iron Cross *(decoration)*.
Eisregen *m* sleet.
Eissporn *m* ice spade *(trail spade)*.
Ekrasit *n* ecrasite *(explosive)*.
E-Latte *f* aiming stake, aiming post (E=Entfernung, *range)*.
Elektrizitätszähler *m* electric meter.
Elektrode *f* electrode; grounded electrode *(spark plug)*.
Elektrodenröhre *f* radio tube.
Elektromechaniker *m* electrician.
Elektron *n* electron; trade name of a magnesium-aluminum alloy.
Elektronbrandbombe *f* electron incendiary bomb.
Elektrotechniker *m* electrical engineer.
Element *n* cell, element *(Elec)*.
Elementbecher *m* cell container *(Elec)*.
Elementekühler *m* cellular-type radiator *(MT)*.
Elementprüfer *m* battery tester *(Elec)*.
Ellbogen *m* elbow.
E.Meßgerät *n* *See* **Entfernungsmeßgerät**.
E.Meßmann *m* *See* **Entfernungsmeßmann**.
E.Messer *m* *See* **Entfernungsmesser**.
Emfang *m* receipt, reception.
Empfänger *m* indicator *(follow-the-pointer mechanism of AA gun)*; indicator *(fuze setter)*; receiver, receiving set *(Rad)*; data receiver, indicator-regulator *(data transmission system of AA gun)*.
Empfangsapparatur *f* receiver chassis, receiving equipment *(Rad)*.
Empfangsberechtigter *m* beneficiary.
Empfangsbescheinigung *f* *See* **Empfangsschein**.
Empfangsbestätigung *f* acknowledgment of receipt *(Sig C)*.
Empfangslautstärke *f* volume of reception *(Rad)*.
Empfangsschaltung *f* receiver circuit *(Rad)*.
Empfangsschein *m* receipt form.
Empfangswelle *f* receiving frequency *(Rad)*.
Empfangszone *f* reception zone *(Rad)*.
empfindlich sensitive.
empfindlicher Aufschlagzünder superquick impact fuze.
empfindlicher Kopfzünder allways fuze.
empfindlicher Zünder superquick fuze.
Endauflager *n* abutment *(Bdg)*.
Endbahnhof *m* railhead, terminal.
Enddrall *m* terminal twist *(Ord)*.
Endgeschwindigkeit *f* terminal velocity.
Endmontage *f* final assembly.
Endverstärker *m* terminal repeater *(Tp)*; final amplifier, power amplifier *(Rad)*.
Endziel *n* final objective.

Drf	Dreifuss	tripod
DRG	Deutsches Reichsgesetz	Law of the German Reich
D.R.H	Doppelrichtungshörer	twin sound locator
Dr.habil		academic degree
Dr.h.c	Dr. honoris causa	honorary doctor's degree
Drhdn	Drahthindernis	wire entanglement
DRK	Deutsches Rotes Kreuz	German Red Cross
Dr.-N	Drahtnachricht	telegram message; telegram
DRP	Deutsche Reichspost	German Postal Service
Drp	Druckpunkt	squeeze-point *(trigger mechanism)*; center of pressure *(aerodynamics)*
D.S	Dampfsäge	steam-powered sawmill
DS	Dampfschifffahrt	steamship service
D.S	Deutsche Seewarte	German Naval Observatory
DS	Deutschlandsender	German transmitter *(official German radio station)*
DS	Dienstsache	official business; pertaining to the service
ds	dieses Monats	of this month
DSM	Deutsches Sportmodell	German sport model *(small caliber rifle)*
Dst	Dienst	duty; service
Dst	Dienststelle	office; authority; duty station
Dst.A	Dienstalter	seniority
Dst.Anz	Dienstanzug	field service uniform
Dst.Aufs	Dienstaufsicht	service supervision
Dst.Ausz	Dienstauszeichnung	service decoration
Dst.Bez	Dienstbezeichnung	service classification; service designation
Dst.Bez	Dienstbezirk	service district
Dst.Fl	Dienstflagge	service flag
Dst.Gr	Dienstgrad	rank; rating
D.St.O	Disziplinarstrafordnung	disciplinary code
D-Stoff	Dimethylsulfat	dimethylsulphate *(poison gas)*
D.-Strafe	Disziplinarstrafe	disciplinary punishment
dt	deutsch	German
D.T.B	Divisions-Tagesbefehl	divisional order of the day
Dt.Gr	Deutscher Gruss	German greeting
dtsch	deutsch	German *(on maps)*
Dtsch.Mil.Miss	Deutsche Militärmission	German Military Mission
Dtzd	Dutzend	dozen
d.u	dauernd untauglich	permanently unfit
d.u	dienstuntauglich	unfit for military service
D.U	Dienstuntauglichkeit	unfitness for military service
D.u.D	Dienstsiegel und Dienststempel	official seal and official stamp
D.-Übertr	Disziplinarübertretung	transgression of discipline
dufg	dienstunfähig	unfit for active service
Dulag	Durchgangslager	transit camp for prisoners of war
Dupl	Duplikat	duplicate
Durchf.Best	Durchführungsbestimmungen	regulations of procedure
Durchf.V.O	Durchführungsverordnung	procedure order
D.U.Verf	Dienstuntauglichkeits-Verfahren	action instituted to determine unfitness for military service
D.U.-Z	Dienstuntauglichkeits-Zeugnis	certificate of unfitness for military service
Dv	Dienstvorschrift	service regulations; training manual
DV	Durchführungsverordnung	procedure order
Dv.Abko	Dienstvorschrift für die Abnahmekommandos des Waffenamts	Regulations for the Acceptance Commissions of the Ordnance Department
D.V.A.V	Dienstvorschrift für die Versuchsabteilungen der Verkehrstruppen	training regulations for the experimental battalions of communication troops
d.Vf	der Verfasser	the author
Dv.f.San.Insp	Dienstvorschriften für die Sanitätsinspektionen	service regulations for medical inspections
D.V.L	Deutsche Volksliste	German public directory
DVO	Durchführungsverordnung	procedure order
D-Vorg	Disziplinarvorgesetzter	summary court officer
Dw	Deckungswinkel	angle-of-site to mask
Dw.M	Deckungswinkelmesser	angle-of-site clinometer
Dyn	Dynamit	dynamite
Dyn Masch	Dynamomaschine	dynamo
dz	Doppelzentner	100 kilograms
DZ	Doppelzünder	combination fuze; double-action fuze
D-Zug	Durchgangszug des öffentlichen Verkehrs	through train for civilian traffic

E

E	eigene Truppe	own troops
E	Eilzug	express train
E	Einschlag	impact *(gunnery)*
E	Einwohner	inhabitant; resident
E	Einzelfeuer	independent fire
E	Einzelschuss	single shot: semiautomatic
E	Einzelwerfer	mortar with single load
E	Eisenbahn	railway
E	Eisenbahngeschütz	railroad gun
E	empfindlich	sensitive; instantaneous *(fuze)*

E	Entfernung	range (*gunnery*)
E	Entfernungsmesser	range finder (*soldier*)
E	Entscheidung	decision
E	Entwurf	draft; rough sketch; project; outline
E	Ergänzungs-	reserve
E	Ergänzungsoffizier	replacement officer
E	Ersatz	reserve; replacement; substitute
e	erster	first
E	Etappe	zone of communications
E.A	Ersatzabteilung	replacement center
E.B	Ersatzbataillon	replacement training battalion
E.Batl	Ergänzungsbataillon	reserve battalion
Ed	Edikt	edict
ED	Eindecker	monoplane
E.D	Ersatzdivision	replacement training division
E-Einheiten	Ergänzungseinheiten	divisional replacement units
E.F	Einzelfeuer	independent fire (*rifle*)
E.F	Eisenbahnfähre	railroad ferry
E.Fd	Erdfeind	hostile ground forces
Eff.St	Effektivstärke	effective strength; effectives
E.F.K	Etappenfuhrparkkolonne	communications zone transport and supply column
40	**Eisenbahn-Flugzeugabwehrkanone**	**railroad antiaircraft gun**
E.Flak Schei	Flugzeugabwehrkanonen-Scheinwerfer auf Eisenbahnwagen	antiaircraft searchlight mounted on railroad car
E.Flu.Wz	Eisenbahn - Flugwarnzentrale	railroad air raid warning center
E.G	Einheitsgruppe	tactical unit
Eg	Entgiftung	decontamination
ehem	ehemalig	former
E.H.K	Vorschrift für die Erhaltung des Heeres in der Kriegsformation	regulation for the maintenance of the army in battle formation
E.H.O	Etappen-Hauptort	field base of communications zone
Ehr.Bez	Ehrenbezeigung, Ehrenbezeichnung	military salute
Ehr.Kr	Ehrenkreuz von 1934	Cross of Honor (1934)
Ehr.V.Off	Verordnung über die Ehrengerichte der Offiziere des Heeres	Order concerning Courts of Honor for Officers of the Army
Ehr.W	Ehrenwache	guard of honor
Ehrz	Ehrenzeichen	decoration
E.H.Z	empfindlicher Haubitszünder	instantaneous howitzer fuse
E.I	Etappenintendant	chief administrative officer in charge of supply for communications zone
eig	eigen	own
eig	eigentlich	actually
eigtl	eigentlich	actually
Eihgr	Eierhandgranate	egg-shaped hand grenade
Eilb	Eilbote	express messenger
Eilg	Eilgut	express freight
Eilm	Eilmarsch	forced march
Einber	Einberufung	call to the colors
Einbr	Einbruch	penetration (*tactics*); raid
eindr	eindringen	break into (*tactics*)
Eindr	Eindringung	penetration; entry (*tactics*)
Eindr.T	Eindringungstiefe	depth to which a raiding plane penetrates into enemy territory
einf.mittl.Dien	einfacher mittlerer Dienst	regular service, middle group officials
Einf.V.O	Einführungsverordnung	introductory regulations
Einf.W	Einfallwinkel	angle of fall; angle of incidence
Eingr.Div	Eingreifdivision	division in reserve
Einh	Einheit	basic arm or service unit
Einh.Gr	Einheitsgruppe	tactical unit
Einh.W	Einheitswaffe	standard weapon
Einkr	Einkreisung	envelopment (*tactics*); encirclement
Einl.Lf	Einlegelauf	sub-caliber barrel
Einl.R	Einlegerohr	sub-caliber barrel; liner
Einqu	Einquartierung	billeting; quartering troops
einr	einrichten	to organize; to arrange; to furnish
einr	einrücken	to install; to lay (*artillery*); to enter military service
Eins	Einsitzer	single seater (*plane*)
Einsch	Einschaltung	switching on
Einsch	Einschiessen	adjustment fire
Einsch	Einschiffung	embarkation
Einsch	Einschuss	point where bullet enters body
einschl	einschliesslich	inclusive
Eins.Geschw	Einsitzergeschwader	single-seater wing
Eint	Einteilung	graduation; scale; classification
Einw	Einwohner	inhabitant; resident

Energieleitung *f* feeder cable (*Elec*).
Energienachfuhr *f* additional supply of power (*Elec*).
Energieverlust *m* power loss (*Elec, Rad*).
Energievorrat *m* power supply.
Enge *f* defile (*Tac*).
Engländer *m* Englishman; monkey wrench.
Engpaß *m* bottleneck, defile.
entblößen uncover (*Tac*).
Ente *f* duck; canard airplane.
Enteiser *m* de-icer (*Ap*).
Enteisungsanlage *f* de-icer system, ice-eliminating system (*Ap*).
Enteisungsgerät *n* de-icer (*Ap*).
Enteisungmittel *n* anti-icer solution.
Entenflugzeug *n* canard airplane.
entfalten develop (*a route column, etc.*); unfold.
entfalteter Anmarsch advance in developed formation (*Tac*).
Entfaltung *f* development (*followed by* Entwicklung, *deployment*).
Entfaltung aus dem Marsch development from march column.
Entfaltungszeit *f* parachute opening time.
Entfernung *f* range, distance; removal; departure.
mittlere Entfernung medium range (*up to 800 m*).
nächste Entfernung close range (*up to 100 m*).
nahe Entfernung close range (*up to 400 m*).
weite Entfernung long range (*beyond 800 m*).
Entfernungsermittlung *f* range determination.
Entfernungsgerät *n* range finder.
Entfernungslineal *n* range ruler (*Arty*).
Entfernungsmarke *f* range indicator (*practice firing*).
Entfernungsmeßgerät *n* range-finder, altimeter, height-finder (*AAA*).
Entfernungsmeßmann *m* range-finder operator; height-finder sergeant (*AAA*).
Entfernungsmeßmann zur Seitenbeobachtung lateral tracker (*AAA*).
Entfernungsmesser *m* range-finder; range-finder operator; height-finder sergeant (*AAA*).
Entfernungsschätzen *n* range estimation.
Entfernungsteilung *f* range scale.
Entfernungstrommel *f* range knob (*G*).
Entfernungsunterschied *m* range difference.
Entfernungsvorhalt *m* linear difference between present slant range (*at instant of range determination*) and future slant range (*AAA*).
Entfettung *f* degreasing.
Entgasung *f* degassing.
entgegenwirken counteract, act against, work against.
Entgiftung *f* decontamination.
Entgiftungsabteilung *f* decontamination battalion.
Entgiftungsdienst *m* decontamination service.
Entgiftungsgerät *n* decontamination apparatus.
Entgiftungskompanie *f* decontamination company.
Entgiftungskraftwagen *m* decontamination truck.
Entgiftungsmittel *n* decontamination agent.
Entgiftungspflug *m* decontamination plow.
Entgiftungsplatz *m* decontamination point.
Entgiftungsstoff *m* decontamination agent.
Entgiftungstrommel *f* perforated decontamination drum.
fahrbare Entgiftungstrommel decontamination cart.
Entgiftungstrupp *m* decontamination squad.
entheben relieve (*of a command, etc.*).
entkeimen sterilize.
entkohlen decarbonize.
entkupfern decopper.
entladen unload, empty; discharge.
Entladestab *m* unloading staff (*harbor*).
Entladung *f* to discharge (*Am, Elec, etc.*).
Entladungsstoß *m* discharge surge (*Elec*).
entlassen to dismiss, discharge; release; disband, demobilize.
Entlassung *f* discharge; dismissal; release.
Entlassung auf Ehrenwort release on parole, home parole.
Entlassungsjahrgang *m* age class due for discharge.
Entlassungsschein *m* certificate of discharge.
Entlassungsstelle *f* demobilization center, discharge center.
entlasten relieve (*of pressure*).
Entlastung *f* relief (*of pressure*).
Entlastungsangriff *m* relief attack (*made to relieve enemy pressure elsewhere*).
entlaufen to escape.
entlausen delouse.
Entlausungsanstalt *f* delousing station.
entlüften ventilate; bleed (*recoil mechanism*).
Entlüfter *m* ventilator.
Entlüftungsstutzen *m* breather (*Mtr*).
Entmagnetisierung *f* de-gaussing.
entrollen to unfurl or uncase (*a flag*).
Entsatz *m* relief (*of a fortress, etc.*).
Entschädigung *f* compensation, reimbursement, allowance, recoupment.
entschärfen disarm (*Am*).
Entscheidung *f* decision.
Entscheidungsgefecht *n* decisive action, decisive battle (*Tac*).
Entschluß *m* decision (*Tac*).
Entschlußfassung *f* formulation of decision(s).
Entschlußkraft *f* power of decision.
entschlüsseln decode, decryptograph.
entsenden to dispatch, send off.
entsetzen relieve (*a fortress, etc.*); be terrified; relieve (*of a command*).
Entsetzung *f* relief (*of a fortress, etc.*).
entseuchen disinfect.
Entseuchungsgerät *n* disinfestor.
Entseuchungsmittel *n* disinfecting agent.
Entseuchungsschrank *m* disinfecting chamber.
entsichern to disengage or release the safety (*SA, R, etc.*); to arm or activate (*a mine, bomb, etc.*).
Entsicherungsflügel *m* arming vane (*bomb*).
entspannen to uncock; to relieve tension.
Entstaubung *f* dust filtering (*MT*).
Entstörkappe *f* ignition shield (*over spark plug*).
Entstörung *f* interference elimination (*Rad*).
enttarnen remove camouflage.
entwaffnen disarm.
Entwarnung *f* "all clear" signal.
Entwässerungsgraben *m* drainage ditch.
Entweichen *n* escape, evasion.
Entwesung *f* sterilization.
entwickeln deploy (*Tac*); develop (*Photo*); generate (*smoke, etc.*).
Entwicklung *f* deployment (*follows* Entfaltung, *development*); development (*Photo*); generation (*of smoke, etc.*).
Entwurf *m* sketch, outline; plan, scheme.
Entzerrer *m* balancing network (*Rad, Tp*).
Entzerrung *f* rectification, restitution (*aerial Photo*); correction, compensation (*of frequency response, Rad, Tp*).
Entzerrungsgerät *n* rectifying camera (*aerial Photo*).
entziehen remove, withdraw, deprive.
sich entziehen avoid, evade, disengage (*Tac*).
entziffern decipher, decryptograph.
Entzifferung *f* deciphering.
entzurren unlock, unclamp.
Episkop *n* reflecting projector, episcope.
erbeuten to capture (*matériel*).
Erdanschluß *m* ground connection (*Elec*).
Erdarbeit *f* excavation work; earthwork (*Ft*).
Erdartillerie *f* artillery used against ground targets (*as distinguished from AAA*).
Erdaufklärung *f* ground reconnaissance (*Tac*).
Erdbeobachtung *f* ground observation.
Erdbeschuß *m* anti-aircraft fire (*as seen from target*).
Erdbildmessung *f* phototopography.
Erde *f* earth, soil; ground (*Elec*).
Erdei *See* **Erdeinschießziel.**
Erdeinschießziel *n* ground adjustment target (*Gunnery*).
erden to ground (*Elec*).
Erder *m* ground (*Elec*).
Erdfernsprechverbindung *f* ground-return telephone circuit.
Erdgegner *m* hostile ground force.
Erdgleiche *f* ground level (*Ft*).
Erdgrube *f* borrow pit.
Erdhörer *m* geophone.
Erdkabel *n* underground cable or wire (*Tp*).
Erdkrümmungslineal *n* altitude-correction ruler.
Erdleitung *f* ground, ground lead (*Elec*).
Erdleitungsdraht *m* ground wire (*Elec*).
Erdleitungsrohr *n* ground pipe, underground pipe.
Erdmine *f* land mine.
Erdöl *n* petroleum.
Erdortung *f* pilotage (*Air Navigation*).
erdrosseln to throttle, strangle.
Erdrückleitung *f* ground-return circuit (*Tp*).
Erdschluß *m* ground leak, ground short (*Elec*).
Erdschwere *f* gravitation, gravity.
Erdsporn *m* trail spade (*G*).
Erdstecker *m* grounding rod (*Elec*).
Erdtelegraphieverbindung *f* ground-return telegraph circuit.
Erdtruppen *fpl* ground forces.
Erdung *f* ground, grounding (*Elec*).
Erdvergleichsziel *n* auxiliary ground target (*Arty*).
Erdvermessung *f* topographic survey.
Erdwinde *f* winch (*for Bln*).
Erdzielbeschuß *m* firing against ground targets (*AAA*).
Erdzuleitung *f* ground lead (*Elec*).
Ergänzung *f* supplement, replacement(s), reserve(s); completion, rounding out, bringing to full strength.
Ergänzungsbedarf *m* deficiency, **shortage, replacement requirements.**
Ergänzungsgruppe *f* replacement training group (*Air Force group composed of 2 or more* Ergänzungsstaffeln).
Ergänzungsstaffel *f* *See* **Ergänzungsgruppe.**
Ergänzungsstelle *f* replacement center.
ergeben, sich to surrender, capitulate.
Ergebnis *n* result; score.
Erhebungswinkel *m* quadrant angle (*Surv*).
Erhöhung *f* quadrant elevation (*Gunnery*).
Erhöhungsskala *f* elevation scale (*G, MG*).
Erhöhungswinkel *m* quadrant angle of elevation (*Gunnery*).
Erholungsurlaub *m* leave; arrest, imprisonment (*slang*).
Erinnerungsmedaille *f* campaign medal.
erkämpfen to force (*a crossing, etc.*).
Erkennungsmarke *f* identification tag, "dog tag."
Erkennungsmunition *f* signal ammunition.
Erkennungstuch *n* identification panel, ground panel.
Erkennungswort *n* countersign, password.
Erkennungszeichen *n* marking, insignia, identification mark; recognition signal.
Erker *m* "bay window" type gun mount in front right sponson (*Tk*).
Erkunder *m* scout; reconnaissance airplane.
Erkundung *f* reconnaissance (*Tac*).
Erkundungsfahrzeug *n* reconnaissance vehicle, scout vehicle.
Erkundungsorgan *n* reconnaissance element.
Erkundungsvorstoß *m* scouting raid.
Erlaubnis *f* permission.
Erlaubnisschein *m* leave pass.
Erledigung *f* accomplishment, completion.
Ermäßigung der Strafe remission of sentence.
ermächtigen empower.
Ermattungsstrategie *f* strategy of attrition.
Ermessen *n* discretion.
Ermüdung *f* **fatigue, exhaustion.**
Ermüdungskampfstoff *m* harassing agent (*CWS*).
Ermüdungsschießen *n* harassing fire, gas-shell fire (*Arty*).
ernannt *See* **Ernennung.**
Ernennung *f* appointment to brevet rank.
Ernstfall *m* emergency.
erobern conquer (*territory or locality*).
Eroberung *f* conquest.
Erreger *m* exciter (*Rad*).
Erregerstrom *m* excitation current (*Elec*).
Erregerwicklung *f* excitation winding (*Elec*).
Ersatz *m* replacement; substitute, synthetic material; spare part; compensation, damages.
Ersatzbataillon *n* replacement training battalion.
Ersatzbatterie *f* spare battery (*Elec*).
Ersatzbedienung *f* gun crew replacements, reserve gun crew.
Ersatzdienststelle *f* recruiting center.
Ersatzeinheit *f* replacement unit, replacement training unit.
Ersatzfunkstelle *f* secondary radio station.
Ersatzheer *n* replacement training Army.
Ersatzkarte *f* provisional map, substitute map.
Ersatzmann *m* replacement.
Ersatzmannschaften *fpl* replacements.
Ersatzpferd *n* remount.
Ersatzregiment *n* replacement training regiment.
Ersatzreifen *m* spare tire.
Ersatzreserve *f* replacement reserves.

E.K.Z	empfindlicher Kanonenzünder	instantaneous gun fuze
E.K.I	Eisernes Kreuz I. Klasse	Iron Cross, 1st Class
E.K.II	Eisernes Kreuz II. Klasse	Iron Cross, 2d Class
El	Einstecklauf	subcaliber barrel
el	elastisch	elastic
el	elektrisch	electric
El	Element	element; cell
El	Elite	élite
E.-L	Elsass-Lothringen	Alsace-Lorraine
El.Abw	elastische Abwehr	elastic defense
elast	elastisch	elastic
elektr	elektrisch	electric
Elektr.W	Elektrizitätswerk	powerhouse (*on maps*)
Elev	Elevation	elevation (*of a gun*)
Els	Elsass	Alsace (*province*)
Els.Loth	Elsass-Lothringen	Alsace-Lorraine
El.Vert	elastische Verteidigung	flexible defense
El.W	Elektrizitätswerk	power plant (*on maps*)
em	emeritiert	retired
E.M	Entfernungsmesser	range finder
E.M	Ergänzungs - Mannschaften	reserves; replacements
E.M.D	evangelische militärkirchliche Dienstordnung für das Reichsheer und die Reichsmarine	Evangelical (Protestant) military church regulations for the army and navy
E.Messer	Entfernungsmesser	stereoscopic range finder
Emigr	Emigrant	emigrant
E.M.K	elektromotorische Kraft	electromotive power
Empf.Ant	Empfänger-Antenne	receiving antenna
Empf.Besch	Empfangsbescheinigung	receipt
E.Mssger	Entfernungsmessgerät	range finder (*instrument*)
EmW	Eilzug mit Wehrmachtteil	civilian train with section for troops
Endkpf	Endkampf	final engagement; final encounter
Ends	Endsieg	final victory
Endz	Endziel	final goal
eng	engagieren	to engage (*in battle*); to enter
engl	**englisch**	**English**
einz	einzeln	single
Eisb	Eisenbahn	railroad
Eisb.Baubtl	**Eisenbahnbaubataillon**	**railroad construction battalion**
Eisb.Brg	Eisenbahnbrigade	railroad brigade
Eis.Best	eiserner Bestand	iron rations
Eis.Brig	Eisenbahnbrigade	railroad brigade
Eisb.Tr	Eisenbahntruppen	railroad troops
Eisenb.Gesch	Eisenbahngeschütz	railroad gun
Eisenb.Tr	Eisenbahntruppen	railroad troops
Eisenb.Verk.O	Eisenbahnverkehrsordnung	railroad traffic regulations
Eis. Krz	Eisernes Kreuz	Iron Cross
Eis. Port	eiserne Portion	iron ration
Eis.Rat	eiserne Ration	iron rations
Ei.Z	Einschiessziel	registration target
E.K	Ersatzkompanie	replacement company
eK	Kartenentfernung	map range (*gunnery*)
Engp	Engpass	pass; defile
ent	entbehren	to do without; to miss
Ent	Entente	entente
ent	entern	to enter
Entd	Entdecker	discoverer
Entf	Entfernung	range; distance
entfl	entflammen	to inflame; to kindle
Entf.M	Entfernungsmesser	range finder
Entg	Entgasung, Entgiftung	degassing; decontamination
Entg.Tr	Entgiftungstrupp	decontamination squad
entk	entkommen	to escape
entl	entladen	to unload; to discharge
Entl.Gr	Entlassungsgrund	reason for dismissal
Entl.St	Entladestab	unloading crew
Entsch	Entscheidung	decision
Entsch	Entschiedenheit	decisiveness
Entsch.RG	Entscheidung des Reichsgericht	decision of the Supreme Court of the Reich
entspr	entsprechend	corresponding
Entv	Entvölkerung	depopulation
Entw	Entwässerung	drainage
Entw	Entwaffnung	disarmament sketch; project; design
Entw.M	Entwässerungsmühle	drainage mill (*on maps*) set at variance
E.O	Eisenbahnoffizier	railroad officer
E.O	Erkundungsoffizier	reconnaissance officer
e.P	eiserne Portion	iron ration
e.R	eiserne Ration	iron ration; reserve forage ration
ER	Exerzier-Reglement	drill regulations
Erd.Abw	Erdabwehr	ground defense
Erd.Art	Erdartillerie	field and coast artillery
Erdtr	Erdtruppen	ground troops
E.R.G	Entscheidung des Reichsgerichts	decision of the Supreme Court of the Reich
Erg	Ergänzung	reserve; supplementary
Erhöhg	Erhöhung	elevation (*of a gun*)
Erk	Erkundung	reconnaissance; inquiry
Erkl	**Erklärung**	**explanation**
Erk.M	Erkennungsmarke	identification tag or disc
Erk.S	Erkennungssignal	identification signal
Erk.St	Erkundungsstab	reconnaissance headquarters

Erk.Tr	Erkundungstrupp	reconnaissance detachment
Erl	Erläuterung	explanation
Erl.Sch	Erlaubnisschein	permit
ern	ernannt	appointed to brevet rank
Ern	Ernennung	appointment to brevet rank
Erob	Eroberer	conqueror
E.R.P	Ersatzröhrenpulver	substitute tubular powder ing; substitute
ers	ersuchen	to request
Ers.Abt	Ersatzabteilung	replacement training center, battalion, or detachment
Ers.B	Ersatzbataillon	training battalion; replacement training battalion
Ers.Div	Ersatzdivision	replacement training division
Ers.Komm	Ersatzkommission	draft commission
Ers.Mag	Ersatzmagazin	reserve magaine; reserve depot
Ers.R	Ersatzregiment	reserve training regiment
Ers.Res	Ersatzreserve	draft registrants
erst	erstürmen	to assault; to storm
Ers.Tr	Ersatztruppen	replacements
Erzw	Erzwingung	enforcement mount
E.S.D	Etappensanitätsdepot	depot of medical supplies in communications zone
E.S.K	Eisenbahnsonderkommando	special railroad service command
Esk	Eskarpe	forward slope of trench
Esk	Eskorte	mounted convoy; escort
E.S.K.A	Etappensanitätskraftwagenabteilung	communications zone ambulance battalion
EStB	Elektrische Strassenbahn	electric trolley car
E.T	eigene Truppen	own troops
Et	Etappe	communications zone
Et.Anf.O	**Etappenanfangsort**	**rear boundary of the communications zone; home base**
Etap	[illegible]	**communications zone** tions zone
Etapp.Mun.Kol	Etappen Munitionskolonne	communications zone ammunition column
Et.B.K	Etappenbäckereikolonne	communications zone bakery column
E.T.D	Etappentelegraphendirektion	telegraph direction of the communications zone
E.Tel.B.Tr	Eisenbahntelegraphenbautrupp	railroad telegraph construction squad
ETelD	Etappentelegraphendirektion	telegraph direction of the communications zone
Et.Fp.K	Etappenfuhrparkkolonne	communications zone transport and supply column
Et.Hpt.O	**Etappenhauptort**	**field base of communications zone**
Et.Insp	**Etappeninspekteur**	**inspector of the communications zone**
Et.Kdt	**Etappenkommandant**	**commandant of the communications zone**
Etkomet Et.Ko.M.u.T	**Kommandeur der Etappen-Munitionskolonnen und Trosse**	**commander of the ammunition columns and trains in the communications zone**
Et.Laz	Etappenlazarett	stationary hospital in the communications zone
Et.Mag	Etappenmagazin	supply depot in the communications zone
Et.Mun.Kol	Etappenmunitionskolonne	communications zone ammunition column
Et.Mun.Verw	Etappenmunitionsverwaltung	administration of ammunition depots in the communications zone
Et.Pf.D	**Etappenpferdedepot**	**remount depot in communications zone**
Et.San.Dep	**Etappensanitätsdepot**	**depot of medical supplies in communications zone**
E. V	**Einführungsverordnung**	**introductory regulations**
E.V	Empfangsverstärker	receiving amplifier (*radio*)
E.V	Etappenverwendungsfähig	suitable for employment in zone of communications
evang	evangelisch	Protestant (*on identity discs*)
E.V.F	Etappenverwendungsfähig im Felde	fit for field service in the communications zone
EVO	Eisenbahnverkehrsordnung	railroad traffic regulations
evtl	eventuell	eventual; possible
Ew	Einwohner	inhabitant; resident
EWGG	Einsatzwehrmachtgebührnisgesetz	law governing special assignment compensation
Ex	Exil	exile; banishment
exerz	exerzieren	to drill
Exerz.Pl	Exerzierplatz	parade ground; drill ground
Exist.K	Existenzkampf	fight for existence
Ex.Mun	Exerziermunition	blank ammunition
exp	exportieren	to export
Ex.Patr	Exerzierpatrone	dummy cartridge; blank
Exped.-K	Expeditionskorps	expeditionary force
Exp.Kr	Expansionskraft	power of expansion
Expl	Exemplar	specimen; copy
Ex.Pl	Exerzierplatz	parade grounds; drill grounds
expl	explosiv	explosive
Expr	Express	express train
Exptr	Expeditionstruppen	expeditionary troops
Ex.R	Exerzierreglement	drill regulations
Ex.Rgl	Exerzierreglement	drill regulations to statute law
Exz	Exzellenz	Excellency
Ez	Eilzug	express train
E.Z	empfindlicher Zünder	instantaneous fuze
E.Zug	Eilzug	express train

F

F	Fähre	ferry (*on maps*)
F	Fahrabteilung	transport section; horsement
F	Fahrenheit	Fahrenheit
F	Fahrtruppe	horse-drawn supply service
F	Feind	enemy
f	feindlich	**hostile**
F	Feld-	field
F	Feldküchenverpflegung	field-kitchen food supply, feeding through field-kit-
F	Fernerkundung	long-distance reconnaissance
F	Fernsprecher	telephone
F	Festung	fort; fortress; fortification
F	Feuer	fire
F	Feuerwerker	ordnance sergeant; artificer
F	F-Flagge	F-flag (*for military telephone stations*)
F	Fläche	area; plane surface (*aviation*)
F	Flug	flight
F	Fluss	river
F	Försterei	forest ranger's house (*on*
f	folgende	following
F	Forst	forest
f	freitragend	cantilever (*airplane*)
F	Frequenz	frequency (*radio*)
F	Friede	peace
F	Führer	leader; commander; driver of vehicle
F	Führungsamt der NSDAP	board for tactical leadership of the National Socialist Party
f	für	for
F	Fuhrpark	wagon park
F	Funk; Funker	radio; radio operator
	Füsilier	fusilier; light-infantry
F.A.	Fahrabteilung	transport section; horse-drawn transport detachment
F.A.	Feldartillerie	field artillery
F.A.	Forstamt	office of the local forest superintendent (*on maps*)
F.A.	Fürsorge - Abteilung des Reichswehrministeriums	Social Service Division of the German War Department
Fab.	Fabrik	factory
Fabr.	Fabrik	factory (*on maps*)
F.A. Brig.	Feldartillerie-Brigade	field artillery brigade
Fachgr.	Fachgruppe	occupational group
FAD	Freiwilliger Arbeitsdienst	voluntary labor service
Fähnr.	Fähnrich	officer candidate (*rank corresponding roughly to U. S. sergeant*)
Fahn.J.	Fahnenjunker	cadet (*rank corresponding roughly to U. S. corporal*)
Fahr.	Fahrenheit	Fahrenheit
fahrb.	fahrbar	passable; navigable; transportable
Fahrb.-D.	Fahrbahndecke	road surface
Fahrtr.Ausb.	Fahrtruppenausbildung	training of personnel of horsedrawn services
Fahrv.	Fahrvorschrift für die Fahrtruppen	driving regulations for the horse-drawn services
Fahrw.	Fahrwerk	landing gear; undercarriage (*aviation*); chassis
FAK	Freiwilliges Automobilkorps	Volunteer Automobile Corps
Fallsch.	Fallschirm	parachute
Fallsch. Spr.	Fallschirmspringer	parachutist
FAR	Feldartillerieregiment	field artillery regiment
farb.	farbig	colored
F.A.S.	Flakartillerieschule	antiaircraft school
Fasch.	Faschine	fascine (*bundle for the strengthening of field fortifications*)
Fasch.	Faschismus, Faschist	fascism; fascist
fb.	fahrbar	passable; navigable; transportable
Fb.	Feldbahn	field railway
F.B.	Feldbefestigungsvorschrift	manual of field fortifications
Fb.	Festungsbau	fortress-construction
Fb.	Fliehbolzen	disappearing firing-pin (*fuze*)
F.B.	Flugzeugbreite	width of plane
F.B.	Füsilierbataillon	fusilier battalion
Fba.	Fahrbahn	roadway
F.B.Abt.	Feldeisenbahnbetriebsabteilung	field railroad operation unit
Fb. A.I.W.m.	Fahrbare Artillerie-Instandsetzungs-Werkstatt mit Motorzug	motor-drawn artillery repair workshop
Fbba.	Feldbahnbetriebsamt	field-railway operations office
Fb.Backof.	fahrbarer Backofen	mobile baking oven
F.B.D.	Feldbahndepot	field railway depot
FbH.	Festungsbauhauptmann	fortress construction captain
F.B.K.	Feldbäckereikolonne	field bakery column
fb.Kwerkst.	fahrbare Kraftwagenwerkstatt	mobile repair shop
FbM.	Festungsbaumajor	fortress construction major
F.B.O.	Festungsbauordnung	manual for the construction of fortifications

Ersatzreserve I reserves comprising untrained men under 35.
Ersatzreserve II reserves comprising physically unfit, untrained men under 35.
Ersatzreserveausbildung *f* training of replacement reserves.
Ersatzschaltschema *n* equivalent circuit (*Elec*).
Ersatzteil *n* reserve unit (*Tac*); spare part.
Ersatztruppen *fpl* replacements.
Ersatzverpflegungsmagazin *n* ration depot (*Z of I*).
Ersatzwesen *n* recruiting and replacement administration.
Erschießen der Tageseinflüsse obtaining metro data by registration (*FA*).
erschöpfen to exhaust, wear out, use up.
Erschütterung *f* concussion, shock.
erstarren become rigid or stiff; "freeze" in position.
Erstausstattung *f* initial issue.
erste Hilfe first aid.
Erster Offizier first officer (*Nav*).
ersticken asphyxiate, choke, stifle, suffocate.
erstickender Kampfstoff lung irritant.
Erststrom *m* primary current.
erstürmen to rush, take by assault (*Tac*).
Erträglichkeitsgrenze *f* harassing concentration (*CWS*).
Erwa-Meldung *f* stand-by message (*preliminary to metro message*) (*Arty*).
Erwiderungsfeuer *n* retaliation fire, counterfire.
erzwingen force (*a crossing, etc.*).
Etappe *f* communications zone (*superseded by* rückwärtiges Armeegebiet, *but still frequently used*).
Etappenmarsch *m* administrative march.
Etat *m* budget.
Etatposten *m* budget item.
Exerzierbombe *f* drill bomb, practice bomb.
Exerzieren *n* drill, practice.
Exerzierform *f* drill formation.
Exerziergeschoß *n* dummy projectile.
Exerzierhalle *f* drill hall.
Exerzierhaus *n* armory.
Exerziermarsch *m* goose step.
Exerziermunition *f* drill ammunition, dummy ammunition.
Exerzierordnung *f* drill formation; drill regulations.
Exerzierpatrone *f* dummy cartridge.
Exerzierplatz *m* drill ground, parade ground.
Exerzierschritt *m* *See* **Exerziermarsch.**
Exerziervorschrift *f* drill regulations.
Exzenterhülse *f* eccentric sleeve

F

Fabrik *f* factory.
Fach *n* field of competency, trade, profession; branch of knowledge; specialty; compartment, pigeonhole.
Fachabteilungen *fpl* professional service units (*Med*).
Facharbeiter *m* technician, skilled workman, specialist.
Fachausdruck *m* technical term.
Fachbearbeiter *m* staff officer or official in charge of some technical branch or administrative department.
Fachberater *m* technical adviser.
Fächermotor *m* fan-type engine, double-V engine.
Fächerturn *m* half-loop wing-over (*Avn*).
Fachmann *m* specialist, expert.
Fachsprache *f* technical terminology.
Fachverständiger *m* specialist, expert.
Fachwerk *n* latticework, grillage; truss.
Fachwerkbrücke *f* truss bridge.
Fachwerkträger *m* truss (*Bdg*).
Fackel *f* flare, torch.
Faden *m* thread, filament; string; fathom (*Nav*); front-sight slit (*aiming circle*); hair (*Optics*).
Fadenkreuz *n* cross hairs, cross wires (*Optics*).
Fadenstück *n* front-sight piece (*aiming circle*).
Fahne *f* colors, flag, guidon.
Fahnenband *n* battle honors.
Fahneneid *m* oath of allegiance, oath of enlistment.
Fahnenflucht *f* desertion.
Fahnenflüchtiger *m* deserter.
Fahnenjunker *m* officer candidate (*from enlistment until promotion to* Fähnrich).
Fahnenjunker-Gefreiter *m* officer candidate (*with grade of* Gefreiter).
Fahnenjunker-Unteroffizier *m* NCO officer candidate (*with grade of Sgt*).
Fahnenkompanie *f* color guard company.
Fahnenmast *m* fixed flagpole.
Fahnenposten *m* color sentinel.
Fahnenschaft *m* flagpole.
Fahnenstange *f* flagpole, pike.
Fahnenträger *m* color bearer, guidon.
Fahnentrupp *m* color guard.
Fahnentuch *n* bunting.
Fahnenwache *f* color guard, color sentinel.
Fähnrich *m* officer candidate (*grade above* Fahnenjunker-Unteroffizier).
Fahrabteilung *f* supply-train battalion (*H-Dr*).
Fahrausweis *m* travel order, traveling permit.
Fahrbahn *f* roadway.
Fahrbahnträger *m* floor beam, roadway girder (*Bdg*).
fahrbar passable (*for vehicles*); mobile; practicable; navigable.
Fahrbefehl *m* transportation order (*MT*).
Fahrbenzin *n* standard gasoline.
Fahrbereich *m* operating range, traveling distance, cruising radius (*MT, Tk*).
Fährbetrieb *m* ferrying operations.
Fahrbremse *f* wheel brake (*G carriage*).
Fähre *f* ferry.
fahren to drive, travel, ride.
fahrendes Ziel moving target (*Tk, vehicle*).
Fahrer *m* driver (*MT, Tk, etc.*); private (*H-Dr Transport*).
Fahrerhaus *n* cab (*Trk*).
Fahreroptik *f* driver's periscope (*Tk*).
Fahrgast *m* passenger.
Fahrgerät *n* propelling equipment (*Engr*).
Fahrgestell *n* chassis (*MT*); landing gear, landing-gear frame (*Ap*).
Fahrkarte *f* transportation ticket (*RR, bus, etc.*).
Fahrkolonne *f* horse-drawn column.
Fahrkostenentschädigung *f* travel allowance (*reimbursement*).
Fahrküche *f* rolling kitchen.
Fahrlässigkeit *f* negligence.
Fahrleistung *f* traveling capacity (*MT, Tk*).
Fahrplan *m* timetable, train schedule.
Fährprahm *m* tank landing craft.
Fahrrad *n* bicycle.
Fahrrinne *f* rut.
Fährseil *n* ferry cable.
Fährstelle *f* ferrying site, ferry embarkation point.
Fahrstellung *f* traveling position (*Ord*).
Fahrt *f* ride, run; trip, journey; speed.
Fahrtenschwimmer *m* qualified swimmer (*on basis of time-endurance test*).
Fahrtliste *f* entraining table.
Fahrtmesser *m* airspeed indicator.
Fahrtrupp *m* boat crew (*Engr*).
Fahrtruppen *fpl* transportation units (*H-Dr*).
Fahrweg *m* dirt road.
Fahrwerk *n* landing gear (*Ap*); running gear, chassis (*MT*); suspensions and tracks (*Tk*).
Fahrwerkachse *f* landing-gear axle (*Ap*).
Fahrwerkrahmen *m* chassis frame (*MT*).
Fahrwerkstrebe *f* landing-gear strut (*Ap*).
Fahrwiderstand *m* tractional resistance (*MT*).
Fahrwind *m* air stream, airflow.
Fahrzeug *n* vehicle; craft.
Fahrzeugüberhang *m* overhang, angle of approach (*MT*).
Fall *m* drop, fall; case, instance.
Fallbahn *f* bomb trajectory.
Fallbenzintank *m* gravity tank (*MT*).
Fallbeschleunigung *f* downward acceleration (*Ballistics*).
Fallbö *f* downdraft (*Met*).
Fallblockverschluß *m* drop-block type breechblock (*G*).
Falle *f* trap, decoy; catch (*MG*).
Fallenachse *f* catch pivot (*MG*).
Fallgeschwindigkeit *f* velocity of fall (*Ballistics*).
Fallgesetz *n* law of falling bodies.
Fallhöhe *f* drop, height of drop.
Fallklappe *f* drop (*Tp switchboard*).
Fallpunkt *m* level point, point of fall (*Ballistics*).
Fallschirm *m* parachute.
Fallschirmabsprung *m* parachute jump.
Fallschirmabsprungturm *m* parachute tower, controlled tower.
Fallschirmbombe *f* parachute bomb.
Fallschirmgerät *n* parachute equipment.
Farb-Spritzanlage *f* spray painting unit.
farbtonrichtig orthochromatic.
Faschine *f* fascine.
Faschinenbahn *f* fascine road.
Faschinendamm *m* raised fascine road.
Faser *f* fiber.
Fassung *f* receptacle, socket (*Elec*); text or wording, version; composure.
Fassungsvermögen *n* volumetric capacity.
fäulnisbekämpfend antiseptic.
Faust *f* fist.
Faustachse *f* Mercedes-type front axle (*MT*).
Fäustel *n* mallet.
Fausthandschuh *m* mitten.
Faustriemen *m* sword knot.
Faustskizze *f* rough sketch.
F-Boot *n* tank landing craft.
Feder *f* pen; spring; feather.
Federantrieb *m* spring action (*clockwork fuze*).
Federaufhängung *f* spring suspension (*MT*).
Federausgleicher *m* spring equilibrator (*G*).
Federbarometer *n* aneroid barometer.
Federbein *n* shock-absorbing strut (*Ap*).
Federbock *m* spring hanger (*MT*).
Federbolzen *m* spring bolt (*MT*).
Federbund *n* spring clip (*MT*).
Federeinrichtung *f* spring mechanism (*MG*).
Federgehänge *n* spring suspension.
Federhand *f* spring bracket (*MT*).
Federkolben *m* breechblock endpiece (*self-loading pistol*).
Federkopf *m* follower-spring stud (*self-loading pistol*).
Federkraft *f* elasticity.
Federlasche *f* shackle, spring shackle (*MT*).
Federluftdruckmesser *m* aneroid barometer.
Federring *m* lockwasher.
Federteller *m* valve-spring retainer (*Mtr*).
Federung *f* suspension (*MT*).
Federvorholer *m* spring counterrecoil mechanism, spring recuperator (*G*).
Federwolke *f* cirrus cloud.
Fallschirmgewehr *n* parachutist's automatic rifle.
Fallschirmgurt *m* parachute harness.
Fallschirmjäger *m* parachutist.
Fallschirmjäger-Abteilung *f* parachute detachment.
Fallschirmjägerbataillon *n* parachute battalion.
Fallschirmlast *f* delivery unit (*airborne operations*).
Fallschirmleuchtbombe *f* aircraft parachute flare.
Fallschirmleuchtkugel *f* parachute flare.
Fallschirmleuchtpatrone *f* parachute-flare cartridge (*for Sig pistol*).
Fallschirmrakete *f* parachute rocket signal.
Fallschirmsack *m* pack assembly, pack (*Prcht*).
Fallschirmschütze *m* parachutist rifleman.
Fallschirmschützen-Abzeichen *n* parachute badge (*decoration*).
Fallschirmspringer *m* parachutist.
Fallschirmtruppen *fpl* parachute troops.
Fallschirmturm *m* parachute tower.
Fallstromvergaser *m* downdraft carburetor.
Falltafel *f* bomb trajectory table.
Falltür *f* trapdoor; escape hatch (*Ap*).
Fallwind *m* katabatic wind (*Met*).
Fallwinkel *m* angle of fall (*Ballistics*).
Fallzeit *f* time of fall (*Bombing*).
Faltboot *n* faltboat, collapsible boat with rubberized-cloth skin.
Familienunterhalt *m* dependency benefits.
Fangleine *f* shroud line (*Prcht*).
Fangnetz *n* anti-submarine net.
Fangschnur *f* aiguillette, fourragere.
Fangstoß *m* parry.
farbenblind color blind.
Farbentüchtigkeit *f* color vision.
farblos colorless.
Fehlbestand *m* shortage, discrepancy (*supplies, etc.*).
Fehler *m* error; defect; miss.
Fehlerdreieck *n* triangle of error (*Surv*).
fehlerhaft defective.
Fehlgänger *m* miss.
Fehlgriff *m* blunder.
Fehlleistung *f* malfunction.
fehlschlagen fail.
Fehlschuß *m* miss.
Fehlstart *m* unsuccessful take-off (*Avn*).
Fehlstelle *f* vacancy (*Adm*).
Fehltreffer *m* near miss.
Fehlweisung *f* deviation (*Rad*).
Fehlzerspringer *m* low-order burst, low-order shell (*Am*).

Fehlzündung *f* backfire *(Mtr)*.
Feigheit *f* cowardice.
Feile *f* file *(tool)*.
Feind *m* enemy.
Feindbeobachtung *f* observation of or by the enemy.
Feindberührung *f* contact with the enemy.
Feindbeschuß *m* enemy fire.
Feindbesetzung *f* occupation by the enemy.
Feinddruck *m* enemy pressure.
Feindeinsicht *f* enemy observation.
Feindeinwirkung *f* enemy action.
Feindesland *n* enemy territory, hostile territory.
Feindflug *m* raid, sortie, combat mission *(Avn)*.
Feindflugausweis *m* special identification card carried on missions during which capture by enemy is likely *(Avn)*.
feindfrei clear of the enemy.
Feindgelände *n* enemy terrain.
Feindnachrichten *fpl* information about the enemy.
Feindnähe *f* closeness to the enemy, nearness to the enemy.
Feindraum *m* enemy zone.
Feindseligkeiten *fpl* hostilities.
Feindsicht *f* enemy observation.
Feindtätigkeit *f* enemy activity.
Feindzusammenstoß *m* collision with the enemy.
Feineinstellung *f* fine tuning *(Rad)*; fine setting, precision adjustment.
Feinhöhenmesser *m* sensitive altimeter *(Ap)*.
Feldflughafen *m* field airdrome.
Feldflugplatz *m* advanced airfield.
Feldfunksprecher *m* See **Feldfunksprechgerät.**
Feldfunksprechgerät *n* field radio set.
Feldgeistlicher *m* chaplain.
Feldgendarm *m* military policeman.
Feldgendarmerie *f* military police.
Feldgendarmerievorschrift *f* military police regulations.
Feldgerät *n* field equipment.
Feldgericht *n* provost court, court-martial.
Feldgeschütz *n* field gun.
Feldhandapparat *m* field handset *(Tp)*.
Feldhaubitze *f* field howitzer.
Feldheer *n* field forces.
Feldherrnkunst *f* strategy, generalship.
Feldinstandsetzung *f* line maintenance.
Feldjustizamt *n* legal branch of army, corps and division general staffs *(consists of civilian officials)*.
Feldkabel *n* field wire *(Tp)*.
Feldkabelader *f* field-wire strand *(Tp)*.
Feldkabelbau *m* field-wire laying *(Tp)*.
Feldkabelleitung *f* field-wire line *(Tp)*.
Feldkanone *f* field gun.
Feldkaplan *m* chaplain.
Feldklappenschrank *m* portable switchboard.
Feldkochherd *m* field range *(cooker)*.
Feldkochunteroffizier *m* cook *(NCO)*.
Feldkommandantur *f* military administration headquarters *(in Com Z and occupied countries)*. Compare **Ortskommandantur, Stadtkommandantur.**
Feldküche *f* field kitchen, rolling kitchen.
Feldlaboratorium *n* field laboratory *(Med)*.
Feldlager *n* bivouac, encampment.
Feldlazarett *n* surgical hospital.
Feldmarschall *m* Field Marshal *(Ger)*.
Feldmeister *m* first sergeant *(Reich Labor Service)*.
Feldmeßkästchen *n* field testing set *(Tp)*.
Feldmütze *f* garrison cap.
Feinkorn *n* fine sight *(R aiming)*; fine grain *(Photo)*.
Feld *n* field *(Top, Elec)*; land *(rifling)*; bay *(Ap)*.
langes Feld chase of gun barrel.
Feldanzug *m* field uniform.
Feldarmee *f* field army.
Feldausbildungsdivision *f* field training division.
Feldausrüstung *f* field equipment.
Feldausstattung *f* field equipment; ammunition reserve.
Feldbäckerei *f* field bakery.
Feldbahn *f* narrow-gage field railway.
Feldbauamt *n* airdrome maintenance office.
Feldbefestigung *f* field fortification.
Feldbischof *m* Chief of Chaplains.
Feldbluse *f* service coat.
feldbrauchbar serviceable for use in the field.
Feldbrunnen *m* field well.
Feldbücherei *f* military field library.
Felddauerlinie *f* permanent field-telephone line.
Felddienst *m* field duty.
felddienstfähig fit for active duty.
Felddienstordnung *f* field service regulations.
Felddienstübung *f* field exercise.
Feldeisenbahn *f* field railway.
Feldeisenbahnbetriebsamt *n* field railway operations office.
Feldeisenbahndirektion *f* field railway command station.
Feldeisenbahner *m* field railway engineer.
Feldeisenbahnmaschinenamt *n* field railway machinery office.
Feldeisenbahnwerkstättenamt *n* field railway workshop office.
Feldelement *n* field cell *(Tp)*.
Felder *npl* lands *(Ord)*; fields *(Top)*.
Feldersatzbataillon *n* replacement training battalion *(assigned to the field forces)*.
Felderscheibe *f* target divided into squares.
Felder und Züge lands and grooves.
Feldfernkabel *n* field trunk wire *(Tp)*.
Feldfernkabeltrupp *m* wire-laying team *(Tp)*.
Feldfernsprecher *m* field telephone; field telephone operator.
Feldflasche *f* canteen *(for water)*.
Feldnachrichtenkommandantur *f* field signal command *(signal Hq for an area of occupied territory or in rear area of T of Opns)*.
Feldpolizei *f* See **Geheime Feldpolizei.**
Feldportion *f* field ration *(for Pers)*.
Feldpost *f* army postal service.
Feldpostamt *n* army post office.
Feldpostbeamter *m* army mail clerk *(Civ official)*.
Feldposteinheit *f* army postal unit.
Feldposten *m* outguard sentinel.
Feldpostwesen *n* army postal service.
Feldprediger *m* chaplain.
Feldprüfschrank *m* field testing box *(Tp)*.
Feldrain *m* uncultivated strip at edge of field.
Feldration *f* field ration *(for animals)*.
Feldschanze *f* field fortification, earthwork.
Feldsicherungskästchen *n* field fuse box *(Tp)*.
Feldsonderbataillon *n* field disciplinary battalion.
Feldstraflager *n* field disciplinary camp.
Feldtrage *f* field litter *(Med)*.
Feldunterarzt *m* acting medical officer.
Feldverpflegung *f* field messing.
Feldwache *f* outguard.
Feldwagen *m* field wagon.
Feldwebel *m* technical sergeant.
Feldweg *m* cross-country dirt road.
Feldwerkstatt *f* field workshop.
Feldwerkstattzug *m* field workshop platoon.
Feldwetterstelle *f* field weather station.
Feldwetterwarte *f* See **Feldwetterstelle.**
Feldzeugbataillon *n* ordnance battalion.
Feldzeugkommando *n* ordnance command *(one in each* Wehrkreis *and some in occupied countries)*.
Feldzeuglager *n* ordnance depot.
Feldzeugstab *m* ordnance staff.
Feldzug *m* campaign.
Felge *f* felloe, rim.
Felgenband *n* tire flap *(MT)*.
Fels *m* rock, cliff.
Felsblock *m* boulder, rock.
Felsenklippe *f* bluff *(Top)*.
Fenster *n* sight peephole *(AA sight)*; window.
Fepo *f* See **Geheime Feldpolizei.**
Ferdinand name of a heavily-armored German self-propelled gun.
Fernantrieb *m* remote drive, remote control.
Fernaufklärer *m* long-range reconnaissance airplane.
Fernaufklärung *f* distant reconnaissance; long-range reconnaissance *(Avn)*.
Fernaufklärungsflugboot *n* patrol bomber, long-range reconnaissance flying boat.
Fernaufklärungsflugzeug *n* See **Fernaufklärer.**
Fernaufklärungsgruppe *f* air force long-range reconnaissance group *(attached to ground forces and composed of two or more* F-Staffeln).
Fernaufklärungsstaffel *f* long-range reconnaissance squadron attached to army ground units *(abbr.* F-Staffel).
Fernbesprechgerät *n* remote control unit *(Rad)*.
Fernbesprechung *f* remote control operation *(Rad)*.
Fernbild *n* telephoto.
Fernbomber *m* long-range bomber.
Ferndrucker *m* teletype, teletypewriter, telegraph printer.
Fernempfang *m* long-distance reception *(Rad)*.
Fernempfangszone *f* reception zone beyond the skip distance *(Rad)*.
Fernerkunder *m* See **Fernaufklärer.**
Fernfahrtmesser *m* remote-reading airspeed indicator *(Ap)*.
ferngelenkt remote-controlled.
Ferngeschütz *n* See **Fernkampfgeschütz.**
Ferngespräch *n* telephone call, telephone conversation.
ferngesteuert remote-controlled.
Fernglas *n* binoculars, field glass.
Fernhörer *m* receiver *(Tp, Rad Tp)*.
Fernkabel *n* trunk wire *(Tp)*.
Fernkampfartillerie *f* long-range artillery.
Fernkampfflugzeug *n* long-range bombardment airplane.
Fernkampfgeschütz *n* long-range gun.
Fernkompaß *m* remote-reading compass *(Ap)*.
Fernkurs *m* correspondence course.
Fernleitung *f* long-distance circuit, interurban line *(Tp)*.
Fernlenkung *f* remote control.
Fernlicht *n* bright light *(on auto headlight)*.
Fernmeßgerät *n* range finder.
Fernmeldeanlage *f* communication station *(Sig C)*.
Fernmesser *m* range finder; range-finder operator.
fernmündlich by telephone.
Fernrichten des Geschützes remote gun control *(CA, Nav)*.
Fernrohr *n* telescope; binoculars *(in this sense, generally* Doppelfernrohr).
Fernrohrarme *mpl* telescope tubes *(BC telescope)*.
Fernrohraufnahme *f* telephoto.
Fernrohraufsatz *m* telescopic sight.
fernrohrbesetzt equipped with telescopic sight *(R)*.
Fernrohrhals *m* telescope center section.
Fernrohrhülse *f* telescope housing.
Fernrohrkopf *m* telescope head.
Fernrohrkörper *m* telescope tube; body *(of binoculars)*.
Fernrohrlager *n* telescope seat.
Fernrohrsteg *m* telescope support.
Fernschreiber *m* teletype, teletypewriter, telegraph printer; teletype operator.
Fernschreibkompanie *f* teletype company, telegraph-printer company.
Fernschreibleitung *f* teletype circuit.
Fernschreibnetz *n* teletype net *(Luftwaffe)*.
Fernschreibwagen *m* teletype truck.
Fernsehen *n* television.
Fernsicht *f* visibility.
Fernsprechanschluß *m* telephone connection.
Fernsprechbaukompanie *f* telephone-construction company.
Fernsprechbautrupp *m* telephone-construction crew.
Fernsprechbauwagen *m* telephone-construction truck.
Fernsprechbetriebstrupp *m* telephone-operations team.
Fernsprechbetriebswagen *m* telephone-operations truck.
Fernsprechbetriebszug *m* telephone operating platoon.
Feuer in der oberen Winkelgruppe high-angle fire.
Feuer in der unteren Winkelgruppe low-angle fire.
Feuerkampf *m* fire fight, fire duel, weapons duel.
Feuerkette *f* line of skirmishers.
Feuerkommando *n* firing command *(Arty)*.
Feuerkraft *f* fire power.
Feuer kreuzen to cross fire.
Feuerleitgerät *n* fire-control equipment, ballistic director *(Arty)*.
Feuerleitung *f* fire direction, fire control.
Feuerleitungsnetz *n* fire control net, fire direction net *(Arty)*.
Feuerleitungsplan *m* fire-control map *(Arty)*.
Feuerleitungsstand *m* fire-direction center.
Feuerleitungsstelle *f* See **Feuerleitungsstand.**
Feuerlinie *f* firing line.
Feuerlöscher *m* fire extinguisher.
Feuerlöschordnung *f* fire plan *(fire prevention measure)*.
Feueröffnung *f* commencement of firing.
Feuerpatsche *f* fire swatter *(used in fire fighting)*.
Feuerpause *f* cessation of fire *(Arty)*.
"Feuerpause!" "Cease firing!"
Feuerplan *m* plan of fire *(Tac)*.
Feuerplattform *f* gun platform.
Feuerregelung *f* fire control, conduct of fire.
Feuerriegel *m* box barrage.
Feuersäule *f* column of flames.
Feuerschiff *n* lightship.
Feuerschlag *m* sudden concentration *(Arty)*.
Feuerschutz *m* covering fire, protective fire; fire support, coverage by supporting fire; artillery protection.
Feuerschütze *m* aerial gunner.
Feuerschutzpolizei *f* fire protection police.
feuersicher fireproof.

Fbr	Fabrik	factory; manufacturing plant
Fbrn	Fabriken	factories *(on maps)*
Fd	Feind	enemy
fd	feindlich	hostile
Fd	Feld	field
f.d	für den, die, das	for the
F.d.D	Führer der Deckungstruppen	commander of covering troops *(bridge construction)*
fdf	felddienstfähig	fit for field duty
Fdg	Fahndung	search for missing person
fdl	feindlich	hostile
Fd.Laz	Feldlazarett	field hospital
FDO	Felddienstordnung	field service regulations
F.d.R	Für die Richtigkeit	a true copy *(certification of accuracy used with signatures)*
F.d.Ü	Führer der Übersetztruppen	leader of river-crossing troops *(bridge construction)*
F.E	Feldeisenbahn	field railroad
Fe	Fernsprech-	telephone
F.E.A	Fliegerersatzabteilung	aviation replacement training center
FeArt	Feldartillerie	field artillery
Febr	Februar	February
Fech	Feldeisenbahnchef, Chef des Feldeisenbahnwesens	chief of the field railroad service
Fech Zetl	Chef des Feldeisenbahnwesens, Zentralstelle	chief of the field railroad service, main office
Fedrawa	Felddrachenwarte	kite-balloon field station *(meteorology)*
feindl	feindlich	hostile
Feka	Fernkampfartillerie	long-range artillery
Fe.Kp	Fernsprechkompanie	telephone company
F.El	Fernmeldetechnik im Heere	long-distance communication technique in army
Felda	Feldartillerie	field artillery
Felda.G	Feldartilleriegerät	field artillery equipment
Felda.G.96 n/A	Feldartilleriegerät 1896 neuer Art	field artillery equipment 1896 (new type)
Feld-AR	Feldartillerie-Regiment	field artillery regiment
Feldausb.Div	Feldausbildungdivision	field training division
Feldb.Kol	Feldbäckerei-Kolonne	field bakery column
Feldb.Wag	Feldbäckerei-Wagen	field bakery wagon
Feld.Ers.Btl	Feldersatzbataillon	field replacement battalion
Feldg	Feldgendarm, Feldgendarmerie	military policeman; military police
Feldgend	Feldgendarm, Feldgendarmerie	military policeman; military police
Feldgend.Tr	Feldgendarmerie-Trupp	military police detachment
Feldg.O	Feldgendarmerie-Ordnung	regulation governing military police
Feld.Hb.Laz.(mot)	Feldhalblazarett (motorisiert)	motorized field hospital, half strength
Feldh.G.98	Feldhaubitzgerät 1898	field howitzer equipment,
Feldk	Feldküche	field kitchen
Feld.Kdtr	Feldkommandantur	Field Administrative Headqua
Feldlaz	Feldlazarett	field hospital
feldm	feldmässig	equipped to take to the quirements
Feldm	Feldmarschall	field marshal
Feldm	Feldmeister	leader in compulsory labor service (seventh rank)
Feldm	Feldmesser	geometer; land-surveyor
Feldm	Feldmütze	field service cap
Feldnachkdtr	Feldnachrichtenkommandatur	field communication headquarters
Feldpola	Feldpolizeiabschnitt der Geheimen Feldpolizei des Oberkommando Nord (Grenzschutz)	field police sector of the Secret Field Police of the Northern High Command (border guard)
Feldtelchef	Chef des Feldtelegrafiewesens	commander of the field telegraphic service
Feldw	Feldwache	picket
Feldw	Feldwebel	*(corresponds roughly to U. S. first sergeant)*
Feld-Wg	Feldwagen	field wagon
Feldz	Feldzeichen	ensign; standard; banner;
Feldz	Feldzug	campaign
Feldzgm	Feldzeugmeister	Chief of Ordnance Department
Fernaufkl.Fl.Sta	Fernaufklärungsfliegerstaffel	long - range reconnaissance squadron
Fernf	Fernfeuer	long-range fire
ferngest	ferngesteuert	guided by remote control *(aviation)*; wireless
Fernk	Fernkampf	battle at long range; long-range fire
Fernl.N	Fernleitungsnetz	station-to-station telephone-line net; trunk system
Ferns.Ap	Fernsehapparat	television apparatus
Fernschr	Fernschreiber	teletype apparatus
Fernspr	Fernsprecher	telephone
Fernst	Fernerkundungsstaffel	long - range reconnaissanc
Ferns.Verb	Fernsehverbindung	television connection
Fe.-Spr	Fernspruch	telephone call;
Fess. B	Fesselballon	captive balloon; sausage balloon
Fest	Festung	fortification; fortress; fort
Fest.Bes	Festungsbesatzung	fortress garrison
Festb.Fw	Festungsbaufeldwebel	*(corresponds roughly to U. S. first sergeant) (fortress construction)*

Fest.B.Hptm	Festungsbauhauptmann	fortress construction captain
Festb.Lehrg	Festungsbaulehrgang	course of instruction in the construction of fortifications
Festb.Sch	Festungsbauschule	training school for the construction of fortifications
Fest.Fernspr.P	Festungs-Fernsprechpark	fortification telephone depot
Fest.Fw	Festungsbaufeldwebel	(*corresponds roughly to U. S. first sergeant*)
Fest.Gef	Festungsgefängnis	fortress prison
Fest.Gef	Festungsgefangener	prisoner in a fortress
Festg.Laz	Festungslazarett	fortress hospital
Fest.Gt	Festungsgürtel	ring of detached forts; ring of forts
festh	festungshaft	restricted to post
Fest.Hptm	Festungsbauhauptmann	fortress construction captain
Fest.Kmdt	Festungskommandant	fortress commander
Festkr	Festungskrieg	siege warfare
Fest.O.Fw	Festungsbauoberfeldwebel	(*corresponds roughly to U. S. staff sergeant*) (*fortress construction*)
Fest.San.K	Festungssanitätskompanie	fortress medical company
Festst	Feststellung	establishing; fixing; settling; discovering; stating; identification; determination
Fest.Üb	Festungsübung	fortress drill
Fest.W	Festungswall	fortress rampart
Feu	Feuer	fire
Feu.A	Feuerart	type of fire
Feuergeschw	Feuergeschwindigkeit	rate of fire
Feuergew	Feuergewicht	density of fire
Feu.Eröff	Feuereröffnung	opening fire
Feuerstg	Feuerstellung	firing position; battery position; emplacement (*artillery*)
Feuerw	Feuerwaffen	firearms
Feuerw	Feuerwerker	ordnance sergeant; artificer
Feu.Flak-Gr	Feuerleitungsstelle für Flakgruppe	fire control post for antiaircraft section
Feu.Fm	Feuerform	types of fire; classification of fire
Feu.Gef	Feuergefecht	fire action
Feu.Ltg	Feuerleitung	fire control
Feu.P	Feuerpause	firing pause; interval in firing
Feu.Übf	Feuerüberfall	surprise fire
Feu.Wlz	Feuerwalze	rolling barrage; creeping barrage
Fewewa	Feldwetterwarte	field meteorological station
FF	Maschinenkanone in die Flügel eines Flugzeugs	rapid-fire cannon in the wing of an airplane
F.F.Kabel	Feldfernkabel	two-strand field cable
F.Fspr	Feldfernsprecher	field telephone
F.Fu	Fernmeldetechnik im Heere	long-distance communication technique in the army
FG	feldgrau	field gray
fg	folgende	following
F.G.A	Feldgendarmerieabteilung	field military police unit
Fgd	Feldgendarm, Feldgendarmerie	military policeman; military police
Fgd.O	Feldgendarmerie-Ordnung	regulation governing military police
F.-Ges.B	Feldgesangbuch	field song book
Fgo	Feldgendarmerieordnung	regulation governing military police
F.Gr	Feldgranate	high-explosive shell
Fh	Fähre	ferry
F.H	Feldhaubitze	field howitzer
F.H	Feldheer	field force; army in the field
F.H	Flugzeughöhe	height of plane
Fh	Forsthaus	forest ranger's house (*on maps*)
F.H.Ger	Feldhaubitzgerät	field howitzer equipment
F.H.Gr	Feldhaubitzgranate	field howitzer shell
F.H.Gr.(N)	Feldhaubitzgranate (Nebel)	field howitzer shell (smoke)
F.H.Gr.Stg	Feldhaubitzgranate(Stahlring)	field howitzer shell (steel band)
Fhj	Fahnenjunker	cadet (*corresponding roughly to U. S. corporal*)
F.H.M.K	Feldhaubitzenmunitionskolonne	field howitzer ammunition column
Fhr	Fähnrich	officer candidate (*corresponding roughly to U. S. sergeant*)
Fhr	Führer	leader; commander; driver of vehicle
Fhr	Fuhrwerk	horse-drawn vehicle
Fhrp	Fuhrpark	wagon park
Fhrws	Fuhrwesen	transport service
Fhrz	Fahrzeug	vehicle; vessel
fix	fixieren	to fix; to hold fast; to establish; to settle; to discover; to state; to identify

Feuersignal *n* fire call.
Feuersperre *f* barrage.
Feuerspritze *f* fire engine.
Feuerspucker *m* Spitfire (*slang*).
Feuerstärke *f* density of fire.
Feuersteigerung *f* increased rate of fire, intensification of fire.
Fesselseil *n* ground cable, mooring cable (*Bln*).
Fesseltau *n* *See* **Fesselseil**.
Fesselung *f* pinning down, containing (*Tac*).
Fesselungsvorstoß *m* containing attack, holding attack.
fest firm, solid, steady; locked; fixed, stationary; fastened.
Festantenne *f* fixed antenna.
festfressen, sich to seize, freeze (*piston, etc.*).
festhalten to contain, hold, immobilize (*Tac*); to track (*a target*).
Festhaltevorrichtung *f* locking device (*MG*).
Festigkeitslehre *f* strength of materials.
Festigkeitsnachweis *m* stress analysis.
Festklemmvorrichtung *f* clamping mechanism (*MG tripod*).
Festland *n* mainland, continent.
festlegen to refer (*Gunnery*); to fix; pinpoint, plot, determine; to sense, spot.
Festlegepunkt *m* reference point.
Festlegezahl *f* deflection reading, new reading (*in referring the piece*) (*Gunnery*).
festmachen to make fast, secure, tie, moor.
Festnahme *f* arrest, seizure.
Festpunkt *m* control point, reference point.
Festpunktnetz *n* control-point net (*Surv*).
festschießen seat the base plate by firing (*Mort*).
Festung *f* fortress, fort.
Festungsartillerie *f* fortress artillery.
Festungsartilleriekommandeur *m* fortress artillery commander.
Festungsbaubataillon *n* fortress construction battalion.
Festungsgraben *m* moat.
Festungsgürtel *m* cordon of forts.
Festungshaft *f* confinement in a fortress.
Festungsingenieur *m* civilian engineer in charge of fortifications.
Festungsinspekteur *m* superintendent of fortress engineering service (*superior of* Festungspionierkommandeur).
Festungskrieg *m* siege warfare.
Festungsnachrichtenkommandantur *f* fortress signal command (*attached to staff of Ft Engr units*).
Festungspionier *m* fortress engineer.
Festungspionierfeldwebel *m* technical sergeant (*Ft Engr*).
Festungspionierkommandeur *m* fortress engineer brigade commander.
Fett *n* grease.
Fettpresse *f* grease gun.
Fettüberzug *m* grease coating.
Feuchtigkeit *f* humidity, moisture, dampness.
Feuchtigkeitsgehalt *m* moisture content, humidity (*Met*).
Feuchtigkeitsmesser *m* hygrometer.
Feuchtigkeitsschreiber *m* hygrograph (*Met*).
Feuer *n* fire.
unter Feuer nehmen to shell, to strafe.
Feuerabriegelung *f* box barrage.
Feuerabriegelung schießen to box in, to lay down a box barrage.
Feuerart *f* method of fire.
Feuerauftrag *m* fire mission (*Arty*).
Feuerbefehl *m* fire order, fire command.
Feuerbegriffe *mpl* fire classification (*Arty*).
Feuerbeobachtung *f* observation of fire (*Gunnery*).
Feuerbereich *m* zone of fire.
feuerbereit in firing position; uncoupled, unlimbered, ready for action (*Arty*).
Feuerdämpfer *m* flash hider.
Feuerdichte *f* density of fire.
Feuereinheit *f* fire unit (*Arty*).
Feuereinheit der Artillerie basic tactical unit of the artillery.
Feuer einstellen to cease fire.
Feuer eröffnen to open fire.
Feuereröffnung *f* commencement of fire, opening of fire.
feuerfest fireproof.
Feuerformen *fpl* types of fire, forms of fire (*Arty, MG*).
"Feuer frei!" "Fire!"
Feuergarbe *f* sheaf of fire, cone of dispersion, cone of fire.
feuergefährlich inflammable.
Feuergefecht *n* fire fight, fire duel.
Feuergeschwindigkeit *f* rate of fire (*MG*).
Feuerhöhe *f* height of muzzle.
Fernsprechdoppelleitung *f* metallic telephone circuit.

Fernsprecher *m* telephone; telephone operator.
Fernsprechfahrzeug *n* telephone-operations vehicle.
Fernsprechgerät *n* telephone equipment.
Fernsprechkompanie *f* telephone-communications company.
Fernsprechkraftwagen *m* telephone motor truck.
Fernsprechleitung *f* telephone line.
Fernsprechnetz *n* wire net (*Tp*).
Fernsprechrelais *n* telephone relay.
Fernsprechstelle *f* telephone station.
Fernsprechtrupp *m* telephone section.
Fernsprechverkehr *m* telephone traffic.
Fernsprechvermittlung *f* telephone central, switching central.
Fernsprechwagen *m* telephone wagon, telephone truck.
Fernspruch *m* telephone transcription, telephone message.
Fernsteuerung *f* remote control.
Fernthermometer *n* water temperature gage (*MT*).
Ferntrauung *f* marriage by proxy (*while on active duty*).
Ferntroß *m* third echelon supply train (*behind the* Mitteltroß).
Fernunterricht *m* instruction by correspondence.
Ferse *f* heel (*Anatomy*).
"Fertig!" "Ready!" (*Arty*).
Fertigaufschlagzünder *m* ready-fixed percussion fuze (*Am*).
Fertigerzeugnis *n* finished product.
Fertigmontage *f* final assembly (*Tech*).
Fertigung *f* production, manufacture, construction.
Fertigungshalle *f* factory shop.
Fertigungsjahr *n* year of manufacture.
Fertigzünder *m* ready-fixed fuze (*Am*).
Fessel *f* pastern (*horse*).
Fesselballon *m* captive balloon.
Fesselgelenk *n* pastern joint (*horse*).
Fesselkabel *n* ground cable, mooring cable (*Bln*).
fesseln to contain, to fix, pin down (*Tac*); to chain, tie up.
Feuerstellung *f* firing position, field emplacement, gun position.
in Feuerstellung in abatage, in firing position.
verdeckte Feuerstellung position defilade.
Feuerstoß *m* burst (*MG*).
Feuerstrahl *m* jet of liquid fire; gun flash.
Feuertaufe *f* baptism of fire.
Feuerüberfall *m* sudden concentration (*Arty*); surprise fire (*Arty, MG*).
Feuerüberlegenheit *f* fire superiority.
Feuer und Bewegung fire and movement, fire and maneuver.
Feuerunterstützung *f* fire support.
Feuervereinigung *f* concentration of fire (*Arty*).
Feuervereinigungswinkel *m* deflection difference (*Btry firing*).
Feuerverlegen *n* shift of fire (*Arty*).
Feuer verlegen to shift fire.
Feuerverteilung *f* fire distribution (*Arty, MG*).
Feuerverteilungswinkel *m* divergence difference (*Btry firing*).
Feuervorbereitung *f* fire preparation (*Tac*).
Feuervorhang *m* fire curtain, curtain of fire.
Feuer vorverlegen to lift fire, to advance fire (*Arty*).
Feuerwaffe *f* firearm.
Feuerwalze *f* rolling barrage.
Feuerwand *f* fire curtain, curtain of fire.
Feuerwehr *f* fire department.
Feuerwerker *m* technical sergeant (*Ord*).
Feuerwerkskörper *m* pyrotechnic composition (*Am*).
Feuerwirkung *f* effect of fire (*Gunnery*).
Feuerzeug *n* cigarette lighter.
Feuerzone *f* zone of fire.
Feuerzucht *f* fire discipline.
F-Haube *f* cowling (*Ap*).
Fieber *n* fever.
Fieseler-Storch *m* a German liaison airplane.
Filmkammer *f* roll-film camera.
Filmkassette *f* film cartridge, film-pack adapter (*Photo*).
Filmstreifen *m* film strip.
Filmvorführapparat *m* motion-picture projector.
Filterbüchse *f* gas mask canister.
Filtereinsatz *m* filter element (*gas mask*).
Filtergehäuse *n* filter container (*gas mask*).
Filterkolonne *f* water purification column.
Filterwechsel *m* filter replacement (*gas mask*).
Filz *m* felt.

Filzstiefel *m* felt boot.
Fingerabdruck *m* fingerprint.
Finnenzelt *n* plywood shelter (*winter operations*).
Finsternis *f* darkness.
Firnis *m* varnish.
Fischgrätenhindernis *n* fishbone obstacle pattern.
Fla *f* antiaircraft defense (*originally abbr. of* Flugabwehr; *now used as independent word*). *Compare* **Flak.**
Flabataillon *n* antiaircraft battalion.
flach flat.
Flachbahngeschütz *n* flat-trajectory gun.
Flachbettfelge *f* flat-base rim (*MT*).
Fläche *f* wing (*Ap*); surface, area.
flache Böschung gentle slope.
Flächenausgleich *m* aerodynamic balance (*Ap*).
Flächenbelastung *f* wing loading.
Flächenbrand *m* area conflagration (*Bombing*).
Flächendrahthindernis *n* multiple-belt entanglement.
Flächenfeuer *n* area fire, zone fire.
Flächeninhalt *m* area.
Flächenmeßplan *m* plotting board (*FR*).
Flächenschießen *n* area fire, zone fire.
flächentreue Projektion equal area projection (*mapping*).
Flächenziel *n* area target.
Flachfeuer *n* flat fire, flat trajectory fire.
Flachfeuergeschütz *n* flat-trajectory gun.
Flachkeilverschluß *m* sliding square-wedge breechblock (*G*).
Flachlasche *f* butt strap.
Flachmeißel *m* flat chisel.
Flachtrudeln *n* flat spin (*Avn*).
Flachzange *f* flat-jawed pliers.
Flackertaste *f* flicker-signal calling key (*Tp*).
Fladdermine *f* land mine.
Fla-Einheit *f* antiaircraft machine-gun unit.
Flagge *f* flag.
Flaggentruppen *fpl* units represented by flags (*in maneuvers*).
Flaggentuch *n* bunting.
Flaggoffizier *m* flag officer (*Nav*).
Flaggschiff *n* flagship.
Flak *f* antiaircraft gun, antiaircraft artillery (*originally abbr. of* Flugabwehrkanone; *now used as independent word*). *Compare* **Fla.**
Flakabteilung *f* antiaircraft artillery battalion.
Flakabwehr *f* antiaircraft defense.
Flakalarm *m* air warning for antiaircraft artillery units.
Flakartillerie *f* antiaircraft artillery.
Flakbatterie *f* antiaircraft battery.
Flakbedienung *f* antiaircraft gun crew.
Flakbrigade *f* antiaircraft brigade (*sometimes known as* Flakdivision).
Flakdivision *f* antiaircraft artillery "division" (*contains two to five* Flakregimenter). *See also* **Flakbrigade.**
Flakfeuer *n* antiaircraft fire.
Flakgeschütz *n* antiaircraft gun.
Flakgranate *f* antiaircraft shell.
Flakgruppe *f* antiaircraft artillery group (*for the defense of an air district*).
Flakgürtel *m* cordon of antiaircraft fire.
Flakhelferin *f* antiaircraft artillery woman auxiliary.
Flak-Kampfgruppe *f* antiaircraft combat group.
Flakkommandeur *m* antiaircraft artillery commander.
Höherer Flakkommandeur antiaircraft artillery commander of a *Luftgau*.
Flakkommandogerät *n* antiaircraft director.
Flakkorps *n* antiaircraft artillery corps (*contains from two to four* Flakdivisionen *or two to three* Flakbrigaden).
Flakkreuzer *m* antiaircraft cruiser.
Flakmaschinengewehr *n* antiaircraft machine gun.
Flakmeßgerät *n* plane spotter and range finder (*AAA*).
Flakmunition *f* ammunition for antiaircraft weapons.
Fla-Kompanie *f* antiaircraft company.
Flakregiment *n* antiaircraft regiment.
Flakscheinwerfer *m* antiaircraft searchlight.
Flakschießen *n* antiaircraft fire.
Flakschießlehre *f* theory of antiaircraft fire.
Flakschutz *m* antiaircraft-artillery protection.
Flaksperre *f* antiaircraft barrage, curtain of antiaircraft fire.
Flakstellung *f* antiaircraft gun emplacement.

Flaksturmabzeichen *n* antiaircraft-artillery assault badge *(decoration)*.
Flaktreffer *m* hit by antiaircraft fire, antiaircraft hit.
Flaktruppe *f* antiaircraft artillery *(as a branch of the Army)*.
Flakuntergruppe *f* subdivision of a *Flakgruppe*.
Flakvierling *m* four-barreled antiaircraft gun.
Flakvisier *n* antiaircraft gun sight.
Fla-Maschinengewehr *n* antiaircraft machine gun.
Fla-Maschinenkanone *f* automatic antiaircraft gun.
Flammendämpfer *m* flash hider *(Ord)*.
Flammenverzehrer *m* flame dampener exhaust stack *(Ap)*.
Flamm(en)öl *n* flame thrower fuel.
Flammenstrahl *m* jet of liquid fire.
Flammenwerfer *m* flame thrower.
Flammenwerfer-Füllwagen *m* recharging trailer for flame throwers.
Flammenwerferpanzerwagen *m* flame-throwing tank.
Flammenwerferschutzanzug *m* flame-thrower operator's protective clothing.
Flandernzaun *m* double-apron entanglement, double-apron fence.
Flanke *f* flank.
Flankenangriff *m* flank attack.
Flankenbewegung *f* flanking movement.
Flankeneinbruch *m* flanking penetration.
Flankenfeuer *n* flanking fire, enfilade fire.
Flankenmarsch *m* flanking march.
Flankenschutz *m* flank protection.
Flankensicherung *f* flank security.
Flankenstellung *f* flanking position.
flankieren to flank, outflank.
Flankierungsdurchbruch *m* flanking break-through.
Flansch *m* flange.
Flaschenhals *m* bottleneck.
Flaschenzug *m* block and tackle.
Flata *m* flame-thrower tank *(probably abbr. of* Flammenwerfertank).
Flattermine *f* *See* **Fladdermine.**
Flattern *n* shimmying *(MT)*.
Fla-Waffe *f* antiaircraft weapon.
Flechtwerk *n* brushwork, brushwood revetment.
Fleckfieber *n* typhus.
Fleischbeschau *m* meat inspection.
Fleischer *m* butcher.
Fleischhackmaschine *f* meat grinder.
Fleischkonserve *f* canned meat.
Flettner-Seitenruder *n* servo rudder *(Ap)*.
fliegen to fly.
fliegendes Personal flying personnel.
Flieger *m* private *(Luftwaffe)*; pilot, flier; airplane *(as seen from ground)*.
Fliegeralarm *m* air alert warning, air raid warning.
Fliegerabwehr *f* antiaircraft defense.
Fliegerabzeichen *n* aviation badge.
Fliegerangriff *m* air attack, air raid.
Fliegerarzt *m* flight surgeon.
Fliegerausbildungsregiment *n* air force preflight training regiment.
Fliegerbenzin *n* aviation gasoline.
Fliegerbluse *f* flight blouse, pilot's blouse.
Fliegerbombe *f* aircraft bomb.
Fliegerdeckung *f* cover from air observation or attack.
Fliegerdivision *f* airborne division, parachute division.
Fliegerei *f* aviation.
Fliegerfilz *m* grenades ejected from airplanes into the path of attacking fighters *(slang)*.
Fliegerformation *f* formation of airplanes.
Fliegerführer *m* air force commander *(commander of a* Luftflotte *or of an area of air operations)*.
Fliegergasbombe *f* chemical bomb *(Avn)*.
Fliegergruppe *f* group *(Avn)*.
Fliegerhandkammer *f* aerial hand camera.
Fliegerhaube *f* helmet *(Avn)*.
Fliegerheld *m* ace.
Fliegerhilfe *f* aviation support.
Fliegerhorizont *m* artificial horizon.
Fliegerhorst *m* airdrome, air base airdrome.
Fliegerhorstkommandant *m* air base commander.
Fliegerhorstkompanie *f* airdrome protection company.
Fliegerkammer *f* aircraft camera, aerial camera.
Fliegerkarte *f* air map, flight map, pilot chart.
Fliegerkorps *n* air force corps *(subordinate operational command of a* Luftflotte).
Fliegerkräfte *fpl* air forces.
Fliegerkraftstoff *m* aviation fuel.
Fliegerkrankheit *f* fliers' sickness *(complex of disorders affecting flying Pers; not to be confused with* Höhenkrankheit).
Fliegerleuchtpistole *f* aircraft signal pistol.
Fliegermarschbreite *f* dispersed formation in width *(AA security)*.
Fliegermarschtiefe *f* dispersed formation in depth *(AA security)*.
Fliegermaske *f* camouflage net *(AA defense)*.
Fliegermütze *f* pilot's garrison cap.
Fliegeroffizier *m* flying officer.
Fliegerschule *f* flying school.
Fliegerschule für technische Ausbildung ground school *(Avn)*.
Fliegerschulung *f* pilot training *(Avn)*.
Fliegerschutz *m* antiaircraft defense.
Fliegerschutzanzug *m* flying suit.
Fliegerschütze *m* aerial gunner.
Fliegerschutzgraben *m* slit trench *(AA security)*.
Fliegersirene *f* air raid siren.
Fliegersoldat *m* enlisted man *(Luftwaffe)*.
Fliegertätigkeit *f* air activity.
Fliegertauglichkeit *f* fitness for flying.
fliegertechnisches Personal ground crew *(Avn)*.
Fliegertruppe *f* flying and maintenance personnel of the *Luftwaffe*.
Fliegertuch *n* ground panel, marking panel.
Fliegerunterstützung *f* aviation support, air support.
Fliegerverband *m* formation of airplanes, air task force.
Fliegerverbindungsoffizier *m* air support officer *(air force liaison officer between* Luftwaffe *and Army; abbr.* Flivo).
Fliegervisier *n* antiaircraft sight.
Fliegervisiereinrichtung *f* antiaircraft sight assembly, aircraft gun sights.
Fliegerwaffenpersonal *n* aircraft armament personnel.
Fliegerwarnung *f* aircraft warning, air raid alarm.
Fliegerwetter *n* good flying weather; bad flying weather *(ironic)*.
Fliegerzeugnis *n* pilot's rating, pilot's certificate.
Fliegerzulage *f* aviation pay, flight pay, flying pay.
Fliehbacke *f* centrifugal arming device *(fuze)*.
Fliehbackenfeder *f* spring of centrifugal arming device *(fuze)*.
Fliehbolzen *m* centrifugal bolt *(fuze)*.
fliehen flee, escape.
Fliehgewicht *n* flyweight *(engine governor)*.
Fliehkraftantrieb *m* centrifugal action *(fuze)*.
Fliehkraftregler *m* centrifugal governor *(Mtr)*.
Fliehkraftzünder *m* centrifugal fuze.
Fließrichtung *f* direction of flow.
Flinte *f* shotgun.
Flivo *m* *See* **Fliegerverbindungsoffizier.**
Floß *n* float, raft.
Floßbrücke *f* floating bridge.
Flosse *f* fin *(Ap)*.
Flossenstummel *m* inboard stabilizing float *(seaplane)*.
Floßsack *m* pneumatic float, pneumatic ponton, pneumatic boat.
Floßsacksteg *m* pneumatic-boat footbridge.
Flotille *f* flotilla.
Flotte *f* fleet *(Nav)*.
Flottenchef *m* Commander-in-Chief of a fleet *(Nav)*.
Flotteneinheit *f* naval unit.
Flottenstützpunkt *m* naval base.
flottmachen to free *(stuck or stalled vehicle)*; to float *(a grounded vessel)*.
Flucht *f* flight, escape.
flüchten flee, escape.
flüchtig hasty *(Ft)*; nonpersistent *(CWS)*; fleeting; volatile.
flüchtige Feldbefestigung hasty field fortification.
flüchtiger Kampfstoff nonpersistent chemical agent.
Flüchtigkeit *f* volatility *(CWS)*.
Fluchtlinie *f* directional traverse.
Flüchtling *m* refugee.
Fluchtstab *m* range pole *(Surv)*.
Fluchtversuch *m* attempt to escape.
Flug *m* flight, flying. *See also terms under* **Flieger** *and* **Luft.**
Flugabwehr *f* antiaircraft defense.
Flugabwehrbezirk *m* air defense region.
Flugabwehrführer *m* antiaircraft commander.
Flugabwehrgeschütz *n* antiaircraft gun
Flugabwehrkanone *f* antiaircraft gun *(abbr.* Flak).
Flugabwehrmaschinengewehr *n* antiaircraft machine gun.
Flugabwehrmaschinenkanone *f* automatic antiaircraft gun.
Flugabwehrmaschinenwaffen *fpl* automatic antiaircraft weapons.
Fluganwärterkompanie *f* pool company for pilot candidates *(waiting for assignment to a pilot school)*.
Flugbahn *f* trajectory.
Flugbahnaufriß *m* *See* **Flugbahnbild.**
Flugbahnbild *n* trajectory diagram.
Flugbahngrundriß *m* *See* **Flugbahnbild.**
Flugbereich *m* range, maximum range *(Ap)*.
flugbereit "on the hangar line" *(after servicing)*.
Flugbereitschaft *f* ground readiness *(Avn)*.
Flugbesprechung *f* orders conference, "briefing" *(Avn)*.
Flugbetrieb *m* airdrome traffic, airdrome activities, routine flying operations.
Flugbetriebsstoffkolonne *f* aviation gasoline, oil and lubricants column.
Flugblatt *n* propaganda leaflet.
Flugboot *n* flying boat.
Flugbuch *n* flight log.
Flugdauer *f* endurance, duration of flight *(Avn)*.
Flugdeck *n* landing deck, flight deck *(aircraft carrier)*.
Flugebene *f* slant plane determined by lines of present and future position *(AA gunnery)*.
Flügel *m* wing *(Ap, Tac)*; fin *(Mort shell, R grenade, bomb)*; vane *(Cml shell, bomb)*; propeller blade.
Flügelangriff *m* frontal attack directed obliquely against one wing.
Flügelanordnung *f* wing setting *(Ap)*.
Flügelblech *n* stabilizing fin *(Mort Am)*.
Flügeleinstellwinkel *m* angle of wing setting *(Ap)*.
Flügeleinteilung *f* classification of wing parts *(Ap)*.
Flügeleintrittskante *f* leading edge *(Ap)*.
Flügelende *n* wing tip.
Flügelgeschütz *n* outside or end gun of a battery.
Flügelhaut *f* wing skin.
Flügelholm *m* wing spar.
Flügelinhalt *m* wing area.
Flügelkanone *f* wing-mounted cannon.
Flügelkolben *m* pump vane.
flügellastig wingheavy.
Flügelleuchtpatrone *f* wing-tip flare.
Flügelmann *m* flank man *(drill)*.
Flügelmann am Drehpunkt fixed pivot, pivot man *(drill)*.
Flügel-Mittelstück *n* wing center section *(Ap)*.
Flügelmutter *f* wing nut.
Flügelnase *f* leading edge *(Ap)*.
Flügelprofil *n* wing profile.
Flügelrippe *f* wing rib.
Flügelschaft *m* fin shaft *(Mort shell)*.
Flügelschiene *f* wing rail *(RR)*.
Flügelschnitt *m* wing section *(Ap)*.
Flügelschraube *f* thumbscrew.
Flügelsehne *f* wing chord.
Flügelsignal *n* wing signal.
Flügelspannweite *f* wing span.
Flügelspitzenkurve *f* ninety-degree turn *(Avn)*.
Flügelstiel *m* interplane strut.
Flügelstrebe *f* wing strut.
Flügelstreckung *f* aspect ratio.
Flügeltiefe *f* depth of wing profile.
Flügelverspannung *f* wing bracing.
Flügelverstrebung *f* wing strut system.
Flügelvorderkante *f* leading edge.
flügelweise in width, in line.
flügelweise Aufstellung disposition in width *(Tac)*.
Flügelwurzel *f* wing root *(Ap)*
Flügelzelle *f* cell, cellule *(Ap)*.
Flugfigur *f* flight maneuver.
Flugform *f* flight formation.
Fluggast *m* airplane passenger.
Fluggerät *n* aircraft instruments.
Fluggeschwindigkeit *f* flying speed.
Fluggewicht *n* gross weight *(Ap)*.
Flughafen *m* airport, airdrome.
Flughafenbautrupp *m* airdrome construction detachment.
Flughafengrenze *f* airdrome boundary.
Flughöhe *f* altitude *(Avn)*; ordinate of trajectory, vertical height *(Ballistics)*.
höchste Flughöhe absolute ceiling *(Avn)*.
Flughöhe über dem Erdboden absolute altitude *(Avn)*.
flugklar airworthy, capable of flying; cleared for take-off.
Fluglage *f* attitude, attitude of flight *(Avn)*.
Fluglehre *f* theory of flight.
Fluglehrer *m* flight instructor.
Flugleistung *f* flight performance *(Ap)*.
Fluglinie *f* flight line.
Flugmeldedienst *m* aircraft warning service.
Flugmeldekommando *n* information center *(AWS, Z of I)*.
Flugmeldenetz *n* aircraft warning net.
Flugmeldeposten *m* antiaircraft lookout, air guard observer *(AWS)*.
Flugmelderose *f* orientation card *(AWS)*; orientation clock *(to indicate target's direction of approach) (AAA)*.
Flugmeldezentrale *f* information center *(AWS, T of Opns)*.

F.K	Feldkanone	field piece; field gun
F.K	Feldkommandantur	Field Administrative Headquarters
F.K	Feldkompanie	field company
FK	Feldküche	field kitchen
FK	Fernkabel	long-distance telephone cable
F.K	Fliegerkammer	aerial camera
FK	Funk; Funker	radio; radio operator
F.Kan.Bttr	Feldkanonenbatterie	field gun battery
F.Kdtr	Festungskommandantur	fortress commander's headquarters
F.K.Gr	Feldkanonengranate	field piece shell
Fkh	Feldkochherd	field range
F.Kl.Abt	Funker-Kleinabteilung	portable radio detail
F.L	Feldlazarett	field hospital
Fl	Fernleitung	station-to-station telephone line; trunk system
Fl	Fernlenkung	remote control; radio control
F.L	Fernlenkwaffe	remote-control weapon
Fl	Fläche	area; plane surface
Fl	Flagg	flag
Fl	Fleck	flaw *(gunnery)*
fl	fliegend	flying
Fl	Flieger	aviator; flyer
Fl	Flottille	flotilla
Fl	Fluss	river *(on maps)*
Fla	Flugzeugabwehr	antiaircraft defense
Fla	Flügelanordnung	wing arrangement *(airplane)*
Flachf	Flachfeuer	flat trajectory fire
Fla-Dr-MG	Fliegerabwehr - Dreifachmaschinengewehr	antiaircraft triple machine gun
Flak	Flugzeugabwehrkanone	antiaircraft gun
Flak-Art	Flugzeugabwehrartillerie	antiaircraft artillery
Flakgruko	Flugzeugabwehrkanonengruppenkommandeur (-kommando)	commander (command) of antiaircraft gun battalion
Flak.Messtr.Wg.	Flakmesstruppwagen	antiaircraft flash and sound ranging truck
Flaksch	Flugzeugabwehrkanonenschule	antiaircraft gun school
Flakzg. 9.9	9.9 cm Flugzeugabwehrkanonenzug	9.9-cm antiaircraft-gun platoon
Flam	Flugabwehrmaschinenwaffen	automatic antiaircraft weapons
Fla.M.G	Flugabwehrmaschinengewehr	antiaircraft machine gun
Flamga	Flugzeugabwehrmaschinengewehrabteilung	antiaircraft machine-gun section
Fla-MGAbt	Flugzeugabwehrmaschinengewehrabteilung	antiaircraft machine-gun section
Fla-MGK	Flugzeugabwehrmaschinengewehrkompanie	antiaircraft machine-gun company
Flaschein	Flugzeugabwehrscheinwerfer	antiaircraft searchlight
Fla-Schw	Flugzeugabwehrscheinwerfer	antiaircraft searchlight
F.Laz	Feldlazarett	field hospital
F.Laz.Insp	Feldlazarettinspektor	field hospital inspector
Flb	Flugbahn	trajectory
Fl.Beob.Sch	Fliegerbeobachterschule	aerial observers' school
Fl.Bt	Flugboot	flying boat
Fld	Feld	field
Fld.Art	Feldartillerie	field artillery
Fldverw.Behl	Feldverwaltungsbehörde	field administrative authority
Fl.E.A	Fliegerersatzabteilung	aviation replacement center
Fl.F	fliegende Fähre	flying ferry
Flg	Flagg-	flag
flgd	folgende	following
Flg.Kan	Flügelkanone	wing cannon
Flgz	Flugzeug	airplane
Fl.H	Flughalle	hangar
Fl.Hf	Flughafen	airfield; airport; seaplane base
Fl. Hst	Fliegerhorst	airbase
Flieg	Flieger	aviator; flyer
Flieg.Tr	Fliegertruppe	air force
Flichb	Fliehbolzen	disappearing firing pin
Fl.In	Inspektion der Fliegertruppen	inspectorate of the air force
Fl.Ing	Flottilleningenieur	flotilla engineer
Fl.Insp	Inspektion der Fliegertruppen	inspectorate of the air force
Flivo	Fliegerverbindungsoffizier	air liaison officer
Fl.K	Flakkompanie	antiaircraft company *(navy)*
Flk	Flanke	flank; side
Flk.M	Flankenmarsch	flank march
Flk.Sch	Flankenschutz	flank protection
Flk.St	Flankenstoss	flank thrust
Flk.Stg	Flankenstellung	flanking position
Fl.Lstg	Flugleistung	flying performance
Fl.M	Flügelmine	finned bomb
Fl.Meld.D	Flugmeldedienst	airplane reporting service
Fl.M.Pl	Flächenmessplan	plotting board *(flash ranging)*
Fl.Mtf	Fliegermarschtiefe	depth of unit flying
Fl.M.Tiefe	Fliegermarschtiefe	depth of unit flying
Fl.M.W	Flügelminenwerfer	trench mortar firing finned bomb

Fl.O.Gr	Fliegerortsgruppe	local air unit
Flot	Flottille	flotilla
F.L.P	Festlegepunkt	reference point (*artillery*)
F.L.R	fahrbaren Eisenbahnladerampen	portable railroad loading ramps
Fl.Sack	Flossack	pneumatic **assault boat**
Fl.Sch	Fliegerschule	flying school
Flsp	Festlegespiegel	sighting mirror
Fl.Stp	Flugstutzpunkt	air base
Fl.T	Fliegertuch	ground panel (*aviation*)
Flugb	Flugboot	flying boat
Fluggew	Fluggewicht	flying weight (*aviation*)
	Flughafen	airport; **airfield**
Flugh	Flugzeughalle	hangar
Flugp	Flugpost	air mail
Fl.UGr	Flieguntergruppe	sub-group of **aviators**
Flugz	Flugzeug	airplane; plane
Flugzeugf	Flugzeugführer	pilot
Flugz.Mu	Flugzeugmutterschiff	seaplane tender rier
Fluko	Flugwachkommando	report center (*aviation*) ment
Fluna	Flugnachrichtenabteilung	air signal detachment
Flu.Wa	**Flugwache**	plane spotting post; **aircraft lookout station**
Fl.V	Flaggenvorschrift	regulations for the use of signal flags
Fl.W	Flammenwerfer	flame thrower
fl.W	fliessendes Wasser	flowing water
Fl.Wirk.Abst	Fliegerwirkungsabstand	interval in march formation attacks
Flz	Flugzeug	airplane
Flzf	Flugzeugführer	pilot
Flzf.Anw	Flugzeugführeranwärter	candidate pilot
Flzg	Flugzeug	airplane
Flzg.-Bes	Flugzeugbesatzung	airplane crew
Flzg.-Bew	Flugzeugbewaffnung	airplane armament
Flzg. Ind.	Flugzeugindustrie	airplane industry
Flzg.-Kan	Flugzeugkanone	airplane cannon
Flzg.-Otg	Flugzeugortung	airplane navigation
Flzg.-Schl	Flugzeugschleuder	catapult (*aviation*)
F.M	Feldmarschall	field marshal
Fm	Feldmeister	leader in compulsory labor service (seventh rank)
Fm^2	Flügelfläche eines Flugzeugs in Quadratmetern	wing area of an airplane in square meters
F.Mag.DO	**Feldmagazindienstordnung**	service regulation for field depots
fmdl	fernmündlich	by telephone
F.M.G	Flugzeugabwehrmaschinengewehr	rapid-fire antiaircraft gun; antiaircraft machine gun
Fm W	Flammenwerfer	flame thrower
Fn	Familienname	family name; **surname**
Fn	Felgen	felloes; wheel rims
Fnd	Feind	enemy
	Feindnachrichtendienst	enemy **communication service**
fndl	fernmündlich	by telephone
F.N.K	**Feldnachrichtenkommandantur**	field signal **headquarters**
F.O	Felddienstordnung	field service regulation
F.O	Fürsorgeoffizier	social service officer
F.O.K	Feldoberkommando	field high command
F.O.K	**Flieger beim Armeeoberkommando**	**aviator with the army high command**
folg	folgende	following
Form	**Formation**	**formation; form; figure; shape; unit**
Form	Formular	form; formulary; schedule; blank
fortl	fortlaufend	continuous; successive
Forts	Fortsetzung	continuation; **carrying on**; prosecution
F.P	Feldpost	field mail; field postal service
F.P	Feldposten	combat outpost; cossack post
F.P	Festlegepunkt	reference point (*artillery*)
Fp	Festungspionier	fortification engineer (*soldier*)
Fp	Füllpulver	powder charge
Fp	Fuhrpark	wagon park
F.P.A	Feldpostamt	field post office
F.Patr	Feldpatrone	field gun cartridge (*fixed ammunition*)
Fp.D.O	Feldpostdienstordnung	field post regulations
F.Pi.D	Feldpionierdienst für alle Waffen	combat engineer service regulations for all branches
Fp.K	Fuhrparkkolonne	wagon park column
F.Pl	Feuerplan	firing chart
F.Plsk	Feuerplanskizze	firing chart sketch
F.P.Nr	Feldpostnummer	field post number
F.Pol	Feldpolizei	military police (*in the field*)
FPS	Funkpeilstelle	radio beam station
F.P.Sek	Feldpostsektor	field post zone
Fpsn	Feuerpausen	intervals in firing; **pauses in firing**
F.P.W	Feldpostwesen	field postal service
Fr	Flammenwerfer	flame thrower
Fr	Frachtflugzeug	freight plane; transport plane
fr	französisch	French
fr	frei angelegt	blasting charge attached to the outside (*engineer demolition service*)

Flugmeldung *f* flight report (*Avn*); report of approaching aircraft (*AWS*).
Flugmotor *m* aircraft engine.
Flugneigungswinkel *m* angle of dive (*AA gunnery*).
Flugordnung *f* flight formation.
Flugpeildienst *m* airways navigation service.
Flugplatz *m* airfield, airdrome.
Flugplatzanlagen *fpl* airdrome installations.
Flugplatzbefeuerung *f* airdrome lighting.
Flugplatzfeld *n* landing field.
Flugplatzzone *f* control zone (*Adrm*).
Flugrichtung *f* direction of flight, course (*Avn*).
Flugrichtungspfeil *m* path-of-flight pointer (*reflector sight*).
Flugschüler *m* pilot trainee.
Flugsicherheit *f* flying safety (*Avn*).
Flugsicherung *f* air-traffic safety control.
Flugsicherungsbereich *m* air-traffic control area.
Flugsicherungsdienst *m* air-traffic control service.
Flugsicherungshauptstelle *f* air-traffic control station.
Flugsicherungsschiff *n* air-traffic safety ship (*vessel employed as radio aid for air navigation and in aircraft rescue service*).
Flugstrecke *f* airway, flight route, flight line, leg of a flight.
Flugstreckenfeuer *n* airway beacon, course light.
Flugstreckenkarte *f* strip map, air navigation map.
Flugstützpunkt *m* air base.
Flugtagebuch *n* flight log.
flugtechnisch pertaining to aeronautical technology or technique of flying.
Flugtorpedoboot *n* torpedo-carrying flying boat.
flugtüchtig airworthy, capable of flying.
Flugwache *f* observation post (*AWS, Z of I*).
Flugwachkommando *n* filter center (*AWS, Z of I*).
Flugweg *m* airway, course, path of flight.
Flugwegbestimmung *f* course determination (*Air Navigation*).
Flugweite *f* range of flight, flying distance.
Flugwesen *n* aviation.
Flugwetter *n* (good) flying weather.
Flugwetterdienst *m* aviation weather reporting service.
Flugwetterwarte *f* aviation weather station.
Flugwinkel *m* angle of approach (*AAA*).
Flugwinkel im Abschußpunkt angle of approach at instant of firing. (*AAA*).
Flugwinkel im Meßpunkt angle of approach at instant of range determination. (*AAA*).
Flugwinkel im Treffpunkt angle of approach at future position. (*AAA*).
Flugwissenschaft *f* aeronautics.
Flugzeit *f* flying time, endurance (*Ap*); time of flight (*of projectile*).
Flugzeitkurve *f* time-of-flight curve (*imaginary curve indicating different points of burst at constant time setting with varying elevation*).
Flugzeitsekunden *fpl* time of flight in seconds (*Ballistics*).
Flugzeug *n* airplane, aircraft.
Flugzeugabwehrscheinwerfer *m* antiaircraft searchlight.
Flugzeugachse *f* axis of an aircraft.
Flugzeugbaumuster *n* airplane model.
Flugzeugbein *n* shock strut (*Ap*).
Flugzeugbesatzung *f* air crew.
Flugzeugbewaffnung *f* airplane armament.
Flugzeug-Flügelkanone *f* wing-mounted cannon (*Ap*).
Flugzeugführer *m* pilot.
zweiter Flugzeugführer co-pilot.
Flugzeugführerschein *m* pilot's certificate.
Flugzeugführerschule *f* pilot school.
Flugzeuggerippe *n* airframe.
Flugzeuggeschwindigkeitslineal *n* airplane speed slide rule (*AAA*).
Flugzeughalle *f* hangar.
Flugzeugkanone *f* aircraft cannon, aircraft automatic gun.
Flugzeugmechaniker *m* air mechanic.
Flugzeugmetaller *m* metalsmith (*Avn*).
Flugzeug-M.G.-Steuerung *f* impulse generator mechanism (*Ap MG*).
Flugzeugmotor *m* aircraft engine.
Flugzeugmutterschiff *n* seaplane tender.
Flugzeugortung *f* air navigation.
Flugzeugrumpf *m* fuselage.
Flugzeugrüstpersonal *n* aircraft armorer-artificers.
Flugzeugschlepp *m* airplane towing.
Flugzeugschleuder *f* catapult (*Avn*).
Flugzeugschleuderschiff *n* seaplane tender with catapult facilities.

Flugzeug-Schwerölmotor *m* Diesel-type aircraft engine.
Flugzeugsteuerung *f* airplane controls, flight control.
Flugzeugtender *m* seaplane tender.
Flugzeugtorpedo *n* aerial torpedo.
Flugzeugträger *m* aircraft carrier.
Flugzeugwart *m* airplane mechanic.
Flugzeug zu Flugzeug air-air (*Sig Com*).
Flugziel *n* air target, air objective.
Flugzielbeschuß *m* firing at air target.
Flugzustand *m* attitude, attitude of flight (*Avn*).
Fluoreszenzfarbe *f* luminous paint.
Fluß *m* river.
Flußbreitenmesser *m* river-width measuring instrument.
Flußerkundung *f* river reconnaissance.
Flüssigkeit *f* liquid.
Flüssigkeitsausgleicher *m* fluid equalizer (*recoil mechanism*).
flüssigkeitsgekühlt liquid-cooled.
Flüssigkeitsgetriebe *n* fluid drive (*MT*).
Flüssigkeitskühlung *f* liquid cooling (*Mtr*).
Flüssigkeitsrücklaufbremse *f* hydraulic recoil brake (*G*).
Flüssigkeitsstoßdämpfer *m* hydraulic shock absorber (*MT*).
Flüssigkeitszerstäuber *m* decontamination sprayer.
Flußkabel *n* marine cable, underwater cable (*Tp*).
Flußpolizei *f* river police.
Flußübergang *m* river crossing, ford.
Flutlicht *n* floodlight.
Folgeladung *f* induced-detonation charge.
Folgezeiger *m* pointer, indicator (*follow-the-pointer mechanism in data transmission system*).
Folgezeigerantrieb *m* follow-the-pointer drive (*AAA*).
Folgezeigereinrichtung *f* follow-the-pointer mechanism (*AAA*).
Folgezeigerempfänger *m* fuze indicator (*follow-the-pointer-type fuze setter*).
Förderbahn *f* miners' tramway.
Formel *f* formula.
Formgebung *f* lofting (*Ap*).
Formular *n* form, blank.
Formveränderung *f* evolution (*Tac*).
Formwert *m* coefficient of form (*Ballistics*).
Forstamt *n* forest service office.
Försterei *f* forest service station.
Fortbewegung *f* propulsion, movement.
Fortbildung *f* advanced training.
Fortschritt *m* effective pitch (*propeller*); progress.
Fracht *f* freight.
Frachtbrief *m* bill of lading.
Frachtdampfer *m* freighter.
Frachtenbeförderung *f* transportation of freight.
Frachter *m* freighter.
Frachtflugzeug *n* cargo-transport plane.
Fragebogen *m* questionnaire.
"fraglich" "doubtful" (*uncertain regarding effect of a projectile*).
Fräsmaschine *f* milling machine.
Fregattenkapitän *m* commander (*Nav*).
Freibord *m* freeboard.
Freigabe *f* clearance.
Freihandnivellierinstrument *n* hand level (*Surv*).
Freiheitsstrafe *f* sentence of confinement.
Freiherr *m* baron.
Freilassung *f* release (*of prisoner*).
Freilassung auf Ehrenwort release on parole.
Freilauf *m* freewheeling (*MT*).
Freileitung *f* overhead line (*Tp*).
Freischärler *m* guerrilla.
Freischwimmer *m* qualified swimmer. *See also* **Fahrtenschwimmer.**
Freischwimmertrupp *m* swimmer detail (*for swimming horses across a stream*).
freitragend cantilever.
Freiübung *f* setting-up exercise.
freiwillig voluntary, volunteer.
sich freiwillig melden to volunteer, enlist, enroll.
Freiwilliger *m* volunteer.
Freiwilligenlegion *f* legion composed of non-German volunteers.
Freizeichen *n* dial hum (*Tp*).
Fremdpeilung *f* direction finding by means of bearings radioed to the aircraft by surface direction-finder stations.
Frequenz *f* frequency.
Frequenzangabe *f* frequency designation (*Rad*).
Frequenzband *n* frequency band (*Rad*).
Frequenzbereich *m* frequency range (*Rad*).
Frequenzeinstellung *f* tuning control (*Rad*).
Frequenzkorrektur *f* calibration adjustment (*Rad*).
Frequenzmesser *m* frequency meter (*Rad*).

Frequenzmodulation *f* frequency modulation (*Rad*).
Freßbeutel *m* feed bag.
Friede *m* peace.
Friedensstärke *f* peace strength.
Friedensstärkenachweisung *f* table of organization (*peacetime*).
Friedensverhandlungen *fpl* peace negotiations.
Friedhof *m* cemetery.
Front *f* front (*Mil, Met*).
innere Front home front.
Frontabschnitt *m* front sector.
Frontalangriff *m* frontal attack.
Frontalfeuer *n* frontal fire.
Frontantrieb *m* front-wheel drive (*MT*).
Frontbogen *m* front arc, curved front line.
Frontdienst *m* service at the front.
Fronteinsatz *m* commitment to the front, employment at the front.
Frontensegeln *n* frontal soaring (*glider*).
Frontflugspange *f* combat aviation clasp (*decoration*).
Frontflugzeug *n* combat airplane.
Frontkämpfer *m* fighter at the front; combatant; veteran.
Frontkämpferkreuz *n* veterans cross (*decoration awarded to all veterans of World War 1*).
Frontingenieur *m* engineer of the Todt Organization (*Ft*).
Frontleitstelle *f* forward directing center for personnel in transit.
Front-MG. *n* bow machine gun (*Tk*).
Frontmitte *f* center of the front (*Tac*).
Frontoffizier *m* line officer.
Frontpanzer *m* front armor (*Tk*).
Frontsammelstelle *f* front collecting point (*for reception of trained replacements and distribution to units*).
Frontsoldat *m* soldier at the front, combatant.
Frontstalag *n* forward prisoner of war camp. *See also* **Stalag.**
Fronturlaub *m* furlough from the combat zone.
Frontverband *m* combat element (*Tac*); support force, formation of support aircraft (*Avn*).
Frontvorsprung *m* salient (*Tac*).
Frontzeitung *f* army newspaper in combat zone.
Frontzulage *f* combat pay (*additional pay for personnel in the combat zone*).
Frostgraupeln *pl* sleet.
Frostschutzmittel *n* antifreeze solution.
Frostschutzsalbe *f* antifrostbite ointment.
frostsicher nonfreezable, frost-resistant.
Frühzerspringer *m* premature burst (*Arty*).
Frühzündung *f* preignition (*Mtr*).
F-Staffel *f* See **Fernaufklärungsstaffel.**
F-Stoff *m* titanium tetrachloride (*a smoke agent*) (*CWS*).
F.T.-Anlage *f* radio installation, radio equipment, radio set (*Ap*).
F.T.-Gerät *n* radiotelegraph set, radio equipment, radio set (*Ap*).
F.T.-Haube *f* helmet with built-in headset and throat-type microphone.
F.T.-Verbindung *f* radiotelegraph communication.
Fuchsloch *n* niche (*Ft*) (*Note:* fox hole = *Schützenloch*).
Fugasse *f* fougasse.
Fühlerlehre *f* thickness gage.
Fühlung *f* contact (*Tac*).
Fühlung aufnehmen to make contact (*with friendly or enemy troops*).
Fühlunghalten *n* contact mission (*Avn*).
Fühlunghalter *m* airplane maintaining contact with enemy force (*Avn, Nav*).
Fühlungnahme *f* establishment of contact (*Tac*).
führen to lead, direct, manage; to drive; to guide; to pilot.
Führer *m* leader; commander, commanding officer; chief; guide; driver; pilot.
Führeranwärter *m* SS officer candidate.
Führerbesprechung *f* conference.
Führer der Luft air liaison officer with the Navy.
Führereigenschaft *f* quality(-ies) of leadership.
Führerflugzeug *n* commander's airplane, leading airplane, command airplane.
Führergehilfe *m* assistant chief of staff.
Führergondel *f* control car (*Ash*).
Führerhauptquartier *n* Hitler's headquarters in the field.
Führerkanzel *f* pilot's cockpit, control cabin (*Ap*).
Führerkompaß *m* pilot's compass (*Ap*).
Führerkurs *m* officer training course.
Führerraum *m* control cabin, pilot's compartment, pilot's cockpit (*Ap*).

Fr.	Freitag	Friday
Fr.	Friede	peace
fr.	früher	earlier; formerly
Fr.	Führer	leader; commander; driver of vehicle
Fr.	Gruppe Franken der S.A.	Franken (Franconia) section of the Storm Troopers
F.R.A.	Funkenrichtungsanlage	directional radio installation
franz	französisch	French
Fr.Arb.D	Frauenarbeitsdienst	compulsory labor service for women
Fr.Bes.V	[illegible] soldungsvor-	peacetime pay regulations
		lines
Freit	Freitag	Friday
Freiw	Freiwilliger	volunteer
Fr.-H	Freihafen	free port
Frhr	Freiherr	Baron
Friedeis	Kommissar für die Demobilmachung und die vorbereitenden Arbeiten für den Frieden	commissioner for demobilization and the preparatory work for peace
Frk	Frühkrepierer	premature burst
Fr.Kprf	Frontkämpfer	combatant; veteran of combat service
Fr.Leg	Fremdenlegion	Foreign Legion
Front-Antr	Frontantrieb	front-wheel drive
Frontstalag	Frontstammlager	forward prisoner-of-war camp
fr.Schr	freier Schritt	route step
Fr.St	Friedenstärke	peacetime strength
F.Rtg.Wg	Feld-Röntgenwagen	field X-ray wagon
frtr	freitragend	cantilever (*airplane*)
Fr.Tr.Teil	Friedenstruppenteil	peacetime unit
Fr.Vertr	Friedensvertrag	peace treaty
Fr.V.V	Friedensverpflegungsvorschrift	ration regulations during peace time
Frw	Feuerwerker	artificer; ordnance sergeant
Frw	Freiwilliger	volunteer
Frw.-Hptm	Feuerwerkshauptmann	ordnance captain
Frw.Krpfl	Freiwillige Krankenpflege	voluntary nursing
Frw.Lab	Feuerwerkslaboratorium	laboratory for ordnance
Frz	Franzose; französisch	Frenchman; French
Frz	Frühzerspringer	premature burst
Fr.Zul	Frontzulage	bonus for front-line troops
F.S	Feldschmiede	mobile forge
Fs	Feldseilbahnbau und -betrieb	cable field-railway construction and operation
Fs	Festung	fortress
FS	Führerschule	school for leaders; motor school
FS	Funkstation; Funkstelle	radio station; wireless station; sending station
Fs.Ball	Fesselballon	captive balloon; sausage balloon
F.Sch	Führerschein	pilot certificate; driver's license
F.Sch.A	Feldschlächtereiabteilung	field slaughter detachment
F.Schm	Fahnenschmied	farrier
Fschm	Fallschirm	parachute
Fschm.Spr	Fallschirmspringer	parachutist; parachute jumper
Fschr	Fernschreiber	teletype apparatus
FSO	Friedenssanitätsordnung	peacetime medical regulations
F.Sp	feindliches Sperrfeuer	hostile barrage fire
Fsp	Fernsprecher	telephone
Fsp.Abt	Fernsprechabteilung	telephone detail
Fsp.Bau-Wg	Fernsprechbauwagen	telephone cart; cable wagon
Fspr	Fernsprecher	telephone
F.Spr.A	Fernsprechabteilung	telephone detachment
F.Sprechltgn	Fernsprechleitungen	telephone lines
Fspr.K	Fernsprechkompanie	telephone company
Fspr.Kb	Fernsprechkabel	telephone cable
Fsp.Wg	Fernsprechwagen	telephone communication wagon
Fssm	Fussmarsch	foot march
Fst	Festung	fortification
F.St	Feuerstellung	firing position; battery position; emplacement
F.St	Flaggenstock	flag pole
Fstg	Festung	fortress
F.St.N	Feindstärkenachweisung	report of actual enemy strength
F.Stoff	Titantetrachlorid	titanium tetrachloride
Ft	Fort	fortification
F.T	Funkentelegraphie	wireless telegraphy
F.T.	Funkturm	radio sending tower (*on maps*)
Ft	Furt	ford (*on maps*)
F.T.B.K	Dienstvorschrift für die Festungs-Telegraphen-baukompanien	regulations for fortress telegraph-construction companies
F.T.K	Feldtransportkommission	field transport commission
F.T.Kpfw	Kampfwagen mit Funkeneinrichtung	tank with radio installation
F.T.-Meldung	Funkentelegraphiemeldung	wireless message; radio message
F.Tr	Fahrtruppe	horse-drawn supply service
F.T.Sperre	Funkentelegrafiesperre	interdiction of radio communication; stop using radio
FT.St	Funkentelegraphiestation	wireless telegraphy station; radio telegraphy station
FT.Stat	Funkentelegraphiestation	wireless telegraphy station; radio telegraphy station
F.T.-Verbindung	Funkentelegraphieverbindung	wireless communication; radio communication
Fu	Funk; Funker	radio; radio operator
Fu	Fuss	foot
F.U.A	Feldunterarzt	medical officer aspirant (in the field)
F.U.Behörden	Familienunterhaltbehörden	family maintenance officials
Fü	Führer	leader; commander
Führ	Führer	leader; commander
Fürs	Fürsorge	public welfare; social service
Fürs.Offz	Fürsorge-Offizier	social service officer
Fürs.St	Fürsorgestelle	public welfare office; social service office
Füs	Füsilier	fusilier; light infantry soldier
Füs.Btl	Füsilierbataillon	fusilier battalion
Fufa	Funkerfeldabteilung	field radio detachment
Fu.Fernschr.Tr	Funken - Fernschreibentruppe	radio teletype section
		ficer
F.U.Fr	Funkunterfeldwebel	(*corresponding roughly to U.S. sergeant, radio*)
Fu.Fw	Funkfeldwebel	radio technical sergeant (*corresponding roughly to U. S. first sergeant*)
F.u.G	Führung und Gefecht der verbundenen Waffen	training manual for leading and combat of combined arms
Fu.Ge	Funkgerät	radio equipment
Fuhrp	Fuhrpark	wagon park
Fuhrp.Kol	Fuhrparkkolonne	wagon park column
FuKl.Abt	Funkerkleinabteilung	portable radio unit
Fu.Kp	Funkkompanie	radio company
Fumstr	Funkmeister	radio sergeant (*corresponding roughly to U. S. first sergeant*)
Fund	Fundament	basis; fundamental principle; base
Funk.Abt	Funkerabteilung	radio detachment
Funkla	Funkerkleinabteilung	portable radio unit
Funkt	Funktion	function; service; duty; execution
Funkt	Funkturm	radio sending tower
Fu.spr	Funkspruch	radiogram; wireless message
Fusta	Funkenstation	radio station; wireless station
Fu.Tel.Abt	Funkentelegraphenabteilung	radio telegraphy detachment
Futtmstr	Futtermeister	forage master
Fu.Tu	Funkturm	radio sending tower
Fu.Überw.Kp	Funküberwachungskompanie	radio supervision company
Fu.Wachtm	Funkwachtmeister	radio sergeant (*corresponding roughly to U. S. first sergeant*)
Fu.Wg	Funkwagen	radio truck
F.V	Fahrvorschrift	driving regulation
F.V	Feldbefestigungsvorschrift	manual of field fortifications
Fv	Fernverbindung	long-distance connection
F.v	Feuer verteilen	to distribute fire
FVO	Funkverordnung	radio regulation
FVS	Fernverkehrsstrasse	long-distance highways
F.V.St	Feldvorschriftenstelle	field order post
F.V.T	Feldverpflegungstabellen	field ration schedule
Fvt	Feuerverteilung	fire distribution
Fvtg	Feuerverteilung	fire distribution
F.W	Feldwache	picket
Fw	Feldwebel	(*corresponds roughly to U. S. first sergeant*)
F.W	Fliegerwarte	air observation tower
F.W.Abt	Feldeisenbahnwerkstättenabteilung	field railroad workshop unit
F.Wg	Feldwagen	field wagon
FwH	Feuerwerkshauptmann	ordnance captain
FwHptm	Feuerwerkshauptmann	ordnance captain
Fwk	Feuerwerker	artificer; ordnance sergeant
Fwk.Uffz	Feuerwerkerunteroffizier	artificer noncommissioned officer
Fw.Lab	Feuerwerkslaboratorium	laboratory for ordnance
Fwp.V	Feuerwerkspersonalvorschrift	ordnance personnel regulations
FWSt	Feldwetterstation	field weather station
F.W.W	Feldwetterwarte	field meteorological station
Fz	Fahrzeug	vehicle; vessel (*navy*)
Fz	Feldzeug	field equipment; ordnance
F.Z	Festlegezahl	reference number (*artillery*)
Fz Jn	Feldzeuginspektion	inspectorate of ordnance
Fz.Pk	Feldzeugpack	field equipment pack
Fzw	Feldzeugwaffenmeister	field ordnance sergeant
F.Zwb	Feldzwieback	field biscuit

G

G	Garnison	garrison
G	Gas	gas
G	Gebirgs-	mountain
G	Gefechtsübungen mit scharfer Munition	maneuvers with live ammunition
G	Gegnerpunkt	present enemy position (*antiaircraft*)
g	geheim	secret
G	Gelände	terrain; ground; region
G	Gendarmerie	local police
G	General	general
G	Generalstab	general staff
G	Gerät	equipment
G	Geschütz	gun; cannon
G	Geschützführer	gun commander
G	Gewehr	rifle
G	Gramm	gram
G	Granate	grenade
g	gross	great; large
G	Gruppe	group; squad (*infantry*)
G	Gruppenkommando	army group command
G	Güterzug	freight train
G.98	Gewehr 1898	rifle, model 1898
G†	gerichtlich für tot erklärt	legally presumed to be dead (*on casualty lists*)
G.A	Gefechtsausbildung	combat training; battle drill
G.A	Generalarzt	(*corresponds to U. S. brigadier general*)
GAB	Gasabwehrdienst	gas protection service
Gam	Gamasche	legging
GAR	Gebirgsartillerieregiment	mountain artillery regiment
Garn	Garnison	garrison
Garn.Arzt	Garnisonarzt	garrison medical officer
Garn.Kom	Garnisonkommando	garrison commander's headquarters
Garn.Laz	Garnisonlazarett	military hospital
Garn.Verw	Garnisonverwaltung	garrison administration
Gas-A	Gasanstalt	gas-works
Gas Kol	Gaskolonne	gas column; balloon service groups
Gasm	Gasmaske	gas mask
Gassch.Ger.Pl	Gasschutz-Gerätepark	antigas equipment park
G.B	Garnisonsbauordnung	garrison building and construction regulations
Gb	Gebirgs-	mountain
G.B	Geschwaderbefehl	squadron order (*navy and air corps*)
Gb.B	Gebirgsbrigade	mountain brigade
Gbd	Gebäude	buildings
Gbg	Gebirgs-	mountain
Gbhf	Güterbahnhof	freight yard
G Blink (m. Zusatz)	grosses Blinkgerät (mit elektrischer Batterie und Azetylen-Sauerstoff Zusatz)	large scale blinker signal (with electric battery and addition of acetylene and oxygen)
G.Bomb	Gasbombe	gas bomb
G-Buch	Gesetzbuch	law book
G-Buch	Gesundheitsbuch	health record (*medical*)
G.D	Geschützdepot	ordnance depot; depot for guns and cannons
GdA	General der Artillerie	general of the artillery (*corresponding to U. S. lieutenant general*)
GdI	General der Infanterie	general of the infantry (*corresponding to U. S. lieutenant general*)
GdK	General der Kavallerie	general of the cavalry
Geb	Gebirgs-	mountain
geb	geboren	born
Geb.Abt	Gebirgsabteilung	battalion of mountain troops
Geb.Batt	Gebirgsbatterie	mountain battery
Geb.Brig	Gebirgsbrigade	mountain brigade
Geb.Btl	Gebirgsbataillon	mountain battalion
Geb.Haub	Gebirgshaubitze	mountain howitzer
Geb.Jäg.Rgt	Gebirgsjägerregiment	mountain rifle regiment
Geb.J.R	Gebirgsjägerregiment	mountain rifle regiment
Geb.K	Gebirgskanone	mountain cannon or gun
Geb.K	Gebirgskorps	mountain corps
Geb.Nachr.Abt	Gebirgsnachrichtenabteilung	mountain signal battalion
Geb.Pi	Gebirgspioniere	mountain combat engineers
Gebr.Anw	Gebrauchsanweisung	printed instructions; directions for use
Geb.Tr	Gebirgstruppe	mountain troops
Geb.Werf.Abt	Gebirgswerferabteilung	mountain mortar battalion
ged	gedeckt	concealed; covered; camouflaged; sheltered
ged.Z	gedecktes Ziel	defiladed target
Gef	Gefallener	dead soldier (*killed in action*)
Gef	Gefangener	prisoner of war
Gef	Gefechts-	combat; battle
Gef.Aufklärung	Gefechtsaufklärung	battle reconnaissance
gefber	gefechtsbereit	prepared for action
Gef.Ber	Gefechtsbereitschaft	preparedness for action
Geferna	Fernsprechabteilung bei Generalkommando *or* Gruppenkommando	telephone detail of the corps general staff or army group headquarters

Führerschaft *f* leadership; group of leaders.
Führerschein *m* operator's permit, driver's permit *(MT)*.
Führersitz *m* cockpit; pilot's seat; driver's seat.
Führerstab *m* command group.
Führerstand *m* control cabin, pilot's cockpit, pilot's compartment *(Ap)*; tank commander's position.
Führerzügel *m* lead rein *(harness)*.
Führung *f* command, conduct, leadership; command post, headquarters; guide *(Mech)*.
obere Führung higher command *(Div and up)*.
untere Führung lower command *(Regt and down)*.
Führungsabteilung *f* tactical group of general staff sections.
Führungsband *n* rotating band *(Am)*.
Führungsfläche *f* flank *(G barrel)*.
Führungshülse *f* traversing slide *(MG)*.
Führungskante *f* edge of land *(G barrel)*.
Führungskette *f* squadron commander's flight, leading flight *(Avn)*.
Führungsklaue *f* assembly guide claw *(G)*.
Führungskunst *f* art of leadership, art of command *(Tac)*.
Führungsleiste *f* ribbed guide *(breechblock)*.
Führungs-Nachrichtenregiment *n* signal regiment which provides communication down to Army Hq.
Führungsring *m* rotating band *(Am)*.
Führungsrolle *f* guide roller *(Tk)*.
Führungsschiene *f* guide rail *(G cradle)*.
Führungsstab *m* operations staff *(Luftwaffe)*.
Führungsstück *n* traversing arc *(MG)*.
Führungsvermittlung *f* command telephone central.
Führungswulst *m* rear bourrelet *(Am)*.
Führungszeichen *n* driving signal.
Füllansatz *m* appendix *(Bln)*.
Füllelement *n* desiccated cell, "add-water" cell *(Elec)*.
Füllfunkspruch *m* dummy radio message.
Füllpulver 02 *n* TNT.
Füllschraube *f* filler cap *(MG)*.
Fülltrichter *m* filling funnel.
Füllung *f* filler *(Am)*; filling *(CWS)*.
Füllzapfen *m* filling plug.
Fundamentring *m* base ring *(Ord)*.
Fünfer-Schwarmwinkel *m* wedge formation of 5 airplanes.
Fünfte Kolonne fifth column.
Funk *m* radio.
Funkabkürzung *f* procedure sign, code group, prosine, prosig.
Funkanlage *f* radio installation.
Funkaufklärung *f* radio intelligence.
Funkauswertekraftwagen *m* radio-intelligence truck.
Funkbake *f* radio beacon.
Funkbefehl *m* radio command, radio order.
Funkbereitschaft *f* radio alert.
Funkbeschickung *f* radio compass calibration *(Air Navigation)*.
Funkbeschickungskurve *f* deviation curve *(Rad)*.
Funkbeschränkung *f* limited radio silence.
Funkbetrieb *m* radio operations.
Funkbetriebskraftwagen *m* radio operations truck.
Funkbetriebsstelle *f* radio operations station.
Funkdauerbereitschaft *f* continuous radio alert.
Funkdienst *m* radio communication service.
Funkdoppelverkehr *m* simultaneous two-way radio traffic.
Funke *m* spark.
Funkeinsatz *m* employment of radio.
Funkempfang *m* radio reception.
Funkempfänger *m* radio receiver.
funken to radio, send by radio.
Funkenbildung *f* production of sparks *(Elec)*.
Funkenstrecke *f* spark gap.
Funkentelegraphie *f* radiotelegraphy.
Funkentelephonie *f* radiotelephony.
Funkentladung *f* spark discharge
Funkentstörer *m* static eliminator
Funker *m* radio operator *(with grade of private)*.
Funkfeuer *n* radio beacon.
Funkgefreiter *m* radio operator *(with grade of* Gefreiter*)*.
Funkgerät *n* radio set, radio equipment.
Funkgerätkraftwagen *m* radio truck, radio-equipment truck.
Funkgerätmechaniker *m* radio repairman.
Funkhorchdienst *m* radio intercept service.
Funkhorchkraftwagen *m* radio intercept truck.
Funkhorchstelle *f* radio intercept station.
Funkkiste *f* radio chest, radio case.
Funkkompanie *f* radio company.
Funkkraftwagen *m* radio car, radio truck, radio command truck.
Funklinie *f* radio line, two-station net.
Funkmast *m* antenna mast, mast-type antenna.
Funkmastkraftwagen *m* radio antenna truck.
Funkmeister *m* technical sergeant *(Rad)*.
Funkmeisterei *f* signal supply and radio maintenance shop.
Funkmeldung *f* radio message.
Funkquerverbindung *f* intercommunication channel *(Rad)*.
Funkrufzeichen *n* radio call signal.
Funksender *m* radio transmitter.
Funksendung *f* radio transmission.
Funksignal *n* radio signal.
Funkskizze *f* radio net diagram.
Funksprechen *n* radio voice transmission, radiotelephone communication, voice-radio communication.
Funksprechgerät *n* radiotelephone.
Funksprechübermittlung *f* voice-radio communication.
Funkspruch *m* radio message.
Funkspruchkopf *m* heading on radio message.
Funkspruchübersicht *f* radio signal unit journal, number sheet.
Funkspruchvermittlung *f* radio-message transmission, radio message relay (station).
Funkspruchweg *m* radio channel.
auf dem Funkspruchweg by radio, via radio.
Funkstaffel *f* echelon of radio units; radio detachment.
Funkstelle *f* radio station.
Funkstille *f* radio silence.
Funkstörung *f* radio interference, radio jamming.
Funktafel *f* radio code table.
Funktasten *n* keying *(Rad)*.
Funktäuschung *f* radio deception.
Funktechnik *f* radio engineering.
Funktechniker *m* radio engineer.
Funktrupp *m* radio section.
Funkturm *m* radio tower.
Funküberwachung *f* radio monitoring.
Funkmeßgerät *n* radar.
Funkmeßturm *m* radar tower, radar station.
Funknachrichten *fpl* radio messages, radio communications.
Funknavigation *f* radio navigation *(Avn)*.
Funknetz *n* radio net.
Funknetz für den Verkehr Boden-Bord air-ground net (Rad).
Funkpanzerkampfwagen *m* radio command tank.
Funkpeiler *m* radio direction finder.
Funkpeilgerät *n* radio direction-finding apparatus.
Funkpeilung *f* radio direction finding.
Funkübung *f* radio-communication exercise.
Funkunteroffizier *m* radio operator *(Sgt)*.
Funkverbindung *f* radio communication.
Funkverbot *n* radio silence.
Funkverkehr *m* radio traffic.
Funkverkehrsabkürzungen *fpl* brevity code, prosigs *(Rad)*.
Funkverkehrsart *f* type of radio-net traffic.
Funkverkehrsform *f* method of radio communication.
Funkwagen *m* radio car, truck, or wagon.
Funkwart *m* radio technician.
Funkwechselsprechen *n* alternate two-way radiophone communication.
Funkwechselverkehr *m* alternate two-way radio traffic.
Funkweg *m* radio channel.
auf dem Funkweg by radio, via radio.
Funkwelle *f* radio wave.
Funkwerkstatt *f* radio maintenance shop.
Funkwetterwarte *f* radio weather station.
Funkzucht *f* radio discipline.
furagieren to forage.
Furagierleine *f* picket line *(for horse)*.
Furche *f* furrow; scour *(river bed)*; groove; white line *(hoof)*.
Furier *m* quartermaster sergeant.
Furnier *n* veneer.
Fürsorge *f* welfare.
Furt *f* ford.
man.
Fußbremshebel *m* brake pedal.
Fußhebel *m* pedal *(Ord, MT)*.
fußkrank footsore.
Fußlappen *m* foot rag, foot cloth; cabbage *(slang)*.
Fußlatscher *m* "foot-slogger," infantryman *(slang)*.
Fußlatte *f* sill *(Bdg)*.
Fußmelder *m* runner.
Fußplatte *f* foot plate, float *(AA gun outrigger)*.
Fußpunkt *m* nadir point.
Fußschalter *m* foot switch *(Elec)*; foot starter *(MT)*.
Fußschaltung *f* foot shifter *(MT)*.
Fußschlingenmine *f* foot snare mine.
Fußstütze *f* footrest.
Fußteller *m* float, float plate, jack float *(AA gun)*.
Fußweg *m* footpath.
Futter *n* forage, fodder; lining *(Clo)*; bushing, liner *(Tech)*; chuck *(of lathe, etc.)*.
Futteral *n* case; scabbard; sheath.
Futterholz *n* frame, shim *(Engr)*.
Futterration *f* forage ration.
Futterrohr *n* removable liner *(G)*.
Futterstück *n* bushing *(breechblock)*.

G

Gabel *f* fork *(utensil)*; bracket *(Arty)*.
eine Gabel bilden to bracket *(Arty)*.
Gabelachse *f* Elliot-type front axle *(MT)*.
Gabelbildung *f* bracketing method, bracket adjustment *(Arty)*.
Gabeldeichsel *f* pair of wagon shafts.
Gabellafette *f* gun carriage with shafts.
Gabelmotor *m* V-engine.
gabeln to bracket *(Arty)*.
Gabelschießen *n* bracket fire.
Gabelschwanz *m* twin tail *(Ap)*.
Gabelstütze *f* bipod *(MG)*.
Gabelumschalter *m* hook switch *(Tp)*.
Gabelung *f* bracket *(Arty)*.
Gamaschen *fpl* leggins, puttees.
Ganasche *f* jaw *(horse)*.
Gang *m* gear, speed, action, play, motion, travel *(Mech)*; passage, gangway.
Gangart *f* gait *(horse)*.
gangbar passable.
Gangrolle *f* pivoted dial *(speedometer)*.
Gangschaltung *f* gearshift *(MT)*.
Gangspill *m* capstan.
Gänsemarsch *m* Indian file, single file.
"Ganze Abteilung, Kehrt!" "About Face!" *(to a detail, squad, company, etc.)*.
Ganzmetallflugzeug *n* all-metal airplane.
Garbe *f* sheaf of fire, cone of dispersion, cone of fire.
Garnison *f* garrison *(now* Standort*)*.
garnisonverwendungsfähig fit for limited service *(i.e., in a garrison post, station or in Com Z) (abbr.* g.v.*)*.
Gasabblaseverfahren *n* gas-release method *(CWS)*.
Gasabdichtung *f* gas check *(breechblock)*.
Gasabwehr *f* gas defense.
Gasabwehrdienst *m* chemical defense service.
Gasabwehrmaßnahmen *fpl* tactical protection *(CWS)*.
Gasabwehrmittel *n* gas-defense equipment.
Gasabwehrwaffe *f* gas-defense weapon.
Gasalarm *m* gas alarm.
Gasalarmsirene *f* gas-alarm siren.
Gasalarmzeichen *n* gas-alarm signal.
Gasangriff *m* gas attack.
Gasanzeiger *m* gas detector kit.
Gasanzug *m* gas-protection suit.
Gasaufklärung *f* gas reconnaissance.
Gasausbildung *f* gas-defense instruction.
Gasbehälter *m* gas container.
Gasbekleidung *f* protective clothing *(CWS)*.
Gasbereitschaft *f* gas alert.
Gasbeschuß *m* gas-shell fire *(Arty)*.
Gasbrand *m* gas gangrene.
Gasbrille *f* gas goggles *(CWS)*.
Gasbrisanzgranate *f* high-explosive chemical shell.
gasdicht gasproof, gastight.
Gasdichte *f* gas concentration.
Gasdichtigkeit *f* impermeability to gas.
Gasdisziplin *f* gas discipline.
Gasdruck *m* blowback, gas pressure *(Ord)*.
Gasdrucklader *m* blowback-operated weapon.
Gasdruckmeßgerät *n* pressure gage *(Arty)*.
Gasdruckprüfung *f* pressure test *(Ord)*.
Gasdüse *f* gas-cylinder nozzle.
Gasentladungsröhre *f* gas tube *(Rad)*.
Gas-Erdmine *f* chemical mine, chemical land mine.
Gaserkennungsdienst *m* gas-detecting service.
Gasflasche *f* chemical cylinder, gas cylinder.
Gasfußhebel *m* accelerator pedal *(Mtr)*.

Gasfußtritt *m* *See* **Gasfußhebel.**
Gasgenerator *m* wood-gas generator *(MT).*
Gasgeschoß *n* chemical projectile.
gasgeschützt gasproofed.
Gasgewehrgranate *f* gas rifle grenade.
Gasgranate *f* chemical shell, gas shell.
Gashandgranate *f* gas hand grenade, chemical hand grenade.
Gashandschuh *m* gas-protection glove.
Gashandwerfer *m* chemical mortar.
Gashebel *m* throttle lever *(Ap);* accelerator *(Mtr).*
Gaskampf *m* chemical warfare.
Gaskampfgerät *n* chemical warfare equipment.
Gaskampfmittel *npl* chemical warfare material.
Gaskrieg *m* chemical warfare.
Gasläufer *m* antigas runner *(roll of impregnated paper on which to cross contaminated ground).*
Gasleitung *f* gas line, gas pipe.
Gasmaske *f* gas mask.
Gasmaskenkörper *m* body of gas mask.
Gasmaskenprüfgerät *n* gas-mask testing apparatus.
Gasmaskentragbüchse *f* gas-mask carrier *(canister type).*
Gasmaskenzubehör *n* gas-mask accessories.
Gasmörser *m* chemical mortar.
Gasmunition *f* chemical munitions.
Gasoffizier *m* gas officer, chemical officer.
Gasöl *n* gas oil, Diesel fuel.
Gasplane *f* antigas paulin, protective awning *(CWS).*
Gasraum *m* gas chamber *(Bln, CWS).*
Gasraumprobe *f* gas-chamber test *(CWS).*
Gasraumprüfung *f* *See* **Gasraumprobe.**
Gasschießen *n* gas-shell fire *(Arty).*
Gasschleuse *f* gas trap, air lock *(CWS).*
Gasschutz *m* chemical defense.
Gasschutzdecke *f* protective mat *(CWS).*
Gasschutzfilm *m* chemical-defense training film.
Gasschutzgerät *n* gas protective equipment.
Gasschutzgerätepark *m* chemical defense equipment park.
Gasschutzgerätwerkstatt *f* repair shop for gas protective equipment.
Gasschutzsalbe *f* protective ointment *(CWS).*
Gassschutzübungsmittel *n* chemical defense training agent.
Gasschutzunteroffizier *m* gas noncommissioned officer.
Gasschutzvorhang *m* gas curtain, blanket door.
Gasschutzvorrat *m* stock of chemical defense equipment.
Gasschutzvorschrift *f* gas-defense regulations.
Gasschwaden *mpl* gas fumes *(CWS).*
Gasse *f* gap *(in obstacle or mine field);* alley, street.
gassicher gasproof.
Gassperre *f* gas barrier, contaminated area.
Gasspüren *n* gas detection.
Gasspürer *m* gas sentry.
Gasspürfähnchen *n* gassed-area marker.
Gasspürgerät *n* gas-detection apparatus.
Gasspürkraftwagen *m* gas-detection car.
Gasspürmittel *npl* gas-detection equipment.
Gasspürstoff *m* gas-detection agent.
Gasspürtrupp *m* gas-detection squad.
Gasstiefel *mpl* gas-protection boots.
Gastruppen *fpl* chemical troops.
Gasüberfall *m* surprise gas attack, surprise gas-shell fire.
Gasumhang *m* gas-protection cloak.
Gasvergifteter *m* gas casualty.
Gasvergiftung *f* gas poisoning, contamination.
Gasverluste *mpl* gas casualties.
Gasvorhang *m* gas curtain.
Gaswarnung *f* gas warning.
Gaswerfen *n* chemical-projector fire.
Gaswerfer *m* chemical projector.
Gaswolke *f* gas cloud.
Gaszelle *f* cell, cellule *(Ash).*
Gaszucht *f* gas discipline.
Gaze *f* gauze.
geballt concentrated.
geballte Ladung concentrated charge *(consisting of several explosive blocks tied together).*
geben to give; transmit *(Rad, Tg).*
Geber *m* sender, transmitter; data transmitter *(data transmission system);* azimuth and elevation indicator *(AA director).*
Gebiet *n* region; territory; zone.
Gebirgsartillerie *f* mountain artillery, pack artillery.
Gebirgsfahrkolonne *f* mountain supply column *(H-Dr).*
Gebirgsgeschütz *n* mountain gun, pack gun.
Gebirgshang *m* mountainside.
Gebirgskanone *f* mountain gun.
Gebirgsinfanteriegeschütz *n* mountain infantry howitzer.
Gebirgsjäger *m* mountain infantryman.
Gebirgsjäger-Bataillon *n* mountain infantry battalion.
Gebirgsjäger-Regiment *n* mountain infantry regiment.
Gebirgskampf *m* mountain combat.
Gebirgskorps *n* mountain corps.
Gebirgskorpskommando *n* mountain corps headquarters.
Gebirgskrieg *m* mountain warfare.
Gebirgsmütze *f* mountain cap.
Gebirgspaß *m* mountain pass.
Gebirgs-Pionier-Regiment *n* mountain engineer regiment.
Gebirgsträgerkompanie *f* mountain carrier company *(on foot).*
Gebirgstruppen *fpl* mountain troops.
Gebiß *n* bit *(harness).*
Gebläse *n* blower, supercharger; ventilator.
Gebläsemotor *m* supercharged engine.
Gebläsewind *m* airflow.
Gebrauch *m* use, custom.
Gebrauchsanweisung *f* instructions for use, operating instructions.
Gebrauchsflugzeug *n* general-purpose airplane.
Gebrauchsladung *f* normal charge.
Gebrauchsstufe *f* the sum of all interior ballistic factors. *See also* **Grundstufe.**
Gebühr *f* charge, rate, allowance, fee.
Gebührnisse *fpl* allowances, rates.
Geburtsjahrgang *m* age class.
Geburtsurkunde *f* birth certificate.
gedämpft damped *(Elec, Mech).*
gedeckt covered, concealed, defiladed, masked, sheltered.
gedeckte Bahn shooting gallery.
gedeckte Batterie masked battery.
gedeckter Raum dead space, safety zone.
gedeckte Stellung cover position.
geeicht calibrated.
geerdet grounded *(Elec).*
Gefahr *f* danger.
gefährden endanger.
gefährlich dangerous.
Gefahrpunkt *m* critical point *(Tac).*
Gefälle *n* gradient *(Met, Top).*
Gefällemesser *m* clinometer *(Engr).*
gefallen fallen, dead, killed.
im Felde gefallen killed in action.
Gefangenenabschub *m* evacuation of prisoners.
Gefangenenaussage *f* prisoner's statement.
Gefangenenaustausch *m* exchange of prisoners.
Gefangenenbewachungskommando *n* prisoner guard detachment.
Gefangenenlager *n* prisoner-of-war camp.
Gefangenensammelkommando *n* prisoner-collecting detachment.
Gefangenensammelstelle *f* prisoner collecting point.
Gefangenenverhör *n* *See* **Gefangenenvernehmung.**
Gefangenenvernehmung *f* interrogation of prisoners.
Gefangener *m* prisoner.
Gefangennahme *f* capture.
Gefängnis *n* prison.
Gefängnisstrafe *f* sentence of confinement to a prison.
Gefecht *n* action, battle, combat, engagement, fight. *See also terms under* **Kampf, Krieg.**
Gefechte unter besonderen Verhältnissen special operations.
Gefecht im Gebirge mountain combat.
Gefechtsabschnitt *m* combat sector, zone of action.
Gefechtsaufgabe *f* combat task.
Gefechtsaufklärung *f* battle reconnaissance, combat reconnaissance.
Gefechtsauftrag *m* combat mission.
Gefechtsausbildung *f* combat practice, tactical training.
Gefechtsbatterie *f* firing battery.
Gefechtsbefehl *m* combat order.
Gefechtsbefehlsstelle *f* command post.
Gefechtsbereich *m* zone of action.
Gefechtsbereitschaft *f* readiness for action.
Gefechtsbericht *m* combat report.
Gefechtsberührung *f* contact with the enemy.
Gefechtsbreite *f* combat frontage.
Gefechtseinheit *f* combat unit.
Gefechtseinsatz *m* employment in action, commitment to action.
Gefechtsentwicklung *f* deployment for action *(Tac).*
Gefechtsfahrzeug *n* combat vehicle.
Gefechtsform *f* combat formation.
Gefechtsgebiet *n* combat zone.
Gefechtsgliederung *f* tactical grouping.
Gefechtsgruppe *f* combat unit; armored support unit.
Gefechtshandlung *f* operation, action, engagement, battle.
Gefechtskarren *m* ammunition and weapons cart *(H-Dr).*
Gefechtskarte *f* battle map.
Gefechtskasten *m* medical supplies and equipment chest.
gefechtsklar cleared for action *(Nav).*
Gefechtskompanie *f* assault company *(Prcht troops).*
Gefechtskopf *m* warhead *(torpedo).*
Gefechtskraftwagen *m* combat car.
Gefechtslage *f* combat situation.
Gefechtslandeplatz *m* advance(d) landing field.
Gefechtslärm *m* noise of battle.
Gefechtslehre *f* tactics.
Gefechtslinie *f* line of battle.
Gefechtsluftaufklärung *f* combat air reconnaissance.
gefechtsmäßig similar to actual combat or conditions in the field.
gefechtsmäßiges Schießen combat practice firing.
Gefechtsmeldung *f* combat message, combat report.
Gefechtspause *f* lull in combat.
Gefechtsraum *m* zone of action, combat area *(Tac);* fighting compartment, turret basket *(Tk).*
Gefechtsscheibe *f* field target, aiming silhouette.
Gefechtsschießen *n* advanced combat practice firing.
Gefechtsschießstand *m* field firing range *(R).*
Gefechtsschlitten *m* combat sled.
Gefechtsschreiber *m* clerk at a command post.
Gefechtsspähtrupp *m* combat patrol.
Gefechtsstab *m* command group; tactical operations staff.
Gefechtsstaffel *f* combat-train echelon.
Gefechtsstand *m* command post *(in combat);* headquarters *(Avn);* gun position, gunner's station *(Ap).*
Gefechtsstellung *f* action station.
Gefechtsstreifen *m* combat sector, zone of action.
Gefechtstätigkeit *f* combat activity.
Gefechtstroß *m* combat train; maintenance section *(Btry).*
Gefechtsübung *f* combat practice.
Gefechtsverlauf *m* progress of action *(Tac).*
Gefechtsverwendung *f* employment in combat.
Gefechtsvorposten *m* combat outpost.
Gefechtswagen *m* ammunition and weapons wagon.
Gefechtszeitangabe *f* chronology of battle.
Gefechtszweck *m* objective of combat, purpose of an action.
Gefecht um Engen combat at defiles.
Gefolgschaft *f* collective term for subordinate officers and/or enlisted personnel.
Gefreitenarmwinkel *m* acting corporal's chevron.
Gefreitenwinkel *m* *See* **Gefreitenarmwinkel.**
Gefreiter *m* acting corporal *(grade between Pvt 1cl and Cpl, strictly not NCO in Ger definition of term, translated as acting Cpl, lance Cpl, etc.).*
Gefrierschutz *m* antifreeze *(MT).*
Gefrierschutzmittel *n* antifreeze solution *(MT).*
Gegenangriff *m* counterattack *(Tac).*
Gegenaufklärung *f* counterreconnaissance.
Gegenbefehl *m* counterorder.
einen Gegenbefehl geben to countermand.
Gegenböschung *f* counterslope.
Gegend *f* region, vicinity, neighborhood.
Gegenfeuer *n* counterfire, retaliation fire.
Gegenfunkstelle *f* called station *(Rad).*
Gegengewicht *n* counterpoise *(Rad);* counterweight, counterbalance.
Gegenhang *m* counterslope.
Gegenkolbenmotor *m* opposed-piston engine.
Gegenlaufgraben *m* counterapproach trench.
gegenläufige Luftschrauben contrarotating propellers.
Gegenlicht *n* "counter-light" *(sunlight against the attacker, defender or observer).*
Gegenlosung *f* countersign.
Gegenmarsch *m* countermarch.
Gegenmaßnahme *f* countermeasure.
Gegenmine *f* countermine.
Gegenmutter *f* lock nut.
Gegenoffensive *f* counteroffensive.
Gegenpropaganda *f* counterpropaganda.
Gegenseil *n* stagger wire *(biplane).*
gegenseitig two-way, mutual, reciprocal.
gegenseitige Sprechverbindung two-way telephone circuit.
Gegensignal *n* answer signal.
Gegensinn *m* counterclockwise direction, opposite direction.
im Gegensinn zum Uhrzeiger counterclockwise.
Gegenspionage *f* counterespionage.

Gef.Gr	Gefechtsgruppe	combat group; combat unit
Gef.Lag	Gefangenenlager	prison camp
Gef.Lpl	Gefechtslandeplatz	combat landing field; advanced landing field
Gefr	Gefreiter	*(corresponds roughly to U. S. acting corporal)*
Gef-Sgn	Gefahrsignale	danger signals *(on maps)*
Gef.St	Gefechtsstand	command post
Gef.Staff	Gefechtsstaffel	field train *(services of supply)*
Gef.Stat	Gefechtsstation	battle station *(navy)*
Gef.Str	Gefechtsstreifen	combat sector
Gef.Tr	Gefechtstross	combat train
Gef.Vorp	Gefechtsvorposten	combat outpost
Gef.Wg	**Gefechtswagen**	combat wagon; company wagon (munition and tool)
Geg.Angr	**Gegenangriff**	**counterattack**
Gegens	Gegensatz	contrast; antithesis; opposition
Gegn	Gegner	opposition
Gegs	Gegensatz	contrast; antithesis; opposition
geh	geheim	secret
Geh	Gehilfe	assistant
Geha	Generaldirektor der Heereswerkstätten	director general of the Army Plants
gehob	gehoben	elevated (in rank)
Geh.Sch	Geheimschrift	code; cipher; secret writing
gel	geladen	loaded
Gel	Gelände	terrain; ground; region
gel	geländegängig	having cross-country traveling ability
Gel	Gelbkreuz	yellow cross *(gas)*
Gel	Gelegenheit	occasion; opportunity
Gel	Geleit	convoy; escort
Gel.Fl	Geleitflottille	convoy flotilla
Gel.W	Geländewelle	curtain; screen; mask *(as regards relation of gun to target)*
Gel.Wink	Geländewinkel	angle of site
gem	gemäss	according to
gem	gemischt	mixed
Gem.Pol	Gemeindepolizei	community police
gem.Pzkw.Kp	gemischte Panzerkraftwagen-Kompanie	mixed tank company
Gem.Vertr	Gemeindevertreter	representative of the community
Gem.Vorst	Gemeindevorsteher	mayor of the community
gen	genannt	mentioned; called
ge.N	geographische Nord	true north
Gen	General	general
Gen.Adj	Generaladjutant	adjutant general
Gen.Arzt	Generalarzt	*(corresponds to U. S. brigadier general, Medical Corps)*
Gen.d.Artl	General der Artillerie	general of the artillery *(corresponding to U. S. lieutenant general)*
Gen.d.Fl	General der Flieger	general of the air corps *(corresponding to U. S. lieutenant general)*
Gen.d.Inf	General der Infantrie	general of the infantry *(corresponding to U. S. lieutenant general)*
Gen.d.Kav	General der Kavallerie	general of the cavalry *(corresponding to U. S. lieutenant general)*
Gen.d.Pi	General der Pioniere	general of the engineers *(corresponding to U. S. lieutenant general)*
Gen.d.Pztr	General der Panzertruppe	general of the armored forces *(corresponding to U. S. lieutenant general)*
Genf.Konv	Genfer Konvention	Geneva Convention
Genfldm	Generalfeldmarschall	field marshal *(no U.S. equivalent)*
Gen.Fm	Generalfeldmarschall	field marshal *(no U. S. equivalent)*
Gen.Insp	Generalinspekteur	inspector general
Gen.Kdo	Generalkommando	corps headquarters
Genko	Generalkommando	corps general staff; corps headquarters
Gen.Lt	Generalleutnant	*(corresponds to U. S. major general)*
Gen.Maj	Generalmajor	*(corresponds to U. S. brigadier general)*
Gen.Obst	Generaloberst	*(corresponds to U. S. general)*
Gen.Ob.St.Arzt	Generaloberstabsarzt	*(corresponds to U. S. lieutenant general,*
Gen.Ob.St.Vet	Generaloberstabsveterinär	*corresponds to U. S. lieutenant general*
Gen.Ord.Komm	Generalordenskommission	General Decorations Commission
Gen.Qu	Generalquartiermeister	quartermaster general
Genst	Generalstab	general staff
Gen.St.Arzt	Generalstabsarzt	*(corresponds to U. S. major general, Medical Corps)*
Genstb	**Generalstab**	**general staff**
Genstb.-Chef	Generalstabschef	chief of the general staff
Genstb.d.H	Generalstab des Heeres	army general staff
Gen.St.Vet	Generalstabsveterinär	*(corresponds to U. S. major general) (Veterinary Corps)*
Gen.Vet	Generalveterinär	*(corresponds to U. S. brigadier general) (Veterinary Corps)*

geogr.Br	geographische Breite	latitude
geogr.L	geographische Länge	longitude
Geopol	Geopolitik	geopolitics
Gep	Gepäck	pack; baggage
Gep.Wg	Gepäckwagen	baggage wagon
Ger	Gerät	equipment
Ger.Fw	Gerätefeldwebel	equipment sergeant (*corresponding roughly to U. S. first sergeant*)
Ger.Uffz	Geräteunteroffizier	equipment non-commissioned officer
Ger.Wg	Gerätwagen	equipment wagon
Gesch	Geschoss	projectile; bullet
Gesch	Geschütz	piece; gun; cannon
gesch.Arrest	geschärfter Arrest	disciplinary arrest for a short period
Gesch.Ex	Geschützexerzieren	gun drill
Gesch.F	Geschützführer	gun commander
Gesch.Fabr	Geschossfabrik	ammunition factory
Gesch.Giess	Geschützgiesserei	gun foundry
Gesch.Kb	Geschosskorb	shell basket; shell case
Geschl.Kr	Geschlechtskrankheit	venereal disease
Gesch.Rei	Geschützreinigen	gun cleaning
geschtl	geschichtlich	historical
Geschw	Geschwader	wing formation (*aviation*); squadron (*navy*)
Geschw.M	Geschwindigkeitsmesser	speedometer
Gesch.Z	Geschäftszimmer	office
gesetzl	gesetzlich	legally
Ges.St	Gesamtstärke	total strength
gest	gestaffelt	echeloned
Gest	Gestalt	figure; shape; form; stature
Gest	Gestellung	summons, calling-up (*of recruits*); provision (*of carts*)
gest	gestorben	died
Gestapa	Geheimes Staatspolizeiamt	office of the secret state police
Gestapo	Geheime Staatspolizei	secret state police
get	getötet	killed
Gew	Gewalt	force; power; might
Gew	Gewehr	rifle
gew	gewerblich	industrial; pertaining to trade
Gew	Gewicht	weight; stress
Gew	Gewinn	profit
gew	gewöhnlich	usual; customary
Gew.98	Gewehr 98	rifle, model 1898
Gew.Fhr	Gewehrführer	gun commander (*heavy machine gun*)
Gew.Gran	Gewehrgranate	rifle grenade
Gew.Gran.Ge	Gewehrgranatengewehr	grenade-rifle
Gew.M	Geländewinkelmesser	angle-of-site instrument
Gew.Mun	Gewehrmunition	rifle ammunition
Gew.Sch	Gewehrschütze	rifleman
Gew.Z.F	Gewehrzielfernrohr	telescopic sight (*rifle*)
gez	gezeichnet	signed
gez	gezogen	rifled; twisted; drawn
Gf	Gefechts-	combat; battle
Gf	Geschossfabrik	shell factory
Gf	Geschützfabrik	gun factory
G.F	Geschützführer	gun commander
Gf	Gruppenführer	SS or SA commander with rank corresponding to U. S. major general; squad leader (*infantry*)
GFM	Generalfeldmarschall	field marshal (*no equivalent U. S. rank*)
G.F.P	Geheime Feldpolizei	secret military police
Gfsch	Gefangenschaft	imprisonment; captivity
Gfuk	grosse Funkstation	large radio station
G.Fuk.Stat	grosse Funkstation	large radio station
Gf.Wg	Gefechtswagen	combat wagon; company wagon (*ammunition and tools*)
Gf.Wg. gr	grosser Gefechtswagen	large combat wagon
Gf.Wg.kl	kleiner Gefechtswagen	small combat wagon
gg	gegen	against; to; towards; opposed to
G.G	Generalgouvernement	General Government (Central Poland)
G.G	Graugussgeschoss	cast iron shell
G.G	grosse goldene Medaille	great gold medal
G.G	Grundgeschütz	base piece (*artillery*)
G.G.I	Garnisongebäude - ordnung I	order I concerning garrison buildings
G.Gr	Gasgranate	gas shell; chemical shell
G.Gr. Ger	Gasgranatgerät	gas shell equipment
G.Gr. Ger	Gewehrgranatgerät	rifle grenade equipment
Ggs	Gegensatz	contrast; antithesis; opposition
G.G.U	Gasschutzgerätunteroffizier	noncommissioned officer in charge of antigas equipment
Ggw	Gegenwart	presence; present time
Ggw	Gegenwert	equivalent
G.H	Gebirgshaubitze	mountain howitzer
G.I	Generalinspekteur(-ion)	Inspector-General; Inspector General's Department
GI	Generalinspekteur der SA	Inspector-General of the Storm Troops

Gegensprechen *n* duplex operation, two-way break-in communication *(Rad)*; duplexing *(Tp)*.
Gegenstand *m* item, object, article.
Gegenstelle *f* called station *(Rad)*.
Gegensteuern *n* trimming *(with one or more engines inoperative) (Avn)*.
Gegenstollen *m* countermine.
Gegenstoß *m* counterthrust, counterattack *(Tac)*.
Gegentakt-Verstärker *m* push-pull amplifier *(Rad)*.
Gegenvorbereitungsfeuer *n* counter preparation, counterpreparation fire.
Gegenwehr *f* resistance *(Tac)*.
Gegenwind *m* head wind.
Gegenzeiger *m* pointer, indicator *(follow-the-pointer mechanism)*.
Gegenzeigersinn *m* counterclockwise direction.
Gegner *m* opponent.
Gegnerpfeil *m* path-of-flight pointer *(reflector sight)*.
Gegnerpunkt *m* future position at moment of burst *(AAA)*.
gegossen cast *(metals, armor, etc.)*.
gegurtet belted *(Am, etc.)*.
Gehalt *m* concentration *(CWS)*; content, volume.
Gehäuse *n* case, casing, housing.
geheim secret, confidential.
Geheime Feldpolizei secret field police *(special MP units attached to armies and Mil Adm of occupied countries; abbr.* G.F.P.).
geheimer Gegenstand classified military item, secret item.
Geheime Staatspolizei secret state police *(political police; abbr.* Gestapo).
Geheimhaltung *f* secrecy.
Geheimnis *n* secret.
Geheimschrift *f* cryptography.
Geheimschriftanalyse *f* cryptanalysis.
Geheimtext *m* cipher text.
Geheimwort *n* cipher key.
Gehilfe *m* aid, assistant.
Gehilfe des Richtschützen assistant gunner *(MG squad)*.
Gehirnerschütterung *f* concussion of the brain.
gehoben raised, lifted, elevated; higher grade *(of* Wehrmachtbeamter).
Gehorsam *m* obedience.
Gehorsamsverweigerung *f* insubordination.
Geisel *f* hostage.
geladen loaded, armed, charged, activated.
geladener Draht live wire.
Gelände *n* terrain, ground, country.
Geländeabschnitt *m* terrain sector, terrain compartment.
Geländeanpassung *f* adaptation to the terrain, blending with the ground *(Cam)*.
Geländeaufnahme *f* terrain photosurvey.
Geländeausbildung *f* field training.
Geländeausnutzung *f* utilization of terrain.
Geländeausschnitt *m* coverage *(aerial Photo)*.
Geländebedeckung *f* mask *(Gunnery)*.
Geländebesprechung *f* tactical ride, tactical walk.
Geländebeurteilung *f* terrain appreciation, estimate of terrain.
Geländedarstellung *f* terrain representation *(Surv)*.
Geländeentgiftung *f* ground decontamination.
Geländeerkundung *f* terrain reconnaissance.
geländefähig capable of cross-country travel *(MT)*.
Geländefahren *n* cross-country driving.
Geländefahrzeug *n* cross-country vehicle *(MT)*.
Geländegang *m* auxiliary gear, underdrive *(MT)*.
geländegängig capable of cross-country travel, having cross-country mobility *(MT)*.
Geländegängigkeit *f* cross-country traveling ability, cross-country mobility *(MT)*.
Geländegegenstand *m* terrain feature, landmark.
Geländegestaltung *f* configuration of terrain, terrain features.
Geländehindernis *n* natural obstacle, terrain obstacle.
Geländekampfstoff *m* ground-contaminating agent, persistent agent *(CWS)*.
Geländekette *f* traction band *(MT)*.
Geländekraftfahrzeug *n* cross-country motor vehicle.
Geländenachbildung *f* simulation of terrain.
Geländeneigung *f* slope.
Geländeorientierung *f* orientation by map.
Geländepunkt *m* terrain point, landmark.
Geländer *n* railing; handrail *(Bdg)*.
Geländeraum *m* terrain area.

Geländerstütze *f* railing post; handrail post *(Bdg)*.
Geländescheibe *f* landscape target *(Tng)*.
Geländeschutz *m* defilade, natural protection.
Geländeskizze *f* military sketch.
Geländestreifen *m* terrain sector.
Geländeübung *f* field exercise.
Geländevergiftung *f* terrain contamination *(CWS)*.
Geländeverhältnisse *npl* terrain conditions.
Geländevermessung *f* terrain survey.
Geländeverstärkung *f* organization of the ground *(Tac)*.
Geländewinkel *m* angle of site *(Gunnery)*; angle of slope *(Top)*.
negativer Geländewinkel angle of depression, negative angle of site.
Geländewinkellibelle *f* angle-of-site level.
Geländewinkelmesser *m* angle-of-site instrument, clinometer.
Geländewinkelmeßvorrichtung *f* angle-of-site mechanism *(telescopic sight)*.
Gelatit *n* a rock-blasting explosive.
gelb yellow.
Gelbkreuz *n* Yellow Cross *(Ger marking for vesicants) (CWS)*.
Gelbkreuzbeschuß *m* chemical-shell fire *(vesicant filler)*.
Geldabfindung *f* money allowance, reimbursement, cash settlement.
Geldstrafe *f* fine *(Law)*.
Geldwert der Verpflegungsersparnisse ration savings.
Gelegenheitsziel *n* target of opportunity.
Geleise *n* track *(RR)*.
Geleit *n* escort, convoy.
Geleitmannschaft *f* escort personnel.
Geleitschiff *n* convoy vessel, escort vessel.
Geleitschutz *m* convoy guard *(Nav)*.
Geleitzug *m* convoy *(Nav)*.
Gelenk *n* knuckle, joint, flexible coupling.
Gelenkbinden *fpl* ankle wrap puttees.
Gelenkbogenbrücke *f* hinged-arch bridge.
Gelenkgehäuse *n* universal-joint housing *(MT)*.
Gelenkstück *n* joint piece *(MG tripod)*.
Gelenkwelle *f* flexible drive shaft, drive shaft and universal joint, propeller shaft.
gelöste Flugordnung route formation *(Avn)*.
Gemeiner *m* private, common soldier or sailor *(in disuse)*.
Gemischbildung *f* mixing, mixture formation *(carburetor)*.
gemischt mixed, combined.
Gemischtbauweise *f* composite construction.
gemischter Verband combined-arms unit.
gemodelte Welle modulated wave.
genau accurate, exact, precise; tight; close; strict.
genaues Einschießen precision adjustment fire.
Gendarm *m* rural policeman.
Gendarmerie *f* rural police.
genehmigen authorize, approve.
General *m* lieutenant general; general; general officer *(specifically,* Lt Gen). *Compare* **Generaloberst.**
Generaladmiral *m* admiral *(commander of a fleet)*.
Generalarzt *m* brigadier general *(Med)*.
Generalarbeitsführer *m* brigadier general *(Reich Labor Service)*.
Generalfeldmarschall *m* Field Marshal.
Generalgouvernement *n* Government General *(administrative region established in occupied territory; specifically, in Central Poland in 1939)*.
Generalinspekteur für die Panzerwaffe Inspector General of Armored Forces.
Generalintendant *m* civilian official in administrative services ranking as brigadier general.
Generalkommando *n* corps headquarters.
Generalleutnant *m* major general.
Generalluftzeugmeister *m* chief of air forces special supply and procurement service.
Generalmajor *m* brigadier general.
Generaloberst *m* general *(full general)*.
Generaloberstabsarzt *m* surgeon general *(lieutenant general)*.
Generaloberstabsveterinär *m* lieutenant general *(Vet)*.
Generalquartiermeister *m* general staff officer Ib in charge of supply and administration at headquarters of field forces.
Generalstab *m* general staff.
Generalstab des Heeres General Staff of the Army.
Generalstabsarzt *m* major general *(Med)*.
Generalstabschef *m* Chief of Staff.
Generalstabskarte *f* strategic map *(1:100,000)*.

Generalstabskorps *n* General Staff Corps.
Generalstabsoffizier *m* general staff officer.
Generalstabsveterinär *m* major general *(Vet)*.
Generalveterinär *m* brigadier general *(Vet)*.
Generatoranhänger *m* wood-gas generator trailer *(MT)*; generator trailer *(Elec)*.
Genesung *f* convalescence.
Genesungskompanie *f* convalescent company, rehabilitation company.
Genesungsurlaub *m* sick leave.
Genfer Abkommen Geneva Convention.
Genfer Rotes Kreuz Geneva Cross.
genormt standardized.
geöffnet open, extended.
geöffnete Ordnung extended order.
geographische Breite latitude.
geographische Karte geographic map.
geographische Koordinaten geographic coordinates.
geographische Länge longitude.
Geographisch-Nord *m* true north.
Gepäck *n* baggage, impedimenta.
Gepäcktroß *m* baggage train.
Gepäckwagen *m* baggage car *(RR)*.
gepanzert armored.
gepflastert paved.
gerade straight.
geradeaus straight ahead.
Geradeausflug *m* horizontal flight, level flight *(Avn)*.
Geradseitfelge *f* straight-side rim *(MT)*.
Gerät *n* nonexpendable supplies, matériel, ordnance, equipment; instrument; apparatus.
Gerätart *f* type of equipment.
Gerätausstattung *f* allotment of equipment.
Gerätbrett *n* instrument panel.
Gerätedurchsicht *f* inspection of equipment or ordnance.
Geräteeinheit *f* unit assemblage *(of equipment, etc.)*.
Geräteentgiftung *f* decontamination of equipment.
Gerätelicht *n* instrument light.
Geräteoffizier *m* ordnance staff officer, ordnance officer, property officer.
Geräteunteroffizier *m* ordnance sergeant.
Geräteverwalter *m* quartermaster sergeant.
Gerätewagen *m* *See* **Gerätwagen.**
Gerätinspizient *m* equipment inspector.
Gerätklasse *f* class of equipment.
Gerätsammelstelle *f* ordnance collecting point.
Gerätsatz *m* unit of equipment.
Gerätstück *n* piece of equipment, item of equipment.
Gerätwagen *m* equipment truck, equipment wagon.
Geräusch *n* noise, sound.
Geräuschtarnung *f* "noise camouflage" *(any noise-producing means intended to deceive enemy as to position of guns, advance of tanks, etc.)*.
Gerbersche Anordnung Gerber design *(a type of cantilever bridge)*.
Gerberträger *m* cantilever span *(two cantilever arms with suspended span)*.
Gericht *n* court.
gerichteter Empfang directional reception *(Rad)*.
Gerichtsherr *m* appointing authority *(Law)*.
Gerippe *n* skeleton, framework, outline.
Gerippeabteil *n* bay *(Ap)*.
Germanisches SS-Panzerkorps SS armored corps composed of non-German volunteers from "Germanic" countries.
Geruch *m* odor.
geruchlos odorless.
Gerücht *n* rumor.
Gerüst *n* scaffold, frame.
Gesamtausfall *m* total loss(es).
Gesamtauswanderungsstrecke *f* linear travel of target from position at instant of range determination to future position *(AA gunnery)*.
Gesamtauswanderungszeit *f* dead time plus time of flight *(AA gunnery)*.
Gesamtbefehl *m* complete order *(Tac)*.
Gesamtdruck *m* total pressure.
Gesamterhöhung *f* quadrant elevation *(Gunnery)*.
Gesamtkilometerzähler *m* total mileage odometer *(on speedometer)*.
Gesamtkriegführung *f* grand strategy, general conduct of the war.
Gesamtlage *f* total situation, over-all situation *(Tac)*.
Gesamtrohrerhöhung *f* total elevation *(G)*.
Gesamtseitenrichtung *f* total traverse, total deflection *(G)*.
Gesamtvorhaltewinkel *m* principal lateral deflection angle *(AA gunnery)*.
Gesandtschaft *f* legation.
Geschirr *n* harness; utensils.
Geschirrtau *n* trace *(harness)*.

Geschlechtskrankheit *f* venereal disease.
geschlossen closed, close; combined; compact.
geschlossene Ordnung close order.
geschlossener Bau close-order construction *(method of Tp line construction by a single crew)*.
geschlossenes Exerzieren close-order drill.
geschlüsselt encoded, secret.
geschlüsselter Funkspruch radio code message.
Geschoß *n* projectile, bullet, shell.
Geschoßabweichung *f* deviation, absolute deviation *(Gunnery)*.
Geschoßanlage *f* clearance space *(R)*.
Geschoßaufschlag *m* impact of projectile, point of impact.
Geschoßbahn *f* trajectory, ballistic curve.
Geschoßbö *f* blast effect of antiaircraft shell.
Geschoßboden *m* base of projectile.
Geschoßdrall *m* spin of projectile.
Geschoßdrehung *f* See **Geschoßdrall.**
Geschoßdurchmesser *m* diameter of projectile.
Geschoßeinschlag *m* impact of projectile, point of impact.
Geschoßflugzeit *f* time of flight of projectile.
Geschoßform *f* shape of projectile.
Geschoßführung *f* seating of projectile.
Geschoßgarbe *f* cone or sheaf of fire, cone of dispersion.
Geschoßgewicht *n* weight of projectile.
Geschoßheber *m* gun hoist.
Geschoßhöhlung *f* shell cavity *(Am)*.
Geschoßhülle *f* body of projectile *(Am)*.
Geschoßhülse *f* cartridge case *(Am)*.
Geschoßkanal *m* bullet tube *(grenade launcher)*.
Geschoßkappe *f* cap of projectile.
Geschoßkern *m* core of bullet.
Geschoßknall *m* report produced by shell wave *(SR)*.
Geschoßkopf *m* head of projectile.
Geschoßkran *m* gun hoist.
Geschoßmantel *m* jacket of bullet.
Geschoßmine *f* improvised antitank mine made of a high-explosive shell.
Geschoßspitze *f* ogive of shell.
Geschoßwagen *m* ammunition truck.
Geschoßwirkung *f* effect of projectile.
Geschoß-Zubringewagen *m* ammunition truck *(for carrying heavy projectile to the piece)*.
Geschütz *n* gun *(Arty piece)*. See **Artillerie** *for classification as light, medium and heavy.*
Geschützart *f* type of gun *(Arty)*.
Geschützbank *f* barbette.
Geschützbedienung *f* gun crew; service of the piece.
Geschützbettung *f* ground platform *(RR gun)*.
Geschützexerzieren *n* service of the piece drill.
Geschützführer *m* chief of section *(FA)*.
Geschützkompanie *f* howitzer company *(Inf)*.
Geschützladung *f* propelling charge *(Am)*.
Geschützmannschaft *f* gun crew.
Geschütznullpunkt *m* position of gun *(on firing charts and diagrams)*.
Geschützort *m* See **Geschütznullpunkt.**
Geschützpark *m* ordnance park.
Geschützplane *f* gun cover.
Geschützrohr *n* gun barrel.
Geschützschlepper *m* prime mover *(Arty)*.
Geschützstaffel *f* gun section.
Geschützstand *m* gun position, gun emplacement, position of the piece *(Arty)*.
Geschützstellung *f* gun position, gun emplacement.
geschützt protected.
geschützter Behälter self-sealing tank *(Ap)*.
Geschützverschluß *m* breech mechanism, breechblock *(Ord)*.
Geschützwagen *m* gun car *(RR)*.
geschützweises Feuer fire by piece at command *(Arty)*.
Geschützwinde *f* firing jack *(G)*.
Geschützzielfeuer *n* simulated fire representing an enemy gun target *(Tng)*.
Geschützzug *m* howitzer platoon *(Inf)*.
Geschwader *n* wing *(air force operational unit consisting of about 100 aircraft organized into from 3 to 5* Gruppen*)*; squadron *(Nav)*.
Geschwaderflugform *f* wing flight formation.
Geschwaderkeil *m* wing wedge formation *(Avn)*.
Geschwaderkolonne *f* wing column formation *(Avn)*.
Geschwaderkommodore *m* wing commander *(Avn)*.
geschweißt welded.
Geschwindigkeit *f* speed, velocity; rate *(of fire)*.
Geschwindigkeitsdreieck *n* triangle of velocities *(Avn)*.
Geschwindigkeitsmesser *m* speedometer *(MT)*.
Geschwindigkeitssteigerung *f* speed increase.
Geschwindigkeitsverlust *m* loss of velocity *(Ballistics)*.
Geschwindigkeit zur Luft indicated airspeed.
Gesellschaftsanzug *m* dress uniform for social occasions.
Gesenk *n* die *(for stamping or punching)*.
Gesetz *n* law, statute.
Gesetze und Gebräuche des Landkrieges Laws and Customs of War on Land *(Hague Convention, 1907)*.
gesichert safe; secured.
Gesichtsfeld *n* field of view *(Optics)*.
Gespann *n* team of horses.
Gespräch *n* conversation; telephone call.
Gesprächsschluß *m* completion of call *(Tp)*.
Gesprächsverbindung *f* call, connection *(Tp)*.
gestaffelt echeloned, staggered.
Gestalt *f* form, shape, figure, configuration.
Gestalt der Flugbahn curve of the trajectory.
Gestänge *n* bars, poles, rods, linkage.
Gestapo *f* See **Geheime Staatspolizei.**
gestattet allowed, allowable, granted, permitted.
gestattete Abweichung tolerance *(Tech)*.
Gesteinssprengmittel *n* rock-blasting explosive.
Gestell *n* stand; mount; frame; block; trestle; carriage; gear.
Gestellungsbefehl *m* induction order.
Gestellungspflicht *f* obligation to appear before draft board.
gesteuert controlled, steered; synchronized.
gesteuertes Maschinengewehr synchronized machine gun *(Ap)*.
Gesträuch *n* underbrush, shrubbery.
gestreckt elongated, extended; stretched; flat.
gestreckte Flugbahn flat trajectory.
gestreckte Ladung elongated charge. See also **Reihenladung.**
gestrichenes Korn medium sight *(R aiming)*.
Gestrüpp *n* underbrush, brush.
Gesuch *n* petition, request, application.
Gesundheit *f* health.
Gesundheitsappell *m* physical inspection.
Gesundheitsdienst *m* Sanitary Corps.
Gesundheitsoffizier *m* health officer.
Gesundheitszustand *m* physical condition.
Getränk *n* beverage.
getrennt separate(d); cut off *(Tp)*.
getrennte Munition separate-loading ammunition.
getrennter Bau extended-order construction *(method of Tp line construction by two separate crews)*.
Getriebe *n* gear, transmission *(MT)*.
Getriebebremse *f* transmission brake *(MT)*.
Getriebefett *n* transmission grease *(MT)*.
Getriebehauptwelle *f* transmission main shaft *(MT)*.
Getriebegehäuse *n* transmission case *(MT)*.
Getriebewelle *f* transmission shaft *(MT)*.
Gewahrsam *m* custody.
Gewaltmarsch *m* forced march.
gewaltsam forceful, in force.
gewaltsame Erkundung reconnaissance in force.
Gewehr *n* rifle.
"Gewehr, ab!" "Order, arms!"
"Gewehr abnehmen!" "Unsling, arms!"
Gewehrappell *m* rifle inspection.
Gewehrauflage *f* fire crest *(Ft)*.
Gewehrfeuer *n* rifle fire.
Gewehrführer *m* machine-gun squad leader, gun leader *(heavy MG)*.
Gewehrgeschoß *n* rifle bullet.
Gewehrgranate *f* rifle grenade.
Gewehrgranatenschütze *m* rifle grenadier.
"Gewehr in die, Hand!" "Take, arms!"
Gewehrkartusche *f* propelling cartridge for rifle grenade.
Gewehrkolben *m* rifle butt.
Gewehrkupplungsstück *n* barrel-locking stud *(MG)*.
Gewehrmieke *f* arms rack.
Gewehrmücke *f* See **Gewehrmieke.**
Gewehrmunition *f* rifle ammunition.
Gewehr-Panzergranate *f* armor-piercing rifle grenade.
Gewehr-Propagandagranate *f* rifle propaganda grenade *(scatters leaflets)*.
Gewehrriemen *m* rifle sling.
Gewehrschaft *m* rifle stock.
Gewehrschießstand *m* rifle range.
Gewehrschuß *m* rifle shot.
Gewehrschütze *m* rifleman.
Gewehrsprenggranate *f* high-explosive rifle grenade.
Gewehrstock *m* cleaning rod *(R)*.
Gewehrstütze *f* arms rack.
Gewehrträger *m* rifleman; machine-gun carrier *(gunner No. 1)*; cradle *(on MG sleigh mount or tripod)*.
Gewehrtragevorrichtung *f* rifle scabbard *(Cav)*.
"Gewehr, über!" "Left shoulder, arms!" *(with tightened sling)*; "Sling arms!" *(with loosened sling)*.
Gewehrübung *f* rifle exercise *(calisthenics)*.
"Gewehr umhängen!" "Sling arms!"
Gewehrzielfeuer *n* simulated fire representing enemy rifle or MG target *(Tng)*.
Gewehrzubehör *n* rifle accessories.
gewerblich industrial.
Gewicht *n* weight; gravity.
Gewichtsverteilung *f* weight distribution, balance.
Gewinde *n* thread *(Tech)*.
Gewindebacken *fpl* die *(for cutting threads)*.
Gewindegang *m* pitch *(of screw thread)*.
Gewindeschablone *f* screw pitch gage.
Gewitter *n* thunderstorm.
gewitterdrohend ugly, threatening sky *(Met)*.
Gewitterflug *m* frontal soaring *(glider)*.
Gewitterstörung *f* atmospherics, static *(Rad)*.
gewöhnliches Ferngespräch routine call *(Tp)*.
gewölbt convex, arched, vaulted.
gewölbte Böschung convex slope.
Gezeiten *pl* tide(s).
Gezeitentafel *f* tide table.
gezogen rifled *(barrel)*; drawn, towed.
gezogene Kurve climbing turn *(Avn)*.
gezogenes Geschütz rifled gun *(Arty)*.
gezogenes Ziel towed target.
Gieren *n* yawing; trail-ferrying.
Gierfähre *f* trail ferry.
Gierungsmesser *m* yawmeter *(Ap)*.
Gierwinkel *m* angle of yaw *(Avn)*.
Gießerei *f* foundry.
Gift *n* poison.
giftig poisonous, toxic.
Giftnebel *m* toxic smoke *(CWS)*.
Giftnebelkerze *f* gas candle, irritant gas candle *(CWS)*.
Giftnebelwolke *f* gas cloud.
Giftrauch *m* irritant smoke *(CWS)*.
Giftrauchkerze *f* toxic-smoke candle, gas candle *(CWS)*.
Giftregen *m* aerial gas spray *(CWS)*.
Giftregenangriff *m* spray attack *(CWS)*.
Giftstoff *m* toxic agent *(CWS)*.
Gipfel *m* peak, summit.
Gipfelentfernung *f* abscissa for maximum ordinate *(of trajectory)*.
Gipfelhöhe *f* maximum ordinate *(of trajectory)*; absolute ceiling *(Avn)*.
Gipfelhöhe mit einem stehenden Motor emergency ceiling *(Avn)*.
Gipfelpunkt *m* summit *(of trajectory, etc.)*.
Gitter *n* grid *(maps, Rad)*; trellis, lattice, grillage.
Gitterantenne *f* parasol-type antenna.
Gitterdrossel *f* grid resistor *(Rad)*.
Gittergleichrichter *m* grid rectifier *(Rad)*.
Gitterkondensator *m* grid condenser, grid capacitor *(Rad)*.
Gitterkreis *m* grid circuit, grid resonant circuit *(Rad)*.
Gitterlinie *f* grid line.
Gittermast *m* trellis mast.
Gitternetz *n* coordinate map grid, grid system, military grid.
Gitternetzkarte *f* gridded map.
Gitternetzlinie *f* See **Gitterlinie.**
Gitter-Nord *m* grid north.
Gitterrichtung *f* grid base-line direction *(Gunnery)*.
Gitterschießplan *m* fire-control grid *(Gunnery)*.
Gitterschwanz *m* open tail *(Ap)*.
Gitterspannung *f* grid voltage *(Rad)*.
Gittervorspannung *f* bias *(Rad)*.
Gitterwerte *mpl* grid coordinates, grid numbers *(maps)*.
Gitterwiderstand *m* grid resistance *(Rad)*.
Glas *n* glass; binoculars, field glass.
glasartig glasslike.
glasartige Vereisung clear ice, glaze *(Avn)*.
Glasbeobachtung *f* observation with field glass or telescope.
Glasgefäß *n* envelope *(of Rad tube)*.
Glasmaßstab *m* glass scale *(Optics)*.
glatt smooth, smooth-bore.
glattes Geschütz smooth-bore gun.
gleichachsig coaxial.
gleichbleibend uniform, constant.
gleichbleibender Drall uniform twist *(Ord)*.
gleichförmiger Drall See **gleichbleibender Drall.**
Gleichgewicht *n* balance, equilibrium.
Gleichlauf *m* synchronism.
Gleichlaufende *f* parallel line.

G.I	Generalintendant	army commissary general *(corresponding to U. S. brigadier general)*
Gi.N	Gitternord	grid north *(maps)*
G.Insp	Generalinspekteur (-ion)	Inspector - General; Inspector-General's Department
G.K	Gebirgskanone	mountain gun
Gk	Generalkommando	corps headquarters
G.K	Genfer Konvention	Geneva Convention
Gk	Gruppenkommando	army group command
G.K.15	Gebirgskanone 15	mountain gun, 1915
G.Kart	Gewehrkartusche	cartridge case
G.Kdo	Generalkommando	corps headquarters
G.K.F	gepanzerte Kampffahrzeuge	armored combat vehicles
G.kg	Gesamtgewicht in Kilogramm	total weight in kilograms *(airplane engines)*
G.K.V	Verfügung des Generalkommandos	corps order
G.Kw	Geschützkraftwagen	self-propelled gun mount
G.L	Garnisonlazarett	military hospital
GL	Gauleiter	district leader
gl	geländegängig	having cross-country traveling ability
GL	Generalleutnant	*(corresponds to U. S. major gene*
gl	glatt	smooth; even; slippery
Gl	Gleichstrom	direct current *(electricity)*
Glash	Glashütte	glass works *(on maps)*
gldg	geländegängig	having cross-country traveling ability
Gleisk	Gleiskette	caterpillar track
Gleisk	Gleiskettenfahrzeug	full-track vehicle
Gleisk.Pr	Gleisketten-Panzerfahrzeug	full-track armored vehicle
Glfl	Gleitflug	glide *(aviation)*
Gl.Kfz	geländegängiges Kraftfahrzeug	cross-country motor vehicle
Gl.St	Gleichstrom	direct current *(electricity)*
Glühl	Glühlicht	incandescent light: electric bulb; incandescent lamp
Glw	Geländewinkel	angle of site shell
glz	gleichzeitig	simultaneous
Gm	Gasmaske	gas mask
GM	Generalmajor	*(corresponds to U. S. brigadier general)*
G.m.b.H	Gesellschaft mit beschränkter Handlung	limited liability company
G.Med	Goldmedaille	gold medal
G.M.G	Grundmaschinengewehr	base piece *(machine gun)*
G.M.K	Gebirgsmunitionskolonne	mountain ammunition column
Gmr	Geschwindigkeitsmesser	speedometer
G.M.Sch.G	grosses Markscheidegerät	large inclinometer *(geology)*
GOA	Generaloberarzt	*(corresponds to U. S. lieutenant colonel, Medical Corps)*
GOK	Generalordenskommission	General Decorations Commission
GOStA	Generaloberstabsarzt	*(corresponds to U.S. lieutenant general, Medical Corps)*
GOSt.V	Generaloberstabsveterinär	*(corresponds to U. S. lieutenant general) (Veterinary Corps)*
Gp	Gepäck	baggage
gp	gepanzerte	armored
G.P	graphischer Punkt	graphic point; topographical point
G.P	Grundrichtungspunkt	base point *(artillery)*; reference point *(gunnery)*
gp. Kw	gepanzerter Kraftwagen	armored car
Gp.Tr	Gepäcktross	baggage train
G.Pzgr	Gewehr-Panzergranate	armor-piercing rifle shell
g/qmo	Querschnittbelastung	ballistic coefficient; average load *(ballistics)*
G.Qu	Generalquartiermeister	Deputy Chief of High Command, General Staff
G.Qu.M	Generalquartiermeister	Deputy Chief of High Command, General Staff
G.Qu.St	Generalquartiermeisterstab	staff of Deputy Chief of Command, General Staff
Gr	Graben	trench; ditch *(on maps)*
Gr	Grad	degree
Gr	Granate	shell; grenade
Gr	Grauguss	cast iron
Gr	Grösse	size; greatness; height
Gr	Gros	main body *(of a unit)*
Gr	Grube	pit; mine; ditch; quarry; grave *(on maps)*
G.R	Grundrichtung	base-line direction *(artillery)*
Gr	Gruppe	section; squad; group;
Gran	Granate	shell; grenade
gr.Bl.P	grobes Blättchenpulver	powder in large flakes
Gr.Br	Grossbritannien	Great Britain
Grd	Grund	ground; soil; terrain
Grdf	Grundfläche	base; basis; area
Grdl	Grundlage	basis; foundation; base
Grdl	Grundlinie	base line; outline; datum line; point of reference
Grd.MG	Grundmaschinengewehr	base piece *(machine gun)*

Grdr	Grundrichtung	base-line direction (*artillery*)
Grdr	Grundriss	design; sketch; outline; plan
Grdwsp	Grundwasserspiegel	water table
Gren	Grenadier	grenadier; infantryman
Grenzm	Grenzmark	Grenzmark (*former German provinces Posnania and West-Prussia*)
Grepola	Grenzpolizeiabschnitt	border police zone
Grf	Granatfüllung	bursting charge
Gr.F	Gruppenführer	squad leader (*infantry*)
gr.Fk	grosse Feldküche	large field kitchen
Gr.G.St	Grosser Generalstab	Grand General Staff (1914–1918)
Gr.H.Qu	Grosses Hauptquartier	general headquarters
Gr.K	Gruppenkommando	army group command
Gr.Kpf	Grosskampf	large-scale fighting
Gr.Kr.Mun	Grünkreuzmunition	green cross (*gas*) shell
Gr.Kw.Kol	grosse Kraftwagenkolonne	heavy motor transport train
Grkz	Grünkreuz	green cross (*gas*): choking gas (*diphosgene*
Grm	Grenzmark	Grenzmark (*former German provinces Posnania and West-Prussia*)
Grm	Grossmacht	Great Power
Gr.m.P	Granate mit Panzerkopf	armor-piercing shell
grosskal	grosskalibrig	(of) large caliber
G.R.P	Grundrichtungspunkt	base point (*artillery*); reference point (*gunnery*)
Grp	Gruppe	section; squad; group; pursuit squadron; bombardment group
Gr.R.Dn	Gruppe von Reservedivisionen	group of reserve divisions
Gr.Sch	Grenzschutz	frontier protective force
Gr.St	Grenzstation	border station
Gr T	Rüstgewicht in Tonnen	structural weight in tons (*airplane*)
Gru	Gruppe	section; squad; group; flying formation
Gruf	Gruppenführer	(SS) Elite Guard corps commander of Storm Troops corps leader
Grufahr	Führer der Fahrtruppen beim Gruppenkommando	commander of horsedrawn supply trains with the army group command
Grufl	Gruppenführer der Flieger	staff air officer
Gru.Kdo	Gruppenkommando	army group command
gr.u.kl.Fz	grosse und kleine Feldküchen	large and small field kitchens
Gruko	Gruppenkommando	army group command
Grutrain	Führer der Fahrtruppen beim Gruppenkommando	commander of horse-drawn supply trains with the army group command
Gru Vet	Gruppenveterinär	chief veterinary officer with army group command
Gr.W	Granatwerfer	mortar
Gr.Z	Granatzünder	shell fuze
Grz	Grenz	border
Grz.Kdo	Grenzkommando	frontier division headquarters
Grzsch	Grenzschutz	frontier protective force
Grz.Sch.Kdo	Grenzschutzkommando	frontier protective force headquarters
Grzst	Grenzstein	boundary marker
GS	Generalinspekteur des Sanitätswesens (SA)	Inspector-General of the Medical Service of the Storm Troops
G.S.L	Gasschutzlager	chemical warfare depot; gas-defense supply depot
G.S.O	Gasschutzoffizier	antigas officer
G.Sp	Grundwasserspiegel	water table (*topography*)
G.Sprgr	Gewehr-Sprenggranate	high explosive rifle shell
G.St	Gefechtsstand	command post
GSt	Generalstab	general staff
GStA	Generalstabsarzt	(*corresponds to U. S. major general, Medical Corps*)
G St V	Generalstabsveterinär	(*corresponds to U. S. major general*) (*Veterinary Corps*)
G.S.U	Gasschutzunteroffizier	anti gas non-commissioned officer
G.S.V	Gasschutzvorschrift	regulations for defense againt chemical warfare
G.t.	Fluggewicht in Tonnen	flying weight in tons (*aviation*); gross weight;
Gt.Br	Gross Britannien	Great Britain
Gtr.Bhf	Güterbahnhof	freight yard
G.Tross	Gepäcktross	baggage train
Gtt	Gitter	grid; fence
Gtt.Br	Gitterbrücke	lattice bridge
Gürt.Wag	Gürtelwagen des langen schweren Mörsers	pedrail truck for the long heavy mortar
Güt.Bhf	Güterbahnhof	freight yard
Güt.W	Güterwagen	freight car
g.v	garnisonverwendungsfähig	fit for garrison duty
GV	Generalveterinär	(*corresponds to U. S. brigadier general*)
Gvb	Gesamtverband	total force
GVE	garnisonverwendungsfähig in der Etappe	fit for garrison duty in the communications zone

Gleichlaufstellung *f* laying pieces reciprocally *(Btry)*.
Gleichlaufverfahren *n* reciprocal laying *(Btry)*.
Gleichrichter *m* rectifier *(Elec)*.
Gleichrichterröhre *f* rectifier tube.
Gleichrichtung *f* rectification *(Rad)*.
Gleichschritt *m* cadence; quick time. "Im Gleichschritt, marsch!" "Forward, march!" *(being at a halt)*. "Im Gleichschritt!" "Quick time, march!" *(being in march in double time)*.
gleichstellen synchronize *(watches)*; equalize.
Gleichstrom *m* direct current.
Gleichung *f* equation.
gleichzeitig simultaneous.
Gleis *n* rail, track *(RR)*.
Gleisanlage *f* railroad yard.
Gleisbalken *m* stringer *(Bdg)*.
Gleiskette *f* caterpillar track.
Gleiskettenantrieb *m* caterpillar drive.
Gleiskettenfahrzeug *n* track-laying vehicle.
Gleiskettenschlepper *m* caterpillar tractor.
Gleiskettenzugmaschine *f* caterpillar prime mover.
Gleiskurve *f* epi, curved spur track *(RR gun)*.
Gleitbahn *f* slide *(G cradle)*.
Gleitbombe *f* glider bomb *(Avn)*.
gleiten to glide.
Gleiter *m* glider.
Gleitfähigkeit *f* gliding ability; sliding ability.
Gleitflug *m* glide, gliding *(Avn)*.
Gleitflugwinkel *m* gliding angle *(Avn)*.
Gleitflugzeug *n* glider.
Gleithebel *m* sliding lever *(breechblock)*.
Gleithebelverschluß *m* sliding-lever breechblock.
Gleitkufe *f* landing ski *(Ap)*.
Gleitlager *n* plain bearing.
Gleitmittel *n* lubricant.
Gleitriegel *m* sliding bolt *(breechblock)*.
Gleitschiene *f* guide slide, guide rail *(G cradle)*; track *(of a catapult)*.
Gleitschuh *m* gun slide.
Gleitschutz *m* nonskid tread *(MT)*.
Gleitschutzkette *f* skid chain *(MT)*.
Gleitschutzmittel *n* nonskid device, traction aid *(MT)*.
Gleitstein *m* cam plate *(G)*.
Gleitstößel *m* tappet rod *(sliding-cam type)*.
Gleitvorrichtung *f* slide mechanism *(MG)*.
Gleitwand *f* slide plate *(MG)*.
Gleitwinkel *m* gliding angle *(Avn)*.
Glied *n* rank *(in formation)*; limb; link; member; unit; penis.
Gliederung *f* formation, organization; distribution; classification, arrangement; composition.
Gliedersäge *f* chain saw.
Glimmer *m* mica.
Glimmlampe *f* neon lamp.
Glühdraht *m* *See* **Glühfaden.**
Glühfaden *m* filament.
Glühkathode *f* hot cathode *(Rad)*.
Glühkathodenröhre *f* vacuum tube, incandescent cathode tube *(Rad)*.
Glühkerze *f* glow plug *(Diesel engine)*.
Glühköpfchen *n* hot-wire-bridge head *(Elec igniting device)*.
Glühlampe *f* incandescent lamp.
Glührohrzündapparat *m* hot-tube igniter.
Glühzündapparat *m* blasting machine, exploder *(Engr)*.
Glühzünder *m* electric igniter *(blasting cap)*.
Glühzündstück *n* electric detonator, electric igniter *(Engr)*.
Glysantin *n* an antifreeze solution *(MT)*.
Gnade *f* quarter, mercy; grace; pardon.
Goerz-Visier *n* bomb sight manufactured by Goerz Company.
Gondel *f* gondola, nacelle *(Ap)*.
Goniometer *n* goniometer *(Surv)*.
Goniometrie *f* goniometry *(Surv)*.
Graben *m* trench; ditch.
Grabenbagger *m* trench excavator.
Grabenbekleidung *f* trench revetment.
Grabendurchfahrt *f* crossing of trenches or ditches *(MT)*.
Grabenkopf *f* saphead *(Ft)*.
Grabenkrieg *m* trench warfare.
Grabenprofil *n* trench profile *(Ft)*; ditch profile *(Engr)*.
Grabenrost *m* trench boards, boardwalk.
Grabensohle *f* trench bottom.
Grabenspiegel *m* trench periscope.
Grabenstellung *f* trench position.
Grabenstufe *f* firing step.
Grabenwehr *f* parapet.
Gräberoffizier *m* graves registration officer.
Grabkreuz *n* grave marker.
Grabtafel *f* grave marker.

Gradabteilung *f* map square.
Gradabzeichen *n* *See* **Dienstgradabzeichen.**
Gradbogen *m* quadrant scale *(G)*.
Gradeinteilung *f* graduation, scale.
Gradfeld *n* map square.
Gradnetz *n* map grid.
Gradzahl *f* number of degrees, number of graduations.
Granatbüchse *f* antitank grenade rifle.
Granate *f* shell *(Am)*.
Granatfüllung *f* shell filler *(Am)*.
Granathülse *f* shell case.
Granatloch *n* shell hole.
Granatsignal *n* projector signal, star shell.
Granatsplitter *m* shell splinter.
Granattreffer *m* hit *(shell fire)*.
Granattrichter *m* shell crater.
Granatwerfer *m* mortar *(Ord)*; gunner *(Mort squad)*.
Granatwerfergeschoß *n* mortar shell.
Granatwerfer-Gruppe *f* mortar section.
Granatwerfernest *n* mortar pit.
Granatwerferstand *m* mortar emplacement.
Granatwerfertrupp *m* mortar team.
Granatwerferzug *m* mortar platoon.
graphisch graphic; mapped, surveyed or plotted.
graphischer Punkt topographical point *(on map)*.
graphische Schußtafel trajectory chart *(not to be confused with US graphical firing table)*.
Graphitschmiermittel *n* graphite lubricant.
Grat *m* ridge *(especially a sharp, rocky ridge)*; scoring *(in bore of gun)*.
Gräte *f* fishbone.
Graupelschauer *m* snow-pellet shower, graupel shower *(Met)*.
Greifer *m* cleat, grouser *(MT, Tk)*.
Greifervorrichtung *f* traction device *(MT)*.
Greifzirkel *m* calipers, dividers.
Grenadier *m* private, infantry rifleman *(historical term reintroduced)*. *See also* **Panzergrenadier.**
Grenadierbataillon *n* rifle battalion.
Grenadierkompanie *f* rifle company.
Grenadier-Panzerwagen *m* armored personnel carrier *(MT)*.
Grenadierregiment *n* rifle regiment, infantry regiment.
Grenzbahnhof *m* frontier station *(RR)*.
Grenzbezirk *m* frontier district.
Grenze *f* frontier, border; boundary; limit.
Grenzfrequenz *f* cut-off frequency *(Rad)*.
Grenzgebiet *n* border area, frontier area.
Grenzlehre *f* fixed gage, plug or snap gage.
Grenzschicht *f* boundary layer *(fluid mechanics)*.
Grenzschraube *f* setscrew.
Grenzschutz *m* frontier guard; frontier protection.
Grenzschutzabschnittskommando *n* frontier guard sector command *(Regtl Hq)*.
Grenzschutzunterabschnitt *m* frontier guard sub-sector *(Bn Hq)*.
Grenzüberschreitung *f* crossing a frontier.
Grenzwache *f* frontier sentry, frontier guard.
Grenzwacht *f* frontier guard.
Grenzwachtdivision *f* frontier guard division.
Grenzzwischenfall *m* border incident, frontier incident.
Griff *m* grip; hold; handle; doorknob.
Griffigkeit *f* grip, traction *(tires)*; traction, ground-gripping ability *(Mt, Tk)*.
Griffplatte *f* holding plate *(G sight)*.
Griffrohr *n* tubular handle *(trail spade)*.
Griffschale *f* stock *(pistol)*.
Griffstück *n* grip *(MG)*; receiver *(pistol)*.
grob approximate, rough, gross, coarse; bad, serious *(mistake)*.
Grobeinstellung *f* frequency selection *(Rad)*; coarse setting *(Optics)*.
grobes Einschießen approximate adjustment fire.
Grobfeile *f* coarse file.
Grobsicherung *f* fuse *(Elec)*.
Grobstufenschalter *m* band switch *(Rad)*.
Grof *m* heavy flame thrower *(on two-wheel carrier)* *(abbr. of* grosser Flammenwerfer*)*.
Gros *n* main body *(Tac)*.
Großadmiral *m* Admiral of the Fleet; Commander-in-Chief *(operational and/or administrative)* *(Nav)*.
Großangriff *m* large-scale attack, major attack, major offensive operation.
Größe *f* quantity *(Math)*; greatness, magnitude, size.

Großeinsatz *m* major commitment, commitment of large forces, employment of great numbers *(Tac)*.
Großer Bär Big Dipper.
Großfertigung *f* mass production.
Großfunkstelle *f* high-power long-distance radio station.
großkalibrig large-caliber.
Großkampfschiff *n* capital ship.
Großkreis *m* great circle.
Großreihenfertigung *f* large-scale series production.
Größtgeschwindigkeit *f* maximum speed.
Großvernebelung *f* extensive smoke screen, large-area screening.
Grube *f* pit.
Grundausbildung *f* basic training.
Grundbegriffe *mpl* fundamentals, basic concepts.
Grundbuchse *f* base bushing *(counterrecoil mechanism)*.
Grundgehalt *n* base pay.
Grundgeschütz *n* base piece, directing gun.
Grundgeschwindigkeit *f* ground speed *(Avn)*.
Grundlagen *fpl* data.
Grundlinie *f* base line.
Grundmaschinengewehr *n* base machine gun.
Grundmine *f* ground mine, controlled mine, observation mine *(Nav)*.
Grundplatte *f* base plate.
Grundrichtung *f* base-line direction *(Gunnery)*.
Grundrichtungslinie *f* base line *(Gunnery)*.
Grundrichtungspunkt *m* base point *(Gunnery)*.
Grundrichtungswinkel *m* base angle *(Gunnery)*.
Grundrißskizze *f* area sketch.
Grundschwelle *f* ground sill *(Bdg)*.
Grundstellung *f* position of attention, position of the soldier *(drill)*.
Grundstufe *f* a factor used for correction of velocity error *(expressed in units — Stufeneinheiten — each equal to ⅓ of 1% of standard muzzle velocity)*.
Grundwasser *n* subsoil water, underground water.
Grundzahl *f* reference-point reading *(Gunnery)*.
Grünkreuz *n* green cross *(Ger marking for lung irritants)* *(CWS)*.
Gruppe *f* group, groupment *(Tac)*; rifle squad *(Inf)*; section *(Cav)*; volley *(Arty)*; group *(air force operational unit of 3* Staffeln, *about 27 aircraft)*.
Gruppenfeuer *n* volley fire *(Arty)*.
Gruppenflugform *f* group formation *(Avn)*.
Gruppenführer *m* squad leader *(Inf)*; section leader *(Cav)*. *See also* **SS-Gruppenführer.**
Gruppenführerabmarsch *m* section-leader half-squad *(Cav)*.
Gruppengefechtsstand *m* group command post *(Avn)*.
Gruppengetriebe *n* auxiliary transmission *(MT)*.
Gruppenkeil *m* group wedge *(Avn)*.
Gruppenkolonne *f* group of squadron javelins *(Avn)*.
Gruppenkolonne aus geschlossenen Winkeln group column of squadron wedges.
Gruppenkolonne links group of squadron javelins echeloned left.
Gruppenkommandeur *m* commander of a *Gruppe* *(Luftwaffe)*.
Gruppenkommando *n* army group headquarters; air force headquarters of a *Gruppe*.
Gruppenschaltung *f* series-parallel connection *(Elec)*.
Gruppenschießen *n* volley fire *(Arty)*.
gruppenweise by squads; by sections; by groups.
Gruppenwinkel *m* group column of squadron V's *(Avn)*.
Gruppe zu Pferde mounted section *(Cav)*.
Gruß *m* hand salute.
Grußpflicht *f* obligation to salute.
Grußweite *f* saluting distance.
Guerillakämpfer *m* guerrilla.
Guerillakrieg *m* guerrilla warfare.
Gulasch *n* beef stew.
Gulaschkanone *f* field kitchen *(slang)*.
Gummi *m-n* rubber; gum.
Gummierung *f* rubberizing, rubber coating; gumming.
Gummifederung *f* rubber shock absorber.
Gummigleiskette *f* rubber track *(Tk)*.
Gummikabel *n* rubber-insulated wire *(Tp)*.
Gummiknüppel *m* rubber truncheon, rubber club.
Gummipolster *n* rubber block *(caterpillar track)*.
Gummirad *n* rubber-tired wheel.
Gummistoff *m* rubberized material.

günstig favorable.
Gurt *m* belt, strap, web *(Clo)*; ammunition belt, feed belt *(MG)*; chord *(of a truss)*.
Gürtel *m* belt, strap; cordon; zone.
Gürtelfestung *f* fortress with an outer cordon of smaller forts.
gurten to load an ammunition belt.
Gurtförderer *m* belt conveyor.
Gurtfüller *m* belt-filling machine, belt-loading machine, link-loading machine.
Gurthebel *m* belt-feed guide *(MG)*.
Gurtladung *f* belt feed.
Gurtschieber *m* belt-feed pawl *(MG)*.
Gurtstrippe *f* rear cinch (pack-saddle).
Gurttrommel *f* belt drum *(MG)*.
Gurtwerk *n* parachute harness.
Gurtzuführer *m* belt feed *(MG)*.
Gußeisen *n* cast iron.
Gußgehäuse *n* cast-metal case or housing.
Gußstahl *m* cast steel.
Güterbahnhof *m* freight station *(RR)*.
Güterwagen *m* freight car *(RR)*.
Güterzug *m* freight train *(RR)*.
Guttaperchapapier *n* gutta-percha paper, waterproof paper.
G.W.-Stand *m* See **Granatwerferstand.**
Gyrorektor *m* gyro flight indicator *(Ap)*.

H

Haager Abkommen Hague Convention.
Haarrohr *n* capillary tube.
Hacke *f* hatchet, ax, pickax; point of hock *(horse)*.
Hackmesser *n* machete; meat cleaver.
Hafen *m* harbor, port.
Hafenanlage *f* port installation.
Hafenarbeiter *m* longshoreman.
Hafenbecken *n* harbor basin.
Hafendamm *m* mole, jetty.
Hafengebiet *n* harbor area.
Hafenoffizier *m* port officer, port control officer.
Hafenschlepper *m* harbor tugboat.
Hafenschutz *m* harbor defense.
Hafenschutzboot *n* harbor defense boat.
Hafenüberwachung *f* port control.
Haft *f* custody, arrest, detention, confinement.
Haft-Hohlladung *f* magnetic antitank hollow charge.
Haftlokal *n* guardhouse, detention room.
Haftpflock *m* steel picket or stake *(Bdg)*.
Haftung *f* adhesion.
Haftung am Erdboden stability, low center of gravity *(of a vehicle)*.
Hagel *m* hail *(Met)*.
Hahn *m* hammer *(SA)*; cock; stopcock, faucet.
Hahnbolzen *m* trigger pin *(MG)*.
Hahngewehr *n* hammer gun *(as distinguished from* hahnloses Gewehr, *hammerless gun)*.
hahnlos hammerless *(Ord)*.
Haken *m* hook; clasp; clamp; catch.
Hakenkreuz *n* swastika.
Hakenumschalter *m* hook switch *(Tp)*.
halbautomatisch semiautomatic.
Halbbildentfernungsmesser *m* split-field coincidence range finder.
Halbflachbettfelge *f* semiflat-base rim *(MT)*.
Halbflachfelge *f* See **Halbflachbettfelge.**
halbfreitragend semicantilever.
Halbholz *n* split post, split log.
Halbinsel *f* peninsula.
Halbkettenantrieb *m* half-track drive *(MT)*.
Halbkettenfahrzeug *n* half-track vehicle.
Halbkettenkraftfahrzeug *n* half-track motor vehicle.
Halbketten-Lastkraftwagen *m* half-track motor truck.
"Halblinks schwenkt, Marsch!" "Column half left, march!"
Halbmesser *m* radius.
"Halbrechts schwenkt, Marsch!" "Column half right, march!"
halbstarr semirigid.
halbstarres Luftschiff semirigid airship.
halbstocks half-mast, half-staff.
Halbzelt *n* lean-to tent.
Halbzug *m* section *(of MG platoon)*.
Halbzugführer *m* section leader *(MG section)*.
Halfter *f* halter *(harness)*.
Halfterkinnkette *f* halter chain *(harness)*.
Halfterriemen *m* halter strap, halter tie *(harness)*.
Halfterstrick *m* picket line.
Halftertasche *f* holster.

Halle *f* hangar; garage; shed; hall.
Hallenvorplatz *m* apron *(Adrm)*.
Halsbinde *f* neckband *(Clo)*.
Halshalfter *f* neck halter *(harness)*.
Halshalfterriemen *m* neck-halter tie *(harness)*.
Halskerbe *f* neck groove *(horse)*.
Halskoppel *f* breast strap *(harness)*.
Halsriemen *m* neck strap *(harness)*.
Halt *m* halt.
Halteleinenbund *m* maneuvering spider *(Bln)*.
halten to hold; to carry *(AA SL)*; to aim.
Halteplatz *m* halt area; stopping place; parking place; loading place.
Haltepunkt *m* point of aim; stop *(halting place)*.
Halterung *f* arms rack, ammunition rack.
Haltestelle *f* halting place, stop.
Haltetau *n* handling line *(Bln)*; guy line.
Haltezeichen *n* stop signal *(MT)*; block signal *(RR)*.
"Halt, wer da!" "Halt! Who is there?"
Handanlasser *m* crank starter, hand starter *(Mtr)*.
Handapparat *m* handset *(Rad, Tp)*.
Handbeil *n* hatchet.
Handbohrmaschine *f* hand drill.
Handbremse *f* hand brake, emergency brake.
Handdrehmaschine *f* hand-crank generator *(Tp)*.
Handelsmarine *f* merchant marine.
Handelsschiff *n* merchantman *(Nav)*.
Handelsschiffsraum *m* merchant tonnage *(Nav)*.
Handelssperre *f* embargo on commerce.
handelsüblich commercial.
Handfäustel *n* mallet.
Handfesseln *fpl* handcuffs, manacles.
Handfeuerlöscher *m* hand fire extinguisher.
Handfeuerwaffen *fpl* small arms.
Handgeld *n* See **Kapitulantenhandgeld.**
Handgemenge *n* hand-to-hand fighting.
Handgranate *f* hand grenade.
Handgranatenwurfstand *m* grenade court.
Handgriff *m* grip, handle; single manual operation.
Handhabungstau *n* prolonge, drag rope *(Arty)*.
Handkammer *f* hand camera.
Handkurbel *f* hand crank.
Handleuchtzeichen *n* ground signal flare.
Handloch *n* hand hole *(G carriage wheel)*.
Handlüfter *m* hand-operated ventilator.
Handpferd off horse, led horse.
Handrad *n* handwheel.
Handrädchen *n* micrometer-scale knob *(angle-of-site Instr)*; small handwheel.
Handrad zur Höhenrichtung elevating handwheel *(G)*.
Handrad zur Seitenrichtung traversing handwheel *(G)*.
Handramme *f* hand piledriver; maul.
Handrauchzeichen *n* hand smoke signal.
Handschellen *fpl* handcuffs, manacles.
Handschuh *m* glove.
Handschutz *m* hand guard.
Handstreich *m* surprise raid; coup de main.
Handstreutrommel *f* hand sprinkler *(CWS)*.
Handstütze *f* pistol grip.
handtätig hand-operated, manually operated, manual *adj.*
Handwaffe *f* hand weapon, hand arm.
Handwagen *m* handcart.
Handwerfer *m* mortar.
Hang *m* slope.
Hängeantenne *f* trailing wire antenna *(Ap)*.
Hängebrücke *f* suspension bridge.
Hängeleine *f* suspension line *(Prcht)*.
Hängematte *f* hammock.
Hängemine *f* hanging mine.
Hängesäule *f* king post.
Hängeventil *n* inverted valve *(Mtr)*.
Hängewerk *n* erect truss *(Bdg)*.
Hangfaktor *m* slope factor *(influence of slope of target surface on longitudinal dispersion) (Ballistics)*.
Hangsegeln *n* ridge soaring *(glider)*.
Hangstellung *f* slope position *(Tac)*.
Hangwind *m* anabatic wind.
Hangwinkel *m* gradient *(Top)*.
Hardyscheibe *f* flexible disk *(MT)*.
Harke *f* rake.
Hartfutter *n* oats and grain.
Hartgummi *n* ebonite.
Haschee *n* hash.
Haube *f* cap *(Am)*; hood *(Mtr)*; spinner *(Ap propeller)*.
Haubenverkleidung *f* engine cowling *(Ap)*.
Haubitze *f* howitzer *(light and medium)*.
Haue *f* pickax.
Haufenwolke *f* cumulus cloud.

Hauptangriff *m* main attack, main effort.
Hauptanschluß *m* trunk station *(Tp)*.
Hauptauswanderungsstrecke *f* linear travel of target during time of flight *(AA gunnery)*.
Hauptbeobachtungsstelle *f* fire direction center *(Arty)*.
Haupteinbruchsstelle *f* main point of penetration *(Tac)*.
Hauptfeldwebel *m* first sergeant.
Hauptfunkstelle *f* net control station *(Rad)*.
Hauptgefreiter *m* a grade in the *Luftwaffe* between *Obergefreiter (Cpl)* and *Unteroffizier (Sgt)*; seaman, 1st class *(highest rated 1st class seaman, with 4½ years' seniority)*.
Hauptgestell *n* headstall *(harness)*.
Hauptgetriebe *n* main transmission gear *(MT)*.
Hauptkampffeld *n* main defensive area, battle position.
Hauptkampflinie *f* main line of resistance.
Hauptladung *f* main charge *(blasting cap)*.
Hauptleute *pl* captains.
Hauptmacht *f* main striking force.
Hauptmann *m* captain.
Hauptmasse *f* main body.
Hauptquartier *n* headquarters.
Hauptreinigung *f* complete cleaning *(R)*.
Hauptschlußmotor *m* series motor *(Elec)*.
Hauptschlußschaltung *f* series connection *(Elec)*.
Hauptschnittverfahren *n* main-station intersection method *(FR)*.
Hauptsender *m* final amplifier, power amplifier *(Rad)*.
Hauptstelle *f* trunk station *(Tp)*.
Hauptsturmführer *m* See SS-Hauptsturmführer.
Hauptträger *m* longeron *(Ap)*; main beam or girder *(Bdg)*.
Haupttrupp *m* advance guard reserve *(in Adv Gd of large unit)*; rear guard reserve *(in rear Gd of large unit)*; advance guard support *(in Adv Gd of smaller unit)*; rear guard support *(in rear Gd of smaller unit)*.
Hauptuhr *f* master watch.
Hauptverbandplatz *m* clearing station *(Med)*.
Hauptvorgelege *n* main reduction gear *(Tk)*.
Hauptwache *f* main guard.
Hauptwachtmeister *m* first sergeant *(Arty, Cav)*.
Hauptwelle *f* mainshaft.
Hauptzündung *f* main ignition lead *(blasting)*.
Haushaltsjahr *n* fiscal year.
Hauswart *m* house warden; janitor.
Hauszelt *n* "house tent" *(a 16-man tent constructed from shelter halves)*.
Haut *f* skin.
hautätzend vesicant *(CWS)*.
Hautentgiftungsmittel *n* skin decontamination agent.
Hautentgiftungssalbe *f* decontamination ointment.
Hautgift *n* blister agent, vesicant agent *(CWS)*.
Hautwirkung *f* skin effect *(Rad)*.
Heavisideschicht *f* Heaviside layer.
Hebebaum *m* crowbar, handspike, lever.
Hebel *m* lever.
heben elevate *(a gun)*; raise, lift.
Hebezeug *n* hoisting gear, hoist.
Heck *n* stern *(Nav, Ash)*; tail *(Ap)*; rear *(Tk)*.
Heckantrieb *m* rear drive *(MT)*.
Hecke *f* hedge.
Heckenschütze *m* sniper.
Heckenspringen *n* hedge-hopping *(Avn)*.
Heckkanzel *f* tail turret *(Ap)*.
Heckmaschinengewehr *n* tail gun *(Ap)*.
Heckmotorwagen *m* rear-engine motor car.
Heckpanzer *m* rear armor *(Tk)*.
Heckschütze *m* tail gunner *(Ap)*.
Heckstand *f* tail-gun position *(Ap)*.
Heckwaffe *f* tail gun *(Ap)*.
Heer *n* Army *(the Army, as distinguished from* Armee, *a tactical unit)*.
Heeresakja *f* See **Akja.**
Heeresamt *n* See **Allgemeines Heeresamt.**
Heeresanstalt *f* Army establishment, organization, or institution.
Heeresartillerie *f* GHQ artillery.
Heeresarzt *m* chief representative of Army Medical Department at *Oberkommando des Heeres (subordinate to* Heeressanitätsinspekteur).
Heeresatmer *m* service oxygen breathing apparatus *(automatically operated)*.
Heeresbaudienst *m* Army construction service.
Heeresbeamter *m* civilian official of the Army.
Heeresbedürfnisse *npl* military necessities.

G.Verw.V.L.	Gerätsverwaltungsvorschrift für die Luftwaffe	equipment administration for the air corps
GVF	garnisonverwendungsfähig im Felde	fit for garrison duty in the field
GVG	garnisonverwendungsfähig in der Garnison	fit for garrison duty in the garrison
GVH	garnisonverwendungsfähig in der Heimat	fit for garrison duty in the interior
GVI	Garnisonverwaltungsinspektor	inspector (supervisor) of garrison administration
GVO	Garnisonverwaltungsordnung	regulations for garrison administration
G.V.O	Gräberverwaltungsoffizier	grave administration officer
GVOI	Garnisonverwaltungsoberinspektor	chief inspector (supervisor) of garrison administration
Gw	Geländewinkel	angle of site
GW	Gruppenwähler	group selector; intermediate selector *(signal service)*
G-Wagen	Güterwagen mit 15 Tonnen Ladungsgewicht	2-3 axle, covered freight car with 15-ton load capacity
G.Wg	Gürtelwagen des langen schweren Mörsers	heavy mortar
GZ	Generalstab - Zentralabteilung	Central Section of the General Staff
G.Z	Granatzünder	shell fuze
GZ	Grundzahl	basic data *(gunnery)*
Gz	Güterzug	freight train
Gz t	Zuladungsgewicht in Tonnen	weight of disposable load in tons *(aviation)*
GZug	Güterzug	freight train

H

h	hängend	inverted *(cylinder arrangement of airplane engine)*
H	Halt!	Halt!
H	Haltestelle	stop; station
H	Handwerker	workman; artisan; craftsman
H	Haubitze	howitzer
H	Haupt-	chief; principal
H	Hauptmann	captain
H	Heckmotor	rear engine *(motor vehicle)*
H	Heer	army
H	Hengst	stallion
H	Hilfs-	auxiliary
H	Hinter-	rear; after; back
H	Hoch-	high
H	Hochdecker	high-wing monoplane
H	Hochleistungssegelflugzeug	high-performance glider
H	Holz	wood
h	horizontal	horizontal
H	Horizontalachse am Theodoliten	horizontal axis of theodolite *(surveying service)*
H	Hütte	hut *(on maps)*
/H	in der Stunde	per hour
H	Reichs-SA-Hochschulamt	Reichs Office of Storm-Trooper Academy
H	Zielhöhe	height of target *(gunnery)*
Ha	Gruppe Hansa (SA)	Hansa Section (Storm Troopers)
Ha	Handgranatenunterstand	hand-grenade shelter
H.A	Hauptabschnitt	main sector
Ha	Hektar	hectare
Ha.B.St	Hauptbeobachtungsstelle	main observation post
Haf	Hafen	port; harbor *(on maps)*
Haf.Pol	Hafenpolizei	harbor police
Haf-St	Hafenstadt	seaport
HAL	Hauptanschlussleitung	main connecting line *(communications)*
halbj	halbjährlich	semiannual
Halbkol	Halbkolonne	half column
halt	halten	to stop; to halt; to hold
haltb	haltbar	tenable; defensible; strong; durable; valid
Handb	Handbuch	handbook; manual
Handgr	Handgranate	hand grenade
Handl.Kr	Handelskrieg	economic warfare
Handschr	Handschrift	signature; manuscript; handwriting
H.A.O	Anzugsordnung für das Reichsheer	clothing regulations for the army
Haub	Haubitze	howitzer
Haupt. B. Stelle	Hauptbeobachtungsstelle	main observation post
Hauptgefr	Hauptgefreiter	*(corresponds roughly to U. S. acting corporal)*
Hauptl	Hauptleute	captains
Hauptm	Hauptmann	captain
Hauwewa	Hauptwetterwarte	main meteorological station; main weather station
hb	halb	half
H.B	Haubitzbatterie	howitzer battery
H.B	Hauptbahn	main railway
H.B	Hauptbeobachtung	main observation
H.B	Heeresbeamter	civilian employee of army
H.B.A	Heeresbauamt	army construction service
H.Bau A	Heeresbauamt	army construction service
H.Bef.Best	Heeresbeförderungsbestimmungen	army promotion regulations

H.Bekl.A	Heeresbekleidungsamt	army clothing service
H.Bekl.A.V	Heeresbekleidungsamtsvorsteher	director of the army clothing office
H.Bes.Best	Heeresbesoldungsbestimmungen	army pay regulations
H.Bes.E.V	Heeresbesoldungsergänzungsvorschrift	army supplementary pay regulations
Hbf Hbhf.	Hauptbahnhof	main depot; main railway station
H.Br.	Heeresbrot	army bread
hbst	halbstarr	semirigid (*aviation*)
hbst	halbstündig	every half hour
Hchfl	Hochflieger	high-altitude flyer
H.D	Hochdecker	high-wing monoplane
Hdb	Handbuch	handbook; manual
Hdbr	Handbremse	hand brake; emergency brake
Hdfw	Handfeuerwaffe	small fire arms
Hdgem	Handgemenge	hand-to-hand fight
Hdgr	Handgriff	handle
H.Dienst	Horchdienst	listening-in service (*radio*)
Hdpfd	Handpferd	led horse
Hd.R	Hunderotte	dog pack (*3 messenger dogs*)
H.Draht Nd	Drahtnachrichtendienst des Reichsheeres	army wire signal service
Hd.Sch.W	Handscheinwerfer	portable searchlight
H.D.St.O	Heeresdisziplinarstrafordnung	army disciplinary regulations
H.Dv	Heeresdienstvorschrift	army service regulation
H.Dv	Heeresdruckvorschrift	printed army regulations; army service regulations; army manual
H.Dv	Heeresdruckvorschriftenverwaltung	army regulations administration
He	Gruppe Hessen (SA)	Hesse Section (Storm Troopers)
He	Helium	helium
H.E.B	Heeresergänzungsbestimmungen	army recruiting regulations
Heeresgr	Heeresgruppe	army group; group of armies
Heer San	Heeressanitätswesen	army medical service
Heerw	Heerwesen	army organization; military affairs
H.E.O	Heeresergänzungsordnung	army recruiting regulations
Heliom	Heliometer	heliometer
H.F	Hochfrequenz	high frequency (*radio*)
H.F.A	Heeresforstamt	army board of woods and forests
H.Fachsch	Heeresfachschule	army technical school
H.Fachsch.D	Heeresfachschuldienst	army technical school service
H.Fachsch.f. Ld.u. Fstw.	Heeresfachschule für Landwirtschaft und Forstwirtschaft	army school for agriculture and forestry
H.F.Auf.A	Heeresforstaufsichtsamt	army forest supervision office
Hfbeschl.Lmst	Hufbeschlaglehrmeister	horseshoeing instructor
H.F.G	Hinterbliebenenfürsorgegesetz	law pertaining to the welfare of survivors
H.F.I	Heeresforstinspektion	army forestry inspection service
H.Filmst	Heeresfilmstelle	army motion picture service
Hfn	Hafen	harbor; port
H.Forst-I	Heeresforstinspektion	army forestry inspection service
H.Forst-Verw.	Heeresforstverwaltung	army forestry administration
H.F.R.A	Heeresforstrevieramt	district office of army forestry service
H.F.Sch	Heeresfachschule	army technical school
H.F.St	Hauptfürsorgestelle	main social service office
Hfst	Hilfstelle	auxiliary station
H.Fürs.St	Hauptfürsorgestelle	main social service office
H.Fz	Heeresfeldzeugmeister(ei)	chief of ordnance; army ordnance department
H.Fzgr	Heeresfeldzeuggruppe	army ordnance group
H.Fz.Gru	Heeresfeldzeuggruppe	army ordnance group
H.Fzm	Heeresfeldzeugmeister(ei)	chief of ordnance; army ordnance department
H.Fz.V	Heeresfeldzeugverwaltung	army ordnance administration
Hg	Handgranate	hand grenade
H.G	Heeresgerät	army equipment; military equipment
Hg	Hügel	hill
H.Geb.O	Heeresgebäudeordnung	army housing regulations
Hgefr	Hauptgefreiter	(*corresponds roughly to U. S. acting corporal*)
H.Ger.Pk	Heeresgerätepark	army equipment park
H.G.I	Heergerätinspizient	army equipment inspector; ordnance inspector
Hgr	Handgranate	hand grenade
H.Gr	Heeresgruppe	army group; group of armies
H. Gren	Handgranate	hand grenade
Hgr.Kdo	Heeresgruppenkommando	headquarters of a group of armies
H.H.A	Heereshundeanstalt	army messenger-dog kennels
H.Handw.Sch	Heereshandwerkerschule	army vocational school
H.Haush	Heereshaushaltsabteilung	Army Administrative Section

Heeresbergführer *m* Army mountain guide (*mountaineer specialist*).
Heeresbericht *m* official Army communiqué.
Heeresbestände *mpl* military stores.
Heeresbetreuungsabteilung *f* Army welfare unit, Army morale unit.
Heeresbetriebsstofflager *n* Army gasoline and lubricant bulk storage plant.
Heeresbildungsanstalt *f* military school.
Heeresbücherei *f* Army library.
Heeresdruckvorschrift *f* Army Manual (*abbr.* H. Dv.).
Heereseinrichtung *f* Army establishment, organization, or institution.
Heeresflak *f* Army antiaircraft artillery (*as distinguished from AAA of the* Luftwaffe).
Heeresgerät *n* Army equipment (*in its broadest sense; to be distinguished from* Heergerät).
Heeresgruppe *f* group of armies.
Heeresgruppenkommando *n* headquarters of a group of armies.
Heereshochgebirgsschule *f* Army training school for mountain warfare.
Heeresintendant *m* See **Intendant.**
Heeresjustizbeamter *m* military law official.
Heereskavallerie *f* GHQ cavalry.
Heereskraftfahrpark *m* GHQ motor transport park.
Heereskrankenschwester *f* Army nurse.
Heeresküstenartillerie *f* Army coast artillery (*as distinguished from the* Marineartillerie).
Heereslazarett *n* general hospital, Army hospital.
Heeresleitung *f* GHQ, Army Command.
Heeresmunitionslager *n* Army ammunition-supply depot.
Heeresnachrichtenregiment *n* GHQ signal regiment.
Heeresnachschubführer *m* GHQ chief of rear services.
Heeresnachschubkolonne *f* GHQ supply column.
Heerespersonalamt *n* Army Personnel Office (*branch of the* Oberkommando des Heeres) (*abbr.* HPA, PA).
Heerespferdelazarett *n* GHQ veterinary hospital.
Heerespsychologe *m* personnel consultant.
Heeresreserve *f* GHQ reserve.
Heeressanitätsabteilung *f* GHQ medical battalion.
Heeres-Sanitätsinspekteur *m* surgeon general (*with rank of* Generaloberstabsarzt).
Heeres-Sauerstoffschutzgerät *n* service oxygen breathing apparatus (*manually operated*).
Heeresstandort *m* army post.
Heeresstandortkasse *f* army post finance office.
Heeresstandortverwaltung *f* army post administration.
Heerestruppen *fpl* GHQ troops.
Heeresversorgung *f* Army supply.
Heeresverwaltung *f* Army administration, administrative services.
Heeresverwaltungsamt *n* Army Administration Office (*branch of the* Oberkommando des Heeres) (*abbr.* HVA, VA).
Heereswaffenamt *n* Army Ordnance Office (*branch of the* Oberkommando des Heeres) (*abbr. HWaA*).
Heeres-Zeugamt *n* Army ordnance supply office or depot.
Heergerät *n* Army transport equipment (*includes transport accessories; to be distinguished from* Heeresgerät).
Heimatgebiet *n* zone of the interior.
Heimatflughafen *m* home base (*Avn*).
Heimat-Pferdelazarett *n* veterinary general hospital (*Z of I*).
Heimathorst *m* home base (*Avn*).
Heimatstaat *m* country of origin (*PW*).
Heimatwachbataillon *n* guard battalion (*Z of I*).
Heimsendung *f* repatriation.
heißen to hoist (*a flag*).
heiter bright, cheerful; scattered (*Met*).
Heizbatterie *f* "A" battery, filament battery (*Rad*).
Heizfaden *m* filament (*Rad*).
Heizkanal *m* hot-air duct (*thermo anti-icer*).
Heizkreis *m* filament circuit (*Rad*).
Heizöl *n* fuel oil (*for heating*).
Heizregler *m* variable filament resistor (*Rad*).
Heizsammler *m* filament battery (*Rad*).
Heizstrom *m* filament current (*Rad*).
Heldenfriedhof *m* military cemetery.
Heldentat *f* heroic deed, exploit.
Helm *m* helmet.
Helmband *n* identification helmet band (*Tng*).
Helmbezug *m* helmet cover.
Helmüberzug *m* See **Helmbezug.**
hemmen to check (*recoil, etc.*); to jam (*a gun, etc.*); to obstruct, hinder, slow down; inhibit.
Hemmung *f* stoppage (*Ord*); obstruction; inhibition.
Beseitigen von Hemmungen immediate action (*Ord*).
herabsetzen reduce (*in rank*).
heranlocken to decoy, to lure.
heranpirschen, sich to creep or stalk up to.
herausmanövrieren to maneuver the enemy out of position.
"Heraustreten!" "Fall out!" (*to men in barracks*).
Herbertgerät *n* Herbert bridge unit (*similar to US Bailey-type bridge*).
Hereinlotsen *n* "piloting-in" by ground-air radio communication.
Hering *m* tent pin.
Hersteller *m* maker, manufacturer.
Hertz *n* cycles per second (*Ger unit of frequency*).
Herzstück *n* switch point (*RR*).
Heulsignal *n* siren.
Hexachloräthan *n* hexachlorethane (*CWS*).
Hieb *m* slash (*bayonet*); cut (*saber, etc.*).
Hiebwaffe *f* slashing weapon.
Hilfe *f* help, aid, assistance.
Hilfsantenne *f* sensing antenna (*Rad direction finder*).
Hilfsbeobachter *m* assistant observer (*Avn*).
Hilfsflügel *m* slat, auxiliary airfoil.
Hilfskette *f* auxiliary track (*MT*).
Hilfskettenfahrzeug *n* combination wheel-track vehicle.
Hilfskreuzer *m* auxiliary cruiser.
Hilfslafette *f* improvised mount (*MG*).
Hilfslandeplatz *m* auxiliary landing field.
Hilfsmaßstab *m* auxiliary scale (*Inst*).
Hilfsmotor *m* auxiliary engine.
Hilfsschirm *m* pilot parachute.
Hilfstruppen *fpl* auxiliary troops. *See also* **Hilfswilliger.**
Hilfswaffe *f* auxiliary arm.
Hilfswilliger *m* auxiliary volunteer (*East-European or PW volunteer for non-combat service with the German Army*).
Hilfsziel *n* auxiliary target; reference point.
Himmelskugel *f* celestial sphere.
Himmelsrichtung *f* point of the compass, cardinal point.
Hindernis *n* obstacle, hurdle, obstruction; accessory defense (*Tac*).
Hindernisbahn *f* obstacle course.
Hindernisfeuer *n* obstacle light, obstruction light (*Avn*).
Hindernisschlagpfahl *m* driving-type obstacle picket (*i.e., set up by driving into ground*).
Hindernisschraubpfahl *m* screw-type obstacle picket (*i.e., set up by screwing into ground*).
Hindernissprengtrupp *m* obstacle demolition squad.
Hindernisstrecke *f* obstacle course.
Hindernistrupp *m* obstacle construction squad.
hinhaltend delaying.
hinhaltender Widerstand delaying action (*in successive positions*).
hinhaltendes Gefecht delaying action.
Hinterachsantrieb *m* rear-axle drive (*MT*).
Hinterachsgehäuse *n* differential housing, differential case (*MT*).
Hintereinanderschaltung *f* series connection (*Elec*).
Hintergelenk *n* rear toggle joint (*pistol*).
Hinterhalt *m* ambush, concealment; trap.
Hinterhand *f* hindquarters (*horse*).
Hinterhang *m* reverse slope.
Hinterhangstellung *f* reverse-slope position.
Hinterholm *m* rear outrigger (*AA gun*).
Hinterkaffe *f* stern compartment (*Pon*).
Hinterkante *f* trailing edge (*Ap wing*).
Hinterradantrieb *m* rear-wheel drive (*MT*).
Hintersielengeschirr *n* wheel harness.
Hintersteven *m* sternpost.
Hinterstütze *f* trail (*MG tripod*).
Hinterwagen *m* caisson.
Hinterzeug *n* breeching (*harness*).
Hinterzwiesel *m* cantle of saddle; rear of packsaddle arch.
Hirnsäge *f* crosscut saw.
Höhenteilung *f* elevation scale (*G, MG*).
Höhentemperatur *f* temperature at various altitudes (*Met*).
Höhentrieb *m* elevating worm (*sight mechanism*).
Höhenunterschied *m* difference in altitude between target and piece (*Gunnery*); elevation difference (*Surv, Top*); vertical interval, vertical offset.
Höhenvorhalt *m* See **Höhenwinkelvorhalt.**
Höhenwinkel *m* angular height, vertical visual angle (*AA gunnery*).
Höhenwinkelverbesserungsknopf *m* vertical correction knob (*AA gun*).
Höhenwinkelvorhalt *m* vertical lead, vertical deflection (*AA gunnery*).
Höherer...Offizier Senior...Officer (*with mention of arm or service*) (*at Army Hq, e.g.* Höh. Kav. Offz., *Senior Cav Officer at Army Hq*).
hohl hollow, concave, sunken.
Höhle *f* cave.
Hohlkopfgeschoß *n* hollow-charge projectile.
Hohlladung *f* hollow charge.
Hohlraumpanzerung *f* spaced armor (*Tk*).
Hohlringladung *f* hollow ring charge.
Hohlweg *m* sunken road.
Holm *m* spar (*Ap*); stringer, spar (*Bdg*); outrigger (*AA gun*); trail (*right or left trail of a split trail*).
die Holme spreizen to spread the trails.
Holmzurrung *f* outrigger lock (*G*).
Holzbunker *m* log bunker, timber shelter (*Ft*).
Holzgasanlage *f* wood-gas generator.
Holzgas-Lastkraftwagen *m* wood-gas motor truck.
Holzgehäuse *n* wooden baffle, cabinet (*Rad*).
Holzgeist *m* wood alcohol.
Holzkohle *f* charcoal.
Holzkohlen-Gasgenerator *m* wood-gas generator (*MT*).
Holzmine *f* wooden box mine.
Holzrost *m* wooden grating; trench flooring, catwalk, boardwalk (*trench*).
Holz-Tankstelle *f* filling station for wood-gas motor vehicles.
Holzverkleidung *f* wood revetment.
Holzweg *m* dead-end loggers' road.
hissen to hoist (*a flag*).
Hitler-Jugend *f* Nazi party youth organization.
hitzebeständig heat-resistant.
Hitzschlag *m* heatstroke.
Hochachse *f* vertical axis (*Ap*).
Hochangriff *m* high-altitude bombing attack (*Avn*).
Hochbau *m* overhead construction (*Tp line*).
hochbrisant high-explosive.
Hochdecker *m* high-wing monoplane.
Hochdruckgebiet *n* high-pressure area (*Met*).
Hochdruckreifen *m* high-pressure tire (*MT*).
Hochdruckschmierung *f* high-pressure lubrication.
Hochebene *f* plateau.
Hochelastikreifen *m* cushion tire (*MT*).
hochempfindlich supersensitive.
hochempfindlicher Aufschlagzünder supersensitive fuze (*AA Am*).
Hochfrequenz *f* radio frequency, high frequency.
Hochfrequenzdrossel *f* radio-frequency choke.
Hochfrequenzstörungen *fpl* high-frequency interference (*Rad*).
Hochfrequenzstufe *f* radio-frequency stage.
Hochfrequenztransformator *m* radio frequency transformer.
Hochfrequenzverstärker *m* radio frequency amplifier.
Hochgebirgsbataillon *n* high-mountain rifle battalion (*consists entirely of mountaineer specialists*).
hochgezogene Kehrkurve Immelmann turn.
Hochleitung *f* overhead line.
Hochofen *m* blast furnace.
Hochseeschlepper *m* ocean-going tugboat.
Hochspannungsleitung *f* high-tension line, power transmission line (*Elec*).
Hochstand *m* high lookout post.
Höchstgasdruck *m* maximum gas pressure (*Ord*).
Höchstgeschwindigkeit *f* maximum speed.
Höchstlast *f* maximum load.
Höchstleistung *f* maximum power, maximum performance.
Höchstschußweite *f* extreme range, maximum range (*Ord*).
Höchstwertverfahren *n* maximum intensity method (*sound locator*).
Höchstzahl *f* maximum number.
Hochwert *m* Y-coordinate number (*map grid or coordinate scale*).
Hochziehen *n* steep climb, zoom (*Ap*).
Höckerhindernisse *npl* "dragon's teeth" (*AT obstacle*).
Hockloch *n* crouching foxhole.
Hof *m* yard, courtyard; farm.
Höhe *f* altitude, elevation, height; hill; rate, amount.
Hoheitsabzeichen *n* nationality marking (*Ap, Tk*); national insignia, national emblem (*Clo*).
Hoheitsgewässer *npl* territorial waters.
Hoheitszeichen *n* See **Hoheitsabzeichen.**

H.Hd	Heereshund	army messenger-dog
H.Hd.Anst	Heereshundeanstalt	army messenger-dog kennels
H.Hg.Stg	Hinterhangstellung	reverse slope position
Hhl	Höhle	cave (*on maps*)
H.I	Halbinsel	peninsula
Hi	Hinterräder	rear wheels
Hi.B.St	Hilfsbeobachtungsstelle	auxiliary observation post
Hilfs-Min.Su	Hilfsminensucher	auxiliary mine sweeper
Hind	Hindernis	obstacle; barrier; barricade; entanglement; impediment
hinh	hinhaltend	delaying
hinh.Gef	hinhaltendes Gefecht	delaying action
hinh.Kpf	hinhaltender Kampf	delaying engagement
Hint.H	Hinterhang	reverse slope
hinw	hinweisen	to indicate; to point (to)
HJ	Hitlerjugend	Hitler Youth
H.K.A	Heeresküstenartillerie	army coast artillery
H.Kav	Heereskavallerie	general headquarters cavalry
H.K.F	Hauptkampffeld	battle position
H.K.F	Heereskraftwagenfachlehrer	instructor in an army motor transport school
H.K.Feld	Hauptkampffeld	battle position
HKL	Hauptkampflinie	main line of resistance
H.Km	Gipfelhöhe in Kilometern	ceiling in kilometers
H.K.O	höherer Kavallerieoffizier	cavalry officer above the rank of captain
H.Körp	Heereskörper	body of an army; army
H.K.P	Heereskraftfahrpark	army motor transport park
H.K.P	Heimatkraftfahrpark	motor transport park in interior
H.K.S	Heereskraftfahrschule	army motor transport school
HL	Heeresleitung	army high command
h.l	hinten links	from behind and to the left (*gunnery, wind direction*)
Hl	Hohlladungsgeschoss	blank shell
H.Laz	Heereslazarett	army hospital
Hlft	Halfter	halter
H.L.Schm	Heereslehrschmiede	army horseshoer's school
Hlst	Heilstätte	health-resort (*on maps*)
HM	Allgemeine Heeresmitteilungen	general army information (*bulletin*); army memorandum
hm	Höhe eines Flugzeuges in Metern	height of an airplane in meters
H.M	Höhenmesser	altimeter; height-finder
H.Ma	Heeresmunitionsanstalt	army ammunition establishment
Hmins	Hilfsminensucher	auxiliary mine sweeper
Hmm	Hub eines Flugzeugmotors in Millimetern	stroke of an airplane in millimeters
H.Mun.Anst	Heeresmunitionsanstalt	office of army ammunition
H.Mus.Insp	Heeresmusikinspizient	superintendent of army music
H Nb	Heeresnachrichtenbetriebsleitung	army signal corps administration
H.N.Ma	Heeres-Nebenmunitionsanstalten	sub-office of army ammunition
H.N.O	höherer Nachrichtenoffizier	signal officer above the rank of captain
H.N.S	Hauptnachschubstelle	main base of supply
H.N.Za	Heeresnachweisungszeugamt	army recording bureau for army equipment
H.N.Za	Heeresnebenzeugamt	army ordnance sub-bureau
H.O	Heeresordnung	army organization; army order
H.O	Hochofen	blast furnace (*on maps*)
höh	höher	higher
Höh.Kdo	Höheres Kommando	corps command
hölz	hölzern	wooden
Hö.Tonn	Höchsttonage	tonnage limit; maximum tonnage
Holzbr	Holzbrücke	wooden bridge (*on maps*)
H.O.Pf	Heeresoberpfarrer	senior army chaplain
H/OQuV	Heeres - Oberquartiermeister V	Army Director of Historical Records
horiz	horizontal	horizontal
Hp	Haltepunkt	aiming point; point of aim; stopping point (*railroad, street car*) (*on maps*)
H.P	Horchposten	listening post
H.P.A	Heerespersonalamt	Army Personnel Office
H.Pf	Heil- und Pflegeanstalt	convalescent sanatorium
H.Pi.O	höherer Pionieroffizier	engineer officer above the rank of captain
Hpt	Haupt-	chief; principal
Hpt	Hauptstadt	capital
Hpt.K.Feld	Hauptkampffeld	battle position
Hptl	Hauptleute	captains
Hptm	Hauptmann	captain
Hpt.Res	Hauptreserve	main body of reserve
Hpt.San.Pk	Hauptsanitätspark	medical supply depot
Hptscha	Hauptscharführer	(SS) first platoon-leader, Elite Guard (*corresponding to U. S. master sergeant*)
Hptst	Hauptstadt	capital city
Hptstuf	Hauptsturmführer	(SS) chief company-commander, Elite Guard
Hpt.Tr	Haupttross	main field train; main supply train
Hpttr	Haupttrupp	reserve (*of advance or rearguard*)
Hpt.Tr.Fhr	Haupttrossführer	commander of main field trains
Hpt.Verb.Pl	Hauptverbandplatz	main dressing station (*medical*)
Hptverw	Hauptverwaltung	main administration
Hpt.V.Pl	Hauptverbandplatz	main dressing station

Hpt.Vet.Pk	Hauptveterinärpark	veterinary supply depot
H.Pz.O	höherer Panzeroffizier	tank officer above the rank of major
H.Qu	Hauptquartier	headquarters
HR	Heeresrechtabteilung	army legal section
H.Ro	Heeresrohstoffabteilung	army raw material section
H.R.P	Hauptrichtungspunkt	base point
hrsg	herausgegeben	edited
H.S	Handscheinwerfer	hand searchlight
Hs	Handschrift	handwriting; signature; manuscript
Hs	Haus	house (*on maps*)
H.San.Inspr	Heeressanitätsinspekteur	inspector of the army medical service
H.San.Lager	Hauptsanitätslager	main medical supply depot
H.Sattlmstr	Heeressattlermeister	army saddle master
hschr	handschriftlich	written by hand
H.Schr.V	Vorschrift für den Schriftund Geschäftsverkehr im Reichsheer	regulations for army correspondence
H.Schuhm.Mstr	Heeresschuhmachermeister	army shoemaker
hsl	handschriftlich	written by hand
H.S.L	Hauptsanitätslager	main medical supply depot
H.S.S.Ger	Heeressauerstoffschutzgerät	military oxygen apparatus
H.SS Pf	Höherer SS und Polizeiführer	Superior SS and Police Commander
H.St	Haltestelle	stop; station
Hst	Hauptstadt	capital city
Hst	Hilfstelle	auxiliary station
H.St.O.K	Heeresstandortkasse	post finance office
H.St.O.V	Heeresstandortsverwaltung	army post administration
H.Stp.V	Handwaffenstempelvorschrift	small arms stamping regulations
H.St.V	Strafvollstreckungsvorschrift für Reichsheer	regulations for the execution of sentences in the army
Ht	Hütte	hut; cottage (*on maps*)
hT	Treffpunkthöhe	altitude of point of impact (*antiaircraft artillery*)
HTA	Haupttelegraphenamt	main telegraph office
Htf	Hinterfessel	pastern
H.Tp	Heereskraftwagentransportgruppe	army truck detachment
Htr	Hinter-	rear; after; back
H.U.A	Heeresunterkunftsamt	army billeting administration
H.U.A.Dir	Heeresunterkunftsamtsdirektor	director of army billeting administration
Hünengr	Hünengrab	prehistoric grave (*on maps*)
Hufbeschl.Lm	Hufbeschlaglehrmeister	horseshoeing instructor
hund	hundert	hundred
hundtsd	hunderttausend	hundred thousand
HV	Heeresverwaltung	army administration
H.V.A	Hauptversorgungsamt	main social service and welfare office (*for dependents of soldiers*)
H.V.A	Heeresverpflegungsamt	army commissary service
H.V.Bl	Heeresverordnungsblatt	army bulletin
H.Verpfg.A	Heeresverpflegungsamt	army commissary service
H.Verpfl.V	Heeresverpflegungsvorschrift	army regulations for commissary service
H.Vers.A	Hauptversorgungsamt	main social service and welfare office
H.Verw	Hauptverwaltung	main administration
H.Vet.Akad	Heeresveterinärakademie	army veterinary school
H.Vet.U.A	Heeresveterinäruntersuchungsamt	army veterinary examining service
H.Vpfl.A	Heeresverpflegungsamt	army commissary service
H.V.Pl	Heeresverbandplatz	army field dressing station
H.V.U.A	Heeresveterinäruntersuchungsamt	army veterinary examining service
H.V.V	Heeresverkehrvorschriften	army traffic regulations
H.V.V	Heeresverwaltungsvorschriften	army administrative regulations
H.V.V	Heeresveterinärvorschrift	army veterinary regulations
H.Wg	Handwagen	handcart
hy	hydraulisch	hydraulic
H.Z	Haubitzzünder	howitzer fuze
H.Z	Heereszeitung	army journal
H.Za	Heeres-Zentralamt	army central bureau
H.Zä	Heereszeugämter	army ordnance departments or depots
H.-Zahlm.Verw	Heereszahlmeisterverwaltung	army finance department
H.Zg.A	Heereszeugamt	army ordnance department
Hzw	Heereszeugverwaltung	army ordnance administration

I

i.	im, in	in; in the
I	Industrie	industry
I	Infanterie	infantry
I	Infanterieziel	infantry target *or* objective
I	Insel	island
I	Inspektor; Inspektion	inspecting officer; inspector; inspection; supervision
I	Institut	institute
Ia	(*pronounced "Einss-ah"*)	operations officer of field unit
i.a	im allgemeinen	generally
I.A	im Auftrage	by order of
i.A	in Abwesenheit	in absence
i.A	in Ausbildung	in training
i.ad.D	im ausserordentlichen Dienst	in extraordinary service
i.allg	im allgemeinen	generally
i.Aufb	im Aufbau	in construction; building up
i.Ausb	im Ausbau	in consolidation; in completion
I.A.W	Inspekteur des Ausbildungswesens	inspector of training
I.B	Infanteriebataillon	infantry battalion
i.bes.A	im besonderen Auftrage	in special mission
I.B.O	Infanterie-Beobachtungs-Offizier	infantry observation officer
id	identisch	identical
I.D	Infanteriedivision	infantry division
i.d.F	in der Fassung	wording (*of document*)
i.d.G	in der Gegend	in the vicinity
i.d.M	in der Minute	per minute
I.d.O	Inspekteur der Ordnungspolizei	Inspector of Regular Police
i.d.R	in der Regel	as a rule
i.d.Res	in der Reserve	in the Reserve
i.d.Sek	in der Sekunde	per second
i.d.Std	in der Stunde	per hour
I.E.B	Infanterieersatzbataillon	infantry replacement training battalion
i.e.F	in erleichterter Form	in simplified form; facilitated
i.Entw	in Entwurf	in draft; outline
i.e.R	im einstweiligen Ruhestande	temporarily retired
I.E.R	Infanterieersatzregiment	infantry replacement training regiment
i.e.S	im engeren Sinne	in a narrower sense
i.F	im Felde	in the field
If	Infanterieführer	infantry commander in a division
I.F.H	internationales Flughandbuch	international aviation manual
I Fhr	Infanterieführer	infantry commander in a division
Ifl	Infanterieflieger	pilot assigned to infantry-support aviation
Iflakheim	Inspekteur der Flugabwehrkanonen in Heimatgebiet	inspector of antiaircraft artillery in the zone of the interior
Iflakop	Inspekteur der Flugabwehrkanonen im Operationsgebiet	inspector of antiaircraft artillery in zone of operations
I.Fü	Infanterieführer	infantry commander in a division
i.G	im Generalstabe	on the general staff
I.G	Infanteriegeräte	infantry equipment
I.G	Infanteriegeschütz	infantry howitzer
Ig	Inspektion für Waffen und Gerät	inspectorate of weapons and equipment
I.Gesch	Infanteriegeschütz	infantry howitzer
I.G.I	Infanteriegerätsinspizient	inspector of infantry equipment
Igr.Z	Infanteriegranatezünder	infantry grenade fuze
i.H.L	in Haubitzlafette	in howitzer gun carriage
i.i.D	im inneren Dienst	on interior duty
i.J	im Jahre	per year; in the year
i.Kas.L	in Kasematten Lafette	on casemate mount
I.K.H.D	immobiles Kraftwagenhilfsdepot	stationary automobile auxiliary depot
I.K.K	immobile Kraftwagenkolonne	stationary motor transport train
I.L.R	Infanterielehrregiment	infantry training regiment
Iluft	Inspektion der Luftschiffertruppen	inspectorate of dirigible troops
Iluk	Inspektion des Militär- Luft- und Kraftfahrwesens	motor transport echelon inspectorate
im	imitiert	imitated
I.M.Kol	Infanteriemunitionskolonne	infantry ammunition column; infantry ammunition train
Imp	Impediment	obstacle
impr	imprägniert	impregnated
imst	imstande	capable
i.N	im Namen	in the name of
In 1	Inspektion der Kriegsschulen	inspectorate of cadet schools
In 2	Inspektion der Infanterie	inspectorate of the infantry

Höhenabstand *m* vertical interval.
Höhenabweichung *f* range deviation, vertical deviation *(Gunnery)*.
Höhenangabe *f* altitude indication, altitude reading.
Höhenänderung *f* change of height *(AA predictor)*.
Höhenatmer *m* oxygen apparatus *(Avn)*.
Höhenbegrenzer *m* elevating stop *(Ord)*.
Höhenbestimmung *f* determination of altitude.
Höhenbombenwurf *m* high-altitude bombing.
Höhenebene *f* horizontal plane through path of target in horizontal flight *(AA gunnery)*.
Höhenempfänger *m* elevation indicator, elevation indicator-regulator *(AA gun)*.
Höhenentfernungsmesser *m* height finder, altimeter *(AAA)*.
Höhenflosse *f* stabilizer *(Ap)*.
Höhenflug *m* high-altitude flight *(Avn)*.
Höhenflugzeug *n* sub-stratoplane.
Höhengradbogen *m* elevating sector *(G)*.
Höhenhebel *m* elevating gear lever *(MG)*.
Höhenkabine *f* pressure cabin *(Ap)*.
Höhenkrankheit *f* aeroembolism, bends *(Avn)*.
Höhenlader *m* supercharger with high blower ratio *(Ap)*.
Höhenleitwerk *n* elevator assembly *(Ap)*.
Höhenlibelle *f* elevation level *(MG sight)*.
Höhenlinie *f* contour line.
Höhenmesser *m* altimeter *(Ap)*; height finder, altimeter *(AAA)*.
Höhenmeßplan *m* elevation plotting board *(Gunnery)*.
Höhenmessung *f* hypsometry *(Surv)*.
Höhenmischregelung *f* high-altitude mixture control *(Ap)*.
Höhenmotor *m* supercharged engine *(Ap)*.
Höhenrichtfeld *n* elevation, total movement in elevation *(Ord)*.
Höhenrichtfernrohr *n* elevation tracking telescope *(height finder)*.
Höhenrichtkanonier *m* elevation setter.
Höhenrichtmaschine *f* elevating mechanism *(Ord)*.
Höhenrichtrad *n* elevating handwheel *(G)*.
Höhenrichtschraube *f* elevation screw *(prismatic sight)*.
Höhenrichttrieb *m* elevating drive, elevating mechanism *(Ord)*.
Höhenrichtung *f* adjusted range; laying for elevation *(Gunnery)*.
Höhenrichtwelle *f* elevating shaft *(G)*.
Höhenrichtwerk *n* elevating mechanism *(Ord)*.
Höhenrichtzeiger *m* elevation indicator *(Ord)*.
Höhenrippe *f* ridge *(Top)*.
Höhenrücken *m* ridge, crest of ridge.
Höhenruder *n* elevator *(Ap)*.
Höhenruderhebel *m* elevator control lever *(Ap)*.
Höhenschicht *f* altitude bracket *(Avn, Met)*.
Höhenschichtlinie *f* contour line.
Höhenschreiber *m* barograph *(Avn)*.
Höhenstaffelung *f* stepped-up formation *(Avn)*.
Höhenstellung *f* position on dominant height.
Höhensteuer *n* elevator *(Ap)*.
Höhensteuerung *f* elevator control *(Ap)*.
Höhenstreuung *f* range dispersion on vertical target *(Ballistics)*.
Holzzwischenlage *f* wood separator *(storage battery)*.
Horchauswertestelle *f* radio intelligence post.
Horchdienst *m* intercept service *(Rad, Tp)*.
Horchempfang *m* stand-by operation *(Rad)*.
Horchempfänger *m* intercept set *(Rad)*.
Horcherprüf- und Übungsgerät *n* binaural trainer, binaural training instrument.
Horchgerät *n* sound locator, sound detector; intercept receiver.
Horchkompanie *f* intercept company *(Sig C)*.
Horchortung *f* sound location, sound ranging *(AAA)*.
Horchposten *m* listening sentry, listening post.
Horchstelle *f* listening post, intercept post.
Hörfrequenz *f* audio frequency.
Hörer *m* telephone receiver, headphone.
Horizont *m* horizon; artificial horizon *(Ap)*.
Horizontalebene *f* horizontal plane.
Horizontalflug *m* horizontal flight, level flight *(Avn)*.
Horizontalgeschwindigkeit *f* ground speed *(of target) (AA gunnery)*.
Horizontiergriff *m* leveling jack handle *(AA gun outrigger)*.
Horizontierung *f* leveling jack *(AA gun outrigger)*.
Horizontierungsvorrichtung *f* leveling device *(AA gun mount)*.
Hörmuschel *f* earpiece *(Tp)*.
Horn *n* bugle, horn.
Hornisse *f* hornet *(name of Ger self-propelled AT gun)*.
Hornist *m* bugler.
Hornsignal *n* bugle call; horn signal *(MT)*.
Hörsaalflugzeug *n* "flying classroom."
Hörsaalsummer *m* oscillator-amplifier *(code practice)*.
Horst *m* *See* **Fliegerhorst.**
H-Staffel *f* tactical reconnaissance squadron attached to army ground units *(Luftwaffe)*.
Hub *m* stroke *(Mtr)*.
Hubhöhe *f* angle of axle displacement *(MT)*.
Hubraum *m* piston displacement *(Mtr)*.
Hubschrauber *m* helicopter.
Hubvolumen *n* *See* **Hubraum.**
Hufbeschlag *m* horseshoeing.
Hufkrone *f* hoof coronet *(horse)*.
Hügel *m* hill.
Hülle *f* case, envelope, skin, cover, shell.
Hüllenbahn *f* panel *(Bln)*.
Hülse *f* hoop *(Mort)*; gas-cylinder plug *(MG)*; receiver *(pistol, R)*; socket *(G carriage)*; cartridge or shell case.
Hülsenauswurf *m* ejection of cartridge case.
Hülsenauszieher *m* extractor *(Ord)*.
Hülsenboden *m* base of cartridge case.
Hülsenbrücke *f* receiver cover *(R)*.
Hülsenfänger *m* deflector bag *(AA gun, MG)*.
Hülsenhals *m* neck of cartridge.
Hülsenkartusche *f* semifixed cartridge.
Hülsenkasten *m* deflector box *(AA gun, MG)*.
Hülsenkopf *m* front end of receiver *(R)*.
Hülsenmantel *m* cartridge-case jacket.
Hülsenrand *m* cartridge-case rim.
Hülsenreißer *m* stoppage caused by broken cartridge case.
Hülsenzapfen *m* recoil lug *(R)*.
Hummel *f* bumblebee *(nickname for Ger self-propelled medium field howitzer)*.
Hundeführer *m* dog handler, dog guard.
Hundeführerrotte *f* dog-handler party.
Hüpflinie *f* short hop, short leg of flight *(Avn)*.
Hurde *f* brush hurdle.
Hütchen *n* blasting cap; cup *(cartridge)*.
Hütte *f* hut, cottage; iron works; rolling mill.
Hüttenlager *n* cantonment.
Hydrozyansäure *f* hydrocyanic acid, prussic acid *(CWS)*.
Igel *m* hedgehog *(AT obstacle)*; all-around defense *(Tac)*.
Igelit *n* a type of electric wire insulation.
Igelstellung *f* "hedgehog" defense position, position of all-around defense.
Ilag *n* *See* **Interniertenlager.**
impfen inoculate, vaccinate.
Impfschein *m* vaccination certificate.
Impfung *f* inoculation, vaccination.
Imprägniermittel *n* impregnite.
Inaktive Offiziere inactive reserve.
Inaugenscheinnahme *f* inspection.
Inausgabegenehmigung *f* authorized permission to delete from stock record items issued.
Inbesitznahme *f* occupation *(Tac)*; act of taking possession.
Indienststellung *f* commissioning *(of a vessel)*.
Indizienbeweis *m* circumstantial evidence.
indizierte Leistung indicated horsepower.
Industrieanlagen *fpl* industrial installations.
Induktor *m* generator *(Tp)*.
Ineinklangbringen *n* harmonization.
Infanterie *f* infantry.
Infanteriebegleitgeschütz *n* infantry accompanying gun.
Infanteriefliegerstaffel *f* air support squadron. *See also* **Staffel.**
Infanterieflug *m* contact patrol *(Avn)*.
Infanteriegeschütz *n* infantry gun, infantry howitzer.
Infanteriegranate *f* shell fired by infantry gun or howitzer.
Infanteriekolonne *f* infantry supply column *(generally prefixed by* leichte).
Infanteriekommandeur *m* infantry commander *(supervises training of Inf units under Div Commander)*.
Infanterienachspitze *f* infantry rear point *(march column)*.
Infanteriepark *m* infantry equipment park.
Infanteriepionier *m* infantry pioneer.
Infanteriepionierzug *m* pioneer platoon *(Inf Regt)*.
Infanterie-Reiterzug *m* mounted rifle platoon *(Inf Regt)*.
Infanteriespitze *f* infantry point *(march column)*.
Infanteriesturmabzeichen *n* infantry assault badge *(decoration)*.
Infanterist *m* infantryman.
Infinitesimalrechnung *f* calculus *(Math)*.
Influenz *f* electrostatic induction.
Ingangsetzen *n* starting.
Ingenieur *m* engineer *(a Civ official with nominal Mil rank serving in technical capacity generally in MT, Ft Engr, or Avn)*.
Initialzünder *m* initiator *(Am)*.
Inklination *f* dip *(compass)*.
Innenauskreuzung *f* interior bracing *(Ap)*.
Innenbackenbremse *f* internal expanding brake.
Innendienst *m* interior duty, duty in barracks.
Innengrenzlehre *f* plug gage.
Innenhafen *m* inner harbor.
Innenhütchen *n* plug, inner cap *(blasting cap)*.
Innenraum *m* interior.
Innenschieber *m* inner sleeve *(sleeve-valve engine)*.
Innenverspannung *f* interior bracing *(Ap)*.
Innenwache *f* interior guard.
innerballistisch pertaining to interior ballistics.
Insel *f* island.
Inspektion *f* inspectorate *(any of the sections devoted to various arms and services in the* Allgemeines Heeresamt).
Inspekteur *m* inspector *(chief of an inspectorate in the* Allgemeines Heeresamt, *as* Waffeninspekteur *[Ord])*.
Inspizient *m* inspector.
Inspizierung *f* inspection.
Installateur *m* plumber; electrician.
Installationsplan *m* wiring diagram; pipe layout.
Instandhaltung *f* maintenance.
Instandsetzung *f* repair.
nach Bedarf durchgeführte Instandsetzung march maintenance, operating maintenance.
regelmäßig durchgeführte Instandsetzung scheduled maintenance.
Instandsetzungsabteilung *f* maintenance unit.
Instandsetzungsdienst *m* damage-clearance and repair service *(Civ defense)*.
Instandsetzungskraftwagen *m* maintenance truck, repair truck.
Instandsetzungsstaffel *f* maintenance echelon.
Instandsetzungswerkstätte *f* repair shop.
Instandsetzung und Unterhaltung repair and maintenance.
Instanz *f* authority, court *(Law)*.
Instellungbringen *n* emplacing *(Arty)*.
Instellunggehen *n* moving into position *(Tac)*.
Instrumentenbrett *n* instrument panel.
Instrumentfehler *m* instrumental error.
Intendant *m* civilian official in administrative services *(ranking as colonel)*.
Intendantur *f* general staff administrative section *(section IV of an army, corps, or Div general staff, dealing mostly with supply)*.
Intendanturassessor *m* civilian official in administrative services *(ranking as captain)*.
Intendanturinspektor *m* civilian official in administrative services *(ranking as 1st Lt)*.
Intendanturrat *m* civilian official in administrative services *(ranking as major)*.
internieren to intern.
Internierter *m* internee.
Interniertenlager *n* internment camp.
Invarol *n* a cold-resistant grease.
Invertentfernungsmesser *m* inverted-image range finder.
Irrung *f* correction *(Rad procedure)*.
Isolator *m* insulator *(Elec)*.
Isolierband *n* friction tape *(Elec)*.
Isolierbecher *m* insulating case *(circuit tester)*.
isolieren to insulate *(Elec)*; isolate *(Med)*.
Isoliergerät *n* oxygen breathing apparatus.
Isolierschutz *m* insulation *(Elec)*.
Isolierstoff *m* insulating material, insulator *(Elec)*.
Isolierstreifen *m* friction tape, insulating tape.
Isolierung *f* isolation, absolute quarantine.
Istbestand *m* equipment on hand.
Iststand *m* *See* **Iststärke.**
Iststärke *f* actual strength, morning-report strength.
Iststärkenachweisung *f* daily strength report.

In 3	Inspektion des Reit- und Fahrwesens	inspectorate of riding and driving training
In 4	Inspektion der Artillerie	inspectorate of the artillery
In 5	**Inspektion der Pioniere**	**inspectorate of combat engineers**
In 6	Waffenabteilung der Panzertruppe, Kavallerie und Heeresmotorisierung	section for the panzer troops, cavalry and army motorization
In 7	...n der Nachrichtentruppen	inspectorate of signal troops
In 8	Inspektion der Fahrtruppen	inspectorate of transport troops
In 9	Inspektion der Nebel- und Gasabwehrtruppen	inspectorate of chemical warfare troops
In 10	Inspektion der Eisenbahnpioniere	inspectorate of railroad engineers
inakt	inaktiv	inactive
ind	indem, indes, indessend	while; meanwhile; however
Ind	Index	index
Ind	Indiz	circumstantial (*evidence*)
Ind	Industrie	industry
Ind.A	Industrieanlage	industrial plant
Ind.B	Industriebahn	industrial railroad
Ind.B	Industriebetrieb	industrial organization; industrial operation
Indust.Mob	industrielle Mobilmachung	industrial mobilization
Inf	Infanterie	infantry
Inf	Information	information
Inf.Abt	Infanterieabteilung	infantry detachment
Inf.Batl	Infanteriebataillon	infantry battalion
Inf.Beob	Infanteriebeobachter; Infanteriebeobachtung	infantry observer; infantry observation
Inf.Br	Infanteriebrigade	infantry brigade
Inf.Btl	Infanteriebataillon	infantry battalion
Inf.Bttr	Infanteriebatterie	infantry howitzer battery
Inf.Div	Infanteriedivision	infantry division
InFest	Inspektion der Festungen	inspectorate of fortresses
Inf.F	Infanterieführer	infantry commander in division
Inf.Kol	Infanteriekolonne	infantry train; infantry column
Inf.Mun.Kol	Infanteriemunitionskolonne	infantry ammunition train; infantry ammunition column
Inf.Nsp	Infanterienachspitze	infantry rear point
Inf.N.Z	Infanterienachrichtenzug	infantry signal platoon
Inf.Regt	Infanterieregiment	infantry regiment
Inf.Sch	Infanterieschule	infantry school
Inf.Sp	Infanteriespitze	infantry point
Infü	Infanterieführer	infantry commander in division
Inf.Wff	Infanteriewaffen	infantry weapons
Ing	Ingenieur	engineer
Ing.O	Ingenieuroffizier	engineer officer
Ing.Offz.Anw	Ingenieuroffizieranwärter	engineer officer candidate
Ing. Tr	Ingenieurtruppen	engineer troops
Inh	Inhaber	possessor; holder; proprietor
Inh	Inhalt	content; capacity; substance
inhib	inhibieren	to hinder; to prevent
Inn	Inneres	inside; interior
innerh	innerhalb	within; on the inside
inoff	inoffiziell	unofficial
Ins	Insel	island
insbes	insbesondere	especially; in particular
Insp	Inspektor; Inspektion	inspecting officer; inspector; inspection; supervision
insp	inspizieren	to inspect; to supervise
Insp.d.Artl	Inspekteur der Artillerie	inspector of artillery
Insp.d.Fest	Inspekteur der Festungen	inspector of fortifications
Insp.d.Inf	Inspekteur der Infanterie	inspector of infantry
Insp.d.Inf.Sch	Inspektion (Inspekteur) der Infanterieschulen	infantry school inspectorate; inspector of infantry schools
Insp.d.Kav	Inspekteur der Kavallerie	inspector of cavalry
Insp.d.Kf.Tr	Inspekteur der Kraftfahrtruppen	inspector of motor transport troops
Insp.d.N	Inspekteur der Nachrichtentruppen	inspector of signal corps troops
Insp.d.OBef	Inspektion der Ostbefestigungen	inspectorate of the Eastern fortifications
Insp.d.Pion	Inspekteur der Pioniere	inspector of combat engineers
Insp.d.WBef	Inspektion der Westbefestigungen	inspectorate of the Western fortifications
InspKdr	Inspektionskommandeur	inspection commander (*state police*)
Insp.O	Inspektionsoffizier	inspecting officer
Inst	Institut	institute
Inst.96 n A	Instandsetzungsanleitung für das Feldartilleriegerät 1896 neuer Art	repair regulations for field field artillery equipment 1896, new type
Inst.98/09 (98)	Instandsetzungsanleitung für das Feldhaubitzgerät 1898/1909	repair regulations for field howitzer equipment 1898/1909
Instand	Instandsetzung	repair
Instr	Instruktion	instruction; order; command
Int	Intendant	intendant; administrative officer (*with higher staff*)
Int	Intendantur	general administrative and provisioning office (*branch of Quartermaster Department*)
Int	international	international
Intdt	Intendant	intendant; administrative officer (*with higher staff*)
Intend	Intendant	intendant; administrative officer (*with higher staff*)
Intend	Intendantur	general administrative and
intern	international	international
Intern	Internierung	internment
Intern.Lag	Internierungslager	internment camp
Interv	Intervention	intervention; mediation
Int.Insp	Intendanturinspektor	inspector in branch of the Quartermaster General's Department
Int.Verw	Intendanturverwaltung	administration of Quartermaster General's branch office
Inv	Invalide	[illegible]; soldier not fit for active service; disabled man
Inv	Invasion	invasion
Invas.A	Invasionsarmee	invading army
InvH	Invalidenhaus	hospital for disabled soldiers
InvR	Invalidenrente	veteran's pension
Inw	Inwohner	inhabitant
IO	Inspekteur Ost (SA)	Inspector, Eastern Section
i.P.L	in Panzerlafette	in an armored carriage; on an armored mount
i.R	im Ruhestand	retired
I.R	Infanterieregiment	infantry regiment
irg	irgend	any
i.R.L	in Radlafette	in wheeled gun carriage
I.R.(mot)	motorisiertes Infanterieregiment	motorized infantry regiment
Irr.A	Irrenanstalt	lunatic asylum (*on maps*)
irreg	irregulär	irregular (*soldier*)
IS	Infanterieschule	infantry school
i.S.L	in Schirmlafette	in carriage with overhead shield
ISO	Inspekteur Südost (SA)	Inspector, South Eastern Section (Storm Troops)
I.St	Iststärke	actual strength
Isth	Isthmus	isthmus
Istus	Internationale Studienkommission für motorlosen Flug	International Commission for the Study of Motorless Flying
Itnach	Inspektion der technischen Abteilung der Nachrichtentruppen	inspectorate of the technical section of the signal corps
i.u.F	im umgekehrten Falle	vice versa
i.V	in Vertretung	for; as the representative of;
i.V	in Vollmacht	acting for; by proxy
i.Verb	in Verbindung	in connection
i.Vorb	in Vorbereitung	in preparation
I.W	Innenwache	interior guard
IW	Inspekteur West (SA)	Inspector, Western Section (Storm Troops)
I.W.G	Inspektion für Waffen und Gerät	in... weapons and equipment
Iz	Innenzünder	internal fuze
I.Z.V	Infanteriezielbauvorschrift	regulations for infantry target construction (*range*)

J

J	Jäger	rifleman (*in a light division*);
j	jährig	annual
J	Jagdflugzeug	pursuit plane
J	Jahr	year
j	jüdisch	Jewish
Jabo	Jagdbomber	pursuit bomber
Jäg	Jäger	rifleman (*in a light division*); pursuit plane
Jäg.B	Jägerbataillon	rifle battalion in a light division
Jäg.K.K	Jägerkraftwagenkolonne	motor transport train in a light division
Jäg.R	Jägerregiment	infantry regiment
JägRzPf	Jägerregiment zu Pferde	infantry regiment in a light division (mounted)
Jagdh	Jagdhaus	hunting lodge (*on maps*)
Jagdkdo	Jagdkommando	raiding detachment
Jagdschl	Jagdschloss	hunting castle (*on maps*)
jed	jeder	each; every
jed	jedoch	however; yet
J.Eins	Jagdeinsitzer	single-seater pursuit plane
jem	jemals	ever; at any time
jem	jemand	someone; anyone
jen	jener	that; that person
jens	jenseitig; jenseits	opposite; beyond; on the other side
jew	jeweils	at times; for the time being
Jg.Hb	Jugendherberge	youth hostel (*on maps*)
Jgr	Jäger	rifleman (*in a light division*); pursuit plane
J. H	Jägerhaus	hunting lodge (*on maps*)
j.J	jeden Jahres	of (in) every year
JR	Jägerregiment	rifle regiment in a light infantry division
JR.zPf	Jägerregiment zu Pferde	rifle regiment in a light infantry division (mounted)
jüd	jüdisch	Jewish
jug	jugoslawisch	Jugoslavian
Jul	Juli	July
Jun	Juni	June

K

K	**Chef des Kraftfahrwesens (SA)**	chief of motor **transport (Storm Troops)**
K	**Feldküche**	**field kitchen**
K	Inspektor und Kontrolleur (Militarbekleid-	inspector and supervisor (military clothing service)
K	Kabel	cable
K	Kammer	room; clothing **depot**
K	Kanal	canal (*on maps*)
K	Kanone	cannon; gun
K	Kanonier	cannoneer
K	Karabiner	carbine
K	Kastenmagazin	box magazine (*rifle*)
K	Katapultdeckflugzeug	catapult deck plane
K	Katapultflugzeug	catapult plane
K	Kavallerie	cavalry
(K.)	Kirche	church (**visible from afar**) (*on maps*)
K	Kirchhof	cemetery (***on maps***)
K	Kolonne	column
K	Kommandant	commander; commandant
k	kommandiert	detached; detailed; commanded
K	Kompanie	company
K	Konstruktionsabteilung	construction **detachment**
K	Konsul; Konsulat	consul; consulate
K	Korps	corps
K	Kraftfahrer	driver; truck driver
K	Krankenhaus	infirmary; hospital
K	Krankenträger der Infanterie	stretcher **bearer of the infantry**
K	Kreis	district
K	Kugellager	ball bearing
K	Schirrmeister bei **Kraftfahrgerät**	supply sergeant, **motor transport** equipment
K.98b	Karabiner 98b	carbine 98b
K.98K	Karabiner 98 kurz	carbine 98 **with short** (600 mm) barrel
KA	**Kabelaufführungspunkt**	point where **overhead** line is **connected to underground cable**
Ka	Kardan	universal coupling (*automobile technical term*)
K.A	Kraftfahrabteilung	motor transport battalion
K.A	Küstenartillerie	coast artillery
K.A	**Luftkriegsakademie**	air force staff school; aerial warfare academy
K.A.B	**Kriegsgefangenenarbeiter-bataillon**	**war prisoners' labor battalion**
Kab.Tr	Kabeltrage	cable **carrier; reel**
Kad	Kader	cadre
Kad	Kadett	cadet
Kad. H	Kadettenhaus	military academy
KAI	Inspektion der Küstenartillerie und des Minenwesens	coast artillery **and mine** inspectorate
K.Ak	Kriegsakademie	war college
Kal	Kaliber	caliber
Kampfgr	Kampfgruppe	combat group
Kan	Kanal	canal
Kan	Kanone	cannon; gun
Kan	Kanonier	cannoneer
K.A.N	Kriegsausrüstungsnachweisung	war equipment **information**
Kand	Kandare	curb bit (***bridle***)
Kand	Kandidat	candidate
Kand.Z	Kandarenzügel	curb rein
Kant	Kantine	canteen; **post exchange**
Kap	Kapazität	capacity; **ability**
Kap	Kapelle	chapel
Kap	Kapitän	captain
Kapit	Kapitulation	capitulation
Kapl	Kaplan	chaplain
Kap.Sch	Kaperschiff	raiding ship; **sea raider**
Kapt	Kapitän	captain
Kar	Karabiner	carbine
Karab	Karabiner	carbine
Kart	Kartätsche	case shot; **canister shot**
Kart	Kartell	cartel
Kart	Kartograph	cartographer; **map draftsman**
Kart	**Kartusche**	**shell (*semifixed ammunition*); cartridge**
K.Art	Korpsartillerie	corps artillery
Kartogr	Kartograph	cartographer
K.Arzt	Korpsarzt	corps area surgeon
Kas	Kasematte	casemate
Kas	Kaserne	barracks
K.A.S	Küstenartillerieschule	coast artillery **school (*Wilhelmshaven*)**
Kasem	Kasematte	casement
Kast	Kasten	case
Kat	Katapult	catapult **plane**
Kath	Katholik	Catholic
Kathol	Katholik	Catholic
Kav	Kavallerie	cavalry
Kav.Br	Kavalleriebrigade	cavalry brigade
Kav.Div	Kavalleriedivision	cavalry division
Kav. Div.-Schwd.	Kavalleriedivisionsnachrichtenschwadron	cavalry division **communications** troop

Jabo *m See* **Jagdbomber.**
Jackenwiege *f* jacket cradle, ring cradle (*G*).
Jafü *m See* **Jagdführer.**
Jagdabwehr *f* fighter defense (*Avn*).
Jagdbomber *m* fighter bomber.
Jagdeinsitzer *m* single-seater fighter (*Avn*).
Jagdflieger *m* fighter pilot (*Avn*) (*same word used in plural to denote fighter aviation*).
Jagdflieger-Ergänzungsstaffel *f* fighter replacement squadron (*Avn*).
Jagdflug *m* fighter patrol, fighter sweep (*Avn*).
Jagdflugzeug *n* single-engine fighter airplane.
Jagdführer *m* commander of all fighter units of a *Luftflotte*.
Jagdgeschwader *n* fighter wing (*Avn*). *See also* **Geschwader.**
Jagdgruppe *f* fighter group (*Avn*). *See also* **Gruppe.**
Jagdmehrsitzer *m* multi-seater fighter airplane.
Jagdraum *m* patrol area for fighter aircraft.
Jagdschutz *m* fighter escort (*Avn*).
Jagdsperre *f* fighter screen (*Avn*).
Jagdstaffel *f* fighter squadron (*Avn*). *See also* **Staffel.**
Jagdverband *m* fighter formation (*Avn*).
Jagen *n* subarea of forest (*for mapping purposes*).
Jäger *m* rifleman (*in a light Mtz Inf Div*, Jägerdivision); private (*in mountain Inf*, Gebirgsjäger); fighter airplane, pursuit airplane.
Jägerbataillon *n* rifle battalion. *See* **Jägerdivision.**
Jägerdivision *f* light infantry division (*so-called "light division" somewhat similar to Ger Mtz Inf Div*).
Jägerplatz *m* fighter airdrome.
Jäger-Regiment *n* rifle regiment. *See* **Jägerdivision.**
Jägerschutz *m* fighter escort (*Avn*).
Jahrgang *m* age class; year (*of a publication, etc.*).
Joch *n* bent, trestle (*Bdg*); yoke.
Jochleiste *f* cheekbone (*horse*).
Jochpfahl *m* pile of pile bent (*Bdg*).
Jod *n* iodine.
Jodessigester *m* ethyliodoacetate (*CWS*).
Jodtinktur *f* tincture of iodine.
Jolle *f* yawl (*Nav*).
Jugendherberge *f* youth hostel.
justieren to adjust, to collimate (*bore-sight alinement, etc.*).
Justiergerät *n* bore sight.

K

Kabel *n* cable, wire (*Tp*).
Kabelader *f* strand, conductor (*of Tp wire*).
Kabelaufführungspunkt *m* wire lead-in point (*Tp*).
Kabelgraben *m* wire trench (*Tp*).
Kabelleitung *f* wire line (*Tp*).
Kabelmantel *m* cable sheath (*Elec, Tp*).
Kabelmeßgerät *n* wire-testing instrument (*Tp*).
Kabelmesser *n* electrician's knife.
Kabelschuh *m* loop-tip terminal (*Elec*).
Kabelseele *f* core conductor (*Tp wire*).
Kabelstecker *m* wire plug (*Elec*).
Kabeltau *n* hawser.
Kabeltrommel *f* reel (*Tp*).
Kabelverbinder *n* connecting sleeve (*Tp wire*).
Kabelverbindung *f* wire splice (*Tp*).
Kabelwachs *n* cable wax, adhesive pitch (*Tp*).
Kabine *f* compartment, cockpit (*Ap*).
Kader *m* cadre.
Kadett *m* cadet.
Kaffe *f* compartment, sponson (*Pon*).
Kahn *m* boat.
Kahnfähre *f* punt ferry, boat ferry.
Kai *m* quay.
Kajüte *f* cabin (*Nav*).
Kaliber *n* caliber.
Kalibereinheit *f* unit load of single-caliber ammunition (*approximately 18-ton unit for one RR car*).
Kaliberlänge *f* barrel length expressed in calibers.
Kaliberring *m* bore gage, breech bore gage.
Kaliberzylinder *m See* **Kaliberring.**
Kalipatrone *f* potassium cartridge (*oxygen breathing apparatus*).
Kaliumpermanganat *n* potassium permanganate.
Kalk *m* lime.
Kalkmilch *f* lime solution (*CWS*).
kältebeständig cold-resistant.
kaltgereckt cold-worked.
Kaltklebekitt *m* cold adhesive putty (*for attaching demolition charges*) (*abbr.* Kat).
Kaltluftfront *f* cold front (*Met*).
Kaltmeißel *m* cold chisel.
Kaltrecken *n* cold-working process, autofrettage (*Ord*).
Kameradschaftsheim *n* service club, canteen.
Kamm *m* crest, ridge; comb.
Kammer *f* bolt (*R, pistol*); camera; chamber; stockroom.
Kammerbahn *f* bolt slide (*R*).
Kammerfang *m* bolt catch (*MG*).
Kammerfangstück *n* bolt-catch piece (*pistol*).
Kammergriff *m* bolt handle (*MG*).
Kammerhülse *f* central tube, flash tube (*shrapnel*).
Kammerhülsenladung *f* flash-tube charge (*shrapnel*).
Kammerhülsenrohr *n* burster tube (*Am*).
Kammerknopf *m* bolt knob (*R*).
Kammerstengel *m* bolt handle (*R*).
Kammerunteroffizier *m* supply sergeant.
Kammerwarze *f* bolt lug (*R*).
Kammkissen *n* back pad (*harness*).
Kammkissengurt *m* back-pad strap (*harness*).
Kammlinie *f* ridge line (*Top*).
Kampf *m* battle, combat, fight. *See also terms under* **Gefecht, Krieg.**
Kampfabschnitt *m* combat sector.
Kampfabteil *m* fighting compartment, turret basket (*Tk*).
Kampfaufgabe *f* combat task (*Tac*).
Kampfauftrag *m* combat mission.
Kampfeinheit *f* combat unit, tactical unit.
kämpfen to fight.
kämpfende Truppe combat element.
Kämpfer *m* fighter; abutment (*of an arch*).
kampferprobt seasoned, battle-tried, having combat experience.
Kampffahrzeug *n* combat vehicle.
Kampffeld *n* field of combat.
Kampfflieger *m* bomber pilot; any member of a combat crew (*same word used in plural to denote bombardment aviation*).
Kampffliegerei *f* bombardment aviation.
Kampffliegergruppe *f* bombardment group (*Avn*). *See also* **Gruppe.**
Kampffliegerstaffel *f* bombardment squadron (*Avn*). *See also* **Staffel.**
Kampffliegerverband *m* bombardment formation (*Avn*).
Kampfflugzeug *n* bombardment airplane.
Kampfführung *f* battle command, conduct of battle.
Kampfgas *n* war gas (*CWS*).
Kampfgebiet *n* combat zone, forward area, combat area.
Kampfgelände *n* battle terrain.
Kampfgemeinschaft *f* combat team.
Kampfgeschwader *n* bombardment wing (*Avn*). *See also* **Geschwader.**
Kampfgeschwader z.b.V. special purpose transport wing (*airborne operations*).
Kampfgruppe *f* bombardment group (*Avn*); combat command (*Armd Comd*); combat team, task force.
Kampfhandlung *f* engagement, action.
Kampfkraft *f* fighting power.
Kampflage *f* tactical situation.
Kampfleistung *f* battle performance, combat performance.
Kampflinie *f* line of battle.
Kampfmehrsitzer *m* multiseater bomber.
Kampfmittel *npl* means of combat, arms and ammunition.
Kampfnachricht *f* combat message (*Rad*).
Kampfpistole *f* rifled Very pistol (*for Sig and/or incendiary cartridges*).
Kampfraum *m* combat zone, forward area, combat area.
Kampfruf *m* password, slogan, battle cry.
Kampfschule *f* bombardment school (*Avn*).
Kampfstaffel *f* combat echelon (*Tac*); bombardment squadron (*Avn*). *See also* **Staffel.**
Kampfstellung *f* battle position.
Kampfstoff *m* chemical warfare agent.
Kampfstoffbelegung *f* gas coverage.
Kampstoffbeschuß *m* chemical-shell fire.
Kampfstoffbombe *f* chemical bomb.
Kampfstoffgehalt *m* gas concentration (*CWS*).
Kampfstoffgruppen *fpl* classification of chemical warfare agents.
Kampfstoffriegel *m* chemical obstacle; chemical-shell box barrage.
Kampfstoffschwaden *mpl* chemical fumes (*CWS*).
Kampfstoffsperre *f* chemical obstacle, contaminated area (*CWS*).
Kampfstoffverwendung *f* employment of chemical warfare agents.
Kampfstoffzerstäuber *m* chemical-spray apparatus.
Kampftätigkeit *f* combat activity, active combat, action.
Kampftruppe *f* combat element.
Kampfverband *m* bomber formation (*Avn*); combined arms unit, combat team.
Kampfwagen *m* tank, combat car.
Kampfwagenfalle *f* tank trap.
Kampfwagengeschütz *n See* **Kampfwagenkanone.**
Kampfwagenkanone *f* tank gun.
Kampfwagennachbildung *f* tank silhouette, dummy tank.
Kampfwagenscheibe *f* tank-silhouette target.
Kampfwagenwerk *n* tank factory.
Kampfwert *m* fighting qualities (*of a unit*).
Kampfwunde *f* battle injury, wound.
Kampfziel *n* objective (*Tac*).
Kampfzone *f* battle zone.
Kampfzweck *m* tactical purpose, intention.
Kandare *f* curb bit (*harness*).
Kandarenzügel *m* curb rein (*harness*).
Kanone *f* gun, cannon.
Kanonenboot *n* gunboat.
Kanonenflugzeug *n* cannon-armed airplane.
Kanonenjagdflieger *m* cannon-armed fighter airplane.
Kanonenrohr *n* gun barrel.
Kanonensalut *m* gun salute.
Kanonenschlag *m* firecracker (*simulated fire*).
Kanonenschlag mit Knallerscheinung firecracker.
Kanonenschlag mit Raucherscheinung smoke-puff charge.
Kanonenschuß *m* gun shot.
Kanonenwagen *m* assault gun car.
Kanonier *m* private (*Arty*); cannoneer.
Kante *f* edge; ridge.
Kantholz *n* squared timber.
Kantine *f* canteen.
Kanzel *f* cockpit, turret (*Ap*); pillbox (*Ft*).
vordere Kanzel nose turret (*Ap*).
Kap *n* cape (*point of land*).
Kapelle *f* band (*music*); chapel.
Kaperfahrt *f* naval raid against enemy merchant shipping.
kapern to capture (*a ship*).
Kapitänleutnant *m* lieutenant (*Nav*).
Kapitän zur See captain (*Nav*).
Kapitulant *m* reenlisted man.
Kapitulantenhandgeld *n* reenlistment bonus.
Kapitulation *f* capitulation, surrender; reenlistment.
kapitulieren capitulate, surrender; reenlist.
Kappagerät *n* predictor (*AA*).
Kappe *f* cap (*of a projectile*).
Kapsel *f* detonator, blasting cap; capsule.
Kapuze *f* hood.
Karabiner *m* carbine.
Karabinertragevorrichtung *f* carbine scabbard carrier.
Karbolsäure *f* carbolic acid, phenol.
Kardangelenk *n* universal joint.
kardanische Aufhängung compass gimbal.
Kardanwelle *f* flexible drive shaft, propeller shaft.
Karosserie *f* body (*MT*).
Kartätsche *f* canister (*separate-loading Am*).
Karte *f* map, chart; card, ticket.
Kartei *f* card file.
Karteikarte *f* filing card.
Kartenausschnitt *m* map section.
Kartenbatterie *f* topographic section, mapping section.
Kartenblatt *n* map sheet, zone map.
Kartenblatt mit Gitter grid sheet.
Kartenblattnummer *f* geographic index number.
Kartenbrett *n* map-mounting board, military sketching board.
Kartendruckerei *f* map-printing office or plant.
Kartenebene *f* horizontal plane through base of trajectory.
Kartenentfernung *f* horizontal range, map range.
Kartenentfernung zum Abschußpunkt horizontal range to present position (*instant of firing*) (*AAA*).
Kartenentfernung zum Meßpunkt horizontal range to present position (*instant of range determination*) (*AAA*).
Kartenentfernung zum Treffpunkt horizontal range to future position (*AAA*).
Kartenentfernung zum Wechselpunkt horizontal range to midpoint, minimum horizontal range (*AAA*).
Kartenentwurf *m* map projection.
Kartengitternetz *n* map grid.
Kartenkurs *m* map course (*Navigation*).
Kartenlesen *n* map reading.
Kartenmaßstab *m* map scale.
Kartenprojektion *f* map projection.
Kartenraum *m* chartroom (*Nav*).
Kartensignatur *f* conventional sign (*on maps*).

Kav.Gesch	Kavalleriegeschütz	cavalry howitzer
Kav.Gesch.Z	Kavalleriegeschützzug	cavalry howitzer platoon
Kav.K	Kavalleriekorps	cavalry corps
Kav.Man	Kavalleriemanöver	cavalry maneuvers
Kav.MG.Zg	Kavalleriemaschinengewehrzug	cavalry machine-gun platoon
Kav.N.Z	Kavallerienachrichtenzug	cavalry signal platoon
Kav.Pi-Esk	Kavalleriepioniereskadron	cavalry combat troop
Kav.Pi-Schwd	Kavalleriepionierschwadron	cavalry combat engineer troop
Kav.Rgt	Kavallerieregiment	cavalry regiment
Kav.San.Wg	Kavalleriesanitätswagen	cavalry ambulance
Kav.Sch	Kavallerieschule	cavalry school
Kav.Schts	Kavallerieschützen	cavalry riflemen
Kav.Sp	Kavalleriespitze	cavalry point (*tactics*);
Kav.Tel	Kavallerietelegraf	cavalry telegraph
K.B	Kavalleriebrigade	cavalry brigade
k.b	kommandiert bei	commanded by; detailed by
Kb	Kriegsbeschädigter	disabled soldier
KBeförd Best	Kriegsbeförderungsbestimmungen	act governing wartime promotions
K.Besold.V	Kriegsbesoldungsvorschrift	wartime pay regulations
K-Blink	kleines Blinkgerät	small blinker signal equipment
kbm	Kubikmeter	cubic meter
KBr	Kavalleriebrigade	cavalry brigade
Kch.V	Vorschrift für die Verwaltung der Truppenküchen	regulations for the administration of troop kitchens
KD	Katapultdeckflugzeug	catapult deck plane
KD	Kavalleriedivision	cavalry division
kdb	kriegsdienstbeschädigt	injured in line of war duty
K.D.B	Kriegsdienstbeschädigter	war invalid; soldier injured in war
K.D.B	Kriegsdienstbeschädigung	war service injury; war serv-
K'deur	Kommandeur	commander; commanding
K.d.F	Kraft durch Freude	Strength through Joy (*German welfare organization*)
K.Div	Kavalleriedivision	cavalry division
K.d.K	Kommandeur der Kraftfahrtruppen	commander of motor-transport troops
K.d.O	Kommandeur der Ordnungspolizei	Commander of Regular Police
Kdo	Kommando	command; headquarters staff
Kdo.Beo	Kommando der Beobachterschulen	observation schools command
Kdo.d.Ps.Tr	Kommando der Panzertruppen	armored troops command
Kdo.Fea	Kommando der Fliegerersatzabteilungen	air-force replacement unit command
Kdo.Ger	Kommandogerät	stereoscopic fire director; station control
Kdo.Gewalt	Kommandogewalt	military authority
Kdo.HGer	Kommandohilfsgerät	auxiliary stereoscopic fire director (*antiaircraft*)
Kdo.L.Sch	Kommando der Luftschiffenschule	airship school command
Kdo.Milgas	Kommando der Militärgasanstalten	military gas works command
Kdos	Kommandosache	matter pertaining to command (*military correspondences*)
Kdo St	Kommandostand	command post; bridge (*navy*)
Kdr	Kommandeur	commander
Kdr.d.Fl	Kommandeur der Flieger	commanding officer of air force with corps headquarters
K.d.Schupo	Kommandeur der Schutzpolizei	commander of the municipal police
K.d.Sipo u.d.SD	Kommandeur der Sicherheitspolizei und des Sicherheitsdienstes	Chief of the Security Police and Security Service (*of the SS*)
Kdt	Kommandant	commander; commandant
kdt	kommandiert	command; detailed
Kdt.H.Q	Kommandant des Haupquartiers	headquarters commandant
Kdtr	Kommandantur	administrative headquarters; commandant's office
Kdt.St.Qu	Kommandant des Stabsquartiers	commandant of staff headquarters
kdt.z	kommandiert zu, zur	ordered to (the); detailed to; detached to
K.E	Kalibereinheit	unit of caliber
Ke	Kette	chain; flight (*aviation*); series
Kea	Kraftfahr-Ersatzabteilung	replacement center for motor-transport forces
K.E.B	Kriegseisenbahnbau	wartime railroad construction
Kek	Kampfeinsitzerkommando	command of single-seater fighter planes
K.E.O	Kriegsetappenordnung	war regulations for the zone of communications
kf	kaltefest	cold resisting
K.F	Kahnfähre	boat ferry; ferry by rowing boat (*on maps*)
K.F	Kompanieführer	company commander
Kf	Kraftfahrabteilung	motor transport battalion
KF	Kraftfahrer	driver
Kf	Kraftfahrtruppen	motor transport troops
K.F.A	Korpsfernsprechabteilung	corps signal detachment (*telephone*)
K.F.A	Kriegsfeuerwerkerei für Artillerie	war ordnance section for artillery
K.f.d.K	Kampfbund für deutsche Kultur	militant association for German culture
Kf.K.Tr	Kraftfahrkampftruppe	mechanized combat force
K.Flak	Flugabwehrkanone auf Kraftwagen	antiaircraft gun mounted on truck
Kf.Lehrst	Kraftfahrlehrstab	motor-transport training staff
K.Flzg	Kanonenflugzeug	cannon-equipped airplane
Kfrw	Kriegsfreiwilliger	wartime volunteer; war vol-
kftechn	kraftfahrtechnischer	motor technical
k.Fuk Station	kleine Funkstation	small radio station
K.F.V	Kraftfahrzeugvorschrift	motor vehicle regulations
KFVO	Kraftfahrzeugverkehrsordnung	motor vehicle traffic regulation
Kfw	Kampfwagen	tank
Kfw	Kriegsfreiwilliger	wartime volunteer; war volunteer
Kfz	Kraftfahrzeug	motor vehicle
Kfzen	Kraftfahrzeugen	motor vehicles
K.G	Kavalleriegeschütz	cavalry howitzer
K.g	Kenntnis genommen	notice taken
kg	Kilogramm	kilogram
K.-Gerät	Kraftfahrgerät	motor transport equipment
Kgf	Kriegsgefangene	prisoners of war
K.G.I	Kraftfahrgerätsinspizient	motor transport equipment inspector
Kgr	Kiesgrube	gravel pit (*on maps*)
Kgtb	Kriegstagebuch	war diary; station and record of events book
Kh	Krankenhaus	hospital
Kh	Kriegshinterbliebene	war widows and other dependents
Khf	Kirchhof	cemetery (*on maps*)
K.H.Qu	Korpshauptquartier	corps headquarters
Ki	Kimme	notch; sight notch; notch of
Ki	Kirche	church (*on maps*)
K.I	Korpsintendant	corps staff administrative officer
K.I	Korpsintendantur	Quartermaster General's Department Corps Office
K.Intdt	Korpsintendant	corps staff administrative officer
K.Intdt	Korpsintendantur	Quartermaster General's Department Corps Office
K.i.R.L	Kanone in Radlafette	cannon on wheeled carriage
K.K	Kavalleriekorps	cavalry corps
K.K	Kompasskurs	compass course
K.K	Kontrollkommission	control commission
KKS	Kleinkaliberschützen	riflemen (*small caliber arms*)
K.K.Schiessen	Kleinkaliberschiessen	small bore target practice
Kkw	Krankenkraftwagen	motor ambulance
kl	Kiloliter	kiloliter
kl	klein	small
Kl	Kloster	monastery; cloister; convent
K.Laf	Kastenlafette	box trail
Klbhf	Kleinbahnhof	small railroad station
kleinkal	kleinkalibrig	of small caliber
kl.Fk	kleine Feldküche	light field kitchen
Kl.Fu.u.E.Wa	kleiner Funk- und Empfangswagen	light radio transmitting and receiving wagon
Klg	Kugellager	ball bearing
Kl.Kpfw	Kleinkampfwagen	light tank
Kl.Krg	Kleinkrieg	guerrilla warfare
Klkw	Kleinkraftwagen	light motor car
kl.Kw.Kol	kleine Kraftwagenkolonne	light motor transport column
kl.Ldg	kleine Ladung	reduced charge; small load
Klop	Chlorpikrin	chloropicrin (*gas*)
Klost	Kloster	cloister; convent; monastery
Klp	Klippe	cliff; reef; crag (*on maps*)
kl.Spl.Bo	kleine Splitterbombe	small splinter bomb; small fragmentation bomb
K.Ltg	Kabelleitung	cable line
kl.Zdg	kleine Zündung	small primer
KM	Kastenmagazin	box magazine (*rifle*)
km	Kilometer	kilometer
K.M	Kriegsmagazin	war magazine; war depot
km^2	Quadratkilometer	square kilometer
Kmdo	Kommando	command; headquarters staff
Kmdr	Kommandeur	commander
Kmdt	Kommandant	commander; commandant
kmdt	kommandiert	commanded; detailed
Kmdtr	Kommandantur	local headquarters
kmdt.z	kommandiert zu, zur	ordered to (the); detailed to; detached to
KMGB	katholisches Militär-Gebet- und Gesangbuch	Catholic military prayer and song book
km/std	Kilometer in der Stunde	kilometers per hour
Kn.P	Knotenpunkt	junction
Kn/Std	Knoten in der Stunde	knots per hour
K.O	Kalkofen	lime kiln (*on maps*)
Ko	Kompass	compass
Ko	Korn	front sight; bead (*gunnery*)
Kof	Kompanieführer	company commander
Kohl.Grb	Kohlengrube	coal mine
Kok	Kokarde	cockade (*a circular metal badge worn on cap*)
Kokampf	Kommandeur der Kampfwagenabteilungen beim Gruppenkommando	commander of the combat car units of the army group command
kol	kolonial	colonial
Kol	Kolonie	colony (*on maps*)
Kol	Kolonne	column

Kol.A	Kolonialarmee	colonial army
KoLa	Konzentrationslager	concentration camp
Kol.Br	Kolonnenbrücke	bridge for all arms
Kolb.Verschl.	Kolbenverschluss	bolt section; cylinder breech
Kol.Rgt	Kolonialregiment	colonial regiment
Koluft	Kommandeur der Luftwaffe	air force commander (*attached to large unit*)
Kol.W	Kolonnenweg	road passable for columns; unimproved country road
Kom	Kommandant	commander; commandant
Kom	Kommissar	commissioner; inspector
Kom	Kraftomnibus	motor bus
Komb	Kombattant	combatant
Komb	Kombination - Arbeitsschutzanzug der Luftwaffe und Kraftfahrtruppen	combination fatigue uniform of the aircorps and the motor transport troops
komb.Kol	kombinierte Kolonne	combined column
Kom.Br	Kommisbrot	army bread
Komdo	Kommando	command
Komdr	Kommandeur	commander; commandant
Komdt	Kommandant	commander; commandant
Komdtr	Kommandantur	local headquarters; commandant's office
kom.Gen	kommandierender General	commanding general of a corps
Komm	Kommissar	commissioner; inspector
Komp	Kompanie	company
Komp	Kompass	compass
Komp.F	Kompanieführer	company commander
Konf	Konfiskation	seizure; confiscation; expropriation
Kons	Konsul; Konsulat	consul; consulate
Konstr	Konstruktion-	construction; type of construction; structure
Kont	Kontingent	contingent
Konting	Kontingent	contingent
Kontr	Kontrolle	control; supervision
Konv	Konvoi	convoy (*naval*)
Konz	Konzentration	concentration
Konz	Konzession	concession; permission; admission
Konz.Lg	Konzentrationslager	concentration camp
Korps-St.Qu	Korpsstabsquartier	Corps staff headquarters
Korück	Kommandant des rückwärtigen Armeegebiets	Commandant of Army Rear Area
Kp	Kapelle	chapel (*on maps*)
Kp	Kolbenpumpe	piston pump
Kp	Kompanie	company
K.P	Panzerkabel	armored cable
Kp.Fhr	Kompanieführer	company commander
Kpf.Tr	Kampftruppe	combat troops
Kpfw	Kampfwagen	tank
Kpfw.Abw	Kampfwagenabwehr-	antitank
Kpfw.Abw.Ge	Kampfwagenabwehrgeschütz	antitank gun
Kpfw.Abw.Kp.	Kampfwagenabwehrkompanie	antitank company
Kpfw.Abw.Z	Kampfwagenabwehrzug	antitank platoon
Kpfw.Begl.Art.	Kampfwagenbegleitartillerie	artillery accompanying tanks
Kpfw.Falle	Kampfwagenfalle	tank trap
Kpfw.Handw.K	Kampfwagenhandwerkerkompanie	tank maintenance company
Kpfw.Kp	Kampfwagenkompanie	tank company
Kpfw.Kr	Kampfwagenkrieg	tank warfare
Kpfw.Nachb	Kampfwagennachbildung	dummy tank
Kpfw.sich.Gel	kampfwagensicheres Gelände	tank-proof zone
Kpfw.Verb	Kampfwagenverband	tank formation; tank unit
Kpfw.Zg	Kampfwagenzug	tank platoon
Kp.-Grs	Kompanieabschnittsgrenze	company sector boundary
Kpl	Kapelle	chapel (*on maps*)
Kp.(mot.gl.)	Kompanie auf geländegängigen Kraftfahrzeugen motorisiert	company motorized on cross-country vehicles
Kp.PW	Kompaniepackwagen	company baggage wagon
Kps	Korps	corps
KPS	Kupferpanzerstahl	copper-steel alloy for armoring
Kpt	Kapitän	captain
Kp.Tr	Kompanietrupp	company headquarters detachment
K.Q	Kasernenquartier	barracks quarters
Kr	Kammer	room; clothing depot
K.R	Kavallerieregiment	cavalry regiment
K.R	Kopframpe	end ramp
Kr	Kraftwagen	motor car
kr	krank	ill; sick
Kr	Kreis	district
Kr	Kreig	war
K.R	Kriegsrecht	martial law
Kr	Krug	inn (*on maps*)
Kr	Krupp	Krupp (*manufacturing company*)
Kr.A	Kraftfahrabteilung	motor transport detachment or battalion

Karten- und Vermessungstruppen *fpl* topographic troops.
Kartenunterlage *f* plane table.
Kartenvervollständigung *f* map compilation.
Kartenwinkelmesser *m* map protractor.
Kartenzeichen *n* conventional sign (*on maps*).
Kartenzeichner *m* cartographer.
kartieren to map.
Karton *m* cardboard.
Kartothek *f* card file.
Kartuschbeutel *m* cartridge bag, powder bag (*Am*).
Kartusche *f* cartridge; cartridge case; powder bag; any container of the propelling charge (*generally for separate-loading Am*); cartridge pouch (*Cav*).
Kartuschenwagen *m* ammunition vehicle for cartridge cases.
Kartuschhülse *f* cartridge case.
Kartuschmunition *f* separate-loading ammunition.
Kartuschraum *m* chamber (*G*).
Kartuschvorlage *f* flash-reducing wad (*Am*).
Kaseinleim *m* casein glue.
Kasematte *f* casemate.
Kasemattenlafette *f* casemate gun mount.
Kaserne *f* permanent barracks.
Kasernenarrest *m* restriction to barracks.
Kasernenhof *m* barracks yard.
kaserniert quartered in barracks.
kasernierungspflichtig obliged to live in barracks.
Kasino *n* officers' mess, officers' club.
Kasino-Ordonnanz *f* dining room orderly.
Kasinovorstand *m* mess council.
Kassenabteilung *f* finance department.
Kassenordnung *f* finance regulations.
Kassenverwaltung *f* finance administration.
Kassenwesen *n* finance.
Kasten *m* receiver (*MG*); magazine (*R*); tank, airplane (*slang*); box, case.
Kastenboden *m* receiver floor plate (*MG*); magazine floor plate (*R*).
Kastendeckel *m* receiver top (*MG*).
Kastenlafette *f* box-trail gun carriage.
Kastenleitwerk *n* box tail unit (*Ap*).
Kastenmagazin *n* box magazine.
Kastenschlüssel *m* transposition cipher (*Sig C*).
Kastenträger *m* box girder.
Kastenwand *f* side of receiver (*MG*).
Kat *m* *See* **Kaltklebekitt.**
Katapultflugzeug *n* catapult airplane.
Kathodenstrahlröhre *f* cathode-ray tube.
Kausche *f* grommet; thimble (*rigging, etc.*).
kaustisches Natron lye, caustic soda, sodium hydroxide.
Kautschuk *m* rubber.
Kavalierstart *m* climbing take-off (*Avn*).
Kavallerie *f* cavalry.
Kavallerist *m* cavalryman.
K.-Blink *n* portable signal lamp.
K-Brückengerät *n* portable bridge unit.
Kegel *m* cone; conical peak (*Top*).
Kegelfeder *f* volute spring.
Kegelkupplung *f* cone clutch (*MT*).
Kegelprojektion *f* conic projection.
Kegelrad *n* bevel gear.
Kegelrollenlager *n* conical roller bearing.
Kegelzahnrad *n* bevel gear.
Kehlriemen *m* throatlatch (*harness*).
Kehlkopfmikrophon *n* throat-type microphone (*Avn*).
Kehrbildentfernungsmesser *m* inverted-image range finder.
Kehrichtofen *m* incinerator.
Kehrkurve *f* turn (*Avn*).
kehrtmachen to face about.
Kehrtwendung *f* turn (*Avn*); about face (*drill*).
Kehrtwendung links left-about (*drill*).
Kehrwert *m* inverse value, reciprocal value.
Keil *m* breech wedge (*G*); wedge formation (*Tac*); wedge; key; cotter pin.
Keilloch *n* breech recess (*G*).
Keillochfläche *f* breech-recess surface (*G*).
Keilnut *f* keyway.
Keilriemen *m* V-type belt (*Tech*).
Keil und Kessel breakthrough and encirclement.
Keilverschluß *m* wedge-type breechblock.
Keilwelle *f* spline shaft (*MT*).
Keim *m* germ.
Keks *m-n* biscuit.
Kelle *f* signaling disk; marking disk; trowel.
Kellerwart *m* shelter warden (*Civ defense*).
Kennbuchstabe *m* identification letter.
Kennfaden *m* tracer thread (*Tp wire*).

Kennkarte *f* civilian identity card.
Kennlicht *n* identification light, navigation light (*Ap*).
Kennscheinwerfer *m* identification light (*Ap*).
Kenntlichmachen *n* marking, identification.
Kennummer *f* identification number.
Kennung *f* identification signal, marker beacon signal (*Avn*).
Kennwort *n* password.
Kennzeichen *n* identification mark.
Kern *m* core.
Kerngarbe *f* effective part of cone (*Ballistics*).
Kerngeschoß *n* armor-piercing bullet.
Kernladung *f* base section (*separate-loading Am*).
Kernrohr *n* liner (*G*).
Kernschußweite *f* point-blank range.
Kerntruppen *fpl* crack troops, picked troops, elite troops.
Kerze *f* candle; spark plug.
Kessel *m* pocket, encircled area (*Tac*); deep hollow (*Top*); meat can (*mess kit*); boiler; kettle.
Kesselhaus *n* boiler house.
Kesselschlacht *f* battle of encirclement.
Kesselwagen *m* tank truck (*MT*).
Kette *f* chain; track (*Tk*); flight (*3 airplanes*).
Kettenabdeckung *f* track shield (*Tk*).
Kettenbolzen *m* track pin (*Tk track*).
Kettenfahrzeug *n* track-laying vehicle (*MT*).
Kettenführer *m* flight commander (*Avn*).
Kettenglied *n* track shoe, track block (*Tk*); chain link.
Kettenhund *m* rear outside airplane in a formation, "tail-end Charlie," "wing man."
Kettenkeil *m* flight wedge (*Avn*). *See* **Kette.**
Kettenkrad *n* half-track motorcycle.
Kettenkraftrad *n* *See* **Kettenkrad.**
Kettenkurbel *f* connector (*MG*).
Kettenlaufräder *npl* bogie wheels (*Tk*).
Kettenreihe *f* flight of airplanes echeloned left or right. *See also* **Kette.**
Kettenspanner *m* track-connecting fixture, track-connecting tool (*for Tk track*).
Kettentriebrad *n* driving sprocket (*Tk*).
Kettenwinde *f* chain winch.
K.-Gerät *n* *See* **Kraftfahrgerät.**
Kiel *m* keel.
Kielflosse *f* keel fin (*of flying-boat hull or seaplane float*).
Kielwasser *n* wake (*of a ship*).
Kiesgrube *f* gravel pit.
Kiesstraße *f* gravel road.
Kilohertz *n* kilocycles per second (*Ger unit of frequency*).
Kilometerzähler *m* mileage indicator, odometer (*MT*).
Kimme *f* sight notch (*MG, R, etc.*).
Kimmtiefe *f* dip (*Avn*).
Kinderzulage *f* dependency allowance for children.
Kinnkette *f* curb chain (*harness*).
Kinnkettengrube *f* chin groove.
Kinnriemen *m* chin strap (*helmet*).
Kinnstößel *m* chin strap (*harness*).
Kinnstütze *f* chin support (*gas mask*).
Kinotheodolit *m* recording theodolite (*practice firing*).
kippen to tip, tilt.
Kippfrequenz *f* sweep frequency (*Rad*).
Kippgerät *n* sweep generator (*Rad*).
Kipphebel *m* rocker arm (*Mtr*).
Kipplore *f* dump car (*field RR*).
Kippneigung *f* tipping gradient (*MT*).
Kippregel *f* alidade (*Surv*).
Kippschalter *m* toggle switch (*Elec*).
Kippschnecke *f* elevating worm (*aiming circle, BC telescope*).
Kippschwingung *f* sawtooth oscillation, relaxation oscillation (*Rad*).
Kippvorrichtung *f* dumping mechanism (*dump truck*).
Kippwagen *m* dump truck.
Kirche *f* church.
Kissen *n* cushion; pad (*Clo, harness, etc.*); gas-check pad (*G*); pillow.
Kiste *f* case, crate, chest, box; airplane (*slang*).
Kitt *m* putty.
Klage *f* complaint.
Klammer *f* butt swivel (*R*); clip, paper clip; clamp, clasp; parenthesis.
Klammerfuß *m* butt-swivel plate (*R*).
Klapparm *m* extension arm (*AA sight*).
Klappblende *f* drop cover (*Ft*).
Klappbrücke *f* drawbridge, bascule bridge.
Klappe *f* drop (*Tp switchboard*); tailboard (*Trk*); flap (*Ap*); landing ramp (*on landing craft*).
Klappenschrank *m* portable switchboard.
Klappflügel *m* folding wing (*Ap*).
Klapphacke *f* pick mattock.

Klapplafette *f* extendable mount (*Ap MG*).
Klappmesser *n* jackknife.
Klappscheibe *f* bobbing target (*practice firing*).
Klappsporn *m* folding trail spade.
Klappvisier *n* leaf sight.
Klarinol *n* a cleaning fluid for optical glass.
Klarscheibe *f* antidim eyeglass.
Klarsichtsalbe *f* antidim compound.
Klartext *m* text in clear (*Sig C*).
Klartextfunken *n* transmitting in clear (*Rad*).
Klaue *f* dog (*clutch*); epi, curved spur track (*RR gun*); claw.
Klauenbeil *n* claw hatchet.
Klauenfutter *n* guide lining (*G*).
Klauenkupplung *f* dog clutch (*MT*).
Klauenring *m* guide ring (*G*).
Klebeflugzeug *n* intruding airplane, intruder (*one which trails an enemy plane back to its home base*).
Klebelack *m* dope (*Ap*).
kleben to adhere, to stick to; to follow closely, to trail.
Klebestreifen *m* adhesive tape.
Klebezettel *m* paster, sticker (*sticker-type baggage tag, etc.*).
Kleiderkarte *f* ration card for clothing.
Kleif *m* portable flame thrower (*abbr. of* kleiner Flammenwerfer).
Kleinbahn *f* substandard-gage railway.
Kleiner Bär Little Dipper.
Kleiner Krieg guerrilla warfare, partisan warfare.
Kleinfunkkraftwagen *m* small radio truck.
Kleinfunktrupp *m* portable-radio section.
Kleinfunkwagen *m* *See* **Kleinfunkkraftwagen.**
Kleinkaliberlauf *m* subcaliber tube (*G*); small-bore barrel (*R*).
Kleinkalibermunition *f* subcaliber ammunition.
Kleinkaliberschießen *n* subcaliber target practice (*Arty*); small-bore target practice (*R*).
Kleinkraftrad *n* light motorcycle.
Kleinkrieg *m* guerrilla warfare.
Kleinluftschiff *n* blimp.
Kleinmaschinensatz *m* portable generating unit (*Elec*).
Klein-Panzerkampfwagen *m* light tank.
Kleinschießplatz *m* miniature range; subcaliber target range (*Arty*); small-bore target range (*R*).
Kleinsendegerät *n* portable radio transmitter.
Kleinvernebelung *f* limited-area smoke screen, local smoke screening.
Kleister *m* adhesive paste.
Klemme *f* clip; clamp; terminal; binding post.
klemmen to hold right or left (*R aiming*); to clamp, to jam, to become wedged.
Klemmenspannung *f* voltage across terminals.
Klemmhebel *m* clamping lever (*MG*).
Klemmplatte *f* clamping plate (*G barrel guide*).
Klemmring *m* clamping ring (*grenade launcher*).
Klemmschraube *f* setscrew; clamping screw (*aiming circle*).
Klemmzange *f* clamp (*blasting-cap fuze*).
Klempner *m* plumber.
Klettereisen *npl* climbers, climbing irons.
Kletterfähigkeit *f* vertical axle displacement (*MT*).
Kletterschuhe *mpl* rock-climbing shoes (*mountain operations*).
Kletterspornm *m* gaff (*of climbers*).
Kletterwalze *f* front roller (*MT*).
Klima *n* climate.
Klimaanlage *f* air conditioning plant.
Klinke *f* pawl, catch; jack (*Tp*).
Klippe *f* bluff. cliff (*Top*).
Klop *n* *See* **Chlorpikrin.**
Klopfen *n* detonation, knock, pinking (*of an engine*).
Klopfer *m* telegraph sounder.
klopffest antiknock.
Klopffestigkeit *f* antiknock quality (*engine fuel*).
Klotz *m* block, log.
Kluppe *f* stock (*die holder*).
Knagge *f* prop, wedge.
Knall *m* report (*G*); bang, crack, detonation.
Knallbild *n* sound track (*on SR film*).
Knalldämpfer *m* silencer (*R, pistol, etc.*).
Knallerscheinung *f* sound effect (*SR*).
Knallkörper *m* firecracker (*simulated fire*).
Knallmeß- *See* **Schallmeß-.**
Knallnetz *n* mine-exploding net, primacord net.
Knallquecksilber *n* mercury fulminate.
Knallzündschnur *f* detonating cord, primacord (*Engr*).
Knebel *m* gag.
Kneifzange *f* pincers.
Knemeyer *m* computer (*circular slide rule used in air navigation*).

Knetlegierung *f* malleable alloy.
Knick *m* break; crack; kink; knee *(Rad).*
knicken to buckle.
Knickfestigkeit *f* resistance to buckling.
Knickflügel *m* gull wing *(Ap).*
Knie *n* knee; salient *(Tac);* stifle joint *(horse);* elbow, bend *(of pipe, etc.).*
Kniegelenk *n* toggle joint *(pistol).*
kniender Anschlag kneeling position *(in firing).*
Kniepausche *f* knee pad *(harness).*
Knieschützer *mpl* knee pads *(Prcht troops).*
Kniestellung *f* salient *(Tac).*
Kniff *m* knack; helpful hint, handy device; "shortcut," trick.
Knochen *m* bone.
Knochenbruch *m* fracture *(Med).*
Knopf *m* button.
Knorrbremse *f* Knorr air brake.
Knoten *m* knot.
Bunde und Knoten knots and ties.
Knotenpunkt *m* intersection, junction.
Knüppel *m* control stick *(Ap);* club, bludgeon; log, round timber.
Knüppeldamm *m* corduroy road.
Knüppelgriff *m* grip of control stick *(Ap).*
Knüppelsteuerung *f* stick control *(Ap).*
Knüppelweg *m* corduroy road.
Kobona chocolate with caffeine *(Prcht ration).*
Kochgeschirr *n* mess kit, mess gear.
Kochgeschirrhülle *f* mess-kit cover.
Kochloch *n* cooking pit.
Kohle *f* carbon, coal; carbon brush, carbon rod *(Elec).*
Kohlebürste *f* carbon brush *(Elec).*
Kohleklotz *m* carbon block *(microphone).*
Kohlenelektrode *f* carbon electrode.
Kohlenkörner *npl* carbon granules *(microphone).*
Kohlenmikrophon *n* carbon microphone.
Kohlenoxyd *n* carbon monoxide.
Kohlensäure *f* carbon dioxide.
Kohlenstoff *m* carbon.
Kohlenstoffträger *m* carbon filler *(in liquid-oxygen blasting charges).*
Kohlepapier *n* carbon paper.
Kohleschicht *f* charcoal layer *(gas mask).*
Kohlestab *m* carbon rod *(Elec).*
Kohle-Zink-Element *n* carbon-zinc cell *(Elec).*
Kohle-Zinksammler *m* carbon-zinc battery.
Koinzidenzentfernungsmesser *m* coincidence range finder.
Koje *f* cabin *(Nav).*
Kokillenguß *m* chilled casting.
Kolben *m* piston *(Mech);* butt *(MG, R).*
Kolbenbolzen *m* piston pin *(Mtr).*
Kolbenbolzenlager *n* piston-pin bushing *(Mtr).*
Kolbenhals *m* small of the stock *(R).*
Kolbenhieb *m* butt stroke.
Kolbenhub *m* piston stroke *(Mtr).*
Kolbenkappe *f* butt plate *(R).*
Kolbenpistole *f* submachine gun consisting of automatic pistol with telescope or skeleton stock.
Kolbenring *m* piston ring *(Mtr).*
Kolbenstange *f* piston rod *(Mtr).*
Kolk *m* scour *(in river bottom).*
Kollektor *m* commutator, collector ring *(Elec).*
Kollimationslinie *f* collimating mark *(Optics).*
Kollodiumwolle *f* pyroxylin *(Am).*
Kolonne *f* column; train *(supply);* javelin *(Avn).*
Kolonnenbrücke *f* portable bridge.
Kolonnenchef *m* column commander *(MT).*
Kolonnengebiet *n* communications zone.
Kolonnenspitze *f* head of column.
Kolonnenstaffel *f* rear echelon train.
Kolonnenverkehr *m* column traffic.
Kolonne zu Einem column of files.
Kolonne zu Zweien column of twos.
Koluft *m* See **Kommandeur der Luftwaffe.**
Kombination *f* flying suit, coverall.
Kombüse *f* galley *(Nav).*
Kommandant *m* commander *(of an Ap, Tk, ship, etc.);* commanding officer *(of a post, garrison, or station).*
Kommandantur *f* commander's office, garrison headquarters. *See also* **Feldkommandantur, Ortskommandantur.**
Kommandeur *m* commander, commanding officer *(Bn and higher units, including entire arm or service);* commandant *(of a service school).*
Kommandeur der Luftwaffe air support commander.
Kommandeurpanzer *m* commander's tank.
kommandieren to command; to detach, to detail.
kommandierender General commanding general *(of a corps or service command).*
Kommandierrolle *f* duty roster.
Kommando *n* order, command; headquarters *(Div and larger units);* detached duty or service; detached unit; party or detail.
Kommandobehörde *f* command, command agency, headquarters *(Div and larger units).*
Kommandoflagge *f* command post flag *(Bn or higher unit).*
Kommandoführer *m* commander of a detachment, leader of a party.
Kommandogerät *n* data computer, ballistic director *(AAA);* command set *(Rad).*
Kommandohilfsgerät *n* auxiliary fire director *(AAA).*
Kommandopanzer *m* command tank.
Kommandosache *f* confidential military document.
Kommandospruch *m* radio message from commander's tank.
Kommandostelle *f* command post, headquarters.
Kommandotafel *f* range conversion table *(Gunnery).*
Kommando- und Ladeverzugszeit dead time *(Gunnery).*
Kommando- und Stabsschwadron headquarters troop *(Cav).*
Kommandowagen *m* command car, command truck.
Kommandowerte *mpl* fire-director data *(AAA).*
"Kommando zurück!" "As you were!"
Kommiß *m* military service, "the service" *(corresponds in many cases to the term "G.I." as used colloquially).*
Kommißbrot *n* G.I. bread.
Kommißstiefel *m* G.I. boot.
Kommodore *m* wing commander *(Avn).*
Kommodor und Lufttransportführer chief of air transport *(at Ger Air Ministry).*
Kompanie *f* company.
Kompanieabschnitt *m* company sector.
Kompaniebezirk *m* company area.
Kompaniebreitkeil *m* company inverted wedge formation.
Kompaniechef *m* company commander.
Kompanieführer *m* officer in charge of company, temporary company commander.
Kompaniegefechtsstand *m* company command post *(in combat).*
Kompaniegelder *npl* company fund.
Kompaniegrenze *f* company boundary.
Kompaniekeil *m* company wedge formation.
Kompanierevier *n* company area.
Kompanieschreiber *m* company clerk.
Kompanietrupp *m* company headquarters (personnel).
Kompanietruppführer *m* leader of company headquarters personnel.
Kompaß *m* compass.
Kompaßablenkung *f* compass error.
Kompaßausgleichung *f* compass compensation.
Kompaßkessel *m* compass bowl *(Ap).*
Kompaßkurs *m* compass heading, compass course *(Avn).*
Kompaßkurswinkel *m* compass azimuth.
Kompaßlenkung *f* compass deviation.
Kompaßmißweisung *f* compass declination.
Kompaßpeilung *f* compass bearing.
Kompaßrose *f* compass rose, compass card.
Kompaßstrich *m* point of the compass.
Kompaßzahl *f* azimuth, compass reading, bearing.
Komplize *m* accomplice *(Law).*
Kompressionsraum *m* compression chamber *(Mtr).*
Kompressor *m* compressor, supercharger.
Kompressormotor *m* supercharged engine.
Kondensationswärme *f* heat of condensation *(Met).*
Kondensator *m* condenser, capacitor *(Rad).*
Kondensatormikrophon *n* condenser microphone.
Kondensstreifen *m* vapor trail *(Avn).*
konisch conical, tapered.
konisches Rohr tapered-bore barrel *(G).*
Konstrukteur *m* technical designer.
Konstruktion *f* design; construction; structure.
Konstruktionsfehler *m* faulty design, structural defect.
Konstruktionszeichner *m* designer, draftsman.
Kontaktmesser *n* knife-switch prong *(Elec).*
Kontaktmine *f* contact mine *(Nav).*
Kontaktstift *m* prong of jack *(Elec).*
Kontaktstück *n* contact, contact piece *(Elec).*
Konteradmiral *m* rear admiral.
Konterbande *f* contraband.
Kontrollkarte *f* intercept board *(AWS).*
Kontrollampe *f* pilot light *(Ap, MT).*
Kontrolliste *f* check list.
Konuskupplung *f* cone clutch *(MT).*
konvergieren to converge.
Konzentrationslager *n* concentration camp.
konzentrisch concentric, converging.
Koordinate *f* coordinate.
Koordinatennetz *n* map grid, coordinate grid system.
Koordinatenschieber *mpl* coordinate cards.
Koordinatenverzeichnis *n* table of coordinates *(Surv).*
Koordinationsausgangspunkt *m* point of origin of coordinates.
Kopf *m* head; heading *(on a message);* nose or point *(of a shell).*
Kopfbahnhof *m* terminal; railhead.
Kopfbänder *npl* head straps *(gas mask).*
Kopfbänderung *f* head harness *(Gas mask).*
Kopfbedeckung *f* headgear, hat or helmet.
Kopffernhörer *m* headphone, headset.
Kopfgestell *n* headstall *(harness).*
Kopfhaube *f* helmet *(Avn).*
Kopfhörer *m* headphone, headset.
kopflastig noseheavy *(Ap).*
Kopfplatte *f* head-strap cushion *(Gas mask).*
Kopframpe *f* end ramp *(RR).*
Kopfschützer *m* woolen cap, winter cap.
Kopfstand *m* nose-over *(Avn).*
Kopfstärke *f* strength *(of a unit).*
Kopfstück *n* crownpiece *(harness);* head *(MG).*
Kopfsturz *m* vertical dive, nose dive *(Avn).*
Kopfteil *n* nose section of shell *(Am).*
Kopfteilung *f* graduation on head of panoramic telescope.
Kopfwelle *f* shell wave, ballistic wave, bow wave *(Ballistics).*
Kopfzünder *m* point-detonating fuze *(Am);* nose fuze *(bomb).*
Koppel *n* belt.
koppeln to determine a course or establish a fix by dead reckoning *(Avn);* to couple *(Arty).*
Koppelnavigation *f* navigation by dead reckoning *(Avn).*
Koppelort *m* fix, dead reckoning position *(Air Navigation).*
Koppelschloß *n* belt buckle.
Koppelzeit *f* time at which exact position is ascertained by means of dead reckoning *(Air Navigation).*
Kopplung *f* coupling *(Arty, Rad).*
Korb *m* basket *(Bln, etc.);* cluster of bombs *(slang).*
Korbring *m* concentration ring *(Bln).*
Kordelmutter *f* knurled nut.
Kordelung *f* knurl, knurling.
kordieren to knurl.
Kordit *n* cordite.
Korkenzieher *m* spiral dive, "corkscrew dive" *(Ap).*
Korn *n* front sight *(R, pistol, etc.);* muzzle sight *(G);* grain; bead; acorn.
das Korn klemmen to hold right or left.
geklemmtes Korn incorrectly centered front sight.
Körnchen *n* granule.
Körner *m* center punch.
Körnerform *f* granular form *(powder).*
Kornfuß *m* front-sight base *(R).*
Kornhalter *m* front-sight holder *(R).*
Kornwarze *f* front-sight stud *(R).*
Körperschutzmittel *n* protective clothing *(CWS).*
Korps *n* corps.
Korpsbezirk *m* corps area.
Korpsführer *m* assistant band leader.
Korpsgeist *m* esprit de corps, group spirit, group morale.
Korpskommando *n* corps headquarters.
Korpsnachschubführer *m* chief of corps supply services.
Korpsstab *m* corps headquarters staff.
Korrekturluftdüse *f* air-adjustment jet *(Mtr).*
Korrosionsbeständigkeit *f* resistance to corrosion.
Korvettenkapitän *m* lieutenant commander *(Nav).*
Kost *f* meal, food; diet.
Kot *m* mud, excrement, filth.
Köte *f* fetlock.
Kotflügel *m* mudguard, fender.
Krad *n* motorcycle *(abbr. of* **Kraftrad***).*
Kradfahrer *m* motorcyclist.
Kradmantel *m* motorcyclist's overcoat.
Kradmelder *m* motorcycle messenger.
Kradmeldetrupp *m* motorcycle messenger detachment.
Kradschütze *m* motorcycle rifleman.
Kradschützen-Bataillon *n* motorcycle battalion.
Kradschützenschwadron *f* motorcycle troop.
Kradschützensteg *m* floating wooden treadway bridge.
Kradschützenzug *m* motorcycle platoon.
Kradspäher *m* motorcycle scout.
Kradspitze *f* motorcycle point of advance guard.

Kr.A	Kriegsanleihe	war loan
Krabus	Kraftomnibus	motor bus
Krad	Kraftrad	motorcycle
Kradf	Kraftradfahrer	motorcyclist
Krad.m.B	Kraftrad mit Beiwagen	motorcycle with side car
Kradsch	Kraftradschütze	motorcycle rifleman
Kradsch.Komp	Kraftradschützenkompanie	motorcycle company
Kräder	Krafträder	motorcycles
Kraft	Regimentskommandeur der Kraftfahrtruppen	regimental commander of the motor transport troops
Kraft Abt	Kraftfahrabteilung	motor transport battalion *or* detachment
Kraftf	Kraftfahrer	motor transport driver
Kraftf.Tr	Kraftfahrtruppen	motor transport troops
Kraftobus	Kraftomnibus	motor bus
Kraftwk	Kraftwerk	power plant; power station
Kr.Ak	Kriegsakademie	military academy
Krak.W	Krankenwagen	ambulance
Kra[illegible]	Kriegsranglistenauszug	war service record of officer
Krankenhs	Krankenhaus	hospital
Krank.Sam.P	Krankensammelpunkt	collecting point (*medical*)
Krank.Wg	Krankenwagen	ambulance
Kr.Art	Kriegsartikel	articles of war
Kr.Ber.Erst	Kriegsberichterstatter	war correspondent
Kr.D	Kraftdivision	motorized division
Krd.-S.Btl	Kradschützenbataillon	motorcycle rifle battalion
Kr.Erf	Kriegserfahrung	war experience
Kr.Erkl	Kriegserklärung	declaration of war
Krf	Kraftfahrer	motor transport driver
Krf	Kraftwagenführer	driver
Krfa.Abt	Kraftfahrabteilung	motor transport battalion *or* detachment
Krfg	Kriegführung	conduct of war
KrfT	Kraftfahrtruppen	motor transport troops
Kr.G	Kraftwagengeschütz	self-propelled gun
Kr.G	Kriegsgericht	court martial
Kr.Geb	Kriegsgebiet	theater of war; war zone; combat zone
Krgef	Kriegsgefangener	prisoner of war
Kr.Ger.R	Kriegsgerichtsrat	civilian judiciary official in the Judge Advocate General's Department
Kr.Gesch.Heer	Kriegsgeschichtliche Abteilung des Heeres	history of the war section of the army
Krgf	Kriegsgefangener	prisoner of war
Kr.Gr	Kriegergräber	war graves (*on maps*)
Kr.GR	Kriegsgerichtsrat	civilian judiciary official in the Judge Advocate General's Department
Krgs	Kriegs-	war
Krgsd	Kriegsdienst	war service
Krgs.Gef.Arb	Kriegsgefangenenarbeit	work done by prisoners of
Krgs.Gef.Arb.Abt	Kriegsgefangenenarbeiterabteilung	detail of workers who are prisoners of war
Krgs.Gef.Arb.Btl	Kriegsgefangenenarbeiterbataillon	battalion of workers who are prisoners of war
Krgs.Gef.L	Kriegsgefangenenlager	prisoner-of-war camp
Krgsgef.Laz	Kriegsgefangenenlazarett	hospital for prisoners of war
Krgsk	Kriegskunst	art of war
Krgs.Laz	Kriegslazarett	station hospital in communications zone
Krgs.Lief	Kriegslieferant	furnisher of war material
Krgs.Rüst	Kriegsrüstungen	war armaments
Krgssch	Kriegsschule	military school
Krgst	Kriegsteilnehmer	participant in war
Krgstln	Kriegsteilnehmer	participant in war
Krgsw	Kriegswesen	warfare
Krgsw	Kriegswirtschaft	wartime economy
Krh	Krankenhaus	hospital
Kr.Hint	Kriegshinterbliebene	war widows and other dependen
Kriegfg	Kriegführung	conduct of war
Kriegsbed	Kriegsbedarf	military requirements
Kriegsbes	Kriegsbesatzung	war garrison
Kriegsbesch	Kriegsbeschädigter	disabled man
Kriegsfin	Kriegsfinanzierung	financing of war
Kriegsfl	Kriegsflüchtling	refugee of war
Kriegs Fürs	Kriegsfürsorge	care for people affected by war
kriegsgesch	kriegsgeschichtlich	pertaining to military history
Kriegsgew	Kriegsgewinn	gains of war
Kriegsgew	Kriegsgewinnler	war profiteer
Kriegskst	Kriegskunst	art of war
Kriegs T	Kriegsteilnehmer	participant in war
Kriegs-W	Kriegswesen	warfare
Kriegs-W	Kriegswirtschaft	wartime economy
Kr.Ind	Kriegsindustrie	war industry
Kripo	Kriminalpolizei	criminal police
Krista	Kriegsstammrollenauszug	war service record (*of an enlisted man or noncommissioned officer*)
Krk.Hs	Krankenhaus	hospital
Kr.Kt	Kriegskarte	war map
Krkw	Krankenkraftwagen	ambulance
Kr.Laz	Kriegslazarett	communications zone station hospital
Kr.Lg	Kriegslage	war situation; strategical situation
Krnk.W	Krankenwagen	ambulance
Krpf	Kriegspfarrer	chaplain

Kr.R	Kriegsrecht	martial law
Kr.R	Kriegsrichter	civilian judiciary official in the Judge Advocate General's Department with rank of captain
Kr.Rat	Kriegsration	war ration
Krs	Kreis	district
Kr.San.Ausr.	Kriegssanitätsausrüstung	wartime medical equipment
Kr.Sch	Kriegsschule	military school
Kr.Schd	Kriegsschaden	war damage
Kr.Schld	Kriegsschulden	war debts
Kr.Schpl	Kriegsschauplatz	theater of war
Kr.Schtz	Kriegsschatz	war chest
Kr.SL	Kriegsschuldlüge	lie of war guilt
Kr.Sp	Kriegsspiel	war game; map maneuver
Kr.St	Kriegsstärke	war strength
Kr.St.N	Kriegsstärkenachweisung	war strength record
Kr.Tb	Kriegstagebuch	war diary; station and record of events book
Kr.Tr.Abt	Krankentransportabteilung	ambulance detachment
Kr.Verl	Kriegsverluste	war casualties
Kr.W	Krankenwagen	ambulance
Krw.G	Kraftwagengeschütz	tractor-drawn gun
Kr.Z	Kriegsziel	aim of war
Kr.Zust	Kriegszustand	state of war
Ks	Kaserne	barracks
K.S	Kavallerieschule	cavalry school
K.San.Kp	Kraftwagensanitätskompanie	medical company (motorized)
Ksgr	Kiesgrube	gravel pit (*on maps*)
K.Sig	kleines Signalgerät	small signal apparatus
K.S.O	Kriegssanitätsordnung	war service regulations for medical corps
KSSVO	Kriegssonderstrafrechtsverordnung	special war penal decree
Kst	Küste, Küsten-	coast; coastal
Kst.Batt	Küstenbatterie	coast defense battery
Kst.H	Küstenhaubitze	coast defense howitzer
Kst.K	Küstenkanone	coast defense gun
Kst.L	Küstenlafette	coast defense mounting
Kst.Mrs	Küstenmörser	coast defense mortar
K.St.N	Kriegsstärkenachweisung	war strength record
K.S.V	Kriegssanitätsvorschrift	war sanitary regulations
K.T	Kabeltelegramm	cablegram
Kt	Kartätsche	case shot
Kt	Karte	map
K.T	Kolonialtauglichkeit	fitness for colonial service
K.T.B	Korpstagesbefehl	army corps order of the day
Ktn.Sk	Kartenskizze	map sketch
Kt.O	Krankenträgerordnung	stretcher-bearer regulations
K.Tr	Korpstruppen	army corps troops
Ktt.Br	Kettenbrücke	suspension bridge
Ku	Kuppe	knoll
Küst.Bttr	Küstenbatterie	coastal battery
K.u.F	Anleitung für den Kampf um Festungen	instructions for warfare on fortified positions
Kuppl	Kupplung	coupling; clutch
kv	kriegsverwendungsfähig	fit for war service
K.Verschl	Keilverschluss	wedge type of breechblock
K.Vet	Korpsveterinär	corps area veterinary
K.Vet.V	Kriegsveterinärvorschriften	army veterinary regulations
kv.f.b.Z	kriegsverwendungsfähig für besondere Zwecke	fit for war service for special purposes
KVL	Kriegsverbindungsleutnant	liaison lieutenant
K.V.O	Kraftfahrtruppenverbindungsoffizier	motor transport liaison officer
K.V.V	Kriegsverpflegungsvorschrift	wartime commissary regulations
K.W	Kartenwinkelmesser	map protractor
kW	Kilowatt	kilowatt
Kw	Kraftwagen	motor car
Kw.AH	Kraftwagenanhänger	trailer truck
Kw.-D	Kampfwagendivision	armored division
Kw.Flak	Kraftwagen-Flugzeugabwehrkanone	motorized antiaircraft gun
Kw.G	Kraftwagengeschütz	gun mounted on a truck
Kr.Kt	Kriegskarte	war map
Krkw	Krankenkraftwagen	ambulance
Kr.Laz	Kriegslazarett	communications zone station hospital
Kr.Lg	Kriegslage	war situation; strategical situation
Krnk.W	Krankenwagen	ambulance
Krpf	Kriegspfarrer	chaplain

Kr.R Kriegsrecht martial law
Kr.R Kriegsrichter civilian judiciary official in the Judge Advocate General's Department with rank of captain
Kr.Rat Kriegsration war ration
Krs Kreis district
Kr.San.Ausr. Kriegssanitätsausrüstung wartime medical equipment
Kr.Sch Kriegsschule military school
Kr.Schd Kriegsschaden war damage

Kraft durch Freude Strength Through Joy (*Ger Civ morale and travel organization*).
Kräfte *fpl* forces; power; strength.
Kräfteersparnis *f* economy of manpower, sparing of personnel.
Kräfteverteilung *f* distribution of forces, tactical grouping (*Tac*).
Kräftezersplitterung *f* splitting up of forces, dissipation of forces (*Tac*).
Kraftfahrabteilung *f* motor transport battalion.
Kraftfahrausbildung *f* driver training (*MT*).
Kraftfahrer *m* driver; private (*MT*).
Kraftfahr-Ersatzteil-Staffel *f* spare parts section (*MT*).
Kraftfahrgerät *n* motor-transport equipment.
Kraftfahrkampftruppen *fpl* armored troops.
Kraftfahrkorps *n* See **Nationalsozialistisches Kraftfahrkorps.**
Kraftfahrlehrstab *m* motor transport training staff.
Kraftfahrpark *m* motor transport park (*GHQ or Army*); motor pool, vehicle park.
Kraftfahrparkkompanie *f* motor transport company (*component unit of a* Kraftfahrpark).
kraftfahrtechnisch pertaining to automotive mechanics.
Kraftfahrtransport *m* motor transport.
Kraftfahrtruppen *fpl* motor transport troops.
Kraftfahrversorgung *f* motor transport supply.
Kraftfahrwesen *n* motor transport service.
Kraftfahrzeug *n* motor vehicle.
Kraftfahrzeugkolonne *f* motor convoy, motor column.
Kraftfahrzeugpark *m* motor vehicle park.
Kraftfahrzeug-Verwertung *f* sorting and classification of motor vehicle salvage.
Kraftfahrzeugzubehör *n* motor-vehicle accessories.
Kraftlinien *fpl* lines of force (*Elec*).
Kraftmoment *n* moment of force.
Kraftomnibus *m* bus.
Kraftquelle *f* power source.
Kraftquellenwagen *m* horse-drawn generating unit.
Kraftrad *n* motorcycle. *For compounds see under* **Krad.**
Kraftsäge *f* power saw.
Kraftschlepper *m* tractor, prime mover.
Kraftspeicher *m* closing spring cylinder (*AA gun*); storage battery.
Kraftstoff *m* fuel, gasoline.
Kraftstoffabstellhahn *m* fuel shut-off valve (*Mtr*).
Kraftstoffanlage *f* fuel system (*Mtr*).
Kraftstoffausgabestelle *f* gasoline distributing point.
Kraftstoffbehälter *m* fuel tank, gasoline tank.
Kraftstoffdruckmesser *m* fuel pressure gage (*Ap*).
Kraftstoffdüse *f* fuel jet (*Mtr*).
Kraftstoffgemisch *n* fuel mixture (*Mtr*).
Kraftstofflager *n* fuel dump.
Kraftstoffleitung *f* fuel line (*MT*).
Kraftstoff-Luftgemisch *n* fuel-air mixture (*Mtr*).
Kraftstoffmeßuhr *f* fuel gage (*Mtr*).
Kraftstoffnachschub *m* fuel supply, gasoline supply.
Kraftstoffnormverbrauch *m* normal fuel consumption (*MT*).
Kraftstoffölmischung *f* gasoline-oil mixture.
Kraftstofförderpumpe *f* fuel pump (*Mtr*).
Kraftstofförderung *f* fuel feed (*Mtr*).
Kraftstoffreiniger *m* fuel filter (*Mtr*).
Kraftstoffsieb *n* See **Kraftstoffreiniger.**
Kraftstoffstaffel *f* gasoline supply section (*Tk Bn*).
Kraftstoffverbrauch *m* fuel consumption (*MT*).
Kraftstoffverbrauchssatz *m* rate of fuel consumption (*MT*).
Kraftstoffversorgung *f* gasoline supply.
Kraftsoffvorratsmesser *m* fuel level gage (*Ap*).
Kraftstoffzufluß *m* fuel feed (*Mtr*).
Kraftstoffzug *m* gasoline-supply train (*RR*).
Kraftübertragung *f* power transmission, power train (*MT*).
Kraftübertragungsteile *mpl* power train (*MT*).
Kraftverstärker *m* power amplifier (*Rad*).
Kraftverstärker-Anlage *f* public-address system (*Elec*).
Kraftwagen *m* automobile, motor vehicle (*occasionally used in sense of* Lastkraftwagen, *truck*).
Kraftwagenanhänger *m* trailer.
Kraftwagenbegleiter *m* assistant driver (*MT*).
Kraftwagenflak *f* mobile antiaircraft artillery.
Kraftwagengeschütz *n* See **Kraftwagenkanone.**
Kraftwagenkanone *f* gun mounted on motor carriage.
Kraftwagenkanonenwagen *m* assault gun car, motor carriage for gun.
Kraftwagenkolonne *f* motor transport column.
große Kraftwagenkolonne heavy motor transport column (*capacity 60 tons*).
kleine Kraftwagenkolonne light motor transport column (*capacity 30 tons*).
Kraftwagenkolonne für Betriebsstoffe gasoline and lubricant supply column.
Kraftwagenküchenkompanie *f* mobile kitchen company.
Kraftwagenmarsch *m* motorized march.
Kraftwagenpark *m* motor park.
Kraftwagentransport *m* motor transport.
Kraftwagentransportabteilung *f* motor transport battalion.
Kraftwagentransportkolonne *f* motor transport column.
Kraftwagenwerkstatt *f* motor vehicle repair shop.
Kraftwagenwerkstattzug *m* motor maintenance repair shop platoon.
Kraftwerk *n* power house, power station.
Kraftzug *m* power traction (*as of a prime mover*).
mit Kraftzug tractor-drawn, truck-drawn.
Kraftzugartillerie *f* motorized artillery.
Kraftzuggeschütz *n* motorized gun.
Kraftzugmaschine *f* prime mover.
Kragen *m* collar (*Clo*).
Kragenlitze *f* collar badge (*facing sewn on the* Kragenpatte).
Kragenpatte *f* collar patch (*cloth backing for the* Kragenlitze).
Kragenspiegel *m* collar patch (*Luftwaffe*).
Kragträger *m* cantilever beam.
Kragträgerbrücke *f* cantilever bridge.
Krähennest *m* "crow's nest," gunner's compartment (*Ap upper turret*).
Krampe *f* staple (*Tech*).
Kran *m* crane, hoist; crane tractor (*used as a power shovel*).
krängen to heel (*Avn*).
Krängungsfehler *m* heeling error (*Avn*).
krank sick, ill.
sich krank melden to go on sick call, to report sick.
Krankenabschub *m* evacuation of the sick.
Kranken-Absonderung *f* medical isolation.
Krankenabteilung *f* ward (*Med*).
Krankenabtransport *m* evacuation of the sick.
Krankenbehandlung *f* treatment of sick.
Krankenblatt *n* clinical record.
Krankenbuch *n* See **Krankenmeldebuch.**
Kranken-Isolierung *f* medical isolation.
Krankenkraftwagen *m* motor ambulance.
Krankenkraftwagenzug *m* motor ambulance platoon.
Krankenmeldebuch *n* sick report book or folder.
Krankenmeldung *f* daily sick report.
Krankenrevier *n* infirmary, dispensary.
Krankensammelpunkt *m* See **Krankensammelstelle.**
Krankensammelstelle *f* collecting station (*Med*).
Krankenschwester *f* nurse.
Krankenstall *m* veterinary hospital.
Krankenstube *f* infirmary, ward.
Krankentrage *m* litter, stretcher.
Krankentragenfahrgerät *n* wheeled litter carrier (*Med*).
Krankenträger *m* litter bearer (*Med*).
Krankentransportabteilung *f* ambulance battalion.
Krankenunterkunft *f* field hospital.
feste Krankenunterkunft fixed hospital.
Krankenurlaub *m* sick leave.
Krankenwärter *m* ward attendant (*Med*).
Kranz *m* circular track (*MG mount*).
Kratze *f* scraper, hoe.
Kraxe *f* wood frame pack carrier.
Kreis *m* circle; area; circuit.
Kreisbogen *m* arc of a circle.
Kreisbogenabsteckung *f* measuring or transferring an arc with dividers.
Kreisel *m* gyroscope.
Kreiselabfeuergerät *n* gyro control, gyro-stabilizer (*Tk*).
Kreiselkompaß *m* gyro compass.
Kreiselkompressor *m* centrifugal compressor.
Kreiselneigungsmesser *m* bank-and-turn indicator (*Ap*).
Kreiselpumpe *f* centrifugal pump.
Kreiselsteuerzeiger *m* gyro indicator, gyroscopic turn indicator (*Ap*).
Kreiselwendezeiger *m* gyro turn indicator, gyroscopic turn indicator (*Ap*).
kreisen to circle, to maneuver in circles.
Kreisflug *m* circular course (*Avn*).
Kreisfunkfeuer *n* fan-marker beacon, omnidirectional beacon (*Rad*).
Kreisfunktion *f* trigonometric function.
Kreiskimme *f* rear ring sight (*MG*).
Kreiskommandantur *f* area headquarters (*Mil Govt*).
Kreiskorn *n* front ring sight (*MG*).
Kreiskornfuß *m* front ring sight base (*MG*).
Kreiskornhalter *m* front ring sight support (*MG*).
Kreiskornrahmen *m* front ring sight frame (*MG*).
Kreislauf *m* cycle.
Kreisleitung *f* series circuit (*demolitions*).
Kreisprozeß *m* cycle.
Kreisverkehr *m* "circular" radio traffic (*radio-net traffic in which stations communicate directly with each other on a common frequency with different call signs and without a net control station*).
Kreisvisier *n* ring sight (*Ord*).
krepieren to explode, burst; to die.
Kresolseifenlösung *f* cresol soap solution.
Kresolwasser *n* cresol solution.

Kreuz *n* cross; crosspiece (*of universal joint*).
Kreuzbund *n* shear lashing (*for diagonal timbers*).
Kreuzen *n* traffic crossing.
kreuzen to cross; to cruise (*Nav*).
Kreuzer *m* cruiser.
Kreuzfeuer *n* cross fire.
Kreuzgelenk *n* universal joint.
Kreuzhacke *f* double-bitted pickax.
Kreuzlafette *f* outrigger-type gun mount.
Kreuzleinen *fpl* cross line (*reins*).
Kreuzlochschraube *f* cross-hole screw.
Kreuzmuffe *f* cross pipe fitting, four-way pipe joint.
Kreuzpeilung *f* determining a fix, taking cross bearings (*Air Navigation*).
Kreuzschraube *f* trigger-guard screw (*R*).
Kreuzteil *n* rear of receiver well (*R*).
Kreuzung *f* intersection.
Kreuzungsbahnhof *m* crossing station (*RR*).
Kreuzverhör *n* cross-examination.
kriechen to creep or crawl.
Kriechgraben *m* crawl trench, shallow communication trench.
Krieg *m* war. *See also terms under* **Gefecht, Kampf.**
kriegführend belligerent.
kriegführende Macht belligerent power.
Kriegführung *f* warfare.
Kriegsakademie *f* war college.
Kriegsartikel *mpl* Articles of War (*now replaced by brief summary of military ideals and obligations called* Pflichten des deutschen Soldaten).
Kriegsausgang *m* outcome of war.
Kriegsausrüstungsnachweisung *f* table of basic allowances (*wartime*).
Kriegsband *n* battle honors.
Kriegsbeorderung *f* See **Kriegsbeordnung.**
Kriegsbeordnung *f* mobilization order for reservists.
Kriegsbericht *m* war communiqué, war news report.
Kriegsberichter *m* accredited correspondent (*in a Ger propaganda Co*).
kriegsbeschädigt disabled on active duty.
Kriegsbeteiligung *f* participation in war.
Kriegsbrauch *m* customs of war.
Kriegsbrücke *f* military bridge.
Kriegsbrückengerät *n* military bridge equipment.
Kriegsdauer *f* duration of war.
auf Kriegsdauer for the duration (*abbr.* a.K.).
Kriegsdenkmünze *f* campaign medal.
Kriegsdienstverweigerer *m* conscientious objector.
Kriegserfordernisse *fpl* military requirements in wartime.
Kriegserklärung *f* declaration of war.
Kriegsflagge *f* ensign.
Kriegsfuß *m* war footing.
Kriegsgebiet *n* theater of operations.
Kriegsgebrauch *m* customs of war.
Kriegsgefangenenbau- und Arbeitsbataillon PW construction and labor battalion (*for guarding PWs working in Germany or rear areas*).
Kriegsgefangeneneinsatz *m* employment of prisoners of war.
Kriegsgefangenensammelstelle *f* prisoner-of-war collecting point.
Kriegsgefangener *m* prisoner of war.
Kriegsgerät *n* war matériel.
Kriegsgericht *n* court-martial.
Kriegsgerichtsrat *m* judge advocate.
Kriegsgerichtsrechtsprechung *f* military justice.

Kriegsgerichtsverfahren *n* court-martial proceedings.
Kriegsgliederung *f* order of battle.
Kriegskasse *f* field safe; war chest.
Kriegskonterbande *f* contraband of war.
Kriegskunst *f* art of war.
Kriegslazarett *n* base hospital.
Kriegslist *f* stratagem, ruse *(Tac)*.
Kriegsmarine *f* navy.
Kriegsmarsch *m* tactical march.
kriegsmäßig warlike, similar to actual conditions in the field.
Kriegsneurose *f* war neurosis.
Kriegsoffizier-Bewerber *m* applicant for wartime commission.
Kriegsrangliste *f* army directory.
Kriegsräson *f* military necessity.
Kriegsrecht *n* military law.
Kriegssanitätsordnung *f* medical field regulations or manual.
Kriegsschauplatz *m* theater of war.
Kriegsschiff *n* warship.
Kriegsschule *f* officer candidate school.
Kriegsspiel *n* war game, map maneuver.
Kriegsstammrolle *f* personnel roster *(wartime)*.
Kriegsstand *m* *See* **Kriegsstärke.**
Kriegsstärke *f* war strength *(of a unit, etc.)*.
Kriegsstärkenachweisung *f* table of organization *(wartime)*.
Kriegstagebuch *n* war diary; journal, daybook.
Kriegsverdienstkreuz *n* War Service Cross *(decoration)*.
Kriegsverrat *m* war treason.
Kriegsverräter *m* war traitor.
kriegsverwendungsfähig fit for active service *(abbr.* k.v.).
Kriegswerft *f* navy yard.
kriegswichtig of military importance.
Kriegswissenschaft *f* military science.
Kriegszahnarzt *m* dental surgeon.
Kriegszustand *m* state of war.
Kriminalpolizei *f* criminal investigation police.
Krimschild *m* Crimea Shield *(decoration on upper left sleeve, worn by all veterans of the battle in the Crimea)*.
Kripo *f* *See* **Kriminalpolizei.**
K.-Rolle *f* plain-wire concertina *(abbr. of* Klaviersaitendraht-Rolle).
Kronenmutter *f* castellated nut.
Kröpfung *f* right-angle bend; throw *(of a crankshaft)*.
Krümmer *m* elbow pipe; manifold.
Krümmung *f* bend; turn; camber; curvature.
Kruppe *f* croup *(horse)*.
K-Stoff *m* diphosgene *(CWS)*.
Kübel *m* bucket; jeep.
Kübelsitzer *m* *See* **Kübelwagen.**
Kübelsitzwagen *m* *See* **Kübelwagen.**
Kübelwagen *m* command car, jeep.
Kubikzahl *f* cube *(Math)*.
Küche *f* kitchen.
Küchendienst *m* kitchen police, KP; mess orderly, mess attendant.
Küchenunteroffizier *m* mess sergeant.
Kufe *f* sled runner; skid.
Kugel *f* bullet; ball; sphere.
Kugelblende *f* mantlet of flexible ball mount, ball mount *(Tk)*.
Kugelfang *m* target butt, range butt.
kugelfest bulletproof.
Kugelfüllung *f* ball filler *(shrapnel)*.
Kugelgelenk *n* ball-and-socket joint.
Kugellafette *f* ball mount *(MG)*.
Kugellager *m* ball bearing.
Kugelpfanne *f* ball socket *(Mort)*.
kugelsicher bulletproof.
Kühlanlage *f* cooling system *(Mtr)*.
Kühler *m* radiator *(Mtr)*.
Kühler-Einfüllverschluß *m* radiator cap *(MT)*.
Kühlerklappe *f* louver *(Mt, Tk)*.
Kühlerschutzhaube *f* radiator guard *(MT)*.
Kühlerverschluß *m* radiator cap *(MT)*.
Kühlflüssigkeit *f* cooling liquid *(Mtr)*.
Kühlmantel *m* water jacket *(Mtr, MG)*.
Kühlmittel *n* coolant *(Mtr)*.
Kühlrippe *f* cooling fin *(Mtr)*.
Kühlstoff *m* coolant.
Kühlung *f* cooling system *(Mtr)*.
Kühlwagen *m* refrigerator truck, refrigerator car.
Kühlwassermantel *m* water jacket.
Kulissenschaltung *f* gate-type gear shift.
Kumpel *m* buddy.
Kumuluswolke *f* cumulus cloud.
Kundschafter *m* spy.
Kunstflug *m* stunt flying.
Kunstflugfigur *f* stunt-flying maneuver.
Kunstleder *n* artificial leather.
künstliche Antenne artificial antenna *(Rad)*.
künstliche Atmung artificial respiration.
künstliche Lüftung artificial ventilation.
künstlicher Gummi synthetic rubber.
künstlicher Horizont absolute inclinometer, gyro horizon indicator, artificial horizon *(Ap Inst)*.
künstlicher Nebel screening smoke *(CWS)*.
künstliches Hindernis artificial obstacle.
künstliche Spur artificial scent *(for army dogs)*.
Kunstschaltung *f* superposed connection *(Tp)*.
Kunstseide *f* rayon.
Kunststoff *m* synthetic plastic.
Kupfer *n* copper.
Kupferdraht *m* copper wire.
Kupferkapsel *f* copper shell *(detonator cap)*.
Kuppe *f* knoll, knob, rounded hilltop.
Kuppel *f* cupola.
Kuppellafette *f* cupola mount *(Ap)*.
Kuppelstange *f* tie rod *(split-trail carriage)*.
Kupplung *f* clutch *(MT)*; coupling *(Mech)*; recoil connection *(pistol)*.
Kupplungsfeder *f* clutch spring *(MT)*.
Kupplungsfußhebel *m* clutch pedal *(MT)*.
Kupplungsgehäuse *n* clutch housing *(MT)*.
Kupplungshebel *m* clutch lever *(MT)*; recoil-spring lever *(pistol)*.
Kupplungskasten *m* junction box, gun junction box, control box *(AA director)*.
Kupplungskegel *m* clutch cone *(MT)*.
Kupplungskopf *m* coupling head *(trailer)*.
Kupplungspedal *n* clutch pedal *(MT)*.
Kupplungsscheibe *f* clutch plate *(MT)*.
Kupplungsstange *f* recoil-spring lever bar *(pistol)*.
Kupplungstritt *m* clutch pedal *(MT)*.
Kupplungswelle *f* clutch shaft *(MT)*.
Kurbel *f* crank.
Kurbelarm *m* crank arm *(of crankshaft)*.
Kurbeldynamo *f* hand-crank generator.
Kurbelgehäuse *n* crankcase *(Mtr)*.
Kurbelgriff *m* crank handle.
Kurbelinduktor *m* hand-crank generator *(Tp)*.
Kurbelkröpfung *f* crankshaft throw.
Kurbellager *n* crankshaft bearing, pillow block.
Kurbelrad *n* crankwheel *(G)*.
Kurbelstange *f* connecting rod *(Mtr)*.
Kurbeltrieb *m* crank mechanism.
Kurbeltriebwerk *n* crankshaft assembly *(Mtr)*.
Kurbelübung *f* crankwheel operation exercise *(gun laying)*.
Kurbelwelle *f* crankshaft *(Mtr)*.
Kurbelzapfen *m* crank pin *(Mtr)*.
Kurier *m* courier, special messenger.
Kurierflugzeug *n* liaison airplane.
Kurierpost *f* courier mail.
Kurier-Staffel *f* special communication squadon *(Luftwaffe)*. *See also* **Staffel.**
Kurs *m* course, heading.
Kursgleiche *f* rhumb line *(Air Navigation)*.
Kurskreisel *m* directional gyro.
Kursscheibe *f* bearing plate *(Avn)*.
Kursstabilität *f* directional stability *(Ap)*.
Kurssteuerung *f* piloting, navigating, pilot control.
automatische Kurssteuerung automatic pilot, mechanical pilot *(Ap)*.
Kursverbesserung *f* off-course correction *(Air Navigation)*.
Kursvisier *n* bomb sight *(Ap)*.
Kurswechsel *m* change of course, change of direction *(Avn)*.
Kurswinkel *m* azimuth of target *(AAA)*.
Kurszeiger *m* navigator's compass *(Ap)*.
Kurve *f* curve, turn.
Kurvenblatt *n* graph.
Kurvenflug *m* curvilinear flight *(Avn)*.
Kurvengleitflug *m* spiral *(Avn)*.
Kurvenkampf *m* turning combat, dogfight *(Avn)*.
Kurvenmesser *m* map measurer *(Inst)*.
Kurvenscheibe *f* cam plate *(Ord)*; curvilinear target *(Tng)*.
Kurvenvisier *n* tangent sight *(SA)*.
Kurzleistung *f* military rating *(of an Ap engine)*.
Kurzschluß *m* short circuit, short *(Elec)*.
Kurzschlußankermotor *m* squirrel-cage motor.
Kurzschuß *m* short *(Gunnery)*.
Kurzsignal *n* code group.
Kurzwelle *f* short wave *(Rad)*.
Kurzwellensender *m* short-wave transmitter.
Küste *f* coast, shore.
Küstenartillerie *f* coast artillery.
Küstenaufklärer *m* coast reconnaissance airplane.
Küstenaufklärung *f* coast reconnaissance.
Küstenbatterie *f* coast battery, shore battery.
Küstenflak *f* coast antiaircraft gun, coast antiaircraft artillery.
Küstenfliegergruppe *f* coast reconnaissance and naval support group *(Avn)*. *See also* **Gruppe.**
Küstengebiet *n* coastal area.
Küstengeschütz *n* coast artillery gun.
Küstengewässer *npl* coastal zone, coastal waters.
Küstenlafette *f* coast artillery gun mount.
Küstenstaffel *f* coastal squadron *(Avn)*. *See also* **Staffel.**
Küstenstation *f* coast guard station.
Küstenverteidigung *f* coast defense.
Küstenvorfeld *n* coastal zone.
Küstenwache *f* coast guard, coast guard station.
Küstenwacht *f* coast patrol.
Küstenwehr *f* coast defense, coast defense troops.
Kutonnase *f* cable cutter on leading edge of wing *(an anti-barrage-balloon device)*.
Kuvi *n* *See* **Kursvisier.**
KWK.-Stand *m* fixed emplacement made of tank gun turret.

L

Ladeleitrad *n* diffuser *(supercharger)*.
Ladeloch *n* loading recess *(G)*.
Ladeluftkühler *m* intercooler *(Ap supercharger)*.
Ladeluke *f* loading hatch *(Ap)*.
Lademaschine *f* battery charger *(Elec)*.
Lademaschinensatz *m* battery charging unit *(Elec)*.
Lademulde *f* loading tray *(G)*.
laden to load *(R, G, etc.)*.
"Laden und sichern!" "Load and lock!"
Ladeplatz *m* pier, wharf, quay.
Lack *m* lacquer, varnish.
Ladebaum *m* boom, derrick, crane.
Ladebrücke *f* loading ramp *(on trailer)*.
Ladedruck *m* manifold pressure *(Mtr)*.
Ladedruckmesser *m* manifold pressure gage *(Ap engine)*.
Ladedruckregler *m* manifold pressure control *(Ap engine)*.
Ladeeinheit *f* load unit, unit load.
Ladefähigkeit *f* load capacity; serviceable condition of ammunition.
Ladegewicht *n* load capacity, weight of load.
Ladegleis *n* loading siding *(RR)*.
Ladegurt *m* cartridge belt.
Ladehemmung *f* stoppage in loading mechanism *(Ord)*.
Ladekanonier *m* gun loader, loader, assistant gunner, cannoneer No. 1.
Ladeklappe *f* breechblock.
Ladekran *m* gun hoist.
Ladelaufrad *n* impeller *(supercharger)*.
Lader *m* stevedore, loader, supercharger *(Mtr)*.
Laderampe *f* loading ramp.
Laderaum *m* chamber, powder chamber *(G)*; hold *(Nav)*.
Laderaumverlängerung *f* advance of forcing cone *(G)*.
Ladergetriebe *n* supercharger drive.
Ladeschale *f* loading tray *(G)*.
Ladeschütze *m* assistant gunner, loader *(Tk)*.
Ladesitz *m* loader's seat *(G)*.
Ladespannung *f* charging voltage *(battery charger)*.
Ladestelle *f* loading point, entraining or entrucking point; battery-charging station.
Ladestock *m* rammer.
Ladestörung *f* stoppage in loading mechanism *(Ord)*.
Ladestraße *f* delivery roadway *(RR freight station)*.
Ladestreifen *m* cartridge clip, ammunition clip.
Ladetätigkeit *f* loading operations *(service of the piece)*.
Ladetisch *m* loading tray *(G)*.
Ladetrommel *f* cartridge drum.
Ladetrupp *m* loading detail.
Ladeverzug *m* loading lag *(Gunnery)*.
Ladeverzugszeit *f* loading lag, loading time *(Gunnery)*.
Ladevorgang *m* loading action *(semi- or full-automatic weapons)*.
Ladevorrichtung *f* breech mechanism, loading device *(Ord)*; feeding device *(SA)*.
Ladezeit *f* loading time, entrucking time, entraining time; charging time *(Elec battery)*.
Ladung *f* cargo, load; charge.
Ladungsbüchse *f* blasting-charge container *(generally of galvanized metal)*.
Ladungsgefäß *n* blasting-charge container.
Ladungskasten *m* blasting-charge box.
Ladungsraum *m* *See* **Laderaum.**

Kr.Schld	Kriegsschulden	war debts
Kr.Schpl	Kriegsschauplatz	theater of war
Kr.Schtz	Kriegsschatz	war chest
Kr.SL	Kriegsschuldlüge	lie of war guilt
Kr.Sp	Kriegsspiel	war game; map maneuver
Kr.St	Kriegsstärke	war strength
Kr.St.N	Kriegsstärkenachweisung	war strength record
Kr.Tb	Kriegstagebuch	war diary; station and record of events book
Kr.Tr.Abt	Krankentransportabteilung	ambulance detachment
Kr.Verl	Kriegsverluste	war casualties
Kr.W	Krankenwagen	ambulance
Krw.G	Kraftwagengeschütz	tractor-drawn gun
Kr.Z	Kriegsziel	aim of war
Kr.Zust	Kriegszustand	state of war
Ks	Kaserne	barracks
K.S	Kavallerieschule	cavalry school
K.San.Kp	Kraftwagensanitätskompanie	medical company (motorized)
Ksgr	Kiesgrube	gravel pit (*on maps*)
K.Sig	kleines Signalgerät	small signal apparatus
K.S.O	Kriegssanitätsordnung	war service regulations for medical corps
KSSVO	Kriegssonderstrafrechtsverordnung	special war penal decree
Kst	Küste, Küsten-	coast; coastal
Kst.Batt	Küstenbatterie	coast defense battery
Kst.H	Küstenhaubitze	coast defense howitzer
Kst.K	Küstenkanone	coast defense gun
Kst.L	Küstenlafette	coast defense mounting
Kst.Mrs	Küstenmörser	coast defense mortar
K.St.N	Kriegsstärkenachweisung	war strength record
K.S.V	Kriegssanitätsvorschrift	war sanitary regulations
K.T	Kabeltelegramm	cablegram
Kt	Kartätsche	case shot
Kt	Karte	map
K.T	Kolonialtauglichkeit	fitness for colonial service
K.T.B	Korpstagesbefehl	army corps order of the day
Ktn.Sk	Kartenskizze	map sketch
Kt.O	Krankenträgerordnung	stretcher-bearer regulations
K.Tr	Korpstruppen	army corps troops
Ktt.Br	Kettenbrücke	suspension bridge
Ku	Kuppe	knoll
Küst.Bttr	Küstenbatterie	coastal battery
K.u.F	Anleitung für den Kampf um Festungen	instructions for warfare on fortified positions
Kuppl	Kupplung	coupling; clutch
kv	kriegsverwendungsfähig	fit for war service
K.Verschl	Keilverschluss	wedge type of breechblock
K.Vet	Korpsveterinär	corps area veterinary
K.Vet.V	Kriegsveterinärvorschriften	army veterinary regulations
kv.f.b.Z	kriegsverwendungsfähig für besondere Zwecke	fit for war service for special purposes
KVL	Kriegsverbindungsleutnant	liaison lieutenant
K.V.O	Kraftfahrtruppenverbindungsoffizier	motor transport liaison officer
K.V.V	Kriegsverpflegungsvorschrift	wartime commissary regulations
K.W	Kartenwinkelmesser	map protractor
kW	Kilowatt	kilowatt
Kw	Kraftwagen	motor car
Kw.AH	Kraftwagenanhänger	trailer truck
Kw.-D	Kampfwagendivision	armored division
Kw.Flak	Kraftwagen-Flugzeugabwehrkanone	motorized antiaircraft gun
Kw.G	Kraftwagengeschütz	gun mounted on a truck
Kw.K	Kraftwagenkanone	tractor-drawn gun; gun mounted on truck
Kw.Kol	Kraftwagenkolonne	motor transport train
Kw.Werkst	Kraftwagenwerkstatt	motor repair shop
K.Z	Kanonenzünder	gun percussion fuze; cannon shell fuze; gun fuze
k.z	kommandiert zu, zur	ordered to (the); detailed to; detached to
K.Z	Konzentrationslager	concentration camp
Kz	Kopfzünder	point detonating fuze
Kz.Flak	Kraftzug-Flugzeugabwehrkanone	motorized antiaircraft gun
Kz.Laf	Kreuzlafette	outrigger-gun platform (*antiaircraft artillery*)

L

L	Ladung	charge; propelling charge;
L	Lafette	g. load age
L	Landes-	land; country; region
L	Landesverteidigung	home defense; national defense
L	Landsturm	reserve (*men over 45*)
L	Landwehr	reserve (*men between 35 and 45*)
l	lang	long
L	Lazarett	hospital
l	ledig	single (*unmarried*)
l	leicht	light
L	Leuchtgeschoss	flare shell
L	Leutnant	2d lieutenant
l	links	left
L	Luftfahrt	aeronautics; aviation

L.	Luftwaffe	air force
Lab.Fl.	Labeflasche	canteen
Ladg.	Ladung	charge; load
Lad.R.	Laderampe	loading ramp
Lad.R.	Laderaum	chamber (*artillery*)
Laf.	Lafette	gun carriage; mount
Lag.	Lager	camp; dump; depot; bearing
Landesvert.	Landesverteidigung	home defense; national defense
Landg.	Landegeschwindigkeit	
Landgs.	Landungs-	landing
L.A.O.	Anzugsordnung für die Luftwaffe	uniform regulations for the air force
L.Ap.	Löhnungsappell	pay call
l.Art.Abt.	leichte Artillerieabteilung	light artillery battalion
Latr.	Latrine	latrine
Laz.	Lazarett	hospital
Laz.Zg.	Lazarettzug	hospital train
l.b.	lange Brennlänge	long burning action (*fuse*)
Lb.	Libelle	level; spirit level
L.B.	Lichtbild	photograph
Lb.	Luftbild	aerial photograph
Lb.Flugzeug.	Flugzeug mit eingebauten Lichtbildgerät	plane with built-in camera
L.Br.	Leiter des Brückenschlages	chief engineer of bridge construction
L.Brig.	Luftbrigade	air brigade
Ld.	Land	country; land; state; region
Ld.	Landungs-	landing
LD.	Landwehrdivision	reserve division (*men between 35 and 45*)
Ldfrt.	Landfront	land front
Ldg.	Ladung	charge; propelling charge
Ldg.	Landungs-	landing
Ldg.Gesch.	Landungsgeschütz	landing gun
Ldg.H.	Landungshafen	landing port
Ldg.K.	Landungskorps	landing detachment; landing force
Ldg.Pl.	Landungsplatz	landing place; landing ground
Ldgs.	Landungs-	landing
L.Div.	Luftdivision	air division
L.Div.	Landwehrdivision	reserve division (*men between 35 and 45*)
L.d.L.	Leutnant der Landwehr	Landwehr (reserve) 2d lieutenant
L.d.R.	Leutnant der Reserve	reserve 2d lieutenant
Lds.	Landes-	land; country; regional
Ldsch.Btl.	Landesschützenbataillon	local defense battalion
Ldschtz.	Landesschützen	local defense unit
Lds.Pol.	Landespolizei	state police
Ldst.	Landsturm	reserve (*men over 45*)
Ldst.Btl.	Landsturmbataillon	Landsturm (reserve) battalion
Ldstm.	Landsturmmann	Landsturm man (*reservist over 45*)
Ld.Tr.	Landtransport	overland transportation
L.Dv.	Druckvorschrift für die Luftwaffe	service regulations for the air force
Ldw.	Landwehr	reservists (*men between 35 and 45*)
Ldw.Div.	Landwehrdivision	Landwehr (reserve) division
Ldw.Dstpfl.	Landwehrdienstpflicht	obligation for service in the Landwehr (reserve)
Ldw.IB.	Landwehrinfanteriebataillon	Landwehr (reserve) infantry battalion
Ldw.IR.	Landwehrinfanterieregiment	Landwehr (reserve) infantry regiment
Ldw.Rgt.	Landwehrregiment	Landwehr (reserve) regiment
le.	leicht	light
leb.Z.	lebendiges Ziel	living target
led.	ledig	single (*unmarried*)
Legit.	Legitimation	identification
legit.	legitimieren	to prove identity
Lehrg.	Lehrgang	training; course of instruction
Lehr-IB.	Lehrinfanteriebataillon	infantry training battalion
Lehrst.	Lehrstab	staff of instructors
le.I.G.	leichtes Infanteriegeschütz	light infantry gun
Leit.	Leiter	leader
le.Kp.Wass. Versorg	leichte Wasserversorgungskompanie	light company for water supply
le.Krad.	leichtes Kraftfahrrad	light motorcycle
L.E.Munition	Lufteinschiessmunition	tracer ammunition
L.Ers.I.	Luftwaffenersatzreserve I	draft registrants assigned to the air corps
l.Ex.M.	leichte Exerziermine	light training mine
l.Ex.m.R.	leichte Exerziermine mit Rauchladung	light training mine with smoke element
L.F.	Lafettenfahrzeug	gun carriage
lfde.	laufende	current
l.Fernspr.Tr.	leichter Fernsprechtrupp	light telephone operations squad
l.F.H.	leichte Feldhaubitze	light field howitzer
l.Fl.F.	vom linken Flügel Feuer	battery left (*artillery*)
Lfschr.	Laufschritt	double time (*march*)
l.F.Tr.	leichter Fernsprechtrupp	light telephone operations squad

Ladungsverhältnis *n* loading ratio (*ratio between weight of charge and weight of projectile*).
Ladungswerfer *m* spigot mortar.
Lafette *f* gun carriage, gun mount.
Lafettenachse *f* gun-carriage axle.
Lafettenart *f* type of gun carriage or mount.
Lafettenaufsatzstück *n* adapter, tripod extension piece (*MG*).
Lafettendreieck *n* triangular base (*AA gun*).
Lafettenfahrzeug *n* trailer mount (*Arty*).
Lafettenholm *m* gun-mount outrigger; gun-trail crosspiece.
Lafettenkasten *m* trail box (*G*).
Lafettenkranz *m* circular track mount (*Ap, Tk*).
Lafettenkreuz *n* outriggers (*AA gun*).
Lafettenschwanz *m* trail (*G*).
Lafettensporn *m* trail spade (*G*).
Lafettenstütze *f* firing base (*G*).
Lafettentisch *m* gun-carriage bed.
Lafettenwand *f* gun-carriage side plate.
Lage *f* situation (*Tac*); position, site; salvo (*pieces fire in succession*); layer, stratum (*Met*).
Lagebericht *m* situation report.
Lagebeurteilung *f* estimate of the situation (*Tac*).
Lagenfeuer *n* salvo fire (*pieces fire in succession*).
Lagenkarte *f* situation map (*Tac*).
Lagenmeldung *f* situation report.
Lager *n* camp; depot, dump; bearing, support.
das Lager abbrechen to strike camp.
das Lager aufschlagen to pitch camp.
Lagerbestand *m* stock, stockage.
Lagerbock *m* support (*for piston rod of counterrecoil mechanism*); pillow block.
Lagergehäuse *n* housing or case enclosing a bearing or bushing.
Lagergeld *n* pay (*PW*).
Lagergerüst *n* storage-closet rack.
Lagerhaus *n* warehouse.
Lagerkommandant *m* prison camp or internment camp commander.
Lagerleitung *f* camp authorities (*PW*).
Lagermetall *n* bearing metal.
Lagern *n* storage.
Lagerort *m* camp site.
Lagerplatz *m* storage place; camp site.
Lagerraum *m* storeroom.
Lagerschale *f* bushing.
Lagerschuppen *m* storage shed.
Lagerstelle *f* camp site.
Lagerung *f* storage, stowage.
Lagerzapfen *m* journal (*crankshaft*); pivot pin (*trail spade*); trunnion (*aiming circle*).
lähmen paralyze, immobilize, neutralize (*Tac*).
lahmlegen neutralize (*an attack*).
Lahmlegung *f* neutralization (*Tac*).
Lähmungsschießen *n* harassing fire (*with Cml shell*).
Lamelle *f* disk; leaf; plate; shim; cooling fin.
Lamellenkupplung *f* multiple-disk clutch (*MT*).
Lamellenschluß *m* armature short (*Elec*).
Lampenfassung *f* lamp socket (*Elec*).
Lampengehäuse *n* lamp case (*Sig lamp*).
Landankertau *n* shore anchor line (*Pon Bdg*).
Landbatterie *f* land-based antiaircraft battery (*as distinguished from ship-based battery*).
Landbord *m* shoreward side.
Landbrücke *f* landing stage (*Engr*).
Landebahn *f* landing strip, runway.
Landebahnfeuer *n* contact light (*Adrm*).
Landedeck *n* landing deck, flight deck (*aircraft carrier*).
Landefackel *f* wing-tip flare (*Ap*).
Landefeuer *n* landing light (*Ap*).
Landefunkfeuer *n* runway localizing beacon (*Rad*).
Landegeschwindigkeit *f* landing speed
Landeklappe *f* landing flap (*Ap*).
Landekopf *m* beachhead.
Landekreuz *n* landing T (*Avn*)
Landelicht *n* landing light (*Ap*).
Landemannschaft *f* ground crew *Bln*).
Landeplatz *m* landing area, landing field (*Avn*).
Landesaufnahme *f* topographic survey, geodetic survey.
landeseigener Verband "native" unit (*composed of inhabitants of German-occupied country who fight, on their own soil, as auxiliaries of German Army*).
Landesschützeneinheit *f* regional defense unit (*such as* Landesschützendivision, -regiment, -bataillon, and -kompanie; *mainly for guard duty in Com Z and Z of I*).

Landesteg *m* landing ramp (*Nav*).
Landesverrat *m* treason.
Landesverteidigung *f* home defense.
Landetrupp *m* landing and saddling detail (*at stream crossing*) (*Cav*).
Landezeichen *n* landing signal.
Landezone *f* landing zone (*Adrm*).
Landfahrwerk *n* wheel-type landing gear (*Ap*).
Landfahrzeug *n* land vehicle; shoreward ponton (*Bdg*).
Landkrieg *m* war on land, land warfare.
Landkriegsordnung *f* Rules of Land Warfare.
Landmeile *f* statute mile (1.609 *km*).
Landmine *f* land mine.
Landser *m* doughboy.
Landstraße *f* road, highway.
Landsturm *m* territorial reserve, replacement reserves (*age over 45*).
Landsturm I trained reserves (*age over 45*).
Landsturm II untrained reserves (*age over 45*).
Landtruppen *fpl* ground troops.
Landung *f* landing.
Landung mit Seitenwind cross-wind landing.
Landungsabteilung *f* beach party or detachment.
Landungsboot *n* landing barge, landing boat.
Landungsfahrzeug *n* landing craft.
Landungsklappe *f* landing ramp (*of a landing craft or ship*).
Landungsplatz *m* landing area.
Landungsrauchzeichen *n* landing smoke signal (*Avn*).
Landungstrupp *m* landing party.
Landungsunternehmung *f* landing operation.
Landverankerung *f* guy-line anchorage (*Pon*).
Landwehr *f* reserves (*age group* 35-45).
Landwehr I trained reserves (35-45).
Landwehr II untrained reserves (35-45).
Landwehroffizier *m* reserve officer. *See* **Landwehr.**
Langbasis *f* horizontal base (*Arty, Surv*).
Langbasisanlage *f* base end station.
Langbasisverfahren *n* horizontal base method, long base method (*Gunnery*).
Länge *f* length.
der Länge nach beschießen to enfilade.
Längenabweichung *f* longitudinal deviation, range deviation (*Gunnery*).
Festlegen der Längenabweichung range sensing, range spotting (*Arty Obsn*).
Längengrad *m* degree of longitude.
Längenkreis *m* circle of longitude.
Längenmessung *f* linear measurement.
Längenstreuung *f* range dispersion on horizontal target (*Ballistics*).
Längenverbesserung *f* range correction (*Gunnery*).
Längenverhältnis *n* aspect ratio (*Ap*).
Länge über alles over-all length.
Längsachse *f* longitudinal axis.
Langsamflug *m* stalling flight (*Ap*).
Längsbestreichung *f* enfilade fire.
Längsfeld *n* chase of gun barrel.
Längsfeuer *n* enfilade fire.
Längslibelle *f* longitudinal level (*sighting mechanism*).
Längsneigungsmesser *m* pitch indicator, fore-and-aft inclinometer (*Ap*).
Längsschnitt *m* longitudinal section.
Längsseitgehen *n* pulling alongside.
Längsstabilität *f* longitudinal stability (*Ap*).
Längsträger *m* stringer, balk (*Bdg*); longitudinal outrigger (*AA gun*); longeron (*Ap*); long channel bar of chassis frame (*MT*).
Langstreckenbomber *m* long-range bomber.
Langstreckenjäger *m* long-range fighter airplane.
Langstrecken-Seeflugzeug *n* long-range seaplane.
Längszapfen *m* axle pivot pin (*split trail carriage*).
Langwellen *fpl* long waves (*Rad*).
Langwellenpeiler *m* long-wave direction finder (*Rad*).
Lasche *f* butt strap (*Engr*).
Last *f* load.
Lastanhänger *m* truck trailer (*MT*).
Lastensegelflugzeug *n* *See* **Lastensegler.**
Lastensegler *m* troop-carrying glider, cargo-carrying glider.
Lastfallschirm *m* cargo parachute.
Lastflugzeug *n* cargo transport airplane.
Lastigkeitsregelung *f* trimming (*Ap*).
Lastigkeitswaage *f* balance indicator (*Ap*).
Lastkraftwagen *m* truck, cargo truck.

Lastwagenschlepper *m* truck-tractor.
Latte *f* batten, lath, board; propeller (*Ap*); stadia rod (*Surv*).
Lattenführung *f* pitch control (*propeller*).
Lattenpunkt *m* place mark (*Surv*).
Lattenrost *m* boardwalk, duckboard (*trench*).
Laubwald *m* deciduous forest, deciduous wood.
Lauerstellung *f* ambush gun emplacement, ambush.
Lauf *m* barrel (*MG, R*); run, course.
Laufbahn *f* career (*as an officer, specialist, etc.*); runway (*Adrm*).
Laufbahnabzeichen *n* specialist's insignia or badge.
Laufbrücke *f* gangplank.
Laufdecke *f* tire casing (*MT*).
laufend running; current; continuous; serial.
laufende Nummer serial number.
Läufer *m* runner, messenger.
Lauffläche *f* tread (*of a tire*); sliding surface (*of a sled runner*) bearing surface, friction surface.
Laufgraben *m* approach trench, communication trench.
Laufinneres *n* bore (*SA*).
Laufmantel *m* jacket (*MG*).
Laufmundstück *n* breech piece (*R*).
Laufrad *n* landing wheel (*Ap*); bogie wheel (*Tk*); impeller (*of pump, etc.*).
Laufring *m* race (*ball bearing*).
Laufrolle *f* bogie wheel (*Tk*).
Laufschritt *m* double time.
"Im Laufschritt, Marsch! Marsch!" "Double time, march!"
Laufseele *f* bore (*SA*).
Laufseelenprüfer *m* barrel reflector (*SA*).
Laufsitzring *m* barrel-locking ring (*MG*)
Laufweite *f* caliber.
Laufwerk *n* tracks and suspensions (*Tk*); running gear (*of a vehicle*).
Laufwerkpanzerung *f* track shield, armored skirting (*Tk*).
Lauschdienst *m* intercept service (*Sig C*).
Lauschempfänger *m* intercept receiver (*Sig C*).
Lauschgerät *n* intercept set (*Rad*).
Lauschstelle *f* intercept station (*Sig C*).
Lauschzange *f* wire-tapping clamp.
Lauthörknopf *m* handset switch, amplifier knob (*Tp*).
Lautsprecher *m* loudspeaker (*Rad*).
Lautsprechertrichter *m* horn, cone, trumpet (*of loud speaker*).
Lautsprechertruhe *f* baffle, speaker cabinet (*Rad*).
Lautstärke *f* signal strength, volume, readability (*Rad*); sound intensity (*sound locator*).
Lautstärkenregler *m* volume control (*Rad*).
Lautverstärker *m* volume amplifier (*Rad*).
Lazarett *n* hospital.
Lazarettaufnahme *f* hospitalization.
Lazarettbehandlung *f* hospital treatment, hospitalization.
Lazarettflagge *f* flag of protection.
Lazarettschiff *n* hospital ship.
Lazarettzug *m* hospital train.
Lebensdauer *f* accuracy life (*G*).
Lebensmittel *npl* subsistence supplies.
Lebensmittelkarte *f* food ration card.
Lederfett *n* dubbin.
Lederring *m* *See* **Lederscheibe.**
Lederscheibe *f* leather washer.
Ledertasche *f* leather case, leather bag.
Leere *f* vacuum.
Leergang *m* backlash, lost motion; neutral gear (*Mtr*).
Leergewicht *m* empty weight.
Leergut *n* empties (*Am*).
Leerlauf *m* idling, neutral, idling speed (*Mtr*).
Leerlaufdüse *f* idler jet (*Mtr*).
Leermaterial *n* train of empties (*RR*).
Leerschraube *f* drain plug.
Legierung *f* alloy.
Legionsschütze *m* non-German rifleman in the *Wehrmacht*.
Lehmgrube *f* clay pit.
Lehrbataillon *n* instruction battalion (*used for demonstrations, etc.*).
Lehre *f* doctrine, theory; gage.
Lehrfilm *m* training film.
Lehrflugwesen *n* training aviation.
Lehrgang *m* course of instruction.
Lehrgangsleiter *m* instructor.
Lehrgruppe *f* instruction group
Lehrregiment *n* instruction regiment (*used for demonstrations, etc.*).
Lehrtruppe *f* instruction unit.
Leibgarde *f* bodyguard.
Leibgurt *m* belt (*Clo*).
Leibgurt mit Schulterriemen Sam Browne belt.
Leibriemen *m* garrison belt (*Clo*).
Leibstandarte *f* *See* **SS-Leibstandarte.**
Leibwache *f* bodyguard.
Leiche *f* corpse; carcass.
leichte Division motorized division, "light division."

Leichtkrankenkriegslazarett *n* base hospital for minor cases *(Com Z)*.

Leichtkrankenschiff *n* hospital ship for minor cases.

Leichtkrankenzug *m* hospital train for minor cases.

Leichtkranker *m* ambulatory case, minor case *(sick, not wounded)*.

Leichtöl *n* light fuel *(as distinguished from Diesel fuel)*.

Leichtverwundetensammelplatz *m* collecting station for walking wounded.

Leichtverwundeter *m* minor casualty.

Leinenbund *n* rope lashing.

Leinöl *n* linseed oil.

Leinwand *f* linen; cloth; projection screen.

Leiste *f* strip; edge; fillet; batten.

Leistenbruch *m* hernia.

Leistengegend *f* groin.

Leistung *f* output, performance, capacity; power *(Rad)*.

Leistungsbelastung *f* power loading

Leistungsfähigkeit *f* efficiency, capacity.

Leistungsgewicht *n* weight per horsepower.

Leistungsregler *m* power control

Leistungsröhre *f* power amplifier

Leistungssegelflugzeug *n* performance-type glider *(Avn)*.

Leistungssteigerung *f* increase of efficiency *(Mtr)*.

Leistungsstufe *f* power amplifier, final amplifier *(of a Rad transmit-*

Leistungswählhebel *m* output selector lever *(Ap engine)*.

leiten conduct, lead, direct, manage.

Leitender *m* director *(maneuvers)*.

Leitender Arzt ward officer *(Med)*.

Leitender Ingenieur chief engineer *(a Civ official in the Armed Forces)*.

Leitender Offizier executive officer.

Leiter *m* leader, director; conductor *(Elec)*.

Leiter *f* ladder.

Leiterschleife *f* armature turn

Leitfähigkeit *f* conductivity *(Elec)*.

Leitfeuer *n* cord fuze, safety fuze.

Leitfeuerzündmittel *n* cord fuze detonator.

Leitfeuerzündung *f* cord fuze detonation.

Leitfunkstelle *f* net control station *(Rad)*.

Leitkante *f* leading edge *(Ap wing)*.

Leitrad *n* idler, idler wheel *(Tk)*; diffuser *(supercharger)*.

Leitradachse *f* idler wheel shaft

Leitstand *m* fire-direction center *(Arty)*; command post.

Leitstelle *f* net control station

Leitstrahl *m* localizer beam *(Inst landing)*.

Leitstrahlverfahren *n* localizer-beam method *(Inst landing)*.

Leitung *f* line *(Tp)*; command; direction; control; management.

Leitungsbau *m* line construction

Leitungsgehilfe *m* director's aide *(maneuvers)*.

Leitungskapazität *f* capacity of a line, traffic capacity of a line *(Elec, Tp, Tg)*.

Leitungsmast *m* telephone pole.

Leitungsmaterial *n* conducting material, electric wire.

Leitungsmittel *n* line wire *(Tp)*.

Leitungsnetz *n* wire net, circuit, wiring system, wire-communication

Leitungsoffizier *m* assistant director *(maneuvers)*.

Leitungsplan *m* wiring diagram.

Leitungsprüfer *m* galvanometer *(Engr)*; circuit tester *(Elec)*.

Leitungsskizze *f* circuit diagram

Leitungssondertruppen *fpl* special troops of director headquarters *(maneuvers)*.

Leitungsstab *m* directing staff *(maneuvers)*.

Leitungssystem *n* wiring system

Leitungstruppen *fpl* troops assigned to director headquarters *(maneuvers)*.

Leitungs- und Schiedsrichterdienst *m* directing and umpiring service *(maneuvers)*.

Leitungswiderstand *m* line resistance *(Elec)*.

Leitverkehr *m* control-station traffic *(Rad)*.

Leitwand *f* baffle.

Leitwellverschluß *m* sliding-wedge-type breechblock *(G)*.

Leitwerk *n* empennage, tail assembly, tail unit *(Ap)*.

Leitwert *m* conductance *(Elec)*.

Leitzaun *m* guide fence *(a type of snow fence)*.

Lenden *fpl* loins *(horse)*.

Lenkballon *m* dirigible

Lenkbremse *f* steering brake *(Tk)*.

Lenkeinrichtung *f* steering mechanism.

Lenkeinschlag *m* maximum angle of turn *(steering wheels)*.

Lenker *m* steering arm *(of a gun wheel)*.

Lenkgehäuse *n* steering-gear housing *(MT)*.

Lenkgestänge *n* tie rods *(MT)*.

Lenkgetriebe *n* steering mechanism *(track-laying vehicles)*.

Lenkhebel *m* steering-knuckle gear-rod arm *(MT)*; steering lever *(track-laying vehicle)*.

Lenkknüppel *m* steering lever *(track-laying vehicle)*.

Lenkluftschiff *n* dirigible.

Lenkrad *n* steering wheel *(MT)*.

Lenksäule *f* steering column *(MT)*.

Lenkschnecke *f* steering worm

Lenkschraube *f* cylindrical cam on steering column *(MT)*.

Lenkschubstange *f* steering gear connecting rod *(MT)*.

Lenksegment *n* steering-worm sector *(MT)*.

Lenkstange *f* tie rod *(MT)*; handle bar *(Mtcl)*.

Lenkstock *m* See **Lenkstockhebel.**

Lenkstockhebel *m* steering arm

Lenkstoßfang *m* steering shock suspension *(MT)*.

Lenkung *f* steering, steering system *(MT)*.

Lettenhaue *f* mattock hoe *(Engr)*.

leuchtbereit ready for action *(SL)*.

Leuchtblatt *n* luminous dial.

Leuchtboje *f* light buoy.

Leuchtbombe *f* aircraft parachute flare.

Leuchtdauer *f* burning time *(of a ground Sig, etc.)*.

Leuchtfallschirm *m* parachute flare *(Avn)*.

Leuchtfarbe *f* luminous paint.

Leuchtfeuer *n* beacon light *(Avn)*.

Leuchtgeschoß *n* See **Leuchtgranate.**

Leuchtgranate *f* star shell *(Am)*.

Leuchtgranatwerfer *m* pyrotechnic projector.

Leuchtkompaß *m* luminous compass.

Leuchtkreuze *npl* reticle image *(reflector sight)*.

Leuchtkugel *f* ground signal, Very signal light.

Leuchtmittel *n* pyrotechnic device.

Leuchtmunition *f* pyrotechnics; tracer ammunition.

Leuchtpatrone *f* signal case; signal cartridge; cartridge-type ground signal.

Leuchtpfad *m* flare path *(Avn)*.

Leuchtpistole *f* pyrotechnic pistol, signal pistol, Very pistol.

Leuchtrakete *f* signal rocket.

Leuchtraketengestell *n* pyrotechnic projector *(for Sig rockets)*.

Leuchtröhre *f* fluorescent tube.

Leuchtsatz *m* pyrotechnic composition, flare composition, illuminant charge; tracer composition.

Leuchtschiff *n* lightship.

Leuchtspur *f* tracer trajectory.

Leuchtspurgeschoß *n* tracer bullet, tracer.

Leuchtspurgranate *f* tracer shell

Leuchtspurmunition *f* tracer ammunition.

Leuchtspursatz *m* tracer composition *(Am)*.

Leuchtstern *m* star *(signal)*.

Leuchttonne *f* light buoy.

Leuchtturm *m* lighthouse.

Leuchtvisier *n* luminous sight.

Leuchtzeichen *n* ground signal, light signal.

Leuchtzifferblatt *n* luminous dial *(Inst)*.

Leukoplast *n* court plaster.

Leute *fpl* personnel.

Leutnant *m* second lieutenant; lieutenant *(specifically, 2nd Lt)*.

Leutnant der Flieger second lieutenant *(Luftwaffe)*.

Leutnant zur See ensign *(Nav)*.

Lewisit *n* Lewisite *(CWS)*.

Libelle *f* level *(Inst)*; clinometer *(Arty, Surv)*.

die Libelle einspielen to center the bubble in a level.

Libelleneinstellung *f* level setting, level adjustment.

Libellengehäuse *n* level housing *(panoramic telescope)*.

Libellenquadrant *m* gunner's quadrant *(with spirit level)*.

"Licht auf!" "In action!" *(AA SL)*.

Lichtbild *n* photograph.

Lichtbildaufnahme *f* See **Lichtbild.**

Lichtbildauswertung *f* interpretation of photographs.

lichtbilden to photograph.

Lichtbildentzerrung *f* rectification of aerial photographs.

Lichtbilderkundung *f* photographic reconnaissance.

Lichtbildmaschinengewehr *n* machine-gun camera.

Lichtbildmessung *f* phototopography.

Lichtbild-MG *n* camera gun *(Avn)*.

Lichtbildner *m* photographer.

Lichtbildpause *f* photographic overlay.

Lichtbildwesen *n* photography.

Lichtbogenschweißung *f* arc welding.

Lichtkegel *m* beam of light, cone of light.

Lichtmaschine *f* generator *(MT)*.

Lichtmeßbatterie *f* flash ranging section *(Obsn Bn)*.

Lichtmeßdienst *m* flash ranging service.

Lichtmessen *n* flash ranging.

Lichtmeßstelle *f* flash ranging station.

Lichtmeßtrupp *m* flash ranging team.

Lichtnetz *n* lighting system.

Lichtpause *f* photostatic reproduction; photocopy; blueprint.

Lichtrufanlage *f* light-signal call system *(in hospitals, etc.)*.

Lichtschallmessen *n* sound and flash ranging.

Lichtschalter *m* light switch.

Lichtsprechgerät *n* modulated light-ray communication set.

Lichtspruch *m* signal-lamp message.

Lichtspur- See **Leuchtspur-.**

Lichtstärke *f* luminous intensity, intensity of light.

Lichtung *f* forest clearing.

lidern to pack, seal, obturate.

Liderung *f* gas check, obturator (G).

Liderungskopf *m* mushroom head *(of obturator)*.

Liderungspolster *n* gas-check pad.

Lieferant *m* supplier, contractor.

Lieferdienst *m* ferrying service

Lieferschein *m* shipping ticket.

Lieferung *f* lot, shipment.

liegend prone, lying; berthed.

Liegeplatz *m* berth *(in port)*.

Linealvisier *n* linear sight *(Ger AA gun)*.

lineares System linear speed method *(AA Gunnery)*.

Linie *f* line, rank.

"In Linie zu einem Gliede, angetreten!" "In single rank, fall in!"

Linie B-Stelle-Ziel OP-target line.

Linie Geschütz-Ziel gun-target line.

Linienaufstellung *f* line formation.

Linienbö *f* line squall.

Linienkarte *f* line route map *(Tp)*.

Linienverkehr *m* "line" traffic *(two-station Rad Com on one or two frequencies)*.

Linie zu einem Glied single rank *(Inf)*; line *(Cav)*.

links left, to the left, on the left.

Linkskurve *f* left turn *(MT)*; left bank *(Avn)*.

linkslaufend counterclockwise.

Linksdrall *m* left-hand twist *(rifling)*.

linksgängig counterclockwise; left-hand *(threads, etc.)*.

Linksgewinde *n* left-hand thread

linkslaufend counterclockwise.

"Links schwenkt, Marsch!" "Column left, march!"

"Links, um!" "Left, face!" *(being at a halt)*; "By the left flank, march!" *(given in marching)*.

Linkswendung *f* left face.

Linse *f* lens.

List *f* cunning, ruse, trick; stratagem *(Tac)*.

Litze *f* stranded wire *(Elec)*; colored facing on collar *(Clo)*.

Litzenspiegel *m* two narrow colored strips on collar *(Clo)*.

Livens-Handwerfer *m* Livens projector *(CWS)*.

l.M.G.-Abmarsch *m* light MG half squad *(Cav)*.

l.M.G.-Trupp *m* light machine-gun team *(of Ger R squad)*.

Ln.-Helferin *f* See **Luftnachrichten-Helferin.**

Ln.-Zugführer *m* See **Luftnachrichten-Zugführer.**

Locken *n* call to quarters.

Löffelbagger *m* power shovel.

Löhnung *f* base pay.

Lokomotivbahnhof *m* engine yard

Lokomotivschuppen *m* engine house, roundhouse *(RR)*.

Looping *m* loop *(Avn)*.

Losantin *n* a German decontaminating agent *(calcium hypochlorite preparation in powder or in tablet form)*.

Losantinbrei *m* calcium hypochlorite slurry *(CWS)*.

löschen to unload *(a ship)*; to extinguish *(a fire)*; to slake *(lime)*.

Löschflüssigkeit *f* extinguisher fluid.

Löschgerät *n* fire extinguisher.

Löschmeister *m* sergeant fireman *(Luftwaffe official ranking as Master Sgt)*.

Löschplatz *m* pier, wharf.

Löschtrupp *m* fire-fighting crew.

lose loose, unlocked.

loslösen, sich disengage *(Tac)*.

Loslösung *f* disengagement *(Tac)*.

Lost *n* mustard gas.

Losung *f* password.

Lösung *f* solution; mixture.

Lösungsmittel *n* solvent.

Losungswort password, countersign

Lot plumb bob, sounding lead; solder.

löten to solder.

Lotfe *n* See **Lofternrohr.**

Lotfernrohr *n* bomb sight.

Lötkolben *m* soldering iron.

Lötlampe *f* blowtorch.

Lftsp	Luftspäher	air scout
Lftsp	Luftsperre	balloon barrage
Lftw	Luftwaffe	air force
l.Fu.Ger.Wg.	Gerätewagen für leichtes Funkgerät	equipment car for light radio apparatus
l.Fu.Wg	Funkwagen für leichtes Funkgerät	radio car for light wireless set
Lfw	Luftfahrwesen	aeronautics; aviation
Lg	Länge	length
lg	lang	long
Lg	Leuchtgeschoss	flare shell
L.G	Luftgau	air territorial district
lg.Bd.Z	langer Bodenzünder	long base percussion fuze
L.Gesch	Leuchtgeschoss	flare shell
lg.F.H.Gr	lange Feldhaubitzgranate	long field howitzer shell
lg.F.H.Gr.(N)	lange Feldhaubitzgranate (Nebel)	long field howitzer shell (smoke)
Lggr	Langgranate	long shell
Lgr	Lager	camp; dump; depot; bearing
l.Gr.W	leichter Granatwerfer	light mortar
Lg.Zdr	Leuchtsgeschosszünder	flare shell fuze
l.Hb	leichte Haubitze	light howitzer
Li	Lichtmessbatterie	flash ranging battery
Lib	Libelle	spirit-level
l.I.G	leichtes Infanteriegeschütz	light infantry gun
Lin	Linie	line
L.Inf.Batl	Lehrinfanteriebataillon	infantry training battalion
L.Inf.R	Lehrinfanterieregiment	infantry training regiment
l.Inf.Wff	leichte Infanteriewaffen	light infantry weapons
Li.Off	Lichtsignaloffizier	lamp signal officer
L.I.R	Lehrinfanterieregiment	infantry training regiment
L.I.R.	Landwehrinfanterieregiment	Landwehr (reserve) infantry regiment
Li.Sign.Off	Lichtsignaloffizier	lamp signal officer
l.K	leichte Kolonne	light column
L.K	Luftkühlung	air cooling
L.Kg	Leuchtkugel	rocket; flare
l.Kol	Leerkolonne	column of empty trucks or cars
l.Kol.Br	leichte Kolonnenbrücke	bridge for carrying troops in file
l.Kpfw	leichter Kampfwagen	light tank
L.Kr	Landkrieg	land warfare
Lkr	Lastkraftwagen	truck
L.Kr	Leichtkrankenzug	hospital train for slightly wounded
L.Kr.AK	Luftkriegsakademie	air force staff school
L.Kr.Sch	Luftkriegsschule	air force school
L.Kt	Landkarte	map
Lkw	Lastkraftwagen	truck
Lkw.f.Betr.& Gerät	Lastkraftwagen für Betriebsstoff und Gerät	motor truck for fuel and equipment
Lkw.f.Fsp.Bau	Lastkraftwagen für Fernsprechbauzug	motor truck for telephone installation platoon
Lkw.f.Fsp.St.Z	Lastkraftwagen für Fernsprechstationszug	motor truck for telephone station platoon
l.K.Z	langer Kanonenzünder	long cannon fuze
l.Lkw	leichter Lastkraftwagen	light truck
L.L.T	Luftlandungstruppen	airborne troops
l.m	Länge eines Flugzeuges in Metern	length of an airplane in meters
l.M.A	leichte Munitionsabteilung	light ammunition detachment
l.mech	leicht mechanisiert	light mechanized
l.M.G	leichtes Maschinengewehr.	light machine gun
l.mot	leicht motorisiert	light motorized
l.mot.Kp	leichte motorisierte Kompanie	light motorized company
L.Mssg	Lichtmessung	flash-ranging
L.M.Tr	Lichtmesstrupp	flash-ranging detail
L.M.V	Lichtmessverfahren	flash-ranging process
l.M.W	leichter Minenwerfer	light mortar
l.Nachr.Ger.K	leichte Nachrichtengerätekolonne	light signal equipment train
Ln.Tr	Luftnachrichtentruppe	air signal troops
lok	lokal	local
Lok	Lokomotive	railroad engine; locomotive
Los	Losung, Losungswort	password
Los.W	Losungswort	password
LP	Landespolizei	state police
L.Pi.Kp. (mot)	Lehr- und Versuchs-Pionierkompanie (motorisiert)	combat engineers training and experimental company (motorized)
Lpl	Ladeplatz	loading place; loading point (*on maps*)
L.P.O	leitender Pionieroffizier	officer in charge of combat engineers (*bridge construction*)
L.Rgt	Luftregiment	regiment of the air force
Ls	Luftschutz	antiaircraft defense
Lsch.Ger	Lauschgerät	listening equipment (*telephone*)
L.Schm	Lehrschmiede	horseshoer's school
L.Sch.Wd	Luftschutzwarndienst	air raid warning service
Lsg	Losungswort	password
L.S.Gesch	Leuchtspurgeschoss	tracer bullet
Lsp	Luftsport	air sport
l.Splitt	leichte Splitterbombe	light splinter bomb; light fragmentation bomb
l.Spr.M	leichte Sprengmine	light blast mine
L.Spur	Leuchtspur	tracer bullet trajectory
L.Stg	Lauerstellung	hidden gun emplacement

Lstr	Landstrasse	highway
lt	laut	according to
L.T	Leuchtturm	lighthouse (*on maps*)
Lt	Leutnant	2d lieutenant
Ltg	Leitung	control; line (*electricity*); administration
L.Th	Lichtmesstheodolit	flash-ranging theodolite
Ltn	Leutnant	2d lieutenant
Luftber	Luftbereit	provided with pneumatic tires
Luftf	Luftfahrt	aviation
Luftna.Tr	Luftnachrichtentruppe	air signal troops
Luftvert	Luftverteidigung	air defense
Luftwi	Luftwiderstand	air resistance
luth	lutherisch	Lutheran
Lv	Ladungsverhältnis	ratio of charge to weight of projectile
L.V	Lautverstärker	amplifier
l.v	leicht verwundet	slightly wounded
l.v	links vorbei	over and to the left
LVBl	Luftverordnungsblatt	air raid protection bulletin
L.Vert	Landesverteidigung	home defense; national defense
L.V.S.St	Leichtverwundetensammelstelle	collecting point for slightly wounded
Lw	Luftwaffe	air force
Lwg	Lastwagen	truck
Lwk	Leitwerk	trail unit; empennage; tail assembly (*aviation*)
L.W.M	leichte Wurfmine	light mine (light mortar shell)
L.W.M.Z	leichter Wurfminenzünder	light mine fuze (*on mortar shell*)
L Z	Lazarettzug	hospital train

M

M	Magazin	magazine; store; dump; depot
M	Magazinverpflegung	depot food supply; provisioning by supply depot
M	Main	the river Main
M	Major	major
M	Mann, Männer	man (soldier), men
M	Manöver	maneuver
M	Mark	mark (*coin*); model; mark
M	Maschine	machine; engine
M	Maschinist	machinist
M	Maske	(gas) mask
M	Medaille	medal
m	mehr	more; additional
M	Messmann	range finder (*infantryman*)
M	Messpunkt	midpoint (*antiaircraft*)
m	Meter	meter
m	militär	military
M	Mine	mine
m	mit	with
M	Mitglied	member
M	Mitteilung	message; report; information
M	Mitteldecker	midwing monoplane
m	mittlerer	medium; mean; average
M	Mörser	mortar
m	monatlich	monthly
M	Motor	motor; engine
M	Mühle	mill (*on maps*)
M	Munitions-	ammunition
M	Muster	pattern; model; sample
m^2	Quadratmeter	square meter
m^3	Kubikmeter	cubic meter
M.17, M.18,	(Gas-) Masken von 1917, 1918 und 1924	(gas) masks of 1917, 1918, and 1924
ma	magnetisch	magnetic
Ma	Mannschaftsunterstand auf dem Handgranatenwurfstand	shelter on hand grenade practice range
M.A	Meldeamt	draft and inactive reserve registration office; message center
Ma	Militärarrestanstalt	
M.A	Militärattaché	military attaché
MA	Mitarbeiter	co-worker
M.A	Mondaufgang	moonrise
Ma	Munitionsanstalt	ammunition loading factory
M.A.A	Militärische Stelle der Nachrichtenabteilung des Auswärtigen Amts,	Military Department of the Intelligence Section of the Foreign Office
M.A.B	militärische Ausführungsbestimmungen	military regulations for execution (of orders)
M.Abw.St	Meldeabwurfstelle	message dropping center
Ma.C	Munitionsanstalt Cassel	ammunition loading factory, Cassel
Ma.F	Mastfernrohr	large observation telescope on special mount
Mag	Magazin	magazine; store; dump; depot (*on maps*)
Mag.Fp.Kol	Magazinfuhrparkkolonne	depot supply train
Mag.Gew	Magazingewehr	magazine rifle
magn	magnetisch	magnetic
Mag.Tasche	Magazintasche am Maschinengewehr Dreyse	magazine pocket of the Dreyse light machine gun

Lötmetall *m* solder.
lotrecht perpendicular.
Lotrechte *f* perpendicular *(line)*.
Lotschnur *f* plumb line.
Lotse *m* pilot *(Nav)*.
Lotsenflagge *f* Union Jack *(Nav)*.
Lötzinn *n* solder.
Loxodrome *f* rhumb line *(Navigation)*.
L'Spur *f* *See* **Leuchtspur.**
Lücke *f* gap.
Luft *f* air *(in compounds: Air Forces, airborne, aircraft, aviation, etc.). See also terms under* **Flieger, Flug.**
Luftabflußklappen *fpl* cowling flaps.
Luftabwehr *f* active air defense.
Luftabwehrdienst air defense service.
Luftabwehrstelle *f* air defense post.
Luftabwehrwaffe *f* antiaircraft weapon.
Luftalarm *m* air-raid alarm.
Luftamt *n* *See* **Allgemeines Luftamt.**
Luftangriff *m* air attack, air raid.
Luftangriffsziel *n* air objective.
Luftanreicherung *f* concentration of gas in the air *(CWS)*.
Luftaufklärung *f* air reconnaissance.
Luftaufklärungsraum *m* air reconnaissance area.
Luftaufsichtsdienst *m* flight control service *(a branch of the Ger Air Ministry)*.
Luftausgleicher *m* pneumatic equilibrator *(G)*.
Luftbauamt *n* Air Ministry construction office.
Luftbehälter *m* compressed-air tank *(Engr, MT)*; air chamber *(counter-recoil mechanism, vehicle brake)*.
Luftbehälter des Vorholers recuperator cylinder *(G)*.
Luftbeobachtung *f* air observation.
Luftbild *n* aerial photograph.
Luftbildauswertung *f* interpretation of aerial photographs.
Luftbildentzerrung *f* rectification of aerial photographs.
Luftbildgerät *n* aircraft camera.
Luftbildkammer *f* aerial camera, aircraft camera.
Luftbildkarte *f* aerial mosaic; photographic map.
Luftbildplan *m* photomap.
Luftbildreihe *f* photographic strip.
Luftbildwesen *n* aerial photography.
luftdicht airtight.
Luftdichte *f* air density.
Luftdienstzulage *f* aviation pay, flying pay.
Luftdraht *m* antenna wire, overhead antenna.
Luftdruck *m* air pressure *(Mech)*; atmospheric pressure *(Met)*; blast *(effect of explosion)*.
Luftdruckbremse *f* air brake.
Luftdruck-Fettpresse *f* grease gun.
Luftdruckgradient *m* pressure gradient *(Met)*.
Luftdruckmesser *m* barometer.
Luftdrucktür *f* blast baffle *(Ft)*.
Luftdruckwirkung *f* blast effect.
Luftdüse *f* air jet *(Mtr)*.
Lufteinschießziel *n* high-burst adjustment target *(Arty)*.
lüften to air, to ventilate.
Lüfter *m* ventilator, fan, blower.
Lufterkundung *f* air reconnaissance.
Luftfahrt *f* aeronautics, aviation.
Luftfahrthindernis *n* airway obstruction.
Luftfahrtmedizin *f* aviation medicine.
Luftfahrtministerium *n* *See* **Reichsluftfahrtministerium.**
Luftfahrwesen *n* aeronautics.
Luftfahrzeug *n* aircraft.
Luftfelddivision *f* air forces field division *(fighting as ground force with Army)*.
Luftfilter *m* air filter.
Luftflasche *f* compressed-air cylinder, oxygen flask.
Luftflotte *f* air force *(a territorial and tactical command of the Luftwaffe)*.
Luftflottenchef *m* air force commander. *See also* **Luftflotte.**
Luftgau *m* air force administrative command *(administrative area of a Luftflotte)*.
Luftgaukommado *n* air force administrative command headquarters. *See also* **Luftgau, Luftflotte.**
Luftgegner *m* hostile aircraft.
luftgekühlt air-cooled.
Luftgeschwader *n* *See* **Geschwader.**
Luftgewicht *n* density of the air.
ballistisches Luftgewicht ballistic density.
Lufthafenbereichkommandantur *f* airdrome regional command *(subdivision of a* Luftgau*)*.
Luftherrschaft *f* air supremacy, mastery of the air, control of air.
Luttnoheit *f* air sovereignty.
Luftinfanterie *f* airborne infantry.
Luftkabel *n* overhead wire *(Tp)*.
Luftkampf *m* air fighting, air attack.
Luftkampfgeschwader *n* bombardment wing. *See also* **Geschwader.**
Luftkampfstoff *m* volatile chemical agent *(as distinguished from* Geländekampfstoff, *ground contaminating agent)*.

Luftkampfübung *f* air fighting or air attack exercise.
Luftkarte *f* air map.
Luftklappenventil *n* choke valve *(carburetor)*.
Luftkraft *f* aerodynamic force.
Luftkreis *m* air force service area.
Luftkreiskommando *n* air force service area headquarters.
Luftkrieg *m* air war, air warfare.
Luftkriegführung *f* air warfare.
Luftkriegsschule *f* officer candidate school *(Luftwaffe)*.
Luftkühlung *f* air cooling.
Luftlager *n* PW camp for air forces personnel.
Luftlandegeschwader *n* glider wing *(strictly, a wing of transport airplanes for towing gliders)*.
Luftlandekette *f* glider flight *(airborne operations)*. *See also* **Luftlandegeschwader.**
Luftlandestaffel *f* glider squadron *(airborne operations)*. *See also* **Luftlandegeschwader.**
Luftlandetruppen *fpl* air landing troops.
Luftleere *f* vacuum.
Luftleiter *m* antenna.
Luftloch *n* air pocket *(Avn)*.
Luftmacht *f* air power.
Luftmarsch *m* "air march" *(flight of airborne troops from departure Adrm to destination)*.
Luftmeer *n* atmosphere.
Luftmeldequadrat *n* grid square *(for reporting locations in air reconnaissance)*.
Luftmine *f* aerial mine.
Luftnachrichten *fpl* signal communication *(Luftwaffe)*.
Luftnachrichtenabteilung *f* signal battalion *(Luftwaffe)*.
Luftnachrichtenhelferin *f* woman signal auxiliary *(Luftwaffe)*.
Luftnachrichtenkompanie *f* signal company *(Luftwaffe)*.
Luftnachrichtenstelle *f* signal center of an airdrome.
Luftnachrichtentruppe *f* signal communication troops *(Luftwaffe)*.
Luftnavigation *f* air navigation.
Luftoffensive *f* air offensive.
Luftparade *f* aerial review, aerial pass in review.
Luftpersonalamt *n* *See* **Luftwaffenpersonalamt.**
Luftpresser *m* air compressor.
Luftraum *m* air area; air space; sky.
Luftreibung *f* air friction.
Luftreifen *m* pneumatic tire.
Luftreiniger *m* air filter.
Luftsack *m* wind sock, wind sleeve, wind cone *(Avn)*; towed-sleeve target *(AAA practice)*; ballonet *(Bln)*. **Luftsackmaul** *n* air scoop *(Bln)*.
Luftsackventil *n* ballonet valve *(Bln)*. **Luftsäule** *f* column of air *(Met)*.
Luftscheibe *f* antiaircraft practice target.
Luftschicht *f* atmospheric layer
Luftschiff *n* airship.
Luftschlacht *f* air battle.
Luftschlauch *m* inner tube *(MT)*.
Luftschlitz *m* louver *(Tk)*.
Luftschraube *f* propeller *(Ap)*. *See also* **Propeller.**
Luftschraubenblatt *n* propeller blade
Luftschraubendrehzahl *f* propeller rpm.
Luftschraubenebene *f* plane of propeller rotation *(Ap)*.
Luftschraubenflügel *m* propeller blade *(Ap)*.
Luftschraubenhaube *f* propeller spinner *(Ap)*.
Luftschraubenkreis *m* propeller-disk area *(Ap)*.
Luftschraubensteigungsmesser *m* propeller pitch indicator.
Luftschraubenstrahl *m* slipstream.
Luftschraubennabenstück *n* propeller boss *(Ap)*.
Luftschraubenverstellgerät *n* pitch-control mechanism *(propeller)*.
Luftschutz *m* air raid protection, passive air defense *(Civ defense)*.
Luftschutzabschnitt *m* civilian defense sector *(air raid protection)*.
Luftschutzbezirk *m* civilian defense district *(air raid protection)*.
Luftschutzbrandspritze *f* stirrup pump.
Luftschutzbund *m* *See* **Reichsluftschutzbund.**
Luftschutzkeller *m* air raid shelter.
Luftschutzleiter *m* chief of air defense *(in a local defense council)*.
Luftschutzmaßnahmen *fpl* air raid precautionary measures.
Luftschutzordnungsdienst *m* civilian defense police service *(air raid protection)*.
Luftschutzpolizei *f* civilian defense police *(air raid protection)*.
Luftschutzraum *m* air raid shelter.
Luftschutzrevier *n* civilian defense zone *(air raid protection)*.
Luftschutzsanitätsdienst *m* civilian defense medical service *(air raid protection)*.
Luftschutzsirene *f* air raid siren.
Luftschutztruppen *fpl* civilian defense troops *(air raid protection)*.
Luftschutzturm *m* air raid tower.

Luftschutzübung *f* air raid drill, practice alert.
Luftschutzveterinärdienst *m* civilian defense veterinary service *(air raid protection)*.
Luftschutzwarndienst *m* aircraft warning service *(Civ defense)*.
Luftschutzwarnstelle *f* district warning center *(AWS)*.
Luftschutzwarnzentrale *f* control center *(AWS)*.
Luftschutzwart *m* air raid warden.
Luftschutzzentrale *f* *See* **Luftschutzwarnzentrale.**
Luftsog *m* vacuum *(resulting from explosion)*.
Luftspäher *m* ground observer *(AWS)*; antiaircraft scout or lookout, air sentinel, air guard.
Luftspäh- und Warndienst *m* aircraft scout and warning service.
Luftsperre *f* antiaircraft defenses *balloon barrage, fighter patrol,*
Luftsperrgebiet *n* prohibited zone, airspace reservation *(Avn)*.
Luftsperrtruppen *fpl* barrage balloon troops.
Luftsprengpunkt *m* point of air burst *(Arty)*.
Luftstörungen *fpl* atmospheric disturbances.
Luftstoß *m* blast, concussion of air *(resulting from an explosion)*.
Luftstreitkräfte *fpl* air forces.
Luftstrom *m* air current.
Luftstromgerät *n* airplane chemical spray apparatus.
Luftstützpunkt *m* air base.
lufttanken to refuel in flight.
Lufttorpedo *n* aerial torpedo.
Lufttransport *m* air transport.
Lufttreffbild *n* air-burst pattern.
Lufttüchtigkeit *f* airworthiness.
Lufttüchtigkeitsschein *m* airworthiness certificate.
Luftüberlegenheit *f* air superiority.
Lüftung *f* ventilation.
Lüftungsrohr *n* ventilation shaft
Luftverankerung *f* overhead cable anchorage *(Pon Bdg)*.
Luftverdichter *m* air compressor.
Luftvergleichsziel *n* high-burst auxiliary target *(Arty)*.
Luftverkehrslinie *f* civil airway.
Luftversorgung *f* supply by air.
Luftverteidigung *f* air defense, antiaircraft defense; air defense system.
Luftverteidigungsgebiet *n* special air defense command in vital areas.
Luftvorholer *m* pneumatic recuperator *(G)*.
Luftwache *f* ground observer *(AWS)*; air sentinel, air guard.
Luftwaffe *f* German Air Forces.
Luftwaffenbautruppe *f* aviation construction engineers.
Luftwaffenbetriebskompanie *f* airdrome maintenance and service unit.
Luftwaffen-Druckvorschrift *f* air forces manual *(abbr. L.Dv.)*.
Luftwaffen-Felddivision *f* air forces field division *(fighting as ground force with the Army)*.
Luftwaffenflak *f* air forces antiaircraft artillery *(as distinguished from Army antiaircraft artillery)*.
Luftwaffengruppenkommando *n* air force headquarters of a *Gruppe*.
Luftwaffenhelfer *m* air forces orderly *(messenger or clerk of premilitary age)*.
Luftwaffenhelferin *f* air forces woman auxiliary.
Luftwaffen-Jäger-Regiment *n* air forces rifle regiment.
Luftwaffenkommando *n* air forces headquarters.
Luftwaffenpersonalamt *n* Air Forces Personnel Office *(a branch of the Ger Air Ministry)*.
Luftwaffenschützenregiment *n* air forces rifle regiment.
Luftwaffen-Sturm-Bataillon *n* Air Forces assault battalion *(air-landing troops)*.
Luftwaffenverordnungsblatt *n* Air Forces Regulations *(a publication)*.
Luftwaffenverwaltungsamt *n* Air Forces Administration Office *(a branch of the Ger Air Ministry)*.
Luftwichte *f* specific gravity of air.
Luftwiderstand *m* air resistance *(Ballistics, MT, etc.)*; drag *(Avn)*.
Luftzielapparat *m* azimuth instrument.
Luger 08 *f* German standard military pistol.
Luke *f* door, hatch *(Ap, Tk)*.
Lukendeckel *m* hatch cover *(Tk)*.
Lungengift *n* *See* **Lungenreizstoff.**
Lungenreizstoff *m* lung irritant *(CWS)*.
Lunte *f* slow match *(fuze lighter)*.
Luv *f* weather side.
Luvwinkel *m* crab, angle of crab, drift angle *(Air Navigation)*.

M

Maat *m* petty officer, third class
Macht *f* power; country.
Maderfelge *f* quick-detachable rim *(with side ring) (MT)*.
Magazin *n* storage depot; magazine.
Magazinfeuer *n* automatic fire.
Magazingehäuse *n* magazine housing

Magazinhaltehebel *m* magazine catch lever *(MG)*.

Magazinhalter *m* magazine holder *(MG)*; magazine catch *(pistol)*.

Magazinlager *n* magazine rack *(Ord)*.

Magnesiumthermit *n* thermit filler *(incendiary bomb)*.

Magnetapparat *m* magneto *(Mtr)*.

Magnetisch-Nord *m* compass north, magnetic north.

Magnetkompaß *m* magnetic compass.

Magnetmine *f* magnetic mine.

Magnetspule *f* solenoid *(Elec)*.

Magnetzündapparat *m* magneto.

Magnetzündung *f* magneto ignition.

Magnus-Effekt *m* Magnus effect *(of air rotation caused by projectile spin)*.

Major *m* major.

Mangan *n* manganese.

Männchen *n* whipstall *(Avn)*.

Manneszucht *f* military discipline.

Mannschaft *f* crew, team, party, squad, "outfit." *See also* **Mannschaften.**

Mannschaften *fpl* enlisted personnel *(up to and including* Obergefreiter, *Cpl)*.

Mannschaftsentgiftungskraftwagen *m* decontamination truck for personnel.

Mannschaftsstube *f* squad room.

Mannschaftswagen *m* personnel carrier *(MT)*.

Manöver *n* maneuver.

Manöverkartusche *f* blank cartridge.

Manövrierfähigkeit *f* maneuverability.

Manövrierventil *n* maneuvering valve *(Bln)*.

Mantel *m* overcoat *(Clo)*; jacket *(MG, Am)*; casing *(of a tire)*.

Mantelboden *m* jacket base *(MG)*.

Mantelkopf *m* jacket end cap *(MG)*.

Mantelringrohr *n* built-up barrel *(G)*; jacketed barrel *(MG)*.

Marine *f* navy.

Marineakademie *f* naval academy.

Marineartillerie *f* naval coast artillery.

Marineartillerieabteilung *f* naval coast artillery battalion.

Marineartilleriemaat *m* petty officer, third class, in naval coast artillery.

Marineattaché *m* naval attaché.

Marinebaubataillon *n* naval construction battalion.

Marine-Flak *f* naval antiaircraft artillery.

Marineflieger *m* naval aviator, naval pilot.

Marineflugwesen *n* naval aviation.

Marinelager *n* *See* **Marlag.**

Marineministerium *n* Admiralty of the German Navy.

Marke *f* mark, index mark, reading on range drum *(Arty)*; label; brand; stamp.

Markenplatte *f* index plate *(on aiming circle or telescopic sight)*.

Markenring *m* index ring *(MG telescopic sight)*.

Marinestation *f* naval base.

Marinestoßtrupp *m* naval landing party.

Marinewaffenamt *n* Bureau of Ordnance *(Nav)*.

Marinewerft *f* navy yard.

Markenstück *n* line-up stud *(on top gun carriage)*.

Marketenderei *f* post exchange.

Marketenderware *f* sales article *(sold at PX)*.

Markscheidegerät *n* mine-surveying set *(Engr)*.

Marlag *n* prisoner-of-war camp for sailors *(abbr. of* Marinelager).

Marschabstand *m* distance between march units.

Marschallstab *m* baton.

Marschbataillon *n* personnel replacement transfer battalion *(conducting replacements from* Wehrkreis *to T of Opns)*.

Marschbefehl *m* march order; official travel order.

Marschbereitschaft *f* march readiness.

Marschbreite *f* width of march column.

Marschdecke *f* blanket.

marschfähig capable of walking, fit for marching.

marschfähige Verwundete walking wounded, ambulant cases.

Marschfähigkeit *f* marching ability.

Marschfolge *f* order of march.

Marschfühlung *f* maintenance of contact on the march.

Marschführer *m* control officer *(march column)*.

Marschgepäck *n* full pack.

Marschgeschwindigkeit *f* cruising speed *(Ap)*; rate of march.

Marschgliederung *f* march formation, organization of march.

Marschgruppe *f* march group, march section, march unit.

Marschhalt *m* march halt.

Marschieren ohne Tritt route march, route step.

Marschkolonne *f* march column, route column.

Marschkompanie *f* trained replacement company.

Marschkompaß *m* prismatic compass.

Marschkontrollstelle *f* control point.

Marschlänge *f* road space *(march column)*.

Marschleistung *f* march capacity, march performance.

Marschlinie *f* line of march.

"**Marsch! Marsch!**" "Double time, march!"; "On the double!"

Marschordnung *f* column of threes *(Inf drill)*; close order march formation; line of march.

"**In Marschordnung, angetreten!**" "In column of threes, fall in!"

"**Marschordnung!**" "March order!"

Marschpause *f* march halt.

Marschrast *f* march rest.

Marschsicherung *f* security on the march.

Marschskizze *f* strip map *(MT)*.

Marschstockung *f* road jam.

Marschstraße *f* march route.

Marschstrecke *f* march route, stretch or leg of a march.

Marschtafel *f* march table.

Marschtiefe *f* road space *(march column)*.

Marschübersicht *f* march schedule.

Marschvorposten *m* march outpost.

Marschweg *m* route of march.

Marschzeit *f* time of march, time distance.

Marschziel *n* march objective, march destination.

Marschzucht *f* march discipline.

Maschendraht *m* woven wire, wire netting, wire mesh.

Maschendrahtzaun *m* woven-wire fence, woven-wire obstacle.

Maschine *f* motor, engine; machine; airplane *(colloquial)*.

Maschinenflak *f* antiaircraft automatic weapons.

Maschinengewehr *n* machine gun. *See also terms under* **MG.**

Maschinengewehrangriff *m* strafing assault, strafing attack *(Avn)*.

Maschinengewehr-Bedienung *f* machine-gun crew.

Maschinengewehrgarbe *f* sheaf of fire *(MG)*.

Maschinengewehrgruppe *f* machine-gun section.

Maschinengewehr-Halbzug *m* machine-gun squad.

Maschinengewehrschlitten *m* machine-gun sleigh mount.

Maschinengewehrschütze *m* machine gunner.

Maschinengewehrstand *m* machine-gun empl ment; machine gunner's station *(Ap)*.

Maschinengewehrsteuerung *f* synchronization *(Ap MG's)*.

Maschinengewehrtrupp *m* light MG team *(of Inf squad)*.

Maschinengewehrzug *m* MG platoon.

Maschinenkanone *f* automatic cannon *(Ap)*; automatic gun.

Maschinenkarabiner *m* automatic rifle.

Maschinenpistole *f* submachine gun.

Maschinensatz *m* generating unit, power unit.

Maschinenschlosser *m* mechanic.

Maschinenschreiber *m* typist.

Maschinenwaffe *f* automatic weapon.

Maschinist *m* machinist *(Nav)*.

Maske *f* mask, screen, camouflage net, flat-top, overhead screen *(Cam)*; gas mask; oxygen mask.

Maskenbrille *f* special type of eyeglasses for wear under gas mask.

Maskenkörper *m* facepiece *(gas mask)*.

Maskenspanner *m* face form *(to prevent gas-mask distortion)*.

Maß *n* measure *(of quantity, etc.)*.

Masse *f* mass.

Massenabwurf *m* salvo release *(Bombing)*.

Massenausgleich *m* counterbalance, counterweight *(Ap)*.

Massenbeschuß *m* concentrated fire.

Masseneinsatz *m* commitment of major forces, employment of major forces *(Tac)*.

Massenfertigung *f* mass production.

Massentaktik *f* grand tactics.

Massenwirkung *f* mass effect *(Tac)*.

massieren to mass, concentrate; to massage.

Massierung *f* mass, massing, line of masses *(Tac)*.

Maßnahme *f* measure; step; enactment.

Maßstab *m* scale; proportion.

maßstabgerecht according to scale.

Mast *m* mast.

Mastwurf *m* clove hitch.

Materialfehler *m* defect of material.

Materialsammelstelle *f* salvage dump.

Materialschlacht *f* battle of matériel.

Materialwirkung *f* effect of fire against material objects *(Gunnery)*.

Matrose *m* apprentice seaman; sailor.

Matrosengefreiter *m* seaman, second class. **obergefreiter** first class.

Matrosenhauptgefreiter *m* seaman, first class *(highest rated, with $4\frac{1}{2}$ years seniority)*.

Mattanstrich *m* lusterless paint.

Mattscheibe *f* ground-glass plate.

Mauer *f* stone, brick or concrete wall. *n* mule.

Maultierkolonne *f* mule train.

Maximaleffekt *m* maximum intensity *(sound locator)*.

M.-Blink *n* portable signal lamp *(abbr. of* mittleres Blinkgerät).

Mechaniker *m* mechanic.

fuze. **scher Zünder** mechanical

mechanisierter Verband mechanized unit.

mechanisiertes Fahrzeug armored combat vehicle.

Mechanisierung *f* mechanization.

Medaille *f* medal.

Meer *n* ocean, sea.

Meeresküste *f* seacoast.

Meeresspiegel *m* sea level.

Mehrachsantrieb *m* multi-axle drive.

Mehrachser *m* multi-axle vehicle.

Mehrbestand *m* surplus stock *(i.e. above authorized basic allowance)*.

Mehrdecker *m* multiplane *(Ap)*.

mehrfach multiple; multiplex; combination.

Mehrfachbetrieb *m* multiplex operation *(Tp)*.

Mehrfach-Reihenbildkammer *f* multiple lens camera *(aerial Photo)*.

Mehrfachsprechen *n* multiplex telephony.

Mehrfachzünder *m* combination fuze *(Am)*.

Mehrgitterröhre *f* multiple-grid tube, multielement tube *(Rad)*.

mehrgleisig multiple-tracked *(RR)*.

Mehrlader *m* magazine-fed rifle or carbine, clip-fed rifle or carbine.

Mehrladevorrichtung *f* magazine feeding device *(R)*.

mehrläufige Fla-Waffe multiple-barrel antiaircraft weapon.

Mehrlauflafette *f* multiple-gun mount.

Mehrlochdüse *f* multiple-hole nozzle *(Mtr)*.

mehrmotorig multiple-engine.

Mehrscheibenkupplung *f* multiple-disk clutch.

Mehrsitzer *m* multiseater airplane.

Mehrzweckfahrzeug *n* general-purpose vehicle.

Mehrzweckflugzeug *n* general-purpose airplane.

Mehrzweckgeschütz *n* multipurpose gun.

Meilenstein *m* milestone.

Meißel *m* chisel.

Meldeabwurf *m* message dropping.

Meldeabwurfhülle *f* drop-message bag.

Meldeabwurfstelle *f* message-dropping ground.

Meldeblatt *n* message blank.

Meldeblock *m* message pad.

Meldebuch *n* field message book.

Meldebüchse *f* message container *(for dropping messages)*.

Meldedienst *m* message communication service.

Meldefahrer *m* mounted messenger *(MT)*; dispatch rider, dispatch driver.

Meldefahrzeug *n* messenger vehicle.

Meldeformular *n* message blank.

Meldegänger *m* runner, messenger.

Meldehund *m* messenger dog.

Meldehundführer *m* messenger-dog handler, messenger-dog guard.

Meldehundtrupp *m* dog-handler team *(for messenger dogs)*.

Meldekapsel *f* message-dropping container.

Meldekarte *f* message blank.

Meldekopf *m* wire head *(line construction)*; advance message center.

Meldelauf *m* message run *(messenger dog)*.

Meldeläufer *m* runner, messenger.

melden to report.

sich melden to report *(to present oneself)*; to register with the police; to volunteer.

sich krank melden to report sick, to go on sick call.

sich freiwillig melden to volunteer, enlist, enroll.

Meldepatrone *f* ground signal cartridge.

Meldepflicht *f* obligation to report to, or register with, the police.

Meldequadrat *n* grid square *(for reporting locations)*.

Melder *m* messenger.

Melderakete *f* message-carrying rocket.

Meldereiter *m* mounted messenger.

Melderose *f* orientation card *(AWS)*; orientation clock *(to indicate target's direction of approach) (AAA)*.

Meldesammelstelle *f* message center.

Meldestelle *f* control point *(march column)*; local reporting office.

Meldetasche *f* dispatch case.

Meldeweg *m* message channel.

Meldung *f* message, report, dispatch.

Membran *f* diaphragm.

Membranmaske *f* diaphragm gas mask.

Membranpumpe *f* diaphragm pump.

mengenmäßig quantitative; volumetric.

Meridiankonvergenz *f* gisement, grid declination *(Surv)*.

Merkblatt *n* supplement *(to a manual)*; instructional pamphlet

Mag.Wff	Magazinwaffe	magazine weapon
Ma.H	Munitionsanstalt Hannover	ammunition loading factory, Hanover
Ma.In	Munitionsanstalt Ingolstadt	ammunition loading factory, Ingolstadt
Maj	Major	major
Ma.J	Munitionsanstalt Jüterbog	ammunition loading factory, Jüterbog
M.Ak	militärärztliche Akademie	military medical school
M.K	Munitionsanstalt Königsberg	ammunition loading factory, Königsberg
Malz-Fabr	Malzfabrik	malt factory *(on maps)*
ma.N	magnetisch Nord	magnetic north
Man	Manöver	maneuver
m.A.n	meiner Ansicht nach	in my opinion
Mand	Mandat	mandate; order; authorization
Man.Kart	Manöverkarten	maneuver maps
Mannsch	Mannschaft	body of men; crew; team
Manöv	Manöver	maneuver
Manöv.Best	Manöverbestimmungen	maneuver regulations
Mar	Marine	navy
Masch	Maschine	machine; engine
Masch	Maschinist	machinist
Mascha	Maschinenamt	locomotive depot; locomotive office
Maschfbr	Maschinenfabrik	machine factory
Masch.Gew	Maschinengewehr	machine gun
Masch.Pist	Maschinenpistole	machine pistol; automatic pistol; submachine gun
massg	massgebend	authoritative; decisive; determining
Ma.Ste	Munitionsanstalt	ammunition loading factory,
Mat	Material	material; matériel; substance
Mault	Maultier	mule
Maus.Gew	Mausergewehr	Mauser rifle
m.a.W	mit anderen Worten	in other words
Max	Maxim	Maxim *(machine gun)*
Max	Maximal-, Maximum-	maximum
Ma.Z	Munitionsanstalt Zeithain	ammunition loading factory, Zeithain
M.B	Manöverbestimmungen	maneuver regulations
M.B	Messband	tape measure
MB	Militärbrieftaube	military carrier pigeon
MB	Motorboot	motorboat
M.Batt	Messbatterie	survey battery
M.Batt	**Mörserbatterie**	**mortar battery**
M.B.d.W	Vorschrift für die militärische Benutzung der Wasserstrassen im Kriege	regulations for the military use of waterways in wartime
M.B.I.(K.)	Militärbrieftaubenanstalt I, Königsberg	military carrier pigeon station I, Königsberg
M-Blink	mittleres Blinkgerät	medium blinker signal apparatus
M-Boot	Minensucherboot	mine sweeper
M-Boot	Motorboot	motorboat
Mbr	Marschbreite	width of marching column; front of marching column
Mbs	Meerbusen	bay
M-Buch	Bestandsbuch bei den Truppen über Munition, Nahkampf-, Spreng- und Zündmittel	troop inventory of ammunition, close-combat weapons, explosives, and priming substances
M.D	Messdreieck	range triangle *(instrument to measure traverse and range of heavy machine gun)*
Md	Milliarde	milliard (1,000,000,000); billion *(American)*
m.d	mit dem,—der	with the
m.D	mit der Kriegsdekoration	with the War Decoration
M.D	Mitteldecker	midwing monoplane
Mdf	Dienstanweisung zur Beurteilung der Militärdienstfähigkeit	service regulations for the judgment of fitness for active military duty
m.d.F.b	mit der Führung beauftragt	authorized to command; commissioned to take charge
Mdg	Mündung	muzzle *(gunnery)*
Mdg.Sch	Mündungsschoner	muzzle and sight cover *(rifle)*
mdl	mündlich	oral; verbal
mdl.Bef	mündlicher Befehl	oral order
Mdlchf	Mündlochfutter	fuze recess *(ammunition)*; gaine *(of fuze)*
m.d.R	mit dem Range	with the rank of
m.d.R.e.GfM	mit dem Range eines Generalfeldmarschalls	with the rank of field marshal
Mdst	Mundstück	mouthpiece
M.Dv	**Marinedienstvorschrift**	**naval service regulations**
me	mechanisch	mechanical
m.E	meines Erachtens	in my opinion
M.E	Militäreisenbahn	military railroad
m.E	mit Erlaubnis	with permission
M.E.Betr.Abt	Militäreisenbahnbetriebsabteilung	military railroad operations section
Mech	Mechanik	mechanics
mech	mechanisiert	mechanized
Mechan	Mechanismus	mechanism
Meckl	Mecklenburg	Mecklenburg
Med	Medaille	medal
med	medizinisch	medical
M.E.D	Militäreisenbahndirektion	Directorate of Military Railroads

Meg	Megaphon	megaphone
Mego	Messgerätoffizier	measuring - instruments officer
Mehrf.Kan.Oe	Mehrfachkanone Oerlikon	Oerlikon multiple gun (*with several tubes*)
Mehrzw	Mehrzweck-	multiple purpose
Mehrzw.Flzg	Mehrzweckflugzeug	multiple-purpose airplane
Mel	Melinit	melinite (*explosive*)
Meld	Melder	runner
Meld	Meldung	message
Meldeh	Meldehund	messenger dog
Meld.St	Meldestelle	message center
Mens	Mensur	student's duel
Merk.Z	Merkator-Funkpeilung	Mercator radio direction finding
Mess.I	Messinstrument	measuring instrument
Messkraft wagen Aft	Messkraftwagen für Anschluss-, Fernleitungs- und Telegrafenkabel der deutschen Telegrafenverwaltung	surveying motor vehicle for connecting, station-to-station and telegraph cables of the German Telegraph Administration
Met	Metall	metal
met	metallisch	metallic
Meteor	Meteorologie	meteorology
Met.St	meteorologische Station	meteorological station
M.E.u.B.W	Militär-Erziehungs- und Bildungswesen	military educational and instructional services
M.E.V.A	Militär-Eisenbahnverkehrsamt	military railroad traffic office
M.E.W.Abt	Militär-Eisenbahnwerkstättenabteilung	military railroad workshop section
m.Ex.M.R	mittlere Exerziermine mit Rauchladung	medium dummy mine with smoke element
M.E.Z	mitteleuropäische Zeit	Central European Time
Mf	Marschfolge	order of march
M.F	Mondfinsternis	moon eclipse
Mf	Motorfahrzeug	motor vehicle
Mfd	Mündungsfeuerdämpfer	flash hider; flash reducer
M-Flak	Flugzeugabwehrmaschinenkanone	antiaircraft rapid-fire cannon
m.folg.W	mit folgenden Worten	with the following words
M.F.S	Marinefunkstelle	naval radio station
M.F.-Schein	Militärführerschein für Kraftfahrzeuge	military driver's license for motor vehicles
m.Fu.Ger.Wg	Gerätewagen für mittleres Funkgerät 17	equipment truck for medium radio equipment 17
m.Fuk.Stat	mittlere Funkstation	medium radio station
m.Fu.Wg	Funkwagen für mittleres Funkgerät 17	radio wagon for medium radio equipment 17
MG	Maschinengewehr	machine gun
mg	Milligramm	milligram
MG.08	(schweres) Maschinengewehr (Maxim), Konstruktion von 1908	(heavy) machine gun (Maxim), 1908 construction
MG.08/15	(leichtes) Maschinengewehr, Konstruktion von 1908 mit Änderungen von 1915	(light) machine gun, 1908 construction with changes of 1915
MGA	Maschinengewehrabteilung	machine-gun detachment
MG.-Batl	Maschinengewehrbataillon	machine-gun battalion
MG.Begl.Zg	Maschinengewehr-Begleitzug	machine-gun escort (accompanying) platoon
MG.-Chef	Chef der Maschinengewehrkompanie	commander of machine-gun company
M.G.E.R	Maschinengewehrexerzierreglement	machine-gun drill rules
M-Gerät	Mörser (auf Kraftzug)	mortar (on motor tractor)
M.G.G	Maschinengewehrgerät	machine-gun equipment
MG.Hd.Wg	Maschinengewehrhandwagen	machine-gun handcart
MG.IAnl	Maschinengewehrgerätinstandsetzungsanleitung	machine-gun equipment repair regulations
MGK	Maschinengewehrkompanie	machine-gun company
MG.-Kam	Maschinengewehrkamera	machine-gun camera
Mg.Kp	Maschinengewehrkompa-	machine-gun company
Mg.Kw	Maschinengewehrkraftwagen	machine-gun truck (carrier)
Mgl	Mitglied	member
m.gl.Lkw.off	mittlerer offener geländegängiger Lastkraftwagen	medium open cross-country motor truck
m.gl.Pkw	mittlerer geländegängiger Personenkraftwagen	medium cross-country passenger car
m.gl.Zkw	mittlerer geländegängiger Zugkraftwagen	medium cross-country truck prime mover
MGMun.-Stelle	Maschinengewehrmunitionsausgabestelle	machine-gun ammunition distributing point
M.G.O	Maschinengewehroffizier	machine-gun officer
Mg.Off.v.Pl	Maschinengewehroffizier vom Platz	machine-gun officer of the fortress
M.Gr	Marschgruppe	march group; marching unit disposed for combat
M.-Gr	Mörsergranate	mortar shell
MG.-R.A	Maschinengewehrrichtaufsatz	machine-gun sight
M.G.Sch	Maschinengewehrschütze	machine gunner
M.G.Sch.V	Maschinengewehr-Schiessvorschrift	regulations for machine-gun fire

Merkzettel *m* data card, memo.
Meßband *n* surveyor's tape.
Meßbatterie *f* survey battery (*Arty*).
Meßbecher *m* dispenser, graduate.
Meßbildpaare *npl* stereoscopic complements (*Photo Surv*).
Meßbildverfahren *n* phototopography.
Meßbrücke *f* measuring bridge circuit, Wheatstone bridge (*Elec*).
Meßdreieck *n* plotting protractor (*Arty*).
Meßdreieckverfahren *n* plotting-protractor method (*protractor compensates for position offset and determines firing range on basis of range-finder and aiming-circle data*).
Meßei *n* pressure gage (*Arty*).
Meßeinheit *f* unit of measurement.
Meßentfernung *f* slant range to present position (*at instant of range determination*) (*AA gunnery*).
Messerflug *m* steep-bank flight.
Messerschalter *m* knife switch
Meßflug *m* test flight (*Avn*).
Meßgerät *m* range-finder; survey equipment or instrument.
Meßhöhe *f* altitude of target at instant of range determination (*AA gunnery*).
Messing *n* brass.
Meßkammer *f* topographic-survey camera.
Meßkartusche *f* test cartridge; charge temperature cartridge (*Arty*).
Meßkette *f* surveyor's chain.
Meßknopf *m* measuring knob (*range finder*).
Meßkreis *m* protractor arc (*plotting protractor*); azimuth circle (*BC telescope*).
Meßlatte *f* stadia rod (*Surv*).
Meßleitung *f* measuring circuit (*SR, FR*).
Meßmann *m* range-finder operator.
Meßmarke *f* measuring mark (*range finder*).
Meßpatrone *f* bore gage (*SA*).
Meßpunkt *m* present position of target (*at instant of range determination*) (*AA gunnery*).
Meßspiegel *m* reference mirror (*river-width measuring Inst*).
Meßstab *m* stadia rod (*Surv*).
Meßstand *m* base end station
Meßstelle *f* ranging station (*SR, FR*).
Meßtisch *m* plane table (*Surv*).
Meßtischblatt *n* plane table sheet.
Meßtrupp *m* survey team, flash or sound ranging team (*Arty*).
Meßwalze *f* measuring knob (*height finder*).
Meßzentrale *f* flash central station, sound central station (*FR, SR*).
Metallgefäß *n* metal container.
Metallgliedergurt *m* metallic-link ammunition belt (*MG*).
Metallgliederkette *f* metallic-link belt (*MG*).
Metallsäge *f* hacksaw.
Meteorograph *m* aerometeorograph, aerograph, meteorograph (*Avn, Met*).
Meteorologe *m* meteorologist.
Meterspur *f* one-meter track gage
Methyldichlorarsin *n* methyldichlorarsine (*CWS*).
Meuterei *f* mutiny.
M.-Flak *f* automatic antiaircraft gun (*abbr. of* Flugabwehrmaschinenkanone).
MG.-Dreifuß *m* tripod (*MG*).
MG.-Gerät *n* machine-gun matériel.
MG.-Gurt *m* machine-gun ammunition belt.
MG.-Mann *m* machine gunner.
MG.-Richtaufsatz *m* machine-gun sight.
MG.-Richtkreis *m* machine-gun aiming circle.
MG.-Staffel *f* heavy machine-gun section (*Cav*).
MG.-Träger *m* machine-gun carrier.
MG.-Wagen *m* machine-gun cart (*H-Dr*).
MG.-Warze *f* blister (*Ap*).
MG.-Zieleinrichtung *f* machine-gun sighting mechanism.
MG.-Zielfernrohr *n* machine-gun telescopic sight.
MG.-Zwilling *m* twin machine gun.
Mikrometerschraube *f* micrometer, micrometer calipers.
Milag *n* *See* **Militärlager.**
Milchglas *n* frosted glass.
Militär *n* military, military forces, soldiery. *See also terms under* **Heer, Wehrmacht.**
Militärärztliche Akademie army medical school.
Militärattaché *m* military attaché.
Militärausschuß *m* military commission.
Militärbefehlshaber *m* military commander in occupied territory.
Militärbehörde *f* military authorities.
Militärbevollmächtigter *m* military plenipotentiary.
Militärbezirk *m* military district.
Militärfriedhof *m* military cemetery.
Militärgefängnis *n* military prison.
Militärgericht *n* military court, military tribunal.

Militärgerichtsbarkeit *f* military jurisdiction.
militärische Besetzung military occupation.
militärische Formen military courtesy.
militärischer Auftrag military mission.
militärischer Schriftverkehr military correspondence.
militärisch räumen demilitarize.
Militärkommission *f* military commission.
Militärlager *n* prisoner of war camp (*abbr.* Milag).
Militärluftfahrt *f* military aviation.
Militärpfarrer *m* chaplain.
Militärstrafgesetzbuch *n* military penal code.
Militärverwaltung *f* military administration; military government.
Militärverwaltungsbezirk *m* military subdistrict.
Miliz *f* militia.
Mindestnutzbreite *f* minimum useful width of roadway.
Mine *f* mine.
Minenabweiser *m* paravane (*Nav*).
Minenanker mit Tiefensteller automatic anchor (*Nav*).
Minenanlage *f* demolition installation (*in a Bdg, etc.*); mine system (*mine warfare*).
Minenboje *f* mine buoy.
Minenbombe *f* aerial mine.
Minenfahrzeug *n* mine layer, mine planter (*Nav*).
Minenfeld *n* mine field.
Minenflugzeug *n* mine-laying airplane.
Minengang *m* mine gallery.
Minengefäß *n* mine case (*container*).
Minenhund *m* miner's tramcar (*Engr*); remote-controlled explosive-laden tank, "robot tank."
Minenkammer *f* demolition chamber (*Bdg, mine*).
Minenkampf *m* military mining, mine warfare.
Minenkratze *f* grub hoe.
Minenkrieg *m* military mining, mine warfare.
Minenlegen *n* mine laying.
Minenleger *m* mine layer, mine planter (*Nav*).
Minenlegermotorboot *n* mine yawl (*Nav*).
Minenlegerpanzerkampfwagen *m* mine-laying tank.
Minenräumboot *m* mine sweeper
Minenräumer *m* mine sweeper (*Nav*).
Minenräumpanzer *m* mine-clearance tank.
Minenräumung *f* mine sweeping; mine clearance.
Minenrohr *n* borehole.
Minenschacht *m* mine shaft.
Minenschleppen *n* mine dragging (*Nav*).
Minensperre *f* mine field, mine obstacle; submarine mine field (*Nav*); mine defense (*Tac*).
Minenstollen *m* gallery, tunnel.
Minensuchboot *n* (*Nav*) mine sweeper
Minensucher *m* mine sweeper (*Nav*).
Minensuchgerät *n* mine detector.
Minensuchstab *m* mine-probing rod.
Minensuchtrupp *m* mine-locating detail.
Minentonne *f* mine buoy.
Minentrichter *m* mine crater.
minenverseuchtes Gebiet mined area, mine-infested area.
Minenwirkung *f* mining effect (*Am*).
Minierdienst *m* mining service (*tunneling*).
Miniergerät *n* mining tools.
Miniergut *n* spoil (*mining*).
Mißbilligung *f* disapproval.
mißlingen fail.
mißweisender Kurs magnetic heading, magnetic course (*Air Navigation*).
mißweisender Kurswinkel magnetic azimuth (*Air Navigation*).
Mißweisung *f* magnetic declination, magnetic variation, declination constant, compass declination.
Mithöreinrichtung *f* sidetone circuit (*Rad, Tp*).
mithören to listen in, to monitor (*Rad, Tp*).
Mithörstelle *f* intercept station.
Mitklingen *n* resonance (*Rad*).
Mitkoppeln *n* determining of course or fix by dead reckoning (*Avn*).
Mitlesen *n* interception (*of visual signals*).
Mitnehmer *m* translating lever (*sight mechanism*); lathe dog; catch; lifter; cam; lug.
Mitschuldiger *m* accomplice.
mitteilen inform.
Mitteilung *f* communication, message, information.
Mittelbalken *m* center balk (*Bdg*).
Mitteldecker *m* midwing monoplane.
Mittelhand *f* barrel (*horse*).
Mittelpferde *npl* swing team.
Mittelpfropfen *m* tompion (*G*).
Mittelrohrrahmen *m* tubular-center chassis (*MT*).

Mittelspiegel *m* a colored center strip between the halves of the Kragenlitze (*Clo*).
Mitteltroß *m* second echelon supply train (*behind the* Gefechtstroß).
Mitteneindruck *m* binaural balance (*sound locating*).
mittlere Flugbahn mean trajectory.
mittlerer Fehler average error, mean error.
mittlerer Panzerkampfwagen medium tank.
mittlerer Sprengpunkt center of burst.
mittlerer Treffpunkt center of impact, center of dispersion.
mittlere Sonnenzeit mean solar time.
Mitwirkung *f* cooperation.
mobil mobilized.
mobil machen to mobilize.
Mobilmachung *f* mobilization.
Mobilmachungsbestimmungen *fpl* mobilization regulations.
Mobilmachungsplan *m* mobilization plan.
Modell *n* model, type, pattern.
Modelung *f* modulation (*Rad, Tp*).
modulierte Welle modulated wave.
Moment *m* moment, instant.
Moment *n* factor, element.
Momentstrom *m* instantaneous current (*Elec*).
Montage *f* assembly, erection, mounting, installation.
Montagehalle *f* assembly shop. (*Tk*).
Montageluke *f* inspection hatch
Montageplatte *f* chassis panel (*Rad*).
Montagewerk *n* assembly plant.
Monteur *m* mechanic, assembler.
montieren to assemble, make up, erect, mount.
Montierhebel *m* tire tool.
Moor *n* bog, marsh, moor.
Morast *m* bog.
Morgenkost *f* breakfast, morning meal.
Morsealphabet *n* Morse code.
Morsen *n* transmitting by Morse code.
Mörser *m* howitzer, (*caliber 210 mm and larger*).
Morsespruch *m* telegraph message.
Morsetaste *f* telegraph key.
Morsezeichen *n* Morse code character.
Motor *m* engine, motor.
Motorblock *m* cylinder block (*Mtr*).
Motorbremse *f* engine brake (*MT*).
Motordrehmoment *n* engine torque.
Motordrehzahl *f* engine rpm.
Motoren-Instandsetzung *f* engine re-
Motorenkühlung *f* engine cooling.
Motorenlüftung *f* engine ventilation, engine louvers (*Tk*).
Motorenraum *m* engine compartment (*Tk*).
Motorgleiter *m* powered glider.
Motorgondel *f* engine nacelle (*Ap*).
Motorhaube *f* engine cowling (*Ap*); hood (*MT*).
motorisiert motorized; mechanized; mobile.
motorisierte Kavallerie mechanized cavalry.
Motorpanne *f* engine failure.
Motorponton *m* ponton with outboard motor.
Motorrad *n* *See* **Kraftrad.**
Motorregler *m* engine governor.
Motorsäge *f* power saw.
Motorschaden *m* engine damage, engine trouble.
Motorschlitten *m* motor sled, aerosled.
Motorschnellboot *n* motor torpedo boat, PT boat.
Motorsegler *m* powered glider.
Motorstörung *f* engine trouble.
Motortorpedoboot *n* motor torpedo boat, PT boat.
Motorverkleidung *f* engine cowling
Motorverschalung *f* *See* **Motorverkleidung.**
Motorwelle *f* engine crankshaft.
m.Pak *f* medium antitank gun.
M.Patrone *f* ground signal cartridge (*abbr. of* **Meldepatrone**).
Mucken *n* flinching (*SA firing*).
Müdigkeit *f* fatigue.
Mudrasteg *m* a type of portable hasty footbridge.
Muffe *f* threaded sleeve (*for pipe connections*).
Mühle *f* mill.
Mulde *f* pit, hole, depression, hollow.
Muldenlinie *f* centerline of depression (*Top*).
mündlich oral.
Mundloch *n* adapter opening (*Am*).
Mundlochfries *m* muzzle bell, muzzle swell (*G*).
Mundlochgewinde *n* adapter thread (*Am*).
Mundlochschraube *f* adapter plug
Mundpfropfen *m* tompion (*G*).
Mundschicht *f* chemical layer (*gas mask*).
Mundstück *n* mouthpiece (*harness*).
Mündung *f* muzzle (*Ord*); mouth, outlet (*of a river*).
Mündungsarbeit *f* kinetic energy at the muzzle.
Mündungsbremse *f* muzzle brake (*G*).

MG.Schwd	Maschinengewehrschwadron	machine-gun troop
MGSS	Maschinengewehrscharfschütze	machine-gun sharpshooter
M.G.S.S.A	Maschinengewehrscharfschützenabteilung	machine-gun sharpshooter detachment
M.G.Stp.V	Maschinengewehrgerätstempelvorschrift	machine-gun equipment stamping regulations
M.G.-T	Maschinengewehrturm	machine-gun turret (*aviation*)
M.G.V	Marschgebührnisvor	march allowances
M.G.V.V	Maschinengewehrgerätverwaltungsvorschrift	technical manual on machine-gun equipment
M.G.Wffm.Wg	Maschinengewehrwaffenmeisterwagen	machine-gun artificer wagon
M.G.Wg(l.)	leichter Maschinengewehrwagen für Dreifussgewehr	light machine-gun cart for guns on tripod
M.G.Wg.(s.)	schwerer Maschinengewehrwagen für Schlittengewehre	heavy machine-gun cart for guns on sleighs
M.G.Z	mittlere Zeit des Meridians von Greenwich	Central Greenwich Meridian Time
MG.-Z.F	Maschinengewehrzielfernrohr	machine-gun telescopic sight
MG.Zg	Maschinengewehrzug	machine-gun platoon
M.H	Meldehund	messenger dog
M.Hbgr	Mörserhaubengranate	high-explosive mortar shell with windshield
Mhd	Meldehund	messenger dog
MHD	Munitionshauptdepot	ammunition main depot
Mhd.Vb	Meldehundverbindung	messenger dog communication
M.H.Tr	Meldehundtrupp	messenger dog section
Mi	Mittagskost	noon meal (*military provisioning*)
Mi	Mitte	middle
Mikr	Mikrometer	micrometer
Mikr	Mikrophon	microphone
Mikr	Mikroskop	microscope
mil	militär	military
Mil	Miliz	militia
Mil.A	Militäranwärter	ex-service man (*after 12 years of military service*)
Mil.Ak	Militärakademie	military academy
Mil.Arr.Anst	Militärarrestanstalt	military guard house
Mil.Att	Militärattaché	military attaché
Mil.Bev	Militärbevollmächtigter	military plenipotentiary
Mil.Bez	Militärbezirk	military district
Mil.Bhf	Militärbahnhof	military railway station (*on maps*)
Mil.DGO	Dienst- und Geschäftsordnung für die Militärgerichte des Reichsheeres	service and business regulations for the military courts of the German army
Mil.Eis	Militäreisenbahn	military railroad
Mil.Eis.Dir	Militäreisenbahndirektion	military railroad direction
mil.Gef	Militärgefangener	military prisoner
mil.Gef	militärisches Gefolge	military retinue
mil.Ger	Militärgericht	military court
Mil.Ger.Ob.Wm	Militärgerichtsoberwachtmeister	military court sergeant (*corresponding roughly to staff sergeant*)
Mil.Gouv	Militärgouverneur	military governor
Mil.Gouv	Militärgouvernment	military government
milit	militär	military
Milit.Eisenb	Militäreisenbahn	military railroad
Milit.Int	Militärintendant	administrative officer (*with higher staff*)
Milit.Int	Militärintendantur	office of administrative officer (*with higher staff*)
Milit.Just.B	Militärjustizbeamter	military court official
Milit.Knab.Erz.Anst.	Militärknabenerziehungsanstalt	military boys educational institution
Milit.L	Militärlehrer	military teacher
Milit.Ob.Pf	Militäroberpfarrer	senior military chaplain
Milit.Techn.Akad	Militärtechnischeakademie	military technical academy
Milit.Veter.Akad	Militärveterinärakademie	military veterinary academy
Milit.Veter.Insp	Militärveterinärinspekteur (-ion)	military veterinary inspector *or* inspection
Mil.Kab	Militärkabinet	military cabinet
Mil.Kfz	Militärkraftfahrzeug	military motor vehicle
Mil.Kr.Wt	Militärkrankenwärter	military hospital orderly
Mil.Lit	Militärliteratur	military literature
Mil.Mus	Militärmusik	military music; band
Mil.Mus	Militärmusiker	military musician; bandsman
Mil.Pers	Militärperson	military person
Mil.Reitanst	Militärreitanstalt	military riding institution
Mil.-Reitinst	Militärreitinstitut	military riding institute
Mil.Reitsch	Militärreitschule	military riding school
Mil.San	Militärsanatorium	military sanatorium
MilStGB	Militärstrafgesetzbuch	military penal code
MilStGerO	Militärstrafgerichtsordnung	manual for court-martial
Mil.Str.Anst	Militärstrafanstalt	military penitentiary
Mil.T.Anst	Militärturnanstalt	military athletic institution
Mil.Url.Zug	Militärurlaubzug	train carrying men on furlough
Mil.Vers	[illegible]	military insurance
Mil.Verw	Militärverwaltung	military administration
Mil.Vet.Insp	Militärveterinärinspekteur	military veterinary inspector
Mil.Wbl	Militärwochenblatt	military weekly bulletin
Mil.Ztg	Militärzeitung	military newspaper
/Min	in der Minute	per minute
Min	Minen-	mine
Min	Ministerium	ministry; department; cabinet
Min.Abt	Minenabteilung	mine detachment
Min.Dep	Minedepot	mine dump
Minens	Minensuch-	minesweeping
Minsbt	Minensucherboot	mine sweeper
Min.-Su	Minensuch-	minesweeping
Minw	Minenwesen	military mining; mine warfare *or* tactics
Min.Wf	Minenwerfer	trench mortar
Mio	million	million
Mipo	Militärpolizei	military police
MIR	Militärintendanturrat	military superintendent (*administrative official*)
Miss	Mission	mission
Missb	Missbilligung	disapproval
Missbr	Missbrauch	misuse
missf	missfallen	displease
Missh	Misshandlung	abuse
Mi.-Stelle	Minenwerferstelle	mortar position
Mitarb	Mitarbeiter	co-worker
Mitbes	Mitbesitzer	co-owner
Mitbew	Mitbewohner	co-occupant; co-inhabitant
Mitgl	Mitglied	member
Mitt	Mitteilungen	communications; information
Mitt	Mittel-	middle
mittl.Bomb	mittlerer Bomber	medium bomber
Mittn	Mitteilungen	communications
Mitw	Mitwirkender	co-operator; participant
Mitw	Mitwirkung	assistance; participation; cooperation
Mk	Marschkolonne	march column
M.-K	Maschinenkanone	machine cannon; automatic cannon
M.K	Meldekopf	advanced message center
M.K	Militärkraftfahr-	military motor transport
m.K	mit Karte	with a map
m.K	mit Klappensicherung	with folding safety device
MK	Munitionskolonne	ammunition column
M.Kab	Militärkabinet	military cabinet
M.-Ko	Marschkompass	lensatic-type march compass
M.Kol	Marschkolonne	march column
M.Kr	Messkreis	map protractor; graduated circle
M-K-Sch	Maschinenkanonenschütze	gunner of rapid-fire cannon
MKw	Munitionskraftwagen	ammunition truck
M.L	Marineleitung	navy department
M.L	Messlatte	surveyor's rod
M.L	Militärliteratur	military literature
Mld	Melder	runner
Mld	Meldung	message
Mld	Milliarde	milliard (1,000,000,000); million (*American*)
M.-Lehrling	Militärlehrling	military apprentice (*in the aviation industry*)
Mlst	Meilenstein	milestone (*on maps*)
mm²	Quadratmillimeter	square millimeter
mm³	Kubikmillimeter	cubic millimeter
m.M.W	mittlerer Minenwerfer	medium mortar
m.M.W.Zg	mittlerer Minenwerferzug	medium mortar platoon
Mn	Minensuch-	mine sweeping
Mob	Mobilisierung	mobilization
Mob.Instr	Mobilmachungsinstruktion	instructions for mobilization
Mobm	Mobilmachung	mobilization
Mob.Tg	Mobilmachungstag	mobilization day; M-day
mob.Tr	mobile Truppen	mobile troops
Mod	Modell	pattern; model
mod	modern	modern
Modellrgt	Modellregiment	model regiment
M-Öl	Mineralöl	mineral oil
Mörs	Mörser	mortar
monatl	monatlich	monthly
Morep.Komp	Motorreparaturkompanie	motor repair company
morg	morgen	tomorrow
Mot	Motor	motor
mot	motorisiert	motorized
mot.gl	auf geländegängigen Fahrzeugen motorisiert	motorized on cross-country vehicles
mot.s.Art	motorisierte schwere Artillerie	motorized medium artillery
mot.Tr	motorisierte Truppen	motorized troops
mot.Z	motorisiert mit Kraftzug	tractor drawn
M.P	Maschinenpistole	machine pistol; automatic pistol
M.P	Militärpension	military pension
M.P	Militärpolizei	military police
m.P	mit Panzerkopf	with armor-piercing head
m.P	mit Pension	with pension
m.Pl	mit Plan	with plans; with map; with
m.R.r	mit Rohrrücklauf	with recoil
Mrs	Mörser	mortar
M.S	Meldesammelstelle	message center
M.S.	Minensuch-	minesweeping
Mschft.Ers	Mannschaftsersatz	troop replacements
M'schftn	Mannschaften	enlisted personnel below rank of noncommissioned officers; rank and file
M.Sch.G	Markscheidegerät	inclinometer
m.sek	Metersekunden	meters per second
m.Sig	mittleres Signalgerät	medium signal apparatus
M.S.O	Meldesammeloffizier	officer in charge of message center
Ms.Offiz	Mobilmachungsoffizier	mobilization officer
mst	meistens, meistenteils	mostly
Mstb	Massstab	scale; standard; rule

MstGB	Marinestandgesetzbuch	naval code
MStGB	Militärstrafgesetzbuch	military penal code
MStGO	Militärstrafgerichtsordnung	manual for court-martial
M.Str	Marschstrasse	route of march
Mstr	Meister	master; chief
Mstr	Muster	pattern; model
M.St.V.V	Militärstrafvollstreckungsvorschrift	army regulations for the execution of disciplinary punishment
M.S.W	Militärsanitätswesen	army medical service
M.T	Marschtag	day of march
MT	**militärtechnisch**	**military technical**
mt	mittlere	medium
M.T	Munitionstragtier	munition pack animal
MTB	Messtischblatt	map, scale 1:25,000
Mtf	Marschtiefe	depth of marching column
M.Tr	Militärtransport	military railroad transportation
M.Tr.O	Militärtransportordnung	transportation regulations
Mttl	Mittel-	middle
M.T.W	Mannschaftstransportwagen	personnel transportation wagon
M.U	Marschunterkunft	march quarters; march billets; march shelter
M.U	Militärurlauber	man on furlough
Mun	Munitions-	ammunition
Mun-Anst	Munitionsanstalt	ammunition factory
Mun.Bed	Munitionsbedarf	ammunition requirement
Mun-Erg	Munitionsergänzung	replenishment of ammunition supplies
Mun.Ers	Munitionsersatz	ammunition replacement
Mun.F	Munitionsfabrik	ammunition factory
Mun.Kol	Munitionskolonne	ammunition column
Mun.Nachsch	Munitionsnachschub	ammunition supply and replacement
Mun.Trgt	Munitionstragtier	ammunition pack animal
Mun.Trsp	Munitionstransport	ammunition transport
Mun.Verbr	Munitionsverbrauch	expenditure of ammunition
Mun.Wg	Munitionswagen	caisson
Mun.Zg	Munitionszug	ammunition train
Mus	Musik	music
Musk	Musketier	musketeer
Must.Kom	Musterungskommission	mustering commission
M.U.Z	Militärurlauberzug	train carrying men on furlough
M.V	Militärversicherung	military insurance
M.V	Militärverwaltung	military administration
m.V	mit Verzögerung	with delay-action (*fuze*)
MVBl	Marineverordnungsblatt	naval regulations publication
m.V.u.K	mit Verzögerung und Klappensicherung	equipped with delayed action and folding safety device
m.W	meines Wissens	as far as I know
M.W	Minenwerfer	mortar
mw	missweisend	deviating
m.W	mittlerer Wasserstand	mean water level
MWB	Militärwochenblatt	military weekly bulletin
M.W.G	Meldewurfgranate	message canister
M.W.O	Minenwerferoffizier	officer in mortar unit
M.W.Pr	Minenwerferprotze	trench-mortar limber
M.W.Tr	Minenwerfertruppe	mortar troops
M.W.Zg (l)	leichter Minenwerferzug	light mortar platoon
M.W.Zg.(m)	mittlerer Minenwerferzug	medium mortar platoon
M.W.Zg.(s)	schwerer Minenwerferzug	heavy mortar platoon
MZ	Maschinengewehrzug	machine-gun platoon
M.Z	Militärzeitung	military newspaper
Mz	Motorenzahl	number of engines (*aviation*)
M.Z.Brücke	mittlere zerlegbare Eisenbahnbrücke	medium portable railroad bridge
M.Zug	Mehlzug	flour train

N

n	nach	in the direction of; following
N	Nachrichten	reports; information; communications; intelligence
N	Nachrichtenabteilung	signal battalion; intelligence section
N	Nachrichtentruppe	signal corps
N	Nachschub-	services of supply
N	Nahkampf	close combat
N	Nebel	smoke; fog (*used to designate gas as well as smoke*)
N	Nebelmunition	smoke ammunition
n	neutral	neutral
n	nördlich	northern
N	Norden	north
N	Nordsee	North Sea
N.A	Nebenanschluss	extension (*telephone*)
n.A	neuer Art	of new type
Nachf	Nachforschung	investigation; search
Nachh	Nachhut	rear guard
Nachkdo	Nachkommando	rear-guard detachment
Nachr	Nachrichten	reports; information; communications; intelligence
Nachr.A	Nachrichtenabteilung	signal battalion; intelligence section
Nachr.D	Nachrichtendienst	signal service; intelligence service

Mündungsdeckel *m* muzzle cover.
Mündungsenergie *f* kinetic energy at the muzzle.
Mündungsfeuer *n* muzzle flash.
Mündungsfeuerdämpfer *m* flash hider.
Mündungsgasdruck *m* muzzle gas pressure.
Mündungsgeschwindigkeit *f* muzzle velocity.
Mündungskappe *f* tompion, muzzle cover *(G)*.
Mündungsknall *m* report produced by gun or muzzle wave *(SR)*.
Mündungspfropfen *m* tompion *(G)*.
Mündungsrauch *m* muzzle-blast smoke.
Mündungsschoner *m* muzzle cover
Mündungswaagerechte *f* base of the trajectory.
Mündungswucht *f* kinetic energy at the muzzle.
Munition *f* ammunition.
Munitionieren *n* loading *(Ap weapons)*.
Munitionsart *f* grade of ammunition.
Munitionsaufzug *m* shell hoist.
Munitionsausgabestelle *f* ammunition distributing point.
Munitionsausstattung *f* issue of ammunition.
Munitionsbestand *m* stock of ammunition.
Munitionseinsatz *m* commitment or employment of ammunition.
Munitionsersatz *m* resupply of ammunition.
Munitionsfahrzeug *n* ammunition carrier *(vehicle)*.
Munitionskammer *f* ammunition sponson *(Tk)*; ammunition storage chamber, magazine.
Munitionskarren *m* loading barrow; ammunition carrier *(H-Dr)*.
Munitionskasten *m* ammunition box.
Munitionskolonne *f* ammunition train, ammunition column.
Munitionslager *n* ammunition dump, ammunition depot.
Munitionslager in Geschütznähe ready magazine *(Arty)*.
Munitionsloch *n* ammunition pit.
Munitionsmangel *m* ammunition shortage.
Munitionsnachschub *m* ammunition supply.
Munitionsnische *f* ammunition niche, hasty ammunition shelter *(Ft)*.
Munitionsschlepper *m* ammunition prime mover *(MT)*.
Munitionsschuppen *m* ammunition storage shed.
Munitionsschütze *m* ammunition bearer, ammunition carrier.
Munitionsstaffel *f* ammunition section *(of firing Btry, Tk Bn, etc.)*.
Munitions-Staffelführer *m* ammunition supply officer.
Munitionsstapelplatz *m* ammunition dump.
Munitionsträger *m* ammunition bearer, ammunition carrier.
Munitionstrommel *f* ammunition drum.
Munitionstrupp *m* ammunition detail.
Munitionsumschlagstelle *f* ammunition supply point.
Munitionsunteroffizier *m* chief of ammunition *(NCO, Arty)*.
Munitionsverbrauch *m* expenditure of ammunition.
Munitionsvergeudung *f* waste of ammunition.
Munitionsverteilungsstelle *f* ammunition distributing point.
Munitionsverwaltung *f* ammunition administrative office *(Div and up)*.
Munitionsverwaltungskompanie *f* ammunition administration company.
Munitionswagen *m* caisson, ammunition wagon, ammunition trailer, ammunition carrier *(H-Dr)*.
Munitionswesen *n* ammunition supply service.
Munitionszug *m* ammunition train
Munitionszugmaschine *f* ammunition prime mover *(MT)*.
mürbe softened up, worn out, demoralized.
M- u. R.-Patronen *fpl* signal and smoke cartridges *(abbr. of* Melde- und Rauchpatronen).
Musikkorps *n* military band.
Musikmeister *m* bandmaster *(2Lt)*.
Muster *n* model, type, pattern.
Musterung *f* registration for the draft *(includes physical examination and tentative classification)*.
Musterungsbezirk *m* draft subdistrict *(subdivision of* Wehrmeldebezirk).
Musterungsstab *m* registration staff *(for the draft)*.
Mutter *f* nut *(Tech)*.
Mutterkompaß *m* master compass
Muttermal *n* birthmark.
Mutterrohr *n* gun tube designed to receive a liner.
Mutterschiff *n* tender *(Nav)*.
Mutterschlüssel *m* wrench.
Mutteruhr *f* master watch.
Mütze *f* cap, hat.
Mützenkordel *f* hat cord.

N

Nabe *f* hub.
Nachbar *m* adjacent unit *(Tac)*; neighbor.
Nachbartruppen *fpl* adjacent troops.
Nachbildung *f* mock-up, model, dummy.
nachbrennen to hang fire *(Am)*.
Nachbrenner *m* hangfire *(Am)*.
Nachdrängen *n* direct pressure in pursuit *(Tac)*.
Nachhinken *n* hysteresis *(Mech)*.
Nachhut *f* rear guard.
Nachlässigkeit *f* negligence.
Nachlauf *m* positive caster *(MT)*.
"Nach links, richt Euch!" "Dress left, dress!"
Nachprüfung *f* verification.
Nachricht *f* information, intelligence, news, message.
Nachrichten *fpl* information, intelligence, signal communication.
Nachrichtenabteilung *f* signal battalion.
Nachrichtenachse *f* axis of signal communication.
Nachrichtenaufklärung *f* signal intelligence.
Nachrichtenbeschaffung *f* procurement of information, intelligence.
Nachrichtenbeurteilung *f* evaluation of information.
Nachrichtenblatt *n* bulletin *(publication)*.
Nachrichtendienst *m* military intelligence service, intelligence service; news service *(Rad)*.
Nachrichteneinsatz *m* commitment or employment of signal units.
Nachrichtenfahrzeug *n* signal vehicle.
Nachrichtenführer *m* signal officer of a *Fliegerkorps* *(in Comd of a* Luftnachrichtenregiment).
Höherer Nachrichtenführer signal officer at a *Luftflotte* headquarters.
Nachrichtengerät *n* signal equipment, signal supplies.
Nachrichtengerätkarren *m* signal-equipment cart.
Nachrichtengerätpark *m* signal-supply dump.
Nachrichtenhelferin *f* signal-communication woman auxiliary.
Nachrichtenkolonne *f* signal-supply column.
Nachrichtenkompanie *f* signal company.
Nachrichtenkopf *m* wire head, advance message center.
Nachrichtenkraftfahrzeug *n* signal motor vehicle.
Nachrichtenmaid *f* woman signal auxiliary of the *SS*.
Nachrichtenmann *m* signal communication man.
Nachrichtenmittel *n* means of signal communication.
Nachrichtennetz *n* communication net.
Nachrichtenoffizier *m* signal officer, communication officer, intelligence officer.
Nachrichtenpark *m* signal-supply depot.
Nachrichtenquerverbindung *f* liaison communication.
Nachrichtensammelstelle *f* signal intelligence center.
Nachrichtenstaffel *f* communication section *(Bn, Btry, etc.)*.
Nachrichtenstelle *f* message center, signal center.
Nachrichtentrupp *m* communication detail.
Nachrichtentruppe *f* Signal Corps.
Nachrichtentruppen *fpl* signal troops.
Nachrichtenübermittlung *f* transmission of communications.
Nachrichtenverband *m* signal unit.
Nachrichtenverbindung *f* signal communication.
Nachrichtenverkehr *m* signal communication traffic.
Nachrichtenwagen *m* signal wagon, signal truck.
Nachrichtenwege *mpl* signal communication channels.
Nachrichtenwerkstattkraftwagen *m* signal repair truck.
Nachrichtenwesen *n* signal communications.
Nachrichtenzentrale *f* signal center, message center.
Nachrichtenzug *m* signal communication platoon.
Nachsatteln *n* readjustment of saddle.
Nachschub *m* supply.
Nachschubabwurf *m* dropping of supplies from aircraft.
Nachschubausgabestelle *f* supply point.
Nachschubbataillon *n* supply battalion.
Nachschubboot *n* supply boat.
Nachschubdienst *m* supply service.
Nachschubdienststelle *f* supply service headquarters, office of supply services.
Nachschubfahrzeug *n* supply vehicle.

Nachschubführer *m* chief of supply services *(Div, corps, army)*.
Nachschubgeleit *n* supply convoy *(Nav)*.
Nachschubgut *n* supply, supplies.
Nachschubkolonne *f* supply column, supply train.
Nachschubkolonnenabteilung *f* supply column battalion.
Nachschubkompanie *f* supply company.
Nachschublage *f* supply situation.
Nachschublager *n* supply depot, supply dump.
Nachschublinie *f* supply line.
Nachschubmittel *n* means of supply movement.
Nachschuboffizier *m* supply officer.
Nachschub-Panzerkampfwagen *m* armored supply and maintenance vehicle.
Nachschubpark *m* supply dump, supply depot.
Nachschubsammelgebiet *n* railhead service area.
Nachschubstab z.b.V. special supply staff.
Nachschubstraße *f* supply route, line of supply, line of communication.
Nachschubstützpunkt *m* supply base.
Nachschubtrupp *m* supply party, supply detail.
Nachschubtruppen *fpl* supply troops, supply units.
Nachschubübung *f* supply service exercise.
Nachschubumschlagstelle *f* supply point.
Nachschubverkehr *m* supply traffic, movement of supplies.
Nachschubverteilungsstelle *f* supply distributing point.
Nachschubweg *m* supply road, supply route.
Nachschubwesen *n* supply services.
Nachschubzug *m* supply train *(RR)*.
Nachsicherung *f* additional security *(Tac)*.
Nachspitze *f* rear point *(march column)*.
Nachspitzenkompanie *f* rear party *(in rear guard of large unit)*.
nachstellen to readjust; to pursue.
Nachstrom *m* slipstream *(Avn)*.
Nachtangriff *m* night attack, night raid.
nachtanken refuel.
Nachtaufklärung *f* night reconnaissance.
Nachtbefeuerung *f* night beacon lighting *(along a flight route or airway)*; lighting facilities for landing at night *(Adrm)*.
Nachtgefecht *n* night combat.
Nachtglas *n* night glasses.
Nachtjagd *f* night fighting, pursuit operations at night *(Avn)*.
Nachtjagdgeschwader *n* wing of night fighters *(Avn)*.
Nachtjagdgruppe *f* night fighter group *(Avn)*.
Nachtjagdschule *f* night fighter school *(Avn)*.
Nachtjäger *m* night fighter *(Avn)*.
Nachtjägergeschwader *n* wing of night fighters *(Avn)*.
Nachtkampfflugzeug *n* night bomber.
Nachtluftkampf *m* night fighting *(Avn)*.
Nachtmarsch *m* night march.
nachträglich supplementary.
Nachtrupp *m* rear guard support *(in rear guard of large unit)*; rear party *(in rear guard of smaller unit)*.
Nachtschießen *n* night firing.
Nachtunternehmung *f* night operation.
Nachurlaub *m* extension of leave.
Nachweis *m* proof, evidence; inventory; list; record.
Nachweisung *f* list, account, record; strength report, stock report.
Nachzügler *m* straggler.
Nachzündung *f* retarded ignition.
Nackenband *n* neck strap *(gas mask)*.
Nackenriemen *m* neck strap *(harness)*.
Nadel *f* needle; firing pin *(fuze)*.
Nadelabweichung *f* magnetic declination.
Nadellager *n* needle bearing *(MT)*.
Nadelschwankungen *fpl* oscillations of compass needle.
Nadelstück *n* firing pin support *(fuze)*.
Nadelverfahren *n* compass method *(of laying guns)*.
Nadelwald *m* coniferous forest, coniferous wood.
Nadelwehr *n* needle dam *(Engr)*.
Nadelzahl *f* magnetic azimuth, azimuth reading.
Nafü *m* See **Nachrichtenführer**.
Nahabwehr *f* close defense.
Nahaufklärer *m* close reconnaissance airplane.
Nahaufklärerstaffel *f* close reconnaissance squadron *(Avn)*.
Nahaufklärung *f* local reconnaissance, close reconnaissance.
Nahaufklärungsflugzeug *n* close-reconnaissance airplane
Nahaufklärungsgruppe *f* close reconnaissance airplane group *(attached to ground forces)*.

Nahbeobachtung *f* local observation.
Naherkunder *m* close reconnaissance airplane, observation airplane.
nähern to approach, close in.
Nahkampf *m* close combat.
Nahkampfartillerie *f* close support artillery.
Nahkämpfer *m* close-combat fighter.
Nahkampffliegerverband *m* formation of close support airplanes.
Nahkampfführer *m* commander of a *Nahkampfgruppe (Luftwaffe)*.
Nahkampfgruppe *f* close support airplane group *(attached to ground forces)*.
Nahkampfmittel *n* close-combat munitions or weapons.
Nahkampfspange *f* close combat clasp *(decoration)*.
Nahkampfwaffe *f* close combat weapon.
Nahkampfweite *f* close range, close-combat range.
Nahkompaß *m* direct-reading compass.
Nah-Packgefäß *n* unit container *(as distinguished from a bulk container)*.
nähren to feed; to reinforce.
Nahrung *f* nourishment, food.
Nahsicherung *f* close-in security, close-in protection.
Naht *f* seam; boundary between units *(Tac)*.
Nahtkompanie *f* contact company *(occupying a boundary position between two units)*.
Nahtreffer *m* near miss.
Nahtstelle *f* boundary position *(between units)*.
Nahunterstützung *f* close support.
Nahverkehr *m* local traffic, short-range traffic.
Nahverteidigung *f* close defense.
Nahwerfer *m* short-range flame thrower.
Nähzeug *n* sewing kit.
Naifagtafel *f* chart showing chemical warfare agents and their properties *(Tng)*.
Narbe *f* scar.
Narvikschild *m* Narvik Shield *(emblem on upper left sleeve, worn by all participants in reconquest of Narvik, 1940)*.
Nase *f* nose; stud; cap; lug.
Nasenklammer *f* nose clamp *(gas mask)*.
Nasenleiste *f* leading edge *(Ap wing)*.
Nasenrachenreizstoff *m* nose and throat irritant, sternutator *(CWS)*.
Nasenriemen *m* noseband *(harness)*.
Nasen- und Rachenreizstoff *m* See **Nasenrachenreizstoff**.
Naßbrandpulver *n* black powder.
Nationale *n* personal data *(birth, occupation, etc.)*.
Nationalsozialistisches Fliegerkorps Nazi party aviation corps *(abbr.* N.S.F.K.).
Nationalsozialistisches Kraftfahrkorps Nazi party motor corps *(abbr.* N.S.K.K.).
Natrium *n* sodium.
Natriumhypochlorit *n* sodium hypochlorite.
Natriumkarbonat *n* washing soda.
Natriumsulfid *n* sodium sulfide.
Natriumsulfit *n* sodium sulfite.
Natur *f* nature.
in **Natur** in kind *(rations, Clo, etc.)*
Naturalleistungsgesetz *n* requisition law.
Naturalverpflegung *f* rations in kind.
Naturgummi *m* See **Naturkautschuk**.
Naturkautschuk *m* natural rubber.
natürliche Deckung accidental cover.
Naturschutzgebiet *n* national park.
Nautiker *m* navigator.
Navigationsfunkfeuer *n* radio marker beacon *(Air Navigation)*.
Navigationskarte *f* navigation chart or map.
Nebel *m* smoke *(CWS)*; fog, mist, haze, vapor.
Nebelabblasen *n* release of smoke *(CWS)*.
Nebelabblasgerät *n* smoke-filled chemical cylinder *(CWS)*.
Nebelabteilung *f* smoke-producing unit *(CWS)*.
Nebelausdehnung *f* smoke coverage.
Nebelbombe *f* smoke bomb.
Nebeldecke *f* smoke blanket, smoke screen.
Nebeleinsatz *m* employment of smoke.
Nebelentwicklung *f* generation of smoke.
Nebelgebiet *n* fog area *(Met)*.
Nebelgerät *n* chemical tank, smoke tank *(for Cml spraying)*.
Nebelgeschoß *n* smoke projectile.
Nebelgewehrgranate *f* smoke rifle grenade.
Nebelgranate *f* smoke shell *(Am)*.
Nebelhandgranate *f* smoke hand grenade.
Nebelkasten *m* box-type smoke container *(CWS)*.
Nebelkerze *f* smoke candle.
Nebelkraftwagen *m* smoke equipment truck.
Nebelmittel *n* smoke agent, smoke equipment.
Nebelmunition *f* smoke munitions.
Nebelpanzerkampfwagen *m* smoke-screen tank.
Nebelpatrone *f* smoke cartridge.
Nebelsäure *f* FS solution, sulfur trioxide-chlorsulfonic acid solution *(CWS)*.
Nebelschießen *n* smoke-shell firing *(Arty)*.
Nebelschleier *m* smoke screen.
Nebelstoff *m* smoke agent, screening agent *(CWS)*.
Nebeltopf *m* smoke pot *(CWS)*.
Nebeltornister *m* pack smoke apparatus *(CWS)*.
Nebeltrommel *f* drum-type smoke container *(CWS)*.
Nebeltrupp *m* smoke party.
Nebeltruppen *fpl* chemical troops, smoke-generator units.
Nebelübung *f* smoke-screening exercise
Nebelwalze *f* creeping barrage of smoke-shell fire *(Arty)*; progressive smoke screening.
Nebelwand *f* smoke curtain, smoke screen.
Nebelwerfer *m* chemical projector *(smoke shell)*; smoke-shell mortar; rocket launcher, rocket mortar. *(Note:* Nebelwerfer 41 *is a six-tube rocket launcher for HE rockets)*.
Nebelwerferabteilung *f* smoke battalion, chemical battalion.
Nebelwerferregiment *n* smoke regiment, chemical regiment.
Nebelwolke *f* smoke cloud *(CWS)*.
Nebelwurfgranate *f* mortar smoke shell
Nebelzerstäuber *m* smoke spray *(smoke-filled Cml cylinder with spray nozzle)*.
Nebelzone *f* smoke-screened area.
Nebelzündmittel *n* smoke-container firing device.
Nebenabschnitt *m* adjacent sector.
Nebenabsicht *f* secondary objective.
Nebenangriff *m* holding attack, secondary attack, secondary effort *(Tac)*.
Nebenanschluß *m* local station, extension *(Tp)*.
Nebenanschlußleitung *f* local-circuit line, extension line *(Tp)*.
Nebeneinanderschaltung *f* parallel connection *(Elec)*.
Nebenfarbe *f* secondary service color *(as distinguished from the basic service color,* Waffenfarbe).
Nebengeräusche *npl* ambient noise *(sound locating)*.
Nebengleis *n* side track, siding *(RR)*.
Nebenkolonne *f* adjacent column, secondary column.
Nebenlager *n* branch camp *(PW)*.
Nebenluft *f* secondary air *(Mtr)*.
Nebenmann *m* man on the left or right *(Drill)*.
Nebenoperationen *fpl* secondary operations *(Tac)*.
Nebenschluß *m* shunt *(Elec)*.
Nebenschlußmotor *m* shunt motor *(Elec)*.
Nebenstachel *m* front sight *(AT gun)*
Nebenstelle *f* local station *(Tp)*.
Nebenstraße *f* side street, side road; secondary road, auxiliary road.
Nebenstromkreis *m* shunt circuit *(Elec)*.
Nebsttreffer *m* near miss.
nehmen to take.
aus der Flanke nehmen to attack on the flank.
unter Feuer nehmen to shell, to fire on.
Nehmestaat *m (PW)* detaining power
nehmestaatliche Behörde detaining authority *(PW)*.
Neigung *f* inclination, slope.
Neigungsmesser *m* clinometer *(Surv, Gunnery)*; flight indicator, inclinometer *(Ap)*.
Neigungswinkel *m* angle of slope.
Nennhöhe *f* rated altitude.
Nennleistung *f* rated horsepower.
Nest *n* nest; emplacement; position consisting of a group of foxholes with shallow connecting trenches.
Netz *n* net, network; grid; wiring system; power system.
Netzanschlußgerät *n* power-line operated radio set *(as distinguished from battery-operated or local power-supply set)*; power-supply unit, power pack *(Rad)*.
Netzleger *m* net-laying vessel.
Netzsperre *f* net obstacle, net-defense obstacle *(coastal defense)*.
Netztransformator *m* power transformer *(Rad)*.
Netzverkehr *m* "net" traffic *(includes several radio stations communicating at will on the frequency of their called stations)*.
Neuaufstellung *f* reorganization, new organization; reorganized or newly activated unit.
Neubearbeitung *f* revision.
neu einrichten re-lay *(Gunnery)*; re-adjust.
Neugrad *m* 1/400th of a circle *(equals 16 artillery mils, as distinguished from Grad, degree.*
Neugradteilung *f* centesimal graduation. *See* Neugrad.
neutrale Nachrichtenverbände neutral communication units *(maneuvers)*.
neutrale Truppen neutral troops *(maneuvers)*.
neutrale Zone taxiway *(Adrm)*.
neutralisieren to neutralize.
Neutralität *f* neutrality.
nichtbrisanter Sprengstoff low explosive.
Nichtkämpfer *m* noncombatant.
Nickelsammler *m* nickel-alkaline cell *(Elec)*.
Niederdruckreifen *m* low-pressure tire *(MT)*.
Niederfrequenz *f* low frequency, audio-frequency *(Rad)*.
Niederfrequenzverstärker *m* audio-frequency amplifier *(Rad)*.
niederhalten to neutralize, immobilize, hold down.
Niederhaltungsschießen *n* neutralization fire *(Arty)*.
niederkämpfen reduce, overpower, put out of action *(Tac)*; to silence *(enemy fire)*.
Niederkämpfung *f* reduction, destruction, putting out of action *(Tac)*; covering with destruction fire *(Arty)*.
Niederlage *f* defeat, reverse.
niedermachen kill, slaughter.
niedermetzeln to massacre, slaughter.
Niederschläge *mpl* precipitation *(Met)*.
Niederspannung *f* low voltage *(Elec)*.
Niederung *f* low country, depression, low ground.
Niedrigantenne *f* low antenna.
Niemandsland *n* no man's land.
Nieseln *n* drizzle *(Met)*.
Niesgas *n* sneeze gas *(CWS)*.
Niet *m* riveted joint, riveted assembly, riveted seam.
Niete *f* rivet.
nieten to rivet.
Niethammer *m* riveter *(tool)*.
Nietung *f* riveting.
Nippel *f* nipple *(Tech)*.
Nitrierung *f* nitration *(Am)*.
Nitroglyzerin *n* nitroglycerin.
Nitroglyzerin-Blättchenpulver *n* nitroglycerin flake powder.
nitroglyzerinhaltiges Nitrozellulosepulver double base powder *(Am)*.
Nitroglyzerinpulver *n* nitroglycerin powder.
Nitrozellulose *f* nitrocellulose, pyrocellulose.
Nitrozellulose-Blättchenpulver *n* nitrocellulose flake powder.
Nitrozellulosepulver *n* blank fire powder, E.C. powder, E.C. smokeless powder, E.C. blank fire *(SA Am)*.
Nivellementspunkt *m* bench mark.
Nivellierinstrument *n* surveyor's level.
Nivellierlibelle *f* sighting level *(plane table)*.
Nocken *m* cam *(also spelled* die Nocke).
Nockenwelle *f* camshaft.
Nonius *m* vernier.
Norden *m* north.
Norm *f* standard *(Tech)*.
Normalbelastung *f* normal load, standard load.
Normalfluglage *f* level flight *(Avn)*.
Normalkette *f* standard caterpillar track.
Normalnull *f* mean sea level *(abbr.* NN).
Normalraupe *f* standard caterpillar track.
Normalspur *f* standard gage *(RR)*.
Normalstellung *f* zero position
Normalvisier stellen to zero a gun sight.
normen standardize.
Normteil *m* standard part.
Normung *f* standardization.
Not *f* emergency.
Notabwurf *m* emergency salvo release *(Bombing)*.
Notbeleuchtung *f* emergency illumination.
Notbremse *f* emergency brake.
Notfall *m* emergency.
Notfeuer *n* barrage, normal barrage *(now called* Sperrfeuer).
Nothilfe *f* See Technische **Nothilfe**.
nötigen compel.
Notlandehafen *m* emergency landing field
notlanden make an emergency landing, make a forced landing *(Avn)*.
Notlandeplatz *m* emergency landing field.
Notlandung *f* emergency landing, forced landing *(Avn)*.
Notleitung *f* emergency line *(Tp)*.
Notpiste *f* emergency trail or path.
Notruf *m* emergency call *(Tp)*.
Notsender *m* emergency radio transmitter *(floatable rescue set)*.
Notsignal *n* distress signal, SOS.
Notverbandpäckchen *n* first-aid packet, first-aid dressing.
Notverbandtasche, *f* first-aid pouch.
Notvisier *n* direct-fire sight *(Ord)*.
notwassern to make an emergency landing on water, to "ditch"
Notwasserung *f* emergency landing on water, "ditching" *(Avn)*.

Nachr.Flg	Nachrichtenflugzeug	communications plane
Nachr.Ger.Kol	Nachrichtengerätkolonne	signal corps equipment col.
Nachrm	Nachrichtenmittel	channel of communications
Nachr.Mine	Nachrichtenmine	message shell
Nachrm.O	Nachrichtenmitteloffizier	communications officer
Nachr.St	Nachrichtenstaffel	signal section
Nachr.Tr	Nachrichtentruppe	signal corps
Nachr.W	Nachrichtenwesen	signal service
Nachsch	Nachschub	supply
Nachsch.D	Nachschubdienst	supply service
Nachsch.Kol	Nachschubkolonne	supply column
Nachsp	Nachspitze	rear point
Nachsp.Kp	Nachspitzenkompanie	rear party
Nacht Bo	Nachtbomber	night bomber
Nachtr	Nachtrupp	support of rear party
Nachtw	Nachtwache	night watch; night guard
näml	nämlich	that is to say
NahAufkl	Nahaufklärung	close reconnaissance
Nah-B-Stelle	Nahbeobachtungsstelle	close-range observation post
Nahgef	Nahgefecht	close combat
Nahk	Nahkampf	close combat
Nahk.Battr	Nahkampfbatterie	close-combat battery
Nahk.M	Nahkampfmittel	close-combat weapons
N.A.L	Nebenanschlussleitung	extension wire
n.ar	nichtarisch	non-aryan
nat	national	national
Nat.Soz	Nationalsozialismus	National Socialism
nat.soz	nationalsozialistisch	National Socialistic
Natur.V	Naturalverpflegung	food supplies in kind
Nav	Navigation	navigation
N.B	Nahbeobachtung	close-range observation
Nb	Nebel	fog; smoke (*used to designate gas as well as smoke*)
n.B	nördliche Breite	northern latitude
N.Bomb	Nebelbombe	smoke bomb
n.Br	nördliche Breite	northern latitude
NbW	Nebelwerfer	chemical projector
Nb.Zst	Nebelzerstäuber	smoke-disperser
Ndn	Norden	north
ndr	nieder-	low; down
Neb	Nebel	smoke; fog (*also gas*)
neb	neben	besides; next to
Neben-A	Nebenabteilung	adjacent formation; flank unit
Neb.Gesch	Nebelgeschoss	smoke shell
Neb.Hgr	Nebelhandgranate	smoke hand grenade
Neb.Kz	Nebelkerze	smoke candle
Neb.Mun	Nebelmunition	smoke ammunition
Neb.St	Nebelstoff	smoke-producing agent
Neg	Neger	negro
Neuform	Neuformation	new formation; re-formation; reorganization; newly organize
Neum	Neumark	Neumark (*German city*)
neutr	neutral	neutral
neutr.Bd	neutraler Boden	neutral ground
Neutr.Bed	Neutralitätsbedingungen	conditions of neutrality
Neutr.Erkl	Neutralitätserklärung	declaration of neutrality
neutr.Geb	neutrales Gebiet	neutral territory
Neutr.Grz	Neutralitätsgrenze	boundary of neutrality
Neutr.Sch	Neutralitätsschutz	protection of neutrality
neutr.St	neutraler Staat	neutral state
Neutr.Verh	Neutralitätsverhandlung	negotiation of neutrality
Neutr.Vertr	Neutralitätsvertrag	neutrality pact; treaty (agreement) of neutrality
neutr.Z	neutrale Zone	zone of neutrality
N.f.d.D	nur für den Dienstgebrauch	only for service use
N.f.L	Nachrichten für Luftfahrer	flight information
NFL	Nachtflug	night flight
N-Fluwa	Nachtflugwache	night flight guard (patrol, spotting post)
N.Gesch	Nebelgeschoss	smoke-shell
N.G.I	Nachrichtengerätinspizient	inspector of signal equipment
Ngl	Nitroglyzerin	nitroglycerine
Ng.PS	höchste Leistung eines Flugzeugmotors in Pferdestärken	maximum performance of an airplane motor in horse power
N.Hgr	Nebelhandgranate	smoke hand grenade
Nitros	Nitrozellulose	nitrocellulose
Niv	Niveau	level; standard
n/K	neuere Konstruktion	of new-type construction
NSBDT	Nationalsozialistischer Bund Deutscher Technik	National Socialist Association of German Technology
NSBO	Nationalsozialistische Betriebszellenorganisation	National Socialist Organization of Cells in Industry
Nsch	Nachschub	supply
NSDAB	Nationalsozialistischer Deutscher Ärztebund	National Socialist Association of German Physicians and Surgeons
NSDAP	Nationalsozialistische Deutsche Arbeiter Partei	National Socialist German Workers Party
NSDFB	Nationalsozialistischer Deutscher Frontkampfbund	National Socialist League of German War Veterans *formerly Stahlhelm*
NSDMB	Nationalsozialistischer Deutscher Marinebund	National Socialist German Naval League

NSDStB	Nationalsozialistischer Deutscher Studentenbund	National Socialist Association of German Students
NSF	Nationalsozialistische Frauenschaft	National Socialist German Women's League
NSFK	Nationalsozialistisches Fliegerkorps	National Socialist Flying Corps
NSG	Nationalsozialistische Gemeinschaft "Kraft durch Freude"	National Socialist Organization "Strength through Joy"
NS Hago	Hauptamt für Handwerk und Handel der NSDAP	National Socialist Central Office of Trades and Commerce
NSK	Nationalsozialistische Parteikorrespondenz	National Socialist Party Bulletin *or* News Agency
NSKK	Nationalsozialistisches Kraftfahrkorps	National Socialist Motor Corps
NSKOV	Nationalsozialistische Kriegsopferversorgung	National Socialist Welfare Department for War Victims
NSLB	Nationalsozialistischer Lehrerbund	National Socialist Teacher's Guild
NSRK	Nationalsozialistisches Reiterkorps	National Socialist Mounted Corps
N.K.A	Nachschubkolonnenabteilung	supply column detachment
NKdo	Nachkommando	rear-guard detachment
N.Kz	Nebelkerze	smoke candle
NL	Naturalleistung	payment in kind
N.M	Nachrichtenmittel	channels of communications
N.M	Nachtmarsch	night march
N.M.A	Nachrichtenmittelabteilung	signal communications detachment
n.Massg	nach Massgabe	according to; in proportion
N.M.O	Nachrichtenmitteloffizier	communications officer
N.Mun	Nebelmunition	smoke ammunition
N.N.O	Nordnordost	north-northeast
N.N.W	Nordnordwest	north-northwest
N.O	Nachrichtenoffizier	signal officer; intelligence officer
N.O	Nordosten	northeast
No	Nordsee	North Sea
Nob	Nachrichtenoffizier Berlin	signal or intelligence officer, Berlin
NöBre	Notbremse	emergency brake
n.ö	nicht öffentlich	not public
nördl	nördlich	northern
Norm.Spb	Normalspurbahn	standard-gauge railroad
Not.F	Notfeuer	barrage; protection fire
Notw	Notwehr	self-defense
NOzN	Nordost zu Nord	northeast by north
NOzO	Nordost zu Ost	northeast by east
NP	Nordpol	North Pole
N.P	Normalprofil	normal profile
N.P	Nullpunkt	zero point; zero
N.Post	Nachtposten	night guard
NR	Nationalsozialistischer Reichskriegerbund (Kyffhäuserbund)	National Socialist Reich League of Veterans (Kyffhäuserbund)
Nr	Nummer	number
N.S	Luftnachrichtenschule	air force communication and signal school
NS	Nachschrift	postscript
N.-S	Nebelsignal	smoke signal
N.-S	Nordsee	North Sea
NSS	Nationalsozialistische Schwesternschaft	National Socialist Sisterhood of Nurses and Social Workers
N.St	Nachschubstab	supply staff
NSV	Nationalsozialistische Volkswohlfahrt	National Socialist Organization for Public Welfare
NSW	Nationalsozialistischer Wirtschaftsdienst	National Socialist Service for Economic Information
NT	Nachrichtentechnik	signal corps communications
n.tdf	nicht tropendienstfähig	not fit for duty in the tropics (*Africa*)
Ntldg	Notlandung	emergency landing
Ntzl	Nutzlast	useful load
N-Url	Nachturlaub	overnight pass
NW	niedrigster Wasserstand	lowest water level
NW	Nordwesten	northwest
Nz	Nachrichtenmittelnetz	network of means of communication
N.Z	Nachrichtenzentrale	communication center
Nz	Nitrozellulose	nitrocellulose
N.-Z	Normalzeit	standard time

O

o	oben	above
o	ober	upper; first; chief
O	Oberkommandierender	high commander
O	Oberkommando	high command
O	Oder	Oder (*river*)
O	Offizier	officer
O	Omnibus	bus
O	Orden	decoration; order
O	Ordnung	order; regulation
O	Osten	east
o	ostwärts	eastwards
o.a	oben angegeben	indicated above
Oa	Oberabschnitt	region or district

Notwehr *f* self-defense.

Notwurf *m* emergency salvo release (*Bombing*).

Notzeichen *n* distress signal, SOS.

Notzug *m* emergency release handle (*Ap*).

NSKK.-Mann *m* private in the Nazi party motor corps.

NSKK.-Transportregiment *n* transportation regiment of the Nazi party motor corps.

Null *f* zero.

auf Null stellen to zero (*on Inst, scale, etc.*).

Nullpunkt *m* zero, freezing point; zero point, aiming point, directing point, point of origin (*Arty, Surv*).

Nullstellung *f* zero position (*of an Inst, scale, etc.*); neutral position, zeroing.

Nullzeit *f* zero hour.

Nummer *f* number.

Nummerscheibe *f* dial (*Tp*).

Nummerscheibenkästchen *n* dial box (*field Tp*).

Nurflügelflugzeug *n* all-wing airplane, "flying wing."

Nüstern *fpl* nostrils.

Nute *f* groove, slot, keyway (*also spelled der Nut*).

Nutzarbeit *f* useful work, brake horsepower.

Nutzfahrzeug *n* commercial vehicle (*MT*).

Nutzfrequenz *f* desired frequency (*Rad*).

Nutzlast *f* useful load, pay load.

Nutzleistung *f* net horsepower.

Nutzwiderstand *n* useful resistance (*Elec*).

O

OB-Betrieb *m* local-battery operation (*Tp*) (*abbr of* Ortsbatteriebetrieb).

Oberarbeitsführer *m* major (*Reich Labor Service*).

Oberarzt *m* first lieutenant (*Med*).

Oberbau *m* permanent way, top of roadbed (*RR*).

Oberbaustab *m* superior construction staff (*equivalent in status to a brigade staff*).

Oberbefehl *m* high command (*function*).

Oberbefehlshaber *m* commander in chief, commander. *See also* **Oberster Befehlshaber.**

Oberbefehlshaber des Heeres Commander-in-Chief of the Army.

Oberbefehlshaber einer Gruppe army group commander.

Oberbeschlagmeister *m* horseshoer (*master Sgt*).

Oberbrieftaubenmeister *m* pigeoneer (*master Sgt*).

obere Führung higher command (*Div and up*); higher command echelon.

Oberfähnrich *m* master sergeant (*officer candidate*).

Oberfähnrich der Flieger aviation cadet (*with rank of master Sgt*).

Oberfahrer *m* private first class (*H-Dr T*).

Oberfeldarzt *m* lieutenant colonel (*Med*).

Oberfeldkommandantur *f* military government area headquarters (*under commander of army group, in a T of Opns; under general commanding officer in charge of Mil Adm, in occupied territories*).

Oberfeldmeister *m* master sergeant (*Reich Labor Service*).

Oberfeldveterinär *m* lieutenant colonel (*Vet*).

Oberfeldwebel *m* master sergeant.

Oberfeldzeugstab *m* higher ordnance staff.

Oberfeuerwerker *m* master sergeant (*Ord*).

Oberfläche *f* surface (*outside or top*).

Oberfunker *m* radioman (*Pvt 1st class*).

Oberfunkmeister *m* radioman (*master Sgt*).

Obergefreiter *m* corporal.

Obergeneralarbeitsführer *m* major general (*Reich Labor Service*).

Obergrenadier *m* private first class (*Inf*).

Obergurt *m* top chord (*truss*); surcingle (*harness*).

Oberjäger *m* private first class (*mountain Inf*).

Oberkanonier *m* private first class

Oberkommandierender *m* commander-in-chief. *See* **Oberster Befehlshaber.**

Oberkommando *n* high command (*agency and function*).

Oberkommando der Kriegsmarine High Command of the Navy

Oberkommando der Luftwaffe High Command of the Air Forces

Oberkommando der Wehrmacht High Command of the Armed Forces (*abbr.* OKW).

Oberkommando des Heeres Army High Command (*abbr.* OKH).

Oberkraftfahrer *m* private first class (*MT*).

Oberlafette *f* top carriage (*G*).

Oberleutnant *m* first lieutenant.

Oberleutnant zur See lieutenant junior grade (*Nav*).

Oberpanzergrenadier *m* armored infantry rifleman (*Pvt 1st class*).

Oberpionier *m* private first class (*Engr*).

Oberquartiermeister *m* Deputy Chief of the General Staff (*at Oberkommando des Heeres; known as* Oberquartiermeister I, *Operations;* Oberquartiermeister II, *Training;* Oberquartiermeister III, *Organization;* Oberquartiermeister IV, *Intelligence;* Oberquartiermeister V, *Historical*); general staff officer at Hq of an army (*in charge of supply* and *Adm*).

Oberreiter *m* private first class

Oberring *m* upper band (*R*).

Oberringfeder *f* upper-band spring

Oberschenkel *m* thigh.

Oberschiedsrichter *m* assistant director (*maneuvers*).

Oberschild *m* upper shield (*G*).

Oberschirrmeister *m* master sergeant (*maintenance*).

Oberschütze *m* private first class (*Inf rifleman*).

Oberschwester *f* chief nurse.

Oberschwingungsfrequenz *f* harmonic frequency (*Rad*).

Oberst *m* colonel.

Oberstabsarzt *m* major (*Med*).

Oberstabsveterinär *m* major (*Vet*).

Oberstarbeitsführer *m* colonel (*Reich Labor Service*).

Oberstarzt *m* colonel (*Med*).

Oberster Befehlshaber der Wehrmacht Commander-in-Chief of the Armed Forces.

oberster Schiedsrichter director (*maneuvers*).

Oberstfeldmeister *m* lieutenant (*Reich Labor Service*).

Oberstintendant *m* civilian official in administrative services ranking as colonel.

Oberstleutnant *m* lieutenant colonel.

oberstrom upstream.

Oberstveterinär *m* colonel (*Vet*).

Obertruppführer *m* sergeant (*Reich Labor Service*).

Oberveterinär *m* (*Vet*) first lieutenant

Obervormann *m* chief foreman (*Reich Labor Service*)

Oberwachtmeister *m* master sergeant (*Arty, Cav*).

Oberzahlmeister *m* paymaster official (Wehrmachtbeamter *ranking as 1st Lt*). *See also* **Zahlmeister.**

Objektschutz *m* air defense of fixed installations.

OB-System *n* local-battery system (*Tp*) (*abbr. for* Ortsbatteriesystem).

Ofen *m* heater, oven, stove.

Ofenrohr *m* stovepipe; "bazooka" (*slang term for* Raketenpanzerbüchse, *rocket launcher*).

offen exposed (*Tac*); in clear (*Sig Com*); open, frank.

offene Flanke open flank (*Tac*).

offener Flügel exposed wing (*Tac*).

offener Funkspruch radio message in clear.

offene Stellung exposed position

Offensive *f* offensive (*Tac*).

offensive Verteidigung offensive defense.

Offizier *m* officer.

Offizierbewerber *m* officer aspirant.

Offizier des Beurlaubtenstandes reserve officer.

Offizierheim *n* officers' mess, officers' club.

Offizierlaufbahn *f* officer's career.

Offizierledigenheim *n* bachelor officers' quarters.

Offiziersanwärter *m* officer candidate.

Offiziersbursche *m* officer's orderly.

Offizierskasino *n* officers' mess.

Offizierslager *n* permanent camp for officer prisoners of war (*abbr.* Oflag).

Offiziersnachwuchs *m* new crop of officers.

Offiziersspähtrupp *m* officer reconnaissance patrol.

Offizierspatent *n* commission.

Offizier vom Biwakdienst bivouac security officer.

Offizier vom Dienst duty officer, officer on duty.

Offizier vom Ortsdienst officer of the guard.

Offizier vom Tagesdienst officer of the day.

Öffnerhebel *m* operating level, operating handle (*G*).

Öffnung *f* aperture, port, opening.

Oflag *n* *See* **Offizierslager.**

Ohnehaltflug *m* nonstop flight (*Avn*).

"Ohne Tritt, Marsch!" "Route step, march!"

Ohrverschlußwatte *f* cotton for ear plugs.

Oktanwert *m* octane rating.

Oktanzahl *f* octane number.

Okular *n* eyepiece.

OKW.-Bericht *m* official communiqué of the *Oberkommando der Wehrmacht.*

Öl *n* oil.

Ölablaß *m* oil drain.

Ölbehälter *m* oil tank.

ölbeständig oil-resistant.

Ölbohrloch *n* oil well.

Ölbombe *f* oil bomb.

Ölbüchse *f* oilcan.

öldicht oiltight.

Öldruckbremse *f* hydraulic brake.

Öleinfüll-Verschraubung *f* oil filler plug (*Mtr*).

Ölfederstrebe *f* oleo strut (*Ap*).

olivgrün olive drab.

Ölkanister *m* oil container (*Ap*,

Ölkohle *f* carbon (*Mtr*).

Öllager *n* oil-storage depot.

Ölmanometer *n* oil pressure gage.

Ölmeßbecher *m* graduated oil dispenser (*MT*).

Ölschlitzring *m* grooved piston ring (*Mtr*).

Ölstand *m* oil level.

Ölstandanzeiger *m* oil level gage

Ölstandschraube *f* oil level plug

Ölstandskontrolle *f* oil level check, oil level indicator (*Mtr*).

Ölthermometer *n* oil temperature gage.

Öltropfer *m* oiler.

Ölüberlauf *m* oil overflow (*Mtr*).

Ölwanne *f* oil pan (*Mtr*).

Operation *f* operation (*Tac, Med*).

Operationsbasis *f* base of operations (*Tac*).

Operationsbefehl *m* operations order.

Operationsgebiet *n* zone of operations, theater of operations.

Operationskarte *f* operations map.

Operationslinie *f* line of operations.

Operationsplan *m* operations plan.

Operationsraum *m* zone of operations, theater of operations.

operativ operational, strategic.

operative Aufklärung strategic reconnaissance.

operative Luftaufklärung strategic air reconnaissance.

operatives Ziel strategic objective.

operative Unterstützung indirect support (*Avn, Tac*).

Opfer *n* victim.

Oppanol *n* a synthetic substance resistant to mustard gas and Lewisite (*CWS*).

Optik *f* optics; lens system, optical system or instruments; telescopic sight (*G*); periscope (*Tk*).

optische Peilung pilotage (*Avn*).

optisches Zielgerät optical sight (*Ord*).

O-Punkt *m* aiming point (*Gunnery*). *See also* **Nullpunkt.**

Orden *m* medal, decoration, order.

Ordensband *n* ribbon (*of a decoration*).

Ordensschnalle *f* bar (*decoration*).

kleine Ordensschnalle miniature (*decoration*).

Ordensspange *f* bar (*decoration*).

Ordinate *f* ordinate, Y-coordinate.

Ordnung *f* order, rule.

Ordnungsdienst *m* provost service, military police service.

Ordnungsgleis *n* make-up track (*RR*).

Ordnungspolizei *f* uniformed regular police.

Ordonnanz *f* orderly.

Ordonnanzoffizier *m* special-missions staff officer.

Organisationsstab *m* organizational staff.

Organisation Todt Todt Organization (*Engr and Ft construction*).

Orientierung *f* orientation.

Orientierungslinie *f* orienting line (*Surv*).

Orientierungspunkt *m* control point (*Surv*).

Orkan *m* hurricane, tropical cyclone.

Orpo *f* See **Ordnungspolizei.**

Orsatapparat *m* Orsat gas-analysis apparatus (*CWS*).

Ort *m* locality, place; locus (*Math*). *See also* **Standort.**

Ortbalken *m* exterior stringer (*on a fixed bridge*); exterior balk (*on a floating bridge*).

orten locate; orient; take bearings.

Orter *m* navigator (*Avn*).

Orterkompaß *m* navigator's compass (*Avn*).

örtlich local.

Ortsbatterie *f* local battery (*Tp*).

Ortsbatterie-Betrieb *m* local-battery operation (*Tp*).

Ortsbesprechung *f* local operation

Ortsbestimmung *f* orientation, position determination.

Ortsbiwak *n* billets, close billets.

Ortschaft *f* village, town, inhabited locality.

Ortscheit *n* doubletree (*limber*).

Ortseindruck *m* sensation of direction (*sound locator*).

Ortsempfang *m* local reception

ortsfest fixed, permanent (*Arty, Ft*).

O.A.	Offizieranwärter	officer candidate
O.A.	Offizieraspirant	probationary cadet; **aspirant** officer
o.A.	ohne Auftrag	without order
o.As	**ohne Aufschlagzündung**	**without percussion system**
ob	ober	upper; **first; chief**
Ob	Oberst	colonel
O.B	Ortsbiwak	close billets
o.b.B	**ohne besonderen Befund**	without any distinct symptoms *(medical)*
Ob.Baustb	Oberbaustab	superior construction staff *(equal in status to a brigade staff)*
Obbfhb	Oberbefehlshaber	commander in chief
Ob.d.H	Oberbefehlshaber des Heeres	commander in chief of the army
Ob.d.L	Oberbefehlshaber der Luftwaffe	commander in chief of the air force
Ob.d.M	Oberbefehlshaber der Kriegsmarine	commander in chief of the navy
Ob.d.W	Oberbefehlshaber der Wehrmacht	commander in chief of the armed forces
Oberf	**Oberführer**	(SA) first regimental leader, Storm Troops *(equivalent U. S. rank: colonel)*; (SS)
Oberfeldkdtr	**Oberfeldkommandantur**	Supreme Field Command
Obergruf	**Obergruppenführer**	(SA) leader of group of Storm Troops corps *(equivalent U. S. rank: general)*; (SS) commander
Oberlt	**Oberleutnant**	first lieutenant
Oberr	**Oberreiter**	*(corresponds roughly to U. S. private first class, cavalry)*
Oberschles	Oberschlesien	Upper Silesia
Oberstlt	Oberstleutnant	lieutenant colonel
Oberstubaf	**Obersturmbannführer**	(SA) first battalion-leader, Storm Troops *(equivalent U. S. rank: major)*; (SS)
Oberstuf	**Obersturmführer**	(SA) first company-leader, Storm Troops *(equivalent U. S. rank: 1st lieutenant)*; (SS)
Obertruf	**Obertruppführer**	first platoon-leader, Storm Troops *(equivalent U. S. rank: master sergeant)*
OBF	Oberbannführer	chief district leader *(Hitler Youth)*
Ob.Fähnr	Oberfähnrich	officer candidate *(corresponding roughly to U. S. staff sergeant)*
Ob.F.Arzt	Oberfeldarzt	lieutenant colonel *(Medical Corps)*
Of.F.Apoth	Oberfeldapotheker	lieutenant colonel *(Pharmacy)*
Ob.F.K	Oberfeldkommandantur	Supreme Field Command
Obfu	Oberfunker	chief radio operator
Ob.F.Vet	Oberfeldveterinär	lieutenant colonel *(Veterinary Corps)*
Ob.Fw	Oberfeldwebel	*(corresponds roughly to U. S. staff sergeant, ordnance)*
Ob.Fw	Oberfeuerwerker	ordnance sergeant; artificer
Ob.Fwrk	Oberfeuerwerker	ordnance sergeant; artificer
Ob.Fw Sch	Oberfeuerwerkerschule	ordnance artificers' school
Ob.Gefr	Obergefreiter	*(corresponds roughly to U. S. acting corporal)*
Obgfr	Obergefreiter	*(corresponds roughly to U. S. acting corporal)*
obh	oberhalb	above
Obj.. Objäg	**Oberjäger**	soldier in light infantry division *(corresponding roughly to U. S. private first class)*
Obkan	**Oberkanonier**	*(corresponds roughly to U. S. private first class in artillery unit)*
Ob.Kom	**Oberkommandierender**	**high commander**
Ob.Kom	Oberkommando	high command
Ob.Kr.Ger	Oberkriegsgericht	general court-martial
Oblt	Oberleutnant	first lieutenant
Ob.Milit.Anw	Obermilitäranwalt	Judge Advocate General
Ob.Pi	Oberpionier	*(corresponds roughly to U. S. private first class, combat engineers)*
Ob.Quartiermstr	Oberquartiermeister	Army Quartermaster (Deputy Chief of Staff)
Ob.Qu.Mstr		
Obr	Ober-	first; chief; upper
Ob.R	Oberreiter	*(corresponds roughly to U. S. private first class, cavalry)*
Obrtr.		
Obs	Observations-	observation
Ob.Schmstr	Oberschirrmeister	supply sergeant *(corresponding roughly to U. S. staff sergeant)*
Obschtz	Oberschütze	*(corresponds roughly to U. S. private first class)*
Obst	Oberst	colonel
ObSta	Oberstabsarzt	major *(Medical Corps)*
Ob.St.Apoth	Oberstabsapotheker	major *(Pharmacy)*
Ob.St.Arzt	Oberstabsarzt	major *(Medical Corps)*
ObstArzt	Oberstarzt	colonel *(Medical Corps)*
Ob.-St.-B.Fhr	Obersturmbannführer	first battalion-leader, Storm Troops; rank of lieutenant
Ob.Stbs.Vet	Oberstabsveterinär	major *(Veterinary Corps)*
Obstlt	Obersleutnant	lieutenant colonel
Ob.St.Vet	Oberstabsveterinär	major *(Veterinary Corps)*
ObstVet	Oberstveterinär	colonel *(Veterinary Corps)*
Obus	Omnibus	motor bus
Ob.Vet	Oberveterinär	first lieutenant *(Veterinary Corps)*
Ob. Wachtmstr	Oberwachtmeister	*(corresponds roughly to U. S staff sergeant)*
Ob.Wm		

Ob.Zahlm	Oberzahlmeister	chief paymaster
Ob.Zm	**Oberzahlmeister**	**chief paymaster**
o.D	**ohne Datum**	**undated**
Od	Ostdeutscher	Eastern German
Od	Ostdeutschland	Eastern Germany
Ö	Ölstation	oil station; **fuel station**
Ö	Österreich	Austria
ö	östlich	eastward
O.E.G	Offizierentschädigungsgesetz	officers' **compensation law**
Ö.M	Ölmühle	oil-mill **(on maps)**
örtl	örtlich	local
Öst	Österreich	Austria
öst	östlich	eastward
Ofeldw	Oberfeldwebel	*(corresponds roughly to U. S. staff sergeant)*
off	offen	open
off	offensiv	offensive
off	offiziell	official
Off	Offizier	officer
Off.Anw	Offizieranwärter	officer candidate
OffEntschG	Offizierentschädigungsgesetz	officer's **compesation law**
Off.Erg.Best	Offizierergänzungsbestimmungen	officers **replacement regulations**
Off.K	Offizierkorps	officers' corps
Offiz	Offizier	officer
Offiz.Reitsch	Offizierreitschule	officers' cavalry **school**
Off.Kr	Offensivkrieg	offensive war
Off.Patr	Offizierpatrouille	officers' patrol
Off.Pf	Offizierpferd	officer's horse
Off.St Off.Stv	Offizierstellvertreter	acting officer *(noncommissioned officer)*
Offz	Offizier	officer
Offz.Anw	Offizieranwärter	officer candidate
Offz.Anw.d.B	Offizieranwärter des Beurlaubtenstandes	candidate for **a commission** as reserve officer
Offz.Asp	Offizieraspirant	probationary **cadet; aspirant** officer
Offz.Aufs	Offizieraufsicht	officer's **supervision**
Offz.d.B	Offizier des Beurlaubtenstandes	**reserve officer**
Offz.d.R	**Offizier der Reserve**	**reserve officer**
Offz.d.Rde	Offizier der Ronde	deputy officer of the guard
Offz.d.S	Offizier der Seewehr	naval reserve officer
Offz.(E)	**Ergänzungsoffizier**	retired officer **recalled to** active duty
Offz.Entl.Best	**Offizier-Entlassungsbestimmungen**	regulations concerning the discharge of officers
Offz.K	**Offizierkorps**	officers' corps; commissioned personnel
Offz.(La E)	**Luftaufsichtergänzungsoffizier**	retired officer recalled to active duty for air traffic control
Offz.Prf	Offizierprüfung	officers' examination
Offz.Sp.A	Offiziersspeiseanstalt	officers' mess
Offzstv	Offizierstellvertreter	acting officer *(noncommis-*
Offz.v.D	Offizier vom Dienst	officer on duty
Offz.Vers	Offizierversammlung	officers' assembly
Offz.Vers.R	**Offizierversammlungsraum**	officers' **assembly room**
Offz.v.Kas.D	Offizier vom Kasernendienst	**officer on barracks duty**
Offz.v.Lag.D	Offizier vom Lagerdienst	officer on camp duty
Offz.v.O	Offizier vom Ortsdienst	officer of the day
Offz.v.O.u.d.Rde	Offizier vom Ortsdienst und der Ronde	officer of the day and deputy officer of the guard
Offz.v.TrD	Offizier vom Truppendienst	deputy officer of the day
Offz.(W.E.)	Waffenergänzungsoffizier	ordnance replacement officer
Oflag	Offizierslager	officers prisoner-of-war camp
O-Flak	ortsfeste Flugzeugabwehrkanone	stationary or fixed antiaircraft gun
O-Flak-Battr	ortsfeste Flugzeugabwehrkanonenbatterie	**stationary or fixed antiaircraft gun battery**
O-Flak-Zg	ortsfester Flugzeugabwehrkanonenzug	**stationary antiaircraft platoon**
OFSchm	Oberfahnenschmied	horseshoer sergeant
Ofw	Oberfeldwebel	*(corresponds roughly to U. S. staff sergeant)*
OGefr	**Obergefreiter**	*acting corporal)*
O.Grenz-Kontr	**Obergrenzkontrolleur**	**chief border supervisor**
O.K	**Oberkommandierender**	**high commander**
O.K	Oberkommando	high command
O.K	Ortskommandant	local **military administrator**
O.K	**Ortskommandantur**	local military **administrative** headquarters
Okdo	Oberkommando	high command
O.K.H	Oberkommando des Heeres	**Army High Command**
Okkup	Okkupation	occupation
O.K.L	Oberkommando der Luftwaffe	**Air Force High Command**
O.K.M	Oberkommando der Kriegsmarine	Navy High Command
O.Kr	Ortskrankenstube	sick bay; hospital ward
O.Kr.Ger	Oberkriegsgericht	general court-martial
Okt	Oktober	October
O.K.W	Oberkommando der Wehrmacht	High Command of the Armed Forces
O.L	Oberste Luftsportkommission	Supreme Aerial Sports Commission
OLandm	Oberlandmesser	chief surveyor
Oldb	Oldenburg	Oldenburg
OLK	Oberste Luftsportkommission	Supreme Aerial Sports Commission
Ölst	Ölstation	oil (fuel) station

O Lt.	Oberleutnant	first lieutenant
O.M.	Ortsmisswelsung	local compass declination
Om	Ostmark	Austria
OMA	Obermilitäranwalt	Judge Advocate General
OMilA	Obermilitäranwalt	Judge Advocate General
OMilBefh	Obermilitärbefehlshaber	commander in chief
Omn	Omnibus	motor bus
ON	Ortsnetz	local telephone network
ONO	Ostnordost	east-northeast
OO	Abort	latrine
OO	Grossgüterwagen	4-axle heavy freight car (*up to 15 tons*)
O.O	Ordonnanzoffizier	administrative officer
o.P	ohne Portepee	without sword knot
Op	Operation	operation
Op	Operationsabteilung	operations section
O.P	Ortspolizei	local police
Op.B	Operationsbasis	base of operations
oper	operativ	operative
Operat	Operation	operation
Op.Flgh	Operationsflughafen	operational airport
Op.L	Operationslinie	line of operations
O.p.l.m	Orden Pour le Mérite	order *Pour le Mérite*
O.p.l.m.E	Orden Pour le Mérite mit Eichenlaub	order *Pour le Mérite* with oak leaf
Op.Pl	Operationsplan	plan of operations
Opt	Optik	optics
Op.Z	Operationsziel	tactical objective
O.Q. O.Qmstr.	Oberquartiermeister	Army Quartermaster
o.R	ohne Rauch	smokeless
Ord	Orden	decoration; order
Ord	Ordnung	order
Ord. Offz	Ordonnanzoffizier	administrative officer
Ordonn.Offis	Ordonnanzoffizier	administrative officer
Org	Organisation	organization
org	organisieren	to organize
org	originell	original
Org.Pl	Organisationsplan	plan of organization
Orpo	Ordnungspolizei	regular police
Ortsbef	Ortsbefestigung	local fortification
Ortsbeh	Ortsbehörde	municipal authorities
Ortsbw	Ortsbiwak	close billet
Ortsgef	Ortsgefecht	local combat;local fighting
Ortskdt	Ortskommandant	local militaryadministrator
Ortskdtr	Ortskommandantur	local militaryadministrative headquarters
Orts San.Offs	Ortssanitätsoffizier	local medical officer
Orts Vet.Offs	Ortsveterinäroffizier	local veterinary officer
OSAF	Oberster SA-Führer	Supreme Commander of the Storm Troops
O.Sch	Oberschütze	(*corresponds roughly to U.S. private first class*)
Oscha (SA)	Oberscharführer	first section-leader, Storm Troops (*equivalent U. S. rank: staff sergeant*)
Oscha(SS)	Oberscharführer	platoon leader, Elite Guard (*equivalent U. S. rank: 1st sergeant*)
O.Schirrm	Oberschirrmeister	supply sergeant(*corresponding roughly to U. S. staff sergeant*)
OSO	Ostsüdost	east-southeast
Ost	Ostland	Eastern Germany
OSta	Oberstabsarzt	major (*Medical Corps*)
OSt.Apoth	Oberstabsapotheker	major (*Pharmacy*)
Ostd	Ostdeutscher	Eastern German
Ostd	Ostdeutschland	Eastern Germany
Ostuf	Obersturmführer	first company-leader(Storm Troops), rank of captain
OStV	Oberstabsveterinär	major (*Veterinary Corps*)
ostw	ostwärts	eastwards
o.T	oberer Totpunkt	upper center of gravity; top dead center
O.T. Org.Todt	Organisation Todt	special construction organization (*Dr. Fritz Todt*)
Otg	Ortung	orientation; location
OTF	Obertruppführer	first platoon-leader (Storm Troops), rank of 2d lt
O.U	Ortsunterkunft	billet
O.u.E	Orden und Ehrenzeichen	decorationand honor badges
O.Untk	Ortsunterkunft	billet
OV	Oberveterinär	first lieutenant (*Veterinary*)
o.V	ohne Verpflegung	without rations
o.V	ohne Verzögerung	without delay
O.v.D	Offizier vom Dienst	officer on duty
O.V.L	oberste Verkehrsleitung	general headquarters, traffic control section
O.v.N	Offizier vom Nachrichtendienst	intelligence officer
O.v.O	Offizier vom Ortsdienst	officer of the day
OW	Oberwachtmeister	(*corresponds roughly to U.S. staff sergeant*)
OWachtmstr	Oberwachtmeister	
O.Z	Oberzahlmeister	chief paymaster
O.Z	Oberzensurstelle	chief censor's office
Oz	Ozean	ocean
O.Zm	Oberzahlmeister	chief paymaster
OzN	Ost zu Nord	east by north
OzS	Ost zu Süd	east by south

ortsfeste Küstenartillerie fixed seacoast artillery.
ortsfeste Lafette stationary gun mount (*G*).
Ortsgefecht *n* *See* Ortskampf.
Ortskampf *m* combat in towns.
Ortskommandant *m* commander of a garrison, post, or station; town commander (*Mil Govt*).
Ortskommandantur *f* garrison, post, or station headquarters; town headquarters (*Mil Govt*) (Ortskommandantur I, *in large and medium-sized cities;* Ortskommandantur II, *in small cities, towns, and villages*).
Ortskrankenlazarett *n* billet hospital. (*Med*).
Ortskrankenstube *f* billet dispensary.
ortskundig familiar with a locality or area.
Ortsmißweisung *f* magnetic declination.
Ortsnetz *n* local net (*Tp*).
Ortsquartier *n* *See* Ortsunterkunft.
Ortssender *m* local station (*Rad*).
Ortsunterkunft *f* billets.
Ortsvorstand *m* local authorities, town authorities.
Ortung *f* position finding, orientation, taking of bearings.
Ortungsanforderung *f* request for a bearing (*Avn, Rad*).
Ortungsleuchtzeichen *n* ground position signal (*ground-air Com*).
Öse *f* lug; ring; lunette; eye (*Tech*).
Ost *m* east (*also spelled* Osten).
Ostlegion *f* legion composed of non-German volunteers and prisoners of war from East-European countries.
Ostmedaille *f* Eastern Campaign Medal (*decoration*).
Ostsee *f* Baltic Sea.
Otter *f* paravane.

P

Packgefäß *n* bulk container.
Packriemen *m* pack strap (*harness*).
Packsattel *m* pack saddle (*harness*).
Packstrick *m* pack rope (*harness*)
Packtasche *f* saddlebag.
Packung *f* packing (*Mech*).
Paddelboot *n* collapsible paddling boat.
Pak *f* antitank gun, antitank artillery (*abbr. of* Panzerabwehrkanone).
Pakethülle *f* wrapping.
Pak-Flak *f* antitank-antiaircraft gun, dual-purpose gun.
Pakgeschütz *n* antitank gun.
Pakgeschütz auf Selbstfahrlafette self-propelled antitank gun, tank destroyer.
Pakstellung *f* antitank gun position, antitank gun emplacement.
Pak-Zug *m* antitank platoon.
Panne *f* breakdown; engine failure; blowout.
Panoramakammer *f* panoramic camera (*Avn*).
Pantograph *m* pantograph (Surv).
Panzer *m* armor; tank.
Panzerabteilung *f* armored battalion.
Panzerabwehr *f* antitank defense, antimechanized defense (*in compounds, now superseded by* Panzerjäger-).
Panzerabwehrgewehr *n* antitank rifle (*now called* Panzerbüchse).
Panzerabwehrgeschütz *n* antitank gun.
Panzerabwehrgraben *m* antitank ditch.
Panzerabwehrkanone *f* antitank gun (*now called* Panzerjägerkanone).
Panzerabwehrmine *f* antitank mine.
Panzerabwehrmittel *npl* means of antitank defense.
Panzerabwehrrakete *f* antitank rocket.
Panzerangriff *m* armored attack, tank attack.
Panzerartillerie *f* armored division artillery, armored artillery.
Panzeraufbau *m* tank hull and turret; armored body of a vehicle.
Panzeraufklärungsabteilung *f* armored reconnaissance battalion.
Panzerbataillon *n* armored battalion.
Panzerbefehlswagen *m* armored command car.
Panzerbekämpfung *f* antitank combat.
Panzerbeobachtungsturm *m* armored observation turret.
Panzerbesatzung *f* tank crew, armored vehicle crew.
Panzerbeschuß *m* firing at tanks; test firing at armor plate.
Panzerbeschußtafel *f* firing table for antitank gun.
Panzerblech *n* armor plate.
Panzerblende *f* tank shutter; tank gun shield, mantlet.
Panzerbombe *f* antitank bomb, armor-piercing bomb, heavy-case bomb.
panzerbrechend armor-piercing.
Panzerbrigade *f* armored brigade, tank brigade.
Panzerbüchse *f* antitank rifle.
Panzerdeckungsloch *n* foxhole (*for AT protection*).
Panzerdivision *f* armored division.
Panzerdrehturm *m* revolving armored turret (*Ft*); revolving tank turret (*Tk*).
panzerdurchschlagend armor-piercing (*Am*).
Panzerdurchschlagsleistung *f* armor-piercing capacity, penetration (*Am*).
Panzereinsatz *m* commitment of armored units.
Panzererkennungsdienst *m* tank identification service.
Panzerfahrer *m* tank driver.
Panzerfahrschule *f* armored vehicle operators' school.
Panzerfahrzeug *n* armored vehicle.
Panzerfahrzeugfalle *f* tank trap.
Panzerfahrzeuggraben *m* antitank ditch.
Panzerfalle *f* tank trap.
Panzerführer *m* tank commander (*NCO*); armored-vehicle commander; armored-unit commander.
Panzerfunker *m* tank radio operator.
Panzerfunktrupp *m* armored radio section.
Panzerfunkwagen *m* armored radio car or truck.
Panzergeschoß *n* armor-piercing projectile.
panzergeschützt armor-protected.
Panzerglas *n* bulletproof glass.
Panzergraben *m* antitank ditch.
Panzergranate *f* armor-piercing shell, armor-piercing rifle grenade.
Panzergranate-Patrone *f* armor-piercing shell (*fixed Am*).
Panzergrenadier *m* armored infantry rifleman, private in armored infantry regiment.
Panzergrenadier-Bataillon *n* armored infantry battalion.
Panzergrenadier-Brigade *f* armored infantry brigade.
Panzergrenadier-Division *f* motorized division. *See also* **SS-Panzergrenadier-Division.**
Panzergrenadier-Ersatzregiment *n* armored infantry replacement regiment.
Panzergrenadier-Personenkraftwagen armored personnel carrier.
Panzergrenadier-Regiment *n* motorized infantry regiment (*of a* Panzerdivision).
Panzergruppe *f* armored group.
Panzergürtel *m* armor belt.
Panzerhindernis *n* antitank obstacle.
Panzerinstandsetzungsabteilung *f* tank repair battalion.
Panzerjäger *m* member of antitank unit.
Panzerjägerabteilung *f* antitank battalion.
Panzerjägergeschütz *n* antitank gun.
Panzerjägerkanone *f* *See* Panzerjägergeschütz.
Panzerjägerkompanie *f* antitank company.
Panzerjägerregiment *n* antitank regiment.
Panzerjägerzug *m* antitank platoon.
Panzerkabel *n* armored cable (*Elec*).
Panzerkampfabzeichen *n* *See* **Panzerkampfwagenabzeichen.**
Panzerkampfwagen *m* tank.
Panzerkampfwagenabzeichen *n* Tank Badge (*decoration awarded to members of armored units after participation in three separate combat actions*).
Panzerkampfwagenhindernis *n* tank obstacle.
Panzerkanone *f* tank gun.
Panzerkasten *m* tank hull.
Panzerkastenoberteil *n* sponson, upper hull (*Tk*).
Panzerkette *f* tank track.
Panzer-Kommandant *m* tank commander.
Panzerkompanie *f* tank company.
Panzerkopf *m* armor-piercing cap (*Am*). **-körper** *m* hull (*Tk*).
Panzerkorps *n* armored corps.
Panzerkorpskommando *n* armored corps headquarters.
Panzerkräfte *fpl* armored forces, armored units.
Panzerkraftfahrzeug *n* armored vehicle.
Panzerkraftwagen *m* armored car.
Panzerkrieg *m* armored warfare.
Panzerkuppel *f* tank cupola, armored cupola (*Ft*).
Panzer-Lehr-Regiment *n* armored demonstration regiment.
Panzermine *f* antitank mine.
Panzermunition *f* armor-piercing ammunition; tank ammunition.
Panzernachrichtenabteilung *f* armored signal battalion.
Panzer-Obergrenadier *m* private first class (*Armd Inf Regt*).
Panzeroberschütze *m* private first class (*in Armd unit*).
Panzeroffizier *m* armored officer.
Panzerpionier *m* armored engineer.
Panzer-Pionier-Bataillon *n* armored engineer battalion.
Panzerplatte *f* armor plate.
Panzerregiment *n* armored regiment.
Panzerrichttafel *f* tank-silhouette aiming target.
Panzerscharte *f* peephole, direct vision slit (*Tk*).
Panzerschild *m* armor-plate shield (*G*). **-schott** *n* armor bulkhead (*Tk*).
Panzerschutz *m* armor protection (*Ft, Tk*); antitank defense.
Panzerschütze *m* private in an armored unit; tank gunner.
panzersicher secure against mechanized attack.
Panzersonderfahrzeug *n* special-purpose armored vehicle.
Panzerspähfahrzeug *n* armored reconnaissance vehicle.
Panzerspähkompanie *f* armored reconnaissance company.
Panzerspäh-Schwadron *f* mechanized cavalry reconnaissance troop.
Panzerspähtrupp *m* armored reconnaissance car section.
Panzerspähwagen *m* armored reconnaissance car, armored scout car.
Panzersperre *f* antitank obstacle.
Panzersperrgraben *m* antitank ditch.
Panzersperrmauer *f* antitank wall obstacle.
Panzerspitze *f* armored point (*Adv Gd*). **-sprenggeschoß** *n* armor-piercing projectile.
Panzersprenggranate *f* armor-piercing shell.
Panzerstärke *f* thickness of armor (*Tk*).
Panzerstoß *m* armored thrust (*Tac*).
Panzersturmabzeichen *n* Armored Assault Badge (*decoration*).
Panzertransportwagen *m* armored personnel carrier.
Panzertruppe *f* Armored Command.
Panzertruppen *fpl* armored troops, armored forces.
Panzerturm *m* tank turret; armored turret (*Ft*).
Panzerung *f* armor, armor plating.
Panzerunterstützung *f* armored support (*Tac*).
Panzerverband *m* armored formation, armored force unit, combined-arms armored force.
Panzerverbände der Heerestruppen GHQ reserve tank groups.
Panzervernichtungsabzeichen *n* decoration awarded for close-combat destruction of at least one enemy tank.
Panzer-Verschwindeturm *m* disappearing armored turret (*Ft*).
Panzerwaffe *f* Armored Command.
Panzerwagen *m* armored car, combat car, tank.
Panzerwagenfalle *f* tank trap.
Panzerwagengraben *m* tank ditch.
Panzerwanne *f* tank hull.
Panzerwarndienst *m* antimechanized warning system.
Panzerwarnung *f* tank warning, antimechanized warning.
Panzerwart, *m* armored maintenance man.
Panzerwerk *n* steel and concrete fortification.
Panzerwerkstattkompanie *f* armored force repair shop company.
Panzerweste *f* body armor (*Avn*).
Panzerzug *m* armored train (*RR*); tank platoon.
Papierstreifenverfahren *n* paper-strip method (*aerial Photo*).
Pappe *f* cardboard (*also called* Pappdeckel *m*).
Parabel-Fachwerkträger *m* curved-chord truss.
Parabellum *n* a type of self-loading pistol.
Parade *f* parade, review.
Paradeanzug *m* full-dress uniform.
Parademarsch *m* march in review, pass in review.
Paradeplatz *m* parade ground.
Parallaxe *f* parallax, azimuth difference.
Parallaxwinkel *m* angle of parallax, azimuth difference.
Parallel-Fachwerkträger *m* parallel-chord truss.
Parallelogrammgestänge *n* parallelogram linkage system (*AA sight*).
Parallelschaltung *f* parallel connection (*Elec*).
Pardon *m* quarter, mercy, clemency.
parieren to parry.
Parierstange *f* bayonet guard.
Park *m* park, depot.
parken to park.
Parklicht *n* parking light (*auto headlight*).
Parlamentär *m* parlementaire, bearer of a flag of truce.
Parlamentärflagge *f* flag of truce.
Parole *f* password.
Parteien *fpl* opposing sides (*maneuvers*).
Parteiführer *m* commander of one of the opposing forces in maneuvers.
Paspel *f* piping or edging on uniform.
Paß *m* pass (*Top*); passport.
Paßgenauigkeit *f* accuracy of fit
Passierschein *m* permit, pass, safe-conduct, military passport.
Paßstück *n* adapter (*Ord*).
Passung *f* fit (*Tech*).

P

P	Panzer	armored
P	Panzergeschoss	armor-piercing shell
P	Panzertruppe	armored troops; armored units; mechanized units; tank forces (*P on shoulder straps*)
P	Park	park; depot
P	Parkplatz	parking lot (*for automobiles*)
P	Parseval	Parseval (*non-rigid airship*)
P	Partei	party; faction
P	Patrone	cartridge; semifixed shell; round of ammunition
P	Patrouille	patrol
P	Pegel	water gauge; watermark post (*on maps*)
P	Personenzug	passenger train
P	Pferd	horse
P	Phosphor	phosphorus ammunition (*tracer*)
P	Pionier	combat engineer
P	Pistole	pistol
p	planmässig	according to plan
P	Platzpatrone	blank cartridge
P	Polizeibeamter	police official; policeman
P	Prallschiff	non-rigid airship
P	Protestant	Protestant
P	Proviant	supplies; provisions; stores
P	Pulver	powder
P	Pumpe	pump
P.A.	Panzerabwehr	antitank defense
P.A.A.	Panzerabwehrabteilung	antitank detachment
PA	Personalamt	Army Personnel Office
PA	Propagandaamt	propaganda office
Packh	Packhülle	carrying case
Packpf	Packpferd	pack horse
Pack-Wg	Packwagen	baggage wagon
Pack-Wg.m F.Schm.	Packwagen mit Feldschmiede	baggage wagon with mobile forge
Pak	Panzerabwehrkanone	antitank gun
PAN	Dringlichkeitsmeldung	emergency message (*aviation*)
Panz.Tr.Pi.Zg	Panzertruppenpionierzug	combat engineer platoon of tank troops
P.A.O.	Proviantamtsordnung	supply office regulations
Pap	Papiergeld	paper money
Pap.M	Papiermühle	paper mill (*on maps*)
Par	Parade	parade; review
Par.Anz	Paradeanzug	parade uniform
Par.Stg	Parierstange	bayonet guard
Part	Partei	party; faction
Pass	Passagier	passenger
Pass.Sch	Passierschein	pass; permit
Pat	Patent	officer's commission; patent
Patr	Patrone	cartridge; semifixed shell;
Patr	Patrouille	patrol
Patr.Mun	Patronenmunition	fixed ammunition
Patr.T	Patronentasche	cartridge pouch
Patr.Tr	Patronentrommel	cartridge drum
Patr.Wg	Patronenwagen	ammunition carrier
P.Auftrag	Patrouillenauftrag	patrol task; patrol mission
PB	Pionierbataillon	combat engineers battalion
PB	Polizeibeamter	police official; policeman
P.B.T.	Panzerbeobachtungsturm	armored observation turret
PEG	Pensionsergänzungsgesetz	law regarding supplementary pension
Pens	Pension	pension
PensV	Pensionierungsvorschrift für das Heer	pension regulations for the army
Perisk	Periskop	periscope
Perm	Permanenz	permanence
perm.Bef	permanente Befestigung	permanent fortification
pers	persönlich	personal
Pers	Person	person; passenger
Pers.Adj	persönlicher Adjutant	personal adjutant; aide de camp
Per-Stoff	Grünkreuz	"green cross" choking gas
Pers.V	Personenverkehr	passenger traffic
Petr.F	Petroleumfeuerung	petroleum firing (*heating*); petroleum fuel
Pf	mit Pferdezug	horse-drawn
P.F	Personenfähre	passenger ferry (*on maps*)
Pf	Pfennig	pfennig (*1/100 of mark*)
Pf	Pferd	horse
Pf	Pferdehalter	groom (*cavalry*)
Pf	Pflege	nursing; care
Pf	Pflicht	duty; obligation
Pf	Pflock	peg; stake; picket
Pf	Pfuhl	pool (*on maps*)
Pf	Pfund	pound (*.5 of a kilogram*)
Pf	Polizeiführer	chief of police
Pf.Aush	Pferdeaushebung	requisitioning of horses
Pf.A.V.	Pferdeaushebungsvorschrift	regulations for the requisitioning of horses
Pfd	Pferd	horse
Pf.D	Pferdedepot	remount depot
Pfd.Kr.Kw	Pferdekrankenkraftwagen	horse ambulance
Pfd.Kr.Kw.Kol	Pferdekrankenkraftwagenkolonne	horse ambulance column (*motorized*)
Pfd.Trsp.Wg	Pferdetransportwagen	horse transport wagon
Pf.Ers	Pferdeersatz	horse replacement
Pf.F	Pfadfinder	scout
PfFB	Pferdefeldbahn	horse field-railroad
Pf.Fz	Pferdefahrzeug	horse-drawn vehicle
Pfg	Pfennig	pfennig (*1/100 of mark*)
Pf.Kr.S.St	Pferdekrankensammelstelle	collecting station for sick horses
Pf.L	Pferdelazarett	horse hospital
Pfl	Pflege	nursing; care
pfl	pflegen	to nurse; to take care of
Pfl	Pflicht	duty; obligation
Pfl	Pflock	peg; stake; picket
Pfl	Pfuhl	pool (*on maps*)
Pf.Laz	Pferdelazarett	horse hospital
Pflegep	Pflegepersonal	nursing personnel
pflgem	pflichtgemäss	duty-bound; loyal
P.F.S	Peilfunkstelle	radio bearing station
Pf.Verb.Pl	Pferdeverbandplatz	dressing station for horses
Pf.W	Pferdewärter	horse-groom
Pf.Zg	mit Pferdezug	horse-drawn
Pg	Parteigenosse	member of the National Socialist Party
P.G	Pensionsgesetz	pension law
P.G.I	Pioniergerätinspizient	combat engineer equipment inspector
PGr	Panzergranate	armor-piercing shell
Ph	Phosphor	phosphorus (*ammunition, tracer*)
Pharm	Pharmazeut	pharmacist; apothecary; druggist
P.H.D	Pionierhauptdepot	combat engineer main depot
Ph.Mun	Phosphormunition	phosphorus (tracer) ammunition
phot	photogrammetrisch	photogrammetric
Phot	Photographie	photography
phot	photographisch	photographic
photogr	photogrammetrisch	photogrammetric
Photom	Photometer	photometer; light meter
phys	physisch	physical
Pi	Pionier	pioneer; combat engineer
Pi	Pistole	pistol
Pi08	Pistole (Modell von 1908)	pistol, model 1908
Pi.A	Pionierabteilung	combat engineer detachment
Pi B	Pionierbataillon	combat engineer battalion
Pi.Br.Kol	Pionierbrückenkolonne	engineer bridge train
Pi.Btl	Pionierbataillon	combat engineer battalion
Pi.Hd.Karr	Pionierhandkarren	combat engineer handcart
Pi.Kp	Pionierkompanie	combat engineer company
Pi.Kp.(mot)	motorisierte Pionierkompanie	motorized combat engineer company
Pi.K.u.F	Pionierdienst im Kampf um Festungen	combat engineers instructions for warfare on fortifications
Pil	Pilot	pilot
Pi.L.Boot	Pionier-Landungsboot	combat engineer assault-boat
Pi.Masch.Zg	Pioniermaschinenzug	engineer repair platoon
Pion	Pionier	pioneer; combat engineer
Pion.Btl	Pionierbataillon	combat engineer battalion
Pion.Kol	Pionierkolonne	combat engineer train
Pion.Min.Komp	Pionierminenkompanie	combat engineer mine company
Pion.u.Nachr.P	Pionier- und Nachrichtenpark	combat engineer and signal equipment depot (*on maps*)
Pion.Vers.K	Pionierversuchskompanie	combat engineer experimental company
Pion.Wg	Pionierwagen	combat engineer wagon
Pi.Park-Kp	Pionierparkkompanie	combat engineer park company
Pi.Rgt	Pionierregiment	combat engineer regiment
Pi.Sch	Pionierschule	combat engineer school
Pi.Schirrm.V	Pionierschirrmeistervorschrift	service regulations for supply sergeants (*combat engineers*)
Pi.Schwd	Pionierschwadron	combat engineer troop (*cavalry*)
Pi.Spr.M	Pioniersprengmittel	explosives used by combat
Pist	Pistole	pistol
Pist. Gr	Pistolengriff	pistol grip
Pist.Sch	Pistolenschiessen	pistol firing
Pist.Sch	Pistolenschütze	pistol sharpshooter
Pi.Üb.Pl	Pionierübungsplatz	combat engineer training
P.Verb.Offz	Pionierverbindungsoffizier	combat engineer liaison officer
Piv.L	Pivotlafette	pivot mounting;
Pi.Wst.Kl	Pionierwerkstatt Klaus-	combat engineer workshop,
Pi.Zg	Pionierzug	combat engineer platoon
Pk	Park	park; depot
P.K	Propagandakompanie	propaganda company
Pkt	Punkt	point; dot; period; aid station
PkW	Packwagen	baggage wagon
Pkw	Panzerkraftwagen	armored car
Pkw	Personenkraftwagen	passenger automobile; passenger car; motor car
Pl	Personen- und Lastauto	combination passenger car and truck
Pl	Plan	plan; map; design; project
pl	planmässig	according to plan
Pl	Plateau	plateau
Pl	Platin	platinum
Pl	Platz	location; place; aid station (*medical*)
planm	planmässig	according to plan
P-Lauf	Platzpatronenlauf am Maschinengewehr	blank-cartridge barrel of machine gun
P Kdo	Platzkommando	garrison headquarters
Pl.Maj	Platzmajor	fortress headquarter's executive officer
Pl.Patr	Platzpatrone	blank cartridge
Pl.Sch	Planschiessen	map fire (*artillery*)
Plu	Planunterlage	plane table
Pl.Vet	Platzveterinär	local veterinary
Pl.W	Planwagen	tilted cart
Plz	Planzeiger	plotting board
Pl. Zchn	Planzeichnen	map making; plotting
PM	Papiermark	paper mark (*currency*)
PM	Platzmajor	fortress headquarter's executive officer

P.M	Pulvermagazin	powder magazine (*on maps*)
Pmk	Papiermark	paper mark (*currency*)
P-Mun	Platzpatronenmunition	blank ammunition
Pm.W	Postzug mit Wehrmachtteil	mail train with section for the armed forces
Pneu	Pneumatik	pneumatics; pneumatic tire
P.O	Personenomnibus	passenger bus
PO	Politische Organisation der NSDAP	political organization of the National Socialist Party
Pol	Polizei	police
Pol B	Polizeibeamter	police official; policeman
Pom	Pommern	Pomerania
Pont	Ponton	ponton
Pont	Pontonnier	ponton-bridge engineer
Pont.Br	Pontonbrücke	ponton bridge
Ponton	Pontonnier	ponton-bridge engineer
Pont.Zg	Pontonzug	ponton platoon
Port	Portepee	officer's sword knot
Port.Uffz	Portepeeunteroffizier	senior noncommissioned officer *with officer's swordknot*
Posit.Art	Positionsartillerie	artillery in permanent emplacements
Pos.Lpn	Positionslampen	navigation lights
Pr	Phosphor	phosphorus (*ammunition*)
P.R	Pionierregiment	combat engineer regiment
Pr	Probe	trial; test
Pr	Proviant	supply; provisions; stores
Pr	Prüfung	test; examination; check
PrA	Proviantamt	supply office; depot
PrAD	Proviantamtsdirektor	supply office director
Präs.St	Präsenzstärke	effectives; effective strength
Pr IA	Proviantamtsinspektor	supply office inspector
prakt	praktisch	practical
prbw	probeweise	by way of trial; experimental
Prf	Prüfung	test; examination; check
Pris R	Prisenrecht	right of capture; law governing prizes (*naval*)
pr.M	preussische Meile	Prussian mile (*7.532 kilometers*)
Pr M	Proviantmeister	rations non-commissioned officer
Pr.Mun	Phosphormunition	phosphorus (tracer) ammunition
Probl	Problem	problem
Proj	Projekt	project
Proj	Projektil	projectile
Prokl	Proklamation	proclamation
Prol	Prolongation	prolongation
Promi	Propagandaministerium	propaganda ministry
Prop	Propaganda	propaganda
Prop	Propeller	propeller
Prop.Min	Propagandaministerium	Propaganda Ministry
Prosp	Prospekt	prospect
Prot	Protektion	protection
Prot	Protektorat	Protectorate
Prot	Protestant	Protestant
Prov	Proviant	supplies; provisions; stores
Prov.Amt	Proviantamt	supply office; depot (*on maps*)
Prov.Anst	Provinzialanstalt	provincial institution
Prov.Ch	Provinzial-Chaussee	provincial highway
Prov.Wsstr	Provinzialwasserstrasse	provincial waterway; provincial canal
Proz	Prozent	per cent
Proz.G	Prozentgehalt	percentage content
Pr.St	Protzenstellung	limber position
Prüf	Prüfung	test; examination; check
Prv	Proviant	supply; provisions; stores
Prv.Amts-Dir	Proviantamtsdirektor	supply office director
Prvmstr	Proviantmeister	rations noncommissioned officer
PS	Pferdestärken	horsepower
P.S	Pionierschule	combat engineer school
PS	Postskriptum	postscript
P.S.Gr	Panzerstahlgranate	steel armor-piercing shell
PSi	Indizierte Pferdestärken	indicated horsepower
PS Std	Pferdestärken pro Stunde	horsepower per hour
PSt	Passstelle	passport office; point on a mountain pass
P.St	Pioniersturmanleitung	combat engineer assault manual
Pt	Pontonnier	ponton-bridge engineer
Pt.V	Pontonniervorschrift	ponton bridging regulations
P.Ü	Post-Überwachung	surveillance of mails
Pulv	Pulver	powder
pulv	pulverisieren	to pulverize
Pulv.Fabr	Pulverfabrik	powder factory
Pulv.Mag	Pulvermagazin	powder magazine (*on maps*)
Pumpst	Pumpstation	pump station (*on maps*)
P.V	Pensionierungsvorschrift	pension regulations
P.V	Pontonniervorschrift	ponton bridging regulations
P.V.V	Patronenverwaltungsvorschrift	ammunition handling regulations
P.V.W	Postvorschrift für die Wehrmacht	postal regulations for the armed forces
pw	paarweise	by pairs; in couples
Pw	Packwagen	baggage wagon
Pw	Personenzuggepäckwagen	passenger-train baggage-car
Pw 4 Ü	4-achziger D-Zuggepäckwagen mit stählerner Übergangsbrücke	4-axle express-train baggage-car with steel footbridge

Patent *n* officer's commission; patent *(Tech)*.
paten[illegible]er [illegible]fficer
Patrone *f* cartridge *(Am)*; round of fixed ammunition *(Arty)*.
Patronenauswerfer *m* ejector.
Patronenauszieher *m* extractor.
Patroneneinlage *f* breech recess *(R)*.
Patronenführungsleisten *fpl* cartridge guides *(MG)*.
Patronengurt *m* cartridge belt *(MG)*; bandoleer.
Patronenhalter *m* cartridge holder *(MG)*.
Patronenhebel *(MG)* cartridge lever
Patronenhülse *f* cartridge case.
Patronenkasten *m* cartridge box, ammunition box.
Patronenkorb *m* shell basket *(for fixed Am)*.
Patronenlager *n* cartridge chamber *(G, R)*.
Patronenmunition *f* fixed ammunition.
Patronenrahmen *m* clip *(R, AA gun)*.
Patronenraum *m* propelling-charge chamber *(Mort shell)*.
Patronenschacht *m* feed funnel *(fixed aircraft MG)*.
Patronenstreifen *m* cartridge clip.
Patronenstützfeder *f* cartridge-support spring *(MG)*.
Patronentasche *f* ammunition pocket, ammunition pouch.
Patronenträger *m* cartridge carrier *(MG)*.
Patronenträgerhebel *m* belt-feed lever *(MG)*.
Patronenzuführung *f* cartridge feed *(SA)*.
Patrouillenflug *m* patrol, patrolling *(Avn)*.
Patte *f* collar patch, cuff patch.
Pause *f* pause; tracing.
Pauspapier *n* tracing paper.
Pech *n* pitch.
Pegel *m* water-level gage *(for rivers, lakes, etc.)*.
Peilanlage *f* direction-finder station *(Air Navigation)*.
Peilantenne *f* direction-finding antenna.
Peilapparat *m* azimuth instrument.
Peilaufsatz *m* pelorus *(Avn)*.
Peilberichtigungskurve *f* deviation curve *(Rad)*.
Peilempfänger *m* radio compass, direction finder *(Air Navigation)*.
Peilen *n* direction finding *(Rad)*.
peilen to take a bearing *(Nav, Rad, Avn)*.
Peilfluglelter *m* chief of direction-finder station *(Avn)*.
Peilfunkempfänger *m* radio compass, direction finder *(Air Navigation)*.
Peilfunkgerät *n* radio direction finder.
Peilfunkstelle *f* radio direction finder station *(Avn)*.
Peilgerät *n* azimuth instrument *(Surv)*; direction-finder equipment or set *(Rad, Avn)*.
Peilkompaß *m* navigator's compass *(Avn)*.
Peilkraftwagen *m* radio direction-finding truck.
Peilleitstelle *f* radio direction-finder control station.
Peillinie *f* line of bearing, bearing line *(Air Navigation)*.
Peillot *n* sounding lead *(Nav)*.
Peilnebenstelle *f* auxiliary direction-finder station *(Air Navigation)*.
Peilrahmen *m* directional loop antenna *(Rad)*.
Peilscheibe *f* azimuth instrument.
Peilsender *m* directional transmitter.
Peilstelle *f* radio direction-finder station.
Peilstrahl *m* beam *(Rad)*.
Peilung *f* bearing, direction finding.
optische Peilung pilotage *(Avn)*.
Peilzeichen *n* direction-finder signal *(Avn)*.
pelzgefüttert fur-lined.
Pelzkombination *f* fur-lined flying suit.
Pendel *n* pendulum.
Pendelfrequenz *f* quenching frequency *(Rad)*.
Pendelfrequenzempfänger *m* super-regenerative receiver.
pendeln oscillate; swerve.
Pendelverkehr *m* shuttle traffic.
Perchlorameisensäuremethylester *m* diphosgene *(CWS)*.
Perlkorn *n* bead sight *(R)*.
Personal *n* personnel.
Personalabteilung *f* personnel section.
Personalamt *n* See **Heerespersonalamt**.
Personalausweis *m* identification papers, certificate of identification.
Personaldaten *npl* personal data *(birth, occupation, etc.)*.
Personalveränderung *f* change of personnel.
Personenbahnhof *m* passenger station *(RR)*.
Personenfähre *f* passenger ferry.
Personenkraftfahrzeug *n* personnel carrier, passenger vehicle *(MT)*.
Personenkraftwagen *m* personnel carrier, passenger car *(MT)*.

perspektivische Projection geometric projection, perspective projection.
Perstoff *m* diphosgene *(CWS)*.
Petroleum *n* kerosene.
Pfad *m* path, trail.
Pfahl *m* picket, stake; pile; post.
Pfahlhindernis *n* See **Pfahlsperre**.
Pfahljoch *n* pile bent *(Bdg)*.
Pfahljochbrücke *f* pile-bent bridge.
Pfahlsperre *f* post obstacle *(AT)*.
Pfeife *f* whistle, pipe.
Pfeifpatrone *f* whistling pyrotechnic signal cartridge *(used as gas alarm)*.
Pfeifsignal *n* whistle signal.
Pfeiler *m* pier *(Bdg)*; column, pillar *(Engr)*.
Pfeilform *f* sweepback *(Ap wing)*; arrow or wedge formation.
Pferd *n* horse.
pferdebespannt horse-drawn.
Pferdeersatz *m* remounts.
Pferdefahrzeug *n* horse-drawn vehicle.
Pferdehalter *m* horseholder *(Cav, Arty)*.
Pferdekrankenkraftwagen *m* veterinary motor ambulance.
Pferdekrankensammelplatz *m* veterinary collecting station.
Pferdelazarett *n* veterinary hospital.
Pferdepark *m* remount depot.
Pferdestärke *f* metric horsepower *(abbr.* PS) *(1 PS = 0.986 HP; 1 HP = 1.014* PS).
Pferdetransportkolonne *f* horse-drawn transport column.
Pferdeverbandplatz *m* veterinary aid station.
Pferdezug *m* draft *(horse traction)*.
Pferdezweigpark *m* branch remount depot.
Pfiff *m* whistle *(sound)*.
Pfiffikus *n* phenyldichlorarsine *(CWS)*. ester *f* nurse.
Pflicht *f* duty, obligation.
Pflichten des deutschen Soldaten *See* **Kriegsartikel**.
Pflock *m* stake, peg, pin, picket.
Pflugbagger *m* tractor plow; bulldozer.
Pfropfen *m* plug, stopper, wad.
Phasenverschiebung *f* phase shift, phase displacement, phase difference *(Elec, Rad)*.
Phenyldichlorarsin *n* phenyldichlorarsine.
Phon *n* decibel.
Phosgen *n* carbonylchloride, phosgene *(CWS)*.
Phosphor *m* phosphorus.
Phosphorfliegerbombe *f* phosphorus bomb.
Phosphorgeschoß *n* phosphorus bullet, incendiary bullet.
Phosphorhandgranate *f* phosphorus grenade.
Photogrammetrie *f* photogrammetry.
Photograph *m* photographer.
Photographie *f* photography.
photographische Kartenaufnahme photographic mapping.
Photokopie *f* photostat.
photokopieren to photostat.
Phototopographie *f* phototopography.
Photozelle *f* photo-electric cell.
Pickettpfahl *m* picket, stake.
Pier *m* pier.
Pi-Kampfmittel *npl* engineer combat equipment.
Pikrinsäure *f* trinitrophenol, picric acid.
Pille *f* pill, pellet, primer.
Pilotballon *m* pilot balloon, trial balloon.
Pilotballonaufstieggerät *n* pibal equipment *(Met)*.
Pilz *m* mushroom head of obturator.
Pinsel *m* paint brush.
Pionier *m* engineer soldier, private in engineer unit.
Pionieraufklärung *f* engineer reconnaissance.
Pionier-Ausbau-Bataillon *n* engineer construction-improvement battalion.
Pionierbataillon *n* engineer battalion.
Pionierdienst *m* engineer service.
Pionier-Erkundungstrupp *m* engineer reconnaissance squad.
Pionierfahrzeug *n* engineer vehicle.
Pionierführer *m* special staff engineer officer and engineer commander *(at Div Hq)*.
Pioniergerät *n* engineer equipment.
Pioniergerätepark *m* engineer equipment depot.
Pionier-Kampfmittel *npl* engineer combat equipment.
Pionierkolonne *f* engineer equipment column.
Pionierlandungskompanie *f* engineer landing company.
Pioniermaschinenzug *m* engineer machine platoon.
Pionieroffizier *m* engineer officer.
Pionierpanzerkampfwagen *m* engineer tank.
Pionierpark *m* engineer park, engineer depot.
Pionierschule *f* engineer school.
Pioniersprengmittel *npl* engineer explosives.

Pionier-Sturmabzeichen *n* Engineer Assault Badge *(decoration)*.
Pioniersturmzug *m* engineer assault platoon.
Pioniertruppe *f* Corps of Engineers.
Pioniertruppen *fpl* engineer troops.
Pionierverband *m* engineer unit.
Pioniervermessungsgerät *n* engineer surveying instrument or equipment.
Pionierwerkzeug *n* engineer tool.
Pionierwerkzeugtasche *f* engineer tool bag.
Pionierzug *m* engineer platoon.
Pionierzwischenpark *m* engineer dump.
Piste *f* trail, path, beaten track.
Pistole *f* pistol.
Pistolengriff *m* pistol grip.
Pistolenöffnung *f* pistol port *(Tk)*.
Pistolentasche *f* pistol holster.
Pi.-Sturmabzeichen *n* *See* **Pionier-Sturmabzeichen**.
Pitotrohr *n* pitot tube.
Pivotgeschütz *n* swivel gun, pedestal-mounted gun.
Pivotlafette *f* pivot-type mount *(MG)*; turntable carriage *(G)*.
Pivotlager *n* trunnion bearing *(G)*.
Pi.-Zug *m* *See* **Pionierzug**.
PK.-Filmberichter *m* propaganda-company moving-picture cameraman.
P.K.-Kriegsberichter *m* propaganda-company war correspondent.
Plan *m* plan, chart, diagram, scheme.
Plane *f* tarpaulin.
Planfeuer *n* concentrated antiaircraft fire within the critical zone.
Planfeuertafel *f* lead chart *(AA firing)*.
Planfeuerwürfel *m* critical zone *(AA firing)*.
Planier-Raupenschlepper *m* bulldozer, angledozer, tractor with angledozer.
Planimeter *n* planimeter *(Surv)*.
Plänkelei *f* skirmish.
Planladung *f* computed charge *(demolitions)*.
planmäßig in accordance with table of organization or basic allowance; according to plan; systematic, deliberate, thorough.
planmäßige Feldbefestigung deliberate field fortification.
planmäßiger Nachschub automatic supply.
Planpause *f* overlay, traced map or firing chart.
Planquadrat *n* grid square.
Planrichten *n* laying by survey *(Arty)*. **-schießen** *n* map fire, unobserved fire *(Gunnery)*.
Plansektor *m* map-protractor set *(Arty, Surv)*.
Planspiel *n* map exercise *(Tng)*.
Planstärke *f* authorized strength, table of organization strength.
Planstelle *f* place authorized by table of organization.
freie Planstelle vacancy.
Planübergang *m(RR)* level crossing
Planübung *f* map maneuver, map exercise *(Tng)*.
Planunterlage *f* plane table *(Arty, Surv)*.
Planzeichnen *n* plotting *(Surv)*.
Planzeiger *m* coordinate scale *(Arty, Surv)*.
plastische Liderung plastic-pad obturator *(G)*.
Platte *f* plate *(Tech)*; phonograph record.
Platteneinsatz *m* storage-battery cell *(Elec)*.
Plattenkondensator *m* parallel plate condenser *(Rad)*.
Plattenpulver *n* flake powder *(Am)*.
Plattensatz *m* storage-battery cell *(Elec)*.
Plattenventil *n* poppet valve *(Mtr)*.
Plattform *f* platform *(Arty, etc.)*.
Plattformwagen *m* flatcar *(RR)*.
Plattfüße *mpl* flat feet.
Platz *m* airdrome, airfield, landing field *(Avn)*; aid station *(Med, Vet)*; place, square *(in a city or town)*; site; locality; station; space; room.
platzen to burst; to blow out *(tire)*.
Platzfeuer *n* airdrome light.
Platzfeuerwehr *f* airdrome fire-fighting unit.
Platzgrenze *f* airdrome boundary.
Platzmembrane *f* bursting diaphragm *(message container)*.
Platzpatrone *f* blank cartridge.
Platzrunde *f* circle flown over airdrome.
Platzwechsel *m* change of station.
Pleuelstange *f* connecting rod, piston rod *(Mtr)*.
Plombe *f* lead seal.
Plünderer *m* marauder, plunderer.
plündern to plunder.
Plünderung *f* plundering, pillage, looting.
Pneumassivreifen *m* cushion tire.
Polarstern *m* North Star.
polieren to polish, to buff *(Tech)*.
Polizei *f* police.
Polizist *m* policeman.
Polklemme *f* battery-terminal binding post *(Elec)*.
Polschuh *m* pole piece *(magnet)*.

Polster *n* pad (*Clo, harness, etc.*); track block (*Tk*); pillow, cushion.
Polwechsler *m* pole changer (*Tp*).
Polygonzug *m(Surv)*closed traverse
Ponton *m* ponton.
Pontonbrücke *f* ponton bridge.
Pontonfähre *f* ponton ferry.
Pontonier *m* pontoneer.
Pontonoberkante *f* gunwale (*Pon*).
Pontonstrecke *f* ponton bay.
Pontonwagen *m(MT)* ponton carrier
Porontoofen m a small liquid-fuel stove
Portepee *n* sword knot (*worn by Ger officers and higher-bracket NCO's*).
Portepeeunteroffizier *m* noncommissioned officer (*from* Feldwebel *up*).
Portion *f* ration; dose (*Med*).
eiserne Portion emergency ration.
Portionenausgabe *f* distribution of rations.
Portionssatz *m* scale of rations, ration quantity.
Positionslicht *n* position light, running light (*Ap*).
Post *f* mail.
Postaufnahmegerät *n* mail pick-up device (*Ap*).
Posten *m* sentry; post; duty station; item (*in a list*); lot (*of goods*).
Postenanweisungen *fpl* guard orders.
allgemeine Postenanweisungen general orders (*guard duty*).
besondere Postenanweisungen special orders (*guard duty*).
Postenkette *f* line of sentries.
Postleitungen *fpl* civil communication lines.
Postprüfungsstelle *f* postal censor's office.
Postüberwachungsstelle *f* *See* **Postprüfungsstelle.**
Potenz *f* power (*Math*).
potenzieren raise (*to a power*) (*Math*).
Prahm *m* barge, lighter (*Engr, Nav*).
Prallhaltevorrichtung *f* ballonet balloon (*airship*).
Prallschuß *m* ricochet.
Prallwand *f* baffle.
Präzisionsschießen *n* precision fire.
Preis *m* price; rate; prize.
Preisübung *f* qualification course.
Prellschuß *m* ricochet.
Presseoffizier *m* public relations officer.
Preßfutter *n* compressed forage.
Preßluft *f* compressed air.
Preßluftanlasser *m* air starter, compressed-air starter (*Mtr*).
Preßluftflasche *f* compressed-air flask.
Preßlufthammer *m* pneumatic hammer.
Preßluft-Niethammer *m* pneumatic riveter.
Preßluftzylinder *m* compressed-air cylinder.
Preßstoff *m* plastic.
Pr.Geschoß *n* *See* **Phosphorgeschoß.**
Primärkreis *m(Rad)* primary circuit
Primärwicklung *f* primary winding (*Elec*).
Prise *f* prize.
Prisenrecht *n* angary.
Prismenkreuz *n* an engineer surveying instrument.
Pritsche *f* wooden-board bed.
Probe *f* test, trial.
Probeflug *m* test flight.
Probelauf *m* test run (*Mtr*).
Probeschießen *n* test firing.
Profil *n* profile, cross section; tread (*of a tire*).
Profildicke *f* profile thickness (*Ap wing*).
Profilhinterkante *f* trailing edge (*Ap wing profile*).
profiliert streamlined, faired.
Profilierung *f* fairing (*Ap*); recapping (*tires*); streamlining.
Profilsehne *f* wing chord (*Ap*).
Profiltiefe *f* depth of profile
Profilvorderkante *f* leading edge (*Ap wing profile*).
Projektion auf die Horizontalebene horizontal projection.
Projektion auf die Senkrechtebene vertical projection.
Propaganda *f* propaganda, publicity.
Propagandakompanie *f* **propaganda** company (*for front-line reporting; composed of writers and cameramen*)
Propeller *m* **propeller.** *See also* **Luftschraube.**
Propellerblatt *n* propeller blade (*Ap*).**erhaube** *f* propeller spinner.
Propellerkreis *m* plane of propeller rotation, propeller-disk area (*Ap*).
Propellernabe *f* propeller hub (*Ap*).
Propellersteigung *f* propeller pitch.
Propellerwind *m* slipstream (*Avn*).
Protzarm *m* limber drawbar (*Arty*).
Protze *f* limber (*Arty*).
Protzgestell *n* limber frame (*Arty*).
Protzhaken *m* limber pintle.
Protzkasten *m* limber ammunition chest (*Arty*).
Protzöse *f* lunette (*G*).
Prozentsatz *m* percentage.
prüfen to check, inspect, test, verify.
Prüfgerät *n* testing apparatus.
Prüfgestell *n* testing stand.
Prüfknopf *m* testing button (*field Tp*).
Prüfröhrchen *n* detector tube (*in CWS detector kit*).
Prüfstand *m* testing block (*Avn*).
Prüftaste *f* testing key (*field Tp*).
Prüfung *f* test, testing, verification.
Prüfungsschießen *n* verification fire.
Puffer *m* buffer (*Ord*).
Puffergehäuse *n* buffer housing (*MG*).
Pufferlager *n* buffer support (*G cradle*).
Pulk *m* boat-type runner (*placed under gun wheels for operations in deep snow*); formation (*Avn slang*).
Pulver *n* powder.
Pulverbrennzündung *f* powder-train ignition (*fuze*).
Pulverbündel *n* powder bag (*Am*).
Pulverhaus *n* powder magazine.
Pulverkammer *f* powder chamber.
Pulverkorn *n* powder grain (*Am*).
Pulverladung *f* powder charge (*Am*).
Pulverraum *m* powder chamber.
Pulverrückstände *mpl* powder fouling (*G*).
Pulversatz *m* powder train, powder pellet (*fuze*).
Pulversprengstoff *m* low explosive.
Pulvertemperaturmessung *f* measurement of powder temperature.
Pulverthermometer *n* powder thermometer (*Am*).
Pulvertreibladung *f* propellent charge.
Pulverzerstäuber *m* decontaminating-powder sprayer (*CWS*).
Pumpenkühlung *f* forced-circulation cooling (*Mtr*).
Punkt *m* point, place; dot (*Tg*).
Punktbestimmung *f* point designation, point location.
Punktfeuer *n* point fire, fixed fire
Punktplan *m* range card (*Gunnery*).
Punktschießen *n* *See* **Punktfeuer.**
Punktschweißung *f* spot welding.
Punkttafel *f* point-designation grid (*Arty*).
Punktziel *n* point target (*Gunnery*).
Pupinspule *f* loading coil (*Tp*).
Puppe *f* dummy (*for bayonet Tng, etc.*).
putzen to clean, polish, shine.
Putzlappen *m* cleaning rag.
Putzwolle *f* cotton waste.
Pz.Kw.-Nachbildung *f* tank silhouette (*practice firing*).

Q

Q-Gruppe *f* Q signal (*Rad*).
Quadrant *m* quadrant.
Quadrantenfläche *f(G)* quadrant plate
Quadrantenvisier *n* leaf-type quadrant sight (*R, MG*).
Quadrat *n* square, grid square.
Quadratwurzel *f* square root.
Qualifikationsbericht *m* qualification card.
Qualm *m* dense smoke.
Quarantäne *f* quarantine (*Med*).
Quartier *n* quarters, billets.
Quartierarrest *m* restriction to quarters.
Quartiermacher *m* quartering officer, billeting officer.
Quartiermacherkommando *n* quartering party, billeting party.
Quartiermachertrupp *m* quartering detail, billeting detail.
Quartiermeister *m* corps or division quartermaster (*general staff officer "Ib" in charge of supply and Adm at corps or Div Hq*).
Quartiermeisterabteilung *f* supply group of staff sections (*comprises* Quartiermeister *and* Intendantur).
Quartier und Verpflegung quarters and subsistence.
Quartier- und Verpflegungsvergütung *f* quarters and subsistence allowance (*reimbursement*).
Quartier- und Verpflegungszuschuß *m* quarters and subsistence allowance.
Quartiervergütung *f* quarters allowance.
quarzgesteuerter Sender crystal-controlled transmitter (*Rad*).
Quarzkristall *n* quartz crystal (*Rad*).
Quarzsteuerung *f* crystal control
Quast *m* tassel.
Qu-Blende *f* *See* **Querschnittblende.**
Quecksilber *n* mercury.
Quelle *f* source, spring, well.
quer across, obliquely.
Querachse *f* lateral axis (*Ap*).
Queraxt *f* adze.
Querbeil *n* *See* **Queraxt.**
Querdeckung *f* traverse (*Ft*).
querfahrendes Ziel target moving parallel to front (*ground target*).
Querfahrt *f* movement parallel to front (*ground target*).
querfeldein cross-country.
Querlibelle *f* cross level (*Surv, Arty*).
Querrinne *f* open culvert (*road*).
Querruder *n* aileron (*Ap*).
Querruderhebel *m* aileron horn (*Ap*).
Quersäge *f* crosscut saw.
Querschläger *m* ricochet.
Querschnitt *m* cross section.
Querschnittbelastung *f* ballistic coefficient.
Querschnittblende *f* transverse shutter (*signal lamp*).
Querstabilität *f* lateral stability
Querstreuung *f* *See* **Breitenstreuung.**
Querträger *m* transverse beam, transom, transverse support (*Bdg*).
Querverbindung *f* intervehicular communication; local circuit; cross bar, transverse bracing.
Querverkehr *m* internet traffic (*Rad*).
Querverstrebung *f* cross bracing (*Bdg*).
Querwall *m* traverse (*Ft*).
quetschen to crush, bruise, squeeze, pinch.
Quetschkondensator *m* trimmer condenser (*Rad*).
Quetschladung *f* camouflet.
Quetschmine *f* *See* **Quetschladung.**
Quetschung *f* contusion (*Med*).
quietschen to screech (*brakes*); to squeal (*Rad*).

R

Rache *f* revenge.
Rachen *m* throat.
Rachenreizstoff *m* *See* **Nasen- und Rachenreizstoff.**
Rad *n* wheel; bicycle.
Radachse *f* axle.
Radauflagepunkt *m* center of tire contact (*MT*).
Raddruck *m* wheel load (*MT*).
Räderantrieb *m* wheel drive (*MT*).
Räderbahre *f* wheeled litter carrier.
Räderfahrzeug *n* wheeled vehicle.
Räder-Gleiskettenantrieb *m* combination wheel-track drive, convertible wheel-track drive.
Räderkettenfahrzeug *n* combination wheel-track vehicle, convertible wheel-track vehicle.
Räderraupenfahrzeug *n* *See* **Räderkettenfahrzeug.**
Räderwerk *n* **tracks and suspensions** (*Tk*).
Radfahrabteilung *f* bicycle battalion.
Radfahrkompanie *f* bicycle company.
Radfahrschwadron *f* bicycle troop.
Radfahrwerk *n* wheel-type landing gear (*Ap*).
Radfahrzug *m* bicycle platoon.
Radflügelflugzeug *n* cyclogiro (*Avn*).
Radgürtel *m* caterpillar band (*G*).
Radiergummi *m* rubber eraser.
Radiosonde *f* radiosonde, radio meteorograph (*Met*).
Radizierung *f* extraction of roots.
Radkappe *f* hub cap.
Radkörper *m* disk spider (*wheel*).
Radlafette *f* wheeled gun carriage.
Radlandung *f* two-point landing
Radlenker *m* guard rail (*RR switch*).
Radnabe *f* hub.
Radreifen *m* tire (*of a wheel*).
Radschlepper *m* wheeled tractor.
Radsporn *m* tail wheel (*Ap*).
Radstand *m* wheelbase; alinement of wheels.
Radstandlibelle *f* cross level (*G*).
Radstandtrieb *m* cross-leveling mechanism (*G sight*).
Radsteuerung *f* wheel control (*as distinguished from stick control*)
Radsturz *m* camber (*MT*).
Radzugmaschine *f* wheeled tractor.
Rahmen *m* frame.
Rahmenantenne *f (Rad)* loop antenna
Rahmenheer *n* enlisted cadre.
Rahmenlafette *f* frame-type gun carriage.
Rahmenspannturm *m* frame cabane
Rahmenübung *f* command-post exercise (*staff Tng*).
Rakete *f* rocket.
Raketenantrieb *m* rocket propulsion.
Raketenbombe *f* rocket bomb (*Avn*).
Raketen-Panzerbüchse *f* antitank rocket launcher.
Raketenstart *m* rocket-assisted take-off (*Avn*).
Raketenwurfmaschine *f* rocket launcher, rocket projector.
Rammbär *m* drop hammer of a pile driver.
Rammbühne *f* pile-driver staging.
Ramme *f* pile driver.
rammen to ram (*Nav*); to drive (*a pile*).
Rammfähre *f* pile-driver raft.
Rammgerüst *n* pile-driver frame.
Rampe *f* ramp.
Rampengerät *n* ramp equipment.
Rampenmine *f* ramp mine (*improvised mine under an inclined board*).
Rampensperre *f* sawhorse ramp obstacle.
Rampenwagen *m* ramp carrier (*MT*).
Rand *m* edge, border, margin, rim; perimeter (*Tac*).
Randbemerkungen *fpl* marginal data.
Randdüsenzünder *m* rimvent fuze
Rändel *m* knurled nut or knob, micrometer knob.

Pyrot	Pyrotechniker	artificer
Pz	Panzer	armor; armor-plate
PZ	Personenzug	passenger train
Pz.Abw	Panzerabwehr-	antitank
Pz.Abw.Abt	Panzerabwehrabteilung	antitank battalion
Pz.Abw.Kp	Panzerabwehrkompanie	antitank company
Pz.Abw.Zg	Panzerabwehrzug	antitank platoon
Pz.A.O.K	Panzerarmeeoberkommando	high command of an armored army
Pz.B	Panzerbüchse	antitank rifle
Pz.B	Panzerbrigade	tank brigade; armored brigade
pzbr	panzerbrechend	armor-piercing
Pz.B.Tr	Panzerbüchsentrupp	antitank rifle section
Pz.D	Panzerdivision	armored division
Pz Ft	Panzerfort	armored fort
Pz.Fu.Wg	Panzerfunkwagen	armored radio car
Pz.Gr	Panzergranate	armor-piercing shell
Pz.Gr	Panzergrenadier-	infantry in a panzer unit
Pz.Jg	Panzerjäger-	antitank
Pz.Jg.Abt	Panzerjägerabteilung	antitank battalion
Pz.Kp	Panzerkompanie	armored company; tank company
Pz.Kpfw	Panzerkampfwagen	tank
Pzkw	Panzerkraftwagen	tank
Pzkw.-Nachb	Panzerkraftwagennachbildung	dummy tank
Pz.Rgt	Panzerregiment	panzer regiment; tank regiment; armored regiment
Pzsch	Panzerschüler	student at armored school
Pz.Spr.Gr	Panzersprenggranate	high-explosive armor-piercing she
Pz.Sp.Wg	Panzerspähwagen	armored reconnaissance car;
Pz.Sp.Wg.Kp	Panzerspähwagenkompanie	tank reconnaissance company
Pz.T	Panzerturm	armored turret
Pz.Tr	Panzertruppen	mechanized units
Pz.Trsp.Wg	Panzertransportwagen	armored transport vehicle;
P-Zug	Postzug	mail train
Pz.Verb	Panzerverband	mechanized tank force; tank force; mechanized force
Pzwff	Panzerwaffe	armored troops; tank troops
Pz.Z	Panzerziel	tank objective
Pz.-Zg	Panzerzug	armored train; tank platoon

Q

Q	Quadrant	quadrant
Q	Quadrat	square
q	qualifiziert	qualified
Q	Quartier	billet; quarters
Q	Querschnittsbelastung	ballistic coefficient
qcm	Quadratzentimeter	square centimeter
qdm	Quadratdezimeter	square decimeter
qkm	Quadratkilometer	square kilometer
ql	querliegend	diagonal
QM	Quadratmeile	square mile
qm	Quadratmeter	square meter
qmm	Quadratmillimeter	square millimeter
Qmstr	Quartiermeister	quartermaster (*general staff offic*
QSL-Karte	Funkverkehrskarte	wireless communication map
Qu	Quartier	billet; quarters
Qu	Quartierverpflegung	rationing in quarters
Qu	Quelle	spring; well; fountainhead
Qu	Querschnitt	profile; section; cross-section
Quadr	Quadrant	quadrant
Quadr	Quadrat	square
quadr	quadratisch	square
Qual	Qualifikation	qualification
qual	qualifiziert	qualified
Qual.Ber	Qualifikationsbericht	qualification report
Quar	Quarantäne	quarantine
Quart	Quartier	billet; quarters
Quartm	Quartiermacher	billeting officer
Quart.Mstr	Quartiermeister	quartermaster (*general staff offi*
Quart W	Quartierwirt	host (*in billets*)
Qu.Bel	Querschnittsbelastung	ballistic coefficient
Qu.-Blende	Querschnittsblende	shutter (*to reduce the size and intensity of blinker beam*)
quitt	quittieren	to quit; to receipt; to give a
Qu.M	Quartiermeister	quartermaster (*general staff officer*)

R

R	Ration	ration
r	rechts	right
R	Regiment	regiment
R	Reglement	regulations; manual; text
R	Reich	R.book
R	Reichsminister	Reich minister
r	reitend	mounted
R	Reiter	cavalryman
R	Rekrut	recruit
R	Reserve	reserve
R	Rettung	rescue
R	Richt-	aiming; sighting
R	Richtung	direction; alignment; aim
R	Rohr	barrel (*gun*); tube (*radio*); pipe
R	Rotationsmotor	engine (*aviation*)
R	Rückstosslader	recoil-operated gun
R	Ruhestand	retirement

R.	Ruine	ruin; ruins (*on maps*)
r.	rund	round; circular
R.	Rundkopfgeschoss	round-headed projectile
R.A.	Regimentsarzt	regimental medical officer
R.A.	Reichsamt	Reich Government Office
R.A.	Remonteamt	remount depot
R.A.	Richtaufsatz	gun sight
R A B	Reichsautobahn	Reich motor highway
Rad	Radio	radio
R.A.D	Reichsarbeitdienst	National Labor Service
Radf	Radfahr-	bicycle
Radf.Btl	Radfahrbataillon	bicycle battalion
Radf.Kp	Radfahrkompanie	bicycle company
Radf.Schwd.	Radfahrschwadron	bicycle troop (*cavalry*)
Radf.Tr	Radfahrtruppe	bicycle troop
Radiogr	Radiogramm	radiogram
R.Adj	Regimentsadjutant	regimental adjutant
r.Ag	rückwärtiges Armeegebiet	rear area under army control
Rah.H	Rahmenheer	cadre army
Rak	Rakete	rocket; flare
R.A.K	Reservearmeekorps	reserve army corps
R Amt	Reichsamt	Reich Government Office
Randst	Randstaat	border state
Rang.Bhf	Rangierbahnhof	shunting station or yard
Rang-Kl	Rangklasse	class; degree of rank; grade
Rangl	Rangliste	officers' register
Rano	Reichsarbeitsnachweis für Offiziere	Reich employment agency for officers
R.A.N.St	**Remonteamtsnebenstelle**	**remount auxiliary depot**
R.Anst.f. Lschts	Reichsanstalt für Luftschutz	(Branch and) Liaison Office of German Air Ministry
R Anw	Reichsanwalt	Assistant Attorney General
r.A.R	reitendes Artillerieregiment	horse artillery regiment
R.Arzt	Regimentsarzt	regimental medical officer
Rat	Ration	ration
Raup	Raupe	caterpillar track
Raup.Fzg	Raupenfahrzeug	full-track vehicle
R Aussch-Ki Fürs	Reichsausschuss der Kriegsbeschädigten- und Kriegshinterbliebenen-Fürsorge	Reich Committee for the Care of War Injured and War Dependents
Rb	Regierungsbezirk	civil administration district; government district
R.B	Regimentsbefehl	regimental order
Rb	Reichsministerium für die besetzten Gebiete	Reich Ministry for Occupied Territories
Rb	Reihenbild	mosaic (*aerial photo*)
R. B	Reiterbrigade	horse cavalry brigade
r.Battr	reitende Batterie	mounted battery
R Bez	Regierungsbezirk	civil administration district; government district
Rbf	Rangierbahnhof	shunting station or yard
Rbf	Reichsbahnhof	railroad station (*on maps*)
RbF. 34	Rundblickfernrohr 34	panoramic sight, M-34 (*artillery*)
R.Bg	Reiterbrigade	horse cavalry brigade
Rbl.F	Rundblickfernrohr	panoramic sight
R.B.St	Regierungsbezirkshauptstadt	capital city of civil administration district
R.B.T.	Richtlinien zur Beurteilung der Tauglichkeit für das Reichsheer und die Marine	directions for the judging of fitness for active duty in the Reich army and navy
r.Bttr	reitende Batterie	horse battery
Rch	Reich	Reich
Rchs	Reichs-	Reich-
Rcklf	Rücklauf	recoil (*of weapons*)
Rd	Rad	wheel; bicycle
R.D	Rekrutendepot	recruit depot
R.D	Reservedivision	reserve division
rd	rund	round; circular
R.D.A	Rangdienstalter	rank and seniority
RDemobA	Reichsdemobilmachungsamt	Reich Demobilization Office
Rdf	Radfahr-	bicycle
R.d.F	Reichsminister der Finanzen	Reich Finance Minister
RDFl	Reichsdienstflagge	German service flag
RDH	Reichsdisziplinärhof	Reich Disciplinary Court
RDisz-Hf	Reichsdisziplinärhof	Reich Disciplinary Court
R Disz Kam.	Reichsdisziplinarkammer	Reich Disciplinary Chamber
R.d.L	Reichsminister der Luftfahrt	Reich Minister of Aviation
RDO	Reichsverband Deutscher Offiziere	Reich Association of German Officers
Rdr	Rechtsdrall	clockwise rifling (*weapons*)
Rdr	Reichsdruckerei	Reich Printing Office
RDStO	Reichsdienststrafordnung	Reich Service Penal Code
reakt	reaktiviert	reactivated
reakt	reaktionär	reactionary
Refl	Reflektor	reflector
Refr	Refraktor	refractor
Reg	Regiment	regiment
Reg	Regiments-	regimental
Reg	Region	region
reg	regulär	regular
reg.A	reguläre Armee	regular army
Reg.Bez	Regierungsbezirk	civil administration district

rändeln to knurl.
Randfeuer *n* boundary light (*Adrm*).
Randstellungen *fpl* perimeter positions (*Tac*).
Rang *m* rank, status.
Rangabzeichen *n* insignia of rank.
Rangältester *m* senior officer.
Rangdienstalter *n* age-in-grade, seniority.
Rangierbahnhof *m* railroad yard.
Rangliste des Heeres army register.
Rasanz der Flugbahn flatness of trajectory.
rasch quick.
Raspel *f* rasp.
Rast *f* rest (*march column*); click, detent (*Tech*).
Rastgruppe *f* rest group
Rasthebel *m* bolt lock (*MG*).
Rastplatz *m* resting place (*march rest*).
Rate *f* rate.
Ration *f* forage ration.
eiserne Ration emergency forage ration.
Rationssatz *m* scale of forage rations.
Rauch *m* smoke.
Rauchentwickler *m* smoke generator.
Rauchentwicklung *f* generation of smoke.
Raucherscheinung *f* smoke effect (*flash ranging*).
Rauchgerät *n* smoke equipment (*Ap*).
Rauchgranate *f* smoke shell (*Am*).
Rauchkerze *f* smoke candle (*CWS*).
Rauchkörper *m* smoke filler (*Am*); smoke-puff charge (*simulated fire*).
Rauchladung *f* smoke charge (*Am*).
regelrecht standard, according to regulations.
Regelröhre *f* variable μ tube, supercontrol tube (*Rad*).
Regelspur *f* standard gage (*RR*).
Regelstange *f* regulator (*G recoil brake*).
Regelvorrichtung *f* governing device (*Mtr*).
Regen *m* rain.
Regendecke *f* tarpaulin.
regenerierter Altgummi reclaimed rubber.
Regengebiet *n* precipitation area (*Met*).
Regenguß *m* shower (*Met*).
Regenklappe *f* rain flap (*on haversack*).
Regenmantel *m* raincoat.
Regenmesser *m* rain gage (*Met*).
Regenschauer *m* shower (*Met*).
Regenwolke *f* rain cloud (*Met*).
Regierung *f* government.
Regiment *n* regiment.
Regimentsabschnitt *n* regimental sector.
Regimentsadjutant *m* aide to regimental commander, regimental executive.
Regimentsarzt *m* regimental surgeon.
Regimentsbefehl *m* regimental order.
Regimentsgefechtsstand *m* regimental command post.
Regimentskommandeur *m* regimental commander.
Regimentsnachrichtenzug *m* regimental communication platoon.
Regimentsstab *m* regimental headquarters, regimental staff.
Regimentstroß *m* regimental train.
Registrier-Chronograph *m* chronograph.
Regler *m* governor; automatic control; automatic corrector.
Reglerdose *f* control aneroid (*Ap engine*).
Reglergabel *f* governor arms (*Mtr*).
Reglergestänge *n* plunger (*engine governor*).
Reglerschalter *m* combination voltage regulator, current regulator and cut-out relay (*Mtr*).
Reglerteilung *f* correction scale on gun sight.
Reglerventil *n* regulating valve.
Rauchmeldepatrone *f* smoke-cartridge message container (*for dropped messages*) (*Avn*).
Rauchofen *m*(*Adrm*) smoke generator
Rauchpatrone *f* smoke signal cartridge.
Rauchsatz *m* pyrotechnic composition (*smoke signal*); smoke composition; smoke pellet (*Am*).
rauchschwach smokeless, semi-smokeless.
rauchschwaches Pulver smokeless powder.
Rauchschwimmer *m* floating smoke pot.
Rauchsignalpatrone *f* smoke signal cartridge.
rauchstark generating much smoke.
Rauchvorhang *m* smoke curtain, smoke screen.
Rauchwolke *f* smoke cloud.
Rauhreif *m* frost (*Met*).
Raum *m* space; room, chamber; sector; area, zone, region.
Raumbild *n* stereoscopic picture.
Raumbildentfernungsmesser *m* stereoscopic range finder.
Räumboot *n* mine sweeper.
räumen to clear mines; to clear out; to evacuate (*a position*).

Raumgehalt *m* See Rauminhalt.
Rauminhalt *m* volume, cubic capacity.
Raumladung *f* space charge (*radio tube*).
Raumlöffel *m* miner's spoon (*Engr tool*).
Raummeßbild *n* stereogram (*Photo survey*).
Räumotter *f* paravane.
Raumstrahlung *f* free-space radiation (*Rad*).
Raumwelle *f* sky wave (*Rad*).
Raupe *f* caterpillar; caterpillar track; plaited shoulder strap.
Raupenantrieb *m* caterpillar drive (*MT*).
Raupenfahrzeug *n* track-laying vehicle.
Raupenkette *f* caterpillar track.
Raupenkrad *n* See Kettenkrad.
Raupenschlepper *m* caterpillar tractor.
R-Boot *n* See Räumboot.
Rechen *m* rake.
Rechengerät *n* computer.
Rechenschieber *m* slide rule.
Rechenschieber zur Entfernungsermittlung logarithmic range scale (*Arty*).
Rechenstelle *f* post of computing section (*firing battery*).
Rechenzettel *m*(*Arty*) firing-data form
rechnen to count, compute.
Rechner *m* computer, plotter (*person*).
Rechnung *f* account, bill; computation.
Rechnungsführer *m* accountant and pay noncommissioned officer.
Rechnungslegung *f* accountability.
Rechnungswesen *n* accounting.
Recht *n* law, jurisprudence.
Rechteck *n* rectangle.
Rechtsabteilung *f* legal branch, legal section.
Rechtsdrall *m* right-hand twist (*rifling*).
rechtsgängig clockwise; right-hand (*threads, etc.*).
Rechtsgewinde *n* right-hand thread.
Rechtskurve *f* right bank (*Avn*).
rechtslaufend clockwise.
"Rechts schwenkt, marsch!" "Column right, march!" (*followed by* "Gerade, aus!").
Rechtsstellung *f* legal status.
"Rechts, um!" "Right, face!"; "By the right flank, march!" (*given in marching*).
Rechtswert *m* X-coordinate (*on coordinate scale in map reading*).
rechtweisender Kurs true course (*Air Navigation*).
rechtweisender Windkurs true heading (*Air Navigation*).
rechtwinklig rectangular.
Reduktionsmaßstab *m* engineer's scale.
Reduziergetriebe *n* reduction gear.
Reede *f* roadstead.
Reflexglas *n* transparent reflector (*reflector sight*).
Reflexvisier *n* reflector sight (*Ap, AA gun*).
Regel *f* rule.
Regellast *f* standard maximum load (*Bdg*).
regellose Flucht rout.
regelmäßig regular.
regelmäßiger Fehler systematic error, determinate error.
regeln to direct, control, regulate.
Reglerwinkel *m* principal vertical deflection angle (*AA gunnery*).
Regulierhebel *m* throttle lever (*carburetor*).
regungslos erstarren freeze in position.
Reibahle *f* reamer.
Reibfläche *f* head (*of SA cartridge*).
Reibung *f* friction, galling, rubbing.
Reibungswiderstand *m* frictional resistance.
Reibzündschraube *f* friction primer.
Reichsarbeitsdienst *m* Reich Labor Service.
Reichsarbeitsführer *m* Lieutenant general (*Reich Labor Service*).
Reichsautobahn *f* Reich automobile express highway.
Reichsflagge *f* German national flag.
Reichsführer SS Reich Leader of SS troops.
Reichskokarde *f* national rosette (*worn on field and mountain cap*).
Reichskriegerbund *m* Veterans Association of the Reich.
Reichskriegsflagge *f* German national ensign (*Nav*).
Reichsluftfahrtministerium *n* German Air Ministry.
Reichsluftfahrtverwaltung *f* German Civil Aeronautics Administration.
Reichsluftschutzbund *f* German national air defense organization.
Reichsmeldedienst *m* German aircraft warning service.
Reichsstraße *f* national highway of the Reich.
Reichweite *f* range, maximum range.
Reif *m* rime ice, frost.
Reifen *m* tire.
Reifenerneuerung *f* recapping, retreading.
Reifenheber *m* tire tool.

Reifen-Luftdruckprüfer *m* tire pressure gage.
Reifenpanne *f* puncture, blowout.
Reihe *f* file, single file (*Inf*); column of troopers (*H Cav*); ladder (*six observed rounds*) (*Arty*); train of bombs.
"In Reihe, angetreten!" "In single file, fall in!"
Reihenabwurf *m* train release, train bombing.
Reihenbild *n* aerial mosaic.
Reihenbildkammer *f* aerial mapping camera.
Reihenbildner *m* See Reihenbildkammer.
Reihenfeuer *n* ladder fire (*Gunnery*).
Reihenkammer *f* See Reihenbildkammer.
Reihenladung *f* elongated charge.
in Rohr gefüllte Reihenladung bangalore torpedo.
Reihenmotor *m* in-line engine.
Reihenschaltung *f* series connection (*Elec*).
Reihenschießen *n* ladder fire (*Gunnery*).
Reihenstandmotor *m* in-line upright engine.
Reihenwurf *m* train release, train bombing.
Reinigungsbürste *f* bore brush, cleaning brush (*Ord*).
Reinigungsdocht *m* (*R*) cleaning patch
Reinigungslappen *m* cleaning rag.
Reisegeld *n* travel allowance.
Reisegeschwindigkeit *f* cruising speed (*Ap*).
Reisekostenvergütung *f* See Reisevergütung.
Reisemarsch *m* administrative march.
Reisevergütung *f* travel allowance, mileage allowance (*reimbursement*).
Reiseverordnung *f* mileage table.
Reiseverpflegung *f* travel ration.
Reisigbündel *n* fascine.
Reißbahn *f* rip panel (*Bln*).
Reißbrett *n* drawing board.
reißen to rip.
Reißleine *f* rip cord (*Prcht, Bln*); static line (*Prcht*).
Reißnadel *f* scriber.
Reißnagel *m* thumbtack.
Reißschnur *f* quick release cord (*Prcht*).
Reißverschluß *m* zipper, slide fastener.
Reißzeug *n* drawing instruments, drawing set.
reitende Artillerie horse artillery.
Reiter *m* private (*Cav*); cavalryman, trooper.
spanischer Reiter cheval-de-frise, knife rest (*Ft*).
Reiteraufklärungsabteilung *f* cavalry reconnaissance detachment (*H Cav*).
Reiterbrigade *f* cavalry brigade (*H Cav*).
Reiterei *f* cavalry.
Reitergruppe *f* cavalry section (*H Cav*).
Reiternachspitze *f* cavalry rear point, rear guard cavalry detachment.
Reiterregiment *n* cavalry regiment (*H Cav*).
Reiterreihe *f* column of troopers (*H Cav*).
Reiterrudel *n* flock (*H Cav*).
Reiterschwadron *f* cavalry troop (*H Cav*).
Reiterspähtrupp *m* cavalry reconnaissance squad, cavalry patrol (*H Cav*).
Reiterspitze *f* cavalry point, advance guard cavalry detachment.
Reiterzug *m* rifle platoon (*H Cav Regt*); mounted platoon (*Inf Regt*).
Reithalfter *f* cavesson (*harness*).
Reithosen *fpl* breeches.
Reitpferd *n* mount, riding horse.
Reitstiefel *mpl* riding boots.
reizender Kampfstoff irritant agent (*lacrimator or nose and throat irritant*).
Reizgeschoß *n* irritant gas projectile.
Reizkerze *f* irritant candle (*CWS*).
Reizkörper *m* CN capsule, lacrimator (*CWS*).
Reizpatrone *f* tear-gas cartridge (*for gas chamber test*).
Reizstoff *m* irritant, harassing agent (*CWS*).
Reiztopf *m* irritant gas candle.
Reizwürfel *m* irritant capsule, CN capsule (*CWS*).
Rekrut *m* recruit.
Rekrutendepot *n* recruit depot.
rekrutieren to recruit.
Relais *n* relay (*Elec*).
Relativgeschwindigkeit *f* indicated air speed (*Avn*).
Relativhöhenmesser *m* sonic altimeter (*Ap*).
Reliefkarte *f* relief map.
Remonteamt *n* remount depot.
Remonteaufkaufskommission *f* remount purchasing board.
Remonteinspektion *f* Remount Division.
Remontekommission *f* See Remonteaufkaufskommission.
Remontewesen *n* remount service.
Repatriierung *f* repatriation.

Reg.Gef.St	Regimentsgefechtsstand	regimental command post
Regl Reglt.	Reglement	regulations; manual; textbook
Reg.Sattl.Mstr	Regimentssattlermeister	regimental saddle master
Regt	Regiment	regiment
reg.Tr	reguläre Truppe	regular troops
regul	regulär	regular
Reichsfrhr	Reichsfreiherr	Barón of the Reich (*title of nobility*)
Reichskok	Reichskokarde	cockade; emblem of the German Reich
Reichskr.Fl	Reichskriegsflagge	Reich war flag
Reichsw	**Reichswehr**	**standing German army (*before 1935*)**
Reihenf	Reihenfolge	order; arrangement
Reinschr	Reinschrift	clean copy
Reisek	Reisekosten	traveling expenses
Reit	Reiter	cavalryman
Reit.Nsp	Reiternachspitze	cavalry rear point
Reit Rgt	Reiterregiment	cavalry regiment
Reitsch	Reitschule	cavalry school; riding school
Reitv	Reitvorschrift	equitation manual
Reit.Zg	Reiterzug	cavalry platoon
rek	rekonstruiert	reconstructed
Rekr	Rekrut	recruit
Rekr.Ausb	Rekruten-Ausbilder, -Ausbildung	recruit trainer *or* training
Rekr.Dep	Rekrutendepot	recruit depot
Rekr.Offz	Rekrutenoffizier	recruit-training officer
Rel	Religion	religion
Rem	Remonte	remount
Rem	Remontierungs-	remounting
Rem.A	Remonteamt	remount depot
Rem.A.Neb.St	Remonteamtsnebenstelle	remount auxiliary depot
Rem.Inspr	Remonteinspekteur	remount inspector
Rem.Kom	Remontekommission	remount commission
Rem.O	Remontierungsordnung	remount regulations
Remowo	Reichsmordwochen	Reich murder weeks
Rep	Reparation	reparation
Rep	Reparatur	repair
Rep	Repartierung	distribution
Rep.Gew	Repetiergewehr	repeating rifle; magazine rifle
Res	Reserve	reserve
Res. A	Reservearmee	reserve army
Res.A.K	Reservearmeekorps	reserve army corps
Res. Div	Reservedivision	reserve division
Res.d.R	Reserve des Regiments	regimental reserve
Res.F	Reserveformation	reserve formation; reserve
Res.F.A	Reservefeldartillerie	reserve field artillery
Res.Fhz	Reservefahrzeug	reserve vehicle
Res.I	Reserveinfanterie	reserve infantry
Res.I.B	Reserveinfanteriebataillon	reserve infantry battalion
Res.I.Br	Reserveinfanteriebrigade	reserve infantry brigade
Res.Inf	Reserveinfanterie	reserve infantry
Res.Inf. Br	Reserveinfanteriebrigade	reserve infantry brigade
Res.Inf.Btl	**Reserveinfanteriebataillon**	**reserve infantry battalion**
Res.Inf.Div	Reserveinfanteriedivision	reserve infantry division
Res.Inf.Mun.Kol	Reserveinfanteriemunitionskolonne	reserve infantry ammunition column
Res.Inf.Regt	Reserveinfanterieregiment	reserve infantry regiment
Res.J.B	Reservejägerbataillon	reserve light infantry battalion
Res.K	Reservekorps	reserve corps
Res.Kav	Reservekavallerie	reserve cavalry
Res.Kav.B	Reservekavalleriebrigade	reserve cavalry brigade
Res.Kol	Reservekolonne	reserve column
Res.Komp	Reservekompanie	reserve company
Res. Kp	Reservekompanie	reserve company
Res.Laz	Reservelazarett	reserve hospital
Res.Mun	Reservemunition	reserve ammunition
Res.Offz	Reserveoffizier	reserve officer
Res.Offz.Anw	Reserveoffiziersanwärter	candidate for a commission in the reserve
Res.Pi.Btl	Reservepionierbataillon	reserve combat engineer battalion
Res.Prov.Kol	Reserveproviantkolonne	reserve supply column
Res.S.K	Reservesanitätskompanie	reserve medical company
Res.Tr	Reservetruppe	reserve troop
Res.Uffz	Reserveunteroffizier	reserve noncommissioned officer
Retr	Retraite	retreat
Rett	Rettung	rescue
Rett.Man	Rettungsmanöver	life-saving maneuvers
Rev	Revier	sick bay; quarter; precinct
Rev	Revolver	revolver
Rev.D	Revierdienst	hospital-attendant duty
Rev.Kan	Revolverkanone	rapid-fire cannon
Rf	Radfahr-	bicycle
Rf	Radfahrbataillon	bicycle battalion
RF	Reichsführer	Führer of the Reich
RF	Reichsführerschule	Reich School for Leaders
RF	Reichsführung	leadership of the Reich
R.f	Rohre frei	barrel empty (*artillery*)
RF	Rundfunk	radio; broadcasting
Rf.B	Radfahrbataillon	bicycle battalion
Rfl	Richtfläche	plane of sighting
r.Fl.F	vom rechten Flügel Feuer!	battery right (*artillery*)
Rf.Sch	Reichsführerschule	Reich School for Leaders
RFSS	Reichsführer SS	Reich Commander of the SS
R.F.W	Reiterfeldwache	mounted picket
Rf.Zg	Radfahrzug	bicycle platoon
RG	Reichsgerät	government-issue equipment
Rg	Ring	ring
R.G.A	Reitergruppenaufgaben	Cavalry Group Problems
Rgbhf	Rangierbahnhof	railroad shunting station or yard (*on maps*)
Rg.K	Ringkanone	built-up gun (*refers to barrel*)
Rgl	Reglement	regulations; manual; textbook
Rg.P	Ringpulver	powder in rings (*propellant*)
R.G.St	Regimentsgefechtsstand	regimental command post
Rgt	Regiment	regiment
Rgt	Regiments-	regimental
Rgt.Grz	Regimentsgrenze	regimental boundary
Rgt.Kdr	Regimentskommandeur	regimental commander
Rgt.N.Zg	Regimentsnachrichtenzug	regimental signal platoon
Rgt.R.Zg	Regimentsreiterzug	regimental mounted platoon
Rgts	Regiments-	regimental
Rgt.Vet	Regimentsveterinär	regimental veterinarian officer
RH	Reichsheer	Army of the Reich
Rh	Rhein	the Rhine
R.I	Reserveinfanterie	reserve infantry
Ri	Richtung	direction; alignment; aim
R.I.Bg	Reserveinfanteriebrigade	reserve infantry brigade
R.I.Br	Reserveinfanteriebrigade	reserve infantry brigade
Richt	Richtung	direction; alignment; aim
Richt-Empf-Tr	Richtungsempfängertrupp	directional reception troop
Richtgswkl	Richtungswinkel	angle of deflection; angle of sighting (*gunnery*)
Richt.H	Richtungshörer	sound locator (*antiaircraft*); direction finder
R.I.D	Reserveinfanteriedivision	reserve infantry division
Ri.Kr.A	Richtlinien für Kraftfahrabteilungen	directions for motor transport units
Rikrs	Richtkreis	aiming circle (*gunnery*)
R.I.R	Reserveinfanterieregiment	reserve infantry regiment
Rittm	Rittmeister	captain (*cavalry*)
R.Jäg.B	**Reservejägerbataillon**	**reserve light infantry battalion**
RK	Reichskriegs-	Reich War-
R.K	Reservekorps	reserve corps
R.K	Revolverkanone	rapid-fire cannon; revolver cannon
R.K	Richtkreis	aiming circle (*gunnery*)
R.K	Ringkanone	built-up gun (*refers to barrel*)
R.K	Rotes Kreuz	Red Cross
R.Kf U	Reichskraftfahrunfallgesetz	motor vehicle accident law
R.K.K.-Scheine	Reichskreditkassenscheine	Reich Credit Office Notes (*occupation marks*)
R.K.O	Regimentskommandoordnung	regimental command regulations
Rkr	Richtkreis	aiming circle (*gunnery*)
Rkr	Rohrkrepierer	barrel burster
Rkr.Felda	Feldartillerierichtkreis	field artillery aiming circle
R.K.U	Richtkreisunteroffizier	non-commissioned officer in charge of aiming circle
RM	Reichsminister	Reich Minister (cabinet officer)
RL	Radlafette	wheeled gun carriage
RL	Reichsluft-	Reich Air
RL	Reichsluftfahrt-	Reich Aeronautical
RL	Reichsluftschutz-	Reich Air Defense
RL	Reichsluftsport-	Reich Aerial Sports
RLAD	Reichsluftaufsichtdienst	Reich Air-Traffic Control Service
R.Laf	Röhrenlafette	tubular gun carriage
RLB	Reichsluftschutzbund	National Air Defense League
RLF	Reichsluftsportführer	Leader of Reich Aerial Sports
RLM	Reichsluftfahrtministerium	Reich Air Ministry
RM	Reichsmarine	German Navy
RM	Reichsmark	Reichsmark
RM	Reichsminister	Reich Minister (cabinet officer)
R M	Reichsministerium	Reich Ministry
Rm.A	Remonteamt	remount commission
RMfVuP	Reichsminister für Volksaufklärung und Propaganda	Reich Minister for Popular Enlightenment and Propaganda
R.M.G	Reichsmilitärgesetz	Reich military law
R.m.O	Ritter mehrerer Orden	knight holding several orders
RMVP	Reichsministerium für Volksaufklärung und Propaganda	Reich Ministry for Popular Enlightenment and Propaganda
R.O	Reiseordnung	travel regulations
ROA	Reichsostwehranordnung	Reich East Army Orders
R.O.A	Reserveoffizieranwärter	reserve officer candidate
Rohrbr	Rohrbremse	recoil brake (*artillery*)
Rot	Rotationsmotor	rotary engine (*aviation*)
rot	rotieren	to rotate
Rot	Rotor	rotor
Rottf	Rottenführer	(SA) file-leader, Storm Troops (*equivalent U. S. rank: corporal*); (SS) file-leader, Elite Guard (*equivalent U. S. rank: corporal*)
Rp	Raupe	caterpillar track
R.-P	Reisepass	passport
Rp	Reparatur	repair
R.P	Richtpunkt	aiming point (*gunnery*)
R.P	Röhrenpulver	tubular powder (*propellant*)
R-Patrone	Rauchpatrone für Messbatterie	smoke-signal cartridge for survey battery
Rp.Fz	Raupenfahrzeug	full-track vehicle
Rp.Schl	Raupenschlepper	caterpillar tractor

Rp.Sl	Raupenschlepper	caterpillar tractor
R.P.V	Reichswehrpostvorschrift	army postal regulations
R.P.-Verf	Richtpunktverfahren	indirect laying (*artillery*)
Rpw	Reparaturwerkstatt	repair workshop
R.Q	Reisequartier	march billet
R R	Reichsrundfunk-	Reich broadcasting
R.R	Reiterregiment	horse cavalry regiment
RRG	Reichsrundfunkgesellschaft	Reich Broadcasting Company; Reich Radio Co.
R.Rp.Fz	Räderraupenfahrzeug	wheel-tracked vehicle (*armored vehicle that can run either on wheels or on a caterpillar track*)
R.R.Zg	Regimentsreiterzug	regimental mounted platoon
Rs	Regimentsuntersattlermeister	regimental assistant saddle master
R.-Sfl.-B.-Schu	Reichs-Segelflugbauschule	Reich Glider Building and Construction School
R.Sp	Reiterspitze	cavalry point; mounted point
R.Sp.Tr	Reiterspähtrupp	cavalry reconnaissance detachment
RSt	Regimentstab	regimental staff
RSt	Reitersturm	mounted troop of Storm Troops or Elite Guard
R.St	Richtstelle	aiming-circle station
R-Sta	Reiterstandarte	mounted regiment of Storm Troops or Elite Guard
RSt GB	Reichstrafgesetzbuch	Reich penal code
R.St.V.O	Reichsstrassenverkehrsordnung	German highway traffic regulations
RT	Reichstag	Reichstag; German Parliament
Rt	Reiter	cavalryman
R.T	Reservetruppe	reserve troops
rtde	reitende	mounted
Rtg	Reichstag	Reichstag; German Parliament
R.T.K	Reservetruppenkommando	reserve troops command
Rtm	Rittmeister	captain (*cavalry*)
Rtr	Reiter	cavalryman
Rtr	Reiterregiment	cavalry regiment (*horse*)
Rttm	Rittmeister	captain (*cavalry*)
R.U	Reiterunteroffizier	cavalry noncommissioned officer
R.U	Reserveunterstand	reserve dugout; shelter
R.U	Richtkreisunteroffizier	noncommissioned officer in charge of aiming circle
Rü	Rüstung	armament; equipment
Rückl	Rücklauf	recoil (*of a gun*)
Rücksp	Rückspiegel	rearview mirror
Rückst	Rückstoss	repulse; recoil
rückw	rückwärtig	behind the line; rearward
rückw	rückwärts	backwards; to the rear
rückw	rückwirkend	retroactive
Rückw	Rückwirkung	reaction; repercussion
rückw.Kr	rückwirkende Kraft	retroactive power
rückw.Verb	rückwärtige Verbindungen	communication in or to the rear
Rücks	Rückzug	retreat; withdrawal
Rüst	Rüstung	armament; equipment
Rüst.Ausg	Rüstungsausgaben	armament expenditure
Rüst.St	Rüstungsstand	state of military preparedness
R.U.P	Reiterunteroffizierposten	mounted cossack post led by noncommissioned officer
russ	russisch	Russian
R.u.V	Verordnung über Rang- und Vorgesetztenverhältnis der Soldaten des Reichsheeres	German Army rank and superiority regulations
r.v	rechts vorbei	too far to the right (*gunnery*)
R.V	Reiseverordnung für die Soldaten	travel regulations for soldiers
R.V	Reitvorschrift	equitation manual
R.V.O	Reichsversicherungsordnung	Reich insurance law
RW	Reichswehr	standing German army (*before 1935*)
R.W	Reparaturwerkstatt	repair workshop
R.W	Richtungsweiser	signpost
Rw	Rollwagen	dray-cart
R.-Wagen	Rungenwagen	heavy freight car (*15 tons*)
RWD	Reichswetterdienst	German weather bureau
RWe	Reichswehr	standing German army (*before 1935*)
R.Wg	Rohrwagen	barrel carriage (*artillery*)
r.w.K	rechtweisender Kurs	true course (*aviation*)
Rw San V	Reichswehrsanitätsvorschrift	regulations regarding the Medical Service of the Reichswehr
Rz	Rohrzerspringer	barrel burster (*artillery*)
R.Zg	Reiterzug	cavalry platoon
R.Zug	Reiterzug	cavalry platoon

Repetitions-Theodolit *m* repeating theodolite (*Surv*).
Repressalien *fpl* reprisals.
requirieren commandeer.
Reserve *f* reserve (Reserve I, *inactive reserve of fully trained men under 35*; Reserve II, *inactive reserve of partly trained men under 35*).
Reservedivision *f* reserve division (*Tng unit in occupied countries*).
Reserveeingreiftrupp *m* reserve detachment (*held in readiness for tactical commitment*).
Reservelazarett *n* general hospital.
Reserveoffizier *m* reserve officer.
Reserveoffizieranwärter *m* reserve officer candidate.
Reserveoffizier-Bewerber *m* reserve officer applicant.
Reservezündung *f* auxiliary ignition lead (*blasting*).
Resonanzkreis *m* resonant circuit
Restflugweite *f* straight-line distance between point of burst and theoretical point of impact (*Ballistics*).
Rettungsboje *f* life buoy.
Rettungsdienst *m* life-saving service, rescue service.
Rettungsfahrzeug *n* lifeboat.
Rettungsgerät *n* life-saving equipment.
Rettungsgürtel *m* life belt.
Rettungsleine *f* life line.
Rettungsmannschaft *f* rescue party.
Rettungsring *m* life preserver.
Rettungsschwimmer *m* qualified swimmer (*holder of life-saver's certificate*).
Rettungsstange *f* boat hook (*for rescue work*).
Rettungstrupp *m* (*CWS*) rescue squad
Revier *n* infirmary; forest range; precinct, district.
Revierkranker *m* infirmary case, dispensary case.
Revierstunde *f* sick call.
Revolver *m* revolver.
Revolvergurt *m* revolver belt.
Revolver mit Wiederspannabzug double-action revolver.
Reynoldszahl *f* Reynolds number (*Aerodynamics*).
Richtantenne *f* directional antenna
Richtaufsatz *m* sight mount, telescope mount.
Richtaufsatzträger *m* sight mount bracket.
Richtausbildung *f* training in sighting and aiming.
Richtbaum *m* trail handspike (*G*).
Richtbefehl *m* aiming order.
Richtbogen *m* clinometer (*Surv, Gunnery*).
Richtempfänger *m* radio compass, direction finder (*Air Navigation*).
Richtempfangsanlage *f* direction-finder station (*Air Navigation*).
Richtempfangsantenne *f* directional receiving antenna (*Rad*).
richten to lay, to aim, to point (*a gun*).
Richter *m* judge.
"Richt Euch!" "Dress right, dress!"
Richtfeld *n* field of fire; extent of traverse and elevation.
Richtfernrohr *n* telescopic sight.
Richtfunkfeuer *f* radio range beacon.
Richtgehäuse *n* elevating-gear housing (*MG*).
Richtgelenk *n* elevating link (*MG*).
Richtgerät *n* laying mechanism, sight equipment (*G*); direction-finding equipment (*Rad*).
Richtglas *n* collimating sight.
Richthebel *m* elevating arm (*MG*).
Richthebelwelle *f* elevating-arm shaft (*MG*).
Richthöhe *f* elevation (*Gunnery*).
Richtkanonier *m* gunner (*Arty*); gun pointer.
Richtkommando *n* aiming order.
Richtkreis *m* aiming circle (*Arty*); azimuth circle (*Surv*).
Richtkreis-Bussole *f* declinator (*aiming circle*).
Richtkreiseinteilung *f* mil graduation (*aiming circle*).
Richtkreisunteroffizier *m* instrument NCO in charge of aiming circle (*Arty*).
Richtlampe *f* aiming light, aiming post light.
Richtlatte *f* aiming stake, aiming post (*Arty*); base stake (*Surv*).
Richtlehre *f* theory of gun pointing.
Richtlehrer *m* instructor in gunnery.
Richtlinien *fpl* guiding principles, directions.
Richtmaschine *f* elevating and traversing mechanism (*G*).
Richtmittel *n* sighting device; laying device.
Richtposten *m* road sign post.
Richtpunkt *m* aiming point
Richtpunktverfahren *n* aiming-point and deflection method (*Gunnery*).
Richtpunktzahl *f* aiming-point azimuth reading.
Richtsäule *f* control column (*for synchronizing sound locator and searchlight*).
Richtscheibe *f* aiming target.

Richtschütze *m* gunner (*MG, Mort, Tk, AT*); gun pointer.
Richtsitz *m* gunner's seat, layer's seat (*G*).
Richtstange *f* alinement stake (*Bdg, Engr*).
Richtstelle *f* aiming-circle station (*MG platoon*).
Richtstock *m* aiming post.
Richtstrahl *m* radio beam.
Richtstrich *m* center line (*on inside of march-compass cover*).
Richtübung *f* aiming practice, aiming exercise (*Gunnery*).
Richtübungsgerät *n* practice sight.
Richtung *f* direction; pointing or laying (*of a gun*).
Richtungsangabe *f* indication of direction.
Richtungsbestimmung *f* determining of direction, orientation.
Richtungsgleis *n* classification track (*RR*).
Richtungshörer *m* (*AAA*) sound locator
Richtungslinie *f* orienting line (*Gunnery, Surv*).
Richtungspunkt *m* orienting point
Richtungsschießen *n* adjustment fire for direction (*Gunnery*).
Richtungsschild *n* road sign.
Richtungsschüsse *mpl* adjustment shots for direction (*Gunnery*).
Richtungsstabilität *f* directional stability (*Ap*).
Richtungswinkel *m* firing angle.
Richtverfahren *n* method of laying (*Gunnery*).
Richtvorrichtung *f* elevating and traversing mechanism.
Richtwirkung *f* (*Rad*) directional effect
Richtzahnbogen *m* elevating rack, elevating arc (*G*).
Riechprobe *f* sniffing test (*CWS*).
Riechprobenkasten *m* gas-identification set, sniff set (*CWS*).
Riechspur *f* artificial scent.
Riechtopf *m* irritant-gas generator, CN generator (*CWS*).
Riechwürfel *m* chemical capsule (*to simulate gas-shell fire*).
Riegel *m* bolt; bar; crossbar; sliding bolt; switch line, oblique defense line (*Tac, Ft*).
Riegelbolzen *m* retaining bolt (*Ord*).
Riegelhebel *m* locking lever (*G*).
Riegelstellung *f* switch position (*Ft, Tac*).
Riemen *m* strap; sling; belt.
Riemenantrieb *m* belt drive.
Riemenbügel *m* sling swivel (*R*).
Riemenscheibe *f* pulley.
Riemenschieber *m* (*R*) gun-sling keeper
Riesenluftreifen *m* giant tire, oversize tire (*MT*).
Rille *f* cannelure (*Am*); groove.
Ringen *n* combat, struggle, wrestling.
Ringfallschirm *m* parachute skirt.
Ringpulver *n* annular powder (*Am*).
Ringrohr *n* built-up barrel (*G*).
Ringtrichterrichtungshörer *m* trumpet-type sound locator (*AAA*).
Ringübertrager *m* repeating coil (*Tg, Tp*).
Ringverkleidung *f* engine ring cowling (*Ap*).
Ringvisier *n* ring sight.
rinnen to leak.
Rippe *f* rib; cooling fin (*air-cooled engine*).
Rippenfläche *f* fin surface (*air-cooled engine*).
Riß *m* rip, tear; split; rupture; laceration; sectional drawing.
Rißwunde *f* lacerated wound.
Ritter *m* knight, noble.
Ritterkreuz *n* Knight's Cross (*decoration*).
Rittmeister *m* captain (*Cav*)
Ritzel *m* pinion.
robben to crawl.
Rödelbalken *m* siderail, curb rail, guard rail (*Bdg*).
Rödelbund *m* siderail lashing (*Bdg*).
Rödelkeil *m* siderail wedge (*Bdg*).
Rödeln *n* siderail lashing (*Bdg*).
Rödelung *f* siderails, guard rails, siderail lashing (*Bdg*).
Rödelzange *f* siderail clamp (*Bdg*).
Rodung *f* logged-off area, cleared woodland.
Rohöl *n* crude oil.
Rohr *n* tube, gun barrel; pipe.
Rohrabnutzung *f* erosion of the bore.
Rohransatz *m* barrel extension.
Rohrbremse *f* recoil brake (*G*).
Rohrbuch *n* gun book.
Röhre *f* tube (*Rad*).
Röhrenheizung *f* filament heating
Röhrenkennlinie *f* characteristic curve, tube characteristic (*Rad*).
Röhrenlafette *f* tubular mount.
Röhrenlibelle *f* tubular spirit level.
Röhrenmast *m* tubular mast.
Röhrenprüfgerät *n* tube tester, tube checker (*Inst, Rad*).
Röhrenpulver *n* perforated powder
Röhrensockel *m* tube base, tube socket (*Rad*).
Röhrenspannungsmesser *m* vacuum-tube voltmeter.

Röhrensummer *m* electronic audio oscillator (*Rad*).
Rohrerhöhung *f* quadrant elevation.
Rohrfestigkeit *f* strength of barrel
Rohrhalter *m* barrel bracket (*G*).
Rohrinneres *n* bore (*G*).
Rohrklaue *f* barrel guide (*G*).
Rohrkrepierer *m* barrel burst.
Rohrlänge *f* length of barrel (*G*).
Rohrleitung *f* pipe line.
Rohrmantel *m* jacket (*G*).
Rohrmündung *f* muzzle (*G*).
Rohrrahmen *m* tubular chassis frame (*MT*).
Rohrrücklauf *m* barrel recoil (*G*).
Rohrschlitten *m* sleigh (*G*); gun-barrel sled (*for carrying barrel of dismantled mountain gun in deep snow*).
Rohrschreiber *m* practice aiming device consisting of pencil mounted on gun barrel and chart on which pencil tracks movement of target.
Rohrseele *f* bore (*G*).
rohrsicherer Zünder bore-safe fuze.
Rohrsicherheit des Zünders bore safety of fuze.
Rohrstütze *f* tubular support (*AA gun outrigger*).
Rohrwagen *m* cannon transport wagon, gun-barrel trailer.
Rohrwandbeobachtungsgerät *n* barrel reflector (*G*).
Rohrwechsel *m* (*Ord*) change of barrel
Rohrweite *f* caliber (*G*).
Rohrwiege *f* cradle (*G*).
Rohrzange *f* Stillson wrench, pipe wrench.
Rohrzeiger *m* gun barrel reference pointer (*matches with* **Aufsatzzeiger** *when gun is laid for elevation*).
Rohrzerspringer *m* barrel burst.
Rollbahn *f* taxiway (*Adrm*); track (*of road*).
Rollbock *m* bogie trailer (*Arty*).
Rolle *f* roll (*Avn, Tech*); roller, pulley; wire roll.
gesteuerte Rolle slow roll (*Avn*).
rollen to taxi (*Avn*); to roll along, to roll forward (*Tks, vehicles*) in rollendem Einsatz in waves (*Tac*).
rollendes Material rolling stock (*RR*).
Rollenlager *n* roller bearing (*Mech*).
Rollenstößel *m* roller-type valve lifter (*Mtr*).
Rollenwagen *m* (*Tk*) bogie suspensions
Rollfeld *n* landing field, cleared zone (*Adrm*).
Rollstraße *f* taxiway (*Adrm*).
Rollwerk *n* landing gear (*Ap*).
Rollwiderstand *m* vehicle resistance (*MT*); rolling friction (*Mech*).
Röntgenbild *n* X-ray photograph.
Röntgenstrahlen *mpl* X-rays.
Rost *m* rust; grate; grill; trench board.
rostig rusty.
Rotes Kreuz Red Cross.
Rotfilterempfangsgerät *n* red-filter receiving attachment (*signal lamp*).
Rotfiltergerät *n* red-filter set (*BC telescope*).
Rotte *f* two-ship element (*formation of two airplanes*); a number of men in file.
R-Patrone *f* *See* **Rauchpatrone**.
Rückbau *m* reconstruction; dismantling.
Rückbeförderung *f* evacuation (*of wounded, etc.*).
Rückblick *m* backsight (*Surv*); rear glance, rear view, retrospect.
Rückblickspiegel *m* rear-view mirror.
Rückdruck *m* reaction pressure
Rücken *m* rear (*Tac*); ridge (*Top*); back.
Rückenangriff *m* attack against the rear; attack from the rear.
Rückendeckung *f* rear covering force, rear cover (*Tac*); parados (*Ft*).
Rückenfallschirm *m* back-pack parachute.
Rückenfeuer *n* enemy fire from the rear.
Rückenflug *m* inverted flight, upside-down flight.
Rückengepäck *n* pack.
Rückenkissen *n* crupper pad (*harness*).
Rückenlehne *f* back rest (*Ap, MT*).
Rückenlinie *f* ridge line (*Top*).
Rückenriemen *m* leadup strap (*harness*).
Rückenring *m* back rest (*AA MG*).
Rückentrage *f* pack reel (*for Tp*
Rückenwehr *f* parados (*Ft*).
Rückenwind *m* tail wind.
Rückfahrlaterne *f* (*MT*) backing light
Rückflug *m* return flight, homing flight (*Avn*).
Rückfrage *f* check-back, tracer.
Rückgrat *n* backbone.
Rückhalt *m* support (*Tac*).
Rückholer *m* connecting arm between firing lever and sear (*light Inf howitzer*).
Rückkehr *f* return.
Rückkopplung *f* feedback, regeneration (*Rad*).
Rücklauf *m* recoil.
Rücklaufbremse *f* recoil brake (*G*).

Rücklaufeinrichtung *f* recoil mechanism *(G)*.
rückläufig retrograde, reverse.
Rücklauffeder *f* recoil spring, buffer spring.
Rücklaufmesser *m* recoil marker *(G)*.
Rücklaufschieber *m* recoil marker slide *(G)*.
Rücklaufwelle *f* reverse idler gear shaft *(MT)*.
Rückleitung *f* return *(Elec, Tp)*; return line *(hydraulics)*.
Rücklicht *n* taillight *(MT)*.
Rückmarsch *m* retrograde march, retirement *(Tac)*.
Rückmarschbewegung *f* retrograde movement.
Rückmarschstraße *f* line of retirement *(Tac)*.
Rückmeldung *f* reply.
Rucksack *m* knapsack, rucksack.
Rückschlag *m* blowback *(Ord)*; back pressure *(Mtr)*; reverse *(Tac)*.
Rückschlagventil *n* check valve, one-way valve.
Rückstände *mpl* fouling *(Ord)*; carbon *(Mtr)*; residue.
Rückstoß *m* recoil, kick *(Ord)*; reaction *(Mech)*.
Rückstoßhülse *f* recoil booster sleeve *(MG)*.
Rückstoßlader *m* recoil-operated weapon.
Rückstoßmotor *m* jet-propulsion engine *(Ap)*.
Rückstoßverstärker *m* recoil booster *(MG)*.
Rückstoßwirkung *f* recoil effect.
Rückstrahler *m* reflector.
Rücktrift *f* trail *(bomb trajectory)*.
Rücktriftwinkel *m* trail angle *(bomb trajectory)*.
rückwärtig rear, rearward, behind the lines.
rückwärtige Dienste rear services, supply services.
rückwärtige Einrichtungen rear installations.
rückwärtiges Armeegebiet communications zone.
rückwärtiges Gebiet rear area, rear zone, communications zone.
rückwärtiges Heeresgebiet communications zone of a group of armies.
rückwärtiges Lazarett base hospital.
rückwärtiges Nachschublager base depot.
rückwärtige Stellung rear position, reserve battle position, rear battle position.
Rückwärtseinschneiden *n* resection *(Surv)*.
Rückwärtsfahrer *m* rear driver *(of a vehicle with double-end control)*.
Rückwärtsfahrt *f* reverse movement *(MT)*.
Rückwärtsgang *m* reverse, reverse gear, reverse speed *(MT)*.
Rückwärtslenkung *f* rear steering system *(of a vehicle with double-end control)*.
Rückwärtsstaffelung *f* negative stagger *(Ap wings)*; echelon formation in depth.
Rückweg *m* withdrawal route *(Tac)*; return, way back.
rückwirkend retroactive.
Rückzug *m* retreat, retirement, withdrawal *(Tac)*.
Rückzugslinie *f* line of retirement, line of retreat *(Tac)*.
Rückzugsstraße *f* withdrawal route, route of retreat.
Rudel *n* *See* **Schützenrudel, Reiterrudel.**
Ruder *n* oar; elevator or rudder *(Ap)*.
Ruderboot *n* rowboat.
Ruderfahrzeug *n* oar-propelled craft.
Ruindersteven *m* stern post *(assault boat, ferry, or barge)*.
Ruf *m* call; ring *(Tp)*; reputation.
Rufbatterie *f* a battery whose observation post is within calling distance of the battalion observation post.
rufen to call; to ring *(Tp)*.
Rufname *m* first name.
Rufstrom *m* signaling current, ringing current *(Tp)*.
Rufzeichen *n* call sign, call signal *(Rad)*; calling signal *(Tp)*.
Ruhe *f* rest, silence, quiet.
Ruhegehalt *n* pension.
Ruhelager *n* rest camp.
Ruhestand *m* retirement.
im Ruhestand retired *(abbr.* i.R.).
Ruhestellung *f* "at ease" position.
Ruhr *f* dysentery.
Ruhrast *f* half cock *(SA)*.
"Rührt, euch!" "At ease!"
Rumpf *m* trunk, torso; fuselage *(Ap)*; hull *(of flying boat)*.
Rumpfbug *m* nose *(Ap)*.
Rumpfende *n* tail *(Ap)*.
Rumpfgerüst *n* fuselage framework *(Ap)*.
Rumpfhaut *f* fuselage skin *(Ap)*.
Rumpfholm *m* longeron *(Ap)*.
Rumpfkanzel *f* cockpit *(Ap)*.
Rumpfklappe *f* bomb doors *(Ap)*.
Rumpflängsachse *f* longitudinal axis of fuselage.
Rumpflängsleiste *f* longeron *(Ap)*.
Rumpfmontage *f* fuselage assembly
Rumpfspant *m* bulkhead *(Ap)*.
Rumpfnase *f* nose *(Ap)*.
Rumpfspitze *f* nose *(Ap)*.
Rumpfverband *m* cadre.
Rundbild *n* panoramic photograph *(Surv)*.
Rundblickfernrohr *n* panoramic telescope, panoramic sight.
Runde *f* tour, round, circle, curve.
Runderneuerung *f* retreading *(MT)*.
Rundflug *m* local flight *(Avn)*.
Rundfunk *m* radio broadcast; broadcasting.
Rundfunkempfang *m* radio broadcast reception.
Rundfunksender *m* radio broadcasting station.
Rundholz *n* round timber, spar.
Rundkeilverschluß *m* cylindrical wedge-type breechblock *(G)*.
Rundschreiben *n* circular.
Rundzelt *n* circular tent.
Rungenwagen *m* flatcar with side racks *(RR)*.
Rüstgewicht *n* structural weight *(plus equipment)* *(Ap)*.
Rüstung *f* armament.
rutschen to slip, slide, skid; to sideslip *(Avn)*.
Rüttelerscheinungen *fpl* flutter *(Ap)*.
R-Wagen *m* *See* **Rungenwagen.**

S

SA *f* *See* **Sturmabteilungen.**
Säbel *m* saber, sword.
Sachbearbeiter *m* technical staff officer; individual in charge of a special administrative department or field of subject matter.
Sachnummer *f* item number.
Sachschaden *m* material damage, damage to property.
Sack *m* bag, sack.
sacken to sag, settle, sink.
Sackgasse *f* dead-end street or road.
Sackleinen *n* burlap, osnaburg.
Saft *m* juice; electric current *(slang)*.
Säge *f* saw.
Sägewerk *n* sawmill.
Salpeter *m* saltpeter.
Salpetersäure *f* nitric acid.
Salut *m* gun salute.
Salve *f* salvo *(pieces fire simultaneously)* *(Arty)*; volley *(fired by riflemen)*.
Salvengeschütz *n* automatic gun.
Salz *n* salt.
Salzkartusche *f* flash-reducing wad *(Am)*.
Salzsäure *f* hydrochloric acid.
Salzvorladung *f* flash-reducing wad.
Salzvorlage *f* *See* **Salzvorladung.**
SA-Mann *m* storm trooper.
Sammelgespräch *n* conference call
Sammelkommando *n* recovery party, salvage collecting party.
Sammelkompanie *f* salvage collecting company.
Sammelmeldung *f* general message
sammeln to salvage, to collect, to gather.
Sammelort *m* assembly place, rendezvous.
Sammelplatz *m* collecting point; assembly point, rallying point, rendezvous *(Tac)*; collecting station *(Med)*.
Sammelpunkt *m* *See* **Sammelplatz.**
Sammelrufzeichen *n* collective call sign, general call sign *(Rad)*.
Sammelschutz *m* collective protection *(CWS)*.
Sammelstelle *f* assembly point.
Sammeltätigkeit *f* collecting; salvage collecting.
Sammelwesen *n* salvage service.
Sammelzug *m* salvage platoon.
Sammler *m* *See* **Sammlerbatterie.**
Sammlerbatterie *f* storage battery.
Sammlerhaube *f* battery cover *(Elec)*.
Sammlerkasten *m* battery box *(Elec)*.
Sandeis *n* "ice concrete" *(a frozen mixture of sand, gravel and water)*.
Sandgrube *f* sand pit.
Sandkasten *m* sand table *(Tng)*.
Sandkastenspiel *n* sand table exercise.
Sandschutzbrille *f* sand goggles.
Sanierung *f* sanitation, introduction of sanitary measures.
Sanierungsmittel *n* prophylactic.
Sanitätsabteilung *f* medical battalion.
Sanitätsausrüstung *f* medical equipment.
Sanitätsdienst *m* medical service.
Sanitätseinrichtung *f* medical installation.
Sanitätsfahrzeug *n* ambulance.
Sanitätsfeldwebel *m* technical sergeant *(Med)*.
Sanitätsflugbereitschaft *f* airplane ambulance unit.
Sanitätsflugzeug *n* airplane ambulance.
Sanitätsgefreiter *m* acting corporal *(Med)*. *See also* **Gefreiter.**
Sanitätsgerät *n* medical equipment.
Sanitätshelferin *f* medical woman auxiliary.
Sanitätshund *m* first-aid dog.
Sanitätskasten *m* medicine chest, surgical chest.
Sanitätskolonne *f* ambulance column.
Sanitätskompanie *f* medical company.
Sanitätskorps *n* Medical Corps.
Sanitätsmaterialpark *m* medical supply depot.
Sanitätsoberfeldwebel *m* master sergeant *(Med)*.
Sanitätsobergefreiter *m(Med)* corporal
Sanitätsobersoldat *m* private first class *(Med)*.
Sanitätsoffizier *m* medical officer.
Sanitätsoffizier (Z) *m* dental officer (Z *is abbr. of* Zahnarzt).
Sanitätsordnung *f* regulations governing organization and operation of Medical Corps.
Sanitätspark *m* medical depot.
Sanitätspersonal *n* medical corps personnel.
Sanitätssoldat *m* private *(Med)*.
Sanitätsstaffel *f* medical unit *(of Div Med Bn)*.
Sanitätstroß *m* medical train.
Sanitätstruppe *f* medical corps.
Sanitätstasche *f* pouch kit.
Sanitätstruppen *fpl* medical troops.
Sanitätsunteroffizier *m(Med)* sergeant
Sanitätswesen *n* medical service.
Sappe *f* sap *(Ft)*.
Sappenkopf *m* saphead *(Ft)*.
Sarg *m* coffin.
Sattel *m* saddle *(harness, Top)*.
Sattelbaum *m* saddletree *(harness)*.
Sattelbefehl *m* field order.
Sattelbekleidung *f* saddle covering.
Sattelgurt *m* girth *(of a saddle)*.
Sattelholz *n* short wooden plate or sill placed on top of a column so as to increase its bearing surface.
Sattelkissen *n* saddle pad.
Sattelpferd *n* near horse.
Sattelschlepper *m* semitrailer *(MT)*.
Sattelsitz *m* seat *(of a saddle)*.
Satteltasche *f* skirt *(saddle)*.
Satteltracht *f* saddle cover *(pack saddle)*.
Sättigung *f* saturation.
Satz *m* sentence, axiom; rate, scale; set, unit; composition, pellet *(Am, CWS)*; jump, bound.
Satzring *m* time train ring *(time fuze)*.
Satzstück *n* powder pellet *(time fuze)*.
säubern to clean; clear up; clean out; mop up *(Tac)*.
Säuberungstrupp *m* mopping-up detachment.
Säuberungsunternehmen *n* mopping-up operation.
Sauerstoff *m* oxygen.
Sauerstoffazetylenschweißung *f* oxyacetylene welding.
Sauerstoffflasche *f* oxygen cylinder.
Sauerstoffgerät *n* oxygen apparatus.
Sauerstoff-Wiederbeleber *m* pulmotor.
Saughub *m* intake stroke, suction stroke *(Mtr)*.
Saugleitung *f* intake duct *(Mtr)*.
Saugluft *f* inflow *(Avn)*.
Saugrohr *n* intake manifold *(Mtr)*.
Saugseite *f* suction surface
Saugsteinbehälter *m* silicic acid gel container *(gas-detection apparatus)*.
Säule *f* column, pile.
Saumpfad *m* path *(for pack animals)*; mountain trail.
Sauna Finnish steam bath.
Säure *f* acid.
Säuremesser *m* hydrometer.
S-Beköstigungsmittel *npl* army post subsistence supplies *(abbr. for* Standort-Beköstigungsmittel).
S-Boot *n* *See* **Schnellboot.**
Schaber *m* scraper.
Schablone *f* stencil, templet.
schablonieren to stencil.
Schacht *m* shaft *(mining)*; bomb rack; conduit *(Elec)*.
Schachtel *f* box.
Schädel *m* skull.
Schaden *m* damage.
Schadenbekämpfung *f* damage control.
Schadenersatz *m* indemnity.
schädlich injurious, harmful, destructive, pernicious, dangerous; prejudicial, disadvantageous.
schädlicher Widerstand parasite drag *(Avn)*.
Schädlichkeitsgrenze *f* point of intolerable concentration *(CWS)*.
Schaft *m* stock *(R)*; forearm *(automatic R)*; leg *(of a jackboot)*; rod, stem, handle, shank, shaft, stick.
Schaftpflegemittel *n* stock preservative *(R)*.
Schäkel *m* clevis, shackle.
Schalenbauweise *f* monocoque construction *(Ap)*.
Schalenkreuzwindmesser *m* cup anemometer *(Met)*.
Schall *m* sound.
Schallaufnahmegerät *n* oscillograph *(sound ranging)*.
Schallblech *n* diaphragm *(Tp)*.
Schalldämpfer *m* muffler *(MT)*; silencer *(Ord)*.
schalldicht soundproof.

S

S	Heeresnachrichtenschule	army signal school *(insignia on shoulder straps)*
S	Luftsprengpunkt	point of burst in air *(mortar)*
S	Sachverständiger	expert
S	Säure	acid
S	Sammelstation	collecting station
S	Sammeltransport	collective transport; combination transport
S	Sanitäts-	medical
S	Sanitätsabteilung	medical battalion; medical officer detachment
S	Sanitätsunteroffizier	medical noncommissioned
S	Schallmessstelle	sound-ranging station
S	scharf	live *(ammunition)*
S	Scheinwerfer	searchlight
S	Scheinwerferzug	searchlight platoon
S	Schirrmeister	supply sergeant *(sleeve insignia)*
S	Schiess-	fire; firing
S	Schiessbaumwolle	gun cotton
S	Schnellzug	express train
S	Schütze	rifleman
S	Schule	school
S	Schutz-	protective
S	Schwefel	sulphur
s	schwer	heavy *(medium in case of artillery weapons)*
s	schwere Panzerwagen	heavy tanks
S	Sehschärfe	sight; clearness of vision
S	Seite	page
S	Seiten-	flank
S	Sekunde	second
s	selbst-	self-
S	Sicherheit	security; safety
s	sichern	to put machine gun at safety by the safety catch
S	Sicherungsstreitkräfte	protecting forces *(navy)*; reserve forces
s	siehe	see, refer to
S	Signal	signal
S	Sold	pay
S	Soldat	soldier
S	Sommer	summer
S	Sonder-	special
S	Sozialist	socialist
S	Spitz-	pointed
S	Sprechstelle	call station *(on sketches)*
Sam.San.P.	Sammelsanitätspark	medical supply collecting depot
Sam.Sch.	Sammelschutz	gas protection measures
Sam.St.	Sammelstelle	salvage dump; collecting
Sam.Tr.	Sammeltransport	collective transport; combination transport
San	Sanitäts-	medical
San	Sanitätslager	medical depot
San.A	Sanitätsamt	medical department
San. Abt.	Sanitätsabteilung	medical battalion; medical detachment
San.Ausr.	Sanitätsausrüstung	medical equipment
San.Bed.	Sanitätsbedarf	needed medical supplies
San.D.	Sanitätsdienst	medical corps; army medical service
San.Dep.	Sanitätsdepot	medical depot
San.D.St.	Sanitätsdienststelle	medical service station
San.Einr.	Sanitätseinrichtung(en)	medical establishment; medical installations
San.Fz.	Sanitätsfahrzeug	medical vehicle; ambulance
San.Ger.Wg.	Sanitätsgerätewagen	medical supply car
San.Hd.	Sanitätshund	ambulance dog
San.Insp.	Sanitätsinspektion	medical inspectorate
Sanit.K.	Sanitätskorps	medical corps
San.K.	Sanitätskarren	ambulance cart
San.K.	Sanitätskraftwagen	ambulance
Sanka	Sanitätskraftwagenabteil-	ambulance detachment
San.Kp.	Sanitätskompanie	medical company
Sankra	Sanitätskraftwagen	ambulance
San.Kst.	Sanitätskasten	medical kit
Sankw	Sanitätskraftwagen	ambulance
San.Mitt.	Sanitätsmittel	medical supplies
San.Ob.Fw.	Sanitätsoberfeldwebel beim Stabe	*(corresponds roughly to U. S. staff sergeant, Medical Corps, at headquarters)*
San.Ob.Gef.	Sanitätsobergefreiter	*(corresponds roughly to U. S. acting corporal, Medical Corps)*
San.P.	Sanitätspark	medical supply depot
San.Pers.	Sanitätspersonal	medical personnel
San.P.Pf.	Sanitätspackpferd	medical pack horse
San.P.T.	Sanitätspacktasche	medical pack
S	Sprengpunkt	point of burst
S	Stahl	steel
S	Streitkräfte	fighting forces
S	Süd-	south
s	südlich	southward; southerly
08/S	Rückstossverstärker für scharfe Munition	recoil booster for live ammunition *(machine-gun)*
S.A	Sanitätsabteilung	medical battalion; medical detachment
S.A	Selbstanschlussamt	automatic central office
S.A	Skiabteilung	ski detachment; ski battalion

SA	Sonnenaufgang	sunrise
SA	Sturmabteilungen der NSDAP	Storm Troopers Organization of the National Socialist Party
SA.-A	Anwärter der Sturmabteilung der NSDAP	candidate for the Storm-Troopers Organization of the National Socialist Party
Sab	Sabotage	sabotage
Sach.B	Sachbearbeiter	specialist
Sachbesch	Sachbeschädigung	damage to property
sachgem	sachgemäss	relevant; pertinent
Sachk	Sachkenntnis	professional knowledge
Sachk	Sachkunde	expertness
Sachl	Sachlage	state of affairs; situation
Sachsch	Sachschaden	damage to property
Sachsch.-V	Sachschadenversicherung	insurance against property damage
Sachv	Sachverständiger	expert; specialist
Sachv.-G	Sachverständigengutachten	expert's opinion; expert's report
Säb	Säbel	saber; sword
Säb.Sch	Säbelscheide	saber sheath
Säb.Tr	Säbeltroddel	sword knot
Säub.Tr	Säuberungstrupp	mopping-up party
SA-M	Sturmabteilungsmann	(SA) Storm Trooper (*equivalent U. S. rank: private*)
Sam	Sammel-	collecting; collective
Sam.Bhf	Sammelbahnhof	railroad collecting point
Sam.Dep	Sammeldepot	collecting depot
Sam.Kp	Sammelkompanie	salvage company
Sam.L	Sammellazarett	collecting hospital
Samml	Sammlung	collection
San.St	Sanitätsstab	medical staff
San.Tr	Sanitätstrupp	medical detail (*navy*)
San.Vorr.Wg	Sanitätsvorratswagen	medical supply car
San.Wg	Sanitätswagen	ambulance
s.Art	schwere Artillerie	medium artillery
s.Art.(mot.)	motorisierte schwere Artillerie	motorized medium artillery
Sas	Sandsack	sandbag
Satt	Sattel	saddle
Sattlmstr	Sattlermeister	master saddler
Sattl.Zg	Sattelzeug	saddle harness
Sauerst	Sauerstoff	oxygen
sb	selbständig	independent
s.b	siehe bei	look under
S.B	Soldbuch	identification book and service record
s.B	südliche Breite	southern latitude
Sbd	Sonnabend	Saturday
Sbst	Selbst-	self-; automatic
Sch	Schaden	damage; injury
Sch	Schaft	shaft; rifle stock
Sch	Schallmess	sound-ranging
Sch	Schanz-	entrenchment; fieldwork
sch	schanzen	to entrench; to dig
Sch	Schar	troop; band; host; multitude
sch	scharf	sharp; live (*ammunition*)
Sch	Scharfschütze	sharpshooter
Sch	Scheibe	target
Sch	Scheide	limit; boundary; sheath
Sch	Scheidung	separation
Sch	Schein	appearance; light; dummy
Sch	Scheinwerfer	searchlight; headlight
Sch	Scheune	barn (*on maps*)
Sch	Schi	ski
Sch	Schieds-	arbitration; umpire
Sch	Schiene	splint; rail
sch	schienen	to put in a splint
Sch	Schiess-	firing; shooting
Sch	Schiff	ship
Sch	Schiffahrt	navigation
Sch	Schilderhaus	sentry box
Sch	Schirm	shelter; screen; umbrella
Sch	Schirr-	harness; trappings
Sch	Schnee	snow
sch	schon	already
Sch	Schornstein	chimney
Sch	Schütze	rifleman
sch	schützen	to protect; to guard; to shelter
Sch	Schule	school
Sch	Schuss	shot
Sch	Schutz	shelter; refuge; protection; cover
Sch	Schutzschild	protective shield
Schalld	Schalldämpfer	muffler; silencer
Schall-Geschw	Schallgeschwindigkeit	velocity of sound
Schallm	Schallmessung	sound-ranging
Schallm.Battr	Schallmessbatterie	sound-ranging battery
Schallm.Ger	Schallmessgerät	sound-ranging equipment
Schallm.Tr	Schallmesstrupp	sound-ranging section
Schallm.Verf	Schallmessverfahren	sound-ranging method
Schaltg	Schaltung	connection; gear shift
Sch.Anl	Scheinanlage	dummy works; camouflage works
Schanz.Wg	Schanzzeugwagen	entrenching-tools wagon

Schalldose *f* pick-up unit (*phonograph*).
Schallgeschwindigkeit *f* velocity of sound.
Schallmeßaufnahmegerät *n* oscillograph (*sound ranging*).
Schallmeßbatterie *f* sound-ranging battery (*Arty*).
Schallmeßfilm *m* oscillogram (*film*) (*sound ranging*).
Schallmeßstelle *f* sound-ranging station (*Arty*).
Schallmeßstellentrupp *m* sound unit (*sound ranging*).
Schallmeßsystem *n* sound-ranging net (*Arty*).
Schallmessung *f* sound ranging.
Schallmikrophon *n* sound-ranging microphone.
Schallmittel *n* sound-communication device.
Schallortung *f* sound location (*AAA*).
Schallplatte *f* phonograph record.
Schallplatten-Abtastdose *f* phonograph pick-up unit, pick-up.
Schallverzug *m* sound lag (*AAA*).
Schallwelle *f* sound wave.
Schalmesser *n* drawknife.
Schaltbrett *n* control panel, dashboard, instrument panel.
Schaltbrettlaterne *f* instrument light.
Schaltdom *m* gearshift-lever housing.
schalten to shift (*MT*); to switch (*Elec*).
Schalter *m* switch (*Elec*).
Schaltgabel *f* shifter fork (*MT*).
Schaltgetriebe *n* gearshift transmission (*MT*).
Schalthebel *m* gearshift lever (*MT*); throwout lever (*panoramic telescope*).
Schaltkästchen *n* portable switchboard (*Tp*); switchbox (*Elec*).
Schaltkasten *m* switchbox (*Elec*); combination switch box (*MT*).
Schaltklaue *f* dog clutch member (*constant-mesh transmission*) (*MT*).
Schaltmuffe *f* gearshift collar (*MT*).
Schaltplan *m* circuit diagram.
Schaltschema *n* See Schaltplan.
Schaltskizze *f* See Schaltplan.
Schaltstange *f* shift rail (*MT*).
Schaltstück *n* throwout (*sight-mount housing*).
Schalttafel *f* control board, control panel, instrument panel.
Schalttisch *m* switchboard (*Tp*).
Schaltung *f* connection (*Elec*); circuit (*Rad, Tp, Tg*); gearshift (*MT*).
Schaltvorrichtung *f* switching device (*Elec*).
Schalung *f* casing; form (*concrete construction*); revetment.
Schandeck *n* gunwale (*Pon*).
Schanzarbeiten *fpl* entrenchments, spadework (*field Ft*).
Schanze *f* earthwork (*Ft*).
schanzen dig, dig in, entrench.
Schanzkorb *m* gabion (*Ft*).
Schanzzeug *n* entrenching tool(s).
scharf armed, live, primed (*Am*); activated (*LM*); sharp.
Schärfe *f* sharpness.
scharfe Munition live ammunition.
scharfe Panzermine activated antitank mine.
scharfe Patrone live cartridge, ball cartridge (*Am*).
scharfgeladene Granate live shell
scharf machen to arm (*Am*); to activate (*a mine*).
Scharfschütze *m* sharpshooter, sniper, marksman.
Scharfschützengewehr *n* sharpshooter's rifle.
Scharfschützennest *n* sniper's post.
scharf stellen to arm (*Am*); to activate (*LM*).
Scharmützel *n* skirmish.
Scharnier *n* hinge.
Scharte *f* port (*Tk*); loophole, embrasure (*Ft*).
Schartenblende *f* firing-port shutter (*Tk*); gun shelter (*Ft*).
Schartenschild *m* shield with sighting ports (*G*); gun shelter (*Ft*).
Schartensprengtrupp *m* pillbox demolition party.
Schatten *m* shadow.
Schattenriß *m* silhouette.
Schattenwirkung *f*(*Cam*) shadow effect
schätzen to estimate.
Schätzung *f* estimation, estimate.
Schaufel *f* shovel.
Schauflug *m* demonstration flight (*Avn*).
Schauloch *n* inspection hole.
Schauzeichen *n* visual signal.
Scheibe *f* disk, plate (*Tech*); practice target; pane (*of glass*); compass card.
Scheibenkupplung *f*(*MT*) plate clutch
Scheibenrahmen *m* target frame.
Scheibenrose *f* compass card.
Scheibenstand *m* target butt.
Scheibentreffbild *n* vertical shot group (*Ballistics*).
Scheibenwischer *m* windshield wiper.
Scheibenzuganlage *f* range unit with moving targets (*Tng*).
Scheide *f* scabbard, sheath.
Scheider *m* separator (*storage battery*).
Schein *m* card, ticket, certificate; illusion, deceptive appearance; light, blaze, flash, halo.
Scheinangriff *m* feint attack, feint, demonstration (*Tac*).
Scheinanlage *f* dummy installation, dummy works.
Scheinflughafen *m* dummy airport.
Scheingas *n* fake gas.
Scheingefecht *n* mock combat, sham battle; feint, demonstration (*Tac*).
Scheingraben *m* dummy trench (*Ft*).
Scheinleitwert *m* admittance (*Elec*).
Scheinmine *f* dummy mine.
Scheinplatz *m* dummy airfield.
Scheinsperre *f* dummy obstacle (*Ft*).
Scheinstellung *f* dummy site, dummy position.
Scheinvergiftung *f* fake contamination (*CWS*).
Scheinverneblung *f* deceptive smoke screen.
Scheinwerfer *m* headlight; searchlight, spotlight, projector.
führender Scheinwerfer carry light (*AAA*).
Scheinwerferabteilung *f* searchlight battalion (*AAA*).
Scheinwerferrichtungsweiser *m* control station (*AA SL*).
Scheinwerferstellung *f* searchlight station (*AAA*).
Scheinwiderstand *m* impedance (*Elec*).
Scheitel *m* apex, summit, vertex, zenith.
Scheitelbogen *m* azimuth (*Surv*).
Scheitelkreis *m* See Scheitelbogen.
Scheitelpunkt *m* apex, vertex, zenith.
Scheitelwert *m* peak value (*Elec*).
Scheitelwinkel *m* vertical angle, opposite angle.
scheitern to be shipwrecked, run aground; fail, miscarry, be frustrated.
Schellband *n* hoop (*G*).
Schelle *f* clamping collar (*Mort*).
Schenkel *m* leg, thigh; side (*of an angle*); leg (*of a tripod, etc.*).
Scherbalken *m* ponton balk.
Scherdraht *m* shear wire (*fuze*).
Schere *f* scissors, shears.
Scherenfernrohr *n* battery commander's telescope.
Scherfestigkeit *f* shearing strength.
Scherspannung *f* shear stress.
Scherwinkel *m* angle of yaw (*Avn*).
Scheune *f* barn.
Schi *m* ski.
Schibataillon *n* ski battalion.
Schicht *f* course, layer, stratum; sheet, coating, film; working shift.
Schichtlinie *f* contour line.
Schichtwolke *f* stratocumulus cloud.
Schiebedach *n* sliding roof (*Ap*).
schieben to push, slide, shove; to drift (*Avn slang*).
Schieber *m* rear sight slide (*R*); keeper (*R sling*); slide; sleeve (*sleeve-type engine*); slide rule.
Schiebermotor *m* sleeve-type engine.
Schieberwiderstand *m* rheostat.
Schiebeschnalle *f* slide buckle.
Schiebewind *m* cross wind (*Avn*).
Schieblehre *f* vernier calipers.
Schiedsrichter *n* umpire (*maneuvers*).
oberster Schiedsrichter director.
Schiedsrichteranweisung *f* instructions to umpires (*maneuvers*).
Schiedsrichtergehilfe *m* umpire's aide.
Schiedsrichterstab *m* umpire staff.
schief oblique; biased; crooked; sloping, inclined.
schiefer Radstand cant (*Arty*); misalignment of wheels (*MT*).
Schieflaufende *f* rhumb line
Schienbein *n* shin.
Schiene *f* rail; surgical splint.
Schienensperre *f* steel rail antimechanized obstacle.
Schießaufgabe *f* fire problem (*Arty Tng*).
Schießauftrag *m* fire mission (*Arty*).
Schießausbildung *f* training in firing.
Schießausbildungshilfe *f* marksmanship training aid.
Schießbahn *f* practice range.
Schießbaumwolle *f* guncotton.
Schießbecher *m*(*R*) grenade launcher
Schießbedarf *m* ammunition requirements.
Schießbehelf *m* fire-control aid (*Gunnery*).
Schießbremse *f* gun-wheel brake.
Schießbuch *n* score book.
Schießen mit Entfernungskommandos fire by command for range.
Schießen mit hohen Sprengpunkten air-burst registration fire.
Schießen mit Karte map fire (*Gunnery*).
Schießen ohne Beobachtung unobserved fire (*Gunnery*).
Schießen während der Bewegung assault fire (*automatic weapons*).
Schießfertigkeit *f* marksmanship.
Schießgerät *n* firing equipment, practice-firing device (*Gunnery*).
Schießgestell *n* firing stand (*MG*).
Schießgrundlagen *fpl* firing data (*Gunnery*).
Schießhilfsmittel *npl* means of fire control (*Gunnery*).
Schießkladde *f* battery emplacement book.
Schießklotz *m* wheel chock (*Arty*).
Schießlehre *f* ballistics.
Schießlehrer *m* gunnery instructor.
Schießlineal *n* straightedge (*SR correction chart*).
Schießliste *f* battery chart.
Schießplan *m* fire-control map (*Gunnery*).
Schießplatz *m* artillery range.
Schießpulver *n* gunpowder.
Schießscharte *f* loophole, embrasure.
Schießstand *m* range, target range.
Schießstock *m* projector rod (*Sig projector*).
Schießtechnik *f* firing technique.
Schießübung *f* firing practice, range practice.
Schießunterlagen *fpl* basic data (*firing*).
Schießverfahren *n* method of fire (*Arty*).
Schießvorschrift *f* firing regulations; gunnery field manual.
Schießvorschule *f* basic training course (*Arty*); elementary marksmanship training.
Schießwagen *m* range car (*on target range*).
Schießwesen *n* gunnery.
Schießwolle *f* See Schießbaumwolle.
Schiffahrt *f* shipping (*Nav*).
Schiffbau *m* shipbuilding.
Schiffbauwerft *f* shipbuilding yard.
Schiffbruch *m* shipwreck.
Schiffsflak *f* ship-based antiaircraft artillery.
Schiffslazarett *n* sick bay.
Schiffsraum *m* tonnage (*Nav*).
Schiffsrumpf *m* hull (*Nav*).
Schiffstaucher *m* diver (*Nav*) See also Torpedotaucher.
Schiffswerft *f* shipyard.
Schiffswesen *n* shipping (*Nav*).
Schild *n* signboard.
Schild *m* shield (*G*).
Schilderhaus *n* sentry box.
Schildlager *n* bracket seat (*G*).
Schildstütze *f* shield support (*G*).
Schildzapfen *m* trunnion (*G*).
Schildzapfenlager *n* trunnion bearing (*G*).
Schildzapfenlagerdeckel *m* trunnion cap (*G*).
Schildzapfenpfanne *f* trunnion socket.
Schippe *f* shovel.
Schirm *m* screen; visor (*of cap*); parachute canopy, parachute; umbrella.
Schirmantenne *f* umbrella antenna (*Rad*).
Schirmeindecker *m* parasol monoplane.
Schirmgitter *n* screen grid (*Rad*).
Schirmgitterröhre *f* screen-grid tube (*Rad*).
Schirmmütze *f* service cap.
Schirrmeister *m* maintenance technical sergeant.
Schirrunteroffizier *m* maintenance sergeant.
Schlacht *f* battle.
Schlächtereiabteilung *f* butchery battalion.
Schlächtereizug *m* butchery platoon.
Schlachtfeld *n* battlefield.
Schlachtflieger *m* close support airplane; ground attack airplane; pilot of close support airplane (*pl: support Avn*).
Schlachtfliegerbombe *f* fragmentation bomb.
Schlachtfliegerunterstützung *f* close aviation support, support by ground attack airplanes.
Schlachtflotte *f* battle fleet.
Schlachtflugzeug *n* close support airplane, ground attack airplane.
Schlachtgeschwader *n* ground attack and antitank wing, support aviation wing. See also Geschwader.
Schlachtkreuzer *m* battle cruiser.
Schlachtlinie *f* battle line.
Schlachtschiff *n* battleship.
Schläfenband *n* temple strap (*gas mask*).
schlaff slack.
Schlafsack *m* sleeping bag.
Schlag *m* shock, stroke, blow; pigeon loft; bay (*of a trench*).
Schlagbolzen *m* firing pin (*Ord*); inertia pellet, inertia striker pellet (*fuze*).
Schlagbolzenfeder *f* main spring (*R*); firing-pin spring (*pistol, fuze*).
Schlagbolzenmutter *f* cocking piece (*R*).
Schlagbolzenspitze *f* striker (*G, R*).
Schlagbolzen-Versager *m* hung striker (*fuze*).
Schlägel *m* mallet; drumstick.
Schlägelstampfer *m* maul (*Tech*).
schlagen to hit, knock, strike; to defeat; to build (*a Bdg*).
Schlagfeder *f* firing-pin spring (*fuze*).
schlagfertig ready for immediate action.

Schlagfertigkeit *f* readiness for action, state of tactical preparedness.
Schlagkraft *f* striking power *(Tac)*.
Schlagladung *f* booster, magazine charge *(fuze)*.
Schlagloch *n* pothole, road hole.
Schlaglot *n* hard solder.
Schlagring *m* brass knuckles.
Schlagschatten *m* shadow cast by an object *(as distinguished from shadow on the object itself) (Cam)*.
Schlagseite *f* list *(of a ship)*.
Schlagstift *m* striker *(fuze)*.
Schlagstück *n* hammer *(SA)*.
Schlagwort *n* slogan.
Schlagzünder *m* impact fuze, percussion fuze.
Schlagzündschraube *f* threaded percussion primer *(fuze)*.
Schlamm *m* mud.
Schlange *f* snake; spiral, coil, helix, worm.
Schlappe *f* reverse, defeat, setback.
Schlauch *m* hose, pipe, tube; inner tube *(MT)*.
Schlauchbinder *m (MT)* hose coupling
Schlauchboot *n* pneumatic raft, pneumatic boat.
Schlauchbootfähre *f* pneumatic boat ferry.
Schlauchbrücke *f* pneumatic boat bridge.
Schlauchschoner *m* tire flap *(MT)*.
Schlaufe *f* keeper *(R sling)*; band, loop.
Schlechtwetter-Landedienst *m* station marker beacon service *(for Inst landing in bad weather) (Avn)*.
Schlechtwetterzone *f* bad-weather zone *(Met)*.
Schleichweg *m* hidden trail.
Schleier *m* screen *(Tac)*.
Schleife *f* loop *(Avn, Elec, etc.)*.
schleifen to grind, sharpen, abrade.
Schleifenflug *m* loop *(Avn)*.
Schleifmaschine *f* grinding machine *(Tech)*.
Schleifmittel *n* abrasive.
Schleifring *m* collector ring *(magneto)*; release ring *(clutch)*.
Schlenke *f* ravine, gully.
Schleppantenne *f* trailing wire antenna *(Ap)*.
schleppen to tow, drag.
Schlepper *m* tractor; tug *(Nav)*.
Schlepphaken *m* pintle *(Trac)*.
Schleppkahn *m* towed boat.
Schleppkante *f* trailing edge *(Ap)*.
Schleppkommando *n* glider-towing detachment, unit of tug airplanes.
Schleppschacht *m* inclined gallery *(Mining)*.
Schleppseil *n* *See* **Schlepptau.**
Schleppscheibe *f* tow target, towed-sleeve target *(AAA)*.
Schlepptau *n* trail rope *(Bln)*; tow rope, tow line.
Schleppwagen *m* beaching gear *(seaplane)*.
Schleppziel *n* flag target, towed-sleeve target *(AAA)*.
Schleppzug *m* column of tractors; train of barges.
Schleuder *f* catapult *(Avn)*.
Schleuderbund *m (Engr)* sling lashing
Schleuderguß *m* centrifugal casting *(foundry)*.
Schleudermine *f* sling mine, sliding mine.
schleudern to skid, to slip, to catapult.
Schleuderstart *m* catapult take-off
Schleuderpsychrometer *n* sling psychrometer *(Met)*.
Schleuderthermometer *n* sling thermometer *(Met)*.
Schleuse *f* lock *(of a canal)*; sluice
schließen to close, lock *(a door, etc.)*.
Schließender *m* file closer; trail officer *(MT column)*.
Schließfeder *f* main spring *(pistol)*; closing spring.
Schließkontakt *(Elec)* contact maker
Schließstelle *f* contact point *(Elec)*.
schlingern to roll.
Schlingerwand *f* baffle *(Ap tank)*.
Schlips *m* necktie.
Schlitten *m* sled; sleigh, sleigh mount *(MG)*.
Schlittenaufsatzstück *n* sleigh-mount extension piece *(MG)*.
Schlittenführer *m* sled driver.
Schlittenkufe *f* sled runner; sleigh-mount runner *(MG)*.
Schlittenstoßtrupp *m* assault detachment with sled-borne weapons and supplies.
Schlittenstütze *f (MG)* sleigh-mount leg
Schlitz *m* slit; slot *(Ap wing)*.
Schlitzflügel *m* slotted wing *(Ap)*.
Schlitzquerruder *n* slotted aileron.
Schloß *n* lock; bolt mechanism, bolt assembly *(MG, R)*; castle.
Schlößchen *n* bolt sleeve *(R)*.
Schlosser *m* mechanic, locksmith, fitter.
Schloßfuß *m* bolt base *(MG)*.
Schloßgehäuse *n* bolt housing *(MG)*.
Schloßhalter *m* bolt support *(MG)*.
Schloßhebel *m* bolt handle *(MG)*.
Schloßkurbel *f* bolt shaft *(MG)*.
Schloßplatte *f* back plate *(G)*.
Schlot *m* smoke stack.
Schlucht *f* gorge *(Top)*.
Schlund *m* throat.
Schlupf *m* slip *(propeller)*.
Schlupfe *f* keeper *(R sling)*.
Schlupfjacke *f* sweater *(Clo)*.
schlüpfrig slippery.
Schluppe *f* *See* **Schlupfe.**
Schlußbesprechung *f* critique.
Schlüssel *m* key; cipher, code; wrench.
Schlüsselbolzen *m* locking pin *(limber)*; retaining pin or bolt.
Schlüsselgraben *m* main trench.
Schlüsselheft *n* code book.
Schlüsselkraftwagen *m* coding truck *(Sig C)*.
Schlüsselmaschine *f* converter, cipher device.
Schlüsselmine *f* key mine *(antivehicle mine laid as road block)*.
schlüsseln encode, encipher.
Schlüsselpunkt *m* key point *(Tac)*.
Schlüsselschieber *m* corrector pointer *(hand fuze setter)*.
Schlüsselstellung *f (Tac)* key position
Schlüsseltext *m* cipher text.
Schlüsseltrupp *m* code section.
Schlüsselungsoffizier *m* cryptographer officer.
Schlüsselunterlage *f* encoding and decoding chart.
Schlüsselwort *n* cipher key.
Schlußklappe *f* disconnect drop *(Tp switchboard)*.
Schlußlicht *n* taillight *(MT)*.
Schlußzeichen *n (Tp)* clearing signal *(indicating party has rung off)*
Schmalspur *f* narrow gage *(RR)*.
Schmalspurbahn *f* narrow-gage railroad.
Schmelzsicherung *f* fuse *(Elec)*.
schmiedbar malleable.
Schmiede *f* forge.
Schmiedeeisen *n* wrought iron, forged iron.
Schmierbüchse *f* grease cup; axle box.
schmieren to grease, lubricate.
Schmiermittel *n* lubricant.
Schmieröl *n* lubricating oil.
Schmierölpumpe *f* lubrication pump.
Schmierölschicht *f* oil film *(Mech)*.
Schmierplan *m* lubrication diagram.
Schmierpresse *f* grease gun.
Schmierstelle *f* lubrication point.
Schmierstoff *m* lubricant.
Schmierstoffanlage *f* lubricating system *(Mtr)*.
Schmierstoffbehälter *m (Ap)* oil tank
Schmierstoffdruckmesser *m* oil pressure gage *(Ap)*.
Schmierstoffkühler *m* oil cooler.
Schmierstoffvorratsmesser *m* oil level gage.
Schmierung *f* lubrication.
Schmirgelleinwand *f* emery cloth.
Schmirgelrad *n* *See* Schmirgelscheibe.
Schmirgelscheibe *f* emery wheel.
Schnabel *m* beak, nose; launching nose *(Bdg)*.
Schnalle *f (R)* buckle; gun sling hook
Schnecke *f* worm *(Mech)*.
Schneckenantrieb *m* worm drive.
Schneckengehäuse *n* worm-gear housing *(panoramic telescope)*.
Schneckenlenkung *f* worm and sector steering system *(MT)*.
Schneckenrad *n* worm gear *(MG, Mech)*.
Schneckenscheibe *f (Tng)* spiral target
Schneckentrieb *m* *See* **Schneckenantrieb.**
Schneckenwelle *f* worm shaft.
Schnee *m* snow.
Schneefräsmaschine *f* rotary snowplow.
Schneehemd *n* parka.
Schneehütte *f* igloo.
Schneekette *f* snow chain, skid chain *(MT)*.
Schneekufe *f* landing ski *(Ap)*.
Schneekufengestell *n* landing ski assembly *(Ap)*.
Schneeloch *n* snow pit.
Schneemann *m* "snow man" *(an improvised road marker constructed of blocks of snow)*.
Schneepflug *m* snowplow.
Schneereifen *m* snowshoe.
Schneeschuh *m* ski; snow boot, overshoe.
Schneestauung *f* impacted snow.
Schneetreiben *n* snow flurries *(Met)*.
Schneewanne *f* boat-type runner *(placed under gun wheels for operations in deep snow)*.
Schneewolke *f* snow cloud *(Met)*.
Schneidbrennen *n* oxyacetylene cutting.
Schneide *f* edge *(of a bayonet, etc.)*.
Schneise *f* straight narrow clearing, forest aisle, firebreak; sector *(Air Navigation)*.
schneidig smart *(in appearance, deportment, etc.)*.
Schneidkluppe *f* stock *(die holder)*.
Schneidkluppe mit Schneidbacken stock and die.
schnell fast, quick, rapid, mobile.
Schnellablaß *m* quick release, jettisoning *(of fuel)*.
Schnelladeverschluß *m* rapid-fire breechblock *(G)*.
Schnelladung *f* emergency demolition charge.
Schnellboot *n* E-boat *(Ger)*, motor torpedo boat, speedboat.
Schnellbrücke *f* hasty bridge.
Schnelle Truppen Mobile Troops *(includes Tk Rgts, AT Bns, Panzergrenadier units, MG Bns, H-Cav Rgts, Div Rcn units, Mecz Rcn units and cyclist units)*.
Schnellfeuer *n* rapid fire, magazine fire.
Schnellfeuergeschütz *n* rapid-fire gun.
Schnellfeuerkanone *f* rapid-fire cannon.
Schrägentfernung *f* slant range *(AA gunnery)*.
schräges Kreuz St. Andrew's cross *(used as road marker to indicate bypass)*.
Schrägfahrt *f* movement at an angle *(ground target)*.
Schrägfeuer *n* oblique fire, flanking fire, enfilade.
Schräglage *f* bank *(Ap)*.
Schräglinie *f* diagonal.
Schrägnocke *f* inclined beveled cam *(Diesel engine)*.
Schrägstellung *f* tilt, lateral tilt.
Schranke *f* railroad gate; barrier.
Schränkung *f* dihedral *(Ap)*.
Schrapnell *n* shrapnel.
Schrapnellkugel *f* shrapnel ball.
Schrapnellmine *f* antipersonnel mine.
Schraube *f* screw *(Mech)*; propeller.
Schraubendruck *m* propeller thrust.
Schraubenantrieb *m* propeller drive.
Schraubenfeder *f* coil spring, helical spring, spiral spring.
Schraubenflugzeug *n* helicopter.
Schraubenganglenkung *f* cam and lever steering system *(MT)*.
Schraubenmutter *f* nut *(Tech)*.
Schraubenschlüssel *m* wrench.
Schraubenspindelrichtmaschine *f* elevating-screw-type elevating mechanism *(G)*.
Schraubensteigung *f* screw pitch; propeller pitch.
Schraubensteven *m (Nav)* propeller post
Schraubenstrahl *m* slipstream *(Ap)*.
Schraubenverschluß *m* interrupted-screw-type breechblock *(G)*.
Schraubenzieher *m* screwdriver.
Schraubenzug *m* propeller thrust.
Schraubpfahl *m* screw-type post *(for obstacle construction)*.
Schraubstock *m* vise *(Tech)*.
Schreckladung *f* booby trap.
Schreckmine *f* booby mine.
Schreibeblock *m* writing pad.
Schreiber *m* clerk; yeoman *(Nav)*.
Schreibmaschine *f* typewriter.
Schreibstube *f* orderly room, office.
schriftlich in writing, written.
Schriftverkehr *m* correspondence.
Schritt *m* pace, step.
den Schritt wechseln to change step.
Schrittmesser *m* pedometer.
schroff steep *(Top)*.
Schrot *m* shot *(for shotgun)*.
Schnellfeuerwaffe *f* rapid-fire weapon.
Schnellgang *m* overdrive *(MT)*.
Schnellganggetriebe *n* overdrive transmission *(MT)*.
Schnellkampfgeschwader *m* ground attack and antitank wing *(Luftwaffe)*.
Schnellschuß *m* hasty shot *(firing)*.
Schnellsperre *f* hasty obstacle.
Schnellsteg *m* hasty footbridge.
Schnelltelegraph *m* teletype, teletypewriter, telegraph printer.
Schnellzünder *m* instantaneous fuze, nondelay fuze.
Schnitt *m* cut *(injury or wound)*; section, intersection; slice; bearing *(Navigation)*.
Schnittbildentfernungsmesser *m* split-field range finder.
Schnittlinie *f* secant; halving line *(coincidence range finder)*.
Schnittpunkt *m* point of intersection.
Schnittzeichnung *f* cut-away view *(sketching)*.
Schnur *f* rope, cord, twine, string.
Schnürbund *m* cord lashing, rope lashing.
Schnürleiste *f* rack stick *(for cord lashing)*.
Schnurrensattelgurt *m* web girth *(saddle)*.
Schnürschuh *m* laced shoe.
Schnürsenkel *m* bootlace, shoelace.
Schnürstiefel *m* lace boot.
Schokokola chocolate with kola *(Prcht ration)*.
schonen to spare, protect.
Schonganggetriebe *n* overdrive transmission *(MT)*.
Schöpfeimer *m* scoop *(excavator)*.
Schornstein *m* chimney, smoke stack.
Schott *n* bulkhead *(also spelled die Schotte)*.
Schotter *m* road metal, broken stone, gravel.
Schotterstraße *f* metalled road, gravel road.
Schottpanzerung *f* spaced armor.
Schraffen *fpl* hachures *(Surv, Top)*.

Scharfsch	Scharfschütze	sharpshooter
Scha (SA)	Scharführer	section leader, Storm Troops
Scha (SS)	**Scharführer**	first section-leader, Elite Guard *(equivalent U. S. rank: staff sergeant)*
Schb	Scheibe	target
Sch.B	Schiessbuch	score book *(gunnery)*
Sch.B	Schützenbrigade	rifle brigade
Sch.Bew	Scheinbewegung	feint; simulated movement
Sch.Biw	Scheinbiwak	dummy bivouac; camouflage bivouac
Schbw	Schiessbaumwolle	gun cotton
Sch.D	Schulterdecker	high-wing monoplane
Schdpfr	Schalldämpfer	muffler; silencer
Scheinanl	Scheinanlage	dummy works; camouflage works
Scheingef	Scheingefecht	sham battle
Scheinst	Scheinstellung	dummy position; camouflage position
Scheinw	Scheinwerfer	searchlight; headlight
Scheinw.Ger.Wg	Scheinwerfergerätewagen	searchlight equipment truck
Scheinw.Zg	Scheinwerferzug	searchlight platoon
Sch.Entf	Schussentfernung	range
Scherf	Scherenfernrohr	battery commander's telescope
Schf	Scharfschütze	sharpshooter
Sch.F	Scherenfernrohr	battery commander's telescope
Sch.Flgz	Schulflugzeug	training plane
Sch.G	Schulgefechtsschiessen	combat practice firing
Schgr	Schottergrube	rubble pit *(on maps)*
Sch.Gr	Schützengraben	trench
Sch.Gr	Schützengruppe	rifle squad
Sch.Grab.Kan	Schützengrabenkanone	trench gun
Schi-Abt	Skiabteilung	ski detachment; ski battalion
Schichtl	Schichtlinien	contour lines *(on maps)*
Schiess-Aufs	Schiessaufsicht	supervision of firing
Schiessf	Schiessfertigkeit	fire proficiency; fire skill
Schiess-G	Schiessgestell	firing stand; firing rest
Schiess-H.M	Schiesshilfsmittel	fire control aids
Schiessl	Schiesslehre	ballistics; gunnery
Schiesspl	Schiessplatz	firing range *(on maps)*
Schiess St	Schiesstand	rifle range *(on maps)*
Schiesst.Aufs	Schiesstandaufseher	rifle range supervisor
Schiess-Üb	Schiessübung	shooting practice
Schiess V	Schiessvorschrift	gunnery manual
Schiess-Verf	Schiessverfahren	method of fire; conduct of fire
Schiessw	Schiesswesen	ballistics; musketry; gunnery
Schildhs	Schilderhaus	sentry box
Schirrm	Schirrmeister	supply sergeant
Sch.K	Schützenkette	skirmish line
Sch.Kl	Schiesskladde	data book
Sch.Kl	Schiessklasse	markmanship rating
Sch.Kp	Schützenkompanie	rifle company
Sch.Kpf	Scheinkampf	sham battle
Schl	Schlacht	battle
Schl	Schlappe	reverse; rebuff
schl	schleichen	to crawl; to creep
Schl	Schleier	screen; veil
Schl	Schlepp-	tow-
Schl	Schlepper	tractor; prime mover; tug
Schl	Schleppflugzeug	tow plane
Schl	Schleuder-	catapult
Schl	Schleuse	sluice; lock
Schl	Schliessender	file closer
Schl	Schlinge	sling; noose
Schl	Schlitten	sled; sleigh
Schl	Schloss	castle *(on maps)*
Schl	Schlucht	ravine; gorge
schl	schlüsseln	to encode; to encipher
Schl	Schluss	end; close; conclusion; termination; finish
Schl	Schützenloch	rifle pit
Schlächt	Schlächterei	butchery, slaughter
Schlächt.Abt	Schlächtereiabteilung	slaughter detachment
Schl.Aussch	Schlichtungsausschuss	arbitration committee
Schl.Bol	Schlagbolzen	firing pin; striker
Schl.Bt	Schlauchboot	pneumatic boat *(combat engineer service)*
Schlchtgs A	Schlichtungsamt	arbitration office
Schl D	Schleppdampfer	tugboat
Sch.Leist	Schussleistung	gun performance
Schles	Schlesien	Silesia
Schl.Flgz	Schlachtflugzeug	fighter plane
Schlf.M	Schleifmühle	grinding-mill *(on maps)*
Schl.Geschw	Schlachtgeschwader	battle wing *(airplane)*
Schlicht.Aussch	Schlichtungsausschuss	arbitration committee
Sch.Lkw	Schienenlastkraftwagen	truck on rails
Schl.M G	Schlittenmaschinengewehr	machine gun on sleigh mount
Schl.O	Schlachtordnung	battle order
Schlp	Schlepp-	tow-
Schlp.Flgz	Schleppflugzeug	tow plane
Schl.Seg	Schleppsegel	landing-apron *(dragged sail for landing airplanes at sea)*
Schl.St	Schlachtstaffel	battle wing *(air planes)*
Schl W	Schleppwagen	tow car *(motor vehicle)*
Schl.Z.Schr	Schlagzündschraube	threaded-base percussion primer

Schm	Schirrmeister	supply sergeant
Sch.M	Schützenmulde	skirmisher's trench (*for prone riflemen*)
Schmalsp.B	Schmalspurbahn	narrow-gauge railroad
Sch.Masch	Schulmaschine	training plane
Sch.M.K	Schallmesskabel	sound-ranging cable
Schn	Schnecken-	worm-
Schn	Schnee	snow
schn	schnell	fast; quick; rapid
Schn	Schnitt	cut; section; intersection; bearing
Schn.Aufs	Schneckenaufsatz	worm-gear sight (*artillery*)
Schn.Br	Schnellbrücke	portable footbridge
Schn.Br.Zg	Schnellbrückenzug	portable footbridge platoon (*combat engineers*)
Schnee.Btl	Schneeschuhläuferbataillon	ski battalion
Schnee-K	Schneeketten	snow chains; nonskid chains (*for motor vehicles*)
Schnefeu	Schnellfeuer	rapid fire
Schnellbr	Schnellbrücke	portable footbridge
Schnellf	Schnellfeuer	rapid fire
Schnellf.Gesch	Schnellfeuergeschütz	rapid-fire gun
Schnellf.Kan	Schnellfeuerkanone	rapid-fire cannon
Schn.Sch.Patr	Schneeschuhpatrouille	ski patrol
Schn.Sch.Sptr	Schneeschuhspähtrupp	ski scout squad
schn.Verb	schneller Verband	mobile task force (*of motorized, mechanized mixed troops*)
Schn.Z	Schnellzug	express train
Sch.O	Schiessstandordnung	rifle range regulations
Sch.P	Scheitelpunkt	zenith of trajectory (*ballistics*)
Schp	Schuppen	shed; hangar (*on maps*)
Sch.Pl	Schiessplatz	firing range
Sch.Pl.J	Schiessplatz Jüterbog	Jüterbog Firing Range
Sch.Pl.K	Schiessplatz Kummersdorf	Kummersdorf Firing Range
Sch.Pl.Kdo	Schiessplatzkommando	firing range command
Schpl.W	Schiessplatzwache	firing range guard
Sch.Pol	Schutzpolizei	police
schr	schräg	oblique
Schr	Schrapnell	shrapnel
Schr	Schraube	screw; propeller
Schr	Schrot	small-shot; buckshot
Schr	Schrott	scrap metal
Sch.R	Schützenregiment	rifle regiment
Sch.R	Schützenreihe	file of riflemen
Schr. A	Schrapnell mit Aufschlagzünder	shrapnel with percussion fuse
Schrapn	Schrapnell	shrapnel
Schrb	Schraube	screw; propeller
Schrbm	Schraubenmutter	nut
Schr. Bz	Schrapnell mit Brennzünder	shrapnel with time fuse
Sch. Rdl	Schützenrudel	rifle squad in combat formation
Schr.Fl	Schrotflinte	small-shot rifle; buckshot rifle; shotgun
Schr.Gew	Schraubengewinde	thread (*mechanics*)
Sch.Rgt	Schützenregiment	rifle regiment
Schrm	Schirrmeister	supply sergeant
Sch.Rm	Schutzraum	shelter (*air raid*)
Schrm.u.Zgw.	Schirrmeister- und Zeughauswaffenmeistervorschrift	manual for supply sergeants and arsenal ordnance noncommissioned officers
Schr.St	Schreibstube	orderly room; office
Sch.S	Schulschiessen	practice fire
Sch.Std	Scheibenstand	butts (*musketry*)
Sch. Tf	Schusstafel	firing table; range table
Sch.Tr	Schützentrupp	rifle squad
Schtz	Schütze	rifleman
Schtz	Schutz	protection; cover
Schtz.Sch	Schutzschild	protective shield
Sch.U	Schiessunteroffizier	marksmanship instructor (noncommissioned officer)
Schütsh	Schützenhaus	shooting lodge; club-house of a rifle-club (*on maps*)
Schultkl	Schulterklappe	shoulder straps (*on uniforms of noncommissioned officers and privates*)
Schultst	Schulterstück	officers' shoulder straps (*on uniforms of officers*)
Schupo	Schutzpolizei	municipal police force
schussf	schussfertig	ready to fire
Schussgeschw	Schussgeschwindigkeit	velocity of fire; rate of fire
Schussl	Schusslinie	gun-target line; line of sighting; line of aim; line of future position (*antiaircraft*)
Schuss/Min	Schuss in der Minute	rounds per minute
Schussw	Schusswaffe	firearm
Schussw	Schussweite	range
SchusswG	Schusswaffengesetz	firearms law
SchussZ	Schusszahl	number of rounds
Schutzbr	Schutzbrille	goggles
SchutzWg	Schutzwagen	protective wagon (*armored train*)

Schraffierung *f* *See* Schraffen.
schräg diagonal, oblique, inclined.
Schrägaufnahme *f* oblique aerial photograph.
Schräge *f* inclination; diagonal line; bevel (*Tech*).
Schrotgewehr *n* shotgun.
Schrotpatrone *f* shotgun shell.
Schrotsäge *f* ripsaw.
Schubkarren *m* wheelbarrow.
Schubkurbelverschluß *m* pusher-handle sliding-wedge-type breechblock (*G*).
Schubstange *f* torque arm, torque rod; piston rod; connecting rod.
Schuh *m* shoe; boot (*SA scabbard or holster*).
Schuhzeug *n* footgear.
Schulflugwesen *n* training aviation.
Schulflugzeug *n* training airplane, trainer.
Schulgefechtsschießen *n* battle service practice (*Arty*).
Schulgefechtsschießstand *m* target range (*Arty Tng*).
Schulschießen *n* record service practice (*Arty*).
Schulschießstand *m* target range.
Schulter *f* shoulder.
Schulterdecker *m* semi-high-wing monoplane.
Schultergurt *m* shoulder strap (*gas mask carrier*).
Schulterklappe *f* shoulder strap (*enlisted men's uniforms*).
Schulterriemen *m* crossbelt (*Clo*).
Schulterstütze *f* shoulder stock (*MG*).
Schulterstück *n* shoulder strap (*officers' uniforms*); shoulder piece (*MG*).
Schulterwehr *f* traverse (*Ft*).
Schulungskursus *m* training course, orientation course.
Schummerung *f* shading (*on maps*).
Schuppen *m* shed, hangar.
Schupo *f* *See* **Schutzpolizei.**
Schürmanneisen *n* butt strap.
Schurzholz *n* trench timber, wooden revetment.
Schurzholzrahmen *m* gallery case (*Engr*).
Schuß *m* shot (*discharge of firearm*); round (*Am*).
Schußbahn *f* line of fire; trajectory.
Schußbeobachtung *f* sensing, spotting, observation of fire (*Arty*).
Schußbereich *m* range of gun; danger area (*on target range*).
schußbereit ready to fire.
Schußbremse *f* recoil brake.
Schußebene *f* plane of departure, plane of fire (*Gunnery*); plane of position at instant of firing (*AAA*).
Schußelemente *npl* basic data, firing data (*Gunnery*).
Schußentfernung *f* range.
schußfertig ready to fire; prepared for firing (*Am*).
Schußfeld *n* field of fire.
Schußfeldlücke *f* gap in field of fire.
schußfest bulletproof; light shell proof.
Schußfolge *f* cyclic rate (*automatic fire*).
Schußgarbe *f* sheaf of fire, cone of fire.
Schußleistung *f* shooting strength
Schußlinie *f* line of site, line of position (*Gunnery*); line of future position (*AAA*).
Schußrichtung *f* direction of fire.
Schußschneise *f* fire lane.
Schußseitenwinkel *m* firing azimuth.
schußsicher bulletproof; light shell proof.
schußsichere Deckung shellproof cover (*Ft*).
schußsicherer Schlauch self-sealing inner tube, bullet-resisting inner tube (*tire*).
schußsicheres Glas bulletproof glass.
Schußtafel *f* firing table, ballistic table.
graphische Schußtafel trajectory chart (*not to be confused with US graphical firing table*).
schußtafelmäßig according to firing-table data, firing-table (*adj*).
schußtafelmäßige Anfangsgeschwindigkeit standard muzzle velocity.
schußtafelmäßige Erhöhung firing-table elevation (*Gunnery*).
schußtafelmäßige Flugzeit theoretical time of flight (*as indicated in firing table*).
schußtafelmäßige Schußweite firing-table range (*Gunnery*).
Schußverbesserung *f* firing correction (*Gunnery*).
Schußwaffe *f* firearm.
Schußweite *f* range (*Gunnery*).
Schußwerte *mpl* basic data, firing data (*Gunnery*).
Schußwirkung *f* (*Arty*) effect of fire
Schußzahl *f* number of rounds.
Schüttkasten *m* bomb magazine, "Molotov breadbasket" (*container with a number of small bombs*).
Schüttwurf *m* salvo release (*bombing*).
Schutz *m* cover, protection.
Schütz *m* relay (*Elec*).
Schutzanlagen *fpl* protective works.
Schutzanstrich *m* camouflage paint (ing); protective paint(ing).
Schutzanzug *m* protective clothing (*CWS*).
Schutzblech *n* fender, mudguard.
Schutzbrille *f* goggles.
Schütze *m* private (*Inf*); rifleman; machine gunner (*Ap, etc.*); marksman.
schützen to cover, protect; to support (*by fire*).
Schützenabmarsch *m* rifle half squad (*Cav*).
Schützenabzeichen *n* marksmanship badge.
Schützenauftritt *m* fire step (*Ft*).
Schützenbank *f* *See* **Schützenauftritt.**
Schützenfeuer *n* rifle fire.
Schützengraben *m* fire trench, trench.
Schützengrabenspiegel *m* trench periscope.
Schützenhöhle *f* dugout.
Schützenkette *f* *See* **Schützenlinie.**
Schützenkompanie (*Inf*) rifle company
Schützenlinie *f* line of skirmishers.
Schützenloch *n* foxhole, rifle pit.
Schützenmine *f* antipersonnel mine (*abbr.* S-Mine).
Schützenmulde *f* skirmisher's trench, prone shelter, shallow rifle pit.
Schützennest *n* rifle-squad entrenchment, nest of riflemen (*Ft*).
Schützenpanzer *m* *See* **Schützenpanzerwagen.**
Schützenpanzerwagen *m* armored personnel carrier.
Schützenreihe *f* squad column, file of riflemen.
Schützenrudel *n* rifle squad in grouped combat formation (*squad leader and light MG team forward, assistant squad leader and rifle team back, echeloned right or left*).
Schützenschnur *f* marksmanship fourragère.
Schützenstand *m* gun position (*Ap*).
Schützentrupp *m* rifle team (*riflemen of a rifle squad as distinguished from the light MG team*).
Schützenzug *m* rifle platoon (*Inf*).
Schutzgebiet *n* protectorate.
Schutzgitter *n* suppressor grid (*Rad tube*).
Schutzglas *n* bulletproof glass; protectoscope (*Tk*).
Schutzhülle *f* hood (*Am*).
Schutzimpfung *f* inoculation, vaccination.
Schutzmacht *f* (*PW*) protecting power
Schutzmann *m* policeman.
Schutzmittel *n* prophylactic.
Schutzmütze *f* crash helmet (*for Tk crew*).
Schutzpolizei *f* municipal police.
Schutzpolsterung *f* crash padding
Schutzraum *m* shelter (*Ft*); air raid shelter.
Schutzsalbe *f* protective ointment (*CWS*).
Schutzscheibe *f* protectoscope (*Tk*).
Schutzschicht *f* burster course (*Ft*).
Schutzschild *m* shield, gun shield.
Schutzsieb *n* mechanical filter (*gas mask*).
Schutzstaffeln *fpl* elite guard of the Nazi party (*abbr.* SS). *See also* Waffen-SS.
Schutzwall *m* protective wall (*system of land defenses, as the* Westwall *on the western frontier of Germany*).
Schutzwallehrenzeichen *n* bronze medal awarded to workers excelling in the construction of German fortifications.
Schutzzaun *m* guard fence.
Schwachstrom *m* low voltage (*current*).
Schwaden *m* gas cloud, smoke cloud.
Schwadenschießen *n* gas or smoke shell fire (*Arty*).
Schwadron *f* troop (*Cav*).
Schwadronschef *m* troop commander (*Cav*).
Schwadronsführer *m* temporary troop commander, troop commander (*Cav*).
Schwadronstrupp *m* troop headquarters detail (*Cav*).
Schwalbennest *n* shoulder patch (*worn by bandsmen*).
Schwamm *m* sponge; mushroom.
Schwankung *f* fluctuation; variation; sway; oscillation.
Schwanz *m* tail; trail (*G*).
Schwanzblech *n* trail float (*G*).
Schwanzlandung *f* (*Avn*) tail landing
schwanzlastig tailheavy (*Avn*).
Schwanzsporn *m* tail skid (*Ap*); trail spade (*G*).
Schwarm *m* tactical formation of about five airplanes (*consists of two* Ketten).
schwärmen to deploy into line of skirmishers.
Schwarmkolonne *f* javelin formation of from 3 to 5 airplanes.
Schwarmwinkel *m* wedge formation of from 3 to 5 airplanes.
Schwarzpulver *n* black powder.
Schwebekreisvisier *n* pivoted ring sight (*AA*).
Schweberiemen *m* hip strap (*harness*).
Schwebstoff *m* nonpersistent chemical agent (*CWS*).
Schwebstoffilter *m* mechanical filter (*gas mask*).
Schwebstoffteilchen *n* nonpersistent chemical particle (*CWS*).
Schwebungsempfang *m* beat-frequency reception (*Rad*).
Schwebungsfrequenz *f* beat frequency (*Rad*).
Schwebungsfrequenzmesser *m* heterodyne frequency meter.
Schwebungslücke *f* *See* **Schwebungsnull.**
Schwebungsnull *f* zero beat (*Rad*).
Schwefel *m* sulphur.
Schwefelantimon *n* antimony sulfide (*Am*).
Schwefelnatrium *n* sodium sulfide.
Schwefelsäure *f* sulfuric acid.
Schwefeltrioxyd *n* sulfur trioxide (*CWS*).
Schwefelwasserstoff *m* hydrogen sulfide.
schwefligsaures Natrium sodium sulfite.
Schweige-MG. *n* ambush machine gun, concealed machine gun.
Schweigewaffen *fpl* concealed weapons which hold their fire until enemy has reached certain points.
Schweiß *m* sweat.
Schweißbrenner *m* welding torch.
Schweißelektrode *f* welding electrode, welding rod.
schweißen to weld.
Schweißer *m* welder.
Schweißnaht *f* welded seam.
Schweißtechnik *f* theory and practice of welding.
Schwelkerze *f* smoke candle (*CWS*).
Schwelle *f* tie (*RR*); sill (*Bdg*); threshold.
Schwellenbahn *f* corduroy road.
Schwelljoch *n* trestle bent with sill (*Bdg*).
schwenkbar traversable; rotatable; flexible (*MG*).
Schwenkbereich *m* extent of traverse, total movement in traverse (*Ord*).
schwenken to wheel, turn (*Tac*); to traverse, to slew (*a gun*).
Schwenkflügel *m* folding wing (*Ap*).
Schwenkwinkel *m* angle of traverse (*Gunnery*).
Schwenkung *f* pivoting or wheeling maneuver (*Tac*); slewing, traversing motion (*of a gun*).
Schwenkungspunkt *m* pivot (*Tac*).
Schwenkungswinkel *m* angle of traverse (*Gunnery*).
schwer medium (*Ord*); heavy; grave, serious. *See also* **schwerst-.**
schwere Artillerie medium artillery.
schwere Kompanie heavy weapons company (*Mtz R Regt*).
schwere Schwadron *f* weapons troop (*Cav*).
Schwerkraft *f* force of gravity.
Schwerkraftstoff *m* Diesel fuel.
Schweröl *n* Diesel fuel.
Schweröl-Flugmotor *m* Diesel-type aircraft engine.
Schwerölmotor *m* Diesel engine.
Schwerpunkt *m* main effort, point of main effort (*Tac*); center of gravity.
schwerst- heavy (*Ord*); heaviest.
schwerste Artillerie heavy artillery.
Schwerverwundeter *m* serious casualty.
Schwesterwaffe *f* related arm, related branch of the service.
Schwimmdock *n* floating dock.
Schwimmer *m* float, pontoon (*Ap*); float (*carburetor, gage, etc*).
Schwimmerflugzeug *n* floatplane.
Schwimmergehäuse *n* float chamber (*carburetor*).
Schwimmergestell *n* float gear (*seaplane*).
Schwimmernadel *f* float needle (*carburetor*).
Schwimmerwagen *m* beaching gear (*seaplane*).
Schwimmerwerk *n* float gear (*seaplane*).
schwimmfähig capable of floating or swimming, amphibian.
Schwimmlastkraftwagen *m* amphibian truck.
Schwimmpanzerkampfwagen *m* amphibian tank.
Schwimmstabilität *f* flotation stability (*seaplane*).
Schwimmwerk *n* float gear, floats.
Schwimmwerk für Landflugzeuge emergency flotation gear (*Avn*).
Schwimmweste *f* life vest, "Mae West."
Schwindelgas *n* fake gas (*CWS*).
schwinden fade (*Rad*).
Schwingachse *f* flexible axle (*MT*).
Schwinge *f* flexible shaft (*follow-the-pointer mechanism*).
Schwingkreis *m* *See* **Schwingungskreis.**
Schwingschenkel *m* (*G*) wheel spindle
Schwingung *f* oscillation (*Elec, Rad*); vibration (*Mech*).
Schwingungsdämpfer *m* vibration damper.
Schwingungserzeuger *m* oscillator (*Rad*). ngskreis *m* oscillating circuit (*Rad*).

Sch.V	Schiessvorschrift	gunnery manual
Schv.f.Gew	Schiessvorschrift für Gewehr (Karabiner), leichtes Maschinengewehr und Pistole, und Bestimmungen für das Werfen scharfer Handgranaten	gunnery manual for rifle (carbine), light machine gun and pistol, and regulations for the throwing of live hand grenades
Schv.s.M.G	Schiessvorschrift für das schwere Maschinengewehr	gunnery manual for the heavy machine gun
Sch.W	Scheinwerfer	searchlight; headlight
Schw	Schutzwache	protective guard
Schw	Schwaden	fumes; vapor
Schw	Schwadron	troop (*cavalry*); squadron
Schw	Schwanz	trail (*gun*); tail
Schw	Schwarm	swarm (*6–7 airplanes, 2 flights*)
schw	schwarz	black
Schw	Schwenkarm	rotating arm
Schw	Schwenkung	turn; turning movement; wheeling
schw	schwer	heavy
Schw	Schwimm	floating
Schw	Schwimmer	swimmer; float; ponton (*aviation*)
Schw	Schwinge	bird's wing (*collar insignia of the air force*)
Schwadr	Schwadron	cavalry troop; squadron (*aviation*)
schw.Art	schwere Artillerie	medium artillery
schw.Art.Abt	schwere Artillerieabteilung	medium artillery battalion
Schw.B	Schwebebahn	suspension railroad
schw.Besch	Schwerbeschädigter	seriously injured person
schw.Bomb	schweres Bombenflugzeug	heavy bomber
schw.Br.Mod	schweres Brückenmodell	heavy bridge model
schw.Bttr	schwere Batterie	medium battery (*artillery*)
Schwd	Schwadron	cavalry troop; squadron (*aviation*)
Schw.D	Schwimmdock	floating dock
Schwd.Ch	Schwadronschef	troop commander (*cavalry*)
Schw.-Dock	Schwimmdock	floating dock
Schwefla	schweres Flachfeuer	heavy flat trajectory fire
Schwerb	Schwerbeschädigter	seriously injured person
Schwerg	Schwergewicht	heavy weight; main stress;
schwerkr	schwerkrank	seriously ill
SchWf	Scheinwerfer	searchlight; headlight
Schwf.Ger	Scheinwerfergerät	searchlight equipment
Schw.Fhr	Scheinwerferführer	searchlight commander
schw.Fu-Sta.(Kr.)	schwere Funkstation auf Kraftwagen	heavy radio station on truck
Sch.WG	Gesetz über Schusswaffen-Munition	law concerning firearms and ammunition
Schwg.Dpfr	Schwingungsdämpfer	vibration damper (*aviation*)
SchwgR	Schwungrad	flywheel
Schw.K	Schwarmkeil	wedge formation (*aviation*)
schw.Kp	schwere Kompanie	heavy weapons company
schw.Kpfw	schwerer Kampfwagen	heavy tank
Schwöl-Mot	Schwerölmotor	heavy oil engine (*aviation*)
Schwp	Schwerpunkt	strong point (*tactics*); center
Schwpv	Schwarzpulver	black powder
schw.v	schwer verwundet	seriously wounded
Schw.W	Schwarmwinkel	wedge formation (*aviation*)
Schw.W	Schwesterwaffe	related branches (*of the armed forces*)
schw.Wff	schwere Waffen	heavy weapons
Schz	Schanzzeug	entrenching tools
Sch.Zg	Scheinwerferzug	searchlight platoon
Sch.Zg	Schützenzug	rifle platoon
Schz.Wg	Schanzzeugwagen	entrenching-tools wagon
SD	Seitendeckung	flank guard; flank security
S.D	Sicherungsdienst	security service
sd	sonder	special
sd	süddeutsch	South German
Sd	Sund	sound; arm of the sea
SDeckg	Seitendeckung	flank guard; flank security
sdl	südlich	southern; southward
sdr	sonder	special
Sdr.Gesch	Sondergeschoss	special projectile
Sdr.Kdo	Sonderkommando	special command; separate command
SdS	Sandsack	sandbag
S.d.S	Soll der Sanitätsausrüstungen	requisition of medical supplies
Seefl	Seeflieger	naval flier
Seeflgz	Seeflugzeug	seaplane; hydroplane
Seegef	Seegefecht	naval engagement; fleet action
Seek	Seekarte	sea chart; hydrographic chart
seekl	seeklar	ready to sail
SeelA	Seelenachse	axis of the bore (*artillery*)
Seeobsdienst	Seebeobachtungsdienst	international nautical weather service
seew	seewärts	seaward
Seg	Segel	sail
Seg.Flgz	Segelflugzeug	glider
Sehr	Sehrohr	periscope (*submarine, tank*); telescope
Seit	Seiten-	flank
Seit.Abw	Seitenabweichung	drift; deflection error; lateral deviation
Seit.D	Seitendeckung	flank guard; flank security
Seit.Fl	Seitenflosse	vertical fin (*aviation*)
Seit.Gew	Seitengewehr	bayonet; side arm
Seit.M	Seitenmarsch	flank march
Seit.Sch	Seitenschutz	flank protection; flank security
Seit.Sich	Seitensicherung	flank protection
seitw	seitwärts	sidewards
Sek	Sekunde	second
/Sek	in der Sekunde	per second
sekr	sekret	secret
Sekr	Sekretär	secretary
Sekt	Sektion	section
Sekt	Sektor	sector
S.E.L	Selbstlade-Einstecklauf	subcaliber barrel for automatic weapon
Selb	Selbst-	self-; automatic
selbst	selbständig	independent
Selbstf.L	Selbstfahrlafette	self-propelled artillery mount
Selbst-St	Selbststeuerung	automatic control (*aviation*)
selbst.Verb	selbständiger Verband	independent unit
Send	Sender	sender; transmitter (*radio*)
Send	Sendung	transmission; broadcasting; shipment
Send.Anl	Sendeanlage	transmitting station
Send.St	Sendestation	transmitting station; sending station; broadcasting station
senkr	senkrecht	vertical
sessh	sesshaft	persistent (*gas*)
Sessh	Sesshaftigkeit	persistency (*of a gas*)
Sext	Sextant	sextant
S.F	Scherenfernrohr	battery commander's telescope
S.-F	Sonnenfinsternis	solar eclipse
s.F.H	schwere Feldhaubitze	medium field howitzer
s.F.H.M.W	Munitionswagen der schweren Feldhaubitze	ammunition wagon for the medium field howitzer
S.F.K	Schnellfeuerkanone	rapid-fire cannon
Sfl	Segelflieger	glider
Sfl	Selbstfahrlafette	self-propelled mount
Sflg	Seeflieger	naval flier
Sflg	Segelflug	glider flight; gliding
SflL	Segelfluglager	glider depot
SflÜ	Segelflugübungsgelände	drill ground for practice gliding
SFR	Schnellfrontzug mit Reisezugteil	express troop train with civilian section
S.F.St	Scherenfernrohrstand	telescope mount
s.F.St	schwere Funkstelle	large radio station
s.Fu.Ger.Kw	Gerätskraftwagen für schweres Funkgerät	heavy radio equipment truck
s.Fu.Ger.Wg	bespannter Gerätwagen für schweres Funkgerät	heavy radio equipment wagon (horse-drawn)
s.Fu.Kw	Kraftwagen für schweres Funkgerät	truck for heavy radio equipment
s.Fu.St	schwere Funkstelle	large radio station
s.Fu.Wg	bespannter Wagen für schweres Funkgerät	wagon for heavy radio equipment (horse-drawn)
S.F.V	Segelflugverein	glider club
s.F.Wg	schwerer Feldwagen	heavy field wagon
SF-Zug	Schnellfrontzug	express troop train
S.-Gerät	Schutzgerät	protective equipment; depot
S-Gesch	Spitzgeschoss	pointed bullet
SGew	Seitengewehr	bayonet; sidearms
Sg.Fl	Segelflieger	glider
s.gl	schwer geländegängig	heavy cross-country
s.gl.LKW	schwerer geländegängiger Lastkraftwagen	heavy cross-country motor truck
s.gl.PKW	schwerer geländegängiger Personenkraftwagen	heavy cross-country personnel carrier
Sgr	Sandgrube	sandpit (*on maps*)
S.H.D	Sicherheits- und Hilfdienste	air-raid protection auxiliary services
Si	Signalstation	signal station
Sich	Sicherheit	security; safety
sich	sichern	to secure; to protect; to put weapon at safety
Sich.Abt	Sicherungsabteilung	security detachment
Sich.B	Sicherheitsbeamter	security official
Sich.Best	Sicherheitsbestimmungen	safety regulations
Sich.D	Sicherheitsdienst	security service
Sich.Fl	Sicherungsflügel	safety catch (*weapons*)
Sich.H	Sicherungshebel	safety lever (*weapons*)
Sich.L	Sicherungslinie	outguard line of resistance
Sich.Massn	Sicherungsmassnahme	safety precaution; protective
Sich.Schl	Sicherungsschleier	safety screen
Sichtb	Sichtbarkeit	visibility
Sichterk	Sichterkundung	visual reconnaissance
Sich.Tr	Sicherheitstruppe	security troops
Sichtv	Sichtvermerk	visa
Sicht–Z	Sichtzeichen	ground signal; ground panel (*aviation*) visual signal
Sich.W	Sicherungswesen	security measures; safety measures
Sieg	Sieger	victor
siegr	siegreich	victorious
Sig	Signal	signal
s.I.G	schweres Infanteriegeschütz	heavy infantry gun
Sign	Signal	signal
Sign	Signatur	conventional sign (*map or troop symbol*)
Sign.H	Signalhorn	signal horn; siren
Sign.Mitt	Signalmittel	signal device
Sign.Off	Signaloffizier	signal officer
Sign.Rak	Signalrakete	signal rocket; flare
Signst	Signalstation	signal station
Sign.W	Signalwerfer	signal flare projector
Sig.Pers	Signalpersonal	signal personnel
Sig.Pist	Signalpistole	signal pistol
Sig.W	Signalwesen	signal system
silb	silbern	silver
S.In	Heeressanitätsinspektion	army medical inspectorate

s.Inf.Wff	schwere Infanteriewaffen	heavy infantry weapons
Sipo	Sicherheitspolizei	security police
Si.Spruch	Signalspruch	signal message
Sist	Sistierung	temporary arrest
SK	Sanitätskolonne	medical column
SK	Schnellfeuerkanone	rapid-fire cannon
Sk	Skizze	sketch; outline
S.K	Sonderkommando	special command; separate command
s.km	Reichweite eines Flugzeugs in Kilometern	range of a plane in kilometers
S.Kol	Sanitätskolonne	medical train
s.Kom	schwerer Kraftomnibus	heavy motor bus
S.Kp	Sanitätskompanie	medical company
Skr	Sekretär	secretary
S.L	Sanitätslager	medical depot
Sl	Sattel	saddle
SL	See- und Landflugzeug	amphibious plane
Slb	Silber	silver
Slg	Sammlung	collection
Slv	Salve	salvo (*artillery*); volley (*rifle*); broadside (*navy*)
S–M	Seemeile	sea mile; nautical mile; geographical mile; knot (*1855*
sm	Sekundenmeter	meters per second
s.Mast-Kw	Mastkraftwagen für schweres Funkgerät auf Kraftwagen	antenna truck for heavy radio apparatus (motorized)
s.Mast-Wg	Mastwagen für bespanntes schweres Funkgerät	antenna wagon for heavy radio equipment (horse-drawn)
s Med	silberne Medaille	silver medal
s.MG	schweres Maschinengewehr	heavy machine gun
Sm/h	Seemeilen in der Stunde	knots; nautical miles per hour
S-Mine	Spreng- *or* Schrapnellmine	anti-personnel mine; "silent soldier"
S.M.K	schwere Munitionskolonne	heavy ammunition column
Smk	Spitzgeschoss mit Stahlkern	pointed bullet with steel core
Sm K L-spur	Spitzgeschoss mit Stahlkern und Leuchtspur	pointed bullet with steel core and tracer effect
Sm/Std	Seemeilen in der Stunde	knots per hour
S.M.Tr	Schallmesstrupp	sound-ranging section
S-Mun	scharfe Munition	live ammunition
s.Mun.Wg.02	schwerer Munitionswagen Modell 1902	heavy ammunition wagon, model 1902
s.Mw	schwerer Minenwerfer	heavy mortar
SO	Signaloffizier	signal officer
SO	Südosten	southeast
so	südostwärts	southeastward; southeasterly
Sock.Laf	Sockellafette	rotating-base mount
Söld	Söldner	hired soldier; mercenary
Söld.H	Söldnerheer	mercenary army
Söld.Tr	Söldnertruppe	mercenary troops
sof	sofort	immediately
Sof	Sofortsache	immediate action (*notice on documents*)
sog	sogenannt	so-called
sogl	sogleich	immediately; at once
sol	solange	so long as
Sold	Soldat	soldier
sold	soldatisch	soldierlike
Sold-B	Soldbuch	identification book and service record
Sold.Frdh	Soldatenfriedhof	soldiers' cemetery
Soldgr	Soldatengrab	soldiers' grave (*on maps*)
Sold.Hm	Soldatenheim	soldiers' home
Sold.Spr	Soldatensprache	soldiers' slang
Sold.St	Soldatenstand	military profession
Sold.Url.O	Soldatenurlaubsordnung	soldiers' leave regulations
Sollbest	Sollbestand	required strength
Somm	Sommer	summer
sond	sonder	special
Sond.Anh	Sonderanhänger	special trailer; extra car (*motor transport*)
Sond.Auftr	Sonderauftrag	special mission
Sond.-Ber	Sonderbericht	special report
Sond.Kl	Sonderklasse	special class
Sond.Url	Sonderurlaub	special leave
Sond.Zw	Sonderzweck	special purpose
Sonnt Url	Sonntagsurlaub	Sunday leave
SOzO	Südost zu Ost	southeast by east
S.P	Signalposten	signal post; signal guard; signal sentry
Sp	Späh-	scout-
sp	spähen	to scout; to observe
Sp	Späher	scout; observer
sp	-spännig	drawn by animals
sp	spät-	late
Sp	Spalte	split; crack
Sp	Spannung	tension; strain; stress; volt-
Sp	Sperre	barricade; blockade
Sp	Sperr-	blocking; arresting
sp	sperren	to block; to arrest
sp	spezifisch	specific
Sp	Spiegel	mirror; reflector
Sp	Spiess	spit; pike; soldier's slang for master sergeant

Schwingungsweite *f* amplitude of oscillations (*Rad*).
Schwingungszahl *f* number of oscillations, frequency (*Elec, Rad*).
schwitzen to sweat.
Schwund *m* fading (*Rad*).
Schwundausgleich *m* automatic volume control (*Rad*).
Schwundwirkung *f* fading effect
Schwungkraft *f* centrifugal force.
Schwungkraftanlasser *m* inertia starter (*Mtr*).
Schwungrad *n* flywheel.
Schwungscheibe *f* *See* Schwungrad.
Sechskantschraube *f* hexagonal-head screw.
Sechsradkraftfahrzeug *n* six-wheel motor vehicle.
See *m* lake (die See = *ocean or sea*).
See *f* sea, ocean (der See = *lake*).
Seeaufklärer *m* naval patrol airplane, patrol bomber, scout bomber.
Seeflieger *m* naval aircraft pilot; naval airplane, seaplane.
Seefliegerei *f* naval aviation.
Seefliegerhorst *m* seaplane base.
Seeflugwesen *n* naval aviation.
Seeflugzeug *n* naval airplane, seaplane.
Seehöhe *f* height above mean sea level.
Seekabel *n* marine cable.
Seekadett *m* midshipman.
Seekarte *f* hydrographic map.
Seele *f* bore (*Ord*).
Seelenachse *f* axis of the bore.
Seelendurchmesser *m* caliber.
Seelenlänge *f* tube length, barrel length (*Ord*).
Seelenmesser *m* star gage (*G*).
Seelenrohr *n* tube, liner (*G*).
Seelenwand *f* bore surface (*G*).
Seelenweite *f* caliber.
seelische Wirkung moral effect (*Tac*).
Seeluftstreitkräfte *fpl* naval aviation.
Seemeile *f* nautical mile (*1.853 km*).
Seemine *f* submarine mine.
Seeminensperre *f* submarine mine field.
Seenenge *f* defile between lakes.
Seenotdienst *m* air forces sea rescue service.
Seenotflugkommando *n* air forces sea rescue command.
Seenotflugzeug *n* sea rescue airplane.
Seestreitkräfte *fpl* naval forces.
Seetransportübung *f* exercise in transportation by water.
seewasserbeständig salt-water resistant.
Seezünder *m* hydrostatic bomb fuze (*antisubmarine bombs and depth charges.*)
Segelflieger *m* glider, sailplane; glider pilot.
Segelflug *m* glide, gliding.
Segelflugzeug *n* glider, sailplane.
segeln to glide, soar; to sail.
Segelstellung *f* feathered position (*propeller*).
Segeltuch *n* canvas.
Segler *m* glider; sail boat.
Segmentlenkung *f* worm and sector steering system (*MT*).
Segmentstück *n* segment (*angle-of-site Inst*).
Sehfehler *m* defect of vision.
Sehfeld *n* field of view (*Optics*).
Sehklappe *f* peephole protector, lookout hole cover (*Tk*).
Sehkraft *f* eyesight, vision.
Sehlinie *f* line of observation; line of sight (*Surv*).
Sehne *f* tendon; chord.
Sehöffnung *f* peephole, lookout hole (*Ft, Tk*).
Sehrohr *n* periscope.
Sehschärfe *f* eyesight, vision; focus.
Sehschärfeneinteilung *f* focusing scale (*Optics*).
Sehschlitz *m* direct vision slot (*Tk*); observation slit, lookout slit (*Ft*).
Sehstreifen *m* sector of view (*from observation point to right and left ends of target*).
Sehverbindung *f* visual communication.
Sehwinkel *m* angle of view.
Sehzeichen *n* visual signal.
seicht shallow (*water*).
Seide *f* silk.
Seife *f* soap.
Seil *n* cord, rope, cable, line.
Seilbahn *f* overhead cable railway.
Seilbahnkommandotruppen *fpl* overhead cable railway troops.
Seilbremse *f* cable brake.
Seilfähre *f* cable ferry, rope ferry.
Seilrolle *f* cable drum.
Seiltrommel *f* cable drum.
Seilwinde *f* cable winch.
Seite *f* azimuth, direction (*Gunnery*); side.
Seitenabgangsfehler *m* lateral jump (*Gunnery*).
Seitenabstand *m* interval (*from left to right*); displacement (*Gunnery*).
Seitenabstand vom Richtpunkt angle of shift (*indirect firing*).
Seitenabweichung *f* drift (*of a projectile*): deflection (*Gunnery*).
Seitenänderung *f* deflection change, deflection correction (*Gunnery*).
Seitenansicht *f* side view.
Seitenbegrenzer *m* traverse stop (*G, MG*).
Seitenbestimmung *f* sensing (*Rad direction finding*).
Seitenbewegung *f* lateral movement.
Seitenblatt *n* skirt (*saddle*).
Seitendeckung *f* flank guard, flank security (*Tac*).
Seitenempfänger *m* azimuth indicator (*AA gun*).
Seitenfehler *m* lateral error (*Gunnery*).
Seitenfeuer *n* enfilade fire.
Seitenflosse *f* tail fin (*Ap*).
Seitenteilring *m* azimuth scale (*AA gun*).
Seitentrieb *m* traversing drive (*G*).
Seitenverankerung *f* apron (*of double-apron fence*).
Seitenverbesserung *f* deflection correction (*Gunnery*).
Seitenverbindung *f* lateral communication (*Sig C*).
Seitenverhältnis *n* aspect ratio (*Ap*).
Seitenverschiebung *f* drift correction (*Gunnery*).
Seitenvorhalt *m* lateral lead (*firing*).
Seitenvorhaltsebene *f* slant plane of lateral lead (*AA gunnery*).
Seitenwagen *m* sidecar (*Mtcl*).
Seitenwelle *f* jack shaft (*MT*).
Seitenwind *m* cross wind.
Seitenwinkel *m* deflection angle (*Gunnery*); horizontal angle (*Surv*).
Seitenwinkelverbesserungsknopf *m* lateral correction knob (*AA gun*).
Seitenwinkelvorhalt *m* lateral angular lead, lateral deflection angle (*AA gunnery*).
seitlich abrutschen to fall off (*Avn*).
seitlich einschwenken pivot to the left or right, fan out (*Tac*).
Seitwärtsbewegung *f* yawing (*Ap*).
Seitwärtseinschneiden *n* lateral resection (*Surv*).
Sektor *m* sector; protractor.
Sekundärkreis *m* secondary circuit (*Rad*).
Sekundärstrom *m* secondary current (*Rad*).
selbständig independent.
Selbstantrieb *m* self-propulsion, automatic drive.
selbstdichtend self-sealing (*Ap tank*).
selbsterregend self-exciting (*Rad*).
Selbstfahrlafette *f* self-propelled mount, gun motor carriage.
Selbstinduktion *f* self-induction (*Elec*).
Selbstinduktionsspule *f* self-induction coil (*Elec*).
Selbstladeeinstecklauf *m* subcaliber barrel (*for semiautomatic weapon*).
Selbstladegewehr *n* self-loading rifle, semiautomatic rifle.
Selbstladepistole *f* self-loading pistol, automatic pistol.
Selbstlader *m* self-loading rifle.
Selbstladewaffe *f* self-loading weapon, semiautomatic weapon.
Seitengewehr *n* bayonet.
"Seitengewehr, an Ort!" "Unfix, bayonets!"
Seitengewehrgriff *m* bayonet grip.
Seitengewehrhalter *m* (*R*) bayonet stud
"Seitengewehr, pflanzt auf!" "Fix, bayonets!"
Seitengewehrtasche *f* bayonet scabbard.
Seitenhebel *m* traversing lever (*MG sleigh mount*).
Seitenholm *m* side outrigger (*AA gun*).
Seitenklappe *f* side door (*Tk*).
Seitenleitwerk *n* (*Ap*) rudder assembly
Seitenlicht *n* running light (*Ap*).
Seiten-MG. *n* waist gun, side gun.
Seitenrampe *f* side-loading ramp.
Seitenrichtbereich *m* total movement in traverse (*G*).
Seitenrichtfeld *n* extent of traverse, total movement in traverse (*G*).
Seitenrichtfeld von 360° all-round traverse.
Seitenrichtfernrohr *n* azimuth tracking telescope (*height finder*).
Seitenrichtkanonier *m* azimuth setter.
Seitenrichtmaschine *f* traversing mechanism (*G*).
Seitenrichtrad *n* traversing handwheel (*G*).
Seitenrichtschieber *m* deflection board (*Arty*).
Seitenrichtschraube *f* traversing screw (*G*).
Seitenrichtteilung *f* deflection scale.
Seitenrichttrieb *m* traversing drive (*G, Mort*).
Seitenrichtung *f* azimuth, direction (*Gunnery*).
Nehmen der Seitenrichtung laying for direction.
Seitenrichtwerk *n* traversing mechanism (*G*).
Seitenrichtwinkel *m* angle of traverse, azimuth (*Gunnery*).
Seitenruder *n* rudder (*Ap*).
Seitenrutsch *m* side slip (*Avn*).
Seitenschwankung *f* lateral sway (*Bde*).
Seitensicherung *f* flank security.
Seitensteuerung *f* rudder controls; lateral control.
Seitenstreuung *f* lateral dispersion, width of dispersion (*Arty*).
Selbstretter *m* oxygen breathing apparatus.
Selbstschutz *m* self-defense; individual air raid precautions.
Selbstschutzmittel *n* prophylactic.
selbstsperrend self-locking.
Selbststeuergerät *n* automatic pilot (*Ap*).
Selbststeuerung *f* automatic control.
selbsttätig automatic (*adj*), automatically operated.
Selbstunterbrecher *m* automatic circuit breaker (*Elec*).
Selbstvernebelung *f* smoke screening (*one's own troops and/or installations*).
Selbstverstümmelung *f* self-mutilation.
Selbstverwaltung *f* self government (*PW*).
Sendeantenne *f* transmitting antenna.
Sendebereitschaft *f* stand-by, readiness to transmit (*Rad*).
Sendegerät *n* radio transmitter.
Sender *m* transmitter (*Rad*).
Senderempfänger *m* transceiver (*Rad*).
Senderöhre *f* transmitting tube (*Rad*).
Sendestelle *f* transmitting station.
Sendung *f* shipment; transmission (*Rad*).
Senfgas *n* mustard gas (*CWS*).
Senkblei *n* plumb bob, sounding lead.
Senke *f* depression (*Top*).
senken to depress (*a gun*); to sink (*a shaft*); to let down, to lower.
Senkfaschine *f* sunken fascine revetment.
Senkfaschinendamm *m* fascine-reveted dam.
Senkfeuer *n* plunging fire (*Arty*).
Senkkasten *m* caisson (*Engr*).
Senklot *n* *See* **Senkblei.**
senkrecht vertical, perpendicular.
Senkrechtaufnahme *f* vertical aerial photograph.
Senkrechtbild *n* *See* **Senkrechtaufnahme.**
Senkrechte *f* perpendicular (*line*).
Senkrechtebene zum Zielweg vertical plane containing course of target (*AA gunnery*).
senkrechte Gitterlinie Y-line (*of map grid*),
senkrechter Abstand vertical interval.
senkrechtes Auftreffen normal impact (*Ballistics*).
Senkrechtgeschwindigkeit *f* vertical speed (*Avn*).
Senkrechtluftaufnahme *f* vertical aerial photograph.
Senkstück *n* sunken fascine mat or cribwork.
Senkungswinkel *m* depression angle (*G*).
Serienschaltung *f* series connection (*Elec*).
Servowirkung *f* servo action (*servo brake*).
seßhafter Kampfstoff persistent chemical warfare agent.
Seßhaftigkeit *f* persistency (*CWS*).
"Setzt die, Gewehre! Zusammen!" "Stack, arms!"
Setzwaage *f* builders' level (*Engr*).
Seuche *f* epidemic, contagious disease.
S-Gerät *n* *See* Suchgerät.
S.-Geschoß *n* *See* Spitzgeschoß.
sicher safe.
Sicherer *mpl* security patrol(s).
Sicherheitsbestimmungen *fpl* safety regulations.
Sicherheitsdienst *m* security measures (*Tac*); SS security service (*abbr.* SD).
Sicherheitsdraht *m* safety wire (*Ord*).
Sicherheitsfunkenstrecke *f* safety spark gap (*magneto ignition*).
Sicherheitsglas *n* safety glass, shatterproof glass.
Sicherheitshöhe *f* safe altitude (*Avn*).
Sicherheitskoeffizient *m* factor of safety.
Sicherheitsmaß *n* clearance, safety angle (*Gunnery*).
Sicherheitsmaßnahme *f* safety measure, security measure.
Sicherheitsoffizier *m* safety officer (*at target range*).
Sicherheitspolizei *f* security police (*comprising* Kriminalpolizei *and* Geheime Staatspolizei).
Sicherheits- und Hilfsdienste *mpl* air raid protection services. (*Also called* Luftschutzpolizei).
Sicherheitsventil *n* safety valve.
Sicherheitszone *f* safety area (*Arty*).
sichern to cover, protect, make secure (*Tac*); to lock, to put at "safe" (*Ord, Am*).
Sicherung *f* security, security detachment, covering party (*Tac*); safety (*SA*); safety lock (*fuze*); safety device; fuse (*Elec*).

Sicherungsabstand *m* security distance *(between march units).*
Sicherungsauftrag *m* security mission *(Tac).*
Sicherungsdienst *m* guard service *(Tac).*
Sicherungs-Division *f* security division *(mobile* Landesschützen *units employed at rear area duties).*
Sicherungsflügel *m* protective wing or flank *(Tac)*; interrupter *(Am).*
Sicherungsflugzeug *n* escort airplane.
Sicherungshaken *m* release hook *(glider).*
Sicherungshebel *m* grip safety *(pistol).*
Sicherungskappe *f* safety device *(fuze)*; safety cap *(hand grenade).*
Sicherungsklappe *f* interrupter *(Am).*
Sicherungslinie *f* line of security.
vorderste Sicherungslinie outpost line.
Sicherungsmaßnahme *f* security measure.
Sicherungsmutter *f* lock nut.
Sicherungsschleier *m* screen *(Tac).*
Sicherungsstift *m* safety pin *(fuze).*
Sicherungsstück *n* safety lug *(on gun cradle).*
Sicherungsvorrichtung *f* interrupter *(Am)*; safety device.
Sicherungsvorstecker *m* arming pin *(fuze)*; safety pin *(bomb).*
Sicherungszuschlag *m* margin of safety *(firing).*
Sicht *f* visibility.
Sichtabstand *m* interval permitting visual contact.
Sichtanzeigegerät *n* visual indicator *(Ap Inst).*
sichtbar visible.
Sichtbarkeit *f* visibility.
Sichtbereich *m* radius of visibility.
Sichtberührung *f* visual contact.
Sichtdeckung *f* sight defilade; smoke and flash defilade *(Arty).*
Sichtigkeit *f* visibility.
Sichtnavigation *f* contact flight, pilotage *(Air Navigation).*
Sichtverhältnisse *npl* visibility conditions.
Sichtweite *f* radius of visibility.
Sichtzeichen *n* visual signal, panel signal.
Sickerschacht *m* drainage ditch, sump *(trench).*
Sieb *n* screen, sifter, filter.
Siebkreis *m* series resonant circuit *(Rad).*
Siebtrichter *m* filter funnel *(MT).*
Siegel *n* seal.
Sieger *m* victor.
siegreich victorious.
Sielengeschirr *n* breast harness.
Signal *n* signal; bugle call.
Signalbombe *f* signal flare.
Signalbuch *n* signal book *(Nav).*
internationales Signalbuch international code *(Nav).*
Signalmittel *n* signal device.
Signalpatrone *f* signal cartridge.
Signalrakete *f* signal rocket.
Signalscheibe *f* signaling disk.
Signalstreifen *m* code panel *(Avn).*
Signaltafel *f* code chart *(Sig C).*
Signaltuch *n* code panel *(Avn).*
Signalwerfer *m* ground signal projector, pyrotechnic projector.
Signatur *f* conventional sign *(on maps).*
Simmerring *m* oil seal *(MT).*
Simulant *m* malingerer.
simulieren malinger.
Simultanschaltung *f* simplexed connection *(Tg, Tp).*
Sinkgeschwindigkeit *f* rate of drop *(Avn).*
Sinn *m* sense, meaning; direction.
Sipo *f* *See* **Sicherheitspolizei.**
Sirene *f* siren.
sitzender Anschlag sitting position *(MG or R firing).*
Sitzfallschirm *m* seat pack parachute.
Sitzriemen *m* seat strap *(saddle).*
Skala *f* scale, dial.
Skalenring *m* micrometer *(angle-of-site Inst).*
Skalenscheibe *f* angle-of-site scale *(Arty)*; dial plate, scale disk *(Rad).*
Skizze *f* sketch.
S-Maske *f* *See* **Staubmaske.**
s.M.G.-Bedienung *m* heavy machine-gun squad.
s.M.G.-Zug *m* heavy machine-gun platoon.
S-Mine *f* antipersonnel mine *(abbr. of* Schützenmine).
Sonderlastkraftwagen *m* special-purpose motor truck.
Sonderlaufbahn *f* specialist's career.
Sondermeldung *f* special message, special announcement *(Rad).*
Sondermunition *f* separate-loading ammunition; special-purpose ammunition.
Sonderstahl *m* special steel.
Sondertruppen *fpl* special units, special troops.
Sonderverband *m* special unit.
Sonderverfügungen *fpl* special orders.
Sonderverpflegung *f* special rations.
Sonderwaffe *f* special weapon.
Sonderzweck *m* special purpose.
Sondiernadel *f* probing rod *(for land mines).*
Sonnenblende *f* sun shield, sun shade.
Sonnengeflecht *n* solar plexus.
Sonnenstich *m* sunstroke.
Sonnenzeit *f* solar time.
spähen to scout.
Späher *m* scout, lookout.
Spähtrupp *m* patrol, reconnaissance patrol.
Spähtruppführer *m* patrol leader.
Spähtrupptätigkeit *f* patrol activity.
Spähtruppvorstoß *m* scouting raid.
Spähwagen *m* scout car.
s.Pak *f* heavy antitank gun.
Spalt *m* crack, split.
Spalte *f* slit; split; crevice, fissure; leak; column *(in tables).*
Spaltflügel *m* slotted wing *(Ap).*
Spaltring *m* split ring *(breechblock).*
Spaltrohr *n* collimator.
Spange *f* clasp *(decoration).*
Spanienkämpfer *m* veteran of Spanish Civil War.
spanischer Reiter knife rest, cheval-de-frise.
Spanndraht *m* tension wire, wire brace.
spannen to cock *(SA)*; to stretch, strain, apply tension, tighten.
Spannfalle *f* firing pin trip *(breechblock).*
Spannfeder *f* cocking spring *(MG).*
Spannhebel *m MG)*cocking lever *(G,*
Spannlack *m* dope *(Ap).*
Spannrast *f* full cock *(SA).*
Spannriegel *m* cocking bolt *(breechblock).*
Spannschieber *m* cocking slide *(MG)*
S-Mittel *npl* *See* **Standort-Beköstigungsmittel.**
S.m.K.Geschoß *n* pointed steel-core armor-piercing bullet.
S.m.K.L'spurgeschoß *n* pointed steel-core tracer bullet.
Sockel *m* pedestal, swivel *(G).*
Sockelgeschütz *n* swivel gun, pedestal-mounted gun.
Sockellafette *f* pedestal mount, swivel mount *(G).*
Sockelschaltung *f* socket connection *(Rad tube).*
Sog *m* suction.
Sohle *f* sole; bottom of trench.
Sold *m* pay.
Soldat *m* soldier, enlisted man.
soldatische Haltung military bearing.
Soldbuch *n* pay book *(soldier's individual pay record).*
Sollbestand *m* authorized basic allowance.
Sollstand *m* *See* **Sollstärke.**
Sollstärke *f* authorized strength.
Sollstelle *f* *See* **Planstelle.**
Solokrad *n* solo motorcycle.
Sommerweg *m* road shoulder.
Sonderanhänger *m* special trailer.
Sonderaufbau *m* special body *(MT).*
Sonderauftrag *m* special mission.
Sonderbataillon *n* special battalion, disciplinary battalion.
Sonderberichterstatter *m* visiting correspondent.
Sonderfahrzeug *n* special-purpose vehicle.
Sonderflugzeug *n* special-purpose airplane.
Sonderfrequenz *f* specially assigned frequency *(Rad).*
Sonderfrieden *m* separate peace.
Sonderführer *m* specialist *(includes interpreters, laboratory technicians, radio specialists, cameramen, etc., serving in the Ger armed forces, with nominal rank up to Bn commander but no actual Mil rank).*
Sonderfunkspruch *m* special radio message *(for Arty metro message and weather reports).*
Sondergasmaske *f* special gas mask.
Sondergespräch *n* special telephone call.
Sonderkriegsgericht *n* special court-martial.
Sonderlafette *f* special gun mount.
Spannschloß *n* idler adjuster rod *(Tk)*; turnbuckle.
Spannschraube *f* threaded breech hoop *(G).*
Spannstollen *m* cocking cam *(breechblock).*
Spannstück *n* sear *(G)*; accelerator *(MG).*
Spannturm *m* cabane *(Ap).*
Spannung *f* voltage, tension *(Elec).*
Spannungsabfall *m* voltage drop, potential drop.
Spannungs-Dehnungs-Diagramm *n* stress-strain diagram.
Spannungsmesser *m* voltmeter.
Spannungsregler *m* voltage regulator.
Spannungsschwankung *f* voltage variation.
Spannungssicherung *f* circuit breaker.
Spannungsteiler *m* voltage divider *(Rad).*
Spannweite *f* span *(Bdg)*; wing span *(Ap).*
Spannwelle *f* recocking shaft *(breechblock).*
Spant *m* vertical frame, vertical ring, bulkhead frame *(Ap).*
Spargelbeete *npl* asparagus-bed obstacle pattern.
Sparschaltung *f* autotransformer circuit *(Elec).*
Sparstoff *m* scarce material, high-priority material.
Spartransformator *m* autotransformer *(Rad, Elec).*
Spaten *m* spade, shovel.
Spätzerspringer *m* retarded burst.
Spätzündung *f* retarded ignition, retarded spark *(Mtr).*
Speiche *f* spoke.
Speicher *m* storeroom.
Speiseleitung *f* feeder line *(Rad).*
Speiseraum *m* mess.
Speisestrom *m* feeder current *(Elec).*
Speisung *f* feed, feeding.
Sperrabschnitt *m* prohibited area; defense sector.
Sperrad *n* locking wheel *(gun cradle)*; ratchet wheel.
Sperramt *n* harbor-defense ordnance depot.
Sperrballon *m* barrage balloon.
Sperrballontruppen *fpl* barrage balloon troops.
Sperrdienst *m* obstacle-construction service.
Sperrdrache *m* barrage kite.
Sperre *f* block, obstacle, barrier, accessory defense; blockade, embargo; air alert, fighter patrol *(Avn).*
Sperre aus Schienen steel-rail obstacle.
Sperre aus Stahlträgern steel-beam obstacle, structural-steel obstacle.
Sperre fliegen to fly on an air alert.
sperren to lock, to bar; interdict *(Tac)*; tune out *(Rad).*
Sperrfeder *f* retard spring *(fuze)*; locking spring *(MG).*
Sperrfeld *n* obstacle field.
Sperrfeuer *n* barrage, barrage fire.
Sperrfeuerskizze *f* barrage chart.
Sperrfeuerwand *f* curtain of antiaircraft fire.
Sperrfeuerzone *f* zone covered by barrage fire *(AAA).*
Sperrgebiet *n* prohibited area, restricted area; blockade zone *(Nav).*
Sperrhebel *m* locking lever *(G carriage).*
Sperrholz *n* plywood.
Sperrholzzelt *n* plywood shelter.
Sperriegel *m* switch position, switch trench; locking bolt *(MG stock).*
Sperrklinke *f* retaining catch *(breechblock)*; safety catch, pawl *(Mech).*
Sperrkreis *m* tank circuit *(Rad).*
Sperrlicht *n* barrier light.
Sperrlinie *f* obstacle line.
Sperrnase *f* catch *(fuze).*
Sperrohr *n* outer steam tube *(MG).*
Sperrstück *n* locking bolt *(pistol).*
Sperrtrupp *m* obstacle-construction detachment; blocking party.
Sperrung *f* obstruction, blocking.
Sperrverband *m* obstacle-construction unit; blocking unit.
Sperrwachboot *n* boom defense vessel.
Sperrzone *f* obstacle zone.
spezifischer Bodendruck ground pressure per unit area *(MT).*
spezifisches Gewicht specific gravity.
Spiegel *m* mirror; level mirror *(panoramic telescope)*; periscope; bull's-eye *(target)*; collar patch.
Spiegeldurchmesser *m* mirror diameter *(SL).*
Spiegelentfernungsmesser *m* macrometer.
Spiegelfrequenz *f* image frequency *(Rad).*
Spiegelhalter *m* mirror support *(MG prismatic sight).*
Spiegelkreuzlibelle *f* reflector-type cross level *(panoramic telescope).*
Spiegelneigungsmesser *m* Abney level.
Spiegelrahmen *m* mirror frame *(MG prismatic sight).*
Spiegeltelegraph *m* heliograph, heliotrope *(Sig C).*
Spiegelvisier *n* mirror sight.
Spiel *n* backlash, clearance, play *(Mech)*; game.
Spielmann *m* bandsman *(pl* Spielleute).
Spielraum *m* clearance, backlash.
Spieß *m* "top sergeant," "top kick."
Spill *n* winch.
Spindel *f* gear shaft *(elevating mechanism)*; spindle, pinion, mandril.
Spindellenkung *f* cam and lever steering system *(MT).*
Spinne *f* multiple road junction; spider.
Spion *m* spy.
Spionage *f* espionage.
Spionageabwehr *f* counterespionage.
Spiralbohrer *m* twist drill.
Spiralfeder *f* spiral spring, helical spring.
Spiralfederausgleicher *m* spiral-spring equilibrator *(AA gun).*
spitz pointed.
Spitze *f* point, advance guard point *(Tac)*; tip, peak, head.
Spitzengruppe *f* point squad; advance element *(Tac).*
Spitzenkompanie *f* advance party *(in Adv Gd of large unit).*

Sp	Spind	locker *(soldier's wardrobe)*
Sp	Spinne	road junction
Sp	Spion(age)	spy; espionage
sp	spionieren	to spy
Sp	Spital	hospital
Sp	Spitzen-	head; point; advance
Sp	Splitter-	splinter
Sp	Sporn	trail spade; tail skid; spur *(artillery, aviation)*
Sp	Spreng-	explosive
Sp	Sprengpunkt	point of burst *(gunnery)*
Sp	Spur	track; trail; scent
Sp.A	Sportabzeichen	badge for achievement in sports
Spann.-W	Spannweite	wingspread; span
Span.R	Spanische Reiter	cheval-de-frise *(wire entanglements)*
Sp.D	Spähdienst	scouting duty
Sperrf	Sperrfeuer	barrage; barrage fire
Sperrh	Sperrholz	plywood
Spez	Spezialität	specialty
spez.Gew	**spezifisches Gewicht**	**specific gravity**
Spez.Tr	Spezialtruppen	special troops
Spez.Verw	Spezialverwendung	special use
Sp.Flg	Spaltflügel	slotted wing
Sp.Flgz	Spezialflugzeug	special airplane
Sp.Flgz	Sportflugzeug	sport plane
Sp.Ft	Sperrfort	outer fort
spg	-spännig	drawn by animals
Spg	Spannung	span; voltage
Sp.Geb	Sperrgebiet	barred zone; blockaded zone
S P.Gesch	Spitzgeschoss mit Phosphor	pointed bullet with tracer effect
Sp.Gr	Sperrgrenze	boundary of blocked zone
Sp.Gr	Spitzengruppe	forward echelon
Sp.Gr	Sprenggranate	high-explosive shell
Spgr.m.K	Sprenggranatenzünder mit Klappensicherung	fuze with centrifugal safety device (high-explosive shell)
Sp-H	Sprengpunkthöhe	height of point of burst
Spion	Spionage	espionage
Spit	Spital	hospital
Spitz	Spitzen-	head; point; advance
Spitz.Komp	Spitzenkompanie	advance party
Sp.Kp	Spitzenkompanie	advance party
Sp.Kps	Sprengkapsel	detonating cap
Spl.Bo	Splitterbombe	fragmentation bomb
Sp.Leist	Spitzenleistung	peak capacity; record
Spl.Gr	Splittergranate	fragmentation shell
Sp.M	Sperrmauer	blocking wall; rampart
Sp.Metalle	Sparmetalle	rare metals
Spr	Sperr-	blocking; mining *(naval)*
S.Pr	Spitzgeschoss mit Phosphor	pointed bullet with tracer effect
spr	spreizen	to spread; to straddle
Spr	Spreng-	explosive
spr	sprengen	to blast
Spr.B	Sprengbüchse	blasting charge
Spr.Bo	Sprengbombe	high-explosive bomb
Sp.Rd	Spornrad	rowel; spur wheel
Sprengm	Sprengmittel	explosive
Sprengm	Sprengmunition	explosive ammunition
Sprengst	Sprengstoff	explosive
Spr.Gr	**Sprenggranate**	**high-explosive shell**
Sprgr.m.K	Sprenggranate mit Klappensicherung	high-explosive shell with folding safety device
Spr.K Spr.Kp	Sprengkörper	blasting charge; explosive charge
Spr.Kab	Sprengkabel	blasting ignition cable
Spr.Kdo	Sprengkommando	demolition party
Spr.Kps	Sprengkapsel	detonating cap; primer cap
Spr.Kps.Zd	Sprengkapselzünder	detonator
Spr.Laf	Spreizlafette	split-trail carriage
Spridg	Sprengladung	high explosive charge
Spr.Mitt	Sprengmittel	explosive
Spr.Mun	Sprengmunition	explosive ammunition
Spr.Mt	Sprengmunition	explosive ammunition
Spr.P	Sprengpunkt	point of burst
Spr.Patr	Sprengpatrone	blasting cartridge
Spr.Patr	Sprengpatrouille	demolition patrol
Spr.St	Sprechstelle	telephone extension; call sta-
Spr.St	Sprengstoff	explosive
Spr.St	Sprengstück	bomb splinter; shell fragment
Sp.Rtr	Spanische Reiter	cheval-de-frise *(wire entanglements)*
Spr.V	Sprengvorschrift	technical manual on blasting
Sprzlaf	Spreizlafette	split-trail carriage
Spt	September	September
Sp.Tr	Spähtrupp	scout squad; patrol
S-Pulver	Pulver für scharfe Munition	powder for live ammunition
Sp.W	Spannweite	wing spread; span
Sp.Zg	Spielmannszug	fife and drum corps
s.Pz.Kpf.Wg	schwerer Panzerkampfwagen	heavy tank
S.Pz.Sp.Wg	schwerer Panzerspähwagen	heavy armored scouting car; heavy armored reconnaissance car

S.R.	Schützenregiment	rifle regiment
S.R.	Sehrohr	periscope; telescope
Ss.	Sandsack	sandbag
S S.	Scharfschütze	sharpshooter; marksman
S.S.	Schutzstaffel der NSDAP	Elite Guard of the National Socialist Party
S S Brücke	schwere Schiffsbrücke	heavy ponton bridge
s S-Gesch	schweres Spitzgeschoss	heavy pointed bullet
S.Sich	Seitensicherung	flank protection
S.Sign	Schallsignal	sound signal
SS-Mann	Schutzstaffelmann	(SS) Elite Guard private
ss.MG	überschweres Maschinengewehr	superheavy (large caliber) machine gun
SSO	Südsüdost	south-southeast
S.S.P.	Sammelsanitätspark	medical collecting depot
SS Pf.	SS und Polizeiführer	SS (Elite Guard) and Police Commander
S.St	Sammelstelle	collecting point; salvage dump
sst	schrägstehend	diagonal
S.St.A	Schiffsstammabteilung	cadre *(naval)*
SSW	Südsüdwest	south southwest
SS.Wagen	besonders schwerer Güterwagen	especially heavy freight car
ST	Schlüsseltrupp zur Bearbeitung von Funksprüchen *(on sketches)*	radiogram deciphering troop
S.T.	schnelle Truppen	mobile troops
St	Stab	staff
st	ständig	permanent
St	Stärke	strength
St	Stafette	dispatch-radio; messenger relay service
St	Staffel	echelon; squadron *(aviation)*; detachment; ammunition section
st	staffelförmig	echeloned
St	Stahl	steel
St	Stahlhelm	Steel Helmet *(organization of war veterans)*
St	Stall	stable *(on maps)*
St	Stamm-	stem; cadre
St	Standarte	standard; regiment of Storm Troopers
St	Stapel	staple; dump
st	stark	strong
st	starr	rigid
St	Station	station; depot
St	Staudruck	dynamic pressure; impact pressure *(aviation)*
st	stehend	standing
st	steif	stiff; rigid
st	steigend	rising; climbing
st	stellen	to put; to place; to set
St	Stellung	position
St	Stellvertreter	deputy
St	Stempel	stamp
st	sterben	to die
St	Sternmotor	radial engine
St	Steuer	rudder; tax; helm controls *(aviation)*
st	steuern	to steer; to navigate; to pilot
St	Stoff	stuff; material
st	stoppen	to stop
St	Stoss-	thrust
St	Straf-	punishment; sentence
St	Strasse	street
St	Stube	room
St	Stück	piece; part
St	Stütze	support
St	Stunde	hour
St	Sturm	storm; assault
St	Sturz	crash; dive; plunge
St	Stutzen	short rifle
Sta	Stabsarzt	captain *(Medical Corps)*
Sta	Standarte	standard; regiment of Storm Troopers
Sta	Station	station; railroad station
St.A	Stubenarrest	confinement to quarters
Staatsb	Staatsbahn	federal railway
Stabsw	Stabswache	headquarters company
St.Abw	Sturmabwehr	defense against assault
Stä	Stärke	strength
Stä.Nchw	Stärkenachweisung	statement of actual strength
Staff	Staffel	echelon; squadron *(aviation)*; detachment; ammunition section
St.Afü	Stab des Artillerieführers	staff of the (divisional) artillery commander
StAG	Sturmabwehrgeschütz	anti-assault gun
Stahlw	Stahlwerk	steel works
St.Al	stiller Alarm	silent alarm
Stalag	Standlager	prisoner-of-war camp for enlisted men
Stamm B	Stammbataillon	cadre battalion
Stammbttr	Stammbatterie	cadre battery
Stamml	Stammliste	muster roll; cadre list

Spitzenpanzer *m* leading tank.
Spitzenwagen *m* leading car, "point" car *(MT)*.
Spitzenzug *m* advance platoon *(Armd Comd)*.
spitzer Winkel acute angle.
Spitzgeschoß *n* pointed bullet.
Spitzgeschoß mit Stahlkern pointed steel-core armor-piercing bullet.
Spitzhacke *f* pickax.
Spleißung *f* splice.
Splint *m* cotter pin, pin.
Splissung *f* splice.
Splitter *m* splinter, fragment.
Splitterbombe *f* fragmentation bomb, antipersonnel bomb.
Splitterdichte *f* density of fragments *(number of shell fragments per unit area)*.
Splittergraben *m* slit trench, trench shelter.
Splittergranate *f* fragmentation shell.
Splitterring *m* fragmentation ring *(fits over casing of the* Stielhandgranate*)*.
Splitterschutz *m* splinterproof protection *(Ft)*.
Splitterschutzbrille *f* protective goggles.
splittersicher splinterproof.
splittersichere Deckung splinterproof cover.
splittersicherer Unterstand splinterproof shelter.
Splitterwirkung *f* fragmentation, spray effect *(Am)*.
Sporn *m* tail skid *(Ap)*; trail spade *(G)*; spike *(MG tripod)*; spur *(Cav)*; gaff.
Spornarm *m* spade arm *(G)*.
Spornblech *n* spade plate *(G)*.
Spornkufe *f* trail-spade runner *(Arty operations in deep snow)*.
Spornrad *n* tail wheel *(Ap)*.
Spornschuh *m* tail skid *(Ap)*.
Spornteller *m* spike plate *(MG tripod)*.
Sportlehrer *m* athletic instructor.
Sprachfrequenzband *n* voice frequency band *(Rad, Tp)*.
Sprachrohr *n* megaphone.
Sprachübertragung *f* voice transmission *(Rad, Tp)*.
Sprechen *n* voice transmission *(Rad, Tp)*.
Sprechfunk *m* voice radio.
Sprechmaschine *f* phonograph.
Sprechschleife *f* loop circuit *(Tp)*.
Sprechspule *f* induction coil *(Tp)*.
Sprechstelle *f* telephone station.
Sprechtaste *f* push-to-talk switch *(Rad, Tp)*.
Sprechverbindung *f* telephone communication, telephone connection, telephone circuit.
Sprechverkehr *m* telephone traffic.
Sprechverständigung *f* talking range *(Tp)*.
Spreizklappe *f* split flap *(Ap)*.
Spreizlafette *f* split-trail gun carriage.
Spreizlafettenholme *mpl* trails *(of split-trail carriage)*.
Spreizlafettenschwanz *m* split trail.
Sprengbombe *f* demolition bomb, high-explosive bomb.
Sprengbrandbombe *f* combination incendiary-demolition bomb.
Sprengbüchse *f* explosive block *(in container)*; demolition block.
Sprengdienst *m* demolition service.
sprengen to blast, blow up, detonate.
Sprengfalle *f* booby trap.
Sprengfüllung *f* filler charge *(Am)*.
Sprenggegenstand *m* object to be blasted or demolished.
Sprenggerät *n* demolition equipment.
Sprenggeschoß *n* explosive projectile, explosive bullet.
Sprenggranate *f* high-explosive shell.
Sprenggranate-Patrone *f* high-explosive shell *(fixed Am)*.
Sprenggrube *f* blasting pit *(Engr)*.
Sprenghöhe *f* height of burst *(Gunnery)*.
Sprengkabel *n* firing wire *(blasting)*.
Sprengkammer *f* mine chamber *(blasting)*.
Sprengkapsel *f* detonator *(Am)*; blasting cap.
Sprengkapselröhrchen *n* detonator tube *(hand grenade)*.
Sprengkapselsicherung *f* detonator safety *(fuze)*.
Sprengkapselzünder *m* detonating-cord unit with blasting cap and fuze lighter.
Sprengkegel *m* spray *(air burst)*.
Sprengkommando *n* bomb disposal unit; demolition party.
Sprengkörper *m* demolition block.
Sprengkraft *f* explosive force *(Am)*.
Sprengladung *f* demolition charge, blasting charge *(Engr)*; bursting charge *(Am)*; burster *(Cml shell)*.
Sprengladungsröhre *f* burster tube.
Sprengluft *f* liquid oxygen.
Sprengmittel *n* explosive *(in prepared form, as distinguished from generic term* Sprengstoff*)*.
Sprengmunition O2 *f* TNT.

Sprengniete *f* explosive rivet.
Sprengöl *n* nitroglycerin, blasting oil.
Sprengölpulver *n* nitroglycerin powder.
Sprengpatrone *f* blasting cartridge *(demolitions)*; explosive bullet.
Sprengplan *m* demolition plan.
Sprengpulver *n* blasting powder *(black powder)*.
Sprengpunkt *m* point of burst *(Gunnery)*.
hoher Sprengpunkt air burst.
mittlerer Sprengpunkt center of burst.
Sprengpunktentfernung *f* straight line from muzzle to point of burst *(Gunnery)*.
Sprengring *m* retaining ring *(gas mask)*.
Sprengsalpeter *m* nitrate explosive.
Sprengsatz *m* bursting charge *(Am)*.
Sprengstange *f* charge-placing pole.
Sprengstelle *f* point of rupture, breaching point; demolition chamber *(Bdg)*.
Sprengstoff *m* explosive.
Sprengstoffgehalt *m* amount of bursting charge *(Am)*.
Sprengstoffüllung *f* explosive filler *(Am)*.
Sprengstück *n* shell fragment, shell splinter.
sprengtechnisch pertaining to technical aspect of demolitions.
Sprengtrichter *m* crater, mine crater.
Sprengtrupp *m* demolition squad.
Sprengung *f* demolition, blasting.
Sprengweite *f* horizontal distance between point of air burst and theoretical point of impact *(Gunnery)*.
Sprengwerk *n* inverted truss; strut-braced construction *(Engr)*.
Sprengwirkung *f* burst effect *(Am)*.
Sprengzünder *m* detonating fuze *(Am)*.
Spreutlage *f* brushwork revetment.
Springschreiber *m* a type of telegraph printer.
Spritzdüse *f* spray nozzle *(carburetor)*.
Spritzer *m* splash.
Spritzschlauch *m* spray nozzle.
Spritzumlaufschmierung *f* splash lubrication *(Mtr)*.
Spritzweite *f* range *(of a flame thrower)*.
Spruch *m* message *(Tp, Rad)*; call *(Tp)*; sentence, verdict.
Sprühbüchse *f* chemical tank for spray contamination.
Sprühpistole *f* spray gun *(lubrication)*.
Sprühregen *m* drizzle *(Met)*.
Sprung *m* bound, rush *(Tac)*; jump *(Prcht)*; crack, split.
Sprunggelenk *n* hock *(horse)*.
Sprungkombination *f* parachute jump suit.
Sprungturm *m* controlled tower *(Prcht jump Tng)*.
sprungweise by bounds, by rushes.
sprungweises Vorgehen advance by bounds.
Spulensatz *m* set of coils, coil unit *(Rad)*.
Spur *f* trail, path; scent *(for messenger dogs)*; track *(of road)*; gage *(RR)*; trace *(of a tracer bullet)*.
Spürbüchse *f* gas-detector set container.
Spürfähnchen *n* gas-detection flag, gas-warning flag.
Spurgeschoß *n* tracer projectile.
Spürhund *m* tracking dog, bloodhound.
Spürmittel *npl* gas-detection equipment.
Spürpapier *n* gas-detection paper.
Spürpulver *n* gas-detection powder.
Spurpunkt *m* caster-angle vertex *(point at which line through inclined kingpin touches road)* *(MT)*.
Spurstange *f* tie rod *(MT)*.
Spurstangenhebel *m* steering-knuckle arm *(MT)*.
Spurtafel *f* treadway, duckboard *(Bdg)*.
Spurtafelbrücke *f* duckboard treadway bridge.
Spurweite *f* track, tread *(MT)*; gage *(RR)*.
S.-Rolle *f* barbed-wire concertina *(abbr. of* Stacheldraht-Rolle*)*.
SS *f* elite guard of the Nazi party *(originally abbr. of* Schutzstaffeln *but now used as independent term; combat units of SS are known as* Die Waffen-SS, *The SS Armed Forces)*.
SS-Abschnitt *m* SS area. *See also* SS-Oberabschnitt.
SS-Anwärter *m* candidate for rank of SS private.
SS-Brigade *f* SS brigade.
SS-Brigadeführer *m* SS brigadier general.
SS-Führer *m* SS officer.
SS-Gebirgs-Division *f* SS mountain division.
SS-Grenadier *m* SS private *(Inf)*.
SS-Gruppenführer *m* SS major general.
SS-Hauptscharführer *m* SS master sergeant.

SS-Hauptsturmführer *m* SS captain.
SS-Heeres-Flakdivision *f* SS antiaircraft artillery division.
SS-Junker *m* SS cadet *(officer candidate)*.
SS-Junkerschule *f* SS officer training school.
SS-Kanonier *m* SS private *(Arty)*.
SS-Kavallerie *f* SS cavalry.
SS-Kradschützen-Bataillon *n* SS motorcycle battalion.
SS-Kriegsberichter *m* SS war correspondent.
SS-Legionär *m* non-German SS man.
SS-Leibstandarte *f* SS Bodyguard Regiment *(formerly Hitler's bodyguard; increased to approximately division strength in 1943)*.
SS-Mann *m* SS private.
SS-Nachrichtensturm *m* SS communication company.
SS-Oberabschnitt *m* SS region *(corresponds in most cases to a* Wehrkreis *and is composed of 2 or 3* SS-Abschnitte, *SS areas)*.
SS-Oberführer *m* SS brigadier general *(below* SS-Brigadeführer*)*.
SS-Obergruppenführer *m* SS lieutenant general.
SS-Oberscharführer *m* SS first sergeant.
SS-Oberschütze *m* SS private first class.
SS-Oberstgruppenführer *m* SS general.
SS-Obersturmbannführer *m* SS lieutenant colonel.
SS-Obersturmführer *m* SS first lieutenant.
SS-Panzergrenadier *m* SS private *(Armd Inf)*.
SS-Panzergrenadier-Division *f* SS armored infantry division.
SS-Panzergrenadier-Regiment *n* SS armored infantry regiment.
SS-Panzerkorps *n* SS armored corps. *See also* **Germanisches SS-Panzerkorps.**
SS-Panzerjäger-Abteilung *f* SS antitank battalion.
SS-Panzerschütze *m* SS private in armored unit.
SS-Pionier *m* SS engineer.
SS-Pionierbataillon *n* SS engineer battalion.
SS-Pionier-Stoßtrupp *m* SS engineer assault detachment.
SS-PK.-Kriegsberichter *m* SS propaganda-company war correspondent.
SS-Polizei-Bataillon *n* SS police battalion.
SS-Polizei-Division *f* SS police division.
SS-Reiterei *f* SS horse cavalry.
SS-Rottenführer *m* SS corporal.
SS-Scharführer *m* SS staff sergeant.
SS-Schütze *m* SS private, SS rifleman.
SS-Sicherheitsdienst *m* SS security service.
SS-Standarte *f* SS regiment.
SS-Standartenführer *m* SS colonel.
SS-Standartenjunker *m* a graduate from *SS-Junkerschule.*
SS-Sturmbannführer *m* SS major.
SS-Sturmmann *m* SS private first class.
S-Stellung *f* dummy position *(abbr. of* Scheinstellung*)*.
SS-Totenkopf-Verbände *mpl* SS "Death's Head" units *(primarily used as concentration camp guards and for terrorizing missions)*.
SS-Unterscharführer *m* SS sergeant.
SS-Untersturmführer *m* SS second lieutenant.
Staat *m* state, country, power.
Staatsangehörigkeit *f* nationality, citizenship.
Staatsbesitz *m* government property.
Staatsbürger *m* citizen.
Staatspolizei *f See* **Geheime Staatspolizei.**
Stab *m* staff; headquarters; headquarters personnel; bar, rod.
Stabantenne *f* rod antenna, "buggy-whip" antenna *(Rad)*.
Stabbrandbombe *f* stick-type incendiary bomb.
Stäbchenpulver *n* cord powder, strip powder *(Am)*.
Stabilisierungsfläche *f* stabilizing surface *(Ap)*.
Stabilisierungsflügel *m* fin *(bomb)*.
Stabilisierungswulst *m* stabilizer lobe *(Bln)*.
Stabilität *f* stability.
Stabo *f See* **Stachelbombe.**
Stabsapotheker *m* pharmacist official *(ranking as captain)*.
Stabsarzt *m* captain *(Med)*.
Stabsbatterie *f* headquarters battery *(Arty)*.
Stabsbefehl *m* staff order.
Stabschef *m* chief of staff.
Stabsfeldwebel *m* master sergeant, regimental sergeant major.
Stabsgefreiter *m* staff lance corporal *(no US equivalent)*.
Stabshelferin *f* woman clerk auxiliary.
Stabs-Kette *f* headquarters flight *(three planes)*.
Stabskompanie *f* headquarters company.

Stabskraftwagen *m* staff car.
Stabsoffizier *m* field officer *(officer of field grade)*; staff officer *(Nav)*.
Stabsordonnanz *f* headquarters orderly.
Stabsquartier *n* headquarters; officers' quarters.
Stabsschiedsrichter *m* umpire at headquarters of a unit *(maneuvers)*.
Stabsschreiber *m* headquarters clerk.
Stabsveterinär *m* captain *(Vet)*.
Stabswache *f* headquarters guard.
Stabswachtmeister *m* master sergeant, regimental sergeant major *(Arty, Cav)*.
Stabszahlmeister *m* paymaster official *(ranking as captain)*.
Stachelbombe *f* bomb with nose spike.
Stacheldraht *m* barbed wire.
Stacheldrahthindernis *n* barbed-wire obstacle.
Stacheldrahtverhau *m* barbed-wire entanglement.
Stacheldrahtzaun *m* double-apron entanglement *(Ft)*.
Stadtkommandantur *m* garrison, post, or station headquarters in a city or large town; military government headquarters in a city or large town.
Stafetten *fpl* relay messengers.
Staffel *f* echelon *(Tac, Adm)*; squadron *(9 to 12 planes)*; section *(Arty, Cav, supply)*.
Staffelform *f* squadron formation *(Avn)*.
Staffelfront *f* squadron line of flight wedges *(Avn)*.
Staffelführer *m* echelon commander; squadron commander *(Avn)*; section leader or commander *(Arty, Cav, supply)*.
Staffelkapitän *m* squadron commander *(Avn)*.
Staffelkeil *m* squadron wedge formation of flight wedges *(Avn)*.
Staffelkolonne *f* squadron javelin formation *(Avn)*.
Staffellinie *f* squadron line formation *(Avn)*.
Staffeltrupp *m* section personnel *(Cav heavy MG section)*.
Staffelung *f* echelonment; stagger *(Ap wings)*; gun displacement *(Arty)*.
Staffelverband *m* squadron formation *(Avn)*.
staffelweise in echelon, by echelon.
Staffelwinkel *m* squadron V-formation *(Avn)*.
Stahl *m* steel.
Stahlblech *n* sheet steel.
Stahlbrücke *f* steel bridge.
Stahldrahtbeklöppelung *f* steel wire armor *(armored cable)*.
Stahlfederring *m* lockwasher.
Stahlflasche *f* steel flask, steel cylinder, steel tank.
Stahlfutter *n* steel bushing *(breech-block wedge)*.
Stahlgurt *m* metallic link belt *(MG)*.
Stahlhelm *m* steel helmet.
Stahligel *m* steel hedgehog antitank obstacle.
Stahlkerngeschoß *n* steel-core bullet, armor-piercing bullet.
Stahllegierung *f* steel alloy.
Stahlmeßband *n* steel measuring tape.
Stahlplatte *f* steel plate.
Stahlröhre *f* metal tube *(Rad)*.
Stahlschwelle *f* steel plank *(Engr)*; steel tie *(RR)*.
Stahlspurbahn *f(Engr)* steel treadway
Stahlstraße *f* steel landing strip.
Staken *n* punting *(with punt pole)*.
Stalag *n* See **Stammlager**.
Stall *m* stable.
Stallhalfter *f* halter headstall *(harness)*.
Stammannschaft *f* cadre personnel.
Stammeinheit *f* parent unit.
Stammkompanie *f* cadre company *(for replacements)*.
Stammlager *n* permanent prisoner-of-war camp for NCO's and privates, base camp for prisoner-of-war labor detachments *(abbr.* Stalag).
Stammleitung *f* trunk line, trunk circuit *(Tp)*.
Stammrolle *f* personnel roster.
Stammtafel *f* record sheet showing the formations to which a unit has belonged.
Stammtruppe *f* cadre.
Stammtruppenteil *m* parent unit.
Stampfwinkel *m* angle of pitch *(Ap)*.
Stand *m* status, state, occupation; position, station *(of crew members) (Ap, Tk, Nav)*; gun position.
Standarte *f* standard; guidon *(Arty, Cav, Armd Comd)*. See also SS-**Standarte**.
Standartenführer *m* See SS-Standartenführer.
Standartenträger *m* guidon *(Pers)*.
Stander *m* pennant.
Ständer *m* bracket, mount, support, stand, pedestal.
Standgericht *n* summary court-martial.
ständig constant, fixed.
ständige Befestigung permanent fortification.
ständige Belastung basic load *(Avn)*.
Standlinie *f* base line *(Surv)*; line of position *(Navigation)*.
Standmotor *m* upright engine.
Standort *m* post, garrison, station; position *(Surv, Navigation)*.
gekoppelter Standort dead-reckoning position *(Air Navigation)*.
Standortältester *m* garrison, post, or station commander.
Standortarzt *m* station surgeon.
Standortkommandantur *f* garrison, post, or station headquarters.
Standortlazarett *n* post hospital, station hospital.
Standortlohnstelle *f* army post pay office.
Standortmeldung *f* position report *(Air Navigation)*.
Standort-Pferdelazarett *n* veterinary station hospital.
Standortwachdienst *m* interior guard duty.
Standrecht *n* martial law.
Standsack *m* hand-grenade bag.
Standsicherheit *f* stability; steadiness *(of mobile gun mount, vehicle, etc.)*.
Standvisier *n* battle sight *(R)*.
Stange *f* pole, post, pillar, bar, rod, spar.
Stangenbau *m* line construction on poles *(Tp)*.
Stangenbild *n* pole-location diagram *(Tp)*.
Stangenbock *m* spar trestle *(Bdg)*.
Stangenhandpferd *n* off horse of wheel team.
Stangenpferde *npl* wheel team.
Stangenvisier *n* pillar-type rear sight *(MG)*.
Stangenvisiereinrichtung *f* MG sights *(blade front sight and pillar-type rear sight)*.
Stanze *f* die *(for stamping or punching)*.
Stapel *m* pile *(regular heap)*; dump; crib *(Bdg)*; launching cradle.
Stapellauf *m* launching *(Nav)*.
Stärke *f* strength.
Stärkebestand *m* actual strength.
Stärkenachweisung *f* table of organization; strength return, strength report.
Starkstrom *m* high voltage *(current)*.
Starkstromleitung *f(Elec)* power line
Starkstromsperre *f* electrified obstacle, high-tension obstacle.
starr stiff, fixed, rigid.
starre Kanone fixed gun *(Ap)*.
starres Luftschiff rigid airship.
starres Maschinengewehr fixed machine gun.
Start *m* take-off *(Avn)*; take-off point *(Adrm)*.
Startbahn *f* runway.
Startbereitschaft *f(Avn)* ground alert
Startdruck *m* propeller thrust at take-off *(Avn)*.
starten to start, to take off.
Starterbatterie *f(MT)* starter battery
Starterklappe *f* choke *(Mtr)*.
Startflagge *f* starter flag *(Avn)*.
Startkatapult *m* catapult *(Avn)*.
startklar ready for take-off *(Avn)*.
Startlänge *f* take-off distance *(Avn)*.
Startleistung *f* power output of engine at take-off *(Avn)*.
Startschiene *f* track *(catapult)*.
Startseil *n* towline *(glider)*.
Startstelle *f* take-off point *(Adrm)*.
Startvorrichtung *f* launching device *(Avn)*; starting device *(Mtr)*.
Startzone *f* take-off zone *(Adrm)*.
statische Berechnung stress analysis.
Stativ *n* tripod, stand.
Statoskop *n* rate-of-climb indicator, climb-and-dive indicator *(Ap)*.
Stau *m* indicated air speed *(Avn)*.
Stauanlage *f* dam.
Staub *m* dust.
Staubdeckel *m* dust cover *(Ord)*.
Stäubchen *n* cloud particle, dust particle *(CWS)*.
Staubmaske *f* respirator, dust-filtering mask.
Staubschutzdeckel *m(Ord)* dust cover
Staubschutzgerät *n* respirator.
Staubschutzmaske *f* See **Staubmaske**.
Stauchlafette *f* telescopic carriage, retractable gun mount.
Staudamm *m* storage dam.
Staudruck *m* dynamic pressure, velocity pressure.
Staudruckfahrtmesser *m* pitot tube.
stauen to stow; to dam up.
Stauer *m* stevedore.
Staufläche *f* area of dammed water.
Stauhöhe *f* height of upstream water.
Stausee *m* reservoir.
Stauwehr *n* weir.
Stecher *m* hair trigger *(SA)*.
Stechruder *n* paddle.
Stechschritt *m* goose step.
Stechzirkel *m* dividers.
Steckdose *f* jack, receptacle, socket.
Stecker *m* plug *(Elec)*.
Steckerstift *m* plug prong *(Elec)*.
Steckmast *m* sectional antenna mast.
Stecknadel *f* pin, plain pin.
Steckschlüssel *m* socket wrench; ignition key.
Steg *m* footbridge, footpath; web *(of girder, etc.)*.
Stegblech *n* web *(of girder, etc.)*.
stehender Spähtrupp stationary patrol.
stehendes Heer standing army.
stehendes Ziel stationary target.
steifer Wind high wind.
Steigbö *f* ascending gust *(Met)*.
Steigbügel *m* stirrup.
Steigeisen *npl* ice creepers; climbers *(Sig C)*.
steigen to climb.
Steigerung *f* intensification, increase.
Steigfähigkeit *f* grade-ascending ability *(vehicles)*; climbing ability *(Ap)*.
Steigflug *m* climb *(Avn)*.
Steighöhe *f* height of rise *(ground signal)*; altitude, ceiling *(Ap)*.
Steigleistung *f* rate of climb *(Avn)*.
Steigriemen *m* stirrup strap.
Steigung *f* gradient, grade, slope; pitch *(Mech.)*
Steigungswinkel *m* blade angle *(propeller)*; gradient angle.
Steigvermögen *(Ap)* climbing ability
Steigzeit *f* rate of climb *(Ap)*.
steil steep.
Steilfeuer *n* high-angle fire.
Steilfeuergeschütz *n* high-angle gun.
Steilfeuerwaffe *f* high-angle weapon.
Steilhang *m* steep slope, steep grade.
Steilheit *f* steepness; transconductance, mutual conductance *(Rad)*.
Steilkurve *(Avn)* steep banked turn
Steinbruch *m* quarry.
Steinflachs *m* asbestos.
Steinkohle *f* anthracite coal.
Steinschlag *m* broken stone, rubble; rock slide.
Steinschotter *m* road metal, broken stone.
Stellbecher *m* mouth of fuze setter.
Stelle *f* point, post, site, station.
Stellmarke *f* index, micrometer index *(Optics)*.
Stellmutter *f* lock nut, regulating nut, adjusting nut.
Stellring *m* adjusting ring *(fuze)*.
Stellschlüssel *m* fuze wrench; adjusting wrench.
Stellschraube *f* set screw, regulating screw, adjusting screw.
Stellung *f* position, emplacement.
Stellungnahme *f* commentary *(Tac)*; expression of opinion.
Stellungsabschnitt *m* sector of occupied position.
Stellungsbau *m* construction of field fortifications.
Stellungskampf *m* position warfare, combat from fortified positions.
Stellungskrieg *m* war of position, position warfare.
Stellungsmeßblatt *n* battery survey chart.
Stellungsunterschied *m* perpendicular distance between two parallel lines of sight *(such as that between the line: base point—aiming circle and the line parallel to it running through the base piece)*.
Stellungswechsel *m* change of position *(Tac)*; gun displacement *(Arty)*.
stellvertretend acting, deputy *(adj)*.
Stellvertretender Chef des Generalstabes Deputy Chief of Staff.
stellvertretender Führer second-in-command.
Stellvertreter *m* deputy; substitute.
Stellwerk *n* switch tower, switch control room *(RR)*.
Stempel *m* stamp, seal; punch *(Tech)*.
Stempelkissen *n* stamp pad.
Stempelplatte *f* inspection-mark plate *(R)*.
Sterbegeld *n* gratuity upon death.
Sternbild *n* constellation.
Sternbündel *n* star cluster *(signal)*.
Sternmotor *m* radial engine.
Sternplatte *f* multiple-connection plate *(stadia rod)*.
Sternschaltung *f* Y-connection *(Elec)*.
Sternsignal *n* signal flare.
Sternverkehr *m* "star" traffic *(radio net traffic in which several stations communicate only one at a time with the net control station, the other stations listening in)*.
Sternwarte *f* observatory.
stetig constant, steady, uniform, continuous.
Steuer *n* control, steering wheel.
Steuer *f* tax.
Steuerbord *m* starboard.
Steuerfläche *f* control surface *(Ap)*; stabilizing fin *(Mort shell)*.
Steuerflügel *m* stabilizing fin *(bomb)*.
Steuergitter *n* control grid *(Rad tube)*.
Steuerhebel *m* elevator control lever *(Ap)*.
Steuerknüppel *m* control stick *(Ap)*.
Steuerkompaß *m* steering compass.
Steuerkurs *m* heading *(Air Navigation)*.
steuern steer, control.
Steuerorgane *npl* controls *(Ap)*.
Steuerrad *n* control wheel *(Ap)*; steering wheel *(MT)*; timing gear *(Mtr)*.
Steuerröhre *f* master oscillator tube *(Rad)*.
Steuerruder *n* rudder *(ship)*.

Stammr	Stammrolle	register of recruits; name roll *(of a formation)*
Stand	Standarte	standard; regiment of Storm Troopers
Stand.F	Standartenführer	(SA) regimental leader, Storm Troops *(equivalent* (SS) regimental commander, Elite Guard *(equivalent U. S. rank: colonel)*
Stand.Ger	Standgericht	court martial
Standorta	Standortarzt	garrison medical officer
Standortlaz	Standortlazarett	garrison hospital
Standr	Standrecht	martial law
standr	standrechtlich	by martial law
St.Angeh	Staatsangehöriger	citizen; subject of a state
St.Angeh	Staatsangehörigkeit	citizenship; nationality
Stap	Stapel	staple; dump
Stapellg	Stapellegung	laying of the keel
St.Apoth	Stabsapotheker	captain *(Pharmacy)*
St.Art	Stellungsartillerie	artillery in permanent emplacements
StaStr	Starkstrom	high voltage
St.B	Stammbatterie	cadre battery
stB	stenographischer Bericht	shorthand report
Stb.Ä	Stubenältester	man in charge of barracks room
St.Batt	Stabsbatterie	headquarters battery
St.Bef	Stabsbefehl	administrative order; headquarters order
Stbr	Steinbruch	quarry
Stbs	Stabs-	staff; headquarters
Stbstr	Stabstrompeter	leader of trumpeter-corps *(cavalry)*
StbsW	Stabswache	headquarters company
St.Ch	Stabschef	(SA) Chief of Staff, Storm Troops *(equivalent U. S. rank; general)*
Stck	Stück	piece; part
Std	Stunde	hour
/Std	in der Stunde	per hour
stdg	ständig	permanent
Std./Geschw	Stundengeschwindigkeit	speed per hour
Stdkm	Stundenkilometer	kilometers per hour
Std.L	Standlinie	radio base line *(air navigation)*
stdl	stündlich	hourly
Stdort	Standort	garrison; station
Stdort-Vet	Standortveterinär	garrison veterinary officer
St.Dr	Stacheldraht	barbed wire
Std/sm	Seemeilen in der Stunde	knots per hour
St.D.V	Standortdienstvorschrift	manual on garrison duty
steh.H	stehendes Heer	standing army
Steig	Steigerung	increase; augmentation
Steig	Steigung	gradient; ascent; rise; pitch *(aviation)*; incline
Steigb	Steigbügel	stirrup
Steigg	Steiggeschwindigkeit	climbing speed; rate of climb
Steilf	Steilfeuer	high-angle fire
Steilf.Gesch	Steilfeuergeschütz	high-angle gun
Steilh	Steilhang	steep bank; precipice
Steinbr	Steinbruch	quarry
St.Eis	Steigeisen	climbing iron
Stell	Stellung	position; emplacement; line; setting; station; post; rank; attitude
Stell.Div	Stellungsdivision	front-line division; division in line
Stell.Kr	Stellungskrieg	war of position
Stellv	Stellvertreter	deputy
stellv.K.A	stellvertretender Korpsarzt	deputy corps area surgeon
St.Ent	Sturmentfernung	assault distance
Sterbl.Z	Sterblichkeitsziffer	mortality rate
St.F	Staffelführer	squadron leader (aviation officer)
St.F	Störungsfeuer	harassing fire *(artillery)*; strafing
Stffstb	Staffelstab	divisional train command
Stfl	Stabsflagge	staff flag
stfr	sturmfrei	unassailable (well-fortified against surprise attack)
St.Fu.St	Standortfunkstelle	garrison radio station
Stg	Stahlring	ring of steel
stg	steigend	climbing; rising
Stg	Stellung	position; emplacement; line; setting; station; post; rank; attitude
Stg.Aufs	Stangenaufsatz	tangent sight; bar sight
St.G.B	Strafgesetzbuch	penal code
St.Gefr	Stabsgefreiter	*(corresponds roughly to U. S. acting corporal)*
St.Gr	Standesgrade	grade
Stg.Vis	Stangenvisier	tangent sight; bar sight
Sthg	Stielhandgranate	stick hand grenade; "potato masher"
Stichpr	Stichprobe	spot check; sample at random
Stickst	Stickstoff	nitrogen
Stielhgr	Stielhandgranate	stick hand grenade; "potato masher"
ST K	schnelle Kavallerietruppen	mobile troops *(cavalry)*

St.K	Staffelkeil	squadron wedge (*aviation*)
St.K	Strassenkommandantur	road traffic control headquarters
St.K	Streitkräfte	combat forces
Stkm	Stundenkilometer	kilometers per hour
St.Kn	Steuerknüppel	joy stick (*airplane*); control column
St.Kol	Staffelkolonne	squadron column (*aviation*)
St.Kol	Sturmkolonne	assault echelon
St.Kp	Stabskompanie	headquarters company
St.Kpf	Stellungskampf	position warfare
St.Kr	Stellungskrieg	war of position
Stllv	Stellvertreter	deputy
St.Ltg	Stammleitung	trunk line (*communications*)
Stm	Sturmmann	(SA) Storm Trooper (*equivalent U. S. private first class*)
St.N	Stärkenachweisung	statement of actual strength
StO	Stabsoffizier	staff officer; field officer
St.O	Standort	garrison; station
St.O.Ä	Standortältester	garrison commander
StOArt	Stabsoffizier der Artillerie	staff officer for artillery
Stofahr	Stabsoffizier der Fahrtruppen	staff officer for horsedrawn supply troops
Stoffgl	Stoffgliederung	classification
St.Offz	Stabsoffizier	staff officer; field officer
Stokraft	Stabsoffizier der Kraftfahrtruppen	staff officer for motor transport troops,
St.O.Laz	Standortlazarett	garrison hospital
Stona	Stabsoffizier der Nach-	staff officer for signal troops
St.O.Pf	Standortpfarrer	garrison chaplain
St.O.Pi	Stabsoffizier der Pioniere	staff officer combat engineers
St.O.V	Standortverwaltung	garrison administration
St.Oz	Stiller Ozean	Pacific Ocean
St.P	Stützpunkt	strong point; base
st.Patr	stehende Patrouille	fixed patrol
St.Pers	Stammpersonal	cadre
St.Pl	Stapelplatz	dump; depot
Stpl	Stempel	stamp
St.PS	Steuerpferdestärken	taxable horse power (*motor*)
St.P.W	Stabspackwagen	headquarters baggage-wagon
ST Pz	schnelle Panzertruppen	mobile troops (*panzer*)
St.Q	Stabsquartier	headquarters
St.R	Stammrolle	register of recruits; nominal roll (*of a formation*)
Str	Steuer	rudder; tax; helm controls
str	strafen	to punish
Str	Strand	shore; beach; coast
Str	Strasse	street
str	strategisch	strategic
Str	Strebe	stay; brace; strut; support (*airplane construction*)
Str	Streife	party; patrol; raiding
Str	Streifen	band; strip; sector; lane
str	streitbar	fit for fighting; warlike; valiant
Str	Streitkräfte	fighting forces
str	streng	severe; strict; stern; harsh
str	streuen	search and traverse
Str	Strom	current; stream; river
Str.A	Strafanstalt	prison; jail; penitentiary
Straf.Anst	Strafanstalt	prison; jail; penitentiary (*on*
Strassb	Strassenbahn	street car
Str	Stratosphäre	stratosphere
strat.B	strategische (Eisen-) Bahn	strategic railroad
Strat.Ball	Stratosphärenballon	stratosphere balloon
Strat.Flgz	Stratosphärenflugzeug	stratosphere plane
strat.L	strategische Linie	strategic line
strat.P	strategischer Punkt	strategic point
strat.Pl	strategischer Plan	strategic plan
strat.Z	strategisches Ziel	strategic objective
Str.-B	Strassenbahn	street car
Str.B	Strassenbau	road construction
StrBef	Strafbefehl	sentence (*by lower court*)
StrBesch	Strafbescheid	sentence (*by government*)
Str.B.Kp	Strassenbaukompanie	road construction company
Strd	Strand	coast
Strd:Bttr	Strandbatterie	shore battery (*coast artillery*)
Streuf	Streufeuer	combined traversing and searching fire (*artillery*)
Str.F	Streufeuer	combined traversing and searching fire (*artillery*)
strf	sturmreif	softened up for assault
Strg	Streuung	dispersion (*ballistics*)
St.Riem	Sturmriemen	chin strap (*of steel helmet*)
Str.Korps	Streifkorps	raiding force; combined unit for patrolling duties
Str.Kr	Strassenkreuzung	street intersection
Str.Kr	Streitkräfte	fighting forces
Str.N	Strassennetz	road network; road system
Str.P.O	Strafprozessordnung	criminal code
Str.Pzkw	Strassenpanzerkraftwagen	armored scout car
Str.Pzkw.Kp	Strassenpanzerkraftwagenkompanie	armored scout-car company
Str.Pzkw.Zg	Strassenpanzerkraftwagenzug	armored scout-car platoon
StrR	Strafrecht	penal law
Str.Sp	Strassenspinne	road junction
Str.Spr	Strassensperre	barricade

Steuersack *m* rudder lobe (*Bln*).
Steuersäule *f* control column (*Ap*); steering column (*MT*).
Steuersender *m* master oscillator (*Rad*).
Steuerstrich *m* lubber line (*Ap com pass*)
Steuerstufe *f* master oscillator stage (*Rad*).
Steuerung *f* controls (*Ap*); timing, synchronization (*Mtr*); steering system (*MT*).
Steuerwelle *f* control shaft (*Ap*); camshaft (*Mtr*).
Steven *m* stem or stern (*Nav*).
Stich *m* thrust, stab; stitch; bite, sting; hitch, knot.
Sticheisen *n* cutting spade (*Engr*).
Stichgleis *n* firing spur (*RR Arty*).
Stichprobe *f* sample taken at random.
Stichwaffe *f* thrusting weapon.
Stichwort *n* cue; catchword; code word.
Stichzähler *m* tachometer (*Ap*).
Stickstoff *m* nitrogen.
Stickstofflost *n* nitrogen mustard gas.
Stiefel *m* boot.
Stiefelschaft *m* leg of boot.
Stiel *m* strut (*Ap*); spar, compression member (*Bdg*); handle, holder; stick.
Stielgranate *f* See Stielhandgranate.
Stielhandgranate *f* stick hand grenade, "potato-masher" hand grenade.
Stift *m* brad, holder, pin, prong, peg, tack.
"Stillgesessen!" "Attention!" (*mounted drill*).
"Stillgestanden!" "Attention!" (*dismounted drill*).
Stimmung *f* morale, mood, atmosphere.
Stirn *f* forehead.
Stirnangriff *m* frontal attack.
Stirnansicht *f* bow-on view (*Tk*); front view.
Stirnband *n* forehead strap (*gas mask*).
Stirnfläche *f* frontal area.
Stirnpanzer *m* front armor.
Stirnrad *n* spur gear.
Stirnriemen *m* brow band (*harness*).
Stirnschattenriß *m* bow-on silhouette (*practice target*).
Stirnseite *f* front (*Tk*).
Stirnwiderstand *m* head resistance.
Stirnwind *m* headwind.
Stock *m* cleaning rod (*R*); stick, baton, picket, pole; floor, story.
Stockmine *f* antipersonnel pickettype mine; stake mine (*concrete antipersonnel mine*).
Stockung *f* block, jam, stoppage.
Stoff *m* fabric, material, substance.
Stoffbahn *f* panel, canopy (*Prcht*).
Stoffbespannung *f* (*Ap*) fabric covering
Stoffgliederung *f* classification of equipment.
Stoffgurt *m* web belt.
Stollen *m* tunnel (*Engr*).
Stolperdraht *m* trip wire.
Stolperdrahtfeld *n* field of trip-wire obstacles.
Stolperdrahthindernis *n* trip-wire entanglement.
Stolperdrahtmine *f* trip-wire mine.
stolpern to trip.
Stopfbüchse *f* gland; stuffing box (*Mech*).
"Stopfen!" "Suspend firing!" *See also* **"Feuerpause!"**
stoppen to stop; to time with a stop watch.
Stoppuhr *f* time interval recorder, stop watch.
Stopp- und Schlußlicht *n* stop and taillight (*MT*).
Stoppzeit *f* time interval, time difference, time lag (*FR*); sound travel time (*SR*).
Stöpsel *m* plug (*Tp*); stopper.
stöpseln to plug in (*Rad, Tp*).
Störangriff *m* nuisance raid.
Storch *m* a German liaison airplane.
Storchschnabel *m* pantograph.
Störeinsatz *m* nuisance raid (*Avn*).
stören harass (*Tac*); jam, interfere (*Rad*).
Störflieger *m* nuisance raider; sneak raider (*Avn*).
Störflug *m* nuisance raid (*Avn*).
Störflugzeug *n* nuisance raider (*Ap*).
Störfrequenz *f* interfering frequency, undesired frequency (*Rad*).
Störfunkstelle (*Rad*) jamming station
Störgeräusch *n* static, interference (*Rad*).
Störschutz *m* radio noise suppressor.
Störstelle *f* See Störfunkstelle.
Störung *f* disturbance, annoyance; interference, static, jamming (*Rad*); stoppage (*MG*); breakdown.
Störungsdienst *m* trouble-shooting service, maintenance service.
Störungsfeuer *n* harassing fire (*Arty*).
Störungsflug *m* nuisance raid.
Störungssucher *m* trouble shooter, maintenance man (*Tp*).
Störungssuchtrupp *m* wire patrol (*field Tp*).
Stoß *m* thrust, lunge, shock, kick, blow, push; burst (*MG fire*).
Stoßarmee *f* main-attack army.

Stoßbalken *m* abutment beam (*Bdg*).
Stoßboden *m* breechblock (*Ord*); diaphragm (*shrapnel*).
Stoßbohle *f* end dam (*Bdg*).
Stoßdämpfer *m* (*MT*) shock absorber
Stößel *m* valve lifter (*Mtr*); rammer (*fuze*).
Stößelführung *f* valve-lifter guide (*Mtr*).
Stößelschraube *f* valve-lifter adjusting nut (*Mtr*).
stoßempfindlich sensitive to shock (*explosives*).
stoßen to push, thrust, lunge, strike.
Stoßfänger *m* bumper (*MT*).
Stoßkappenmine *f* contact mine (*Nav*).
Stoßkeil *m* spearhead (*Tac*).
Stoßkraft *f* shock power, striking power.
Stoßlinie *f* thrust line, line of attack (*Tac*).
Stoßmine *f* contact mine (*Nav*).
Stoßrad *n* (*Tk*) shock-absorber wheel
Stoßreserve *f* local supports in assault (*Tac*).
Stoßscheibe *f* diaphragm (*shrapnel*); lock washer (*for wheel bearing*).
stoßsicher insensitive to shock (*explosives*).
Stoßstange *f* push rod; bumper.
Stoßtrupp *m* combat patrol, assault detachment.
Stoßtruppen *fpl* shock troops, assault troops.
Stoßtruppspioniere *mpl* assault engineers.
Stoßtruppunternehmung *f* (*Tac*) raid
Stoßwaffe *f* thrusting weapon.
stoßweises Feuer intermittent fire, interrupted fire, fire by bursts or volleys.
Stoßzündung *f* contact fire (*Nav*).
Strafbuch *n* punishment book.
Strafdienst *m* extra duty.
Strafe *f* punishment.
Straffeuer *n* retaliation fire.
Strahl *m* ray, beam (*of light, etc.*); jet, squirt (*of a liquid, etc.*); frog (*of hoof*).
Strahldrehung *f* rotation of the slipstream (*propeller*).
Strahlenzieher *m* protractor.
Strahlung *f* radiation.
Strahlungsablenkung *f* radio wave deflection.
Strand *m* beach, shore.
Strang *m* strand, rope, strap.
Stranglaufe *f* lazy strap (*harness*).
Strangträger *m* See Stranglaufe.
Straße *f* street, road, highway, route.
Straßenbaubataillon *n* road-construction battalion.
Straßenbaudienst *m* road-construction and maintenance service.
Straßenbiegung *f* road curve, road bend.
Straßendamm *m* causeway, embanked road.
Straßendecke *f* road surface.
Straßendisziplin *f* road discipline.
Straßendreieck *n* triangular road junction.
Straßeneinmündung *f* side road joining main highway.
Straßen-Entgiftungsabteilung *f* road decontamination battalion.
Straßengabel *f* road fork.
straßengängig roadbound.
Straßengraben *m* road ditch.
Straßenkampf *m* street fighting.
Straßenknie *n* V-turn (*road*).
Straßenknotenpunkt *m* road intersection, road junction, road center.
Straßenkommandant *m* traffic control officer.
Straßenkommandantur *f* area road traffic control headquarters.
Straßenkreuzung *f* crossroads, intersection.
Straßennetz *n* road net.
Straßensperre *f* road block.
Straßenspinne *f* multiple road junction.
Straßensprengung *f* road demolition.
Straßenstreife *f* street patrol.
Straßenüberführung *f* overpass.
Straßenunterführung *f* underpass.
Straßenverhältnisse *npl* road conditions.
Straßenwalze *f* road roller.
Straßenzucht *f* road discipline.
Stratege *m* strategist.
Strategie *f* strategy.
strategisch strategic.
strategische Einheit large unit (*USA: Div and up; Ger: corps and up*).
strategischer Rückzug strategic withdrawal.
Strauch *m* bush, shrub.
Strauchbündel *n* fascine.
Strauchdamm *m* fascine road, brush road.
Strauchmaske *f* shrubbery screen, brushwood screen (*Cam*).
Strauchpackung *f* See Strauchwerk.
Strauchwerk *n* brushwork.
Strauchwerkbekleidung *f* fascine revetment.
Strebe *f* diagonal strut (*Ap*); brace, tension member (*Bdg*).

Streckbalken *m* stringer (*Bdg*).
Strecke *f* span, bay, section (*Bdg*); stretch, length, distance; leg (*of a route*).
Streckenfeuer *n* course light, airway beacon.
Streckenzug *m* traverse (*Surv*).
Streich *m* cut, slash; coup; blow; trick.
streichen cross out, strike out, eliminate; strike (*a flag*); to back water.
Streichholz *n* match.
Streifabteilung *f* raiding party.
Streife *f* patrol, raiding party; guard sentinel (*guard duty*).
Streifen *m* band, strip, belt, sector.
streifen to patrol, reconnoiter; to graze.
Streifenplan *m* diagram of patrol posts.
Streifenweg *m* patrol post.
Streifkommando *n* raiding party.
streitig machen to contest.
Streubrandbombe *f* scatter bomb.
streuen to cover with zone fire (*Arty*); to cover with searching and traversing fire (*MG*); to strew, scatter; to be erratic, to have dispersion (*G*).
Streufeuer *n* zone fire (*Arty*); searching and traversing fire (*MG*).
Streukegel *m* sheaf of fire, cone of dispersion, cone of fire.
Streumine *f* uncontrolled mine; stray mine (*not laid according to regular pattern*).
Streuschießen *n* zone fire (*Gunnery*).
Streutrommel *f* sprinkler drum or cart (*for ground decontamination*).
Streuung *f* dispersion (*Ballistics*).
Streuungsbereich *m* zone of dispersion (*Ballistics*).
Streuungsbild *n* dispersion diagram (*Ballistics*).
Streuungsfeuer *n* See Streufeuer.
Streuungsfläche *f* dispersion area (*Ballistics*).
Streuungsgarbe *f* See Streukegel.
Strich *m* artillery mil; stroke, line; dash (*Tg*); point (*of compass*); graduation, index line.
Stricheinteilung *f* graduation (*specifically, mil graduation*).
Strichfeuer *n* grazing fire (*MG*).
Strichmaß *n* marking gage.
Strichplatte *f* graduated range plate (*MG mount*); reticle (*Optics*).
Strick *m* rope, cord.
Strickjacke *f* knitted sweater (*Clo*).
Strickleiter *f* rope ladder.
Striegel *m* currycomb.
Stroboskop *n* stroboscope; protectoscope (*based on stroboscope principle*) (*Tk*).
Stroh *n* straw.
Strohpuppe *f* dummy (*Tng*).
Strom *m* current (*Elec*); stream, river.
Stromaggregat *n* generating unit.
Stromanker *m* (*Bdg*) upstream anchor
Stromaufnahme *f* current draw (*Elec*).
Strombord *m* offshore side.
Stromerzeuger *m* generator (*Elec*).
Stromfahrzeug *n* river craft (*Pon, assault boat, etc.*).
Stromfluß *m* current flow (*Elec*).
Stromform *f* See Stromlinienform.
Stromgeschwindigkeit *f* speed of current.
Stromkreis *m* circuit (*Elec*).
Stromleine *f* upstream tension line (*Bdg*).
Stromlinienform *f* streamline shape.
Strommesser *m* ammeter.
Strommeßgerät *n* current measuring instrument (*Elec*).
Stromquelle *f* source of current (*Elec*); power source (*Rad*).
Stromschiene *f* live rail, third rail (*RR*); bus bar (*Elec*).
Stromsicherungsbataillon *n* electric cable maintenance battalion.
Stromstärke *f* amperage.
Stromstoß *m* current impulse, current surge (*Elec*).
Stromstrich *m* course of current (*line joining points of greatest surface speed of a river current*).
Strömung *f* current, flow.
Strömungslehre *f* fluid mechanics.
Stromunterbrecher *m* circuit breaker
Stromverbraucher *m* outlet, current consumer (*Elec*).
Stromzufuhr *f* current supply, power supply (*Elec*).
Strumpf *m* stocking.
Stubenältester *m* barracks leader, squad-room leader.
Stubenarrest *m* arrest in quarters.
Stufe *f* stage, step; muzzle-velocity correction value (*Ballistics*).
Stufeneinheit *f* See Grundstufe.
Stufenfallschirm *m* lobe parachute.
Stufenformation *f* stepped-up (or stepped-down) formation (*Avn*).
Stufenlader *m* multistage supercharger.
Stufensender *m* multistage transmitter.
Stufung *f* step-up (-down) distance, staggering, stagger distance (*formation flying*).

Stuhl *m* chair; excrement, feces.
Stuka *n* dive bomber *(abbr. of* Sturzkampfflugzeug).
Stukaangriff *m* dive-bombing attack.
Stukabremse *f* diving brake *(Ap)*.
Stukaflieger *m* dive-bomber pilot.
Stumpf *m* stump.
stumpf *adj* blunt, dull; worn out; obtuse.
stumpfer Winkel obtuse angle.
Stundenwinkel *m* hour angle.
Sturm *m* assault, onrush, onslaught; storm; an SS company.
Sturmabteilung *f* storm trooper detachment of Nazi party *(abbr.* SA).
Sturmabteilungsmann *m* storm trooper.
Sturmabzeichen *n* assault badge *(decoration)*.
Sturmangriff *m* assault, onrush, onslaught.
Sturmartillerie *f* assault artillery.
Sturmausgangsstellung *f* assault position, jump-off position.
Sturmbann *m* SS or SA battalion.
Sturmbannführer *m* *See* **SS-Sturmbannführer.**
Sturmbataillon *n* assault battalion, shock battalion.
Sturmboot *n* assault boat.
Sturmbootkommando *n* assault boat detachment.
Sturmdivision *f* assault division *(honorary title for division with reduced Inf Pers and heavy firepower)*.
stürmen to assault, storm, rush.
Sturmgasse *f* assault gap *(through obstacles)*.
Sturmgepäck *n* light equipment carried in assault *(as distinguished from field pack)*.
Sturmgeschütz *n* assault gun *(self-propelled)*.
Sturmgeschützabteilung *f* assault-gun battalion.
Sturmgeschützbatterie *f* assault-gun battery.
Sturmgeschützführer *m* assault-gun commander.
Sturmhaubitze *f* assault howitzer *(self-propelled)*.
Sturmkanone *f* assault gun *(self-propelled)*.
Sturmleiter *f* scaling ladder.
Sturmlücke *f* assault gap.
Sturmpanzer *m* assault tank.
Sturmpionier *m* combat engineer.
Sturmregiment *n* airborne assault regiment.
Sturmreifmachung *f* "softening up" *(by bombing or Arty fire)*.
Sturmreifschießen *n* artillery preparation, "softening up."
Sturmriemen *m* chin strap *(headgear)*.
Sturmschritt *m* fast run.
Sturmtrupp *m* assault detachment.
Sturmwelle *f* assault wave *(Tac)*.
Sturmwind *m* gale.
Sturz *m* plunge, dive, fall; camber, caster *(MT)*.
Sturzangriff *m* diving attack *(Avn)*.
Sturzbett *n* streambed at downstream base of dam.
Sturzbomben *n* dive bombing.
stürzen to dive, crash, plunge; to rush, assault; to fall.
Sturzflug *m* dive.
Sturzflug-Automatik *f* automatic dive control *(Ap)*.
Sturzflugbremse *f* diving brake *(Ap)*.
Sturzflug mit Endgeschwindigkeit terminal velocity dive *(Avn)*.
Sturzgeschwindigkeit *f* diving speed *(Ap)*.
Sturzhelm *m* crash helmet.
Sturzkampfflieger *m* dive-bomber pilot.
Sturzkampfflugzeug *n* dive bomber *(abbr.* Stuka).
Sturzkampfgeschwader *n* wing of dive bombers *(Avn)*.
Sturzsirene *f* dive siren *(dive bomber)*.
Sturzspirale *f* spiral dive *(Avn)*.
Sturzvisier *n* dive-bombing sight *(Avn)*.
Sturzwehr *n* spillway weir.
Sturzwinkel *m* angle of dive, diving angle *(Avn)*.
Stütze *f* support, prop.
Stützflosse *f* inboard stabilizing float *(seaplane)*.
Stützpunkt *m* organized tactical locality, strong point; base; point of support *(structures)*.
Stützpunktschiff *n* aircraft tender.
Stützrolle *f* track-supporting roller *(Tk)*.
Stützschwimmer *m* fixed wing float *(flying boat)*.
Stützweite *f* span between supports *(Bdg)*.
Stuvi *n* dive-bombing sight *(abbr. for* Sturzvisier).
Suchanker *m* grapnel.
suchen to search.
Sucher *m* spotlight *(MT)*; view finder *(Optics)*.
Sucherde *f* ground detector for telephone interception.
Sucherfernrohr *n* finder telescope *(height finder)*.
Suchgerätsempfänger *m* search receiver *(Ap, Rad)*.
Süden *m* south.
Summer *m* buzzer.
Summeranruf *m* buzzer signal *(Tp)*.
Summerknopf *m* buzzer button *(Tp)*.
Summerzusatz *m* buzzer set *(Tp)*.
Sumpf *m* marsh, swamp, bog.
Sumpffieber *n* malaria.
Synchrongetriebe *n* synchro-mesh transmission *(MT)*.
Synchronisator *m* impulse generator mechanism *(Ap)*.

T

Tabelle *f* chart.
Tabellenzeichner *m* cartographer.
Tachodynamo *m* generator voltmeter tachometer *(AA gun)*.
Tachograph *m* speedometer combined with odometer *(MT)*.
Tafel *f* table; list; chart, diagram; blackboard.
Tagebuch *n* log book, diary, journal.
Tagegeld *n* per diem allowance.
Tagesanbruch *m* daybreak.
Tagesangriff *m* daylight attack; daylight raid *(Avn)*.
Tagesbefehl *m* order of the day; special orders.
Tageseinflüsse *mpl* ballistic density and wind factors.
Tageskilometerzähler *m* trip mileage odometer *(speedometer)*.
Tageskost *f* day's rations, food for one day.
Tagesmarsch *m* day's march.
Tagesrate *f* basic load *(Am)*.
Tagessatz *m* daily scale or quantity; daily ration quantity.
Tagestiefangriff *m* daylight low-level attack *(Avn)*.
Tagesverpflegung *f* daily ration.
Tagesversorgung *f* daily automatic supply.
Tagesvorstoß *m* daylight raid, daylight thrust or advance.
Tagesziel *n* day's objective, day's destination; target of the day.
Tagjagd *f* daylight pursuit, daylight fighting, daylight interception *(Avn)*.
Tagmarsch *m* day march.
Takt *m* stroke *(Mtr)*.
Taktfeuer *n* blinker light.
Taktik *f* tactics.
Taktiker *m* tactician.
taktisch tactical.
taktische Feuerbegriffe tactical fire classification *(Arty)*.
taktische Unterstützung direct support *(Avn, Tac)*.
taktischer Einsatz tactical employment.
taktischer Verband tactical unit.
taktisches Hindernis tactical obstacle.
taktisches Zeichen tactical symbol.
Tal *n* valley.
Talnebel *m* ground fog *(Met)*.
Talsperre *f* dam *(large storage dam)*; reservoir.
Tambourstock *m* baton.
Tangens *m* tangent *(trigonometrical function)*.
Tangente *f* tangent *(geometry)*.
Tank *m* tank.
Tankanlagen *fpl* fuel tank installations.
Tankbüchse *f* antitank rifle.
Tankdampfer *m* tanker *(Nav)*.
tanken to fuel, refuel, to fill *(a gasoline tank)*.
Tankfalle *f* tank trap.
Tankgraben *m* antitank ditch.
Tankprahm *m* fuel tender *(Nav)*.
Tankschiff *n* tanker *(Nav)*.
Tankstelle *f* filling station *(MT)*.
Tankwagen *m* tank truck *(MT)*; tank car *(RR)*.
Tapferkeitsmedaille *f* medal awarded for bravery.
Tarnanstrich *m* camouflage painting.
Tarnausweis *m* special deceptive identification card *(carried on missions where capture by the enemy is likely)*.
Tarndecke *f* covering, flat-top *(Cam)*.
Tarndisziplin *f* camouflage discipline.
tarnen to camouflage.
Tarnjacke *f* camouflage jacket.
Tarnkappe *f* helmet cover *(Cam)*.
Tarnmittel *n* camouflage material.
Tarnnetz *n* camouflage net, drape; apron *(G emplacement, Cam)*.
Tarnscheinwerfer *m* blackout driving light *(MT)*.
Tarnüberwachung *f* camouflage inspection.
Tarnung *f* camouflage.
Tarnungsfarbe *f* camouflage paint.
Tarnungsgeflecht *n* netting *(Cam)*.
Tarnungstruppe *f* camouflage troops.
Tarnzeltbahn *f* camouflage cape.
Tasche *f* bag, pocket, pouch; link *(of cartridge belt)*; boot *(SA)*; carrier, case.
Taschenbehälter *m* pocket flask.
Taschenlampe *f* flashlight.
Taschenmesser *n* pocket knife.
Taschenmunition *f* small arms ammunition in pouches.
Taste *f* key *(Rad, Tg)*.
tasten to key, send by key *(Tg, Rad)*.
Tastfunk *m* cw transmission *(Rad)*.
Tastgerät *n* keyer *(Rad)*.
Tastverkehr *m* cw communication *(Rad)*.
Tatbericht *m* detailed report, bill of particulars.
Tätigkeit *f* activity.
tatsächliche Schußweite actual range *(Gunnery)*.
Tau *n* rope, tow rope; trace *(harness)*.
Tau *m* dew.
Taube *f* pigeon.
Taubenschießen *n* skeet shooting.
Taucher *m* diver *(Nav)*. *See also* **Torpedotaucher.**
Tauchgerät *n* diving apparatus *(Nav)*.
Tauchrohr *n* spray-nozzle tube *(carburetor)*.
tauglich physically fit, able-bodied.
Taukranz *m* grommet.
Taupunkt *m* dew point.
Tausch *m* exchange.
täuschen deceive.
Täuschung *f* deception.
Täuschungsangriff *m* feint attack, diversion.
Täuschungsmanöver *n* demonstration, feint *(Tac)*.
Tauträger *m* lazy strap *(harness)*.
Techniker *m* technician.
technische Dienstzweige technical services.
technische Eignungsprüfung mechanical aptitude test.
technische Kompanie BT mining company *(Mil)*.
technische Kompanie E electricity company *(Mil)*.
technische Kompanie GW gas and water company *(Mil)*.
Technische Nothilfe Technical Emergency Corps *(used for Civ defense in Z of I and for maintenance, bomb disposal, restoration of public utilities, etc., in T of Opns and occupied territory)*.
Technisches Amt Technical Office *(department of Ger Air Ministry, dealing with research, procurement and testing)*.
Teer *m* tar.
Teich *m* pond.
Teileinheit *f* basic, self-sufficient element of a unit. *See also* **Einheitsprinzip.**
teilen to divide.
Teilgebiet *n* subarea.
Teilkreis des Höhenrichttriebs elevation circle *(G)*.
Teilladung *f* increment, increment section *(separate-loading Am)*.
teilmotorisiert semi-motorized.
Teilplatte *f* graduated scale.
Teilring *m* azimuth micrometer *(telescopic sight)*.
Teilringänderung *f* azimuth change *(telescopic sight)*.
Teilringeinstellung *f* azimuth adjustment, azimuth setting.
Teilringzahl *f* azimuth reading.
Teilscheibe *f* graduated scale; interpupillary-distance scale *(binocular)*; elevation micrometer *(panoramic telescope)*; graduated disk *(plotting protractor)*.
Teilstrich *m* mil *(Arty)*; dial division *(Rad)*; scale division *(Inst)*.
Teilstrichteilung *f* mil graduation.
Teiltrommel *f* micrometer knob *(on (panoramic or BC telescope)*; range drum.
Teilung *f* graduation, scale; division, separation.
Telefunken trade name of German company manufacturing electronic equipment.
Telegraphenleitung *f* telegraph line.
Telegraphennetz *n* wire net *(Tg)*.
Telegraphenstange *f* telegraph pole.
Tellermine *f* antitank mine.
Tellersäule *f* float column *(AA gun outrigger)*.
Tellertrudeln *n* flat spin *(Avn)*.
Tellerventil *n* poppet valve *(Mtr)*.
Temperatureinflüsse *mpl* elasticity effect; temperature factors *(Ballistics)*.
Temperaturgradient *m* temperature gradient *(Met)*.
vertikaler Temperaturgradient lapse rate.
Temperaturmesser *m* temperature gage *(Mtr)*.
Temperaturschwankung *f* temperature variation.
Teno *f* *See* **Technische Nothilfe.**
Termin *m* dead line.
Terrorangriff *m* terror raid *(Avn)*.
Tetrachlorkohlenstoff *m* carbon tetrachloride.
Thermiksegeln *n* thermal soaring *(glider)*.
Thermitbombe *f* thermite bomb.
Thermitladung *f* thermite charge *(incendiary bomb)*.
Thermokreuzinstrument *n* thermocouple meter.
Thermosyphonkühlung *f* gravity-system water cooling *(Mtr)*.
Tief *n* cyclone, depression *(Met)*.
Tiefanflug *m* low-level approach *(Avn)*.

Str.T	Streckenzugtafel	traverse table *(gunnery)*
Str.V	Strafvollstreckung	execution of sentence
ST Sch	schnelle Schützentruppen	mobile troops *(infantry)*
St.Schl	Stellungsschlacht	position warfare
st.Sptr	stehender Spähtrupp	fixed scout squad
St.St.	Staffelstab	divisional train command
St.Stellg	Sturmstellung	assault position
St.Str	Starkstrom	high voltage
St.Tr	Stosstrupp	shock detachment; assault detachment
St.Trt	Stammtruppenteil	cadre unit
St.U	Stellungsunterschied	perpendicular from base piece—aiming circle—target line *(artillery)*
St.U	Stoppuhr	stop watch
Stub.A	Stubenarrest	confinement to quarters
Stub.Ä	Stubenältester	man in charge of barracks room
Stubaf	Sturmbannführer	(SA) battalion leader, Storm Troops (SS) battalion commander, Elite Guard *(equivalent U. S. major)*
Stützp	Stützpunkt	strong point; base
Stuf	Sturmführer	(SA) company leader, Storm Troops *(equivalent U. S. rank: 1st lieutenant)*
Stu.Gesch	Sturmgeschütz	assault gun
Stu.H.	Sturmhaubitze	assault howitzer
Stuka	Sturzkampfflugzeug	dive bomber
Sturmhptf	Sturmhauptführer	(SA) chief company-leader, Storm Troops *(equivalent U. S. rank: captain)*
Sturminf	Sturminfanterie	shock infantry; assault infantry
StV	Stabsveterinär	captain *(Veterinary Corps)*
Stv	Stellvertreter	deputy
St.V.O	Strassenverkehrsordnung	traffic regulations
St.V.Z.O	Strassenverkehrszulassungsordnung	ordinance for the operation of motor vehicles
Stw	Stabswache	headquarters company
St.W	Staffelwinkel	open squadron angle *(aviation)*
St.W	Stallwache	stable guard
St.W	Stellungswechsel	shift of position; change of position
St.Z	Stabszahlmeister	civilian official of the Army Finance Department with equivalent rank of captain
Stzbomb	Sturzbomber	dive bomber
St.Zm	Stabszahlmeister	civilian official of the Army Finance Department with equivalent rank of captain
St.Zt	Steigzeit	time of climb
s.u	siehe unten	see below
S.U	Sonnenuntergang	sunset
subm	submarin	submarine
südd	süddeutsch	South German
südl	südlich	southern
südl.Br	südliche Breite	southern latitude
südw	südwärts	southward
Südw	Südwesten	southwest
S.u.E.-Gerät	Sende- und Empfangsgerät	transmitting and receiving apparat
S.V	Selbstverwaltung	autonomy
s.v.a	soviel als	as much as
S.Verst	Selbstverstümmelung	self-mutilation
SVG	Soldatenversicherungsgesetz	soldiers' insurance law
s.v.w	soviel wie	as much as
S.W	Scheinwerfer	searchlight; headlight
S.W	Scheinwerferzug	searchlight platoon
S.W	Schmiedewagen	forge wagon
SW	Südwest	southwest
sw	südwestlich	southwestern
S.W.Abt	Scheinwerferabteilung	searchlight detachment
S-Wagen	Güterwagen	2-axle freight car with iron side-supporting-bars, detachable wall, suitable for carrying rails
s.W.G	schweres Wurfergerät	heavy mortar equipment
s.w.u	siehe weiter unten	see further down
S.W.Zg	Scheinwerferzug	searchlight platoon
SWzS	Südwest zu Süd	southwest by south
SWzW	Südwest zu West	southwest by west
SZ	Schnellzug	express train
S.Z. S-Zerl	Selbstzerleger	self-destruction charge *(projectiles)*
Sz	Sitzzahl	seating capacity *(aviation)*
SZ	Spielmannszug	fife and drum corps
S.Zg	Sekundenzeiger	second hand *(timepiece)*

T

T		air base *(conventional sign in double circle)*
T	Güterwagen mit Selbstladeeinrichtung	freight car with self-loading installation
T	Täuschung	deception; fraud; illusion
T	Tag	day
T	Tagesbefehl	order of the day
T	Tank	tank
T	Tapferkeits - Medaille; Tapferkeitsorden	medal *or* decoration for valor

T	Tasche	pocket
T	Technik	technique; technology
T	Techniker	technician
t	technisch	technical
T	Teil	part; element; component; piece
T	Teilring	graduated ring; azimuth drum; micrometer ring
T	Telefon	telephone
T	Telegraf	telegraph
t	telegrafisch	telegraphic
T	Temperatur	temperature
T	Tender	tender (*boat or train*)
T	Termin	term; date; hearing (*law*)
t	tief	deep; low
T	Tiefdecker	low-wing monoplane
T	Titel	title
t	Tonne	metric ton (*2,205 pounds*)
T	Topograf	topographer
T Top.	Topographie; topographisch	topography; topographic
T	Torpedo	torpedo
T	Torpedoboot	torpedo boat
T	Torpedoflugzeug	torpedo plane
T	Touren	revolutions
T	Tross	train
T	Transport	transport; conveyance
T	Treffpunkt	point of impact (*ballistics*)
T	Treib-	propelling; driving
T	Trieb-	driving
T	Triebwagen	self-propelled railroad car
T	Trupp	party; detail; troop
T	Truppendienst	duty with troops
T	Truppengerät	troop equipment
T	Turbine	turbine
T	Turm	tower (*on maps*); turret
T.A	Lufttechnische Akademie	Technical Aeronautic Academy (*insignia on straps*)
Ta	Tank	tank
Ta	Tarnung	camouflage
Tab	Tabelle	table; list
tägl	täglich	daily
Täusch	Täuschung	deception; fraud; illusion
Taf	Tafel	table; chart; index; diagram
Tag	Tag	day
Tageg	Tagegeld	daily allowance
Tag-P	Tagposten	day post
Tak	Tankabwehrkanone	antitank gun
Tak-Kp	Tak-Kompanie	antitank company
Takt	Taktik	tactics
Takt.L	Taktiklehrer	teacher of tactics
takt.L	taktische Lage	tactical situation
takt. Üb.R	taktische Übungsreise	tactical route march
takt. Üb.R	taktische Übungsritt	tactical practice ride
Tak-Zg	Takzug	antitank platoon
Tals	Talsohle	bottom of valley
Talsp	Talsperre	dam
Talsp.-S	Talsperrensee	lake formed by dam
Ta.M	Tarnmittel	camouflage material
Ta.N	Tarnnetz	camouflage net
Tarn	Tarnung	camouflage
Tasch	Tasche	pocket
Tasch.M	Taschenmunition	small arms ammunition in pouches
Taus	Tausend	thousand
T.B	Tuberkulose	tuberculosis
Tb	Turbine	turbine
T.-Bed	Tagesbedarf	daily requirements
T.B.F	Turmbeobachtungsfernrohr	turret observation telescope
T.Br	Tankbrigade	tank brigade
tch	technisch	technical
T.D	Tiefdecker	low-wing monoplane
tdf	tropendienstfähig	fit for service in the tropics
T.D.F	Tropendienstfähigkeit	availability for tropical service
Tdr	Tender	tender (*boat or train*)
t.E	taktische Einheit	tactical unit
t.E.Ball.Zug	technischer Ersatzballonzug	technical replacement training balloon platoon
Techn	Technik	technique; technology
Techn.Insp	Technischer Inspektor	technical inspector
Techn.Nh	Technische Nothilfe	Technical Emergency Service
Techn.Ob.Insp.	Technischer Oberinspektor	chief technical inspector
Techn.Offz	Technischer Offizier	technical officer
techn.Schwd	technische Schwadron	technical troop (*cavalry*)
techn.Tr	technische Truppen	technical troops
Teilg	Teilung	division; separation
Teilm	Teilmantel	semi-jacketed (*bullet*)
Teiln	Teilnehmer	participant
teilw	teilweise	partial; in part; partly
Teilz	Teilzahlung	part-payment
T.-Einn	Tageseinnahme	receipts of the day
Tel	Telefon	telephone
Tel	Telegraf	telegraph
tel	telegrafisch	telegraphic
Tel	Telegramm	telegram
TelA	Telegrafenamt	telegraph office
Tel.Insp	Telegrafeninspektor	telegraph inspector
Tel.Kp	Telegrafenkompanie	telegraph company
Tel-Ob-Bauf	Telegrafen-Oberbauführer	telegraph construction squad engineer

Tiefangriff *m* low-level attack *(Avn)*.
Tiefbau *m* surface construction *(Tp line)*; subsurface construction *(Engr)*.
Tiefbettfelge *f* drop-base rim *(MT)*.
Tiefdecker *m* low-wing monoplane.
Tiefe *f* depth.
Tiefenabstand *m* distance *(from front to rear)*.
Tiefenausdehnung *f* extension in depth *(Tac)*.
Tiefenfeuer *n* searching fire *(MG)*.
Tiefenfeuereinrichtung *f* searching-fire device *(MG)*.
Tiefenfeuertafel *f* searching-fire table *(MG)*.
Tiefengliederung *f* distribution in depth, disposition in depth *(Tac)*.
Tiefenkreuzverspannung *f* longitudinal cross bracing *(Ap)*.
Tiefenlehre *f* depth micrometer, depth gage.
Tiefenstaffelung *f* echelonment in depth *(Tac)*.
Tiefenstreuung *f* range dispersion on horizontal target *(Ballistics)*.
Tiefenverspannung *f* longitudinal cross bracing *(Ap)*.
Tiefenwinkel *m* angle of depression *(Surv)*.
Tiefenzone *f* zone of resistance *(organized in depth)*.
Tiefflieger *m* low-flying airplane.
Tiefflug *m* low-level flight, hedge-hopping *(Avn)*.
Tiefflugangriff *m* low-level attack.
Tiefgang *m* draught *(Nav)*.
tiefgegliedert distributed in depth.
tiefgestaffelt echeloned in depth.
Tiefladeanhänger *m* flatbed trailer, tank transporter trailer.
Tiefladelinie *f* load line *(Nav)*.
Tiefseekabel *n* marine cable.
Tiegelgußstahl *m* crucible steel.
Tierarzt *m* veterinarian.
Titantetrachlorid *n* titanium tetrachloride *(CWS)*.
T-Mine *f* See **Tellermine**.
Tochterkompaß *m* repeater compass *(Ap)*.
tödliche Menge killing concentration *(CWS)*.
Toleranz *f* tolerance *(Tech)*.
Tolit *n* trinitrotoluol.
Tolita *n* See **Tolit**.
Ton *m* sound; tone *(Photo)*; clay.
Tonarm *m* pick-up arm *(phonograph)*.
tönend icw *(marking on Rad set)*.
Tonfrequenz *f* audio frequency *(Rad)*.
Tonfrequenzbereich *m* audio-frequency range *(Rad)*.
Tonhacke *f* mattock.
Tonhöhe *f* pitch *(sound)*.
tonlos cw *(marking on Rad set)*.
Tonne *f* metric ton (=1.102 *short tons*); buoy *(Nav)*; barrel, cask, drum.
Tonnenbrücke *f* improvised floating bridge of barrels or drums.
Tonnenfähre *f* barrel raft.
Tonnenfloß *n* barrel float.
Tonnenlager *n* spherical roller bearing.
Tontaubenschießen *n* skeet shooting.
Tontaubenschießstand *m* skeet range.
Tönung *f* tone *(Photo)*.
Tonwagen *m* sound truck *(film unit)*.
Tonwiedergabe *f* sound reproduction.
Topf *m* pot; container *(hand grenade)*.
Tor *n* large gate.
Tornister *m* pack, field pack, knapsack, haversack.
Tornisterempfänger *m* portable receiver, pack receiver *(Rad)*.
Tornisterfiltergerät *n* pack-type water purification unit.
Tornisterfunkgerät *n* pack radio set, portable radio set.
Tornisterfunktrupp *m* portable-radio section.
Tornisterklappe *f* pack flap.
torpedieren to torpedo.
Torpedo *n* torpedo.
Torpedoabwurf *m* torpedo release *(Avn)*.
Torpedoausstoßrohr *n* torpedo tube.
Torpedobootzerstörer *m* destroyer
Torpedoflieger *m* torpedo bomber; torpedo-bomber pilot.
Torpedoflugzeug *n* torpedo bomber.
Torpedojäger *m* fighter-type torpedo bomber *(Ap)*.
Torpedorohr *n* torpedo tube.
Torpedoschnellboot *n* motor torpedo boat.
Torpedoschutznetz *n* torpedo defense net.
Torpedotaucher *m* deep-sea diver
Torpedotreffer *m* torpedo hit.
Torpedo-Waffenleitvormann *m* torpedoman *(Nav)*.
Torpedowulst *m* blister *(Nav)*.
Torpedowurf *m* torpedo release *(Avn)*.
Torsionsstab *m* torsion rod *(MT)*.
tot dead.
Totalausfall *m* total loss.
totaler Krieg total war.
töten to kill.
Totenkopfverbände *mpl* See **SS-Totenkopfverbände**.
toter Gang steering play *(MT)*; backlash, play, lost motion *(Mech)*; free travel *(of clutch pedal)*.
toter Schußraum dead area, dead space.
toter Trichter dead space *(AA gun)*.
toter Winkel dead space.
tote Zone skip zone *(Rad)*.
Totpunkt *m* dead center *(Mtr)*.
Totschläger *m* blackjack.
Tracht *f* saddle cover *(pack saddle)*.
Trachte *f* wall, periople *(hoof)*.
Trachtenkissen *n* saddle pad.
Tragbalken *m* balk, stringer *(Bdg)*.
Tragband *n* carrying strap *(gas mask)*.
tragbar portable.
Tragbeutel *m* gas-mask carrier.
Tragbüchse *f* gas-mask carrier *(metal type)*.
Tragdeck *n* wing *(Ap)*.
Trage *f* litter, stretcher *(Med)*.
Tragegestell *n* pack frame *(pack saddle)*.
Tragegurt *m* carrying strap, supporting strap.
Tragepolster *n* carrying pad *(MG)*.
Träger *m* carrier, mount, support, beam.
Tragerand *m* bearing surface *(hoof)*.
Transportführer *m* transportation officer, train commander *(RR)*.
Transportgeschwader *n* transport wing, transport command *(Avn)*.
Transportglied *n* ferry element *(one of a train of towed ferries)*.
Transportkolonne *f* motor transport column.
Transportkommandantur *f* transport control headquarters *(RR)*.
Transportluftfahrt *f* transport aviation.
Transportmittel *n* means of transportation.
Transportoffizier *m* transportation officer *(RR)*.
transportsicherer Zünder shipment-safe fuze *(Am)*.
Transportsperre *f* embargo *(on truck, RR, and ship movements)*.
Transportstaffel *f* transport squadron *(Avn)*.
Transporttau *n* handling line *(Bln)*.
Transportübersicht *f* transportation table, table of movements.
Transportverbot *n* embargo *(on truck, RR, and ship movements)*.
Transportwesen *n* transportation system.
Transversalmaßstab *m* interpolating scale *(Surv)*.
Trapez *n* trapezoid *(Math)*; suspension frame *(Bln)*.
Trapez-Fachwerkträger *m* Warren truss, trapezoidal truss.
Trassierband *n* tracing tape *(CWS, Engr)*.
Trauerfeier *f* funeral; commemoration services.
Trauergefolge *n* funeral escort.
Traverse *f* crossbar *(split-trail carriage)*; traverse *(Ft)*.
Trecker *m* tractor *(MT)*.
Treffaussicht *f* probability of hit.
Treffbild *n* shot group, dispersion pattern; recording target *(Tng)*.
Treffen *n* encounter, shock of assault; wave of tanks; phase of attack.
treffen to hit, meet, strike; guess; take *(measures)*.
Treffentfernung *f* slant range to future position *(AAA)*.
treffenweise in depth, in echelon.
treffenweise Aufstellung disposition in depth *(Tac)*.
Treffer *m* hit.
Treffer erzielen to score hits.
Trageriemen *m* carrying strap, carrying sling.
Trägerstrom *m* carrier current *(Tp)*.
Trägerwelle *f* carrier wave *(Rad)*.
Tragesattel *m* pack saddle.
Trageschiene *f* frame rib *(pack saddle)*.
Tragevorrichtung *f* scabbard *(R)*.
Tragfähigkeit *f* load capacity *(Bdg)*; ton capacity, passenger capacity *(MT, Ap)*; gallon capacity *(tank Trk)*.
Tragfeder *f* suspension spring *(split-trail carriage)*.
Tragfläche *f* airfoil *(Ap)*.
Tragflächenumriß *m* airfoil profile.
Tragflügel *m* wing *(Ap)*.
Tragflügelende *n* wing tip *(Ap)*.
Tragflügelhinterkante *f* trailing edge of wing *(Ap)*.
Tragflügelprofil *n* wing profile.
Trägheit *f* inertia *(Mech)*.
Trägheitsmoment *n* moment of inertia.
Traglast *f* load *(Ap, MT)*; pack *(pack animals)*.
Tragpferd *n* pack horse.
Tragriemen *m* neck strap *(pack saddle)*.
Tragrolle *f* See **Laufrolle**.
Tragschrauber *m* autogiro, gyroplane.
Tragtier *n* pack animal.
Tragtierbeförderung *f* pack transportation.
Tragtierkolonne *f* pack train.
Tragvorrichtung *f* bomb shackle
Tragwerk *n* wing assembly *(Ap)*.
Tragzapfen *m* trunnion.
Trampelpfad *m* beaten path, beaten track.
Trampelweg *m* See **Trampelpfad**.
Tränengas *n* lacrimator gas, tear gas.
Tränengaskerze *f* tear-gas candle *(CWS)*.
Tränengasstoff *m* CN solution.
Tränenstoffkerze *f* tear gas pot *(CWS)*.
Tränken *n* watering *(of animals)*.
Transportbefehl *m* movement order.
Transporter *m* transport *(Avn, Nav)*.
Transportflugwesen *n* transport aviation.
Transportflugzeug *n* transport airplane.
Treffergebnis *n* score *(firing or bombing)*.
Trefferraum *m* zone of dispersion *(Ballistics)*.
Treffer verzeichnen to register hits.
Treffgenauigkeit *f* accuracy of fire; accuracy of practice.
Treffhöhe *f* altitude of target at future position *(AA gunnery)*.
Treffläche *f* target area.
Treffpunkt *m* point of impact, objective point *(Arty)*; future position *(AAA)*; meeting point, rendezvous.
Treffpunktentfernung *f* slant range to future position of target *(AA gunnery)*.
Treffsicherheit *f* accuracy of fire.
Treffwahrscheinlichkeit *f* expectancy or probability of hitting *(Arty)*.
Treffwahrscheinlichkeit der Waffe developed armament probable error.
treiben impel, drive, propel; drift.
Treibachse *f* driving axle *(MT)*.
Treibgas *n* wood gas *(MT)*; propellent gas *(Bln)*.
Treibgasmotor *m* wood-gas engine
Treibholz *n* driftwood.
Treibladung *f* propellent charge
Treibmine *f* floating mine, unanchored automatic contact mine.
Treibmittel *n* propellant *(Am)*.
Treibscheibe *f* diaphragm *(case shot)*.
Treibstoff *m* engine fuel.
Treibstoffbehälter *m* fuel tank
Treibstofflager *n* fuel dump.
treideln to tow boats from land.
trennen disconnect, cut off, divide, separate.
Trennklinke *f* disconnect jack *(Tp)*.
Trennschärfe *f* selectivity *(Rad)*.
Trennschnitt *m* line of breach *(demolitions)*.
Trennung *f* break *(Rad procedure)*; disconnection, separation.
Trennungsbahnhof *m* junction *(RR)*.
Trennungslinie *f* boundary *(Tac)*.
Trense *f* bit, snaffle *(harness)*.
Trensengebiß *n* snaffle bit *(harness)*.
Trensenzügel *m* snaffle rein *(harness)*.
Tresse *f* braid *(Clo)*.
"Treten Sie ab!" "Dismissed!" *(formal style, to an individual)*.
Tretmine *f* tread mine *(pressure-ignited antipersonnel mine)*.
Tretmotor *m* pedal-operated generator.
Tretsatz *m* pedal-operated generating unit.
Trichter *m* crater; funnel; cone; horn collector *(AA sound locator)*.
Trichterlautsprecher *m* horn-type speaker, cone speaker *(Rad)*.
Trichterfeld *n* shelled area, area pitted with shell craters.
Trichtergelände *n* shelled terrain, terrain pitted with shell craters.
Trichterladung *f* crater charge *(Engr)*.
Trieb *m* drive; drift; impulse; instinct.
Triebrad *n* driving sprocket *(Tk)*.
Triebsand *m* drift sand, loose sand, silt.
Triebscheibe *f* knob, micrometer head *(Optics, Ord)*.
Triebscheibe zur Höhenrichtung elevating knob *(Optics, Ord)*.
Triebscheibe zur Seitenrichtung azimuth knob *(Optics, Ord)*.
Triebschraube *f* upper prism micrometer head *(panoramic sight)*.
Triebwerk *n* power plant *(Ap, MT)*.
Triebzahn *m* connector *(caterpillar track)*.
trigonometrischer Punkt triangulation point, primary traverse station.
Trilit *n* trinitrotoluol.
Trimmklappe *f* trim tab *(Ap)*.
Trimmruder *n* trim tab, balance tab, servo tab *(Ap)*.
Trimmvorrichtung *f* flight control surfaces used for trimming *(Ap)*.
trinkbar potable.
Trinkbecher *m* drinking cup.
Trinkwasser *n* drinking water.
Trinkwasserbereiter *m* water purification unit.
Tripelstreifen *m* special prism used to direct the beam of a signal lamp.
Tripper *m* gonorrhea.
Tritt *m* step, pace, tread.
Trittbrett *n* running board *(MT)*.
Trockendock *n* dry dock.
Trockenelement *n* dry cell *(Elec)*.
Trockengelenk *n* flexible-disk joint *(MT)*.
Trockengleichrichter *m* dry cell rectifier *(Rad)*.
Trockensumpfschmierung *f* dry-sump lubrication *(Mtr)*.
Troddel *f* bayonet tassel.
Trog *m* trough.

Tel. St.	Telegrafenstation	telegraph station
Tel.Vt.	Telegrafenverwaltung	telegraph administration
Temp	Temperatur	temperature
Tend	Tendenz	tendency
Tend	Tender	tender (*boat or train*)
Teno	Technische Nothilfe	Technical Emergency Service.
Term	Termin	term; date; hearing (*law*)
Terr	Terrasse	terrace
Terr	Territorium	territory
Terr.Gl	territoriale Gliederung	territorial organization
TF	Telefunken	trade name of German wireless-telegraph company
tf	tief	deep; low
T.F	Tiefenfeuer	searching fire
TF	Tragtierführer	pack animal leader
T.F	Transportführer	officer in charge of a military transport
T.F	Truppenführer	commander of a task force
T.F	Truppenführung	tactical command; leadership
TF	Truppführer	troop leader
T-Falle	Tankfalle	tank trap
T.f.d.Gstb	Taschenbuch für den Generalstabsoffizier	pocket manual for the general staff officer
T-Flugzeug	Torpedoflugzeug	torpedo plane
T-Fluwa	Tagflugwache	daylight spotting post
Tg	Tag	day
Tg.B	Tagbomber	daylight bomber
Tg.Bef	Tagesbefehl	order of the day
Tg.Bo	Tagbomber	daylight bomber
tgl	täglich	daily
Tg.M	Tagmarsch; Tagesmarsch	day march; day's march
Tgr	Telegrafie	telegraph
Tgt	Tragtier	pack animal
T.H	Technische Nothilfe	Technical Emergency Service
Th	Theodolit	theodolite
Th	Theorie	theory
T.H	Turmhaubitze	howitzer in turret
Therm	Thermometer	thermometer
Thür	Thüringien	Thuringia
Tief	Tiefen-	depth
Tiefangr	Tiefangriff	low-flying attack
Tiefd	Tiefdecker	low-wing monoplane
Tief.Gl	Tiefgliederung	distribution in depth
Tief.St	Tiefenstaffelung	echelonment in depth
Tief.Z	Tiefenzone	defensive zone
Tilg	Tilgung	extermination; eradication
Tit	Titel	title
T.I.W	Train - Instandsetzungs-Werkstatt	train-repair workshop
Tk	Tank	tank
TK	Turmkanone	gun in turret
Tkst	Tankstelle	filling station; gas station
TL	Taschenlampe	flashlight
Tl	Teil	part; element; component;
T.L	Torpedolaboratorium	torpedo laboratory (*Kiel*)
T.L	Truppenlehrer	military instructor
TLBlatt	Taschenlampenbatterie	flashlight battery
Tlbn	Taschenlampenbatterien	flashlight batteries
Tln	Taschenlampen	flashlights
Tln	Teilnehmer	participant
TM	Tapferkeitsmedaille	medal for valor
tm	teilmotorisiert	partly motorized
TM	Torpedomechaniker	torpedo mechanic
T/Min	Touren in der Minute	revolutions per minute
T-Mine	Tellermine	flat percussion-type antitank mine
tmot	teilmotorisiert	partly motorized
T-Mun	Tank-Munition	tank ammunition
T.N	Technische Nothilfe	Technical Emergency Service
T.N.A	Truppennachrichtenabteilung	signal communications battalion
T.N.V	Truppennachrichtenverband	signal communications unit
T.O	Technischer Offizier	technical officer
T.O	Teerofen	tar works (*on maps*)
To	Tonne	ton (*1000 kilograms or about 2205 pounds avoirdupois*)
TO	Transportoffizier	transport officer
TOBF	Telegrafen-Oberbauführer	telegraph construction squad engineer
Tonn	Tonnage	tonnage
Top	Topograph	topographer
Torn	Tornister	pack; knapsack
Torn.Fu.Ger	Tornisterfunkgerät	portable radio set
Torn.Fu.Tr	Tornisterfunktrupp	portable radio detachment
Torp	Torpedo	torpedo
Torp.Flgz	Torpedoflugzeug	torpedo plane
Torp.Lab	Torpedolaboratorium	torpedo laboratory (*Kiel*)
Torp.Mot.Bt	Torpedomotorboot	torpedo motor boat
tot	total	total; complete
Tot	Toter	dead person
tot.Kr	totaler Krieg	total war
tot.Mob	totale Mobilmachung	total mobilization
tot.P	toter Punkt	dead center; dead point
Tot-V	Totalverlust	total loss
tot.W	toter Winkel	dead angle
Tp	Torpedo	torpedo
t.P	trigonometrischer Punkt	trigonometrical point maps)
tp	tropenfest	heat-resisting
Tp	Tropenmunition	tropical ammunition
T.p.M	Teile pro Million	parts per million
T.p.Min	Touren in der Minute	revolutions per minute
Tpp	Trupp	troop; party; detail
T.R	Tankregiment	tank regiment
Tr	Trab; Traber	trot; trotter
Tr	Träger	carrier; prop; girder
tr	tragbar	portable
Tr	Train	train
Tr	Traktor	tractor
Tr	Transformator	transformer
Tr	Transport	transport; conveyance
tr	treffen	to hit (*gunnery*); to meet
Tr	Treffer	hit (*gunnery*)
Tr	Treib-	propelling; driving
Tr	Treibladung	propellant charge
Tr	Trennschnitt	cross section; chamber
Tr	Trennung	division; dividing
Tr	Tross	supply train; field train
Tr	Trupp	party; detail; troop
Träg	Träger	carrier; prop; girder
Tragf	Tragfähigkeit	carrying capacity
Tragfl	Tragflügel	wing (*aviation*)
Tragschr	Tragschrauber	gyroplane; autogyro
Tragt	Tragtier	pack animal
Tragw	Tragweite	range; significance; bearings
train	trainieren	to train
Traj	Trajekt	ferry
Trakt	Traktor	tractor
transatl	transatlantisch	transatlantic
Transp	Transport	transport; conveyance
Transp.F	Transportführer	officer in charge of a military transport
Tr.Arzt	Truppenarzt	medical officer with troops
Tr.Ausw	Truppenausweis	military identification paper
Tr.B	Trefferbild	plotted hits
Tr.Bef	Truppenbefehl	military order
Tr.Befh	Truppenbefehlshaber	commander
T.Rbl.F	Turmrundblickfernrohr	turret panoramic telescope
Trbst	Treibstoff	fuel
Tr.Dst	Truppendienst	duty with troops
Tr.E. Tr.Eint	Truppeneinteilung	disposition of troops; tactical organization; organization for combat
Treff	Treffer	hit (*gunnery*)
Treffähigk	Treffähigkeit	accuracy of fire; striking
Treffwahrsch	Treffwahrscheinlichkeit	hitting probability; probable percentage of hits
Trens.Z	Trensenzügel	snaffle rein
Tr.F	Truppenführer	commander
Tr.Fl	Tragflügel	wing (*aviation*)
Tr.Fz	Truppenfahrzeug	troop carrier
Trgf	Tragfähigkeit	carrying capacity
Tr.Gl	Truppengliederung	organization of troops; formation of troops
Trgw	Tragweite	range; significance; bearings; span (*of bridge*)
Triebkr	Triebkraft	driving power
trig.P	trigonometrischer Punkt	trigonometrical point
Tr.Kch	Truppenküche	troop kitchen; field kitchen
Tr.Kdr	Truppenkommandeur	commander
Tr.L	Trennungslinie	line of demarcation
Tr.Ldg	Treibladung	propelling charge
Tr.Lehr	Truppenlehrer	military instructor
Tr.Lsch	Truppenluftschutz	military air protection; aerial defense
Tr. Mldg	Truppenmeldung	unit report
Tr.Nachr.V	Truppennachrichtenverband	communications detachment
Trop	Tropen	tropics
trop.df	tropendienstfähig	fit for service in the tropics
Trop.Hm	Tropenhelm	sun helmet
Tr.P	Treffpunkt	point of impact
Trsp	Transport	transport; carrier
Trsp.Bew	Transportbewegung	transport movement
Trsp.F	Transportführer	officer in charge of a military transport
Trt	Tragtier	pack animal
Trt.Kol	Tragtierkolonne	pack animal train
Tr.T	Truppenteil	unit
Tr.Trsp	Truppentransport	transportation of troops
Tr.Ü.Pl	Truppenübungsplatz	drill ground; training area
Truf	Truppführer	(SA) platoon leader, Storm Troops (*equivalent U. S. rank: 1st sergeant*)
Tr.V.Pl	Truppenverbandplatz	dressing station
Trw	Treffwahrscheinlichkeit	hitting probability; probable percentage of hits
TrWg	Triebwagen	self-propelled railroad car
Tr.Z	Truppenzeichen	conventional signs or troop symbols
T-S	Talsperre	dam
Tsd	Tausend	thousand
Tsp	Talsperre	dam
T-Staffel	Torpedoflugzeugstaffel	torpedo plane squadron
T.St.R.Nr	Truppenstammrollnummer	unit roll number
TTT	Sicherheitsmeldung	weather warning signal
Tuberk	Tuberkulose	tuberculosis
T.Üb.Pl	Truppenübungsplatz	drill ground; raining area
tunl	tunlich, tunlichst	feasible; most feasible
Turb	Turbine	turbine
Turm-MG	Turmmaschinengewehr	turret machine gun
T.V	Truppentransportvorschrift	troop transportation regulations

T.V	Truppenvermessungsdienst	surveying service (*artillery*)
T.V.P	Truppenverbandplatz	aid station (*combat*)
T.W	Turmwarte	observation tower (*on maps*)
T.Z	Tagesziel	day's objective
T.Z	Teilringzahl	micrometer setting
T.Z.F	Turmzielfernrohr	turret telescopic sight

U

u	um	about; around
U	Umlaufmotor	rotary engine
u	und	and
U	Unfall	accident
U	Uniform	uniform
U	untauglich für Wehrdienst	unfit for military service
U	Unter-	under; beneath; subordinate
U	Unterkunft	billet; accommodation
U	Unteroffizier	noncommissioned officer; sergeant (*corresponding roughly to U. S. sergeant*)
U	Unterrichtsmunition	practice ammunition; drill ammunition
U	Unterschied	difference
U	Unterseeboot	submarine; U-boat
U	Unterstand	dugout; shelter
u.a	und andere	and others
U.A	Unterabschnitt	subdivision of a sector
u.a	unter anderen	among others
U.A	Unterseebootsabwehr	defense against submarines
U.Abt	Unterabteilung	subdivision
U.Abt	Unterseebootsabteilung	submarine detachment
u.ä	und ähnliches	and the like
U.A.K	Unterabschnittskommandeur	sub-sector commander
U.Arzt	Unterarzt	medical officer aspirant
Ubtsabt	Unterseebootsabteilung	submarine detachment
u.dgl	und dergleichen	and the like
u.d.M	unter dem Meeresspiegel	below sea level
Ud.S.S.R	Union der Sozialisten Sowjetrepubliken	Union of Socialist Soviet Republics
ü	über	above; over
ü	überschwer	superheavy
üb	über	above; over
Üb	Übereinkommen	agreement
Üb	Übergang	crossing; level crossing (*railroad*); transition
Üb	Überschreitung	crossing; transgression
Üb	Übersicht	survey; synopsis; summary
Üb	Übung	drill; maneuver; exercise; practice
Üb	Übungsmunition	blank ammunition; practice ammunition
ÜbAnl	Übungsanlage	planning of field practice
Üb.Anl	Übungsanleitung	field practice regulations
Üb.Beg	Übungsbeginn	start of practice drills
Üb.Best	Übungsbestimmungen	field practice regulations
Übereink	Übereinkommen	agreement
Übereink	Übereinkunft	arrangement
Überf	Überfahrt	crossing; passage
Überf	Überfall	raid; surprise attack
Überf	Überführung	crossing; transfer
Überfl	Überflügelung	outflanking
Überfl	Überfluss	abundance
Überg	Übergabe	surrender; capitulation
Übergew	Übergewicht	overweight; preponderance
Überg.z.R	Übergang zur Ruhe	transition to rest period
Überl	Überläufer	deserter
Überl	Überlassung	cession; yielding
Überl	Überlastung	overstrain; overburdening
Überl	Überlegenheit	superiority
Überl	Überlieferung	tradition; surrender
Übern	Übernachtung	spending the night
Übern	Übernahme	taking over; taking possession
Überpr	Überpreis	overprice; excessive price
Überpr	Überprüfung	examination; check-up
Überr	Überraschung	surprise
Überr	Überredung	persuasion
Überr	Überreichung	presentation; handing over
Übers	Übersee	overseas
übers	übersetzen	to cross (*a river*); to translate
Übers	Übersetzer	translator
Übersch	Überschätzung	overestimation; overrating
Übersch	Überschiessen	firing beyond the target
Überschw	Überschwemmung	flooding; overflowing
überschw.MG	überschweres Maschinengewehr	superheavy machine gun
Übers.K	Übersichtskarte	index map (*to a series*)
Übertr	Übertragung	transmission; transcription
Übertr	Übertreibung	exaggeration
Übertr	Übertretung	violation; transgression
Überv	Übervölkerung	excess of population; overpopulation
Überv	Übervorteilung	imposition; overreaching
Überw	Überweisung	transfer; conviction
Überw	Überwinterung	hibernation
Überw.Bttr	Überwachungsbatterie	observation battery
überz	überzählige	surplus; supernumerary

Trombe *f* cyclone, tornado.
Trommel *f* drum; dial; range drum (*sight mount*); micrometer drum (*panoramic sight*); metal drum (*for belt Am*).
Trommelfell *n* eardrum.
Trommelfellverletzter *m* person with punctured eardrums.
Trommelfeuer *n* drum fire, heavy barrage (*Arty*).
Trommelmagazin *n* drum magazine (*MG*).
Trommelmagazinzuführung *f* drum feed (*MG*).
Trommelwirbel *m* drum roll.
Trommelzeiger *m* drum index (*sight mount, panoramic sight*).
Trommler *m* drummer.
Trompete *f* bugle.
Trompetensignal *n* bugle call.
Trompeter *m* bugler.
tropenbeständig suitable for use in tropical climates.
Tropenhelm *m* pith helmet, sun helmet.
Tropenkraftstoff *m* tropical gasoline.
Tröpfchen *n* droplet, vapor particle (*CWS*).
Tropfen *m* drop (*of water, etc.*).
tropische Warmluft tropical air
Troß *m* train (*combat, supply, or baggage*).
Trosse *f* hawser.
Troßfahrzeug *n* train vehicle (*supply, baggage, etc.*).
Trotyl *n* trinitrotoluol.
trudeln to spin (*Ap*).
Trümmer *pl* debris.
Trupp *m* detachment, section, squad, team, detail, party (*pl* Trupps) (*to be distinguished from* Truppe).
Truppe *f* collective term for field elements of armed forces; unit; arm or branch of service (*to be distinguished from* Trupp).
Truppen *fpl* troops.
Truppenansammlung *f* concentration of troops.
Truppenarzt *m* medical officer.
Truppenausladung *f* detraining of troops.
Truppenausweis *f* soldier's identification card.
Truppenbefehlshaber *m* commander of troops.
Truppenbeförderung *f* transportation of troops.
Truppenbereitstellung *f* assembly of troops.
Truppenbewegung *f* troop movement.
Truppendienst *m* service with troops, duty with troops.
Truppeneinheit *f* troop unit (*usually has uniform type of weapons, as distinguished from* Truppenverband, *combined-arms unit*).
Truppeneinladung *f* entraining of troops.
Truppeneinteilung *f* order of battle; disposition of troops; allotment or allocation of troops; conventional sequence by arms and services (*in orders*).
Truppenentgiftung *f* decontamination of personnel (*CWS*).
Truppenentgiftungskompanie *f* personnel decontamination company.
Truppenführer *m* commander, commanding officer (*generally of a combined-arms force*); task force commander.
Truppenführung *f* leading of troops, conduct of field operations (*title of Ger manual corresponding to Field Service Regulations: Operations*).
Truppengattung *f* branch of service.
Truppengebrauch *m* military usage, military custom.
Truppengeländebesprechung *f* junior-command field critique (*maneuvers*).
Truppengeneralstab *m* general staff with troops.
Truppenlager *n* camp.
Truppenmarketenderei *f* post exchange.
Truppenmasse *f* troop concentration.
Truppennachrichtenoffizier *m* unit communication officer.
Truppennachrichtenverband *m* communication unit.
Truppennachrichtenzug *m* unit communication platoon.
Truppenoffizier *m* line officer, officer of the line.
Truppenschiedsrichter *m* unit umpire (*maneuvers*).
Truppenteil *m* unit.
Truppentransport *m* troop transport.
Truppentransporter *m* troop carrier (*Ap*); troop transport (*Ap, Nav*).
Truppentransport-Flugzeug *n* troop carrier airplane.
Truppentransportschiff *n* troop transport, troopship.
Truppentransportzug *m* troop train.
Truppenübungen *fpl* field maneuvers.
Truppenübungsplatz *m* troop training camp, troop training grounds.
Truppenunterkunft *f* barracks, quarters, billet.
Truppenverband *m* mixed force, combined-arms unit.
Truppenverbandplatz *m* aid station (*Med*).
Truppenvermessungsdienst *m* field survey service.
Truppenwetterdienst *m* field meteorological service.
Truppführer *m* leader of a *Trupp*; corporal (*Reich Labor Service*).
l.MG-Truppführer light MG team leader (*R squad*).
T-Stoff *m* lacrimator (*abbr.* of Tränenstoff).
Tucheinsatz *m* cloth filter.
Tuchzeichen *n* ground panel, code panel.
Turbokompressor *m* centrifugal compressor, turbosupercharger.
Turm *m* tower; turret.
Turmanschluß *m* turret connection (*Ap, Tk*).
Turmaufsatz *m* cupola (*Tk*).
Turmgeschütz *n* turret gun.
Turmklappe *f* turret hatch (*Tk*).
Turmlafette *f* turret mount.
Turmluke *f* turret hatch (*Tk*).
Turmlukendeckel *m* turret hatch cover (*Tk*).
Turmschwenkwerk *n* turret traversing mechanism (*Ap, Tk*).
Turmzurrung *f* turret locking clamp (*Ap, Tk*).
Tutol *n* trinitrotoluol.
Typenbezeichnung *f* model designation.
Typennummer *f* model number.
Typenschild *n* name plate.

Ü

üben to practice, exercise, train.
Überbau *m* superstructure.
Überbeanspruchung *f* overload (*Mech*).
Überbelichtung *f* overexposure (*Photo*).
Überbestand *m* surplus stock (*i.e., above authorized basic allowance*).
Überdeckung *f* overlap (*aerial Photo*).
seitliche Überdeckung sidelap (*aerial Photo*).
Überdruck *m* pressure above atmospheric pressure; pressure difference, excess pressure.
Überfall *m* raid, surprise attack (*Tac*); spillway (*dam*).
Überfallkommando *n* raiding party.
Überfallkrone *f* spillway crest (*dam*).
Überfallwehr *n* spillway weir, overfall dam.
überflügeln outflank.
Überflügelung *f* outflanking.
überfluten to flood, inundate.
Überflutung *f* flood, flooding, inundation.
überführen to ferry (*Avn*); to transport.
Überführung *f* overpass (*RR*).
Überführungsdienst *m* ferry service (*Avn*).
Überführungsflug *m* ferrying flight.
Übergabe *f* surrender, capitulation; handing over; giving up.
Übergabeverhandlungen *fpl* negotiations for surrender.
Übergang *m* transition; shifting; crossing.
Übergangsbahnhof *m* crossing station (*RR*).
Übergangsgebührnisse *npl* temporary monthly allowance paid on discharge (*to ease transition to civilian life*).
Übergangsgerät *n* stream-crossing equipment.
Übergangskegel *m* forcing cone (*G tube*).
Übergangsmittel *npl* stream-crossing means.
Übergangsstellung *f* intermediate position.
Übergangstruppe *f* stream-crossing troops.
übergeben hand over, surrender.
sich übergeben to vomit.
Überhang *m* overhang (*Top, etc.*); angle of approach (*MT*).
überhitzen overheat (*an engine*); superheat (*steam*).
Überhitzer *m* superheater.
überholen overtake; overhaul.
überholende Verfolgung encircling maneuver in pursuit.
Überholung *f* passing, overtaking (*MT*); encirclement (*in pursuit*) (*Tac*); overhauling (*maintenance*).
Überholungsabteilung *f* encircling detachment (*in pursuit*).
Überholungsgleis *n* passing siding
Überlagerungsempfänger *m* superheterodyne receiver (*Rad*).
Überlagerungsfrequenz *f* heterodyne frequency.
Überlandflug *m* cross-country flight.
überlasten to overload.
Überläufer *m* deserter (*to the enemy*).
Überlaufrohr *n* overflow pipe.
Überlegenheit *f* superiority.
Übermacht *f* superior strength, superiority.
übermannen overcome, overpower.
Übermantel *m* overcoat.
Übernahme *f* taking over, assuming (*a command, etc.*); acceptance (*of matériel, etc.*).
überplanmäßig in excess of authorized strength or allowance.
überqueren to cross (*a river, etc.*).
Überraschung *f* surprise.
Übersättigung *f* supersaturation (*Met*).
überschießen to fire over the heads of friendly troops; to fire beyond the target.
Überschießen eigener Truppen overhead firing (*Gunnery*).
Überschießen von Deckungen clearance of masks (*Gunnery*).
Überschießgrenze *f* corresponding range (*Gunnery*).
Überschießtafel *f* overhead firing table.
Überschlag *m* loop (*Avn*).
Überschlag auf dem Boden ground loop (*Avn*).
überschlagen, sich to tumble (*projectile*); to roll over (*Avn*); to turn over (*vehicles*).
Überschlag über den Flügel barrel roll (*Avn*).
überschreiten to cross (*a Bdg, road, etc.*).
Überschreitfähigkeit *f* trench-crossing ability (*Tk*).
Überschrift *f* heading.
Überschußwasser *n* overflow water (*dam*).
überschwemmen to flood.
Überschwemmung *f* flood.
überschwer heavy (*.50 caliber MG as distinguished from German "heavy" MG, which is .30 caliber and on tripod mount*).
übersetzen to translate; to cross, to ferry.
Übersetzen über Wasserläufe stream crossing.
Übersetzer *m* translator.
Übersetzfähre *f* ferry.
Übersetzgruppe *f* crossing detail.
Übersetzmittel *n* stream-crossing equipment.
Übersetzstelle *f* stream-crossing point, ferrying point, crossing site.
Übersetzung *f* translation; gear ratio, gear transmission (*to increase speed*).
Übersetzungsgetriebe *n* gear transmission (*to increase speed*).
Übersetzungsverhältnis *n* gear ratio.
Übersicht *f* survey; chart, plan, table; summary; synoptic view.
Übersichtsbild *n* index map (*aerial Photo*).
Übersteuerung *f* over bias (*Rad*); overloading (*Elec, Rad*).
Überstromkanal *m* bypass (*Mtr*).
Übertrager *m* transformer (*Elec*); repeating coil (*Tp*).
Übertragerkästchen *n* repeating coil unit (*Tp*).
Übertragungsgerät *n* data transmission system (*AAA*).
Übertragungskörper *m* induced-detonation charge.
Übertragungsladung *f* primer charge.
Übertrommel *f* range drum (*sight mount*).
überwachen to supervise, monitor, guard, police.
Überwachung *f* surveillance, observation; monitoring; guarding, policing.
überwältigen overcome, overpower.
Überwasserstreitkräfte *fpl* surface forces (*Nav*).
überweisen to allot; send, convey; to refer.
Überweisungsamt *n* toll station (*Tp*).
überwinden to overcome; surmount (*obstacles*); to force (*a crossing, etc.*); to conquer (*the enemy, etc.*).
überziehen to stall (*Ap*).
Überzug *m* cover, hood.
U-Boot *n* submarine, U-boat (*abbr.* of Unterseeboot).
U-Boot-Bunker *m* submarine pen.
U-Bootjäger *m* submarine chaser.
U-Bootkrieg *m* submarine warfare.
U-Boot-Mutterschiff *n* submarine tender.
U-Bootnetz *n* submarine net.
U-Boot-Werft *f* submarine construction yard.
Übung *f* practice, exercise, training, drill, training maneuver.
Übungsflug *m* practice flight.
Übungsflugzeug *n* training airplane, trainer.
Übungsgerät *n* practice device, practice equipment.
Übungsgeschoß *n* training projectile, target-practice projectile.
Übungsgranate *f* practice shell (*Am*).
Übungshandgranate *f* practice grenade, training grenade.
Übungsladung *f* practice charge (*Am*).
Übungsleitung *f* director headquarters (*maneuvers*).
Übungsmaske *f* training mask (*CWS*).
Übungsmine *f* practice mine.
Übungsmunition *f* practice ammunition, training munitions.

Übungsreizstoff *m* irritant training agent *(CWS)*.
Übungsriechstoff *m* odor-detection training agent *(CWS)*.
Übungsschießen *n* practice firing.
Übungsverband *m* training unit.
Ufer *n* shore, bank.
Uferbalken *m* shore sill *(Bdg)*.
Uferbrücke *f* single-span stringer bridge.
Uferschnellsteg *m* hasty single-span footbridge.
Uhr *f* watch, clock, timepiece; instrument dial.
Uhrenscheibe *f* target consisting of circle of silhouettes.
Uhrvergleich *m* synchronization of watches.
Uhrwerkantrieb *m* clockwork action *(fuze)*.
Uhrwerkzünder *m* clockwork fuze
Uhrzeiger *m* clock hand; indicator *(Inst)*.
im Gegensinn zum Uhrzeiger counterclockwise.
im Sinne des Uhrzeigers clockwise.
Uhrzeit *f* clock time *(such as 1345; as distinguished from* Zeit, *time, in sense of "time length")*.
Uhrzeitangabe *f* time announcement, time signal.
Ultrakurzwelle *f* ultrashort wave, ultrahigh frequency *(in strict sense, very high frequency, 30 mc. to 300 mc.)*.
Ultrakurzwellenempfänger *m* ultrahigh frequency receiver. *See also* **Ultrakurzwelle.**
Ultrakurzwellensender *m* ultrahigh frequency transmitter. *See also* **Ultrakurzwelle.**
umbilden reorganize.
Umbildung *f* reorganization.
Umdrehung *f* revolution *(Mech)*.
Umdrehungszahl *f* number of revolutions, rpm.
Umdrehungszähler *m* tachometer.
Umdruck *m* mimeograph or offset reproduction.
Umfang *m* perimeter, scope, circumference.
umfassen to envelop *(Tac)*.
Umfassung *f* envelopment *(Tac)*.
Umformer *m* converter *(Elec)*.
Umformersatz *m* converter unit *(Elec)*.
Umgang *m* breeching *(harness)*.
umgehen to turn, outflank *(Tac)*; to detour, go around, bypass.
Umgehung *f* turning, outflanking *(Tac)*; bypass(ing), detour(ing).
Umgehungsbewegung *f* turning movement, outflanking movement.
umgliedern to reorganize.
Umgruppierung *f* regrouping.
Umhang *m* cape, cloak.
umhängen to sling *(arms)*; take up *(packs)*.
umkehren to reverse, turn over.
Umkehrgetriebe *n* **reversing gear** ***(in rear-axle differential of half-track vehicle)*.**
umkippen to tip over, to dump.
Umklammerung *f* envelopment, encirclement *(Tac)*.
Umkreis *m* perimeter, circumference, periphery; radius.
Umladung *f* transshipment.
Umlauf *m* rotation; cycle; circulation; circular; side spillway *(dam)*.
in Umlauf to be circulated *(documents)*.
Umlaufgetriebe *n* planetary gear.
Umlaufmotor *m* rotary engine *(Ap)*.
umleiten to reroute *(traffic, etc.)*; to divert *(a stream)*.
Umlenkrolle *f* deflecting pulley.
Umpolung *f* pole reversal *(Elec)*.
Umrandung *f* edge, edging, border, border strip.
Umrandungsfeuer *n* boundary light *(Adrm)*.
Umrechnung *f* conversion *(Math)*.
Umrechnungstafel *f* conversion table.
Umschalteklinke *f* throwout *(MG tripod)*.
umschalten to switch over; to change gear.
Umschaltepause *f* switch interval, answer lag *(interphone)*.
Umschalter *m* change-over switch, selector switch *(Elec)*.
Umschalthebel *m* change lever *(automatic R)*.
Umschlag *m* application *(Med)*.
umschlagen to transload; to fell *(a tree)*; to break down from bulk to unit containers; to capsize *(a boat)*; to change suddenly *(wind, etc.)*.
Umschlagshafen *m* transshipment port.
Umschlagstelle *f* bulk reduction point, transloading point, relay point.
umschulen to retrain.
umschwingen to veer.
Umweg *m* detour.
Umzäunung *f* enclosure.
unabhängig independent.
unabkömmlich irreplaceable, indispensable.
unangelehnte Flanke exposed flank.
unbefestigte Straße dirt road.
unbenutzbar unserviceable.
unbewaffnet unarmed.
unbrauchbar unserviceable.
Unbrauchbarmachung *f* destruction, rendering useless.
undicht leaky, permeable, not gas-proof or waterproof.
Undichtigkeit *f* permeability, leakage.
undurchdringlich impermeable, impenetrable.
Undurchdringlichkeit *f* impermeability, impenetrability.
unentzündbar inert *(Am)*.
unerlaubte Entfernung absence without leave.
Unfallbearbeitung *f* accident investigation.
ungedämpft undamped *(Tech)*.
ungeeignet unqualified, unsuited, unsuitable.
ungefähr approximate.
Ungehorsam *m* disobedience.
ungeklärte Lage obscure situation *(Tac)*.
ungepflastert unpaved.
ungeschützt exposed *(Tac)*.
ungünstig unfavorable.
Uniform *f* uniform *(Clo)*.
Uniformbezugschein *m* individual clothing slip.
Universalinstrument *n* transit *(Surv)*.
unmittelbare Unterstützung direct support *(Arty, Tac)*.
unregelmäßig irregular.
unscharf unarmed *(fuze, etc.)*; blurred, out of focus *(Optics)*.
unscharf machen disarm *(Am)*.
unstarres Luftschiff nonrigid airship.
untauglich physically unfit for active service.
Unterabschnitt *m* subsector.
Unterarzt *m* medical noncommissioned officer *(with rank of Master Sgt)*.
Unterbau *m* subgrade, foundation, substructure.
Unterbindung *f* choking off, forestalling, preventing *(Tac)*.
unterbrechen interrupt.
Unterbrecher *m* contact breaker, interrupter *(Elec)*.
Unterbrechung *f* interruption; cessation; suspension *(of traffic)*.
unterbringen to billet, quarter; to store, stow.
Unterbringung *f* **sheltering, quartering, billeting; quarters, billets; stowage position** ***(of equipment in vehicle)*.**
Unterbringungsgebiet *n* **quartering area.**
Unterdruck *m* **vacuum, low pressure** ***(below atmospheric pressure)*.**
Unterdruckförderer *m* **vacuum tank** ***(MT)*.**
Unterdruckkammer *f* **low-pressure chamber.**
Unterfeldmeister *m* **staff sergeant** ***(Reich Labor Service)*.**
Unterfeldwebel *m* **staff sergeant.**
Unterführer *m* **enlisted man tentatively selected for subsequent officer's training; subordinate commander.**
untere Führung **lower command** ***(Regt and down)*.**
Unterführung *f* underpass *(RR)*.
untergebene Stellen lower commands.
untergeordnet **inferior in rank, subordinate.**
Untergurt *m* **cincha** ***(saddle)*;** **bottom chord** ***(truss)*.**
unterhaltener Fahrweg **improved road.**
Unterhaltsberechtigter *m* dependent *(entitled to dependency benefits)*.
Unterhaltung *f* maintenance; conversation; recreation, entertainment.
Unterhändler *m* negotiator, bearer of a flag of truce, parlementaire.
Unterhandlung *f* parley.
Unterholz *n* underbrush, undergrowth.
Unterkalibergeschoß *n* subcaliber projectile *(Am)*.
Unterkunft *f* shelter, quarters, billets.
freie Unterkunft quarters in kind.
Unterkunftsbezirk *m* shelter area, quartering area, billeting area.
Unterkunftsgruppe *f* billeting group.
Unterkunftsraum *m* shelter area, cantonment area.
Unterlafette *f* bottom gun carriage.
Unterlage *f* plane table *(Arty, Surv)*; datum; basis; document, record.
Unterlagerungstelegraphie *f* simplexed telegraphy.
Unterlegbohlen *fpl* dunnage.
unterlegen inferior *(in numbers)*.
Unterlegenheit *f* inferiority *(Tac)*.
Unterlegeplane *f* ground cloth *(Bln)*.
Unterlegscheibe *f* washer.
Unternehmen *n* operation *(Tac)*.
Unternehmung *f* operation *(Tac)*.
Unteroffizier *m* noncommissioned officer; sergeant.
Unteroffizieranwärter *m* candidate for noncommissioned rank.
Unteroffiziere mit Portepee noncommissioned officers from *Feldwebel* up.
Unteroffiziere ohne Portepee noncommissioned officers from *Unteroffizier* down.
Unteroffiziere und Mannschaften enlisted men.
unterpolstert padded.
Unterredung *f* parley.
Unterricht *m* instruction.
unterrichten instruct, teach.
Unterrichtstafel *f* demonstration chart *(Tng)*.
Unterring *m* lower band *(R)*.
Unterringfeder *f* lower band spring.
Unterschenkel *m* gaskin *(horse)*.
Unterschied *m* difference.
Unter-Schiedsrichter *m* umpire assigned to a subordinate unit *(generally an NCO)*.
Unterschild *m* apron shield, lower shield *(G)*.
Unterschildträger *m* lower shield bracket *(G)*.
Unterschlupf *m* cut-and-cover shelter, dugout.
Unterseeboot *n* U-boat, submarine.
Unterseite *f* underside, lower side; belly *(Tk)*.
Untersetzung *f* reduction *(Mech)*.
Untersetzungsgetriebe *n* reduction gear *(MT)*.
Unterstand *m* shelter, protected shelter, dugout *(Ft)*.
unterstellt inferior in rank, subordinate.
unterstrom downstream.
Untersturmführer *m* *See* **SS-Untersturmführer.**
unterstützen to support.
Unterstützung *f* support *(Tac)*.
Unterstützungsartillerie *f* supporting artillery.
Unterstützungsfeuer *n* supporting fire.
untersuchen inspect, examine; test; investigate.
Untersuchung *f* investigation, examination; surveillance *(of Am and CWS supplies, etc.)*; inspection.
Untersuchungsstelle *f* test station *(Tp)*.
Unterveterinär *m* veterinary noncommissioned officer *(with rank of Master Sgt)*.
Unterwachtmeister *m* staff sergeant *(Arty, Cav)*.
Unterwasserbombe *f* depth bomb, depth charge.
Unterwasserhorchgerät *n* hydrophone *(Nav)*.
Unterwasserschneidetrupp *m* underwater cutting and welding detachment.
Unterweisung *f* indoctrination, instruction.
Unterwerfung *f* subjection, subjugation, submission, surrender.
Unterzug *m* transom *(Bdg)*.
Untiefen *fpl* shoals.
unverzüglich immediate.
unvorschriftsmäßig contrary to regulations, not prescribed, irregular.
Unwetter *n* bad weather, storm.
U-Rahmen *m* U-frame *(tubular chassis)*.
Urbaumuster *n* original model, prototype *(Ap, Tk, etc.)*.
Urkunde *f* document, permanent record.
Urkundenbeweis *m* documentary evidence.
Urlaub *m* leave, furlough, leave of absence.
Urlauber *m* man on leave, furlough, or pass.
Urlaubsschein *m* furlough certificate; leave; pass.
Ursprung *m* origin.
Urteilsmilderung *f* mitigation of sentence.
Urwald *m* jungle.
Urwaldkrieg *m* jungle warfare.

Ubers	Überzahl	surplus; superior number (*of*
Überz	Überzeugung	conviction
Üb.Flgz	Übungsflugzeug	training plane
Üb.Fz	Übungsfahrzeug	training vehicle
Üb.Gr	Übungsgranate	practice shell
übl	überland	overland
Üb.Ldg	Übungsladung	practice charge
Üb.Lg	Übungslager	training camp
Üb.M	Übungsmarsch	practice march; route march
Üb.M	Übungsmine	dummy (training) mine
Üb.Mun	Übungsmunition	blank ammunition
Üb.Pl	Übungsplatz	drill ground; training ground
Üb.Pl.Kdo	Übungsplatzkommando	drill ground headquarters
Üb.Pl.Kdt	Kommandant des Truppenübungsplatzes	commander of the drill ground
Üb.Pse	Übungspause	rest period during training
Üb.R	Übungsreise	tactical ride
Übs	Übersetzung	translation; crossing (*a river*)
Üb.Spr.K	**Übungssprengkörper**	**dummy blasting charge**
Übst	Übergangsstelle	crossing point
Üb.S.hg	Übungsstielhandgranate	practice stick hand grenade
Üb.Tg	Übungstag	drill day
Üb.Tp	Übungstorpedo	training torpedo; dummy torpedo
Übtr	Übertragung	transmission; transcription
Übtr	Übertreibung	exaggeration
Übtr	Übertretung	violation; transgression
Üf	Überlagerungsfrequenz	heterodyne frequency
ü.MG	überschweres Maschinengewehr	superheavy machine gun
Ü.Pl	Übungsplatz	drill ground; training ground
üschw	überschwer	superheavy
Uf	Unterfeldwebel	(*corresponds roughly to U. S. serg*
U.F	Unterführer	subordinate commander
Uffz	Unteroffizier	noncommissioned officer
Uffz.Anw	Unteroffizieranwärter	noncommissioned officer as-
Uffz.D.R	Unteroffizier der Reserve	reserve noncommissioned officer
Uffz.v.D	Unteroffizier vom Dienst	noncommissioned officer on du
Uf.Schn.St	Uferschnellsteg	hasty landing bridge
U.Fw	Unterfeldwebel	(*corresponds roughly to U. S. ser*
ugesch	ungeschützt	unprotected
ugf	ungefähr	approximately; about
U.K	Umgebungskarte	position sketch; map of immediate vicinity
Uk	Umzugskosten	moving costs
uk	unabkömmlich	indispensable; subject to occupational deferment
u.M	unter dem Meeresspiegel	below sea level
umf	umfangreich	voluminous
umf	umfassend	extensive; comprehensive;
Umg	Umgang	detour
umg	umgeändert	changed; altered; converted
Umg	**Umgebung**	**vicinity**
Umg.Bew	Umgehungsbewegung	turning movement
Umg.K	Umgebungskarte	position sketch; map of immediate vicinity
Umg.Man	Umgehungsmanöver	outflanking maneuver
Umgr	Umgruppierung	regrouping; redistribution of force
umh	umhängen	to sling (*packs or rifles*)
U/Min	Umdrehungen in der Min	revolutions per minute
Umkr	Umkreis	surrounding environment
Uml	Umlauf	circulation; rotation
Uml.Mot	Umlaufmotor	rotary engine
Umw	Umweg	detour
Un	Uniform	uniform
Unabh	Unabhängigkeit	independence
unangr	unangreifbar	unassailable; impregnable
unausg	unausgebildet	untrained
unbed	unbedeutend	insignificant
unbed	unbedingt	unconditional; absolute
unbef	unbefestigt	unfortified; open
unbek	unbekannt	unknown
Unbek.Sold	Unbekannter Soldat	unknown soldier
unbem	unbemannt	unmanned
unbem	unbemerkt	unnoticed
unbeob	unbeobachtet	unobserved
unbes	unbesetzt	unoccupied
unbesch	unbeschädigt	uninjured; undamaged
unbesch	unbeschäftigt	unemployed
unbesch	unbeschützt	unprotected
unerl	unerlaubt	forbidden
unerl	unerledigt	unsettled
unerpr	unerprobt	not tested; untried
unerr	unerreichbar	unattainable; inaccessible
uners	unersetzlich	irreparable
unerw	unerwartet	unexpected
Unf	Unfall	accident
unf	unfahrbar	impassable
ung	ungünstig	unfavorable
ungb	ungangbar	impassable
ungeh	ungehorsam	disobedient
ungen	**ungenau**	**inaccurate**
ungep	ungepanzert	without armor; unarmored
unges	ungesetzlich	unlawful; illegal
unges	ungesichert	unsecure
unges	ungesund	unhealthy

ungesch	ungeschützt	unprotected
ungez	ungezielt	unaimed
ungez	ungezogen	unrifled
ungf	ungefähr	approximately; about
unh	unhaltbar	untenable; indefensible
Unif	Uniform	uniform
unk	unkundig	ignorant
unl	unlöslich	insoluble
unpass	unpassierbar	impassable
unt	unter	under
Unterg	Untergang	decline; fall; ruin
Untergb	Untergebener	subordinate
unterh	unterhalb	below; beyond
Unterk.Gr	Unterkunftsgruppe	billeting party
Untern	Unternehmung	enterprise
Unterord	Unterordnung	subordination
Unterr	Unterredung	conversation
Unterr	Unterrichtsmunition	practice ammunition
Untersch	Unterschied	difference; distinction
Unterst	Unterstand	shelter; dugout
Unt.F	Unterführer	subordinate commander
Untffz	Unteroffizier	noncommissioned officer
Untffz-Sch	Unteroffiziersschule	school for noncommissioned officers
untgl	untauglich	unfit
unv	unvollständig	incomplete
unvert	unverteidigt	undefended
unverz	unverzagt	undaunted; fearless
unvors	unvorsichtig	careless; unwise
unzug	unzugänglich	inaccessible
unzul	unzulänglich	insufficient
unzul	unzulässig	inadmissible
unzuv	unzuverlässig	unreliable
Uoffz	Unteroffizier	noncommissioned officer
U.P	Unteroffizierposten	noncommissioned officer command post
u.R	unter Rückerbittung	request return (*on documents*)
Url	Urlaub	furlough; leave
Url.Antr	Urlaubsantritt	date of start of furlough
Url.Ges	Urlaubsgesuch	request for furlough
Url.Sch	Urlaubschein	furlough paper or pass
Url.Sp	Urlaubssperre	(temporary) discontinuance for furloughs
Urs	Ursache	cause; reason
Urschr	Urschrift	original (*as opposed to copy*)
Urspr	Ursprung	origin
Urs.u	Ursache unbekannt	cause unknown
U.S	Unteroffiziersschule	school for noncomsioned officers
Uscha	Unterscharführer	(SS) section leader
Uschla	Untersuchungs- und Schlichtungsausschuss der ReichsleitungNSDAP	National Socialist Supreme Party Board of Investigation and Arbitration
Ustuf	Untersturmführer	(SS) company commander
usw	und so weiter	and so forth
u.U	unterirdischer Unterstand	subterranean shelter or dugout
u.U	unter Umständen	under certain conditions
u.V	unter Vorbehalt	with the proviso or reservation
U.V.D	Unteroffizier vom Dienst	noncommissioned officer on duty
uverh	unverheiratet	single (*unmarried*)
U.Wm	Unterwachtmeister	(*corresponds roughly to U. S sergeant*)
U.z.b.V	Unteroffizier zur besonderen Verwendung	noncommissioned officer specialist

V

V	Vater	father
V	Veränderung	change; alteration; modification; variation
V	Verband	formation; task force; unit; surgical dressing
V	Verbindung	connection; junction; combination; communication; contact; liaison
v	verboten	forbidden; prohibited
v	verdeckt	defiladed; camouflaged; screened; masked; covered
V	Verdienst	earnings; gain; profit; merit
V	Verein	association; society; union
v	vereinigte	united; combined
V	Vereinigung	unification; union; association; fusion; junction
V	Verfassung	state; condition; constitution; situation
V	Verfügung	decree; order; disposition; disposal
V	Vergütung	compensation; indemnity
V	Verkehr	traffic; communication; intercourse
V	Vermessungs-Batterie	survey battery
V	(Fernsprech)-Vermittlung	telephone exchange
V	Vermögen	wealth; ability; power; capacity; faculty
V	Vernehmung	examination; hearing; interrogation; questioning
V	Veröffentlichung	publication; promulgation
V	Verordnung	order; ordinance; decree; in-
V	Verpflegung	food supply; ration
V	Verpflegungsunteroffizier	supply noncom

V

veraltet obsolete.
verankern to moor.
Verankerung *f* anchorage, holdfast.
Verankerungsgurt *m* mooring band *(Bln).*
Verankerungskabel *n* guy; mooring cable.
Verankerungsmast *m* mooring mast *(Bln).*
Verankerungstau *n* ground cable, mooring cable *(Bln).*
Verankerungsturm *m* mooring tower *(Bln).*
veranlassen to cause, bring about, call forth.
veranschaulichen illustrate.
verantwortlich responsible.
Verantwortlichkeit *f* responsibility.
verausgaben to issue.
Verausgabung *f* issue.
Verband *m* combined-arms unit, force, task force; air force unit, force, formation *(Avn)*; bandage, dressing.
Verband aller Waffen combined-arms unit.
Verbandflug *m* formation flying.
Vakuumröhre *f* vacuum tube.
V-Boot *n* launch *(abbr. of* Verkehrsboot*).*
Velozitätsmeßzug *m* velocity measurement platoon *(Arty).*
Ventil *n* valve.
Ventilanordnung *f* valve arrangement *(Mtr).*
Ventilfeder *f* valve spring *(Mtr).*
Ventilkammer *f* valve chamber *(Mtr).*
Ventilkegel *m* valve ball *(MT)*; valve head *(pneumatic counterrecoil mechanism).*
Ventilleine *f* valve cord, gas-valve operating line *(Bln).*
ventilloser Motor sleeve-type engine.
Ventilschaft *m* valve stem *(Mtr).*
Ventilschaftführung *f* valve guide *(Mtr).*
Ventilsitz *m* valve seat *(Mtr).*
Ventilsteuerung *f* valve-timing system *(Mtr).*
Ventilstößel *m* valve lifter *(Mtr).*
Ventilteller *m* valve head *(Mtr).*
Verachtung *f* contempt, disregard.
Verbandkasten *m* first-aid box.
Verbandmittel *npl* dressing equipment *(Med).*
Verbandpäckchen *n* first-aid packet.
Verbandplatz *m* aid station, dressing station.
Verbandsabwurf *m* formation release *(bombing).*
Verbandsflug *m* flying in formation, formation flying.
Verbandswurf *m* *See* **Verbandsabwurf.**
Verbandtasche *f* first-aid bag.
Verbandzeug *n* first-aid kit, first-aid supplies.
verbergen to mask, conceal, hide.
Verbesserung *f* correction *(Gunnery).*
Verbesserung für Länge range correction *(Gunnery).*
Verbesserung für Seite lateral correction *(Gunnery).*
Verbesserung für Witterungseinflüsse metro correction *(Arty).*
Verbesserungsgerät *n* parallax offset mechanism *(sound locator).*
Verbesserungswert *m* correction factor *(Gunnery).*
Verbesserungswinkel *m* correction angle *(Gunnery).*
verbeulte Patrone battered round.
Verbiegen *n* droop *(Mech).*
verbieten to prohibit, forbid.
Verbindung *f* liaison, communication, contact *(Tac)*; connection *(Tp)*; compound *(Cml).*
Verbindung aufnehmen make contact, establish communication *(with friendly troops).*
Verbindungsachse *f* axis of communication.
Verbindungsaufnahme *f* establishment of communication, liaison, or contact *(with friendly troops).*
Verbindungsdienst *m* liaison service, liaison duty.
Verbindungsflugzeug *n* liaison airplane.
Verbindungsgraben *m* communication trench, connecting trench.
Verbindungshülse *f* connecting sleeve, casing, collar.
Verbindungsleute *mpl* connecting file, communicating file; liaison agents.
Verbindungslinie *f* line of communication.
Verbindungsmann *m* liaison agent.
Verbindungsmittel *n* means of communication.
Verbindungsnetz *n* liaison net *(Rad).*
Verbindungsoffizier *m* liaison officer.
Verbindungsorgane *npl* connecting elements *(march column).*
Verbindungspatrouille *f* contact patrol *(Tac).*
Verbindungsriemen *m* turnback *(harness).*
Verbindungsschnur *f* connecting cord *(Tp).*
Verbindungsschraube *f* floor plate screw *(R).*
Verbindungsstaffel *f* liaison squadron *(Avn).*
Verbindungsstraße *f* communication road, communication route.
Verbindungstrupp *m* liaison party, liaison detachment; connecting group; contact patrol.
Verbindungsweg *m* channel of communication *(Tp, Rad).*
verblenden to dim or black out *(lights).*
verbogen bent, twisted, warped.
Verbot *n* prohibition, off-limits declaration; exclusion; restriction.
Verbotstafel *f* "prohibited" sign.
Verbrauch *m* consumption, expenditure.
verbrauchbar expendable.
Verbraucherstelle *f* outlet *(Elec).*
Verbrauchsgüter *npl* expendable supplies.
Verbrauchssatz *m* consumption per 100 kilometers *(of gasoline, oil, and lubricants).*
Verbrauchsstoffe *mpl* *See* Verbrauchsgüter.
Verbrennung *f* combustion; deflagration *(of powder).*
Verbrennungskraftmaschine *f* internal-combustion engine.
Verbrennungsraum *m* combustion chamber; powder chamber *(G).*
Verbrennungsrückstand *m* carbon *(Mtr).*
verbundene Waffen combined arms *(Tac).*
Verbündete(r) *m* ally.
Verbundmaschine *f* compound-wound motor.
Verbundröhre *f* multi-unit tube *(Rad).*
verchromt chromium-plated.
Verdämmen *n* tamping, mud capping *(demolitions)*; damming up *(a stream).*
verdampfen to vaporize, evaporate.
Verdampfungswärme *f* heat of vaporization *(Met).*
Verdeck *n* cover; hood; deck.
verdecken to cover, mask, conceal, defilade.
Verdeckung *f* concealment, defilade.
Verdichtung *f* compression *(Mtr).*
Verdichtungshub *m* compression stroke *(Mtr).*
Verdichtungsverhältnis *n* compression ratio *(Mtr).*
Verdichtungswelle *f* burst wave, detonation wave *(SR)*; compression wave *(Physics).*
Verdienstkreuz *n* Meritorious Service Cross *(decoration).*
verdolmetschen interpret, translate.
verdrahten to wire, to block with wire obstacles.
Verdrängung *f* displacement.
Verdrängungszylinder *m* compression cylinder *(counterrecoil mechanism).*
Verdunkelung *f* blackout.
Verdunkelungslampe *f* blackout lamp, blackout light.
vereinigtes Feuer collective fire *(SA).*
Vereinheitlichung *f* standardization.
Vereisung *f* icing, formation of ice *(Avn).*
Vereisungsschutzgerät *n* de-icer *(Ap).*
vereiteln nullify, foil, render useless, fail.
Verfahren *n* method, procedure, process.
verfehlen to miss.
verfertigen to make, manufacture.
Verfolgung *f* pursuit *(Tac).*
Verfolgungsabteilung *f* direct pressure detachment *(in pursuit).*
verfügbar available.
Verfügung *f* disposal, disposition; availability; instruction, order.
zur Verfügung available for duty *(abbr.* z.V.*).*
Verfügungsfrequenzen *fpl* assigned frequencies *(Rad).*
vergasen to gas *(CWS).*
Vergaser *m* carburetor.
Vergaseranordnung *f* carburetion *(Mtr).*
Vergasermotor *m* carburetor engine.
Vergatterung *f* guard mount *(bugle call).*
Vergehen *n* offense, breach *(of discipline)*, infraction *(of regulations).*
Vergeltung *f* retaliation, reprisal.
Vergeltungsangriff *m* retaliation attack; reprisal raid *(Avn).*
Vergeltungsmaßnahme *f* reprisal.
vergiften to poison; to contaminate, to gas *(CWS).*
Vergiftung *f* contamination *(CWS).*
Vergiftungsschießen *n* gas-shell fire *(Arty).*
Vergleichsschießen *n* calibration firing *(Arty).*
Vergleichsziel *n* auxiliary target *(Gunnery).*
Vergrößerung *f* enlargement, magnification.
Vergrößerungsapparat *m* enlarger, enlarging projector *(Photo).*
Vergütung *f* reimbursement, recoupment; compensation, award, allowance; heat treatment *(of metals).*
Vergütungsanlage *f* soaking pit *(Ord).*
Vergütungsstahl *m* heat-treated steel.
Verhaftung *f* arrest.
Verhältnis *n* relation; proportion, ratio; condition, situation.
verhandeln negotiate.
Verhandlung *f* parley, negotiation.
Verhängung von Strafen imposition of punishment *(Law, PW).*
Verhau *m* abatis, hurdle, entanglement.
Verheerung *f* devastation.
verhindern prevent.
Verhör *n* interrogation.
verhören to interrogate.
verjüngt tapered; reduced.
Verjüngung *f* taper; reduction *(of scale).*
verkanten to cant *(G, R)*; to tilt, incline; to become misalined.
Verkantung *f* cant *(Arty)*; misalinement of wheels *(MT).*
Verkantungslibelle *f* cross level.
Verkantungstrieb *m* cross-level drive.
Verkehr *m* traffic; communication.
Verkehrsbestimmung *f* traffic regulation.
Verkehrsboot *n* launch *(Nav).*
Verkehrsfliegerei *f* commercial aviation.
Verkehrsflugzeug *n* commercial airplane.
Verkehrskreis *m* traffic area.
Verkehrslast *f* bridge capacity.
Verkehrsleitung *f* traffic control.
Verkehrslinien *fpl* lines of communication *(Tac).*
Verkehrsposten *m* traffic control point.
Verkehrspunkt *m* traffic center.
Verkehrsregel *f* traffic rule, traffic regulation, rule for road procedure, rule of the road.
Verkehrsregelung *f* traffic control.
Verkehrsregelungsbataillon *n* traffic control battalion.
Verkehrsschild *n* traffic sign.
Verkehrsstockung *f* traffic congestion, jam, tie-up.
Verkehrsstreife *f* traffic patrol.
Verkehrsteilnehmer *m* traffic element.
Verkehrsüberwachung *f* traffic supervision.
Verkehrszeichen *n* traffic sign, traffic symbol.
verkehrt reverse, inverse; wrong.
verkitten fasten or seal with putty or other adhesive.
verkleiden to revet; to mask, camouflage, disguise.
Verkleidung *f* cowling, fairing *(Ap)*; revetment; camouflage, disguise.
verklemmen to jam, to wedge.
Verladebahnhof *m* loading station, entraining station *(RR).*
Verladehafen *m* loading port, port of embarkation.
verladen to load, entrain, entruck, embark.
Verladeoffizier *m* entraining officer, entrucking officer, loading officer.
Verladeplan *m* loading table; entraining or entrucking table.
Verladeplatz *m* loading point; entraining or entrucking point.
Verladerampe *f* loading platform, loading ramp.
Verladestab *m* loading staff *(sea port).*
Verladestelle *f* *See* **Verladeplatz.**
Verladezeit *f* loading time, entrucking time, entraining time.
Verladung *f* loading, entrucking, entraining.
Verladungsoffizier *m* *See* **Verladeoffizier.**
Verladungsschein *m* bill of lading.
Verlängerungsstück *n* extension; sight extension *(G sight).*
verlasten to pack or load on vehicles or horses *(specifically, to load on pack animals).*
verlastete Artillerie portée artillery.
verlastete Truppen motorized troops.
Verlauf *m* sequence of events, course, progress *(of an attack, etc.).*
verlegen to transfer; shift *(fire, etc.).*
Verlegenheit *f* confusion, embarrassment, perplexity.
Verlegewagen *m* reel cart *(for Tp wire).*
Verlegung *f* transfer, shift.
Verlegungsbefehl *m* movement order; order to shift fire *(Arty).*
Verlust *m* casualty, loss; forfeiture *(of pay, etc.).*
Verlustliste *f* casualty list.
Verlustmeldung *f* casualty report.
Verlustrate *f* casualty rate.
tägliche Verlustrate casualty day.
vermessen to survey, to locate.
Vermessung *f* survey, surveying, locating *(Arty, Engr).*
Vermessung durch Anhängen survey by controlled traverse *(Surv).*
Vermessungsbatterie *f* survey battery *(Arty).*

V	Verschlagwagen	crate car; freight car with latticed walls for small cattle
V	Versicherung	insurance; assurance
V	Versorgung	supply; provisioning
v	verspannt	braced
V	Verstärkung	reinforcement; amplification
V	Versuch	attempt; experiment; trial
V	Verteidigung	defense
v	verteilen	to distribute; to divide
v	vertikal	vertical
V	Vertikalachse	vertical axis of theodolite
V	Vertrag	treaty; contract; agreement
V	Vertreter	representative; agent
V	Verwaltung	administration; management
V	Verwaltungsamt	administrative office
V	Verwaltungsdienst	civil service
V	Verwaltungsunteroffizier der Luft	administrative noncommissioned officer of the air
V	Verwendung	use; application
v	verwundet	wounded
V	Verzögerung	delay; delay-action
V	Veterinär	veterinary
V	Viertel	quarter; fourth
V	Vize-	vice-
V	Völker	peoples; nations
V	Volks-	people's
V	Voll	full
V	Vollzug	execution (*of orders*); carry-
V	Volt	volt
v	vom	of the
v	von	from; of
v	vor-	before; in front of
v	vorbei	missed! (*gunnery*)
V	Vorder-	front; forward
V	Vorderrad	front wheel
V	Vorgang	event; occurrence
V	Vorhaltepunkt	lead point
V	Vormittag	morning; forenoon
v	vormittags	in the morning; before noon
V	Vorn-	front
V	Vorposten	outpost
V	Vorschriften	regulations; instructions; manual; provisions
V	Vorwerk	advanced work; outwork
v	verwendungsfähig	fit for duty; employable
1.V	erste Verzögerung	short delay
2.V	zweite Verzögerung	long delay
vl	Landegeschwindigkeit von Flugzeugen	landing speed
VA	Heeresverwaltungsamt	Army Administration Office
V.A	Vermessungsabteilung	survey detachment
VA	Versicherungsanstalt	insurance office
VA	Versuchsanstalt	experimental station; research laboratory
V.A	Verteidigungsanleitung	defense regulations
VAbd	Vorabend	eve; evening before
VAbz	Verwundetenabzeichen	wound stripe
var	variabel	variable
Var	Variation	variation
vat	vaterländisch	national; patriotic
vaterl	vaterländisch	national; patriotic
Vb	Verband	formation; unit; task force
Vb	Verbindung	connection; junction; combination; communication
Vb	Vereinbarung	agreement; arrangement; ac-
VB	Visierbereich	danger zone (*gunnery*)
V.B	Völkerbund	League of Nations
VB	Vollzugsbestimmungen	regulations for the execution of orders
VB	vorgeschobene Beobachtung	advanced observation
V.Battr	Vermessungsbatterie	survey battery
Vbd	Verband	formation; unit; task force; surgical dressing
Vbd	Verbindung	connection; junction; combination; communication; contact; liaison
vbd	verbunden	joined; combined; connected; dressed (*medical*)
VBef	Vollstreckungsbefehl	writ of execution; execution-warrant
Vb.G	Verbindungsgraben	communication trench
vbl	variabel	variable
V.Bl	Verordnungsblatt	published orders
Vbr	Verbrauch	expenditure (*ammunition*)
V.B.St	vorgeschobene Beobachtungsstelle	advanced observation post
V.D	Veterinärdepot	veterinary depot
v.D	vom Dienst	on duty; of the service
v.d	von der	of the
v.d	vor dem	before the
VDA	Volksbund für das Deutschtum im Ausland	National Association for the German Element Abroad
V.d.F.H	Anleitung zur Verpflegung des Feldheeres	field commissary regulations for the army
Vdg	Verordnung	decree
ve	Endgeschwindigkeit der Geschosse	final velocity; striking velocity of projectiles
V.E	Verpflegungseinheit	ration unit
VE	Volksempfänger	people's radio receiver
Ver	Verein	association; society; union
ver	vereinigte	united; combined
verabsch	verabschiedet	discharged; retired
Verabsch	Verabschiedung	dismissal; discharge; farewell
Veränd	Veränderung	change; alteration
Verantw	Verantwortlicher	responsible person
verb	verbessert	corrected; improved
Verb	Verbesserung	correction; improvement; adjustment
Verb	Verbindung	connection; junction; combination; communication
verb	verboten	forbidden; prohibited
verb	verbündete	allied; united; confederate
verb	verbunden	joined; combined; connected
Verbd	Verband	formation; unit
Verbd	Verbindung	connection; junction; combination; communication;
Verb.Flgz	Verbindungsflugzeug	communication plane
Verb.Gr	Verbindungsgruppe	connecting group
Verb.Grb	Verbindungsgraben	communication trench
Verb.Kradf	Verbindungskraftradfahrer	communication motorcyclist
Verb.Kst	Verbandkasten	surgeon's dressing case; med-
Verb.L	Verbindungslinie	line of communication
Verb.Lte	Verbindungsleute	connecting file
Verb.M	Verbindungsmann	contact man (*march security*)
Verb.Offz	Verbindungsoffizier	liaison officer; agent officer
Verb.P	Verbandpäckchen	first-aid kit
Verb.Pl	Verbandplatz	field dressing station
Verb.R	Verbindungsrotte	connecting file
verbr	verbrannt	burned; consumed by fire
Verbr	Verbrauch	expenditure (*of ammunition*);
verbr	verbraucht	consumed; spent; used; expended (*of ammunition*)
Verbr	Verbrechen	crime; felony
verbr	verbrecherisch	criminal
Verbr	Verbrennung	combustion
Verbr.Geschw	Verbrennungsgeschwindigkeit	rate of combustion (*gunnery*)
Verbr.Mot	Verbrennungsmotor	combustion engine
Verbr.R	Verbrennungsraum	combustion chamber
Verbr.Temp	Verbrennungstemperatur	combustion temperature (*gunnery*)
Verbst	Verbandstoff	bandage; dressing
Verb.St	Verbindungsstab	liaison staff
Verb.Uffz	Verbindungsunteroffizier	liaison non-commissioned officer
Verbzg	Verbandzeug	bandage; dressing (*medical*)
Verd	Verdacht	suspicion
verd	verdächtig	suspected; suspicious
verd	verdämmt	tamped (*combat engineer blasting service*)
Verd	Verdämmung	tamping (*combat engineer blasting service*)
verd	verdeckt	defiladed; camouflaged; screened; masked
verd	verdichtet	condensed; compressed
Verd	Verdichtung	compression; condensation; concentration; packing; solidification; thickening
Verd	Verdichtungsverhältnis	compression ratio; degree of compression (*engine*)
Verd	Verdienst	earnings; gain; profit; merit
verd	verdient	deserved; earned; merited
verd	verdorben	spoiled; rotten
verd	verdunkelt	blacked out
Verd	Verdunkelung	black-out
Verd.Med	Verdienstmedaille	medal of merit
Verd.Üb	Verdunkelungsübung	black-out practice
vereid	vereidigen	to swear (a person) in; to administer an oath
Vereid	Vereidigter	person under oath
Vereid	Vereidigung	swearing-in; attestation
verein	vereinigen	to concentrate (*fire*)
Vereinf	Vereinfachung	simplification
verf	verfahren	to act; to proceed; to manage
Verf	Verfahren	procedure; process; practice
Verf	Verfall	decay; decadence; decline
verf	verfallen	to decay; to decline; to
Verf	Verfassung	state (condition); constitution; situation
verf	verfehlen	to fail; to miss
Verf	Verfehlung	lapse
verf	verfeuern	to burn; to use up
verf	verfeuert	burned; used up
verf	verfolgen	to pursue, to persecute
verf	verfolgt	pursued; persecuted; trailed
Verf	Verfolgung	persecution; pursuit
verf	verfügen	to decree; to dispose
Verf	Verfügung	decree; order; disposition;
Verf.Fl	Verfolgungsflieger	pursuit flier
Verf.Tr	Verfügungstruppe	reserves; maneuver force; permanently militarized SS units
Verg	Vergangenheit	past
verg	vergasen	to gas; to attack with gas
Verg	Vergaser	carburetor
Verg	Vergasung	gassing; carburetion
verg	vergattern	assemble for change of the guard

Verg	Vergatterung	change of the guard
Verg	Vergehen	misdemeanor
verg	vergelten	to repay; to retaliate
Verg	Vergeltung	retaliation; reprisal
verg	vergiften	to poison
Verg	Vergiftung	poisoning; contamination
Verg	Vergütung	compensation; indemnity
Verg.F	Vergeltungsfeuer	retaliatory fire
Vergl	Vergleich	comparison
Vergl.Sch	Vergleichsschiessen	registration fire
Vergl.Z	Vergleichsziel	auxiliary target (*artillery*)
Verg.M	Vergeltungsmassnahme	retaliatory measure
Verg.Mot	Vergasermotor	carburetor engine
Vergr	Vergrösserung	enlargement; increase
Verh	Verhältnis	relation; proportion; ratio
verh	verhängnisvoll	fatal; fateful; ominous; portentous; disastrous
verh	verhaftet	arrested; apprehended
Verh	Verhaftung	arrest; imprisonment
Verh	Verhalten	behavior; attitude
verh	verhandelt	negotiated; treated
Verh	Verhau	abatis; barbed-wire obstacle
verh	verhindert	hindered; prevented
Verh	Verhinderung	hindering; prevention; obstacle; impediment
Verh	Verhör	hearing; interrogation; examination; questioning
verh	verhört	examined; interrogated
verj	verjudet	Judaized
Verj	Verjüngung	tapering (*form of projectile*)
verk	verkantet	tilted; canted (*sighting error*)
Verk	Verkehr	traffic; communication; in-
Verk	Verkündigung	announcement; publication
Verk	Verkürzung	shortening; abridgmentunr
Verk.Fl	Verkehrsflieger	commercial flier
Verk.Flzg	Verkehrsflugzeug	commercial plane
Verkl	Verkleidung	cowling (*airplane and automobile construction*); casing; camouflage; disguise
Verkl	Verkleinerung	reduction; diminution
Verk.Tr	Verkehrstruppen	communication troops
Verkzg	Verkürzung	shortening; abridgment
verl	verladen	to load; to entrain (*troops*)
Verl	Verladung	entraining; embarkation
Verl	Verlängerung	prolongation; extension
verl	verlastet	loaded (*pack animals*)
Verl	Verlastung	loading of pack animals
Verl	Verlauf	course; progress; process
verl	verlegen	to shift fire (*artillery*)
Verl	Verlegung	shift; transfer; transport
verl	verlesen	to call the roll
verl	verletzt	wounded; injured; hurt
Verl	Verletzung	injury; violation
verl	verloren	lost
Verl	Verlust	loss; casualty
Verl.Bhf	Verladebahnhof	loading station (*railway*)
Verl.Kdo	Verladekommando	entraining command post
Verl.L	Verlustliste	casualty list
Verl.Offz	Verladeoffizier	entraining officer
Verl.R	Verladerampe	loading ramp
Verl.St	Verladestab	loading crew
Verl.St	Verladestation	entraining station
Verl.St	Verladestelle	entraining point
Verl.St	Verlängerungsstück	extension piece
Verl.Üb	Verladeübung	entraining practice
Verl.Z	Verladezeit	entraining time
verm	vermacht	bequeathed
Verm	Vermächtnis	testament
Verm	Vermahlung	grinding
verm	vermehrt	increased; multiplied
Verm	Vermehrung	increase; multiplication
Verm	Vermerk	observation; note; remark
verm	vermessen	to measure; to survey
Verm	Vermessung	survey; measurement
verm	vermindert	lessened; diminished; abated
Verm	Verminderung	reduction; diminution
verm	vermisst	missing
Verm	Vermisste	missing men
verm	vermitteln	mediate; arrange
Verm	Vermittlung	intervention; mediation
Verm	Vermittlungsstelle	telephone exchange
Verm	Vermögen	wealth; ability; power
verm	vermutet	conjectured; supposed
verm	vermutlich	presumable; probable; likely
Verm	Vermutung	supposition; conjecture
Verm.Abt	Vermessungsabteilung	survey detachment
Verm.Battr	Vermessungsbatterie	survey battery
Verm.Tr	Vermessungstrupp	survey detachment
Vern	Vernachlässigung	negligence; neglect
Vern	Vernehmung	questioning; interrogation
vern	verneint	denied; contradicted
Vern	Verneinung	denial; contradiction
vern	vernichtet	destroyed; annihilated
Vern	Vernichtung	annihilation; destruction
vern	vernachlässigt	neglected; slighted
vern	vernagelt	spiked (*weapon*)
vern	vernommen	questioned; interrogated

Vermessungs- und Kartenabteilung *f* survey and mapping unit.
Vermessung von Feuerstellungen field artillery survey (*Arty*).
verminderte Ladung reduced charge.
verminen to mine, to lay mines.
vermißt missing, missing in action.
vermitteln to connect, to communicate (*Tp*); to convey or impart (*information*).
Vermittlung *f* connection; switching central, telephone central.
Vermittlungskästchen *n* portable switchboard (*Tp*).
Vermittlungsklinke *f* connecting jack (*Tp*).
Vermittlungsschnur *f* patching cord (*Tp*).
Vermittlungsstelle *f* switching central, telephone central.
Vernachlässigung *f* neglect, negligence.
Vernebelung *f* smoke screening.
vernehmen to question, interrogate (*PW, etc.*).
Vernehmung *f* questioning, interrogation.
Vernehmungsoffizier *m* interrogation officer (*PW*).
Vernichtung *f* destruction, annihilation.
Vernichtungsfeuer *n* fire for destruction (*Arty*).
Vernichtungskampf *m* battle of extermination.
vernieten to rivet.
verordnen to order; prescribe (*Med*).
Verordnung *f* regulation, order.
Verpackungsgeschosse *npl* dummy ammunition (*for vehicle-loading practice*).
Verpassung *f* fitting (*of uniforms, gas masks, etc.*).
Verpflegung *f* feeding, messing, rationing; rations, food; food supply.
Verpflegung in Natur rations in kind.
Verpflegungsabrechnung *f* ration and savings account.
Verpflegungsabteilung *f* ration supply section.
Verpflegungsamt *n* ration supply office.
Verpflegungsausgabestelle *f* ration distribution point.
Verpflegungsbedarf *m* ration requirements.
Verpflegungsbestände *mpl* ration stores, ration stockage.
Verpflegungsbezugsschein *m* ration return.
Verpflegungsbombe *f* rations delivery unit (*airborne operations*).
Verpflegungsdienst *m* ration supply service.
Verpflegungsersparnisse *fpl* ration savings.
Verpflegungsgebührnisse *fpl* ration allowances.
Verpflegungsgegenstände *mpl* ration articles.
Verpflegungsgeld *n* ration allowance.
Verpflegungslager *n* ration supply depot.
Verpflegungslagerausgabestelle *f* ration distributing point (*Div*).
Verpflegungsmittel *npl* rations, subsistence supplies.
Verpflegungsnachschub *m* ration supply.
Verpflegungsoffizier *m* mess officer.
Verpflegungsportion *f* ration.
Verpflegungssatz *m* ration quantity, ration scale.
Verpflegungsstärke *f* ration strength.
Verpflegungsstroß *m* ration supply train (*H-Dr or Mtz*).
Verpflegungsunteroffizier *m* mess sergeant.
Verpflegungszug *m* ration supply train (*RR*).
Verpflegungszuschuß *m* commutation of rations.
Verpflegung und Unterkunft rations and quarters.
verraten betray.
Verräter *m* traitor.
verriegeln to lock, cut off, block, box in.
verrostet rusty.
versacken bog down.
versagen fail.
Versager *m* misfire; dud.
Versammlung *f* assembly, concentration (*Tac*); meeting, gathering.
Versand *m* shipment, transportation, forwarding.
verschaffen procure.
Verschalung *f* covering, skin, fairing (*Ap*); revetment.
Verschanzung *f* entrenchment.
Verschickung *f* shipment, transportation.
Verschiebebahnhof *m* switching yard.
verschieben shift, move, displace, switch; postpone.
Verschiebung *f* displacement (*of troops, etc.*); postponement.
verschießen to expend (*Am*).
verschleiern to mask, screen, blanket, conceal, camouflage.
Verschleierung *f* screening, concealment (*Tac*).
Verschleierungsfähigkeit *f* screening capacity, density of coverage (*screening smoke*).
Verschleierungsfeuer *n* deception fire, diversion fire; smoke-shell fire.
Verschleierungsverkehr *m* deception signal traffic.
Verschleißteil *m* part subject to wear (*Mech*).
Verschluß *m* breechblock, breech mechanism (*Ord*); bolt mechanism (*R, pistol*); locking action (*Tech*); lock; shutter.
Verschlußabstand *m* head space (*Ord*).
Verschlußblock *m* breechblock (*screw-type breech*).
Verschlußkeil *m* wedge-type breechblock
verschlüsseln encode, encipher.
verschlüsselter Text secret text.
Verschlüsselung *f* coding, enciphering.
Verschlüsselungsscheibe *f* cipher disk.
Verschlußkammer *f* bolt (*R*).
Verschlußkappe *f* filler cover (*MG*).
Verschlußleiste *f* back plate (*MG*).
Verschlußleistenachse *f* back plate hinge pin (*MG*).
Verschlußplatte *f* front plate (*breechblock*).
Verschlußring *m* breech ring (*G*).
Verschlußschlitten *m* lock frame (*Ord*).
Verschlußschraube *f* threaded closing cap (*fuze*).
Verschlußstück *n* breechblock (*G, MG*).
Verschlußträger *m* breechblock carrier (*G*).
Verschlußüberzug *m* breech cover (*G*).
Verschlußzylinder *m* bolt (*SA*).
Verschränkbarkeit der Achsen compression-and-rebound range of spring suspension (*MT*).
Verschraubung *f* threaded plug, screw.
Verschraubungsstück *n* breech ring.
Verschubbahn *f* launching track (*Bdg*).
Verschuß *m* expenditure (*of Am*).
Verschwertung *f* lateral truss, sway brace (*Bdg*).
Verschwindeturm *m* disappearing turret (*Ft*).
Verschwindlafette *f* disappearing carriage (*G*).
Verschwindscheibe *f* bobbing target, disappearing target (*Tng*).
Verschwörung *f* conspiracy.
Versehrtengeld *n* disability allowance or pension.
versenken to sink; to countersink.
Versenknietung *f* flush riveting.
versetzen to transfer (*Pers*); to shift, move; to stagger (*obstacles, etc.*).
versetzt staggered; displaced, transferred.
Versetzung *f* transfer (*Pers*); deviation, drift (*Avn*); stagger(ing).
Versorgung *f* supply; care (*for ex-service men*).
Versorgungsbehälter *m* aerial delivery unit.
Versorgungsbombe *f* aerial delivery unit.
Versorgungsdienst *m* supply service.
Versorgungsfahrzeug *n* supply vehicle, train vehicle.
Versorgungsgebiet *n* supply area.
Versorgungsgüter *npl* supplies.
verspannen to brace, tighten, stretch.
Verspannung *f* bracing, fastening, tightening, stretching.
Versprengter *m* straggler; man separated from his unit in action.
versprühen to spray (*CWS*).
verständigen inform, make known.
Verständigung *f* communication; readability, audibility (*Sig Com*).
Verständigungsgerät *n* interphone equipment (*Ap*).
Verständigungsmittel *n* password.
Verständigung von Bord zu Bord interaircraft communication.
Verständlichkeit *f* readability (*Sig Com*).
verstärken reinforce, strengthen; amplify, boost, increase.
Verstärker *m* amplifier (*Rad*).
Verstärkung *f* amplification (*Rad*); reinforcement.
Verstärkungsfaktor *m* amplification factor (*Rad*).
Verstärkungsring *m* hoop (*gun barrel*).
Verstauchung *f* sprain (*Med*).
verstauen to stow.
verstecken to hide, conceal, mask.
verstellbar controllable (*Ap propeller*); adjustable (*tools, etc.*).
Verstell-Luftschraube *f* controllable-pitch propeller (*Ap*).
Verstellschlüssel *m* adjustable wrench.
Verstellschraube *f* adjusting screw (*Tech*); controllable-pitch propeller.
Verstellung *f* adjustment, regulation, control.
Verstellwelle *f* control rod (*Ap*).
Verstoß *m* infraction, irregularity.
Verstrebung *f* spar bracing (*Bdg*); bracing.
verstümmeln mutilate.
Versuch *m* experiment, attempt, test, trial.
Versuchsflugzeug *n* test airplane, experimental airplane.
Versuchsladung *f* test charge (*Arty*).
Versuchslauf *m* test run, trial run.
Versuchsschießen *n* test firing (*Ord*).
Versuchstruppen *fpl* experimental troops.
vertäuen to moor.
Vertäumast *m* mooring mast.
Verteidigung *f* defense, defensive.
Verteidigungsabschnitt *m* defense area, defensive area, defensive sector.
Verteidigungsanlagen *fpl* defensive installations.
Verteidigungslinie *f* line of defense.
Verteidigungsnest *n* nest of resistance.
Verteidigungsplan *m* defense plan.
Verteidigungsstellung *f* defensive position.
Verteidigungszone *f* defensive zone.
verteilen to distribute, to issue.
Verteiler *m* distributor (*Mtr*); distribution box (*data transmission system*).
Verteilerbahnhof *m* regulating station (*RR*).
Verteilerfinger *m* distributor arm (*Mtr*).
Verwaltungsdienste *mpl* administrative and supply services.
Verwaltungsgebäude *n* administration building.
Verwaltungsordnung *f* administrative plan.
Verwaltungstruppenteil *m* administrative unit.
Verwaltungsübersichtskarte *f* administrative map.
Verwaltungswesen *n* administration.
Verwendung *f* employment (*Tac*); use, utilization.
zu besonderer Verwendung on special assignment (*abbr.* z.b.V.).
verwickeln involve, complicate; engage (*Tac*).
verwinden to warp, to twist.
Verwirrung *f* confusion.
verwundbar vulnerable.
verwunden to wound.
Verwundetenabschub *m* evacuation of wounded.
Verwundetenabschublinie *f* chain of evacuation.
Verwundetenabtransport *m* evacuation of wounded.
Verwundetenabzeichen *n* Wound Badge (*decoration*).
Verwundetenbetreuung *f* care of casualties.
Verwundetennest *n* aid station.
Verwüstung *f* devastation.
Verzerrung *f* distortion (*Rad*).
verzinkt galvanized.
verzinnt tin-plated.
Verzögerung *f* delay.
verzögerungsfrei immediate, nondelay.
Verzögerungsmine *f* delayed-action mine.
Verzögerungssatz *m* delay pellet (*electric igniter*); delay powder train (*fuze*).
Verzögerungsschütz *m* time-delay relay (*Elec, Rad*).
Verzögerungszünder *m* delayed-action fuze, delay fuze.
Verzug *m* delay, lag.
Verzugsrechner *m* acoustic corrector (*sound locator*).
Veterinär *m* veterinary officer (*2nd Lt*).
Veterinärdienst *m* veterinary service.
Veterinärgehilfe *m* veterinary aid man.
Veterinärgerät *n* veterinary equipment.
Veterinärkompanie *f* veterinary company.
Veterinärpark *m* veterinary depot.
V-Form der Tragflügel wing dihedral (*Ap*).
V-Formwinkel *m* dihedral angle (*Ap*).
Vieh *n* cattle, livestock.
Vielfache *n* multiple (*Math*).
Vielfachschaltung *f* multiple connection (*Tp*).

Viereck *n* square.
Viererleitung *f* phantom circuit (*Tp*).
Viererschaltung *f* phantom connection (*Tp*).
Viererzelt *n* four-man tent.
viergliedrige Division square division.
Vierlings-MG. *n* four-barreled machine gun.
Vierradantrieb *m* four-wheel drive.
Vierradlenkung *f* four-wheel steering.
Vierspitz *m* crowsfoot, four-pointed knife rest (*obstacle*).
Viertaktmotor *m* four-cycle engine.
Viertelkreis *m* quadrant (*of a circle*).
Visier *n* sight, rear sight (*Ord*).
Visierbereich *m* danger space (*MG firing*).
Visierebene *f* plane of present position (*AA gunnery*).

verneb	vernebeln	to screen by smoke
Verneb	Vernebelung	smoke screening
Vern.F	Vernichtungsfeuer	destructive fire; annihilating fire (*artillery*)
Vern.i.D	Vernachlässigung im Dienst	neglect of duty
Vern.Kr	Vernichtungskrieg	war of annihilation
Veröff	Veröffentlichung	publication; promulgation
verordn	verordnet	ordered; decreed
Verordn	Verordnung	ordnance; decree; order; instruction
Verp	Verpackung	packing; loading
verp	verpasst	missed; adjusted (*gas mask*)
verp	verpestet	infected; poisoned
verp	verpönt	forbidden; prohibited
verp	verpufft	fired away (uselessly); wasted
verpfl	verpflanzt	transplanted; replanted
verpfl	verpflegt	fed; cared for; nourished
Verpfl	Verpflegung	rations; food supply; rationing
Verpfl	Verpflichtung	obligation; duty
Verpfl.Auf	Verpflegungsaufenthalt	food stop
Verpfl.Ausg.(St.)	Verpflegungsausgabestelle	rations distribution point
Verpfl.B	Verpflegungsbasis	rations base
Verpfl.Empf	Verpflegungsempfang	receipt of rations
Verpfl.Fz	Verpflegungsfahrzeug	commissary wagon
Verpfl.Kfs	Verpflegungskraftfahrzeug	rations motor truck
Verpfl.Kol	Verpflegungskolonne	commissary train; supply column
Verpfl.L	Verpflegungsliste	ration list
Verp.Lg	Verpflegungslager	commissary depot
Verpfl.Mag	Verpflegungsmagazin	food depot
Verpfl.Nachsch	Verpflegungsnachschub	supply replacement
Verpfl.Offs	Verpflegungsoffizier	commissary officer; mess officer
Verpfl.P	Verpflegungsportion	individual rations
Verpfl.Tr	Verpflegungstross	supply train; ration train; commissary train
Verpfl.Uffs	Verpflegungsunteroffizier	supply noncommissioned officer; mess sergeant
Verpfl.V	Verpflegungsvorschrift	rations regulations
Verpfl.Wg	Verpflegungswagen	supply wagon
Verpfl.Zg	Verpflegungszug	supply train (*railway*)
Verr	Verräter	traitor
Verr	Verrat	treason
verr	verraten	to betray
verr	verrechnet	placed to account; settled
Verr	Verrechnung	placing to account; settlement; miscalculation
verr	verringert	diminished; reduced
verr	verrückt	insane; crazy; deranged
Verrgl	Verriegelung	barricade; locking mechanism (*weapons*)
Vers	Versäumnis	neglect; negligence
vers	versäumt	missed; neglected
vers	versagen	to fail; misfire; refuse; deny
Vers	Versager	misfire
vers	versammelt	assembled
Vers	Versammlung	convention; assembly; gathering
vers	versandt	dispatched
Vers	Versandung	sanding up; choking up with sand
vers	versehen	provided; furnished with
Vers	Versehen	provisioning; furnishing with; supply; mistake
vers	versetzt	transferred; removed
Vers	Versetzung	transfer; removal
vers	versichert	insured; guaranteed
Vers	Versicherung	insurance; assurance
vers	versorgt	provided for; cared for
Vers	Versorgung	provision; maintenance; supply
Vers	Versorgungswesen	supply system; state provision for the deserving
Vers	Versuch	attempt; experiment; trial
vers	versuchsweise	by way of trial; as an experiment; experimental
Vers.Abt	Versuchsabteilung	experimental department
Vers.Abt.d.Verk.-Tr	Versuchsabteilung der Verkehrstruppen	experimental detachment of the communication troops
Vers.Anst	Versicherungsanstalt	insurance office
Vers.Anst	Versuchsanstalt	experimental station; research laboratory
Vers.Anst.f.Hdfw	Versuchsanstalt für Handfeuerwaffen	experimental station for small weapons
Vers.B	Versuchsballon	experimental balloon
Vers.Batt	Versuchsbatterie	experimental battery
Vers.Beh	Versorgungsbehörde	state administration for veterans
Vers.Bt	Versuchsboot	experimental boat
Vers.Bttr	Versuchsbatterie	experimental battery
versch	verschalt	boarded; revetted
versch	verschanzt	entrenched
Versch	Verschanzung	entrenchment; entrenching
versch	verscharrt	covered with earth
Versch	Verschiebung	shifting; displacement; delay
versch	verschieden	died; various
Versch	Verschiedenes	sundry; various
Versch	Verschiedenheit	difference; variety
versch	verschifft	shipped out; exported
Versch	Verschiffung	shipping; shipment
versch	verschoben	removed; shifted; delayed
versch	verschollen	presumed dead; sunk into oblivion
Versch	Verschollene	missing person
versch	verschont	protected; spared; immune
versch	verschossen	out of ammunition

Versch	Verschüttung	burial alive
versch	verschulden	to be in debt; to be indebted
Versch.H	Verschiffungshafen	port of embarkation
Verschl	Verschlammung	silt
verschl	verschlechtert	deteriorated; made worse
Verschl	Verschlechterung	deterioration
verschl	verschleiert	screened
verschl	verschleppt	removed; misplaced
verschl	verschleudert	thrown away; wasted
verschl	verschlossen	locked; uncommunicative
verschl	verschlungen	swallowed; interwoven
Verschl	Verschluss	bolt; breechblock lock
Verschl.K	Verschlusskappe	locking cap; breechblock cover
Verschl.St	Verschlusstück	breechblock
Verschl.Tr	Verschleierungtruppen	camouflaging troops; smoke troops
Verschr	Verschraubung	screwing
Verschr	Verschrottung	scrapping
verschw	verschwiegen	secretive
verschw	verschwinden	to disappear
Verschw	Verschwörung	conspiracy; plot
verschw	verschwunden	disappeared
Verschw.Laf	Verschwindlafette	retractable gun mount
Vers.Fst	Vorschrift für die wirtschaftliche Versorgung der Festungen	regulations for the provisioning of fortresses
Vers.Fz	Versuchsfahrzeug	test vehicle
Vers.Geb	Versammlungsgebiet	assembly area
Vers.Kdo	Versuchskommando	experimental unit
Vers.Kdo.Flak	Versuchskommando für Flugzeugabwehrkanonen	experimental detachment of antiaircraft artillery
Vers.Komp	Versuchskompanie	experimental company
Vers.Lg	Versammlungslager	reception center; assembly camp
Vers.Mschft	versammelte Mannschaft	assembled personnel (*of a unit*)
Versorg	Versorgung	provisioning; supply; social security
Versp	Verspätung	delay
versp	verspannt	braced (*aviation*)
Versp	Verspannung	bracing (*airplane*)
versp	versperrt	blocked; barricaded; blockaded
Versp	Versperrung	barring; barricading; blockade (*of a port*)
Vers.Pl	Versammlungsplatz	assembly point
Verspr	Versprechung	promise
Verspr	Versprengter	straggler
Verspr	Versprengung	dispersal; isolation
Verspr.S.St	Versprengtensammelstelle	straggler collecting point
Vers.Sch	Versuchschiessen	test firing
Vers.St	Versorgungstelle	supply station; social welfare
Ver.St	Verladestelle	entraining point; loading point
Ver.St	Verlängerungsstück	extension piece
Verst	Verstärker	amplifier (*radio*)
verst	verstärkt	reinforced; intensified
Verst	Verstärkung	reinforcement; amplification
verst	verstanden	understood
Verst	Versteck	hiding place
verst	versteckt	hidden
Verst	Verstopfung	stoppage; obstruction
verst	verstorben	deceased
Verst	Verstorbener	deceased person
verst	verstümmelt	mutilated; maimed
Verst	Verstümmelung	mutilation
Vers.St	Versuchsstelle	testing station
Verst.Art	Verstärkerungsartillerie	reinforcement artillery
verst.F.P	verstärkter Feldposten	reinforced combat outpost
Verstkg	Verstärkung	reinforcement; amplification
Verstzg	Versetzung	transfer
Verst.Zul	Verstümmeltenzulage	allowance for mutilated
Vers.Vbd	Versuchsverband	experimental unit
Vers.Vg	Versailler Vertrag	Versailles Treaty
Vers.Zw	Versuchszweck	experimental purpose
vert	vertagt	adjourned
Vert	Verteidiger	defender
vert	verteidigt	defended
Vert	Verteidigung	defense
vert	verteilen	to distribute
Vert	Verteiler	distributor
vert	vertikal	vertical
Vert	Vertreter	representative; agent
Vert.Abschn	Verteidigungsabschnitt	defense sector
Vert.Anl	Verteidigungsanlage	defenses; defensive works
Vert.Anl	Verteidigungsanleitung	defense instructions
Vert.Art	Verteidigungsartillerie	defensive artillery
Vert.Bhf	Verteilungsbahnhof	distribution railroad station
Vert.Fr	Verteidigungsfront	defense front; frontage of defensive position
Vert.L	Verteidigungslinie	line of defense
Vert.P	Verteidigungspunkt	defense point
Vertr	Vertrag	treaty; contract; agreement
vertr	vertreten	to represent
Vertr	Vertreter	representative; agent
Vertr.P	Vertrauensposten	confidential position; place of trust
Vertr.Tr.Arzt	Vertragstruppenarzt	contract surgeon
Vert.St	Verteidigungsstellung	defensive position
Vert.Syst	Verteidigungssystem	defensive system
Vert.Z	Verteidigungszone	defense zone
Vert.Zust	Verteidigungszustand	defense condition
verurs	verursacht	caused
Verurt	Verurteilter	condemned person; convicted person; sentenced person

Verurt.	Verurteilung	condemnation; sentence
Verv.	Vervielfältigung	reproduction; multiplication
Vervollst.	Vervollständigung	completion
Verw.	Verwalter	administrator
verw.	verwaltet	administered; managed
Verw.	Verwaltung	administration; management
verw.	verwandt	related
Verw.	Verwarnung	caution; reprimand
Verw.	Verwechselung	confusion; mistake
Verw.	Verweigerung	refusal; denial
Verw.	Verweis	reprimand; rebuke
Verw.	Verwendung	use; employment
Verw.	Verwüstung	devastation
Verw.	Verwundeter	wounded person
verw.	verwundet	wounded
Verw.	Verwundung	wound; injury
Verw.Abbef.	Verwundetenabbeförderung	evacuation of wounded men
Verw.Absch.	Verwundetenabschub	evacuation of wounded men
Verw.Abz.	Verwundetenabzeichen	wound stripe
Verw.B.	Verwaltungsbeämter	administrative official
Verwdg.	Verwendung	use; employment; application; appropriation
Verw.Geb.	Verwaltungsgebäude	administration building
Verw.N.	Verwundetennest	forward collecting point for wounded
Verw.Pers.	Verwaltungspersonal	administrative personnel
Verw.S.St.	Verwundetensammelstelle	collecting point (*medical*)
Verw.Tr.	Verwundetentransport	transportation of wounded
verz.	verzeichnet	listed; registered
Verz.	Verzeichnis	index; list; register
Verz.	Verzettelung	waste; scattering
verz.	verzögert	delayed
Verz.	Verzögerung	delay; delay-action
Verz.	Verzug	delay; postponement
Verzw.	Verzweiflung	despair
Verzw.	Verzweigung	ramification
Verz.Z.	Verzögerungszünder	delay-action fuze
Vet.	Veterinär	veterinary
Vet.	Veterinärmittel	veterinary supplies and remedies
Vet.D.	Veterinärdienst	veterinary service
Vet.Ger.	Veterinärgerät	veterinary equipment
Vet.Insp.	Veterinärinspektion	inspectorate of veterinary services
Vet.K.	Veterinärkorps	Veterinary Corps
Vet.Offz.	Veterinäroffizier	veterinary officer
Vet.R.	Veterinärrat	senior veterinary officer in government service
Vf.	Verfassung	state; condition
Vf.	Verfolgung	persecution; pursuit
Vf.	Verfügung	decree; order; disposition;
V.F.	Vernichtungsfeuer	destructive fire (*artillery*); annihilating fire
V.F.	Vorschrift für—	regulations for—
Vfg.	Verfügung	decree; order; disposition;
Vg.	Höchstgeschwindigkeit	top speed (*airplane*)
Vg.	Vereinigung	association; union
Vg.	Verordnung	decree
Vg.	Vertrag	treaty; contract; agreement
Vg.	Volksgenosse	fellow countryman; co-national
Vg.	Vorgang	event; occurrence
VgKm/h.	Höchstgeschwindigkeit in Stundenkilometern	top speed in kilometers per hour
Vgl.	Vergleich	comparison
vgl.	vergleiche	compare; see
Vgr.	Vergaser	carburetor
v.g.u.	vorgelesen, genehmigt, unterschrieben	read, approved, signed
v.H.	vom Hundert	per cent
V.I.	Veterinärinspektion	inspectorate of veterinary services
viell.	vielleicht	perhaps
Vierr.Antr.	Vierradantrieb	four-wheel drive
Vierr.Br.	Vierradbremse	four-wheel brake
viersp.	vierspännig	drawn by four horses
Vjn.	Veterinärinspektion	veterinary inspectorate
Vis.	Visier	rear sight
Vis.	Visum	visa
Vis.Ber.	Visierbereich	danger zone
Vis.Eb.	Visierebene	plane of sighting
Vis.Einr.	Visiereinrichtung	sighting mechanism
Vis.L.	Visierlinie	line of sighting; line of present position (*antiaircraft*)
Vis.Sch.	Visierschuss	sighting shot
Vis.Sch.W.	Visierschussweite	sighting range
Vis.St.	Visierstellung	sight setting
Vis.W.	Visierwinkel	elevation setting; angle of elevation (*rifle*)
vit.	vital	vital
V.K.	Verkehrskontrolle	traffic control
V.K.	Vorpostenkompanie	outpost company
VKG.	Verkehrsgraben	communication trench
VLF.	Vereinigung für Luftforschung	association for aeronautical research

Verteilerkasten *m* distribution box *(Elec, Nav)*; junction box *(data transmission system)*.
Verteilerlaufstück *n* distributor rotor, distributor arm *(Mtr)*.
Verteilerscheibe *f* distributor plate.
Verteilung *f* distribution.
Verteilungsstelle *f* distributing point.
Vertrag *m* treaty, contract, compact.
Vertragsarzt *m* contract surgeon.
vertraulich confidential.
Vertretung *f* deputy; proxy; representation.
verursachen to cause.
vervielfältigen multiply; multigraph; mimeograph; duplicate.
verwalten administer, administrate, manage.
Verwaltung *f* administration.
Verwaltungsamt *n* See **Heeresverwaltungsamt.**
Visiereinrichtung *f* sighting mechanism, sighting device, sight assembly; quadrant sight *(G)*.
visieren to sight.
Visierfeder *f* rear-sight spring *(MG, R)*.
Visierfernrohr *n* telescopic sight.
Visierfuß *m* rear-sight base *(MG, R)*.
Visiergestänge *n* parallelogram linkage system *(AA sight)*.
Visierhaltestift *m* rear-sight pin *(MG, R)*.
Visierkimme *f* rear sight; rear sight notch.
Visierklappe *f* rear-sight leaf *(MG, R)*; sight-port cover *(gun shield)*.
Visierkorn *n* front sight; bead.
Visierlinie *f* line of sight *(Ord)*; line of present position *(AA gunnery)*.
Visierlupe *f* magnifying sight lens *(site-to-mask clinometer)*.
Visierschieber *m* sight slide *(MG, R)*.
Visierschild *m* sight shield *(G)*.
Visierschuß *m* direct-fire shot.
Visierschußweite *f* direct-fire range.
Visierstange *f* rear sight pillar *(MG)*.
Visierstift *m* rear-sight pin *(MG, R)*.
Visierträger *m* sight bracket *(Ord)*.
Visiervorrichtung *f* sight mechanism *(Ord)*.
Visierwinkel *m* angle of elevation *(Gunnery)*; angular difference between present and future position *(AAA)*.
Visierzeiger *m* telescope mount reference pointer *(matches with* Rohrzeiger *when gun is laid for elevation)*.
Vizeadmiral *m* vice admiral.
V-Motor *m* V-engine.
V-Null *f* muzzle velocity *(abbr.* Vo).
Völkerrecht *n* international law.
Volksdeutscher *m* German who is a citizen of another country.
Volkswagen *m* "people's car" *(general purpose car, somewhat lighter than the jeep)*.
Vollbahn *f* See **Vollspurbahn.**
Vollgas *n* wide-open throttle.
vollgeländegängig having complete cross-country ability *(vehicles)*.
Vollgeschoß *n* shot *(solid projectile)*; ball projectile; solid nonexplosive projectile.
Vollgummireifen *m* solid tire.
Vollkettenfahrzeug *n* full-track vehicle.
Vollkorn *n* full sight *(R aiming)*.
vollmotorisiert fully mechanized.
Vollreifen *m* solid tire.
Vollrohr *n* monobloc gun barrel.
Vollsichtkanzel *f* turret with full field of view *(Ap)*.
Vollsichtkuppel *f* See **Vollsichtkanzel.**
Vollspurbahn *f* standard-gage railroad *(1.435 meters)*.
vollständiger Schuß complete round *(Am)*.
Volltraghöhe *f* service ceiling *(Ap)*.
Volltreffer *m* direct hit.
vorarbeiten, sich work one's way forward *(by rushes, or crawling)*.
Vorausabteilung *f* advance detachment.
Vorausaufgabe *f* preliminary mission *(Tac)*.
Voraussage *f* prediction, forecast.
Vorauswanderungsstrecke *f* linear travel of target during dead time, linear travel of target from position at instant of range determination to present position *(AA gunnery)*.
Vorbauschnabel *m* launching nose *(Bdg)*.
Vorbefehl *m* warning order *(Tac)*.
vorbeifahren roll by, ride by.
Vorbeiflug *m* side-view flight, passing flight *(AAA)*.
Vorbeimarsch *m* pass in review, march in review.
vorbeirollen roll by, pass by.
Vorbeischlagen der Pulvergase flareback *(G)*.
vorbereiten to prearrange, prepare in advance, to schedule in advance *(Arty fire, etc.)*.
Vorbereitung *f* preparation.
Vorbereitungsfeuer *n* preparation *(Arty)*.
vorbeugen prevent, anticipate.
Vorbeugung *f* prophylaxis.
Vorbeugungsmittel *n* prophylactic.
Vorderachsantrieb *m* front-axle drive *(MT)*.
Vorderachse *f* front axle *(MT)*.
Vordergelenk *n* front piece of toggle joint *(pistol)*.
Vorderhang *m* forward slope *(Top)*.
Vorderhangstellung *f* forward slope position *(Tac)*.
Vorderholm *m* front outrigger *(AA gun mount)*.
Vorderkaffe *f* bow compartment *(Pon)*.
Vorderkante *f* leading edge *(Ap)*.
Vorderlader *m* muzzle loader.
vorderlastig noseheavy *(Ap)*.
Vordermann *m* the man in front *(drill)*.
auf Vordermann stehen to be covered in file.
"**Vordermann!**" "Cover off!"
Vordermann nehmen to cover off, to cover in file *(drill)*.
Vorderpferd *n* lead horse.
Vorderradantrieb *m* front-wheel drive.
Vordersteven *m* stem *(Nav)*.
Vorderstützen *fpl* front legs *(MG tripod)*.
Vorderzeug *n* martingale, breastplate harness, body of breast collar *(harness)*.
Vorderzwiesel *m* pommel *(saddle)*; front arch *(pack-saddle frame)*.
vordringen to push forward, press forward.
Vordruck *m* printed form, blank.
Vorfahrt *f* right-of-way, priority.
Vorfahrterberechtigter *m* one who has right-of-way.
Vorfahrterlaubnis *f* permission to pass *(vehicles in column)*.
Vorfahrtregelung *f* priority regulations, traffic regulations regarding right-of-way or priority.
Vorfahrtsrecht *n* priority, right-of-way.
Vorfahrtszeichen *n* priority sign *(on a vehicle)*.
Vorfeld *n* foreground; outpost area *(Tac)*; apron *(Adrm)*.
Vorflügel *m* slat *(Ap wing)*.
vorfühlen, sich to feel one's way forward, to try to establish contact.
Vorführung *f* demonstration.
Vorgang *m* occurrence, incident, event; process.
vorgehen to advance.
Vorgelegewelle *f* countershaft *(MT)*.
vorgeschoben advance(d); forward.
vorgeschobene Beobachtungsstelle forward observation post.
vorgeschobener Gefechtsstand advance command post.
vorgeschobene Stellungen position of advanced covering forces *(Tac)*.
vorgeschrieben prescribed.
Vorgesetzter *m* superior, superior officer or NCO.
Vorhaben *n* intent, intention, plan.
Vorhalt *m* lead *(firing)*.
Vorhalteeinrichtung *f* lead computer *(AA and AT guns)*.
Vorhalteeinstellung *f* positioning device for leads *(sight mechanism)*.
Vorhaltemaß *n* See **Vorhaltsmaß.**
vorhalten to take a lead, apply a lead *(Gunnery)*.
Vorhaltepunkt *m* future position of target *(AA gunnery)*; predicted position of target, set-forward point.
Vorhaltestrecke *f* predicting interval *(AA gunnery)*.
Vorhaltewinkel *m* lead angle, angle between line of present position and line of future position *(AA gunnery)*; angle of lateral lead *(Gunnery)*; range angle *(bombing)*; drift angle *(Air Navigation)*.
Vorhaltsmaß *n* amount of lead, lead factor *(in firing at moving targets)*.
Vorhaltswert *m* See **Vorhaltsmaß.**
Vorhand *f* forequarters *(horse)*.
Vorhersage *f* prediction, forecast.
Vorholeinrichtung *f* counterrecoil mechanism, recuperator mechanism.
Vorholer *m* recuperator, counterrecoil mechanism.
Vorholerkolben *m* recuperator piston, counterrecoil piston.
Vorholerlager *n* counterrecoil-mechanism bushing.
Vorholerstütze *f* counterrecoil-mechanism support.
Vorhut *f* advance guard.
Vorhutführer *m* advance guard commander.
Vorhutgefecht *n* advance guard action or engagement.
Vorkammer *f* precombustion chamber *(Diesel engine)*.
Vorlage *f* flash-reducing wad *(Arty)*; text, copy, pattern.
Vorlauf *m* counterrecoil *(G)*; negative caster *(MT)*.
Vorlaufbewegung *f* counterrecoil motion.
Vorlaufhemmstange *f* counterrecoil piston rod *(G)*.
Vormann *m* foreman *(Reich Labor Service)*.
Vormarsch *m* advance.
Vormarschlinie *f* line of advance, axis of advance.
Vormarschstraße *f* road of advance, route of advance.
Vormarschweg *m* line of advance, route of advance.
Vorposten *m* outpost.
Vorpostenabschnitt *m* outpost sector.
Vorpostenabschnittsgrenze *f* outpost-sector boundary.
Vorpostenaufstellung *f* setting up of outposts, disposition of outposts.
Vorpostenboot *n* outpost patrol boat *(Nav)*.
Vorpostendienst *m* outpost duty.
Vorpostenführer *m* outpost commander.
Vorpostengefecht *n* outpost engagement.
Vorpostenkette *f* line of outguards *(Tac)*.
Vorpostenkompanie *f* outpost company.
Vorpostenreserve *f* outpost reserve.
Vorpostensicherungslinie *f* outpost line of security *(Tac)*.
Vorpostenstellung *f* outpost position *(Tac)*.
Vorposten-Widerstandslinie *f* outpost line of resistance *(Tac)*.
vorprellen to rush forward.
Vorrang *m* precedence, priority.
Vorrat *m* stock, stores, supply.
Vorratshaltung *f* maintenance of stocks or supplies.
Vorratslauf *m* spare barrel *(MG)*.
Vorratsteil *n* spare part *(MT)*.
Vorratszug *m* supply platoon *(Tk Bn)*.
Vorrichtung *f* device, mechanism, fixture.
vorrobben, sich to crawl forward.
vorrücken to advance.
Vorschlaghammer *m* sledge hammer.
vorschreiben prescribe.
Vorschrift *f* regulation, instruction, rule; manual.
vorschiftsmäßig according to regulations.
Vorsicht *f* caution, care; foresight *(Surv)*.
Vorsignal *n* preliminary signal, warning signal.
vorspringend projecting, salient.
Vorsprung *m* salient *(Tac)*; start, head start, lead.
Vorspur *f* toe-in *(MT)*.
Vorstecker *m* safety pin *(bombs, mines, etc.)*; lug *(fuze)*.
Vorsteckriemen *m* pommel-pad strap *(saddle)*.
Vorstoß *m* assault, thrust, lunge; piping, edging *(along seams of uniform)*.
Vorstrom *m* inflow *(Avn)*.
vortäuschen to deceive, simulate, feign.
Vortäuschung von Krankheiten malingering.
Vortrag *m* lecture; verbal report and consultation *(with commanding officer)*.
vortreten to step forward, to step out of the ranks.
Vortriebskraft *f* propelling power.
Vortrupp *m* advance guard support *(in Adv Gd of large unit)*; advance party *(in Adv Gd of smaller unit)*.
Vorverdichter *m* supercharger.
vorverlegen to lift *(Arty fire)*.
Vorwähler *m* preselector *(Tp)*.
Vorwärmer *m* preheater.
Vorwarner *m* outpost observer *(SR)*.
Vorwarnerstelle *f* outpost station *(SR)*.
Vorwärtseinschneiden *n* intersection *(Surv)*.
Vorwärtsfahrer *m* front driver *(of a vehicle with double-ended drive)*.
Vorwärtsgang *m* forward speed *(MT)*.
Vorwärtsgeschwindigkeit *f* forward velocity *(bombing)*.
Vorwärtsstaffelung *f* positive stagger *(Ap wings)*.
Vorzündung *f* preignition *(Mtr)*.
V-Stellung *f* dihedral setting *(Ap wings)*.

Vlkrbd	Völkerbund	League of Nations
V.Lkw	Verpflegungslastkraftwagen	commissary truck
VM	Verdienstmedaille	merit medal
Vm	Verminderung	reduction; diminution
v.M	vorigen Monats	last month
Vm	Vormittag	morning; forenoon
vm	vormittags	in the morning; before noon
V-M-Stoff		mustard gas
vnull	Anfangsgeschwindigkeit der Geschosse	initial velocity; muzzle velocity of projectiles
Vn	Vorname	first name
vo	Anfangsgeschwindigkeit der Geschosse	initial velocity; muzzle velocity of projectiles
vo	velocitäts-	velocity
VO	Verkehrsordnung	traffic regulation
VO	Verordnung	decree
Vo	Vorderrad	front wheel
Vol	Volumen	volume
Volks-Vertr	Volksvertretung	representation of the people;
vollaut. Wff	vollautomatische Waffe	automatic weapon
vollber	vollberechtigt	fully authorized; qualified
vollj	volljährig	of age
Vollk	Vollkommenheit	perfection
Vollm	Vollmacht	authority; power of attorney
Vollsp.B	Vollspurbahn	standard-gauge railroad
vollst	vollständig	complete; entire
Vollstr	Vollstreckung	execution; accomplishment
Vollstr.Bef	Vollstreckungsbefehl	writ of execution
vollz	vollzählig	complete
Vomi	Volksdeutsche Mittelstelle	agency for repatriation of racial Germans
Vor	Vorrat	supply; stores; provisions
Voranschl	Voranschlag	estimate; provisional calculation
Vorbef	Vorbefehl	warning order
Vorb.F	Vorbeifahrt	driving past; passing by
Vorb.Fl	Vorbeiflug	passing flight (*antiaircraft*)
Vorb.M	Vorbeimarsch	passing review
vorb.M	vorbereitende Massnahme	preparatory measure
Vorb.M	Vorbeugungsmassnahme	preventive measure
Vord	Vorder-	fore; front
Vordgr	Vordergrund	foreground
Vord.H	Vorderhang	forward slope
Vord L	Vorderlader	muzzle loader
Vord.M	Vordermann	front-rank man
vordr	vordringend	advancing; forging ahead
vordr	vordringlich	forward; urgent
Vord.S	Vorderseite	front; frontispiece
Vord.T	Vorderteil	front part; front
Vord.Wg	Vorderwagen	limber
Vorf	Vorfahren	ancestors
Vorf	Vorfahrt	driving up
Vorf	Vorfall	occurrence; incident
Vorf	Vorfeld	foreground
Vorf	Vorführung	demonstration; bringing forth
Vor.Fz	Vorratsfahrzeug	supply wagon
Vorg	Vorgänger	predecessor
Vorg	Vorgang	event; occurrence
Vorg	Vorgehen	advance
vorg	vorgehen	to proceed; to advance; to precede
Vorg	Vorgelände	foreground
vorg	vorgeschoben	advanced
vorg	vorgesetzt	superior; set ahead
Vorg	Vorgesetzter	superior
vorg.Beob	vorgeschobener Beobachter	advanced observer
vorg.B.St	vorgeschobener Beobachtungsstelle	advanced observation post
vorg.D.St	vorgesetzte Dienststelle	superior office or post
vorg.P	vorgeschobener Posten	advanced post
vorg.St	vorgeschobene Stellung	advanced position
Vorh	Vorhalt	lead (*artillery*)
vorh	vorhalten	to take a lead (*antiaircraft and artillery*)
vorh	vorhanden	at hand; available
vorh	vorher	before; previously
vorh	vorhergehend	previous
vorh	vorherrschend	predominant
Vorh	Vorholer	counterrecoil mechanism
Vorh	Vorhut	advance guard
Vorh.M	Vorhaltemass	amount of lead (*antiaircraft*)
Vork	Vorkehrungen	provisions; precautions
Vorkdo	Vorkommando	advance detail
Vork	Vorkommnis	occurrence; event
Vorkr.Zt	Vorkriegszeit	prewar time
vorl	vorläufig	meanwhile; temporarily
Vorl	Vorlage	flash hider
Vorl	Vorlauf	counterrecoil
vorm	vormals	formerly
Vorm	Vormarsch	advance
vorm	vormilitärisch	premilitary
Vorm	Vormittag	forenoon; morning
vorm	vormittags	in the morning; before noon
Vorm	Vormusterung	inspection; examination
Vorm.Bef	Vormarschbefehl	advance march order
vormil	vormilitärisch	premilitary
Vorm.Str	Vormarschstrasse	advance route; approach
Vorn	Vorname	first name
vorn	vornehmlich	chiefly; mainly
Vorp	Vorposten	outpost
Vorp.Abschn	Vorpostenabschnitt	outpost sector
Vorp.Aufst	Vorpostenaufstellung	posting of outposts
Vorp.Bef	Vorpostenbefehl	outpost order
Vorp.D	Vorpostendienst	outpost duty
Vorp.Gef	Vorpostengefecht	outpost skirmish
Vorp.Gr	Vorpostengros	main body of outpost
Vorp.Kp	Vorpostenkompanie	outpost company
Vorp.L	Vorpostenlinie	line of outposts
Vorp.Res	Vorpostenreserve	outpost reserve
Vorp.St	Vorpostenstellung	outpost position
Vorr	Vorrang	precedence; superiority
vorr	vorrätig	in stock; on hand
Vorr	Vorrat	supply; store; stock
Vorr	Vorrecht	privilege
Vorr	Vorrichtung	mechanism; device
vors	vorsätzlich	intentional
Vors	Vorsatz	plan; design; project; resolution
vors	vorsichtig	cautious; careful
Vors	Vorsitzender	president; chairman
Vors	Vorsorge	care; foresight
Vorschl	Vorschlag	proposition; proposal
vorschm	vorschriftsmässig	according to directions
Vorschr	Vorschrift	regulation; instruction; manual
vorschrm	vorschriftsmässig	according to directions
vorschrw	vorschriftswidrig	contrary to directions
Vorsp	Vorspann	team of horses
vorspr	vorspringend	projecting
Vorspr	Vorsprung	lead; salient; head start
Vorst	Vorstadt	suburb
Vorst	Vorstecker	tension lock (*fuze*); fuze safety pin
vorst	vorstellen	present; represent; introduce
Vorst	Vorstellung	advanced position
Vorst	Vorstoss	forward movement; advance; thrust; raid
vorst	vorstossen	to thrust; to push forward
vort	vortäuschen	to simulate; to feign
Vort	Vortäuschung	simulation; feigning
Vort	Vorteil	advantage; benefit; profit
vortr	vortraben	to trot ahead
Vortr	Vortrupp	advance party and support
vorw	vorwärts	forward
Vorw	Vorwerk	advanced work; outworks
vorz	vorzeitig	premature
vorz	vorziehen	to move up; to prefer
Vp	Vorposten	outpost
Vpfl	Verpflegung	rations; food supply; rationing
Vpfl.E	Verpflegungsempfang	receipt of rations
Vrmtg	Vermutung	supposition; conjecture; surmise
vrmtl	vermutlich	presumable; probable; likely
Vs	Versorgung	supply; provisioning
Vs	Vorderseite	front; frontispiece
Vschr	Vorschrift	regulation; instruction; manual; provision
v.S.d	von Seiten des	on the part of
VSt	Vermittlungsstelle	switchboard exchange
V.St	Vorderstütze	front tripod leg
V.St.A	Vereinigte Staaten von Amerika	United States of America
vst.St	versteckte Stellung	masked or camouflaged position; hidden emplacement
V.S.V	Vorschrift für den Schriftverkehr	correspondence regulations
Vt	Verteiler	distributor
v.T	vom Tage	of the day
V.T	Vorderteil	front part; front
V.Tr	Verpflegungstross	supply train; commissary train
v.u	völlig untauglich	absolutely unfit
V.u.G.Tr	Verpflegungs- und Gepäcktross	commissary and baggage train
V.U.Wm	Vorschrift über militärärztliche Untersuchungen der Wehrmacht	medical examination regulations
V.V	Versailler Vertrag	Treaty of Versailles
V.V.St	Verkehrsvorschriftstab	traffic regulation headquarters
V.V.St	Vorschriftenverwaltungsstelle	administrative office of regulations
Vw	Verwaltung	administration
Vw	Verwendung	use; application; employment; appropriation
Vw	Verwundetenabzeichen	wound stripe
Vw	Vorwerk	advanced work; outworks (*on maps*)
Vwz	Verwendungszweck	purpose of use; use to be put to
V.Z	Verzögerungszünder	delay-action fuze
V-Zug	Verpflegungszug	supply train (*railway*)
Vz	Vize-	vice-

W

W	Wache	guard; watch; sentinel
W	Wachregiment Berlin	Berlin Guard Regiment (*in-*
W	Waffe	arm; weapon; branch *raps*)
W	Waffenmeister	civilian armorer with rank of
W	Waffenmeistergehilfe	assistant artificer (*used in*
W	Waffenoffizier	ordnance officer
W	Waffen- und Gasschutz-unteroffizier	ordnance and antigas protection noncom officer
W	Waffenunteroffizier	ordnance noncom officer *on*
W	Wagen	wagon; vehicle
W	Wagenführer	driver
W	Wald	wood; forest; woodland
Wachst	Wachstube	guard room
Wachtm	Wachtmeister	(*corresponds roughly to U. S. first sergeant*)
Wachtr	Wachtruppe	guard detachment
W.A.d. K.	Wachabteilung der Kommandantur Berlin	Guard Detachment of Berlin Local Headquarters
WaF	Forschungabteilung des Heeres-Waffenamts	Research Section of Army Ordnance Office
Waff	Waffen-	ordnance; weapon; arm of service
WaffDA	Dienstanweisung für den Waffengebrauch	service regulations for the use of arms
waffenf	waffenfähig	able-bodied; capable of bearing arms
Waffenf	Waffenfähigkeit	ability to bear arms
Waffenf	Waffenfarbe	color on uniform, indicating branch of service
WaffFw	Waffenfeldwebel	ordnance sergeant (*corresponding roughly to U. S. first sergeant*)
WaffGebrG	Gesetz über den Waffengebrauch	law concerning the use of arms
Waff.L	Waffenlehre	science of arms and weapons
Waffm	Waffenmeister	civilian ordnance technician (*army official*)
Waffm.Sch	Waffenmeisterschule	ordnance maintenance school
WaffOFw	Waffenoberfeldwebel	(*corresponds roughly to U. S. staff sergeant, ordnance*)
WaffOWm	Waffenoberwachtmeister	ordnance sergeant (*corresponding roughly to U. S staff sergeant*)
Waff.Pl	Waffenplatz	large fortress; alarm post in a fortification
WaffR	Waffenrock	blouse; tunic
Waff.Rev	Waffenrevision	arms revision; arms check-up
Waff.Rev	Waffenrevisor	army civilian ordnance inspector with rank of 1st lieutenant (*army official*)
Waff.St	Waffenstillstand	armistice
Waff.St.Bed.	Waffenstillstandsbedingungen	armistice terms
W	Wallmeister	civilian official with the fortification maintenance service, rank of 2d lieutenant (*sleeve insignia*)
W	Warte	observatory; watchtower
W	Wasser	water
W	Wasserflugzeug	hydroplane; seaplane
W	Watt	shallows (*on maps*)
W	Wechsel	change; variation; oscillation (*electricity*)
W	Wechselpunkt	reference point (*antiaircraft artillery*)
W	Wechselstrom	alternating current
W	Wehr-	army; defense; resistance
W	Wehrkreis	military district
W	Wehrkreiskommando	military district headquarters (*with Roman numerals*)
W	Wehrmacht	armed forces
w	weiss	white
W	Werfer	mortar; projector
W	Werkstatt	workshop
W	West	west
w	westlich	western; westerly
w	wider	against; contrary to
w	wieder	again; once more
W	Windwinkel	angle of drift (*aeronautics*)
W	Woche	week
w	wochentags	weekdays
w	wöchentlich	weekly
W.A	Wachabteilung	guard detachment
Wa	Waffen-	ordnance; weapon; arm of service
Wa	Wasser	water
WaA	Heeres-Waffenamt	Army Ordnance Office
WaAbn	Abnahmeabteilung des Heeres-Waffenamts	Acceptance Section of Army Ordnance Office
WachAbt	Wachabteilung	guard detachment
WachD	Wachdienst	guard duty
WaChefing	Chefingenieur des Heeres-Waffenamts	Chief Engineer of the Army Ordnance Office
Wachhab	Wachhabender	commander of a guard detail

W

Waage *f* scales, balance.
waagerecht horizontal.
Waagerechtbombenwurf *m* level-flight bombardment.
waagerechte Gitterlinie X-line (*of map grid*).
waagerechte Schußweite level-point range (*Gunnery*).
Waagerechtflug *m* level flight, horizontal flight.
Wabo *f* *See* **Wasserbombe.**
Wachanzug *m* guard uniform (*prescribed for guard duty*).
Wachbataillon *n* guard battalion (*in rear areas and Z of I*).
Wachboot *n* patrol vessel.
Wachbuch *n* guard book (*guard duty*).
Wachdienst *m* guard duty.
Wache *f* guard; watch (*Nav*).
die Wache aufziehen to mount the guard.
die Wache ablösen to relieve the guard.
Wachgebäude *n* guardhouse.
Wachhabender *m* commander of the guard.
Wachkompanie *f* guard company (*one providing the detail for guard duty*).
Wachlokal *n* guardroom.
Wachmannschaft *f* guard detail.
Wachposten *m* sentry.
Wachradfahrerkompanie *f* bicycle company of a *Wachbataillon.*
Wachregiment *n* guard regiment (*in rear areas and Z of I*).
Wachsamkeit *f* vigilance.
Wachschiff *n* patrol vessel.
wachsender Drall increasing twist (*Ord*).
Wachstaffet *m* oilskin.
Wachstube *f* guardroom.
Wachstuch *n* oilcloth.
Wacht *f* radar station (*Luftwaffe*).
Wachtleitstelle *f* radar control station (*Luftwaffe*).
Wachtmeister *m* technical sergeant (*Arty, Cav, AAA of the* Luftwaffe).
Wachtruppen *fpl* guard troops (*in rear areas and Z of I*).
Wachtturm *m* watchtower.
Wachvorgesetzter *m* commander of the guard.
Wachwelle *f* stand-by frequency (*Rad*).
Wackelkontakt *m* loose contact (*Elec*).
wackeln to rock (*Ap wings*); to shake, to be loose.
Wade *f* calf (*of leg*).
Waffe *f* weapon; arm.
Waffenamt *n* ordnance office (*a branch of the* Oberkommando des Heeres).
Waffenaufnahme *f* gun holder (*multiple AA gun mount*).
Waffenblende *f* gun shield, gun mantlet (*Tk*).
Waffenentgiftung *f* decontamination of weapons.
Waffenentgiftungsmittel *n* weapons decontaminating agent.
Waffenfarbe *f* service color.
Waffenfeldwebel *m* technical sergeant (*armorer-artificer*).
Waffenfett *n* gun grease, rifle grease.
Waffenführung *f* tactics and technique.
Waffengattung *f* arm or branch of the service.
Waffengruppe *f* group (*Ord, SA*).
die Waffengruppen auseinandernehmen to field strip (*a R, etc.*).
Waffeninspektion *f* ordnance inspectorate (*a branch of the* Allgemeines Heeresamt).
Waffenkasten *m* arms container (*aerial delivery unit*).
Waffenlager *n* ordnance depot.
waffenlos unarmed.
Waffenmeister *m* armorer-artificer official (*Civ official ranking as 2nd Lt*).
Waffenmeistergehilfe *m* assistant armorer-artificer.
Waffenmeisterei *f* armory, ordnance shop; armorer-artificer's staff or function.
Waffenmeisterschule *f* armorer-artificer school, ordnance school.
Waffenoffizier *m* ordnance staff officer, ordnance officer.
Waffenprüfung *f* ordnance proving or testing.
Waffenrock *m* blouse.
Waffenruhe *f* truce.
Waffenschule *f* service school.
Waffen-SS *f* SS Armed Forces.
Waffenstillstand *m* armistice.
örtlicher Waffenstillstand truce.
Waffenstillstandsbedingungen *fpl* armistice terms.
Waffenstreckung *f* surrender.
Waffenstreuung *f* armament error.
Waffentechnik *f* tactics and technique.
waffentechnisch pertaining to ordnance engineering or mechanics.
Waffenüberlegenheit *f* superiority of arms and equipment.
Waffen und Gerät ordnance matériel.
Waffen- und Gerätenachweis *m* property book.
Waffen- und Gerätuntersuchung *f* technical inspection.
Waffen-Unteroffizier *m* ordnance sergeant.
Waffenwagen *m* armament car (*armored RR train*).
Waffenwart *m* armorer-artificer.
Wagen *m* wagon; car (*MT, RR*).
Wagenfähre *f* ferry for vehicles.
Wagenführer *m* car commander (*MT*).
Wagenhalteplatz *m* ambulance loading post.
Wagenheber *m* jack.
Wagenplane *f* tarpaulin for vehicle.
Wagenzugführer *m* caisson section leader (*Arty*).
wählen to dial (*Tp*); to select, choose; to vote.
Wähler *m* dial (*Tp*); selector (*switchboard mechanism*).
Wählerbetrieb *m* dial system (*Tp*).
Wählscheibe *f* dial (*Tp*); selector dis'. (*switchboard mechanism*).
wahrscheinlicher Fehler probable error.
Wahrscheinlichkeitsfaktor *m* probability factor (*Ballistics*).
Waldblöße *f* forest clearing.
Waldgefecht *n* combat in woods.
Waldgelände *n* wooded area, woodland.
Waldlichtung *f* forest clearing.
Waldrand *m* edge of woods or forest.
Waldschneise *f* fire break, straight narrow forest clearing.
Waldweg *m* forest road.
Wall *m* rampart, wall (*Ft*); embankment.
Wallfeldwebel *m* technical sergeant (*Ft troops*).
Wallgraben *m* moat, ditch.
Wallmeister *m* technical official of fortifications (*Civ official ranking as 2nd Lt*).
Walloberfeldwebel *m* master sergeant (*Ft troops*).
Wallstabsfeldwebel *m* regimental sergeant major (*Ft troops*).
Walze *f* roller; body (*of a shell*); cylinder.
Walzenblende *f* cylindrical mount, mantlet for cylindrical mount (*Tk gun*).
walzenförmig cylindrical.
Wälzlager *n* antifriction bearing, ball or roller bearing.
Walzwerk *n* rolling mill.
Wand *f* interior wall; baffle; bulkhead; interior side.
Wanderbatterie *f* roving battery (*Arty*).
Wandergeschütz *n* roving gun.
Wanderungsgeschwindigkeit *f* rate of travel.
Wange *f* cheek.
Wanne *f* trough, tub; hull (*Tk*); ventral turret (*Ap*).
Wanze *f* bedbug.
Warenlager *n* warehouse.
Wärme *f* heat.
Wärmebeständigkeit *f* resistance to heat.
Wärmegleichwert *m* mechanical equivalent of heat.
Wärmeunterschied *m* temperature difference (*Met*).
Warmluftenteisung *f* thermo ice elimination (*Ap*).
Warmluftfront *f* warm front (*Met*).
Warnflagge *f* danger flag.
Warnsignal *n* danger signal.
Warnstelle *f* lookout post; district warning center (*AWS*).
Warnung *f* warning.
Warnzentrale *f* control center (*AWS*).
Wart *m* ground mechanic, maintenance man (*Avn*); mechanic, rigger; man in charge; warden, lookout.
Warte *f* watchtower; observatory.
warten to wait; to service (*Ap, Mtr, etc.*).
Wartestellung *f* stand-by position, waiting position.
Wartung *f* servicing, maintenance.
Warze *f* lug, stud.
Waschbenzin *n* gasoline used for cleaning purposes.
Wäschesack *m* laundry bag, barrack(s) bag.
Wäschetasche *f* laundry pocket (*pack*).
Wäschewechsel *m* change of underclothing.
wasserabstoßend water-repellent.
Wasserbehälter *m* water chest; water tank.
Wasserbombe *f* depth bomb, depth charge.
Wasserdestillationskompanie *f* water distillation company.
wasserdicht waterproof, watertight.
Wasserdichtigkeit *f* impermeability to water.
Wasserfahrzeug *n* craft, vessel (*stream crossing*).
Wasserflugzeug *n* seaplane.
wassergekühlt water-cooled.
wassergierig hygroscopic (*powder*).
Wasserlandflugzeug *n* amphibian airplane.
Wasserlandung *f* landing on water (*Avn*).
Wasserlauf *m* stream, watercourse.
Wasserleitung *f* water pipes, water main.
Wasserlinie *f* waterline.
Wassermantel *m* water jacket (*MG, Mtr*).
wassern to land on water (*Avn*).
Wasserpumpe *f* water pump.
Wasserpumpenkühlung *f* force-circulation cooling system (*Mtr*).
Wasserreinigungssack *m* water-sterilizing bag.
Wassersäulen-Druckmesser *m* water-column pressure gage.
Wassersperre *f* water obstacle.
Wasserspiegel *m* water level, water surface.
Wasserstand *m* water level.
Wasserstandsmesser *m* water-level gage.
Wasserstoff *m* hydrogen.
Wasserstraße *f* waterway.
Wassertransport *m* transportation by water.
Wassertrense *f* watering bridle (*harness*).
Wasserturm *m* water tower.
Wasserumlauf *m* water circulation (*Mtr*).
Wasserung *f* landing on water (*Avn*).
Wasserverankerung *f* anchorage in water (*Pon Bdg*).
Wasserversorgungskompanie *f* water supply company (*Mil*).
Wasserversorgungsstelle *f* water supply point.
Wasserverteilungsstelle *f* water distributing point.
Wasserwaage *f* builder's level, water level (*Inst*).
wasserwärts streamward.
Wasserwerk *n* waterworks.
waten to wade.
Watfähigkeit *f* fording ability, stream-crossing ability (*MT*).
Watte *f* absorbent cotton.
Weberknoten *m* weaver's knot.
Wechsel *m* change; displacement (*Arty*); alternation, one-half cycle (*Elec*); exchange, currency.
Wechselbeziehung *f* correlation.
Wechselfälle des Gefechts fortunes of war.
Wechselfestigkeit *f* fatigue strength (*Mech*).
Wechselfeuer *n* intermittent light.
Wechselgetriebe *n* gear transmission.
Wechselpunkt *m* midpoint (*AA gunnery*); critical point (*Top*).
Wechselpunktentfernung *f* slant range to midpoint (*AA gunnery*).
Wechselrichter *m* vibrator (*Rad*).
Wechselstellung *f* alternate emplacement, alternate firing position.
Wechselstrom *m* alternating current.
Wechselstromerzeuger *m* alternating-current generator, alternator (*Elec*).
Wechselstromwecker *m* alternating-current buzzer or ringer (*Tp*).
Wechselverkehr *m* alternate two-way traffic (*Rad*).
Wecken *n* reveille.
Wecker *m* buzzer, ringer (*Tp*).
Weckerfallklappe *f* drop, shutter (*Tp*).
Weg *m* road, route, passage, way, channel.
Wegebau *m* road construction.
Wegebiegung *f* road curve, road bend.
Wegedreieck *n* triangular road junction.
Wegeeinmündung *f* junction of side road with main road.
Wegeerkundung *f* road reconnaissance, reconnaissance of route.
Wegegabel *f* road fork.
Wegekarte *f* circulation map, road map.
Wegeknie *n* V-turn (*road*).
Wegekreuzung *f* crossroads, intersection.
Wegenetz *n* road net, network of roads.
Wegeposten *m* marker (*traffic control*).
Wegesperre *f* road block.
Wegespinne *f* multiple road junction.
Wegestrecke *f* stretch of road.
Wegeverhältnisse *npl* road conditions.
Wegflugpeilung *f* back bearing (*Air Navigation*).
"Weggetreten!" "Dismissed!"
Wegskizze *f* strip map, sketched road map.
Wegsperre *f* road block.
wegtreten to break ranks.
wegtreten lassen to dismiss.
Wegweiser *m* road sign.
Wehr *n* weir (*Engr*).
Wehr *f* defense; parapet (*G emplacement*).
Wehrausbildung *f* military training.
Wehrbarmachung *f* activation.
Wehrbezirk *m* recruiting district (*subdivision of a* Wehrersatzbezirk).
Wehrbezirkskommandeur *m* recruiting district commander.
Wehrbezirkskommando *n* recruiting district headquarters.
Wehrdienst *m* military service; service with the armed forces.
Wehrdienstbeschädigung *f* nonbattle injury.
Wehrdienst im Beurlaubtenstande military service with reserve status.
Wehrdienstverhältnis *n* service status.

WaffUFW	Waffenunterfeldwebel	ordnance sergeant
Waff.Uffz	Waffenunteroffizier	ordnance non-commissioned
Wag	Wagen	wagon; vehicle
wahrsch	wahrscheinlich	probable
WaJRü	Amtsgruppe für Industrielle Rüstung des Heeres-Waffenamts	Industrial Mobilization Section of Army Ordnance Office
Wako	Waffenstillstandskommission	armistice commission
Wallm	Wallmeister	civilian army official with the fortification maintenance service, with equivalent rank of 2d lieutenant
Wallm.Lehrg	Wallmeisterlehrgang	fortification maintenance course of instruction
Wall Uffz	Wallunteroffizier	fortification noncommissioned officer
Wall UFw	Wallunterfeldwebel	fortification sergeant
Wand.Patr	Wanderpatrouille	roving patrol
WaPrüf	Amtsgruppe für Entwicklung und Prüfung des Heeres-Waffenamts	Development and Testing Section of Army Ordnance Office
Wa Prüf 1	Ballistische und Munitionsabteilung	Ballistics and Munition Section of Army Ordnance Office
Wa Prüf 2	Infanterieabteilung	Infantry Section
Wa Prüf 4	Artillerieabteilung	Artillery Section of Army Ordnance Office
Wa Prüf 5	Pionier- und Festungspionierabteilung	Engineer and Fortification Engineer Section of Army
Wa Prüf 6	Kraftfahr- und Motorisie-	Motor transport and Motorization Section
Wa Prüf 7	Nachrichtenabteilung	Signal Section of Army Ordnance Office
Wa Prüf 8	Abteilung für Optik, Messwesen und Heereswetterdienst	Section for Optical and Measuring Equipment and Army Weather Service Section
Wa Prüf 9	Gasschutzabteilung	Chemical Warfare Section of Office
Wa Prüf 11	Abteilung für Sondergerät	Section for Miscellaneous Equipment of Army Ordnance Office
Wa Prüf 12	Abteilung für Versuchsplätze	Section for Experimental Stations of Army Ordnance Office
Wa Pr W	Prüfwesenabteilung des Heeres-Waffenamts	Ordnance Inspection Service of Army Ordnance Office
Warn-D	Warndienst	warning service (*antiaircraft*)
Wa Ro	Rohstoffstelle des Heeres-Waffenamts	Raw Materials Section of the Army Ordnance Office
Wass	Wasser	water
Wasserb	Wasserbombe	depth charge
wassergek	wassergekühlt	water-cooled
Wass.Flgz	Wasserflugzeug	hydroplane; seaplane
Wass.Kr	Wasserkraft	water power
Wass.Kühl	Wasserkühlung	water cooling; water cooling system
Wassmss	Wassermesser	hydrometer
Wass.Sch	Wasserscheide	watershed; divide
Wass.Str	Wasserstrasse	canal; waterway
Wass.Vers	Wasserversorgung	water supply
Wass.Wg	Wasserweg	waterway
WaVs	Vorschriftenabteilung des Heeres-Waffenamts	Regulations Section of Army Ordnance Office
W.B	Wehrbezirk	recruitment district
W.Bez	Wehrbezirk	recruitment district
W.B.Kdo	Wehrbezirkskommando	recruitment district headquarters
W.B.Kd	Wehrbezirkskommandeur	commanding officer of recruitment district
W.B.O	Wehrbezirksoffizier	recruitment officer
Wchs	Wechsel	change; variation; oscillation
Wchs.Str	Wechselstrom	alternating current
wd	wieder	again; once more
W.D.B	Wehrdienstbeschädigung	injuries received in line of duty
W.d.E	Wahrung der Ehre	preservation of honor
Wdg	Wendung	turn
Wdh	Wiederholung	repetition
Wdr	Wider-	against; contrary to
Wdr.-Aufn	Wideraufnahme	resumption
Wdrhst	Wiederherstellung	repair; reconstruction
Wdst	Wandstärke	wall thickness (*of projectiles and barrels*)
Wdst	Widerstand	resistance; opposition
Wdst.Kr	Widerstandskraft	power of resistance; magnitude of resistance; defensive power
Wdst.L	Widerstandslinie	line of resistance
Wdst.N	Widerstandsnest	point of resistance
Wdst.Z	Widerstandszone	zone of resistance
Wdst.Zentr	Widerstandszentrum	center of resistance
W.Dv	Waffenmeisterdienstvorschrift	ordnance technical manual
W(E)	Waffen - Ergänzungsoffizier	designation of retired ordnance officer recalled to active duty
We	Wehr-	defense; resistance; arms
W.E	Wehrersatz	draft registrants
W.E	Witterungseinflüsse	atmospheric influences; error of the moment
weg	wegen	on account of
wegl	weglegen	to file
Wegw	Wegweiser	signpost; road sign; guide
Wehr-Bez	Wehrbezirk	recruitment district
Wehrd	Wehrdienst	active service
wehrf	wehrfähig	fit for army service
Wehrf	Wehrform	system of national defense
Wehrg	Wehrgesetz	basic law pertaining to national defense
Wehrkde	Wehrkunde	military science
Wehrkr	Wehrkraft	total military potential
Wehrkr	Wehrkreis	military district
Wehrkr.Apoth	Wehrkreisapotheker	military district pharmacist
Wehrkr.Int	Wehrkreisintendant	civilian official in the Quartermaster General's Department with rank of brigadier general
Wehrkr.Kdo	Wehrkreiskommando	military district headquarters
Wehrkr.Kdr	Wehrkreiskommandeur	commander of military district
Wehrkr.Pf	Wehrkreispfarrer	military district chaplain
Wehrkr.Rem.Sch	Wehrkreisremonteschule	military district remount school
Wehrkrs	Wehrkreis	military district
Wehrkr.Verw	Wehrkreisverwaltung	military district administration
Wehrkr.Verw.A	Wehrkreisverwaltungsamt	military district administrative office
Wehrkr.Vet	Wehrkreisveterinär	military district veterinary
Wehrm	Wehrmacht	armed forces
Wehrm.Ak	Wehrmachtakademie	staff college
Wehrm.Laz	Wehrmachtlazarett	military hospital
Wehrm.Sp	Wehrmachtsport	military sports
WehrP	Wehrpass	service and conduct book; service record
Wehrpfl	Wehrpflicht	liability for military service
wehrtgl	wehrtauglich	fit for military service
Wehrtglkt	Wehrtauglichkeit	fit for military service
Wehrverb	Wehrverband	semi-military nationalist organization
WehrVerf	Wehrverfassung	military system as established by law
WehrVers	Wehrversammlung	annual control assembly of reservists
WehrWirtsch	Wehrwirtschaft	military economy
Wehrwiss	Wehrwissenschaft	military science
W.E.I	Wehrersatzinspektion	recruitment replacement district headquarters
W.E.Inspr	Wehrersatzinspekteur	inspector of recruitment replacement district
W.Einst.Best	Bestimmungen für Einstellung in die Wehrmacht zur Erfüllung der aktiven Wehrpflicht	regulations pertaining to the recruitment into the armed forces for active military service
Weis	Weisung	mission-type order (*tactics*); instruction
Weiterl.St	Weiterleitungsstelle	forwarding office (*railway*); supply reloading station
W.E.M	Waffenentgiftungsmittel	liquid preparation for decontamination of weapons
Wend	Wendung	turn
Wend.P	Wendepunkt	critical moment; turning point
WE-Offz	Waffenergänzungsoffizier	ordnance replacement officer
werf	werfen	to throw; to cast; to fling
Werf	Werfer	mortar; projector
Werkst	Werkstatt	workshop
W.Ers.Insp	Wehrersatzinspektion	recruitment replacement district headquarters
W.Ers.Ispr	Wehrersatzinspekteur	inspector of recruitment replacement district
West	Westen	west
Westd	Westdeutschland	Western Germany
Westf	Westfalen	Westphalia
westl	westlich	western; westerly
WESZ	Westeuropäische - Sommerzeit	Western European Summer Time
Wett	Wetter	weather
Wett.-D	Wetterdienst	weather service; meteorological service
Wett.M	Wetterkraftwagen	meteorological truck
Wett.M	Wettermessung	meteorological measurement
Wett.St	Wetterstelle	weather station
Wett.Tr	Wettertrupp	meteorological detachment
WettW	Wetterwarte	weather station
Wett.Zg	Wetterzug	meteorological platoon
Weva	Wehrkreisverwaltungsamt	military district headquarters office
WeWi	Wehrwirtschaft	defense economics
WEZ	Westeuropäische Zeit	Western European Time
W.F	Wagenfähre	ferry for vehicles (*on maps*)
W.F	Wahrscheinlichkeitsfaktor	factor of probability
W.F	Werferführer	leader of trench mortar detachment
WFA	Amtsgruppe Führungsstab	Armed Forces Operations Staff
Wff	Waffe	arm; weapon; branch of service
Wff.Fw	Waffenfeldwebel	ordnance sergeant
Wff.G	Waffengattung	arm of the service
Wffm	Waffenmeister	civilian armorer with rank of 2d lieutenant
Wffm	Waffenmeisterei	maintenance section armorers workshop
Wffm.Geh	Waffenmeistergehilfe	assistant artificer
Wffm.Wg	Waffenmeisterwagen	maintenance wagon (*ordnance*)
Wff.Ob	Waffenoberwachtmeister	ordnance sergeant
Wff.Ob.Fw	Waffenoberfeldwebel	(*corresponding roughly to U.S. staff sergeant, ordnance*)
Wff.Rev	Waffenrevisor	army civilian ordnance inspector with rank of 1st lieutenant (*army official*)
Wff.Sch	Waffenschule	branch-of-service school (*for young officers and officer-aspirants*)
Wff.Str	Waffenstreuung	gun dispersion
Wff.Uffz	Waffenunteroffizier	ordnance noncommissioned officer
Wff.UFw	Waffenunterfeldwebel	ordnance sergeant
Wff.U-Wachtm	Waffenunterwachtmeis-	ordnance sergeant
Wff.Wirk	Waffenwirkung	effectiveness of a weapon
Wff.Wirk.Uffz	Waffenwirkungsunteroffizier	noncommissioned officer umpire for effectiveness of weapons
WFO	Wehrmachtfürsorgeoffizier	officer in charge of the social service of the armed forces Staff
W.F.Sch	Wehrmachtsführerschein	army driver's license

W.F.St	**Wehrmachtsführungsstab**	**Armed Forces Operations**
WFVA	Wehrmachtfürsorge- und Versorgungsamt	Social Service and Employment Department of the Armed Forces
WFVDst	Wehrmachtfürsorge- und Versorgungsdienststellen	Offices of the Social Service and Employment Department of the Armed Forces
WFVG	Wehrmachtfürsorge- und Versorgungsgesetz	Law concerning Social Service and Employment of the Armed Forces
Wg	Wagen	wagon; vehicle; freight car
wg	wegen	on account of
W.G	Wehrgesetz	basic law pertaining to national defense
Wg.f.Hd.Schei	Wagen für Handscheinwerfer	wagon for portable searchlight
Wg.H.Pl	Wagenhalteplatz	park; ambulance station
Wg.Kr	Wegekreuzung	road crossing
Wgl	Wagenladung	wagon load; car loading
Wg.N	Wegenetz	road network
Wg.Pk	Wagenpark	wagon park
Wgr	Winkelgruppe	firing angles (*gunnery*)
Wgr.Z	Werfergranatzünder	mortar shell fuze
Wg.Sp	Wegespinne	road junction
WGZ	Wohnungsgeldzuschuss	rent allowance
WH	Wehrmachthaushalt-und Verwaltungsabteilung	Armed Forces Budget and Administration Section
Widersetzl	Widersetzlichkeit	refusal to obey orders; insubordination
Willk	Willkür	discretion; arbitrary action
willk	willkürlich	arbitrary; despotic
Wimp	Wimpel	pennant; streamer
Winddr	Winddruck	wind pressure
Winddr.M	Winddruckmesser	wind pressure gauge
Wink	Winken	signalling (*with flags or rods*)
Wink	Winker	flag signalman
Winkelgr	Winkelgruppe	firing angles (*gunnery*)
Wink.Fl	Winkerflagge	signaling flag
Wink.St	Winkerstab	signaling rod
Wink.Z	Winkerzeichen	flag signal; wigwag signal
Wirk	Wirkung	effect; result
Wirk.Kr	Wirkungskreis	radius of action; effective radius (*blasting*)
Wirk.Sch	**Wirkungsschiessen**	**fire for effect**
wirtsch	wirtschaftlich	economic
Wirtsch.Bl	Wirtschaftsblockade	economic blockade
Wirtsch.Kr	Wirtschaftskrieg	economic war
Witt	Witterung	weather; temperature; weather conditions
Witt.Einfl	Witterungseinflüsse	atmospheric influences; error of the moment
Witt.K	Witterungskunde	meteorology
WK-W.Kdo	Wehrkreiskommando	military district headquarters
W.K	Windkurs	wind direction
Wk	Winker	flag signalman
WKdo	Wachkommando	guard detail
W.Kdr	Wehrkreiskommandeur	military district commander
WKK	Wehrkreiskommando	military district headquarters
Wk.Lftsch	Werkluftschutz	antiaircraft defense of industrial plants
Wkmstr	Werkmeister	motor transport repair-shop foreman
W.Kp	Wachkompanie	guard company
Wkr	Wasserkraft	water power; hydraulic power
Wkr	Wehrkreis	military district
W.Kr	Wirtschaftskrieg	economic war
W.K.S	Wehrmachtkraftfahrsachverständiger	army motor vehicle operations expert
Wkst	Werkstatt	workshop
Wk.V	Winkervorschrift	signal communication manual
Wkz	Werkzeug	tool; implement
WL	Wachtruppe der Luftwaffe, Berlin	air corps guard detachment, Berlin
W.L	Widerstandslinie	line of resistance
Wld	Wald	wood; forest; woodland
W.L.R	Werferlehrregiment	mortar training regiment
W.L.St	**Weiterleitungsstelle**	forwarding office (*railroad*);
Wm	Wachtmeister	(*corresponds roughly to U. S. first sergeant*)
Wm	Wallmeister	civilian official with the fortification maintenance service
WM	Wegemarke	trail marker
Wm	Wehrmacht	armed forces
W.M	Wehrmelde-	recruitment reporting
W.M	Winkelmesser	clinometer (*instrument for measuring angles*)
W.M.A	Wehrmeldeamt	recruitment reporting office
W.M.Bez	Wehrmeldebezirk	recruitment reporting district
Wm.San.V	Wehrmachtsanitätsvorschrift	regulations for the medical service of the armed forces
Wm.Sch	Wallmeisterschule	fortification maintenance school
Wm.Verw	Wehrmachtverwaltung	central administration of the armed forces

Wehrersatz *m* recruiting and replacement for the armed forces.
Wehrersatzbezirk *m* recruiting area (*subdivision of a* Wehrkreis).
Wehrersatzdienststelle *f* recruiting office.
Wehrersatzinspekteur *m* recruiting area commander.
Wehrersatzinspektion *f* recruiting area headquarters.
Wehrersatzwesen *n* armed forces recruiting and replacement administration.
Wehrertüchtigung *f* military training.
Wehrerziehung *f* military education.
wehrfähig fit for military service, eligible for military service; able-bodied.
Wehrform *f* national defense system.
Wehrgeographie *f* military geography.
Wehrgeologie *f* military geology.
Wehrgeopolitik *f* military geopolitics.
Wehrgesetz *n* compulsory service law, national defense act.
Wehrhoheit *f* military sovereignty (*right of a country to have armed forces of any strength and type*).
Wehrkreis *m* military area (*corresponds roughly to corps area or service command; territorial Germany is divided into about 15* Wehrkreise *which form the basis for recruitment and replacements*).
Wehrkreisbefehlshaber *m* military area commander.
Wehrkreis-Ersatzdepot *n* recruit reception center of a *Wehrkreis*.
Wehrkreiskommando *n* military area headquarters.
Wehrmacht *f* Armed Forces.
Wehrmachtakademie *f* armed forces war college.
Wehrmachtauskunftstelle *f* armed forces information office (*supplies information regarding casualties, missing, etc., upon inquiry by next of kin*).
Wehrmachtbeamter *m* civilian official of the armed forces (Wehrmachtbeamte *have nominal rank and wear uniforms; they are classified as combatants*).
Wehrmachtbefehlshaber *m* military district commander in occupied territory (*directly responsible to the* Oberkommando der Wehrmacht).
Wehrmachtbericht *m* communiqué of the High Command.
Wehrmachtbevollmächtigter *m* Armed Forces Plenipotentiary (*commander of a protectorate or other occupied territory*).
Wehrmachtfahrkarte *f* soldier's reduced-rate railroad ticket.
Wehrmachtführerschein *m* military motor vehicle operator's permit.
Wehrmachtführungsstab *m* armed forces operations staff (*a joint operations staff under the* Oberkommando der Wehrmacht).
Wehrmachtgefängnis *n* disciplinary barracks.
Wehrmachtgeistlicher *m* chaplain.
Wehrmachtgelände *n* military reservation.
Wehrmachtgericht *n* military court.
Wehrmachtgesundheitsdienst *m* military hygiene service.
Wehrmachtrundfunkempfänger *m* standard broadcast receiver issued to armed forces personnel.
Wehrmachtseelsorgedienst *m* chaplains' service of the armed forces.
Wehrmachtsfahrlehrerschein *m* military motor vehicle instructor's license.
Wehrmacht-Standort *m* military post, garrison or station.
Wehrmacht-Strafgesetzbuch *n* military penal code.
Wehrmachtteil *m* branch of the armed forces (*such as Army or Navy*).
Wehrmeldeamt *n* draft board.
Wehrmeldebezirk *m* draft district (*subdivision of a* Wehrbezirk).
Wehrnummer *f* personal number (*appears on identification tag and in pay book; does not correspond to US Army Serial Number*).
Wehrordnung *f* compulsory service law regulations.
Wehrorganisation *f* armed-defense system.
Wehrpapiere *npl* military service documents.
Wehrpaß *m* service record book.
Wehrpflicht *f* obligation to serve in the armed forces.
Wehrpflichtiger *m* one who is subject to the draft.
Wehrrecht *n* military law.
Wehrsold *m* army pay.
Höhe des Wehrsoldes rate of pay.
Wehrsoldgruppe *f* pay grade.
Wehrstammblatt *n* document giving personal details (*made out at local induction center*).
Wehrstammbuch *n* service record book.
Wehrstammkarte *f* locator card.
Wehrstammrolle *f* roster of draftees (*arranged according to age groups*).
Wehrstrafrecht *n* military penal law.
Wehrsystem *n* national defense system.
wehrtauglich fit for military service.
wehrunwürdig unworthy to bear arms (*classification given to criminals, etc.*).
Wehrvergehen *n* military offense.
Wehrversammlung *f* annual assembly of reservists.
wehrwichtige Güter essential items.
wehrwichtige Nachrichten military information.
Wehrwirtschaft *f* war economy, military economics.
Wehrwissenschaft *f* military science.
wehrwürdig worthy to bear arms. *See also* **wehrunwürdig.**
Weiche *f* switch (*RR*); filter (*Rad*); flank (*horse*).
Weicheisen *n* soft iron, mild steel.
weichen give ground, give way, fall back.
Weichenbock *m* switch stand (*RR*).
Weichenhebel *m* switch lever (*RR*).
Weichenlaterne *f* switch lamp (*RR*).
Weingarten *m* vineyard.
Weingeist *m* alcohol.
Weise *f* manner, method, way.
Weißkreuz *n* lacrimator (*Ger marking "White Cross"*).
Weisung *f* directive, instruction, letter of instruction.
Weite *f* width; distance.
Weiterbildung *f* advanced training.
weitergeben to forward, pass along, relay.
Weiterleitungsstelle *f* forwarding point, forwarding station.
"Weitermachen!" "As you were!" (*In the sense of "Carry on!"*).
Weitermarsch *m* resumed march.
Weitschuß *m* over (*Gunnery*).
Weitwerfer *m* long-range flame thrower.
Weitwinkelaufnahme *f* wide-angle photograph.
Wellblech *n* corrugated sheet metal.
Welle *f* wave; frequency (*Rad*); shaft, axle, spindle.
in rollenden Wellen in waves (*Tac*).
Wellenausbreitung *f* wave propagation (*Rad*).
Wellenband *n* wave band, frequency band (*Rad*).
Wellenbereich *m* wave range (*Rad*).
Wellenbrecher *m* breakwater.
Wellenlänge *f* wave length (*Rad*).
Wellenleistung *f* brake horsepower.
Wellenmesser *m* wavemeter, frequency meter (*Rad*).
Wellenspektrum *n* frequency spectrum (*Rad*).
Wellenwechsel *m* change of frequency (*Rad*).
Wellenwiderstand *m* characteristic impedance, surge impedance
Wellenzapfen *m* journal (*Mech*).
wellig wavy, undulating; pulsating (*Elec*).
Wellpappe *f* corrugated paper.
Weltkrieg *m* World War I.
Weltkriegsteilnehmer *m* veteran of World War I.
Wendegetriebe *n* reversing gear.
Wendekreis *m* turning radius (*MT*).
wenden to turn, veer.
Wendepunkt *m* turning point, critical point.
Wendeturm *m* pylon (*Adrm*).
Wendewinkel *m* angle of yaw (*Avn*).
Wendezeiger *m* bank and turn indicator (*Ap*).
Wendigkeit *f* maneuverability (*Ap*); ease in steering or turning, mobility (*vehicles*).
Wendung *f* turn (*Avn*); **facing** (*drill*); reversal; change.
werfen to throw.
Werfer *m* smoke-shell mortar; signal projector; rocket projector. *See also* **Nebelwerfer.**
Werferabteilung *f* chemical battalion, smoke battalion; rocket projector battalion.
Werferrahmen *m* projector frame; frame-type rocket projector.
Werferregiment *n* chemical regiment, smoke regiment; rocket projector regiment.
Werferschütze *m* mortar gunner.
Werft *f* shipyard, dockyard; workshop (*Adrm*).
Werfthalle *f* repair hangar (*Adrm*).
Werg *n* oakum.
Werk *n* work (*Ft, etc.*); plant, factory.
Werkbank *f* workbench.
Werkflugplatz *m* factory airfield.
Werkluftschutz *m* factory air-defense system.
Werkmeister *m* shop foreman (*Civ official ranking as Master Sgt*).
Werkstatt *f* workshop, machine shop.
Werkstattauftrag *m* work order.
Werkstattgerätkraftwagen *m* spare parts truck (*MT*).
Werkstattkompanie *f* repair-shop company, workshop company.
Werkstattkraftwagen *m* repair-shop truck, mobile machine shop (*MT*).
Werkstattrupp *m* repair-shop detachment, maintenance party.
Werkstattzug *m* maintenance platoon (*Tk Bn*).
Werkstoff *m* material.
Werkzeug *n* tool.
Werkzeugkasten *m* tool box.
Werkzeugmaschine *f* machine tool.
Werkzeugstahl *m* tool steel.
Werkzeugtasche *f* tool bag, tool kit.
Wert *m* value, factor.
Wespe *f* wasp (*also nickname for Ger self-propelled light field howitzer*).
Westa *f See* **Wettererkundungsstaffel.**
Westwall *m* West Wall (*a system of fortifications along Germany's western frontier*).
Westwallabzeichen *n* West Wall Badge (*decoration*).
Wetter *n* weather.
Wetterbeobachtung *f* weather observation.
Wetterberatung *f See* **Wetterbericht.**
Wetterberatungszentrale *f* air forces weather reporting center.
Wetterbericht *m* weather report.
Wetterbericht vom Pilotballon pibal (*Met*).
Wetterbezirk *m* weather region, control region.
Wetterdienst *m* weather service.
Wetterdienstgeräte *npl* weather instruments (*Met*).
Wetterdiensthelferin *f* air forces weather service woman auxiliary.
Wetterelement *n* weather factor (*Ballistics, Met*).
Wettererkundung *f* weather reconnaissance (*Avn*).
Wettererkundungsstaffel *f* weather reconnaissance squadron (*Avn*).
Wetterfahne *f* weather vane.
Wetterführung *f* ventilating system (*mine*).
Wetterfunkmeldung *f* weather message, meteorological message (*Rad*).
Wetterfunkspruch *m See* **Wetterfunkmeldung.**
Wetterkarte *f* weather map (*Met*).
Wetterkunde *f* meteorology.
Wetterlage *f* weather conditions.
Wetterleuchten *n* lightning (*Met*).
Wettermeldung *f* weather report (*Avn*); metro message (*Arty*).
Wettermessung *f* meteorological measurement.
Wetterpeilzug *m* meteorological and direction-finding platoon.
Wetterschlüssel *m* weather code.
Wetterspinne *f* wind-component indicator (*Gunnery*).
Wettersprengmittel *n* safety mining explosive.
Wetterstelle *f* weather station.
Wetterstörung *f* meteorological disturbance.
Wettervoraussage *f* weather forecast.
Wettervorhersage *f See* **Wettervoraussage.**
Wetterwarte *f* weather station.
Wetterzug *m* metro platoon (*Arty*).
wetzen to sharpen, hone.
Wezu-Gerät *n* wind corrector and time scale (*SR*) (*Wezu* = *Wetterzug*).
wichsen to polish (*leather, etc.*).
Wickelgamaschen *fpl* wrapped leggins, wrap puttees.
Wicklung *f* winding, wrapping.
Widerlager *n* abutment (*Bdg*).
Widerrist *m* withers (*horse*).
Widerstand *m* resistance (*Elec, Tac*); drag (*Avn*).
Widerstandsgruppe *f* unit assigned to one sector of main line of resistance (*Tac*).
Widerstandskessel *m* pocket of resistance.
Widerstandslinie *f* line of resistance.
Widerstandslinie der Vorposten outpost line of resistance (*Tac*).
Widerstandsmesser *m* ohmmeter.
Widerstandsmoment *n* section modulus (*Engr*).
Widerstandsnest *n* island of resistance, pocket of resistance.
Widerstandsstellung *f* delaying position.
Widerstandstruppe *f* delaying unit (*Tac*).
Widerstandszentrum *n* center of resistance (*Tac*).
widerstehen to withstand, resist.
wiederherstellen to repair, restore, reconstruct.
Wiederherstellung *f* reconstruction, repair, restoration.
wiederholen to repeat.
Wiederholungsunterricht *m* refresher instruction.
wieder richten to re-lay (*Gunnery*).
Wiederspannabzug *m* double action (*SA*).
Wiege *f* cradle (*G*).
wiegen to weigh.
Wiegengleitbahn *f* cradle guide rails (*G*).
Wiegenträger *m* cradle frame (*G*).
Wiegentrog *m* cradle trough (*G*).
Wiegenzurrung *f* cradle lock (*G*).
Wiese und Weide grassland.
Wimpel *m* pennant.
Windabtrift *f* wind drift.
windabwärts downwind, leeward.

Windanker *m* downstream anchor cable *(Pon Bdg).*
Windankerleine *f* downstream anchor cable *(Pon Bdg).*
Windankerlinie *f* downstream line of anchors *(Pon Bdg).*
Windankertau *n* downstream anchor cable *(Pon Bdg).*
Windanzeiger *m* wind indicator.
Winddruck *m* wind pressure.
Winde *f* winch.
Windenkasten *m* winch box.
Windewagen *m* winch truck.
Windfahne *f* wind vane.
Windfahnenkorn *n* wind vane front sight *(Ap MG).*
Windflügel *m* fan *(MT);* arming vane *(bomb).*
Windjacke *f* double-breasted field jacket.
Windkanal *m* wind tunnel *(Avn).*
Windkegel *m* wind cone.
Windmesser *m* *See* **Windmeßgerät.**
Windmeßgerät *n* anemometer.
Windmessung *f* wind test *(Met).*
Windmühle *f* windmill.
Windpfeil *m* wind arrow *(Met).*
Windrichtungsanzeiger *m* wind-direction indicator *(Avn).*
Windsack *m* wind cone, windsock.
windschief twisted, warped.
windschiefer Flug crabbing *(Avn).*
Windschlüssel *m* key to weather code numbers and symbols *(Met).*
Windschutz *m* windbreak.
Windschutzscheibe *f* windshield.
windseitig windward.
Windstärke *f* wind velocity *(Met).*
Windstoß *m* squall, gust, bump.
Windung *f* twist *(Ord).*
Windverband *m* lateral bracing *(Bdg).*
Windverhältnisse *npl* wind factors *(Ballistics).*
windwärts upwind, windward.
Windziffer *f* wind reference number *(Gunnery).*
Winkel *m* angle; V-formation, wedge formation *(Avn);* chevron.
Winkelauswanderung *f* angular movement, angular travel.
Winkelbeschleunigung *f* angular acceleration.
Winkel der Schräglage angle of bank, angle of roll *(Avn).*
Winkelfernrohr *n* elbow telescope.
Winkelgeschwindigkeit *f* angular speed, angular velocity, angular travel.
Winkelgruppe *f* firing angles.
untere Winkelgruppe low firing angles (0° to 45°).
obere Winkelgruppe high firing angles (45° to 90°).
Winkelhebel *m* angle cam *(MG lock).*
Winkelkopf *m* head of static rod *(river-width measuring Inst).*
Winkellasche *f* butt strap *(made of angle iron).*
Winkelmaß *n* angular measurement; phase constant *(Rad).*
Winkelmesser *m* gunner's quadrant; clinometer *(Surv, Arty);* goniometer *(Surv);* protractor.
Winkelmesserebene *f* quadrant plate *(G).*
Winkelmeßgerät *n* protractor.
Winkelmessung *f* goniometry *(Surv).*
Winkelspiegel *m* periscope, protectoscope *(Tk).*
Winkeltrommel *f* cross staff *(Surv Inst for laying out right angles).*
Winker *m* flagman; signaler using a signal disk; signal arm or light indicating direction of turn *(MT).*
Winkerflagge *f* *See* **Winkflagge.**
Winkerkelle *f* *See* **Winkerstab.**
Winkerstab *m* signaling disk.
Winkflagge *f* semaphore flag, control flag, signal flag.
Winkspruch *m* semaphore message, message transmitted by signaling disk or hand signals.
Winkverbindung *f* visual communication by flag or hand signals.
Winkzeichen *n* hand signal, flag signal.
Winterausrüstung *f* winter equipment.
Winterbeweglichkeit *f* mobility in winter.
Winterkettenglied *n* oversize track shoe for operations in deep snow *(MT, Tk).*
Winterkrieg *m* winter warfare.
Winterlost *n* 50-50 mixture of lewisite and mustard *(CWS).*
Wintermedaille des Ostkrieges Eastern Campaign Winter Medal *(decoration).*
Wirbel *m* vortex, eddy, whirl; whirlpool; drum roll; spine.
Wirbelbildung *f* formation of eddies *(Ballistics).*
Wirbelkammer *f* turbulence chamber *(Diesel engine).*
Wirbelsäule *f* spinal column.
Wirbelstrom *m* eddy current *(Elec).*
Wirbelsturm *m* cyclone, tornado.
wirksam effective.
wirksame Schußweite effective range.
wirksame Steigung effective pitch *(propeller).*
Wirkungsbereich *m* effective range *(Ord);* field of fire *(Ord);* radius of action *(Ap).*
Wirkungsdauer *f* persistence *(of a Cml agent).*
Wirkungsfeuer *n* fire for effect *(Arty).*
Wirkungshalbmesser *m* radius of rupture *(demolitions).*
Wirkungskreis *m* circle of rupture *(demolitions).*
Wirkungsschießen *n* fire for effect *(Gunnery).*
Wirtschaft *f* economy; tavern.
wirtschaftlich economical.
Wirtschaftskrieg *m* economic warfare.
Wirtshaus *n* tavern, inn.
Wischer *m* wiper; sponge; cleaning patch; windshield wiper.
Wischstock *m* cleaning rod *(G).*
Wischstrick *m* pull-through rope *(for pulling brush or sponge through G barrel).*
Witterung *f* atmospheric conditions, weather.
Witterungseinflüsse *mpl* exterior ballistic factors, weather factors.
W-Motor *m* three-bank upright engine.
Wohnungsgeldzuschuß *m* commutation of quarters, rental allowance.
Wohnviertel *n* residential quarter.
Woilach *m* saddle blanket.
Wölbung *f* droop; camber.
Wolfram *n* tungsten.
Wolfsgrube *f* obstacle pit *(Ft).*
Wolke *f* cloud.
Wolkendecke *f* cloud cover.
Wolkenfeld *n* cloud bank.
Wolkenhöhe *f* ceiling *(Met).*
wolkenlos clear *(Met).*
Wolkenscheinwerfer *m* ceiling light *(Met).*
Wolkensegeln *n* cloud soaring *(glider).*
Wolkenspiegel *m* nephoscope *(Met).*
Wolkenuntergrenze *f* base of cloud.
wolkig broken *(Met).*
Wolldecke *f* wool blanket.
Wolle *f* wool.
Wolokusche *f* boat-type runner *(placed under gun wheels for operations in deep snow).*
Wortlaut *m* text, wording.
Wriggeln *n* sculling.
Wucht *f* kinetic energy; striking power, force of impact.
Wulstband *n* rim band *(MT).*
Wulstfelge *f* clincher rim *(MT).*
Wundbrand *m* gangrene.
Wunde *f* wound.
Wundstarrkrampf *m* lockjaw, tetanus.
Wundverband *m* dressing, bandage.
Wurf *m* cast, throw; bomb release.
"Wurf!" "Bombs away!"
Wurfarten *fpl* types of release *(bombing).*
Wurfbahn *f* bomb trajectory.
Würfel *m* cube; capsule, pellet.
Wurfgerät *n* projector.
schweres Wurfgerät chemical rocket projector.
Wurfgranate *f* mortar shell.
Wurfgranatzünder *m* mortar-shell fuze.
Wurfkörper *m* special projectile for signal pistols.
Wurfparabel *f* bomb trajectory.
Wurfrahmen *m* framework-type projector for high-explosive or incendiary rockets.
Wurftaubenschießstand *m* skeet range.
Wurfweite *f* mortar range; throwing range *(hand grenades);* bombing range.
Würgebohrung *f* tapered bore, choke *(barrel) (Ord).*
Würgezange *f* cap crimper *(Engr).*
Würgung *f* crimp *(Am).*
Wurzel *f* root.
Wüste *f* desert.

X

X-Uhr *f* H-hour, zero hour.
X-Tag *m* M-day, mobilization day.

Y

Yperit *n* mustard gas.

Wm.Verw.V	Wehrmachtverwaltungsvorschrift	manual for administration of the armed forces (Army Regulation 320; Navy Regulation 530; Air Corps Regulation 402)
W.M.Z	Wurfminenzünder	fuze of mortar shell
WNW	Westnordwest	west-northwest
W.O.	Waffenoffizier	ordnance officer
WO	Wehrordnung	regulations for execution of the law pertaining to national defense
W.O.	Werferoffizier	mortar officer
W.Ob.Fw	Waffenoberfeldwebel	*(corresponds roughly to U. S. staff sergeant, ordnance)*
W.Ob.Wm	Waffenoberwachtmeister	ordnance sergeant *(corresponding roughly to U. S. staff sergeant)*
wöch	wöchentlich	weekly
Wo km/min	Steiggeschwindigkeit eines Flugzeugs in Kilometern in der Minute	climbing speed of an airplane in kilometers per minute
Wolfsgr	Wolfsgrube	pit with pointed stakes; trap hole
W.P	Wachposten	sentry post
W.P	Würfelpulver	flaked powder *(propellant in small rectangular tablets)*
WR	Wehrmachtrechtsabteilung	Armed Forces Legal Section
W.Rgt.Bln	Wachregiment Berlin	Berlin Guard Regiment
Wrt.Kr	Wirtschaftskrieg	economic war
Wsp	Wehrsport	military sport
Wss	Wasser	water
Wssb	Wasserbombe	depth charge
Wss.Üb.Pl	Wasserübungsplatz	water training area *(combat engineers)*
W.St	Wartestellung	position in readiness
W.St	Wechselstellung	alternate position
Wst	Werkstatt	workshop
WStb	Amtsgruppe Wehrwirtschaftsstab	Defense Economic Staff
W.-Str	Wasserstrasse	canal; waterway
Wstr	Wechselstrom	alternating current
Wstr.-M	Wechselstrommotor	alternating current engine
WStVZV	Wehrmachtstrafvollzugsvorschrift	regulations for the execution of sentences in the armed forces
WSW	Westsüdwest	west-southwest
W.T	Wasserturm	water tower *(on maps)*
W.Tr	Wachtruppe	guard detachment
W.Tr	Wassertransport	water transportation
w.u	wehruntauglich	unfit for military service
W.Uffz	Waffenunteroffizier	ordnance noncommissioned officer
W.UFw	Waffenunterfeldwebel	ordnance sergeant *(corresponding roughly to U. S. sergeant)*
W.u.G	Abteilung Waffen und Gerät beim Wehrkreiskommando	weapons and equipment department of the military district headquarters
W.V	Wehrkreisverordnung	military district orders
W.V	Wehrkreisverwaltung	military district headquarters
W.V	Wehrmachtversorgung	social service for members of the armed forces
W.V	Wehrverwaltung	army administration
W.V.A	Wehrkreisverwaltungsamt	military district administrative office
W.W	Waffenwerkstatt	weapon repair shop
Ww	Wegweiser	signpost; road sign; guide
Wz	Warnzentrale	warning center *(antiaircraft defense)*
W.Z	Wetterzug	meteorological platoon
WZ	Zentralabteilung des Oberkommandos der Wehrmacht	Central Section of Armed Forces High Command
Wzg	Werkzeug	tool; implement
Wzgm	Werkzeugmaschine	machine tool
WzN	West zu Nord	west by north
WzS	West zu Süd	west by south

X

X	nicht sonderlich dringend	not particularly urgent *(sign on message blank)*
XX	dringend	urgent *(sign on message blank)*

Z

Z	Zahlmeister	paymaster
(Z)	Zahlmeisterlaufbahn	paymaster career *(added to designation of rank)*
Z	Zeichen	sign; symbol
Z	Zeichnung	drawing; design; sketch
Z	Zeile	line
Z	Zeit	time; period
Z	Zelt	tent
Z	Zentral-	central
Z	Zentralamt	central office
Z	Zentrum	center
Z	Zerstörer	destroyer *(navy)*
Z	Ziel	target; objective; goal; destination; aim; scope
Z	Zielachse am Theodoliten	sighting axis on theodolite
Z	Zielbau	construction of target
Z	Zielbezeichnung	target designation
z	zielen	to aim; to sight
Z	Ziffer	cipher; numeral
Z	Zoll	inch
Z	Zone	zone
z	zu, zum, zur	to; to the; at; for: by
Z	Zubehör	accessories; fittings
Z	Zünder	fuze; detonator
Z	Zug	train *(railroad)*; platoon; section; pull *(mechanics)*
Z	Zugführer	platoon leader
Z	Zugkraftwagen	prime mover truck
Z	Zugschiessen	platoon fire *(mortar)*
Z	Zugschraube	tractor propeller *(airplane)*
Z.A	Zentralamt	central office
Z.A	Zeugamt	ordnance department
Za	Zündapparat	magneto; ignition apparatus
Z.A.B	Zivilarbeiterbataillon	civilian workers' battalion
Za C	Zeugamt Cassel	ordnance department, Cassel
Zahlm	Zahlmeister	paymaster
Zahlm	Zahlmeisterei	paymaster's office
Zahlm.Anw	Zahlmeisteranwärter	candidate for paymaster
Zahlm.Asp	Zahlmeisteraspirant	candidate for paymaster
Zahlmstr	Zahlmeister	paymaster.
Zahlm.V	Vorschrift über die Zahlmeisterlaufbahn	regulations concerning the career of paymaster
Zahlm.Verw	Zahlmeisterverwaltung	paymaster administration; administration by paymaster's office
ZAK	Zentralnachweiseamt für Kriegerverluste und Kriegergräber	Central Information Bureau for War Casualties and Soldiers' Graves
Za S	Zeugamt Spandau	ordnance depart., Spandau
Z-Aufkl	Zielaufklärung	target reconnaissance
ZB	Zentralbatterie	central battery
z.B	zum Beispiel	for example
Z-Büro	Zentralbüro	central office
z.b.V	zur besonderen Verwendung	for special use
Z.D	Zivildienst	civil service
Zd	Zünd-	ignition; detonating
Zd	Zünder	fuze; detonator
Zdg	Zündung	ignition; priming; detonation
Zdht	Zündhütchen	primer; percussion cap
Zdlg	Zündladung	detonation charge
Zd.Mitt	Zündmittel	priming substance; means of detonation *(explosive)*
Zdr	Zünder	fuze; detonator
Zdschn	Zündschnur	fuze
Zdschn.Anz	Zündschnuranzünder	fuze cord
Zdschr	Zündschraube	threaded percussion primer
Zd.St	Zünderstreuung	dispersion caused by fuze differences
Zeich	Zeichen	sign; symbol
Zeichn	Zeichner	draftsman
Zeichng	Zeichnung	drawing; design; sketch
Zeitlp	Zeitlupe	slow-motion lens
Z.E.L	Zentralersatzteillager	central spare parts depot
Zellst	Zellstoff	cellulose
Zens	Zensor	censor
Zentr	Zentral	central
Zentr	Zentrum	center
Zentra.A	Zentralamt	central office
Zentr.W	Zentrierwulst	bourrelet
Zepp	Zeppelin	Zeppelin
Z-Erk	Zielerkundung	target spotting
zerm	zermürbt	worn down; ground down; crushed
Zerm	Zermürbung	attrition
zerr	zerreissen	to split
Zerspl	Zersplitterung	dispersion *(of forces)*
zerspr	zersprengt	dispersed; scattered; blown
Zerst	Zerstäuber	sprayer; spray diffuser; spraying apparatus
zerst	zerstören	to destroy
Zerst	Zerstörer	destroyer *(navy)*
Zerst	Zerstörung	destruction; demolition
Zerst.F	Zerstörungsfeuer	destructive fire

Z

zäh tough, tenacious; viscous; stubborn.
Zahl *f* number.
Zahlenwert *m* numerical value.
Zahlmeister *m* paymaster official (Wehrmachtbeamter, *generally ranking as 2nd Lt, responsible for pay and allowances, ration, messing, clothing accounts and company finances).*
Zahlmeisterei *f* office and function of the *Zahlmeister.*
Zahn *m* tooth.
Zahnarzt *m* dentist. *See also* Sanitätsoffizier(Z).
Zahnbehandlung *f* dental treatment.
Zahnbogen *m* elevating arc, elevating rack *(G).*
Zahnbogenrichtmaschine *f* arc-type elevating mechanism *(G).*
Zahnkette *f* driving chain *(MT).*
Zahnkranz *m* traversing rack *(Tk turret, AA gun).*
Zahnkranzlenkung *f* worm and sector steering system *(MT).*
Zahnrad *n* gear, gear wheel; pinion.
Zahnradgetriebe *n* gear transmission *(MT).*
Zahnradpumpe *f* gear pump *(Mtr).*
Zahnstange *f* rack *(Tech).*
Zahnstangenlenkung *f* pinion and sector steering system *(MT).*
Zahntechniker *m* dental technician.
Zange *f* pliers, tongs.
Zangenangriff *m* pincer attack, double envelopment *(Tac).*
Zangenbewegung *f* pincer movement.
Zapfen *m* pin; journal; trunnion; pivot; plug; tap; spigot; tenon.
Zapfendüse *f* pintle nozzle, pin nozzle *(Mtr).*
Zapfenkreuz *n* cross *(of a universal joint).*
Zapfenlager *n* pillow block, bushing.
Zapfenstreich *m* taps.
Zapfstelle *f* standpipe.
Zaum *m* bridle.
Zaun *m* fence.
Zehe *f* toe.
Zeichen *n* sign; signal; call; military symbol.
Zeichenbrett *n* drawing board.
Zeichenerklärung *f* legend, key to map signs.
Zeichengerät *n* plotting instrument, drawing instrument.
Zeichenpapier *n* drawing paper.
Zeichenverbindung *f* visual communication.
zeichnen to draw, sketch.
Zeichnung *f* drawing, blueprint, plan.
Zeigefinger *m* forefinger.
Zeiger *m* indicator, pointer; hand, needle *(on Inst dial).*
Zeigerzieleinrichtung *f* follow-the-pointer sight mechanism *(G).*
Zeitabstand *m* headway, time interval.
Zeitbombe *f* time bomb.
Zeiteinteilung *f* timetable *(Tac).*
Zeitgruppe *f* time heading *(on Rad messages).*
Zeitmaß *n* cadence *(marching).*
Zeitschnur *f* safety fuze, blasting fuze.
Zeittafel *f* timetable, schedule.
Zeitunterschied *m* time difference *(SR)*; time interval *(AAA).*
Zeitunterschiedverfahren *n* time-difference method *(SR).*
Zeitzeichen *n* time signal.
Zeitzünder *m* time fuze *(Am).*
Zeitzünderschuß *m* time fire *(Gunnery).*
Zeitzündschnur *f* safety fuze, blasting fuze.
Zelle *f* cell, cellule.
Zellon *n* cellulose acetate.
Zellophan *n* cellophane.
Zellophanüberzug *m* cellophane cover.
Zellstoff *m* cellulose.
Zelluloidtafel *f* celluloid disk; protractor; templet.
Zellwolle *f* cellulose fiber.
Zelt *n* tent.
Zeltausrüstung *f* tent equipment.
Zeltbahn *f* shelter half.
Zeltbau *m* tent pitching.
Zeltlager *n* tent camp.
Zeltleine *f* guy rope *(tent).*
Zeltpflock *m* tent pin, guy pin, guy-line stake.
Zeltstock *m* tent pole.
Zementfliese *f* concrete paving block.
Zensor *m* censor.
Zensur *f* censorship.
Zentralbatterie *f* common battery
Zentrale *f* central *(Tp)*; central station *(Arty).*
zentrale Projektion gnomonic projection.
Zentralrichtgerät *n* director *(AAA).*
Zentralschmierung *f* central lubrication *(MT).*
Zentrierwulst *m* bourrelet *(Am).*
Zentrum *n* center; bull's eye.
zerbrechen to crack, break into pieces.
zerdrücken crush, crumple, squash, squeeze.
zerfallen disintegrate.
Zerfallgurt *m* disintegrating belt *(MG).*
Zerknallstoß *m* blast, concussion.
zerlegen disassemble, dismantle, strip; decentralize, disperse; disintegrate.
Zerlegerzünder *m* self-destroying fuze *(AA Am).*
zerlegte Formen broken outlines *(Cam).*
Zerlegung *f* dispersal, decentralization; disintegration; dismantling, stripping.
zermalmen crush, crunch, smash, dash to pieces.
zermürben wear down.
Zermürbung *f* attrition.
Zermürbungskrieg *m* war of attrition.
Zermürbungsstrategie *f* strategy of attrition.
Zerschellerschicht *f* burster course, bursting layer, detonating slab *(Ft).*
Zerschneidezünder *m* *See* Zug- und Zerschneidezünder.
zerspalten to split up.
zersplittern to shatter; to split up, dissipate *(forces, etc.).*
zersprengen to crack, burst into pieces, shatter; to blow up; to rout.
zerspringen to explode, burst.
Zerstäuber *m* atomizer, spray.
Zerstäuberdüse *f* spray nozzle; Diesel fuel injector.
Zerstäubergerät *n* chemical spray apparatus; sprayer-type decontaminating apparatus.
Zerstörangriff *m* hit-and-run raid *(Avn).*
zerstören destroy, demolish.
Zerstörer *m* destroyer *(Nav)*; twin-engine fighter, long-range fighter *(Ap).*
Zerstörerflugzeug *n* twin-engine fighter airplane.
Zerstörergeschwader *n* twin-engine fighter wing.
Zerstörerschule *f* twin-engine fighter pilot school.
Zerstörung *f* destruction, demolition.
Zerstörungsarbeiten *fpl* demolitions.
Zerstörungsfeuer *n* destruction fire *(Arty).*
Zettel *m* card, tag, ticket, slip.
Zeug *n* ordnance supplies; gear, equipment.
Zeugamt *n* ordnance office.
Zeughaus *n* arsenal.
Zeugnis *n* certificate.
Zickzackscheibe *f* zigzag target *(Tng).*
Ziegelei *f* brickyard.
ziehen to draw, pull, drag, tow; to pull up *(Ap)*; to be drafty.
Ziehzünder *m* pull firing device *(land mine).*
Ziel *n* target, objective, goal.
ins Ziel gehen to hold into the target.
das Ziel aufsitzen lassen to hold at bottom edge of target.
das Ziel verschwinden lassen to hold at upper edge of target.
Zielabschnitt *m* sector of fire, target sector.
Zielachse *f* sighting axis *(plane table alidade).*
Zielanflug *m* approach flight, approach run *(Avn).*
Zielansprache *f* target designation.
Zielaufklärung *f* artillery target reconnaissance.
Zielaufnahme mit Langbasisanlage horizontal base method.
Zielausbildung *f* training in aiming, training in laying.
Zielbild *n* target image *(telescopic sight).*
Zielbreite *f* target length *(moving targets).*
"Ziel dreht!" "Target changing course!" *(AA predictor).*
Zieldreieck *n* shot group, aiming group *(sighting and aiming exercise).*
Zieleinrichtung *f* sighting mechanism *(Ord).*
zielen to aim, sight.
Zielentfernung *f* range to target *(Gunnery).*
Zielerkundung *f* target reconnaissance.
Zielfehler *m* aiming error.
Zielfernrohr *n* telescopic sight, direct sighting telescope.
Zielfernrohrträger *m* telescopic sight mount.
Zielfeststellung *f* locating of target *(Gunnery).*
Zielfläche *f* objective plane *(Gunnery)*; target area *(bombing).*
Zielflug *m* homing *(Air Navigation).*
Zielgelände *n* target area.
zielgenau accurate, precise.
Zielgerät *n* sight, sighting mechanism *(Ord)*; bomb sight.
Zielgeschwindigkeit *f* speed of target.
Zielgevierttafel *f* target-designation grid *(Arty Surv).*
Zielhöhe *f* height of target, altitude of target.
Zielhöhenwinkel *m* angle of site *(Gunnery)*; angular height of target *(AAA).*
Zielhöhenwinkel zum Abschußpunkt angular height of target at present position *(AAA).*
Zielhöhenwinkel zum Meßpunkt angular height of target at instant of range determination *(AAA).*
Zielhöhenwinkel zum Treffpunkt angular height of target at future position *(AAA).*
Zielhöhenwinkel zum Wechselpunkt angular height of target at midpoint *(AAA).*
Zielkelle *f* *See* Ziellöffel.
Zielkontrollspiegel *m* aim-checking device.
Zielkreis *m* target area *(bombing).*
Ziellandung *f* spot landing *(Avn).*
Ziellineal *n* orienting straightedge *(MG aiming circle).*
Ziellinie *f* line of sight.
Ziellinienprüfer *m* bore sight *(Ord).*
Ziellöffel *m* aiming disk, sighting disk, marking disk.
Zielmarke *f* lead mark *(telescopic sight).*
Zielmunition *f* subcaliber ammunition.
Zielpunkt *m* target point, objective point.
Zielpunktkarte *f* battle map or firing chart showing location of probable targets.
Zielpuppe *f* dummy.
Zielraum *m* target area, sector of fire.
Zielrechenmaschine *f* predictor, prediction mechanism *(AA)*; ballistic director *(Arty).*
Zielrichtung *f* direction of the target.
Zielscheibe *f* practice target.
Zielschiene *f* sighting bar.
Zielschiff *n* target ship.
Zielschwarze *n* bull's-eye.
Zielseitenwinkel *m* azimuth of target.
Zielseitenwinkel zum Abschußpunkt azimuth of target at present position *(AAA).*
Zielseitenwinkel zum Treffpunkt azimuth of target at future position *(AAA).*
Zielsetzung *f* designation of objective.
Zielsicherheit *f* accuracy of fire, marksmanship.
Zielspinne *f* range-deflection fan *(Gunnery).*
Zielstachel *m* pointed-post [illegible]cle *(telescopic sight).*
Zieltafel *f* data sheet *(Gunnery).*
Zielteil *m* target sector.
Ziel- und Anschlagsübungen *fpl* aiming drill.
Zielunterlagen *fpl* information of objectives, target data.
Zielvorrichtung *f* aiming mechanism.
Zielwaagerechte *f* horizontal through base of target *(Arty).*
Zielwechsel *m* change of target, engaging of successive targets.
Zielweg *m* course of target *(AAA).*
Zielwurf *m* precision bombing.
Zielzuweisung *f* allocation of targets.
Ziffer *f* cipher, figure, numeral.
Zifferblatt *n* dial *(on Inst).*
ziffern to cipher, encipher, encrypt.
Zimmerantenne *f* indoor antenna.
Zimmermann *m* carpenter.
Zimmerschießgerät *n* field artillery trainer.
Zinkbecher *m* zinc container *(dry cell).*
Zinknebel *m* HC mixture, HC smoke mixture *(CWS).*
Zinn *n* tin.
Zirkel *m* compasses, dividers.
Zirruswolke *f* cirrus cloud *(Met).*
Zisternenfahrzeug *n* vehicle fitted with chemical spray apparatus.
Zisternenflugzeug *n* airplane fitted with chemical-spray apparatus.
Zivil *n* civilian clothing.
Zivilbevölkerung *f* civilian population.
Zivilgericht *n* civil court.
Zivilinternierter *m* civilian internee.
Zivilist *m* civilian.
Zivilkleidung *f* civilian clothing.
Zivilluftfahrt *f* civil aviation, commercial aviation.
Zivilperson *f* civilian.
Zivilvergehen *n* civil offense.
Zoll *m* inch *(2.54 cm)*; duty, tariff, toll.
Zollhaus *n* custom house.
Zollschranke *f* tollgate.
Zonenzeit *f* standard time.
Zubehör *n* accessories.
Zubehörteil *m* part, accessory.
Zubehörtornister *m* accessories case *(portable Rad).*
Zubringer *m* follower *(SA).*
Zubringerfeder *f* follower spring *(SA).*
Zubringerhebel *m* belt-feed lever *(MG).*
Zucht *f* discipline.
Zuchthaus *n* penitentiary.
Zuchthausstrafe *f* sentence of confinement to a penitentiary.
Zufahrtstraße *f* access road, approach road.
zufälliger Fehler nonsystematic error *(Arty)*; accidental error *(Mech, Optics).*
Zufallstreffer *m* accidental hit.
Zufuhr *f* supply, bringing up of supplies.
Zuführer *m* belt feed *(MG)*; feed mechanism *(automatic weapon).*
Zufuhrstraße *f* line or road of communication, line or road of supply.
Zuführung *f* feed *(MG)*; lead-in *(Rad).*
Zuführungsdraht *m* lead-in *(Rad).*

Zuführungsgehäuse *n* feed box *(AA gun).*
Zuführungsweg *m* route for bringing up supplies, etc.
Zug *m* platoon; groove *(rifling)*; train *(RR)*; pull; tension; draft.
Zugang *m* access, approach; increase, addition.
Zugangsweg *m* access road, approach road.
Zugbewachung *f* train guard.
Zugbreitkeil *m* platoon in inverted-wedge formation.
Zugbrücke *f* drawbridge.
Zugdämpfer *m* baffle *(engine muffler).*
Zugdruckzünder *m* pull-pressure igniter *(mine).*
Zügel *m* bridle; rein.
zugelassen authorized, permitted; admitted.
Zügelring *m* bit ring *(harness).*
zugeteilt attached; allotted.
Zugfähre *f* rope ferry *(Engr).*
Zugfeder *f* safety spring *(MG).*
Zugfederhaken *m* safety-spring catch *(MG).*
Zugfederschraube *f* See Zugfederspannschraube.
Zugfederspannschraube *f* safety-spring tension screw *(MG).*
Zugfestigkeit *f* tensile strength.
Zugführer *m* platoon leader.
Zuggrenze *f* platoon boundary.
Zuggurt *m* tension chord *(truss).*
Zughaken *m* pintle *(Trac)*; singletree attachment hook *(limber).*
Zugkeil *m* platoon in wedge formation.
Zugkolonne *f* column of platoons.
Zugkraft *f* tractive power; tension force; drawbar pull *(prime mover).*
Zugkraftwagen *m* prime mover, half-track carrier and prime mover.
Zugleistung *f* tractive power; drawbar pull *(Trac)*; draft efficiency *(of animals).*
Zugmaschine *f* prime mover *(MT).*
Zugöse *f* drag washer *(wheel)*; lunette *(limber, trailer).*
Zugramme *f* drop-hammer-type pile driver.
Zugriemen *m* brake cable; trace *(harness).*
Zugschraube *f* tractor propeller *(Ap).*
Zugschrauber *m* tractor airplane.
Zugspannung *f* tensile stress.
Zugstange *f* brake rod *(vehicle brake)*; pintle drawbar *(MT, Trac)*; drawbar *(trailer).*
Zugstreife *f* train patrol.
Zugtau *n* tow rope.
Zugtrupp *m* platoon headquarters personnel, platoon command group personnel.
Zug- und Zerschneidezünder *m* pull and cut igniter, tension release igniter *(LM).*
Zugverkehr *m* railroad traffic.
Zugwache *f* train guard.
Zugzünder *m* pull igniter *(LM).*
Zuladung *f* useful load *(Ap).*
Zulage *f* additional pay or allowance; addition; appendix.
zulässig permissible; admissible.
Zulassung *f* registration certificate *(MT)*; registration and airworthiness certificate *(Avn)*; admission; permission.
Zulegeplatte *f* attachable base plate *(mine-surveying set).*
zulegen to add to.
Zuleitung *f* lead-in *(Rad).*
Zuleitungskabel *n* lead-in cord *(signal lamp).*
Zunahme *f* increase, gain, addition.
Zündachse *f* operating-piston sleeve *(blasting machine).*
Zündapparat *m* magneto; igniter; exploder, blasting machine.
Zündbolzen *m* concussion plunger, percussion plunger, plunger *(powder-train time fuze).*
Zündeinstellung *f* timing *(ignition).*
zünden ignite, detonate; fire *(a demolition charge).*
Zünder *m* fuze *(Am)*; igniter *(land mine).*
den Zünder einstellen set the fuze.
Zünderdeckel *m* false ogive *(Am).*
Zünderdraht *m* firing wire, lead wire *(demolitions).*
Zündereinstellung *f* fuze setting.
Zündereinteilung *f* fuze scale.
Zündergehäuse *n* fuze body *(Am)*; fuze cover *(bomb).*
Zünderhalter *m* shell *(of blasting cap).*
Zünderhülse *f* hood *(of fuze).*
Zünderkappe *f* closing cap *(time fuze)*; head *(point-detonating fuze)*; upper cap *(clockwork fuze).*
Zünderkörper *m* body *(fuze).*
Zünderlaufzeit *f* time of functioning *(fuze)*, fuze range.
Zünderstellmaschine *f* automatic fuze setter *(AA gun).*
Zünderstellschlüssel *m* manual fuze setter.
Zünderstellsitz *m* fuze-setter support *(AA gun).*
Zünderstellung *f* fuze setting *(Gunnery).*
Zünderteller *m* body *(powder-train time fuze).*

zündfertig armed, fuzed, ready for firing.
Zündfolge *f* firing order *(of engine cylinders).*
Zündfunke *m* ignition spark *(Mtr).*
Zündgerät *n* demolition equipment.
Zündglocke *f* inside bottom of cartridge case *(SA Am).*
Zündhebel *m* spark control *(Ap).*
Zündholz *n* match.
Zündhütchen *n* primer *(SA Am)*; percussion primer *(fuze)*; percussion cap, propellent primer *(Am).*
Zündhütchenausfall *m* blown primer.
Zündhütchenhülse *f* primer cup *(Am).*
Zündkabel *n* spark plug cable *(Mtr).*
Zündkanal *m* vent hole *(obturator)*; primer vent *(cartridge)*; flash hole *(fuze)*; cap hole *(blasting cartridge).*
Zündkapsel *f* detonator.
Zündkerze *f* spark plug.
Zündladung *f* primer, primer charge, igniting charge.
Zündladungskapsel *f* detonator casing *(fuze).*
Zündladungskörper *m* detonator charge *(fuze).*
Zündlage *f* ignition system *(Mtr).*
Zündlichtmaschine *f* generator *(MT).*
Zündloch *n* vent, flash vent.
Zündmagnet *m* magneto.
Zündmittel *n* detonation agent, primer, igniter, igniting mixture.
Zündnadel *f* firing pin *(fuze).*
Zündpatrone *f* ignition cartridge *(Am).*
Zündpunkt *m* flash point.
Zündpunktverstellung *f* timing *(engine ignition).*
Zündsatz *m* powder train, primer *(Am, demolitions)*; igniter train *(pyrotechnic Sig)*; detonating composition.
Zündschalter *m* ignition switch *(Ap, MT).*
Zündschlüssel *m* ignition key *(MT).*
Zündschnur *f* safety fuze.
Zündschnuranzünder *m* fuze lighter.
Zündschraube *f* threaded primer *(Am).*
Zündschraubengehäuse *n* case *(threaded percussion primer).*
Zündspule *f* ignition coil *(Mtr).*
Zündstift *m* insulated electrode *(spark plug).*
Zündstrahl *m* igniting flash, priming flash *(Am).*
Zündstrom *m* ignition current *(Mtr).*
Zündübertragung *f* induced detonation *(demolitions).*
Zündung *f* firing, detonation *(Am, demolitions)*; ignition *(Mtr).*
"Zündung eingestellt!" "Contact!" *(Avn).*
Zündverstellung *f* spark control, spark adjustment *(Mtr).*
Zündverteiler *m* distributor *(Mtr).*
Zündvorrichtung *f* firing device *(LM)*; ignition system *(Mtr).*
Zündwilligkeit *f* ignition quality *(Diesel fuel).*
Zündzeitpunkt *m* instant of firing *(engine ignition).*
zunehmender Drall increasing twist *(Ord).*
Zungenschiene *f* point of switch rail *(RR).*
Zungenstuhl *m* knee *(RR switch).*
Zurrbolzen *m* locking pin *(G).*
Zurrbrücke *f* cradle lock frame *(G).*
Zurrgriff *m* cradle lock handle *(G).*
Zurrhaken *m* locking hook *(G carriage).*
Zurrhebel *m* lock lever.
Zurrlager *n* lock support *(cradle lock).*
Zurrstange *f* lock rod.
Zurrstellung *f* locked position *(Ord).*
Zurrstück *n* back plate latch lock *(MG).*
Zurrung *f* locking mechanism *(G, Tk, MG)*; anchorage; lashing; holdfast.
Zurückstellung *f* deferment.
Zurückstellungsantrag *m* request for deferment.
zurückweichen give ground, give way.
zurückziehen, sich fall back, retire, withdraw.
Zusammenarbeit *f* cooperation, mutual support.

Zusammenballung *f* concentration *(Tac).*
Zusammenfassung *f* concentration *(Arty)*; abridgment, summary.
zusammengefaßtes Feuer concentrated fire *(Arty)*; collective fire *(SA).*
zusammenlaufen converge.
zusammensetzen assemble; compile; compound; collect, bring together; fit together.
Zusammensetzung *f* composition.
Zusammenstoß *m* collision; clash.
Zusammenwirken *n* synchronization; coordination; liaison; cooperation.
zusammenziehen tighten, draw together, contract.
Zusatz *m* addition; supplement; appendix.
Zusatzfallschirm *m* parachute lobe.
Zusatzflügel *m* auxiliary airfoil, slat *(Ap).*
Zusatzgetriebe *n* auxiliary transmission *(MT).*
Zustand *m* state, condition, situation.
zuständig competent; authorized.
Zustellung *f* delivery.
zuteilen allot, attach.
Zutritt *m* entrance; admittance.
zuverlässig reliable.
zuwiderhandeln act in opposition, act against, counteract; break, violate *(a regulation, etc.).*
zuziehen tighten, draw together.
Zwangsauslösung *f* static line device *(Prcht).*
Zweiachser *m* two-axle vehicle, four-wheel vehicle.
zweiadrig two-stranded *(Elec).*
zweiäugig binocular *adj.*
Zweibein *n* bipod *(MG).*
Zweidecker *m* biplane.
Zweielektrodenröhre *f* diode tube *(Rad).*
Zweierzelt *n* two-man shelter tent.
Zweiflügel-Luftschraube *f* two-blade propeller *(Ap).*
Zweiglager *n* branch depot; branch camp *(PW).*
zweigleisig double-tracked *(RR).*
Zweiglinie *f* junction line *(RR).*
Zweigpark *m* branch depot.
Zweigstelle *f* branch, branch office, substation.
zweimotorig twin-engine.
Zwei-Ohr-Verfahren *n* binaural method *(sound locating).*

Zweipolröhre *f* diode tube *(Rad).*
Zweipunktverfahren *n* two-point resection *(Surv).*
Zweischwimmer-Seeflugzeug *n* twin-float seaplane.
Zweisitzer *m* two-place airplane; two-seater *(vehicle).*
Zweitaktmotor *m* two-cycle engine.
Zweisternmotor *m* double-row radial engine.
Zweistieler *m* double-bay biplane.
zweistufig two-stage *(Elec, Rad).*
Zweitaktsystem *n* two-cycle principle.
Zweiwegeatmung *f* two-way respiration *(gas mask).*
Zwickzange *f* cutter, cutting pliers.
Zwillingslafette *f* twin mount *(Ord).*
Zwillingsläufe *mpl* twin barrels *(MG).*
Zwillingsmachinengewehr *n* twin-barreled machine gun.
Zwillings-MG.-Drehturm *m* revolving turret with twin-barreled machine gun *(Ap).*
Zwillingswaffe *f* twin-barreled weapon.
zwingen compel, force.
Zwischenbahnhof *m* intermediate station *(RR).*
Zwischenentfernung *f* intermediate range *(Gunnery).*
Zwischenfeld *n* ground between delaying positions, area between successive positions, intermediate area.
Zwischenfrequenz *f* intermediate frequency *(Rad).*
Zwischenfrequenzempfänger *m* superheterodyne receiver.
Zwischengebläse *n* auxiliary stage supercharger, turbosupercharger.
Zwischengetriebe *n* auxiliary transmission *(MT).*
Zwischenlandung *f* intermediate landing.
Zwischenlandungsplatz *m* intermediate landing field.
Zwischenraum *m* interval *(from left to right).*
Zwischenstecker *m* adapter plug *(Elec).*
Zwischenstelle *f* linking station; relay station *(Sig Com).*
Zwischenstellung *f* intermediate position.
Zwischenstück *n* adapter.
Zwischenwelle *f* intermediate shaft, propeller shaft.
Zwischenziel *n* intermediate objective; reference point *(Arty, R fire).*
Zwitterfahrzeug *n* half-track vehicle.
zwo two *(used in voice transmission to avoid confusion with* drei, *three).*
Zyanwasserstoffsäure *f* hydrocyanic acid, prussic acid *(CWS).*
Zylinderblock *m* cylinder block *(Mtr).*
Zylinderinhalt *m* total volume of cylinder *(Mtr).*
Zylinderkopf *m* cylinder head *(Mtr).*

Zylinderlaufbüchse *f* cylinder liner *(Mtr).*
Zylinderschleifen *n* cylinder grinding *(Mtr).*
Zylinderverschluß *m* bolt mechanism *(R).*
Zylinderwand *f* cylinder wall *(Mtr).*
ZZ-Verfahren *n* method of radio approach landing *(the main let-down signal is ZZ with last letter of airport station signal in between).*

Zertr	Zertrümmerung	demolition; destruction
Zeugh	Zeughaus	arsenal; armory
Zeugh.Verw	Zeughausverwaltung	arsenal administration
Z.F	Zielfernrohr	telescopic sight
Zf	Ziffer	cipher; numeral
z.F	**zu Fuss**	**afoot; on foot**
ZF	Zugführer	platoon leader
ZF	Zwischenfrequenz	intermediate frequency
Z.F.-Gew	**Zielfernrohrgewehr**	rifle with telescopic sight
Z-Fl	Zielflug	flight toward a fixed objective
ZFw	**Zeugfeldwebel**	ordnance sergeant
Zg	**Zehrgeld**	money for provisions; traveling expenses or allowan[ce]
Zg	**Zug**	train *(railroad)*; platoon; section; groove *(ordnance)*;
Zg.A	Zeugamt	ordnance department
Z-Gel	Zielgelände	target area
Zgf	**Zugführer**	platoon leader
Zgflg	**Zugfolge**	order (sequence, succession) of trains *(military transpor[t])*
Zg.Hs	Zeughaus	arsenal; armory
Zgkw	Zugkraftwagen	prime mover truck
Zgl	Ziegelei	brick kiln
zgl	zugleich	at the same time
Zgpf	Zugpferd	draught horse
Z.G.T	Zielgeviertlafel	combination protractor and
Zgtr	**Zugtrupp**	platoon headquarters detachment *(infantry)*
Zgw	Zeughauswaffenmeister	arsenal artificer
zgw.Eins	zugweiser Einsatz	employment by platoons
zickz	zickzack	zigzag
Zickz.K	Zickzackkurs	zigzag course
Ziegelhe	Ziegelhütte	brick kiln; tile kiln
Zielb	Zielbau	construction of targets
Zielbeweg	Zielbewegung	movement of target
Zielbez	Zielbezeichnung	target designation
Ziel.-F	**Zielfehler**	**sighting error**
Ziel.-F	Zielfernrohr	telescopic sight
Zielf	Zielfeuer	fire representing target
Zielgel	Zielgelände	target area
Zielgev.T	Zielgeviertlafel	combination protractor and
Zielgew	Zielgewehr	subcaliber rifle
Zielmun	Zielmunition	subcaliber ammunition
Ziff	Ziffer	cipher; numeral
Zit	Zitadelle	citadel
Ziv	Zivilist	civilian
Ziv.Arb.Btl	Zivilarbeiterbataillon	civilian worker's battalion
Ziv.B	Zivilbeamter	civilian official
Ziv.Beh	Zivilbehörde	civilian authorities
Zk	Zündkerze	spark plug
zk	zurück	back; backwards
Zkw	Zugkraftwagen	prime mover truck
Zl	im linken Zieldrittel	in the left-hand third of target
ZL	Zickzack- und Leiterkette	zigzag and ladder chain
Z.L	Zwischenladung	intermediate blasting charge
Z-Ldg	Ziellandung	precision landing *(aviation)*
Zlmstr	Zahlmeister	pay master
Zm	im mittleren Zieldrittel	in the middle third of target
Zm	Zahlmeister	paymaster
ZM	Zugmaschine	prime mover
Z.m.V	Zünder mit Verzögerung	delay-action fuze
Zp	Zahnradpumpe	geared pump
Z.P	Zielpunkt	aiming point; goal
z.Pf	zu Pferde	on horseback; mounted
Zpfstr	Zapfenstreich	retreat; tattoo *(bugle call)*
Zr	im rechten Zieldrittel	in right-hand third of target
z.Rd	zu Rad	on bicycle
zs	zusammen	together
Z-Schlüssel	Zünderstellschlüssel	hand fuze setter *(artillery)*
Z-Schw	Zentralschwimmer	central float; central pontoon
zsf	zusammenfassen	to combine; to summarize
Zst	Zusammenstellung	organization *(of a unit)*
Z.St.M	**Zünderstellmaschine**	**fuze setter**
Zt	Zeit	time; period
z.T	zum Teil	partly
ztl	zeitlich	timely; temporarily
Z.tr	Zentner	hundredweight; 50 kilograms
Ztschr	Wehrmachtzeitschriftenabteilung	Periodicals Section of the Army Ordnance Office
Ztschr	Zeitschrift	periodical; publication
ztws	zeitweise	from time to time
Zt.Z	Zeitzünder	time fuze
Zt.Zdschn	Zeitzündschnur	time fuze; long fuze cord
Zub	Zubehör	accessories; fittings
Zubr	Zubringer	follower *(magazine)*
Züg	Zügel	reins; bridle
Zuf	Zufahrt	approach
Zuf	Zuführer	feeder; belt pawl supplies
Zuf	Zufuhr	supplies; bringing up
Zufl	Zuflucht	refuge; shelter; recourse
Zuf.Tr	Zufallstreffer	accidental hit
zug	zugänglich	accessible
Zug	Zugang	access; approach; entry
zugeh	zugehörig	belonging to; attached to
zuget	zugeteilt	attached to
zugew	zugewiesen	allotted; assigned to
Zug-F	Zugführer	platoon leader; platoon commander

Zul	Zulage	allowance
Zul	Zulassung	permission
zur	zurück	back; backwards
Zurr	Zurrung	lashing; latch
Zur.St	Zurückstellung	deferment
zus	zusammen	together; in connection with
Zus	Zusammensetzung	organization (*of a unit*); composition; combination
Zusch	Zuschuss	allowance; extra pay
Zus.Ger	Zusatzgerät	supplementary equipment
Zus.Wk	Zusammenwirken	cooperation
zut	zuteilen	to attach; to allot; to assign
Zut	Zuteilung	allotment; attachment; assignment
Zuw	Zuwachs	increase
Zuw	Zuweisung	allotment; assignment
Zuw	Zuwiderhandlung	infringement; violation; contravention
z.V	zur Verfügung	available
ZvD	Zivildienst	civil service
ZVerw	Zentralverwaltung	central administration
ZVerw	Zeugverwaltung	ordnance department administration
Zw	Zwang	compulsion; coercion
Zw	Zweck	purpose; objective; aim
Zw	Zweifel	doubt
Zw	Zweig	branch
zw	zwischen	between; among; amongst
Zw	Zwischenwerk	intermediate work; redoubt
Zw	Zwitterfahrzeug	half-track vehicle
Zw.Bttr	Zwischenbatterie	intermediate battery (*fortification*)
Zwg	Zweig	branch
Zwgst	Zweigstelle	branch
ZwillMG	Zwillingsmaschinengewehr	double-barreled machine gun
Zwisch	Zwischen-	intermediate; between
Zwisch.Bttr	Zwischenbatterie	intermediate battery (*fortification*)
Zw.F	Zwischenfeld	intermediate delaying position; covering position
Zwisch.R	Zwischenraum	interval; intermediate space
Zwisch.W	Zwischenwerk	intermediate work; redoubt
Zwitt.Fz	Zwitterfahrzeug	half-track vehicle
Zw.L.Pl	Zwischenlandeplatz	intermediate landing field
Zw.MG	Zwillingsmaschinengewehr	double-barreled machine gun
Zw.P	Zwischenpunkt	intermediate point
Zyl	Zylinder	cylinder
Zyl.P	Zylinderpulver	powder in cylindrical pellets
Zyl.Verschl	Zylinderverschluss	cylinder locking; bolt action
Z.Z	Zeitzünder	time fuze
z.Z	zur Zeit	at the moment, at this time
Zz	Zylinderzahl	number of cylinders
Z.Z.E	Zeigerzieleinrichtung	dial sight (*artillery*)

EXAMPLES

A./A.R.6	Ausbildungsbatterie, Artillerieregiment 6	Training Battery of Artillery Regiment No. 6
A./I.R.12	Ausbildungsbataillon, Infanterieregiment 12	Training Battalion, 12th Infantry Regiment
14.(A.)/I.R.13	14 (Ausbildungs-) Kompanie, Infanterieregiment 13	14th (Training) Company, 13th Infantry Regiment
A.K./A.R.6	leichte Artilleriekolonne des Artillerieregiments 6	Light Artillery Transport Column of the 6th Artillery Regiment
III./A.R.4	III. Abteilung, Artillerieregiment 4	3d Battalion of the 4th Field Artillery Regiment
1./A.R.5	1. Batterie, Artillerieregiment 5	1st Battery, 5th Artillery Regiment
A./R.R.17	Ausbildungsschwadron, Reiterregiment 17	Training Troop of the 17th Cavalry Regiment
1.Div	1.Division	1st Division
Div.N.(tm) 6	Nachrichtenabteilung (teilmotorisiert) der 6. Division	Signal Battalion of the 6th Division (partly motorized)
F.6	Fahrabteilung 6	Transport Section 6
2.F.5	2. Schwadron Fahrabteilung 5	2d Troop, Transport Section 5
F.A.6	Fahrabteilung 6	Transport Section 6
6.(Geb.)A.R.7	6. (Gebirgs-) Batterie, Artillerieregiment 7	6th Mountain Battery of the 7th Artillery Regiment
4.(Geb.) F.7	4. (Gebirgs-) Schwadron, Fahrabteilung 7	4th Troop of the 7th Mountain Transport Detachment
G./I.R.1	Geschützkompanie, Infanterieregiment 1	Howitzer Company, 1st Infantry Regiment
G./I.R.3	Geschützkompanie, Infanterieregiment 3	Howitzer Company, 3d Infantry Regiment
G./R.R.8	Geschützschwadron, Reiterregiment 8	Howitzer Troop, 8th Horse Cavalry Regiment
I.K./I.R.19	leichte Infanteriekolonne des Infanterieregiments 19	light infantry column of the 19th Infantry Regiment
4./I.R.9	4. Kompanie, Infanterieregiment 9	4th Company, 9th Infantry Regiment
I./I.R.15	1. Bataillon, Infanterieregiment 15	1st Battalion, 15th Infantry Regiment
5./Kav.R.10	5. Schwadron, Kavallerieregiment 10	5th Troop of 10th Cavalry Regiment
2.K.D	2. Kavalleriedivision	2d Cavalry Division
Kdo sb.I.Bg.(m) 2	Kommando der selbständigen 2. Infanteriebrigade (motorisiert)	Command of the independent 2d Infantry Brigade (motorized)
Kdr.I.R.24	Kommandeur des Infanterieregiments 24	24th Infantry Regimental Commander
Kf.3	Kraftfahrabteilung 3	Motor Transport Battalion 3
1.Kf.7	1. Kompanie, Kraftfahrabteilung 7	1st Company, Motor Transport Battalion 7
Korps.Kdo.VI	Korpskommando VI	VI Corps Headquarters
2.Kradsch.Btl.3	2. Kompanie, Kradschützenbataillon 3	2d Company of 3d Motorcycle Battalion
4.(M.G.)/I.R.19	4 (Maschinengewehr-) Kompanie, Infanterieregiment 19	4th (Machine-Gun) Company, 19th Infantry Regiment
MG./R.R.9	Maschinengewehrschwadron des Reiter-Regiments 9	Machine-Gun Troop of the 9th Horse Cavalry Regiment
Nachr.Z.I/I.R.8	Nachrichtenzug, I. Bataillon, Infanterieregiment 8	Signal Platoon of 1st Battalion of 8th Infantry Regiment
Pi.4	Pionierbataillon 4	4th Combat Engineer Bat-
II./Pz.Rgt.4	II. Abteilung, Panzerregiment 4	2d Battalion of 4th Panzer Regiment
IV.(r)/A.R.3	IV. (reitende) Abteilung, Artillerieregiment 3	4th Horse Battalion, 3d Artillery Regiment
11.(r.)/A.R.6	11. (reitende) Batterie, Artillerieregiment 6	11th Horse Battery, 6th Artillery Regiment
Rf.4	Radfahrbataillon 4	4th Bicycle Battalion
2./Rf.4	2. Kompanie, Radfahrbataillon 4	2d Company, 4th Bicycle Battalion
R./F.A.R.5	Reitende Abteilung des Feldartillerieregiments 5	Horse Battalion of 5th Field Artillery Regiment
Rf.(tm) 3	Teilmotorisiertes Radfahrbataillon 3	3d Bicycle Battalion (part motorized)
R.R.14	Reiterregiment 14	14th Horse Cavalry Regiment
5.R.R.9	5. Schwadron Reiterregiment 9	Troop 5, 9th Horse Cavalry Regiment
S.A.1 K	Sanitätsabteilung 1, Kraftwagenpersonal	1st Medical Battalion (Motor Transport Personnel)
Sch.1	Schütze 1	machine-gunner No. 1
Sch.2	Schütze 2	machine-gunner No. 2
I./Sch.Rgt.2	I. Bataillon Schützenregiment 2	1st Battalion of 2d Rifle Regiment
St.I	Stab des I. Bataillons	Headquarters of the 1st Battalion
St./A.R.15	Stab des Artillerieregiments 15	Headquarters, 15th Artillery Regiment
St.I/A.R.23	Stab der I. Abteilung des 23. Artillerieregiments	Headquarters 1st Battalion, 23d Artillery Regiment
St./I.Fü.I	Stab des Infanterieführers I	Staff of Infantry Commander I
St.I./I.R.19	Stab des I. Bataillons, Infanterieregiment 19	Headquarters of the 1st Battalion, 19th Infantry Regiment
St./I.R.37	Stab des Infanterieregiments 37	Headquarters of 37th Infantry Regiment
St.II./I.R.(m)5	Stab des II. Bataillons des motorisierten Infanterieregiments 5	Headquarters of the 2d Battalion, 5th Infantry Regiment (motorized)
St./Kf.7	Stab der Kraftfahrabteilung 7	Headquarters of 7th Motor Transport Battalion
St./MG.3	Stab der Maschinengewehrabteilung 3	Headquarters of 3d Machine-Gun Detachment
St./MG.(m)2	Stab der motorisierten Maschinengewehrabteilung 2	Headquarters of 2d Machine-Gun Detachment (motorized)
St./N.A.Div.5 (tmot)	Stab der teilmotorisierten Divisionsnachrichtenabteilung 5	Headquarters of 5th Divisional Communications Battalion (part motorized)
St./Pi.3	Stab des Pionierbataillons 3	Headquarters of the 3d Combat Engineer Battalion
St./R.A.A.5	Stab der Reiteraufklärungsabteilung 5	Headquarters of the 5th (Horse) Cavalry Reconnaissance Battalion
St.III.(r.)/A.R.3	Stab der III. (reitenden) Abteilung, Artillerieregiment 3	Headquarters of the 3d (Horse) Battalion of the 3d Artillery Regiment
St.R.Bg.1	Stab der Reiterbrigade 1.	Staff of the 1st (Horse) Cavalry Brigade
St./Rf.3	Stab des Radfahrbataillons 3	Headquarters of the 3d Bicycle Battalion

Numbers, Weights, Measures, Temperatures, Amounts

Cardinal Numbers (Grundzahlen)		Ordinal Numbers (Ordnungszahlen)
Ein(s) (One)	1	(First) Der, Die, Das, Erste
Zwei	2	Zweite
Drei	3	Dritte
Vier	4	Vierte
Fünf	5	Fünfte
Sechs	6	Sechste
Sieben	7	Sieb(en)te
Acht	8	Achte
Neun	9	Neunte
Zehn	10	Zehnte
Elf	11	Elfte
Zwölf	12	Zwölfte
Dreizehn	13	Dreizehnte
Vierzehn	14	Vierzehnte
Fünfzehn	15	Fünfzehnte
Sechzehn	16	Sechzehnte
Siebzehn	17	Siebzehnte
Achtzehn	18	Achtzehnte
Neunzehn	19	Neunzehnte
Zwanzig	20	Zwanzigste
Einundzwanzig	21	Einundzwanzigste
Dreißig	30	Dreißigste
Vierzig	40	Vierzigste
Fünfzig	50	Fünfzigste
Sechzig	60	Sechzigste
Siebzig	70	Siebzigste
Achtzig	80	Achtzigste
Neunzig	90	Neunzigste
Hundert; Einhundert	100	(Ein)hundertste
Hundertundeins	101	Hundertunderste
Tausend; Eintausend	1,000	(Ein)tausendste
Tausendundeins	1,001	Tausendunderste
Hunderttausend	100,000	(Ein)hunderttausendste
Hunderttausendundeins	100,001	Hunderttausendunderste
Eine Million	1,000,000	(Ein)million(s)te

Weight

German — U.S.		*U.S. — German*	
1 Gramm	= 0.035 ounce	1 ounce	= 28.35 Gramm
1 Pfund	= 1.102 pounds (= 500 Gramm)		= 0.014 Pfund
1 Kilogramm	= 2.205 pounds (= 1,000 Gramm)	1 pound	= 453.6 Gramm = 0.454 Kilogramm = 0.908 Pfund
1 Zentner	= 110.25 pounds (= 100 Pfund) (= 50 Kilogramm)		
1 Doppelzentner	= 220.50 pounds (= 100 Kilogramm)		
1 Tonne (metric)	= 1.102 tons (short) (= 1,000 Kilogramm)	1 ton (short)	= 0.907 Tonnen (metric) = 907.2 Kilogramm

Length

1 Kilometer	(= 1,000 Meter) = 0.621 mile = 1,094 yards = 3,281 feet	1 mile	= 1.609 Kilometer = 1,609 Meter
1 Meter	(= 100 Zentimeter) = 1.09 yards = 3.28 feet	1 yard	= 0.914 Meter = 91.44 Zentimeter
1 Zentimeter	(= 10 Millimeter) = 0.393 inch	1 foot	= 0.305 Meter = 30.48 Zentimeter
1 Millimeter	= 0.039 inch	1 inch	= 2.54 Zentimeter = 25.4 Millimeter

Area

1 Quadratmeter	= 1.196 square yards = 10.76 square feet	1 square inch	= 6.452 Quadratzentimeter = 645.2 Quadratmillimeter
1 Quadratzentimeter	= 0.155 square inch	1 square foot	= 0.093 Quadratmeter
1 Quadratmillimeter	= 0.00155 square inch	1 square yard	= 0.836 Quadratmeter
1 Hektar	(= 100 Ar) (= 10,000 Quadratmeter) = 2.471 acres	1 acre	= 0.405 Hektar

Convenient Approximate Conversions

Kilometers into miles:	Multiply by 6/10
Meters into yards:	Add 10%
Meters into feet:	Multiply by 3 and add 10%.
Centimeters into inches:	Multiply by 4/10
Kilograms into pounds:	Multiply by 2 and add 10%
Liters into gallons:	Divide by 4 and add 5%

Volume

1 Kubikzentimeter	= 0.061 cubic inch
1 Kubikmeter	= 35.31 cubic feet = 1.308 cubic yards
1 Liter	(= 1 Kubikdezimeter) = 0.264 gallons = 1.057 quarts (liquid)
1 Hektoliter	(= 100 Liter) = 26.42 gallons
1 gallon	= 3.785 Liter
1 liquid quart	= 0.946 Liter
1 cubic inch	= 16.39 Kubikzentimeter
1 cubic foot	= 0.0283 Kubikmeter
1 cubic yard	= 0.764 Kubikmeter
1 fluid ounce	= 29.58 Kubikzentimeter

Temperature Conversion

Fahrenheit into Centigrade

Subtract 32 and multiply by 5/9

Centigrade (or Celsius) into Fahrenheit

Multiply by 9/5 and add 32

Amounts

high / low	hoch / niedrig
heavy / light	schwer / leicht
few / lot	einige / menge
several / many	mehrere / viele
not many / very many	nicht viele / sehr viele
more / less	mehr / weniger

Rank Equivalents Between Army and Various Paramilitary Units

Army	*SS*	*Police*	*TN (and other auxiliary police)*	*RAD*	*OT*	*NSKK*	*Party-Officials#*	*SA and NSFK*	*HJ*
Gren.	SS-Mann	Anwärter	Anwärter	Arbeitsmann	Arbeiter	Sturmmann	Helfer	Sturmmann##	Hitlerjunge
Ob. Gren.	Sturmmann			Vormann	Vormann	Obersturmmann	Oberhelfer	Obersturmmann##	Rottenführer
Gefr.	Rottenführer	Unterwachtmeister	Unterwachtmeister	Obervormann	Meister	Rottenführer	Arbeitsleiter	Rottenführer	Oberrottenführer
							Oberarbeitsleiter		
Ob. Gefr.		Rottwachtmeister	Rottwachtmeister	Hauptvormann	Obermeister				
							Hauptarbeitsleiter		
Stabsgefr.				Untertruppführer					
Unt. Offz.	Unterscharführer	Wachtmeister	Wachtmeister	Truppführer	Truppführer	Scharführer		Scharführer	Kameradschaftsführer
Unt. Feldw.	Scharführer	Oberwachtmeister	Oberwachtmeister			Oberscharführer		Oberscharführer	Oberkameradschaftsführer
Feldw.	Oberscharführer	Zugwachtmeister	Zugwachtmeister	Obertruppführer	Obertruppführer	Truppführer	Bereitschaftsleiter	Truppführer	Scharführer
Ob. Feldw.	Hauptscharführer	Hauptwachtmeister	Hauptwachtmeister		Haupttruppführer	Obertruppführer	Oberbereitschaftsleiter	Obertruppführer	Oberscharführer
Stabsfeldw.	Sturmscharführer		Bereitschaftswachtmeister			Haupttruppführer	Hauptbereitschaftsleiter	Haupttruppführer	
		Meister	Meister	Unterfeldmeister					
		Obermeister							
Lt.	Untersturmführer	Leutnan	Zugführer	Feldmeister	Frontführer	Sturmführer	Einsatzleiter	Sturmführer	Gefolgschaftsführer
Ob. Lt.	Obersturmführer	Oberleutnant	Oberzugführer	Oberfeldmeister	Oberfrontführer	Obersturmführer	Obereinsatzleiter	Obersturmführer	Obergefolgschaftsführer
Hauptmann	Hauptsturmführer	Hauptmann	Bereitschaftsführer	Oberstfeldmeister	Hauptfrontführer	Hauptsturmführer	Haupteinsatzleiter	Hauptsturmführer	Hauptgefolgschaftsführer
Major	Sturmbannführer	Major	Abteilungsführer	Arbeitsführer	Stabsfrontführer	Staffelführer	Gemeinschaftsleiter	Sturmbannführer	Stammführer
Obst. Lt.	Obersturmbannführer	Oberstleutnant	Oberabteilungsführer	Oberarbeitsführer	Oberstabsfrontführer	Oberstaffelführer	Hauptgemeinschaftsleiter	Obersturmbannführer	Oberstammführer
Oberst	Standartenführer	Oberst	Landesführer	Oberstarbeitsführer	Ob[illegible]frontführer	Standartenführer	Hauptabschnittsführer	Standartenführer	Bannführer
	Oberführer					Oberführer	Hauptbereichsleiter	Oberführer	Hauptbannführer
Gen. Maj.	Brigadeführer	Generalmajor		Generalarbeitsführer	Einsatzleiter	Brigadeführer	Hauptdienstleiter	Brigadeführer	Gebeitsführer
Gen. Lt.	Gruppenführer	Generalleutnant	(Chef der TN)	Obergeneralarbeitsführer	Einsatzgruppenleiter II	Gruppenführer	Hauptbefehlsleiter	Gruppenführer	Obergebeitsführer
General	Obergruppenführer	General			Einsatzgruppenleiter I	Obergruppenführer	(Gauleiter	Obergruppenführer	Stabsführer
Gen. Obst.	Oberstgruppenführer	Generaloberst		Reichsarbeitsführer	Chef der OT	Korpsführer	kReichsleiter	Stabschef der SA	Reichsjugendführer
Gen. Feldm.	Reichsführer-SS								

This is only a selection of the many Party ranks.

SA-Sturmmann equals NSFK-Mann.
SA-Obersturmmann equals NSFK-Sturmmann.

Chapter II: English - German Terms

A

abandon *v* räumen *(a locality)*; verlassen *(a position, etc.)*; zurücklassen *(equipment, wounded, etc.)*.
abatage *(G)* Stellung auf Fußtellern
abatis Baumsperre *f*.
"A" battery Heizbatterie *f (Rad)*.
abbreviation Abkürzung *f*.
authorized abbreviation amtlich festgelegte Abkürzung.
able-bodied wehrfähig, tauglich, wehrtauglich *(fit for Mil service)*.
Abney level Spiegelneigungsmesser *m (Surv)*.
about face Kehrtwendung *f*.
"About, face!" "Ganze Abteilung, Kehrt!"
abrasive Schleifmittel *n*.
abreast nebeneinander, Seite an Seite, in Linie.
abscissa Abszisse *f*.
abscissa for maximum ordinate Gipfelentfernung *f (Ballistics)*.
absence without leave unerlaubte Entfernung, eigenmächtige Entfernung.
absent abwesend.
absent without leave abwesend ohne Urlaub.
absolute altitude Flughöhe *f*, Flughöhe über dem Erdboden *(Avn)*.
absolute ceiling Gipfelhöhe *f (Avn)*.
absolute deviation Geschoßabweichung *f (Arty)*.
absolute quarantine *(Med)* Isolierung *f*
absorbent cotton Watte *f*.
abutment Widerlager *n*, Brückenwiderlager *n*, Endauflager *n (Bdg)*; Kämpfer *m (of an arch)*.
abutment beam Stoßbalken *m (Bdg)*.
abutment section Pioniertrupp beauftragt mit Errichtung der Brückenendwiderlager *(Engr)*.
accelerate beschleunigen.
accelerating pump Beschleunigungspumpe *f*.
acceleration Beschleunigung *f*.
acceleration downward Fallbeschleunigung *f (of projectile)*.
accelerator Spannstück *n (MG)*; Gashebel *m*, Beschleuniger *m (Mtr)*.
accelerometer Beschleunigungsmesser *m (Ap)*.
acceptance test Abnahmeprüfung *f*.
accessories Ausrüstung *f*, Zubehör *n*, Zubehörteile *mpl*.
accessories case Zubehörtornister *m (portable Rad)*.
accessory Ausrüstungsstück *n*, Zubehör *n (part)*; Komplize *m*, Mitschuldiger *m (Law)*.
accessory defense Hindernis *n*, Sperre *f*.
accelerator pedal Gasfußtritt *m*, Gasfußhebel *m*.
access road Zufahrtstraße *f*.
accident Unfall *m*.
accidental cover natürliche Deckung.
accidental error zufälliger Fehler.
accidental hit Zufallstreffer *m*.
accompanying artillery Begleitartillerie *f*.
accompanying battery Begleitbatterie *f*.
accompanying fire Begleitfeuer *n*.
accompanying gun Begleitgeschütz *n*.
accompanying tank Begleitpanzer *m*, Begleitpanzerkampfwagen *m*.
accomplice Mitschuldiger *m*, Komplize *m (Law)*.
accomplish erledigen, erfüllen, vollenden.
accomplishment Erledigung *f (completion)*; Leistung *f (feat)*.
accordion action wechselnder Fahrzeugabstand, Aufschließen und Abhängen *(MT)*.
accordion effect *See* **accordion action.**
accountability Buchungspflicht *f*, Verantwortlichkeit *f*.
accountable zur Buchung verpflichtet.
accountable officer Verwaltungsoffizier *m*.
accouterments *npl*. Ausrüstungsstücke
accredited aviation school behördlich anerkannte Fliegerschule.
accredited correspondent Kriegsberichter *m*.
accrued leave zustehender Gesamturlaub.
accumulated leave akkumulierter Urlaub.
accuracy Genauigkeit *f*.
accuracy life Lebensdauer *f (G)*.
accuracy of fire Zielsicherheit *f*, Treffähigkeit *f*, Treffgenauigkeit *f*, Treffsicherheit *f*.
accuracy of fit Paßgenauigkeit *f*.
accuracy of practice Treffgenauigkeit *f*.
accurate genau, zielgenau.
ace Fliegerheld *m*, erfolgreicher Jagdflieger.
acetone Azeton *m*.
acetylene Azetylen *n*.
acetylene torch *See* **oxyacetylene torch.**
a-c generator Wechselstromerzeuger *m*.
acid Säure *f*.
acknowledge Bitte Quittung, Bitte Bestätigung *(Rad procedure)*.
acknowledgment of receipt Empfangsbestätigung *f (Rad, Tg, Tp)*.
acoustic correction Ausschalten des Schallverzuges *(sound locator)*.
acoustic corrector Verzugsrechner *m (sound locator)*.
acoustic orientation akustische Ortung *(sound locator)*.
act *v* wirken, handeln.
acting stellvertretend.
action Gefecht *n*, Gefechtshandlung *f*, Kampftätigkeit *f (Tac)*; Arbeitsspiel *n (Mech)*.
"In action!" "Licht auf!" *(AA SL)*.
"Action front!" "Zum Feuern nach vorwärts, protzt ab!"
"Action left!" "Zum Feuern nach links, protzt ab!"
"Action rear!" "Zum Feuern nach rückwärts, protzt ab!"
"Action right!" "Zum Feuern nach rechts, protzt ab!"
action station Gefechtsstation *f (Nav)*; Gefechtsstellung *f*.
activate wehrbar machen, aufstellen *(a unit)*; scharf machen *(a mine)*.
activated mine scharfe Panzermine.
activation Wehrbarmachung *f*; Aufstellung *f (of a unit)*.
active air defense Luftabwehr *f*, aktive Luftabwehr.
active defense Abwehr *f*.
active duty aktiver Dienst.
active list Liste der aktiven Offiziere und Mannschaften.
active service aktiver Wehrdienst.
act of sabotage Sabotageakt *m*.
actual range tatsächliche Schußweite *(Arty)*.
acute angle spitzer Winkel.
adamsite Adamsit *m*, Diphenylaminchlorarsin *n*.
adaptable anwendbar, paßlich.
adapter Lafettenaufsatzstück *n (MG)*; Mundlocheinschraubvorrichtung *f*, Paßstück *n (Ord)*; Zwischenstück *n (Mech)*.
adapter opening Mundloch *n (Am)*.
adapter plug Mundlochschraube *f (AM)*; Zwischenstecker *m (Elec)*.
adapter thread Mundlochgewinde *n (Am)*.
add zusammenzählen, addieren *(Math)*; hinzufügen, beifügen.
adding machine Rechengerät *n*.
adhesive paste Kleister *m*.
adhesive pitch Kabelwachs *n (Engr, Tp)*.
adhesive tape Klebestreifen *m (Tech)*; Leukoplast *n (court plaster)*; Isolierband *n (friction tape)*.
adjacent angrenzend, Nachbar—, Neben—.
adjacent unit Nachbar *m (Tac)*.
adjust einschießen *(G fire)*; justieren *(bore-sight alinement)*; einstellen, verstellen *(Tech)*.
adjustable verstellbar, regulierbar, verschiebbar, einstellbar.
adjustable holder Einstellhülse *f (panoramic telescope)*.
adjustable marker Einstellmarke *f*.
adjustable-pitch propeller einstellbare Luftschraube.
adjustable wrench verstellbarer Schraubenschlüssel.
adjusted elevation Erhöhungseinstellung *f*.
adjusted range Höhenrichtung *f (Arty)*.
adjusting nut Stößelschraube *f (on valve-lifter)*.
adjusting point Einschießpunkt *m (Arty)*.
adjusting ring Stellring *m*, Einstellring *m (fuze)*.
adjusting screw Verstellschraube *f*.
adjustment Einstellung *f*, Eichung *f*, Verstellung *f*; Berichtigung *f (correction)*.
adjustment drum Berichtigungswalze *f (range finder)*.
adjustment fire Richtungsschießen *n*, Einschießen *n*.
adjustment nut Einstellmutter *f*.
adjustment of fire Einschießen *n*.
adjustment shots Richtungsschüsse *mpl (for direction)*.
adjustment target Einschießziel *n*, Lufteinschießziel *n (high burst)*.
adjutant Adjutant *m*.
adjutant general Generaladjutant *m*.
The Adjutant General Der Chef des Heeresverwaltungsamts *(USA)*.
Adjutant General Board Die Abteilungsleiter des Heeresverwaltungsamts *(USA)*.
Adjutant General's Department Heeresverwaltungsamt *n (USA)*.
adjutant's office Schreibstube *f*.
administration Verwaltung *f*, Verwaltungswesen *n*.
administration building Verwaltungsgebäude *n*.
administrative inspector Verwaltungsinspektor *m*.
administrative map Verwaltungsübersichtskarte *f*.
administrative march Reisemarsch *m*, Etappenmarsch *m*.
administrative order besondere Anordnung.
administrative plan Verwaltungsordnung *f*.
administrative services Verwaltungsdienste *mpl*.
administrative unit Verwaltungstruppenteil *m*.
administrative vehicle Heeresfahrzeug *n*.
admiral Generaladmiral *m (Nav)*.
advance *n* Vormarsch *m*, Vorgehen
advance *v* vorrücken, vorgehen, vordringen, vormarschieren, sich vorwärtsbewegen.
advance base Ausgabestelle im Operationsgebiet.
advance by bounds sprungweises Vorgehen.
advance by echelon staffelweises Vorgehen.
advance by rushes *See* **advance by bounds.**
advance command post vorgeschobener Gefechtsstand, vorderer Gefechtsstand.
advanced airfield Feldflugplatz *m*.
advanced detachment Vorausabteilung *f*.
advance depot Umschlagstelle *f*.
advanced specialized training militärische Sonderausbildung.
advanced training Weiterbildung *f*, Fortbildung *f*.
advance element Spitzengruppe *f (Tac)*.
advance guard Vorhut *f*.
advance guard action Vorhutgefecht *n*.
advance guard cavalry detachment Reiterspitze *f*.
advance guard commander Vorhutführer *m*.
advance guard company Vorauskompanie *f*.
advance guard engagement Vorhutgefecht *n*.
advance guard point Spitze *f*.
advance guard reserve Haupttrupp *m (in Adv Gd of large unit)*.
advance guard support Vortrupp *m (in Adv Gd of large unit)*; Haupttrupp *m (in Adv Gd of smaller unit)*.
advance in phases abschnittweises Vorgehen.
advance landing field Feldflugplatz *m*, Gefechtslandeplatz *m*.
advance message center Meldekopf, *m*.
advance of forcing cone Laderaumverlängerung *f (G)*.
advance party Spitzenkompanie *f (in Adv Gd of large unit)*; Vortrupp *m (in Adv Gd of smaller unit)*.
advance position vorgeschobene Stellung.
advance post vorgeschobener Posten.
advance the attack sich an den Feind heranarbeiten.
"Advance to be recognized!" "Kommen Sie näher! Wer sind Sie?"
adviser Berater *m*.
adze Querbeil *n*, Queraxt *f*.
aerial *See* **antenna.**
aerial acrobatics Kunstflug *m*.
aerial barrage Luftsperre *f*.
aerial barrage equipment Luftsperrmittel *n*.
aerial camera Luftbildkammer *f*.
aerial combat exercise Luftkampfübung *f*.
aerial delivery container Abwurfkiste *f*.
aerial gas spray Giftregen *m*.
aerial gunner Fliegerschütze *m*, Bordschütze *m*, Feuerschütze *m*.
aerial gunnery Schießen aus der Luft.
aerial hand camera Fliegerhandkammer *f*.
aerial mapping camera Reihenkammer *f*, Reihenbildner *m*, Reihenbildkammer *f*.
aerial mine Minenbombe *f*, Luftmine *f*.
aerial mosaic Reihenbild *n*, Luftbildkarte *f*.
aerial objective Flugziel *n*.
aerial observation Luftbeobachtung *f*.
aerial observer Beobachter *m*, Beobachtungsflieger *m*.
aerial photograph Luftbild *n*.
aerial photographer Bildflieger *m*.
aerial photographic crew Flugzeugbildpersonal *n*.
aerial photograph interpretation Luftbildauswertung *f*.
aerial photography Luftbildwesen *n*, Luftphotographie *f*.
aerial photomapping camera Reihenmeßkammer *f*.
aerial review Luftparade *f*.
aerial sound ranging Horchortung von Flugzielen *(AAA)*.
aerial spraying Abregnen *n (CWS)*.
aerial target Flugziel *n*.
aerial torpedo Lufttorpedo *n*, Flugzeugtorpedo *n*.
aerial warfare Luftkrieg *m*.
aerobatics *See* **aerial acrobatics.**
aerocartograph Aerokartograph *m*.
aerodynamic force Luftkraft *f*.
aerodynamics Aerodynamik *f*.
aeroembolism Höhenkrankheit *f*.
aerograph *See* **aerometeorograph.**
aerographer Meteorologe im Unteroffiziersrang *(Nav)*.
aerologist Meteorologe im Offiziersrang *(Nav)*.
aerometeorograph Meteorograph *m (Met)*.
aerometer Dichtemesser *m*, Dichtigkeitsmesser *m*.
aeronautical chart Fliegerkarte *f*.
aeronautical mile Flugmeile *f (1853.25 meters)*.
aeronautics Luftfahrt *f*, Luftfahrwesen *n*, Flugwissenschaft *f*.
aerosled Motorschlitten *m*.
aerostat Aerostat *m*.
affidavit beglaubigte Bescheinigung, eidliche Erklärung.
age Alter *n*.
age-in-grade Rangdienstalter *m*.
age limit Dienstaltersgrenze *f*.
agent Verbindungsmann *m*, Vertrauensmann *m*.
agent officer Verbindungsoffizier *m*.
aggressive angriffsfreudig, angriffslustig.
aggressiveness Einsatzbereitschaft *f*.
aggressor Angreifer *m*.
agonic line Agone *f*.
aide *See* **aide-de-camp.**
aide-de-camp Adjutant *m*.
aid man Sanitäter *m*.
aid station Truppenverbandplatz *m (Med)*.
aiguillette Fangschnur *f*.
aileron Querruder *n*.
aileron horn Querruderhebel *m*.
aim *v* zielen, richten, anlegen.
aim-checking device Zielkontrollspiegel *m*.
aiming circle Richtkreis *m*.
aiming-circle station Richtstelle *f*.
aiming device Zielspiegel *m*.
aiming disk Ziellöffel *m*.
aiming drill Ziel- und Anschlagsübungen *fpl*.
aiming error Zielfehler *m*.
aiming exercise Richtübung *f*.
aiming group Zieldreieck *n (aiming triangle)*.
aiming light Richtlampe *f*.
aiming mechanism Richtgerät *n*, Zieleinrichtung *f*, Zielvorrichtung *f*.
aiming order Richtkommando *n*, Richtbefehl *m*.
aiming point Richtpunkt *m*, Haltepunkt *m*, Anlegepunkt *m*, Zielpunkt
aiming-point azimuth reading Richtpunktzahl *f*.
aiming-point and deflection method Richtpunktverfahren *n*.
aiming point offset Beobachtungswinkel *m*.
aiming post Richtlatte *f*, E-Latte *f*.
aiming post light Richtlampe *f*.
aiming practice Richtübung *f*.
aiming silhouette Gefechtsscheibe *f (target)*.
aiming stake Richtlatte *f*, E-Latte *f*.
aiming target Richtscheibe *f*.
air *n* Luft *f*.
air *v* lüften.
"Air!" "Hoch!" *(firing)*.
air-adjustment jet Korrekturluftdüse *f (Mtr)*.
air adviser Fliegerverbindungsoffizier *m*.
air-air Flugzeug zu Flugzeug *(Sig Com)*.
air alert Jagdpatrouille in Kampfbereitschaft *(Avn)*; Fliegeralarm *m (AWS)*.
air ambulance Sanitätsflugzeug *n*.
air area Luftraum *m*.
air attack Luftangriff *m*.
air base Luftstützpunkt *m*, Flugstützpunkt *m (Tac)*; Fliegerhorst *m*, Horst *m (Adrm in Z of I)*.
air base airdrome Fliegerhorst *m*, Horst *m (Z of I)*.
air base commander Fliegerhorstkommandant *m*, Horstkommandant *m*.
air base service area Bodenanlage der Luftwaffe.
air base troops Bodenpersonal *n*.
air battle Luftschlacht *f*.
airborne auf dem Luftwege befördert.
airborne infantry Luftinfanterie *f*.
airborne troops Luftlande- und Fallschirmtruppen *fpl*.
air brake Luftdruckbremse *f (Mech)*; Landeklappe *f (Ap)*.
air burst Luftsprengpunkt *m*, hoher Sprengpunkt, Sprengpunkt *m (Arty)*.
air-burst pattern Lufttreffbild *n (Arty)*.
air-burst registration fire Schießen mit hohen Sprengpunkten.
air chamber Luftbehälter *m (counterrecoil mechanism, vehicle brake)*.
air combat Luftgefecht *n*, Luftkampf *m*.
air command communication Funkverbindung von Flugzeug zu Flugzeug.
air command headquarters Luftwaffengruppenkommando *n*.
air compressor Drucklufterzeuger *m*, Luftverdichter *m*, Luftpresser *m*.
air conditioning plant Klimaanlage *f*.
air-cooled luftgekühlt, mit Luftkühlung.
air-cooled engine luftgekühlter Motor, Motor mit Luftkühlung.
air-cooled weapon luftgekühlte Waffe.
Air Corps *See* **Army Air Forces.**
aircraft Luftfahrzeug *n*.
aircraft ammunition Flugzeugmunition *f*, Bordmunition *f*.
aircraft armament Bordwaffen *fpl*.
aircraft automatic gun *See* **aircraft cannon.**
aircraft camera Luftbildkammer *f*, Luftbildgerät *n*, Fliegerkammer *f*.
aircraft cannon Flugzeugkanone *f*.
aircraft carrier Flugzeugträger *m*.
aircraft engine Flugmotor *m*.
aircraft equipment Bordgeräte *npl*.
aircraft factory Flugzeugwerk *n*, Flugzeugfabrik *f*.
aircraft gun sights Fliegervisiereinrichtung *f*.
aircraft industry Luftfahrzeugindustrie *f*.
aircraft instruments Bordgeräte *npl*.
aircraft landing flare Bordlandefackel *f*.
aircraft log Flugbuch *n*, Flugtagebuch *n*.
aircraft machine gun Bord-Maschinengewehr *n*.
aircraft observer Aufklärungsflieger *m*, Beobachter *m*.
aircraft parachute flare Fallschirmleuchtbombe *f*, Leuchtbombe *f*.
aircraft signal Leuchtpatrone *f*, Signalpatrone *f (ground-air Com)*.
aircraft signal pistol Fliegerleuchtpistole *f*.
aircraft tender Flugzeugmutterschiff *n*, Stützpunktschiff *n*.
aircraft warning Fliegerwarnung *f*.
aircraft warning company Flugmeldekompanie *f*.
aircraft warning officer Flugmeldeoffizier *m*.
aircraft warning service Flugmeldedienst *m*.
air crew Bordbesatzung *f*, Bordmannschaft *f*, fliegende Besatzung, Flugzeugbesatzung *f*.
air current Luftstrom *m*.
air defense Luftverteidigung *f*; Luftabwehr *f (active)*; Luftschutz *m (passive)*.
air defense area Flugabwehrgebiet *n*.
air defense region Flugabwehrbezirk *m*.
air density Luftdichte *f*.
air depot Nachschubstelle der Luftwaffe.
airdrome Flugplatz *m*.
airdrome boundary Flughafengrenze *f*, Platzgrenze *f*.
airdrome construction detachment Flughafenbautrupp *m*.
airdrome light Platzfeuer *n*.
airdrome lighting Flugplatzbefeuerung *f*.
airdrome traffic Flugbetrieb *m*.
airfield *See* **airdrome.**
air fight *See* **air combat.**
air filter Luftfilter *m*, Luftreiniger *m (Mtr)*.
airflow Fahr(t)wind *m*, Gebläsewind *m (Avn)*.
airfoil Tragfläche *f (Ap)*.
airfoil section Flügelprofil *n*, Tragflügelprofil *n*.
air force Luftflotte *f (tactical and territorial unit)*.
air force commander Flottenchef *m*, Luftflottenchef *m*, Fliegerführer *m*.
air forces Fliegerkräfte *fpl*, Luftstreitkräfte *fpl*.
Air Forces *See* **Army Air Forces.**
Air Forces Headquarters Luftwaffenkommando *n*.

airframe Flugzeuggerippe n.
air friction Luftreibung f (Ballistics).
air-ground Bord zu Boden (Sig Com)
air-ground communication Nachrichtenverbindung Boden-Bord.
air-ground liaison code Funkverkehrsabkürzungen fpl.
air-ground net Funknetz für den Verkehr Boden-Bord.
air guard Luftspäher m.
air-intake duct (Ft) Ansaugleitung f
air-intake horn Ansaugkrümmer m (carburetor).
air jet Luftdüse f (Mtr).
air landing troops Luftlandetruppen fpl.
airline Fluglinie f, Flugstrecke f.
air lock Gasschleuse f (CWS).
air mechanic Flugzeugmechaniker m, Bordmonteur m.
air mile Luftmeile f (1,853.25 meters or 6,080 feet).
air navigation Flugzeugortung f, Luftnavigation f.
air navigation map Flugstreckenkarte f.
air objective Luftangriffsziel n.
air observation Luftbeobachtung f.
air observer Beobachter m (Avn); Luftspäher m (AWS).
air obstacle Luftsperre f (Avn).
air offensive Luftoffensive f.
air officer Fliegerverbindungsoffizier
airplane Flugzeug n; Flieger m (as seen from ground).
airplane ambulance Sanitätsflugzeug
airplane armament Flugzeugbewaffnung f, Bordwaffen fpl.
airplane chemical spray apparatus Luftstromgerät n, Zerstäubungsgerät n.
airplane construction m Flugzeugbau
airplane controls Flugzeugsteuerung
airplane direction finding Flugzeugortung f.
airplane engine Flugzeugmotor m.
airplane flare Fallschirmleuchtbombe f.
airplane mechanic Flugzeugwart m, Bordwart m, Bordmonteur m, Flugzeugmechaniker m.
airplane model n Flugzeugbaumuster
airplane passenger Fluggast m.
airplane production Flugzeugbau m, Flugzeugproduktion f.
airplane signal Fliegerverständigungszeichen n.
airplane-speed slide rule Flugzeuggeschwindigkeitslineal n (AAA).
airplane spotter Luftspäher m, Flugmeldeposten m.
airplane towing Flugzeugschlepp m.
air pocket Luftloch n.
airport Flughafen m.
air power Luftmacht f, Luftgeltung
air pressure Luftdruck m.
air raid Luftangriff m.
air raid alarm Fliegeralarm m, Luftalarm m.
air raid drill Luftschutzübung f (civilian defense).
air raid shelter Luftschutzkeller m, Luftschutzraum m.
air raid siren Fliegersirene f, Luftschutzsirene f.
air raid warden Luftschutzwart m.
air raid warning district Luftwarnbezirk m.
air reconnaissance Luftaufklärung f.
air reconnaissance area Luftaufklärungsraum m.
air resistance Luftwiderstand m (Ballistics, Avn).
air scoop Luftsackmaul n (captive Bln).
air scout Luftspäher m.
air sentinel See air scout.
Air Service Command Luftgau m.
airship Luftschiff n.
airspace Luftraum m (Avn, etc.); leerer Raum (Am).
airspace reservation Luftsperrgebiet n (Avn).
air speed Eigengeschwindigkeit f, Geschwindigkeit zur Luft (Ap).
air speed indicator Fahrtmesser m (Ap).
Air Staff Führungsstab der Luftwaffe (USA).
air starter Preßluftanlasser m (Mtr).
airstream Fahrwind m (Avn).
air superiority Luftüberlegenheit f.
air support Fliegerunterstützung f.
Air Support Command Schlachtfliegerverband m.
air support party Luftnachrichtenverbindungsoffiziere mpl.
air target Flugziel n.
air task force fliegerischer Verband, Fliegerverband m.
airtight luftdicht.
air-traffic safety control Flugsicherung f.
air transport Transportflugzeug n.
air transportation Lufttransport m.
Air Transport Command Lufttransportkommando n (USA). See also Ferry Command.
air umpire Schiedsrichter m (Avn).
air warfare Luftkriegführung f.
air warning net Flugmeldenetz n.
airway Flugweg m, Flugstrecke f.
airway beacon Flugstreckenfeuer n, Streckenfeuer n.
airway obstruction Luftfahrthindernis n.
airway traffic control area Flugsicherungsbereich m.
airworthiness (Ap) Lufttüchtigkeit f
airworthy flugklar, flugtüchtig.
alarm Alarm m.
alarm station Alarmplatz m.
alcohol Alkohol m, Weingeist m.
alert n Startbereitschaft f (Avn); Bereitschaft f, Alarmbereitschaft f.
alert v alarmieren, in Bereitschaft stellen.
alert hut Bereitschaftsbaracke f (Avn).
alert station Jagdpatrouille f, Bereitschaftsstellung f (Avn).
alidade Kippregel f (Surv).
alidade ruler Diopterlineal n (aiming circle).
alignment See alinement.
alinement Nachstellung des Radstands (of vehicle wheels); Ausrichten n, Richtung f (of sights).
alinement stake Richtstange f (Bdg, Engr).
aliquot part charge aus zwei gleichen Teilladungen bestehende Treibladung (Am).
aliquot propelling charge See aliquot part charge.
alkali cartridge Alkalipatrone f (in oxygen breathing apparatus).
all-around defense Igelverteidigung f.
all-around traverse Seitenrichtfeld von 360°; mit Sockellafette.
all clear Beendigung der Luftgefahr. "All clear!" "Alarm aus!"
all clear signal Entwarnung f.
all-metal airplane Ganzmetallflugzeug n.
allocation Zuteilung f (of men, supplies, etc.); Zuweisung f, Anweisung f (of funds).
allocation of targets Zielzuweisung
allot anweisen.
allotment Anweisung f.
allotment of equipment Geräteausstattung f.
allowance See authorized basic allowance.
allow for berücksichtigen.
alloy Legierung f.
allways fuze empfindlicher Kopfzünder (Am).
all-wheel drive Räderantrieb m, Allradantrieb m (MT).
all-wing airplane Nurflügelflugzeug n.
ally Bundesgenosse m, Verbündete(r) m.
alphabet code flag Signalflagge f, internationale Signalflagge (Nav).
alpine cap Bergmütze f (Clo).
alternate v wechseln, abwechseln.
alternate airport Ausweichhafen m.
alternate emplacement Wechselstellung f (G, MG).
alternate firing position See alternate emplacement.
alternate routing Ausweichvermittlung f (emergency Tp Com).
alternate target Ausweichziel n (bombing).
alternate traversing fire Breitenfeuer n (Arty).
alternate two-way radiophone communication Funkwechselsprechen n.
alternate two-way radio traffic Funkwechselverkehr m.
alternating current Wechselstrom m; Drehstrom m (three-phase).
alternating-current generator Wechselstromerzeuger m.
alternation Wechsel m (Elec).
alternator See alternating-current generator.
altimeter Höhenmesser m; Höhenentfernungsmesser m, Höhenmesser m, Entfernungsmeßgerät n (AA height finder).
altitude Höhe f.
altitude bracket Höhenschicht f (Avn, Met).
altitude-correction ruler Erdkrümmungslineal n.
altitude indication Höhenangabe f.
altitude lead Höhenvorhalt m (AAA).
altitude of flight Flughöhe f.
altitude of target Meßhöhe f (instant of range determination); Zielhöhe f (present position); Treffhöhe f (future position).
altitude reading Höhenangabe f.
aluminum Aluminium n.
aluminum alloy f Aluminiumlegierung
amatol Amatol n (Am).
ambient noise störende Nebengeräusche.
ambulance Krankenkraftwagen m; Sanitätsfahrzeug n (any Med vehicle).
ambulance battalion Krankentransportabteilung f.
ambulance loading post Wagenhalteplatz m.
ambulance station Krankentransportstelle f.
ambulant marschfähiger Verwundeter.
ambush n Hinterhalt m, Lauerstellung f.
ambush v aus dem Hinterhalt überfallen.
American Red Cross Amerikanisches Rotes Kreuz.
ammeter Amperemeter n, Strommesser m.
ammonal Ammonpulver n, Ammonal n (Am).
ammonia Ammoniak n; Salmiakgeist m (spirits of ammonia).
ammonium nitrate explosive Ammonsalpeter-Sprengmittel n.
ammonium picrate Ammoniumpikrat n (Am).
ammunition Munition f. See also munitions.
ammunition bearer Munitionsschütze m.
ammunition belt Gurt m, Patronengurt m.
ammunition box Munitionskasten m.
ammunition branch depot Munitionszweiglager n.
ammunition carrier Munitionsfahrzeug n; Munitionswagen m, Munitionskarren m (H Dr), Gefechtskarren m (includes weapons); Munitionsschütze m, Munitionsträger m (bearer).
ammunition chest Protzkasten m (on limber).
ammunition clip Ladestreifen m.
ammunition company Munitionsnachschub-Kompanie f.
ammunition depot Munitionslager n.
ammunition detail Munitionstrupp m.
ammunition distributing point Munitionsausgabestelle f, Munitionsverteilungsstelle f.
ammunition drum Munitionstrommel f.
ammunition dump Munitionslager n.
ammunition lot number laufende Nummer der Munitionslieferung.
ammunition niche Munitionsnische f (Ft).
ammunition pit Munitionsloch n.
ammunition pocket Patronentasche f (Clo).
ammunition point Munitionsausgabestelle f.
ammunition requirements Schießbedarf m.
ammunition section Munitionsstaffel f (firing Btry).
ammunition shelter Munitionsnische f (Ft).
ammunition shortage Munitionsmangel m.
ammunition sponson Munitionskammer f (Tk).
ammunition stock Munitionsbestand
ammunition supply Munitionsnachschub m, Munitionsausstattung f, Munitionsbestand m.
ammunition supply point Munitionsumschlagstelle f.
ammunition supply service Munitionswesen n.
ammunition trailer Munitionswagen
ammunition train Munitionszug m (RR); Munitionskolonne f.
ammunition transloading point Munitionsumschlagstelle f.
ammunition truck Geschoß-Zubringewagen m, Geschoßwagen m.
ammunition wagon Munitionswagen
amnesty allgemeine Begnadigung, Amnestie f.
amount Betrag m, Bestand m; Menge f (quantity); Summe f (sum).
amperage Amperezahl f.
ampere Ampere n.
amphibian airplane Wasserlandflugzeug n, Amphibienflugzeug n.
amphibian tank Schwimmpanzerkampfwagen m, Amphibienkampfwagen m.
amphibian tractor See tracked landing vehicle.
amphibian truck Schwimm-Lastkraftwagen m; Schwimmwagen m.
amplification Verstärkung f (Rad).
amplifier Lautverstärker m (volume); Kraftverstärker m (power).
amplifier tube Verstärkerröhre f (Rad).
amplitude of oscillations Schwingungsweite f (Rad).
amputate amputieren, abnehmen.
anabatic wind Aufwind m, Hangwind m (Met).
anaglyph Anaglyphe f, Anaglypt n (Photo Surv).
anchor Anker m.
anchorage Verankerung f, Ankergrund m, Ankerplatz m, Ankerstelle f (Nav); Verankerung f, Zurrung f.
anchor cable Ankertau n.
anchored mine Ankermine f.
anchor hitch Ankerstich m (Engr).
anchoring Verankerung f (Nav).
anchor light Ankerlicht n.
anchor pin Bremsträger m (of brakeshoes).
anchor plate Ankerplatte f (of clockwork fuze).
anchor rack stick Ankerrödel m (Bdg, Engr).
anchor stake Ankerpfahl m.
anemometer Windmesser m, Anemometer n, Windmeßgerät n.
aneroid barometer Dosenbarometer n, Federbarometer n, Federluftdruckmesser m, Aneroid-Barometer
anesthetic Betäubungsmittel n.
angary Prisenrecht n.
angle Winkel m.
angledozer Planier-Raupenschlepper
angle of approach Flugwinkel m (AAA); Flugwinkel im Abschußpunkt (present position); Flugwinkel im Treffpunkt (future position); Anflugwinkel m (Avn); Fahrzeugüberhang m, Überhang m (MT).
angle of attack Anstellwinkel m (Avn).
angle of axle displacement Hubhöhe f (MT).
angle of axle swing Achsenverschränkbarkeit f (MT).
angle of bank Winkel der Schräglage (Avn).
angle of clearance Differenz zwischen Abgangswinkel und Deckungswinkel (Ballistics).
angle of convergence Parallaxwinkel m (Optics); Winkel zur Ausschaltung des Stellungsunterschiedes (Arty, Surv).
angle of crab Luvwinkel m (Avn).
angle of departure Abgangswinkel m (Ballistics).
angle of depression negativer Geländewinkel (Gunnery); Tiefenwinkel m (Surv).
angle of dive Flugneigungswinkel m (AA gunnery); Sturzwinkel m (Avn).
angle of elevation Visierwinkel m, Aufsatzwinkel m, Erhöhungswinkel
angle-of-elevation dial Aufsatztrommel f (G).
angle-of-elevation mechanism Aufsatzwinkeltrieb m (G).
angle of fall Fallwinkel m (Ballistics).
angle-offset method Kreisbogenabsteckung von einer Tangente aus (Btry Surv).
angle of glide Gleitwinkel m (Avn).
angle of impact Aufschlagwinkel m, Auftreffwinkel m (Ballistics).
angle of incidence Einstellwinkel m (Ap wing); Ergänzungswinkel des Auftreffwinkels (Ballistics); Einfallwinkel m.
angle of jump Abgangsfehlerwinkel m (Gunnery).
angle of parallax Parallaxe f, Parallaxwinkel m (Optics).
angle of pitch Steigungswinkel m, Anstellwinkel m (propeller); Stampfwinkel m (Ap).
angle of ricochet Abprallwinkel m.
angle of roll Winkel der Schräglage (Avn).
angle of safety Erhöhung einschließlich der Sicherheitsteilstriche (overhead firing).
angle of shift Seitenabstand vom Richtpunkt (indirect firing)
angle of site Geländewinkel m, Zielhöhenwinkel m (Gunnery).
angle-of-site instrument Geländewinkelmesser m.
angle-of-site level Geländewinkellibelle f.
angel-of-site mechanism Geländewinkelmeßvorrichtung f (on telescopic sight).
angle-of-site micrometer Geländewinkelmesser m (G).
angle-of-site scale Skalenscheibe f.
angle-of-site table Libellentafel f (Gunnery).
angle of site to mask Deckungswinkel m (Gunnery).
angle of slope Böschungswinkel m (Top).
angle of traverse Schwenkwinkel m, Schwenkungswinkel m, Seitenrichtwinkel m (Gunnery)
angle of twist Drallwinkel m (rifling).
angle of view Sehwinkel m.
angle of wing setting Flügeleinstellwinkel m (Ap).
angle of yaw Wendewinkel m, Gierwinkel m, Scherwinkel m (Avn).
angular acceleration Winkelbeschleunigung f.
angular height (AAA) Höhenwinkel m
angular height of target Zielhöhenwinkel m (AAA); Zielhöhenwinkel zum Abschußpunkt (present position); Zielhöhenwinkel zum Wechselpunkt (midpoint); Zielhöhenwinkel zum Treffpunkt
angular measurement Winkelmaß n
angular movement Winkelauswanderung f; Winkelgeschwindigkeit f (rate).
angular travel See angular movement.
angular velocity Winkelgeschwindigkeit f.
animal-drawn bespannt.
ankle Fußknöchel m, Knöchel m.
A.N. method of instrument landing A.N.-Verfahren n (beam bracketing) (Avn).
anneal ausglühen.
annex Anlage f.
annihilation fire Vernichtungsfeuer n.
announcement Ankündigung f, Bekanntgabe f.
anode Anode f.
answering jack Abtrageklinke f (Tp) signal Gegensignal n.
answer to call-up Anrufantwort f (Rad). adj antarktisch, den Südpol betreffend.
antenna Luftleiter m, Antenne f.
antenna ammeter Antennenstromanzeiger m.
antenna array Antennengebilde n.
antenna binding post Antennenanschluß m.
antenna capacitance Antennenkapazität f.
antenna circuit Antennenkreis m.
antenna coupling Antennenkopplung f.
antenna jack Antennenbuchse f, Antennen-Anschlußbuchse f.
antenna mast Antennenstab m (portable Rad set); Antennenmast m, Funkmast m.
antenna outfit Antennengerät n.
antenna reel (Ap) Antennenhaspel f
antenna resistance Antennenwiderstand m.
antenna truck Funkmastkraftwagen m. nna tuning coil Antennenspule f. nna wire Luftdraht m.
anthracite coal Steinkohle f.
antiaircraft artillery Flakartillerie f, Flak f.
antiaircraft artillery battalion Flakabteilung f.
antiaircraft artillery regiment Flakregiment n.
antiaircraft automatic weapons Maschinenflak f.
antiaircraft barrage Flaksperre f.
antiaircraft battery Flakbatterie f.
antiaircraft company Fla-Kompanie f. aircraft cruiser Flakkreuzer m (Nav).
antiaircraft defense Flugabwehr f, Flakabwehr f, Fliegerabwehr f, Luftverteidigung f.
antiaircraft director Kommandogerät n, Flakkommandogerät n.
antiaircraft emplacement Flakstellung f.
antiaircraft fire Flakfeuer n, Flakschießen n.
antiaircraft fire director Flakkommandogerät n.
antiaircraft gun Flugabwehrgeschütz n, Flakgeschütz n, Flugabwehrkanone f, Abwehrgeschütz n.
antiaircraft gun crew Flakbedienung f.
antiaircraft lookout Luftspäher m.
antiaircraft machine gun Flugabwehrmaschinengewehr n, Flakmaschinengewehr n, Flamaschinengewehr n, Fla-MG. n.
antiaircraft MG unit Fla-Einheit f.
antiaircraft protection Flakschutz m.
antiaircraft scout Luftspäher m.
antiaircraft searchlight Flugzeugabwehrscheinwerfer m, Flakscheinwerfer m.
antiaircraft security Sicherung gegen den Luftgegner (Tac).
antiaircraft sight Fliegervisier n, Flakvisier n.
antiaircraft weapon Luftabwehrwaffe f, Fla-Waffe f.
anticyclone Antizyklon m, Hoch n (Met).
antidim compound Klarsichtsalbe f, Brillenglassalbe f.
antidim eyeglass Klarscheibe f (gas mask).
antifreeze Gefrierschutz m, Gefrierschutzmittel n (MT).
antifreeze solution Frostschutzmittel
antifriction bearing Wälzlager n.
anti-glare windshield Blendschutzscheibe f.
anti-icer solution Enteisungsmittel n.
antiknock klopffest (MT).
antiknock quality Klopffestigkeit f (of engine fuel).
antimechanized defense Panzerabwehr f.
antimechanized security Sicherung gegen Panzer.
antimechanized warning Panzerwarnung f.
antimechanized warning system Panzerwarndienst m.
antimechanized weapon Panzerabwehrwaffe f.
antimony sulfide Schwefelantimon n (Am).
antipersonnel bomb Splitterbombe f.
antipersonnel mine S-Mine f, Schrapnellmine f, Schützenmine f.
antipersonnel rifle grenade Gewehrsprenggranate f.
antiseptic fäulnisbekämpfendes Mittel, Antiseptikum n.
antisubmarine net Fangnetz n.
antitank Pak-, Panzerabwehr-, Panzerjäger-. See also tank destroyer.
antitank artillery Pak f.
antitank battalion Panzerjägerabteilung f, Panzerabwehrabteilung f.
antitank bomb Panzerbombe f.
antitank company Panzerabwehrkompanie f, Panzerjägerkompanie f.

antitank defense Panzerabwehr *f*.
antitank ditch Panzerfahrzeuggraben *m*, Panzergraben *m*, Panzersperrgraben *m*, Tankgraben *m*.
antitank gun Pak *f*, Pak-Geschütz *n*, Panzerabwehrgeschütz *n*, Panzerabwehrkanone *f*, Panzerjägerkanone *f*, Panzerjägergeschütz *n*.
antitank gun emplacement Pakstellung *f*.
antitank hedgehog Igel *m*.
antitank lookout *m* Panzerwarnposten
antitank mine Panzerabwehrmine *f*, Panzermine *f*.
antitank obstacle Panzersperre *f*, Panzerhindernis *n*.
antitank platoon Panzerabwehrzug *m*, Pak-Zug *m*, Panzerjägerzug *m*.
antitank regiment Panzerabwehrregiment *n*, Panzerjägerregiment *n*.
antitank rifle Panzerabwehrgewehr *n*, Tankbüchse *f*, Panzerbüchse *f*.
antitank rifle grenade panzerbrechende Gewehrgranate.
antitank rifle grenadier Gewehr-Panzergranatenschütze *m* *(USA)*.
antitank rocket Panzerabwehrrakete *f*.
antitank rocket launcher Raketen-Panzerbüchse *f*.
antitank squad Pak-Halbzug *m*.
antitank tetrahedron Igel *m*.
antitank wall Panzersperrmauer *f*.
antitank weapon Panzerabwehrwaffe *f*.
anvil Amboß *m* *(Am, blacksmith's)*.
aparejo mexikanischer Packsattel.
aperiodic compass aperiodischer Kompaß.
aperture Öffnung *f* *(opening)*; Loch *n* *(hole)*; Spalt *m*, Schlitz *m* *(slit)*; Scharte *f* *(port or peephole, Ft, Tk, etc.)*.
apparatus Gerät *n*, Apparat *m*.
appeal Berufung *f* *(Law)*; dringende Bitte *(earnest request)*; Aufruf *m* *(public appeal)*.
appendix Füllansatz *m* *(Bln)*; Blinddarm *m* *(anatomy)*; Anhang *m* *(in a manual, etc.)*.
application Bewerbung *f*, Gesuch *n* *(request)*; Umschlag *m* *(Med)*.
appoint bestallen, ernennen.
appointing authority Gerichtsherr *m* *(Law)*.
appointment Dienststellung *f*; Ernennung *f* *(to brevet rank)*.
approach *n* Annäherung *f*, Herangehen an den Feind *(Tac)*; Anmarschweg *m* *(road)*; Anflug *m* *(bombing)*; Einflug *m* *(of a target)* *(AWS)*.
approach *v* anfliegen *(Avn)*; sich nähern.
approach angle Anflugwinkel *m* *(Avn)*; Fahrzeugüberhang *m*, Überhang *m* *(MT)*.
approach embankment Brückendamm *m* *(Bdg)*.
approaching course Anflugkurs *m* *(Avn)*.
approaching target kommendes Ziel.
approach march Anmarsch *m*, Annäherungsmarsch *m* *(Tac)*.
approach route Anmarschweg *m*.
approach trench Laufgraben *m*.
approach zone Anflugsektor *m* *(Adrm)*.
appropriation Bewilligung *f* *(of funds, etc.)*.
approximate *v* sich nähern, nahebringen, schätzen.
approximate *adj* ungefähr, annähernd, grob.
approximate adjustment fire grobes Einschießen *(Arty)*.
apron Hallenvorplatz *m*, Vorfeld *n* *(Adrm)*; Tarnnetz *n* *(of G emplacement)*; Seitenverankerung *f* *(of double-apron fence)*.
apron shield Unterschild *m* *(G)*.
aptitude test Eignungsprüfung *f*.
aquadag Aquadag *m* *(lubricant)*.
arc Kreisbogen *m* *(of a circle)*; Bogen *m*.
arch Brückenbogen *m* *(Bdg)*.
arched bridge Bogenbrücke *f*.
arc lamp Bogenlampe *f* *(SL)*.
arctic *adj* arktisch; den Nordpol betreffend.
arctic circle nördlicher Polarkreis.
arctic zone Nordpolgebiet *n*.
arc-type elevating mechanism Zahnbogenrichtmaschine *f* *(G)*.
arc welding Lichtbogenschweißung *f*.
area Raum *m*, Gebiet *n*, Fläche *f*, Flächeninhalt *m*.
area bombing Bombenabwurf auf Flächenziel.
area contamination Geländevergiftung *f* *(CWS)*.
area fire Flächenschießen *n*, Flächenfeuer *n* *(Arty)*.
area sketch Grundrißskizze *f*.
area target Flächenziel *n* *(Gunnery)*.
arm *n* Arm *m* *(Anatomy)*; Waffe *f* *(weapon)*; Waffengattung *f* *(branch of the Army)*.
arm *v* bewaffnen, bestücken *(provide armament)*; scharf machen, entsichern *(Am, mine)*; scharf stellen *(bomb)*.
armament Rüstung *f*; Bewaffnung *f*, Bestückung *f*.
armament error Waffenstreuung *f*.
armament officer Waffenoffizier *m*.
armament plant Rüstungswerk *n*.
arm and hand signal Armzeichen *n*.
armature Anker *m*.
armature shaft Ankerwelle *f* *(Elec)*; Ankerachse *f* *(field Tp)*.
armature short Lamellenschluß *m*.
armature turn Leiterschleife *f*.
armature winding Ankerwicklung *f*.
armband Armbinde *f*.
armed bewaffnet; scharf gemacht, scharf gestellt *(Am)*.
armed-defense system Wehrorganisation *f*.
Armed Forces Wehrmacht *f*.
armed merchantman bewaffnetes Handelsschiff.
armed reconnaissance bewaffnete Aufklärung.
armes blanches blanke Waffen, Handwaffen *fpl*.
arming device Fliehbacke *f* *(centrifugal type device in fuze)*.
arming pin Sicherungsvorstecker *m* *(fuze)*.
arming vane Entsicherungsflügel *m*, Windflügel *m* *(bomb)*.
arming wire Entsicherungsdraht *m* *(bomb)*.
armistice Waffenstillstand *m*.
armistice terms Waffenstillstandsbedingungen *fpl*.
armor Panzer *m*, Panzerung *f* *(Tk, etc.)*; Bewehrung *f* *(Tp cable)*.
armor belt Panzergürtel *m*.
armored gepanzert, Panzer—.
armored artillery Panzerartillerie *f*.
armored attack Panzerangriff *m*.
armored battalion Panzerbataillon *n*, Panzerabteilung *f*.
armored cable armiertes Kabel, Panzerkabel *n*.
armored car Panzerwagen *m*, Panzerkraftwagen *m*.
armored cargo carrier Panzertransportwagen *m* *(MT)*.
armored combat Panzerkampf *m*, Panzergefecht *n*.
armored combat vehicle gepanzertes Gefechtsfahrzeug, mechanisiertes Fahrzeug.
Armored Command Panzertruppe *f*, Panzerwaffe *f*.
armored corps Panzerkorps *n*.
armored division Panzerdivision *f*.
armored engagement Panzergefecht
armored engineer Panzerpionier *m*.
armored engineer battalion Panzer-Pionier-Bataillon *n*.
Armored Force Panzerwaffe *f*, Panzertruppe *f*.
armored force officer *m* Panzeroffizier
armored forces Panzertruppen *fpl*, Panzerkräfte *fpl*.
armored formation Panzerverband *m*, Panzerformation *f*.
armored infantry battalion Panzergrenadier-Bataillon *n*.
armored infantry regiment Panzergrenadier-Regiment *n*, Panzer-Infanterieregiment *n*.
armored personnel carrier Panzertransportwagen *m*, Schützenpanzer *m*, Schützenpanzerwagen *m*, Grenadier-Panzerwagen *m* *(MT)*.
armored platoon Panzerkraftwagenzug *m*.
armored point Panzerspitze *f* *(Adv Gd)*.
armored radio car Panzerfunkwagen *m*.
armored radio truck Panzerfunkwagen *m*.
armored reconnaissance battalion Panzeraufklärungsabteilung *f*.
armored reconnaissance car Panzerspähwagen *m*.
armored reconnaissance company Panzerspähkompanie *f*.
armored reconnaissance vehicle Panzerspähfahrzeug *n*.
armored regiment Panzerregiment *n*.
armored rifleman *m* Panzergrenadier
Armored School Panzertruppenschule *f*.
armored scout car Panzerspähwagen *m*.
armored signal battalion Panzernachrichtenabteilung *f*.
armored skirting Laufwerkpanzerung *f* *(Tk)*.
armored support Panzerunterstützung *f* *(Tac)*.
armored train Eisenbahnpanzerzug *m*, Panzerzug *m* *(RR)*.
armored troops Panzertruppen *fpl*, Kraftfahrkampftruppen *fpl*.
armored turret Panzerturm *m*; Panzerdrehturm *m* *(revolving)*; Panzer-Verschwindeturm *m* *(disappearing)*.
armored-unit commander Panzerführer *m*.
armored vehicle Panzerfahrzeug *n*, Panzerkraftfahrzeug *n*.
armored warfare Panzerkriegführung *f*, Panzerkrieg *m*.
armorer Waffenwart *m*.
armorer-artificer Waffenmeisterunteroffizier *m* *(NCO)*.
armor-piercing panzerbrechend, panzerdurchschlagend *(Am)*.
armor-piercing ammunition Panzermunition *f*.
armor-piercing bomb Panzerbombe *f*.
armor-piercing bullet Stahlkerngeschoß *n*, Spitzgeschoß mit Stahlkern, Panzersprenggeschoß *n*.
armor-piercing cap Panzerkopf *m*.
armor-piercing grenade Panzergranate *f* *(R)*.
armor-piercing projectile Stahlkerngeschoß *n*, Spitzgeschoß mit Stahlkern, Panzersprenggeschoß *n*, Panzergeschoß *n*.
armor-piercing rifle grenade Gewehr-Panzergranate *f*.
armor-piercing shell Panzersprenggranate *f*, Panzergranate *f* *(Am)*.
armor-piercing shot Stahlkerngeschoß *n*, Spitzgeschoß mit Stahlkern, Panzersprenggeschoß *n*.
armor plate Panzerplatte *f*, Panzerblech *n*.
armor-plate shield *(G)* Panzerschild *m*
armor-protected panzergeschützt.
armor protection Panzerschutz *m* *(Ft, Tk)*.
armor thickness Panzerstärke *f* *(Tk)*.
armory Exerzierhaus *n*, Waffenmeisterei *f*.
arms Waffen *fpl* *(weapons)*; Waffengattungen *fpl* *(branches of the Army)*.
arms depot Arsenal *n*, Waffenlager *n*.
arm signal Armzeichen *n*.
arms rack Gewehrstütze *f*.
army Armee *f* *(a tactical unit)*; Heer *n* *(the Army)*.
army air defense Heeresluftabwehr *f*.
Army Air Forces Heeresfliegertruppe *f*, Heeresluftwaffe *f* *(USA)*.
Army Air Forces Weather Service Wetterdienst der Luftwaffe.
army ammunition depot Armeemunitionslager *n*, Heeresmunitionslager *n*.
army area Armeegebiet *n*.
Army Command Heeresleitung *f*.
army corps Armeekorps *n*.
army depot Heergerätepark *m*.
Army Directory Kriegsrangliste *f*.
army dog Heereshund *m*.
army engineer Pionier *m*.
army field order Armeebefehl *m*.
Army Ground Forces Heer *n*.
army headquarters Armeeoberkommando *n*.
Army High Command Oberkommando des Heeres *(Ger)*.
army hospital Heereslazarett *n*.
army mail clerk Feldpostbeamter *m* *(USA: enlisted man; Ger: civilian official)*.
army medical battalion Armeesanitätsabteilung *f*.
Army Medical School Militärärztliche Akademie.
army newspaper Frontzeitung *f* *(T of Opns)*.
army nurse Pflegeschwester *f*, Heereskrankenschwester *f*.
Army Nurse Corps Heeres-Krankenschwesternkorps *n* *(USA)*.
army of occupation Besatzungsheer *n*, Besatzungsarmee *f*.
Army of the United States Das Heer der Vereinigten Staaten. *Compare* **United States Army.**
Army Ordnance Department Heereswaffenamt *n*.
army post Standort *m*, Heeresstandort *m*.
army post administration Heeresstandortverwaltung *f*.
army postal service Feldpostwesen *n*, Feldpost *f*.
army post office Feldpostamt *n*.
army quartermaster Höherer Kommandeur der Armeenachschubtruppen *(USA)*.
army ration depot Heeresverpflegungslager *n*, Armeeverpflegungslager *n*.
Army Register Rangliste des Heeres.
army remount depot Armeepferdepark *m*.
army saddle Armeesattel *m*.
army serial number Wehrnummer *f*.
army service area Versorgungsraum *m*.
Army Service Forces Heeresversorgungs- und Nachschubdienste *mpl* *(USA)*.
army signal unit Armeenachrichtenabteilung *f*.
army supply Heeresversorgung *f*.
army supply train Armeenachschubkolonne *f*.
army surgeon Armeearzt *m*.
army surgical hospital Armeefeldlazarett *n*.
army troops Armeetruppen *fpl*.
army veterinary hospital Armeepferdelazarett *n*.
Army War College Kriegsakademie *f*.
arrest *n* Festnahme *f*, Arrest *m*, Verhaftung *f*.
arrest *v* festnehmen, verhaften, in Haft nehmen; anhalten, aufhalten, abbremsen, hemmen *(stop)*.
arresting gear Abbremsvorrichtung *f* *(Ap)*.
arrest in quarters Stubenarrest *m*.
arrival Ankunft *f*.
arrival time Eintreffzeit *f*, Ankunftzeit *f*.
arrive ankommen, eintreffen.
arsenal Zeughaus *n*, Zeugamt *n*.
arsine Arsin *n* *(CWS)*.
artery Arterie *f*.
article of clothing Bekleidungsstück *n*.
Articles of War Kriegsartikel *mpl*.
artificer Feuerwerker *m* *(NCO)*.
artificial antenna künstliche Antenne *(Rad)*.
artificial horizon Horizont *m*, künstlicher Horizont, Fliegerhorizont *m* *(Ap)*.
artificial leather Kunstleder *n*.
artificial respiration künstliche Atmung.
artificial scent Riechspur *f*, künstliche Spur.
artificial ventilation künstliche Lüftung.
artillery Artillerie *f*.
heavy artillery schwerste Artillerie.
medium artillery schwere Artillerie.
light artillery leichte Artillerie.
artillery ammunition Artilleriemunition *f*.
artillery barrage Artilleriesperrfeuer *n*.
artillery battalion Artillerieabteilung *f*.
artillery commander Artillerieführer *m* *(corps and Div)*.
artillery duel Artillerieduell *n*.
artillery fire Artilleriebeschuß *m*, Artilleriefeuer *n*.
artillery fire-control instruments Artillerie-Beobachtungs- und Vermessungsgerät *n*.
artillery group Artilleriegruppe *f*.
artillery intelligence center Artillerienachrichtenstelle *f*.
artillery intelligence section Artillerienachrichtentrupp *m*.
artillery liaison command post Artillerieverbindungskommando *n*.
artillery liaison officer Artillerieverbindungsoffizier *m*.
artilleryman Artillerist *m*.
artillery mechanic Artilleriemechaniker *m*.
artillery mil Strich *m*.
artillery mission Artillerieflug *m* *(Avn)*.
artillery observation airplane Artilleriebeobachtungsflugzeug *n*.
artillery observation post Artilleriebeobachtungsstelle *f*.
artillery observer Artilleriebeobachter *m*.
artillery officer Höherer Artilleriekommandeur *(army and higher Hq)*.
artillery order Artilleriebefehl *m*.
artillery park Artilleriepark *m*.
artillery preparation Artillerievorbereitung *f*.
artillery prime mover Artilleriezugmaschine *f*.
artillery protection Feuerschutz *m*.
artillery reconnaissance artilleristische Aufklärung.
artillery reconnaissance aviation Artillerieflieger *mpl*.
artillery reconnaissance detail Artilleriespähtrupp *m*.
artillery reference points artilleristische Punkte *mpl*.
artillery regiment Artillerieregiment *n*.
artillery support Artillerieunterstützung *f*.
artillery survey section Artillerievermessungstrupp *m*.
artillery target reconnaissance Zielaufklärung *f*.
artillery train Artilleriestaffel *f*.
art of leadership Führungskunst *f*.
art of war Kriegskunst *f*.
asbestos Asbest *m*, Steinflachs *m*.
ascending air current Aufwind *m* *(Met)*.
ascending branch aufsteigender Ast *(of trajectory)*.
ascending gust Steigbö *f* *(Met)*.
ashore am Ufer, an der Küste *(being ashore)*; ans Land, ans Ufer *(going ashore)*.
aspect ratio Längenverhältnis *n*, Seitenverhältnis *n*, Flügelstreckung *f* *(Ap)*.
asphalt Asphalt *m*.
asphyxiate ersticken.
aspirin Aspirin *n*.
assault *n* Sturmangriff *m*, Sturm *m*, Vorstoß *m*, Vorstoßen *n*, Erstürmung *f* *(Tac)*.
assault *v* erstürmen, stürmen *(Tac)*.
to take by assault im Sturm nehmen.
assault battalion Sturmbataillon *n*.
assault boat Sturmboot *n*.
assault detachment Stoßtrupp *m*.
assault fire Schießen während der Bewegung *(automatic weapons)*; Einbruchsfeuer *n* *(Tac)*.
assault fire position Anschlag zum Schießen während der Bewegung.
assault gap Sturmgasse *f* *(through obstacles)*.
assault gun Sturmgeschütz *n* *(self-propelled)*.
assault-gun car Kraftwagenkanonenwagen *m*, Kanonenwagen *m*.
assault howitzer Sturmhaubitze *f* *(self-propelled)*.
assault position Ausgangslage *f*, Sturmausgangsstellung *f*.
assault trench Angriffsgraben *m*.
assemble (sich) versammeln *(to gather)*; montieren *(an Ap, Tk, etc.)*; zusammensetzen *(a weapon)*.
assembly Bereitstellung *f*, Versammlung *f* *(Tac)*; Montage *f* *(Tech)*.
assembly area Bereitstellungsraum *m* *(Tac)*.
assembly formation Versammlungsform *f*.
assembly of troops Truppenbereitstellung *f*.
assembly order Bereitstellungsbefehl *m*.
assembly plant Montagewerk *n*.
assembly point Sammelpunkt *m*, Sammelplatz *m*, Sammelstelle *f*, Sammelort *m*, Bereitstellungsplatz *m*.
assembly shop Montagehalle *f*.
assign eingliedern *(to a unit)*; zuweisen *(a task, etc.)*. *See also* **attach.**
assigned frequencies Verfügungsfrequenzen *fpl* *(Rad)*.
assignment Eingliederung *f*, Auftrag *m*, Aufgabe *f*.
assignment of missions Auftragserteilung *f*.
assistant Gehilfe *m*, Helfer *m*, Assistent *m*.
Assistant Chief of Staff Abteilungschef im Generalstab.
assistant chief of staff Führergehilfe *m*.
assistant director Oberschiedsrichter *m*, Leitungsoffizier *m* *(maneuvers)*.
assistant driver Begleiter *m*, Kraftwagenbegleiter *m*, Beifahrer *m* *(MT)*.
assistant gunner Ladeschütze *m* *(Tk)*; Ladekanonier *m* *(Arty)*; Gehilfe des Richtschützen *(MG squad)*.
Assistant Secretary of War Abteilungsleiter im Kriegsministerium *(USA)*.
asymptote correction chart Hyperbelplan *m* *(sound ranging)*.
"As you were!" "Kommando zurück!" *(to revoke a command)*; "Weitermachen!" *(carry on)*.
"At ease!" "Rührt Euch!" *(silence not required)*.
athletics Athletik *f*.
Atlantic Charter Atlantik-Charta *f*.
Atlantic Wall Atlantikwall *m* *(Ger Ft)*.
atlas grid Kartengitternetz *n* *(aerial Photo)*.
atmosphere Luftmeer *n* *(air)*; Atmosphäre *f* *(unit of pressure)*.
atmospheric layer Luftschicht *f* *(Met)*.
atmospheric pressure Luftdruck *m* *(Met)*.
atmospherics Gewitterstörung *f* *(Rad)*.
attach zuteilen *(to a unit)*; befestigen *(fasten)*. *See also* **assign.**
attaché Attaché *m*.
attached zugeteilt *(to a unit)*; befestigt *(fastened)*.
attack *n* Angriff *m*.
attack *v* angreifen.
attack airplane Kampfflugzeug *n*.
attacker Angreifer *m*.
attack formation Angriffsform *f*.
attack from march formation Angriff aus der Bewegung.
attack from the rear Rückenangriff *m*.
attack frontage Angriffsbreite *f*.
attack group Angriffsgruppe *f*.
attacking flank Angriffsflügel *m*.
attack of organized positions Angriff auf Stellungen.
attack on the flank *v* aus der Flanke nehmen.
attack order Angriffsbefehl *m*, Befehl zum Angriff.
attack sector Angriffsstreifen *m*.
attack troops Stoßtruppen *fpl*, Angriffstruppen *fpl*, Sturmtruppen *fpl*.
attack wave Angriffswelle *f*, Sturmwelle *f* *(Tac)*.
attempt *n* Versuch *m*.
attention Grundstellung *f*.
"Attention!" "Achtung!" *(on approach of an officer)*; "Abteilung, Stillgestanden!" *(for formations)*; "Stillgesessen!" *(mounted drill)*.
attitude Fluglage *f*, Flugzustand *m* *(Avn)*.
attrition Abnutzung *f*, Ermattung *f*, Zermürbung *f*.
audible hörbar.
audio frequency Tonfrequenz *f*.

audio-frequency amplifier Niederfrequenzverstärker *m.*
audio-frequency range Tonfrequenzbereich *m.*
audit *n* Rechnungsprüfung *f*, Buchprüfung *f.*
audit *v* Rechnungen prüfen, buchprüfen.
auger Lochbohrer *m*, Holzbohrer *m.*
authentication Beglaubigung *f*, Bescheinigung *f.*
authority Befehlsbefugnis *f (Mil)*; Behörde *f*, Instanz *f (Law).*
authorization Berechtigung *f*, Genehmigung *f.*
authorize genehmigen *(approve)*; bevollmächtigen *(empower).*
authorized behördlich zugelassen *(officially permitted)*; dienstlich *(regulation)*; genehmigt *(approved)*; bevollmächtigt *(empowered)*; Soll-, Plan- *(in tables of basic allowances or organization).*
authorized abbreviation amtlich festgelegte Abkürzung.
authorized basic allowance Sollbestand *m.*
authorized strength Sollstärke *f.* Compare **Iststärke.**
autofrettage Kaltrecken *n*, Autofrettage *f (Ord).*
autogiro Tragschrauber *m*, Autogiro *m.*
autoloader Selbstlader *m (Small Arms).*
automatic *n* Selbstladepistole *f.*
automatically operated selbsttätig.
automatic anchor Minenanker mit Tiefensteller *(Nav).*
automatic antiaircraft gun Flugabwehrmaschinenkanone *f*, Fla-Maschinenkanone *f.*
automatic antiaircraft weapons Flugabwehrmaschinenwaffen *fpl.*
automatic breech mechanism selbsttätiger Verschluß.
automatic cannon Maschinenkanone *f (Ap).*
automatic circuit breaker Selbstunterbrecher *m (Elec).*
automatic control Selbststeuerung *f*, Regler *m.*
automatic direction finder selbstweisendes Peilgerät *(Ap).*
automatic feed mechanism Zuführer *m (automatic weapon).*
automatic fire Dauerfeuer *n (MG, R).*
automatic fuze setter Zünderstellmaschine *f (AA gun).*
automatic gun Maschinenkanone *f*, Salvengeschütz *n.*
automatic pilot automatische Kurssteuerung, automatischer Pilot, Selbststeuergerät *n (Ap).*
automatic pistol Selbstladepistole *f.*
automatic-pitch propeller vollautomatische Verstell-Luftschraube.
automatic rifle Maschinenkarabiner *m*, automatisches Gewehr.
automatic supply planmäßiger Nachschub.
automatic volume control Schwundausgleich *m.*
automatic weapon Maschinenwaffe *f*, Schnellfeuerwaffe *f (Small Arms).*
automobile Kraftwagen *m.*
automobile engine Wagenmotor *m.*
automobile express highway Autobahn *f.*
automobile flag Kraftwagenflagge *f.*
automobile jack Wagenheber *m.*
auto-tow take-off Autoschleppstart *m (glider).*
autotransformer Spartransformator *m (Rad, Elec).*
autotransformer circuit Sparschaltung *f (Elec).*
autumn Herbst *m.*
auxiliary Hilfs-, Behelfs-. See also **woman auxiliary.**
auxiliary air Nebenluft *f (Mtr).*
auxiliary airfoil Zusatzflügel *m*, Hilfsflügel *m (Ap).*
auxiliary arm Hilfswaffe *f.*
auxiliary cruiser Hilfskreuzer *m.*
auxiliary engine Hilfsmotor *m.*
auxiliary equipment Hilfsgerät *n.*
auxiliary gear Geländegang *m (MT).*
auxiliary ground target Erdvergleichsziel *n (Gunnery).*
auxiliary ignition lead Reservezündung *f (Blasting).*
auxiliary landing field Hilfslandeplatz *m.*
auxiliary scale Hilfsmaßstab *m (Inst).*
auxiliary stage supercharger Zwischengebläse *n (Ap engine).*
auxiliary target Vergleichsziel *n*, Hilfsziel *n*; Luftvergleichsziel *n (high burst).*
auxiliary track Hilfskette *f (MT).*
auxiliary transmission Gruppengetriebe *n*, Zwischengetriebe *n*, Zusatzgetriebe *n (MT).*
auxiliary troops Hilfstruppen *fpl.*
auxiliary vessel Hilfsschiff *n.*
auxiliary wing Hilfsflügel *m (Ap).*
available verfügbar, zur Verwendung.
available for commitment einsatzfähig.
AVC See **automatic volume control.**
average *n* Durchschnitt *m.*
average *v* den Durchschnitt berechnen *(Math)*; im Durchschnitt machen *(in marching, etc).*
average *adj* durchschnittlich, Durchschnitts-.
average error mittlerer Fehler, durchschnittlicher Fehler.
average performance Durchschnittsleistung *f.*
aviation Flugwesen *n*, Luftfahrt *f*, Fliegerei *f*; Flieger *mpl (collective term for any number of airplanes).*
aviation badge Fliegerabzeichen *n.*
aviation cadet Fähnrich der Flieger *(USA).*
aviation engineers Luftwaffenbautruppe *f.*
aviation fuel Fliegerkraftstoff *m.*
aviation gasoline Fliegerbenzin *n.*
aviation medicine Luftfahrtmedizin *f.*
aviation pay Luftdienstzulage *f*, Fliegerzulage *f.*
aviation support Fliegerhilfe *f*, Fliegerunterstützung *f*, Schlachtfliegerunterstützung *f (Tac).*
aviation weather service Flugwetterdienst *m.*
aviation weather station Flugwetterwarte *f.*
aviator Flieger *m.*
aviator's helmet Fliegerhaube *f.*
award Auszeichnung *f (citation)*; Orden *m*, Ehrenzeichen *n (decoration)*; Ehrensold *m (payment).*
ax Axt *f*, Beil *n.*
axial observation Beobachtung aus der Schußlinie *(Arty).*
axial road direkte Zufuhrstraße, direkte Anmarschstraße.
axial spotting Beobachtung in der Schußrichtung *(Arty).*
axis Achse *f*, Hauptlinie *f.*
Axis forces Achsenstreitkräfte *fpl.*
axis of advance Vormarschlinie *f.*
axis of an aircraft Flugzeugachse *f.*
axis of communication Verbindungsachse *f.*
axis of signal communication Nachrichtenachse *f.*
axis of supply Nachschublinie *f.*
axis of supply and evacuation Hauptnachschublinie *f.*
axis of the bore Seelenachse *f.*
axis of trunnions Schildzapfenachse *f (G).*
axle Radachse *f*, Achse *f.*
axle bearing Achslager *n.*
axle displacement Kletterfähigkeit *f (MT).*
axle drive Achsantrieb *m (MT).*
axle load Achsdruck *m (MT).*
axle nut Achsmutter *f.*
axle pivot pin Längszapfen *m (split-trail carriage).*
axle seats Achssitze *mpl (for gunners, G).*
axle spring Achsfeder *f (G).*
azimuth Seite *f*, Seitenrichtung *f*, Richtung *f (Gunnery)*; Azimut *m*, Scheitelkreis *m*, Scheitelbogen *m (Surv)*; Kompaßzahl *f*, Nadelzahl *f (compass)*; Kurs *m (Nav).*
azimuthal projection Azimutalprojektion *f.*
azimuth and elevation indicator Seiten- und Höhenempfänger *m (AA).*
azimuth change Teilringänderung *f (telescopic sight).*
azimuth circle Meßkreis *m (BC telescope)*, Richtkreis *m (Surv).*
azimuth controller Seitenrichtmann *m (AAA).*
azimuth difference Parallaxe *f*, Parallaxenwinkel *m (Optics).*
azimuth indicator Seitenempfänger *m (AA gun).*
azimuth instrument Peilapparat *m*, Peilgerät *n*, Peilscheibe *f*, Luftzielapparat *m*; Theodolit *m (Surv).*
azimuth knob Triebscheibe zur Seitenrichtung *(Ord).*
azimuth micrometer Teilring *m (telescopic sight).*
azimuth of target Kurswinkel *m*, Zielseitenwinkel in der Horizontalebene *(AAA)*; Zielseitenwinkel zum Abschußpunkt *(present position)*; Zielseitenwinkel zum Treffpunkt *(future position).*
azimuth reading Teilringzahl *f*, Nadelzahl *f (magnetic)*; Richtpunktzahl *f (aiming point).*
azimuth scale Teilring *m (panoramic sight)*; Seitenteilring *m (AA gun).*
azimuth setter Seitenrichtkanonier *m.*
azimuth tracking telescope Seitenrichtfernrohr *n (height finder).*

B

back-pack parachute Rückenfallschirm *m.*
back pad Kammkissen *n (harness).*
back-pad strap Kammkissengurt *m (harness).*
back plate Verschlußleiste *f (MG)*; Schloßplatte *f (G).*
back plate hinge pin Verschlußleistenachse *f (MG).*
back plate latch lock Zurrstück *n (MG).*
back rest Rückenlehne *f (Ap, MT)*; Rückenring *m (AA MG).*
backsight Rückblick *m (Surv).*
back step Schritt zurück.
bacteriological examination bakteriologische Untersuchung.
bachelor officers' quarters Offizierledigenheim *n.*
back Rücken *m.*
back azimuth der um 180° vermehrte (oder verminderte) Richtungswinkel *(Surv).*
back azimuth method Messen der rückwärtigen Verlängerung *(Surv)*; "Durchschlagen" *n (of a surveyor's transit).*
back bearing Wegflugpeilung *f (Air Navigation).*
backbone Rückgrat *n.*
backfire Fehlzündung *f (Mtr).*
backing light Rückfahrlaterne *f (MT).*
backlash Spiel *n*, Spielraum *m*, toter Gang.
bacteriological warfare Bakterienkrieg *m.*
bacteriologist Bakteriologe *m.*
badge Abzeichen *n.*
bad weather Unwetter *n.*
baffle Truhe *f*, Lautsprechertruhe *f (Rad)*; Schlingerwand *f (Ap tank)*; Zugdämpfer *m (engine muffler)*; Prallwand *f*, Leitwand *f.*
bag Sack *m*, Beutel *m*, Tasche *f.*
baggage Gepäck *n.*
baggage car Gepäckwagen *m (RR).*
baggage train Gepäcktroß *m.*
bail out abspringen, aussteigen *(Avn)*; ausschöpfen *(a boat).*
bakery Bäckerei *f.*
bakery company Bäckereikompanie *f.*
balance *n* Gewichtsverteilung *f*, Gleichgewicht *n (equilibrium)*; Waage *f (Inst).*
balance *v* ausgleichen.
balanced profile ausgeglichenes Profil.
balanced rudder ausgeglichenes Seitenruder, entlastetes Seitenruder *(Ap).*
balanced stock vorschriftsmäßige Bestände.
balanced surface ausgeglichene Tragfläche *(Ap).*
balance tab Ausgleichfläche *f*, Trimmruder *n (Ap).*
bale *n* Ballen *m.*
bale *v* in Ballen verpacken.
baling machine Ballenpresse *f.*
balk Längsträger *m*, Tragbalken *m (Bdg)*; Scherbalken *m (Pon).*
ball ammunition scharfe Munition.
ball-and-socket joint Kugelgelenk *n.*
ballast Ballast *m.*
ball bearing Kugellager *n.*
ball cartridge scharfe Patrone.
ball filler Kugelfüllung *f (shrapnel).*
ballistic ballistisch.
ballistic coefficient ballistischer Beiwert, Querschnittbelastung *f.*
ballistic correction Ausschalten der besonderen und Witterungseinflüsse.
ballistic curve Flugbahn *f*, Geschoßbahn *f*, ballistische Kurve.
ballistic density ballistisches Luftgewicht.
ballistic director Feuerleitgerät *n*, Kommandogerät *n*, Zielrechenmaschine *f (Gunnery).*
ballistic efficiency ballistische Leistungsfähigkeit *(Am).*
ballistics Schießlehre *f*, Ballistik *f.*
ballistic table Schußtafel *f.*
ballistic wave Kopfwelle *f.*
ballistic wind ballistischer Wind.
ballistite Ballistit *n (Am).*
ball mount Kugellafette *f*, Kugelblende *f (Tk).*
ballonet Luftsack *m (Bln).*
ballonet balloon Prallhaltevorrichtung *f.*
ballonet valve Luftsackventil *n.*
balloon Ballon *m.*
balloon barrage Ballonsperre *f.*
balloon basket Ballonkorb *m.*
balloon chief Ballontruppführer *m.*
balloon cover Ballonhülle *f.*
balloon crew Ballonmannschaft *f.*
balloon envelope Ballonhülle *f.*
balloon fabric Ballonstoff *m.*
balloon interval Ballonabstand *m.*
balloon net Ballonnetz *n.*
balloon observation Ballonbeobachtung *f.*
balloon observer Ballonbeobachter *m.*
balloon pilot Ballonführer *m.*
balloon position Verankerungsstelle *f (captive Bln).*
balloon site Ballonaufstiegplatz *m.*
balloon squad Ballontrupp *m.*
balloon tire Ballonreifen *m.*
ball projectile Vollgeschoß *n.*
ball socket Kugelpfanne *f (Mort).*
ball turret Bodenkanzel *f.*
ball turret gunner Bodenschütze *m.*
band Musikkorps *n*; Frequenzband *n (Rad)*; Band *n*, Binde *f (Clo, etc.).*
bandage *n* Verband *m*, Binde *f*, Bandage *f.*
bandage *v* verbinden.
band brake Bandbremse *f (MT).*
bandmaster Musikmeister *m (Ger: 2nd Lt).*
band of fire Feuerstrahl *m (MG).*
bandoleer Patronengurt *m.*
band saw Bandsäge *f.*
bandsman Spielmann *m (pl: Spielleute).*
bandspread Bandspreizung *f (Rad).*
band switch Grobstufenschalter *m (Rad).*
band width Bandbreite *f (Rad).*
bangalore torpedo in Rohr gefüllte Reihenladung.
bank *n* Schräglage *f (Ap)*; Ufer *n (river).*
bank *v* sich in die Kurve legen *(Avn).*
bank-and-turn indicator Kreiselneigungsmesser *m*, Wendezeiger *m (Ap).*
banner Banner *n.*
baptism of fire Feuertaufe *f.*
bar Rangabzeichen *n*, Ordensschnalle *f*, Ordensspange *f (insigne or decoration)*; Stab *m*, Stange *f (Tech)*; Sandbank *f*, Barre *f (rivers, etc.).*
barbed wire Stacheldraht *m.*
barbed-wire concertina S.-Rolle *f*, Stacheldrahtrolle *f.*
barbed-wire entanglement Stacheldrahtverhau *m*, Stacheldrahthindernis *n.*
barbette Geschützbank *f*, Barbette *f.*
barbette carriage Barbettelafette *f (G).*
bare wire blanker Draht *(Tp).*
barge Prahm *m.*
barn Scheune *f.*
barogram Barogramm *n.*
barograph Barograph *m.*
barometer Barometer *n*, Luftdruckmesser *m*; Federbarometer *n*, Federluftdruckmesser *m (aneroid).*
barometric pressure Außenluftdruck *m (Avn)*; Luftdruck *m (Met).*
barracks Kaserne *f.*
barrack(s) bag Bekleidungssack *m*, Wäschesack *m.*
barrage Sperre *f*; Feuersperre *f*, Sperrfeuer *n (Arty).*
barrage balloon Sperrballon *m.*
barrage chart Sperrfeuerskizze *f.*
barrage fire Sperrfeuer *n.*
barrage kite Sperrdrache *m.*
barrel Rohr *n (G)*; Lauf *m (SA)*; Mittelhand *f (horse)*; Faß *n*, Tonne *f (container).* See also **tube.**
barrel bracket Rohrhalter *m (G).*
barrel burst Rohrzerspringer *m.*
barrel erosion Ausbrennung *f*, Rohrabnutzung *f.*
barrel extension Rohransatz *m*, Rohransatzstück *n.*
barrel float Tonnenfloß *n.*
barrel guide Rohrklaue *f (G).*
barrel length Rohrlänge *f*, Seelenlänge *f (Ord).*
barrel-locking ring Laufsitzring *m (MG).*
barrel-locking stud Gewehrkupplungsstück *n (MG).*
barrel raft Tonnenfähre *f.*
barrel recoil Rohrrücklauf *m (G).*
barrel reflector Rohrwandbeobachtungsgerät *n (G)*; Laufseelenprüfer *m (R).*
barrel roll Rolle *f*, Überschlag über den Flügel *(Avn).*
barricade Barrikade *f.*
barrier Hindernis *n*, Sperre *f (Ft)*; Sperriegel *m (Tac).*
barrier detachment Sperrtrupp *m*, Sperrverband *m.*
barrier light Sperrlicht *n.*
barrier line Straßensperrung *f (MP).*
barrier zone Sperrzone *f.*
bascule bridge Klappbrücke *f.*
base Bettung *f (fixed gun)*; Boden *m*, Geschoßboden *m (Am)*; Stützpunkt *m (Tac)*; Visierfuß *m (of rear sight)*; Hülsenboden *m (of cartridge case)*; Wolkenuntergrenze *f (of cloud).*
base angle Grundrichtungswinkel *m (Gunnery)*; Winkel zwischen Grundrichtungslinie und Orientierungslinie *(Surv).*
base bushing Grundbuchse *f (of counterrecoil mechanism).*
base charge Bodenkammerladung *f (Am).*
base cover Abschlußplättchen *n (Am).*
base deflection die vom Grundgeschütz aus gemessene Seitenänderung *(Gunnery).*
base delay-action fuze Bodenabstandszünder *m (Am).*
base depot rückwärtiges Nachschublager.
base detonating fuze Bodenzünder *m.*
base end station Stand einer Langbasisanlage *(CA)*; Meßstand *m (AAA).*
base fuze Bodenzünder *m (Am).*
base hospital Kriegslazarett *n.*
base line Grundrichtungslinie *f (Gunnery)*; Standlinie *f (Surv).*
base-line arm Basislineal *n (plotting protractor).*
base-line direction Grundrichtung *f (Gunnery).*
base machine gun Grundmaschinengewehr *n*, Leit-Maschinengewehr *n.*
base of operations Operationsbasis *f (Tac).*
base of the trajectory Mündungswaagerechte *f.*
base pay Grundgehalt *n*, Löhnung *f.*
base piece Grundgeschütz *n (Arty).*
base plate Bodenplatte *f (Mort)*; Grundplatte *f (Tech).*
base point Grundrichtungspunkt *m (Gunnery).*
base ring Fundamentring *m (Ord).*
base section hinterer Abschnitt des rückwärtigen Gebiets.
base services Bodendienst *m (Avn).*
base stake Richtlatte *f (Surv).*
basic allowance Sollbestand *m.*
basic data Schußwerte *mpl*, Schußelemente *npl*, Schießunterlagen *fpl*, Schießgrundlagen *fpl.*
basic load Tagesrate *f (Am)*; ständige Belastung, bleibende Belastung *(Avn).*
basic tactical unit taktische Einheit; Feuereinheit der Artillerie *(Arty).*
basic training Grundausbildung *f.*
basic training course Schießvorschule *f (Arty).*
basic unit See **basic tactical unit.**
basket Korb *m.*
bastion Bastion *f.*
baton Marschallstab *m*; Tambourstock *m*, Bataillonstambourstock *m.*
battalion Bataillon *n*, Abteilung *f.*
battalion aid station Bataillonsverbandplatz *m.*
battalion combat train Gefechtstroß eines Bataillons.
battalion commander Abteilungskommandeur *m*, Bataillonsführer *m*, Bataillonskommandeur *m.*
battalion command post Abteilungsgefechtsstand *m*, Bataillonsgefechtsstand *m.*
battalion communication section Bataillonsnachrichtenstaffel *f*, Abteilungsnachrichtenstaffel *f.*
battalion headquarters Bataillonsstab *m*, Abteilungsstab *m.*
battalion sector Bataillonsabschnitt *m.*
battalion train Bataillonstroß *m*, Bataillonskolonne *f.*
batter Böschungsanlage *f (Ft).*
battered round verbeulte Patrone *(Am).*
battery Batterie *f (Arty, Elec)*; Element *n (cell)*; Sammlerbatterie *f*, Sammler *m (storage).*
battery box Batteriekasten *m*, Sammlerkasten *m (Elec).*
battery charger Lademaschine *f.*
battery-charging unit Lademaschinensatz *m.*
battery chart Schießliste *f.*
battery commander Batteriechef *m*, Batterieführer *m.*
battery commander's telescope Scherenfernrohr *n.*
battery cover Sammlerhaube *f*, Zellendeckel *m (Elec).*
battery detail See **battery headquarters detail.**
battery emplacement book Schießkladde *f.*
battery executive Batterieoffizier *m.*
battery front Batteriefront *f.*
battery headquarters detail Batterietrupp *m.*
battery ignition Batteriezündung *f (Mtr).*
battery-location plot Batteriebild *n (sound ranging).*
battery manning table Batterietafel *f.*
battery position Geschützstellung *f*, Batteriestand *m*, Batteriestellung *f (Arty).*
battery survey chart Stellungsmeßblatt *n.*
battery-target line Linie Grundgeschütz-Ziel.
battery tester Elementprüfer *m (Elec).*
battle Schlacht *f*, Kampf *m*, Gefecht *n.*
battle casualty Ausfall *m*, Gefechtsausfall *m.*
battle casualty report Verlustmeldung *f.*
battle chart Einschießplan *m (Arty).*
battle clasp Erinnerungsspange *f.*

battle command Kampfführung f.
battle cruiser Schlachtkreuzer m.
battle fatigue Kriegsneurose f.
battlefield Schlachtfeld n, Kampffeld n.
battle flag Sturmfahne f.
battle fleet Schlachtflotte f.
battle honor Kriegsband n, Fahnenband n.
battle injury Kampfwunde f.
battle line Schlachtlinie f, Kampflinie f.
battle map Gefechtskarte f.
battle of attrition Abnutzungskampf m.
battle of encirclement Einkreisungsschlacht f.
battle of extermination Vernichtungskampf m.
battle performance Kampfleistung f.
battle position Hauptkampffeld n, Kampfstellung f.
battle reconnaissance Gefechtsaufklärung f.
battle reserves Reserve f.
battle service practice Schulgefechtsschießen n (Arty).
battleship Schlachtschiff n.
battle sight Standvisier n (R); Fliegervisier n (MG).
battle star Erinnerungsstern m.
battle terrain Kampfgelände n.
battle zone Kampfzone f.
bay Feld n, Gerippeabteil n, Zelle f (Ap); Strecke f, Brückenstrecke f, Brückenglied n (Bdg); Bucht f (sea inlet).
bayonet Seitengewehr n, Bajonett n.
bayonet charge Bajonettangriff m.
bayonet fighting Bajonettfechten n.
bayonet grip Seitengewehrgriff m, Bayonettgriff m.
bayonet guard Parierstange f.
bayonet joint Bajonettkupplung f (Mech).
bayonet lock Seitengewehrverschluß m (R).
bayonet practice Übung im Bajonettfechten.
bayonet scabbard Seitengewehrtasche f.
bayonet stud Seitengewehrhalter m (R).
bayonet thrust Bajonettstoß m.
"bazooka" "Ofenrohr" n. See also **antitank rocket launcher.**
"B" battery Anodenbatterie f (Rad).
BC telescope Scherenfernrohr n.
beach Strand m.
beach defense Strandsperre f, Strandverteidigung f.
beachhead Landekopf m.
beaching gear Schwimmerwagen m, Schleppwagen m (seaplane).
beaching party Landungsabteilung f.
beacon Bake f, Feuer n; Funkbake f, Funkfeuer n (Rad).
beacon light Leuchtfeuer n (Avn).
beacon lighting Nachtbefeuerung f (Avn).
bead sight Perlkorn n (R).
beam Balken m, Träger m (Engr); Strahl m (ray); Peilstrahl m (Rad); Lichtkegel m, Lichtstrahl m (SL).
bearing Peilung f, Peilrichtung f, Peillinie f (Navigation); Lager n (Mech).
bearing line Peillinie f (Air Navigation).
bearing metal Lagermetall n.
bearing plate Peilscheibe f, Peilaufsatz m, Kursscheibe f (Air Navigation).
bearing station Peilort m, Peilstelle f (Air Navigation).
bearing surface Lauffläche f (Mech); Auflagefläche f (Engr); Tragerand m (hoof).
beaten track Trampelweg m.
beaten zone bestrichener Raum (firing).
beat frequency Schwebungsfrequenz f (Rad).
Beaufort scale Beaufortskala f (Met).
beaver dam Biberwehr n (Engr).
bed Bett n.
bedbug Wanze f.
bedding Bettzeug n (for Pers); Streu f (for animals).
bedding roll Bettzeugrolle f.
bed sheets Bettbezug m.
beef Rindfleisch n, Ochsenfleisch n.
beef stew Gulasch n.
beer Bier n.
Behm sound-ranging altimeter Behmlot n (Avn).
belligerent n kriegführende Macht.
belligerent adj. kriegführend.
belly Bauch m; Unterseite f (Tk).
belly landing Bauchlandung f (Avn).
belly tank Abwurfbehälter m (Ap).
belly turret Bodenkanzel f (Ap).
belt Gurt m (MG); Streifen m (Top); Gürtel m, Koppel n (Clo).
belt buckel Koppelschloß n.
belt conveyor Gurtförderer m.
belt drive Riemenantrieb m.
belted ammunition gegurtete Munition (MG).
belt-fed mit Gurtzuführung (MG).
belt feed Gurtladung f, Zuführer m, Gurtzuführer m (MG).
belt-feed guide Gurthebel m (MG).
belt-feed lever Zubringerhebel m, Patronenträgerhebel m (MG).
belt-feed pawl Gurtschieber m (MG).
belt-filling machine See **belt-loading machine.**
belt-loaded mit Gurtzuführung (MG).
belt-loading machine Gurtfüller m.
belt road Querverbindungsstraße f.
bench Bank f; Werkbank f (Tech).
bench mark Nivellementspunkt m.
bend Straßenbiegung f (road).
bending machine Biegemaschine f.
bends Höhenkrankheit f (aeroembolism); Caisson-Krankheit f (caisson disease).
beneficiary Nutznießer m, Empfangsberechtigter m.
bent Joch n, Bock m (Bdg).
benzol Benzol n.
benzyl bromide Benzylbromid n, T-Stoff m (CWS).
berm Berme f (Ft).
berth Bett n (Nav, RR); Liegeplatz m (of a ship).
besiege belagern.
Bessel method Rückwärtseinschneiden n (Surv).
betray verraten.
bevel Schräge f.
bevel drive pinion Antriebskegelrad n (differential gear) (MT).
bevel gear Kegelrad n, Kegelzahnrad n.
bevel-gear rear-axle drive Kegelrad-Hinterachsantrieb m.
beverage Getränk n.
bias Gittervorspannung f (Rad); schräger Schnitt (slant cut); Voreingenommenheit f (prejudice).
bible Bibel f.
bicarbonate of soda doppelkohlensaures Natrium.
Bickford fuze Bickford-Leitfeuer n (Engr).
bicycle Fahrrad n, Rad n.
Big Dipper Großer Bär.
bilateral observation Beobachten mit zwei Beobachtungsstellen (Arty).
bill Rechnung f.
billet dispensary Ortskrankenstube f (Med).
billet hospital Ortskrankenlazarett n (Med).
billeting Unterbringung f.
billeting area Unterkunftsbezirk m.
billeting detail See **billeting party.**
billeting equipment Unterkunftsgerät n.
billeting officer Quartiermacher m.
billeting party Quartiermachertrupp m.
billets Unterbringung f, Ortsunterkunft f, Ortsbiwak n.
bill of lading Frachtbrief m, Verladungsschein m.
bill of particulars Tatbericht m.
binaural balance Mitteneindruck m (Sound Locating).
binaural method Zwei-Ohr-Verfahren n, Binauralverfahren n (Sound Locating).
binaural trainer Horcherprüf- und Übungsgerät n.
binder Einbanddeckel für lose Blätter (loose-leaf cover).
binder ring Dichtring m (gas mask).
binding post Anschlußklemme f, Polklemme f (Elec).
binocular adj binokular, zweiäugig (Optics).
binocular n Glas n, Fernglas n, Doppelglas n.
biplane Doppeldecker m.
bipod Zweibein n, Gabelstütze f (MG).
birth certificate Geburtsurkunde f.
birthmark Muttermal n.
biscuit Keks m-n, Biskuit m-n.
bit Gebiß n, Trense f, Kandare f (curb bit, harness); Bohrer m, Schneide f (carpenter's drill).
bite Stich m (of insect); Biß m (of animal).
biting angle kleinster Panzerdurchschlagswinkel (Am).
bit ring Zügelring m (harness).
bitumen Bitumen n.
bivouac Biwak n, Feldlager n.
bivouac commander Biwakskommandant m (ranking officer at a bivouac).
bivouac security officer Offizier vom Biwakdienst.
bivouac site Biwakplatz m.
black schwarz.
blackboard schwarze Tafel, schwarzes Brett.
blackjack Totschläger m.
blackout n Verdunkelung f.
black-out v schwarz vor den Augen werden (Avn); verdunkeln (lights).
blackout light Tarnscheinwerfer m (MT).
blackout measures Verdunkelungsmaßnahmen fpl (AA defense).
black powder Schwarzpulver n, Naßbrandpulver n.
blacksmith Schmied m. See also **horseshoer.**
blade Blatt n, Flügel m (propeller); Klinge f (of knife, etc.).
blade angle Steigungswinkel m, Anstellwinkel m (propeller).
blank Platzpatrone (Am); Vordruck m, Formular n (printed form).
blank ammunition Platzpatronen fpl.
blank cartridge Platzpatrone f, Manöverkartusche f.
blanket n Decke f, Marschdecke f; Wolldecke f (woolen); Woilach m (saddle); künstlicher Nebel, Nebeldecke f (CWS).
blanket v verschleiern, vernebeln, einnebeln, abschirmen.
blanket door Gasschutzvorhang m.
blanketing smoke Nebelwand f, Nebelschleier m (CWS).
blanket roll Bettzeugrolle f.
blank fire powder Nitrozellulosepulver n (Small Arms).
blank form Formular n.
blank shell blindgeladene Granate (Am).
blast n Luftdruck m, Detonationsdruck m, Luftstoß m, Zerknallstoß m (pressure); Sprengung f, Explosion f (explosion).
blast v sprengen.
blast effect Luftdruckwirkung f, Luftstoß m.
blast furnace Hochofen m.
blasting Sprengen n.
blasting cap Sprengkapsel f.
blasting cartridge Sprengpatrone f, Bohrpatrone f.
blasting charge Sprengladung f; Bohrladung f (borehole); Schnellladung f (emergency).
blasting-charge box Ladungskasten m.
blasting-charge can Ladungsbüchse f.
blasting-charge container Ladungsgefäß n.
blasting fuze Zeitzündschnur f, Zeitschnur f (Engr).
blasting machine Glühzündapparat m (Engr).
blasting oil Sprengöl n (nitroglycerin).
blasting pit Sprenggrube f (Engr).
blasting powder Sprengpulver n (black powder).
bleach Bleichmittel n.
bleaching powder Chlorkalk m.
bleed bluten; entlüften (recoil mechanism).
blend anpassen (Cam).
blimp unstarres Kleinluftschiff.
blind v blind machen, blenden.
blind adj blind.
blind flying See **instrument flying.**
blinker Blinklampe f. See also **signal lamp.**
blinker light Blinkfeuer n, Taktfeuer n.
blinker signal Blinkzeichen n.
blister Torpedowulst m (Nav); MG.-Warze f (Ap); Blase f (Med).
blister agent ätzender Kampfstoff (CWS).
blister gas Hautgift n, ätzender Kampfstoff (CWS).
block Sperre f (Ft); Block m, Klotz m (Engr); Kettenglied n (Tk, Trac); Haltezeichen n (RR block signal); Bremsklotz m (wheel); Sprengkörper m (explosive).
blockade Blockade f, Sperre f.
block and tackle Flaschenzug m.
"blockbuster" schwere Sprengbombe.
blockhouse Blockhaus n (Ft).
blocking Sperrung f (by means of obstacles).
block warden Blockwart m (Civ Defense).
blood Blut n.
blood donor Blutspender m.
blood group See **blood type.**
blood plasma Blutplasma n.
blood-poisoning Blutvergiftung f.
blood type Blutgruppe f.
blouse See **service coat.**
blowback Rückschlag m (Ord).
blowback-operated weapon Gasdrucklader m.
blower Gebläse n (Ap engine).
blown primer Zündhütchenausfall m.
blowtorch Lötlampe f.
blow up sprengen (blast); aufblasen (inflate).
bludgeon Knüppel m.
blue blau.
blueprint Blaupause f.
bluff Felsenklippe f, Klippe f (Top).
board n Brett n (wood); Ausschuß m (committee).
board v einsteigen (a vehicle); beköstigen, verköstigen (to supply meals); in Kost sein (to receive meals).
board of officers Ehrenrat m; Offiziersausschuß m.
boardwalk Bretterbahn f.
boat Boot n, Kahn m.
boat crew Fahrtrupp m (Engr).
boat ferry Kahnfähre f (Engr).
boat hook Bootshaken m.
boatswain Bootsmann m (Nav).
boat-tail Verjüngung nach hinten (Am).
bobbing target Klappscheibe f, Verschwindscheibe f (practice firing).
body Körper m; Walze f (Am); Zünderkörper m, Zündergehäuse n (fuze); Zünderteller m (powder-train time fuze); Aufbau m (MT); Fernrohrkörper m (binocular); Geschoßhülle f (projectile); Gasmaskenkörper m (gas mask).
body armor Panzerweste f (Avn).
bodyguard Leibgarde f, Leibwache f.
Bofors gun Bofors-Maschinenkanone f.
bog Sumpf m, Moor n, Morast m.
bog down versacken.
bogie Rollenwagen m (Tk); Rollbock m (Arty).
bogie trailer Rollbock m (Arty).
bogie wheel Laufrad n, Laufrolle f (Tk).
boil v kochen.
boiler Kessel m.
bolo philippinisches Hackmesser.
bolt Verschluß m, Kammer f (R, pistol); Verschlußzylinder m (Small Arms); Bolzen m (Mech).
bolt assembly Schloß n (MG, R).
bolt base Schloßfuß m (MG).
bolt catch Kammerfang m (MG).
bolt-catch piece Kammerfangstück n (pistol).
bolt handle Kammerstengel m (R); Kammergriff m, Schloßhebel m (MG).
bolt housing Schloßgehäuse n (MG).
bolt knob Kammerknopf m (R).
bolt lock Rasthebel m (MG).
bolt lug Kammerwarze f (R).
bolt mechanism Zylinderverschluß m, Schloß n (R).
bolt sleeve Schlößchen n (R).
bolt slide Kammerbahn f (R).
bolt support Schloßhalter m (MG).
bolt thread Bolzengewinde (MT).
bomb n Bombe f, Fliegerbombe f.
bomb v bombardieren, bomben.
bombard bombardieren, bomben.
bombardier Bombenschütze m.
bombardier's compartment Bombenschützenstand m (Ap).
bombardment Bombardierung f, Kanonade f (Arty); Bombenangriff m (Avn).
bombardment airplane Bomber m, Bombenflugzeug n, Kampfflugzeug n, Kampfmaschine f.
bombardment aviation Kampffliegerei f; Bombenflieger mpl, Kampfflieger mpl.
bombardment formation Kampffliegerverband m (Avn).
bombardment group Kampfgruppe f, Kampffliegergruppe f (Avn).
bombardment school Kampfschule f (Avn).
bombardment squadron Kampfstaffel f, Kampffliegerstaffel f (Avn).
bombardment wing Kampfgeschwader n, Luftkampfgeschwader n (Avn).
bomb bay Bombenkammer f, Bombenmagazin n (Ap).
bomb-bay doors Bombenklappe f (Ap).
bomb case Bombenhülle f.
bomb control Bombenabzughebel m (Ap).
bomb control mechanism Bombenabwurfvorrichtung f, Bombenauslösungsvorrichtung f (Ap).
bomb crater Bombenloch n.
bomb disposal officer Bombenräumoffizier m.
bomb disposal unit Bombenräumtrupp m, Sprengkommando n.
bomber Bomber m, Bombenflugzeug n, Kampfflugzeug n.
bomber command Kampffliegerkommando n (USA).
bomber-fighter See **fighter-bomber.**
bomber formation Kampfverband m (Avn).
bomber pilot Kampfflieger m.
bomber squadron Kampfstaffel f.
bomber wing Kampfgeschwader n, Bombengeschwader n.
bomb fuze Bombenzünder m.
bomb hit Bombeneinschlag m, Bombentreffer m.
bomb hoist Bombeneinhängevorrichtung f.
bomb hole Bombenloch n.
bombing Bomben n, Bombenwurf m, Bombardierung f.
bombing altitude Angriffshöhe f, Abwurfhöhe f.
bombing approach Anflug m.
bombing attack Bombenangriff m.
bombing formation Kampfverband m (Avn).
bombing raid Bombenangriff m.
bomb load Bombenlast f.
bomb nose Bombenkopf m.
bombproof bombensicher, bombenfest.
bombproof shelter bombensichere Deckung.
bomb rack Schacht m, Bombenschacht m, Abwurfschacht m (Ap).
bomb rack control Bombenabzughebel m (Ap).
bomb release Wurf m, Abwurf m, Bombenwurf m, Bombenauslösung f.
bomb release altitude Abwurfhöhe f.
bomb release controls Bombenabwurfgerät n.
bomb release handle Bombenhebel m.
bomb release line Auslöselinie f.
bomb release mechanism Bombenabwurfvorrichtung f, Bombenauslösungsvorrichtung f.
bomb release point Auslösepunkt m.
bomb-resistant bombensicher, bombenfest.
"Bombs away!" "Wurf!"
bomb shackle Tragvorrichtung f (Ap).
bomb sight Zielgerät n, Abwurfzielgerät n, Bombenzielgerät n, Bombenzielvorrichtung f, Bombenzielapparat m, Bombenvisier n, Bombenrichtgerät n.
bomb target area Bombenwurfplatz m.
bomb trailer Bomben-Zubringewagen m.
bomb train Bombenreihe f.
bomb trajectory Fallbahn f, Wurfbahn f, Wurfparabel f, Bombenflugbahn f, Bombenfallkurve f, Bombenabwurfkurve f.
bone Knochen m; Gräte f (of fish).
bonus Handgeld n.
booby trap Sprengfalle f, Schreckladung f, Schreckmine f.
boom Ladebaum m (of a crane); schwimmende Balkensperre (water obstacle).
boom defense vessel Sperrwachboot n.
boost aufladen, verstärken.
booster Schlagladung f (fuze).
booster charge Beiladung f, Anfeuerungssatz m (Am).
boot Stiefel m (Clo); Tasche f, Schuh m (holster).
border Grenze f.
border area Grenzgebiet n.
border incident Grenzzwischenfall m.
bore n Rohrseele f, Seele f (Ord); Rohrinneres n (G); Laufinneres n (Small Arms); Bohrung f (Mech).
bore v bohren.
bore brush Reinigungsbürste f (Ord).
bore gage Meßpatrone f (Small Arms); Kaliberzylinder m, Kaliberring m.
borehole Minenrohr n, Bohrloch n.
borehole blasting charge Bohrladung f.
bore-safe and detonator-safe fuze rohrsicherer Zünder mit Sprengkapselsicherung (Am).
bore-safe fuze rohrsicherer Zünder.
bore sight Ziellinienprüfer m, Justiergerät n (Ord).
bore-sight adjustment Justieren n (G).
boric acid Borsäure f.
borrow pit Erdgrube f.
bottleneck Flaschenhals m (figuratively and literally); Engpaß m (Top).
bottom chord Untergurt m (truss).
bottom gun carriage Unterlafette f.
boulder Felsblock m, großer Stein.
"bouncing baby" See **bounding mine.**
bound Sprung m (jump).
boundary Grenze f, Abschnittsgrenze f, Nahtstelle f (between units), Trennungslinie f.
boundary layer Grenzschicht f (fluid mechanics).
boundary light Umrandungsfeuer n, Randfeuer n (Adrm).
bounding mine S-Mine f, Schrapnellmine f.
bounds Einzelsprünge mpl (method of advancing).
by bounds sprungweise.
bourrelet Zentrierwulst m; Führungswulst m (rear).
bow Bug m (Ap, Nav, Tk).
bow compartment Vorderkaffe f (Pon).
bowden control cable Bowdenzug m.
bow gun Buggeschütz n, Bugfeuergeschütz n (Tk).
bow gunner Bugschütze m (Ap, Tk).
bow-on Stirnansicht f.
bow-on silhouette Stirnschattenriß m (practice target).
bow wave Kopfwelle f (Ballistics).
box Kasten m, Schachtel f.
box barrage Feuerabriegelung f.
box car gedeckter Güterwagen (RR).
box girder Kastenträger m.
box in Feuerabriegelung schießen.
box level Dosenlibelle f.
box magazine Kastenmagazin n.
box-trail gun carriage Kastenlafette f.
brace n Strebe f (structures); Bohrwinde f (a tool).
brace v abspreizen, absteifen.
braced verspannt.
bracing Auskreuzung f, Verspannung f, Verstrebung f.
bracket n Gabelung f, Eingabelung f (Arty).

bracket *v* gabeln, eingabeln *(Arty)*.
bracket adjustment Gabelbilden *n*.
bracket fire Gabelschießen *n*.
bracketing Gabelbildung *f*, Eingabeln *n*.
bracketing correction Gabelschießen *n*.
bracketing elevation Erhöhung zum Gabelbilden.
bracketing method Gabelbilden *n*.
bracketing salvo gabelbildende Salve.
bracket seat Schildlager *n (G)*.
braid Borte *f*, Tresse *f (Clo)*.
brake *n* Bremse *f (MT, Ord)*.
brake *v* abbremsen.
brake arm Bremsarm *m (gun-carriage wheel brake)*.
brake band Bremsband *n (MT)*.
brake bushing Bremsbuchse *f (recoil mechanism)*.
brake cable Zugriemen *m*.
brake cylinder Bremszylinder *m (MT)*.
brake drum Bremstrommel *f*, Bremsscheibe *f*.
brake equalization Bremsausgleich *m (MT)*.
brake fluid Bremsflüssigkeit *f*.
brake horsepower Bremsleistung *f*, Nutzleistung *f*.
brake lever Bremshebel *m (G, MT)*.
brake lining Bremsbelag *m*.
brake pedal Fußbremshebel *m*, Bremsfußhebel *m*, Bremstritt *m*, Bremspedal *n (MT)*.
brake release spring Bremsfeder *f (MT)*.
brake rod Bremsgestänge *n (MT)*.
brakeshoe Bremsklaue *f (gun-carriage wheel)*; Bremsbacke *f*, Bremsklotz *m*.
braking effect Bremswirkung *f*.
branch Waffengattung *f (of the Army)*; Ast *m*, Zweig *m (of a tree)*; Filiale *f*, Zweigstelle *f (of a bank, business)*; Nebenstelle *f (of a post office)*; Abteilung *f (Adm)*.
branch depot Zweigpark *m*, Zweiglager *n*.
branch of the service Dienstzweig *m*, Waffengattung *f*, Truppengattung *f*.
brand Marke *f*, Sorte *f (of commercial product)*.
brass Messing *n*.
brassard Armbinde *f*.
brass knuckles Schlagring *m*.
breach *n* Bresche *f*, Sturmlücke *f*, Einbruchstelle *f*.
breach *v* einbrechen *(a line)*; eine Bresche schießen *(a wall, etc.)*.
breaching charge Sprengladung *f*.
breaching line Trennschnitt *m (demolitions)*.
breaching point Sprengstelle *f (demolitions)*.
breach of discipline Disziplinarvergehen *n*, Übertretung *f*, Vergehen *n*, Verfehlung *f*.
bread Brot *n*.
break *n* Bruch *m*; Trennung *f (Rad procedure)*.
break *v* brechen; degradieren, herabsetzen *(demote)*.
breakage Bruch *m*.
break camp das Lager abbrechen.
breakdown Zusammenbruch *m (collapse)*; Panne *f (of vehicle)*; Betriebsstörung *f (Tp, Com, etc.)*; Gliederung *f (analysis)*.
break down eine Panne erleiden *(MT)*; zusammenbrechen *(physical collapse)*; zerlegen, zergliedern *(analyze, decompose)*.
break in einfahren *(a vehicle)*; einarbeiten *(Pers)*; zureiten, abrichten *(a horse)*.
break-in procedure Dazwischensprechen *n (Rad)*.
break loose losbrechen.
break off combat das Gefecht abbrechen.
break ranks wegtreten.
break-through Durchbruch *m (Tac)*.
break up abschlagen, abweisen *(an attack)*; auseinandertreiben *(a crowd)*; zerschlagen, zersplittern *(into pieces)*; aufklären *(of clouds, weather)*.
breakwater Wellenbrecher *m*.
breast harness Sielengeschirr *n*.
breastplate Brustblatt *n (harness)*.
breastplate harness Vorderzeug *n*.
breast strap Halskoppel *f (harness)*.
breastwork Brustwehr *f*.
breather Entlüftungsstutzen *m (Mtr)*.
breech Bodenstück *n (G)*.
breechblock Verschlußblock *m (screw-type breech)*; Verschlußkeil *m (wedge-type breech)*; Verschlußstück *n*, Kartuschestück *n*, Ladeklappe *f*, Stoßboden *m (Ord)*.
breechblock carrier Verschlußträger *m (G)*.
breechblock wedge Verschlußkeil *m (G)*.
breech bore gage Kaliberzylinder *m*, Kaliberring *m*.
breech cover Verschlußüberzug *m (G)*.
breeches Reithosen *fpl*.
breeching Umgang *m*, Hinterzeug *n (harness)*.
breechlock Verschluß *m*, Geschützverschluß *m (Ord)*.
breech mechanism Verschluß *m*, Verschlußsystem *n*, Geschützverschluß *m*, Ladevorrichtung *f (Ord)*.
breech piece Laufmundstück *n (R)*.
breech recess Patroneneinlage *f (R)*; Keilloch *n (G)*.
breech ring Verschlußring *m*, Verschraubungsstück *n (G)*.
breech wedge Verschlußkeil *m*.
Bren gun Bren-Maschinengewehr *n*.
brevet rank Rang eines charakterisierten oder ernannten Offiziers.
brevity code Funkverkehrsabkürzungen *fpl (Rad)*.
bribe *v* bestechen; schmieren *(slang)*.
bribery Bestechung *f*.
brickyard Ziegelei *f*.
bridge *n* Brücke *f*; Floßbrücke *f (floating)*; Schnellbrücke *f (hasty)*.
bridge *v* eine Brücke schlagen, eine Brücke bauen.
bridge bay Brückenstrecke *f*.
bridge capacity Verkehrslast *f*.
bridge center line Brückenachse *f*, Brückenlinie *f*.
bridge commander Brückenkommandant *m*.
bridge construction Brückenschlag *m*, Brückenbau *m*.
bridge-construction party Brückentrupp *m*.
bridge diagram Brückenskizze *f*.
bridge equipage *See* **bridge equipment.**
bridge equipment Brückengerät *n*, Kriegsbrückengerät *n*, Brückenbaugerät *n*, Übergangsgerät *n*.
bridge foundation Brückenunterbau *m*.
bridgehead Brückenkopf *m*, Brückenkopfstellung *f (Tac)*.
bridgehead line Brückenkopflinie *f*.
bridge railing Brückengeländer *n*.
bridge roadway Brückenbahn *f*.
bridge site Brückenstelle *f*.
bridge span Brückenstützweite *f*.
bridge structure Brückenbau *m*.
bridge superstructure Brückenüberbau *m*.
bridge traffic control post Ablaufposten *m*.
bridge train Brückenkolonne *f (Engr)*.
bridge trestle Brückenbock *m*.
bridle Zaumzeug *n (harness)*.
brief *v* den Flug besprechen *(Avn)*.
briefing Flugbesprechung *f*, Einsatzbesprechung *f*; Befehlsausgabe *f (issuance of orders)*.
brigade Brigade *f*.
brigade commander Brigadeführer *m*, Brigadekommandeur *m*.
brigade headquarters Brigadekommando *n*.
brigadier general Generalmajor *m*; Generalmajor der Flieger *(Luftwaffe)*; Generalarzt *m (Med)*; Generalveterinär *m (Vet)*.
bright light Fernlicht *n (on auto headlight)*.
bring down abschießen *(an Ap)*.
brisance Brisanz *f*.
broadcast *n* Rundfunk *m*.
broadcast *v* rundfunken.
broadcasting Rundfunk *m*.
broadcasting station Rundfunksender *m*.
broadside Breitseite *f (Nav)*.
broken wolkig, fast bedeckt *(Met)*.
broken outlines zerlegte Formen *(Cam)*.
broken stone Steinschlag *m*.
bromacetone Bromazeton *n*, B-Stoff *m (CWS)*.
brombenzylcyanide Brombenzylzyanid *n*, T-Stoff *m (CWS)*.
bronchitis Luftröhrenkatarrh *m*, Bronchialkatarrh *m*.
bronze Bronze *f*.
brow band Stirnriemen *m* (harness).
Browning automatic rifle Browning-Selbstladegewehr *n*.
Browning machine gun Browning-Maschinengewehr *n*.
brush Bürste *f*, Pinsel *m*; Anstrichpinsel *m (paint)*; Gebüsch *n (undergrowth)*; Strauch *m (brushwood)*; Scharmützel *n (skirmish)*.
brush hurdle Hurde *f*.
brush road Strauchdamm *m*.
brushwood Dickicht *n (thicket)*; Strauch *m (broken branches, bushes, etc.)*.
brushwork Flechtwerk *n*, Strauchwerk *n*, Strauchpackung *f*.
brushwork revetment Spreutlage *f*.
bucket Kübel *m*, Eimer *m*.
buckle *n* Koppelschloß *n*.
buckle *v* knicken.
buckling Knicken *n (march column)*.
"buddy" "Kumpel" *m*.
budget Etat *m*.
budget item Etatposten *m*.
buffer Auffangvorrichtung des Rückstoßes, Puffer *m (Ord)*.
buffer spring Rücklauffeder *f (MG)*.
buffing Polieren *n*.
buggy whip antenna Stabantenne *f*.
bugle Horn *n*, Trompete *f*.
bugle call Trompetensignal *n*, Hornsignal *n*.
bugler Hornist *m*, Trompeter *m*.
building Gebäude *n*.
built-up area bebautes Gelände.
built-up barrel Ringrohr *n*, Mantelringrohr *n (G)*.
bulb Glühbirne *f*, Birne *f (Elec)*; Ballen *m (horse)*.
bulk container Packgefäß *n*.
bulkhead Spant *m*, Rumpfspant *m*, Schott *n (Ap)*.
bulk reduction point Eisenbahntankstelle *f (RR)*.
bulldozer Planier-Raupenschlepper *m*, mechanischer Pflugbagger.
bullet Geschoß *n*, Kugel *f*.
bullet drop Geschoßfall *m (Ballistics)*.
bulletin Ankündigung *f*, Bekanntmachung *f (notice)*; Nachrichtenblatt *n (publication)*.
bulletin board Anschlagtafel *f*.
bulletproof kugelsicher, kugelfest, schußfest, schußsicher.
bulletproof glass schußsicheres Glas, beschußsicheres Glas, Panzerglas *n*.
bullet-resisting inner tube schußsicherer Schlauch *(MT)*.
bullet tube Geschoßkanal *m (grenade launcher)*.
bullet wound Schußwunde *f*, Schußverletzung *f*.
bull's eye Spiegel *m*, Zentrum *n*, Zielschwarze *n*, "Das Schwarze."
bump Windstoß *m (Avn)*; Höcker *m*, Rast *f (road)*.
bumper Stoßfänger *m* Stoßstange *f (MT)*.
buna tire Bunareifen *m (MT)*.
bungee mechanische Hilfsvorrichtung *(Ap)*.
bunk Koje *f*.
bunker Bunker *m*.
bunting Fahnentuch *n*, Flaggentuch *n*; Flaggenschmuck *m*.
buoy Boje *f*, Tonne *f*.
buoyancy Auftrieb *m*, Hubkraft *f (Avn)*; Schwimmkraft *f (Nav)*.
bureau Amt *n*, Bureau *n*, Büro *n*.
burial Begräbnis *n*, Beerdigung *f*, Bestattung *f*.
burial detail Bestattungskommando *n*.
burlap Sackleinen *n*.
burn *n* Brandwunde *f*.
burn *v* brennen, verbrennen.
burning rate Brenngeschwindigkeit *f (cord fuze)*.
burning time Leuchtdauer *f (Sig)*.
burst *n* Stoß *m*, Feuerstoß *m (MG)*.
burst *v* bersten, zerspringen, platzen.
burst center mittlerer Sprengpunkt.
burst effect Zerknallstoß *m*, Sprengwirkung *f (Am)*.
burster Sprengladung *f (Am)*.
burster course Zerschellerschicht *f (Ft)*.
burster tube Kammerhülsenrohr *n*, Sprengladungsröhre *f (Am)*.
bursting charge Sprengladung *f*, Sprengstoffgehalt *m*, Sprengsatz *m (Am)*.
burst interval Aufschlagweite *f (Gunnery)*.
burst of fire Feuerstoß *m (MG)*.
burst wave Verdichtungswelle *f (Sound Ranging)*.
bury begraben, beerdigen; vergraben, verbergen *(to hide)*.
bus Kraftomnibus *m*.
bush fighting Buschgefecht *n*, Waldgefecht *n*.
bushing Buchsring *m (G)*; Futterstück *n (breechblock)*; Lagerschale *f*, Buchse *f*, Futter *n (Tech)*.
busy besetzt *(Tp)*.
busy signal Besetztzeichen *n*, Besetztschauzeichen *n (Tp)*.
butcher Fleischer *m*, Metzger *m*, Schlächter *m*.
butchery platoon Schlächtereizug *m (QMC)*.
butt Kolben *m (MG, R)*; Kugelfang *m (target range)*.
butt assembly Bodenstück *n (MG)*.
butter Butter *f*.
buttock Gesäßbacke *f*.
button Knopf *m*.
butt plate Kolbenkappe *f (R)*.
butt strap Lasche *f (Engr)*.
butt stroke Kolbenhieb *m*.
butt swivel Klammer *f (R)*.
butt-swivel plate Klammerfuß *m (R)*.
buzzer Wecker *m*, Summer *m (Tp)*.
buzzer button Summerknopf *m (Tp)*.
buzzer set Summerzusatz *m (Tp)*.
buzzer signal Summeranruf *m (Tp)*.
bypass *n* Überstromkanal *m (Mtr)*; Ausweichstelle *f (road)*.
by-pass *v* aussparen *(Tac)*.
"By the left flank, march!" "Links, um!"
"By the right flank, march!" "Rechts, um!"

C

cab Fahrerhaus *n (of truck)*.
cabane Spannturm *m*, Rahmenspannturm *m (Ap)*.
cabbage Kraut *n*.
cabin Kabine *f (Ap, Nav)*; Hütte *f (hut)*.
cabinet Truhe *f*, Gehäuse *n (Rad)*.
cable Seil *n*, Tau *n (Nav, etc.)*; Kabel *n (Elec, Tp)*; Drahtzug *m (flexible steel, Ap)*; Drahtseil *n (wire)*. *See also* **wire.**
cable armor Bewehrung *f*.
cable block Drahtseilhindernis *n (obstacle)*.
cable brake Seilbremse *f*.
cable drum Seilrolle *f*, Seiltrommel *f*.
cable ferry Seilfähre *f*.
cablegram Kabeldepesche *f*.
cable knife Kabelmesser *n*.
cable lead-in point Kabelaufführungspunkt *m (Elec, Tp)*.
cable line Kabelleitung *f (Tp)*.
cable ship Kabelschiff *n*.
cable sleeve Kabelverbinder *m (Tp)*.
cable splice Kabelverbindung *f (Tp)*.
cable-testing instrument Kabelmeßgerät *n (Tp)*.
cable trench Kabelgraben *m (Tp)*.
cable wax Kabelwachs *n (Engr, Tp)*.
cable winch Seilwinde *f*.
cadence Gleichschritt *m*, Zeitmaß *n (Marching)*.
cadet Kadett *m*; Fahnenjunker *m*, Fahnenjunker-Gefreiter *m (junior cadet)*; Fahnenjunker-Unteroffizier *m (cadet Sgt)*.
cadre Cadre *m*, Kader *m*, Stammtruppe *f*.
cadreman Soldat einer Stammannschaft.
cadre personnel Stammannschaft *f*.
caduceus Äskulapstab *m (insigne)*.
caisson Hinterwagen *m*, Munitionswagen *m (Arty)*; Senkkasten *m (Engr)*.
caisson section leader Wagenzugführer *m (Arty)*.
calcium bleach Chlorkalk *m*.
calcium chloride Chlorkalk *m*.
calculate rechnen, berechnen, ausrechnen.
calculation Berechnung *f*.
calculator Rechenmaschine *f*, Rechengerät *n*.
calculus Infinitesimalrechnung *f*.
calf Wade *f (of leg)*.
caliber Rohrweite *f*, Kaliber *n*, Waffenkaliber *n (Ord)*.
calibrate eichen.
calibrated geeicht.
calibration Höhenrichtverbesserung nach Einschießgeschütz *(Gunnery)*; Eichung *f (Tech)*; Funkbeschickung *f (Rad compass)*.
calibration adjustment Frequenzkorrektur *f (Rad)*.
calibration correction Ausschalten der Grundstufe *(Gunnery)*.
calibration firing Vergleichsschießen *n (Arty)*.
calipers Greifzirkel *m*.
calk dichten.
call *n* Ruf *m*, Zeichen *n*, Signal *n*, Anruf *m*, Gesprächsverbindung *f (Sig C)*; Ferngespräch *n*, Gespräch *n*, Spruch *m (Tp)*.
call *v* rufen; anrufen *(Tp)*.
called station Gegenstelle *f (Rad, Tp)*.
call key Flackertaste *f (Tp)*.
call letters Buchstaben des Rufzeichens *(Rad)*.
call sign Rufzeichen *n (Rad)*.
call signal Rufzeichen *n (Rad, Tp)*; Anrufzeichen *n (Tp)*.
call the roll Namen aufrufen.
call the shot das Abkommen melden.
call to quarters Locken *n*.
call to the colors *See* **induction.**
call-up Anruf *m (Rad)*.
call up aufrufen, anrufen.
calm *adj* still, ruhig, windstill *(Met)*.
cam Daumen *m*, Nocken *m (Tech)*; Drucknase *f (trigger)*; Lenkschraube *f (steering column, MT)*.
cam and lever steering system Schraubenganglenkung *f*, Spindellenkung *f (MT)*.
camber Radsturz *m (MT)*; Wölbung *f*, Krümmung *f*.
camera Kammer *f*.
camera gun Lichtbild-MG *n (Avn)*.
cameraman Photograph *m*.
camera spotting Artillerie-Bildbeobachtung *f*.
camouflage *n* Tarnung *f*, Tarnen *n*.
camouflage *v* tarnen.
camouflage discipline Tarndisziplin *f*.
camouflage jacket Tarnjacke *f*.
camouflage material Tarnmittel *n*.
camouflage net Maske *f*, Fliegermaske *f*, Tarnnetz *n*.
camouflage paint Tarnungsfarbe *f*, Tarnanstrich *m*.
camouflage troops Tarnungstruppe *f*.
camouflet Quetschladung *f*, Quetschmine *f*.
camp *n* Lager *n*, Lagerplatz *m*, Lagerort *m*, Truppenlager *n*; Gefangenenlager *n (PW)*.
camp *v* das Lager aufschlagen.
campaign Feldzug *m*.
campaign medal Kriegsdenkmünze *f*, Erinnerungsmedaille *f*.
camp hospital *See* **station hospital.**
camp kitchen Lagerküche *f*.
cam plate Kurvenscheibe *f (Ord)*.
camp site Lagerstelle *f*.
camshaft Nockenwelle *f*, Steuerwelle *f*, Daumenwelle *f*.
can Büchse *f*, Blechbüchse *f*, Dose *f*.
canal Kanal *m*.
canard airplane Ente *f*, Entenflugzeug *n*.
cancel ausstreichen, durchstreichen *(cross out)*; aufheben, absagen, annullieren *(annul)*; widerrufen *(revoke)*.
cancellation Streichung *f (crossing out)*; Aufhebung *f*, Annullierung *f (annulment)*.
candle Kerze *f*.
canister Kartätsche *f (separate-loading Am)*; Filterbüchse *f (gas mask)*.
canister filter Büchsenfilter *m (gas mask)*.
canned food Büchsenkonserven *fpl*.
canned meat Fleischkonserve *f*, Büchsenfleisch *n*.
canned ration Büchsenkonserven *fpl*.
cannelure Rille *f (Am)*.
cannibalization Wiederinstandsetzung unter Verwendung von Teilen beschädigten Kriegsgeräts *(Ord)*.
cannon Kanone *f*.
cannonade Bombardierung *f*, Kanonade *f*.
cannoneer Schütze *m*, Kanonier *m*.
cannon salute Kanonensalut *m*.
cannon transport wagon Rohrwagen *m*.
canopy Baldachin *m (Ap)*; Stoffbahn *f (Prcht)*.
cant *n* schiefer Radstand, Verkantung *f (Arty)*.
cant *v* verkanten *(G, R)*.
canteen Feldflasche *f (water container)*; Kantine *f*, Kamaradschaftsheim *n (place)*.
canteen cover Feldflaschenhülle *f*.
canteen cup Trinkbecher *m*, Becher *m*.
cantilever freitragend.
cantilever beam Kragträger *m*.
cantilever bridge Kragträgerbrücke *f*, Auslegerbrücke *f*.
cantilever wing freitragender Flügel.
cantle Hinterzwiesel *m (saddle)*.
cantonment Barackenlager *n*.
cantonment area Unterkunftsraum *m*.
cantonment building Militärbaracke *f*, Baracke *f*.
canvas Segeltuch *n*.
cap Haube *f*, Kappe *f*, Kopf *m (Am)*; Mütze *f (Clo)*; Geschoßkappe *f (projectile)*; Sprengkapsel *f (blasting)*.
capacitance Kapazität *f (Elec)*.
capacitor Kondensator *m (Rad)*.
capacity Leistung *f*, Leistungsfähigkeit *f (performance)*; Vermögen *n (capability)*; Fähigkeit *f (ability)*; Eigenschaft *f (function)*; Verkehrslast *f (Bdg)*; Fassungsvermögen *n (volume)*.
cap crimper Würgezange *f*.
cape Umhang *m (cloak)*; Kap *n (point of land)*.
cap hole Zündkanal *m (blasting cartridge)*.
capillary tube Haarröhre *f*.
capital Hauptstadt *f (of a country)*; großer Buchstabe *(letter)*.
capital offense Kapitalverbrechen *n*.
capital ship Großkampfschiff *n*.
capitulate sich ergeben, kapitulieren.
capitulation Übergabe *f*, Kapitulation *f*.
capsize kentern, umkippen.
capstan Gangspill *m*, Ankerwinde *f (Nav)*; Erdwinde *f (Engr)*.
captain Hauptmann *m (plural: Hauptleute)*; Rittmeister *m (Cav, H Arty)*; Stabsarzt *m (Med)*; Stabsveterinär *m (Vet)*; Kapitän zur See *(Nav)*.
captive balloon Fesselballon *m*.
capture *n* Einnahme *f (of a locality)*; Gefangennahme *f (of a person)*.
capture *v* fangen, gefangennehmen *(a person)*; erbeuten *(matériel)*; aufbringen *(a ship)*; einnehmen *(a locality)*.
captured gun Beutegeschütz *n*.
captured matériel erbeutetes Kriegsgerät.
captured officer kriegsgefangener Offizier.
car Wagen *m (MT, RR)*.
carbine Karabiner *m*.
carbine scabbard carrier Karabinertragevorrichtung *f*.
carbolic acid Karbolsäure *f*.
carbon Kohle *f*, Kohlenstoff *m*; Ölkohle *f (Mtr)*.
carbon block Kohleklotz *m (microphone)*.
carbon brush Kohle *f*, Kohlebürste *f (Elec)*.
carbon copy Durchschlag *m (typed)*; Durchschrift *f (written)*.
carbon-copy pad Durchschreibeblock *m*.
carbon dioxide Kohlensäure *f*.
carbon electrode Kohlenelektrode *f*.

carbon filler Kohlenstoffträger *m (in liquid-oxygen blasting charges).*
carbon lightning arrester Kohleblitzableiter *m.*
carbon microphone Kohlenmikrophon *n.*
carbon monoxide Kohlenoxyd *n.*
carbon paper Kohlepapier *n.*
carbon residue Verbrennungsrückstand *m (Mtr).*
carbon rod Kohle *f,* Kohlestab *m (Elec).*
carbon tetrachloride Tetrachlorkohlenstoff *m.*
carbonylchloride Chlorkohlenoxyd *n,* Phosgen *n (CWS).*
carbon-zinc battery Kohle-Zinksammler *m.*
carbon-zinc cell Kohle-Zink-Element *n (Elec).*
carburetion Vergaseranordnung *f,* Gemischbildung im Vergaser *(Mtr).*
carburetor Vergaser *m.*
carburetor engine Vergasermotor *m.*
carcass Kadaver *m,* Leiche *f.*
card Karte *f,* Schein *m,* Zettel *m.*
cardboard Pappe *f,* Pappdeckel *m,* Karton *m.*
card file Kartei *f.*
cardinal point Himmelsrichtung *f.*
care Pflege *f (of wounded, equipment, etc.);* Verwundetenbetreuung *f (of casualties);* Fürsorge *f (welfare);* Vorsicht *f (caution).*
cargo Last *f,* Ladung *f (load);* Fracht *f (freight);* Schiffsladung *f (Nav).*
cargo carrier Lastkraftwagen *m,* Transportwagen *m (MT).*
cargo-carrying glider Lastensegler *m,* Lastensegelflugzeug *n.*
cargo parachute Lastfallschirm *m.*
cargo tonnage Ladefähigkeit *f (capacity);* Ladegewicht *n (weight).*
cargo-transport plane Frachtflugzeug *n.*
cargo truck Lastkraftwagen *m.*
carload Wagenladung *f.*
carpenter Zimmermann *m.*
carriage Lafette *f,* Lafettierung *f (G).*
carrier Beförderungsmittel *n,* Fahrzeug *n (vehicle);* Träger *m (Pers);* Flugzeugträger *m (Nav);* Tragbeutel *m,* Büchse *f,* Tasche *f (container).*
carrier current Trägerstrom *m (Tp).*
carrier pigeon Brieftaube *f,* Heeresbrieftaube *f.*
carrier wave Trägerwelle *f (Rad).*
carry tragen; halten *(AA SL).*
carrying capacity Tragfähigkeit *f.*
carrying pad Tragepolster *n (MG).*
carrying strap Tragband *n (gas mask).*
carry light führender Scheinwerfer *(AAA).*
carry out ausführen, durchführen.
cartel ship Austauschschiff *n.*
cartographer Kartenzeichner *m,* Tabellenzeichner *m.*
cartographical sketching Anfertigung von Grundrißskizzen.
cartridge Patrone *f (Am);* Kartusche *f (semifixed and fixed Am);* **scharfe** Patrone *(ball);* Anlaßpatrone *f (for cartridge starter).*
cartridge bag Kartuschbeutel *m.*
cartridge belt Patronengurt *m (MG).*
cartridge case Hülse *f,* Patronenhülse *f,* Geschoßhülse *f (Am);* Kartusche *f,* Kartuschhülse *f (semifixed and fixed Am).*
cartridge chamber Patronenlager *n (R).*
cartridge clip Patronenstreifen *m,* Ladestreifen *m (Am).*
cartridge feed Patronenzuführung *f (Small Arms).*
cartridge starter Anlaßpistole *f (Mtr).*
cartridge-type ground signal Leuchtpatrone *f.*
cartwheel Wagenrad *n.*
case Gehäuse *n,* Hülse *f,* Büchse *f (Tech);* Kiste *f,* Kasten *m (box);* Futteral *n,* Tasche *f;* Kartusche *f (semifixed and fixed Am);* Zündschraubengehäuse *n (threaded percussion primer) (Am);* Fall *m (instance);* Schurholzrahmen *m (gallery case);* Patronenhülse *f (cartridge);* Bombenhülle *f (bomb).*
casein glue Kaseinleim *m.*
casemate Kasemate *f (Ft, Nav).*
casemate gun mount Kasemattenlafette *f.*
case I pointing direktes Richten *(Gunnery).*
case II pointing Richten mit direkter Seitenrichtung und indirekter Höhenrichtung *(Gunnery).*
case III pointing indirektes Richten *(Gunnery).*
case IV pointing Richten mit vorgeschobener Beobachtungsstelle *(Gunnery).*
cash Bargeld *n.*
cashier *v* aus dem Heere ausstoßen.
casing Deckplatte *f (MG telescopic sight);* Laufdecke *f,* Decke *f,* Mantel *m (tire);* Gehäuse *n,* Hülle *f,* Hülse *f,* Schalung *f.*
castellated nut Kronenmutter *f.*
caster Nachlauf *m,* Vorlauf *m (MT);* Schwenkrolle *f (roller).*
casting Guß *m,* Gießen *n (action);* Abguß *m (thing cast).*
cast iron Gußeisen *n.*
cast-metal case Gußgehäuse *n.*
cast-steel Gußstahl *m.*
casuals zur Verwendung stehendes Militärpersonal.
casualty Verlust *m,* Ausfall *m.*
casualty agent *(CWS)* Kampfstoff *m*
casualty day tägliche Verlustrate.
casualty list Verlustliste *f.*
casualty report Verlustmeldung *f.*
catalog Katalog *m.*
catapult *n* Katapult *m,* Startkatapult *m,* Schleuder *f,* Flugzeugschleuder *f (Avn).*
catapult *v* katapultieren *(an Ap).*
catapult airplane Katapultflugzeug
catapult take-off Schleuderstart *m (Avn).*
catch *n* Falle *f (MG);* Kammerfang *m (MG bolt catch);* Sperrnase *f (fuze);* Sperrklinke *f (pawl).*
catch *v* fangen, einfangen, auffangen; ergreifen *(seize);* sich zuziehen, anstecken *(a disease).*
catch pivot Fallenachse *f (MG).*
caterpillar band Radgürtel *m (G).*
caterpillar drive Raupenantrieb *m,* Gleiskettenantrieb *m (MT).*
caterpillar prime mover Gleiskettenschlepper *m,* Gleiskettenzugmaschine
caterpillar track Raupe *f,* Raupenkette *f,* Gleiskette *f (MT, Tk).*
caterpillar tractor Gleiskettenschlepper *m,* Gleiskettenzugmaschine *f,* Raupenschlepper *m.*
cathode Kathode *f.*
cathode-ray tube Kathodenstrahlröhre *f,* Elektronenstrahlröhre *f,* Braunsche Röhre.
cattle Vieh *n.*
catwalk Lattenrost *m,* Holzrost *m.*
cause *v* verursachen, veranlassen, bewirken.
causeway Straßendamm *m.*
caustic *n* Ätzmittel *n.*
caustic soda kaustisches Natron, Ätznatron *n.*
caution Vorsicht *f,* Achtung *f.*
cavalry Kavallerie *f,* Reiterei *f (H Cav);* motorisierte Kavallerie *(Mecz).*
cavalry brigade Reiterbrigade *f,* Kavalleriebrigade *f.*
cavalry corps Kavalleriekorps *n.*
cavalry division Kavalleriedivision *f.*
cavalryman Kavallerist *m,* Reiter *m.*
cavalry patrol Reiterspähtrupp *m.*
cavalry pioneer Kavalleriepionier *m.*
cavalry reconnaissance detachment Reiteraufklärungsabteilung *f.*
cavalry regiment Reiterregiment *n,* Kavallerieregiment *n.*
Cavalry School Kavallerieschule *f,* Reitschule *f.*
cavalry troop Reiterschwadron *f.*
cave Höhle *f.*
cave in einstürzen.
cave shelter minierter Unterstand *(Ft).*
cavesson Reithalfter *f (harness).*
cavity Loch *n,* Vertiefung *f,* Höhle *f.*
cease aufhören, einstellen.
"Cease firing!" "Feuerpause!"
ceiling Wolkenhöhe *f (Met);* Gipfelhöhe *f (Ap);* Decke *f (of a room).*
ceiling light Wolkenscheinwerfer *m (Met).*
ceiling ventilator Deckenventilator *m (MT).*
celestial navigation astronomische Navigation.
celestial sphere Himmelskugel *f (Navigation, Surv).*
cell Zelle *f,* Flügelzelle *f (Ap);* Gaszelle *f (Airship);* Element *n (Elec).*
cell container Elementbecher *m (Elec).*
cellophane Zellophan *n.*
cellophane cover Zellophanüberzug *m (CWS).*
cellular-type radiator Elementekühler *m (MT).*
cellule Zelle *f,* Flügelzelle *f (Ap);* Gaszelle *f (Airship).*
celluloid Zelluloid *n.*
celluloid templet Zelluloidtafel *f.*
cellulose Zellulose *f.*
cellulose acetate Zellon *n.*
cellulose fiber Zellwolle *f.*
cement Mörtel *m,* Zement *m.*
cemetery Friedhof *m.*
censor Zensor *m.*
censorship Zensur *f.*
center Mitte *f,* Mittelpunkt *m,* Zentrum *n.*
center balk Mittelbalken *m (Bdg).*
center line Brückenlinie *f (Bdg).*
center of burst mittlerer Sprengpunkt.
center of dispersion *See* **center of impact.**
center of impact mittlerer Treffpunkt.
center of lift Auftriebsmittelpunkt *m (Aerodynamics).*
center of resistance Widerstandszentrum *n (Tac).*
center of the front *(Tac)* Frontmitte *f*
center point of target Zielpunkt *m.*
center punch Körner *m.*
centigrade Celsius.
central Vermittlung *f,* Vermittlungsstelle *f (Tp).*
central control zentrale Feuerleitung *(Arty).*
Central European time mitteleuropäische Zeit *(15° E standard meridian).*
central station Zentrale *f (sound ranging).*
central tube Kammerhülse *f (shrapnel).*
centrifugal action Fliehkraftantrieb *m (fuze).*
centrifugal arming device Fliehbacke *f (fuze).*
centrifugal bolt Fliehbolzen *m (fuze).*
centrifugal casting Schleuderguß *m (foundry).*
centrifugal compressor Turbokompressor *m,* Kreiselkompressor *m.*
centrifugal force Fliehkraft *f,* Zentrifugalkraft *f.*
centrifugal fuze Fliehkraftzünder *m.*
centrifugal governor Fliehkraftregler *m (Mtr).*
centrifugal pump Kreiselpumpe *f,* Zentrifugalpumpe *f,* Schleuderpumpe *f.*
centripetal force Zentripetalkraft *f.*
ceremonial detachment Ehrenwache *f.*
ceremony Zeremoniell *n,* Feierlichkeit *f,* besondere Veranstaltung; Trauerfeier *f (Mil funeral).*
certificate Bescheinigung *f,* Zeugnis *n,* Schein *m.*
certificate of discharge Entlassungsschein *m.*
certificate of identification Personalausweis *m.*
certificate of rejection Ausmusterungsschein *m.*
certificate of service Dienstbescheinigung *f.*
certified beglaubigt *(documents).*
certify bescheinigen, bezeugen, beglaubigen.
cessation Einstellung *f.*
cetane rating Cetenzahl *f (Diesel fuel).*
chain Kette *f;* Gleitschutzkette *f (skid);* Meßkette *f (Surv).*
chaining Messen mit Meßkette
chain link Kettenglied *n.*
chain of command Befehlsweg *m,* Befehlsverhältnisse *npl.*
chain of evacuation Verwundetenabschublinie *f.*
challenge Anruf *m,* Einspruch *m,* Herausforderung *f.*
chamber Kartuschraum *m (G);* Patronenlager *n (R);* Kammer *f,* Raum *m.*
change *v* ändern, sich ändern, umändern; verändern *(to alter);* wechseln *(money);* tauschen *(to exchange);* sich umziehen *(clothes);* umsteigen *(trains).*
change lever Umschalthebel *m (automatic R).*
change of course Kurswechsel *m (Avn).*
change of height Höhenänderung *f (AA predictor).*
change of personnel Personalveränderung *f.*
change of position Stellungswechsel *m (Tac).*
change of station Platzwechsel *m.*
change-over switch Umschalter *m (Elec).*
change step den Schritt wechseln, den Tritt wechseln.
channel Dienstweg *m (Adm);* Frequenzbereich *m (Rad);* Verbindungsweg *m (Com).*
through channels auf dem Dienstweg.
channel marker Bake *f (Nav).*
channel of communication Verbindungsweg *m (Tp, Rad).*
chapel Kapelle *f.*
chaplain Wehrmachtgeistlicher *m,* Feldgeistlicher *m.*
character Buchstabe *m,* Schriftzeichen *n (letter);* Charakter *m (of a person).*
characteristic curve Röhrenkennlinie *f (Rad tube).*
characteristic impedance Wellenwiderstand *m (Elec, Rad).*
charcoal Holzkohle *f.*
charcoal layer Kohleschicht *f (gas mask).*
charge *n* Ladung *f (Am, blasting, Elec);* Attacke *f,* Angriff *m (Cav);* Betrauung *f (trust);* Anklage *f (accusation);* Gebühr *f (rate).*
charge *v* anstürmen *(Inf);* attackieren *(Cav);* laden *(Am, Elec);* verlangen, anfordern *(money);* beschuldigen *(accuse).*
charge-placing pole Sprengstange *f.*
charging unit Lademaschinensatz *m,* Aggregat *n (Elec).*
charging voltage Ladespannung *f (battery charger).*
chart *n* Plan *m,* Tabelle *f,* Übersicht *f;* Karte *f (map).*
chartroom Feuerleitstelle *f (Arty);* Kartenraum *m (Nav).*
chase *n* langes Feld *(G).*
chassis Fahrwerk *n,* Fahrgestell *n (MT);* Apparatur *f (Rad).*
chassis clearance Bauchfreiheit *f (MT).*
chassis frame Fahrwerkrahmen *m (MT).*
chassis panel Montageplatte *f (Rad).*
chauffeur Kraftfahrer *m (MT).*
check *n* Scheck *m (banking);* Kontrolle *f (supervision);* Zeichen *n (mark).*
check *v* hemmen, verhindern *(to hinder);* prüfen, nachprüfen, überprüfen *(to test, to verify);* überwachen, kontrollieren *(to supervise).*
check list Kontrolliste *f.*
check point Anhaltspunkt *m,* Bezugspunkt *m.*
check valve Reglerventil *n.*
cheek Backe *f,* Wange *f.*
cheekbone Jochleiste *f (horse).*
cheek strap Backenstück *n (harness).*
cheese Käse *m.*
chemical agent Kampfstoff *m.*
chemical-agent detector kit Gasanzeiger *m.*
chemical barrier Kampfstoffsperre *f,* Kampfstoffriegel *m (CWS).*
chemical battalion Werferabteilung *f (Ger).*
chemical bomb Kampfstoffbombe *f,* Fliegergasbombe *f (Avn).*
chemical candle Giftrauchkerze *f,* Giftnebelkerze *f (CWS).*
chemical cylinder Gasflasche *f,* Gasbehälter *m;* Nebelabblasgerät *n (smoke).*
chemical decontamination *See* **decontamination.**
chemical decontamination company Entgiftungskompanie *f.*
chemical defense Gasschutz *m.*
chemical defense school Heeresgasschutzschule *f.*
chemical fumes Kampfstoffschwaden *mpl (CWS).*
chemical hand grenade Gashandgranate *f.*
chemical land mine chemische Erdmine, Gas-Erdmine *f.*
chemical layer Mundschicht *f (gas mask).*
chemical mine chemische Erdmine, Gas-Erdmine *f.*
chemical mortar Gashandwerfer *m,* Gasmörser *m.*
chemical munitions Gasmunition *f,* chemische Kampfmittel.
chemical officer Gasoffizier *m.*
chemical projectile Gasgeschoß *n.*
chemical projector Werfer *m,* Nebelwerfer *m,* Gaswerfer *m (CWS).*
chemical-projector fire Gaswerfen *n.*
chemical regiment Nebelwerferregiment *n,* Werferregiment *n (Ger).*
chemical security Gasschutz *m.*
chemical shell Gasgranate *f;* Gasbrisanzgranate *f (HE).*
chemical-shell fire Kampfstoffbeschuß *m (CWS);* Gelbkreuzbeschuß *m (vesicant filler, CWS).*
chemical spray apparatus Kampfstoffzerstäuber *m;* Luftstromgerät *n,* Zerstäubungsgerät *n (Ap).*
chemical spraying Versprühen von Kampfstoffen *(CWS).*
chemical tank Nebelgerät *n (for air Cml spraying).*
chemical troops chemische Truppen, Gastruppen *fpl,* Nebeltruppen *fpl.*
chemical warfare chemischer Krieg; Gaskampf *m,* Gaskrieg *m.*
chemical warfare agent chemischer Kampfstoff.
Chemical Warfare Board Gastechnischer Forschungsausschuß *(USA).*
chemical warfare depot Gasschutzpark *m.*
chemical warfare material Gaskampfmittel *npl,* Gaskampfgerät *n.*
chemical warfare officer Gasoffizier *m.*
Chemical Warfare School Gaskriegsschule *f (USA).*
Chemical Warfare Service chemischer Kriegsdienst *(USA).*
chemist Chemiker *m.*
chess Brückenbelag *m (Bdg).*
chest Brust *f (anatomy);* Kiste *f,* Kasten *m (box).*
chest pack parachute Brustfallschirm *m.*
cheval-de-frise spanischer Reiter
chevron Uniformwinkel *m.*
chewing gum Kaugummi *m.*
chicken wire Maschendraht *m.*
chief Chef *m.*
chief engineer Leitender Ingenieur, Chefingenieur *m,* Oberingenieur *m.*
chief nurse Oberschwester *f.*
chief of ammunition Munitionsunteroffizier *m (Arty).*
Chief of Chaplains Feldbischof *m.*
Chief of Chemical Warfare Service Chef des chemischen Kriegsdienstes *(USA).*
chief of civil affairs section Chef der Zivilverwaltung *(at army Hq).*
Chief of Coast Artillery Chef der Küstenartillerie *(USA).*
chief of corps supply services Korpsnachschubführer *m (Ger).*
chief of division supply services Divisionsnachschubführer *m (Ger).*
Chief of Engineers Inspekteur der Pioniere.
Chief of Naval Operations Chef des Admiralstabs *(USA).*
Chief of Ordnance Chef des Heeres-Waffenamtes.
chief of staff Stabschef *m,* Generalstabschef *m.*
Chief of Staff Chef des Generalstabes.
chief of supply services Nachschubführer *m.*
Chief of the Air Staff Chef des Führungsstabes der **Luftwaffe**
Chief of the Veterinary Service Chefveterinär *m.*
chief of transportation Chef des Transportwesens *(Tac, RR).*
chief petty officer Portepeeunteroffizier *m (Nav).*
Chief Signal Officer Inspekteur der Nachrichtentruppen.
Chief Surgeon Armeearzt *m.*
chief transportation officer bevollmächtigter Transportoffizier.
chilled casting Kokillenguß *m.*
chimney Schornstein *m.*
chin Kinn *n.*
chinaware Porzellan *n.*
chin groove Kinnkettengrube *f (horse).*
chin strap Sturmriemen *m,* Kinnriemen *m (headgear);* Kinnstößel *m (harness).*
chin support Kinnstütze *f (gas mask).*
chisel Meißel *m.*
chloracetophenone Chlorazetophenon *n (CWS).*
chloracetophenone solution Chlorazetophenon - Chlorpikrin - Lösung *f,* Tränenstoff *m (CWS).*
chloramine-T Chloramin *n (CWS).*
chlorate explosive Chlorat-Sprengmittel *n.*
chloride of lime Chlorkalk *m.*
chlorination Chlorbeimischung *f,* Chlorzusetzung *f.*
chlorine Chlor *n,* Chlorgas *n (CWS).*
chlorpicrin Chlorpikrin *n (CWS).*
chlorsulfonic acid Chlorsulfonsäure *f (CWS).*
chock Bremsklotz *m.*
chocolate Schokolade *f.*
choke *n* Starterklappe *f (Mtr);* Würgebohrung *f (barrel) (Ord).*
choke *v* ersticken *(suffocate);* erwürgen *(strangle).*
choke coil Drosselspule *f (Elec).*
choke valve Luftklappenventil *n (carburetor).*
cholera Cholera *f.*
chord Gurt *m (truss);* Sehne *f (Geometry).*
Christie tank Christie-Panzerkraftwagen *m.*
chromium Chrom *n.*
chromium-plated verchromt.
chronograph Chronograph *m,* Registrier-Chronograph *m.*
chronology of battle Gefechtszeitangabe *f.*
chronometer Chronometer *n.*
chuck Futter *n (of lathe, etc.).*
church Kirche *f.*
cigarette Zigarette *f.*
cigarette lighter Feuerzeug *n.*
cincha Untergurt *m (saddle).*
cipher *n* Schlüssel *m,* Chiffre *f.*
cipher *v* schlüsseln, chiffrieren, ziffern.
cipher device Chiffriermaschine *f,* Schlüsselmaschine *f.*
cipher disk Verschlüsselungsscheibe *f.*
cipher key Geheimwort *n,* Schlüsselwort *n.*
cipher text Geheimtext *m,* Schlüsseltext *m.*
circle *n* Kreis *m.*
circle *v* Runde(n) fliegen *(Avn).*
circle of rupture Wirkungskreis *m (blasting).*
circling target kreisendes Ziel *(AAA).*
circuit Stromkreis *m,* Leitungsnetz *n,* Schaltung *f (Elec).*
circuit arrangement Leitergebilde *n (Elec).*
circuit breaker Stromunterbrecher *m,* Spannungssicherung *f (Elec).*
circuit diagram Schaltplan *m,* Schaltungsschema *n;* Leitungsskizze *f,* Schaltskizze *f (Tp).*
circuit tester Leitungsprüfer *m (Elec).*
circular *n* Rundschreiben *n,* Umlauf *m.*
circular course Kreisflug *m (Avn).*
circular track Kranz *m,* Drehkranz *m (MG mount).*
circular track mount Lafettenkranz *m (Ap, Tk).*
circulation Umlauf *m (of money, fluids);* Kreislauf *m (of blood);* Auflage *f (of a newspaper);* Verbreitung *f (of news).*
circulation map Wegekarte *f.*
circumference Umkreis *m.*

circumstance Sachlage *f*, Zustand *m*.
circumstantial evidence Indizienbeweis *m*.
cirrocumulus Zirrokumulus *m*.
cirrostratus Zirrostratus *m*.
cirrus cloud Cirruswolke *f*, Zirruswolke *f*, Federwolke *f*.
citation Auszeichnung *f*, ehrenvolle Erwähnung.
citizen Staatsbürger *m*, Bürger *m*.
citizenship Staatsangehörigkeit *f*.
city Stadt *f*.
civil staatlich, Staats- *(pertaining to government)*; höflich, anständig *(polite)*.
civil affairs section Zivilverwaltung *f (Mil Govt)*.
civil airway Luftverkehrslinie *f*.
civil aviation Zivilluftfahrt *f*.
civil communication lines Postleitungen *fpl*.
civil court Zivilgericht *n*.
civilian *n* Zivilist *m*, Zivilperson *f*.
civilian clothes Zivil *n*, Zivilkleidung *f*, bürgerliche Kleidung.
civilian defense ziviler Luftschutz.
civilian internee Zivilinternierter *m*.
civilian population Zivilbevölkerung *f*.
civil offense Zivilvergehen *n*, nichtmilitärisches Vergehen.
civil service Staatsdienst *m*.
civil war Bürgerkrieg *m*.
claim *n* Anspruch *m*, Anrecht *n*.
clamp *n* Klammer *f (Tech)*; Klemmzange *f (blasting-cap fuze)*.
clamping collar Schelle *f (Mort)*.
clamping lever Klemmhebel *m*, Begrenzungshebel *m (MG)*.
clamping mechanism Festklemmvorrichtung *f (MG tripod)*.
clamping plate Klemmplatte *f (G barrel guide)*.
clamping ring Klemmring *m (grenade launcher)*.
clamping screw Klemmschraube *f (aiming circle)*.
clarity of sound Klangreinheit *f (Rad)*.
clash Zusammenstoß *m (Tac)*.
clasp Spange *f (decoration)*.
class Klasse *f*; Jahrgang *m (age class)*.
classification Einteilung *f*, Gliederung *f*.
classification of artillery fire Feuerformen der Artillerie.
classification of chemical agents Kampfstoffgruppen *fpl*.
classification of equipment Stoffgliederung *f*.
classification of machine-gun fire Feuerformen des Maschinengewehrs.
classification track Richtungsgleis *n*, Abstellgleis *n (RR)*.
classified military information geheime Gegenstände.
class of equipment Gerätklasse *f*.
claw hatchet Klauenbeil *n*.
clay pit Lehmgrube *f*.
clean *v* reinigen, säubern, putzen.
cleaning and preserving material Reinigungsgerät *n*.
cleaning brush *(G)* Reinigungsbürste *f*
cleaning patch *(R)* Reinigungsdocht *m*
cleaning rag Reinigungslappen *m*, Putzlappen *m*.
cleaning rod Stock *m*, Gewehrstock *m (R)*; Wischstock *m (G)*.
clean-up party Säuberungstrupp *m*.
clean out säubern *(Tac)*.
clear *v* räumen, säubern.
clear *adj.* wolkenlos *(Met)*; frei *(of obstructions)*.
in clear im Klartext *(Com)*.
clearance Spielraum *m (Mech)*; Sicherheitsmaß *n (Gunnery)*; Entlastung *f (of responsibility)*; Freigabe *f (permit)*; Bauchfreiheit *f (chassis)*.
clearance of masks Überschießen von Deckungen *(Gunnery)*.
clearance of the enemy Feindfreiheit *f*.
clearance space Geschoßanlage *f (R)*.
cleared for action gefechtsklar *(Nav)*.
cleared zone Rollfeld *n (Adrm)*.
clear ice glasartige Vereisung.
clearing Waldblöße *f*, Waldlichtung *f (forest or wood)*.
clearing signal Schlußzeichen *n (Tp)*.
clearing station Hauptverbandplatz *m (Med)*.
clearing unit Krankenträgertrupp *m (Med)*.
clear up säubern *(Tac)*.
cleat Greifer *m (MT)*.
clergyman Geistlicher *m*, Pfarrer *m*; Pastor *m (Protestant)*; Priester *m (Catholic)*; Rabbiner *m (Jewish)*.
clerical aptitude test Schreibereignungsprüfung *f*.
clerk Schreiber *m*, Schriftführer *m*, Gefechtsschreiber *m*.
clevis Schäkel *m*.
click *n* Rast *f (Mech)*.
cliff Klippe *f*, Kliff *n*.
climate Klima *n*.
climatic klimatisch.
climb *n* Steigflug *m*, Steigen *n (Avn)*.
climb *v* steigen, besteigen, klettern.
climb-and-dive indicator Statoskop *n (Ap)*.
climbers Steigeisen *npl (for Tp lineman)*.
climbing ability Steigvermögen *n (Ap)*.
climbing iron Klettereisen *n*, Kletterspom *m*.
climbing take-off Kavalierstart *m (Avn)*.
climbing turn gezogene Kurve *(Avn)*.
clincher rim Wulstfelge *f (MT)*.
clinical record Krankenblatt *n*.
clinometer Gefällemesser *m*, Neigungsmesser *m (Arty, Surv)*; Geländewinkelmesser *m (for angle of site, Arty)*; Richtbogen *m (G)*.
clip *n* Patronenrahmen *m*, Ladestreifen *m (R, AA gun)*; Klammer *f (paper clip)*.
clip-fed rifle Mehrlader *m*.
clip loading machine Ladestreifenfüller *m*.
clock Uhr *f (timepiece)*; Borduhr *f (Ap)*; Melderose *f (AWS)*.
clock method Melderoseverfahren *n (Gunnery, AWS)*.
clockwise im Sinne des Uhrzeigers, im Uhrzeigersinn, rechtsgängig, rechtslaufend.
clockwork action Uhrwerkantrieb *m (fuze)*.
clockwork fuze Uhrwerkzünder *m*.
close *v* schließen, zuschließen, zumachen *(a door, etc.)*; abschließen *(an account)*; beenden *(conclude)*.
close billets Ortsbiwak *n*.
close column aufgeschlossene Marschfolge.
close combat Nahkampf *m*.
close-combat range Nahkampfweite *f*.
close-combat weapon Nahkampfwaffe *f*.
closed airdrome Flugplatz außer Betrieb.
close defense Nahabwehr *f*, Nahverteidigung *f*.
closed traverse geschlossener Zug, Polygonzug *m (Surv)*.
closed weather ungünstiges Fliegerwetter *(Avn)*.
close-in security Nahsicherung *f*.
close order geschlossene Ordnung.
close-order drill Exerzieren in der geschlossenen Ordnung.
close range Nahkampfweite *f*; nächste Entfernung *(up to 100 meters)*; nahe Entfernung *(up to 400 meters)*.
close-range fighting Nahkampf *m*.
close-range weapon Nahkampfwaffe *f*.
close reconnaissance Nahaufklärung *f*.
close-reconnaissance airplane Nahaufklärungsflugzeug *n*, Nahaufklärer *m*, Naherkunder *m*.
close support Nahunterstützung *f (Tac)*.
close terrain bewachsenes Gelände.
closing cap Zünderkappe *f*, Verschlußschraube *f (fuze)*.
closing spring cylinder Kraftspeicher *m (AA gun)*.
cloth filter Tucheinsatz *m (MT)*.
cloth garnish bunte Lappen *(Cam)*.
clothing Bekleidung *f*.
clothing account Bekleidungsnachweis *m*.
clothing allowance verabfolgte Kleidungsstücke
clothing slip Bekleidungsschein *m*.
cloud Wolke *f*.
cloud attack Blasangriff *m (CWS)*.
cloud bank Wolkenfeld *n*.
cloud cover Wolkendecke *f*.
cloud formation Wolkenform *f*.
cloud gas attack Blasangriff *m*.
cloud particle Stäubchen *n (CWS)*.
cloud soaring Wolkensegeln *n (glider)*.
clove hitch Mastwurf *m*.
club Knüppel *m (weapon)*.
cluster Sternbündel *n (Sig)*; Bündel *n (Bombing)*.
cluster adapter Bombenbündelträger *m*.
clutch Kupplung *f (MT)*.
throw in the clutch einkuppeln.
throw out the clutch auskuppeln.
clutch cone Kupplungskegel *m*.
clutch housing Kupplungsgehäuse *n*.
clutch lever Kupplungshebel *m*.
clutch pedal Kupplungsfußhebel *m*, Kupplungspedal *n*, Kupplungstritt
clutch plate Kupplungsscheibe *f*.
clutch shaft Kupplungswelle *f*.
clutch spring Kupplungsfeder *f*.
CN Chlorazetophenon *n (CWS)*.
CNB Tränengasstoff *m*.
CN candle Universalkerze CN *f (CWS, USA)*.
CN capsule Reizwürfel *m (CWS)*.
CN generator Riechtopf *m (CWS)*.
CNS Chlorazetophenon-Chlorpikrin-Lösung *f (CWS)*.
CN solution Tränengasstoff *m*.
coal Kohle *f*.
coarse file Grobfeile *f*.
coarse setting Grobeinstellung *f*.
coarse sight Vollkorn *n*, volles Korn *(R)*.
coast Küste *f*.
coastal area Küstengebiet *n*.
Coast Artillery Corps Küstenartilleriekorps *n (USA)*.
coastal force Küstenverband *m*.
coastal reconnaissance airplane Küstenaufklärer *m*.
coastal squadron Küstenstaffel *f (Avn)*.
coastal waters Küstengewässer *npl*.
coastal zone Küstenvorfeld *n*.
coast artillery Küstenartillerie *f*.
coast artillery district Küstenartilleriebezirk *m (USA)*.
Coast Artillery School Küstenartillerieschule *f (USA)*.
coast battery Küstenbatterie *f (CA)*.
coast defense Küstenverteidigung *f*, Küstenwehr *f*, Küstenwacht *f*.
Coast Guard Küstenwache *f*, Küstenwachkorps *n (USA)*.
coast guard station Küstenstation *f*.
coast reconnaissance Küstenaufklärung *f*.
coat Jacke *f*, Rock *m (of a suit)*; Mantel *m*, Überzieher *m (overcoat)*; Schicht *f (of paint, grease, etc.)*. *See also* **service coat**.
coaxial gleichachsig, mit gemeinschaftlicher Achse, Doppel-.
coaxial counterrotating propellers Doppelpropeller *m (Ap)*.
cobalt Kobalt *m*.
cock *v* spannen *(Small Arms)*.
cocking bolt Spannriegel *m (breechblock)*.
cocking cam Spannstollen *m (breechblock)*.
cocking lever Spannhebel *m (G, MG)*.
cocking piece Schlagbolzenmutter *f (R)*.
cocking slide *(MG)* Spannschieber *m*
cockpit Kabine *f*, Kanzel *f*, Führerraum *m*, Führersitz *m*, Führerstand *m (Ap)*.
code Schlüssel *m*, Geheimschrift *f*.
code book Schlüsselheft *n*.
code call Deckanruf *m (Tp)*.
code chart Signaltafel *f*.
code group Funkabkürzung *f*, Kurzsignal *n*, Schlüsselgruppe *f*.
code name Deckname *m*.
code panel Signaltuch *n*, Signalstreifen *m*, Tuchzeichen *n (Avn)*.
code section Schlüsseltrupp *m*.
code sign Deckzeichen *n*.
code word Deckwort *n*.
coding Verschlüsselung *f*, Schlüsseln *n*.
coefficient Beiwert *m*.
coefficient of form Formwert *m (Ballistics)*.
coffee Kaffee *m*.
coffin Sarg *m*.
coil Spule *f (Elec, Rad)*.
coil spring Schraubenfeder *f (MT)*.
coil unit Spulensatz *m (Rad)*.
coincidence range finder Halbbildentfernungsmesser *m*, Schnittbildentfernungsmesser *m*, Koinzidenzentfernungsmesser *m*.
cold Erkältung *f*, Schnupfen *m (Med)*.
cold chisel Kaltmeißel *m*.
cold front Kaltluftfront *f*, Einbruchsfront *f (Met)*.
cold-resistant kältebeständig.
cold working Kaltrecken *n (Ord)*.
collapsible boat Faltboot *n*.
collar Kragen *m (Clo)*.
collar patch Patte *f*, Kragenpatte *f*, Kragenspiegel *m*.
collation of information Nachrichtenbearbeitung *f*.
collecting depot Sammelplatz *m (Salvage)*.
collecting point Krankensammelpunkt *m (Med)*.
collecting station Verwundetensammelstelle *f (Med)*; Leichtverwundetensammelplatz *m (for walking wounded)*.
collecting unit Bergekommando *n*, Sammelkommando *n (Salvage)*.
collective call sign Sammelrufzeichen *n (Rad)*.
collective fire vereinigtes Feuer, zusammengefaßtes Feuer.
collective protection Sammelschutz *m (CWS)*.
collector ring Kollektor *m*, Schleifring *m (Elec)*.
collimate berichtigen *(Surv)*; justieren *(G)*.
collimating mark Kollimationslinie *f*.
collimating sight Richtglas *n*.
collimation Kollimation *f (G)*; Berichtigung *f (Surv)*.
collimator Kollimator *m*, Spaltrohr *n*.
collision Zusammenstoß *m*.
collision course Zielanflugkurs *m (Avn)*.
colonel Oberst *m*; Oberst der Flieger *(AAF)*; Oberstarzt *m (Med)*; Oberstveterinär *m (Vet)*.
color Farbe *f*.
color bearer Fahnenträger *m*.
color blind farbenblind.
colored cloth bunte Lappen *(Cam)*.
color guard Fahnenkompanie *f*, Fahnentrupp *m*, Fahnenwache *f*.
colorless farblos.
colors Fahne *f*.
color salute Senken der Fahne.
color sentinel Fahnenposten *m*, Fahnenwache *f*.
color vision Farbentüchtigkeit *f*.
column Kolonne *f (Tac)*; Reihe *f (Inf drill, Cav)*; Pfeiler *m*, Säule *f (Engr)*.
column commander Kolonnenchef *m (MT)*.
"Column half left, march!" "Halblinks schwenkt, marsch!"
"Column half right, march!" "Halbrechts schwenkt, marsch!"
"Column left, march!" "Links schwenkt, marsch!" *(followed by* "Augen gerade, aus!"*)*.
column of companies Kompaniekolonne *f*.
column of files Kolonne zu Einem.
column of fours Kolonne zu Vieren.
column of groups Gruppenkolonne *f*.
column of platoons Zugkolonne *f*.
column of refugees Flüchtlingskolonne *f*.
column of threes Marschordnung *f (Inf drill)*; Kolonne zu Dreien *(march Clm)*. *See also* **"Fall in!"**
column of troopers Reihe *f*, Reiterreihe *f (Cav)*.
column of twos Doppelreihe *f (Inf drill)*; Kolonne zu Zweien *(march Clm)*. *See also* **"Fall in!"**
"Column right, march!" "Rechts schwenkt, marsch!" *(followed by* "Augen gerade, aus!"*)*.
column traffic Kolonnenverkehr *m*.
comb Kamm *m*.
combat Kampf *m*, Kampfhandlung *f*, Gefecht *n*; Luftkampf *m (Avn)*.
combat activity Kampftätigkeit *f*, Gefechtstätigkeit *f*.
combat airplane Kriegsflugzeug *n*, Frontflugzeug *n*.
combat air reconnaissance Gefechtsluftaufklärung *f*.
combatant Frontkämpfer *m*, Frontsoldat *m*.
combat area Kampfraum *m*.
combat at defiles Gefecht um Engen.
combat aviation Kampf- und Jagdflieger *mpl*.
combat car Kampfwagen *m*, Kampffahrzeug *n*, Panzerwagen *m*.
combat command Kampfgruppe *f (Armd Comd)*.
combat conditions Kampfbedingungen *fpl*.
combat crew fliegendes Personal *(Ap)*.
combat exercise Kampfübung *f*.
combat echelon Kampfstaffel *f*.
combat element Kampftruppe *f*, kämpfende Truppe, Frontverband *m*.
combat engineer regiment Sturmpionier-Regiment *n*.
combat engineers Sturmpioniere *mpl*.
combat firing Gefechtsschießen *n*.
combat formation Gefechtsform *f*, Gefechtsformation *f*.
combat from fortified positions Stellungskampf *m*.
combat frontage Gefechtsbreite *f*.
combat in snow Gefecht bei tiefem Schnee.
combat intelligence Ergebnisse der Gefechtsaufklärung.
combat in towns Ortskampf *m*.
combat in woods Waldgefecht *n*.
combat liaison Gefechtsanschluß *m*.
combat message Gefechtsmeldung *f*; Kampfnachricht *f (Rad)*.
combat mission Gefechtsauftrag *m*, Kampfauftrag *m (Tac)*; Feindflug *m (Avn)*.
combat operation Kampfhandlung *f (Tac)*.
combat order Gefechtsbefehl *m*, Operationsbefehl *m (Tac)*.
combat outpost Gefechtsvorposten *m*.
combat patrol Gefechtsspähtrupp *m*, Stoßtrupp *m*.
combat performance Kampfleistung *f*.
combat practice Gefechtsexerzieren *n*, Gefechtsausbildung *f*, Gefechtsübung *f*, Gefechtsdrill *m*.
combat practice firing gefechtsmäßiges Schießen; Gefechtsschießen *n (advanced)*; Schulgefechtsschießen *n (elementary)*.
combat preparation Bereitstellung *f (Tac)*.
combat reconnaissance Gefechtsaufklärung *f*.
combat report Gefechtsbericht *m*.
combat sector Gefechtsstreifen *m*, Gefechtsabschnitt *m*, Kampfabschnitt *m*.
combat situation Gefechtslage *f*.
combat station *(Ap)* Gefechtsstand *m*
combat team Kampfgruppe *f*, Kampfgemeinschaft *f*.
combat train Gefechtstroß *m*.
combat-train echelon Gefechtsstaffel *f*.
combat troops Kampftruppen *fpl*, Gefechtstruppen *fpl*, Frontverbände *mpl*.
combat unit Kampfeinheit *f*, Gefechtseinheit *f*, Gefechtsgruppe *f*, Kampfgruppe *f*.
combat unit loading gefechtsmäßiges Verladen.
combat vehicle Kampffahrzeug *n*, Gefechtsfahrzeug *n*.
combat zone Gefechtsgebiet *n*.
combination Vereinigung *f*, Zusammenschluß *m (group)*; Verbindung *f (of group, Cmls, etc.)*; Kombination *f (Math)*.
combination fuze Dreifachzünder *m (superquick, delay and time)*; Mehrfachzünder *m*, Doppelzünder *m*.
combination tool Mehrfachwerkzeug *n*.
combination wheel-track car Räder-Raupen-Wagen *m*.
combination wheel-track drive Räder-Gleiskettenantrieb *m (MT)*.
combination wheel-track vehicle Hilfskettenfahrzeug *n*, Räder-Raupen-Fahrzeug *n (MT)*.
combine *v* kombinieren, (sich) vereinigen, zusammensetzen, verbinden *(forces, etc.)*; kombinieren *(Math)*.
combined arms Verband *m*, Kampfverband *m*, gemischter Verband, verbundene Waffen *(Tac)*.
combined-arms armored force Panzerverband *m*.
combined-arms force gemischter Verband.
combined-arms unit Verband aller Waffen, gemischter Verband, Truppenverband *m*.
combined force Kampfgruppe *f*.
combined observation Artilleriebeobachtung mit seitlicher Beobachtungsstelle.
combined operations Operationen der verbundenen Waffen.
combustible composition Anfeuerung *f (Sig cartridge)*.
combustion Verbrennung *f*.
combustion chamber Verbrennungsraum *m (Mtr)*; Laderaum *m (G)*.
"come in" signal Einflugzeichen *n (Inst landing)*.
coming flight Anflug *m*.
command Befehl *m*, Kommando *n (order) (Tac)*; Führung *f (leadership)*; Kommandobehörde *f (agency)*; Befehlsgewalt *f (authority)*.
command airplane Führermaschine *f*.
Command and General Staff School Führer- und Führergehilfen-Schule *f (USA)*.
commandant Kommandeur *m (Mil school)*.
command car Befehlswagen *m*, Kommandowagen *m*.
command channel Befehlsweg *m*.
commandeer requirieren, beitreiben.
command element Stab *m*, Führungsstab *m*, Truppenführer *mpl*.
commander Truppenführer *m*, Befehlshaber *m*; Kommandeur *m (battalion and higher units)*; Kommandant *m (Ap, Tk)*; Fregattenkapitän *m (Nav)*.
commander-in-chief Oberbefehlshaber *m*, Oberkommandierender *m*.
Commander-in-Chief Oberster Befehlshaber.
Commander-in-Chief of the Armed Forces Oberster Befehlshaber der Wehrmacht.
commander of a unit Einheitsführer *m*.
commander of communications zone Kommandant des rückwärtigen Armeegebiets.
commander of the guard Wachvorgesetzter *m*, Wachhabender *m*.
commander of troops Truppenbefehlshaber *m*.
commander's armored truck Panzerbefehlswagen *m (Armd Comd)*.
commander's car Befehlswagen *m*.
commanding officer Führer *m*, Vorgesetzter *m*, Befehlshaber *m*, Truppenführer *m*.
commander's tank Kommandeurpanzer *m*.
command group Führerstab *m*, Befehlsgruppe *f*.
command headquarters Dienststelle *f*.
commanding general Oberbefehlshaber *m*, Kommandierender General.
commanding ground beherrschendes Gelände *(Tac)*.
commanding height beherrschende Höhe *(Top)*.
commanding position Höhenstellung *f*.
command liaison Zusammenwirken mit benachbarten Kommandostellen.
command net Befehlsnetz *n*.
Commando Stoßtrupp *m*, Commando *n (British)*.
command of execution Operationsbefehl *m (Tac)*; Ausführungskommando *n (drill)*.
command pilot Flugzeugführer mit über 10 Dienstjahren.
command post Gefechtsstand *m*, Befehlsstelle *f*, Kommandostelle *f*.
command-post exercise Rahmenübung *f (staff training)*.
command-post flag Kommandoflagge *f (battalion or higher unit)*.
command-post shelter Befehlsstand *m*.
command set Funkanlage für Verkehr von Bord zu Bord, Kommandogerät *n (Ap, Rad)*.
command tank Befehlspanzer *m*,

Kommandopanzer *m.*
command telephone central Führungsvermittlung *f.*
command truck Befehlswagen *m,* Kommandowagen *m (MT).*
"Commence firing!" "Feuer frei!"
commencement of firing Feueröffnung *f.*
commencement of hostilities Ausbruch der Feindseligkeiten.
commendation Anerkennungsschreiben *n.*
comment *n* Erklärung *f,* Deutung *f,* Auslegung *f (interpretation);* Bemerkung *f (remark);* Anmerkung *f (note).*
comment *v* Erklärungen geben *(interpret);* Bemerkungen machen *(remark);* mit Anmerkungen versehen *(annotate).*
commentary Stellungnahme *f (Tac).*
commercial handelsüblich *(vehicles, etc.);* kaufmännisch, kommerziell.
commercial airplane Verkehrsflugzeug *n.*
commercial aviation Zivilluftfahrt *f,* Verkehrsfliegerei *f.*
commercial loading Verladen mit bestmöglicher Raumausnutzung.
commercial motor truck handelsüblicher Lastkraftwagen.
commercial vehicle Nutzfahrzeug *n.*
commissary Verpflegungsamt *n.*
commissary officer Verpflegungsoffizier *m.*
commission *n* Patent *n,* Offizierspatent *n (written order);* Offiziersrang *m (rank and authority).*
commission *v* das Patent verleihen *(as an officer);* in Dienst stellen *(a vessel).*
commissioned officer patentierter Offizier, Offizier *m.*
commit einsetzen, ansetzen *(Tac);* begehen *(a crime).*
commitment Einsatz *m (Tac).*
commitment of armored units Panzereinsatz *m.*
commitment of major forces Großeinsatz *m,* Masseneinsatz *m (Tac).*
commitment order Einsatzbefehl *m.*
commodore Konteradmiral *m (Nav).*
common battery Zentralbatterie *f (Tp).*
common battery system Zentralbatteriesystem *n (Tp).*
communicable disease ansteckende Krankheit.
communicating file Anschlußmann *m,* Verbindungsleute *mpl.*
communicating trench *See* **communication trench.**
communication Mitteilung *f,* Nachricht *f;* Verbindung *f.*
communication battalion Nachrichtenabteilung *f.*
communication chief Nachrichtenunteroffizier *m.*
communication detail Nachrichtentrupp *m.*
communication facilities Nachrichtenanlagen *fpl.*
communication lines Verbindungslinien *fpl.*
communication net Nachrichtennetz *n.*
communication officer Nachrichtenoffizier *m.*
communication platoon Nachrichtenzug *m.*
communication repair truck Nachrichtenwerkstattkraftwagen *m.*
communication route Verbindungsstraße *f.*
communications Nachrichtenmittel *npl,* Nachrichtenverbindung *f,* Nachrichtenwege *mpl.*
communication section Nachrichtenstaffel *f.*
communication station Fernmeldeanlage *f (Rad, Tg, Tp).*
communications zone rückwärtiges Armeegebiet, rückwärtiges Gebiet, Etappe *f.*
communications zone depot rückwärtiges Nachschublager.
communication transmission Nachrichtenübermittlung *f.*
communication trench Verbindungsgraben *m.*
communication truck Nachrichtenwagen *m.*
communication unit Truppennachrichtenverband *m.*
communiqué Kriegsbericht *m;* Heeresbericht *m (official, Army).*
community Gemeinde *f (religious, territorial);* Gemeinschaft *f (social, political).*
commutation of quarters Wohnungsgeldzuschuß *m.*
commutation of rations Verpflegungszuschuß *m.*
commutation value Vergütungswert *m.*
commutator Kollektor *m (Elec).*
compact *adj* dicht, fest, kompakt; kurz, gedrängt *(figurative).*
company Kompanie *f.*
company aid man Sanitätsunteroffizier *m,* Sanitäter *m.*
company area Kompanierevier *n,* Kompaniebezirk *m.*
company boundary Kompaniegrenze *f.*
company clerk Kompanieschreiber *m.*
company commander Kompaniechef *m,* Kompanieführer *m.*
company command post Kompaniegefechtsstand *m.*
company fund Kompaniegelder *npl.*
company grade Kompanieoffiziersrang *m.*
"Company, halt!" "Abteilung, halt!"
company headquarters Kompanieführung *f.*
company headquarters personnel Kompanietrupp *m.*
company litter bearer Kompaniekrankenträger *m.*
company order Kompaniebefehl *m.*
company orderly room Schreibstube *f.*
company street Lagerstraße *f.*
company transport Kompaniefahrzeuge *npl.*
company wedge formation Kompaniekeil *m.*
compartment Kabine *f (Ap).*
compartment of terrain Geländeabschnitt *m.*
compass Bussole *f,* Kompaß *m (magnetic);* Zirkel *m (drawing).*
compass azimuth Kompaßkurswinkel *m.*
compass azimuth ring Bussolenring *m.*
compass bearing Kompaßpeilung *f,* Kompaßzahl *f.*
compass bowl Kompaßkessel *m (Ap).*
compass card Kompaßrose *f,* Scheibenrose *f.*
compass case Bussolengehäuse *n.*
compass compensation Kompaßausgleichung *f.*
compass course Kompaßkurs *m (Avn).*
compass declination Mißweisung, Kompaßmißweisung *f,* Deklination *f.*
compass error Deviation *f,* Kompaßablenkung *f.*
compass heading Kompaßkurs *m.*
compass north magnetische Nordrichtung, Kompaßnord *m.*
compass rose Kompaßrose *f.*
compass traverse Bussolenzug *m (Arty, Surv).*
compel zwingen, nötigen.
compensate ausschalten *(for error, etc.) (Gunnery).*
compensating jet Ausgleichdüse *f.*
compensation Entschädigung *f (reimbursement);* Ersatz *m (damages);* Vergütung *f (award).*
compensator Ausgleicher *m,* Kompensator *m (Ord, Mech).*
compilation Sammlung *f,* Kompilation *f.*
complaint Beschwerde *f,* Klage *f.* Klageschrift *f (Law).*
complement Bemannung *f,* Besatzung *f,* Stärke *f.*
complete *adj* vollzählig, vollständig; vollkommen *(perfect);* ganz *(whole);* vollendet *(finished).*
complete cleaning Hauptreinigung *f (R).*
complete order Gesamtbefehl *m (Tac).*
complete round vollständiger Schuß, kompletter Schuß *(Am).*
completion Erledigung *f.*
component *n* Bestandteil *m,* Einzelteil *m,* Komponente *f.*
component *adj* einen Teil ausmachend, Teil-.
composite connection Doppelbetriebsschaltung *f (Tp).*
composite construction Gemischtbauweise *f.*
compound *n* Einzäunung *f (PW);* Verbindung *f (Cml).*
compound-wound motor Verbundmaschine *f.*
compressed air Druckluft *f,* Preßluft *f.*
compressed-air cleaner Blaspistole *f (MT).*
compressed-air cylinder Preßluftzylinder *m.*
compressed-air equilibrator Luftausgleicher *m (G).*
compressed-air flask Preßluftflasche *f.*
compressed-air starter Preßluftanlasser *m (Mtr).*
compressed-air tank Luftbehälter *m.*
compression Verdichtung *f,* Verdichten *n (Mtr).*
compression-and-rebound range Verschränkbarkeit der Achsen *(of spring suspension) (MT).*
compression chamber Kompressionsraum *m (Mtr).*
compression chord *(Bdg)* Druckgurt *m*
compression cylinder Verdrängungszylinder *m (counterrecoil mechanism).*
compression ratio Verdichtungsverhältnis *n (Mtr).*
compression stroke Verdichtungshub *m (Mtr).*
compressor Drucklufterzeuger *m.*
compulsory zwingend, verbindlich, Zwangs-, Pflicht-.
computation Berechnung *f.*
compute berechnen; schätzen *(estimate).*
computed charge Planladung *f (Engr).*
computer Dreieckrechner *m (circular slide rule, Air Navigation);* Rechner *m (Pers);* Rechengerät *n,* Rechenmaschine *f (Inst).*
computing instrument Rechengerät *n.*
computing slide rule Auswertelineal *n (flash ranging).*
computing station Auswertestelle *f (sound ranging).*
concave hohl, ausgehöhlt, konkav.
concave slope hohle Böschung, konkave Böschung, konkave Geländeneigung *(Top).*
conceal tarnen *(Cam);* verbergen *(an object or person);* verhehlen, verheimlichen *(a fact).*
concealed verdeckt, verschleiert.
concealed machine gun Schweige-MG. *n.*
concealed position verdeckte Stellung.
concealment Deckung *f,* Verdeckung *f,* Verschleierung *f (Tac).*
concentrate *v* massieren.
concentrated attack geballter Angriff, massierter Angriff.
concentrated charge geballte Ladung *(Engr).*
concentrated fire zusammengefaßtes Feuer.
concentration Zusammenballung *f,* Zusammenfassung *f,* Ansammlung *f (Tac);* Dichte *f,* Gehalt *m,* Kampfstoffgehalt *m,* Anreicherung *f,* Luftanreicherung *f (CWS);* Feuerschlag *m,* Feuerüberfall *m (Arty).*
concentration area Aufmarschgebiet *n (Tac).*
concentration camp Konzentrationslager *n.*
concentration fire *See* **concentrated fire.**
concentration march Aufmarsch *m.*
concentration of fire Feuervereinigung *f (Arty).*
concentration of troops Truppenansammlung *f.*
concentration ring Korbring *m (Bln).*
concentric konzentrisch.
concertina Drahtrolle *f;* Stacheldrahtrolle *f,* S.-Rolle *f (barbed wire);* Klaviersaitendrahtrolle *f,* K.-Rolle *f (plain wire).*
conclusion Folge *f,* Folgerung *f,* Schluß *m (deduction, inference);* Beschluß *m,* Entscheidung *f (decision);* Abschluß *m (of a treaty).*
concrete Beton *m (Engr).*
concrete bridge Betonbrücke *f.*
concrete bunker Betonbunker *m.*
concrete dugout Betonunterstand *m.*
concrete emplacement Bunker *m,* Bunkerstand *m.*
concrete mixer Betonmischmaschine *f.*
concrete obstacle Betonsperre *f.*
concrete paving block Zementfliese *f.*
concrete pillbox Betonbunker *m.*
concrete shelter Bunker *m,* Betonunterstand *m.*
concrete turret Betonturm *m (Ft).*
concur übereinstimmen.
concurrent gleichzeitig *(at same time);* übereinstimmend *(corresponding);* zustimmend *(Law).*
concussion Luftstoß *m;* Erschütterung *f.*
concussion of the brain Gehirnerschütterung *f.*
concussion plunger Zündbolzen *m (power-train time fuze) (Am).*
condemn verurteilen *(to sentence);* tadeln, mißbilligen *(disapprove);* beschlagnahmen *(Law).*
condenser Kondensator *m (Rad).*
condenser microphone Kondensatormikrophon *n.*
condenser plates Belegungen *fpl*
condition Zustand *m,* Beschaffenheit *f (state);* Bedingung *f (stipulation).*
condom Vorbeugungsmittel *n,* Schutzmittel *n,* Selbstschutzmittel *n.*
conduct *n* Benehmen *n,* Betragen *n (behavior);* Führung *f,* Leitung *f (direction, management).*
conductivity Leitfähigkeit *f (Elec).*
conduct of battle Kampfführung *f.*
conduction capacitance Leitungskapazität *f (Elec).*
conduct of field operations Truppenführung *f.*
conduct of fire Feuerregelung *f.*
conductor Leiter *m (Elec);* Schaffner *m (RR).*
conduit Schacht *m,* Durchlaß *m.*
cone Kegel *m;* Garbe *f (Ballistics);* Lautsprechertrichter *m (Rad).*
cone clutch Kegelkupplung *f,* Konuskupplung *f (MT).*
cone of dispersion Garbe *f,* Feuergarbe *f,* Schußgarbe *f,* Streukegel *m.*
cone of fire *See* **cone of dispersion.**
cone of light Lichtkegel *m.*
cone speaker Trichterlautsprecher *m (Rad).*
conference Besprechung *f,* Führerbesprechung *f.*
conference call Sammelgespräch *n (Tp).*
confidence Zuversicht *f (reasonable certainty);* Vertrauen *n (trust).*
confidential vertraulich, geheim.
confidential document Kommandosache *f.*
configuration of terrain Geländegestaltung *f,* Bodengestaltung *f.*
confine begrenzen, einschränken *(restrict);* einsperren, einschließen *(imprison).*
confinement Arrest *m,* Arreststrafe *f,* Haft *f,* Beschränkung *f.*
confirm bestätigen.
confirmatory order Befehlsbestätigung *f.*
confiscation Beschlagnahme *f.*
confuse verwirren, aus der Fassung bringen, bestürzt machen *(bewilder);* verwirren, durcheinanderbringen *(create disorder).*
confusion Verwirrung *f,* Unordnung *f,* Durcheinander *n (disorder);* Verlegenheit *f (embarrassment, perplexity).*
congestion Verkehrsstockung *f (traffic);* Anhäufung *f,* Überfüllung *f.*
Congressional Medal of Honor Ehrenmedaille *f (USA).*
conical peak Kegel *m (Top).*
conical roller bearing Kegelrollenlager *n.*
conic projection Kegelprojektion *f.*
connect vermitteln *(Tp);* verbinden, anschließen *(Tech).*
connecting cord Verbindungsschnur *f (Tp).*
connecting elements Verbindungsorgane *npl (march column).*
connecting file Anschlußmann *m,* Verbindungsleute *mpl.*
connecting group Verbindungstrupp *m.*
connecting jack Vermittlungsklinke *f (Tp).*
connecting piece Anschlußstück *n (gas mask).*
connecting plug Anschlußstecker *m (Elec).*
connecting point Anschlußpunkt *m (in axes of Sig Com) (Tp).*
connecting rod Kurbelstange *f,* Pleuelstange *f.*
connecting sleeve Kabelverbinder *m (Tp).*
connecting thread Anschlußgewinde *n (Mech).*
connecting trench Verbindungsgraben *m.*
connecting wire Drahtverbindung *f,* Anschlußschnur *f (Elec).*
connection Vermittlung *f,* Gesprächsverbindung *f (Tp);* Schaltung *f (Elec).*
connector Kettenkurbel *f (MG);* Triebzahn *m (caterpillar track).*
conquer erobern *(territory or locality);* besiegen *(the enemy).*
conquest Eroberung *f.*
conscientious objector Kriegsdienstverweigerer *m.*
conscript *v* ausheben.
conscription Aushebung *f.*
consent *v* genehmigen *(approve);* beistimmen, einwilligen *(agree to).*
consider bedenken, erwägen *(ponder);* in Betracht ziehen, berücksichtigen *(take into account);* schätzen, halten für, ansehen für *(to regard).*
consideration Betrachtung *f,* Erwägung *f;* Bedeutung *f,* Wichtigkeit *f (importance);* Rücksicht *f (thoughtfulness).*
consolidate vereinigen, zusammenbringen; ausbauen *(a position).*
consolidation of position Einrichten einer Stellung.
conspiracy Verschwörung *f.*
conspire sich verschwören.
constant *n* Konstante *f (Math).*
constant *adj* beständig, unverändert, unveränderlich *(unchangeable);* fortwährend *(continuous);* konstant, gleichbleibend *(Math).*
constant-mesh transmission Aphongetriebe *n (MT).*
constellation Sternbild *n,* Konstellation *f.*
constitute aufstellen *(a unit).*
construct (er)bauen *(build);* errichten *(erect);* konstruieren, entwerfen *(geometry).*
construction Bau *m,* Ausbau *m,* Bauausführung *f,* Fertigung *f.*
construction battalion Baubataillon *n.*
construction company Baukompanie *f (Mil).*
construction detail Bautrupp *m.*
construction float Einbaufähre *f.*
construction troops Bautruppen *fpl.*
construction zone Baubezirk *m.*
contact Berührung *f,* Fühlung *f,* Verbindung *f,* Anschluß *m (Tac);* Kontaktstück *n (Elec).*
"Contact!" "Ein!", "Zündung eingestellt!" *(Avn).*
contact fire Stoßzündung *f,* Berührungszündung *f (Nav).*
contact flight Sichtnavigation *f (Air Navigation).*
contact light Landebahnfeuer *n (Adrm).*
contact mine Kontaktmine *f,* Stoßmine *f,* Stoßkappenmine *f (Nav).*
contact mission Fühlunghalten *n (Avn).*
contact party Werkstatt-Trupp *m.*
contact patrol Verbindungspatrouille *f (Tac);* Infanterieflug *m (Avn).*
contact piece Druckstück *n (R trigger);* Kontaktstück *n (Elec).*
contact point Schließstelle *f (Elec).*
contact print Abzug *m (Photo).*
contact surface Auflagefläche *f.*
contact with the enemy Feindberührung *f.*
contagious disease ansteckende Krankheit.
contain fesseln, festhalten, binden, hinhalten *(Tac).*
container Topf *m (hand grenade);* Behälter *m (gasoline tank, etc.);* Blechkanister *m (metal container for gasoline, water, etc.);* Faß *n,* Tonne *f, (barrel or drum).*
containing attack Fesselungsvorstoß *m.*
contaminate vergiften *(CWS).*
contaminated area Gassperre *f,* Kampfstoffsperre *f,* vergiftetes Gelände *(CWS).*
contamination Vergiftung *f (CWS).*
contempt Verachtung *f;* Mißachtung *f (of court).*
contest *v* streitig machen.
contiguous Nachbar-.
contingent *n* Kontingent *n (quota of troops, etc.).*
contingent *adj* abhängig, bedingt.
continuance Aussetzung *f,* Aufschub *m (Law).*
continuous fire Dauerfeuer *n (MG, AAA).*
continuous interference Dauerstörung *f (Rad).*
continuous note Dauerton *m (Rad).*
continuous radio alert Funkdauerbereitschaft *f.*
contour *n* Höhenlinie *f,* Höhenschichtlinie *f (Top).*
contour interval senkrechter Abstand der Schichtlinien *(Top).*
contour line Höhenlinie *f,* Höhenschichtlinie *f,* Schichtlinie *f (Top).*
contour map Höhenlinienkarte *f.*
contraband of war Bannware *f,* Konterbande *f,* Kriegskonterbande *f.*
contract *n* Vertrag *m.*
contract *v* einen Vertrag abschließen *(business);* anstecken *(a disease);* (sich) zusammenziehen, einschrumpfen, eingehen *(shrink).*
contracting powers Vertragsstaaten *mpl (treaties, etc.).*
contracting officer zu Vertragsabschlüssen bevollmächtigter Offizier.
contracting parties vertragschließende Teile *(Law).*
contractor Vertragsschließende(r) *m,* Kontrahent *m;* Bauunternehmer *m (builder);* Lieferant *m (supplier).*
contract surgeon Vertragsarzt *m.*
contradiction Widerspruch *m.*
contrast Gegensatz *m,* Kontrast *m.*
control *n* Kontrolle *f,* Oberaufsicht *f,* Leitung *f;* Kontroll-; Leit-.
control *v* beaufsichtigen, überwachen, kontrollieren; nachprüfen *(check up);* (be)herrschen *(govern);* sich beherrschen *(restrain oneself).*
control airport Flughafen mit Flugsicherungsanlagen.
control aneroid barometrische Reglerdose *(Ap engine).*
control board Schalttafel *f (Elec).*
control box Kupplungskasten *m (AA director).*
control buoy Minenmarkierboje *f (Nav).*
control cabin Führerraum *m,* Führerkanzel *f,* Führerstand *f (Ap).*
control cable Bowdenzug *m (in flexible steel conduit).*
control car Führergondel *f (airship).*
control center Luftschutzwarnzentrale *f (AWS).*
control column Steuersäule *f (Ap).*
control device Bedienungseinrichtung *f.*
control flag Winkflagge *f,* Winkerflagge *f.*
control grid Steuergitter *n (Rad tube).*
control grip Drehgriff *m (Mtcl).*
controllable kontrollierbar *(capable of supervision);* steuerbar *(Tech);* verstellbar *(Ap propeller).*
controllable-pitch propeller Verstellschraube *f,* Verstell-Luftschraube *f,* Dreiblattverstellschraube *f (three-blade) (Ap).*
controlled mine Grundmine *f,* Beobachtungsmine *f (Nav).*
controlled mosaic Bildplan *m (aerial Photo).*
controlled tower Sprungturm *m,* Fallschirm-Absprungturm *m (Prcht Tng).*
controller Bediener *m (AA searchlight).*
controlling Steuern *n.*
control officer Marschführer *m (march column).*

control of the air Luftherrschaft *f.*
control panel Schalttafel *f (Elec).*
control point Orientierungspunkt *m,* Festpunkt *m (Surv);* Verkehrsposten *m,* Marschkontrollstelle *f (traffic);* Auskunftstelle *f,* Meldestelle *f (Sig C).*
control rod Verstellwelle *f (Ap).*
controls Flugzeugsteuerung *f,* Steuerung *f,* Steuerorgane *npl (Ap).*
control servo Hilfsvorrichtung *f,* Servomotor *m,* Trimmklappe *f (Ap).*
control shaft Steuerwelle *f (Ap).*
control station Scheinwerferrichtungsweiser *m (AA SL);* Leitfunkstelle *f,* Hauptfunkstelle *f (Rad).*
control-station traffic Leitverkehr *m (Rad).*
control stick Knüppel *m,* Steuerknüppel *m (Ap).*
control surface Steuerfläche *f (Ap).*
control system Steuerung *f (Ap).*
control tower Abfertigungsgebäude *n,* Aufsichtsturm *m,* Befehlsgebäude *n,* Befehlsstelle *f (Adrm).*
control wheel Steuerrad *n (Ap).*
cooling system Kühlung *f,* Kühlanlage *f (Mtr).*
cooperate mitwirken, zusammenarbeiten; beitragen *(contribute to);* unterstützen *(support).*
cooperation Mitwirkung *f,* Zusammenarbeit *f;* Unterstützung *f (support).*
cooperative *adj* mitwirkend; behilflich.
coordinate *n* Koordinate *f.*
coordinate *v* beiordnen, koordinieren, zum Zusammenwirken bringen.
coordinate cards Koordinatenschieber *mpl (Surv).*
coordinated attack planmäßiger Angriff, einheitlich angesetzter Angriff *(Tac).*
coordinate map grid Gitternetz *n.*
coordinate scale Planzeiger *m (Arty, Surv).*
coordinate system Koordinatensystem *n.*
coordination Zusammenwirken *n.*
co-pilot zweiter Flugzeugführer.
copper Kupfer *n.*
copper cup kupfernes Hütchen *(cartridge).*
copper shell Kupferkapsel *f (detonator cap).*
copper wire Kupferdraht *m.*
copy *n* Abschrift *f,* Kopie *f;* Durchschlag *m (carbon copy);* Exemplar *n,* Abdruck *m (of a book);* Manuskript *n (for printer);* Nummer *f (of a newspaper);* Nachahmung *f (imitation).*
cord Seil *n,* Strick *m (rope);* Schnur *f (twine);* Klafter *f (of wood).*
cord fuze Leitfeuer *n (Engr).*
cord-fuze detonation Leitfeuerzündung *f (Engr).*
cord-fuze detonator Leitfeuerzündmittel *n (Engr).*
cordite Kordit *n (explosive).*
cord lashing Schnürbund *m (Engr).*
cordon Gürtel *m (Tac).*
cord powder Stäbchenpulver *n (Am).*
corduroy road Knüppelweg *m,* Knüppeldamm *m,* Schwellenbahn *f.*
core of bullet Geschoßkern *m.*
cork Kork *m (substance);* Kork(en) *m,* Pfropfen *m,* Stöpsel *m (stopper).*
corkscrew Korkenzieher *m.*
coronet Hufkrone *f (of hoof).*
corporal Obergefreiter *m.*
control zone Flugplatzzone *f (Adrm).*
contusion Quetschung *f,* Quetschwunde *f (Med).*
convalescence Genesung *f,* Konvaleszenz *f.*
convalescent *n* Rekonvaleszent *m.*
convalescent camp Genesungsanstalt *f,* Genesungsheim *n.*
convalescent hospital Leichtkrankenkriegslazarett *n.*
convection Strahlung *f,* Konvektion *f.*
conventional sign Kartenzeichen *n,* Kartensignatur *f,* Signatur *f (Top).*
converge zusammenlaufen, konvergieren.
convergence Zusammenlaufen *n,* Zusammenstrahlen *n.*
convergent zusammenlaufend, konvergierend.
converging attack konzentrischer Angriff *(Tac).*
converging fire konzentrisches Feuer *(Arty).*
conversion Umrechnung *f (Math).*
conversion table Umrechnungstabelle *f,* Umrechnungstafel *f.*
convert *v* umrechnen *(Math);* umändern, umwandeln *(change);* bekehren *(to a party, religion).*
converter Umformer *m (Elec);* Chiffriermaschine *f,* Schlüsselmaschine *f (cipher device).*
converter unit Umformersatz *m (Elec).*
convertible umrechenbar *(Math);* vertauschbar, umwechselbar, umwandelbar.
convex konvex, gewölbt.
convex slope gewölbte Böschung *(Top).*
convoy Begleitzug *m,* Geleitzug *m.*
convoy commander Kraftfahrzeugkolonnenführer *m (MT).*
convoy guard Geleitschutz *m (Nav).*
cook *n* Feldkochunteroffizier *m (NCO).*
cooking pit Kochloch *n.*
cool *v* kühlen, abkühlen.
cool *adj* kühl, frisch; ruhig *(calm).*
coolant Kühlmittel *n (Mtr).*
cooling fin Kühlrippe *f,* Lamelle *f (Mtr).*
cooling liquid Kühlflüssigkeit *f (Mtr).*
corporal of the guard Aufführender *m.*
corps Korps *n.*
corps area Korpsbezirk *m.*
corps artillery Korpsartillerie *f.*
corps artillery commander Artilleriekommandeur *m.*
corps cavalry regiment Korps-Kavallerieregiment *n.*
corps combat order Korpsbefehl *m.*
corps communication battalion Korpsnachrichtenabteilung *f.*
corpse Leiche *f.*
corps engineer Kommandeur der Pioniere.
corps headquarters Generalkommando *n,* Korpskommando *n.*
Corps of Chaplains Wehrmachtseelsorgedienst *m.*
Corps of Engineers Pionierkorps *n,* Pioniertruppe *f.*
corps quartermaster Kommandeur der Korpsnachschubtruppen *(USA).*
corps supply column Korpsnachschubkolonne *f.*
corps troops Korpstruppen *fpl.*
corrected azimuth berichtigte Teilringeinstellung *(Gunnery).*
corrected deflection berichtigte Seitenrichtung *(Gunnery).*
corrected elevation Aufsatzerhöhung *f (Gunnery).*
corrected range Aufsatzentfernung *f (Gunnery).*
correction Berichtigung *f,* Verbesserung *f (Gunnery);* Irrung *f (Rad procedure).*
correction angle Verbesserungswinkel *m (Gunnery).*
correction factor Verbesserungswert *m (Ballistics).*
corrector Brennlängenschieber *m (fuze).*
corrector pointer Schlüsselschieber *m (hand fuze setter).*
correlation Wechselbeziehung *f,* Korrelation *f.*
correspondence Schriftverkehr *m.*
correspondence course Fernkurs *m.*
correspondent Kriegsberichter *m (in Ger propaganda Co);* Berichter *m,* Berichterstatter *m,* Korrespondent *m.*
corresponding range Überschießgrenze *f.*
corridor Geländestreifen *m.*
corroboration Bekräftigung *f,* Bestätigung *f.*
corrugated paper Wellpappe *f.*
cosecant Kosekante *f.*
cosine Kosinus *m.*
cost *n* Preis *m,* Kosten *pl.*
cot Feldbett *n,* Pritsche *f.*
cotangent Kotangens *m (function);* Kotangente *f (line).*
cotter pin Splint *m.*
cotton Baumwolle *f;* Watte *f (Med).*
cotton linters Baumwollabfall *m.*
cotton waste Putzwolle *f (for cleaning).*
counsel Anwalt *m,* Rechtsbeistand *m (Law);* Rat *m (advice).*
count *n* Graf *m (title);* Zahl *f (number).*
count *v* zählen *(enumerate);* rechnen *(compute).*
counteract zuwiderhandeln, entgegenwirken; verhindern *(prevent);* vereiteln *(nullify).*
counterapproach trench Gegenlaufgraben *m.*
counterattack Gegenangriff *m (Tac).*
counterbalance Massenausgleich *m (Ap);* Gegengewicht *n (Mech).*
counterbattery fire Artilleriebekämpfung *f.*
counterclockwise im Gegensinn zum Uhrzeiger, im Gegenzeigersinn, linksgängig, linkslaufend.
counterespionage Spionageabwehr *f,* Gegenspionage *f.*
counterfire Erwiderungsfeuer *n,* Gegenfeuer *n,* Feuerkampf *m.*
counterintelligence Abwehrdienst *m.*
countermand Gegenbefehl geben.
countermarch Gegenmarsch *m.*
countermeasure Gegenmaßnahme *f.*
countermine Gegenmine *f,* Gegenstollen *m.*
counteroffensive Gegenoffensive *f.*
counterorder Gegenbefehl *m.*
counterpoise Gegengewicht *n (Rad, Mech);* Beschwerungsstück *n,* Beschwerungsrohr *n (G).*
counterpreparation Gegenvorbereitungsfeuer *n.*
counterpropaganda Gegenpropaganda *f.*
counterrecoil Vorlauf *m,* Vorlaufbewegung *f.*
counterrecoil mechanism Vorholeinrichtung *f,* Vorholer *m (G).*
counterrecoil piston rod Vorlaufhemmstange *f (G).*
counterreconnaissance Gegenaufklärung *f.*
counterreconnaissance screen Gegenaufklärungsstreifen *m.*
counterrotating propellers gegenläufige Luftschrauben *(Ap).*
countershaft Vorgelegewelle *f (MT).*
countersign Erkennungswort *n,* Gegenlosung *f.*
counterslope Gegenböschung *f,* Gegenhang *m.*
counterthrust Gegenstoß *m (Tac).*
counterweight Beschwerungsstück *n,* Beschwerungsrohr *n (G);* Massenausgleich *m (Ap);* Gegengewicht *n (Mech).*
"Count off!" "Abzählen!"
country Land *n;* Gelände *n (terrain);* Gegend *f (region).*
country of origin Heimatstaat *m.*
couple *v* aufprotzen *(Arty).*
coupling Kopplung *f (Mech, Rad);* Kupplung *f (Mech);* Anschluß *m (Ord).*
courier Kurier *m.*
courier mail Kurierpost *f.*
course Kurs *m (Nav, Avn);* Flugweg *m,* Flugrichtung *f (Avn);* Lehrgang *m (instruction).*
course determination Flugwegbestimmung *f (Air Navigation).*
course light Streckenfeuer *n,* Flugstreckenfeuer *n.*
course of target Zielweg *m (AA gunnery).*
court Gericht *n. See also* **military court.**
courtesy Höflichkeit *f,* höfliche Formen. *See also* **military courtesy.**
court-martial Kriegsgericht *n.*
court-martial proceedings Kriegsgerichtsverfahren *n.*
court plaster Leukoplast *n.*
cover *n* Schutz *m;* Decke *f;* Deckel *m;* Überzug *m;* Deckung *f,* Eindeckung *f (Ft);* Aufnahme *f (for withdrawal in delaying action, Tac);* Hülsenbrücke *f (R receiver).*
cover *v* durch Feuer decken, decken, schützen.
coverage Bedeckung *f (Met);* Feuerschutz *m,* Feuerunterstützung *f (Tac);* Geländeausschnitt *m (aerial Photo).*
covering Tarndecke *f (Cam);* Außenhaut *f,* Bespannung *f (Ap);* Verschalung *f.*
covering fire Feuerschutz *m.*
covering force Deckungstruppe *f;* Aufnahme *f (reserve force covering withdrawal from action).*
covering party Deckungstrupp *m.*
covering position vorgeschobene Stellung *(in defense);* Aufnahmestellung *f (covering withdrawal from action).*
"Cover off!" "Vordermann!"; "Auf Vordermann gehen!" *(behind file leaders when in platoon front).*
cover off auf Vordermann gehen, auf Vordermann stehen, Vordermann nehmen.
cover plate Abdeckplatte *f (G).*
cover-plate latch Deckelriegel *m (MG).*
cover-plate lock Deckelsperre *f (MG).*
cover position gedeckte Stellung.
cover trench Deckungsgraben *m.*
cowardice Feigheit *f.*
cowl flaps Luftabflußklappen *fpl (Ap).*
cowling Haube *f,* Verkleidung *f (Ap).*
crab Luvwinkel *m (Avn).*
crabbing windschiefer Flug *(Avn).*
crack *n* Riß *m,* Sprung *m,* Spalt *m (split);* Krach *m,* Knall *m (sound).*
crack *v* zerspalten, zersprengen, zerbrechen.
crack-up Bruch *m (Avn).*
cradle Wiege *f,* Rohrwiege *f (G);* Gewehrträger *m (on MG sleigh mount or tripod).*
cradle frame Wiegenträger *m (G).*
cradle guide rails Wiegengleitbahn *f (G).*
cradle lock Wiegenzurrung *f (G).*
craft Wasserfahrzeug *n (stream crossing).*
crane Kran *m (Engr).*
crank *n* Kurbel *f.*
crank *v* andrehen, ankurbeln, anwerfen.
crank arm Kurbelarm *m (crank shaft).*
crankcase Kurbelgehäuse *n (Mtr).*
crank handle Andrehkurbel *f (MT).*
crank mechanism Kurbeltrieb *m (Mech).*
crankpin Kurbelzapfen *m (Mtr).*
crankshaft Kurbelwelle *f (Mtr).*
crankshaft assembly Kurbeltriebwerk *n (Mtr).*
crankshaft throw Kröpfung der Kurbelwelle *(Mtr).*
crank starter Handanlasser *m (Mtr).*
crankwheel Kurbelrad *n (G).*
crankwheel operation exercise Kurbelübung *f (gun laying).*
crash *n* Bruch *m (Avn).*
crash boat Fliegerrettungsboot *n.*
crash helmet Schutzmütze *f (Armd Comd);* Sturzhelm *m.*
crash landing Bruchlandung *f (Avn).*
crash padding Schutzpolsterung *f.*
crater Trichter *m,* Sprengtrichter *m.*
crater charge Trichterladung *f (Engr).*
crawl *v* robben *(on land);* kraulen *(swimming).*
crawl forward sich vorrobben.
crawl trench Kriechgraben *m.*
credit *n* Kredit *m,* Guthaben *n (financial);* Anerkennung *f (acknowledgment).*
creep kriechen.
creeping barrage Feuerwalze *f.*
cremation Einäscherung *f.*
creosote Kreosot *n.*
cresol soap solution Kresolseifenlösung *f,* Kresolwasser *n.*
crest Kamm *m,* Kammlinie *f (Top);* Gewehrauflage *f,* Brustwehrkrone *f (trench);* Krone *f.*
crew Besatzung *f,* Mannschaft *f (Ap, Tk);* Bedienung *f (G, SL).*
crib Stapel *m (Bdg).*
crime Verbrechen *n.*
criminal Verbrecher *m.*
crimp Würgung *f (Am).*
crimper Würgezange *f.*
critical item Sparstoff *m.*
critical point Gefahrpunkt *m,* kritischer Punkt *(Tac);* Wechselpunkt *m (Top).*
critical speed kritische Geschwindigkeit; Durchsackgeschwindigkeit *f (Avn);* kritische Drehzahl *(Mech).*
critical zone Planfeuerwürfel *m (AA firing).*
critique Schlußbesprechung *f.*
cross *n* Kreuz *n;* Zapfenkreuz *n (universal joint) (MT).*
cross *v* überqueren *(a river, etc.);* überschreiten *(a bridge, road, etc.).*
crossbar Traverse *f (split-trail carriage);* Querverbindung *f (log sled).*
crossbelt Schulterriemen *m (Clo).*
cross bracing Auskreuzung *f (Ap);* Querverstrebung *f (Bdg).*
cross-country querfeldein; geländegängig; Überland-, Gelände-.
cross-country driving Geländefahren *n.*
cross-country flight Überlandflug *m.*
cross-country mobility Geländegängigkeit *f.*
cross-country vehicle Geländefahrzeug *n (MT).*
crosscut saw Hirnsäge *f,* Quersäge *f.*
cross-examination Kreuzverhör *n.*
cross-examine einem Kreuzverhör unterwerfen.
cross fire *n* Kreuzfeuer *n.*
cross-fire *v* Feuer kreuzen *(firing).*
cross hairs Fadenkreuz *n (Optics).*
cross hole screw Kreuzlochschraube *f.*
crossing Übergang *m.*
crossing of ditches Grabendurchfahrt *f (MT).*
crossing of rivers Überwinden von Flüssen.
crossing point Übersetzstelle *f.*
crossing station Übergangsbahnhof *m,* Kreuzungsbahnhof *m (RR).*
crossing target querfahrendes Ziel.
cross level *n* Querlibelle *f,* Verkantungslibelle *f (Optics, Surv, Arty);* Radstandlibelle *f (G).*
cross-level *v* die Libelle einspielen.
cross-level drive Verkantungstrieb *m (Optics, Ord).*
cross leveling Libelleneinstellung *f (firing).*
cross-leveling mechanism Radstandtrieb *m (G sight).*
cross lines Kreuzleinen *fpl (of harness).*
crosspiece Ducht *f (boat).*
cross pipe fitting Kreuzmuffe *f.*
crossroads Wegekreuzung *f,* Straßenkreuzung *f.*
cross section Profil *n,* Querschnitt *m.*
cross wind seitlicher Schiebewind *(Avn).*
cross-wind landing Landung mit Seitenwind.
cross-wind takeoff Start mit Seitenwind.
cross wires Fadenkreuz *n (Optics).*
crouching fox hole Hockloch *n.*
croup Kruppe *f (horse).*
crowbar Brechstange *f,* Hebebaum *m.*
crown of roadbed Bahnkrone *f (RR).*
crownpiece Kopfstück *n (harness).*
crucible steel Tiegelgußstahl *m.*
crude oil Rohöl *n.*
cruise *v* fahren *(vehicle or ship);* kreuzen *(ship);* fliegen *(Ap).*
cruiser Kreuzer *m.*
cruising power rating Reisedauerleistung *f.*
cruising radius Fahrbereich *m (MT, Tk).*
cruising speed Reisegeschwindigkeit *f (Ap);* Marschgeschwindigkeit *f (MT).*
crush (zer)quetschen, zerdrücken, zermalmen.
cryptanalysis Entzifferung *f,* Geheimschriftanalyse *f.*
cryptogram Kryptogramm *n.*
cryptograph *See* **cryptogram.**
cryptography Geheimschrift *f.*
crystal Kristall *m.*
crystal control Quarzsteuerung *f (Rad).*
crystal-controlled transmitter quarzgesteuerter Sender *(Rad).*
crystal detector Kristalldetektor *m (Rad).*
cube *n* Würfel *m,* Kubus *m;* Kubikzahl *f,* dritte Potenz *(Math).*
cubed zur dritten Potenz erhoben.
cubic centimeter Kubikzentimeter *n.*
cultivated fields bebaute Felder.
culvert Durchlaß *m.*
cumulus cloud Haufenwolke *f,* Kumuluswolke *f.*
cup Trinkbecher *m (drinking);* Schmierbüchse *f (grease);* Hütchen *n (cartridge).*
cup anemometer Schalenkreuzwindmesser *m (Met).*
cupola Kuppel *f,* Beobachtungskuppel *f,* Turmkuppel *f,* Beobachtungstürmchen *n,* Turmaufsatz *m (Tk).*
cupola mount Kuppellafette *f (Ap).*
curb bit Kandare *f (harness).*
curb chain Kinnkette *f (harness).*
curbing Rödelung *f (Bdg).*
curb lashing Rödeln *n (Bdg).*
curb rail Rödelbalken *m (Bdg).*
curb rein Kandarenzügel *m (harness).*
cure *v* heilen.
curfew Ausgehverbot *n (Mil Govt).*
currency Währung *f;* Geld *n (money).*
current *n* Strom *m,* Strömung *f.*
current capacity Stromaufnahme *f (Rad).*
current consumer Stromverbraucher *m (Elec).*
current flow Stromfluß *m (Elec).*
current generator unit Stromaggregat *n (Elec).*
current intensity Stromstärke *f (Elec.)*
current-measuring instrument Strommeßgerät *n (Elec).*
current supplies laufender Nachschub.
current supply Stromzufuhr *f* Stromvorrat *m (Elec).*
current surge Stromstoß *m (Elec).*
currycomb Striegel *m.*
curtain door Gasschutzvorhang *m.*
curtain of antiaircraft fire Flaksperre *f,* Sperrfeuerwand *f.*
curtain of fire Feuerwand *f,* Feuervorhang *m.*
curvature Krümmung *f,* Biegung *f.*
curve *n* Straßenbiegung *f (road);* Krümmung *f,* Kurve *f,* Bogen *m.*
curved-chord truss Parabel-Fachwerkträger *m (Engr).*
curved spur track Gleiskurve *f,* Klaue *f (RR gun).*
curve of the trajectory Gestalt der Flugbahn.
curvilinear flight Kurvenflug *m.*
cushion tire Pneumassivreifen *m,* Hochelastikreifen *m (MT).*
custodian Urkundenbewahrer *m (of documents).*
custody Haft *f,* Gewahrsam *m;* Aufsicht *f,* Hut *f,* Verwahrung *f (care);* Schutz *m (protection).*
custom Gebrauch *m.*
custom house Zollhaus *n.*
customs of the service Truppenbrauch *m.*
customs of war Kriegsbrauch *m,* Kriegsgebrauch *m.*
cut *n* Durchstich *m,* Einschnitt *m (Engr, RR);* Schnitt *m (injury or wound);* Hieb *m (slash).*
cut *v* schneiden, abschneiden *(wire, etc.);* hauen, abhauen *(trees, etc.).*
cut a fuze Zünder einstellen.
cut-and-cover shelter Unterschlupf *m.*
cut film Schnittfilm *m.*
cut off trennen *(Elec, Tp).*
cut-off frequency Grenzfrequenz *f (Rad).*
cutout Auspuffklappe *f (Mtr).*
cutter *See* **cutting pliers.**
cutting pliers Zwickzange *f (Engr).*
cw tonlos *(marking on Rad set).*
cw transmission Telegraphiesendung *f (Rad).*
cyanogen bromide Bromzyan *n,* Ce-Stoff *m (CWS).*
cyanogen chloride Chlorzyan *n,* Cyanogenchlorid *n (CWS).*
cycle Periode *f,* Hertz *n (Elec);* Kreisprozeß *m (Mtr);* Kreislauf *m.*
cyclic change mechanism Vorrichtung zur Verlangsamung der Schußfolge *(automatic R).*
cyclic rate Schußfolge *f.*
cyclic rate mechanism *See* **cyclic change mechanism.**
cyclogiro Radflügelflugzeug *n (Avn).*
cyclone Zyklon *m,* Tief *n (low);* Orkan *m,* Taifun *m (tropical);* Wirbelsturm *m,* Tornado *m,* Trombe *f (tornado).*
cylinder Zylinder *m.*

cylinder block Motorblock *m*, Zylinderblock *m* *(Mtr)*.

cylinder grinding Zylinderschleifen *n* *(Mtr)*.

cylinder head Zylinderkopf *m* *(Mtr)*.

cylinder liner Zylinderlaufbüchse *f* *(Mtr)*.

cylinder wall Zylinderwand *f* *(Mtr)*.

cylindrical zylindrisch, walzenförmig.

cylindrical cam Lenkschraube *f* *(steering column, MT)*.

cylindrical grid Zylinderelektrode *f* *(Rad tube)*.

cylindrical mount Walzenblende *f* *(Tk gun)*.

D

dagger Dolch *m*.

daily automatic supply Tagesversorgung *f*.

daily ration Tagesverpflegung *f*.

daily ration strength return Stärkenachweis für die Tagesverpflegung.

daily sick report Krankenmeldung *f*.

daily stock record Bestandsnachweisung *f*.

daily strength report Iststärkenachweisung *f*.

daily telegram tägliche Stärke- und Bedarfsmeldung.

daily train tägliche Nachschubkolonne *(MT)*.

dam Damm *m*, Stauanlage *f*; Talsperre *f* *(across a valley)*; Buhne *f* *(diversion)*.

damage *n* Beschädigung *f*, Schaden *m*.

damage *v* beschädigen.

damage control Schadenbekämpfung *f*.

damming Anstauung *f* *(Engr)*.

damped oscillations gedämpfte Schwingungen *(Rad)*.

damped waves gedämpfte Wellen *(Rad)*.

damping Dämpfung *f* *(Elec, Rad)*.

damping device Dämpfungsvorrichtung *f*.

danger Gefahr *f*.

danger area Schußbereich *m*.

danger flag Warnflagge *f*.

danger of icing Vereisungsgefahr *f* *(Avn)*.

danger of interception Abhörgefahr *f* *(Tp)*.

dangerous gefährlich.

danger signal Warnsignal *n*.

danger space Visierbereich *m* *(MG firing)*.

darkness Dunkelheit *f*, Finsternis *f*.

darkroom Dunkelkammer *f*.

dash *n* Strich *m* *(Tg)*.

dashboard Instrumentenbrett *n*.

data Grundlagen *fpl*, Unterlagen *fpl*, Angaben *fpl*, Daten *npl*.

data board Schreibbrett *n* *(Arty)*.

data card Merkzettel *m*.

data computer Kommandogerät *n*.

data receiver Empfänger *m* *(data transmission system)*.

data transmission system Übertragungsgerät *n* *(AAA)*.

data transmitter Geber *m* *(data transmission system)*.

date Datum *n*.

datum Unterlage *f*, Angabe *f*, Datum *n*.

datum level Bezugsebene *f* *(Surv)*.

datum line Bezugslinie *f* *(Surv)*.

datum plane Bezugsebene *f*, Bezugsfläche *f* *(Surv)*.

datum point Bezugspunkt *m* *(Surv)*.

davit Davit *m*, Schwenkdavit *m* *(Nav)*.

daybook Kriegstagebuch *n*.

daybreak Tagesanbruch *m*.

daylight attack Tagesangriff *m*, Tagesvorstoß *m*.

day march Tagmarsch *m*.

day of fire Munition für einen Tag.

day of supply Tagesverbrauch *m*, Vorratsbestand für einen Tag.

day's destination Tagesziel *n*.

day's march Tagesmarsch *m*.

day's objective Tagesziel *n*.

dazzle-painted bunt bemalt *(Cam)*.

dazzle painting Buntfarbenanstrich *m* *(Cam)*.

DB boat Hilfsfahrzeug zum Legen von Grundminen *(Nav)*.

d-c generator Gleichstromerzeuger *m*.

dead tot.

dead abatis schwere Baumsperre.

dead area toter Schußraum.

dead center Totpunkt *m* *(Mtr)*.

dead-end road Sackgasse *f*; Holzweg *m* *(in a forest)*.

dead-end station Kopfbahnhof *m* *(RR)*.

dead-end street Sackgasse *f*.

dead file erledigte Akten.

deadline Termin *m*.

deadman eingebetteter waagerecht liegender Verankerungspfahl *(Engr)*.

dead reckoning Koppeln *n* *(Avn)*.

dead reckoning navigation Koppelnavigation *f* *(Avn)*.

dead reckoning position Koppelort *m* *(Air Navigation)*.

dead space toter Schußraum, toter Trichter, gedeckter Raum, toter Winkel *(Gunnery)*.

dead-stick landing Landung mit abgestelltem Motor *(Avn)*.

dead time Kommando- und Ladeverzugszeit *f* *(Gunnery)*.

death Tod *m*.

death sentence Todesurteil *n*.

debarkation Ausbooten *n*, Ausbootung *f*.

debarkation officer Landungsoffizier *m*.

debris Trümmer *pl*.

debt Schuld *f*.

deceive täuschen, vortäuschen.

deception Täuschung *f*.

deceptive irreführend, Täuschungs-, Schein-.

deceptive smoke screen Scheinvernebelung *f*.

decibel Phon *n*, Dezibel *n*.

decipher entschlüsseln, entziffern, dechiffrieren.

decision Entschluß *m* *(Tac)*.

decisive ausschlaggebend, entscheidend.

decisive action Entscheidungsgefecht *n* *(Tac)*.

decisive battle Entscheidungskampf *m* *(Tac)*.

deck Deck *n* *(Tk, Nav)*; Oberseite *f*.

declaration of war Kriegserklärung *f*.

declinate Ortsmißweisung bestimmen *(compass)*.

declination Mißweisung *f*, Kompaßmißweisung *f* *(compass)*.

declination constant Mißweisung, Ortsmißweisung *f*.

declinator Richtkreis-Bussole *f*, Bussole *f* *(aiming circle)*.

decode entschlüsseln.

decontaminate entgiften *(CWS)*.

decontaminating agent Entgiftungsmittel *n*, Entgiftungsstoff *m*.

decontaminating apparatus Entgiftungsgerät *n*; Zerstäubergerät *(spray)*.

decontaminating-powder sprayer Pulverzerstäuber *m* *(CWS)*.

decontaminating sprayer Flüssigkeitszerstäuber für Entgiftung.

decontamination Entgiftung *f*.

decontamination agent Entgiftungsstoff *m* *(CWS)*.

decontamination battalion Entgiftungsabteilung *f*.

decontamination cart fahrbare Entgiftungstrommel.

decontamination drum Entgiftungstrommel *f*.

decontamination point Entgiftungsplatz *m* *(CWS)*.

decontamination service Entgiftungsdienst *m*.

decontamination squad Entgiftungstrupp *m*.

decontamination troops Entgiftungstruppen *fpl*.

decopper entkupfern.

decoppering agent Entkupferungsmittel *n*.

decoration Auszeichnung *f*, Ehrenzeichen *n*.

decoy *n* Lockmittel *n*, Falle *f*.

decoy *v* heranlocken.

decryptograph entziffern, entschlüsseln, dechiffrieren.

deduct abziehen, subtrahieren.

deep-sea diver Torpedotaucher *m*.

deep thrust tiefer Vorstoß *(Tac)*.

defeat *n* Niederlage *f*.

defeat *v* schlagen, besiegen.

defecate den Darm entleeren; scheißen *(vulgar)*.

defect Fehler *m*; Materialfehler *m* *(structural)*; Konstruktionsfehler *m* *(design)*; Sehfehler *m* *(vision)*.

defective fehlerhaft.

defense Verteidigung *f*, Abwehr *f* *(as distinguished from Schutz, protection, Tac)*.

defense area Verteidigungsraum *m*.

Defense Command Landesverteidigungsbezirk *m* *(USA)*.

defense in depth nach Tiefe gegliederte Verteidigung.

defense plan Verteidigungsplan *m*.

defense system Wehrorganisation *f* *(total armed defense system of a country)*; Landesverteidigungsorganisation *f* *(home defense)*; Befestigungsanlagen *fpl* *(Ft)*.

defensive *n* Defensive *f*, Verteidigung *f* *(Tac)*.

defensive *adj* defensiv, in der Verteidigung.

defensive area Verteidigungsraum *m*.

defensive arm Abwehrwaffe *f*.

defensive battle Abwehrschlacht *f*.

defensive coastal area Küstenverteidigungsabschnitt *m*.

defensive combat Abwehrkampf *m*, Abwehrgefecht *n* *(Tac)*.

defensive fire Abwehrfeuer *n*, Notfeuer *n* *(Arty, MG)*.

defensive front Abwehrfront *f*.

defensive installations Verteidigungsanlagen *fpl*.

defensive line Verteidigungslinie *f*.

defensively abwehrweise.

defensive measure Abwehrmaßnahme *f*.

defensive-offensive offensive Verteidigung.

defensive operations Verteidigungsoperationen *fpl*.

defensive position Verteidigungsstellung *f*.

defensive preparation Abwehrvorbereitung *f*.

defensive sector Verteidigungsabschnitt *m*.

defensive weapon Abwehrwaffe *f*.

defensive zone Abwehrzone *f*, Verteidigungszone *f*.

defer zurückstellen.

deferment Zurückstellung *f*.

defilade Geländeschutz *m*.

defiladed area gedeckter Raum.

defile Enge *f*, Engpaß *m* *(Tac)*.

defile between lakes Seenenge *f*.

definition Linsenschärfe *f* *(of a lens)*; Definition *f*, Begriffsbestimmung *f* *(of a word)*.

deflagration Verbrennung *f*, Deflagration *f* *(powder)*.

deflection Seitenabweichung *f* *(Gunnery)*; Ablenkung *f*; Strahlungsablenkung *f* *(of Rad waves)*; Durchbiegung *f* *(of a beam or girder)*.

deflection angle Seitenwinkel *m* *(Gunnery)*.

deflection board Seitenrichtschieber *m* *(CA)*.

deflection change Seitenänderung *f* *(Gunnery)*.

deflection correction Seitenänderung *f*, Seitenverbesserung *f* *(Gunnery)*.

deflection difference Feuervereinigungswinkel *m* *(Btry firing)*.

deflection dispersion Breitenstreuung *f* *(Ballistics)*.

deflection reading Festlegezahl *f* *(Gunnery)*.

deflection scale Seitenrichtteilung *f*.

deflector box Hülsenkasten *m* *(AA gun)*.

degassing Entgasung *f*, Entgasen *n*.

de-gaussing Entmagnetisierung *f* *(Nav)*.

degreasing Entfettung *f* *(MT)*.

degree Grad *m* *(of circle, temperature)*; Stufe *f* *(stage or step)*; Grad *m*, Maß *n* *(extent)*.

dehydrated meat Dörrfleisch *n*.

dehydrated vegetables Dörrgemüse *n*.

de-icer Enteiser *m*, Enteisungsgerät *n*, Vereisungsschutzgerät *n* *(Ap)*.

de-icing system Enteisungsanlage *f*.

delay *v* hinhalten *(Tac)*.

delay *n* Verzögerung *f*, Verzug *m*; Aufschub *m*.

delayed-action bomb Bombe mit Verzugszeit.

delayed-action fuze Aufschlagzünder mit Verzögerung, Verzögerungszünder *m*.

delayed-action mine Verzögerungsmine *f* *(Engr)*.

delayed jump Absprung mit verzögerter Öffnung *(Prcht)*.

delay fuze Aufschlagzünder mit Verzögerung, Verzögerungszünder *m*.

delaying action hinhaltendes Gefecht *(Tac)*.

delaying position Widerstandsstellung im hinhaltenden Gefecht, Aufnahmestellung *f* *(Tac)*.

delaying unit Widerstandsgruppe *f* *(Tac)*.

delay pellet Verzögerungssatz *m*.

delay powder train Verzögerungssatz *m* *(fuze)*.

delegation of authority Übertragung einer Amtsgewalt.

deliberate field fortification planmäßige Feldbefestigung.

deliver liefern, abliefern.

delivery Auslieferung *f*.

delivery container Abwurfkiste *f* *(airborne operations)*.

delivery roadway Ladestraße *f* *(RR freight station)*.

delivery unit Fallschirmlast *f*, Versorgungsbehälter *m* *(airborne supply)*.

delouse entlausen.

delousing Entlausung *f*.

delousing station Entlausungsstation *f*.

delta connection Dreieckschaltung *f* *(Elec)*.

demarcation Abgrenzung *f*.

demilitarize militärisch räumen, entmilitarisieren.

demobilization Demobilmachung *f*.

demobilize demobilmachen.

demolish sprengen *(blow up)*; niederreißen, abreißen, abbrechen *(tear down)*; zerstören, vernichten *(to ruin)*.

demolition Sprengung *f*, Zerstörung *f*, Demolierung *f*.

demolition block Sprengbüchse *f* *(Engr)*.

demolition bomb Sprengbombe *f*.

demolition chamber Minenkammer *f* *(Bdg, mine)*; Sprengstelle *f* *(Bdg)*.

demolition detail Sprengtrupp *m*.

demolition equipment Sprenggerät *n*, Zündgerät *n* *(Engr)*.

demolition installation Minenanlage *f*.

demolition mission Sprengauftrag *m*.

demolition order Sprengbefehl *m*, Sprengauftrag *m*.

demolition party Sprengkommando *n*.

demolition plan Sprengplan *m* *(Engr)*.

demolition service Sprengdienst *m*.

demolition squad Sprengtrupp *m*.

demonstration Täuschungsmanöver *n*, Scheingefecht *n*, Scheinangriff *m* *(Tac)*; Vorführung *f*.

demonstration chart Unterrichtstafel *f* *(Tng)*.

demonstration flight Schauflug *m* *(Avn)*.

demonstration material Anschauungsmittel *npl* *(Tng aids)*.

demoralize demoralisieren, entmutigen.

demotion Degradation *f*, Dienstgradherabsetzung *f*.

denim Drillich *m*, Drilch *m*.

densimeter Dichtemesser *m*, Dichtigkeitsmesser *m*.

density Dichte *f*.

density of fire Feuerdichte *f*.

density of fragments Splitterdichte *f* *(Arty)*.

density of gas coverage Belegungsstärke *f* *(CWS)*.

density of loading Ladedichte *f* *(Am)*.

Dental Corps zahnärztliches Korps *(USA)*.

dental officer Sanitätsoffizier *(Z)* *m*.

dental surgeon Kriegszahnarzt *m*.

dental technician Zahntechniker *m*.

dental treatment Zahnbehandlung *f*.

dentist Zahnarzt *m*.

depart abrücken, abmarschieren, aufbrechen.

departing flight Abflug *m* *(AA)*.

department Abteilung *f* *(branch, section)*; Verwaltungsbereich *m* *(sphere)*; Behörde *f* *(Adm)*; Ministerium *n* *(of government)*.

departure Abfahrt *f*, Ausrücken *n*, Abrücken *n*.

departure point Aufbruchsort *m*.

departure time Aufbruchszeit *f*.

dependency benefits Familienunterhalt *m*.

dependent Unterhaltsberechtigter *m*.

deploy entwickeln, ausschwärmen.

deployed riflemen Schützen in Entwicklung.

deployment Entwicklung *f* *(Tac)*.

deployment for action Gefechtsentwicklung *f* *(Tac)*.

deport verschicken, verbannen, deportieren; abschieben *(aliens)*.

depot Lager *n*, Park *m* *(Mil)*; Bahnhof *m* *(RR station)*; Zweiglager *n* *(branch depot)*.

depot quartermaster Lagermeister *m* *(Ger: civilian official)*.

depress senken *(G)*.

depression Mulde *f* *(Top)*; Tief *n* *(Met)*.

depression angle Senkungswinkel *m* *(G)*.

depression position finder Azimutentfernungsmesser *m*.

depth Tiefe *f* *(Tac)*.

in depth tiefgegliedert, treffenweise.

depth bomb Wasserbombe *f*, Unterwasserbombe *f*.

depth of penetration Eindringtiefe *f*, Eindringungstiefe *f* *(Tac)*.

depth of profile Profiltiefe *f* *(Ap wing)*.

depth of wing profile Flügeltiefe *f* *(Ap)*.

deputy Stellvertreter *m*.

Deputy Chief of Staff Stellvertretender Chef des Generalstabes.

descending air current Abwind *m* *(Met)*.

descending branch of trajectory absteigender Ast *(Ballistics)*.

description Beschreibung *f*, Schilderung *f*, Darstellung *f*.

desert *n* Wüste *f*.

desert *v* desertieren, fahnenflüchtig werden, Fahnenflucht begehen.

desert area Wüstenzone *f*.

deserter Fahnenflüchtiger *m*, Deserteur *m*; Überläufer *m* *(to the enemy)*.

desertion Fahnenflucht *f*, Desertion *f*.

desiccated cell Füllelement *n* *(Elec)*.

design *n* Ausführung *f* *(Mech)*.

designated target Punktziel *n* *(Arty)*.

designation of objective Zielsetzung *f*.

designer Konstrukteur *m* *(Mech)*.

design load Normalbelastung *f* *(Mech)*.

desired frequency Nutzfrequenz *f* *(Rad)*.

desk Schreibtisch *m*.

destination Ziel *n*.

destroy zerstören, vernichten.

destroyer Zerstörer *m*, Torpedobootzerstörer *m* *(Nav)*.

destroyer escort Korvette *f* *(Nav)*.

destruction Vernichtung *f*, Zerstörung *f*.

destruction fire Niederkämpfen *n* *(Arty)*.

detach abkommandieren, ausscheiden, absondern.

detached duty *See* **detached service**.

detached post Vorpostenverband *m*.

detached service Kommando *n*.

on detached service abkommandiert.

detached unit Kommando *n*.

detachment Trupp *m*, Abteilung *f*.

detachment commander Truppführer *m*.

detail *n* Trupp *m*, Kommando *n*, Abteilung *f* *(Pers)*; Dienst *m* *(duty)*.

detail *v* kommandieren.

detailed report Tatbericht *m*, Tatsachenbericht *m*.

"Detail, halt!" "Abteilung, halt!" *(given on right foot)*.

detain aufhalten *(to delay)*; abhalten, verhindern *(withhold)*; in Haft behalten, festhalten *(under arrest)*.

detaining authority nehmestaatliche Behörde *(PW)*.

detaining power Nehmestaat *m* *(PW)*.

detect auffangen *(Rad)*; entdecken *(discover)*; aufdecken *(an action)*; ertappen *(to catch)*.

detector Audion *n*, Detektor *m* *(Rad)*.

detector crayon Gasspürkreide *f* *(CWS)*.

detector kit Spürgerät *n*, Gasanzeiger *m* *(CWS)*.

detector paint Gasspürfarbe *f* *(CWS)*.

detent Rast *f* *(Mech)*.

detention Haft *f* *(arrest)*; Einbehaltung *f* *(of pay, etc.)*.

detention of pay Besoldungseinbehaltung *f*.

detention room Haftlokal *n*.

detention ward Arrestraum im Lazarett.

deteriorating supplies begrenzt lagerungsfähige Vorräte.

determinate error regelmäßiger Fehler, systematischer Fehler.

determination of altitude Höhenbestimmung *f* *(Avn)*.

determination of course Flugwegbestimmung *f* *(Air Navigation)*.

determination of direction Richtungsbestimmung *f* *(Avn, Rad)*.

determination of fix Kreuzpeilung *f* *(Air Navigation)*.

determination of position Ortsbestimmung *f* *(Avn)*.

determine a fix anschneiden *(Air Navigation)*.

detonate detonieren, sprengen, zünden *(Engr.)*

detonating agent Zündmittel *n* *(Engr)*.

detonating charge Aufladung *f* *(blasting cap)*.

detonating cord Knallzündschnur *f*.

detonating explosive Brisanzsprengstoff *m*.

detonating fuze Sprengzünder *m*.

detonating net Knallennetz *n*.

detonating slab Zerschellerschicht *f* *(Ft)*.

detonation Klopfen *n* *(Mtr)*; Zünden *n*, Zündung *f* *(blasting)*; Detonation *f*.

detonation wave Verdichtungswelle *f* *(Ballistics)*.

detonator Sprengkapsel *f* *(Am)*.

detonator-safe fuze Zünder mit Sprengkapselsicherung *(Am)*.

detour *n* Umweg *m*.

detour *v* umgehen.

detraining of troops Truppenausladung *f*.

detraining point Ausladebahnhof *m*.

detrucking area Ausladegebiet *n*.

detrucking point Ausladeplatz *m*, Ausladestelle *f*.

devastate verwüsten, verheeren.

devastation Verwüstung *f*, Verheerung *f*.

develop entfalten *(Tac)*; entwickeln *(Photo)*.

developed armament probable error Treffwahrscheinlichkeit der Waffe.

development Entfaltung *f* *(Tac)*.

development from march column Entfaltung aus dem Marsch *(Tac)*.

development order Befehl zur Entfaltung *(Tac)*.

deviate abweichen, abkommen.

deviation Geschoßabweichung *f* *(Gunnery)*; Fehlweisung *f* *(Rad)*; Versetzung *f* *(Avn)*; Kompaßablenkung *f*, Deviation *f*.

deviation curve Funkbeschickungskurve *f*, Peilberichtigungskurve *f* *(Rad)*.

device Vorrichtung *f* *(Mech, Engr)*; Abzeichen *n* *(insigne)*.

dew Tau *m*.

dew point Taupunkt *m*.

diagonal *n* Schräglinie *f*.

diagonal *adj* schräg, querlaufend.
diagonal strut Strebe *f (Ap).*
diagram Plan *m,* Schema *n,* Figur *f;* Abbildung *f (illustration).*
dial *n* Zifferblatt *n (on Inst);* Nummernscheibe *f,* Wählerscheibe *f (Tp);* Gangrolle *f (pivoted dial of speedometer).*
dial *v* einstellen, wählen *(Tp).*
dial box Nummernscheibenkästchen *n (field Tp).*
dial hum Amtszeichen *n,* Freizeichen *n,* Summton *m (Tp).*
dialing central Wählamt *n (Tp).*
dial plate Skalenscheibe *f (Rad).*
dial system Wählerbetrieb *m (Tp).*
diameter Durchmesser *m.*
diameter of projectile Geschoßdurchmesser *m (Ballistics).*
diamond formation Rautenformation *f.*
diaphragm Schallblech *n (Tp);* Membran *f (microphone);* Stoßboden *m,* Stoßscheibe *f (shrapnel); Blende f (Photo).*
diaphragm gas mask Membranmaske *f.*
diaphragm pump Membranpumpe *f (Mtr).*
diarrhea Durchfall *m,* Diarrhöe *f.*
diary Tagebuch *n.*
diatomite layer Diatomitschicht *f (gas filter, CWS).*
dichloramine-T Dichloramin *n (CWS).*
die *n* Gewindebacken *fpl (for cutting threads);* Stanze *f,* Gesenke *n (for stamping or punching).*
stock and die Schneidkluppe *f.*
die *v* sterben.
die down ausschwingen *(Elec oscillations).*
dielectric Dielektrikum *n (Rad).*
Diesel-electric drive dieselelektrischer Antrieb.
Diesel engine Dieselmotor *m,* Dieselmaschine *f,* Schwerölmotor *m.*
Diesel fuel Dieselkraftstoff *m,* Gasöl *n,* Schweröl *n,* Schwerkraftstoff *m.*
Diesel motor *See* **Diesel engine.**
Diesel tractor Dieselschlepper *m*
Diesel truck Diesel-Lastwagen *m (MT).*
dietitian Diätschwester *f.*
difference Unterschied *m;* Differenz *f (Math).*
difference chart graphische Schußtafel.
difference in altitude Höhenunterschied *m.*
differential Differential *n (MT).*
differential calculus Differentialrechnung *f.*
differential case Hinterachsengehäuse *n (MT).*
differential effects Werte zum Ausschalten der Witterungseinflüsse *(Gunnery).*
differential gear Ausgleichgetriebe *n (MT).*
differential lock Ausgleichsperre *f (MT).*
difficult terrain schwieriges Gelände.
difficulty Schwierigkeit *f;* Verlegenheit *f (trouble);* Geländeschwierigkeit *f (of terrain).*
diffuser plate Ladeleitrad *n (Ap engine).*
dig *v* graben; ausgraben *(excavate).*
dig in schanzen, einschanzen, sich eingraben.
diglycolnitrate flaked powder Diglykolnitrat-Blättchenpulver *n.*
dihedral V-Form *f,* V-Stellung *f,* Schränkung *f (Ap).*
dihedral angle V-Formwinkel *m (Ap).*
dike Deich *m.*
dim *v* abblenden *(a light).*
dimension Ausmaß *n.*
dimethylsulfate D-Stoff *m (CWS).*
dim headlights *v* abblenden *(MT).*
dim light *n* Abblendelicht *n (headlight, MT).*
dim-out *n* Halbverdunkelung *f (Air Defense).*
dim out *v* abblenden *(Air Defense).*
diode Diode *f (Rad).*
diode tube Zweielektrodenröhre *f,* Zweipolröhre *f (Rad).*
diopter hair Diopterfaden *m (Optics).*
diopter slit Diopterschlitz *m (Optics).*
dip *n* Inklinationswinkel *m (compass);* Kimmtiefe *f (Avn).*
dip *v* dippen, senken.
diphenylaminechlorarsine Adamsit *m,* Diphenylaminchlorarsin *n (CWS).*
diphenylchlorarsine Diphenylchlorarsin *n,* Chlorarsinkampfstoff *m (CWS).*
diphenylcyanarsine Cyan-Chlorarsinkampfstoff *m (CWS).*
diphosgene Chlorameisensäurechlormethylester *m,* Perchlorameisensäuremethylester *m,* Perstoff *m,* K-Stoff *m (CWS).*
dipole antenna Dipolantenne *f.*
direct-climbing target Flugziel im Steigflug *(AA gunnery).*
direct current Gleichstrom *m.*
direct-current ammeter Gleichstrommeßgerät *n.*
direct-current generator Gleichstromerzeuger *m.*
direct-current meter Gleichstrommeßgerät *n.*
direct-current motor Gleichstromelektromotor *m.*
directed net Nachrichtennetz mit Leitfunkstelle *(Rad).*
direct fire direktes Feuer.
direct-fire range Visierschußweite *f.*
direct-fire shot Visierschuß *m.*
direct-fire sight Notvisier *n,* Flakvisier *n.*
direct hit Volltreffer *m;* Artillerievolltreffer *m (Arty).*
directing gun Grundgeschütz *n.*
directing point Nullpunkt *m (CA).*
directing staff Leitungsstab *m (maneuvers).*
direction Seite *f,* Seitenrichtung *f,* Richtung *f (Gunnery).*
directional antenna Richtantenne *f (Rad).*
directional effect Richtwirkung *f (Rad).*
directional gyro Kurskreisel *m.*
directional loop antenna Peilrahmen *m (Rad).*
directional position Antennenstellung *f (of antenna).*
directional receiving antenna Richtempfangsantenne *f (Rad).*
directional stability Richtungsstabilität *f,* Kursstabilität *f (Ap).*
directional traverse Fluchtlinie *f (Surv).*
direction board Richtungsanzeiger *m (AAA).*
direction dispersion Breitenstreuung *f (Ballistics).*
direction finder Peilfunkempfänger *m,* Richtempfänger *m,* Peilempfänger *m,* Bordpeiler *m,* Funkpeiler *m (Air Navigation).*
direction-finder equipment Peilgerät *n (Rad, Avn).*
direction-finder signal Peilzeichen *n (Avn).*
direction-finder station Richtempfangsanlage *f,* Peilanlage *f,* Peilstelle *f (Air Navigation);* Bodenpeilstelle *f (surface).*
direction finding Peilen *n,* Peilung *f (Avn);* Funkpeilung *f (Rad).*
direction-finding equipment Richtgerät *n (Rad).*
direction-finding set Richtempfänger *m,* Peilempfänger *m (Rad).*
direction of air flow Anströmrichtung *f,* Anblasrichtung *f (in a wind tunnel, Avn).*
direction of approach Anflugrichtung *f (Avn).*
direction of attack Angriffsrichtung *f.*
direction of flight Flugrichtung *f (Avn).*
direction of the target Zielrichtung *f.*
directive Weisung *f,* Anweisung *f,* Verfügung *f.*
direct laying direktes Richten *(Gunnery).*
director Leitender *m,* oberster Schiedsrichter *m (maneuvers);* Kommandogerät *n (Arty);* Zentralrichtgerät *n (AAA).*
director headquarters Übungsleitung *f (maneuvers).*
director's aide Leitungsgehilfe *m (maneuvers).*
direct plate voltage Anodengleichspannung *f (Rad).*
direct pointing direktes Richten *(Gunnery).*
direct pressure Nachdrängen *n (in pursuit, Tac).*
direct pressure detachment Verfolgungsabteilung *f (in pursuit, Tac).*
direct-reading compass Nahkompaß *m.*
directrix Nullstrahl des Schußfeldes *(Gunnery).*
direct-sighting telescope Zielfernrohr *n.*
direct support unmittelbare Unterstützung *(Arty, Tac);* taktische Unterstützung *(Avn, Tac).*
direct vision slit Panzerscharte *f (Tk).*
direct vision slot Sehschlitz *m (Tk).*
dirigible Lenkluftschiff *n.*
dirt Schmutz *m,* Dreck *m;* Erde *f (earth).*
dirt road unbefestigte Straße, ungepflasterte Straße.
disability Kriegsbeschädigung *f (war injury);* Dienstunfähigkeit *f (unfitness for service).*
disability pension Versehrtengeld *n.*
disabled kriegsbeschädigt *(injured in war);* dienstunfähig, untauglich *(unfit for service).*
disadvantage Nachteil *m.*
disappearing armored turret Panzer-Verschwindeturm *m (Ft).*
disappearing carriage Verschwindlafette *f (G).*
disappearing target Verschwindscheibe *f.*
disappearing turret Verschwindeturm *m (Ft).*
disapproval Mißbilligung *f.*
disapprove mißbilligen, tadeln; verwerfen, zurückweisen *(reject).*
disarm entschärfen, unscharf machen *(Am);* entwaffnen, abrüsten.
disarmament Abrüstung *f.*
disassemble auseinandernehmen, zerlegen.
disband entlassen, auflösen.
disbursement Auszahlung *f.*
disbursing agent Zahlmeister *m (Ger: civilian official).*
disbursing officer Oberfeldzahlmeister *m (Ger: civilian official).*
discharge *n* Entlassung *f (from service);* Entladung *f (Am, Elec, etc.).*
discharge *v* entlassen, verabschieden *(dismiss);* abfeuern, losschießen *(shoot);* entladen *(a gun, Elec);* abladen, ausladen *(supplies);* löschen *(ship's cargo).*
discharge certificate Entlassungsschein *m,* Entlassungspapier *n.*
discharge surge Entladungsstoß *m (Elec).*
discharge without honor Dienstentlassung *f.*
disciplinary action Disziplinarverfahren *n.*
disciplinary barracks Militärgefängnis *n,* Wehrmachtgefängnis *n,* militärische Strafanstalt.
disciplinary exercises charakterschulendes Exerzieren.
discipline *n* Disziplin *f,* Manneszucht *f;* Zucht *f.*
disconnect ausschalten, trennen.
disconnect drop Schlußklappe *f (Tp switchboard).*
disconnect from binding post abklemmen *(Elec).*
discrepancy Fehlbestand *m (in supplies, etc.);* Widerspruch *m (contradiction);* Unregelmäßigkeit *f (irregularity);* Vorschriftswidrigkeit *f (infraction of regulations).*
discretion Ermessen *n.*
disease Krankheit *f.*
disembark ausschiffen.
disembarkation Ausschiffung *f.*
disengage from the enemy sich vom Feinde loslösen.
disengagement Absetzen *n,* Absetzbewegung *f,* Loslösung *f (Tac).*
disengage the clutch auskuppeln *(MT).*
dishonorable discharge Wehrunwürdigkeitserklärung *f.*
disinfect entseuchen *(Med).*
disinfectant Desinfektionsmittel *n.*
disinfecting agent Entseuchungsmittel *n.*
disinfecting chamber Desinfektionskammer *f,* Entseuchungsschrank *m (Med).*
disinfection Entseuchen *n.*
disinfestor Entlausungsgerät *n,* Entlausungsapparat *m.*
disintegrate auflösen, zerteilen, zerfallen, zerlegen.
disintegrating belt Zerfallgurt *m (MG).*
disk Scheibe *f,* Lamelle *f (Mech);* Schallplatte *f (phonograph).*
disk spider Radkörper *m (wheel).*
dismantle abbauen, ausbauen; abbrücken *(a bridge).*
dismantling Abbau *m.*
dismiss abtreten lassen, wegtreten lassen.
dismissal Dienstentlassung *f.*
"Dismissed!" "Weggetreten!" *(to a formation);* "Abtreten!", "Treten Sie ab!" *(formal style, to an individual);* "Sie können gehen" *(informal, to an individual).*
dismount absitzen; ausbauen *(Ord).*
dismounted abgesessen, zu Fuß *(Pers).*
dismounted defilade mannshohe Deckung.
dismounted drill Exerzieren zu Fuß.
dismounting Absitzen *n (Pers).*
disobedience Ungehorsam *m.*
disobey nicht gehorchen, den Gehorsam verweigern *(a superior);* verletzen, nicht befolgen, mißachten *(orders).*
disorder Unordnung *f,* Verwirrung *f (confusion);* Aufruhr *m (rioting);* Störung *f (Med).*
disorganized in Unordnung gebracht, in Verwirrung gebracht; zerrüttet *(ruined);* aufgelöst *(disbanded, dispersed).*
dispatch *n* Meldung *f,* Mitteilung *f,* Nachricht *f.*
dispatch *v* aussenden, entsenden, schicken.
dispatch case Meldetasche *f.*
dispensary Krankenrevier *n.*
dispensary case Revierkranker *m.*
dispersal Zerlegung *f (Tac).*
dispersal area Abstellplatz *m (Adrm).*
dispersal landing field Ausweichflugplatz *m.*
dispersed formation in depth Fliegermarschtiefe *f (AA security).*
dispersed formation in width Fliegermarschbreite *f (AA security).*
dispersion Auseinanderziehen *n (Tac);* Streuung *f (Ballistics).*
dispersion diagram prozentmäßiges Streuungsbild.
dispersion error Streuung *f.*
dispersion ladder prozentmäßiges Streuungsbild.
dispersion pattern Bodentreffbild *n (Ballistics).*
dispersion zone Streuungsfläche *f (Ballistics).*
displaced versetzt.
displacement Verschiebung *f (troops, etc.);* Verdrängung *f;* Seitenabstand *m (Arty);* Hubraum *m (piston).*
displacement volume Hubvolumen *n,* Hubraum *m (Mtr).*
display board Anschlagbrett *n,* schwarzes Brett.
disposition Aufstellung *f (Tac);* Verfügung *f (availability).*
disposition in depth treffenweise Aufstellung *(Tac).*
disposition in width flügelweise Aufstellung *(Tac).*
disposition of outposts Vorpostenaufstellung *f.*
disposition of troops Truppeneinteilung *f (Tac).*
disrespect unehrerbietiges Verhalten.
disrupt unterbrechen, sprengen *(enemy communications, etc.).*
dissemination of information Verbreitung von Nachrichten.
distance Abstand *m (Tac, close order drill);* Tiefenabstand *m (Tac);* Entfernung *f.*
distance between march units Marschabstand *m.*
distant control Fernsteuerung *f.*
distant reconnaissance Fernaufklärung *f.*
Distinguished Flying Cross Fliegerverdienstkreuz *n (USA).*
distinguished marksman Scharfschütze *m.*
Distinguished Service Cross Kriegsverdienstkreuz *n (USA).*
Distinguished Service Medal Verdienstmedaille *f (USA).*
distortion Verzerrung *f (Rad).*
distress landing Notlandung *f.*
distress signal Notsignal *n.*
distribute verteilen; ausgeben *(issue).*
distributed fire Breitenfeuer *n (R, MG).*
distributing point Ausgabestelle *f,* Verteilungsstelle *f.*
distribution Verteilung *f,* Gliederung *f,* Aufstellung *f.*
distribution box Verteiler *m,* Verteilerkasten *m (data transmission system) (Elec, Nav).*
distribution box boat Hilfsfahrzeug zum Legen von Grundminen *(Nav).*
distribution in depth Tiefengliederung *f.*
distribution in width Breitengliederung *f.*
distribution of artillery for attack Artillerieaufmarsch *m.*
distribution of forces Kräfteverteilung *f (Tac).*
distribution of rations Portionenausgabe *f.*
distributor Verteiler *m,* Zündverteiler *m (Mtr).*
distributor arm Verteilerlaufstück *n,* Verteilerfinger *m (Mtr).*
distributor cock Brandhahn *m (Ap fire extinguisher).*
distributor head Batteriezündverteilerkopf *m (Mtr).*
distributor plate Verteilerscheibe *f (Mtr).*
distributor rotor Verteilerlaufstück *n (Mtr).*
district Bezirk *m,* Distrikt *m.*
district warning center Luftschutzwarnstelle *f (Civ defense).*
disturbance Störung *f;* Aufregung *f,* Unruhe *f (confusion);* Aufruhr *f (rioting).*
ditch Graben *m;* Entwässerungsgraben *m (drainage);* Straßengraben *m (road);* Panzergraben *m (AT).*
ditching Notwassern *n,* Notwasserung *f (Avn).*
ditch profile Grabenprofil *n (Engr).*
dive *n* Sturzflug *m (Avn).*
dive *v* stürzen, einen Sturzflug machen *(Avn).*
dive-bomb *v* sturzbomben *(Avn).*
dive bomber Sturzkampfflugzeug *n,* Stuka *n.*
dive bomber pilot Sturzkampfflieger *m,* Stukaflieger *m.*
dive bomber wing Sturzkampfgeschwader *n (Avn).*
dive bombing Sturzbomben *n.*
dive-bombing attack Sturzangriff *m,* Stukaangriff *m.*
dive-bombing sight Sturzvisier *n (Avn).*
diver Schiffstaucher *m,* Taucher *m (Nav). See also* **deep-sea diver.**
diverge auseinandergehen.
divergence difference Feuerverteilungswinkel *m (Btry firing).*
diversion Ablenkung *f (of enemy forces);* Ablenkungsangriff *m (feint attack).*
diversion dam Buhne *f (Engr).*
divert ablenken; ableiten *(a stream, etc).*
dive siren Sturzsirene *f (dive bomber).*
divide *v* teilen, absondern, trennen.
dividers Stechzirkel *m.*
diving angle Sturzwinkel *m (Avn).*
diving apparatus Tauchgerät *n (Nav).*
diving brake Stukabremse *f,* Sturzflugbremse *f (Ap).*
diving qualities Sturzflugeigenschaften *fpl (Ap).*
diving speed Sturzgeschwindigkeit *f (Ap).*
division Division *f (Mil).*
division antitank battalion Divisionspanzerabwehrabteilung *f.*
division artillery Divisionsartillerie *f.*
division artillery commander Artillerieführer *m;* Artilleriekommandeur *m (when GHQ artillery is attached).*
division commander Divisionskommandeur *m.*
division command post Divisionsgefechtsstand *m.*
division engineer Pionierführer bei der Division.
division headquarters Divisionsstab *m.*
division order Divisionsbefehl *m.*
division signal battalion Divisionsnachrichtenabteilung *f.*
division supply column Divisionsnachschubkolonne *f.*
division surgeon Divisionsarzt *m,* Divisionschefarzt *m.*
division surgical hospital Divisionsfeldlazarett *n.*
division trains Troß der Division.
division trunk line Divisionsstammleitung *f.*
DM Adamsit *m (CWS).*
DM irritant gas candle Giftnebelkerze DM *f (USA).*
dock *n* Dock *n.*
dock installations Dockanlagen *fpl.*
dockyard Werft *f.*
doctor Arzt *m.*
document Akt *m,* Akte *f (plural: Akten);* Urkunde *f (permanent record).*
documentary data schriftliche Unterlagen.
documentary evidence Urkundenbeweis *m;* urkundliches Beweistück *(document).*
dog Hund *m;* Mitnehmer *m (lathe);* Klaue *f (clutch);* Sanitätshund *m (first-aid).*
dog clutch Klauenkupplung *f (MT).*
dog clutch member Schaltklaue *f (constant-mesh transmission, MT).*
dogfight Kurvenkampf *m (Avn).*
dog handler Hundeführer *m.*
dog-handler party Hundeführerrotte *f (for messenger dogs).*
"dog tag" Erkennungsmarke *f.*
dome light Deckenlicht *n (MT).*
door Tür *f;* Luke *f (Ap, Tk).*
dope Klebelack *m,* Spannlack *m (for Ap fabric);* Betriebsstoffzusatzmittel *n (for Avn gasoline).*
dose Portion *f (Med).*
dot Punkt *m (Tg).*
dots and dashes Punkte und Striche.
double action revolver Revolver mit Wiederspannabzug.
double anchor hitch doppelter Ankerstich *(cow hitch, Engr).*
double-apron entanglement Drahtzaun *m,* Stacheldrahtzaun *m,* Flanderzaun *m (Ft).*
double banking Benutzung beider Fahrbahnen in gleicher Richtung.
double-barreled machine gun Zwillingsmaschinengewehr *n.*
double base powder nitroglyzerinhaltiges Nitrozellulosepulver *(Am).*
double-bay biplane Zweistieler *m.*
double envelopment Doppelumfassung *f,* Zangenangriff *m (Tac).*
double file Doppelreihe *f.*
double rank Linie zu 2 Gliedern.
double-ring snaffle bit Doppelringtrensengebiß *n (harness).*
double-row radial engine Doppelsternmotor *m,* Zweisternmotor *m.*
double sentry Doppelposten *m.*
double slide Doppelschieber *m (plotting protractor).*
double tent Doppelzelt *n.*
double time Laufschritt *m,* Sturmschritt *m (march).*
"Double time, march!" "Im Laufschritt, Marsch! Marsch!"
double-tracked zweigleisig *(RR).*
doubletree Ortscheit *n (limber).*
double V-type engine Fächermotor *m.*
doubtful fraglich *(Arty Obsn).*
dough Teig *m.*
doughboy Landser *m.*
down *v* zum Absturz bringen, herunterholen, abschießen *(an Ap).*
downdraft Fallbö *f (Met).*
downdraft carburetor Fallstromvergaser *m (Mtr).*
downhill abwärts, bergab.

downstream unterstrom (place); stromabwärts (action).
downstream anchor Windanker m (Pon Bdg).
downstream anchor cable Windankertau n, Windankerleine f (Pon Bdg).
downwind adv leewärts, windabwärts.
draft Aushebung f (conscription); Pferdezug m, Zugkraft f (horse); Tiefgang m (Nav).
draftee Ausgehobener m.
draft efficiency Zugleistung f (horse).
drafting equipment Zeichengerät n; Reißzeug n (set).
draftsman Konstruktionszeichner m.
drag Widerstand m, Luftwiderstand m (Avn).
"dragon's teeth" Höckerhindernisse npl (AT obstacle).
drag washer Zugöse f (wheel).
drain n Ölablaß m (Mtr).
drain v abwässern (water).
drainage Abwässern n (Ft).
drainage ditch Entwässerungsgraben m.
drainage pit Sickerschacht m (Ft).
drain plug Leerschraube f.
drape n Tarnnetz n (Cam).
draw v ziehen (pull); zeichnen (sketch).
drawbar Zugstange f (MT); Protzarm m (limber).
drawing board Reißbrett n, Zeichenbrett n.
drawbridge Klappbrücke f.
drawing instrument Zeichengerät n; Reißzeug n (a set).
drawing paper Zeichenpapier n.
drawknife Schalmesser n.
dredge n Bagger m (Engr).
dress v ausrichten (close order drill); Toppflaggen setzen (Nav); verbinden (a wound); sich anziehen (put on Clo).
dressing Verband m (Med).
dressing bag Verbandtasche f (Med).
dressing equipment Verbandmittel npl (Med).
dressing station Verbandplatz m, Truppenverbandplatz m (Med).
"Dress left, dress!" "Nach links, Richt Euch!"
dress parade Ehrenparade f.
"Dress right, dress!" "Richt Euch!"
dress uniform Ausgehanzug m; Paradeanzug m (for ceremonies); Gesellschaftsanzug m (for social occasions).
drift n Durchschlag m (pin); Versetzung f, Abdrift f (Avn, Nav); Drallabweichung f, Seitenabweichung f (Ballistics).
drift angle Luvwinkel m, Abtriftwinkel m (Avn).
drift correction Seitenverschiebung f (Gunnery).
drift meter Abdriftvisier n, Abdriftmesser m (Ap).
drift sand Triebsand m.
driftwood Treibholz n.
drill n Exerzieren n, Ausbildung f; Bohrer m (Mech).
drill v exerzieren (practice); bohren (Mech).
drill ammunition Exerziermunition f.
drill bomb Exerzierbombe f.
drill formation Exerzierordnung f, Exerzierform f.
drill ground Exerzierplatz m.
drill regulations Exerzierordnung f, Exerziervorschrift f.
drinking cup Trinkbecher m.
drinking water Trinkwasser n.
drive n Antrieb m (Mech).
drive v fahren (a vehicle); einschlagen (a nail).
drive gear Antriebszahnrad n (gear-shift transmission, MT).
driver Fahrer m, Kraftfahrer m (MT); Fahrer m (Tk).
driver's cab Fahrerhaus n (Trk).
driver's permit Führerschein m, Wehrmachtführerschein m (MT).
drive shaft Antriebswelle f.
drive wheel Antriebsrad n (MT).
driving axle Treibachse f, Antriebsachse f (MT).
driving chain Zahnkette f (MT).
driving range Fahrbereich m (MT).
driving sprocket Triebrad n (Tk).
drizzle n Nieseln n, Sprühregen m (Met).
droop n Wölbung f, Durchhängen n, Verbiegen n (Mech).
drop n Klappe f, Fallklappe f, Weckerfallklappe f (Tp); Fall m (action); Fallhöhe f (distance); Tropfen m (of water, etc.).
drop v absacken (Avn); fallen lassen (an object); fallen, abnehmen (temperature, etc.).
drop-base rim Tiefbettfelge f (MT).
drop-block type breechblock Fallblockverschluß m (G).
drop cover Klappblende f (Ft).
drophammer Rammbär m (of pile-driver); Fallhammer m (Tech).
droplet Tröpfchen n (CWS, Met).
drop message Abwurfmeldung f.
drop-message bag Meldeabwurfhülle f.
dropping angle Bombenabwurfwinkel m (bombing).
dropping ground Meldeabwurfstelle f.
drop point Abwurfstelle f (airborne supply).
drop tank Abwurfbehälter m (Ap).
drop-type switchboard Klappenschrank m.
drug n Arznei f, Droge f; Rauschgift n (narcotic).
drum n Trommel f (Am, music, etc.); Ölfaß n (container).
drum feed Trommelmagazinzuführung f (MG).
drum fire Trommelfeuer n.
drum index Trommelzeiger m (sight mount, panoramic sight).
drum magazine Trommelmagazin n (MG).
drum major Bataillonshornist m, Tambourmajor m.
drummer Trommler m.
drum-type smoke container Nebeltrommel f (CWS).
drunk betrunken; besoffen (slang).
dry-bulb thermometer trockenes Thermometer (Met).
dry cell Trockenelement n (Elec).
dry cell rectifier Trockengleichrichter (Rad).
dry dock Trockendock n.
dry-sump lubrication Trockensumpfschmierung f (Mtr).
dual controls Doppelsteuerung f.
dual-purpose gun Einheitsgeschütz n.
dual tires Doppelbereifung f (MT).
dubbin Lederfett n.
duckboard Lattenrost m, Holzrost m; Bretterbahn f (trench); Spurtafel f (Bdg).
dud Blindgänger m, Bodenkrepierer m (Arty).
duffle bag Bekleidungssack m.
dugout Unterschlupf m (Ft).
dumdum bullet Dumdum-Geschoß n.
dummy Puppe f, Zielpuppe f, Strohpuppe f (bayonet Tng); Attrappe f (of a Tk, vehicle, etc.).
dummy airfield Scheinplatz m.
dummy airport Scheinflughafen m.
dummy ammunition Exerziermunition f (drill); Verpackungsgeschosse npl (for vehicle-loading practice).
dummy cartridge Exerzierpatrone f (MG, R).
dummy installation Scheinanlage f (Cam, Ft).
dummy mine Scheinmine f.
dummy obstacle Scheinsperre f (Ft).
dummy position Scheinanlage f, Scheinstellung f.
dummy projectile Exerziergeschoß n.
dummy site Scheinstellung f.
dummy trench Scheingraben m (Ft)
dummy works Scheinanlagen fpl.
dump n Lager n, Sammelstelle f.
dump v Ballast abwerfen (Avn).
dump car Kipplore f (field RR).
dumping mechanism Kippvorrichtung f (dump Trk).
dump truck Kippwagen m.
dunnage Unterlegbohlen fpl.
dunnite Dunnit n (Am).
duplex operation Gegensprechen n (Rad).
duplicate n Duplikat n, Kopie f.
duplicate v eine Kopie machen, vervielfältigen.
duplicate adj zweit-, zweifach-, doppelt.
in duplicate in zweifacher Ausführung.
duralumin Duralumin n (Ap).
duration Dauer f.
dust Staub m.
dust filtering Entstaubung f (MT).
dust particle Stäubchen n (CWS).
dust respirator Staubschutzmaske f.
duty Dienst m (service); Pflicht f (obligation); Steuer f (tax).
on duty im Dienst, diensttuend.
duty officer Offizier vom Dienst.
duty roster Diensteinteilung f, Dienstplan m, Kommandierrolle f.
duty station Dienststelle f, Posten, m.
duty with troops Truppendienst m, Dienst bei der Truppe.
dynamic speaker elektrodynamischer Lautsprecher (Rad).
dynamite Dynamit n.
dynamo Dynamomaschine f, Stromerzeuger m.
dynamotor Einankerumformer m (Elec, Rad).
dysentery Ruhr f, Dysenterie f.

E

eagle Adler m.
ear Ohr n; Öse f (Mech).
ear cup Hörmuschel f (sound locator).
eardrum Trommelfell n.
earpiece Hörmuschel f (Rad, Tp).
ear-plug Ohrenverschlußwatte f, Ohrenwatte f (cotton).
earth Erde f.
earth-bleach mixture Chlorkalk-Sand-Gemisch n (CWS).
earth inductor compass Erdinduktionskompaß m.
earthwork Erdwerk n, Schanze f (Ft).
east Osten m, Ost m.
easterlies Ostwinde mpl (Met).
Eastern European time osteuropäische Zeit (30° E standard meridian).
E-boat Schnellboot n, Motorschnellboot n, Motortorpedoboot n (Ger).
ebonite Hartgummi m-n.
eccentric sleeve Exzenterhülse f (aiming circle).
echelon Staffel f (Tac).
echelonment Staffelung f.
echo depth sounder Behmlot n, Echolot n (Nav).
economic warfare Wirtschaftskrieg m.
economy of force Kraftersparnis f, Kräftebemessung f.
economy of manpower Kräfteersparnis f.
E. C. powder Nitrozellulosepulver n.
ecrasite Ekrasit n (explosive).
E.C. smokeless powder See E.C. powder.
ED Äthyldichlorarsin n, Äthylarsindichlorid n (CWS).
edge Schneide f (of a bayonet, etc.); Kante f, Rand m (Mech, Top).
edge of land Führungskante f (G barrel).
edge of slope Böschungskante f (Top).
edge of woods Waldrand m.
edible eßbar.
Edison storage battery Edisonsammler m.
eduction tube Auslaßrohr n (Cml cylinder).
effective wirksam, tatsächlich.
effective beaten zone bestrichener Raum der Kerngarbe (MG).
effective fire Wirkungsfeuer n, Wirkungsschießen n (Gunnery).
effective output Nutzleistung f (Mech).
effective part of cone Kerngarbe f (Ballistics); MG.-Kerngarbe f (MG fire).
effective pattern See effective beaten zone.
effective pitch Fortschritt m, Fortschrittsteigung f, wirksame Steigung (propeller).
effective range wirksame Schußweite, Wirkungsbereich m (Ord).
effective resistance Nutzwiderstand m (Elec).
effective strength Iststärke f, Iststand m.
effective wind Durchschnittswind m (Ballistics).
effect of fire Feuerwirkung, f, Schußwirkung f (Arty).
effect of projectile Geschoßwirkung f.
effect of ricochet burst Splitterwirkung des Abprallers.
effect of shell burst Splitterwirkung der Granate.
efficiency Wirkungsgrad m (Tech); Leistungsfähigkeit f (of performance); Wirtschaftlichkeit f (economy).
egg Ei n (plural: Eier).
eight-man tent Achterzelt n.
eight-speed transmission Achtganggetriebe n (MT).
eighty-five percent zone bestrichener Raum der Kerngarbe (MG).
ejector Auswerfer m (Ord).
ejector mechanism Auswerfervorrichtung f (Ord).
elastic n Gummiband n.
elastic adj spannkräftig, federnd, elastisch.
elasticity Spannkraft f, Federkraft f, Elastizität f.
elasticity correction Ausschalten der Temperatureinflüsse (Gunnery).
elasticity effect Temperatureinflüsse mpl (Ballistics).
elbow Ellbogen m.
elbow pipe Krümmer m.
elbow rest Armauflage f (trench).
elbow telescope Winkelfernrohr n.
electric elektrisch.
electrical detonation elektrische Zündung (Engr).
electrical engineer Elektrotechniker m.
electrically-charged obstacle Starkstromsperre f, elektrisches Hindernis (Ft).
electric circuit Stromkreis m.
electric detonator Glühzündstück n.
electrician Elektromechaniker m.
electrician's knife Kabelmesser n.
electric igniter Glühzünder m (blasting cap); Glühzündstück n (Engr).
electric meter Elektrizitätszähler m.
electric motor Elektromotor m.
electric primer elektrische Zündschraube (G).
electric wiring Leitungsmaterial n (equipment); Leitungsnetz n (installed).
electrified obstacle Starkstromsperre f.
electrode Elektrode f (in a spark plug, the grounded electrode; the insulated electrode is called Zündstift).
electromagnet Elektromagnet m.
electromagnetism Elektromagnetismus m.
electron Elektron n.
electron bomb Elektronbrandbombe f.
electron-ray tube magisches Auge (Rad).
electrostatic induction Influenz f (Elec).
element Element n (Elec); Einheit f, Truppenteil n (Tac).
elementary marksmanship training Schießvorschule f.
elephant halbtonnenförmiges Wellblech (Ft, USA).
elephant steel shelter Wellblech-Hütte f (USA).
elevate nach der Höhe richten, heben (G).
elevating and traversing mechanism Richtmaschine f (G).
elevating arc Zahnbogen m (G).
elevating arm Richthebel m (MG).
elevating-arm shaft Richthebelwelle f (MG).
elevating-gear housing Richtgehäuse n (MG).
elevating-gear lever Höhenhebel m (MG).
elevating handwheel Handrad zur Höhenrichtung, Höhenrichtrad n (G).
elevating knob Triebscheibe zur Höhenrichtung (Optics, Ord).
elevating link Richtgelenk n (MG).
elevating mechanism Höhenrichttrieb m, Höhenrichtwerk n, Höhenrichtmaschine f (G, MG); Schraubenspindelrichtmaschine f (elevating-screw type) (G).
elevating rack Zahnbogen m (G).
elevating sector Höhengradbogen m (G).
elevating shaft Höhenrichtwelle f (G).
elevating stop Höhenbegrenzer m (MG).
elevating worm Kippschnecke f (aiming circle, BC telescope); Höhentrieb m (sighting mechanism).
elevation Erhöhung f (Ballistics, G, MG); Rohrerhöhung f (G); Höhe f, Richthöhe f (Gunnery); Höhe f, Bodenerhebung f (Top); Höhenrichtfeld n (total movement in elevation) (G).
elevation above sea level Höhe über dem Meeresspiegel.
elevation angle Visierwinkel m, Aufsatzwinkel m, Erhöhungswinkel m.
elevation circle Teilkreis des Höhenrichttriebs (G).
elevation controller Höhenrichtmann m (AAA).
elevation difference Höhenunterschied m.
elevation graduations Aufsatzeinteilung f (sight mount).
elevation indicator Höhenempfänger m (AA gun).
elevation level Höhenlibelle f (MG sight).
elevation mechanism Höhenrichttrieb m, Höhenrichtwerk n (G, MG); Aufsatztrieb m (G).
elevation micrometer Teilscheibe f (panoramic telescope).
elevation plotting board Höhenmeßplan m (Gunnery).
elevation quadrant Winkelmesser m, Libellenquadrant m.
elevation scale Erhöhungsskala f, Höhenteilung f (G, MG).
elevation screw Höhenrichtschraube f (prismatic sight).
elevation setter Höhenrichtkanonier m.
elevation setting Erhöhungseinstellung f (Gunnery).
elevation table Schußtafel zum Bestimmen der Erhöhung.
elevation tracking telescope Höhenrichtfernrohr n (height finder).
elevator Höhenruder n, Höhensteuer n (Ap); Aufzug m (for personnel and freight); Fahrstuhl m (for personnel only).
elevator assembly Höhenleitwerk n (Ap).
elevator control Höhensteuerung f (Ap).
elevator control lever Steuerhebel m. Höhenruderhebel m (Ap).
eliminate ausschalten (errors, etc.); ausscheiden (impurities); ausmerzen (eradicate); ausstoßen (expel); streichen (cross out); eliminieren (Math).
elite troops Kerntruppen fpl.
embankment Bahndamm m (RR); Dammkörper m (dam).
embargo Embargo n, Handelssperre f (on commerce); Transportsperre f, Transportverbot n (on truck, RR and ship movements).
embark einschiffen (Pers); verladen (equipment, etc.).
embarkation Einschiffen n, Einschiffung f (Pers); Verladung f (equipment, etc.).
embassy Botschaft f.
emblem Wahrzeichen n, Sinnbild n, Emblem n; Abzeichen n (insigne).
embrasure Schießscharte f (Ft).
emergency Not f, Notfall m, Ernstfall m.
emergency antenna Behelfsantenne f.
emergency blasting charge Schnellladung f (Engr).
emergency brake Notbremse f, Handbremse f.
emergency bridge Behelfsbrücke f.
emergency call Notruf m (Tp).
emergency ceiling Gipfelhöhe mit einem stehenden Motor (Ap).
emergency construction material Behelfsmaterial n (Engr).
emergency flotation gear Schwimmwerk für Landflugzeuge (Avn).
emergency gas protection Behelfsgasschutz m.
emergency illumination Notbeleuchtung f.
emergency landing Notlandung f (on land), Notwasserung f (on water).
make an emergency landing notlanden.
emergency landing field Notlandehafen m, Notlandungsplatz m, Notlandeplatz m.
emergency landing flare Notlandefackel f (Avn).
emergency line Notleitung f (Tp).
emergency medical tag Begleitzettel m.
emergency pneumatic boat Behelfsfloßsack m.
emergency ration eiserne Portion.
emergency release Blindabwurf m (bombing).
emergency release handle Notzug m (Ap).
emergency salvo release Notwurf m, Notabwurf m (bombing).
emery cloth Schmirgelleinwand f.
emery paper Schmirgelpapier n.
emery wheel Schmirgelscheibe f, Schmirgelrad n.
emigrant Emigrant m, Auswanderer m.
empennage Leitwerk n (Ap).
empire Reich n; Kaiserreich n (country ruled by an emperor).
emplace in Feuerstellung bringen.
emplacement Stellung f (Tac); Nest n (Ft); Feuerstellung f (Mort, AT gun, etc.).
emplacing Instellungbringen n (Arty).
employment Einsatz m, Verwendung f (Tac).
employment of armored units Panzerverwendung f.
employment of chemical agents Kampfstoffverwendung f.
employment of major forces Masseneinsatz m (Tac).
employment of prisoners of war Kriegsgefangeneneinsatz m.
employment reconnaissance Einsatz-Aufklärung f.
empower ermächtigen, bevollmächtigen.
empties Leergut n (Am); Leermaterial n (RR).
empty weight Leergewicht n.
encampment Feldlager n.
encipher chiffrieren, verschlüsseln, ziffern.
encipherment Verschlüsselung f, Chiffrierung f.
encircle einkesseln (Tac).
encircled area Kessel m (Tac).
encirclement Einkreisung f, Einkesselung f, Umklammerung f (Tac).
encircling maneuver Einkreisungsmanöver n; überholende Verfolgung (in pursuit).
enclosure Einzäunung f, Umzäunung f.
encode schlüsseln, verschlüsseln.
encoding Schlüsseln n (Rad, Tg).
encoding and decoding chart Schlüsselunterlage f.
encoding section Schlüsseltrupp m.
encounter n Treffen n, Begegnung f, Zusammenstoß m.
encrypt See encipher.
endanger gefährden, in Gefahr bringen.
end cap Mantelkopf m (MG jacket).
end dam Stoßbohle f (Bdg).
end plate Endscheibe f (Ap wing).
end ramp Kopframpe f (RR).

end station Meßstand *m (Gunnery)*.
endurance Flugdauer *f*, Flugzeit *f (Avn)*; Ausdauer *f (Pers)*.
enemy Feind *m*.
enemy action Feindeinwirkung *f (Tac)*.
enemy activity Feindtätigkeit *f*.
enemy alien feindlicher Ausländer.
enemy fire Feindfeuer *n*, Feindbeschuß *m*.
enemy forces Feindkräfte *fpl*, Feindstreitkräfte *fpl*.
enemy movement Feindbewegung *f*.
enemy observation Feindsicht *f*, Feindeinsicht *f*.
enemy pressure Feinddruck *m*.
enemy resistance Feindwiderstand *m*.
enemy terrain Feindgelände *n*.
enemy territory Feindesland *n*.
enemy zone Feindraum *m*.
energy Energie *f*, Kraft *f*.
Enfield rifle Enfield-Gewehr *n*.
enfilade *v* der Länge nach beschießen.
enfilade fire Seitenfeuer *n*, flankierendes Feuer, bestreichendes Feuer, Längsbestreichung *f*, Längsfeuer *n*.
engage in ein Gefecht verwickeln *(Tac)*; einkuppeln *(the clutch) (MT)*.
engagement Gefecht *n*, Gefechtshandlung *f*, Kampfhandlung *f (Tac)*.
engaging of successive targets Zielwechsel *m*.
engine Motor *m*, Maschine *f (MT)*; Lokomotive *f (RR)*.
engine brake Motorbremse *f (MT)*.
engine compartment Motorenraum *m (Tk)*.
engine cowling Motorhaube *f*, Motorverkleidung *f*, Haubenverkleidung *f (Ap)*.
engineer Pionier *m (Army)*; Ingenieur *m (Nav) (also civilian official in Ger Army)*
Engineer Amphibian Command Pionier-Landungstruppen *fpl (USA)*.
engineer assault platoon Pioniersturmzug *m*.
engineer combat equipment Pionier-Kampfmittel *npl*.
engineer commander Pionierführer *m*.
Engineer Corps Pionierkorps *n*, Pioniertruppe *f*.
engineer depot Pionierpark *m*.
engineer dump Pionierzwischenpark *m*.
engineer equipment Pioniergerät *n*.
engineer explosives Pioniersprengmittel *npl*.
engineer headquarters Pionierstab *m*.
engineer officer Pionieroffizier *m*.
engineer reconnaissance Pionieraufklärung *f*.
Engineer School Pionierschule *f*.
engineer soldier Pionier *m*.
engineer's scale Reduktionsmaßstab *m*.
engineer tool Pionierwerkzeug *n*.
engineer troops Pioniere *mpl*, Pioniertruppen *fpl*.
engineer vehicle Pionierfahrzeug *n*.
engine failure Motorpanne *f*.
engine house Lokomotivschuppen *m (RR)*.
engine preheater Vorwärmer *m*.
engine repair Motoren-Instandsetzung *f*.
engine rpm Motordrehzahl *f*.
engine torque Motordrehmoment *n*.
engine trouble Motorstörung *f*.
engine yard Lokomotivbahnhof *m*
enlarge vergrößern.
enlargement Vergrößerung *f*.
enlarging projector Vergrößerungsapparat *m*.
enlist sich freiwillig melden.
enlisted cadre Rahmenheer *n*, Stammtruppen *fpl*.
enlisted man Soldat *m*, Mann *m*; Fliegersoldat *m (Luftwaffe)*.
enlisted men *See* **enlisted personnel.**
enlisted personnel Unteroffiziere und Mannschaften.
enlisted specialists Unteroffiziere und Mannschaften der Sonderlaufbahnen.
enlistment Eintreten als Freiwilliger.
enroll sich freiwillig melden.
en route unterwegs.
ensign Leutnant zur See *(Nav)*; Kriegsflagge *f (flag)*.
entanglement Verhau *m*, Drahtverhau *m*.
entertainment Unterhaltung *f*.
entrain verladen *(RR)*.
entraining officer Verladeoffizier *m*
entraining of troops Truppeneinladung *f*.
entraining point Verladeplatz *m (RR)*.
entraining table Fahrtliste *f*, Verladeplan *m (RR)*.
entrance Eingang *m*, Eintritt *m*, Zutritt *m*.
entrance hatch Einsteigluke *f (Tk)*.
entrench schanzen, einschanzen, sich eingraben.
entrenching tools Schanzzeug *n*.
entrenchment Nest *n*, Verschanzung
entruck verladen *(MT)*.
entrucking point *(MT)* Verladeplatz *m*
entrucking table *(MT)* Verladeplan *m*
envelop umfassen *(Tac)*.
envelope Ballonhülle *f (Bln)*; Glasgefäß *n (Rad tube)*; Umschlag *m (for a letter)*.
enveloping attack umfassender Angriff.
envelopment Umfassung *f*, Umklammerung *f (Tac)*.
epaulet Epaulette *f*.
epi Gleiskurve *f*, Klaue *f (for RR gun)*.
epidemic *n* Seuche *f*, Epidemie *f*.
episcope Episkop *n*.
equal area projection flächentreue Projektion *(mapping)*.
equal section charge aus zwei gleichen Teilladungen bestehende Treibladung *(Am)*.
equation Gleichung *f (Math)*.
equator Äquator *m*.
equilibrator Ausgleicher *m (G)*.
equilibrator anchor *m* Ausgleicherarm
equip ausstatten.
equipage Ausrüstungsstücke *npl*.
equipment Gerät *n*, Ausrüstung *f*.
equipment car Gerätewagen *m*.
equipment on hand Istbestand *m*.
equipment truck Gerätekraftwagen *m*.
equipment wagon Gerätewagen *m*.
equivalent circuit Ersatzschaltschema *n (Elec)*.
eraser Radiergummi *m*.
erect *v* errichten, bauen.
erect *adj* aufrecht.
erect truss Hängewerk *n (Bdg)*.
erosion Abnutzung *f*, Ausbrennung *f (Ord)*.
erosion of the bore Rohrabnutzung *f*, Ausbrennung *f (Ord)*.
error Fehler *m*.
escape *n* Entweichen *n (Tac)*; Flucht *f*.
escape *v* entlaufen, entweichen.
escape hatch Bodenluke *f (Ap, Tk)*; Falltür *f (Ap)*.
escarpment Böschung *f*.
escort *n* Geleit *n*, Geleitmannschaft *f*, Bedeckung *f*, Bedeckungsmannschaft *f*; Begleitschutz *m (Avn)*.
escort airplane Sicherungsflugzeug *n*.
escort of honor Ehrengeleit *n*.
escort party Begleitkommando *n*.
escort vessel Begleitschiff *n*, Geleitschiff *n*.
escutcheon Abzeichen *f*, Hoheitsabzeichen *n*.
espionage Spionage *f*, Ausspähung *f*.
esprit de corps Korpsgeist *m*.
essential items wehrwichtige Güter.
establishment Heereseinrichtung *f*, Heeresanstalt *f (organization or institution)*.
establishment of communication Verbindungsaufnahme *f*.
establishment of contact Fühlungnahme *f (Tac)*.
establishment of liaison Verbindungsaufnahme *f*.
estimate *n* Schätzung *f*, Beurteilung *f*.
estimate *v* schätzen, beurteilen.
estimate of terrain Geländebeurteilung *f*.
estimate of the situation Beurteilung der Lage, Lagebeurteilung *f (Tac)*.
estimation Schätzung *f (Gunnery)*.
ether Äther *m*.
ethyldichlorarsine Äthydichlorarsin *n*, Äthylarsindichlorid *n (CWS)*.
ethyliodoacetate Jodessigester *m (CWS)*.
evacuate abbefördern *(PW, wounded, etc.)*; abtransportieren, abschieben *(supplies, equipment, etc.)*.
evacuating officer Abschuboffizier *m*.
evacuation Abschub *m*, Abtransport *m*, Abbeförderung *f*.
evacuation hospital Kriegslazarett *n*.
evacuation hospital battalion Kriegslazarettabteilung *f*.
evacuation of prisoners Gefangenenabschub *m*.
evacuation of the sick Krankenabtransport *m*.
evacuation of wounded Abschub von Verwundeten, Verwundetenabschub *m*, Verwundetenabtransport *m*.
evacue(e) Evakuierter *m*, Abgeschobener *m*.
evade ausweichen.
evading movement Ausweichbewegung *f*.
evaluation Auswertung *f*, Beurteilung *f*.
evaluation of information Nachrichtenbeurteilung *f*.
evaluation of terrain Geländebeurteilung *f*.
evidence Beweismaterial *n (Law)*.
evolution Formveränderung *f (Tac)*.
examine prüfen, untersuchen; vernehmen, verhören, ausfragen *(question)*.
excavator Baggerwerk *n*, Bagger *m (Engr)*.
excess stock Mehrbestand *m*.
exchange *n* Austausch *m*, Tausch *m*; Amt *n*, Telephonamt *n (Tp)*; Wechsel *m (currency)*; Wechselkurs *m (rate)*; Marketenderei *f (PX)*.
exchange of prisoners Gefangenenaustausch *m*.
exchange ship Austauschschiff *n*.
excitation current Erregerstrom *m*
excitation winding Erregerwicklung *f (Elec)*.
excite erregen *(Elec)*.
exciter Erreger *m (Rad)*.
excrement Kot *m*, Stuhl *m*.
excused from duty vom Dienst entschuldigt.
execute durchführen, ausführen, vollstrecken *(carry out)*; hinrichten *(put to death)*.
execution Durchführung *f*, Ausführung *f (carrying out)*; Hinrichtung *f (putting to death)*.
executive Batterieoffizier *m (firing Btry)*.
executive officer Adjutant *m*.
executive order Notverordnung *f*.
exempt *adj* befreit, verschont, frei; zurückgestellt *(deferred)*.
exercise *n* Übung *f (drill, Tng maneuver)*; Leibesübung *f (physical)*.
exhaust *n* Auspuff *m (Mtr)*.
exhaust *v* erschöpfen *(tire out, use up)*; aufbrauchen *(use up)*.
exhaust valve Auslaßventil *n*.
exile *n* Verbannung *f*, Exil *n*; Verbannte(r) *m (person)*.
exile *v* verbannen.
exonerate freisprechen, entlasten.
expedient Behelf *m*, Aushilfe *f (aid)*; List *f (clever act)*.
expeditionary force Expeditionsarmee *f*.
expendable verbrauchbar, verzehrbar
exhaust duct Auspuffleitung *f*, Auspuffkanal *m (Mtr)*.
exhaust gases Abgase *npl*.
exhaust manifold Auspuffkrümmer *m*.
exhaust port Auslaßventilkammer *f*.
exhaust stroke Auspuffhub *m*, Auspufftakt *m*.
exhaust turbine *(Ap)* Abgasturbine *f*
expendable supplies Mittel *npl*, Verbrauchsstoffe *mpl*, Verbrauchsgüter
expenditure of ammunition Munitionsverbrauch *m*.
experiment *n* Versuch *m*, Experiment *n*.
experiment *v* Versuche anstellen, experimentieren.
experimental airplane Versuchsflugzeug *n*.
expert *n* Fachmann *m*, Sachverständiger *m*.
expert *adj* ausgezeichnet *(excellent)*; qualifiziert *(qualified)*.
expiration Ablauf *m*, Beendigung *f (termination)*; Verfall *m (lapse)*.
explode bersten, krepieren, explodieren.
exploder Glühzündapparat *m (Engr)*.
exploit *n* Heldentat *f*.
exploit *v* ausnutzen *(Tac)*.
exploitation Ausnutzung *f (Tac)*.
explosion Explosion *f*.
explosive Sprengstoff *m (generic term)*; Sprengmittel *n*
explosive block Sprengkörper *m*; Sprengbüchse *f (in container)*.
explosive bomb Sprengbombe *f*.
explosive bullet Sprenggeschoß *n (projectile)*; Sprengpatrone *f (cartridge)*.
explosive charge Sprengladung *f (Engr.)*
explosive D Ammoniumpikrat *n*.
explosive filler Sprengstoffüllung *f*
explosive force Sprengkraft *f (Am)*.
explosive rivet Sprengniete *f*.
explosive train Zündsatz *m*.
exposed offen, ungeschützt, unangelehnt *(Tac)*.
exposed flank unangelehnte Flanke, ungeschützte Flanke.
exposed position offene Stellung
exposed wing offener Flügel *(Tac)*.
exposure Aussetzung *f (to danger, cold, disease)*; Belichtung *f (Photo)*; Enthüllung *f (revelation)*.
exposure time Belichtungszeit *f (Photo)*.
express highway Autobahn *f*.
extend auseinanderziehen *(Tac)*; ausfahren *(Ap landing gear)*.
extendable mount Klapplafette *f (Ap MG)*.
extended formation geöffnete Flugordnung *(Avn)*.
extended order geöffnete Ordnung *(Tac)*; geöffnete Linie *(in width)*.
extension arm Klapparm *m (AA sight)*.
extension in depth Tiefenausdehnung *f (Tac)*.
extension in width Breitenausdehnung *f (Tac)*.
extensive smoke screen Großvernebelung *f*.
exterior balk Ortbalken *m (floating Bdg)*.
exterior ballistic factors Witterungseinflüsse *mpl*.
exterior ballistics äußere Ballistik, äußere Schießlehre.
exterior guard Außenwache *f*.
exterior stringer Ortbalken *m (fixed Bdg)*.
exterminate ausrotten, vertilgen, vernichten.
external contracting brake Außenbackenbremse *f (MT)*.
external suspension Außenaufhängung *f (of bombs)*.
extinguish löschen.
extinguisher Feuerlöscher *m*.
extinguisher fluid Löschflüssigkeit *f*.
extract *v* ausziehen.
extraction of root Radizierung *f (Math)*.
extractor Auszieher *m (Ord)*.
extract order Einzelbefehl *m*.
extra duty Strafdienst *m*.
extreme range Höchstschußweite *f (Ord)*.
eye Auge *n*.
eyeguard Augenmuschel *f*.
eyepiece Einblick *m*, Okular *n (Optics)*; Augenfenster *n (gas mask)*.
eyepiece frame Augenring *m (gas mask)*.
eyepiece lens Einblicklinse *f*.
eyepiece mount Einblickstutzen *m*.
eyepiece tube Einblickrohr *n*.
eyesight Sehkraft *f*, Sehvermögen *n*, Sehschärfe *f*.
"Eyes, left!" "Die Augen, links!"
"Eyes, right!" "Augen, rechts!"

F

fabric Stoff *m*.
fabric covering Bespannung *f (Ap)*.
face *n* Gesicht *n*.
face form Maskenspanner *m (to prevent gas-mask distortion)*.
facepiece Maskenkörper *m (gas mask)*.
facing Wendung *f (drill)*.
facing distance Wendungsabstand *m*.
facsimile equipment Bildtelegraphie-Gerät *n (Tg)*; Bildfunkgerät *n (Rad)*.
fact Tatsache *f*.
factor Faktor *m*, Koeffizient *m*; Wert *m (value)*.
factor of safety Sicherheitskoeffizient *m (Mech)*.
factory Fabrik *f*.
fade schwinden, abnehmen *(Rad)*.
fading Fading *n*, Schwund *m (Rad)*.
fading effect Schwundwirkung *f (Rad)*.
fail mißlingen, scheitern, fehlschlagen, versagen.
failure Mißerfolg *m*, Mißlingen *n*; Betriebsstörung *f (Elec, Tp)*; Panne *f (Mtr)*; Unterlassung *f*, Versäumnis *n (neglect)*.
Fairey gun mount Fairey-Sonderlafette *f (Ap)*.
fairing Verkleidung *f*, Profilierung *f (Ap)*.
fake gas "Scheingas" *n*, "Schwindelgas" *n (CWS)*.
fall *n* Herbst *m (season)*; Fall *m (drop)*.
fall *v* fallen; sinken *(of prices, temperature, etc.)*.
fall back ausweichen, sich absetzen, sich zurückziehen, zurückgehen.
fell in antreten.
"**Fall in!**" "Antreten!" *(not at attention)*; "Angetreten!" *(at attention)*; "In Marschordnung, angetreten!" *(in column of threes)*; "In Doppelreihe, angetreten!" *(in column of twos)*; "In Linie, angetreten!" *(in three ranks)*; "In Linie zu zwei Gliedern, angetreten!" *(in two ranks)*; "In Linie zu einem Glied, angetreten!" *(in one rank)*; "In Reihe, angetreten!" *(in single file)*.
fall off sich seitlich abrutschen lassen, sich über den Flügel abrutschen lassen *(Avn)*.
fall out wegtreten *(drill)*.
"**Fall out!**" "Weggetreten!" *(dismissed)*; "Heraustreten!" *(to men in barracks)*.
false attack Scheinangriff *m*.
false ogive Zünderdeckel *m (Am)*.
family allowance Familienunterhalt *m*.
famine Hungersnot *f*, Nahrungsmangel *m*.
fan *n* Windflügel *m (MT)*.
fan-marker beacon Kreisfunkfeuer *n (Rad)*.
fanning out seitliches Einschwenken *(Tac)*.
fan out seitlich einschwenken *(Tac)*.
fan-type engine Fächermotor *m*.
far fern, weit, entfernt.
farad Farad *n (Elec)*.
fare Fahrpreis *m (RR, etc.)*.
fascine Faschine *f*, Reisigbündel *n*.
fascine revetment Strauchwerkbekleidung *f*, Strauchbündelbekleidung *f*; Senkfaschine *f (sunken)*.
fascine road Strauchdamm *m*, Faschinenbahn *f*; Faschinendamm *m (raised)*.
fasten verbinden *(tie)*; leimen *(glue)*; verkitten, ankleben *(with adhesives)*; anstecken *(hitch)*.
fathom Faden *m (Nav)*.
fathometer Behmlot *n*, Echolot *n (Nav)*.
fatigue Arbeitsdienst *m (duty)*; Müdigkeit *f*, Ermüdung *f (exhaustion)*.
fatigue detail Arbeitskommando *n*.
fatigue duty Arbeitsdienst *m (Mil)*.
fatigue strength Dauerfestigkeit *f (Engr)*.
fatigue uniform Arbeitsanzug *m*, Drillichanzug *m*.
feathered position Segelstellung *f (propeller)*.
feces Kot *m*, Stuhl *m*.
feed *n* Speisung *f (Elec, MT)*; Futter *n (for horses)*.
feed *v* abfüttern *(horses, etc.)*; zu essen geben *(Pers)*.
feedback Rückkopplung *f (Rad)*.
feed bag Freßbeutel *m*.
feed belt Patronengurt *m*, Gurt *m (MG)*.
feed box Zuführungsgehäuse *n (AA gun)*.
feeder current Speisestrom *m (Elec)*.
feed funnel Patronenschacht *m (Ap MG)*.
feeding Verpflegung *f (Pers)*; Füttern *n (horses, etc.)*; Zuführung *f (Am)*.
feeding device Ladevorrichtung *f (Small Arms)*; Mehrladevorrichtung *f (magazine) (R)*.
feed mechanism Zuführer *m (Ord)*.
feint *n* Täuschungsmanöver *n*, Scheinangriff *m*, Scheingefecht *n (Tac)*.
feint *v* vortäuschen.
felloe Felge *f*.
felt Filz *m*.
felt boot Filzstiefel *m*.
felt hat Filzhut *m*.
fence Zaun *m*.
fender Abweiser *m (G)*; Kotflügel *m (MT)*.
ferro-concrete *See* **reinforced concrete.**
ferrule Beschlag *m*.
ferry *n* Fähre *f*, Übersetzfähre *f*.
ferry *v* überführen *(Avn)*.
ferryboat Fähre *f*.
ferry cable Fährseil *n (Engr)*.
Ferry Command Abholkommando *n*, Überführungskommando *n*, Lieferkommando *n (USA)*.
ferry embarkation point Fährstelle *f*.
ferry for vehicles Wagenfähre *f*.
ferrying flight Überführungsflug *n*
ferrying operations Fährbetrieb *m*.
ferrying point Übersetzstelle *f*.
ferrying service Lieferdienst *(Avn)*.
ferrying site Fährstelle *f*.
fetlock Köte *f (horse)*.
fever Fieber *n*.
fiber Faser *f*.
field Feld *n*.
field airdrome Feldflugplatz *m*, Feldflughafen *m*.
field army Feldarmee *f*.
Field Artillery Artillerie *f*.
field artillery intelligence Nachrichtensammeln über den Gegner *(Arty)*.
Field Artillery School Artillerieschule *f*.
field artillery survey Vermessung von Feuerstellungen *(Arty)*.
field artillery trainer Zimmerschießgerät *n*.
field bag Brotbeutel *m*.
field bakery Feldbäckerei *f*.
field cap Feldmütze *f*.
field cell Feldelement *n (Tp)*.
field development Verbesserung auf Grund von Kampferfahrungen.
field duty Dienst bei der Truppe, Felddienst *m*.
field emplacement Feuerstellung *f*.
field equipment Feldgerät *n*.
field exercise Geländeübung *f*, Felddienstübung *f*.
field firing Gefechtsschießen *n (R)*.
field firing range Gefechtsschießstand *m (R)*.
field forces Feldheer *n*.
field fortification Feldbefestigung *f*, befestigte Feldstellung.
fieldglass Glas *n*, Fernglas *n*, Doppelglas *n*.
field grade Stabsoffiziersrang *m*.
field gun Feldkanone *f*, Feldgeschütz *n*.
field hospital Hauptverbandplatz *m*.
field jacket Windjacke *f (Clo)*.
field kit Wäsche, Putz- und Nähzeug.
field kitchen Feldküche *f*.
field laboratory Feldlaboratorium *n*, chemische und hygienische Untersuchungsstelle *(Med)*.
field magazine Munitionslager in Geschützenähe, Munitionsnische *f*.
field magnet Feldmagnet *m*.
field maneuvers Truppenübungen *fpl*.
field manual Druckvorschrift *f*.
Field Marshal Feldmarschall *m*, Generalfeldmarschall *m (Ger)*.
field medical record Krankenblatt *n*.
field mess Feldverpflegung *f*.
field message book Meldeblock *m*.
field officer Stabsoffizier *m*.
field of fire Schußfeld *n*, Wirkungsbereich *m*.
field of view Blickfeld *n*, Sehfeld *n*, Gesichtsfeld *n (Optics)*.
field order Sattelbefehl *m*.
field pack Tornister *m*.

field piece Feldkanone *f*, Feldgeschütz *n (G)*.
field position Feldstellung *f*.
field radio *See* **field radio set.**
field radio section Kleinfunktrupp *m*.
field radio set Feldfunksprechgerät *n*.
field radio truck Kleinfunkkraftwagen *m*.
field railroad Feldbahn *f*.
field range Feldkochherd *m (field kitchen)*.
field ration Feldportion *f*, Feldration
field safe Kriegskasse *f*.
Field Service Regulations Felddienstordnung *f*, Druckvorschriften für Führung und Gefecht der verbundenen Waffen.
field shop Feldwerkstatt *f*.
field strip *v* Waffengruppen auseinandernehmen.
field target Gefechtsscheibe *f*.
field target firing Gefechtsschießen *n (R)*.
field telegraph tragbarer Telegraph.
field telephone Feldfernsprecher *m*.
field telephone line Feldlinie *f*, Feldkabelleitung *f*; Felddauerlinie *f (permanent)*.
field-telephone operator Feldfernsprecher *m*.
field testing box Feldprüfschrank *m (Tp)*.
field testing set Feldmeßkästchen *n*.
field training Geländeausbildung *f*.
field trunk cable *(Tp)* Feldfernkabel *n*
field uniform Feldanzug *m*.
field wagon Feldwagen *m*.
field well Feldbrunnen *m*.
field wire Feldkabel *n (Tp)*.
field-wire laying *(Tp)* Feldkabelbau *m*
field-wire line Feldkabelleitung *f (Tp)*.
field-wire strand *(Tp)* Feldkabelader *f*
fifth column Fünfte Kolonne.
fifth-wheel steering Drehschemellenkung *f*.
fifty percent zone Streifen der 50 %igen oder mittleren Streuung.
fight *v* kämpfen, fechten.
fighter *See* **fighter airplane.**
fighter airdrome Jägerplatz *m*.
fighter airplane Jäger *m*, Jagdflugzeug *n*; Zerstörer *m (long range)*.
fighter aviation Jagdflieger *mpl*.
fighter-bomber Jagdbomber *m*, Jabo
fighter command Kommando der Jagdflieger *(USA)*.
fighter defense Jagdabwehr *f (Avn)*.
fighter escort Jägerschutz *m*, Jagdschutz *m*, Begleitschutz *m (Avn)*.
fighter formation Jagdverband *m (Avn)*.
fighter group Jagdgruppe *f (Avn)*.
fighter pilot Jagdflieger *m (Avn)*.
fighter school Jagdfliegerschule *f (Avn)*.
fighter screen Jagdsperre *f (Avn)*.
fighter squadron *(Avn)* Jagdstaffel *f*
fighter wing Jagdgeschwader *n (Avn)*.
fighting compartment Kampfabteil *m (Tk)*.
fighting control Flugführung und Feuerleitung *(bombardment formation)*.
fighting power Kampfkraft *f*.
fighting qualities Kampfwert *m (of a unit)*.
fighting spirit Kampfgeist *m*.
filament Glühfaden *m (Elec)*.
filament battery Heizsammler *m*, Heizbatterie *f (Rad)*.
filament circuit Heizkreis *m (Rad)*.
filament current Heizstrom *m (Rad)*.
file Reihe *f (formation)*; Feile *f (Tech)*; Kartothek *f (card file)*.
  in file treffenweise, in Reihe.
file closer Schließender *m*.
final objective Endziel *n*.
final protective line letzte Widerstandslinie *(Tac)*.
final stage of amplification Leistungsstufe *f (Rad transmitter)*.
finance *n* Kassenwesen *n*.
Finance Department Kassenabteilung *f*.
finance officer Offizier der Kassenabteilung.
finder telescope Sucherfernrohr *n (height finder)*.
findings Untersuchungsergebnis *n*, Beschluß *m (Law)*.
fine *n* Geldstrafe *f (Law)*.
fine grain Feinkorn *n (Photo)*.
fine setting Feineinstellung *f (optical Inst)*.
fine sight Feinkorn *n (R aiming)*.
fine tuning Feineinstellung *f (Rad)*.
finger Finger *m*.
fingernail Nagel *m*, Fingernagel *m*.
fingerprint *n* Fingerabdruck *m*.
fingerprint *v* Fingerabdrücke machen, daktyloskopieren.
fin shaft Flügelschaft *f (Mort shell)*.
fin surface Rippenfläche *f (air-cooled engine)*.
fire *n* Schießen *n*, Feuer *n*, Beschuß
fire *v* schießen, feuern, abfeuern; abdrücken *(press the trigger)*.
"Fire!" "Feuer frei!" *(R)*; "Feuer!" *(Arty)*.
fire adjustment Einschießen *n*, Einrichten *n*, Richt- oder Zündereinstellung beim Einschießen.
fire against personnel Schießen gegen lebende Ziele *(Gunnery)*.
fire and maneuver *See* **fire and movement.**
fire and movement Feuer und Bewegung *(Tac)*.
firearm Feuerwaffe *f*, Schußwaffe *f*.
fire barrage Sperrfeuer *n*.
fire bay Feuerstellung *f (trench)*.
firebreak Schneise *f*, Waldschneise *f*.
fire by a battalion Abteilungsschießen *n (Arty)*.
fire by command for range Schießen mit Entfernungskommandos.
fire by piece at command geschützweises Feuer *(Arty)*.
fire call Feuersignal *n*.
fire command Feuerbefehl *m*.
fire control Feuerregelung *f (Arty)*.
fire-control aid Schießbehelf *m (Gunnery)*.
fire-control car Gerätewagen *m (RR)*.
fire-control code Zeichen für die Feuerleitung *(Arty)*.
fire-control equipment Feuerleitgerät *n (Arty)*.
fire-control grid Gitterschießplan *m (Gunnery)*.
fire-control instruments Beobachtungs- und Vermessungsgerät *n (Arty)*.
fire-control map Schießplan *m*, Feuerleitungsplan *m (Gunnery)*.
fire-control net Feuerleitungsnetz *n (Arty)*.
firecracker Knallkörper *m*, Kanonenschlag *m (simulated fire)*.
fire crest Brustwehrkrone *f (trench)*; Gewehrauflage *f (Ft)*.
fire curtain Feuervorhang *m*, Feuerwand *f*, Feuerschutz *m*.
fire department Feuerwehr *f*.
fire detector selbsttätiger Feuermelder *(Tk)*.
fire direction Feuerleitung *f*.
fire-direction center Feuerleitungsstelle *f*, Leitstand *m (Arty)*.
fire-direction net Feuerleitungsnetz *n (Arty)*.
fire director Kommandogerät *n*, Flakkommandogerät *n (AAA)*.
fire-director data Kommandowerte *mpl (AAA)*.
fire discipline Feuerzucht *f (Arty)*.
fire distribution Feuerverteilung *f (Arty, MG)*.
fire duel Feuergefecht *n*, Feuerkampf *m*.
fire effect Feuerwirkung *f*.
fire engine Feuerspritze *f*.
fire extinguisher Feuerlöscher *m*.
fire fight Feuergefecht *n*, Feuerkampf *m*.
fire for destruction Zerstörungsfeuer *n*, Vernichtungsfeuer *n (Arty)*.
fire for effect Wirkungsschießen *n (Gunnery)*.
fire lane Schußschneise *f*.
fire marshal Brandmeister *m*.
fire mission Schießauftrag *m*, Feuerauftrag *m (Arty)*.
fire order Feuerbefehl *m*.
fire plan Feuerplan *m (Tac)*; Feuerlöschordnung *f (firefighting)*.
fire position Feuerstellung *f*.
firepower Feuerkraft *f*.
fire preparation Feuervorbereitung *f (Tac)*.
fire prevention Brandschutz *m*.
fireproof feuerfest, feuersicher.
fire raft Brander *m*.
fire sector Beobachtungs- und Wirkungsstreifen *m*, Zielraum *m*, Zielabschnitt *m (Small Arms)*.
fire step Schützenauftritt *m (Ft)*.
fire superiority Feuerüberlegenheit *f*.
fire support Feuerunterstützung *f*.
fire trench Schützengraben *m (Ft)*.
fire unit Feuereinheit *f (Arty)*.
firewall Brandschott *n*, Brandspant *m (Ap)*.
firing Schießen *n*, Feuern *n*, Abfeuern *n*; Zünden *n*, Zündung *f (a blasting charge)*; Erdzielbeschuß *m (at ground targets)*; Flugzielbeschuß *m (at aerial targets)*.
firing angle Richtungswinkel *m*.
firing azimuth Seitenrichtung *f*.
firing base Lafettenstütze *f*.
firing battery Gefechtsbatterie *f*.
firing bay Feuerstellung *f (trench)*.
firing chart Batterieplan *m*, Planpause *f (Arty)*.
firing circuit Abfeuerungsverbindung *f (Tk MG or G)*.
firing command Feuerkommando *n (Arty)*.
firing correction Schußverbesserung *f (Gunnery)*.
firing data Schießgrundlagen *fpl*, Schußwerte *mpl*, Schußelemente *npl (Gunnery)*.
firing device Zündvorrichtung *f (mines)*.
firing elevation Rohrerhöhung *f*.
firing interval Zeitabstand *m*, Pause
firing jack Geschützwinde *f*.
firing lever Abzugsstück *n*, Abfeuerungshebel *m*, Abzugshebel *m (G)*.
firing line Feuerlinie *f*; Feuerkette *f (Pers)*.
firing mechanism Abzugsvorrichtung *f*, Abfeuerungsvorrichtung *f*.
firing order Zündfolge *f (of engine cylinders)*.
firing party für die Ehrensalven bestimmte Abteilung *(at graveside service)*.
firing pin Nadel *f*, Zündnadel *f (fuze)*; Schlagbolzen *m (Ord)*.
firing-pin spring Schlagbolzenfeder *f (pistol, fuze)*.
firing-pin support Nadelstück *n (fuze)*.
firing-pin trip Spannfalle *f (breech-block)*.
firing-port shutter Schartenblende *f*.
firing position Feuerstellung *f (place)*; Anschlagsart *f (standing, kneeling, etc.)*.
  in firing position feuerbereit, in Feuerstellung.
firing practice Schießübung *f*.
firing procedure Schießverfahren *n*.
firing range Schußweite *f (distance)*; Schießstand *m (place)*.
firing regulations Schießvorschrift *f*.
firing spur Stichgleis *n (RR Arty)*.
firing squad Erschießungskommando *n (at an execution)*.
firing stand Schießgestell *n (MG)*.
firing step *See* **fire step.**
firing table Schußtafel *f*; Artillerierechenschieber *m (graphical)*.
firing-table elevation schußtafelmäßige Erhöhung *(Gunnery)*.
firing-table range schußtafelmäßige Schußweite *(Gunnery)*.
firing technique Schießtechnik *f*.
firing wire Zünderdraht *m*, Sprengkabel *n (blasting)*.
first aid erste Hilfe, erster Wundverband.
first-aid dog Sanitätshund *m*.
first-aid kit Verbandzeug *n*.
first-aid packet Verbandpäckchen *n*.
first-aid pouch Notverbandtasche *f*.
first-aid supplies Verbandzeug *n*.
first lieutenant Oberleutnant *m*; Oberleutnant der Flieger *(Luftwaffe)*; Oberarzt *m (Med)*; Oberveterinär *m (Vet)*.
first name Rufname *m*.
first officer Erster Offizier *(Nav)*.
first sergeant Hauptfeldwebel *m*; Hauptwachtmeister *m (Arty, Cav)*.
first sergeant's call Versammlung der Hauptfeldwebel zur Befehlsausgabe.
fiscal year Haushaltsjahr *n*.
fish *n* Fisch *m*.
fish net Fischnetz *n (Cam)*.
fishtail Abbremsen des Flugzeuges bei der Landung durch dauerndes Bewegen des Seitenruders *(Avn)*.
fishtail wind ständig wechselnder Wind.
fist Faust *f*.
fit *v* passen; montieren *(assemble)*.
fit for duty dienstfähig.
fitting Verpassung *f*, Verpassen *n (of uniforms, etc.)*; Zubehörteil *m*, Armatur *f*, Paßstück *n (Tech)*.
fix *n* Koppelort *m (Air Navigation)*.
fix *v* fesseln *(Tac)*.
"Fix bayonets!" "Seitengewehr, pflanzt auf!"
fixed ortsfest, ständig *(Arty, Ft)*.
fixed ammunition Einheitsmunition *f*, Patronenmunition *f*.
fixed antenna Festantenne *f*.
fixed antiaircraft artillery ortsfeste Flak.
fixed bayonet aufgepflanztes Seitengewehr.
fixed bridge Brücke mit festen Stützen.
fixed emplacement fest eingebaute Geschützstellung, ortsfeste Geschützstellung.
fixed fire Punktfeuer *n (MG)*.
fixed gun starre Kanone *(Ap)*.
fixed gun mount starre Lafette.
fixed hospital feste Krankenunterkunft.
fixed liner festes Seelenrohr *(G)*.
fixed machine gun starres Maschinengewehr.
fixed objective festes Ziel.
fixed obstacle fest eingebautes Hindernis.
fixed-pitch propeller Luftschraube mit gleichbleibender Steigung.
fixed pivot Drehpunkt *m*; Flügelmann am Drehpunkt *(drill)*.
fixed round ein Schuß Patronenmunition.
fixed seacoast artillery ortsfeste Küstenartillerie.
fixed target festes Ziel.
flag Flagge *f*, Fahne *f*.
flagman Winker *m*.
flag officer Flaggoffizier *m (Nav)*.
flag of protection Lazarettflagge *f*.
flag of truce Parlamentärflagge *f*, weiße Flagge.
bearer of a flag of truce Unterhändler *m*, Parlamentär *m*.
flagpole Fahnenschaft *m*, Fahnenstange *f*; Fahnenmast *m (fixed)*.
flag semaphore Nachrichtenübermittlung durch Winkflaggen.
flagship Flaggschiff *n*.
flag signal Flaggensignal *n*.
file leader Anführer *m*.
filing cabinet Aktenschrank *m*.
filing card Karteikarte *f*.
fill *n* Damm *m*, Aufschüttung *f (Engr, Top)*.
fill *v* füllen.
filler Füllung *f*; Sprengstoffüllung *f (explosive)*.
filler cap Füllschraube *f (MG)*.
filler charge Sprengfüllung *f (Am)*.
filler cover Verschlußkappe *f (MG)*.
filling Füllung *f (Am, CWS)*.
filling plug Füllzapfen *m*.
filling station Tankstelle *f (MT)*.
film Film *m*.
film-pack adapter Filmkassette *f (Photo)*.
film strip Filmstreifen *m*.
filter *n* Filter *m*; Weiche *f (Rad)*; Sieb *n (Mtr, Rad)*; Kraftstoffreiniger *m (Mtr)*.
filter *v* filtern, filtrieren.
filter area von einem Flugwachkommando überwachtes Gebiet *(AWS)*.
filter board Kartentisch des Flugmeldedienstes.
filter center Flugwachkommando *n (AWS)*.
filter circuit Sperrkreis *m (Rad)*.
filter container Filtergehäuse *n (gas mask)*.
filter element Filtereinsatz *m*, Atemeinsatz *m (gas mask)*.
filter-element container Einsatztopf *m (gas mask)*.
filter funnel Siebtrichter *m (MT)*.
filtering Sammeln, Auswerten und Weitergeben der eingehenden Flugmeldungen *(AWS)*.
filter officer leitender Offizier beim Flugwachkommando.
filter replacement Filterwechsel *m (gas mask)*.
fin Flügel *m (Mort shell, R grenade, bomb)*; Stabilisierungsflügel *m*, Steuerflügel *m (bomb)*; Flosse *f*, Seitenflosse *f (Ap)*; Kühlrippe *f (cooling fin of engine)*; Steuerfläche *f (stabilizing fin of Mort shell)*.
final amplifier Hauptsender *m*, Leistungsstufe *f (of a Rad transmitter)*.
final assembly Bereitstellung *f (Tac)*; Fertigmontage *f*, Endmontage *f (Tech)*.
final assembly area Bereitstellungsraum *m*.
flag target Schleppziel *n*, Schleppscheibe *f*, Luftsack *m (AAA)*.
flake powder Blättchenpulver *n*, Plattenpulver *n (Am)*.
flaksuit Panzerweste *f (Avn)*.
flame Flamme *f*.
flame dampener exhaust stack Flammenverzehrer *m (Ap)*.
flame-thrower Flammenwerfer *m*; Nahwerfer *m (short-range)*; Weitwerfer *m (long-range)*.
flame-throwing tank Flammenwerferpanzerwagen *m (Ger)*.
flange Flansch *m*.
flank *n* Flanke *f*, Breitseite *f (Tac)*; Führungsfläche *f (G tube)*; Weiche *f*, Flanke *f (of horse)*.
flank *v* flankieren, umgehen.
flank attack Flankenangriff *m*.
flank guard Seitendeckung *f (Tac)*.
flanking fire Flankenfeuer *n*, flankierendes Feuer.
flanking march Flankenmarsch *m*.
flank man Flügelmann *m (drill)*.
flank observation Beobachtung von seitlicher Beobachtungsstelle *(Arty)*.
flank patrol Spähtrupp zur Flankensicherung.
flank protection Flankenschutz *m*.
flank protective fire Artilleriefeuer zur Flankensicherung.
flank security Flankensicherung *f*, Seitendeckung *f (Tac)*.
flank spotting Beobachtung von seitlicher Beobachtungsstelle *(Arty)*.
flap Klappe *f (Ap, Clo)*; Tornisterklappe *f (pack)*.
flare Fackel *f*, Leuchtkugel *f (Sig)*.
flareback Vorbeischlagen der Pulvergase *(G)*.
flare composition Leuchtsatz *m*.
flare path Leuchtpfad *m (Avn)*.
flash Mündungsfeuer *n*, Aufblitzen *n (G)*; Zündstrahl *m (Am)*; Blitzstrahl *m (lightning)*.
flash defilade Sichtdeckung *f (Arty)*.
flash fuze elektrischer Glühzünder *(CWS)*.
flash hider Feuerdämpfer *m*, Flammendämpfer *m*, Mündungsfeuerdämpfer *m (Ord)*.
flash hole Zündkanal *m (fuze)*.
flashing light Blinkfeuer *n (Avn)*.
flashlight Taschenlampe *f*.
flashlight battery Taschenlampenbatterie *f*.
flash message dringende Meldung.
flash point Zündpunkt *m (fuels)*.
flash ranging Lichtmessen *n*.
flash-ranging adjustment Einschießen der eigenen Artillerie durch die Lichtmeßbatterie *(Arty)*.
flash-ranging battery Lichtmeßbatterie *f*.
flash-ranging location *See* **flash ranging.**
flash-ranging section Lichtmeßtrupp *m (Arty)*.
flash-ranging station Lichtmeßstelle *f*, Meßstelle *f*.
flash-ranging system Lichtmeßsystem *n*.
flash reconnaissance Gefechtsaufklärung durch Lichtmeßbatterie oder vom Flugzeug aus.
flash-reducing wad Kartuschvorlage *f (Am)*.
flash signal Blinkzeichen *n*.
flash tube Kammerhülse *f (shrapnel)*.
flash-tube charge Kammerhülsenladung *f (shrapnel)*.
flat-base rim Flachbettfelge *f (MT)*.
flat butt strap Flachlasche *f*.
flatcar Plattformwagen *m (RR)*.
flat coil spring Bandfeder *f (fuze)*.
flat feet Plattfüße *mpl*.
flat fire *See* **flat-trajectory fire.**
flat-jawed pliers Flachzange *f*.
flatness of trajectory Rasanz der Flugbahn.
flat spin Flachtrudeln *n*, Tellertrudeln *n (Avn)*.
flatten out abfangen *(Avn)*.
flat-top Maske *f*, Tarndecke *f (Cam)*. *See also* **aircraft carrier.**
flat trajectory gestreckte Flugbahn, gestreckte Geschoßbahn *(Ballistics)*.
flat-trajectory fire Flachfeuer *n*.
flat-trajectory gun Flachfeuergeschütz *n*, Flachbahngeschütz *n*.
flat-trajectory weapon Flachbahnwaffe *f*, Flachfeuerwaffe *f*.
fleet Flotte *f (Nav)*.
fleeting target Augenblicksziel *n*.
flexible schwenkbar *(Ap MG)*; biegsam *(Tech)*.
flexible axle Schwingachse *f (MT)*.
flexible ball mount Kugelblende *f (Tk gun)*.
flexible disk Hardyscheibe *f (MT)*.
flexible-disk joint Trockengelenk *n (MT)*.
flexible drive shaft Gelenkwelle *f*.
flexible gun bewegliches Geschütz.
flexible machine gun bewegliches Maschinengewehr.
flexible shaft Schwinge *f (follow-the-pointer mechanism)*; biegsame Welle *(Tech)*.
flexible steel cable *(Ap)* Drahtzug *m*
flexure Durchbiegen *n (Mech)*.
flick Erfassung des Zieles, kurzdauerndes Halten eines erfaßten Zieles *(AA searchlight)*.
flier Flieger *m*.
flight Kette *f (Avn unit)*; Flug *m*.
flight commander Kettenführer *m (Avn)*.
flight control Flugzeugsteuerung *f (Ap)*; Bewegungskontrolle *f (by operations office)*.
flight deck Flugdeck *n*, Landedeck *n (aircraft carrier)*.
flight diagram Auftragskarte *f (aerial Photo)*.
flight echelon fliegendes Personal.
flight engineer Bordwart *m*, Bordmechaniker *m*, Bordmonteur *m (Avn)*.
flight formation Flugform *f*.
flight indicator Neigungsmesser *m*, Gyrorektor *m (Ap)*.
flight instructor Fluglehrer *m*.
flight line Fluglinie *f*, Flugstrecke *f*.
flight log Flugbuch *n*, Flugtagebuch
flight maneuver Flugfigur *f*.
flight map Fliegerkarte *f*.
flight officer Feldwebelleutnant der Flieger *(USA)*.
flight pay Luftdienstzulage *f*, Fliegerzulage *f*.
flight performance Flugleistung *f*.
flight personnel fliegendes Personal.
flight position Flugrichtung *f*, Fluglage *f*.
flight ration Bordverpflegung *f*.
flight report Flugmeldung *f*.
flight route Flugstrecke *f*.
flight surgeon Sanitätsoffizier bei fliegenden Verbänden, Fliegerarzt *m*.
flinching Mucken *n (Small Arms firing)*.
float Schwimmer *m (Ap, carburetor, gage, etc.)*; Floß *n (Engr)*; Fußplatte *f*, Fußteller *m (AA gun)*; Schwanzblech *n (G trail)*.
float chamber Schwimmergehäuse *n (carburetor)*.
float column Tellersäule *f (AA gun outrigger)*.
float gear Schwimmwerk *n*, Schwimmerwerk *n*, Schwimmergestell *n (seaplane)*.
floating bridge Brücke mit schwimmenden Stützen, Floßbrücke *f*.
floating dock Schwimmdock *n*.
floating mine Treibmine *f*.
float needle Schwimmernadel *f (carburetor)*.
floatplane Schwimmerflugzeug *n*.
float plate Ansteckblech *n (G trail spade)*; Fußplatte *f*, Fußteller *m (AA gun)*.
floats Schwimmwerk *n (Ap)*.
flock Reiterrudel *n (Cav)*.
flood *n* Überflutung *f*, Überschwemmung *f*.
flood *v* überfluten, überschwemmen; anstauen *(dam up)*.

flooded area Anstauung f (Engr).
flooding Anstauung f, Überflutung f (Engr).
floodlight Flutlicht n.
floor Boden m, Fußboden m (buildings); Fahrbahn f, Brückenbahn f (Bdg); Stock m (story).
floor beam Fahrbahnträger m (Bdg).
floor board Bodenbrett n (MT).
floor plate Bodenstück n (MG).
floor-plate lock Bodenstücksperre f (MG).
flotation gear Schwimmwerk n (Ap).
flotation stability Schwimmstabilität f (seaplane).
flour Mehl n.
fluid drive Flüssigkeitsgetriebe n (MT).
fluid equalizer Flüssigkeitsausgleicher m (recoil mechanism).
fluke Ankerflunken m (of an anchor).
fluorescent tube Leuchtröhre f.
flush riveting Versenknietung f.
flutter n Rüttelerscheinungen fpl (Ap).
fly v fliegen.
fly a sortie Einsatz fliegen (Avn).
flying boat Flugboot n; Fernaufklärungsflugboot n (long-range reconnaissance).
flying bridge See flying ferry.
flying cadet Fähnrich der Flieger (USA).
flying distance Flugweite f.
flying ferry Gierfähre mit nur an einem Ufer verankertem Fährseil (Engr).
flying field Flugplatz m.
Flying Fortress Fliegende Festung.
flying in formation Verbandsflug m (Avn).
flying officer Fliegeroffizier m.
flying pay Fliegerzulage f, Luftdienstzulage f.
flying school Fliegerschule f.
flying suit Fliegerschutzanzug m; Pelzkombination f (fur-lined coverall).
flying time Flugzeit f (Avn).
fly on instruments blindfliegen.
flyweight Fliehgewicht n (engine governor).
flywheel Schwungrad n, Schwungmasse f, Schwungscheibe f (Mtr).
FM Titantetrachlorid n (CWS).
FM grenade Nebelhandgranate mit Titantetrachlorid-Füllung (CWS).
FM smoke Titantetrachlorid-Nebel m (CWS).
focal center Flugmeldekommando n (AWS).
focal distance Brennweite f (Optics).
focal length See focal distance.
focal plane Brennebene f (Optics).
focus n Brennpunkt m (Optics).
focusing scale Sehschärfeneinteilung f (Optics).
fog Nebel m.
fog area Nebelgebiet n (Met).
folding wings beiklappbare Tragflügel, Schwenkflügel mpl, Klappflügel mpl (Ap).
follower Zubringer m (Small Arms).
follower spring Zubringerfeder f (Small Arms).
follower-spring stud Federkopf m (self-loading pistol).
follow-the-pointer drive Folgezeigerantrieb m (AAA).
follow-the-pointer indicator Folgezeiger m.
follow-the-pointer sight mechanism Zeigerzieleinrichtung f (G).
follow-the-pointer system Folgezeigereinrichtung f.
follow up v nachdrängen (Tac); anfragen nach (inquire).
food Lebensmittel npl, Nahrungsmittel npl (any means of nutrition); Essen n, Kost f, Verpflegung f (meals in general); Eßwaren fpl (food products).
food ration card Lebensmittelkarte f.
foot Fuß m.
footbridge Steg m, Beselersteg m; Schnellsteg m (hasty); Floßsacksteg m (of pneumatic boats); Uferschnellsteg m (single span).
foot-firing mechanism Abzugsvorrichtung mit Fußhebel (AA gun).
footgear Schuhzeug n.
footpath Fußweg m.
foot plate Fußplatte f, Fußteller m (AA gun).
footrest Fußstütze f (AA gun).
foot shifter Fußschaltung f (MT).
footsore fußkrank.
foot starter Fußschalter m (MT).
foot switch Fußschalter m (Elec).
foot troops Fußtruppen fpl.
forage n Futter n.
forage v furagieren, verpflegen, Futter und Nahrungsmittel beschaffen.
forage ration Futterration f.
foragers Reiter in geöffneter Linie (Cav).
force n Kraft f (power); Kräfte f pl (Pers); Kampfeinheit f (unit); Kräftegruppe f (group); Verband m (formation).
in force mit starken Kräften, mit Einsatz aller Kräfte (Tac).
force v erkämpfen, erzwingen, überwinden (Tac).
forced-circulation cooling Pumpenkühlung f, Wasserpumpenkühlung f (Mtr).
forced crossing Überschreiten des Flusses unter Kampf (Tac).
forced landing Notlandung f (Avn); Truppenlandung unter Feuer (Tac).
make a forced landing notlanden (Avn).
forced march Dauermarsch m, Gewaltmarsch m.
forcing cone Übergangskegel m (G).
ford n Furt f.
ford v durchwaten.
fordable durchwatbar.
fording ability (MT) Watfähigkeit f
fore-and-aft inclinometer Längsneigungsmesser m (Ap).
forearm Schaft m (automatic R); Vorarm m (horse).
forecast See weather forecast.
forefinger Zeigefinger m.
foreground Vorfeld n (Tac).
forehead Stirn f.
forehead strap Stirnband n (gas mask).
foreign ausländisch, fremd, auswärtig.
foreign country Ausland n, fremdes Land.
foreigner Ausländer m, Fremde(r) m.
foreign port Auslandshafen m, ausländischer Hafen.
foreign service Dienst außerhalb der Landesgrenze.
forequarters Vorhand f (horse).
foresight Vorsicht f (Surv).
forest Wald m.
forestalling Unterbindung f (Tac).
forest clearing Waldblöße f, Waldlichtung f.
forest road Waldweg m; Waldschneise f, Schneise f (along a firebreak).
forfeiture Verlust des Wehrsoldes.
forfeiture of pay Verwirkung des Wehrsoldes.
forge n Schmiede f.
forged iron Schmiedeeisen n.
fork Verlegung des mittleren Treffpunktes um die Hälfte des Treffbildes (Gunnery); Wegegabel f (road); Gabel f (utensil).
form Schalung f (concrete construction); Vordruck m, Formular n (printed form); Gestalt f (shape).
formation Form f, Formation f, Gliederung f (drill, Tac); Verband m (Avn); Flugform f (flight formation).
formation flying Verband(s)flug m, Fliegen im Verbande.
formation in depth Tiefengliederung f (Tac).
formation in width Breitengliederung f (Tac).
formation of airplanes Fliegerformation f, Fliegerverband m.
formation of bombardment airplanes Kampfverband m.
formation of dive bombers Sturzkampfverband m, Stukaverband m.
formation of eddies Wirbelbildung f (Ballistics).
formation of pursuit airplanes Jagdverband m (Avn).
formation of reconnaissance airplanes Aufklärungsverband m.
formation of torpedo bombers Torpedoflugzeugverband m.
formation release Verbandswurf m, Verbandsabwurf m (Bombing).
formula Formel f.
formulation of decisions Entschlußfassung f.
fort Werk n, Festung f.
fortification Befestigung f.
fortified defense system Befestigungsanlage f.
fortified line Stützpunktlinie f.
fortified locality Stützpunkt m (Tac).
fortified position befestigte Stellung.
fortress Festung f.
fortress artillery Festungsartillerie f.
fortunes of war Wechselfälle des Gefechts (Tac).
forward v befördern (supplies, etc.); nachsenden (a letter).
forward area Kampfgebiet n, Kampfraum m.
forward echelon I. Staffel (Hq).
forward gunner's compartment Bugkanzel f (Ap).
forwarding point Weiterleitungsstelle f.
"Forward, march!" "Im Gleichschritt, Marsch!"
forward observation post vorgeschobene Beobachtungsstelle (Tac).
forward observer vorgeschobener Beobachter (Arty).
forward PW camp Frontstalag n.
forward slope Vorderhang m (Top).
forward slope position Vorderhangstellung f (Tac).
forward speed Vorwärtsgang m (MT).
forward velocity Vorwärtsgeschwindigkeit f (Bombing).
fougasse Flattermine f, Fugasse f.
fouling Rückstände im Laufinnern (Ord).
fouling shot erster Schuß zum Entölen des Laufinnern.
foundation Bettung f (G emplacement); Unterbau m (Engr).
foundry Gießerei f.
fountain pen Füllfeder f.
four-cycle engine Viertaktmotor m.
four-man tent Viererzelt n.
fourragère Fangschnur f; Schützenschnur f (marksmanship).
four-way pipe joint Kreuzmuffe f.
four-wheel vehicle Zweiachser m.
foxhole Schützenloch n; Hockloch n (crouching); Schützenloch für stehenden Anschlag (standing).
fraction Bruch m (Math).
fractional charge (Am) Teilladung f
fracture Knochenbruch m (Med).
fracture of the skull m Schädelbruch
fragment Bruchstück n, Splitter m, Sprengstück n.
fragmentary order Einzelbefehl m, besondere Anordnung (Tac).
fragmentation(Am) Splitterwirkung f
fragmentation bomb Splitterbombe f.
fragmentation effect f Splitterwirkung
fragmentation hand grenade Eierhandgranate f (egg-shaped).
fragmentation shell f Splittergranate
frame n Rahmen m; Fahrwerkrahmen m (MT); Protzgestell n (limber); Tragegestell n (pack saddle).
frame rib Trageschiene f (pack saddle).
frame-type gun carriage Rahmenlafette f.
frangible grenade Brandflasche f.
fraudulent enlistment freiwilliges Eintreten mit falschen Angaben oder Verschweigen wichtiger Tatbestände.
fraudulent induction Diensteintritt mit falschen Angaben oder Verschweigen wichtiger Tatbestände.
free air thermometer Außenluft-Thermometer n (Ap).
free balloon Freiballon m.
freeboard Freibord m.
freedom Freiheit f.
free-space radiation Raumstrahlung f (Rad).
free travel toter Gang (clutch pedal).
freewheeling Freilauf m (MT).
freeze frieren; erfrieren (to death); sich festfressen (piston, etc.).
freeze in position regungslos erstarren.
freight Fracht f.
freight car Güterwagen m (RR).
freighter Frachter m, Frachtdampfer m (Nav).
freight station (RR) Güterbahnhof m
freight train Güterzug m (RR).
frequency Schwingungszahl f, Frequenz f (Elec, Rad).
frequency band Frequenzband n.
frequency-control element Steuersender m, Steuerstufe f (Rad transmitter).
frequency designation Frequenzangabe f (Rad).
frequency meter Wellenmesser m, Frequenzmesser m (Elec, Rad).
frequency modulation Frequenzmodulation f (Rad).
frequency selection Grobeinstellung f (Rad).
frequency spectrum Wellenspektrum n (Rad).
friction Reibung f.
frictional resistance Reibungswiderstand m.
friction igniter Abreißzünder m, Zündschnuranzünder m.
friction primer Reibzündschraube f.
friction surface Lauffläche f (Mech).
friction tape Isolierstreifen m, Isolierband n.
friendly troops eigene Truppen.
frog Strahl m (hoof); Weichenstück n (RR switch).
front Front f (Met, Mil); Bug m, Stirnseite f (Tk).
frontage Ausdehnung f, Breite f, Gefechtsbreite f (Tac).
frontage in attack Angriffsbreite f.
frontal area Stirnfläche f (Mech).
frontal attack frontaler Angriff, Frontalangriff m, Stirnangriff m.
frontal fire Frontalfeuer n.
frontal security Sicherung nach vorne (Tac).
frontal soaring Frontensegeln n, Gewitterflug m (glider).
front arch Vorderzwiesel m (packsaddle frame).
front armor Bugpanzer m (Tk).
front axle Vorderachse f (MT).
front-axle drive Vorderachsantrieb m (MT).
front cinch Bauchgurt m (pack saddle).
front gunner Bugschütze m (Tk).
frontier Grenze f.
frontier area Grenzgebiet n.
frontier district Grenzbezirk m.
frontier force Grenzschutz m (Tac).
frontier guard Grenzwache f, Grenzwacht f.
frontier protection Grenzschutz m (Tac).
frontier station Grenzbahnhof m (RR).
front line Frontlinie f, vorderste Kampflinie (Tac).
front outrigger Vorderholm m (AA gun mount).
front ring sight Kreiskorn n (MG).
front ring sight base Kreiskornfuß m (MG).
front ring sight frame Kreiskornrahmen m (MG).
front ring sight support Kreiskornhalter m (MG).
front roller Kletterwalze f, Abfangwalze f (MT).
front sector Frontabschnitt m.
front sight Korn n (Small Arms); Nebenstachel m (AT gun).
front-sight base Kornfuß m (R).
front-sight cover Kornschoner m (R).
front-sight holder Kornhalter m (R).
front-sight stud Kornwarze f (R).
front-wheel drive Frontantrieb m, Vorderradantrieb m (MT).
frost Reif m, Rauhreif m (Met).
frostbite Frostbeule f.
frosted glass Milchglas n.
frozen gefroren (of water, etc., frostbitten); erfroren (frozen to death or to point of serious danger).
fruit Frucht f; Obst n (collective).
FS solution Nebelsäure f (CWS).
fuel Brennstoff m, Kraftstoff m, Treibstoff m, Betriebsstoff m (Mtr). See also gasoline.
fuel-air mixture Kraftstoff-Luftgemisch n (Mtr).
fuel cake Brennstoff m (DM irritant gas candle).
fuel consumption Brennstoffverbrauch m, Kraftstoffverbrauch m (MT).
fuel distributing point Kraftstoffausgabestelle f.
fuel dump Brennstofflager n, Treibstofflager n, Kraftstofflager n.
fuel economy Kraftstoffersparnis f (MT).
fuel feed Kraftstoffzufluß m, Kraftstofförderung f.
fuel filter Kraftstoffilter m, Kraftstoffreiniger m.
fuel gage Benzinstandmesser m, Kraftstoffmeßuhr f, Kraftstoffstandanzeige f.
fuel injector Einspritzdüse f.
fuel jet Kraftstoffdüse f.
fuel level gage Kraftstoffvorratsmesser m (Ap).
fuel line Kraftstoffleitung f (MT).
fuel mixture Brenngemisch n, Kraftstoffgemisch n.
fuel oil Heizöl n.
fuel pressure gage Kraftstoffdruckmesser m (Ap).
fuel pump Kraftstofförderpumpe f, Kraftstoffpumpe f.
fuel shut-off valve Kraftstoffabstellhahn m.
fuel supply Brennstoffvorrat m, Kraftstoffnachschub m, Betriebsstoffversorgung f, Kraftstoffversorgung f.
fuel-supply column Betriebsstoffkolonne f.
fuel-supply dump Treibstofflager n.
fuel-supply truck Betriebsstoff-Lastkraftwagen m.
fuel system Kraftstoffanlage f (Mtr).
fuel tank Kraftstofftank m, Kraftstoffbehälter m, Treibstoffbehälter m (MT, Ap).
fuel tender Tankprahm m (Nav).
fuel train Kraftstoffzug m (RR).
fulcrum Drehpunkt m.
full-automatic fire Dauerfeuer n (MG, R).
full cock Spannrast f (Small Arms).
full dress uniform Paradeanzug m.
full pack Marschgepäck n.
full sight Vollkorn n (R aiming).
full-track vehicle n Vollkettenfahrzeug
fulminate of mercury Knallquecksilber n.
fumigate (aus)räuchern, desinfizieren.
functioning Arbeitsspiel n (Mech).
funeral Trauerfeier f.
funeral escort Begleitkommando n, Trauergefolge n.
funnel Trichter m.
fur-lined pelzgefüttert.
fur-lined flying suit Pelzkombination f.
furlough Urlaub m.
furlough allowance See furlough ration allowance.
furlough ration allowance Verpflegungsgebührnisse bei Urlaub.
furrow Furche f, Bodenfalte f
fuse Sicherung f, Schmelzsicherung f, Grobsicherung f (Elec). See also fuze.
fuselage Rumpf m, Flugzeugrumpf m (Ap).
fuselage assembly Rumpfmontage f (Ap).
fuselage framework Rumpfgerüst n (Ap).
fuselage skin Rumpfhaut f (Ap).
future position Treffpunkt m, Vorhaltepunkt m (AA gunnery).
fuze Zünder m (Am); Zeitzündschnur f (blasting). See also fuse.
fuze body Zündergehäuse n.
fuze composition Zündsatz m.
fuze cord Abreißschnur f (hand grenade).
fuze-cord button Abreißknopf m (hand grenade).
fuze-indicator Folgezeigerempfänger m (follow-the-pointer-type fuze setter).
fuze-lighter Zündschnuranzünder m.
fuze-range Zünderlaufzeit f.
fuze-setter Zünderstellschlüssel m (manual); Zünderstellmaschine f (automatic).
fuze-setter support Zünderstellsitz m (AA gun).
fuze setting Zündereinstellung f, Zünderstellung f (Gunnery).

G

gabion Schanzkorb m (Ft).
gag Knebel m.
gage Spurweite f (RR); Lehre f (Tech).
gain n Gewinn m.
gain v gewinnen.
gait Gangart f (of horse).
gait of march Marschgeschwindigkeit f (H Cav).
gale Sturmwind m, stürmischer Wind.
gallery Minengang m, Minenstollen m (mining); Schießhalle f, gedeckte Bahn (shooting).
gallery case Schurholzrahmen m (Engr).
gallery of departure Ausgangsstollen m, Hauptstollen m (mine warfare).
gallery practice ammunition Zielmunition f.
galley Kombüse f (Nav).
galling Reibung f.
gallon Gallone f (3.785 liters).
gallon capacity Tragfähigkeit f (tank Trk).
galvanize verzinken.
galvanized verzinkt.
galvanometer Leitungsprüfer m, Galvanometer n.
galvanoscope Galvanoskop n.
gangplank Laufbrücke f.
gangrene Brand m, Wundbrand m.
gap Lücke f; Gasse f (in mine field); Sturmgasse f (through obstacles); Schußfeldlücke f (in field of fire).
garbage Müll n.
garbage can Mülleimer m.
garlands bunte Lappen (Cam).
garnishing Einflechten bunter Lappenstreifen in ein Tarnnetz (Cam).
garrison Standort m (place); Besatzung f (Pers).
garrison belt Leibriemen m (Clo).
garrison cap Feldmütze f.
garrison gin behelfsmäßiges Hebezeug aus Dreibock und Winde.
garrison prisoner Garnisonhäftling m.
garrison ration Verpflegungsgebührnisse fpl, Beköstigungsgeld n.
gas n Kampfgas n (CWS).
gas v vergasen, begasen, mit Kampfstoff vergiften (CWS).
gas alarm Alarm m, Gasalarm m (CWS).
gas-alarm signal Gasalarmzeichen n.
gas-alarm siren Gasalarmsirene f.
gas alert Gasbereitschaft f.
gas alert line Gasbereitschaftslinie f (CWS).
gas ammunition Gasmunition f.
gas attack Gasangriff m.
gas bag Ballonhülle f (Bln).
gas barrier Gassperre f (CWS).
gas bomb Gasbombe f.
gas candle Giftnebelkerze f, Giftrauchkerze f (CWS).
gas casualty Gasvergifteter m (plural: Gasverluste mpl).
gas chamber Gasraum m (CWS, Bln).
gas chamber test Gasraumprobe f, Gasraumprüfung f.
gas check Gasabdichtung f, Liderung f (breechblock).
gas-check pad Kissen n, Liderungspolster n (breechblock).
gas-check seat Liderungsplatte f (breechblock).
gas cloud Gaswolke f, Giftnebelwolke
gas concentration Kampfstoffgehalt m, Luftanreicherung f (CWS).
gas coverage Kampfstoffbelegung f (CWS).
gas curtain Gasschutzvorhang m (Ft).
gas cylinder Blasflasche f, Gasflasche f (CWS).
gas-cylinder attack Blasangriff m (CWS).
gas-cylinder method Blasverfahren n (CWS).
gas-cylinder nozzle Gasdüse f (CWS).
gas-cylinder plug Hülse f (MG).
gas defense Gasabwehr f.

gas-defense equipment Gasabwehrmittel *n.*
gas-defense instruction Gasausbildung *f.*
gas-defense regulations Gasschutzvorschrift *f.*
gas-defense weapon Gasabwehrwaffe *f.*
gas detection Gasspüren *n*, Abspüren *n (CWS).*
gas-detection apparatus Gasspürgerät *n.*
gas-detection equipment Gasspürmittel *npl*, Spürmittel *npl.*
gas-detection paper Spürpapier *n (CWS).*
gas-detection service Gaserkennungsdienst *m.*
gas detector Gasanzeiger *m.*
gas-detector powder Spürpulver *n (CWS).*
gas discipline Gasdisziplin *f*, Gaszucht *f.*
gas filter Gasfilter *n (gas mask).*
gas fumes Gasschwaden *mpl (CWS).*
gas gangrene Gasbrand *m.*
gas goggles Gasbrille *f (CWS).*
gas hand grenade Gashandgranate *f.*
gas-identification set Riechprobenkasten *m (CWS).*
gas-impervious gasdicht, gassicher.
gasket Dichtung *f.*
gaskin Unterschenkel *m (horse).*
gas line Gasleitung *f.*
gas main Hauptgasleitung *f.*
gas mask Gasmaske *f*, Maske *f*; Sondergasmaske *f (special).*
gas-mask accessories Gasmaskenzubehör *n.*
gas-mask carrier Gasmaskentragbüchse *f*, Tragbüchse *f (metal type).*
gas-mask testing apparatus Gasmaskenprüfgerät *n.*
gas noncommissioned officer Gasschutzunteroffizier *m.*
gas officer Gasoffizier *m.*
gas oil Gasöl *n.*
gasoline Kraftstoff *m*, Betriebsstoff *m*, Benzin *n*, Brennstoff *m*, Treibstoff *m*; Waschbenzin *n (for cleaning). See also* **fuel.**
gasoline-air mixture Kraftstoff-Luftgemisch *n.*
gasoline consumption Brennstoffverbrauch *m*, Kraftstoffverbrauch *m.*
gasoline container Benzinkanister *m (Ap, MT).*
gasoline distributing point Kraftstoffausgabestelle *f.*
gasoline filling station Tankstelle *f (MT).*
gasoline filter Kraftstoffilter *m*, Kraftstoffreiniger *m.*
gasoline-oil mixture Kraftstofföl-mischung *f.*
gasoline pressure gage Benzinmanometer *n (Mtr).*
gasoline pump Benzinpumpe *f*, Kraftstofförderpumpe *f (Mtr).*
gasoline supply Kraftstoffversorgung *f*, Kraftstoffnachschub *m*, Kraftstoffvorrat *m.*
gasoline supply depot Betriebsstofflager *n.*
gasoline supply section Kraftstoffstaffel *f (Tk Bn).*
gasoline supply truck Betriebsstoff-Lastkraftwagen *m.*
gasoline tank Benzinbehälter *m*, Benzintank *m*, Kraftstoffbehälter *m.*
gas-operated durch Gasdruck betätigt *(Ord).*
gas-operated machine gun Gasdrucklader *m.*
gas pipe Gasleitung *f.*
gas pliers Rohrzange *f.*
gas pot Tränenstoffkerze *f (CWS).*
gas pressure Gasdruck *m (Ballistics, Ord).*
gas projectile Gasgeschoß *n.*
gasproof gassicher.
gas proofing Abdichtung gegen Kampfgas *(CWS).*
gasproof shelter gassicherer Unterstand, gasgeschützter Unterstand.
gas-protection boots Gasstiefel *mpl.*
gas-protection cloak Gasumhang *m.*
gas-protection equipment Gasschutzgerät *n.*
gas-protection glove *m* Gashandschuh
gas-protection service Gasabwehrdienst *m.*
gas-protection suit Gasanzug *m.*
gas reconnaissance Gasaufklärung *f.*
gas release Abblasen *n (CWS).*
gas-release method Gasabblasever-fahren *n (CWS).*
gas rifle grenade Gasgewehrgranate *f.*
gassed-area marker Gasspürfähnchen *n.*
gas sentry Gasspürer *m.*
gas shell Gasgranate *f.*
gas-shell fire Gasschießen *n*, Vergiftungsschießen *n (Arty).*
gassing Begasung *f (CWS).*
gas situation map Kampfstoff-Lagenkarte *f (CWS).*
gas-spraying apparatus Aus- und Abgießgerät *n (Ap, CWS).*
gas tank Gasbehälter *m.*
gas trap Gasschleuse *f (CWS).*
gas tube Gasentladungsröhre *f (Rad).*
gas valve Ballonventil *n (Bln).*
gas-valve operating line Ventilleine *f (Bln).*
gas warfare Gaskrieg *m*
gas warning Gaswarnung *f.*
gate Tor *n (large)*; Tür *f (small).*
gate-type gear shift Kulissenschaltung *f.*
gauge *See* **gage.**
gauze Gaze *f.*
gear Zahnrad *n (toothed wheel)*; Gang *m (gear ratio)*; Zeug *n (equipment).*
in gear eingerückt, eingeschaltet.
out of gear außer Eingriff.
gear pump Zahnradpumpe *f (Mtr).*
gear ratio Übersetzungsverhältnis *n*, Übersetzung *f.*
gear shaft Spindel *f (elevating mechanism) (G).*
gearshift Gangschaltung *f*, Schaltung *f.*
gearshift collar Schaltmuffe *f (MT).*
gearshift lever Schalthebel *m (MT).*
gearshift-lever housing Schaltdom *m (MT).*
gearshift transmission Schaltgetriebe *n (MT).*
gear transmission Zahnradgetriebe *n (MT).*
gear wheel Zahnrad *n.*
general *n* General *m*; Generaloberst *m (full general).*
general *adj* allgemein.
general air defense Gesamtheit aller Luftschutzmaßnahmen.
general call sign Sammelrufzeichen *n (Rad).*
general counterpreparation Masseneinsatz der Artillerie zum Gegenvorbereitungsfeuer.
general court-martial Oberkriegsgericht *n.*
general depot Heeresfeldzeugdienststelle *f.*
General Headquarters Oberkommando des Heeres. *See also* **GHQ.**
general hospital Heereslazarett *n*, Reservelazarett *n.*
general message Sammelmeldung *f (Rad).*
general military service allgemeiner Wehrdienst.
general officer General *m.*
General of the Armies Generalfeldmarschall *m.*
general orders allgemeingültige Anordnungen *(Adm)*; allgemeine Postenanweisungen *(guard orders).*
general outpost Vorposten *m.*
general-purpose airplane Mehrzweckflugzeug *n.*
general-purpose bomb Sprengbombe *f (Avn).*
general-purpose gun Mehrzweckgeschütz *n.*
general-purpose vehicle Mehrzweckfahrzeug *n (MT).*
general service allgemeiner Wehrdienst.
generalship Feldherrnkunst *f.*
general staff Generalstab *m.*
General Staff Corps Generalstabskorps *n.*
general staff officer Generalstabsoffizier *m.*
general staff with troops Truppengeneralstab *m.*
general support Unterstützung durch angewiesene Artillerie *(Arty, Tac).*
generate erzeugen.
generating unit Maschinensatz *m*, Stromaggregat *n*; Kraftquellenwagen *m (mobile)*; Tretsatz *m (pedal-operated)*; Kleinmaschinensatz *m (portable).*
generation Erzeugung *f*, Entwicklung *f (Tech)*; Generation *f (age group).*
generator Stromerzeuger *m*, Dynamomaschine *f*, Generator *m (Elec)*; Lichtmaschine *f (for lighting)*; Zündlichtmaschine *f (MT)*; Induktor *m (Tp).*
generator-starter *(MT)* Lichtanlasser *m*
Geneva Convention Genfer Abkommen.
Geneva Cross Genfer Rotes Kreuz.
gentle slope flache Böschung *(Top).*
geodetic survey Landesaufnahme *f.*
geographic code Schlüssel für Ortsnamen *(Sig C).*
geographic coordinates geographische Koordinaten.
geographic index number Kartenblattnummer *f.*
geographic map geographische Karte.
geographic north geographisch Nord.
geometrical pitch geometrische Schraubensteigung *(Ap propeller).*
geometric projection perspektivische Projektion.
geophone Erdhörer *m.*
germ Bazille *f*, Keim *m.*
German Cross Deutsches Kreuz *(decoration).*
getaway man Gefechtsmelder *m.*
GHQ air force dem Heer unterstellte Fliegerverbände.
GHQ artillery Heeresartillerie *f.*
GHQ cavalry Heereskavallerie *f.*
GHQ medical battalion Heeressanitätsabteilung *f.*
GHQ motor vehicle park Heereskraftfahrpark *m.*
GHQ pool *See* **GHQ troops.**
GHQ reserve Heeresreserven *fpl.*
GHQ reserve tank groups Panzerverbände der Heerestruppen.
GHQ signal communication section Heeresnachrichtenverband *m.*
GHQ supply column Heeresnachschubkolonne *f.*
GHQ troops Heerestruppen *fpl.*
giant tire Riesenluftreifen *m (MT).*
gimbal kardanische Aufhängung *(compass).*
girder Balken *m*, Träger *m*, Unterzug *m.*
girth Sattelgurt *m (of saddle).*
gisement Meridiankonvergenz *f (Surv).*
give ground weichen, zurückweichen.
give way ausweichen.
gland Düse *f (MG)*; Stopfbüchse *f (Mech)*; Durchführung *f*, Stopfbuchsdeckel *m (Bln)*; Drüse *f (Med).*
glare Blendung *f.*
glass Glas *n.*
glass scale Glasmaßstab *m (Optics).*
glaze glasartige Vereisung *(Avn).*
glide *n* Gleitflug *m (Avn).*
glide *v* gleiten, segeln.
glide bombing Angriff aus dem Gleitflug.
glide landing Landung in flachem Gleitflug.
glider Segelflugzeug *n*, Segler *m*, Gleiter *m*, Gleitflugzeug *n*; Motorsegler *m (powered).*
glider bomb Gleitbombe *f (Avn).*
glider flight Luftlandekette *f.*
glider pilot Segelflieger *m.*
glider squadron Luftlandestaffel *f.*
gliding Gleitflug *m*, Gleiten *n (Ap)*; Segelflug *m*, Segeln *n (glider).*
gliding ability Gleitfähigkeit *f.*
gliding angle Gleitwinkel *m*, Gleitflugwinkel *m.*
gliding turn Kurve im Gleitflug *(Avn).*
glove Handschuh *m.*
glow plug Glühkerze *f (Diesel engine).*
glue Leim *m*, Fischleim *m.*
glycerin Glyzerin *n.*
gnomonic projection gnomonischer Kartenentwurf, gnomonische Projektion, zentrale Projektion.
goggles Schutzbrille *f.*
going flight Abflug *m.*
gondola Gondel *f (Avn).*
gondola car offener Güterwagen, Bordwandwagen *m (RR).*
goniometer Winkelmesser *m*, Goniometer *n (Surv).*
goniometry Winkelmessung *f*, Goniometrie *f (Surv).*
gonorrhea Tripper *m.*
gooseberry Drahtigel *m (obstacle).*
goose step Exerziermarsch *m*, Stechschritt *m.*
gorge Schlucht *f (Top).*
governing device Regelvorrichtung *f (Mtr).*
government Regierung *f (of a state)*; Verwaltung *f (administration)*; Militärverwaltung *f (Mil Govt).*
government property Staatsbesitz *m.*
governor Drehzahlregler *m*, Motorregler *m*, Regler *m (Mtr).*
governor arms Reglergabel *f (Mtr).*
governor drive Reglerantrieb *m (Mtr).*
governor housing Drehzahlregler-Gehäuse *n*, Reglergehäuse *n (Mtr).*
governor spring Reglerfeder *f (Mtr).*
grade Dienstgrad *m*; Munitionsart *f (Am)*; Steigung *f (Top).*
grade chevron *n* Dienstgradabzeichen
grade crossing Planübergang *m.*
gradient Steigung *f*, Böschungswinkel *m*, Hangwinkel *m (Top)*; Gefälle *n*, Gradient *m (Met).*
graduate *n* Mensur *f*, Meßbecher *m*, Meßglas *n (container)*; Absolvent *m (from a school).*
graduate *v* abstufen, einteilen *(into degrees)*; absolvieren *(from a school).*
graduated disk Teilscheibe *f (plotting protractor).*
graduated oil dispenser Ölmeßbecher *m (MT).*
graduation Eichstrich *m*, Gradeinteilung *f*, Strich *m.*
grand strategy Gesamtkriegführung *f.*
grand tactics Massentaktik *f.*
granular form Körnerform *f (powder).*
granulation Granulation *f*, Granulieren *n*, Gestalt und Dichte der Pulverkörner *(Am).*
granule Körnchen *n.*
graph Kurvenblatt *n.*
graphical firing table Artillerierechenschieber *m.*
graphite Graphit *m.*
graphite grease Graphitfett *n.*
graphite lubricant Graphitschmiermittel *n.*
grapnel Ankersucher *m*, Dragge *f*, Suchanker *m.*
grapple den Suchanker über den Grund schleppen *(Engr, Nav).*
grassland Wiese und Weide.
gratuity Zulage *f.*
gratuity upon death Sterbegeld *n.*
graupel shower Graupelschauer *m (Met).*
gravel pit Kiesgrube *f.*
gravel road Kiesstraße *f*, Schotterstraße *f.*
grave marker Grabkreuz *n*, Grabtafel *f.*
graveside service Ehrenbezeigungen bei Beerdigung *(Mil funeral).*
Graves Registration Service Kriegsgräberfürsorge *f.*
gravitation Erdschwere *f (Physics).*
gravity *See* **gravitation.**
gravity-system water cooling Thermosyphonkühlung *f (Mtr).*
gravity tank Fallbenzintank *m (MT).*
graze *n* Auftreffpunkt eines Geschosses oder Abpralles bei Flachfeuer *(Gunnery).*
graze *v* bestreichen.
graze burst Zerspringen des Geschosses im Augenblick des Aufschlags beim Schießen mit Zeitzünder.
grazing fire bestreichendes Feuer, Strichfeuer *n (MG).*
grease *n* Fett *n.*
grease *v* einfetten.
grease coating Fettüberzug *m.*
grease cup Schmierbüchse *f.*
grease gun Luftdruck-Fettpresse *f*, Fettpresse *f (Mech).*
great circle Großkreis *m.*
great-circle chart Karte nach dem gnomonischen Kartenentwurf.
great-circle course Kurs auf dem größten Kreis.
green grün.
Greenwich hour angle Greenwicher Stundenwinkel.
Greenwich Time Greenwicher Zeit.
grenade Handgranate *f (hand)*; Gewehrgranate *f (R).*
grenade court Handgranatenwurfstand *m.*
grenade launcher Schießbecher *m.*
grid Gitter *n (map, Rad).*
grid azimuth Richtungswinkel *m (Surv).*
grid base-line direction Gitterrichtung *f (Gunnery).*
grid capacitor Gitterkondensator *m (Rad).*
grid circuit Gitterkreis *m (Rad).*
grid condenser Gitterkondensator *m (Rad).*
grid control Steuerwirkung des Gitters *(Rad).*
grid coordinates Koordinaten des Gitters *(Surv).*
grid declination Meridiankonvergenz *f (Surv).*
gridded map Gitternetzkarte *f.*
grid-leak detector Audion *n (Rad).*
grid line Gitterlinie *f*, Gitternetzlinie *f.*
grid north Gitter-Nord *m (Surv).*
grid rectifier Gittergleichrichter *m (Rad).*
grid resistance Gitterwiderstand *m (Rad).*
grid resistor Gitterdrossel *f (Rad).*
grid sheet Kartenblatt mit Gitter.
grid square Quadrat *n*, Planquadrat *n (map).*
grid system Gitternetz *n.*
grid voltage Gitterspannung *f (Rad).*
grinding Schleifen *n (Tech)*; Hacken *n (meat, etc.).*
grinding machine Schleifmaschine *f (Tech)*; Fleischhackmaschine *f (meat grinder).*
grip *n* Griff *m*, Griffstück *n*, Handgriff *m*; Griffigkeit *f (of tires)*; Handstütze *f (pistol)*; Knüppelgriff *m (of control stick, Ap).*
grip safety Sicherungshebel *m (pistol).*
groin Leistengegend *f.*
grommet Kausche *f.*
groove Nut(e) *m(f)*; Zug *m (rifling).*
grooved piston ring Ölschlitzring *m (Mtr).*
gross tonnage Bruttotonnengehalt *m (Nav).*
gross weight Fluggewicht *n*, Gesamtgewicht *n (Ap).*
ground *n* Boden *m*, Erde *f*, Gelände *n*, Grund *m (Top)*; Erdleitung *f*, Erdschluß *m*, Erdung *f*, Erde *f*, Erder *m (Elec).*
ground *v* am Boden festhalten *(Avn)*; erden *(Elec).*
ground adjustment target Erdeinschießziel *n (Gunnery).*
ground alert Bereitschaft zum unverzüglichen Start *(Avn).*
ground cable Fesselkabel *n*, Fesselseil *n*, Verankerungstau *n (Bln).*
ground cloth Unterlegeplane *f (Bln).*
ground commander Befehlshaber von Erdtruppen.
ground crew fliegertechnisches Personal, Bodenbedienung *f*, Bodenpersonal *n (Avn)*; Landemannschaft *f (Bln).*
ground decontamination Geländeentgiftung *f (CWS).*
grounded geerdet *(Elec)*; gestrandet *(ship).*
grounded electrode Elektrode *f (spark plug).*
ground elevation Bodenerhebung *f (Top).*
ground fog Bodennebel *m (Met).*
ground forces Erdtruppen *fpl*, Erdwaffen *fpl.*
ground form Geländegestaltung *f (Top).*
ground gear Landevorrichtung *f (Bln).*
ground-glass plate Mattscheibe *f.*
grounding Erdung *f (Elec).*
grounding rod Erdstecker *m (Elec, Tp).*
ground installations Bodenanlagen *fpl.*
ground lead Erdleitung *f*, Erdzuleitung *f (Elec).*
ground leak Erdschluß *m*, Ableitung *f (Elec).*
ground level Erdgleiche *f (Ft).*
ground loop Überschlag auf dem Boden *(Avn).*
ground mechanic Wart *m (Avn).*
ground mine Grundmine *f (Nav).*
ground observation Erdbeobachtung *f (Arty).*
ground observer Luftspäher *m*, Luftwache *f (AWS).*
ground panel Auslegezeichen *n*, Tuchzeichen *n (Sig C).*
ground personnel Bodenpersonal *n*, Bodenorganisation *f (Avn).*
group column of squadron V's Gruppenwinkel *m (Avn).*
group column of squadron wedges Gruppenkolonne aus geschlossenen Winkeln *(Avn).*
group commander Gruppenkommandeur *m (Avn).*
group command post Gruppengefechtsstand *m (Avn).*
group firing zusammengefaßtes Feuer mehrerer Schützen.
group formation Gruppenflugform *f (Avn).*
groupment Gruppe *f.*
group of armies Heeresgruppe *f.*
group of squadron javelins Gruppenkolonne *f (Avn).*
group of squadron javelins echeloned left Gruppenkolonne links *(Avn).*
group wedge Gruppenkeil *m (Avn).*
grouser Greifer *m (MT).*
grub hoe Minenkratze *f (Engr).*
guard *n* Wache *f*, Posten *m*; Streife *f (patrol)*; Parierstange *f (bayonet guard)*; Abzugsbügel *m (trigger guard).*
on guard auf Wache *(guard duty)*; auf der Hut *(alert).*
guard *v* bewachen, Wachdienst ausüben.
guard detail Wachmannschaft *f*, Wache *f.*
guard duty Feldwachdienst *m*, "Wacheschieben" *n.*
guard fence Schutzzaun *m.*
guardhouse Arrestlokal *n*, Wachgebäude *n.*
guarding mission Auftrag zur dauernden Überwachung des feindlichen Funkverkehrs *(Rad, Sig C).*
guard mount Aufziehen der Wache; Vergatterung *f (bugle call).*
guard of honor Ehrenwache *f*, Ehrenposten *m.*
guard rail Rödelbalken *m (Bdg)*; Radlenker *m (RR).*
guardroom Wachstube *f.*
guerrilla Partisane *m*, Freischärler *m*, Guerillakämpfer *m.*
guerrilla warfare Kleinkrieg *m*, kleiner Krieg, Guerillakrieg *m.*
guide *n* ortskundiger Führer, Einweiser *m (Tac)*; Führer *m*, Anführer *m (file)*; Flügelmann *m (line)*; Anhalt *m (guiding principle).*
ground pipe Erdleitungsrohr *n (Elec).*
ground platform Geschützbettung *f*, Bettung *f (RR gun).*
ground position signal Ortungsleuchtzeichen *n (ground-air Com).*
ground pressure spezifischer Bodendruck *(per unit area, MT).*
ground projector Signalwerfer *m.*
ground radiation Bodenstrahlung *f (Rad).*
ground radio service Bodenfunkdienst *m (Avn).*
ground radio station Bodenstelle *f (Avn).*
ground readiness Flugbereitschaft *f*, Startbereitschaft *f (Avn).*
ground reconnaissance Erdaufklärung *f*, Geländeerkundung *f (Tac).*
ground reference points Bodenpunkte *mpl (Surv).*

ground-return circuit Einfachleitung f, Erdrückleitung f (Tp).
ground-return telephone circuit Erdtelegraphieverbindung f.
ground-return telephone circuit Erdfernsprechverbindung f.
ground school Fliegerschule für technische Ausbildung (Avn).
ground signal Leuchtkugel f, Leuchtzeichen n, Handleuchtzeichen n.
ground signal cartridge Leuchtpatrone f, Meldepatrone f.
ground signal projector Signalwerfer m.
ground sill Grundschwell f (Bdg).
ground speed Zielgeschwindigkeit über Grund, Horizontalgeschwindigkeit des Zieles (AA Gunnery); Grundgeschwindigkeit f (Avn).
ground strafing Maschinengewehrangriff gegen Erdziele (Avn).
ground target Bodenziel n.
ground troops Landtruppen fpl.
ground visibility Bodensicht f (Avn).
ground wave Bodenwelle f (Rad).
ground-wave reception zone Bodenwellenempfangszone f (Rad).
ground wire Erdleitungsdraht m (Elec).
group Gruppe f (Avn); Waffengruppe f (Ord, Small Arms); Gruppe f (Tac) (generally in compounds, i.e., Artilleriegruppe, Flakgruppe, etc.).
party of guides Einweisungskommando n.
guide lining Klauenfutter n (G).
guide rail Führungsschiene f, Gleitschiene f (G cradle).
guide ring Klauenring m (G).
guide roller Führungsrolle f (Tk).
guide slide Gleitschiene f (G cradle).
guidon Standarte f (Arty, Cav, Armd Comd); Fahne f (Inf); Standartenträger m, Fahnenträger m (Pers).
guilty schuldig.
gull wing Knickflügel m (Ap).
gully Schlenke f.
gun Geschütz n, Kanone f (G); Gewehr n (R); Maschinengewehr n (MG).
gun arm Entfernungslineal n (plotting board).
gun barrel Geschützrohr n, Kanonenrohr n.
gun battery Geschützbatterie f.
gunboat Kanonenboot n.
gun book Rohrbuch n.
gun car Geschützwagen m (RR).
gun carriage Lafette f. See also **gun mount.**
gun-carriage axle Lafettenachse f.
gun-carriage bed Lafettentisch m.
gun-carriage side plate Lafettenwand f.
gun commander Geschützführer m.
guncotton Schießbaumwolle f, Schießwolle f.
guncotton powder Schießwollpulver n.
gun cover Geschützplane f.
gun cradle Wiege f.
gun crew Bedienungsmannschaft f, Geschützbedienung f.
gun difference Entfernungsunterschied zwischen Richtkreis-Ziel und Feuerstellung-Ziel.
gun displacement Staffelung f (within a battery); Stellungswechsel m (change of position).
gun emplacement Geschützstellung f, Geschützstand m.
gunfire Geschützfeuer n.
gun grease Waffenfett n.
gun group Geschützteile npl, Waffengruppe f.
gun hoist Ladekran m, Geschoßkran m, Batteriekran m.
gun junction box Kupplungskasten m (AA director).
gun loader Ladekanonier m.
gun motor carriage Selbstfahrlafette f.
gun mount Lafette f; Bordlafette f (on Ap or ship). See also terms under **gun carriage.**
gun-mount outrigger m Lafettenholm
gunner Kanonier m (in a general sense, FA); Richtkanonier m (gunner, FA); Richtschütze m (gunner, MG, AT or Tk G); Panzerschütze m (Tk); Bordschütze m, Fliegerschütze m (Avn); Granatwerfer m (Mort squad).
gunner's quadrant Winkelmesser m, Libellenquadrant m.
gunner's seat Richtsitz m (G).
gunner's station Schützenstand m, Gefechtsstand m (Ap).
gunnery Schießwesen n.
gunnery instructor Schießlehrer m.
gun park Geschützpark m.
gun platform Feuerplattform f.
gun platform excavation Bettungsloch n (RR gun).
gun pointer Richtschütze m, Richtkanonier m.
gun pointer's platform Plattform f (RR gun).
gun pointer's shield Schutzschild m (G).
gun pointing data Schießgrundlagen fpl, Schußelemente npl, Schußwerte mpl (Gunnery).
gun position Geschützstellung f (Arty); Schützenstand m, Gefechtsstand m (Ap).
gunpowder Schießpulver n, Schwarzpulver n.
gun rack Gewehrmieke f, Gewehrmücke f, Gewehrstütze f.
gun rail Lafettenschiene f (MG mount).
gun section Geschützstaffel f (Btry).
gun shelter Schartenblende f, Schartenschild m, Klappblende f (Ft).
gun shield Schutzschild m (G); Blende f (Tk).
gun shot Kanonenschuß m, Schuß m.
gun slide Gleitschuh m (G); Schieber m.
gun sling Gewehrriemen m, Riemen m (R).
gun sling hook Schnalle f (R).
gun sling keeper Riemenschieber m (R).
gun squad Geschützbedienung f, Bedienung f, Geschützmannschaft f, Bedienungsmannschaft f.
gun-target line Linie Geschütz-Ziel.
gunwale Dollbord n (rowboat); Pontonoberkante f (Pon).
gun wave Schallwelle des Mündungsknalls (Sound Ranging).
gun-wheel brake Schießbremse f.
gusset Eckplatte f (Engr).
gust Windstoß m, Bö f (Met).
guy line Ankerseil n, Haltetau n, Verankerungskabel n (Engr).
guy pin Zeltpflock m (tent).
guy rope Zeltleine f (tent).
gyro compass Kreiselkompaß m.
gyro control Kreiselabfeuergerät n (Tk).
gyro flight indicator Gyrorektor m.
gyro horizon indicator Horizont m, künstlicher Horizont (Ap Inst).
gyro instrument Kreiselgerät n.
gyropilot Selbststeuergerät n (Ap).
gyroplane Tragschrauber m, Autogiro m.
gyroscope Kreisel m.
gyroscopic turn indicator Kreiselwendezeiger m, Kreiselsteuerzeiger m (Ap).
gyro-stabilizer Kreiselabfeuergerät n (Tk).

H

hachures Bergstriche mpl, Schraffen fpl (map).
hacksaw Metallsäge f.
Hague Convention Haager Abkommen.
hail n Hagel m (Met).
hailstorm Hagelschlag m.
hair Haar n.
hairpin curve Spitzkehre f.
hair trigger Stecher m (Small Arms).
half cock Ruhrast f (Small Arms).
half left halblinks.
half-loop wingover Fächerturn m.
half-mast halbmast, halbstocks.
half right halbrechts.
half roll halbe Rolle (Avn).
half-squad Abmarsch m (Cav).
half-staff halbstocks.
half step halber Schritt (drill).
half-track carrier Zugkraftwagen m (also used as prime mover).
half-track drive Halbkettenantrieb m (MT).
half-track motorcycle Kettenkrad n.
half-track motor truck Halbketten-Lastkraftwagen m.
half-track motor vehicle Halbkettenkraftfahrzeug n.
half-track vehicle Halbkettenfahrzeug n, Zwitterfahrzeug n.
halt n Halt m, Marschhalt m, Marschpause f; Beobachtungshalt m (for Obsn).
halt v halten, anhalten.
"Halt!" "Halt!" (to an individual); "Abteilung, halt!" (to detail, squad, etc.).
halt area Halteplatz m (Tac).
halter Halfter f (for horse).
halter chain Halfterkinnkette f.
halter headstall Stallhalfter f.
halter tie Halfterriemen m.
halt order Befehl zum Halten.
"Halt! who is there?" "Halt, wer da!"
halving Bildteilung im Schnittbild-Entfernungsmesser (coincidence range finder).
halving adjustment Ausschalten der Schnittbildversetzung (coincidence range finder).
halving line Schnittlinie f (coincidence range finder).
ham Schinken m.
hammer Hahn m, Hammer m, Schlagstück n (Small Arms).
hammer gun Hahngewehr n.
hammerless gun hahnloses Gewehr, Hammerleßgewehr n.
hammock Hängematte f.
hand Hand f.
hand arm Handwaffe f.
handbook Handbuch n.
hand brake Handbremse f.
hand camera Handkammer f.
handcart Handwagen m.
hand crank Handkurbel f (MT).
hand-crank generator Kurbeldynamo m, Handdrehmaschine f (Elec); Kurbelinduktor m (Tp).
handcuff Handfessel f.
hand drill Handbohrmaschine f, Brustbohrer m.
hand extinguisher Handfeuerlöscher m.
hand grenade Handgranate f.
hand-grenade bag Standsack m.
hand-grenade range Handgranatenwurfweite f.
hand guard Handschutz m (R).
hand hole Handloch n (G wheel).
handle n Griff m, Handgriff m, Stiel
handle bar Lenkstange f (Mtcl).
hand level Freihandnivellierinstrument n (Surv).
handling line Haltetau n, Transporttau n (Bln).
hand-operated handtätig.
hand-operated ventilator Handlüfter m.
hand reel tragbare Kabeltrommel (Tp).
hand salute Gruß m.
handset Handapparat m (Tp, Rad (Tp).
handset switch Lauthörknopf m (Tp).
handspike Richtbaum m (G trail).
hand sprinkler Handstreutrommel f (CWS).
hand starter Handanlasser m (Mtr).
hand-to-hand fighting Kampf von Mann gegen Mann, Handgemenge
hand weapon Handwaffe f, blanke Waffe.
handwheel Handrad n.
hang einhaken (hook on); aufhängen (a picture, etc.); hängen (a criminal).
hangar Flugzeughalle f, Halle f.
hanger bar Auflager n (harness).
hangfire Nachbrenner m (Am).
hang fire nachbrennen (Am).
hangwire Entsicherungsdraht m.
harass stören, beunruhigen (Tac).
harassing Beunruhigung f, Störung
harassing agent Ermüdungskampfstoff m, Reizstoff m (CWS).
harassing concentration Erträglichkeitsgrenze f (CWS).
harassing fire Beunruhigungsfeuer n, Ermüdungsschießen n, Störungsfeuer n; Lähmungsschießen n (with Cml shell).
harassing tactics Störungsangriffe mpl, Ermattungstaktik f.
harbor n Hafen m.
harbor v Schutz gewähren, beherbergen.
harbor area Hafengebiet n.
harbor defense Hafenschutz m.
harbor defense craft Hafenschutzboot n (Nav).
harbor-defense ordnance depot Sperramt n.
hard labor Strafarbeit f.
hard solder Schlaglot n.
harmonic frequency Oberschwingungsfrequenz f (Rad).
harmonization Ineinklangbringen n; Anschießen n (Ord).
harness n Bandgestell n (gas mask); Geschirr n (horse); Gurtwerk n (Prcht).
harness v aufschirren.
hash Haschee n.
hasty flüchtig, schnell, behelfsmäßig, Behelfs-.
hasty ammunition shelter Munitionsnische f (Ft).
hasty bridge Behelfsbrücke f, Schnellbrücke f.
hasty field fortification flüchtige Feldbefestigung.
hasty footbridge Schnellsteg m.
hasty intrenchment flüchtige Feldbefestigung.
hasty landing stage Behelfslandbrücke f (Engr).
hasty meteorological message Barbarabehelfsmeldung f (Arty).
hasty obstacle Schnellsperre f.
hasty profile Höhenumrißskizze f (Top).
hasty single-span footbridge Uferschnellsteg m.
hasty trestle bridge Bockschnellsteg m.
hat Hut m; Mütze f (cap).
hatch Luke f, Einstiegluke f, Einsteigklappe f (Ap); Einsteigluke f (Tk).
hatch cover Lukendeckel m (Tk).
hatchet Handbeil n.
hatching Schummerung f (map).
hat cord Mützenkordel f.
haul v ziehen, schleppen.
haversack Tornister m.
haversack-type radio set Tornister-Funkgerät n.
haversack-type receiver Tornisterempfänger m (Rad).
hawser Trosse f, Kabeltau n.
haystack Heuschober m.
haze Dunst m (Met).
hazy diesig, dunstig.
HC mixture See **HC smoke mixture**
HC smoke mixture Zinknebel m, amerikanische Bergermischung (CWS).
head Kopf m (anatomy); Geschoßspitze f (shell); Zünderkappe f (point-detonating fuze); Patronenboden m (cartridge); Reibfläche f (Small Arms Am); Kopfstück n (MG); Geschoßkopf m (projectile); Kolonnenspitze f, Spitze f (of a column); Haupt n (chief, especially in compounds).
head and chest set Brustfernsprecher m (Tp).
head harness Kopfbänderung f (gas mask).
heading Steuerkurs m (Air Navigation); Überschrift f (on messages, etc.).
headlight Scheinwerfer m.
head nurse Oberschwester f.
headphone Hörer m, Kopfhörer m, Kopffernhörer m (Tp, Rad).
headquarters Stab m, Kommando n, Hauptquartier n, Stabsquartier n, Kommandostelle f, Kommandobehörde f; Gefechtsstand m (Avn).
headquarters and service company Stabs- und Betriebskompanie f (USA).
headquarters battery Stabsbatterie f (Arty).
headquarters clerk Stabsschreiber m.
headquarters company Stabskompanie f.
headquarters detachment Stabstrupp m.
headquarters net Nachrichtennetz der Kommandostellen (Rad).
headquarters platoon Stabszug m.
headquarters section Stabsgruppe f.
headquarters squadron Stabsstaffel f (Avn).
headquarters troop Kommando- und Stabsschwadron f (Cav).
head resistance Stirnwiderstand m.
headset Kopfhörer mpl.
head space Verschlußabstand m (Ord). Hauptgestell n, Kopfgestell n (harness).
head-strap cushion Kopfplatte f (gas mask).
head straps Kopfbänder npl (gas mask).
headway Zeitabstand m (time interval, MT, RR).
head wind Gegenwind m.
heal heilen.
health Gesundheit f.
heart Herz n.
heat n Wärme f, Hitze f.
heat v erwärmen, erhitzen; heizen (a room, etc.).
heater Ofen m.
heat of condensation Kondensationswärme f (Met).
heat of vaporization Verdampfungswärme f (Met).
heat-resistant hitzebeständig.
heat shrinking Aufschrumpfen n (Ord).
heatstroke Hitzschlag m.
heat-treated steel m Vergütungsstahl
heavier-than-air aircraft Luftfahrzeuge schwerer als Luft.
heavily armored schwergepanzert.
Heaviside layer Heavisideschicht f (Rad).
heavy schwerst- (Ord).
heavy antitank gun s.Pak f.
heavy artillery schwerste Artillerie.
heavy-case bomb Panzerbombe f.
heavy cruiser schwerer Kreuzer (Nav).
heavy machine gun überschweres Maschinengewehr, s.S.MG. n.
heavy machine-gun section MG.-Staffel f (Cav).
heavy machine-gun squad s.M.G.-Bedienung f.
heavy ponton battalion schweres Pontonier-Bataillon.
heavy tank schwerer Panzerkampfwagen.
heavy weapons schwere Infanteriewaffen.
heavy weapons company Maschinengewehrkompanie f (Inf); schwere Kompanie (Mtz R Regt).
hedge Hecke f.
hedgehog Igel m (AT obstacle).
hedge-hopping Heckenspringen n, Tiefflug m (Avn).
heel n Ballen m (harness); Ferse f (anatomy); Absatz m (of shoe).
heel v krängen (Avn, Nav).
heeling error Krängungsfehler m (Avn, Nav).
height Anhöhe f, Höhe f (Top).
height finder Höhenmesser m, Höhenentfernungsmesser m, Entfernungsmeßgerät n (AAA).
height of burst Sprenghöhe f (Gunnery).
height of mask Deckungshöhe f (Ballistics).
height of muzzle Feuerhöhe f (Arty).
height-of-range setter Höhenrichtkanonier m.
height of rise Steighöhe f (ground Sig).
height of site Höhe über Normalnull (CA).
height of target Zielhöhe f (Gunnery).
helical spring Schraubenfeder f, Spiralfeder f (MT).
helical wire Drahtspirale f.
helicopter Schraubenflugzeug n, Hubschrauber m.
heliograph Spiegeltelegraph m (Sig C).
heliotrope See **heliograph.**
helium Helium n.
helmet Helm m; Stahlhelm m (steel); Fliegerhaube f, Kopfhaube f (Avn); F.T.-Haube f (with built-in headset and throat-type microphone); Tropenhelm m (sun helmet); Sturzhelm m (crash helmet).
helmet cover Helmbezug m, Helmüberzug m; Tarnkappe f (Cam).
hemorrhage Blutung f.
hernia Bruch m, Leistenbruch m.
heterodyne frequency Überlagerungsfrequenz f.
heterodyne frequency meter Schwebungsfrequenzmesser m.
hexachlorethane Hexachloräthan n (CWS).
hexagonal-head screw Sechskantschraube f (MT).
H-hour X-Uhr.
high-altitude bombing Höhenbombenwurf m.
high-altitude flight Höhenflug m.
high-altitude mixture control Höhenmischregelung f (Ap).
high-angle fire Steilfeuer n, Feuer in der oberen Winkelgruppe.
high-angle gun Steilfeuergeschütz n.
high-angle weapon Steilfeuerwaffe f.
high-burst adjustment target Lufteinschießziel n (Arty).
high-burst auxiliary target Luftvergleichsziel n (Arty).
high-burst ranging Einschießen mit hohen Sprengpunkten (Gunnery).
high command obere Kommandobehörde (agency); Oberbefehl m (function); Oberkommando n (agency and function).
High Command of the Air Forces Oberkommando der Luftwaffe (Ger).
High Command of the Armed Forces Oberkommando der Wehrmacht (Ger).
High Command of the Army Oberkommando des Heeres (Ger).
High Command of the Navy Oberkommando der Kriegsmarine (Ger).
higher echelon obere Führung (collective); übergeordneter Truppenteil (unit); übergeordnetes Kommando (command).
high explosive hochbrisanter Sprengstoff.
high-explosive chemical shell Gasbrisanzgranate f.
high-explosive rifle grenade Gewehr-Sprenggranate f.
high-explosive shell Brisanzgranate f, Sprenggranate f (Am); Sprenggranaten-Patrone f (fixed Am).
high-explosive shrapnel Brisanzschrapnell n.
high frequency Hochfrequenz f.
high-frequency interference Hochfrequenzstörungen fpl (Rad).
high-frequency oscillator tube Überlagerröhre f.
high-octane gasoline Benzin mit hoher Oktanzahl.
high-power radio station Großfunkstelle f.
high-pressure area Hochdruckgebiet n (Met).
high-pressure lubrication Hochdruckschmierung f.
high-pressure tire Hochdruckreifen m (MT).
high-priority material Sparstoff m.
high reference point Hochpunkt m (Surv).
high-tension line Hochspannungsleitung f (Elec).
high-tension obstacle Starkstromsperre f.
high-tension wire Hochspannungsleitung f (Elec).
high terrain Höhengelände n (Top).
high tide Hochwasser n.
high voltage Hochspannung f (Elec).
high-voltage line Hochspannungsleitung f.
high-voltage obstacle Starkstromsperre f.
high-voltage power lines Starkstromnetz n (Elec).
high-voltage warning device Berührungswarngerät n.
highway Landstraße f; Autobahn f.
high wind steifer Wind.
high-wing monoplane Hochdecker m.
high wire entanglement Flandernzaun m, Drahtzaun m (Engr).
hill Hügel m (Top).
hilltop Gipfel des Hügels, Bergspitze f.
hindquarters Hinterhand f (horse).
hinge Scharnier n.
hinged-arch bridge Gelenkbogenbrücke f.
hip Hüfte f.
hip strap Schweberiemen m (harness).

hit Treffer *m*, Einschuß *m*; Granattreffer *m (shell fire)*; Bombentreffer *m (bombing)*; Torpedotreffer *m (torpedo)*; Flaktreffer *m (AA fire)*.

hit-and-run raid Zerstörangriff *m (Avn)*.

hitch *n* Stich *m (rope)*.

hitch *v* anstecken *(attach)*; einhaken *(hook up)*; festmachen *(tie)*; anschirren *(harness)*.

hock Sprunggelenk *n (horse)*.

hoe Kratze *f (Engr)*.

hoist *n* Kran *m*, Munitionsaufzug *m*.

hoist *v* heißen, hissen *(a flag)*; in die Höhe ziehen, heben *(lift)*.

hold *n* Laderaum *m (Nav)*; Griff *m (grip)*.

hold *v* halten, standhalten *(Tac)*.

holdfast Verankerung *f (Engr)*.

holding attack Fesselungsvorstoß *m*, Nebenangriff *m*.

holding garrison Verteidigungstruppen *fpl*.

holding plate Griffplatte *f (G sight)*.

hold off abfangen, ausschweben *(Avn)*.

hold right or left das Korn klemmen *(R aiming)*.

hole Loch *n*, Mulde *f (Top)*; Öffnung *f (opening)*; Lücke *f (gap)*.

holster Halftertasche *f*.

home Heim *n*, Heimat *f*; Haus *n*, Wohnung *f (dwelling)*.

home base Heimatflughafen *m*, Heimathorst *m (Avn)*.

home defense Landesverteidigung *f*.

home-defense system Landesverteidigungsorganisation *f*.

home field Einsatzhafen *m (Avn)*.

home front innere Front.

home parole Entlassung auf Ehrenwort.

home port Heimatshafen *m*.

home station Standort *m*.

homing Zielflug *m (Air Navigation)*; Rückflug *m (Avn)*.

homing instinct Ortsgedächtnis *n*.

homing pigeon Brieftaube *f*.

honor Ehre *f*.

honorable discharge ehrenvoller Abschied.

honorary rank Ehrenrang *m*.

honor guard Ehrenwache *f*.

hood Motorhaube *f (MT)*; Zünderhülse *f (fuze)*; Schutzhülle *f*, Überzug *m*, Kapuze *f*.

hoof Huf *m*.

hoof coronet Hufkrone *f (horse)*.

hook Haken *m*.

hook switch Gabelumschalter *m*, Hakenumschalter *m (Tp)*.

hoop Schellband *n*, Verstärkungsring *m (G)*; Hülse *f (Mort)*; Eisenreifen *m (wooden barrel or cask)*.

horizon Kimm *f*, Horizont *m*.

horizontal horizontal, waagerecht.

horizontal angle Seitenwinkel *m (Surv)*.

horizontal base Langbasis *f*, Basis *f (Arty Surv)*.

horizontal base method Zielaufnahme mit Langbasisanlage, Langbasisverfahren *n*.

horizontal bombing Waagerechtbombenwurf *m*.

horizontal clock system Windrichtungsangabe nach Melderose *(Gunnery)*.

horizontal fire Flachfeuer *n*, Feuer in der unteren Winkelgruppe *(Gunnery)*.

horizontal-fire table Tafel für das Schießen in der Mündungswaagerechten *(Gunnery)*.

horizontal flight Horizontalflug *m*, Geradeausflug *m*, Waagerechtflug *m (Avn)*.

horizontal plane Horizontalebene *f*, Kartenebene *f (Gunnery)*.

horizontal projection Projektion auf die Horizontalebene.

horizontal range Kartenentfernung *f (Gunnery)*.

horizontal range to future position Kartenentfernung zum Treffpunkt *(AAA)*.

horizontal range to midpoint Kartenentfernung zum Wechselpunkt *(AAA)*.

horizontal range to present position Kartenentfernung zum Abschußpunkt *(at instant of firing, AAA)*.

horizontal shot group Bodentreffbild *n (Ballistics)*.

horizontal target waagerechte Trefffläche *(Ballistics)*.

horn Lautsprechertrichter *m (Rad)*; Trichter *m (AA sound locator)*.

horn collector Trichter *m (AA sound locator)*.

horn-type speaker Trichterlautsprecher *m (Rad)*.

horse Pferd *n*.

horse ambulance Pferdetransportwagen *m*.

horse artillery berittene Artillerie, reitende Artillerie.

horse blanket Pferdedecke *f*.

horse cavalry Kavallerie *f*.

horse-drawn pferdebespannt, bespannt.

horse-drawn artillery bespannte Artillerie.

horse-drawn generating unit Kraftquellenwagen *m*.

horse-drawn vehicle Pferdefahrzeug *n*.

horsehide Pferdehaut *f*.

horseholder Pferdehalter *m (Cav, Arty)*.

horsepower Pferdestärke *f (Mech)*.

horseshoe Hufeisen *n*.

horseshoe magnet Hufeisenmagnet *m*.

horseshoer Beschlagschmied *m*.

hose Schlauch *m*; Atemschlauch *m (gas mask, oxygen breathing apparatus)*.

hose coupling Schlauchbinder *m (MT)*.

hospital Krankenhaus *n*, Lazarett *n*.

hospital boat Lazarettschiff *n*.

hospitalization Lazarettaufnahme *f*, Lazarettbehandlung *f*, Hospitalisierung *f*.

hospital ship Lazarettschiff *n*; Leichtkrankenschiff *n (for sitting wounded)*.

hospital train Lazarettzug *m*; Leichtkrankenzug *m (for sitting wounded)*.

hospital transport Lazarettschiff *n*.

hospital treatment Lazarettbehandlung *f*.

hostage Geisel *m-f*.

hostile feindlich. *See also* **enemy**.

hostile forces Feindstreitkräfte *fpl*.

hostile territory Feindesland *n*.

hostilities Feindseligkeiten *fpl*.

hot cathode Glühkathode *f (Rad)*.

hot-wire-bridge head Glühköpfchen *n (electric igniting device) (Engr)*.

hour Stunde *f*.

hour angle Stundenwinkel *m*.

hour of operation Betriebsstunde *f (Mech)*.

house Haus *n*.

house warden Hauswart *m (Civ Defense)*.

housewife Nähzeug *n (personal equipment)*.

housing Gehäuse *n (Mech)*.

howitzer Haubitze *f (105 mm and 150 mm)*; Mörser *m (210 mm and larger)*.

howitzer barrel Mörserrohr *n*.

howitzer carriage Haubitzlafette *f*.

HS vapor detector kit Senfgas-Spürgerät *n (CWS)*.

hub Nabe *f*.

hub cap Radkappe *f (Arty, MT)*.

hub flange Nabenscheibe *f (G wheel)*; Nabenflansch *m (MT)*.

hull Kasten *m*, Panzerkasten *m*, Panzerkörper *m*, Wanne *f (Tk)*; Rumpf *m*, Boot *n (flying boat)*; Schiffsrumpf *m (Nav)*.

humidity Feuchtigkeitsgehalt *m*, Feuchtigkeit *f (Met)*.

hump Ablaufberg *m (RR)*.

hung striker Schlagbolzen-Versager *m (fuze)*.

hunt *v* schwingen, wandern *(Mech)*.

hurdle *n* Hurde *f*, Verhau *m*, Hindernis *n*.

hurricane Orkan *m*, Taifun *m*.

hut Hütte *f*.

hydraulic brake Öldruckbremse *f (MT)*.

hydraulic shock absorber Flüssigkeits-Stoßdämpfer *m (MT)*.

hydrochloric acid Salzsäure *f*.

hydrocyanic acid Hydrozyansäure *f*, Blausäure *f*, Zyanwasserstoff *m*, Zyanwasserstoffsäure *f (CWS)*.

hydrogen Wasserstoff *m*.

hydrogen peroxide Wasserstoffsuperoxyd *n*.

hydrogen sulfide Schwefelwasserstoff *m*.

hydrographic map Seekarte *f (Nav)*.

hydrometer Aräometer *n*, Säuremesser *m*.

hydrophone Unterwasserhorchgerät *n (Nav)*.

hydrostatic bomb fuze hydrostatische Zündvorrichtung, Seezünder *m (antisubmarine bombs and depth charges)*.

hygiene Hygiene *f*, Gesundheitspflege *f (care)*; Gesundheitslehre *f (science)*.

hygrograph Feuchtigkeitsschreiber *m*.

hygrometer Feuchtigkeitsmesser *m*.

hygroscopic hygroskopisch, wassergierig.

hypothetical target angenommenes Ziel *(Gunnery)*.

hypsometry Höhenmessung *f (Surv)*.

hysteresis Hysterese *f*, Nachhinken *n (Inst, Mech)*.

I

ice Eis *n*.

ice apron Eisbrecher *m (Bdg)*.

ice creepers Steigeisen *npl*.

ice eliminating Enteisung *f*; Warmluftenteisung *f (thermo method) (Avn)*.

ice-eliminating system Enteisungsanlage *f (Ap)*.

ice formation Eisansatz *m (Avn)*.

ice spade Eissporn *m (trail spade) (G)*.

icing Vereisung *f (Avn)*.

icw tönend *(marking on Rad set)*.

identification Identifikation *f*, Identifizierung *f*, Erkennen *n*.

identification card Ausweiskarte *f*.

identification helmet band Helmband *n (maneuvers)*.

identification light Kennlicht *n*, Kennscheinwerfer *m (Ap)*.

identification mark Erkennungszeichen *n*, Kennzeichen *n*.

identification panel Erkennungstuch *n*.

identification papers Personalausweis *m*, Ausweispapier *n*.

identification signal Kennung *f (Avn)*.

identification tag Erkennungsmarke *f*.

identify identifizieren *(a person, thing)*; erkennen *(a Cml agent)*; sich ausweisen *(identify oneself)*.

idle *v* leerlaufen *(Mtr)*.

idler Leitrad *n (Tk)*.

idler adjuster rod Spannschloß *n (Tk)*.

idler jet Leerlaufdüse *f (Mtr)*.

idler wheel Leitrad *n (Tk)*.

idler wheel shaft Leitradachse *f (Tk)*.

idling speed Leerlauf *m (Mtr)*.

igloo Schneehütte *f*.

igloo magazine Munitionsbunker *m*.

ignite zünden *(a charge, etc.)*; anzünden, in Brand setzen *(set on fire)*; sich entzünden, Feuer fangen *(begin to burn)*.

igniter Beiladung *f (Am)*; Zünder *m (land mine)*; Glühzündstück *n (Elec igniter)*.

igniter train Zündsatz *m (pyrotechnic Sig)*.

igniting Zünden *n (Mtr)*.

igniting charge Beiladung *f (Am)*; Zündladung *f*.

igniting flash Zündstrahl *m (Am)*.

igniting fuze Brennzünder *m (hand grenade)*.

igniting mixture Zündmasse *f*.

igniting powder Beiladung *f (Am)*.

ignition Zünden *n*, Zündung *f (Mtr)*.

ignition cartridge Zündpatrone *f (Am)*.

ignition charge Zündladung *f (Am)*.

ignition coil Zündspule *f (Mtr)*.

ignition current Zündstrom *m (Mtr)*.

ignition key Zündschlüssel *m (MT)*.

ignition quality Zündwilligkeit *f (Diesel fuel)*.

ignition spark Zündfunke *m (Mtr)*.

ignition switch Zündschalter *m (Ap, MT)*.

ignition system Zündanlage *f*, Zündvorrichtung *f (Mtr)*.

ill krank.

illegal illegal, ungesetzlich, gesetzwidrig.

illegible unleserlich, unlesbar.

illiterate *n* Analphabet *m*.

illiterate *adj* des Schreibens und Lesens unkundig.

illuminant charge Leuchtsatz *m*.

illuminating shell Leuchtgranate *f*.

illuminating window Beleuchtungsfenster *n (panoramic sight)*.

illumination Anleuchten *n*, Beleuchtung *f*.

illustrate veranschaulichen.

illustration Abbildung *f (visual)*; Erläuterung *f (explanation)*; Beispiel *n (example)*.

illustrative material Anschauungsmittel *npl (training aids)*.

immediate verzögerungsfrei *(Ord)*; augenblicklich, unverzüglich.

immediate action Beseitigen von Hemmungen.

immediate action letter Vordruck für dringende Meldungen.

immediate objective erstes Angriffsziel.

Immelmann turn hochgezogene Kehrkurve, Immelmann-Turn *m (Avn)*.

immobilize festhalten, lähmen, niederhalten *(Tac)*.

immune geschützt, immun.

immunization Immunisierung *f*.

impact Aufschlag *m*, Auftreffen *n*, Einschlag *m*, Geschoßeinschlag *m*.

impact area Aufschlaggelände *n*.

impacted snow Schneestauung *f*

impact fuze *(Am)* Aufschlagzünder *m*

impedance Scheinwiderstand *m*, Impedanz *f (Elec)*.

impedimenta Gepäck *n*.

impel treiben, antreiben.

impeller Ladelaufrad *n (Ap engine)*; Laufrad *n (of pump, etc.)*.

impermeability Wasserdichtigkeit *f (to water)*; Gasdichtigkeit *f (to gas)*; Dichtigkeit *f*, Undurchdringlichkeit *f*.

impermeable wasserdicht *(to water)*; gasdicht *(to gas)*; undurchdringlich *(impenetrable)*.

impermeable protective clothing Gasschutzkleidung *f*.

impetigo Eiterflechte *f*, Blasengrind *m*, Impetigo *f*.

impregnate imprägnieren.

impregnite Imprägniermittel *n*.

impress zum Dienst pressen.

imprison ins Gefängnis stecken.

improper uniform unvorschriftsmäßige Uniform.

improve ausbauen *(Ft)*; ausbessern, bessern *(a road, etc.)*.

improved road unterhaltener Fahrweg.

improvised mount Hilfslafette *f (MG)*.

improvised road behelfsmäßige Fahrbahn *(Engr)*.

impulse generator mechanism Flugzeug-M.G.-Steuerung *f*, Synchronisator *m (Ap)*.

inaccessible unerreichbar *(of a place)*; nicht zu sprechen *(said of a busy person)*.

inaccurate ungenau *(not precise)*; fehlerhaft *(erroneous)*.

inactivate aus dem aktiven Dienst entlassen.

inactive inaktiv, nicht aktiv.

Inactive Reserve Inaktive Offiziere.

inadequate unzulänglich, unangemessen.

inboard stabilizing float Stützflosse *f*, Flossenstummel *m (seaplane)*.

incandescent cathode tube Glühkathodenröhre *f (Rad)*.

incandescent lamp Glühlampe *f*.

incapable unfähig, ungeeignet; untauglich *(unfit)*.

incendiary *adj* brandwirkend, Brand-.

incendiary agent Brandstoff *m*, Brandmittel *n*.

incendiary ammunition Brandmunition *f*.

incendiary bomb Brandbombe *f*; Stabbrandbombe *f (stick-type)*.

incendiary bottle Brandflasche *f*, Molotowcocktail *m*.

incendiary bullet Phosphorgeschoß *n*, Brandgeschoß *n*.

incendiary cluster Brandbombenbündel *n (bombing)*.

incendiary composition Brandmasse *f (Am)*.

incendiary grenade Brandgranate *f*, Brand-Handgranate *f*.

incendiary projectile Brandgeschoß *n*.

incendiary shell Brandgranate *f*.

inch Zoll *m (2.54 cm)*.

incineration Abbrennen *n (CWS)*.

incinerator Kehrichtofen *m*.

incision Einschnitt *m*, Schnitt *m*.

incite aufhetzen.

inclination Neigung *f*, Steigung *f*.

incline *n* Ablaufberg *m (RR)*; Steigung *f*, Hang *m (Top)*.

inclined sights verkantetes Visier *(Small Arms)*.

inclinometer Neigungsmesser *m*.

inclosure Beilage *f*.

income tax Einkommensteuer *f*.

incoming-call signal light Anrufsschauzeichen *n (Tp)*.

incoming track Einfahrgleis *n (RR)*.

increase *n* Zunahme *f (addition)*; Gewinn *m (gain)*; Steigerung *f (intensification)*; Vermehrung *f*, Erhöhung *f (in numbers)*; Wachsen *n*, Anwachsen *n (growing)*.

increase in range Vorverlegung des Feuers *(Arty)*.

increase of efficiency Leistungssteigerung *f (Mtr)*.

increasing twist wachsender Drall, zunehmender Drall *(Ord)*.

increment Teilladung *f (separate-loading Am)*.

increment section *See* **increment**.

indecision Unentschlossenheit *f*.

indelible pencil Tintenstift *m*, Kopierstift *m*.

indemnity Schadenersatz *m*.

independent unabhängig, selbständig.

independent suspension Einzelaufhängung *f (of wheels, MT)*.

independent units selbständige Verbände *(Tac)*.

index Marke *f*, Stellmarke *f (optical Inst)*.

index error Ablesefehler *m*.

index line Ablesemarke *f*.

index map Übersichtsbild *n (aerial Photo)*.

inductance Belastung *f (Rad)*.

induction Einberufung *f (Mil)*; Induktion *f (Elec)*.

induction coil Sprechspule *f (Tp)*.

induction order Gestellungsbefehl *m*.

induction station Einberufungsort *m*.

industrial gewerblich, industriell.

industrial installations Industrieanlagen *fpl*.

industry Industrie *f*.

inefficient untüchtig, unfähig.

inert träge, unentzündbar, neutral.

inertia Beharrungsvermögen *n*, Trägheit *f (Ballistics, Mech)*.

inertia pellet Schlagbolzen *m (fuze)*.

inertia starter Schwungkraftanlasser *m (Mtr)*.

inertia striker pellet Schlagbolzen *m (fuze)*.

inert material Gaskampf- und Schutzgerät *n (CWS)*.

inexcusable unverzeihlich, unentschuldbar.

infantry Infanterie *f*.

infantry-accompanying gun Infanteriebegleitgeschütz *n*.

infantry assault Infanteriesturm *m*.

infantry battalion Infanteriebataillon *n*.

infantry commander Infanteriekommandeur *m*.

infantry company Grenadierkompanie *f*, Infanteriekompanie *f*.

infantry division Infanteriedivision *f*; Jägerdivision *f (Ger light Mtz Inf Div)*.

infantry equipment park Infanteriepark *m*.

infantry howitzer Infanteriegeschütz *n*.

infantryman Grenadier *m*, Infanterist *m*; Landser *m (Slang)*.

infantry mil Einheit der 6283-Teilung des Vollkreises *(Gunnery)*.

infantry pack Tornister *m*, Rückengepäck *n*.

infantry pioneer Infanteriepionier *m*.

infantry point Infanteriespitze *f (march column)*.

infantry rear point Infanterienachspitze *f (march column)*.

infantry regiment Grenadierregiment *n*, Infanterieregiment *n*.

Infantry School Infanterieschule *f*.

infantry weapon Infanteriewaffe *f*.

infection Ansteckung *f*, Infektion *f*.

inferior niedriger, unter *(lower)*; unterlegen, schwächer *(in numbers)*; untergeordnet, unterstellt *(in rank)*; minderwertig *(in quality)*.

inferiority Unterlegenheit *f (Tac)*.

infiltrate einsickern *(Tac)*.

infiltration Einsickern *n*, Eindringen *n (Tac)*.

infirmary Krankenstube *f*, Krankenrevier *n*.

infirmary case Revierkranker *m (Med)*.

inflammable feuergefährlich, entzündbar.

inflate aufblasen.

inflow Vorstrom *m*, Saugluft *f (Avn)*.

influenza Grippe *f*.

in force mit starken Kräften, mit Einsatz aller Kräfte *(Tac)*.

inform benachrichtigen, in Kenntnis setzen, mitteilen, informieren.

information Auskunft *f*; Auskunftstelle *f (place)*; Nachricht *f (intelligence)*.

information center Flugmeldekommando *n (AWS, Z of I)*; Flugmeldezentrale *f (AWS, T of Opns)*.

information of objectives Zielunterlagen *fpl (bombing)*.

"Information please" "Bitte Auskunft" *(Tp)*.

initial *n* Initiale *f*, Anfangsbuchstabe *m*.

initial *adj* anfänglich, Anfangs-.

initial charge Anfangsladung *f (Engr)*.

initial data Eingangswerte *mpl (AAA)*.

initial fire order Einschieß-Kommando *n*.

initial issue erste Ausstattung.

initial phase Auftakt *m (of an operation)*.

initial point Anfangspunkt *m*, Ausgangspunkt *m*; Bereitstellung *f (Tac)*.

initial position Ausgangsstellung *f*, Anfangsstellung *f (Tac)*.

initial return Iststärkenachweis *m*.

initial twist Anfangsdrall *m (Ord)*.

initial velocity Anfangsgeschwindigkeit *f*, Mündungsgeschwindigkeit *f (Ballistics)*.

initiate anfangen, beginnen *(begin)*; einführen *(introduce)*; einweihen *(initiate into)*.

index mark Ablesemarke *f (optical Inst)*.

index plate Markenplatte *f (on aiming circle or telescopic sight)*.

index ring Markenring *m (MG telescopic sight)*.

Indian file Gänsemarsch *m*.

indicated air speed Eigengeschwindigkeit *f*, Relativgeschwindigkeit *f*, Geschwindigkeit zur Luft *(Avn)*.

indicated horsepower indizierte Leistung.

indicator Anzeiger *m*, Zeiger *m*; Empfänger *m (fuze setter, follow-the-pointer mechanism on AA gun)*; Folgezeiger *m*, Gegenzeiger *m (follow-the-pointer mechanism on data transmission system)*.

indicator-regulator Empfänger *m (data transmission system) (AA gun)*.

indicator slide Anzeigerschiene *f (MG).*
indirect fire indirektes Feuer, indirektes Schießen *(Gunnery).*
indirect laying indirektes Richten *(Gunnery).*
indirect pointing *See* **indirect laying.**
indirect support operative Unterstützung *(Avn, Tac).*
indispensable unabkömmlich, unentbehrlich.
individual *n* der Einzelne.
individual *adj* Einzel-, persönlich.
individual air raid precautions Selbstschutz *m (Civ defense).*
individual attack Einzelangriff *m.*
individual clothing slip Uniformbezugschein *m.*
individual equipment Einzelausrüstung *f.*
individual pay record Soldbuch *n.*
individual protection Einzelschutz *m.*
individual release Einzel(ab)wurf *m (bombing).*
individual suspension Einzelabfederung *f (of wheels, MT).*
indoctrination Unterweisung *f.*
indoor antenna Zimmerantenne *f.*
indoors in geschlossenen Räumen.
induced detonation Zündübertragung *f (blasting).*
induced-detonation charge Folgeladung *f (Engr).*
induced drag induzierter Widerstand *(Avn).*
induct einberufen.
initiate an action das Gefecht einleiten *(Tac).*
initiate an assault zum Sturm antreten.
initiative Initiative *f (Tac);* Einsatzbereitschaft *f (quality).*
take the initiative die Initiative ergreifen *(Tac).*
initiator Initialzünder *m (Am).*
injection nozzle Einspritzdüse *f,* Zerstäuberdüse *f (Diesel engine).*
injection pump Einspritzpumpe *f.*
injury Verletzung *f,* Verwundung *f.*
ink Tinte *f.*
in kind in Natur.
inland waterway Binnenwasserstraße *f.*
inlet Einlaß *m;* Bucht *f (creek).*
inlet valve Einatemventil *n (gas mask, oxygen breathing apparatus);* Einlaßventil *n (Tech).*
in-line engine Reihenmotor *m.*
in-line upright engine Reihenstandmotor *m.*
inner cap Innenhütchen *n (blasting cap).*
inner harbor Innenhafen *m.*
inner sleeve Innenschieber *m (sleeve-valve engine).*
inner tube Luftschlauch *m,* Schlauch *m;* schußsicherer Schlauch *(bullet-resisting).*
innocent unschuldig, schuldlos.
inoculate impfen.
inoculation Impfung *f,* Schutzimpfung *f.*
inquire fragen, nachfragen, sich erkundigen.
inquire as to party desired abfragen *(Tp).*
inquire one's way sich nach dem Wege erkundigen.
inquiry Frage *f,* Nachfrage *f,* Erkundigung *f.*
insensitive to shock stoßsicher *(explosives).*
inshore patrol Küstenpatrouille *f.*
insignia Abzeichen *n;* Rangabzeichen *n (rank);* Hoheitsabzeichen *n (national);* Erkennungszeichen *n (for identification of Ap, Tk, etc.).*
inspect untersuchen, prüfen, besichtigen.
inspection Inspizierung *f,* Inspektion *f,* Inaugenscheinnahme *f,* Besichtigung *f.*
inspection hole Schauloch *n (Mtr).*
inspection-mark plate Stempelplatte *f (R).*
inspector Inspekteur *m.*
inspectorate Inspektion *f (Ger).*
inspector general Heeresinspekteur *m (USA).*
Inspector General's Department Generalinspektion *f (USA).*
installation Anlage *f,* Einrichtung *f.*
instant Moment *m,* Augenblick *m.*
instantaneous current Momentstrom *m (Elec).*
instantaneous fuze Schnellzünder *m,* Augenblickszünder *m,* Aufschlagzünder ohne Verzögerung.
instruct unterrichten *(teach);* anweisen *(direct).*
instruction Unterricht *m (teaching);* Weisung *f (directive);* Anhaltspunkt *m (in orders, etc., generally in plural).*
instructional aid Ausbildungsbehelf *m.*
instruction firing Belehrungsschießen *n.*
instructor Ausbilder *m,* Lehrer *m.*
instructor's license Fahrlehrerschein *m (MT).*
instrument Gerät *n,* Instrument *n.*
instrumental error Instrument-Fehler *m.*
instrument board Armaturenbrett *n.*
instrument case Apparattornister *m (portable Rad).*
instrument flying Blindflug *m.*
instrument-flying equipment Blindfluggerät *n,* Blindfluginstrumentierung *f.*
instrument landing Blindlandung *f;* A.N.-Verfahren *n (A.N. method of beam bracketing) (Avn).*
instrument-landing equipment Blindlandungsgerät *n (Avn).*
instrument-landing receiver Blindlandungsempfänger *m (Rad).*
instrument light Schaltbrettlaterne *f,* Gerätelicht *n.*
instrument panel Armaturenbrett *n,* Gerätebrett *n,* Instrumentenbrett *n (Ap, MT).*
insubordination Gehorsamsverweigerung *f.*
insulate isolieren.
insulated electrode Zündstift *m (spark plug).*
insulating material Isolierstoff *m.*
insulating tape Isolierband *n,* Isolierstreifen *m (Elec).*
insulation Isolierschutz *m (Elec);* Dichtung *f (sealing).*
insulator Isolator *m;* Isolierstoff *m (insulating substance) (Elec).*
insurance Versicherung *f.*
intake duct Ansaugleitung *f,* Saugleitung *f (Mtr).*
intake line Einlaßkanal *m (Mtr).*
intake manifold Saugrohr *n (Mtr).*
intake pipe Ansaugrohr *n (Mtr).*
intake stroke Ansaughub *m,* Saughub *m,* Ansaugetakt *m (Mtr).*
intake valve Einlaßventil *n,* Saugventil *n (Mtr).*
intake-valve chamber Einlaßventilkammer *f (Mtr).*
integral calculus Integralrechnung *f.*
intelligence Nachricht *f (information);* Nachrichtenwesen *n (organization);* Nachrichtenbeschaffung *f (gathering of information);* Nachrichtendienst *m (service).*
intelligence map vom Nachrichtendienst vorbereitete Lagenkarte.
intelligence net Netz des Nachrichtendienstes.
intelligence officer Nachrichtenoffizier *m.*
intelligence section Nachrichtenabteilung *f.*
intelligence service Nachrichtendienst *m.*
intelligence situation map vom Nachrichtendienst vorbereitete Lagenkarte.
intensity Intensität *f,* Stärke *f,* Heftigkeit *f.*
intensity of light Lichtstärke *f.*
intent Absicht *f,* Vorhaben *n.*
interaircraft communication Verständigung von Bord zu Bord *(Avn).*
intercept ablauschen *(Rad);* abfangen *(Tac).*
intercept apparatus Lauschgerät *n (Tg, Tp).*
intercept board Kontrollkarte *f (AWS).*
interception Abhören *n (Tp);* Abfangen *n (Tac).*
interceptor airplane Jäger *m,* Jagdflugzeug *n,* Zerstörer *m.*
interceptor group Jagdgruppe *f (Avn).*
intercept post Lauschstelle *f (Tg, Tp).*
intercept receiver Lauschempfänger *m (Tg, Tp).*
intercept service Horchdienst *m,* Lauschdienst *m (Rad, Tp).*
intercept station Mithörstelle *f,* Abhörstelle *f,* Lauschstelle *f (Rad, Tp);* Funkhorchstelle *f (Rad).*
interchangeable austauschbar, wechselbar.
interchangeability Austauschbarkeit *f.*
intercommunication Querverbindung *f (intervehicular);* Eigenverständigung *f (intravehicular).*
intercommunication channel Funkquerverbindung *f (Rad).*
intercommunication line Querverbindung *f (Tp).*
intercommunication system Bordsprechanlage *f,* Bordverständigungsanlage *f (Ap, Tk).*
intercommunication telephone Bordsprechgerät *n,* Bordgerät *n (Ap, Tk).*
intercooler Ladeluftkühler *m (Ap supercharger).*
interdict abriegeln, sperren, ausschließen.
interdiction fire Behinderungsschießen *n,* Feuerriegel *m.*
interfere stören *(Rad).*
interference Störung *f;* Störgeräusch *n (Rad).*
interference elimination Entstörung *f (Rad).*
interior Innenraum *m.*
interior ballistic factors besondere Einflüsse.
interior ballistics innere Ballistik, innere Schießlehre.
interior bracing Innenauskreuzung *f,* Innenverspannung *f (Ap).*
interior guard Innenwache *f.*
interior guard duty Standortwachdienst *m.*
intermediate circuit Zwischenkreis *m (Rad).*
intermediate depot rückwärtiges Zweiglager.
intermediate frequency Zwischenfrequenz *f (Rad).*
intermediate landing field Zwischenlandungsplatz *m.*
intermediate objective Angriffszwischenziel *n,* Zwischenziel *n.*
intermediate position Übergangsstellung *f,* Zwischenstellung *f.*
intermediate range Zwischenentfernung *f (Gunnery).*
intermediate scale map Karte im Maßstab 1 : 200,000 bis 1 : 500,000.
intermediate section mittlerer Abschnitt des rückwärtigen Gebietes.
intermediate station Zwischenbahnhof *m (RR).*
intermittent fire stoßweises Feuer.
intermittent light Wechselfeuer *n.*
intern internieren.
internal-combustion engine Brennermotor *m,* Verbrennungsmotor *m,* Verbrennungskraftmaschine *f.*
internal expanding brake Innenbackenbremse *f.*
internal resistance innerer Widerstand *(Elec).*
international code internationales Signalbuch *(Nav). See also* **International Morse Code.**
international law Völkerrecht *n,* internationales Recht.
International Morse Code internationales Morsealphabet.
International Red Cross Internationales Rotes Kreuz.
internee Internierter *m.*
internet traffic Querverkehr *m (Rad).*
internment camp Interniertenlager *n.*
internment camp commander Lagerkommandant *m.*
interphone Bordtelephon *n,* Bordsprechanlage *f,* Eigenverständigung *f (Ap, Tk);* Hausleitung *f,* Haustelephon *n (in a building).*
interphone communication Bordverständigung *f.*
interphone equipment Verständigungsgerät *n (Ap).*
interplane strut Flügelstiel *m.*
interpolating scale Transversalmaßstab *m (Surv).*
interpolation Interpolieren *n.*
interpret auswerten *(evaluate);* beurteilen *(estimate, judge);* verdolmetschen *(translate);* auslegen, erklären, deuten *(explain).*
interpretation Auswertung *f,* Verwertung *f.*
interpretation of aerial photographs Luftbildauswertung *f.*
interpretation of photographs Bildauswertung *f.*
interpreter Dolmetscher *m.*
interpupillary distance Augenabstand *m (Optics).*
interpupillary-distance scale Teilscheibe *f (binocular).*
interrogate ausfragen, vernehmen, verhören.
interrogation Befragung *f,* Ausfragen *n,* Verhör *n,* Vernehmung *f.*
interrogation officer Vernehmungsoffizier *m (PW).*
interrogation of prisoners Gefangenenverhör *n,* Gefangenenvernehmung *f.*
interrupt unterbrechen.
interrupted fire stoßweises Feuer.
interrupted-screw-type breechblock Schraubenverschluß *m (G).*
interrupter Sicherungsklappe *f,* Sicherungsflügel *m,* Sicherungsvorrichtung *f (Am);* Unterbrecher *m (Elec).*
interruption Unterbrechung *f.*
intersect anschneiden.
intersection Kreuzung *f,* Straßenkreuzung *f,* Wegekreuzung *f (road);* Anschneiden *n (Surv).*
interstation communication Bordverständigung *f (Ap).*
interurban line Fernleitung *f (Tp).*
interval Zwischenraum *m (close order drill);* Pause *f,* Zwischenzeit *f,* Zeitabstand *m (time).*
intervehicular communication Querverbindung *f.*
intervehicular distance Marschabstand zwischen den einzelnen Fahrzeugen.
interview Unterredung *f,* Interview *n.*
intolerable concentration Schädlichkeitsgrenze *f (CWS).*
intoxication Trunkenheit *f,* Rausch *m.*
intravehicular communication Eigenverständigung *f,* Bordverständigung *f.*
intrench schanzen, einschanzen, (sich) eingraben.
intrenching tool kleines Schanzzeug.
intrenchment Verschanzung *f.*
intruder Klebeflugzeug *n (Ap).*
intruding Kleben *n (Avn).*
intruding airplane Klebeflugzeug *n.*
intrusion Kleben *n (Avn).*
inundated area Anstauung *f (map).*
inundation Überflutung *f,* Überschwemmung *f (flooding);* Anstauung *f (by damming).*
invade einmarschieren, einbrechen, invahieren.
invasion Invasion *f.*
inventory Bestand *m,* Inventar *n,* Bestandsnachweisung *f.*
inverse ratio umgekehrtes Verhältnis.
inverse value Kehrwert *m.*
inverted flight Rückenflug *m.*
inverted-image range finder Invertentfernungsmesser *m,* Kehrbildentfernungsmesser *m.*
inverted truss Sprengwerk *n (Engr).*
inverted valve Hängeventil *n (Mtr).*
inverted wedge formation Breitkeil *m (Tac).*
investigate untersuchen.
investigating officer Untersuchungsoffizier *m.*
investigation Untersuchung *f.*
involuntary unfreiwillig.
involuntary absence without leave unverschuldete Abwesenheit.
iodine Jod *n;* Jodtinktur *f (tincture of iodine).*
iron Eisen *n.*
iron core Eisenkern *m (Elec).*
Iron Cross Eisernes Kreuz *(decoration).*
iron ration eiserne Portion *(for Pers);* eiserne Ration *(for horses).*
iron reinforcement Bewehrung *f,* Eiseneinlage *f (in ferro-concrete).*
iron roller Eisenwalze *f (mine clearing).*
irregular unregelmäßig; unvorschriftsmäßig *(contrary to regulations).*
irregularity Verstoß *m (Law);* Unregelmäßigkeit *f.*
irreplaceable unabkömmlich, unentbehrlich.
irritant *n* Reizstoff *m (CWS).*
irritant agent reizender Kampfstoff *(CWS).*
irritant candle Reizkerze *f (CWS).*
irritant capsule Reizwürfel *m (CWS).*
irritant gas Giftnebel *m (CWS).*
irritant-gas candle Giftrauchkerze *f,* Giftnebelkerze *f (CWS).*
irritant-gas generator Riechtopf *m (CWS).*
irritant smoke Giftrauch *m (CWS).*
irritant training agent Übungsreizstoff *m (CWS).*
irritating concentration Reizkonzentration *f.*
island Insel *f.*
island of resistance Widerstandsnest *n (Tac).*
isobar Isobare *f (Met).*
isolate isolieren; abtrennen *(separate);* abschneiden *(cut off);* absondern *(Med).*
isolated internment Einzelhaft *f.*
isolation Abtrennen *n,* Abschneiden *n,* Isolierung *f (Tac);* Absonderung *f (Med).*
isolation quarters Absonderungsabteilung *f (Med).*
issuance of order(s) Befehlsausgabe *f,* Befehlserteilung *f.*
issue *n* Verausgabung *f,* Verteilen *n,* Ausgabe *f.*
issue *v* verausgaben.
Italian method Rückwärtseinschneiden *n (Surv).*
item Stück *n,* Gegenstand *m,* Artikel *m.*
item of equipment Ausrüstungsstück *n,* Gerätstück *n.*

J

jack Wagenheber *m (MT);* Klinke *f (Tp);* Buchse *f,* Steckdose *f (Elec, Rad).*
jacket Mantel *m (Tech);* Jacke *f (Clo);* Hülsenmantel *m (of cartridge case);* Geschoßmantel *m (of bullet);* Rohrmantel *m (of G);* Wassermantel *m,* Kühlmantel *m (Mtr, MG).*
jacket base Mantelboden *m (MG).*
jacket cradle Jackenwiege *f (G).*
jacket end cap Mantelkopf *m (MG).*
jack float Fußteller *m (AA gun).*
jackknife Klappmesser *n.*
jack shaft Seitenwelle *f (MT).*
jail *n* Gefängnis *n.*
jam *n* Hemmung *f (stoppage, Ord);* Verkehrsstockung *f (traffic).*
jam *v* hemmen *(Ord);* verklemmen *(Mech);* stören *(Rad).*
jamming station Störstelle *f (Rad).*
javelin Kolonne *f (Avn).*
jaw Kiefer *m (man);* Ganasche *f (horse).*
"jeep" "Kübel" *m,* Kübelsitzer *m,* Kübelwagen *m,* Kübelsitzwagen *m.*
jeopardy Gefahr *f.*
jet Strahl *m (of a liquid);* Düse *f (Inst).*
jet-propulsion engine Rückstoßmotor *m (Ap).*
jettison abwerfen *(Avn);* über Bord werfen *(Nav).*
jetty Mole *f,* Hafendamm *m.*
jiu-jitsu Jiu-Jitsu *n.*
jockey box Gerätekasten *m.*
joint *n* Gelenk *n,* Verbindung *f.*
joint operations Operationen der verbundenen Waffen.
joint piece Gelenkstück *n (MG tripod).*
joint plan Operationsplan für Zusammenwirken von Armee und Flotte.
journal Zapfen *m;* Wellenzapfen *m (shaft);* Lagerzapfen *m (crankshaft);* Tagebuch *n,* Kriegstagebuch *n (diary).*
judge Richter *m.*
judge advocate Kriegsgerichtsrat *m.*
Judge Advocate General Chef des Heeresjustizwesens *(USA).*
judo Judo *n.*
jugular groove Drosselrinne *f (horse).*
jump Abgangsfehlerwinkel *m (Gunnery);* Absprung *m,* Sprung *m (Prcht).*
jump area Abdriftplatz *m (Prcht troops).*
jumpmaster Absetzer *m (Prcht troops).*
jump-off Antreten zum Sturm
jump off zum Sturm vorgehen *(Tac).*
jump-off line Ausgangslinie *f.*
jump-off point Absprungpunkt *m (Prcht).*
jungle Dschungel *f,* Urwald *m.*
jungle warfare Dschungelkrieg *m,* Urwaldkriegführung *f,* Urwaldkrieg *m.*
junior officers Hauptleute und Leutnants.
junior umpire Unterschiedsrichter *m (maneuvers).*
jurisdiction Gerichtsbereich *m,* Gerichtsbarkeit *f.*
jump-off position Ausgangsstellung *f (Tac).*
junction Anschlußbahnhof *m,* Trennungsbahnhof *m (RR);* Straßenspinne *f,* Straßenknotenpunkt *m (road).*
junction box Kupplungskasten *m (AA director);* Verteilerkasten *m (data transmission system).*
junction line Abzweigung *f,* Zweiglinie *f (RR).*

K

K Wert zur Verbesserung der Kartenentfernung auf Grund der erschossenen B.W.E. *(FA).*
katabatic wind Fallwind *m (Met).*
keel Kiel *m.*
keel fin Kielflosse *f (flying-boat hull or seaplane float).*
keeper Schieber *m,* Schlaufe *f,* Schluppe *f,* Schlupfe *f (for straps, etc.).*
kerosene Petroleum *n.*
key Schlüssel *m (to a lock, code, etc.);* Taste *f,* Morsetaste *f (Rad, Tg);* Zündschlüssel *m (ignition);* Keil *m (Mech).*
keyer Tastgerät *n (Rad).*
keying Tasten *n.*
key point Schlüsselpunkt *m (Tac).*
key position Schlüsselstellung *f (Tac).*
keyway Keilnut *f,* Nut(e) *m(f).*
khaki Khakituch *n,* Khaki *n.*
kick Rückstoß *m (Ord);* Fußtritt *m (with the foot).*
kick starter Kickstarter *m (Mtcl).*
kill töten; erschießen *(by shooting);* erschlagen *(by blows);* erstechen *(by stabbing);* abschlachten, niedermetzeln, niedermachen *(massacre, slaughter);* umbringen, ermorden *(murder);* sich umbringen, Selbstmord begehen *(commit suicide).*
killed in action im Felde gefallen, vor dem Feind gefallen.
killing concentration tödliche Menge *(CWS).*
kilocycle Kilohertz *n.*
kind *n* Art *f,* Sorte *f.*
in kind in Natur, Natural-.
kinetic energy kinetische Energie.
kingpin Achszapfen *m.*
kingpost Hängesäule *f.*
kit Tasche *f.*
kitchen Küche *f,* Feldküche *f.*
kitchen car Eisenbahnküchenwagen *m (RR).*
kitchen police Küchendienst *m.*
kitchen truck Küchenlastwagen *m.*
kite Drache(n) *m.*
kite balloon Drachenballon *m.*
knapsack Rucksack *m,* Tornister *m.*
knee Knie *n;* Zungenstuhl *m (RR switch).*
kneeling position Anschlag kniend, kniender Anschlag *(in firing).*
kneeling trench Schützenloch für knienden Schützen, Hockloch *n (Ft).*
knee pad Kniepausche *f (harness).*
knife Messer *n.*
knife rest spanischer Reiter *(Engr).*
knife switch Messerschalter *m (Elec).*

knife-switch prong Kontaktmesser *n (Elec).*
knob Knopf *m,* Knagge *f (Tech);* Triebscheibe *f,* Handrädchen *n (optical Inst, Ord);* Griff *m (door);* Kuppe *f (Top);* Kammerknopf *m (R bolt);* Abstimmkondensatorgriff *m (tuning knob, Rad).*
knoll Kupe *f.*
knot Knoten *m (of rope, wood; unit of speed).*
knots and ties Bunde und Knoten *(Engr, Tp).*
knuckle Knöchel *m,* Gelenk *n.*
knuckle lug Auflaufstück *n (G).*
knurl kordieren, rändeln.
knurled nut Kordelmutter *f.*
knurling Kordierung *f,* Kordelung *f (Mech).*
KP Küchendienst *m.*
K-transfer Erschießen der B.W.E. bei Planschießen *(FA).*

L

labor camp Arbeitslager *n.*
lace Schnürsenkel *m (of shoe or boot).*
lace boot Schnürstiefel *m.*
lacerated wound Rißwunde *f.*
lack Mangel *m.*
lacquer Lack *m.*
lacrimator Augenreizstoff *m,* Reizkörper *m.*
lacrimator gas Tränengas *n (CWS).*
ladder Leiter *f (Engr);* Reihe *f (Gunnery).*
ladder fire Reihenfeuer *n,* Reiheschießen *n (Gunnery).*
lake See *m.*
lamb Schöpsenfleisch *n,* Hammelfleisch *n (meat).*
Lambert projection Lamberts flächentreue Azimutalprojektion *(Mapping).*
lamp Lampe *f;* Laterne *f (lantern).*
lamp case Lampengehäuse *n (Sig lamp).*
lamp signal Blinkzeichen *n,* Blinksignal *n,* Lichtsignal *n.*
lamp socket Lampenfassung *f (Elec).*
lance Fahnenstange *f (flagpole).*
lance pole Baustange *f (Tp).*
land *n* Land *n;* Feld *n (rifling).*
land *v* landen *(on land);* wassern *(on water, Avn).*
land-based aircraft von Land operierende Luftstreitkräfte.
landing Landung *f.*
landing area Landeplatz *m,* Landungsplatz *m (Avn);* Abdriftplatz *m (Prcht troops).*
landing attack Landungsangriff *m.*
landing boat Landungsboot *n.*
landing craft Landungsfahrzeug *n.*
landing deck Flugdeck *n,* Landedeck *n (aircraft carrier).*
landing-direction light Landelicht *n (Avn).*
landing field Landeplatz *m (Avn);* Flugplatzfeld *n,* Rollfeld *n (Adrm).*
landing flap Landeklappe *f (Ap).*
landing flare Bordlandefackel *f (Avn).*
landing gear Fahrwerk *n,* Fahrgestell *n (Ap).*
landing-gear axle Fahrwerkachse *f (Ap).*
landing-gear frame Fahrgestell *n (Ap).*
landing-gear strut Fahrwerkstrebe *f (Ap).*
landing light Landefeuer *n,* Landelicht *n (Ap).*
landing operation Landungsunternehmung *f.*
landing party Landungstrupp *m.*
landing ramp Landungsklappe *f,* Klappe *f,* Landesteg *m (landing craft);* Ablaufbahn *f (for seaplanes).*
landing run Ausrollen *n (Avn).*
landing runway Landebahn *f (Avn).*
landing ski Gleitkufe *f (Ap).*
landing ski assembly Schneekufengestell *n (Ap).*
landing smoke signal Landungsrauchzeichen *n (Avn).*
landing speed Landegeschwindigkeit *f (Ap).*
landing stage Landbrücke *f (Engr).*
landing strip Landebahn *f (Adrm);* Stahlstraße *f (steel).*
landing T Landekreuz *n (Avn).*
landing wheel Laufrad *n (Ap).*
landing zone Landezone *f (Adrm).*
landmark Geländepunkt *m (Surv);* Bake *f (Nav).*
land mine Landmine *f (Engr).*
lands Felder *npl (Ord).*
lands and grooves Felder und Züge *(Ord).*
landscape sketch Ansichtsskizze *f.*
landscape target Geländescheibe *f (Tng).*
land vehicle Landfahrzeug *n.*
land warfare Landkrieg *m.*
L-antenna L-Antenne *f.*
lantern Laterne *f.*
lanyard Abzugsschnur *f (Ord);* Pistolengurt *m (pistol).*
lanyard handle Abzugsgriff *m (G).*
lapse rate vertikaler Temperaturgradient *(Met).*
large-caliber machine gun überschweres Maschinengewehr *(Cal .50).*
large-caliber projectile großkalibriges Geschoß.
large-scale attack Großangriff *m.*
large-scale map Karte im Maßstab 1:20,000 oder größer *(Surv).*
large unit strategische Einheit *(USA: Div and up; Ger: corps and up).*
lashing Bund *n (Engr, Tp).*
lateral axis Querachse *f (Ap).*
lateral communication Querverbindung *f,* Seitenverbindung *f (Sig C).*
lateral conduct of fire Einschießen mit Beobachtung von seitlicher Beobachtungsstelle *(Gunnery).*
lateral correction Verbesserung für Seite *(Gunnery).*
lateral deflection angle Seitenwinkelvorhalt in der Horizontalebene *(AA Gunnery).*
lateral error Seitenfehler *m (Gunnery).*
lateral fire *See* lateral conduct of fire.
lateral jump Seitenabgangsfehler *m,* Seitenabweichung *f (Gunnery).*
lateral lead Seitenvorhalt *m (Gunnery);* Seitenwinkelvorhalt der Seitenvorhaltsebene *(AA Gunnery).*
lateral march Seitenbewegung *f (Tac).*
lateral road *f* Querverbindungsstraße
lateral stability *(Ap)* Querstabilität *f*
lateral sway Seitenschwankung *f*
lateral tilt Schrägstellung *f.*
lath Latte *f.*
lathe Drehbank *f.*
lathe operator Dreher *m.*
latitude geographische Breite, Breitenkreis *m,* Breitengrad *m.*
latrine Latrine *f.*
launch *n* Verkehrsboot *n (Nav).*
launch *v* ansetzen *(an attack);* vom Stapel lassen *(a ship).*
launcher Werfer *m.*
launching device Startvorrichtung *f (Avn).*
launching nose *(Bdg)* Brückenspitze *f*
laundry Wäsche *f;* schmutzige Wäsche *(soiled clothes);* Wäscherei *f (place).*
law Recht *n (jurisprudence);* Gesetz *n (statute, scientific formulation);* Kriegsrecht *n (Mil law).*
law member Beisitzer *m.*
Laws and Customs of War on Land Gesetze und Gebräuche des Landkrieges *(Hague convention, 1907).*
laws of war Kriegsrecht *n.*
lay richten *(Gunnery);* stellen, setzen *(place).*
layer Schicht *f,* Lage *f (stratum).*
layer's seat Richtsitz *m (G).*
laying Richten *n (Gunnery).*
laying by survey Planrichten *n*
laying for direction Nehmen der Seitenrichtung *(Gunnery).*
laying for elevation Nehmen der Höhenrichtung *(Gunnery).*
laying mechanism Richtgerät *n,* Richtmaschine *f,* Richtmittel *n (G).*
lazy strap Strangträger *m,* Tauträger *m,* Stranglaufe *f (harness).*
lead *n* Blei *n (metal).*
lead *n* Vorhalt *m (firing).*
take a lead vorhalten.
amount of lead Vorhaltsmaß *n,* Vorhaltswert *m.*
lead *v* führen; vorhalten *(Gunnery).*
lead azide Bleiazid *n.*
lead chart Planfeuertafel *f (AA firing).*
lead computer Auswanderungsmesser *m (AA gun);* Vorhalteeinrichtung *f (AT gun, AA gun).*
lead curve Vorhaltekurve *f.*
leader Leiter *m,* Führer *m.*
leadership Führerschaft *f,* Führung *f.*
lead graduations Vorhaltemaße *npl (firing at moving targets).*
lead horse Vorderpferd *n.*
lead-in Einführungsdraht *m,* Zuführungsdraht *m (Rad).*
lead-in cord Zuleitungskabel *n (Sig lamp).*
leading airplane Führerflugzeug *n.*
leading car Spitzenwagen *m (MT).*
leading edge Flügelvorderkante *f,* Flügeleintrittskante *f,* Leitkante *f,* Flügelnase *f (Ap).*
leading element *(Tac)* Spitzengruppe *f*
leading fire Vorhaltefeuer *n.*
leading flight Führungskette *f*
leading tank Spitzenpanzer *m.*
lead-in point Kabelaufführungspunkt *m (Tp).*
lead jacket Bleimantel *m (Am).*
lead mark Zielmarke *f (telescopic sight).*
lead-plate storage battery Bleisammler *m.*
lead rein Führerzügel *m (harness).*
lead seal Bleiplombe *f.*
lead sheath Bleimantel *m (Armd cable).*
lead spatter Bleispritzer *m.*
lead team Vorderpferde *npl.*
lead track Ausziehgleis *n (RR).*
leadup strap Rückenriemen *m (harness).*
lead wire Zünderdraht *m (blasting);* Zuführungsdraht *m (Rad);* Bleidraht *m (wire made of metallic lead).*
leaf Lamelle *f (Tech);* Blatt *n (of a spring);* Klappe *f (of a sight);* Visierklappe *f (of rear sight).*
leaflet Flugblatt *n (propaganda).*
leaf sight Klappvisier *n.*
leaf spring Blattfeder *f (MT).*
leak *n* Leck *n (ship);* Spalte *f,* Loch *n (container).*
to spring a leak leck werden.
leak *v* leck sein *(ship);* undicht sein *(gas container);* rinnen *(liquid container).*
leakage Undichtigkeit *f (of a container);* Ableitung *f,* Stromverlust *m,* Streuung *f (Elec).*
leakproof dicht, wasserdicht.
lean-to tent Halbzelt *n.*
leather Leder *n.*
leather bag Ledertasche *f.*
leather leggins Beinleder *npl.*
leave *n* Urlaub *m*
on leave beurlaubt, auf Urlaub.
leave area Ruhequartier *n.*
lecture Vortrag *m.*
led horse Handpferd *n.*
leeward leewärts, windabwärts.
leeway Abdrift *f (Avn).*
left-about Kehrtwendung links *(drill).*
left bank Linkskurve *f (Avn).*
left dress sich nach links ausrichten *(drill).*
left face Linkswendung *f.*
"Left, face!" "Links, um!"
left-handed thread Linksgewinde *n.*
left-handed twist Linksdrall *m (rifling).*
leg Bein *n (limb);* Strecke *f (distance);* Schenkel *m (diagrams, Inst).*
legal legal, gesetzlich, gesetzmäßig; rechtsgültig, rechtskräftig *(valid).*
legal status Rechtsstellung *f,* rechtliche Stellung.
legation Gesandtschaft *f.*
legend Zeichenerklärung *f (key to map signs).*
leggins Gamaschen *fpl;* Beinleder *npl (leather);* Wickelgamaschen *fpl (wrapped).*
lemon Zitrone *f.*
length Länge *f.*
length of barrel Rohrlänge *f (G).*
length of rifling Dralllänge *f (Ord).*
lens Linse *f.*
lensatic compass Marschkompaß *m.*
lethal chemical agent tödlicher chemischer Kampfstoff.
lethal concentration tödliche Menge *(CWS).*
letter Brief *m,* Schreiben *n (written message);* Buchstabe *m (of the alphabet).*
letter of instruction Weisung *f.*
letter of transmittal Begleitschreiben *n.*
letter order schriftlicher Befehl.
levee Schutzdamm *m.*
levée en masse allgemeines Aufgebot.
level *n* Libelle *f (Inst);* Setzwaage *f (builder's);* Nivellierinstrument *n*
level *adj* eben, flach.
level crossing Planübergang *m.*
level flight Horizontalflug *m,* Geradeausflug *m,* Waagerechtflug *m,* Normalfluglage *f (Avn).*
level flight bombardment Waagerechtbombenwurf *m.*
level housing Libellengehäuse *n (panoramic telescope).*
leveling Einspielen der Libellen *(Gunnery).*
leveling device Horizontierungsvorrichtung *f (AA gun mount).*
leveling jack Horizontierung *f (AA gun outrigger).*
leveling-jack handle Horizontiergriff *m (AA gun outrigger).*
leveling mechanism Einkipptrieb *m (Mort).*
level off abfangen *(Avn).*
level party Nivellier-Meßtrupp *m*
level point Fallpunkt *m (Ballistics).*
level-point range waagerechte Schußweite *(Gunnery).*
level setting Libelleneinstellung *f.*
lever Hebel *m.*
lewisite Lewisit *n,* Chlorvinyldichlorarsin *n (CWS).*
liaison Anschluß *m,* Verbindung *f,* Verbindungsdienst *m (Tac).*
liaison agent Verbindungsmann *m.*
liaison airplane Kurierflugzeug *n,* Verbindungsflugzeug *n.*
liaison communication Nachrichtenquerverbindung *f.*
liaison detachment Verbindungstrupp *m.*
liaison net Verbindungsnetz *n (Rad).*
liaison officer Verbindungsoffizier *m.*
liaison party Verbindungstrupp *m.*
liaison pilot Verbindungsflieger *m.*
liberate befreien, freilassen.
librarian Bücherwart *m,* Bibliothekar *m.*
library Bibliothek *f,* Bücherei *f.*
license Fahrerschein *m,* Führerschein *f (driver's).*
lieutenant Leutnant *m;* Kapitänleutnant *m (Nav). See also* second lieutenant, first lieutenant, lieutenant junior grade.
lieutenant colonel Oberstleutnant *m;* Oberstleutnant der Flieger *(Luftwaffe);* Oberfeldarzt *m (Med);* Oberfeldveterinär *m (Vet).*
lieutenant commander Korvettenkapitän *m (Nav).*
lieutenant general General der Infanterie *(Inf);* General der Artillerie *(Arty);* General der Kavallerie *(Cav);* General der Flieger *(Luftwaffe);* General der Panzertruppen *(Armd Comd);* General der Flakartillerie *(AAA);* General der Nachrichtentruppen *(Sig C);* etc.
lieutenant junior grade Oberleutnant zur See *(Nav).*
life belt Rettungsring *m.*
lifeboat Rettungsfahrzeug *n.*
lifebuoy Rettungsboje *f.*
lifeguards Rettungsleute *mpl.*
life insurance Lebensversicherung *f.*
life line Rettungsleine *f (for rescue work in river operations)*
life preserver Rettungsring *m.*
life-saving equipment Rettungsgerät *n.*
life-saving service Rettungsdienst *m.*
life vest Schwimmweste *f.*
lift *n* Auftrieb *m (Avn).*
lift *v* heben.
lift fire *(Arty)* das Feuer vorverlegen
lifting capacity *(Ap)* Tragfähigkeit *f*
light *n* Licht *n.*
light *v* beleuchten, erleuchten *(illuminate);* anzünden *(ignite);* befeuern *(with beacon lights).*
light artillery leichte Artillerie.
light buoy Leuchtboje *f,* Leuchttonne
light elephant steel shelter leichte Wellblech-Hütte *(USA).*
lighter Prahm *m (Engr, Nav).*
lighter-than-air aircraft Luftfahrzeuge leichter als Luft.
light fuel Leichtöl *n (as distinguished from Diesel fuel).*
lighthouse Leuchtturm *m.*
light infantry weapons leichte Infanteriewaffen.
light machine gun leichtes Maschinengewehr.
light machine-gun squad leichtes MG.-Halbzug *m.*
lightning Blitz *m;* Wetterleuchten *n (distant lighting) (Met).*
lightning arrester Blitzschutzsicherung *f.*
light shelter leichter Unterstand.
lightship Leuchtschiff *n,* Feuerschiff *n.*
light signal Leuchtzeichen *n;* Leuchtpatrone *f.*
lights out!" "Lichter aus!"
light switch Lichtschalter *m (Elec).*
light tank Klein-Panzerkampfwagen *m,* leichter Panzerkampfwagen.
lignite Braunkohle *f.*
limber *n* Protze *f (Arty).*
limber *v* aufprotzen *(Arty).*
limber ammunition chest Protzkasten *m (Arty).*
limber drawbar Protzarm *m (Arty).*
limber frame Protzgestell *n (Arty).*
limber position *(Arty)* Protzenstellung *f*
limber wheel Protzenrad *n (Arty)*
lime Kalk *m.*
lime solution Kalkmilch *f (CWS).*
limit *n* Grenze *f.*
limit *v* begrenzen, beschränken.
limited-area smoke screen Kleinvernebelung *f.*
limited attack Angriff mit begrenztem Ziel *(Tac).*
limited objective begrenztes Ziel.
limited radio alert Funkbereitschaft für begrenzte Zeit.
limited radio silence Funkbeschränkung *f.*
limited service Wehrdienst für bedingt Taugliche.
line Linie *f (formations, etc.);* Leitung *f (Tg, Tp);* Leine *f,* Seil *n,* Tau *n (rope).*
in line flügelweise, in Linie.
lineal promotion Aufrücken in eine höhere Rang- und Gehaltsklasse nach dem Dienstalter.
linear measurement *f* Längenmessung
linear speed method lineares System *(AA Gunnery).*
linear target Breitenziel *n*
linear travel of target Auswanderungsstrecke *f;* Vorauswanderungsstrecke *f (during dead time),* Hauptauswanderungsstrecke *f (during time of flight of projectile, AA Gunnery).*
line construction Leitungsbau *m (Tp).* struction unit Leitungsbaueinheit *f (Tp).*
line formation Linienform *f,* Linienaufstellung *f.*
line jack Anchlußklinke *f (Tp).*
line maintenance *f* Feldinstandsetzung
lineman Fernsprecher *m (Tp).*
line of aim Visierlinie zum Richtpunkt *(Gunnery).*
line of anchors Ankerlinie *f (Bdg).*
line of battalions Regiment in Linie.
line of battle Kampflinie *f,* Gefechtslinie *f.*
line of bearing Peillinie *f (Air Navigation).*
line of breach Trennschnitt *m (demolitions).*
line of collimation *f* Kollimationslinie
line of communication Zufuhrstraße *f,* Nachschubstraße *f.*
line of companies Bataillon in Linie.
line of defense Verteidigungslinie *f.*
line of departure Ausgangslinie *f (Tac);* Abgangsrichtung *f (Ballistics).*
line of duty Dienst *m,* Pflichterfüllung *f.*
line of elevation verlängerte Seelenachse, Seelenachse am Ende des Einrichtens *(Gunnery).*
line of fall Tangente an die Flugbahn im Fallpunkt *(Ballistics).*
line officer Frontoffizier *m,* Truppenoffizier *m.*
line of fire Schußlinie *f,* Schußbahn *f.*
line-offset method Kreisbogen-Absteckung von einer Sehne aus *(Surv).*
line of future position Schußlinie *f (AA Gunnery).*
line of impact Tangente an die Flugbahn im Aufschlagpunkt *(Ballistics).*
line of interception Auffanglinie *f (Avn).*
line of intersection Anschneidelinie *f.*
line of march Marschlinie *f,* Marschstrecke *f;* Marschordnung *f (formation);* Marschrichtung *f (direction).*
line of masses Massierung *f (Tac).*
line of observation Sehlinie *f.*
line of operations Operationslinie *f.*
line of outguards Vorpostenkette *f (Tac).*
line of platoons Kompanie in Linie.
line of position Visierlinie *f (Ballistics);* Standlinie *f (Navigation).*
line of present position Visierlinie *f (AA Gunnery).*
line of resistance Widerstandslinie *f.*
line of retirement Rückzugslinie *f (Tac).*
line of retreat Rückzugslinie *f,* Rückzugsstraße *f,* Rückmarschstraße *f (Tac).*
line of security Sicherungslinie *f.*
line of sight Visierlinie *f (Gunnery);* Sehlinie *f (Surv).*
line of site Schußlinie *f (Gunnery);* Visierlinie *f (Ballistics);* Standlinie *f (Navigation).*
line of skirmishers Feuerkette *f,* Schützenlinie *f.*
line of squads Zug in Linie zu einem Glied.
line of supply Zufuhrstraße *f,* Nachschubstraße *f.*
line of the Army Truppe *f.*
line of wedges Keillinie *f (Tac).*
line of withdrawal Rückzugslinie *f (Tac).*
liner Kernrohr *n,* Seelenrohr *n (G).*
line route map Linienkarte *f (Tp).*
lines of advance Operationslinien *fpl (Tac).*
lines of communication Verkehrslinien *fpl (Tac).*
lines of force Kraftlinien *fpl (Elec).*
line squall Linienbö *f (Met).*
line-up stud Markenstück *n (on top gun carriage).*
line wire Leitungsmittel *n (Tp).*
link Tasche *f (cartridge belt);* Kettenglied *n (chain).*
link belt Metallgliedergurt *m,* Stahlgurt *m (MG).*
linking station Zwischenstelle *f.*
link-loading machine Gurtfüller *m.*
Link trainer Linktrainer *m (Avn).*
linseed oil Leinöl *n.*
lip Lippe *f.*
liquid Flüssigkeit *f.*
liquid air flüssige Luft.
liquid-cooled flüssigkeitsgekühlt.
liquid-cooled engine flüssigkeitsgekühlter Motor, Motor mit Flüssigkeitskühlung.
liquid fire Flammenstrahl *m (flame thrower).*
liquid oxygen flüssige Luft, Sprengluft *f.*
liquid vesicant detector paint Gasspürfarbe *f.*
liquor Schnaps *m (brandy, gin, etc.).*
list Liste *f (of items);* Schlagseite *f (of a ship).*
listener Horchposten *m.*
listen in ablauschen, abhören, mithören *(Rad, Tp).*
listening post Horchposten *m,* Horchstelle *f.*
Lister bag Listerscher Wasserreinigungssack.
list of balances Bestandliste *f.*
lithographic ink Lithographentinte *f.*
litter Krankentrage *m,* Trage *f*
litter bearer Krankenträger *m*
litter carrier Räderbahre *f (Med).*
little dipper Kleiner Bär.
live *adj (Elec)* charf *(Am);* geladen
live abatis Baumverhau *m.*
live ammunition scharfe Munition.
Livens projector Livens-Handwerfer *m (CWS).*
live shell scharfgeladene Granate.

livestock Viehbestand *m*.
live wire geladener Draht.
load *n* Ladung *f (Ord)*; Ladung *f*, Last *f*, Traglast *f (Ap, MT)*; Beanspruchung *f (Mech)*.
load *v* laden; einladen *(a truck, etc.)*.
"Load!" "Laden!"
"Load and lock!" "Laden und sichern!"
load capacity Ladefähigkeit *f*.
load coefficient Belastungsfaktor *m*.
loader Ladekanonier *m (Arty)*; Ladeschütze *m (Tk)*.
loader's seat Ladesitz *m (G)*.
loading Verladung *f (supplies, etc.)*; Munitionieren *n (Ap weapons)*.
loading action Ladevorgang *m (semi- or full-automatic weapons)*.
loading barrow Munitionskarren *m*.
loading belt Patronengurt *m*.
loading coil Pupinspule *f (Tp)*.
loading crane *(Arty)* Batteriekran *m*
loading device Ladevorrichtung *f*.
loading lag Ladeverzug *m*, Ladeverzugszeit *f (Gunnery)*.
loading officer Verladeoffizier *m*, Verladungsoffizier *m (Transportation)*.
loading operations Ladetätigkeit *f (service of the piece)*.
loading party Aufladekommando *n*.
loading platform Laderampe *f*, Verladerampe *f*.
loading point Verladestelle *f*, Verladeplatz *m*.
loading port Verladehafen *m (Nav)*.
loading ramp Rampe *f*.
loading recess Ladeloch *n (G)*.
loading siding Ladegleis *n (RR)*.
loading station *(RR)* Verladebahnhof *m*
loading table Verladeplan *m*.
loading time Ladezeit *f*, Verladezeit
loading tray Lademulde *f*, Ladeschale *f*, Ladetisch *m (G)*.
load line Tiefladelinie *f (Nav)*.
load test Belastungsprobe *f*.
load unit Ladeeinheit *f*.
lobe parachute Stufenfallschirm *m*.
local örtlich, Orts-.
local air defense örtliche Luftabwehr.
local battery Ortsbatterie *f (Tp)*.
local-battery operation Ortsbatterie-Betrieb *m (Tp)*.
local-battery system Ortsbatterie-System *n (Tp)*.
local circuit Querverbindung *f (Tp)*.
local circuit line Nebenanschlußleitung *f (Tp)*.
local counterattack Gegenstoß *m*, örtlicher Gegenangriff.
local engagement lokales Gefecht, örtliches Gefecht, Teilkampf *m*.
local flight Rundflug *m (Avn)*.
locality Ort *m*, Punkt *m*.
localizer beam Leitstrahl *m (Inst landing)*.
localizer-beam method Leitstrahlverfahren *n (Inst landing)*.
local mobilization *f* Teilmobilmachung.
local net Ortsnetz *n (Tp)*.
local observation Nahbeobachtung *f*.
local protection örtliche Sicherung.
local reception *(Rad)* Ortsempfang *m*
local reconnaissance *f* Nahaufklärung
local security Nahsicherung *f*, örtliche Sicherung.
local smoke screening Kleinvernebelung *f*.
local station Nebenanschluß *m*, Nebenstelle *f (Tp)*; Ortssender *m (Rad)*.
local support Stoßreserve *f (in assault, Tac)*.
locate auffinden *(find)*; orten *(establish position)*; bestimmen, feststellen *(a point on a map, a shell burst, etc.)*.
locate a target das Ziel auffinden.
locator card Wehrstammblatt *n*, Wehrstammkarte *f*.
lock *n* Schloß *n (on door, etc.)*; Schleuse *f (of a canal)*.
lock *v* absperren, zusperren, schließen, zuschließen *(a door, etc.)*; sichern *(Ord)*.
locked position Zurrstellung *f (Ord)*.
lock frame Verschlußschlitten *m (Ord)*.
lock handle Zurrgriff *m (G cradle)*.
locking bolt Sperrstück *n (pistol)*; Sperriegel *m (MG stock)*.
locking device Festhaltevorrichtung *f (MG)*.
locking lever Sperrhebel *m*; Bremshebel *m (panoramic telescope)*.
locking mechanism Zurrung *f (G, Tk, MG)*.
locking pin Schlüsselbolzen *m (limber)*.
locking spring Sperrfeder *f (MG)*.
locking washer Stoßscheibe *f (wheel bearing, MT)*.
locking wheel Sperrad *n (G cradle)*.
lockjaw Wundstarrkrampf *m (Med)*.
lock lever Zurrhebel *m*.
lock nut Gegenmutter *f*, Sicherungsmutter *f*.
lock rod Zurrstange *f*.
lock-spar support [illegible]sprengwerk *n (Bdg)*.
lock support Zurrlager *n (cradle lock)*.
lockwasher Federring *m*, Stahlfederring *m (Mech)*.
locomotive Lokomotive *f*.
loft Brieftaubenschlag *m*, Brieftaubenstelle *f (Sig C)*.
lofting Formgebung *f (Ap)*.
log Baumstamm *m (tree trunk)*; Klotz *m (wood)*; Log *n (Nav)*. *See also* **log book**.
logarithm Logarithmus *m*.
logarithmic range scale Rechenschieber zur Entfernungsermittlung *(Arty)*.
log book Bordbuch *n (Ap)*; Tagebuch *n*.
log crib Balkenstapel *m (Bdg)*.
logistics Transport- und Nachschubplanung *f*.
log runner Baumstammkufe *f (log sled)*.
loins Lenden *fpl (horse)*.
long lang.
long-barreled gun Langrohrkanone *f*, Langrohrgeschütz *n*.
long-base method Langbasisverfahren *n (Gunnery)*.
long dash Dauerstrich *m (Tg)*.
long-delay fuze Aufschlagzünder mit erhöhter Verzögerung.
long-distance circuit *(Tp)* Fernleitung *f*
long-distance reception Fernempfang *m (Rad)*.
long-distance telephone call Ferngespräch *n*, Durchgangsfernspruch
longitudinal deviation Längenabweichung *f (Gunnery)*.
longitudinal level Längslibelle *f (sighting mechanism)*.
longitudinal outrigger Längsträger *m (AA gun)*.
longitudinal stability Längsstabilität *f (Ap)*.
long lunge Ausfall *m (bayonet thrust)*.
long range weite Entfernung *(beyond 800 meters)*.
long-range artillery Fernkampfartillerie *f*.
long-range battery Fernkampfbatterie *f (Arty)*.
long-range bomber Fernbomber *m*, Fernkampfbomber *m*, Langstreckenbomber *m*, Fernkampfflugzeug *n*.
long-range fighter Langstreckenjäger *m*, Zerstörer *m*, Zerstörerflugzeug *n (Avn)*.
long-range fighter wing Zerstörergeschwader *n (Avn)*.
long-range gun Fernkampfgeschütz
long-range seaplane Langstrecken-Seeflugzeug *n*.
longshoreman Hafenarbeiter *m*.
long thrust Ausfall *m (bayonet thrust)*.
long-wave direction finder Langwellenpeiler *m (Rad)*.
long waves Langwellen *fpl (Rad)*.
lookout Späher *m*.
lookout hole Sehöffnung *f (Ft, Tk)*.
lookout hole cover Sehklappe *f (Tk)*.
lookout post Hochstand *m*.
lookout slit Sehschlitz *m (Tk)*.
loop Looping *m*, Schleife *f*, Überschlag *m (Avn)*.
loop antenna Rahmenantenne *f*; Peilrahmen *m (directional)*; Drehrahmenantenne *f (rotating)*.
loophole Schießscharte *f (Ft)*.
loop maneuver Schleifenflug *m*
longeron Hauptträger *m*, Rumpfholm *m*, Rumpflängsleiste *f (Ap)*.
longevity pay Besoldungszulage nach dem Dienstalter.
longhorn Trichter-Richtungshörer *m (AAA)*.
longitude geographische Länge, Längenkreis *m*, Längengrad *m*.
longitudinal axis Längsachse *f*, Rumpflängsachse *f (Ap)*.
longitudinal cross bracing Tiefenverspannung *f*, Tiefenkreuzverspannung *f (Ap)*.
loop-tip terminal Kabelschuh *m (Elec)*.
loose contact Wackelkontakt *m*
loose round Patrone mit locker sitzendem Geschoß *(Am)*.
loot *n* Beute *f*.
looting Plünderung *f*.
loss Verlust *m*.
loss of altitude Höhenverlust *m*
loss of velocity Geschwindigkeitsverlust *m (Ballistics)*.
loss replacements Auffülltruppen *fpl*.
lost motion toter Gang *(Mech)*.
lot Lieferung *f (shipment)*.
lot number laufende Nummer der Lieferung.
loud speaker Lautsprecher *m (Rad)*.
louse Laus *f (plural*: Läuse).
louver Kühlerklappe *f*, Luftschlitz
low-altitude flight Tiefflug *m (Avn)*.
low-angle fire Flachfeuer *n*, Feuer in der unteren Winkelgruppe *(Gunnery)*.
low entanglement niedriger Drahtzaun, n i e d r i g e r Flanderenzaun *(Engr)*.
lower *v* herunterlassen *(let down)*; ausfahren *(landing gear, etc., Avn)*.
lower band Unterring *m (R)*.
lower chord Untergurt *m (truss)*.
lower gun carriage Unterlafette *f*.
lower shield Unterschild *m (G)*.
lower shield bracket Unterschildträger *m (G)*.
low explosive nichtbrisanter Sprengstoff.
low-flying attack *See* **low-level attack**.
low frequency *(Rad)* Niederfrequenz *f*
low-frequency interference Niederfrequenzstörungen *fpl (Rad)*.
low gear Anfahrtsgang *m (MT, Tk)*.
low-level approach Tiefanflug *m*
low-level attack Tiefangriff *m*, Tieffliegerangriff *m*, Tiefflugangriff *m (Avn)*.
low-level bombing attack Bombentiefangriff *m (Avn)*.
low-level flight Tiefflug *m (Avn)*.
low-order burst Fehlzerspringer *m (Am)*.
low position *(MG)* liegender Anschlag
low-pressure area Tiefdruckgebiet *n*, Tief *n (Met)*.
low-pressure chamber Unterdruckkammer *f*.
low-pressure tire Niederdruckreifen *m (MT)*.
low voltage Niederspannung *f*.
low-wing monoplane Tiefdecker *m*.
low wire entanglement niedriger Drahtzaun, niedriger Flanderenzaun *(Engr)*.
loyal loyal, treu, pflichttreu.
lubber line Steuerstrich *m (aircraft compass)*.
lubricant Schmiermittel *n*, Gleitmittel *n*.
lubricate schmieren; einfetten *(grease)*; einölen *(oil)*.
lubricating oil Schmieröl *n*.
lubricating spray Sprühpistole *f (MT)*.
lubricating system Schmierstoffanlage *f (Mtr)*.
lubrication Schmierung *f*.
lubrication point Schmierstelle *f*.
lubrication pump Schmierölpumpe *f (Mtr)*.
lug Vorstecker *m (fuze)*; Dübel *m (G)*; Warze *f*, Kammerwarze *f (R)*; Aufhängeöse *f (suspension lug of bomb)*.
lull Gefechtspause *f (in combat)*.
lumber Bauholz *n*.
luminous compass Leuchtkompaß *m*.
luminous dial Leuchtblatt *n*, Leuchtzifferblatt *n (Inst)*.
luminous paint Leuchtfarbe *f*, Fluoreszenzfarbe *f*.
lunette Zugöse *f*, Protzöse *f (limber, trailer)*.
lung Lunge *f*.
lunge *n* Stoß *m*, Vorstoß *m*.
lunge *v* ausholen.
lung irritant Lungengift *n*, Lungenreizstoff *m*, erstickender Kampfstoff.
lusterless paint Mattanstrich *m*.
lye kaustisches Natron, Ätznatron *n*.
lysol Lysol *n*.
Lyster bag Listerscher Wasserreinigungssack.

M

macadam Makadam *m-n*.
machete Hackmesser *n*.
machine Maschine *f*.
machine gun Maschinengewehr *n*.
machine-gun *v* mit Maschinengewehrfeuer belegen, unter Maschinengewehrfeuer nehmen.
machine-gun ammunition Maschinengewehrmunition *f*.
machine-gun ammunition belt MG.-Gurt *m*.
machine-gun barrel MG.-Lauf *m*.
machine-gun bolt MG.-Schloß *n*.
machine-gun camera Lichtbildmaschinengewehr *n*.
machine-gun carrier Gewehrträger *m (Pers)*; MG.-Träger *m (vehicle)*.
machine-gun cart MG.-Wagen *m*.
machine-gun company Maschinengewehrkompanie *f*, MG.-Kompanie *f*.
machine-gun crew MG.-Bedienung *f*.
machine-gun detail Maschinengewehr-Bedienung *f*, Maschinengewehr-Bemannung *f*.
machine-gun emplacement Maschinengewehrstand *m*, MG.-Stand *m*.
machine-gun fire Maschinengewehrfeuer *n*, MG.-Feuer *n*.
machine-gunner Maschinengewehrschütze *m*, MG.-Schütze *m*, MG.-Mann *m*.
machine-gun nest MG.-Nest *m*.
machine-gun platoon MG.-Zug *m*.
machine-gun sight MG.-Richtaufsatz
machine-gun squad Maschinengewehr-Halbzug *m*, MG.-Halbzug *m*.
machine-gun station MG.-Stand *m (Ap)*.
machine-gun telescopic sight MG.-Zielfernrohr *n*.
machine-gun tripod MG.-Dreifuß *m*.
machinery Maschinerie *f*, Maschinen *fpl*; Mechanismus *m (mechanism)*; Maschinenteile *mpl (parts)*.
machine shop Werkstatt *f*.
machine tool Werkzeugmaschine *f*.
machinist Maschinist *m (Nav)*.
macrometer Makrometer *n*, Spiegelentfernungsmesser *m*.
"Mae West" Schwimmweste *f*.
magazine Magazin *n*, Munitionslager *n (Ord)*; Kasten *m (R)*.
magazine belt Patronengurt *m*.
magazine catch Magazinhalter *m (pistol)*.
magazine charge Schlagladung *f (fuze)*.
magazine-fed rifle Mehrlader *m*.
magazine feeding device Mehrladevorrichtung *f (R)*.
magazine fire Schnellfeuer *n*, Magazinfeuer *n*.
magazine floor plate Kastenboden *m (R)*.
magazine holder Magazinhalter *m (MG)*.
magazine housing Magazingehäuse *n (pistol)*.
magazine pocket Patronentasche *f*.
magazine rack *(Ord)* Magazinlager *n*
magazine release Magazinhaltehebel *m (automatic weapons)*.
magazine weapon Mehrlader *m*.
magnesium Magnesium *n*.
magnesium bomb *f* Magnesiumbombe
magnesium powder Magnesiumpulver *n*.
magnesium thermit Magnesiumthermit *n (incendiary bomb)*.
magnet Magnet *m*.
magnetic magnetisch.
magnetic azimuth mißweisender Kurswinkel *(Navigation)*.
magnetic azimuth reading Nadelzahl
magnetic compass Magnetkompaß *m*.
magnetic course mißweisender Kurs *(Air Navigation)*.
magnetic declination Mißweisung *f*, Ortsmißweisung *f*, Nadelabweichung *f*, Deviation *f*.
magnetic field Magnetfeld *n*, magnetisches Feld *(Elec)*.
magnetic heading mißweisender Kurs *(Air Navigation)*.
magnetic mine Magnetmine *f*.
magnetic north Magnetisch-Nord *m*.
magnetic tachometer Wirbelstromtachometer *n*.
magnetic variation Mißweisung *f*, Deklination *f*.
magneto Magnetzündapparat *m*, Magnetapparat *m*, Zündmagnet *m*.
magneto ignition Magnetzündung *f*.
magnification Vergrößerung *f*.
magnify vergrößern.
magnitude Größe *f*.
magnitude of oscillation Schwingungsgröße *f (Rad)*.
Magnus effect Magnus-Effekt *m (Ballistics)*.
mail Post *f*.
mail call Postaufruf *m*.
mail clerk Postmeister *m*.
mail orderly *See* **mail clerk**.
main attack Hauptangriff *m*.
main body Gros *n (march column) (Tac)*; Hauptmasse *f (Tac)*.
main bore gezogener Teil *(G tube)*.
main charge Hauptladung *f (blasting cap)*.
main clutch Hauptkupplung *f (MT, Tk)*.
main column Hauptkolonne *f*.
main deck Hauptdeck *n*, Batteriedeck *n (Nav)*.
main effort Hauptangriff *m (Tac)*.
main girder Hauptträger *m (Bdg)*.
main guard Hauptwache *f*.
main ignition lead Hauptzündung *f (Blasting)*.
main jet Hauptdüse *f (Mtr)*.
main line of resistance Hauptkampflinie *f*.
main mooring line Haupt-Ankertau *n*, Haupt-Fesseltau *n (Bln)*.
main reduction gear Hauptvorgelege *n (Tk)*.
main shaft Getriebehauptwelle *f (transmission) (MT)*.
main spring Schlagbolzenfeder *f (R)*; Schließfeder *f (pistol)*.
main-station intersection method Hauptschnittverfahren *n (Flash Ranging)*.
main supply road Hauptzufuhrstraße *f*, Hauptnachschubstraße *f*.
maintain instandhalten *(vehicles, etc.)*; unterhalten *(roads)*; behaupten, aufrechterhalten *(an opinion, position)*.
maintenance Instandhaltung *f*, Instandsetzung *f*, Unterhaltung *f*, Wartung *f*.
maintenance and repair Unterhaltung und Instandsetzung.
maintenance area Feldwerkstattsbereich *m*.
maintenance company Werkstattkompanie, *f*.
maintenance crew Instandsetzungsmannschaft *f*.
maintenance detachment Instandsetzungsabteilung *f*.
maintenance man Wart *m (Avn)*; Störungssucher *m (Tp)*.
maintenance officer Instandsetzungsoffizier *m*.
maintenance of supply Vorratshaltung *f*.
maintenance park Werkstattplatz *m*.
maintenance party Instandsetzungstrupp *m*, Werkstatt-Trupp *m*.
maintenance personnel Bodenpersonal *n (Avn)*.
maintenance plan Instandsetzungsplan *m*.
maintenance platoon Abschleppzug *m (MT)*; Werkstattzug *m (Tk Bn)*.
maintenance section Gefechtstroß *m (Btry)*; Instandsetzungshalbzug *m*.
maintenance service Instandsetzungsdienst *m*, Störungsdienst *m*.
maintenance truck Instandsetzungskraftwagen *m*.
maintenance vehicle Instandsetzungsfahrzeug *n*, Instandsetzungswagen *m*.
main transmission gear Hauptgetriebe *n (MT)*.
main trench Hauptgraben *m (Ft)*.
major Major *m*; Oberstabsarzt *m (Med)*; Oberstabsveterinär *m (Vet)*.
major attack Großangriff *m*.
major general Generalleutnant *m*; Generalleutnant der Flieger *(Luftwaffe)*; Generalstabsarzt *m (Med)*; Generalstabsveterinär *m (Vet)*.
major operation Operation in großem Maßstabe *(Tac)*; schwere Operation *(Med)*.
major repair größere Reparatur.
make machen; verfertigen, herstellen *(manufacture)*.
make-and-break device Schaltvorrichtung *f*.
make an emergency landing notlanden *(Avn)*.
make contact Verbindung aufnehmen *(with friendly troops)*; Fühlung aufnehmen *(with friendly or enemy troops)*.
make fast festmachen.
make port in einen Hafen einlaufen *(Nav)*.
maker Hersteller *m*, Verfertiger *m (manufacturer)*.
make tight dichten *(seal)*; zuziehen *(tighten)*.
make up montieren, zusammensetzen *(assemble)*.
make-up track Aufstellgleis *n*, Ordnungsgleis *n (RR)*.
make-up yard Aufstellbahnhof *m (RR)*.
malaria Malaria *f*, Sumpffieber *n*.
malfunction Fehlleistung *f*.
malingerer Simulant *m*.
malingering Vortäuschung v o n Krankheiten, Simulieren *n*.
malleable hämmerbar, schmiedbar.
malleable alloy Knetlegierung *f*.
mallet Fäustel *n*, Handfäustel *n (Engr)*.
manage verwalten, führen, leiten *(direct)*; auskommen *(get along)*.
manager Verwalter *m*, Leiter *m*.
mandatory zwingend, obligatorisch.
maneuver Manöver *n (Tac)*; Truppenübung *f (Tng)*.
maneuverability Manövrierfähigkeit *f (Tac)*; Wendigkeit *f (Ap)*.
maneuvering force vordere Angriffstruppen *(Tac)*.
maneuvering spider Halteleinenbund *m (Bln)*.
maneuvering target kurvendes Ziel *(AAA)*; bewegliche Scheibe *(Tng)*.
maneuvering valve Manövrierventil *n (Bln)*.
manganese Mangan *n*.
manganese dioxide Braunstein *m*.
manhandle mit der Hand bewegen, mit den Händen bewegen.
manhole Kabelbrunnen *m (Tp)*; Mannloch *n*, Einsteigöffnung *f*.
manifold Auspuffkrümmer *m (exhaust) (Mtr)*.
manifold pressure Ladedruck *m*.
manifold pressure control Ladedruckregler *m (Ap engine)*.
manifold pressure gage Ladedruckmesser *m (Ap)*.
manipulation Handhabung *f*; Zielwechsel *m*, Zielverlegung *f (Gunnery)*.
manning detail Geschützbedienung *f (CA)*.
manning table Bemannungsliste *f*.
manometer Manometer *n*.
manta Gepäckdecke *f*.
manual *n* Handbuch *n*, Vorschrift *f*.
manual *adj* handtätig, Hand-.
manual fuze setter Zünderstellschlüssel *m*.
manually-operated handtätig.
manufacture *n* Fertigung *f*.
manufacture *v* verfertigen, herstellen, fabrizieren.
map *n* Karte *f*.
map *v* kartieren.
map code *See* **map coordinate code**.
map compilation Kartenvervollständigung *f*.
map coordinate code Kartenschlüssel
map correction Kartenverbesserung
map course Kartenkurs *m (Navigation)*.
map data Kartenunterlagen *fpl (for making maps)*; Kartenwerte *mpl (as read from maps)*.
map exercise Planspiel *n*, Planübung *f (Tng)*.
map fire Punktfeuer *n*, Planschießen *n*, Schießen mit Karte *(Gunnery)*.
map maneuver Planübung *f (Tng)*.

map measurer Kartenentferungsmesser *m.*
mapping Kartierung *f.*
mapping camera Reihenbildner *m (aerial Photo).*
mapping photography Reihenbildaufnahme *f (aerial Photo).*
mapping unit Kartenabteilung *f.*
map problem Planübung *f (Tng).*
map projection Kartenentwurf *m,* Kartenprojektion *f.*
map protractor Kartenwinkelmesser *m,* Meßdreieck *n.*
map-protractor set Plansektor *m (Arty, Surv).*
map range Kartenentfernung *f (Gunnery).*
map reading Kartenlesen *n.*
map reconnaissance Kartenerkundung *f,* Kartenaufklärung *f.*
map scale Kartenmaßstab *m.*
map section Kartenausschnitt *m.*
map sheet Kartenblatt *n.*
map square Gradabteilung *f,* Gradfeld *n.*
map substitute Ersatzkarte *f.*
marauder Plünderer *m,* Marodeur *m.*
march *n* Marsch *m.*
march *v* marschieren.
march collecting post Marsch-Krankensammelstelle *f.*
march column Marschkolonne *f.*
march destination Marschziel *n.*
march discipline Marschdisziplin *f,* Marschzucht *f.*
march formation Marschform *f;* Marschordnung *f (close order);* Marschgliederung *f (organization of march units);* Marschfolge *f (sequence of units).*
march graph Marsch-Diagramm *n,* Marschtafel *f.*
march group Marschgruppe *f.*
march halt Marschhalt *m,* Marschpause *f.*
marching ability Marschfähigkeit *f.*
marching speed Marschgeschwindigkeit *f,* Marschtempo *n.*
march in review Parademarsch *m,* Vorbeimarsch *m.*
march maintenance nach Bedarf durchgeführte Instandsetzung.
march movement Marschbewegung *f (Tac).*
march objective Marschziel *n.*
march order Marschbefehl *m.*
"March order!" "Marschordnung!" *(Arty).*
march outpost Marschvorposten *m.*
march performance *f* Marschleistung
march plan Marschplan *m.*
march readiness *f* Marschbereitschaft
march rest Marschrast *f.*
march route Marschstraße *f,* Marschstrecke *f.*
march schedule Marschübersicht *f.*
march table Marschtafel *f.*
march unit Marschgruppe *f,* Marschverband *m.*
Marconi antenna Einpolluftleiter *m (Rad).*
marginal data Randnoten *fpl,* Randbemerkungen *fpl.*
margin of safety Sicherungszuschlag *m (Firing).*
margin of the sheaf of fire Anschlußteil der Garbe *(Ballistics).*
marine Seesoldat *m (USA).*
marine cable Flußkabel *n (river);* Seekabel *n,* Tiefseekabel *n (ocean).*
Marine Corps Seesoldatenkorps *n (USA).*
mark Marke *f,* Kennzeichen *n.*
marker Anzeiger *m (Inst);* Wegeposten *m (traffic control).*
marker beacon signal Kennung *f*
marker light Abstandslicht *n (MT).*
marking Abzeichen *n,* Erkennungszeichen *n,* Kennzeichen *n (Ap, Tk);* Hoheitsabzeichen *n (national insignia) (Ap, Tk).*
marking disk Zielkelle *f,* Ziellöffel *m.*
marking gage Strichmaß *n (Woodworking).*
marking out Einfluchten *n (Surv).*
marking panel Fliegertuch *n.*
mark number Kennummer *f.*
marksman Scharfschütze *m.*
marksmanship Schießfertigkeit *f,* Zielsicherheit *f.*
marksmanship fourragère Schützenschnur *f.*
marksmanship training Schießausbildung *f.*
mark time auf der Stelle treten.
marsh Morast *m,* Sumpf *m.*
martial law Standrecht *n.*
martingale Vorderzeug *n (harness).*
mask *n* Deckung *f,* Geländebedeckung *f (Gunnery);* Maske *f (Cam);* Atemmaske *f (oxygen equipment);* Gasmaske *f (gas).*
mask *v* verschleiern, verbergen, verdecken.
mask-clearance table Tafel zum Überschießen von Deckungen *(Gunnery).*
masked area gedeckter Raum.
masked battery gedeckte Batterie.
mason Maurer *m.*
mass *n* Masse *f,* Massierung *f,* Truppenzusammenziehung *f (Tac).*
mass *v* massieren, zusammenziehen, zusammenbringen *(Tac).*
mass athletics Massenturnen *n.*
mass attack massierter Angriff.
massed fire Feuerschlag *m (Arty).*
mass effect Massenwirkung *f (Tac).*
massive attack Massenangriff *m,* massierter Angriff *(Tac).*
mass of maneuver vordere Angriffstruppen *(Tac).*
mass production Großfertigung *f,* Massenfertigung *f,* Großserienfabrikation *f.*
mast Mast *m.*
master Meister *m,* Kapitän *m,* Kommandant *m (Nav).*
master compass Mutterkompaß *m (Avn).*
master cylinder Druckzylinder *m (hydraulic brake).*
master oscillator Steuerstufe *f,* Schwingungserzeugerstufe *f.*
master oscillator tube Steuerröhre *f.*
master sergeant Oberfeldwebel *m;* Oberwachtmeister *m (Arty, Cav);* Stabsfeldwebel *m (Rgtl Sgt Maj).*
master watch Hauptuhr *f,* Mutteruhr *f (timepiece).*
mastery of the air Luftherrschaft *f.*
match *n* Streichholz *n,* Zündholz *n.*
mate Maat *m (Nav).*
material Material *n,* Werkstoff *m,* Stoff *m.*
material damage Sachschaden *m.*
matériel Gerät *n,* Kriegsmaterial *n.*
Matériel Command Technisches Amt *(AAF).*
matrix Mischung von Schwarzpulver und Kollophonium *(shrapnel).*
mattock Tonhacke *f.*
mattock hoe Lettenhaue *f (Engr).*
maul Handramme *f (Engr).*
maximum elevation größte Rohrerhöhung *(Gunnery).*
maximum gas pressure Höchstgasdruck *m (Ballistics, Ord).*
maximum intensity Maximaleffekt *m (sound locator).*
maximum intensity method Höchstwertverfahren *n (sound locator).*
maximum load Belastung *f,* Höchstlast *f (Engr).*
maximum number Höchstzahl *f.*
maximum ordinate Gipfelhöhe *f (Ballistics).*
maximum power Höchstleistung *f.*
maximum punishment Höchststrafe
maximum range Flugbereich *m,* Reichweite *f (Ap);* Höchstschußweite *f (Firing).*
maximum speed Größtgeschwindigkeit *f,* Höchstgeschwindigkeit *f.*
maximum thermometer Maximumthermometer *n.*
M-day Mobilmachungstag *m,* X-Tag
meadow Weide *f,* Wiese *f.*
meal ticket Eßmarke *f.*
mean *adj* mittel, mittler, mittelmäßig; durchschnittlich *(average).*
mean chord mittlere (Flügel-)Tiefe *(Ap wing).*
mean deviation mittlere Streuung *(Gunnery).*
mean error mittlerer Fehler, durchschnittlicher Fehler.
mean height of burst mittlere Sprenghöhe *(Ballistics).*
mean point of impact mittlerer Treffpunkt *(Ballistics).*
mean range mittlere Länge *(Gunnery).*
mean sea level Normalnullpunkt *m,* Normalnull *f.*
means of communication Nachrichtenmittel *n,* Verbindungsmittel *n.*
means of fire control Schießhilfsmittel *npl (Arty).*
means of identification Erkennungszeichen *n.*
means of supply movement Nachschubmittel *m.*
means of traction Zugmittel *n.*
means of transportation Beförderungsmittel *n,* Transportmittel *n.*
means of wire communication Drahtnachrichtenmittel *n.*
mean solar time mittlere Sonnenzeit.
mean trajectory mittlere Flugbahn.
measure *n* Maß *n (of quantity, etc.);* Maßnahme *f (step or enactment).*
measure *v* messen.
measurement Maß *n (measure);* Messung *f.*
measuring apparatus Meßgerät *n (Inst or equipment).*
measuring circuit Meßleitung *f (Sound Ranging, Flash Ranging).*
measuring knob Meßknopf *m,* Meßwalze *f (range finder).*
measuring line Eichstrich *m (Inst).*
measuring mark Meßmarke *f*
meat Fleisch *n.*
meat can Kessel *m (mess kit).*
meat grinder Fleischhackmaschine *f.*
meat inspection Fleischbeschau *f.*
meat loaf Hackbraten *m.*
mechanic Mechaniker *m,* Maschinenschlosser *m.*
mechanical aptitude test technische Eignungsprüfung.
mechanical filter Schwebstoffilter *m,* Schutzsieb *n (gas mask).*
mechanical fuze mechanischer Zünder.
mechanical pick-up unit Schalldose *f (phonograph).*
mechanical pilot automatischer Pilot, automatische Kurssteuerung, Selbststeuergerät *n (Ap).*
mechanical time fuze mechanischer Zeitzünder *(Am).*
mechanical training technische Ausbildung.
mechanism Vorrichtung *f.*
mechanization Motorisierung *f*
mechanized motorisiert, mechanisiert.
mechanized attack Panzerangriff *m.*
mechanized battalion Schnelle Abteilung.
mechanized cavalry motorisierte Kavallerie.
mechanized gun Geschütz auf Selbstfahrlafette, Sturmgeschütz *n.*
mechanized troops Schnelle Truppen.
mechanized unit motorisierter Verband, moto-mechanisierter Verband.
medal Medaille *f,* Orden *m,* Auszeichnung *f.*
Medal of Honor Ehrenmedaille *f*
medical attendance ärztliche Behandlung.
medical battalion Sanitätsabteilung *f.*
medical company Sanitätskompanie *f.*
Medical Corps Sanitätskorps *n.*
medical corps personnel Sanitätspersonal *n.*
medical corps unit Sanitätstruppe *f.*
Medical Department Amt für Gesundheitsdienst *(USA).*
medical depot Sanitätspark *m.*
medical detachment Sanitätstruppe *f.*
medical equipment Sanitätsausrüstung *f,* Sanitätsgerät *n.*
medical examination ärztliche Untersuchung.
medical examiner Truppenarzt *m.*
medical field manual Kriegssanitätsordnung *f.*
medical inspector Sanitätsinspekteur *m.*
medical installation Sanitätseinrichtung *f.*
medical isolation Kranken-Absonderung *f,* Kranken-Isolierung *f.*
medical laboratory medizinisches Laboratorium.
medical officer Sanitätsoffizier *m,* Truppenarzt *m.*
medical service Sanitätsdienst *m.*
medical supply depot Sanitätsmaterialpark *m.*
medical train Sanitätstroß *m.*
medical treatment ärztliche Behandlung.
medical troops Sanitätstruppen *fpl,* Sanitätspersonal *n.*
medical unit Sanitätstruppe *f.*
medicine Medizin *f (science, drug);* Arznei *f (drug).*
medium schwer *(Ord);* mittler, Mittel-.
medium artillery schwere Artillerie.
medium range mittlere Entfernung *(up to 800 meters).*
medium-scale map Karte im Maßstab 1:50,000 bis 1:125,000.
medium sight gestrichenes Korn *(R aiming).*
medium tank mittlerer Panzerkampfwagen.
medium tractor mittelschwerer Schlepper *(MT).*
meet begegnen, treffen.
meeting engagement Begegnungsgefecht *n.*
meeting point Treffpunkt *m (Tac).*
megaphone Sprachrohr *n,* Megaphon
member Mitglied *n (of an organization);* Angehöriger *m (of a unit);* Glied *n (of the body).*
memorandum Merkblatt *n,* Mitteilung *f,* Denkschrift *f.*
meningitis Gehirnhautentzündung *f.*
méplat abgeflachter Teil *(Small Arms Am).*
Mercator chart Mercatorkarte *f.*
Mercator projection Mercatorprojektion *f.*
merchantman Handelsschiff *n.*
Merchant Marine Handelsmarine *f.*
mercury Quecksilber *n.*
mercury fulminate Knallquecksilber
meridian Meridian *m.*
meridian altitude Breitenhöhe *f (Celestial Navigation).*
mesh road Drahtstraße *f (Engr).*
mess Kantine *f,* Kasino *n,* Speiseraum *m.*
message Meldung *f,* Nachricht *f,* Botschaft *f,* Mitteilung *f.*
message blank Meldeblatt *n,* Meldekarte *f.*
message book Meldeblock *m.*
message center Meldesammelstelle *f,* Nachrichtenstelle *f,* Nachrichtenzentrale *f.*
message channel Meldeweg *m.*
message container Meldebüchse *f,* Abwurfpatrone *f (Avn, Sig C).*
message dropping Meldeabwurf *m (Avn, Sig C).*
message dropping ground Abwurfstelle *f,* Meldeabwurfstelle *f (Avn, Sig C).*
message form Vordruck für dringende Meldungen.
message pad Meldeblock *m.*
message pick-up Aufhaken *n (Avn).*
message relay service Meldedienst *m.*
message transmission service Meldedienst *m.*
mess attendant zum Küchendienst kommandierter Soldat.
mess council Kasinovorstand *m.*
messenger Melder *m;* Meldegänger *m,* Läufer *m (on foot);* Meldereiter *m (on horse);* Meldefahrer *m (on vehicle);* Kradmelder *m (on Mtcl).*
messenger dog Meldehund *m.*
messenger-dog detail Meldehundtrupp *m.*
messenger-dog handler Meldehundführer *m.*
messenger pigeon Brieftaube *f,* Heeresbrieftaube *f.*
messenger team Meldehundegespann
messenger vehicle Meldefahrzeug *n.*
mess gear *See* **mess kit.**
messing Verpflegung *f.*
mess kit Kochgeschirr *n,* Eßgeschirr und -Besteck.
mess-kit cover Kochgeschirrhülle *f.*
mess officer Verpflegungsoffizier *m.*
mess orderly *See* **mess attendant.**
mess sergeant Küchenunteroffizier *m,* Verpflegungsunteroffizier *m.*
metal Metall *n.*
metal cabinet Metallgehäuse *n*
metal container Blechbehälter *m,* Blechgefäß *n,* Blechkanister *m.*
metal drum Blechtrommel *f;* Trommel *f (for belt Am).*
metal fittings Beschlag *m (R).*
metal fouling Metallrückstände im Rohr *(G).*
metallic circuit *(Tp)* Doppelleitung *f*
metallic-link ammunition belt Metallgliedergurt *m,* Stahlgurt *m (MG).*
metallic telephone circuit Fernsprechdoppelleitung *f.*
metal mesh road *(Engr)* Drahtstraße *f*
metalsmith Flugzeugmetaller *m (Nav, Avn).*
metal tube Stahlröhre *f (Rad).*
meteorograph Meteorograph *m (Avn, Met).*
meteorological Wetter-. *See also* **metro.**
meteorological disturbance Wetterstörung *f.*
meteorological measurement Wettermessung *f.*
meteorological message Wetterfunkmeldung *f,* Wetterfunkspruch *m (Rad);* Barbarameldung *f (Arty).*
meteorological service Truppenwetterdienst *m (T of Opns).*
meteorological station Wetterwarte
meteorologist Meteorologe *m.*
meteorology Wetterkunde *f.*
method Methode *f,* Verfahren *n,* Weise *f,* Art *f.*
method of attack Angriffsart *f.*
method of combat Kampfmethode *f.*
method of execution Art der Durchführung *(Tac).*
method of fire Feuerart *f,* Schießverfahren *n (Arty).*
method of movement Bewegungsart
method of radio communication Funkverkehrsform *f.*
method of survey Vermessungsart *f (Engr).*
method of warfare Kampfmethode *f.*
methyldichlorarsine Methyldichlorarsin *n (CWS).*
metro Wetter-, Witterungs-, Barbara-. *See also* **meteorological.**
metro correction Verbesserung für Witterungseinflüsse *(Arty).*
metro data Witterungseinflüsse *mpl. (Gunnery).*
metro message Barbarameldung *f,* Wettermeldung *f (Arty).*
metro platoon Wetterzug *m (Arty).*
mica Glimmer *m.*
microbarograph Mikrobarograph *m.*
microfilm Mikrofilm *m.*
micrometer Teilring *m (optical Inst);* Skalenring *m (angle-of-site Inst);* Mikrometerschraube *f (calipers).*
micrometer calipers Mikrometerschraube *f.*
micrometer drum Trommel *f (panoramic sight).*
micrometer head Triebscheibe *f (optical, Ord).*
micrometer index Stellmarke *f (optical Inst).*
micrometer knob Rändel *m,* Teiltrommel *f (panoramic telescope, BC telescope).*
micrometer scale Skalenring *m,* Teiltrommel *f (telescopic sight).*
microphone Mikrophon *n.*
middle Mitte *f.*
midpoint Mittelpunkt *m (center);* Wechselpunkt *m (AAA).*
midrange *See* **medium range.**
midshipman Seekadett *m.*
midwing monoplane Mitteldecker *m.*
mil Teilstrich *n,* Strich *m (Gunnery). See also* **Neugrad.**
mildew Meltau *m.*
mild steel Weicheisen *n.*
mile Landmeile *f (statute mile of 1.609 km);* Seemeile *f (nautical mile of 1.853 km).*
mileage Kilometerzahl *f. See also* **mileage allowance.**
mileage allowance Reisekostenvergütung *f.*
mileage indicator Kilometerzähler *m.*
mileage table Reiseverordnung *f.*
milestone Meilenstein *m.*
mil formula *(Arty)* Teilstrich-Formel *f*
mil graduation Stricheinteilung *f,* Teilstricheinteilung *f;* Richtkreiseinteilung *f (on aiming circle).*
military *n* Militär *n.*
military *adj* militärisch, Wehr-, Heeres-, Kriegs-.
military academy Militärakademie *f.*
military age wehrpflichtiges Alter.
military area Militärbezirk *m (any area under military control);* Wehrersatzbezirk *m (recruiting area, subdivision of a* Wehrkreis).
military attaché Militärattaché *m.*
military authorities Militärbehörde *f.*
military aviation Militärluftfahrt *f.*
military bearing soldatische Haltung.
military bridge Kriegsbrücke *f.*
military bridge equipment Kriegsbrückengerät *n.*
military cemetery Militärfriedhof *m.*
military censorship Militärzensur *f.*
military channel Dienstweg *m.*
military chart Generalstabskarte *f.*
military commission Militärausschuß *m,* Militärkommission *f.*
military correspondence militärischer Schriftverkehr.
military court Militärgericht *n,* Wehrmachtgericht *n.*
military courtesy militärische Formen.
military crest *(Top)* Böschungskante *f*
military custom Truppengebrauch *m.*
military discipline militärische Disziplin, Manneszucht *f.*
military district Militärbezirk *m;* Wehrbezirk *m (subdivision of a* Wehrersatzbezirk).
military district headquarters Feldkommandantur *f (Com Z).*
military education Wehrerziehung *f,* Wehrertüchtigung *f.*
military equipment Heergerät *n,* Kriegsmaterial *n.*
military establishment Wehrmacht-Einrichtung *f.*
military funeral Militärbegräbnis *n;* Trauerfeier *f (service);* Trauerparade *f (procession).*
military geography Wehrgeographie
military geology Wehrgeologie *f.*
military government Militärverwaltung *f.*
military governor Militärbefehlshaber *m.*
military grid Gitternetz *n.*
military hospital Heereslazarett *n.*
military hygiene Wehrmachtgesundheitsdienst *m,* Gesundheitswesen *n.*
military information wehrwichtige Nachrichten.
military intelligence militärisches Nachrichtenwesen.
Military Intelligence Division Amt für den Militärischen Nachrichtendienst im Generalstab des Heeres *(USA).*
Military Intelligence Service Nachrichtendienst *m (USA).*
military internee Internierter *m.*
military jurisdiction Militärgerichtsbarkeit *f.*
military justice Kriegsgerichtsrechtsprechung *f.*
military law Kriegsrecht *n,* Wehrrecht *n;* Wehrstrafrecht *n (penal code).*
military map Generalstabskarte *f.*
military mining Minenkrieg *m,* Minenkampf *m.*
military mission militärischer Auftrag; Militärmission *f.*
military necessity Kriegsräson *f.*
military objective militärisches Ziel.
military occupation militärische Besetzung.
military offense Wehrvergehen *n,* militärisches Vergehen, militärisches Verbrechen.
military order Heeresbefehl *m.*
military passport Passierschein *m.*
military penal code Wehrmacht-Strafgesetzbuch *n,* Militärstrafgesetzbuch *n (Ger).*
military police Feldgendarmerie *f.*
military policeman Feldgendarm *m.*
military police regulations Feldgendarmerievorschrift *f.*
military police service Ordnungsdienst *m.*
military policy Wehrpolitik *f.*
military post Wehrmacht-Standort
military prison Arrestanstalt *f.*
military prisoner Arrestant *m,* Militärgefangener *m,* Militärhäftling *m.*
military railroad Militäreisenbahn *f,* Feldeisenbahn *f.*
military railway engineer Feldeisenbahner *m.*
military rank militärischer Rang.

military rating Kurzleistung f (of an Ap engine).
military requirements Belange der Truppe, Kriegserfordernisse npl.
military reservation Wehrmachtgelände n.
military school Heeresbildungsanstalt f, Waffenschule f.
military science Kriegswissenschaft f, Wehrwissenschaft f.
military service Wehrdienst m.
military sketch Geländeskizze f.
military specialist Wehrmachts-Sachverständiger m, Angehöriger einer Sonderlaufbahn.
military subdistrict Militärverwaltungsbezirk m.
military symbol Kartenzeichen n, taktisches Zeichen.
military train Militärzug m (RR).
military training Wehrausbildung f, Wehrertüchtigung f.
military tribunal Militärgericht n, Wehrmachtgericht n.
military usage Truppengebrauch m.
militia Miliz f.
milk Milch f.
mill Mühle f.
milliammeter Milliamperemeter n.
milling Fräsen n (Tech).
milling machine Fräsmaschine f, Fräswerk n.
mil relation Teilstrich-Formel f (Arty).
mine n Mine f (Mil, Nav); Bergwerk n (coal, iron, etc.).
mine v Minen legen, verminen (laying mines); minieren, unterminieren (Mil tunneling); abbauen (coal, iron, etc.).
mine barrier Minensperre f.
mine buoy Minenboje f, Minentonne
mine case Minengefäß n.
mine chamber Sprengkammer f (Blasting).
mine clearance Minenräumung f.
mine-clearance roller Minenräumwalze f.
mine-clearance tank Minenräumpanzer m.
mine crater Minentrichter m.
mine defense Minensperre f.
mine detector Minensuchgerät n.
mine dragging Minenschleppen n
mine field Minenfeld n.
mine gallery Minengang m (Engr).
mine group Minenabteilung f (harbor defense).
mine-infested area minenverseuchtes Gebiet (Nav).
mine layer Minenfahrzeug n, Minenleger m, Minendampfer m (Nav).
mine-laying airplane Minenflugzeug n, Minenflieger m.
mine-laying tank Minenlegerpanzerkampfwagen m.
mine-locating detail Minensuchtrupp
mine planter See mine layer.
mine planting flotilla Minenlegerflottille f (Nav).
mine-probing rod Minensuchstab m.
mine road block Straßensperre mit Minen.
miner's spoon Raumlöffel m (Engr).
miner's tramcar (Engr) Minenhund m
mine shaft Minenschacht m (Engr).
mine-surveying set Markscheidegerät n (Engr).
mine sweeper Minenräumer m, Minenräumboot n, Minensucher m, Minensuchboot n (Nav).
mine sweeping Minenräumung f.
mine tunnel Minenstollen m (Engr).
mine ventilation (Engr) Bewetterung f
mine yawl Minenlegermotorboot n
miniature kleine Ordensschnalle f (decoration).
miniature range Kleinschießplatz m.
minimum Minimum n, Kleinste n.
minimum altitude attack Tieffangriff m, Tieffliegerangriff m, Tiefflugangriff m (Avn).
minimum-altitude flight Tiefflug m (Avn).
minimum elevation kleinste Rohrerhöhung (Gunnery).
minimum horizontal range Kartenentfernung zum Wechselpunkt (AA Gunnery).
minimum number Mindestzahl f.
minimum range kürzeste Schußentfernung (Firing).
minimum thermometer Minimumthermometer n.
mining effect Minenwirkung f (Am).
mining gallery Minengang m.
mining system Minenanlage f.
mining tools Miniergerät n (Engr).
minor casualty Leichtverwundeter m.
mirror Spiegel m.
mirror diameter Spiegeldurchmesser m (searchlight).
mirror sight Spiegelvisier n.
misalignment of wheels schiefer Radstand, Verkantung f (MT).
misappropriation unrechtmäßige Aneignung.
misbehavior before the enemy militärisches Verbrechen vor dem Feinde, militärisches Vergehen vor dem Feinde.
miscalculate falsch rechnen, sich verrechnen.
misfeed Zufuhrhemmung f.
misfire Versager m.
miss n Fehlgänger m, Fehlschuß m.
miss v verfehlen.
missile Geschoß n.
missing in action vermißt.
mission Auftrag m, Aufgabe f; Gefechtsaufgabe f; Einsatz m (Avn).
"Mission accomplished!" "Auftrag erledigt!"
mist Nebel m.
mistake grober Fehler.
mister Herr m.
mitigation of sentence Urteilsmilderung f.
mitten Fausthandschuh m.
mixed force Truppenverband m, gemischter Verband.
mixed medical commission gemischte ärztliche Kommission.
mixed train gemischter Zug (RR).
mixture Gemisch n; Lösung f (solution).
mixture control Düsenkorrektor m (Inst); Gemischregelung f (process).
moat Festungsgraben m, Wallgraben
mobile fahrbar, fahrend, beweglich, schnell, motorisiert.
mobile antiaircraft artillery Kraftwagenflak f.
mobile artillery fahrende Artillerie, bewegliche Artillerie.
mobile generating unit fahrbarer Stromerzeuger, Kraftquellenwagen
mobile hospital Feldlazarett n.
mobile machine shop fahrbare Werkstatt, Werkstattkraftwagen m.
mobile reserve bewegliche Reserve
mobile reserves beweglich gehaltene Vorräte (supplies).
mobile seacoast artillery bewegliche Küstenartillerie.
mobile surgical unit motorisiertes Bereitschaftslazarett.
mobile troops Schnelle Truppen.
mobile warfare Bewegungskrieg m.
mobility Wendigkeit f (MT, Tk).
mobilization Mobilmachung f.
mobilization camp Mobilmachungslager n.
mobilization center Mobilmachungslager n.
mobilization day Mobilmachungstag m, X-Tag m.
mobilization plan Mobilmachungsplan m.
mobilization point Mobilmachungslager n.
Mobilization Regulations Mobilmachungsbestimmungen fpl.
mobilize mobilisieren, mobilmachen, aufbieten.
mock combat Scheingefecht n.
mock-up Nachbildung f.
model Baumuster n, Modell n, Muster n, Typ m (Ap, MT).
model designation Typenbezeichnung
model number Typennummer f, Modellnummer f.
modulated wave modulierte Welle, gemodelte Welle.
moisture Feuchtigkeit f.
moisture content Feuchtigkeitsgehalt m (Met).
"Molotov breadbasket" Schüttkasten m (Avn).
"Molotov cocktail" Brandflasche f.
moment of force Kraftmoment n.
moment of inertia Trägheitsmoment
momentum Bewegungsgröße f, Impuls m.
monitor v überwachen (Com).
monitoring station Überwachungsstelle f (Com).
monkey wrench Schraubenschlüssel
monobloc gun barrel Vollrohr n.
monocoque construction Schalenbauweise f (Ap).
monocular adj einäugig, monokular (optical Inst).
monoplane Eindecker m.
monsoon Monsun m.
monument Denkmal n.
moon Mond m.
moor v ankern, verankern, festmachen, vertäuen.
moored mine Ankermine f.
mooring band Verankerungsgurt m (Bln).
mooring cable Fesselkabel n, Fesselseil n, Verankerungstau n (Bln).
mooring line See mooring cable.
mooring mast Ankermast m, Verankerungsmast m, Vertäumast m.
mooring tower Ankerturm m, Verankerungsturm m.
mop Mop m.
mopping-up detachment Säuberungstrupp m.
mopping-up operation Säuberungsunternehmen n.
mop up säubern (Tac).
morale Moral f, Stimmung f.
Morale Branch Truppenbetreuung f.
moral effect (Tac) seelische Wirkung
morning Morgen m; Vormittag m (forenoon).
morning report Iststärkenachweisung f.
morning-report strength Iststärke f.
morphine Morphin n, Morphium n.
Morse code Morsealphabet n.
Morse code character n Morsezeichen
mortar Granatwerfer m (Ord); Mörtel m (building material).
mortar ammunition Granatwerfermunition f.
mortar cart Gasmörser-Karren m (CWS).
mortar emplacement Granatwerferstand m.
mortar equipment Granatwerfergerät n.
mortar fire Granatwerferfeuer n, Granatwerferbeschuß m.
mortar gunner Werferschütze m.
mortar pit Granatwerfernest n.
mortar platoon Granatwerferzug m.
mortar projectile Granatwerfergeschoß n.
mortar section Granatwerfer-Gruppe f.
mortar shell Wurfgranate f.
mortar-shell fuze Wurfgranatzünder m.
mortar smoke shell Nebelwurfgranate f.
mortar squad Granatwerfertrupp m.
mosaic Reihenbild n (Photo).
mosaic assembly Zusammensetzen von Reihenbildern (Photo).
mosquito Moskito m, Mücke f.
mosquito bar See mosquito net.
mosquito fleet Schnellboot-Flottille f (Nav).
mosquito net Moskitonetz n.
motor Motor m, Maschine f.
motor ambulance Krankenkraftwagen m.
motor ambulance train Krankenkraftwagenzug m.
motor carriage Selbstfahrlafette f (G).
motor column Kraftfahrzeugkolonne f.
motor convoy Kraftfahrzeugkolonne f, Kraftwagenkolonne f.
motorcycle Kraftrad n, Krad n.
motorcycle infantry Kradschützen mpl.
motorcycle messenger Kradmelder
motorcycle point Kradspitze f (Adv Gd).
motorcycle rifle company Kradschützenkompanie f.
motorcycle rifleman Kradschütze m.
motorcycle scout Kradspäher m, Kraftradspäher m.
motorcycle troop Kradschützenschwadron f, Kraftradschützenschwadron f.
motorcycle troops Kradschützen mpl.
motorcyclist Kradfahrer m, Kraftradfahrer m.
motor dispatch service Kraftfahr-Verbindungsdienst m.
motor ferry Motorfähre f.
motor fuel Kraftstoff m, Treibstoff m, Betriebsstoff m.
motorization Motorisierung f.
motorize motorisieren.
motorized motorisiert, verlastet.
motorized artillery Kraftzugartillerie f, motorisierte Artillerie.
motorized division leichte Division, schnelle Division, motorisierte Division.
motorized gun Kraftzuggeschütz n.
motorized infantry motorisierte Infanterie.
motorized infantry division Panzergrenadierdivision f.
motorized march Kraftwagenmarsch m.
motorized riflemen motorisierte Schützen.
motorized troops verlastete Truppen, schnelle Truppen.
motorized unit motorisierter Verband.
motor messenger Meldefahrer m.
motor officer Kraftfahrtransportoffizier m (USA).
motor oil Motorenöl n.
motor park Kraftwagenpark m.
motor pool Kraftfahrpark m.
motor torpedo boat Schnellboot n, Motorschnellboot n, Motortorpedoboot n, Torpedoschnellboot n.
motor transport Kraftwagentransport m.
motor transport equipment Kraftfahrgerät n.
motor transport officer See motor officer.
Motor Transport Service Kraftfahrwesen n.
motor truck Lastkraftwagen m.
motor vehicle Kraftfahrzeug n.
motor-vehicle column Kraftfahrkolonne f.
motor-vehicle concentration Kraftfahrzeugansammlung f.
motor-vehicle maintenance unit Kraftfahrzeuginstandsetzungseinheit f.
motor-vehicle park Kraftfahrzeugpark m, Kraftwagenpark m.
motor-vehicle repair shop Kraftwagenwerkstatt f.
mount n Träger m (Mech); Lafette f (Ord); Reitpferd n (horse). See also gun mount.
mount v aufsteigen, besteigen; aufziehen (Photo).
mountain Berg m.
mountain artillery Gebirgsartillerie f.
mountain battery Gebirgsbatterie f.
mountain cannon Gebirgskanone f.
mountain cap Bergmütze f (Clo).
mountain combat Gefecht im Gebirge, Gebirgskampf m.
mountain corps Gebirgskorps n.
mountain gun Gebirgsgeschütz n.
mountain infantryman Gebirgsjäger m, Jäger m.
mountain pack company Gebirgsträgerkompanie f.
mountain pass Gebirgspaß m.
mountain range Gebirge n.
mountain supply column Gebirgsfahrkolonne f (H-Dr).
mountain troops Gebirgstruppen fpl.
mountain warfare Gebirgskrieg m.
mounted aufgesessen (on horse or vehicle); beritten (on horse); verlastet (porté).
mounted combat Gefecht zu Pferde.
mounted defilade Sichtdeckung für Reiter (Cav).
mounted drill Ausbildung zu Pferd (Cav).
mounted infantry berittene Infanterie.
mounted maneuver Reitmanöver n.
mounted messenger Meldereiter m (on horse); Meldefahrer m (on vehicle).
mounted officer berittener Offizier, Offizier zu Pferde.
mounted platoon Reiterzug m (Inf Regt).
mounted reconnaissance berittene Aufklärung, Aufklärung zu Pferd
mounted rifle half squad Schützenabmarsch m (Cav).
mounted section Gruppe zu Pferde
mount guard v Wache beziehen.
mouth Mund m (Pers); Maul n (animal); Mündung f (river, G muzzle); Stellbecher m (of fuze setter).
mouthpiece Atemmundstück n (oxygen breathing apparatus); Einsprache f (Tp); Mundstück n (harness).
movement Bewegung f, Fortbewegung f; Verlegung f (from one point to another); Transport m (of troops, etc.).
movement at an angle Schrägfahrt f (ground target).
movement by air Lufttransport m.
movement by rail Eisenbahntransport m.
movement by road Marschbewegungen fpl; Kraftfahrzeugtransport m.
movement by water Seetransport m.
movement order Transportbefehl m, Verlegungsbefehl m.
moving coil Drehspule f (Elec).
moving-coil instrument Drehspulinstrument n.
moving picture Film m.
moving pivot Drehpunkt m (drill).
moving screen Verschleierungsabteilung f.
moving target bewegliches Ziel, fahrendes Ziel.
"moving up" Ausrücken n.
mud Schlamm m.
mud capping Verdämmen n (blasting).
mudguard Schutzblech n, Kotflügel
muffler Auspufftopf m, Schalldämpfer m (Mtr).
mule Maultier n, Maulesel m.
mule train Maultierkolonne f.
multi-axle drive Mehrachsantrieb m.
multi-axle vehicle Mehrachser m.
multielement tube Verbundröhre f.
multiplace mehrsitzig.
multiplace fighter Jagdmehrsitzer m.
multiplane Mehrdecker m (Ap).
multiple Vielfache n (Math).
multiple antiaircraft weapon mehrläufige Fla-Waffe.
multiple-belt entanglement Flächendrahthindernis n.
multiple connection Vielfachschaltung f, zusammengesetzte Vermittlung (Tp).
multiple disk clutch Lamellenkupplung f, Mehrscheibenkupplung f.
multiple-engine mehrmotorig.
multiple-grid tube Mehrgitterröhre f.
multiple-gun mount Mehrlauflafette
multiple-hole nozzle Mehrlochdüse f (Mtr).
multiple-lens camera Mehrfach-Reihenbildkammer f (aerial Photo).
multiplex operation Mehrfachbetrieb m (Tp).
multiplex telephony Mehrfachsprechen n.
multiplex utilization Mehrfachausnutzung f (Tp).
multipurpose gun Mehrzweckgeschütz n.
multiseater mehrsitzig.
multiseater airplane Mehrsitzer m.
multisection charge aus Teilladungen bestehende Triebladung (Am).
municipal police Schutzpolizei f.
munitions Munition f, Kriegsgerät n, Kampfmittel npl.
munitions officer Munitionsoffizier m.
munitions storage shed Munitionsschuppen m.
muscle Muskel m.
musette bag Brotbeutel m.
mushroom head of obturator Liderungskopf m, Pilz m (G).
mustache Schnurrbart m.
mustard Senf m, Mostrich m.
mustard gas Senfgas n, Lost n, Yperit n (CWS).
mustard gas shell Senfgas-Granate f (CWS).
mustardization Vergasung mit Senfgas (CWS).
muster Appell m, Musterung f.
muster roll Stammrolle f.
mutilate verstümmeln.
mutiny Meuterei f.
mutton Hammelfleisch n.
mutual fire support gegenseitige Feuerunterstützung.
mutual support gegenseitige Unterstützung.
muzzle Mündung f (Ord).
muzzle bell Mundlochfries m (G).
muzzle blast Stoß der Mündungsgase (G).
muzzle-blast smoke Mündungsrauch
muzzle brake Mündungsbremse f
muzzle cover Mündungsschoner m.
muzzle energy Mündungsarbeit f, Mündungswucht f, Mündungsenergie
muzzle flash Mündungsfeuer n.
muzzle gas pressure Mündungsgasdruck m.
muzzle-loader Vorderlader m.
muzzle sight Korn n (Ord).
muzzle swell Mundlochfries m (G).
muzzle velocity Anfangsgeschwindigkeit f, Mündungsgeschwindigkeit f.
muzzle wave Schallwelle des Mündungsknalls (Sound Ranging).

N

N.A.C.A. cowling NACA-Haube f (Ap).
nacelle Gondel f (Ap).
nadir point Fußpunkt m.
nail Nagel m.
name plate Typenschild n.
narrow eng, schmal.
narrow gage Schmalspur f (RR).
narrow-gage railroad Schmalspurbahn f, Kleinbahn f.
national anthem Nationalhymne f.
National Defense Act Wehrgesetz n.
national emblem Hoheitszeichen n.
national ensign Reichskriegsflagge f (Ger Nav); Nationalflagge f (other countries) (Nav).
national flag Reichsflagge f, Nationalflagge f.
National Guard Nationalgarde f (USA).
national insignia Hoheitsabzeichen n, Hoheitszeichen n.
nationality Nationalität f, Staatsangehörigkeit f.
national salute Flaggensalut m.
natural obstacle Geländehindernis n.
natural oscillation Eigenschwingung f (Rad).
natural rubber Naturkautschuk m, Naturgummi m.
nausea Brechreiz m.
nautical mile Seemeile f (1.853 km).
naval Marine-, See-. See also navy.
Naval Academy Marineakademie f.
naval aircraft pilot Seeflieger m.
Naval Air Forces Marineluftwaffe f (USA).
naval airplane Seeflieger m, Seeflugzeug n.
naval antiaircraft artillery Marineflak f.
naval attaché Marineattaché m.
naval aviation Marineflugwesen n, Seeluftstreitkräfte fpl, Seeflieger mpl, Marineflieger mpl.
naval aviator Marineflieger m.
naval base Flottenstützpunkt m, Marinestation f.
naval district Marinebezirk m (USA).
naval forces Seestreitkräfte fpl.
naval patrol airplane Seeaufklärer
naval pilot Marineflieger m.
Naval Reserve Marinereserve f (USA).
naval unit Marineeinheit f, Flotteneinheit f.
navigate orten.
navigation Navigation f (Avn, Nav).
navigational chart Navigationskarte
navigation guide Bake f (Nav).
navigation head Schiffsausladestelle f, Endhafen m.
navigation instrument Navigationsinstrument n (Avn).
navigator Orter m (Avn).
navigator's compass Kurszeiger m, Orterkompaß m, Peilkompaß m
navy Kriegsmarine f, Marine f.
navy airplane Seeflugzeug n, Seeflieger m.
Navy Department Marineamt n (USA).
navy patrol airplane Seeaufklärer
navy yard Marinewerft f, Kriegswerft f.
NCO Unteroffizier m.
NCO training course Unterführerkurs m.

near nahe.
near horse Sattelpferd *n.*
near miss Fehltreffer *m*, Nebsttreffer *m.*
neck Hals *m*; Hülsenhals *m* *(cartridge).*
neckband Halsbinde *f* *(Clo).*
neck groove Halskerbe *f* *(horse).*
neck halter Halshalfter *f* *(harness).*
neck-halter tie Halshalfterriemen *m* *(harness).*
neck strap Nackenband *n* *(gas mask)*; Nackenriemen *m*, Halsriemen *m* *(harness)*; Tragriemen *m* *(pack saddle).*
necktie Binder *m* *(Clo).*
needle Nadel *f.*
needle bearing Nadellager *n* *(MT).*
needle dam Nadelwehr *n* *(Engr).*
negative stagger Rückwärtsstaffelung *f*, Staffelung nach hinten *(Ap wings).*
neglect of duty Pflichtverletzung *f*, Pflichtversäumnis *f.*
negligence Fahrlässigkeit *f*, Nachlässigkeit *f*, Vernachlässigung *f.*
negotiate verhandeln.
negotiations for surrender Übergabeverhandlungen *fpl.*
negotiator Unterhändler *m.*
neon lamp Glimmlampe *f.*
nephoscope Wolkenspiegel *m* *(Met).*
nest Nest *n* *(Ft).*
nest of resistance Widerstandsnest *n*, Verteidigungsnest *n.*
nest of riflemen Schützennest *n.*
net Netz *n* *(Rad, Eng, Cam).*
net barrier Netzsperre *f* *(coast defense).*
net control station Funküberwachungsstelle *f*, Hauptfunkstelle *f*, Leitfunkstelle *f* *(Rad).*
net diagram Funkskizze *f* *(Rad).*
netting Tarnungsgeflecht *n* *(Cam).*
net weight Nettogewicht *n.*
network Stromnetz *n* *(Elec).*
neutral *adj* neutral.
neutral *n* Leerlauf *m* *(Mtr).*
neutrality Neutralität *f.*
neutralization Niederkämpfung *f*, Lahmlegung *f* *(Tac)*; Neutralisierung *f*, Neutralisation *f* *(CWS).*
neutralization fire Niederhaltungsschießen *n*, Niederhalten *n* *(Arty).*
neutralize neutralisieren; lähmen, lahmlegen *(an attack)*; niederhalten, niederkämpfen *(fire).*
neutral position Nullstellung *f* *(Mech).*
neutral power neutrale Macht.
neutral troops neutrale Truppen *(Tng).*
news broadcast Nachrichtenübertragung *f.*
newspaper Zeitung *f*; Frontzeitung *f* *(T of Opns).*
newsreel Wochenschau *f.*
news service Nachrichtendienst *m* *(Rad).*
next of kin die nächsten Angehörigen.
NH powder nichthygroskopisches Pulver.
niche Munitionsnische *f*, Fuchsloch *n* *(Ft).*
nickel Nickel *m-n.*
nickel-alkaline cell Nickelsammler *m.*
night attack Nachtangriff *m.*
night beacon lighting Nachtbefeuerung *f* *(Avn).*
night bomber Nachtbomber *m.*
night bombing flare Leuchtbombe *f.*
night combat Nachtgefecht *n.*
night fighter Nachtjäger *m* *(Avn).*
night fighting Nachtjagd *f*, Nachtluftkampf *m* *(Avn).*
night firing Nachtschießen *n.*
night flying chart Nachtflug-Karte *f* *(Avn).*
night glasses Nachtglas *n.*
night march Nachtmarsch *m.*
night operation Nachtunternehmung
night raid Nachtangriff *m* *(Avn).*
night reconnaissance Nachtaufklärung *f.*
ninety-degree turn Flügelspitzenkurve *f* *(Avn).*
nippers Beißzange *f.*
nipple Nippel *f* *(Tech).*
nitrate explosive Sprengsalpeter *m.*
nitration Nitrierung *f* *(Am).*
nitric acid Salpetersäure *f.*
nitrocellulose Nitrozellulose *f.*
nitrocellulose powder Nitrozellulosepulver *n.*
nitrocotton Schießwolle *f*, Schießbaumwolle *f.*
nitrogen Stickstoff *m.*
nitrogen mustard gas Stickstofflost *n* *(CWS).*
nitroglycerin Sprengöl *n*, Nitroglyzerin *n.*
nitroglycerin powder Nitroglyzerinpulver *n*, Sprengölpulver *n.*
noise Geräusch *n*, Lärm *m*; Gefechtslärm *m* *(of battle)*; Motorengeräusch
no man's land Niemandsland *n.*
nomenclature Benennung *f.*
nonbattle injury Wehrdienstbeschädigung *f.*
noncombatant Nichtkämpfer *m*, Nichtkombattant *m.*
noncommissioned officer Unteroffizier *m.*
noncorrosive nichtätzend.
nondelay fuze Schnellzünder *m*, Augenblickszünder *m*, Aufschlagzünder ohne Verzögerung.
nondeteriorating supplies lagerungsfähige Vorräte.
noneffective *n* Dienstunfähiger *m.*
nonexpendable nicht verbrauchbar.
nonexpendable supplies Gerät *n.*
nonhygroscopic powder nichthygroskopisches Pulver.
nonlethal agent nicht tödlich wirkender Kampfstoff, Reizstoff *m* *(CWS).*
nonmilitary objectives nichtmilitärische Ziele.
nonpersistent chemical agent flüchtiger Kampfstoff.
nonpersistent chemical munitions Luftkampfstoffmunition *f.*
nonrecoverable unbrauchbar, nicht instandsetzbar.
non-rigid airship unstarres Luftschiff.
nonskid chain Gleitschutzkette *f*
nonskid device Gleitschutzmittel *n* *(MT).*
nonskid tread Gleitschutz *m* *(MT).*
nonstop flight Ohnehaltflug *m* *(Avn).*
nonsystematic error zufälliger Fehler.
nontoxic agent nicht giftig wirkender Kampfstoff, Reizstoff *m* *(CWS).*
nontransportable nicht transportfähig.
normal barrage Sperrfeuer *n* *(Arty).*
normal height of burst richtige Sprenghöhe, normale Sprenghöhe *(Gunnery).*
normal impact senkrechtes Auftreffen *(Ballistics).*
normal landing Dreipunktlandung *f*
normal position Normalstellung *f* *(Mech).*
normal rating *(Mtr)* Dauerleistung *f*
normal sitting position sitzender Anschlag *(MG).*
north Norden *m* *(point of compass)*; Nordrichtung *f* *(direction).*
North Star Polarstern *m.*
nose Bug *m*, Rumpfbug *m*, Rumpfspitze *f*, Rumpfnase *f* *(Ap fuselage)*; Nase *f* *(anatomy).*
noseband Nasenriemen *m* *(harness).*
nosebleed Nasenbluten *n.*
nose clamp Nasenklammer *f* *(gas mask).*
nose compartment vordere Kanzel, Bugkanzel *f* *(Ap).*
nose dive Kopfsturz *m* *(Avn).*
nose fuze Kopfzünder *m* *(bomb).*
nose gun Bug-Maschinengewehr *n.*
nose gunner Bugschütze *m* *(Ap, Tk).*
nose-gun station Bugstand *m* *(Ap).*
noseheavy kopflastig, vorderlastig
nose irritant Nasenrachenreizstoff *m* *(sternutator)* *(CWS).*
nose-over Kopfstand *m* *(Avn).*
nose section of shell Kopfteil *n*
nose spray vorderer Sprengkegel *(air burst).*
nose turret vordere Kanzel, Bugkanzel *f* *(Ap).*
nostrils Nüstern *fpl* *(horse).*
notarized beglaubigt *(documents).*
notice of induction Einberufungskarte *f.*
notify benachrichtigen.
notify next of kin die nächsten Angehörigen verständigen, die nächsten Verwandten verständigen.
nozzle Düse *f*, Spritzdüse *f.*
nuisance raid Störungsflug *m*, Störflug *m*, Störeinsatz *m* *(Avn).*
nuisance raider Störflugzeug *n*, Störflieger *m* *(Ap).*
number Nummer *f*, Zahl *f*, Ziffer *f.*
number of personnel Kopfstärke *f* *(of a unit).*
number of prisoners Gefangenenziffer *f.*
numerical value Zahlenwert *m.*
nurse Krankenschwester *f.*
nurse balloon Ballonamme *f* *(for supplying gas).*
Nurse Corps *See* Army Nurse Corps.
nut Schraubenmutter *f*, Mutter *f* *(Mech).*

O

Oak Leaf Cluster Eichenlaub *n* *(decoration).*
oakum Werg *n.*
oar Ruder *n.*
oath of enlistment Diensteid *m*, Fahneneid *m.*
obedience Gehorsam *m.*
objective Ziel *n*, Kampfziel *n*; Angriffsziel *n* *(of an attack)*; Zweck *m* *(purpose).*
objective lens Ausblick *m.*
objective-lens socket Ausblickstutzen
objective plane Zielfläche *f* *(Gunnery).*
objective point Treffpunkt *m*, Aufschlagpunkt *m* *(point of impact)*; Zielpunkt *m* *(Tac).*
objective-prism housing Ausblickprismengehäuse *n* *(BC telescope).*
obligation Pflicht *f.*
oblique schräg, schief.
oblique fire Schrägfeuer *n.*
oblique photograph Schrägaufnahme *f* *(aerial Photo).*
obscure situation ungeklärte Lage *(Tac).*
observation Beobachtung *f*, Nahaufklärung *f*; Glasbeobachtung *f* *(with field glass or telescope).*
observation airplane Naherkunder *m*, Nahaufklärungsflugzeug *n.*
observation area Beobachtungsbereich *m* *(Arty).*
observation aviation Nahaufklärungsflieger *mpl.*
observation balloon Beobachtungsballon *m.*
observation battalion Beobachtungsabteilung *f* *(Arty).*
observation battery Beobachtungsbatterie *f* *(Arty).*
observation camp Beobachtungslager *n*, Beobachtungsstation *f.*
observation car Beobachtungswagen *m* *(MT)*; Aussichtswagen *m* *(RR).*
observation group Nahaufklärungsgruppe *f* *(Avn).*
observation mine Beobachtungsmine *f*, Grundmine *f* *(Nav).*
observation mission Aufklärungsaufgabe *f*, Aufklärungsauftrag *m.*
observation of fire Feuerbeobachtung *f*, Schußbeobachtung *f* *(Arty).*
observation of the enemy Feindbeobachtung *f.*
observation point Beobachtungspunkt *m.*
observation post Beobachtungsstelle *f* *(Arty)*; Flugwache *f* *(AWS)*; Beobachtungsstand *m* *(station or position)*; Baumbeobachtungsstand *m* *(in a tree).*
observation post system Beobachtungsnetz *n* *(Arty).*
observation post—target line Linie Beobachtungsstelle-Ziel *(Gunnery).*
observation slit Sehschlitz *m.*
observation squadron Nahaufklärerstaffel *f* *(Avn).*
observation station Beobachtungsstelle *f* *(Arty)*; Flugwache *f* *(AWS).*
observation tower Aussichtsturm *m.*
observatory Warte *f*, Sternwarte *f.*
observe beobachten.
observed fire beobachtetes Feuer, beobachtetes Schießen.
observed-fire chart Zieltafel für beobachtetes Schießen.
observer Beobachter *m*; Orter *m* *(navigator-observer, Avn)*; Luftspäher *m* *(AWS).*
observer's basket Beobachtungskorb *m* *(Bln).*
observer telescope Beobachterfernrohr *n.*
obsolete veraltet.
obstacle Hindernis *n*, Sperre *f.*
obstacle construction Hindernisbau
obstacle-construction equipment Sperrmittel *n.*
obstacle construction squad Hindernistrupp *m.*
obstacle course Hindernisstrecke *f*, Hindernisbahn *f.*
obstacle demolition party Hindernissprengtrupp *m* *(Engr).*
obstacle field Sperrfeld *n.*
obstacle light Hindernisfeuer *n* *(Avn).*
obstacle line Sperrlinie *f.*
obstruction Hindernis *n*, Sperre *f* *(obstacle)*; Hemmung *f*, Sperrung *f* *(Mech).*
obstruction light Hindernisfeuer *n* *(Avn).*
obturation Lidern *n.*
obturator Liderung *f* *(G).*
obtuse angle stumpfer Winkel.
occluded front Okklusion *f* *(Met).*
occlusion Okklusion *f* *(Met).*
occulter Blende *f* *(SL).*
occupation Besetzung *f*, Okkupation *f*; Einnahme *f* *(capture or conquest)*; Inbesitznahme *f* *(taking possession).*
occupation of position Instellunggehen *n* *(Tac).*
occupation troops Besatzungstruppen
occupied area Stellung *f* *(Tac)*; besetztes Gebiet *(territory).*
occupied territory besetztes Gebiet.
occupy besetzen, einnehmen *(a locality).*
ocean Ozean *m*, Meer *n*, See *f.*
ocean-going tug Hochseeschlepper *m.*
octane number Oktanzahl *f.*
octane rating Oktanwert *m.*
octant Oktant *m*, Libellensextant *m* *(Air Navigation).*
odometer Kilometerzähler *m* *(MT).*
odor Geruch *m.*
odor-detection training agent Übungsriechstoff *m* *(CWS).*
odorless geruchlos.
off aus *(a switch, etc.).*
off-carrier position Ausladeplatz *m.*
off-course correction Kursverbesserung *f* *(Air Navigation).*
off duty wachfrei, dienstfrei.
offense Übertretung *f*, Vergehen *n*, Verfehlung *f.*
offensive Offensive *f*, Angriff *m.*
offensive action Angriffsaktion *f*, Angriffshandlung *f* *(Tac).*
offensive combat Angriffsgefecht *n.*
offensive defense aktive Abwehr, offensive Verteidigung.
offensive mission Angriffsaufgabe *f.*
offensive operations Angriffsoperationen *fpl.*
offensively angriffsweise *(Tac).*
off-field landing Außenlandung *f*
off horse Handpferd *n.*
office Amt *n* *(function and place)*; Bureau *n* *(place).*
Office of Civilian Defense Luftschutzamt *n* *(USA).*
officer Offizier *m.*
officer candidate Offiziersanwärter *m.*
Officer Candidate School Kriegsschule *f.*
officer of the day Offizier vom Tagesdienst.
officer of the guard Offizier vom Ortsdienst.
officer of the line Truppenoffizier *m.*
officer on duty Offizier vom Dienst.
officer prisoner kriegsgefangener Offizier.
officers' mess Offizierskasino *n*, Kasino *n*; Offizierheim *n* *(mess and quarters).*
officers' quarters Offizierheim *n* *(quarters and mess).*
Officers' Reserve Corps Reserveoffizierkorps *n* *(USA).*
officer training course Führerkurs *m.*
office supplies Büromaterial *n.*
official *n* Beamter *m.*
official *adj* amtlich, dienstlich.
official correspondence amtlicher Schriftverkehr.
official envelope amtlicher Briefumschlag.
official papers Aktenmaterial *n.*
off limits verbotenes Lokal.
being off limits Besuch eines verbotenen Lokals.
offset Höhenunterschied *m* *(Surv).*
offshore side Strombord *m* *(Pon).*
ogive Bogenspitze *f* *(Am).*
ogive of shell Geschoßspitze *f.*
ohmmeter Ohmmeter *n*, Widerstandsmesser *m.*
oil *n* Öl *n.*
oil *v* ölen, einölen.
oil bomb Ölbombe *f.*
oilcan Ölbüchse *f.*
oilcloth Wachstuch *n.*
oil container Ölkanister *m* *(Ap, MT).*
oil cooler Ölkühler *m*, Schmierstoffkühler *m* *(Mtr).*
oil drain Ölablaß *m* *(Mtr).*
oiler Öltropfer *m* *(R cleaning).*
oil-filler plug Einfüllstutzen *m* *(recoil mechanism)*; Öleinfüll-Verschraubung *f* *(Mtr).*
oil film Ölfilm *m*, Schmierölschicht *f.*
oil gage Öldruckmesser *m* *(pressure)*; Öldstandanzeiger *m* *(level)*; Ölthermometer *n* *(temperature).*
oil level Ölstand *m* *(Mtr).*
oil level gage Schmierstoffvorratsmesser *m* *(Ap).*
oil level plug Ölstandschraube *f* *(Mtr).*
oil overflow Ölüberlauf *m* *(Mtr).*
oil overflow outlet Öl-Überlaufbohrung *f* *(Mtr).*
oil pan Ölwanne *f* *(Mtr).*
oil pressure gage Schmierstoffdruckmesser *m*, Ölmanometer *n* *(Ap, Mtr).*
oil pump Ölpumpe *f.*
oil refinery Ölraffinerie *f.*
oil-resistant ölbeständig.
oilskin Wachstaffet *m.*
oil-storage depot Öllager *n.*
oil tank Ölbehälter *m*, Schmierstoffbehälter *m*, Öltank *m* *(Ap, Mtr).*
oil temperature gage Ölthermometer *n* *(Mtr).*
oiltight öldicht.
oil well Ölbohrloch *n.*
ointment Salbe *f.*
old guard alte Wache.
oleo strut Ölfederstrebe *f* *(Ap).*
olive drab olivgrün.
omnidirectional antenna Antenne mit Rundwirkung.
omnidirectional beacon Kreisfunkfeuer *n* *(Rad).*
on ein *(a switch, etc.).*
on-course zone Anflugsektor *m* *(Inst landing).*
on duty diensttuend, im Dienst.
one-man shelter tent Einerzelt *n.*
one-way Morse-code transmission einseitiges Tasten *(Rad, Tg).*
one-way (radio) telephone transmission einseitiges Sprechen.
one-way radio traffic einseitiger Funkverkehr.
one-way street Einbahnstraße *f.*
one-way telegraphy einseitige Telegraphie.
one-way traffic Einbahnverkehr *m* *(MT).*
on guard auf Wache *(guard duty)*; auf der Hut *(alert, watchful).*
onion Zwiebel *f.*
on leave beurlaubt, auf Urlaub.
"On the double!" "Marsch! Marsch!"
open city offene Stadt.
open column zerlegte Marschkolonne.
open culvert Querrinne *f* *(road).*
open fire Feuer eröffnen.
open flank offene Flanke, nicht geschützte Flanke *(Tac).*
open formation geöffnete Marschordnung.
opening Durchlaß *m*, Öffnung *f.*
opening of fire Feuereröffnung *f* *(Arty).*
open position offene Stellung, nicht geschützte Stellung *(Tac).*
open tail Gitterschwanz *m* *(Ap).*
open traverse Streckenzug *m* *(Surv).*
operating building Operationsbaracke *f* *(surgical unit).*
operating current Betriebsstrom *m* *(Elec).*
operating device Bedienungseinrichtung *f.*
operating directions Bedienungsanweisung *f.*
operating handle Öffnerhebel *m* *(G).*
operating instructions Bedienungsvorschrift *f.*
operating lever Öffnerhebel *m* *(G).*
operating maintenance nach Bedarf durchgeführte Instandsetzung.
operating panel Bedienungsplatte *f* *(Rad).*
operating range Fahrbereich *m* *(MT, Tk).*
operating switch Bedienungsschalter *m* *(Elec)*; Betriebsschalter *m* *(Tp).*
operation Unternehmung *f*, Operation *f*, Gefechtshandlung *f* *(Tac)*; Betrieb *m* *(Rad, Tp, Mech)*; Operation *f* *(Med).*
operational operativ *(Tac).*
operational line Operationslinie *f.*
operations Operationen *fpl* *(Tac).*
Operations Division Operationsabteilung *f* *(USA)* *(corresponds roughly to the department of* Oberquartiermeister I *in the German General Staff).*
operations map Operationskarte *f.*
operations order Operationsbefehl *m.*
operations plan Operationsplan *m.*
operator Fernsprecher *m* *(Tp).*
operator's answering jack Abfrageklinke *f* *(Tp).*
operator's permit Führerschein *m* *(MT)*; Wehrmachtsführerschein *m* *(Mil).*
operator's telephone Abfrageapparat
opiate schmerzstillendes Mittel.
opponent Gegner *m.*
oppose Widerstand leisten.
opposed-piston engine Gegenkolbenmotor *m*, Boxermotor *m.*
opposing sides Parteien *fpl* *(Tng).*
opposition Widerstand *m.*
optical sight optisches Zielgerät *(Ord).*
optician Optiker *m.*
oral message mündliche Mitteilung, mündliche Meldung.
oral order mündlicher Befehl.
order *n* Befehl *m*; Sonderverfügungen *fpl* *(special orders)*; besondere Anordnungen *fpl* *(administrative details in combat orders, fragmentary orders in this sense).*
order *v* befehlen *(command)*; verordnen, anordnen, bestimmen *(prescribe)*; bestellen *(goods, meals).*
"Order, arms!" "Gewehr, ab!"
orderly Ordonnanz *f.*
orderly officer Ordonnanzoffizier *m.*
orderly room Schreibstube *f.*
order of battle Kriegsgliederung *f.*
order of march Marschfolge *f.*
order of the day Tagesbefehl *m.*
Order of the Purple Heart Purpurherz *n* *(USA).*
orders conference Flugbesprechung *f*, Einsatzbesprechung *f* *(Avn).*
ordinary telephone call gewöhnliches Ferngespräch.
ordinate Ordinate *f*, Achse *f.*
ordinate of the trajectory Flughöhe *f* *(Ballistics).*
ordnance Waffen und Gerät.
ordnance battalion Feldzeugbataillon
ordnance collecting point Gerätesammelstelle *f.*
Ordnance Department Waffenamt *n.*
ordnance depot Arsenal *n*, Feldzeuglager *n.*
ordnance matériel Waffen und Gerät.
ordnance officer Waffenoffizier *m*, Geräteoffizier *m.*
ordnance park Geschützpark *m.*
Ordnance School Heereswaffenmeister- und Heeresfeuerwerkerschule
ordnance service Geräte-, Waffen- und Munitionsabteilung *f* *(USA).*
ordnance stores Lagerbestände der Feldzeuginspektion.
organic Stamm-.
organization Organisation *f*, Gliederung *f*, Einrichtung *f.*
organizational equipment Kriegsausrüstung einer Einheit.
Organization and Training Division Organisations- und Ausbildungsamt im Generalstab des Heeres *(USA).*
organization chart Gliederungsübersicht *f.*
organization commander Kommandeur eines Truppenteils.
organization of march Marschgliederung *f.*

organization of the ground Geländeverstärkung *f (Tac).*
organized position befestigte Feldstellung.
Organized Reserves Organisierte Reserve *(USA).*
organized resistance organisierter Widerstand, planmäßiger Widerstand.
organized tactical locality Stützpunkt *m.*
orient *v* sich zurechtfinden, sich orientieren *(get one's bearings)*; ausrichten, einstellen *(an Inst)*; eine Karte in die Nordrichtung einstellen *(a map).*
orientation Orientierung *f*, Ausrichtung *f*; Einrichten *n (of a map).*
orientation by map Geländeorientierung *f (Surv).*
orientation card Flugmelderose *f*, Melderose *f (AWS).*
orientation course Schulungskursus
orientation point Richtungspunkt *m*, Orientierungspunkt *m (Surv).*
orienting line Richtungslinie *f*, Orientierungslinie *f (Gunnery) (Surv).*
orienting point *See* **orientation point.**
origin Ursprung *m*, Ausgangspunkt
original model Urbaumuster *n (Ap, Tk, etc.).*
original position Ausgangslage *f (Mech).*
origin of the trajectory Mündung *f (Ballistics).*
orographic orographisch *(Met).*
orthochromatic farbtonrichtig, orthochromatisch.
orthographic projection orthographische Projektion.
oscillate pendeln, schwingen.
oscillating circuit Schwingungskreis *m (Rad).*
oscillation Schwingung *f (Elec, Rad)*; Nadelschwankungen *fpl (oscillations of compass needle).*
oscillator Schwingungserzeuger *m (Rad).*
oscillator-amplifier Hörsaalsummer *m (code practice).*
oscillator-amplifier transmitter zweistufiger Sender *(Rad).*
oscillogram Knallbild *n*, Oszillogramm *n (sound ranging).*
oscillograph Schallaufnahmegerät *n*, Schallmeßaufnahmegerät *n (sound ranging).*
oscilloscope Oszilloskop *n (Elec, Rad).*
osnaburg Sackleinen *n.*
Otto engine Ottomotor *m (Mtr).*
outboard motor Aubomotor *m*, Außenbordmotor *m.*
outbreak Aufruhr *f (riot)*; Ausbruch *m (of an epidemic, hostilities).*
outcome of battle Ausgang des Kampfes, Schlachtentscheidung *f (Tac).*
outdoors im Freien.
outer cover Ballonhülle *f (Bln).*
outer harbor äußerer Hafen, außenhafen *m.*
outer sleeve Außenschieber *m (sleeve-type engine).*
outer steam tube Sperrohr *n (MG).*
outfit *n* Ausrüstung *f (equipment, etc.)*; Mannschaft *f (crew)*; Truppenteil *m (unit).*
outflank flankieren, überflügeln, umgehen.
outflanking maneuver Überflügelung
outgoing track Ausfahrgleis *n (RR).*
outguard Feldwache *f*, Feldposten *m.*
outlet Steckdose *f (Elec)*; Auslaß *m*, Auslauf *m*, Durchlaß *m (for liquids, etc.).*
outlet valve Ausatemventil *n (gas mask).*
outline *n* Umriß *m*; Entwurf *m (sketch).*
outlying picket Außenwache *f.*
outnumber an Zahl übertreffen, zahlenmäßig überlegen sein.
out of action außer Gefecht (gesetzt).
"Out of action!" "Abblenden!" *(AA searchlight).*
out of alignment dejustiert *(boresight adjustment).*
out of gear außer Eingriff *(MT).*
out of order außer Betrieb.
out of range außer Schußweite.
out of sight außer Sicht.
outpost Vorposten *m.*
outpost area Vorpostengelände *n*, Vorfeld *n*, Vorgelände *n (Tac).*
outpost duty Vorpostendienst *m.*
outpost engagement Vorpostengefecht *n.*
outpost line vorderste Sicherungslinie.
outpost line of resistance Widerstandslinie der Vorposten *(Tac).*
outpost observer Vorwarner *m (sound ranging).*
outpost position Vorpostenstellung *f.*
outpost reserve Vorpostenreserve *f.*
outpost-sector boundary Vorpostenabschnittsgrenze *f.*
outpost station Vorwarnerstelle *f (sound ranging).*
outpost system Vorpostendienst *m.*
output Leistung *f (Mech).*
output transformer Ausgangstransformator *m (Rad).*
output voltage Ausgangsspannung *f.*
outrank einen höheren Rang bekleiden, den Vorrang haben.
outrigger Ausleger *m (for water craft)*; Holm *m (AA gun; plural:* Holme *or* Lafettenkreuz).
outrigger lock Holmzurrung *f (G).*
outrigger-type gun mount Kreuzlafette *f.*
outside antenna Außenantenne *f.*
outworks Außenbefestigungen *fpl*, Außenwerke *npl (Ft).*
oven Ofen *m*, Backofen *m.*
over *n* Weitschuß *m (Gunnery).*
over-all length Länge über alles.
overboard über Bord.
overcast bedeckt *(Met).*
overcoat Mantel *m*, Übermantel *m.*
overcome überwinden, überwältigen, übermannen.
overdrive Schnellgang *m (MT).*
overdrive transmission Schnellganggetriebe *n*, Schonganggetriebe *n (MT).*
overended shot Bodentreffer *m.*
overexposure Überbelichtung *f (Photo).*
overfall dam Überfallwehr *n.*
overflow *n* Überlauf *m.*
overflow pipe Überlaufrohr *n.*
overflow water Überschußwasser *n (dam).*
overhang *n* Überhang *m (MT).*
overhaul *v* überholen.
overhead antenna Luftdraht *m.*
overhead construction Hochbau *m (Tp line).*
overhead firing Überschießen eigener Truppen *(Gunnery).*
overhead firing table Überschießtafel *f (MG tripod).*
overhead line Freileitung *f (Tp).*
overhead line construction Hochbau von Leitungen *(Tp).*
overhead wire Luftkabel *n (Tp).*
overlap *n* Überdeckung *f (aerial Photo).*
overlay Planpause *f.*
overload überlasten.
overloading Übersteuerung *f (Elec, Rad)*; Überbeanspruchung *f (Mech).*
overpass Bahnüberführung *f*, Überführung *f (RR).*
overprint *n* Aufdruck *m.*
overseas cap Feldmütze *f.*
overseas expedition Übersee-Expedition *f.*
overseas operation Übersee-Unternehmung *f.*
overshoes Überschuhe *mpl.*
overshoot über etwas hinausschießen.
oversize tire Riesenluftreifen *m.*
overtake überholen, einholen.
overwhelm niederkämpfen.
oxyacetylene cutting Schneidbrennen
oxyacetylene torch Azetylensauerstoffbrenner *m.*
oxyacetylene welding Sauerstoffazetylenschweißung *f.*
oxygen Sauerstoff *m.*
oxygen apparatus Atemgerät *n*, Höhenatmer *m*, Sauerstoffgerät *n (Avn).*
oxygen breathing apparatus Sauerstoffschutzgerät *n*, Isoliergerät *n*, Selbstretter *m.*
oxygen cylinder Sauerstofflasche *f.*
oxygen mask Atemmaske *f (Avn).*

P

pace *n* Schritt *m.*
pace off abschreiten.
pack *n* Tornister *m*, Rückengepäck *n*; Traglast *f (Animal Transportation)*; Fallschirmsack *m (Prcht).*
pack *v* dichten, abdichten *(seal)*; packen *(a trunk, etc.).*
package Bündel *n*, Paket *n.*
pack animal Tragtier *n.*
pack-animal train Tragtierkolonne *f.*
pack artillery Gebirgsartillerie *f.*
pack assembly Fallschirmsack *m (Prcht).*
pack frame Tragegestell *n.*
pack horse Tragpferd *n.*
pack howitzer Gebirgskanone *f.*
packing Packung *f*, Dichtung *f (Mech).*
pack reel Rückentrage für Feldkabel.
pack rest Ausleger *m (harness).*
pack rope Packstrick *m (harness).*
pack saddle Packsattel *m*, Tragsattel *m.*
pack strap Packriemen *m (harness).*
pack train Tragtierkolonne *f.*
pack transportation Tragtierbeförderung *f.*
pad Block *m*, Schreibeblock *m (writing)*; Kissen *n*, Polster *n (Clo, harness, etc.).*
padded unterpolstert.
paddle *n* Stechruder *n.*
padlock Vorhängeschloß *n.*
pail Eimer *m*, Kübel *m.*
paint *n* Farbe *f*, Anstrich *m.*
paint *v* anstreichen.
paint brush Pinsel *m*, Anstrichpinsel *m.*
palm Handfläche *f.*
pan Pfanne *f.*
pancake *v (Avn)* absacken, durchsacken
pancake landing "Bumslandung" *f.*
panel Signaltuch *n*, Tuchzeichen *n (Sig C)*; Hüllenbahn *f (Bln)*; Stoffbahn *f (Prcht).*
panel code Schlüssel für Tuchzeichen.
panel signal Sichtzeichen *n*, Tuchzeichen *n.*
panoramic camera Panoramakammer
panoramic photograph Rundbild *n.*
panoramic sight Rundblickfernrohr
panoramic sketch Ansichtsskizze *f.*
panoramic telescope Rundblickfernrohr *n.*
pantograph Storchschnabel *m*, Pantograph *n.*
paper Papier *n.*
paper-strip method Papierstreifenverfahren *n (aerial Photo).*
paper work Schreibarbeit *f.*
parabola Parabel *f.*
parabolic parabelförmig, parabelähnlich.
parabolic mirror Parabolspiegel *m.*
parachute Fallschirm *m*, Schirm *m.*
parachute battalion Fallschirmjägerbataillon *n.*
parachute canopy Schirm *m.*
parachute equipment Fallschirmgerät *n.*
parachute flare Fallschirmleuchtkugel *f*, Fallschirmrakete *f (ground Sig)*; Leuchtfallschirm *m*, Fallschirmleuchtbombe *f (Ap Sig).*
parachute harness Fallschirmgurt *m*, Gurtwerk *n.*
parachute jump Fallschirmabsprung
parachute jump suit Sprungkombination *f.*
parachute lobe Zusatzfallschirm *m.*
parachute pack Fallschirmsack *m.*
parachute regiment Fallschirmjägerregiment *n.*
parachute rigger Fallschirmwart *m.*
parachute skirt Ringfallschirm *m.*
parachute tower Fallschirmturm *m*, Fallschirmabsprungturm *m.*
parachute troops Fallschirmjäger *mpl*, Fallschirmtruppen *fpl.*
parachutist Fallschirmjäger *m*, Fallschirmschütze *m*, Fallschirmspringer
parade Parade *f.*
parade ground Paradeplatz *m*, Exerzierplatz *m.*
parados Rückendeckung *f*, Rückenwehr *f (Ft).*
parallax Parallaxe *f.*
parallax offset mechanism Verbesserungsgerät *n (sound locator).*
parallel *adj* gleichlaufend, parallel; e n t s p r e c h e n d *(corresponding)*; gleich, ähnlich *(similar).*
parallel-chord truss Parallel-Fachwerkträger *m (Engr).*
parallel connection Nebeneinanderschaltung *f*, Parallelschaltung *f (Elec).*
parallel line Gleichlaufende *f.*
parallel of latitude Breitenkreis *m.*
parallelogram linkage system Visiergestänge *n*, Parallelogrammgestänge *n (AA sight).*
paralyze lähmen *(Tac).*
parapet Brustwehr *f (trench)*; Wehr *f (G emplacement).*
parasite drag schädlicher Widerstand *(Avn).*
parasol monoplane Schirmeindecker
parasol-type antenna Gitterantenne *f.*
paratrooper *See* **parachutist.**
paratroops *See* **parachute troops.**
paravane Minenabweiser *m*, Räumotter *f*, Otter *f.*
parent unit Stammtruppenteil *m*, Stammeinheit *f.*
park *n* Park *m.*
park *v* parken, abstellen.
parka Anorak *m*, Schneehemd *n (Clo).*
parking area Abstellplatz *m (Adrm, MT).*
parking light Parklicht *n (MT).*
parking place Abstellplatz *m.*
parlementaire Unterhändler *m.*
parley Unterredung *f*, Verhandlung *f*, Unterhandlung *f.*
parole *n* Ehrenwort *n.*
parry *n* Abwehr *f*, Fangstoß *m.*
parry *v* parieren.
part *n* Teil *m (portion)*; Zubehörteil *m (Tech).*
participation Beteiligung *f*, Teilnahme *f.*
partisan warfare kleiner Krieg.
party Kommando *n (Tac)*; Teilnehmer *m (Tp).*
party of guides Einweisungskommando *n.*
pass Erlaubnisschein *m*, Urlaubsschein *m (leave)*; Paß *m (Top)*; Vorbeiflug *m (Avn).*
passable gangbar; fahrbar *(for vehicles).*
passage Durchlaß *m*, Durchgang *m*; Gasse *f (through a mine field, etc.).*
passenger Fahrgast *m*, Passagier *m*, Fluggast *m (Avn).*
passenger capacity Tragfähigkeit *f (MT).*
passenger car Personenkraftwagen *m (MT).*
passenger ferry Personenfähre *f.*
passenger seat Fluggastsitz *m (Ap).*
passenger station Personenbahnhof *m (RR).*
passenger vehicle Personenkraftfahrzeug *n (MT).*
passing Überholung *f (MT).*
passing flight Vorbeiflug *m.*
pass in review *n* Vorbeimarsch *m*, Parademarsch *m.*
pass in review *v* vorbeimarschieren, defilieren.
passive air defense Luftschutz *m.*
passport Paß *m.*
password Kennwort *n*, Parole *f*, Losung *f*, Kampfruf *m*, Verständigungsmittel *n.*
paste Klebstoff *m*, Klebemittel *n*; Kleister *m (starch)*; Fischleim *m (fish glue)*; Kitt *m (putty).*
pastern Fessel *f (horse).*
pastern joint Fesselgelenk *n (horse).*
patching cord Vermittlungsschnur *f (Tp).*
path Pfad *m*, Weg *m*; Bahn *f (of a projectile)*; Fußweg *m (footpath)*; Saumpfad *m (for pack animals)*; Schleichweg *m (hidden trail)*; Fahrweg *m (for carts)*; Holzweg *m (dead-end loggers' road).*
path-of-flight pointer Gegnerpfeil *m*, Flugrichtungspfeil *m (reflector sight).*
patient *n* Patient *m*, Kranker *m.*
patrol *n* Spähtrupp *m*; Patrouillenflug *m (Avn).*
patrol *v* abstreifen *(a road, area, etc.).*
patrol activity Aufklärertätigkeit *f*, Spähtrupptätigkeit *f*, Patrouillentätigkeit *f.*
patrol boat Wachboot *n.*
patrol bomber Seeaufklärer *m.*
patrol leader Spähtruppführer *m.*
patrolling Patrouillenflug *m (Avn).*
patrol message Spähtruppmeldung *f.*
patrol vessel Bewachungsfahrzeug *n*, Wachschiff *n (Nav).*
pattern Streuungsbild *n*, Treffbild *n (Gunnery)*; Modell *n (foundry).*
pattern bombing Abstandwerfen *n.*
paulin Decke *f*, Plane *f.*
paved road gepflasterte Straße, Straße mit fester Decke.
pawl Sperrklinke *f (Mech).*
pay *n* Sold *m*, Besoldung *f*; Lagergeld *n (PW).*
pay grade Wehrsoldgruppe *f.*
pay load Nutzlast *f.*
payment Zahlung *f*, Bezahlung *f*; Besoldung *f (wages).*
pay out auslegen *(a rope, etc.).*
pay roll Soldliste *f.*
PD *See* **phenyldichlorarsine.**
peace Friede *m.*
peace negotations Friedensverhandlungen *fpl.*
peace organization Friedensorganisation *f (of Armed Forces).*
peace strength Friedensstärke *f (of Armed Forces).*
peace training Friedensausbildung *f.*
peak Gipfel *m*, Spitze *f (pointed)*, Kuppe *f (rounded).*
peak value Scheitelwert *m*, Höchstwert *m (Elec).*
pedal Fußhebel *m (Ord, MT).*
pedal-operated generating unit Tretsatz *m (Elec).*
pedal-operated generator Tretmotor *m.*
pedestal Auflager *n (Bdg)*; Sockel *m (G).*
pedestal mount Sockellafette *f (G).*
pedometer Schrittmesser *m.*
"peep" "Kübel" *m.*
peephole Panzerscharte *f*, Sehöffnung *f (Ft, Tk).*
peephole protector Sehklappe *f (Tk).*
peep sight Diopterloch *n.*
peep slit Sehschlitz *m (Tk).*
pelorus Peilaufsatz *m (Avn).*
pen Feder *f.*
penalty Strafe *f.*
penalty envelope frankierter Dienstumschlag.
pencil Bleistift *m.*
pencil sharpener Bleistiftspitzer *m*, Bleistiftspitzmaschine *f.*
penetrate eindringen, durchdringen, durchstoßen *(Tac)*; durchbrechen, durchschlagen *(armor, etc.)*; einfliegen *(Avn).*
penetrating power Durchschlagskraft *f (Am).*
penetration Einbruch *m (Tac)*;
penetration and mining effect Durchschlags- und Minenwirkung *f (Am).*
penetration by assault Durchstoß *m.*
penetration in depth Tiefenstoß *m (Tac).*
peninsula Halbinsel *f.*
penis Penis *m*, Glied *n*, männliches Glied.
penitentiary Zuchthaus *n.*
pennant Stander *m*, Wimpel *m.*
pension Ruhegehalt *n.*
pepper Pfeffer *m.*
per cent Prozent, vom Hundert.
percentage Prozentsatz *m.*
percussion Aufschlag *m.*
percussion cap Zündhütchen *n (Am).*
percussion charge Schlagladung *f.*
percussion composition Zündsatz *m.*
percussion fuze Aufschlagzünder *m*
percussion plunger Zündbolzen *m (powder-train time fuze, Am).*
percussion primer Zündhütchen *n (fuze).*
per diem allowance Tagegeld *n.*
perforated powder Röhrenpulver *n (Am).*
performance Leistung *f*; Nutzleistung *f (Mech)*; Schußleistung *f (Ord)*; Zugleistung *f (Trac)*; Aufführung *f (theater).*
performance-type glider Leistungssegelflugzeug *n (Avn).*
perimeter Umkreis *m*, Umfang *m.*
perimeter positions Randstellungen *fpl (Tac).*
period Periode *f (Elec).*
periople Trachte *f (hoof).*
periphery Umkreis *m.*
periscope Periskop *n*, Sehrohr *n*; Winkelspiegel *m*, Optik *f (Tk).*
permanent ortsfest, fest eingebaut, dauernd, ständig.
permanent emplacement ortsfeste Geschützstellung.
permanent ferrying operations Dauerfährbetrieb *m.*
permanent field-telephone line Felddauerlinie *f.*
permanent fortification ständige Befestigung, Befestigungswerk *n*, Werk *n.*
permanent line Dauerleitung *f*, Dauerlinie *f (Tp).*
permanent magnet Dauermagnet *m.*
permanent rank Dienstgrad mit Patent.
permanent way Oberbau *m (RR).*
permission Erlaubnis *f*, Bewilligung *f*; Einwilligung *f (consent).*
permit *n* Fahrausweis *m (traveling)*; Passierschein *m (pass)*; Urlaubsschein *m (leave pass).*
permit *v* erlauben, gestatten, zulassen; dürfen *(to be allowed).*
perpendicular *n* Senkrechte *f*, Lotrechte *f.*
perpendicular *adj* senkrecht, lotrecht.
persistency Seßhaftigkeit *f*, Wirkungsdauer *f (CWS).*
persistent chemical warfare agent seßhafter Kampfstoff, Geländekampfstoff *m.*
personal effects persönliche Sachen, persönliche Gegenstände.
personal salute persönlicher Salut.
personal staff persönliche Adjutanten.
personnel Personal *n*, Leute *pl*; Mannschaften *fpl (enlisted Pers below the rank of Cpl).*
personnel carrier Mannschaftstransportwagen *m*, Mannschaftswagen *m*, Personenkraftwagen *m*, Personenkraftfahrzeug *n (MT).*
personnel consultant Heerespsychologe *m.*
Personnel Division Heerespersonalamt *n*, Personalamt *n.*
personnel error Beobachtungsfehler
personnel roster Stammrolle *f.*
personnel section Personalabteilung
perspective projection perspektivische Projektion.
perspective spatial model Raumbildmodell *n (aerial Photo).*
petition *n* Gesuch *n*, Bittschrift *f.*
petroleum Erdöl *n.*
petty officer Maat *m (Nav).*
phantom circuit Doppelsprechschaltung *f*, Viererleitung *f (Tp).*
phantom connection Viererschaltung *f (Tp).*
phantoming Doppelsprechen *n (Tp).*
pharmacist Apotheker *m.*
phase Abschnitt *m (Tac)*; Phase *f (Elec)*; Ausbildungsstufe *f (Tng)*; Entwicklungsstufe *f (of development).*
initial phase Auftakt *m (Tac).*
in phases abschnittsweise *(Tac).*
phase difference Phasendifferenz *f*, Phasenunterschied *m.*
phase line *(Tac)* Angriffszwischenziel *n*
phenol Karbolsäure *f.*
phenyldichlorarsine Phenyldichlorarsin *n*, Pfiffikus *n (CWS).*
phonetic alphabet Buchstabiertafel *f (Com).*
phonograph Grammophon *n*, Sprechmaschine *f.*
phonograph pick-up unit Schallplatten-Abtastdose *f.*
phonograph record Schallplatte *f.*
phosgene Chlorkohlenoxyd *n*, Phosgen *n (CWS).*
phosphorus Phosphor *m.*
phosphorus bomb Phosphorbombe *f*, Phosphorfliegerbombe *f.*

phosphorus grenade Phosphorhandgranate *f.*
photo-charting Luftbildherstellung *f (aerial Photo).*
photo-electric cell Photozelle *f.*
photoflash bomb Blitzlichtbombe *f.*
photogrammetry Bildmeßwesen *n,* Photogrammetrie *f.*
photograph *n* Lichtbild *n.*
photograph *v* lichtbilden, photographieren; eine Aufnahme machen *(take a snapshot).*
photographer Photograph *m,* Lichtbildner *m.*
photographic interpretation Luftbildauswertung *f.*
photographic map Luftbildkarte *f.*
photographic mapping photographische Kartenaufnahme.
photographic officer Bildoffizier *m.*
photographic overlay Lichtbildpause
photographic reconnaissance Bildaufklärung *f,* Bilderkundung *f.*
photographic strip Luftbildreihe *f,* Filmstreifen *m.*
photography Photographie *f,* Lichtbildwesen *n.*
photomap Luftbildplan *m.*
photostat *n* Photokopie *f.*
photostat *v* photokopieren.
photo-survey Geländeaufnahme *f.*
phototopography Meßbildverfahren *n,* Lichtbildmessung *f,* Erdmessung *f,* Phototopographie *f.*
physical condition Gesundheitszustand *m.*
physical examination ärztliche Untersuchung.
physical fitness Tauglichkeit *f.*
physical inspection Gesundheitsappell *m.*
pibal Wetterbericht vom Pilotballon *(Met).*
pibal equipment Pilotballonaufstieggerät *n (Met).*
pickaxe Beilpicke *f,* Spitzhacke *f.*
picked troops Kerntruppen *fpl.*
picket Pfahl *m,* Pikettpfahl *m (stake).*
picket line Furagierleine *f,* Halfterstrick *m.*
pick mattock Klapphacke *f.*
pick-up Schallplatten-Abtastdose *f (phonograph).*
pick-up arm Tonarm *m (phonograph).*
pick-up assembly Aufnahmegerät *n (Ap).*
pick-up hook Aufnahmehaken *m (Ap).*
pick-up unit Abtastdose *f (phonograph).*
picric acid Pikrinsäure *f.*
picture Bild *n.*
picture point Bildpunkt *m (aerial Photo).*
piece Artilleriegeschütz *n,* Feldgeschütz *n (Arty);* Gewehr *n (R);* Stück *n (fragment).*
piece of equipment Ausrüstungsstück *n,* Gerätstück *n,* Ausrüstungsgegenstand *m.*
pier Pfeiler *m (Bdg);* Pier *m,* Ladeplatz *m,* Anlegestelle *f;* Löschplatz *m (for unloading cargo).*
pierce durchbrechen, durchlöchern, durchstoßen.
pigeon Taube *f.*
pigeoneer Brieftaubenpfleger *m;* Brieftaubenmeister *m (with rank of Tech Sgt).*
pigeon loft Brieftaubenschlag *m,* Brieftaubenstelle *f.*
Pigeon Service Brieftaubendienst *m.*
pike Fahnenstange *f (flagpole).*
pile *n* Pfahl *m (Engr);* Brückenpfeiler *m (Bdg);* Haufen *m (irregular heap);* Stapel *m (regular heap).*
pile bent Pfahljoch *n (Bdg).*
pile-bent bridge Pfahljochbrücke *f.*
pile driver Ramme *f;* Zugramme *f*
pile-driver drophammer Rammbär *m (Engr).*
pile-driver frame Rammgerüst *n (Engr).*
pile-driver raft Rammfähre *f (Engr).*
pile-driver staging Rammbühne *f (Engr).*
pile-post obstacle Pfahlsperre *f (AT).*
pillage *n* Beute *f,* Plünderung *f.*
pillar Pfeiler *m (Engr).*
pill box betoniertes Maschinengewehrnest, Bunker *m (Ft).*
pill-box demolition party Schartensprengtrupp *m (Engr).*
pillow Kissen *n.*
pilot *n* Flieger *m,* Flugzeugführer *m (Avn);* Lotse *m (Nav).*
pilotage Bodennavigation *f,* Sichtnavigation *f,* Erdortung *f,* optische Peilung *(Air Navigation).*
pilot balloon Pilotballon *m (Met).*
pilot chart Fliegerkarte *f (Avn).*
pilot light Kontrollampe *f (Ap, MT).*
pilot parachute Hilfsschirm *m.*
pilot's certificate Fliegerzeugnis *n.*
pilot's cockpit Führersitz *m,* Führerstand *m,* Führerkanzel *f (Ap).*
pilot's compartment Führerraum *m (Ap).*
pilot's rating Fliegerzeugnis *n.*
pilot trainee Flugschüler *m.*
pilot training Fliegerschulung *f*
pin Stecknadel *f (plain pin);* Sicherheitsnadel *f (safety pin);* Stift *m,* Bolzen *m (Tech);* Pflock *m (stake).*
pincer attack Zangenangriff *m (Tac).*
pincer movement Zangenbewegung *f (Tac).*
pincers Kneifzange *f.*
pinch-bar Brechstange *f.*
pinion Ritzel *m (Mech).*
pinion and sector steering system Zahnstangenlenkung *f (MT).*
pinion shaft Ritzelwelle *f (Mech).*
pinning Fesselung *f (Tac).*
pin nozzle Zapfendüse *f (Mtr).*
pinpointing Herstellung von Einzelbildern *(aerial Photo).*
pinpoint photograph einzelnes Senkrechtbild *(aerial Photo).*
pintle Zughaken *m.*
pintle drawbar Zugstange *f.*
pintle nozzle Zapfendüse *f (Mtr).*
pioneer Pionier *m.*
pioneer and demolition platoon Pionierzug *m.*
pioneer tools Pionierwerkzeug *n.*
pioneer work Pionierarbeit *f.*
pipe *n* Rohr *n,* Leitung *f;* Schlauch *m (hose);* Pfeife *f (smoking).*
pipe cable Röhrenkabel *n*
pipe wrench Rohrzange *f.*
pistol Pistole *f.*
pistol ammunition Pistolenmunition
pistol belt Pistolengurt *m.*
pistol cartridge Pistolenpatrone *f.*
pistol course Pistolenausbildungskurs *m.*
pistol grip Handstütze *f.*
pistol holster Pistolentasche *f.*
pistol port Pistolenöffnung *f (Tk).*
pistol sharpshooter Pistolenscharfschütze *m.*
piston Kolben *m (Mech).*
piston displacement Hubraum *m,* Hubvolumen *n (Mtr).*
piston pin Kolbenbolzen *m (Mtr).*
piston ring Kolbenring *m.*
piston rod Kolbenstange *f,* Pleuelstange *f.*
piston stroke Kolbenhub *m.*
pit Grube *f.*
pitch *n* Gewindegang *m,* Steigung *f (Mech);* Propellersteigung *f (propeller);* Pech *n (tar-like substance);* Tonhöhe *f (sound).*
pitch-control mechanism Luftschraubenverstellgerät *n (propeller).*
pitch indicator Längsneigungsmesser *m (Ap).*
pith helmet Tropenhelm *m.*
pitot tube Pitotrohr *n,* Staudruckfahrtmesser *m.*
pivot *n* Drehzapfen *m (Mech);* Schwenkungspunkt *m (Tac).*
pivot *v* einschwenken *(Tac, drill).*
pivot inclination Achs(zapfen)sturz *m (MT).*
pivot man Flügelmann am Drehpunkt *(drill).*
pivot pin Lagerzapfen *m (trail spade);* Drehbolzen *m (Tech).*
pivot-type mount Pivotlafette *f (MG).*
place *n* Punkt *m (Tac);* Ort *m (locality).*
place mark Bodenpunkt *m,* Pfahl *m (Surv).*
plain text Klartext *m.*
plain-wire concertina Klaviersaitendrahtrolle *f,* K.-Rolle *f.*
plan *n* Plan *m;* Zeichnung *f (Tech).*
plan *v* planen, beabsichtigen.
plane *n* Ebene *f (surface);* Hobel *m (carpentry);* Flugzeug *n (Ap). See also* **airplane.**
plane of departure Schußebene *f (Gunnery).*
plane of fire Schußebene *f (Gunnery).*
plane of position Schußebene *f (at instant of firing) (AA Gunnery).*
plane of present position Visierebene *f (AA Gunnery).*
plane of propeller rotation Luftschraubenebene *f (Ap).*
plane table Kartenunterlage *f,* Meßtisch *m,* Planunterlage *f (Arty, Surv).*
plane table sheet Meßtischblatt *n.*
planetary gear Planetengetriebe *n,* Umlaufgetriebe *n (MT).*
planimeter Planimeter *n (Surv).*
planimetry Planimetrie *f.*
plank Bohle *f.*
plank crib Bretterstapel *m (Bdg).*
plank floor Brettertafel *f (Bdg).*
plank flooring Bretterteppich *m (rope Bdg).*
planking Brückenbelag *m,* Belag *m* (Bdg).
plank road Bohlenbahn *f.*
plank scaffolding Aufrüstung *f (Pon, Engr).*
plank trestle Bretterbock *m.*
plan of attack Angriffsplan *m.*
plan of campaign Feldzugsplan *m,* Operationsplan *m.*
plan of fire Feuerplan *m (Tac).*
plan of operations Operationsplan *m (Tac).*
plan of telephone communication Betriebsunterlagen *fpl.*
plastic Preßstoff *m;* Kunststoff *m (synthetic).*
plastic-pad obturator plastische Liderung *(G).*
plate Lamelle *f,* Platte *f,* Tafel *f (Tech);* Anode *f (Elec);* Teller *m (dish).*
plateau Hochebene *f,* Plateau *n.*
plate battery *(Rad)* Anodenbatterie *f*
plate circuit Anodenkreis *m (Rad).*
plate clutch Scheibenkupplung *f (MT).*
plate dissipation Anodenverlustleistung *f (Rad).*
platform Plattform *f,* Bettung *f (Arty);* Bahnsteig *m (RR).*
platform underpass Bahnsteigunterführung *f (RR).*
platoon Zug *m.*
platoon boundary Zuggrenze *f.*
"**Platoon, halt!**" "Abteilung, halt!"
platoon headquarters detail Zugtrupp *m.*
platoon leader Zugführer *m.*
play *n* Spiel *n (Mech).*
plead guilty sich schuldig erklären.
plead not guilty sich nicht schuldig erklären.
plexiglas Plexiglas *n.*
pliers Zange *f.*
plot *v* abstecken *(a course on a map);* abgreifen *(transfer distance with dividers);* zeichnen *(draw);* Eintragungen machen *(enter data on a map);* sich verschwören *(conspire).*
plotter Rechner *m (Pers).*
plotting Planzeichnen *n,* Festlegen von Zielpunkten *(Surv).*
plotting board Flächenmeßplan *m (flash ranging).*
plotting instrument Zeichengerät *n.*
plotting protractor Meßdreieck *n (Arty).*
plotting scale Reduktionsmaßstab *m,* Lineal *n (FA).*
plug *n* Stecker *m (Elec);* Stöpsel *m,* Anschlußstecker *m (Tp);* Innenhütchen *n (detonator cap);* Pfropfen *m (stopper).*
plug gage Innengrenzlehre *f.*
plug in stöpseln, einstöpseln *(Rad, Tp).*
plug prong Steckerstift *m (Elec).*
plumb bob Lot *n,* Senkblei *n.*
plumber Klempner *m,* Installateur *m.*
plumb line Lotschnur *f.*
plunder *v* plündern, ausplündern.
plundering Plünderung *f.*
plunge *n* Absturz *m.*
plunger Zündbolzen *m (powder-train time fuze, Am);* Reglergestänge *n (engine governor).*
plunging fire Senkfeuer *n,* Steilfeuer
plus *n* Plus *n,* Mehr *n;* Pluszeichen *n (plus sign).*
plywood Sperrholz *n.*
pneumatic boat Floßsack *m,* Schlauchboot *n.*
pneumatic-boat ferry Schlauchbootfähre *f.*
pneumatic-boat footbridge Floßsacksteg *m.*
pneumatic equilibrator Luftausgleicher *m (G).*
pneumatic float Floßsack *m.*
pneumatic hammer Drucklufthammer *m,* Preßlufthammer *m.*
pneumatic pile driver Druckluftramme *f (Engr).*
pneumatic ponton Floßsack *m.*
pneumatic raft Floßsack *m,* Schlauchboot *n.*
pneumatic-raft footbridge Floßsacksteg *m.*
pneumatic recuperator Luftvorholer *m (G).*
pneumatic riveter Druckluft-Niethammer *m,* Preßluft-Niethammer *m.*
pneumatic tire Luftreifen *m.*
pneumonia Lungenentzündung *f.*
pocket *n* Kessel *m (Tac);* Tasche *f*
pocket *v* einkesseln *(Tac).*
pocket battleship Panzerschiff *n,* Westentaschenschlachtschiff *n.*
pocket knife Taschenmesser *n.*
pocket of resistance Widerstandskessel *m.*
point *n* Punkt *m (Tac);* Spitze *f (Adv Gd);* Himmelsrichtung *f (of the compass).*
point *v* richten *(a gun);* zeigen, deuten, weisen *(indicate).*
point-blank range Kernschußweite *f.*
"**point**" **car** Spitzenwagen *m (MT).*
point designation Punktbestimmung *f.*
point-designation grid Artilleriepunkttafel *f.*
point-detonating fuze Kopfzünder *m.*
pointed-post reticle Zielstachel *m (telescopic sight).*
pointer Gegenzeiger *m,* Folgezeiger *m (follow-the-pointer mechanism in data transmission system).*
point fire Punktschießen *n,* Punktfeuer *n.*
pointing Richten *n,* Richtung *f (Gunnery).*
point location Punktbestimmung *f.*
point of aim Haltepunkt *m (Arty, R);* Abkommpunkt *m (R).*
point of air burst Luftsprengpunkt *m (Ballistics).*
point of burst Sprengpunkt *m (Gunnery).*
point of contact Berührungspunkt *m.*
point of departure Ausgangsstellung *f (in attack);* Ausgangsort *m (Air Navigation, Trans).*
point of fall Fallpunkt *m (Ballistics).*
point of hock Hacke *f (horse).*
point of impact Aufschlagpunkt *m,* Auftreffpunkt *m,* Treffpunkt *m (Ballistics).*
point of intersection Schnittpunkt *m (in plotting, etc.).*
point of main effort Schwerpunkt *m (Tac).*
point of origin Ausgangspunkt *m (Arty, Surv).*
point of penetration Einbruchstelle *f.*
point of rupture Sprengstelle *f (Demolitions);* Bruchgrenze *f (Mech).*
point target Einzelziel *n (bombing);* Punktziel *n (Gunnery).*
poison *n* Gift *n.*
poisoned vergiftet.
polar air arktische Kaltluft *(Met).*
polar coordinate Polarkoordinate *f.*
Polaris Polarstern *m,* Nordstern *m.*
pole Stange *f,* Mast *m;* Deichsel *f (limber);* Pol *m (Elec).*
pole changer Polwechsler *m (Tp).*
pole charge Sprengstange mit geballter Ladung *(Engr).*
pole-location diagram Stangenbild *n (Tp).*
pole piece Polschuh *m (magnet).*
pole pin Deichselbolzen *m (limber).*
pole prop Deichselstütze *f (limber).*
pole reversal Umpolung *f (Elec).*
police *n* Polizei *f;* Feldgendarmerie *f (MP).*
police *v* überwachen, in Ordnung halten.
policeman Polizist *m,* Schutzmann *m;* Gendarm *m (rural);* Feldgendarm *m (MP).*
polish *v* putzen, wichsen *(leather, etc.);* polieren *(Tech);* putzen *(equipment).*
polyconic projection polykonische Projektion.
pommel Vorderzwiesel *m (saddle).*
pommel-pad strap Vorsteckriemen *m.*
poncho Poncho *m.*
pond Teich *m.*
ponton Ponton *m (Bdg). See also* **pontoon.**
ponton balk Scherbalken *m (Engr).*
ponton bay Pontonstrecke *f (Pon Bdg).*
ponton bridge Pontonbrücke *f.*
ponton carrier Pontonwagen *m (MT).*
pontoneer Pontonier *m.*
ponton ferry Pontonfähre *f.*
ponton train Brückenkolonne *f.*
pontoon Schwimmer *m (Ap float). See also* **ponton.**
pool *n* gemeinsame Reserve an Truppen und Gerät *(Tac).*
pool *v* vereinigen, zusammenlegen *(Tac).*
poppet valve Plattenventil *n,* Tellerventil *n (Mtr).*
population Bevölkerung *f,* Einwohnerschaft *f (of a town).*
pork Schweinefleisch *n.*
port Hafen *m (harbor);* Scharte *f,* Blende *f (Tk);* Öffnung *f (Mech).*
portable bridge Kolonnenbrücke *f.*
portable generator tragbarer Stromerzeuger.
portable obstacle bewegliches Hindernis.
portable-radio section Tornisterfunktrupp *m.*
portable radio set Tornister-Funkgerät *n (haversack type).*
portable receiver Tornisterempfänger *m (Rad, haversack type).*
portable signal-lamp case Blinktornister *m.*
portable switchboard Klappenschrank *m,* Schaltkästchen *n,* Vermittlungskästchen *n (Tp).*
porté verlastet.
porté artillery verlastete Artillerie.
port engine Backbordmotor *m.*
porter Gepäckträger *m,* Träger *m (RR).*
porthole Bullauge *n.*
port installation Hafenanlage *f.*
port of debarkation Ausschiffungshafen *m.*
port of embarkation Einschiffungshafen *m.*
port of entry Einfuhrhafen *m*
port officer Hafenoffizier *m.*
port side Backbord *m (Nav).*
position Stellung *f (Tac);* Standort *m (location).*
position and aiming drill Ausbildung in den Anschlagsarten.
position defilade verdeckte Feuerstellung *(Tac).*
position determination Ortsbestimmung *f (Air Navigation).*
position finder station Peilfunkstelle *f.*
position finding Ortung *f,* Ortsbestimmung *f.*
positioning device for leads Vorhalteeinstellung *f (sight mechanism).*
position in readiness Bereitstellung *f.*
position light Positionslicht *n (Avn).*
position of departure Ausgangsstellung *f (Tac).*
position of target Meßpunkt *m (at instant of range determination),* Abschußpunkt *m (at instant of firing),* Treffpunkt *m (at instant of impact),* Gegnerpunkt *m,* Sprengpunkt *m (at instant of burst),* Wechselpunkt *m (at midpoint) (AA Gunnery).*
position of the gun Geschütznullpunkt *m,* Geschützort *m (on firing charts and diagrams).*
position of the piece Geschützstand *m (Arty).*
position report Standortmeldung *f (Air Navigation).*
position warfare Stellungskrieg *m,* Stellungskampf *m.*
positive stagger Vorwärtsstaffelung *f,* Staffelung nach vorne *(Ap wings).*
post *n* Pfahl *m (Engr);* Standort *m (station).*
post *v* aufstellen *(a guard, etc.);* anschlagen *(a notice, etc.).*
postage Porto *n.*
postal censor's office Postprüfungsstelle *f,* Postüberwachungsstelle *f.*
post commander Standortältester *m.*
post exchange Marketenderei *f,* Truppenmarketenderei *f.*
poster Plakat *n,* Anschlagzettel *m.*
post hospital Standortlazarett *n.*
posting Aussetzen *n (of guards).*
postmaster Postmeister *m.*
post obstacle Pfahlsperre *f.*
post office Postamt *n,* Post *f.*
postpone aufschieben, verschieben.
potable trinkbar.
potassium cartridge Kalipatrone *f (oxygen breathing apparatus).*
potassium permanganate Kaliumpermanganat *n.*
potato Kartoffel *f.*
"**potato-masher**" **hand grenade** Stielhandgranate *f.*
pothole Schlagloch *n (road).*
potentiometer Potentiometer *n.*
pouch Beutel *m,* Tasche *f.*
pouch kit Sanitätstasche *f.*
powder Pulver *n (Am).*
powder bag Kartuschbeutel *m.*
powder chamber Pulverraum *m,* Ladungsraum *m,* Pulverkammer *f.*
powder charge Pulverladung *f (Am).*
powder fouling Pulverrückstände *mpl (G).*
powder grain Pulverkorn *n (Am).*
powder magazine Pulverhaus *n.*
powder pellet Pulversatz *m (fuze);* Satzring *m (time fuze).*
powder thermometer Pulverthermometer *n (Am).*
powder train Pulversatz *m (fuze),* Zündsatz *m (blasting).*
powder-train fuze *See* **powder-train time fuze.**
powder-train ignition Pulverbrennzündung *f (fuze).*
powder-train time fuze Brennzünder
power Energie *f,* Kraft *f (Mech);* Macht *f,* Staat *m (country);* Potenz *f (Math);* Gewalt *f (authority).*
power amplifier Leistungsstufe *f (Rad).*
power amplifier tube Leistungsröhre
power control Leistungsregler *m (Rad).*
powered glider Motorgleiter *m,* Motorsegler *m.*
powerful mächtig, gewaltig; einflußreich *(influential).*
power house Kraftwerk *n.*
power lead-in Anzapfleitung *f (Rad).*
power line Starkstromleitung *f,* Hochspannungsleitung *f (Elec).*
power loading Leistungsbelastung *f (Ap).*
power loss Energieverlust *m (Elec, Rad).*
power pack Speiseteil *m (Rad).*
power plant Triebwerk *n,* Triebwerksanlage *f (Ap, MT);* Maschinensatz *m (generating unit);* Kraftwerk *n (power house).*
power saw Kraftsäge *f,* Motorsäge *f*
power shovel Bagger *m,* Löffelbagger *m (Engr).*
power source Kraftquelle *f,* Stromquelle *f.*
power station Kraftwerk *n,* Elektrizitätswerk *n.*
power stroke Arbeitshub *m,* Arbeitstakt *m (Mtr).*
power supply Energievorrat *m (Mech);* Speisung *f (Rad).*
power traction Kraftzug *m (MT).*
power train Kraftübertragung *f,* Kraftübertragungsteile *mpl (MT).*
power transformer Netztransformator *m (Rad).*
power transmission Kraftübertragung *f.*
power transmission line Hochspannungsleitung *f (Elec).*
power transmission unit Kraftübertragungsteil *m (MT).*

power unit Maschinensatz m.
practice n Übung f (Tng); Verfahren n (procedure); Praxis f (as distinguished from theory).
practice v üben.
practice alert Luftschutzübung f (Civ defense).
practice ammunition Übungsmunition f.
practice bomb Exerzierbombe f.
practice-bombing panel Bombenteppich m.
practice charge Übungsladung f (Am).
practice firing Schulschießen n, Übungsschießen n.
practice flight Übungsflug m.
practice grenade Übungshandgranate
practice mine Übungsmine f.
practice range Schießstand m.
practice shell Übungsgranate f (Am).
practice sight Richtübungsgerät n (G, MG).
prearranged fire vorbereitetes Feuer (Arty).
precedence Vorrang m.
precipitation Niederschläge mpl.
precipitation area Regengebiet n (rain), Schneefallgebiet, n fall).
precise genau, zielgenau, präzis.
precision Genauigkeit f, Präzision f.
precision adjustment Feineinstellung
precision adjustment fire genaues Einschießen (Arty).
precision bombing Zielwurf m, gezielter Bombenwurf.
precision fire Präzisionsschießen n.
precombustion chamber Vorkammer f (Diesel engine).
predict voraussagen, vorhersagen (forecast); den Vorhalt errechnen (calculate the lead, Gunnery).
predicted position of target Vorhaltepunkt m (Gunnery).
predicting interval Vorhaltestrecke f (AA Gunnery).
prediction Voraussage f, Vorhersage f (forecast); Errechnung des Vorhalts (Gunnery).
predictor Zielrechenmaschine f (AA).
preflight training theoretische Ausbildung.
preheater Vorwärmer m.
preignition Frühzündung f (Mtr).
preliminary action einleitendes Gefecht (Tac).
preliminary mission Vorausaufgabe f (Tac).
preliminary signal Vorsignal n.
premature air burst Frühzerspringer m (Arty).
premature ignition Vorzündung f.
premium Treugeld n.
preparation Vorbereitung f; Vorbereitungsfeuer n (Arty).
preparation of fire Vorbereitung des Schießens.
preparatory command Ankündigungskommando n.
preparatory marksmanship training Schießvorschule f.
preparedness Bereitschaft f.
prescribe vorschreiben; verschreiben, verordnen (Med).
prescribed vorgeschrieben; vorschriftsmäßig (according to regulations).
prescribed load vorgesehene Menge, vorgeschriebene Last.
preselector Vorwähler m (Tp).
"Present, arms!" "Achtung! Präsentiert das, Gewehr!"
present position of target Meßpunkt m (at instant of range determination), Abschußpunkt m (at instant of firing, AA Gunnery).
preserved meat Dauerfleisch n.
press v drücken, pressen.
press report Pressemeldung f (Rad).
pressure Druck m.
pressure-board mine Druckbrettmine Brettstückmine f.
pressure cabin Druckkabine f (Ap).
pressure change Betrag der Druckänderung (Met).
pressure equalizer Druckausgleicher
pressure firing device Druckzünder m (land mine).
pressure gage Gasdruckmeßgerät n, Meßei n (Arty).
pressure gradient barometrisches Gefälle, Luftdruckgradient m (Met).
pressure igniter Druckzünder m.
pressure line Druckleitung f (Hydraulics).
pressure lubrication Druckschmierung f, Druckumlaufschmierung f (Mtr).
pressure plate Druckplatte f (clutch).
pressure plug Druckstempel m (Arty).
pressure point Druckstelle f.
pressure regulator Druckregler m.
pressure surface Druckseite f (Ap wing).
pressure test Gasdruckprüfung f (Ord).
prevailing wind vorherrschende Winde.
prevent hindern, verhindern (hinder or stop); vorbeugen (by measures taken in advance).
preventive maintenance Pflege f.
primacord Knallzündschnur f (Engr).
primacord net Knallnetz n.
primary circuit Primärkreis m (Rad).
primary current Primärstrom m, Erststrom m.
primary target Hauptziel n.
primary trainer Schulflugzeug n.
primary traverse station trigonometrischer Punkt.
primary weapon Hauptwaffe f.
primary winding Primärwicklung f (Elec).
prime mover Kraftzugmaschine f, Zugmaschine f; Zugkraftwagen m (Trk); Kraftschlepper m (Trac).
primer Zündhütchen n (SA Am); Zündmittel n (Am); Zündsatz m (Am, blasting); Zündladung f (primer charge); Zündschraube f (threaded primer) (Am).
primer charge Zündladung f.
primer cup Zündhütchenhülse f (Am).
primer vent Zündkanal m (cartridge).
priming charge Eingangszündung f, Zündladung f (Engr).
priming composition Zündsatz m.
priming flash Zündstrahl m (Am).
principal course of approach Anfluggrundlinie f (Inst landing).
principal lateral deflection angle Gesamtvorhaltewinkel m (AA gunnery).
principal vertical deflection angle Reglerwinkel m (AA gunnery).
principle Grundsatz m Prinzip n.
principles of war Grundprinzipien des Krieges.
print n Abzug m, Lichtpause f (Photo).
print v drucken; kopieren, abziehen (Photo).
printed form Vordruck m.
priority Vorrang m (precedence); Vorfahrtsrecht n (Trans).
priority list Dringlichkeitsliste f.
priority message dringende Meldung.
prismatic compass Marschkompaß m.
prison Gefängnis n; Arrestanstalt f (Mil); Zuchthaus n (penitentiary).
prisoner Gefangener m.
prisoner guard detachment Gefangenenbewachungskommando n (MP).
prisoner of war Kriegsgefangener m.
prisoner of war camp Gefangenenlager n.
prisoner-of-war collection point Kriegsgefangenensammelstelle f.
private Grenadier m (Inf); Jäger m (in Gebirgsjäger or Jäger unit); Panzergrenadier m (Armd Inf Regt); Reiter m (Cav); Kanonier m (Arty); Pionier m (Engr); Fahrer m (H-Dr Trans); Kraftfahrer m (MT); Funker m (radioman); Sanitätssoldat m (Med); Schütze m (rifleman).
private first class Obergrenadier m (Inf); Oberjäger m (in Gebirgsjäger or Jäger unit); Panzer-Obergrenadier m (Armd Inf Regt); Oberreiter m (Cav); Oberkanonier m (Arty); Oberpionier m (Engr); Oberfahrer m (H-Dr Trans); Oberkraftfahrer m (MT); Oberfunker m (radioman); Oberschütze m (rifleman); Sanitätsobersoldat m (Med).
prize Prise f, Beute f.
probability factor Wahrscheinlichkeitsfaktor m (Ballistics).
probability of hit Treffwahrscheinlichkeit f (Gunnery); Treffaussicht f (bombing).
probable error wahrscheinlicher Fehler.
probing rod Minensuchstab m (for land mines).
problem Aufgabe f (Tng); Problem
procedure Verfahren n.
procedure sign Funkabkürzung f.
procedure signal See procedure sign.
proceed weitergehen, weiterfahren; fortfahren (continue).
process v bearbeiten, fertigstellen.
proclamation Proklamation f, Verkündigung f, Bekanntmachung f (public notice); Verordnung f (decree).
procure anschaffen, beschaffen, verschaffen, besorgen.
procurement Anschaffung f, Beschaffung f, Besorgung f.
produce v erzeugen, hervorbringen; herstellen (manufacture).
product Erzeugnis n, Produkt n.
production Erzeugung f, Herstellung f, Fertigung f, Produktion f.
profile Profil n, Umriß m.
profile map Höhenumrißkarte f.
profile thickness Profildicke f (Ap wing).
profit n Gewinn m.
progress n Fortschritt m.
progress of action Gefechtsverlauf m (Tac).
progress of an attack Angriffsverlauf m.
prohibit verbieten.
prohibited zone Luftsperrgebiet n (Avn).
projectile Geschoß n.
projection Entwurf m, Projektion f.
projector Abschußrohr n, Werfer m, Wurfgerät n (CWS, Sig); Filmvorführapparat m, Filmprojektor m (movies); Bildwerfer m (stills).
projector signal Granatsignal n.
prolonge Abschlepptau n, Handhabungstau n (Arty).
promote befördern.
promotion Beförderung f.
promotion list Beförderungsliste f.
prone position Anschlag liegend (firing).
prone shelter Schützenmulde f.
prong Streckerstift m (of a plug), Kontaktstift m (of a jack) (Elec).
proof Beweis m; Probebild n (Photo); Probeabzug m, Probedruck m (printing).
prop Stütze f, Knagge f (Engr).
propaganda Propaganda f.
propellant Treibmittel n (Am).
propellent treibend, antreibend.
propellent gases Treibgase npl (Ballistics).
propellent primer Zündhütchen n
propeller Luftschraube f, Propeller m (Ap).
propeller blade Luftschraubenblatt n, Luftschraubenflügel m (Ap).
propeller boss Luftschraubennabenstück n (Ap).
propeller-disk area Propellerkreis m, Luftschraubenkreis m (Ap).
propeller drive Schraubenantrieb m (amphibian vehicle).
propeller hub Propellernabe f (Ap).
propeller pitch indicator Luftschraubensteigungsmesser m.
propeller post Schraubensteven m (Nav).
propeller rpm Luftschraubendrehzahl f.
propeller shaft Gelenkwelle f, Zwischenwelle f (MT).
propeller spinner Luftschraubenhaube f (Ap).
propeller thrust Schraubenzug m
propelling charge Treibladung f, Geschützladung f (Am).
propelling-charge chamber Patronenraum m (Mort shell).
propelling-charge increment Teilladung f (Am).
propelling equipment Fahrgerät n (Engr).
property Eigentum n, Besitz m.
property book Bestandsliste f, Waffen- und Gerätenachweis m.
property officer Geräteoffizier m.
prophylactic Sanierungsmittel n.
prophylactic station Sanitätsstelle für Schutzbehandlung gegen Geschlechtskrankheiten.
prophylaxis Prophylaxe f, Vorbeugung f.
propulsion Fortbewegung f; Antrieb m (drive).
prosig Funkabkürzung f.
prosine Funkabkürzung f.
protect beschützen, schützen.
protected shelter Unterstand m (Ft).
protecting power Schutzmacht f (PW).
protection Schutz m.
protective awning Gasplane f (CWS).
protective clothing Körperschutzmittel n, Gasbekleidung f (CWS).
protective fire Feuerschutz m, Notfeuer n (Arty, MG).
protective mat Gasschutzdecke f (CWS).
protective ointment Schutzsalbe f (CWS).
protective wire Drahthindernis n.
protectorate Schutzgebiet n, Protektorat n.
protectoscope Winkelspiegel m, Schutzglas n, Schutzscheibe f (Tk).
prototype Urbaumuster n (Ap, Tk, etc.).
protractor Strahlenzieher m, Sektor m, Winkelmeßgerät n, Winkelmesser m; Zelluloidtafel f (transparent template).
prove beweisen; sich erweisen, sich bestätigen (one's ability, etc.); prüfen, erproben (test).
provide versehen, versorgen (to supply); besorgen, beschaffen (to get).
proving ground Waffenprüfungsplatz
provisional map Ersatzkarte f.
provisional organization Spezialverband m.
provisions Proviant m, Lebensmittel npl, Nahrungsmittel npl, Verpflegung f.
provost court Feldgericht n.
provost marshal Stabsoffizier bei der Feldgendarmerie (USA).
prussic acid Hydrozyansäure f, Blausäure f, Zyanwasserstoff m, Zyanwasserstoffsäure f (CWS).
psychrometer Psychrometer n.
PT boat Schnellboot n.
public-address system Kraftverstärker-Anlage f (Elec).
public relations officer Presseoffizier m.
pull v abziehen (trigger); ziehen, schleppen.
pulley Riemenscheibe f, Rolle f.
pull firing device Ziehzünder m
pull igniter Zugzünder m (mine).
pull out durchziehen (dive bombing).
pull-pressure igniter Zugdruckzünder m (mine).
pull up abheben (Avn).
pulmotor Pulmotor m, Sauerstoff-Wiederbeleber m.
pulsating direct current welliger Gleichstrom.
pulse Puls m, Pulsschlag m.
pump n Pumpe f.
punch Durchschläger m (tool); Faustschlag m, heftiger Stoß, Schlag m (blow).
puncture v stechen, zerstechen, durchlöchern (pierce); platzen (said of a tire).
punish strafen, bestrafen.
punishment Strafe f, Bestrafung f.
punishment book Strafbuch n.
punt ferry Kahnfähre f (Engr).
punting Staken n (with punt pole).
pup tent Einerzelt n.
purification unit Trinkwasserbereiterwagen m (vehicle).
Purple Heart Purpurherz n (USA).
purpose Zweck m; Absicht f (intention); Ziel n (aim).
pursue verfolgen, nachsetzen.
pursuit Verfolgung f (Tac).
pursuit airplane Jäger m, Jagdflugzeug n.
pursuit group Jagdgruppe f (Avn).
pursuit squadron Jagdstaffel f (Avn).
pursuit troops Verfolgungstruppen fpl.
pursuit wing Jagdgeschwader n
push v schieben (shove); drücken (press); drängen (crowd); stoßen (thrust).
pushbutton Druckknopf m.
pusher airplane Flugzeug mit Druckschraube, Druckschrauber m.
pusher propeller Druckschraube f (Ap).
push-pull amplifier Gegentakt-Verstärker m (Rad).
push rod Stoßstange f (Mtr).
puttees Gamaschen fpl.
putty Kitt m.
pylon Wendeturm m (Adrm).
pyrocellulose Nitrozellulose f.
pyrocellulose powder Schießwollpulver n.
pyrocotton Schießbaumwolle f, Schießwolle f.
pyro powder Nitrozellulosepulver m.
pyro smokeless powder rauchloses Nitrozellulosepulver n.
pyrotechnic code Leuchtzeichenschlüssel m.
pyrotechnic composition Leuchtsatz m (illuminant); Rauchsatz m (smoke).
pyrotechnic device Leuchtmittel n.
pyrotechnic pistol Leuchtpistole f.
pyrotechnic projector Leuchtraketengestell n, Leuchtgranatwerfer m.
pyrotechnics Leuchtmunition f.
pyroxylin Kollodiumwolle f (Am).

Q

Q signal Q-Gruppe f (Com).
quadrant Quadrant m; Libellenquadrant m (with spirit level, G); Viertelkreis m (of a circle); Winkelmesser m (G).
quadrant angle Erhebungswinkel m.
quadrant angle of departure Abgangswinkel m (Ballistics).
quadrant angle of elevation Erhöhungswinkel m (Arty).
quadrant elevation Gesamterhöhung f, Erhöhung f (Arty).
quadrant plate Quadrantenfläche f, Winkelmesserebene f (G).
quadrant scale Gradbogen m (G).
quadrant sight Quadrantenvisier n (leaf-type) (R, MG); Visiereinrichtung f (G).
qualification Qualifikation f, Fähigkeit f.
qualification as a lawful belligerent Charakter einer kriegführenden Macht.
qualification card Qualifikationsbericht m.
qualification course Preisübung f.
qualification in arms Qualifizierung auf Grund erfolgreich beendeter Ausbildung.
qualified qualifiziert, geeignet, befähigt (fitted); berechtigt (entitled).
qualify qualifizieren.
quality Eigenschaft f (characteristic); Qualität f, Beschaffenheit f, Güte f (degree of excellence).
quantity Größe f (Math); Menge f (amount).
quarantine n Quarantäne f (Med).
quarantine v isolieren, in Quarantäne stellen.
quarry Steinbruch m.
quarter Viertel n (fourth); Stadtviertel n (of a city); Gnade f, Pardon m (mercy).
quartering Unterbringung f.
quartering area Unterbringungsgebiet n, Unterkunftsbezirk m.
quartering officer Quartiermacher m.
quartering party Quartiermacherkommando n.
Quartermaster Quartiermeister m (USA).
Quartermaster Corps Quartiermeisterkorps n (USA).
quartermaster depot Quartiermeisterlager n (USA).
Quartermaster General Generalquartiermeister m (USA).
quartermaster unit Quartiermeistereinheit f (USA).
quarters Unterbringung f, Unterkunft f.
quarters allowance Quartiervergütung f.
quarters and subsistence allowance Quartier- und Verpflegungszuschuß m.
quarters in kind freie Unterkunft.
quartz crystal Quarzkristall m (Rad).
quay Kai m.
quenching frequency Pendelfrequenz f (Rad).
question n Frage f.
question v ausfragen, befragen, verhören, vernehmen; bezweifeln (doubt).
questioning Vernehmung f.
questioning of prisoners Gefangenenverhör n, Gefangenenvernehmung f.
questionnaire Fragebogen m.
quick schnell, rasch.
quick-detachable rim Maderfelge f (MT).
quick fire Schnellfeuer gegen bewegliche Ziele.
quick fuze Augenblickszünder m
quiet n Ruhe f, Stille f.
quiet adj ruhig, still.
quinine Chinin n.
quit verlassen (leave); aufhören (stop).
quota Quote f.
quotient Quotient m.
quicklime ungelöschter Kalk.
quickmatch Zündschnur f (Prcht flare).
quick time Gleichschritt m.
"Quick time, march!" "Im Gleichschritt!" (being in march in double time).

R

race n Laufring m (ball bearing).
racer Drehring m (AA gun).
rack Zahnstange f, Zahnbogen m (Mech, Ord); Gewehrstütze f (R); Bombenschacht m (Ap); Lagergerüst n (for storage of supplies).
rack stick Schnürleiste f (for cord lashing, Bdg).
radar Funkmeßgerät n.
radar station Funkmeßturm m.
radial engine Sternmotor m.
radian Radian m, Bogeneinheit f.
radiation Ausstrahlung f, Strahlung f (Rad).
radiator Kühler m (Mtr); Heizkörper m (for heating).
radiator cap Kühler-Einfüllverschluß m (MT).
radiator guard Kühlerschutzhaube f (MT).
radio n Funk m; Funkgerät n (set).
by radio auf dem Funkwege, auf dem Funkspruchwege.
radio v funken, senden.
radio address Rundfunkrede f.
radio alert Funkbereitschaft f.
radio antenna truck Funkmastkraftwagen m.
radio beacon Funkbake f, Funkfeuer n.
radio beam Funkstrahl m, Leitstrahl m, Ansteuerungsfunkfeuer n.
radio-bearing signal Peilzeichen n.
radio broadcasting station Rundfunkstation f, Rundfunksender m.
radio-broadcast reception Rundfunkempfang m.
radio call sign Funkrufzeichen n.
radio car Funkkraftwagen m.
radio case Funkkiste f.
radio chest See radio case.
radio command Funkbefehl m.
radio command tank Funkpanzerkampfwagen m.
radio command truck Funkkraftwagen m.
radio communication Funkverbindung f, Funkverkehr m.
radio communications Funknachrichten fpl.
radio compass Bordpeiler m, Peilfunkempfänger m, Richtempfänger m, Peilempfänger m (Air Navigation).
radio compass calibration Funkbeschickung f (Air Navigation).
radio deception Funktäuschung f.
radio detector See radar.
radio direction finder Funkpeiler m.
radio direction finder station Bodenpeilfunkstelle f, Peilfunkstelle f, Peilstelle f (Avn).

radio direction finding Funkpeilung f.
radio direction-finding truck Peilkraftwagen m.
radio discipline Funkzucht f.
radio engineer Funktechniker m.
radio engineering Funktechnik f.
radio equipment Funkgerät n, F.T.-Gerät n; F.T.-Anlage f (Ap, Tk).
radio-equipment truck Funkgerätekraftwagen m.
radio exercise Funkübung f.
radio facility chart Fliegerkarte mit für die Funknavigation notwendigen Angaben (Avn).
radio fix Schnittpunkt zweier Peilstrahlen, Standort m (Air Navigation).
radio frequency Hochfrequenz f.
radio-frequency amplifier Hochfrequenzverstärker m.
radio-frequency choke Hochfrequenzdrossel f.
radio-frequency stage Hochfrequenzstufe f (Rad).
radio-frequency transformer Hochfrequenztransformator m.
radio goniometer Funkpeilanlage f.
radiogram Funkfelegramm n.
radio intelligence Funkaufklärung f.
radio intercept Funkhorchen n.
radio intercept station Funkhorchstelle f.
radio jamming Funkstörung f.
radio landing beam Leitstrahl des Landefunkfeuers (Avn).
radio log Funkbetriebsbuch n.
radioman Funker m.
radio marker beacon Navigationsfunkfeuer n (Air Navigation).
radio mast Funkmast m.
radio message Funkmeldung f, Funkspruch m.
radio meteorograph Radiosonde f.
radio monitoring Funküberwachung f.
radio motor vehicle Funkkraftfahrzeug n.
radio navigation Funknavigation f (Avn).
radio net Funknetz n.
radio noise suppressor Störungsschutz m, Störschutz m, Störsperre f.
radio officer Funknachrichtenoffizier
radio operations Funkbetrieb m.
radio operator Funker m; Bordfunker m (Avn); Funkunteroffizier m (Sgt); Funkgefreiter m (Cpl).
radio operator's station Stand des Funkers (Ap).
radio order Funkbefehl m.
radiophoto transmission Bildfunk m.
radio position finding Feststellen des Standortes eines feindlichen Senders durch Funkpeilung (Rad).
radio procedure Funkbetriebsverfahren n.
radio range Funknavigationsanlage f.
radio range beacon Richtfunkfeuer f.
radio range station Bodenstelle für Funknavigation, Richtfunkstelle f.
radio receiver Funkempfänger m.
radio reception Funkempfang m.
radio repairman Funkgerätmechaniker m.
radio section Funktrupp m.
radio set Funkgerät n.
radio shield Entstörkappe f (Mtr).
radio signal Funksignal n.
radio silence Funkstille f, Funkverbot n.
radiosonde Radiosonde f (Met).
radio station Funkstelle f.
radio technician Funkwart m.
radio technology Funktechnik f.
radiotelegraph communication funkentelegraphische Verbindung.
radiotelegraph set F.T.-Gerät n (Ap).
radiotelegraphy Funkentelegraphie f.
radiotelephone Funksprechgerät n.
radiotelephone communication Funksprechen n.
radiotelephony Funkentelephonie f.
radio tower Funkturm m.
radio traffic Funkverkehr m.
radio transmission Funksendung f; Funktasten n (keying).
radio transmitter Funksender m, Sendegerät n.
radio truck Funkkraftwagen m, Funkwagen m.
radio tube Elektronenröhre f.
radio voice transmission Funksprechen n.
radio wave Funkwelle f.
radio wave deflection Strahlungsablenkung f.
radio weather station Funkwetterwarte f.
radius Halbmesser m, Radius m.
radius of action Aktionsradius m, Wirkungsbereich m (Ap).
radius of rupture Wirkungshalbmesser m (blasting).
radius of visibility Sichtweite f.
raft Floß n.
raid n Streifzug m, Überfall m, Stoßtruppunternehmung f (Tac); Razzia f (police); Luftangriff m, Angriffsflug m, Feindflug m (Avn).
raiding party Streifabteilung f, Streifkommando n.
rail Schiene f (RR, etc.); Holm m (spar); Stange f (pole); Runge f (rack bar or pole, MT).
by rail mit der Eisenbahn.
railhead Eisenbahnendpunkt m, Ausladebahnhof m, Ausladespitze f.
railhead distribution Verteilung der Nachschubgüter vom Ausladebahnhof aus.
railhead reserve area Nachschubsammelgebiet n.
railing Geländer n (Bdg).
railing support Geländerstütze f.
railroad Eisenbahn f. See also railway.
railroad antiaircraft artillery Eisenbahnflak f.
railroad artillery See railway artillery.
railroad car Eisenbahnwagen m.
railroad crossing Bahnübergang m; Überführung f (overpass); Unterführung f (underpass); Planübergang m (level).
railroad depot Bahnhof m.
railroad embankment Bahndamm m.
railroad engineer troops Eisenbahnpioniere mpl.
railroad gun Eisenbahngeschütz n.
railroad installation Bahnanlage f, Eisenbahnanlage f.
railroad junction Eisenbahnknotenpunkt m.
railroad line Eisenbahnlinie f, Bahnverbindung f.
railroad station Bahnhof m.
railroad station traffic officer Bahnhofsoffizier m.
railroad supply line Eisenbahnnachschublinie f.
railroad track Eisenbahngleis n.
railroad traffic Zugverkehr m.
railroad train Eisenbahnzug m, Zug m.
railroad transportation Eisenbahnbeförderung f, Bahntransport m.
railroad transportation timetable Eisenbahntransportfolge f.
railroad yard Gleisanlage f.
railway Eisenbahn f. See also railroad.
railway artillery Eisenbahnartillerie f.
railway artillery battery Eisenbahnbatterie f.
railway engineer regiment Eisenbahn-Pionierregiment n.
railway gun Eisenbahngeschütz n.
railway gun car Geschützwagen m (RR).
railway howitzer Eisenbahnhaubitze
railway mortar Eisenbahnmörser m.
railway operating company Betriebskompanie f.
rain n Regen m.
raincoat Regenmantel m.
rain gage Regenmesser m (Met).
raise v heben (lift); erhöhen (increase); potenzieren (to a power) (Math).
rake n Rechen m, Harke f.
rake v beschießen, bestreichen (firing).
rally v sammeln, vereinigen, wiederversammeln (Tac).
rallying point Sammelplatz m (Tac).
ram v ansetzen (G); rammen (Nav).
rammer Ansetzer m (G); Stößel m (fuze).
ramp Rampe f.
ramp carrier Rampenwagen m (Bdg train).
ramp equipment Rampengerät n (Bdg).
range Entfernung f, Schußweite f (distance); Schießplatz m, Schießstand m (place); Flugbereich m (Avn); Wurfweite f (bombing); Reichweite f (of a Rad set); Bodenstelle für Funknavigation (Rad range station).
range adjustment Einschießen nach der Länge (firing).
range angle Vorhaltewinkel m (bombing).
range butt Kugelfang m.
range car Schießwagen m (on target range).
range card Punktplan m (Gunnery).
range conversion table Kommandotafel f (Gunnery).
range correction Längenverbesserung f, Verbesserung für Länge (Gunnery).
range-deflection fan Zielspinne f (Gunnery).
range determination Entfernungsermittlung f.
range deviation Höhenabweichung f, Längenabweichung f (Gunnery).
range difference Entfernungsunterschied m.
range dispersion Längenstreuung f, Tiefenstreuung f (on horizontal target); Höhenstreuung f (on vertical target).
range drum Trommel f, Übertrommel f (sight mount).
range estimation Entfernungsschätzen n.
range finder Entfernungsgerät n, Entfernungsmeßgerät n, Entfernungsmesser m, Fernmesser m, Fernmeßgerät n.
range-finder operator Entfernungsmeßmann m, Entfernungsmesser m.
range finding Entfernungsmessen n.
range indicator Entfernungsmarke f (practice firing).
range knob Entfernungstrommel f (G).
range plate Strichplatte f (MG mount).
range pole Fluchtstab m (Surv).
range practice Schießübung f.
range quadrant Winkelmesser m, Libellenquadrant m (G).
Ranger Soldat der Landungstruppen (USA).
range ruler Entfernungslineal n (Arty).
range scale Entfernungsteilung f.
range sensing Festlegen der Längenabweichung (Arty Obsn).
range setting Entfernungseinstellung f (Gunnery).
range spotting Festlegen der Längenabweichung (Arty Obsn).
range table Schußtafel für Erhöhung.
range to target Zielentfernung f (Gunnery).
ranging fire Einschießen nach der Länge (CA).
ranging station Meßstelle f (sound ranging, flash ranging).
rank n Glied n (in formation); Rang m (status).
ranking adj rangältest.
ranks Unteroffiziere und Mannschaften (Pers).
rape n Notzucht f, Vergewaltigung f.
rapid fire Schnellfeuer n.
rapid-fire breechblock Schnelladeverschluß m (G).
rapid-fire cannon Schnellfeuerkanone f.
rapid-fire gun Schnellfeuergeschütz n.
rasp Raspel f.
rat Ratte f.
ratchet Knarre f (wheel and pawl); Klinke f (pawl).
ratchet wheel Sperrad n.
rate Satz m, Rate f; Geschwindigkeit f (speed); Gebühr f (charge); Preis m (price); Tarif m (classified rate); Honorar n (fee).
rated horsepower Nennleistung f.
rate of angular movement Winkelgeschwindigkeit f (Ord).
rate of burning Brenngeschwindigkeit f (time blasting fuze).
rate of climb Steigleistung f, Steigzeit f (Avn).
rate-of-climb indicator Statoskop n.
rate of drop Sinkgeschwindigkeit f (Avn).
rate of fall Fallgeschwindigkeit f, Sinkgeschwindigkeit f.
rate of fire Feuergeschwindigkeit f (MG).
rate of fuel consumption Kraftstoffverbrauchssatz m (MT).
rate of march Marschgeschwindigkeit f, Marschtempo n.
rate of pay Höhe des Wehrsoldes (Mil).
rating Dienstgrad m (Nav).
ration n Portion f, Portionssatz m, Verpflegungssatz m, Verpflegungsportion f.
ration v rationieren.
ration allowances Verpflegungsgebührnisse fpl.
ration and savings account Verpflegungsabrechnung f.
ration articles Verpflegungsgegenstände mpl.
ration card Kleiderkarte f (Clo); Lebensmittelkarte f (food).
ration distributing point Verpflegungsausgabestelle f.
ration requirements Verpflegungsbedarf m.
ration return Verpflegungsbezugsschein m.
rations Verpflegungsmittel npl, Verpflegung f.
rations and quarters Verpflegung und Unterkunft.
ration savings Geldwert der Verpflegungsersparnisse.
rations delivery unit Verpflegungsbombe f (airborne Opns).
rations in kind Verpflegung in Natur, Naturalverpflegung f.
ration stockage Verpflegungsbestände mpl.
ration strength Verpflegungsstärke f.
ration supplies Verpflegungsmittel npl, Lebensmittel npl.
ration supply depot Verpflegungslager n.
ration train Verpflegungstroß m; Verpflegungszug m (RR).
ravine Schlenke f.
ray Strahl m.
rayon Kunstseide f.
razor Rasiermesser n (barber's); Rasierapparat m (safety).
razor blade Rasierklinge f.
reaction Reaktion f, Rückstoß m.
reaction pressure Rückdruck m (rocket).
read lesen, ablesen.
readability Lautstärke f (Rad, Tp); Lesbarkeit f, Verständlichkeit f.
readiness Bereitschaft f.
readiness for action Gefechtsbereitschaft f.
ready bereit, fertig.
"Ready!" "Fertig!" (Arty).
ready-fixed fuze Fertigzünder m.
ready-fixed percussion fuze Fertigaufschlagzünder m (Am).
ready for take-off startklar (Avn).
"Ready, front!" "Augen gerade, aus!"
ready to fire schußfertig.
reamer Reibahle f.
rear n Rücken m (Tac); Heck n (Tk).
to the rear nach hinten.
rear adj rückwärtig.
rear admiral Vizeadmiral m (Nav).
rear area rückwärtiges Gebiet.
rear armor plate Heckpanzer m (Tk).
rear attack Rückenangriff m (Tac).
rear-axle drive Hinterachsantrieb m (MT).
rear bourrelet Führungswulst m (Am).
rear cinch Gurtstrippe f (pack saddle).
rear communications rückwärtige Verbindungen.
rear cover Rückendeckung f (Tac).
rear covering force Rückendeckung f (Tac).
rear drive Heckantrieb m (MT).
rear driver Rückwärtsfahrer m (of a vehicle with double-end control).
rear echelon II. Staffel (Hq).
rear echelon train Kolonnenstaffel f.
rear guard Nachhut f.
rear-guard action Nachhutgefecht n.
rear guard reserve Haupttrupp m (in rear guard of large unit).
rear guard support Nachtrupp m (in rear guard of large unit); Haupttrupp m (in rear guard of smaller unit).
rear gunner Heckschütze m (Avn).
rear installations rückwärtige Einrichtungen.
rear outrigger Hinterholm m (AA gun).
rear party Nachspitzenkompanie f (in rear guard of large unit); Nachtrupp m (in rear guard of smaller unit).
rear point Nachspitze f (Tac).
rear position rückwärtige Stellung (Tac).
rear rider Beifahrer m (Mtcl).
rear ring sight Kreiskimme f (MG).
rear services rückwärtige Dienste.
rear sight Visier n (Ord).
rear-sight base Visierfuß m (MG, R).
rear-sight leaf Visierklappe f (MG, R).
rear-sight pin Visierhaltestift m, Visierstift m (MG, R).
rear-sight spring Visierfeder f (MG, R).
rear toggle joint Hintergelenk n (pistol).
rear-view mirror Rückblickspiegel m.
rearward rückwärtig.
rearward position rückwärtige Stellung (Tac).
rear-wheel drive Hinterradantrieb m (MT).
rear zone rückwärtiges Gebiet.
recapping Profilieren n, Reifenerneuerung f (MT).
recapture wiedereinnehmen (a locality); wiedergefangennehmen (a prisoner).
receding flight Abflug m (AA).
receding leg Abflugstrecke f, Wegflugstrecke f (AA target).
receding target gehendes Ziel.
receipt n Empfangsschein m, Einnahmeschein m.
receiver Empfänger m (data transmission system) (Rad); Hülse f (pistol) (R); Griffstück n (pistol); Kasten m (MG); Fernhörer m, Hörer m (Rad Tp, Tp).
receiver chassis Empfangsapparatur f, Empfängerchassis n (Rad).
receiver circuit Empfangsschaltung f (Rad).
receiver cover Hülsenbrücke f (R).
receiver floor plate Kastenboden m (MG).
receiver top Kastendeckel m (MG).
receiving antenna Empfangsantenne f.
receiving frequency Empfangsfrequenz f (Rad).
receiving set Empfangsgerät n, Empfänger m (Rad).
receptacle Steckdose f (Elec).
reception Aufnahme f, Empfang m; Funkempfang m (Rad).
reception center Rekrutendepot n.
reception zone Empfangszone f (Rad).
recess Keilloch n (G breech).
reciprocal laying Gleichlaufverfahren n (Btry).
reciprocating motion Vor- und Rückgang m.
reclaim wieder nutzbar machen, instandsetzen, verwerten.
reclaimed rubber regenerierter Altgummi.
reclamation Wiederinstandsetzung f (of equipment).
recocking shaft Spannwelle f (breechblock).
recognition Erkennen n (identification); Anerkennung f (acknowledgment).
recognition signal Erkennungszeichen n.
recoil Rücklauf m, Rückstoß m.
recoil booster Rückstoßverstärker m (MG).
recoil brake Rohrbremse f, Rücklaufbremse f (G).
recoil connection Kupplung f (pistol).
recoil cylinder Bremszylinder m (G).
recoil lug Hülsenzapfen m (R).
recoil marker Rücklaufmesser m (G).
recoil mechanism Bremsvorrichtung f, Rücklaufeinrichtung f (G).
recoil oil Bremsflüssigkeit f (G).
recoil-operated mit Rückstoß betätigt.
recoil-operated weapon Rückstoßlader m.
recoil piston Bremskolben m (G).
recoil spring Rücklauffeder f.
recoil-spring lever Kupplungshebel m (pistol).
recoil-spring lever bar Kupplungsstange f (pistol).
reconnaissance Aufklärung f, Erkundung f (Tac).
reconnaissance airplane Aufklärer m, Aufklärerflugzeug n, Aufklärungsflugzeug n; Nahaufklärer m, Naherkunder m (close reconnaissance).
reconnaissance area Aufklärungsgebiet n, Aufklärungsraum m.
reconnaissance aviation Aufklärungsflieger mpl.
reconnaissance boat Floßsack zur Erkundung der Übersetzstellen.
reconnaissance car Spähwagen m; Panzerspähwagen m (Armd).
reconnaissance company Aufklärungskompanie f.
reconnaissance depth Aufklärungstiefe f.
reconnaissance detachment Aufklärungstrupp m; Reiteraufklärungsabteilung f (Cav).
reconnaissance element Erkundungsorgan n.
reconnaissance exercise Aufklärungsübung f.
reconnaissance flare Fallschirmleuchtbombe f (Avn).
reconnaissance flight Aufklärungsflug m (Avn).
reconnaissance float airplane Aufklärungsseeflugzeug n.
reconnaissance in force gewaltsame Erkundung.
reconnaissance information Aufklärungsmaterial n.
reconnaissance mission Aufklärungsflug m (Avn).
reconnaissance of position Geländeerkundung f.
reconnaissance of route Wegeerkundung f (Tac).
reconnaissance party See reconnaissance patrol.
reconnaissance patrol Aufklärungsspähtrupp m, Spähtrupp m.
reconnaissance platoon Aufklärungszug m.
reconnaissance sector Aufklärungsstreifen m.
reconnaissance squadron Aufklärungsstaffel f (Avn).
reconnaissance troop Aufklärungsschwadron f (Cav).
reconnaissance vehicle Erkundungsfahrzeug n.
reconnoiter aufklären.
reconstruction Wiederherstellung f.
record n Aufzeichnung f, Niederschrift f (notation); Akt m, Urkunde f (document); Rekord m, Höchstleistung f, Bestleistung f (feat); Schallplatte f (phonograph).
record v aufzeichnen, aufschreiben (write); aufnehmen (sound, etc.).
recorder Aufschreiber m (Arty).
recording target Treffbild n (practice firing).
recording theodolite Kinotheodolit m (practice firing).
record of transactions Bewegungsbuch n (QMC).
record service practice Schulschießen n (Arty).
recoupment Entschädigung f, Vergütung f.
recoverable wiederverwendbar, instandsetzbar.
recoverable item wiederinstandsetzbarer Gegenstand.
recovery Bergen n, Bergung f (of matériel, etc.); Genesung f (from sickness); Erholung f (from fatigue).
recovery equipment Bergegerät n.
recovery party Sammelkommando n.
recovery service Bergedienst m.
recreation Unterhaltung f, Zeitvertreib m.
recruit n Rekrut m.
recruit v rekrutieren.
recruit depot Rekrutendepot n.
recruit drill Rekrutenexerzieren n.
recruiting center Ersatzdienststelle f.
recruiting office Annahmestelle f.
rectangle Rechteck n.
rectangular coordinates rechtwinklige Koordinaten.

rectification Gleichrichtung f (Rad); Entzerrung f (aerial Photo).
rectifier Gleichrichter m (Rad).
rectifier tube Gleichrichterröhre f.
recuperator Vorholer m, Luftvorholer m (pneumatic) (Ord.).
recuperator cylinder Luftbehälter des Vorholers (G).
recuperator mechanism Vorholeinrichtung f (Ord).
red rot.
Red Cross Rotes Kreuz.
redesigning Umkonstruktion f.
redline ausstreichen.
reduce degradieren, herabsetzen (in rank); bezwingen, niederkämpfen (Tac); abschwächen (Photo); reduzieren (chemistry); beseitigen (a stoppage) (Ord).
reduced charge verminderte Ladung (Am).
reduction Untersetzung f (Mech).
reduction coefficient Verbesserungswert zum Ausschalten des Stellungsunterschiedes (Gunnery).
reduction gear Untersetzungsgetriebe n, Reduziergetriebe n (MT).
reel Aufspuler m (Tp).
reel cart Handwagen mit Kabeltrommel, Verlegswagen m (Sig C).
reenlist kapitulieren, sich zu einer längeren Dienstzeit verpflichten, freiwillig weiterdienen.
reenlistment Kapitulation f, Verpflichtung zu einer längeren Dienstzeit.
reentrant einspringender Winkel (Ft).
refer festlegen, Teilringzahlen zum Festlegepunkt ermitteln (Gunnery).
reference Hinweis m (in books, etc.); Erwähnung f (mention); Empfehlung f (recommendation); Bezug m (relation).
reference line Bezugslinie f, Null-Linie f (Surv).
reference number Kennummer f, Kennziffer f; Windziffer f (wind reference number) (Ballistics).
reference piece Geschütz, auf das die Grundstufe bezogen wird.
reference point Hilfsziel n, Zwischenziel n (R fire); Festlegepunkt m (Gunnery); Festpunkt m (Surv).
reference-point reading Grundzahl f (Gunnery).
referring point Festlegepunkt m, Nahfestlegepunkt m (close at hand) (Gunnery).
reflecting projector Episkop n.
reflecting sight See reflector sight.
reflector Rückstrahler m.
reflector sight Reflexvisier n.
refresher instruction Wiederholungsunterricht m.
refrigerator Kühlschrank m.
refrigerator car Kühlwagen m.
refrigerator truck Kühlwagen m, Sonderlastkraftwagen mit Kühleinrichtung.
refuel nachtanken, auftanken.
refueling station Tankstelle f (MT).
refugee Flüchtling m.
refugee evacuation center Flüchtlingssammelstelle f.
regeneration Rückkopplung f (Rad); Regeneration f (of rubber, etc.).
regiment Regiment n.
regimental adjutant Regimentsadjutant m.
regimental commander Regimentskommandeur m.
regimental command post Regimentsgefechtsstand m.
regimental communication officer Regimentsnachrichtenoffizier m.
regimental communication platoon Regimentsnachrichtenzug m.
regimental defense area Regimentsabschnitt m.
regimental headquarters Regimentsstab m.
regimental sector Regimentsabschnitt
regimental sergeant major Stabsfeldwebel m; Stabswachtmeister m (Arty, Cav).
regimental staff Regimentsstab m.
regimental surgeon Regimentsarzt
regimental train Regimentstroß m.
region Gebiet n, Raum m, Region f; Gegend f (vicinity).
regional charts Fliegerkartenblätter npl (USA).
register v auf ein Ziel einschießen (Gunnery); aufgeben (baggage, etc.); sich einschreiben (enroll); sich melden (with the authorities).
registration Einschießen auf ein bestimmtes Ziel (Gunnery); Musterung f (for the draft).
registration and airworthiness certificate Zulassung f (Avn).
registration certificate Zulassung f (MT).
registration district Musterungsbezirk m (for the draft).
registration target Einschießziel n, Hilfsziel n.
regrouping Umgruppierung f.
regular regelmäßig.
Regular Army Reguläre Armee (USA); langdienendes Berufsheer.
regulate regeln, regulieren; verstellen, einstellen (adjust).
regulating nut Einstellmutter f.
regulating point Umleitungsstelle f (MT).
regulating station Verteilerbahnhof m (RR).
regulation Regelung f; Verstellung f (Mech); Dienstvorschrift f (service regulation).
regulation of fire Feuerregelung f (Arty).
regulation of traffic Regelung des Verkehrs, Verkehrsregelung f.
regulator Regelstange f (G recoil brake).
rein Zügel m (harness).
reinforce verstärken, nähren (Tac).
reinforced concertina roll Drahtwalze
reinforced concrete Eisenbeton m.
reinforcements Verstärkungen fpl.
reinforcing strap Belag m (harness).
related arm Schwesterwaffe f.
relative humidity relative Feuchtigkeit (Met)
relative rank entsprechender Rang.
relaxation oscillation Kippschwingung f (Rad).
relay Schütz m, Relais n (Elec).
re-lay neu einrichten, wieder richten (Gunnery).
relay coil Relaisspule f (Elec).
relay message weitergegebene Meldung.
relay messengers Stafetten fpl.
relay point See relay station.
relay station Zwischenstelle f (Sig C); Umschlagstelle (Trans).
release n Abwurf m, Auslösung f (of bombs, etc.); Freilassung f (of a prisoner); Presseaussendung f (news); Verzicht m (Law).
release button Auslöseknopf m.
release hook Sicherungshaken m (glider).
release mechanism Auslöseeinrichtung f, Abwurfvorrichtung f, Abwurfgerät n (bombing); Abdrückvorrichtung f (G); Abfeuerungseinrichtung f (Mort).
release of smoke Nebelabblasen n (CWS).
release on parole Freilassung auf Ehrenwort.
release point Auslösepunkt m (bombing).
reliable verläßlich, zuverlässig.
reliability Verläßlichkeit f, Zuverlässigkeit f.
reliability of operation Betriebssicherheit f (Mech).
relief Ablösung f (taking over); Entlastung f (of enemy pressure); Entsatz m, Entsetzung f (of a besieged garrison); Relief n (Top); Abspannung f (of tension or strain).
relief map Reliefkarte f.
relief valve Entlastungsventil n.
relieve ablösen (take over); entheben (of a command, etc.); entsetzen (a besieged garrison); entlasten (of enemy pressure); abspannen (of tension or strain).
relieve oneself austreten.
religion Religion f.
remain bleiben.
remaining velocity Änderungsgeschwindigkeit f (Ballistics).
remission of sentence Ermäßigung der Strafe.
remote control Fernsteuerung f, Fernantrieb m, Fernlenkung f.
remote control system Fernrichtanlage f (AA).
remote control unit Fernbesprechgerät n (Rad).
remote-reading compass Fernkompaß m (Ap).
remote-reading compass assembly Fernkompaßanlage f (Ap).
remount n Ersatzpferd n.
remount v remontieren.
remount area Zuchtgebiet für Truppenpferde und Maultiere.
remount depot Remonteamt n, Pferdepark m.
Remount Division Remonteinspektion f.
remount purchasing board Remonteaufkaufskommission f, Remontekommission f.
remount service Remontewesen n.
removable liner Futterrohr n, auswechselbares Seelenrohr (G).
removal of obstacles Beseitigung von Sperren.
remove abnehmen, ausbauen (Mech).
rendezvous Treffpunkt m, Versammlung f, Rendezvous n.
rendezvous point Versammlungsplatz m.
rental allowance Wohnungsgeldzuschuß m.
reorganization Reorganisation f, Umbildung f.
reorganize reorganisieren, umbilden.
repair n Instandsetzung f, Wiederherstellung f.
repair v instandsetzen, wiederherstellen, ausbessern.
repair and maintenance Instandsetzung und Unterhaltung.
repair hangar Werfthalle f (Adrm).
repair shop Instandsetzungswerkstätte f.
repair shop company Werkstattkompanie f (Inf); Panzerwerkstattkompanie f (Armd Comd).
repair shop truck Werkstattkraftwagen m (MT).
repatriation Heimbeförderung f, Heimsendung f, Repatriierung f.
repeat wiederholen; "Bitte wiederholen" (Rad procedure).
repeater compass Tochterkompaß m (Ap).
repeating coil Übertrager m; Ringübertrager m (ring-through type), (Tg, Tp).
repeating coil unit Übertragerkästchen n (Tp).
repeating theodolite Repetitions-Theodolit m (Surv).
repel abschlagen, abweisen (Tac).
replace ersetzen.
replacement n Ersatz m, Ersatzmann m.
replacement adj Ersatz-.
replacement center Ergänzungsstelle f.
replacement part Ersatzteil m.
replacements Ersatzmannschaften fpl, Ersatztruppen fpl.
replacement unit Ersatzeinheit f.
report n Bericht m, Meldung f; Knall m (explosive sound); Mündungsknall m (produced by gun or muzzle wave), Geschoßknall m (produced by shell wave) (Sound Ranging).
report v sich melden (present oneself); melden, berichten (a message, etc.); melden (a person).
report for duty sich zum Dienst melden.
report of approaching target. Einflugsmeldung f (AWS).
report of survey Ergebnis der Waffen- und Gerätuntersuchungen (Ord).
report sick sich krank melden.
reprimand Verweis m.
reprisal Vergeltung f, Vergeltungsmaßnahme f.
repulse v See repel.
request n Gesuch n, Antrag m.
request v bitten, erbitten, ansuchen, einen Antrag stellen.
request for deferment Zurückstellungsantrag m.
request for transfer Gesuch um Versetzung, Antrag auf Versetzung.
require erfordern, bedürfen.
requirements Bedarf m (Ord); Erfordernisse npl.
requisition n Anforderung f, Bestellung f.
requisition v anfordern (Adm); beitreiben (from civilians).
requisitioning Beitreibung f.
requisition number Anforderungszeichen n, Bestellnummer f.
requisition receipt Beitreibungsschein m (for goods requisitioned from civilians).
requisition ticket Bestellschein m.
re-route umleiten.
rescind aufheben, für ungültig erklären.
rescue n Bergung f, Rettung f.
rescue personnel Rettungsleute mpl.
rescue service Rettungsdienst m.
rescue squad Rettungsmannschaft f; Rettungstrupp m (CWS).
rescue vehicle Abschleppfahrzeug
rescue vessel Bergungsschiff n.
resection Rückwärtseinschneiden n, Rückwärtseinschnitt m (Surv).
reserve Reserve f (Tac); Haupttrupp m (Adv or rear Gd of march column).
reserve officer Reserveoffizier m.
Reserve Officers' Training Corps Reserveoffiziere-Ausbildungskorps n (USA).
reserve unit Reserveteil m, Ersatzteil m.
reservist Reservist m (USA).
reservoir Stausee m, Reservoir n, Wasserreservoir n (water supply); Behälter m (container).
residence ständiger Wohnsitz.
resident Einwohner m.
residential quarter Wohnviertel n.
resistance Widerstand m (Elec, Tac); Gegenwehr f (Tac); Beständigkeit f (of materials).
resistance to aging Alterungsbeständigkeit f.
resistance to corrosion Korrosionsbeständigkeit f.
resistance to heat Wärmebeständigkeit f.
resonance Resonanz f, Mitklingen n (Rad).
resonant circuit Resonanzkreis m (Rad).
respirator Staubmaske f, Staubschutzgerät n, Respirator m.
respirator bag Atemsack m (oxygen breathing apparatus).
responsible verantwortlich.
responsibility Verantwortlichkeit f, Verantwortung f.
rest n Rast f, Marschrast f (march column); Rest m (remainder); Stütze f (prop).
"Rest!" "Rührt Euch!"
rest group Rastgruppe f (march rest).
resting command ruhende Truppe.
restitution Entzerrung f (aerial Photo).
restricted nur für den Dienstgebrauch (manuals, etc.).
restricted area Sperrgebiet n.
restriction Strafmaßnahme f, Verbot
result n Ergebnis n, Resultat n.
retainer Federteller m (valve spring) (Mtr).
retaining catch Sperrklinke f (breechlock).
retaining ring Sprengring m (gas mask).
retaliate vergelten.
retaliation Vergeltung f.
retaliation attack Vergeltungsangriff
retaliation fire Erwiderungsfeuer n, Gegenfeuer n.
retard aufhalten (stop); verlangsamen (slow up); verzögern (delay).
retardation Geschwindigkeitsänderung f, negative Beschleunigung (Ballistics).
retarded ignition Spätzündung f.
retard spring Sperrfeder f (fuze).
reticle Strichplatte f (Optics).
reticle image Leuchtkreuz n (reflector sight).
reticule See reticle.
retire den Rückzug antreten, sich zurückziehen.
retired im Ruhestand, außer Dienst.
retirement Rückmarsch m, Rückzug m, planmäßiger Rückzug m (Tac); Ruhestand m (from active service).
retirement route Rückzugslinie f, Rückzugsstraße f (Tac).
retractable einziehbar.
retractable landing gear Einziehfahrgestell n, Einziehfahrwerk n, einziehbares Fahrgestell (Ap).
retreading Reifenerneuerung f, Runderneuerung f (MT).
retreat n Rückzug m (Tac); Abend-Flaggenparade f (service call).
retreat v zurückgehen, zurückweichen, sich zurückziehen.
retriever boat Rettungsboot n, Bergungsboot n.
retroactive rückwirkend.
retrograde Rück-, rückläufig.
retrograde march Rückmarsch m.
retrograde movement Rückmarschbewegung f.
return n Rückkehr f; Bericht m (report).
return flight Rückflug m (Avn).
return line Rückleitung f.
reveille Wecken n.
revenge n Rache f.
reverse n Rückschlag m (repulse); Niederlage f (defeat); Unglück n (misfortune); Rückseite f (opposite side); Rückwärtsgang m (MT).
reverse v umkehren.
reverse idler gear shaft Rücklaufwelle f (MT).
reverse movement Rückwärtsfahrt f (MT).
reverse slope Hinterhang m (Top).
reverse-slope position Hinterhangstellung f.
reverse speed Rückwärtsgang m (MT).
reversing gear Wendegetriebe n.
revet bekleiden, verkleiden.
revetment Bekleidung f (Ft).
review n Besichtigung f, Parade f.
revised neubearbeitet (manuals, etc.).
revision neubearbeitete Auflage (of a manual, etc.).
revolution Umdrehung f (Mech); Revolution f (political).
revolutions per minute Umdrehungen per Minute; Motorendrehzahl f, Drehzahl f.
revolve sich umdrehen.
revolver Revolver m (Small Arms).
revolver belt Revolvergurt m.
revolving armored turret Panzerdrehturm m (Ft).
revolving beacon light See revolving searchlight.
revolving searchlight Drehlichtscheinwerfer m (Avn).
revolving tank turret Panzerdrehturm m (Tk).
revolving turret Drehturm m, Drehkuppel f (Ap, Ft, Tk).
Reynolds number Reynoldszahl f (Aerodynamics).
r-f See radio frequency.
rheostat Schieberwiderstand m.
rhumb line Schieflaufende f, Loxodrome f (navigation).
rib Rippe f.
ribbed guide Führungsleiste f (breechblock).
ribbon Band n, Ordensband n.
ribbon microphone Bandmikrophon n.
ricochet n Abpraller m, Prallschuß m, Prellschuß n.
ricochet v abprallen.
ricochet fire Abprallerschießen n.
ride n Fahrt f (on vehicle); Ritt m (on animal).
ride v fahren (on vehicle); reiten (on animal).
ridge Kamm m, Rücken m, Höhenrippe f (Top).
ridge line Kammlinie f, Rückenlinie f (Top).
ridge soaring Hangsegeln n (glider).
riding boots Reitstiefel mpl.
riding horse Reitpferd n.
rifle Gewehr n (R); Rohr n (G).
rifle accessories Gewehrzubehör n.
rifle ammunition Gewehrmunition f.
rifle battalion Grenadierbataillon n, Schützenbataillon n.
rifle bullet Gewehrgeschoß n.
rifle butt Gewehrkolben m.
rifle company Grenadierkompanie f, Schützenkompanie f.
rifled gezogen (Ord).
rifle fire Gewehrfeuer n, Schützenfeuer n.
rifle grease Waffenfett n.
rifle grenade Gewehrgranate f.
rifle inspection Gewehrappell m.
rifleman Schütze m, Gewehrschütze m, Gewehrträger m; Grenadier m, Füsilier m (Inf rifleman).
rifle pit Schützenloch n, Schützenmulde f.
rifle platoon Zug m (Inf, Cav); Schützenzug m (Inf); Reiterzug m (H Cav).
rifle rack Gewehrstütze f, Gewehrmieke f, Gewehrmücke f.
rifle range Schießstand m, Gewehrschießstand m.
rifle regiment Grenadierregiment n, Schützenregiment n.
rifle scabbard Gewehrtragevorrichtung f (Cav).
rifle shot Gewehrschuß m.
rifle sling Gewehrriemen m.
rifle squad Gruppe f (Inf).
rifle stock Gewehrschaft m.
rifle unit Schützenverband m.
rifling Drall m (Ord).
rifling grooves Drallzüge mpl (Ord).
rigging band Ballongurt m (Bln).
right recht, richtig; rechts (to the right).
right angle rechter Winkel.
right bank Rechtskurve f (Avn); rechtes Ufer (of a stream).
"Right, face!" "Rechts, Um!"
right-hand thread Rechtsgewinde n (MT).
right-hand twist Rechtsdrall m (rifling).
right of way Vorfahrt f, Vorfahrtsrecht n, Vorfahrtserlaubnis f.
right-of-way regulations Vorfahrtregelung f.
"Right shoulder, arms!" "Das Gewehr, über!"
rigid airship starres Luftschiff.
rim Felge f (MT); Hülsenrand m (of cartridge case).
rim band Wulstband n (MT).
rime ice Reif m.
ring v anläuten, rufen (Tp).
ring and bead sight mechanisches Visier (Ap).
ring cowling Ringverkleidung f (Ap).
ring cradle Jackenwiege f (G).
ringer Wecker m (Tp).
ringing current Rufstrom m (Tp).
ring off abrufen (Tp).
ring sight Kreisvisier n (Ord).
ringworm Ringelflechte f, Ringflechte
riot Aufruhr m.
rip n Riß m.
rip v reißen, aufreißen, abreißen, zerreißen.
rip cord Abreißschnur f, Reißleine f (Bln, Prcht).
rip panel Reißbahn f (Bln).
ripsaw Schrotsäge f.
rise n Bodenerhebung f, Anhöhe f (Top).
river Fluß m, Strom m.
river bed Flußbett n.
river craft Stromfahrzeug n.
river crossing Flußübergang m.
river-crossing equipment Übersetzmittel npl, Werkzeug für Behelfsbrückenbau.
river reconnaissance Flußerkundung
river-width measuring instrument Flußbreitenmesser m.
rivet n Niete f.
rivet v nieten, vernieten.
riveted seam Niet m.
riveter Niethammer m (tool).
riveting Nietung f; Sprengnietung f (with explosive rivets).
road Straße f, Weg m.
roadbed Bahnkörper m, Bettung f (RR).
road bend Wegebiegung f.
road block Straßensperre f, Wegsperre f.
roadbound straßengängig.
road capacity Kapazität f, Aufnahmefähigkeit einer Straße.
road center Straßenknotenpunkt m (junction).
road clearance Bodenfreiheit f (MT).
road conditions Straßenverhältnisse npl, Wegeverhältnisse npl.
road construction Straßenbau m, Wegebau m.
road curve Wegebiegung f.
road discipline Straßenzucht f, Straßendisziplin f.
road ditch Straßengraben m.
road fork Straßengabel f.
road grader and tamper Bodenverdichter m (Engr).
road hole Schlagloch n (MT).
road intersection Wegekreuzung f.
road jam Marschstockung f.

road junction Straßenspinne *f*, Spinne *f*, Straßenknotenpunkt *m*.
road metal Schotter *m*.
road net Straßennetz *n*, Wegenetz *n*.
road reconnaissance Wegeerkundung
road roller Straßenwalze *f*, Chausseewalze *f*.
road rule Verkehrsregel *f*.
road screen Straßentarnung *f (Cam)*.
road sign Richtungsschild *n*.
road space Marschlänge *f*, Marschtiefe *f (march column)*.
road surface Straßendecke *f*.
road traction Bodenhaftung *f (MT)*.
roadway Fahrbahn *f*; Brückenbahn *f (Bdg)*.
roadway girder Fahrbahnträger *m (Bdg)*.
rock *n* Fels *m (geology)*; Felsblock *m (boulder)*; Stein *m (stone)*.
rock-blasting explosive Gesteinsprengmittel *n*.
rocker arm Kipphebel *m (Mtr)*.
rocket-assisted take-off Raketenstart *m (Avn)*.
rocket bomb Raketenbombe *f (Avn)*.
rocketeer *See* **rocket gunner**.
rocket gunner Raketenschütze *m*.
rocket launcher Raketenwurfmaschine *f*; Panzer-Raketenbüchse *f (AT)*.
rocket mortar Werfer *m*, Nebelwerfer *m*.
rocket projector Raketenwurfmaschine *f*.
rocket propulsion Raketenantrieb *m*.
rod Stab *m*.
rod antenna Stabantenne *f (Rad)*.
roll *n* Trommelwirbel *m*, Wirbel *m (drum)*; Rolle *f (Avn)*; Stammrolle *f (list)*; Schlingern *n (Nav, Avn)*.
roll *v* rollen; anrollen *(along runway on take-off run)*.
roll back aufrollen *(Tac)*.
roll by vorbeirollen.
roll call Appell *m*.
roller Rolle *f*, Walze *f*.
roller bearing Rollenlager *n*.
roller bumper Abfangwalze *f*, Kletterwalze *f (MT)*.
roll film Rollfilm *m*.
roll-film camera Filmkammer *f*.
rolling barrage Feuerwalze *f*.
rolling kitchen Feldküche *f*, Fahrküche *f*.
rolling mill Walzwerk *n*.
rolling stock *(RR)* rollendes Material
roll up aufrollen *(Tac)*.
roof Dach *n*.
roof antenna Dachantenne *f*.
roofing paper Dachpappe *f*.
room Zimmer *n (in a house)*; Raum *m (space)*.
root Wurzel *f*.
rope Seil *n*, Strick *m*, Schnur *f*, Leine *f*, Tau *n*.
rope ferry Seilfähre *f*, Zugfähre *f*.
rope ladder Strickleiter *f*.
rope lashing Schnürbund *n*, Leinenbund *n (Engr)*.
roster Kommandierrolle *f*.
rotary engine Umlaufmotor *m (Ap)*.
rotary snowplow Schneefräsmaschine
rotary sweeper Aufrauhbürste *f (road construction)*.
rotate umlaufen, rotieren, sich drehen.
rotating band Führungsring *m*, Führungsband *n (Am)*.
rotating beacon Drehlichtsignal *n*.
rotating crank Drehkurbel *f*.
rotation Drehbewegung *f (Ballistics)*.
rotations per minute Umdrehungszahl *f*.
rotor Anker *m (Elec)*.
rotor airplane Drehflügelflugzeug *n*.
rotor-type valve Drehschieber *m (Mech)*.
rough ground unebenes Gelände.
round *n* Patrone *f (fixed Am)*; Schuß *m (Am)*; vollständiger Schuß *(complete round)*.
round *adj* rund.
roundhouse Lokomotivschuppen *m (RR)*.
round timber Rundholz *n*.
rout *n* wilde Flucht, regellose Flucht.
route *n* Route *f*, Strecke *f*, Weg *m*, Straße *f*.
route *v* leiten, regeln.
route column Marschkolonne *f (MT)*.
route formation gelöste Flugordnung *(Avn)*.
route march Marschieren ohne Tritt.
route of advance Vormarschstraße *f*.
route of approach Anmarschstraße *f*, Anmarschweg *m*, Annäherungsweg *m*.
route of march Marschweg *m*.
route reconnaissance Straßenaufklärung *f*.
route step Marschieren ohne Tritt.
"Route step, march!" "Ohne Tritt, Marsch!"
routine message gewöhnliche Meldung.
routine order Dienstbefehl *m*.
routine radio message Betriebsfunkspruch *m*.
roving gun Arbeitsgeschütz *n (Arty)*.
rowboat Ruderboot *n*.
rpm Umdr./Min.; U/Min. *(Umdrehungen per Minute)*.
rub reiben.
rubber Gummi *m-n*, Kautschuk *m*; Radiergummi *m (eraser)*.
rubber band Gummiband *n*.
rubber block Gummipolster *n (caterpillar track)*.
rubber cable Gummikabel *n (Tp)*.
rubber coating Gummierung *f*.
rubberized material Gummistoff *m*.
rubber-tired wheel Gummirad *n*.
rubber track Gummigleiskette *f (Tk)*.
rubber truncheon Gummiknüppel *m*.
rubble Steinschlag *m*.
rucksack Rucksack *m*.
rudder Seitenruder *n (Ap)*; Steuerruder *n (Nav)*.
rudder assembly Seitenleitwerk *n (Ap)*.
rudder lobe Steuersack *m (Bln)*.
ruffles gedämpfter Trommelwirbel.
rule Regel *f*, Vorschrift *f*, Ordnung *f*.
Rules of Land Warfare Landkriegsordnung *f*.
rules of war Kriegsrecht *n*.
rumor Gerücht *n*.
run *n* Lauf *m*, Gang *m (Mech)*; waagerechter Anflug *(Avn)*.
run *v* rennen, laufen; fahren, rollen *(vehicles)*; laufen *(Mech)*; führen *(drive, manage)*.
run aground auflaufen, auffahren, auf den Grund laufen.
runner Fußmelder *m*, Läufer *m*, Meldeläufer *m (messenger)*; Kufe *f (sled)*.
runner surface Lauffläche *f (sled)*.
running board Trittbrett *n (MT)*.
running fight laufendes Gefecht.
running gear Fahrwerk *n*, Laufwerk *n*, Räderwerk *n (MT, Tk)*.
running light Seitenlicht *n*, Positionslicht *n (Ap)*.
runway Laufbahn *f*, Startbahn *f*, Landebahn *f*, Ablaufbahn *f (Adrm)*.
runway localizer beacon Landefunkfeuer *n (Rad)*.
rupture Bruch *m*, Riß *m*.
rural police Gendarmerie *f*.
ruse Kriegslist *f (Tac)*.
rush *v* erstürmen, vorprellen *(Tac)*.
by rushes sprungweise.
rust Rost *m*.
rusty rostig, verrostet.
rut Fahrrinne *f*, Spur *f*.

S

saber Säbel *m*.
sabotage Sabotage *f*.
saboteur Saboteur *m*.
saddle Sattel *m (harness) (Top)*; Bergjoch *n (Top)*.
saddlebag Packtasche *f*.
saddle blanket Woilach *m*.
saddle cover Satteltracht *f*, Tracht *f (for pack saddle)*.
saddle covering Sattelbekleidung *f*.
saddle pad Trachtenkissen *n*, Sattelkissen *n*.
saddler Sattler *m*.
saddletree Sattelbaum *m (harness)*.
safe gesichert, sicher.
put at safe sichern *(a pistol, etc.)*.
safe altitude Sicherheitshöhe *f (Avn)*.
safe-conduct Passierschein *m*.
safeguard Schutzschein *m (document)*; Schutzwache *f (guard)*.
safety Sicherung *f (Small Arms)*.
safety angle Erhöhung einschließlich der Sicherheitsteilstriche *(overhead firing)*.
safety area Sicherheitszone *f (Arty)*.
safety belt Anschnallgurt *m (Avn)*.
safety cap Sicherungskappe *f (hand grenade)*.
safety catch Sperrklinke *f (Mech)*.
safety device Sicherungsvorrichtung *f*; Sicherungskappe *f (fuze)*.
safety factor Sicherheitskoeffizient *m*.
safety fuze Leitfeuer *n*, Zeitzündschnur *f (Engr)*.
safety glass Sicherheitsglas *n*.
safety lever Sicherungshebel *m (pistol)*.
safety limit Grenze des Sicherheitsbereiches *(practice firing)*.
safety lock Sicherung *f (fuze)*.
safety measure Sicherheitsmaßnahme
safety officer Sicherheitsoffizier *m*.
safety of operation Betriebssicherheit *f (Mech)*.
safety pin Sicherungsvorstecker *m*, Vorstecker *m (bombs, mines, etc.)*; Sicherungsstift *m (fuze)*; Sicherheitsnadel *f (Clo)*.
safety pointing observer Sicherheitsunteroffizier *m (practice firing)*.
safety regulations Sicherheitsbestimmungen *fpl*.
safety spark gap Sicherheitsfunkenstrecke *f (magneto ignition)*.
safety wire Sicherheitsdraht *m (Ord)*.
safety zone gedeckter Raum *(firing)*.
sag Durchhang *m*.
sailor Matrose *m*, Seemann *m*.
sailplane Segelflugzeug *n*, Segelflieger *m (Avn)*.
sales article Marketenderware *f (at PX)*.
salient Frontvorsprung *m*, Vorsprung *m*, Kniestellung *f*, Knie *n*, Ausbuchtung *f (Tac)*; ausspringender Winkel *(Ft)*.
sally Ausfall *m (Tac)*.
salt Salz *n*.
saltpeter Salpeter *m*.
salt tablet Kochsalztablette *f*.
salt-water resistant seewasserbeständig.
salute *n* Ehrenbezeugung *f*; Gruß *m (hand salute)*; Salut *m (G)*.
salute *v* Ehrenbezeugung erweisen, grüßen.
saluting distance Grußweite *f*.
saluting gun Salutgeschütz *n*.
salvage *n* Bergung *f*, Bergen *n*.
salvage *v* sammeln, bergen.
salvage collecting Sammeltätigkeit *f*.
salvage collecting service Bergedienst *m*.
salvage dump Gerätsammelstelle *f*; Beutestelle *f (for enemy matériel)*.
salvage service Sammelwesen *n*.
salvage vessel Bergungsschiff *n*.
salvo Lage *f (pieces fire in succession)*; Salve *f (pieces fire simultaneously)*.
salvo fire Lagenfeuer *n*.
salvo release Massenabwurf *m*, Schüttwurf *m (bombing)*.
Sam Browne belt Leibgurt mit Schulterriemen.
sandbag Sandsack *m (Ft)*.
sandpaper Sandpapier *n*.
sand pit Sandgrube *f*.
sand table Sandkasten *m (Tng)*.
sand-table exercise Sandkastenspiel *n (Tng)*.
sand-table instruction Sandkastenunterricht *m (Tng)*.
sanitary sanitär, gesundheitlich, Gesundheits-.
Sanitary Corps Gesundheitsdienst *m*.
sanitary inspector Sanitätsinspekteur *m*.
sanitary survey Erkundung der hygienischen Verhältnisse eines Gebietes.
sap Sappe *f (Ft)*.
sap end *See* saphead.
saphead Sappenkopf *m*, Grabenkopf *m (Ft)*.
saturation Sättigung *f (Met)*.
sausage Wurst *f*.
saw Säge *f*.
sawhorse ramp obstacle Rampensperre *f (Engr)*.
sawmill Sägewerk *n*.
scabbard Scheide *f (saber, bayonet)*; Futteral *n (saber)*; Tragevorrichtung *f (R)*.
scaffold Baugerüst *n*, Gerüst *n*.
scale Skala *f*, Einteilung *f*; Maßstab *m (proportion)*; Lineal *n (ruler)*.
according to scale maßstabgerecht.
scale disk Skalenscheibe *f (Rad.)*
scalp Kopfhaut *f*.
scar Narbe *f*.
scarp Böschung *f (Top)*.
scatter bomb Streubrandbombe *f*.
scattered heiter *(Met)*.
scattering of fire Zersplitterung des Feuers *(Arty)*.
schedule Zeittafel *f*.
scheduled maintenance regelmäßig durchgeführte Instandsetzung.
schedule fire vorbereitetes Feuer *(Arty)*.
scheme Plan *m*.
scheme of maneuver Gefechtsplan *m*, Operationsplan *m*.
school Schule *f*.
scoop Schöpfeimer *m (excavator)*.
scorched earth tactics Brand- und Asche-Taktik *f*.
score *n* Treffergebnis *n (firing or bombing)*.
score *v* Treffer erzielen, Treffer verzeichnen *(to score hits)*.
score book Schießbuch *n*.
scotch tape Klebestreifen *m*.
scour Auskolkung *f*, Kolk *m*, Furche *f (in river bed)*.
scout *n* Späher *m*, Erkunder *m*.
scout *v* spähen, erkunden, aufklären *(Tac)*; aufklären *(Nav, Avn)*.
scout bomber Seeaufklärer *m*.
scout car Spähwagen *m*; leichter Panzerspähwagen *(Armd)*.
scout car platoon Aufklärungszug *m*.
scouting party Spähtrupp *m*.
scouting raid Erkundungsvorstoß *m*, Spähtruppvorstoß *m*.
scout vehicle Erkundungsfahrzeug *n*.
scraper Kratze *f (Engr)*.
scrap metal Altmetall *n*.
screen *n* Schleier *m*, Aufklärungsschleier *m*, Sicherungsschleier *m (Tac)*; Maske *f (Cam)*; Drahtnetz *n (wire)*; Sieb *n (sifter)*.
screen *v* verschleiern *(Tac)*.
screen grid Schirmgitter *n (Rad)*.
screen-grid tube Schirmgitterröhre *f (Rad)*.
screening Tarnung *f*, Verschleierung *f (Cam)*; Vernebelung *f (smoke)*.
screening agent Nebelstoff *m (CWS)*.
screening force Verschleierungsabteilung *f (Tac)*.
screening smoke künstlicher Nebel *(CWS)*.
screw Schraube *f*.
screwdriver Schraubenzieher *m*.
screw pitch gage Gewindeschablone *f*.
scriber Reißnadel *f*.
scud roll Böenkragen *m (Met)*.
sculling Wriggeln *n*.
sea See *f*, Meer *n*.
seacoast Küste *f*, Meeresküste *f*.
seacoast gun Küstengeschütz *n*.
seal *n* Siegel *n*, Stempel *m*.
seal *v* dichten *(Mech)*; siegeln, versiegeln *(documents, etc.)*.
sealed orders versiegelte Anordnung, versiegelter Befehl.
sea level Meeresspiegel *m*, Meereshöhe *f*.
sealing band Dichtlinie *f (gas mask)*.
sealing frame Dichtrahmen *m (gas mask)*.
sealing pitch Pech *n*.
seaman Matrose *m (apprentice seaman)*.
seaman first class Matrosenobergefreiter *m*; Matrosenhauptgefreiter *m (highest rated, with 4½ years seniority)*.
seaman second class Matrosengefreiter *m*.
sea mile *See* **nautical mile**.
seaplane Seeflugzeug *n*, Wasserflugzeug *n*, Seeflieger *m*.
seaplane base Seefliegerhorst *m*.
seaplane tender Flugzeugmutterschiff *n*, Flugzeugtender *m*.
sear Abzugsstollen *m (R)*; Abzugsstange *f (pistol)*; Spannstück *n (G)*.
section Staffel *f (Arty, Cav)*; Halbzug *m*, MG-Halbzug *m (of MG platoon)*; Gruppe *f (Cav)*; Granatwerfergruppe *f (Mort section)*; Abteilung *f (Adm department)*; Schnitt *m (cut or sectional view)*; Brückenglied *n (Bdg)*; Zelle *f (Ap)*.
sectional antenna mast Steckmast *m (Rad)*.
sectional liner geteiltes Seelenrohr *(G)*.
section leader Gruppenführer *m (Cav)*; Staffelführer *m (Cav MG section)*; Halbzugführer *m (MG section)*.
section personnel Staffeltrupp *m (Cav MG section)*.
section security officer Offizier vom Ortsdienst.
sector Abschnitt *m*, Streifen *m*, Raum *m (Tac)*.
sector boundary Abschnittsgrenze *f*.
sector of fire Beobachtungs- und Wirkungsstreifen *m*, Zielraum *m*, Zielabschnitt *m (Small Arms)*.
sector reserve Abschnittsreserve *f*.
security Sicherung *f (Tac)*.
security detachment Sicherung *f*.
security measure Sicherungsmaßnahme *f*.
security mission Sicherungsauftrag *m (Tac)*.
security on the march Marschsicherung *f*.
security patrol(s) Sicherer *mpl (Tac)*.
sedative *n* beruhigendes Mittel.
sedition Aufruhr *f*, Aufstand *m*; Meuterei *f (mutiny)*.
segregate absondern.
seize sich festfressen *(piston) (Mtr)*.
seizure Festnahme *f (arrest)*; Einnahme *f (of a locality)*; Beschlagnahme *f (confiscation)*.
selectee Ausgehobener *m*.
Selective Service Act Wehrpflichtgesetz *n (USA)*.
selectivity Trennschärfe *f (Rad)*.
selector Wähler *m (switchboard mechanism)*.
selector disk Wahlscheibe *f (switchboard mechanism)*.
selector switch Umschalter *m (Elec)*; Auslöseknopf *m (aircraft armament control)*.
self-destroying fuze Zerlegerzünder *m (AA Am)*.
self-exciting selbsterregend *(Rad)*.
search *v* suchen, absuchen, durchsuchen.
searching and traversing fire Breitenfeuer mit Tiefenfeuer *(MG)*.
searching fire Tiefenfeuer *n (MG)*.
searching sector Beobachtungsraum *m*, Luftraumausschnitt *m (AAA)*.
searchlight Scheinwerfer *m*.
searchlight battalion Scheinwerferabteilung *f (AAA)*.
searchlight battery Scheinwerferbatterie *f*.
searchlight station Scheinwerferstellung *f (AAA)*.
search patrol method Luftabwehr durch Jagdpatrouillen *(Avn)*.
sea rescue airplane Seenotflugzeug *n*.
sear nose Abzugsstollen *m (R)*.
sear spring Abzugsfeder *f (R)*.
seat Sitz *m*; Sattelsitz *m (saddle)*.
seating of projectile Geschoßführung *f (Ballistics)*.
seat pack parachute Sitzfallschirm *m*.
seat strap Sitzriemen *m (saddle)*.
seat-type parachute Sitzfallschirm *m*.
secant Schnittlinie *f*.
second Sekunde *f (time)*; an zweiter Stelle, zweit *(in order)*.
secondary air Nebenluft *f (Mtr)*.
secondary attack Nebenangriff *m*.
secondary circuit Nebenstromkreis *m*, Sekundärkreis *m (Rad)*.
secondary current Sekundärstrom *m*
secondary effort Nebenangriff *m (Tac)*.
secondary objective Ausweichsziel *n (bombing)*.
secondary operations Nebenoperationen *fpl (Tac)*.
second-in-command stellvertretender Führer.
second lieutenant Leutnant *m*; Panzerleutnant *m (Armd Comd)*; Leutnant der Flieger *(Luftwaffe)*; Assistenzarzt *m (Med)*; Veterinär *m*
secrecy Geheimhaltung *f*, Verschwiegenheit *f*.
secret *n* Geheimnis *n*.
secret *adj* geheim.
secretary Sekretär *m*, Sekretärin *f*.
Secretary of War Kriegsminister *m*
secret code Geheimschlüssel *m*.
secret text verschlüsselter Text, geschlüsselter Text, Geheimtext *m*.
self-government Selbstverwaltung *f (PW)*.
self-induction Selbstinduktion *f (Elec)*.
self-induction coil Selbstinduktionsspule *f (Elec)*.
self-loading pistol Selbstladepistole *f*.
self-loading rifle Selbstladegewehr *n*, Selbstlader *m*.
self-loading weapon Selbstladewaffe *f*.
self-locking differential gear selbstsperrendes Ausgleichgetriebe *(MT)*.
self-mutilation Selbstverstümmelung *f*.
self-propelled auf Selbstfahrlafette.
self-propelled gun Geschütz auf Selbstfahrlafette.
self-propelled mount Selbstfahrlafette *f*.
self-propulsion Selbstantrieb *m*.
self-sealing selbstdichtend.
self-seal tank geschützer Behälter.
semaphore flag Winkflagge *f*.
semiautomatic Selbstlade-, halbautomatisch.
semiautomatic fire Einzelfeuer *n*.
semiautomatic rifle Selbtladegewehr *n*.
semiautomatic weapon Selbstladewaffe *f*.
semicantilever halbfreitragend.
semifixed cartridge Hülsenkartusche *f*.
semiflat-base rim Halbflachbettfelge *f*, Halbflachfelge *f (MT)*.
semihigh-wing monoplane Schulterdecker *m*.
semi-motorized teilmotorisiert.
semiparabolic truss Halbparabel-Fachwerkträger *m (Bdg)*.
semirigid airship halbstarres Luftschiff.
semi-smokeless rauchschwach.
semitrailer Sattelschlepper *m (MT)*.
send schicken, senden; aufgeben *(a telegram, etc.)*; funken, senden *(Rad)*; tasten *(key Rad)*.
sending key Taste *f (Tg)*; Drucktaster *m (Sig lamp)*.
senior Rangältester *m*; Dienstältester
seniority Dienstalter *n*; Rangdienstalter *n (age-in-grade)*.
senior officer Rangältester *m*.
senior pilot Flugzeugführer mit über fünf Dienstjahren.
sense *n* Sinn *m*.
sense *v* die Abweichung der Schüsse vom Ziel beobachten *(Gunnery)*.
sense of direction Ortsgedächtnis *n*.
sensing Schußbeobachtung *f (Arty)*; Seitenbestimmung *f (Rad Direction Finding)*.
sensing antenna Hilfsantenne *f (Rad direction finder)*.
sensitive empfindlich; stoßempfindlich *(to shock)*; lichtempfindlich *(to light)*.
sensitive altimeter Feinhöhenmesser *m (Ap)*.
sentence of confinement Freiheitsstrafe *f*.
sentence of confinement to a penitentiary Zuchthausstrafe *f*.
sentence of confinement to a prison Gefängnisstrafe *f*.
sentry Posten *m*, Wachposten *m*.
sentry box Schilderhaus *n*.
separate-loading ammunition getrennte Munition, Kartuschmunition *f*.
separator Scheider *m (storage battery)*.
sequence of events Verlauf *m (Tac)*.
sergeant Unteroffizier *m*.
sergeant major *See* **regimental sergeant major**.
sergeant of the guard dienstältester Unteroffizier der Wache *(interior guard)*.
serial number laufende Nummer.
series circuit Kreisleitung *f (Elec)*.
series connection Hauptschlußschaltung *f*, Hintereinanderschaltung *f*, Reihenschaltung *f (Elec)*.
series motor Hauptschlußmotor *m (Elec)*.
series-parallel connection Gruppenschaltung *f (Elec)*.
serious casualty Schwerverwundeter *m*.

serum Serum n.
service n Dienst m; Wartung f (maintenance).
service v warten (Ap, MT).
service cap Schirmmütze f.
service ceiling Dienstgipfelhöhe f, Volltraghöhe f (Avn).
service coat Feldbluse f.
service color Waffenfarbe f.
Service Command Wehrkreis m.
service commander Wehrkreisbefehlshaber m, kommandierender General eines Wehrkreises.
service company Nachschub- und Instandhaltungskompanie f (USA).
service gas mask Dienstmaske f.
service manual Dienstvorschrift f.
service of the piece Geschützbedienung f, Bedienung f.
service of the piece drill Geschützexerzieren n.
service personnel Bodenpersonal n (Avn).
service pilot Transportflieger m.
service practice Ausbildungsschießen n (Arty).
service record Wehrstammbuch n.
service regulation Dienstvorschrift f.
Services of Supply See Army Service Forces.
service status Wehrdienstverhältnis n.
service stripe Ärmelborte für je drei Dienstjahre (USA).
service troop Nachschub- und Instandhaltungsschwadron eines Kavallerieregiments (USA).
service uniform Dienstanzug m.
service with troops Truppendienst m, Dienst bei der Truppe.
servicing Wartung f.
servo action Servowirkung f (servo brake) (MT).
servo control Hilfsvorrichtung f, Servomotor m, Trimmklappe f (Ap).
servo tab Trimmklappe f (Ap).
sesquiplane Anderthalbdecker m, Eineinhalbdecker m (Ap).
set v einstellen, verstellen (adjust); setzen, stellen (place).
setback Rückstoß m (Tech); Rückschlag m (Tac).
set-forward point Vorhaltepunkt m (Gunnery).
setscrew Klemmschraube f, Grenzschraube f.
setting Einstellung f (adjusting); Ablesung f (reading).
setting-up exercise Freiübung f.
sextant Sextant m.
shackle Schäkel m (chain); Federlasche f (vehicle spring); Tragvorrichtung f (Ap bomb rack).
shadow Schatten m.
shadow effect Schattenwirkung f (Cam).
shaft Welle f (Mech); Schacht m (mining); Deichsel f (wagon).
shallow seicht (water); flach (container).
shallow trench Kriechgraben m.
sham battle Scheingefecht n.
shank Ankerrute f (of an anchor).
shape Form f, Gestalt f.
sharp scharf (blade); spitz (point).
sharpen schärfen; schleifen (grind); wetzen, abziehen (hone); spitzen, zuspitzen (a point).
sharpness Schärfe f.
sharpness of resonance Abstimmschärfe f (Rad).
sharpshooter Scharfschütze m.
sharp turn kurze Kehrtwendung, Turn m (Avn).
shatter splittern, zersplittern.
shatterproof glass splittersicheres Glas, Sicherheitsglas n.
shaving cream Rasiercreme f.
shaving soap Rasierseife f.
sheaf Garbe f (Ballistics).
sheaf of fire Feuergarbe f, Geschoßgarbe f, Schußgarbe f.
shear n Abscheren n, Abscherung f.
shear lashing Kreuzbund m (for diagonal timbers).
shears Schere f (Inst).
shear strength Scherfestigkeit f.
shear stress Scherspannung f.
shear wire Scherdraht m (fuze).
shed Schuppen m.
sheet Bogen m, Blatt n, (paper); Bettuch n, Leintuch n (bed); Blech n (metal); Schicht f (coating or layer); Kartenblatt n (map).
sheet metal Blech n.
sheet-metal case Eisenblechgehäuse n, Blechgehäuse n (Rad).
sheet steel Stahlblech n.
shell n Granate f (Am); Zünderhalter m (blasting cap); Hülse f (casing).
shell v mit Artillerie beschießen, unter Artilleriefeuer nehmen, mit Artilleriefeuer belegen.
shellac Schellack m.
shell case Granathülse f (Am).
shell cavity Geschoßhöhlung f (Am).
shell crater Granattrichter m.
shell filler Granatfüllung f (Am).
shell fragment Sprengstück n.
shell hoist Munitionsaufzug m.
shell hole Granatloch n.
shellproof bombensicher (heavy); schußsicher (light).
shellproof cover bombensichere Deckung (heavy), schußsichere Deckung (light) (Ft).
shellshock See battle fatigue.
shell splinter Granatsplitter m.
shell wave Kopfwelle f (Ballistics).
shelter Deckung f (cover); Unterstand m, Schutzraum m (Ft); Unterkunft f (billets); Luftschutzraum m (air raid).
shelter area Unterkunftsbezirk m, Unterkunftsraum m.
shelter half Zeltbahn f.
sheltering Unterbringung f.
shelter tent Zelt n.
shield Schild m, Brustschild m, Schutzschild m (G).
shielding Abschirmung f (Rad).
shield support Schildstütze f (G).
shift n Schicht f (of workmen); Feuerverlegen n (of fire).
shift v schalten (MT); verlegen, verschieben, versetzen (move).
shifter fork Schaltgabel f (MT).
shift rail Schaltstange f (MT).
shim Lamelle f (Mech); Futterholz n (Engr).
shimmying Flattern n (MT).
shin Schienbein n.
shine v leuchten, glänzen (glisten); putzen (to polish).
ship Schiff n.
ship-based antiaircraft artillery Schiffsflak f.
shipboard airplane Bordflugzeug n.
shipboard antiaircraft artillery Bordflak f (Nav).
shipboard reconnaissance airplane Bordaufklärer m.
shipbuilding Schiffbau m.
shipbuilding yard Schiffswerft f, Schiffbauwerft f.
ship concentration Schiffsansammlung f.
shipment Lieferung f, Sendung f, Versand m.
shipment-safe fuze transportsicherer Zünder (Am).
shipping Schiffahrt f, Schiffswesen n (Nav).
shipping ticket Lieferschein m.
shipwreck Schiffbruch m.
shipyard Werft f, Schiffswerft f.
shipyard installation Werftanlage f.
shirt Hemd n.
shoals Untiefen fpl.
shock Stoß m; Schock m (Med); Schlag m (Elec).
shock absorber Stoßdämpfer m (MT).
shock-absorbing strut Federbein n (Ap).
shock power Stoßkraft f.
shock strut Flugzeugbein n (Ap).
shock troops Stoßtruppen fpl.
shoe Schuh m (Clo, Tech); Decke f (tire); Kettenglied n (Trac); Backe f, Klotz m (brake); Hufeisen n (of horse).
shoe brake Backenbremse f (MT).
shoeing Hufbeschlag m (horse).
shoelace Schnürsenkel m.
shoot schießen, feuern.
shoot down abschießen.
shooting gallery Schießhalle f, gedeckte Bahn.
shop Werkstatt f (Tech); Laden m (store).
shop foreman Werkmeister m.
shore Ufer n (bank); Küste f (coast); Strand m (beach); Land n
shore anchor line Landankertau n.
shore battery Küstenbatterie f (Arty).
shore sill Uferbalken m (Bdg).
shoreward ponton Landfahrzeug n.
shoreward side Landbord m.
short n Kurzschuß m (Gunnery); Kurzschluß m (Elec).
short adj kurz.
shortage Fehlbestand m.
short circuit Kurzschluß m (Elec).
short range nächste Entfernung (up to 100 meters); nahe Entfernung (up to 400 meters).
shorts kurze Unterhose (Clo).
short wave Kurzwelle f (Rad).
short-wave switch Wellenstufenschalter m (Rad).
short-wave transmitter Kurzwellensender m.
shot n Schuß m (discharge of firearms); Schrot m (for shotgun); Vollgeschoß n (solid projectile).
shot group Zieldreieck n (marksmanship Tng); Einschlagsgruppe f (Arty).
shotgun Flinte f, Schrotgewehr n.
shotgun shell Schrotpatrone f.
shot pattern See shot group.
shoulder n Schulter f; Sommerweg m (of road).
shoulder v schultern (rifle, etc.).
shoulder arms das Gewehr übernehmen.
shoulder blade Schulterblatt n.
shoulder loop Schulterstück n (officers), Schulterklappe f (enlisted men, Ger).
shoulder piece Schulterstück n (MG).
shoulder stock Schulterstütze f (MG).
shoulder strap Schultergurt m (gas mask carrier). See also shoulder loop.
shovel Schaufel f, Schippe f (hand); Bagger m, Löffelbagger m (power); Spaten m (spade).
shower Regenschauer m, Regenguß m (Met).
shower bath Duschanlage f.
shower-bath truck Badewagen m.
shrapnel Schrapnell n (Am).
shrapnel ball Schrapnellkugel f (Am).
shroud line Fangleine f (Prcht).
shrubbery screen Strauchmaske f (Cam).
shunt Nebenschluß m (Elec).
shunt motor Nebenschlußmotor m (Elec).
shut-off valve Abstellhahn m.
shutter Weckerfallklappe f (Tp); Blende f (Tk, searchlight, camera).
shutter cover Blendabdeckung f (Tk).
shutter lever Blendenhebel m (searchlight).
shuttle traffic Pendelverkehr m.
sick krank.
sick bay Schiffslazarett n (Nav).
sick call Krankenappell m.
go on sick call sich krank melden.
sick leave Krankenurlaub m.
sick report book Krankenmeldebuch n, Krankenbuch n.
side Seite f.
sidecar Beiwagen m, Seitenwagen m.
sidecar motorcycle Beiwagenkrad n, Beiwagenmaschine f.
sidecar rider Beifahrer m (Mtcl).
side door Seitenklappe f (Tk).
sidelap seitliche Überdeckung (aerial Photo).
side-loading ramp Seitenrampe f.
side of receiver Kastenwand f (MG).
side outrigger Seitenholm m (AA gun).
side plate Lafettenwand f (G carriage).
siderail Rödelbalken m (Bdg).
siderail clamp Rödelzange f (Bdg).
side slip seitliches Abrutschen (Avn).
side spillway Umlauf m (dam).
side spray seitlicher Sprengkegel (air burst).
side street Nebenstraße f, Seitenstraße f.
sidetone circuit Mithöreinrichtung f (Rad, Tp).
side view Seitenansicht f.
side view flight Vorbeiflug m (AA).
sidewise-striking projectile Bauchtreffer m.
siding Ausweichgleis n, Ausweichstelle f, Nebengleis n, Überholungsgleis f (for passing) (RR).
siege Belagerung f.
siege warfare Festungskrieg m.
Siegfried Line See West Wall.
sight n Visier n, Zielgerät n (Ord); Gesichtssinn m (sense).
sight v visieren, anvisieren; zielen, anzielen (aim); anrichten (point); erblicken (see).
sight adjustment rod Aufsatzstange f (G).
sight assembly Visiereinrichtung f.
sight base Visierfuß m.
sight bracket Visierträger m, Aufsatzträger m (Ord).
sight defilade Sichtdeckung f.
sight equipment Richtgerät n (G).
sight extension Verlängerungsstück n (G sight).
sight in anschießen.
sighting device Visiereinrichtung f.
sighting disk Ziellöffel m.
sighting level Nivellierlibelle f (plane table).
sighting mechanism Zieleinrichtung f, Visiereinrichtung f, Visiervorrichtung f, Zielgerät n (Ord).
sighting shot Anschuß m.
sighting-triangle aiming exercise Dreieckzielen n (Gunnery).
sight leaf Visierklappe f (Small Arms).
sight mount Aufsatz m, Richtaufsatz m.
sight-mount bracket Richtaufsatzträger m.
sight-mount housing Aufsatzgehäuse n (G).
sight notch Kimme f (MG, R).
sight peephole Fenster n (AA sight).
sight-port cover Visierklappe f (G shield).
sight shield Visierschild m (G).
sight slide Visierschieber m (MG, R).
sight support Aufsatzträger m (G).
sign Zeichen n (symbol, signal); Schild n, Richtungsschild n (road).
signal n Signal n, Zeichen n.
signal ammunition Erkennungsmunition f.
signal battalion Nachrichtenabteilung f.
signal book Signalbuch n (Nav).
signal cartridge Signalpatrone f, Leuchtpatrone f.
signal center Nachrichtenzentrale f.
signal communication Nachrichtenverbindung f. See also communication.
signal communications Nachrichtenwesen n.
signal communication traffic Nachrichtenverkehr f.
signal company Nachrichtenkompanie f.
Signal Corps Nachrichtentruppen fpl.
Signal Corps School Nachrichtenschule f (USA).
signal depot Nachrichtenpark m.
signal equipment Nachrichtengerät n.
signal flag Signalflagge f (Nav); Winkflagge f (semaphore).
signaling current Rufstrom m (Tp).
signaling panel Tuchzeichen n (airground Com).
signal intelligence Nachrichtenaufklärung f.
signal lamp Blinkgerät n, Blinklampe f.
signal-lamp apparatus Blinkgerät n.
signal-lamp communication Blinkverbindung f.
signal-lamp message Blinkspruch m.
signal-lamp spotting squad Blinksuchtrupp m.
signal-lamp squad Blinktrupp m.
signal-lamp station Blinkstelle f.
signal-lamp transmission Blinken n; Tasten n (keying).
signal motor vehicle Nachrichtenkraftfahrzeug n.
signal officer Nachrichtenoffizier m, Nachrichtenführer m.
signal operation instructions dem Operationsbefehl beigefügte besondere Anordnung des Nachrichtenführers.
signal order Befehl für den Nachrichteneinsatz.
signal personnel Nachrichtenleute mpl.
signal pistol Leuchtpistole f; Kampfpistole f (for Sig and/or incendiary cartridges).
signal pistol ammunition Leuchtpistolenmunition f.
signal projector Signalwerfer m.
signal rocket Leuchtrakete f, Signalrakete f.
signal strength Lautstärke f (Rad).
signal supplies Nachrichtengerät n.
signal-supply dump Nachrichtengerätpark m.
signal troops Nachrichtentruppen fpl.
signal vehicle Nachrichtenfahrzeug n.
signal wagon Nachrichtenwagen m.
signature Unterschrift f (written name); Kartenzeichen n (maps).
sign post Richtposten m (road).
silence Schweigen n, Stille f, Ruhe f.
silencer Knalldämpfer m (R, pistol, etc.).
silent alarm stiller Alarm.
"silent soldier" S-Mine f, Schützenmine f.
silhouette Schattenriß m.
silhouette target Kampfwagenscheibe f (Tk).
silk Seide f.
sill Schwelle f, Fußlatte f (Bdg).
silt Triebsand m.
silver Silber n.
Silver Star Silberstern m (decoration, USA).
simple einfach.
simple anchor hitch einfacher Ankerstich (with bowline).
simplex coil Ringübertrager m (Tg, Tp).
simplexed connection Simultanschaltung f (Tg, Tp).
simplexed telegraphy Unterlagerungstelegraphie f.
simulate vortäuschen (Tac).
simulated agent Übungsreizstoff m (CWS).
simulated fire Geschützzielfeuer n (representing an enemy gun target); Gewehrzielfeuer n (representing an enemy R or MG target).
simulated mine Scheinmine f.
simultaneous gleichzeitig.
simultaneous two-way radio traffic Funkdoppelverkehr m.
sine Sinus m (Math).
single einzeln (one); allein (alone); ledig (unmarried).
single-barreled einläufig.
single connection einfache Vermittlung
single-cylinder engine Einzylindermotor m.
single-engine einmotorig.
single file Reihe f.
single-fuselage airplane Einrumpfflugzeug n.
single-grid tube Eingitterröhre f (Rad).
single-intersection method Einzelschnittverfahren n (Flash Ranging).
single-line charge gestreckte Ladung, Reihenladung f (Engr).
single loader Einzellader m.
single-place fighter Jagdeinsitzer m.
single-plate clutch Einscheibenkupplung f (MT).
single rank Linie zu 1 Glied (Inf).
single release Einzel(ab)wurf m (Bombing).
single-seater einsitzig.
single-seater airplane Einsitzer m.
single-seater fighter Jagdeinsitzer m
single shot Einzelschuß m.
single-shot fire Einzelfeuer n (MG).
single-shot weapon Einzellader m.
single-slot wing einschlitziger Schlitzflügel (Ap).
single-span stringer bridge Uferbrücke f.
single-station spotting Einfachanschnitt m.
singletree attachment hook Zughaken m (limber).
sinking Versenkung f (Nav).
siren Sirene f, Heulsignal n.
site Stelle f, Platz m, Ort m. See also angle of site.
site scale See angle of site scale.
sitting position Anschlag sitzend (firing).
situation Lage f, Zustand m.
situation map Lagenkarte f (Tac).
six-engine sechsmotorig.
six-wheel motor vehicle Sechsradkraftfahrzeug n.
six-wheel vehicle Dreiachser m.
size Grösse f; Nummer f (of shoes, gloves).
skeet range Wurftaubenschießstand m, Tontaubenschießstand m.
skeet shooting Taubenschießen n, Tontaubenschießen n.
sketch Skizze f.
ski n Ski m, Schi m.
ski v Ski laufen.
ski battalion Schibataillon n.
skid n Kufe f (sled runner).
skid chain Gleitschutzkette f, Schneekette f (MT).
skidding Schleudern n (MT).
skid mark Bremsspur f (MT).
skill Geschicklichkeit f.
skilled ausgebildet (Mil).
skin Haut f, Außenhaut f, Bespannung f (Ap).
skin decontamination agent Hautentgiftungsmittel n.
skin effect Hautwirkung f (Rad).
skip zone tote Zone (Rad).
skirmish Scharmützel n, Plänkelei f.
skirmisher's trench Schützenmulde f.
skirmishing Plänkeln n.
skirt Seitenblatt n, Satteltasche f (saddle).
skirting Laufwerkpanzerung f (Tk).
ski troops Skitruppen fpl.
skull Schädel m.
sky Himmel m; Luftraum m (Avn).
sky wave Raumwelle f (Rad).
sky-wave effect Raumwellenwirkung f (Rad).
slack schlaff, locker.
slant plane Seitenvorhaltsebene f (AA gunnery).
slant range Schrägentfernung f (AA Gunnery).
slant range to future position Treffpunktentfernung f (AA Gunnery).
slant range to midpoint Wechselpunktentfernung f (AA Gunnery).
slant range to present position Meßentfernung f (instant of range determination), Abschußentfernung f (instant of firing) (AA Gunnery).
slash n Streich m, Hieb m (bayonet).
slashing weapon Hiebwaffe f.
slat Hilfsflügel m, Vorflügel m, Zusatzflügel m (Ap wing).
sled Schlitten m.
sledge hammer Vorschlaghammer m.
sled runner Kufe f.
sleeping bag Schlafsack m.
sleet Frostgraupeln fpl, Eisregen m.
sleeve Ärmel m (Clo); Schieber m (sleeve-type engine); Kabelverbinder m (cable connector); Muffe f (pipe connector).
sleeve cuff Ärmelaufschlag m (Clo).
sleeve insignia Ärmelabzeichen n.
sleeve target Luftsack m (AAA target practice).
sleeve-type engine Schiebermotor m, ventilloser Motor.
sleigh Rohrschlitten m (G).
sleigh mount Schlitten m (MG).
slew schwenken (gun laying).
slide Gleitbahn f (G cradle).
slide bearing Gleitlager n (Mech).
slide buckle Schiebeschnalle f.
slide fastener Reißverschluß m.
slide mechanism Gleitvorrichtung f (MG).
slide plate Gleitwand f (MG).
slide rule Rechenschieber m.
sliding bolt Gleitriegel m (breechblock).
sliding lever Gleithebel m (breechblock).
sliding-lever breechblock Gleithebelverschluß m.
sliding roof Schiebedach n (Ap).
sliding surface Lauffläche f (sled).
sliding-type breechblock Schubkurbelverschluß m, Leitwellverschluß m
sling Gewehrriemen m (R).
"Sling arms!" "Gewehr umhängen!"
sling lashing Schleuderbund m (Engr).
sling psychrometer Schleuderpsychrometer n (Met).
sling swivel Riemenbügel m (R).
slip Abrutschen n, Slip m (Ap); Schlupf m (propeller).
slipstream Luftschraubenstrahl m, Propellerwind m, Nachstrom m (Avn).
slip tank Abwurfbehälter m (Ap).
slit Schlitz m.
slit trench Deckungsgraben m, Splittergraben m, Fliegerschutzgraben m.
slogan Schlagwort n.
slope n Böschung f, Abdachung f, Geländeneigung f, Neigung f, Hang m, Abhang m, Steigung f (Top).
slope v abfallen (Top).

slope of fall Tangens des Fallwinkels *(Ballistics)*.
slope position Hangstellung *f (Ft)*.
sloping terrain abfallendes Gelände.
slot Nut(e) *m(f) (Tech)*; Schlitz *m (Ap wing)*; Sehschlitz *m (direct-vision slot, Tk)*.
slotted aileron Schlitzquerruder *n*
slotted wing Schlitzflügel *m*, Spaltflügel *m (Ap)*.
slow langsam.
slow match Lunte *f (fuze lighter)*.
slow roll gesteuerte Rolle *(Avn)*.
sluice Schleuse *f*.
slurry Losantinbrei *m (calcium hypochlorite, CWS)*.
small klein.
small arms Handfeuerwaffen *fpl (Ord)*.
small-bore barrel Kleinkaliberlauf *m*
small-bore practice Kleinkaliberschießen *n*.
small-bore target range Kleinschießplatz *m (R)*.
small of the stock Kolbenhals *m (R)*.
smallpox Pocken *fpl*, Blattern *fpl*.
smash zerschmettern.
smoke Rauch *m*; Nebel *m (CWS)*.
smoke agent Nebelstoff *m*, Nebelmittel *n (CWS)*.
smoke and flash defilade Sichtdeckung *f (Arty)*.
smoke apparatus Nebelgerät *n (CWS)*.
smoke battalion Werferabteilung *f*.
smoke blanket Nebeldecke *f (CWS)*.
smoke bomb Nebelbombe *f (Avn)*.
smoke candle Schwelkerze *f*, Nebelkerze *f*, Rauchkerze *f (CWS)*.
smoke cartridge Nebelpatrone *f*.
smoke charge Rauchladung *f (Am)*.
smoke cloud Nebelwolke *f*, Rauchwolke *f (CWS)*.
smoke composition Rauchsatz *m*.
smoke container Nebelkasten *m (case)*, Nebeltrommel *f (drum) (CWS)*.
smoke-container firing device Nebelzündmittel *n (CWS)*.
smoke coverage Nebelausdehnung *f (CWS)*.
smoke curtain Nebelwand *f (CWS)*.
smoke effect Raucherscheinung *f (Flash Ranging)*.
smoke equipment Nebelgerät *n (CWS)*.
smoke-filled chemical cylinder Nebelabblasgerät *n (CWS)*.
smoke filler Rauchkörper *m (Am)*.
smoke generator Rauchentwickler *m*; Rauchofen *m (Adrm)*.
smoke grenade Nebelhandgranate *f*.
smokeless rauchschwach, rauchlos.
smokeless powder rauchschwaches Pulver.
smoke party Nebeltrupp *m (Engr)*.
smoke pellet Rauchsatz *m (Am)*.
smoke pot Nebeltopf *m (CWS)*.
smoke-producing unit Nebelabteilung *f (CWS) (Pers)*.
smoke projectile Nebelgeschoß *n*.
smoke-puff charge Kanonenschlag mit Raucherscheinung, Rauchkörper *m (simulated fire)*.
smoke screen Nebelschleier *m*; Nebelwand *f*, Rauchwand *f*, Rauchvorhang *m (vertical)*; Nebeldecke *f (horizontal)*.
smoke-screened area Nebelzone *f (CWS)*.
smoke screening Vernebelung *f*, Blenden *n*; Feindvernebelung *f (against enemy Obsn)*.
smoke-screening fire Blendungsschießen *n (Arty)*.
smoke-screening tank Nebelpanzerkampfwagen *m*.
smoke shell Nebelgranate *f*, Rauchgranate *f (Arty)*; Nebelwurfgranate *f (Mort)*.
smoke-shell firing Nebelschießen *n (Arty)*.
smoke-shell mortar Nebelwerfer *m*.
smoke signal cartridge Rauchpatrone *f*.
smoke tank Nebelgerät *n (for air Cml spraying)*.
smooth glatt; eben *(even)*; flach *(flat)*.
smooth-bore *adj* glatt *(Ord)*.
snaffle Trense *f (harness)*.
snaffle bit Trensengebiß *n (harness)*.
snaffle rein Trensenzügel *m (harness)*.
snap fastener Druckknopf *m*.
snap gage Außengrenzlehre *f*.
sneak raider Störflieger *m (Avn)*.
sneeze gas Niesgas *n (CWS)*.
sniffing test Riechprobe *f (CWS)*.
sniff set Riechprobenkasten *m (CWS)*.
sniper Heckenschütze *m*, Scharfschütze *m*; Baumschütze *m (in a tree)*.
sniping Schießen aus dem Hinterhalt.
sniping post Scharfschützennest *n*.
snow Schnee *m*.
snow chain Schneekette *f (MT)*.
snow flurries Schneetreiben *n (Met)*.
snow-pellet shower Graupelschauer *m (Met)*.
snow pit Schneeloch *n*.
snowplow Schneepflug *m*.
snowshoe Schneereifen *m*, Schneeschuh *m*.
soakage pit Müllgrube *f (for refuse)*.
soaking pit Vergütungsanlage *f (Ord)*.
soap Seife *f*.
soaring Segeln *n (glider)*.
socket Hülse *f (G carriage)*; Kugelpfanne *f (Mort)*; Lampenfassung *f*, Fassung *f (Elec)*; Buchse *f*, Stutzen *m*, Zapfenlager *n (Tech)*.
socket connection Sockelschaltung *f (Rad tube)*.
socket wrench Steckschlüssel *m*, Aufsteckschlüssel *m*.
sodium Natrium *n*.
sodium chloride tablet Natriumchloridtablette *f*.
sodium hydroxide kaustisches Natron, Ätznatron *n*.
sodium hypochlorite Chlornatron *n*, Natriumhypochlorit *n*.
sodium sulfide Schwefelnatrium *n*, Natriumsulfid *n*.
sodium sulfite schwefligsaures Natrium, Natriumsulfit *n*.
"softening up" Sturmreifmachung *f*.
soil Erde *f*, Boden *m*, Grund *m*.
solar plexus Sonnengeflecht *n*, Solarplexus *m*.
solder *n* Lötzinn *n*, Lötmetall *n*.
solder *v* löten.
soldering iron Lötkolben *m*.
soldier Soldat *m*.
soldierly qualities Soldatentum *n*.
sole Sohle *f*.
solenoid Magnetspule *f*, Solenoid *n (Elec)*.
solid tire Vollgummireifen *m*, Vollreifen *m*.
solitary confinement Einzelhaft *f*.
solo flight Alleinflug *m*.
solo motorcycle Einzelkrad *n*, Solokrad *n*.
solution Lösung *f*.
solvent Lösungsmittel *n*.
sonic altimeter Echolot *n*, Behmlot *n*, Relativhöhenmesser *m (Ap)*.
sort *v* sortieren, aussondern.
sortie Ausfall *m (Tac)*; Einsatz *m*, Feindflug *m (Avn)*.
sound Ton *m*, Schall *m*, Laut *m*; Geräusch *n (noise)*; Knall *m (report)*.
sound and flash ranging Lichtschallmessen *n*.
sound communication Verbindung durch Schallzeichen.
sound-communication device Schallmittel *n*.
sound effect Knallerscheinung *f (Sound Ranging)*.
sounding lotbare Wassertiefe *(depth of water)*.
sounding lead Lot *n*, Peillot *n*, Senkblei *n (Nav)*.
sound intensity Lautstärke *f*.
sound lag Schallverzug *m (AA Gunnery)*.
sound-lag correction Ausschalten des Schallverzugs.
sound location akustische Ortung, Schallortung *f (AAA)*.
sound locator Richtungshörer *m*, Horchgerät *n (AAA)*.
soundproof schalldicht.
sound ranging Schallmessung *f (Arty)*.
sound-ranging altimeter Echolot *n (Avn)*.
sound-ranging microphone Schallmikrophon *n (Arty)*.
sound-ranging net Schallmeßsystem *n (Arty)*.
sound-ranging section Schallmeßtrupp *m*, Meßtrupp *m (Arty)*.
sound-ranging station Schallmeßstelle *f (Arty)*.
sound-recording apparatus Schallaufnahmegerät *n* (Sound Ranging).
sound reproduction Tonwiedergabe *f (Elec)*.
sound signaling *See* sound communication.
sound track Knallbild *n (Sound Ranging)*.
sound travel time Stoppzeit *f (Sound Ranging)*.
sound truck Tonwagen *m (film unit)*.
sound wave Schallwelle *f*.
soup Suppe *f*.
source Quelle *f*.
south Süden *m*.
sovereignty of the air Lufthoheit *f*.
soya-bean flour Bratlingspulver *n*.
space Raum *m*; Abstand *m (distance)*; Zwischenraum *m (interval)*.
space charge Raumladung *f (Rad tube)*.
spaced armor Hohlraumpanzerung *f*, Schottpanzerung *f (Tk)*.
spade Sporn *m (G)*; Spaten *m (tool)*.
spade arm Spornarm *m (G)*.
spade plate Spornblech *n (G)*.
spadework Schanzarbeiten *fpl (field* ...
span Spannweite *f (Ap, Bdg)*; Brückenstützweite *f*, Stützweite *f (span between supports)*; Brückenbogen *m (arch)*; Strecke *f (bay)*.
spar Holm *m (Ap, Bdg)*; Stange *f (pole)*; Rundholz *n (round timber)*; Stiel *m (compression member)*; Strebe *f (tension member)*.
spar bracing Verstrebung *f (Bdg)*.
spare *adj* Ersatz-, Vorrats-.
spare *v* ersparen *(save)*; schonen *(keep intact)*; aufheben, aufbewahren *(keep for future use)*.
spare barrel Vorratslauf *m (MG)*.
spare part Ersatzteil *m*, Vorratsteil *m*.
spare parts truck Werkstattgerätkraftwagen *m (MT)*.
spark Funke *m*.
spark adjustment Zündverstellung *f (Mtr)*.
spark control Zündhebel *m (lever)*; Zündverstellung *f (action or function)*.
spark discharge Funkentladung *f*.
spark gap Funkenstrecke *f*.
spark plug Zündkerze *f*.
spark-plug cable Zündkabel *n*.
spark-plug point Elektrode *f*.
spar trestle Stangenbock *m (Bdg)*.
speaker Lautsprecher *m (Rad)*.
speaker cabinet Lautsprechertruhe *f (Rad)*.
spearhead Stoßkeil *m (Tac)*.
special *adj* besonder, Sonder-.
special agreement Sonderabkommen *n (Law)*.
special announcement Sondermeldung *f (Rad)*.
special court-martial Sonderkriegsgericht *n*.
special gas mask Sondergasmaske *f*.
specialist Fachmann *m*, Fachverständiger *m*; Sonderführer *m (uniformed specialist in Ger Armed Forces with nominal rank up to Bn commander but no actual Mil rank)*.
special message Sondermeldung *f (Rad)*.
special mission Sonderauftrag *m*.
special-missions staff officer Ordonnanzoffizier *m*.
special operations Gefechte unter besonderen Verhältnissen *(Tac)*.
special orders Sonderverfügungen *fpl*, Tagesbefehl *m (Adm)*; besondere Postenanweisung *(guard duty)*.
special-purpose airplane Sonderflugzeug *n*.
special-purpose motor truck Sonderlastkraftwagen *m*.
special-purpose vehicle Sonderfahrzeug *n*.
special radio message Sonderfunkspruch *m*.
special service practice Belehrungs- und Versuchsschießen *n (Arty)*.
special services besondere Dienstzweige.
special telephone call Sondergespräch *n*.
specifications Angaben *fpl*, Beschreibung *f*.
specific gravity spezifisches Gewicht, Einheitsgewicht *n*.
speed Geschwindigkeit *f*; Gang *m (gear shifting)*.
speedboat Schnellboot *n*.
speed increase Geschwindigkeitssteigerung *f*.
speed of current Stromgeschwindigkeit *f*.
speed of target Zielgeschwindigkeit
speedometer Geschwindigkeitsmesser *m*; Tachograph *m (with odometer)*.
spike Sporn *m (MG tripod)*; Spiker *m*, Stift *m (long nail)*.
spillway Überfall *m (dam)*.
spillway crest Überfallkrone *f (dam)*.
spillway weir Überfallwehr *n*, Sturzwehr *n*.
spin Trudeln *n (Ap)*; Geschoßdrall *m*, Geschoßdrehung *f (of projectile)*.
go into a spin abtrudeln.
spinal column Wirbelsäule *f*.
spindle Schwingschenkel *m (steering-knuckle) (MT)*.
spine Wirbel *m*.
spinner Luftschraubenhaube *f*, Propellerhaube *f*, Haube *f (Ap propeller)*.
spiral Kurvengleitflug *m (Avn)*.
spiral dive Sturzspirale *f*; Korkenzieher *m (Avn)*.
spiral spring Spiralfeder *f*, Wickelfeder *f*.
spiral-spring equilibrator Spiralfederausgleicher *m (AA gun)*.
spiral wire Drahtspirale *f*.
splash Spritzer *m*.
splash lubrication Spritzumlaufschmierung *f (Mtr)*.
splice *n* Splissung *f*, Spleißung *f*; Kabelverbindung *f (Tp wire)*.
splice *v* spleißen, splissen.
spline shaft Keilwelle *f (MT)*.
splint Armschiene *f*, Schiene *f (Med)*.
splinter Splitter *m*; Bombensplitter *m (bomb)*; Granatsplitter *m (shell)*; Sprengstück *n (fragment)*.
splinterproof splittersicher.
splinterproof cover splittersichere Deckung.
splinterproof shelter splittersicherer Unterstand *m*.
split-field range finder Schnittbildentfernungsmesser *m*, Halbbildentfernungsmesser *m*.
split flap Spreizklappe *f (Ap)*.
split ring Spaltring *m (breechblock)*.
split trail Spreizlafettenholme *mpl*, Spreizlafettenschwanz *m (G)*.
split-trail gun carriage Spreizlafette *f*.
spoil Bodenaushub *m (Ft)*; Minierguṭ *n (Mining)*.
spoke Speiche *f (wheel)*.
sponge Schwamm *m*.
sponson Panzerkastenoberteil *m (Tk)*; Stabilisierungsschwimmer *m (Ap)*.
spoon Löffel *m*.
spot *v* orten *(locate)*; sichten *(see)*; entdecken *(discover)*.
spot landing Ziellandung *f (Avn)*.
spotlight Sucher *m (MT)*.
spotter Artilleriebeobachter *m*.
spotting Schußbeobachtung *f (Arty)*.
spot welding Punktschweißung *f*.
sprain Verstauchung *f (Med)*.
spray *n* Sprengkegel *m (air burst)*; Zerstäuber *m (Inst)*.
spray attack Giftregenangriff *m (CWS)*.
spray effect Splitterwirkung *f (Gunnery)*.
spray gun Druckzerstäuber *m (CWS)*.
spraying Versprühen *n (CWS)*.
spray nozzle Spritzdüse *f (carburetor)*; Spritzschlauch *m (hose)*.
spray-nozzle tube Tauchrohr *n (carburetor)*.
spray painting unit Farb-Spritzanlage *f*.
spray-type decontaminating apparatus Zerstäubergerät *n (CWS)*.
spread *v* auf Streulicht gehen *(searchlight beam)*: ausstreuen, ausbreiten.
spread-out formation auseinandergezogene Formation *(Avn)*.
spread the trails die Holme spreizen *(split-trail gun carriage)*.
spring Quelle *f (water)*; Feder *f (Tech)*; Frühling *m (season)*.
spring action Federantrieb *m (clockwork fuze)*.
spring bolt Federbolzen *m (MT)*.
spring bracket Federhand *f (MT)*.
spring clip Federbund *m (split-trail G carriage)*.
spring counterrecoil mechanism Federvorholer *m*.
spring equilibrator Federausgleicher *m (G)*.
spring hanger Federbock *m (MT)*.
spring mechanism Federeinrichtung
spring recuperator Federvorholer *m (G)*.
spring shackle Federlasche *f (MT)*.
spring suspension Federaufhängung *f (MT)*; Federgehänge *n (G carriage)*.
spring system Abfederung *f*, Federung *f (MT)*.
sprinkling can Tropfkanne *f*.
sprocket Triebrad *n (driving sprocket) (Tk)*.
spur Sporn *m (Cav)*.
spur gear Stirnrad *n*.
spur track Eisenbahnklaue *f*.
spy *n* Spion *m*, Kundschafter *m*.
spy *v* auskundschaften, ausspähen.
squad Gruppe *f (Inf)*; Trupp *m (detail, team)*; Kommando *n (party)*.
squad column Schützenreihe *f*.
"Squad, halt!" "Abteilung, halt!"
squad leader Gruppenführer *m*.
squadron Staffel *f (Avn)*; Geschwader *n (Nav)*. *Note: No Ger equivalent in Cav.*
squadron commander Staffelführer *m*, Staffelkapitän *m (Avn)*.
squadron commander's flight Führungskette *f (Avn)*.
squadron formation Staffelform *f*, Staffelverband *m (Avn)*.
squadron javelin formation Staffelkolonne *f (Avn)*.
squadron V formation Staffelwinkel *m (Avn)*.
squad room Mannschaftsstube *f*.
squall Bö *f*, Windstoß *m*.
squall line Bölinie *f*.
square *n* Viereck *n*, Quadrat *n*; Platz *m (in city or town)*.
square *adj* viereckig, quadratisch; rechtwinklig *(having right angles)*.
square centimeter Quadratzentimeter
squared quadratisch; quadriert, (zum) Quadrat, hoch zwei *(raised to second power)*.
square division viergliedrige Division.
square lashing Bockschnürbund *m (Bdg)*.
square root Quadratwurzel *f*.
square-wedge breechblock Flachkeilverschluß *m (G)*.
squeeze abkrümmen, durchkrümmen *(trigger)*; drängen *(Tac)*.
squirrel-cage motor Kurzschlußankermotor *m*.
stability Stabilität *f*.
stabilizer Höhenflosse *f (Ap)*; Kreiselabfeuergerät *n (Tk)*.
stabilizer lobe Stabilisierungswulst *m (Bln)*.
stabilizing fin Steuerflügel *m (bomb)*; Flügelblech *n (Am)*; Steuerfläche *f (Mort shell)*.
stabilizing surface Dämpfungsfläche *f*, Stabilisierungsfläche *f (Ap)*.
stable *n* Stall *m*.
stable *adj* stabil, fest, dauerhaft, haltbar, stark; beständig *(durable)*.
"Stack, arms!" "Setzt die, Gewehre! Zusammen!"
stadia rod Meßlatte *f*, Meßstab *m (Surv)*.
staff Stab *m*.
staff administrative order Stabsbefehl *m*.
staff car Befehlswagen *m*.
staff officer Stabsoffizier *m*.
staff order Stabsbefehl *m*.
staff sergeant Unterfeldwebel *m*; Unterwachtmeister *m (Arty, Cav)*.
stage Stufe *f (Rad, etc.)*; Landbrücke *f (landing stage)*.
stagger Staffelung *f (Ap wings)*.
stagger distance Stufung *f (formation flying)*.
staggered gegeneinander verschoben, gegeneinander versetzt.
staggered biplane gestaffelter Doppeldecker *m*.
stagger formation zerlegter Verband, gestaffelter Verband *(Tac)*.
staggering Stufung *f (formation flying)*.
stagger wire Gegenseil *n (biplane)*.
stake *n* Absteckpfahl *m (Surv)*; Stock *m*, Pfahl *m*, Pflock *m*.
stake mine Stockmine *f (Ger concrete antipersonnel mine)*.
stake off abstecken *(Engr, Surv)*.
stall *n* Überziehen *n (Ap)*.
stall *v* abwürgen *(Mtr)*.
stalled bewegungsunfähig *(MT)*.
stalling Überziehen *n (Avn)*.
stalling flight Langsamflug *m (Ap)*.
stalling speed Durchsackgeschwindigkeit *(Avn)*.
stamp Stempel *m*· Briefmarke *f (postage)*.
stamp pad Stempelkissen *n*.
standard *n* Standarte *f (flag)*; Norm *f (Tech)*.
standard *adj* Einheits-, Normal-, Regel-, genormt, vorschriftsmäßig, regelrecht.
standard fuze Einheitszünder *m (Am)*.
standard gage Normalspur *f*, Regelspur *f*, Vollbahn *f (RR)*.
standard-gage railroad Vollspurbahn *f*.
standardization Normung *f*, Vereinheitlichung *f*.
standardize normen, vereinheitlichen.
standard maximum load Regellast *f (Bdg)*.
standard muzzle velocity schußtafelmäßige Anfangsgeschwindigkeit.
standard nomenclature einheitliche Benennung.
standard operating procedure vorschriftsmäßiges Verfahren.
standard part Normteil *m (MT)*.
standard time Zonenzeit *f*, Einheitszeit *f*.
stand-by Alarmbereitschaft *f*.
stand-by message Erwa-Meldung *f (preliminary to metro message) (Arty)*.
stand-by operation Horchempfang *m (Rad)*.
standing army stehendes Heer.
standing barrage Notfeuer *n*, Sperrfeuer *n*, Feuerriegel *m (Arty)*.
standing foxhole Schützenloch für stehenden Anschlag.
standing order Dauerbefehl *m*.
standing position Anschlag stehend
staple *n* Krampe *f (Tech)*.
stapler Hefter *m*.
star Stern *m*; Leuchtstern *m (Sig)*.
starboard Steuerbord *m*.
starboard engine Steuerbordmotor *m (Ap)*.
star cluster Sternbündel *n (Sig)*.
star gage Seelenmesser *m (G)*.
star shell Leuchtgeschoß *n*, Leuchtgranate *f (Am)*; Granatsignal *n (Sig)*.
start aufbrechen *(set out)*; starten *(Ap take-off)*; anlassen, anwerfen *(an engine)*; abrücken, abmarschieren *(start a march)*.
starter Anlasser *m*, Starter *m (MT)*.
starter battery Starterbatterie *f (MT)*.
starter button Anlaßdruckknopf *m*, Anlaßknopf *m (MT)*.
starter-generator Dynastart *m (MT)*.
starter motor Anlaßmotor *m*.
starter pinion Antriebsritzel *m (on armature shaft of starter)*.
starter switch Anlaßschalter *m (Mtr)*.
starting Anlassen *n*, Ingangsetzen *n (MT)*.
starting equipment Anlaßvorrichtung *f (Mtr)*.
starting point Aufbruchsort *m*.
starting time Aufbruchszeit *f*.
state Staat *m (country)*; Zustand *m (condition)*.
state of emergency Ausnahmezustand *m*.
state of siege Belagerungszustand *m*.
state of war Kriegszustand *m*.

static Störgeräusch n, Gewitterstörung f (Rad).
static eliminator Funkentstörer m (Rad).
static line Aufziehleine f, Reißleine f (Prcht).
station Bahnhof m, Station f (RR); Standort m (post or garrison); Stand m (position in Ap or vehicle); Funkstelle f (Rad).
stationary fest, ortsfest, stehend.
stationary generating unit ortsfester Stromerzeuger.
stationary gun mount ortsfeste Lafette (G).
stationary patrol stehender Spähtrupp.
stationary target stehendes Ziel.
station capacity Bahnhofleistung f (number of trains loaded or unloaded per day).
stationery Briefpapier n.
station hospital Standortlazarett n.
station list Kommandostellenverzeichnis n.
station log Betriebsbuch n (Rad).
station surgeon Standortarzt m.
statistics Statistik f.
stator Stator m (Elec).
statoscope Variometer n.
status Wehrdienstverhältnis n (service status); Rechtsstellung f, rechtliche Stellung (Law).
statute Statut n, Satzung f, Grundgesetz n, Gesetz n.
statute mile Landmeile f (1.609 km).
statute of limitations Verjährungsgesetz n.
stave Daube f (of a barrel).
steadiness Standsicherheit f (of a mobile G mount, vehicle, etc.).
steady fest (firm); anhaltend (continuous); gleichmäßig (even).
steal stehlen.
steam Dampf m.
steamboat Dampfschiff n.
steam engine Dampfmaschine f.
steam roller Dampfwalze f (Engr).
steam tube Dampfrohr n (MG).
steel Stahl m.
steel alloy Stahllegierung f.
steel and concrete fortification Panzerwerk n.
steel-beam obstacle Sperre aus Stahlträgern.
steel bridge Stahlbrücke f.
steel bushing Stahlfutter n (breechblock wedge).
steel-core bullet Stahlkerngeschoß n.
steel cylinder Stahlflasche f (container).
steel flask See **steel cylinder.**
steel helmet Stahlhelm m.
steel measuring tape Stahlmeßband n.
steel mill Stahlwerk n.
steel plank Stahlschwelle f (Engr).
steel plate Stahlplatte f.
steel-rail obstacle Sperre aus Schienen.
steel tetrahedron Stahligel m (AT obstacle).
steel tie Stahlschwelle f (RR).
steel treadway Stahlspurbahn f.
steel wire armor Stahldrahtbeklöppelung f (armored cable).
steep abschüssig, schroff, steil (Top).
steep-banked turn Steilkurve f (Avn).
steep-bank flight Messerflug m (Avn).
steep climb Hochziehen n (Ap).
steep grade Steilhang m (Top).
steep hill Steigung f (Top).
steep slope Steilhang m (Top).
steering Steuern n, Lenken n.
steering arm Lenkstock m, Lenkstockhebel m (MT); Lenker m (of a G wheel).
steering brake Lenkbremse f (Tk).
steering column Lenksäule f, Steuersäule f (MT).
steering-column cam Lenkschraube f (MT).
steering gear Lenkung f, Lenkgetriebe n (MT).
steering-gear connecting rod Lenkschubstange f (MT).
steering-gear housing Lenkgehäuse n (MT).
steering-knuckle arm Spurstangenhebel m (MT).
steering-knuckle gear-rod arm Lenkhebel m (MT).
steering-knuckle pivot Achszapfen m (MT).
steering-knuckle type steering Achsschenkellenkung f (MT).
steering lever Lenkhebel m, Lenkknüppel m (Tk, Trac).
steering mechanism Lenkeinrichtung f, Lenkgetriebe n (Tk, Trac).
steering play toter Gang (MT).
steering shock suspension Lenkstoßfang m (MT).
steering system Lenkung f, Steuerung f (MT).
steering wheel Steuer n, Steuerrad n, Lenkrad n (MT).
steering worm Lenkschnecke f (MT).
steering-worm sector Lenksegment n (MT).
stem Vordersteven m (Nav): Aufziehachse f, Aufziehwelle f
stencil n Matrize f (typing); Schablone f (Tech).
stencil v schablonieren, aufschablonieren.
stenographer Stenograph m, Stenographin f.
step Stufe f; Schritt m, Tritt m (pace); Stufe f (Ap float or pontoon).
stepped-up (-down) formation Stufenformation f (Avn).
stereogram Raummeßbild n (Photo survey).
stereo-pair See **stereoscopic pair.**
stereo-photogrammetry Raumbildmessung f.
stereo range finder See **stereoscopic range finder.**
stereoscope Stereoskop n.
stereoscopic complements stereoskopische Meßbildpaare (Photo survey).
stereoscopic height finder See **stereoscopic range finder.**
stereoscopic image Raumbild n.
stereoscopic pair Raumbildpaar n.
stereoscopic range finder Raumbildentfernungsmesser m.
sterilization Entwesung f (of clothing, etc.).
sterilization truck Sterilisationswagen m (Med).
sterilize entkeimen, sterilisieren
stern Heck n.
stern compartment Hinterkaffe f (Pon).
sternpost Hintersteven m, Rudersteven m.
sternutator Nasenrachenreizstoff m, Blaukreuz n (CWS).
stevedore Stauer m, Lader m, Auslader m, Hafenarbeiter m.
stick Stock m Knüppel m.
stick control Knüppelsteuerung f (Ap).
stick hand grenade Stielhandgranate f.
stick-type incendiary bomb Stabbrandbombe f.
sticky klebrig.
stiff steif, starr.
stifle joint Knie n (horse).
still projector Bildwerfer m (Photo).
Stillson wrench Rohrzange f.
stimulant Anregungsmittel n.
stirrup Steigbügel m.
stirrup pump Luftschutzbrandspritze f (Civ defense).
stirrup strap Steigriemen m.
stock Schaft m (R); Griffschale f (pistol); Schulterstütze f (MG); Bestand m, Lagerbestand m, Vorrat m (of supplies, equipment, etc.); Schneidkluppe f, Kluppe f (die holder); Ankerbalken m (of an anchor).
stockade Einzäunung f (PW).
stock and die Schneidkluppe mit Schneidbacken.
stock book Bestandsbuch n (QM).
stocking Strumpf m (Clo).
stock inventory Bestandsnachweisung f.
stock preservative Schaftpflegemittel n (R).
stock rail Backenschiene f (RR).
Stokes mortar Stokes-Granatwerfer m.
stop Aufenthaltspunkt m, Haltepunkt m, Haltestelle f (RR, MT); Anschlag m (Ord).
stop and taillight Stopp- und Schlußlicht n (MT).
stop light Bremslicht n (MT).
stoppage Hemmung f, Ladehemmung f (Ord).
stopping distance Bremsweg m (MT).
stopwatch Stoppuhr f.
storage Lagern n, Lagerung f, Aufbewahrung f.
storage battery Sammlerbatterie f, Sammler m, Kraftspeicher m.
storage-battery cell Platteneinsatz m, Plattensatz m (Elec).
storage-battery truck Sammlerkraftwagen m (Rad).
storage dam Staudamm m.
storage depot Magazin n.
storage rack Lagergerüst n.
storage shed Lagerschuppen m.
storeroom Lagerraum m, Speicher m.
storm n Sturm m, Unwetter n.
storm v stürmen, erstürmen (Tac).
storm trooper SA-Mann m, Sturmabteilungsmann m.
stove Ofen m.
stow unterbringen, verstauen.
stowage chart Beladeplan m (for vehicle).
stowage position Unterbringung f (equipment in vehicle).
strafe unter Feuer nehmen, mit Maschinengewehrfeuer belegen (Avn).
strafing attack Maschinengewehrangriff m (Avn).
straggler Versprengter m, Nachzügler m.
straggler collecting point See **straggler post.**
straggler post Versprengtensammelstelle f.
straight gerade.
straight ahead geradeaus.
straightedge Lineal n.
straight flight Geradeausflug m (Avn).
straight-side rim Geradseitfelge f (MT).
strain Dehnung f (Mech); Beanspruchung f, Belastung f, Anstrengung f.
strand Kabelader f (Tp wire); Strang m (rope).
strangle erwürgen, erdrosseln.
strap Gurt m, Gürtel m, Riemen m.
stratagem Kriegslist f, List f (Tac).
strategic strategisch, operativ.
strategic advance guard Vorausabteilung f.
strategic air reconnaissance operative Luftaufklärung.
strategic concentration Aufmarsch m.
strategic reconnaissance operative Aufklärung.
strategic withdrawal strategischer Rückzug.
strategist Stratege m.
strategy Kriegskunst f, Feldherrnkunst f, Strategie f.
strategy of attrition Ermattungsstrategie f, Zermürbungsstrategie f.
stratocumulus cloud Stratokumulus m.
stratosphere Stratosphäre f (Avn, Met).
stratum Lage f (Met).
stratus cloud Stratus-Wolke f, Schichtwolke f.
straw Stroh n.
stream Bach m, Strom m, Wasserlauf m.
stream crossing Übergang m, Übersetzen über Wasserläufe, Bachübergang m.
stream-crossing ability Watfähigkeit f (MT).
stream-crossing equipment Übergangsmittel npl, Übersetzmittel npl.
stream-crossing point Übersetzstelle f.
stream-crossing troops Übergangstruppe f.
streamlined stromlinienförmig.
streamline shape Stromform f, Stromlinienform f.
streamward wasserwärts.
street Straße f, Gasse f.
street fighting Straßenkampf m.
strength Stärke f, Kopfstärke f (of a unit); Kraft f (of an individual).
strength of barrel Rohrfestigkeit f
strength of cover Deckungsstärke f (Ft).
strength of materials Festigkeitslehre f.
strength report Stärkenachweisung f; Iststärkenachweisung f (daily strength report).
stress n Spannung f, Belastung f.
stress analysis statische Berechnung, Festigkeitsnachweis m.
stress-strain diagram Spannungs-Dehnungs-Diagramm n.
stretch Strecke f (distance); Ausdehnung f (expansion); Verspannung f, Spannung f (tension).
stretcher Feldtrage f, Krankentrage f, Trage f (Med).
stride Doppelschritt m (2 paces).
strike Aufschlag m, Einschlag m, Treffer m (firing); Streik m (labor).
strike a flag die Flagge streichen (in token of surrender); die Flagge niederholen (at retreat, etc.).
strike a tent das Zelt abbrechen.
strike camp das Lager abbrechen.
striker Schlagbolzenspitze f (G, R).
striking force Frontverband m (Avn).
striking power Schlagkraft f (Tac).
striking velocity Auftreffgeschwindigkeit f, Aufschlaggeschwindigkeit f (of a projectile).
string hochgestufte Reihe (formation flying); Schnur f, Bindfaden m (cord).
stringer Längsträger m, Streckbalken m, Tragbalken m; Holm m (spar); Gleisbalken m (rail support) (Bdg).
strip n Streifen m, Band n.
strip v auseinandernehmen, zerlegen (Ord); Waffengruppen auseinandernehmen (field strip); ausschalen (concrete forms).
strip map Flugstreckenkarte f (Avn); Marschskizze f, Wegskizze f (MT).
strip mosaic Bildreihe f.
strip powder Stäbchenpulver n (Am).
stroke Hub m, Takt m (Mtr).
strong stark, kräftig.
strong point Stützpunkt m.
structural defect Materialfehler m (of material); Baufehler m (of construction).
structural dimensions Baumaß n.
structural-steel obstacle Sperre aus Stahlträgern.
structural unit Bauglied n.
structural weight Rüstgewicht n (plus equipment, Ap).
structure Gebäude n (building); Zusammensetzung f (composition); Bau m (type of construction); Gliederung f (organization); Gestaltung f (configuration).
strut Stiel m (compression member); Strebe f (tension member).
strut-braced construction Sprengwerk n (Engr).
stub wing Ansatzflügel m (Ap).
stuck bewegungsunfähig (MT).
to get stuck stecken bleiben (MT).
stud Seitengewehrhalter m (R).
stuffing box Stopfbuchse f.
stump Baumstumpf m, Stumpf m.
stunt flying Kunstflug m.
stunt-flying maneuver Kunstflugfigur f.
styptic n blutstillendes Mittel.
subarea Teilgebiet n, Unterabschnitt m.
subcaliber ammunition Kleinkalibermunition f, Zielmunition f.
subcaliber barrel See **subcaliber tube.**
subcaliber firing Abkommschießen n.
subcaliber target practice Kleinkaliberschießen n (Arty).
subcaliber target range Kleinschießplatz m (Arty).
subcaliber tube Einstecklauf m, Einlegerohr n, Abkommrohr n, Kleinkaliberlauf m (G).
subchaser See **submarine chaser.**
subdepot Zweiglager n, Zweigdepot n, Nebendepot n.
subdue bezwingen (the enemy); unterwerfen (to subject); unterdrücken (to suppress).
sub-grade Bahnplanum n (RR); Unterbau m (road).
submachine gun Maschinenpistole f.
submarine Unterseeboot n, U-Boot n.
submarine chaser U-Bootjäger m.
submarine commander Unterseebootkommandant m.
submarine construction yard U-Boot-Werft f.
submarine mine Seemine f.
submarine mine field Seeminensperre f, Minensperre f, Minenfeld n (Nav).
submarine mine planter Minenfahrzeug n, Minenleger m, Minendampfer m.
submarine mining Minenlegen n.
submarine net U-Bootnetz n.
submarine pen U-Boot-Bunker m.
submarine tender U-Boot-Mutterschiff n.
submarine warfare U-Bootkrieg m.
subordinate unterstellt.
sub-port Nebenhafen m.
subsector Unterabschnitt m.
subsector reserve Unterabschnitts-Reserve f (Tac).
subsistence Quartier und Verpflegung.
subsistence allowance Quartier- und Verpflegungsvergütung f.
subsistence stores Verpflegungsgegenstände mpl.
subsoil water Grundwasser n (Engr).
substitute Ersatz m (thing); Stellvertreter m (Pers).
sub-stratosphere airplane Höhenflugzeug n, Substratosphärenflugzeug n.
substructure Unterbau m.
subtract abziehen.
succeed Erfolg haben, gelingen (make good); folgen, nachfolgen (follow, replace).
success Erfolg m.
suction Sog m, Ansaugung f, Ansaugen n.
suction line Saugleitung f (MT).
suction stroke Saughub m, Ansaugetakt m (Mtr).
suction surface Saugseite f (Ap wing).
suffocate ersticken.
sugar Zucker m.
sulfur Schwefel m.
sulfuric acid Schwefelsäure f.
sulfur trioxide Schwefeltrioxyd n (CWS).
sulfur trioxide-chlorsulfonic acid solution Nebelsäure f (CWS).
sulphur See **sulfur.**
summary court-martial Standgericht n (in USA for noncapital offenses).
summit Gipfel m.
summit of trajectory Gipfelpunkt m (Ballistics).
sump Sickerschacht m (Ft); Schmierstoffbehälter m (Mtr).
sun Sonne f.
sun-blindness Blendung durch Sonnenlicht.
sunburn Sonnenbrand m.
sun helmet Tropenhelm m.
sunken road Hohlweg m.
sunrise Sonnenaufgang m.
sunset Sonnenuntergang m.
sunshade Sonnenblende f.
sunstroke Sonnenstich m.
supercharge vorverdichten (Mtr).
supercharged engine Auflademotor m, Gebläsemotor m, Kompressormotor m (Avn).
supercharger Gebläse n, Kompressor m, Lader m, Vorverdichter m; Bodenlader m (with low blower ratio); Höhenlader m (with high blower ratio).
supercontrol tube Regelröhre f (Rad).
superelevation Aufsatzwinkel m (AA gunnery).
superheterodyne receiver Überlagerungsempfänger m, Zwischenfrequenzempfänger m (Rad).
superior n Vorgesetzter m.
superior adj überlegen (in strength, etc.); vorgesetzt (in command, etc.); höher (higher).
superiority Überlegenheit f, Übermacht f.
superior officer Vorgesetzter m.
superior provost court Oberfeldgericht n (USA).
superior strength Übermacht f (Tac).
supernumerary überzählig, überplanmäßig.
superposed circuit Kunstschaltung f (Tp).
superquick fuze empfindlicher Zünder, empfindlicher Aufschlagzünder (Am).
superregenerative receiver Pendelfrequenzempfänger m.
supersaturation Übersättigung f (Met).
supersede ersetzen.
supersensitive fuze hochempfindlicher Aufschlagzünder (AA Am).
superstructure Überbau m.
stranded wire Litze f (Elec).
supervise beaufsichtigen, überwachen.
supplementary ergänzend, nachträglich, Ergänzungs-.
supplies Nachschubgüter npl, Versorgungsgüter npl.
supply Nachschub m, Versorgung f, Heeresversorgung f.
supply v versorgen, beliefern, liefern.
supply adj Nachschub-, Versorgungs-.
supply area Nachschubgebiet n, Versorgungsgebiet n, Versorgungsbezirk m.
supply balloon See **nurse balloon.**
supply base Nachschubstützpunkt m.
supply boat Nachschubboot n.
supply by air Luftversorgung f.
supply column Nachschubkolonne f.
supply convoy Nachschubgeleit n (Nav).
supply delivery unit Versorgungsbombe f (airborne Opns).
supply depot Nachschublager n, Lager n.
Supply Division Heeresnachschubamt im Generalstab des Heeres (USA).
supply dump Nachschublager n, Materiallager n.
supply line Nachschublinie f.
supply party Nachschubtrupp m.
supply point Nachschublager n (depot); Nachschubumschlagstelle f, (rail or truck head); Nachschubausgabestelle f (distributing point).
supply port Versorgungshafen m.
supply road Nachschubweg m.
supply route Nachschubstraße f.
supply sergeant Kammerunteroffizier m.
supply service Nachschubdienst m, Versorgungsdienst m.
supply shortage Nachschubmangel m.
supply tank Nachschubpanzerkampfwagen m (vehicle).
supply traffic Nachschubverkehr f.
supply train Nachschubzug m (RR); Fahrkolonne f (H-Dr); Kraftfahrkolonne f (MT); Gefechtstroß m (combat); Verpflegungstroß m (rations).
supply vehicle Nachschubfahrzeug n, Versorgungsfahrzeug n.
support Rückhalt m, Unterstützung f (Tac); Aufnahmen fpl (in delaying maneuver); Stütze f, Lager n, Träger m (Tech).
support v unterstützen, Rückhalt geben, schützen (by fire), decken (Tac).
support aviation Schlachtflieger mpl.
supported flank angelehnter Flügel.
support force Frontverband m (Avn).
supporting artillery Unterstützungsartillerie f.
supporting fire Unterstützungsfeuer n.
support party Deckungstrupp m.
suppressor grid Bremsgitter n, Schutzgitter n (Rad tube).
supreme command Oberbefehl m.
surcingle Deckengurt m, Obergurt m, (harness).
surface Oberfläche f (outside or top); Fläche f (area); Boden m (ground).
surface area Flächeninhalt m (Surv).
surface construction Tiefbau m (Tp line).
surface direction-finder station Bodenpeilstelle f (Avn).
surface forces Überwasserstreitkräfte fpl (Nav).
surface line Bodenleitung f (Tp).
surface wind Bodenwind m.
surge Stromstoß m (Elec).
surge chamber Druckraum m (hydraulics).
surgeon Sanitätsoffizier m (Mil); Chirurg m.
Surgeon General Heeres-Sanitätsinspekteur m.
surgery Chirurgie f.
surgical hospital Feldlazarett n, Armeefeldlazarett n.
surname Familienname m, Zuname m.
surplus stock Mehrbestand m.
surprise Überraschung f (Tac).
surprise attack Überraschungsangriff m, Überfall m (Tac).
surprise fire Feuerüberfall m (Arty, MG).
surprise raid Handstreich m.
surrender n Kapitulation f, Übergabe f, Waffenstreckung f.
surrender v sich ergeben, kapitulieren.
surveillance Überwachung f (Obsn); Untersuchung f (Am and CWS supplies).
surveillance of fire Feuerbeobachtung f (Arty).
survey n Vermessung f, Vermessung durch Anhängen (by controlled

traverse) (Arty, Engr).
survey *v* vermessen *(measure)*; besichtigen *(inspect)*.
surveying Vermessung *f*, Einmessen *n (Arty, Engr)*.
survey map sheet Meßtischblatt *n*.
surveyor's chain Meßkette *f (Surv)*.
surveyor's level Nivellierinstrument *n (Engr)*.
surveyor's tape Meßband *n*.
suspend zeitweilig vom Dienst entheben *(from duty)*; hängen *(hang)*; einhängen *(a bomb)*.
suspended camouflage net hängende Fliegermaske *(AA defense)*.
"suspend firing!" "Stopfen!"
suspension zeitweilige Dienstenthebung *(from duty)*; Aufhängung *f (of bombs)*; Federung *f (MT)*; Laufwerk *n (Tk)*; Pause *f (of activity)*.
suspension bridge Hängebrücke *f*.
suspension frame Trapez *n (Bln)*.
suspension line Hängeleine *f (Prcht)*.
suspension lug Aufhängeöse *f (bomb)*.
suspension of arms örtliche vorübergehende Waffenruhe.
suspension of fire Feuerpause *f*.
suspension of traffic Verkehrsunterbrechung *f*.
suspensions Laufwerk *n (Tk)*.
suspensions and tracks Fahrwerk *n (Tk)*.
suspension spring Tragfeder *f (split-trail carriage)*.
sustained fire Dauerfeuer *n*.
swamp Sumpf *m*.
swamp atmosphere Sumpfklima *n*.
swamp sector Sumpfstreifen *m*.
swastika Hakenkreuz *n*.
sway brace Verschwertung *f (Engr)*.
swear in vereidigen.
sweat *n* Schweiß *m*.
sweat *v* schwitzen.
sweater Schlupfjacke *f (Clo)*.
sweep *v* absuchen *(searching for mines)*; räumen *(clearing of mines)*; bestreichen *(Gunnery)*; fegen.
sweepback Pfeilform *f (Ap wing)*.
sweeping fire Breitenfeuer *n (MG)*.
swerve pendeln.
swim schwimmen.
swimmer Schwimmer *m*; Freischwimmer *m (qualified swimmer)*.
swing team Mittelpferde *npl*.
switch Schalter *m (Elec)*; Weiche *f (RR)*.
switchboard Klappenschrank *m*, Schalttafel *f*, Schalttisch *m*, Vermittlungseinrichtung *f (Tp)*.
switchboard drop Anrufklappe *f (Tp)*.
switchboard operator Fernsprecher *m*.
switch box Schaltkasten *m (Elec, MT)*; Schaltkästchen *n (sound ranging apparatus)*.
switching Verschieben *n (RR)*.
switching central Vermittlungsstelle *f*, Vermittlung *f*, Fernsprechvermittlung *f (Tp)*.
switching off Ausschaltung *f (Elec)*.
switching on Einschaltung *f (Elec)*.
switch knob Schaltgriff *m (Elec)*.
switch lamp Weichenlaterne *f (RR)*.
switch lever Weichenhebel *m (RR)*.
switch point Herzstück *n (RR switch)*.
switch position Wechselstellung *f (Tac)*.
switch stand Weichenbock *m (RR)*.
switch tower Stellwerk *n (RR)*.
swivel Riemenbügel *m (R)*.
swivel gun Pivotgeschütz *n*, Sockelgeschütz *n*.
sword Degen *m*.
sword knot Faustriemen *m*; Portepee *n (worn by Ger officers and higher NCO's)*.
symbol Zeichen *n*.
sympathetic detonation übertragene Zündung.
synchro-mesh transmission Synchrongetriebe *n (MT)*.
synchronism Gleichlauf *m*.
synchronization Synchronisierung *f*, Steuerung *f*, Zusammenwirken *n*; Maschinengewehrsteuerung *f (Ap MGs)*.
synchronize synchronisieren; gleichstellen *(watches)*.
synchronized machine gun synchronisiertes Maschinengewehr, gesteuertes Maschinengewehr *(Ap)*.
synchroscope Synchronoskop *n (Ap)*.
synthetic *n* Kunststoff *m*.
synthetic material Ersatz *m*, Ersatzstoff *m*.
synthetic rubber künstlicher Gummi, synthetischer Gummi.
syphilis Syphilis *f*.
systematic error regelmäßiger Fehler, systematischer Fehler.

T

table of coordinates Koordinatenverzeichnis *n (Surv)*.
table of equipment Ausrüstungsnachweisung *f*.
table Tafel *f (list)*; Tisch *m (furniture)*.
table of basic allowances Ausrüstungsnachweisung *f*.
table of maximum punishment Verzeichnis der Höchststrafe.
table of organization Stärkenachweisung *f*; Friedensstärkenachweisung *f (peacetime)*; Kriegsstärkenachweisung *f (wartime)*.
tachometer Drehzahlmesser *m*, Umdrehungszähler *m*, Stichzähler *m*.
tack *n* Stiftzwecke *f (carpet, etc.)*; Reißnagel *m (thumbtack)*.
tackle *n* Flaschenzug *m*.
tactical taktisch.
tactical airplane Kriegsflugzeug *n*.
tactical employment taktische Verwendung, taktischer Einsatz.
tactical exercise taktische Übung.
tactical fire classification taktische Feuerbegriffe *(Arty)*.
tactical grouping taktische Gruppengliederung, Kräfteverteilung *f*, Gefechtsgliederung *f*.
tactical maneuver taktisches Manöver.
tactical march Kriegsmarsch *m*.
tactical obstacle taktisches Hindernis.
tactical offensive taktischer Angriff.
tactical operation Gefechtshandlung *f*, Kampfhandlung *f*.
tactical operations staff Gefechtsstab *m*.
tactical plan taktischer Plan.
tactical protection Gasabwehrmaßnahmen *fpl (CWS)*.
tactical reconnaissance taktische Aufklärung.
tactical retreat planmäßiger Rückzug.
tactical ride Geländebesprechung *f (maneuvers)*.
tactical situation Kampflage *f*, Kampfverhältnisse *npl*, taktische Lage.
tactical smoke künstlicher Nebel.
tactical symbol taktisches Zeichen.
tactical training Gefechtsausbildung *f*.
tactical unit Kampfeinheit *f*, taktischer Verband.
tactical walk Geländebesprechung *f (maneuvers)*.
tactician Taktiker *m*.
tactics Taktik *f*, Gefechtslehre *f*.
tactics and technique Waffenführung *f*, Waffentechnik *f*.
tag Anhänger *m*, Anhängezettel *m (tie-on type)*, Klebezettel *m (stick-on type)*.
tail Heck *n*, Rumpfende *n*, Schwanz *m (Ap)*; Bodenschwanz *m (bomb)*; Schweif *m (horse)*.
tail assembly Leitwerk *n (Ap)*.
tail fin Seitenflosse *f (Ap)*.
tail gun Heckwaffe *f (Ap)*.
tail gunner Heckschütze *m (Avn)*.
tail gun position Heckstand *m (Ap)*.
tailheavy schwanzlastig *(Ap)*.
tail landing Schwanzlandung *f (Avn)*.
taillight Rücklicht *n*, Schlußlicht *n (MT)*.
tail skid Sporn *m*, Schwanzsporn *m*, Spornschuh *m (Ap)*.
tail spin Trudeln *n*.
tail surface Dämpfungsflosse *f (Ap)*.
tail turret Heckkanzel *f (Ap)*.
tail turret gun Heckmaschinengewehr *n*, Heckwaffe *f*.
tail unit Leitwerk *n (Ap)*.
tail wheel Radsporn *m*, Spornrad *n (Ap)*.
tail wind Rückenwind *m*.
"Take, Arms!" "Gewehr in die, Hand!"
take bearings anpeilen, peilen *(Air Navigation) (Rad)*.
take-off Abflug *m*, Start *m (Avn)*.
take off starten *(Avn)*.
take-off distance Startlänge *f*, Anlaufstrecke *f (Avn)*.
take-off point Start *m*, Startstelle *f (Adrm)*.
take-off rating Abflugleistung *f*.
take-off run Anlauf *m (Avn)*.
take-off speed Abfluggeschwindigkeit *f (Avn)*.
take-off zone Startzone *f (Adrm)*.
take up the slack Druckpunkt nehmen *(Small Arms)*.
talking range Sprechverständigung *f (Tp)*.
tamping Verdämmen *n (blasting)*.
tampion *See* **tompion.**
tandem airplane Tandemflugzeug *n*.
tangent Berührungslinie *f*, Tangente *f (geometry)*; Tangens *m (trigonometrical function)*.
tangent sight Kurvenvisier *n (MG)*.
tank Kampfwagen *m*, Panzerkampfwagen *m*, Panzerwagen *m*, Panzer *m*, Tank *m (Tk)*; Behälter *m (container)*.
tank ammunition Panzermunition *f*.
tank armament Bordwaffen *fpl*.
tank barrier Panzersperre *f*, Panzerkampfwagenhindernis *n*.
tank battle Panzerkampf *m*, Panzerschlacht *f*.
tank car Eisenbahnkesselwagen *m*, Tankwagen *m (RR)*.
tank commander Panzerführer *m*, Panzerkommandant *m*.
tank crew Panzerbesatzung *f*.
tank cupola Panzerkuppel *f*.
tank destroyer Pakgeschütz auf Selbstfahrlafette *(USA)*.
tank destroyer gun Panzerjägergeschütz *n*.
Tank Destroyer School Panzerjägerschule *f (USA)*.
tank ditch Panzerwagengraben *m*.
tank driver Panzerfahrer *m*.
tank engagement Panzerkampf *m*.
tank engine Panzermotor *m*.
tanker Tanker *m*, Tankschiff *n*, Tankdampfer *m (Nav)*.
tank factory Kampfwagenwerk *n*.
tank gun Kampfwagenkanone *f*, Kampfwagengeschütz *n*, Panzerkanone *f*.
tank gunner Panzerschütze *m*.
tank hull Panzerkasten *m*, Panzerwanne *f*; Panzeraufbau *m (hull and turret)*.
tank landing craft Fährprahm *m*, F-Boot *n*.
tank mine Panzermine *f*.
tank obstacle Panzerkampfwagenhindernis *n*.
tank radio operator Panzerfunker *m*.
tank shutter Panzerblende *f*.
tank silhouette Pz.Kw.-Nachbildung *f*, Kampfwagennachbildung *f (practice firing)*.
tank-silhouette aiming target Panzerrichttafel *f*.
tank-silhouette target Kampfwagenscheibe *f*.
tank track Panzerkette *f*.
tank trap Panzerwagenfalle *f*, Panzerfalle *f*, Panzerfahrzeugfalle *f*, Tankfalle *f*.
tank truck Tankwagen *m*, Brennstofftankwagen *m*, Kesselwagen *m*, Kraftstoff-Kesselkraftwagen *m (MT)*.
tank turret Panzerturm *m*.
tank warfare Panzerkriegführung *f*.
tank warning Panzerwarnung *f*.
T-antenna T-Antenne *f (Rad)*.
tap *n* Anzapfung *f (Elec)*; Gewindebohrer *m (Tech)*.
tap *v* anzapfen *(a wire, etc.) (Elec)*; ein (Innen) Gewinde schneiden *(Tech)*.
tape *n* Aufnahmestreifen *m (teletype)*; Klebestreifen *m (adhesive tape)*; Trassierband *n (tracing tape)*.
taper Verjüngung *f (Mech)*.
tapered bore Würgebohrung *f (barrel) (Ord)*.
tappet rod Stößel *m*, Stoßstange *f*; Abwälzstößel *m (eccentric-cam type)*; Gleitstößel *m (sliding-cam type)*.
taps Zapfenstreich *m*.
tar Teer *m*.
target Ziel *n (combat)*; Scheibe *f (Tng)*.
target area Zielgelände *n*, Zielraumfläche *f*, Zielkreis *m*, Bombenwurfraum *m (Arty)*; Zielgebiet *n*, Zielplatz *m (bombing)*.
target butt Kugelfang *m*.
target course Zielweg *m (AA)*.
target designation Zielansprache *f*.
target-designation grid Zielgeviert-tafel *f (Arty Surv)*.
target frame Scheibenrahmen *m*.
target image Zielbild *n (telescopic sight)*.
target length Zielbreite *f (moving targets)*.
target location Zielfeststellung *f (Gunnery)*.
target moving at an angle schrägfahrendes Ziel *(ground target)*.
target moving parallel to front querfahrendes Ziel *(ground target)*.
target of opportunity Gelegenheitsziel *n*.
target practice Schulschießen *n*, Übungsschießen *n*.
target range Schießplatz *m*, Schulschießstand *m*, Schulgefechtschießstand *m*.
target reconnaissance Zielerkundung *f*, Zielaufklärung *f*.
target sector Zielteil *m*.
target ship Zielschiff *n*.
target sled Zielschlitten *m*.
tarpaulin Decke *f*, Plane *f*.
task Auftrag *m*, Aufgabe *f*.
task air force Fliegerverband *m*.
task force Armeegruppe *f (usually an army plus miscellaneous units)*; Kampfgruppe *f (smaller)*.
tassel Quast *m*.
taste Geschmack *m*.
tattoo Signal "Lichter aus!"
taxi *v* rollen *(Avn)*.
taxiway neutrale Zone, Rollbahn *f*. Rollstraße *f (Adrm)*.
team Mannschaft *f (Pers)*; Gespann *n*, Bespannung *f (horses, etc.)*.
team of horses Gespann *n*.
tear gas Tränengas *n*, Tränenstoff *m*, Reizkörper *m (CWS)*.
tear-gas candle Tränengaskerze *f (CWS)*.
tear-gas pot Tränenstoffkerze *f (CWS)*.
technical adviser Fachberater *m*.
technical designer Konstrukteur *m*.
technical inspection Waffen- und Gerätuntersuchung *f*.
Technical Manual Bedienungsanleitung *f*, Merkblatt zur Bedienung, Gebrauchsanleitung *f*.
technical sergeant Feldwebel *m*; Wachtmeister *m (Arty, Cav)*; Feuerwerker *m (Ord)*; Funkmeister *m (Rad)*; Schirrmeister *m (maintenance)*; Brieftaubenmeister *m (pigeoneer)*; Festungspionierfeldwebel *m (Ft Engr)*.
technical services technische Dienstzweige.
technician Techniker *m*.
telegram Telegramm *n*.
telegraph Telegraph *m*, Fernschreiber *m*.
telegraph key Morsetaste *f*.
telegraph line Telegraphenleitung *f*.
telegraph pole Telegraphenstange *f*.
telegraph printer Schnelltelegraph *m*, Ferndrucker *m*, Fernschreiber *m*.
telegraphy Telegraphie *f*.
telephone Fernsprecher *m*, Telephon *n*.
by telephone fernmündlich.
telephone call Ferngespräch *n*, Gespräch *n*, Spruch *m*.
telephone central Fernsprechvermittlung *f*, Vermittlung *f*, Vermittlungsstelle *f*.
telephone circuit Sprechverbindung *f*.
telephone communication Sprechverbindung *f*.
telephone - communications company Fernsprechkompanie *f*.
telephone connection Sprechverbindung *f*.
telephone-construction company Fernsprechbaukompanie *f*.
telephone-construction detail Fernsprechbautrupp *m*.
telephone construction truck Fernsprechbauwagen *m*.
telephone equipment Fernsprechgerät *n*.
telephone line Fernsprechleitung *f*.
telephone motor truck Fernsprechkraftwagen *m*.
telephone motor vehicle Fernsprechkraftfahrzeug *n*.
telephone operations truck Fernsprechbetriebskraftwagen *m*.
telephone operations vehicle Fernsprechfahrzeug *n*.
telephone operator Fernsprecher *m*.
telephone pole Leitungsmast *m*.
telephone receiver Hörer *m*.
telephone relay Fernsprechrelais *n*.
telephone section Fernsprechtrupp *m*.
telephone station Fernsprechstelle *f*, Sprechstelle *f*.
telephone traffic Fernsprechverkehr *m*, Sprechverkehr *m*.
telephone transcription Fernspruch *m*.
telephoto Fernbild *n*, Fernrohraufnahme *f*.
telescope Fernrohr *n*.
telescope center section Fernrohrhals *m*.
telescope head Fernrohrkopf *m*.
telescope holder Zielfernrohrträger *m (AT gun, R)*.
telescope housing Fernrohrhülse *f*.
telescope mount Aufsatz *m*, Richtaufsatz *m (Ord)*.
telescope seat Fernrohrlager *n*.
telescope support Fernrohrsteg *m*.
telescope tube Fernrohrkörper *m*; Fernrohrarm *m (BC telescope)*.
telescopic sight Zielfernrohr *n*, Richtfernrohr *n*, Fernrohraufsatz *m*, Optik *f*.
with telescopic sight fernrohrbesetzt.
telescopic sight mount Zielfernrohrträger *m*.
teletype Schnelltelegraph *m*, Ferndrucker *m*, Fernschreiber *m*.
teletype circuit Fernschreibleitung *f*.
teletype net Fernschreibnetz *n*.
teletype operator Fernschreiber *m*.
teletype truck Fernschreibwagen *m*.
teletypewriter Schnelltelegraph *m*, Ferndrucker *m*, Fernschreiber *m*.
television Fernsehen *n*.
temperature Temperatur *f*.
temperature difference Wärmeunterschied *m (Met)*.
temperature gage Temperaturmesser *m (Mtr)*.
temperature gradient Temperaturgradient *m (Met)*.
temperature variation Temperaturschwankung *f*.
tempered steel gehärteter Stahl.
template *See* templet.
temple Schläfe *f (anatomy)*.
temple strap Schläfenband *n (gas mask)*.
templet Schablone *f (Tech)*; Zelluloidplatte mit Einteilung *(Surv)*.
temporary grade zeitweiliger Rang.
tenacious zäh.
tender Anhänger *m (RR)*; Mutterschiff *n*, Tender *m (Nav)*.
tendon Sehne *f*.
tensile strength Zugfestigkeit *f*.
tensile stress Zugspannung *f*.
tension Spannung *f*.
tension chord Zuggurt *m (truss)*.
tension line Stromleine *f (Bdg)*.
tension member Strebe *f*.
tension wire Spanndraht *m*.
tent Zelt *n*.
tent camp Zeltlager *n*.
tent equipment Zeltausrüstung *f*.
tent pin Zeltpflock *m*, Hering *m*.
tent pitching Zeltbau *m*.
tent pole Zeltstock *m*.
terminal Kabelschuh *m (Elec)*; Endbahnhof *m (RR)*.
terminal binding post Polklemme *f*.
terminal plate Endplatte *f (Elec)*.
terminal repeater Endverstärker *m (Tp)*.
terminal station Endbahnhof *m (RR)*.
terminal twist Enddrall *m (Ord)*.
terminal velocity Endgeschwindigkeit *f (Ballistics)*.
terminal velocity dive Sturzflug mit Endgeschwindigkeit *(Avn)*.
terminology of orders Befehlssprache *f*.
terrain Gelände *n*.
terrain appreciation Geländebeurteilung *f (Tac)*.
terrain area Geländeraum *m*.
terrain compartment Geländeabschnitt *m*.
terrain conditions Geländeverhältnisse *npl*.
terrain contamination Geländevergiftung *f*.
terrain corridor Geländestreifen *m*.
terrain exercise Rahmenübung *f*.
terrain feature Geländegegenstand *m*, auffallender Geländepunkt.
terrain intelligence Geländeerkundung *f*.
terrain obstacle Geländehindernis *n*.
terrain photo-survey Geländeaufnahme *f*.
terrain problem Geländeaufgabe *f (maneuvers)*.
terrain representation Geländedarstellung *f (Surv)*.
terrain sector Geländeabschnitt *m*.
terrain surveying Geländevermessung *f*.
terrestrial fire Flachfeuer *n*, Feuer in der unteren Winkelgruppe *(Gunnery)*.
terrestrial observation Erdbeobachtung *f (Arty)*.
territory Gebiet *n*.
test Prüfung *f*, Versuch *m*, Probe *f*.
test airplane Versuchsflugzeug *n*.
test button Prüfknopf *m (field Tp)*.
test cartridge Meßkartusche *f (Am)*.
test firing Probeschießen *n*, Versuchsschießen *n (Ord)*.
test flight Probeflug *m*, Einfliegen *n*.
testicle Hoden *m*.
testing apparatus Prüfgerät *n*.
testing block Prüfstand *m (Avn, MT)*.
testing stand Prüfgestell *n*, Prüfstand *m*.
test key Prüftaste *f (field Tp)*.
test pilot Einflieger *m*.
test run Probelauf *m*, Versuchslauf *m (Mtr)*.
test station Untersuchungsstelle *f (Tp)*.
tetanus Wundstarrkrampf *m (Med)*.
tetraethyl lead Bleitetraäthyl *n*.
tetrahedron Igel *m (AT)*.
tetryl Tetryl *n*.
text Wortlaut *m*, Text *m*.
text in clear Klartext *m (Sig C)*.
theater commander kommandierender General eines Operationsgebiets.
theater of operations Operationsgebiet *n*, Kriegsgebiet *n*.
theater of war Kriegsschauplatz *m*.
theater reserve Hauptreserve des Operationsgebiets.
theodolite Theodolit *m (Surv)*.
theoretical deflection shift schußtafelmäßige Seitenverschiebung.
theoretical range schußtafelmäßige Schußweite *(Gunnery)*.
three-phase alternating current Drehstrom *m*.
three-point landing Dreipunktlandung *f (Avn)*.
three-point resection Einschneiden nach drei Punkten *(Surv)*.
three-seater dreisitzig.
three-speed transmission Dreiganggetriebe *n (MT)*.
three-way selector cock Dreiwegehahn *m*.
throat Kehle *f*, Rachen *m*, Schlund *m*.
throatlatch Kehlriemen *m (harness)*.
throat-type microphone Kehlkopfmicrophon *n (Avn)*.
throttle *n* Drossel *f (Mtr)*.
throttle *v* abdrosseln *(Mtr)*.
throttle grip Drosselgriff *m*.
throttle lever Drosselhebel *m*, Gashebel *m*, Regulierhebel *m*.
throttle shaft Drosselklappenwelle *f*.
throttle unit Drosselorgan *n*.
throttle valve Drosselklappe *f*.
throttling Drosselung *f*.
through channels auf dem Dienstweg.
through station Durchgangsbahnhof *m (RR)*.
through track Durchlaufgleis *n (RR)*.
throw *n* Wurf *m*.

throw v werfen.
throwing pit Wurfgrube f.
throwing range Wurfweite f.
throw in the clutch einkuppeln (MT).
throwout Schaltstück n (sight-mount housing).
throwout lever Ausschaltehebel m (aiming circle); Schalthebel m (panoramic telescope).
throw out the clutch auskuppeln (MT).
thrust Schraubendruck m, Schraubenzug m (propeller); Stich m, Stoß m (with a weapon); Vorstoß m (Tac).
thrusting weapon Stichwaffe f, Stoßwaffe f.
thrust line Stoßlinie f (Tac).
thumb Daumen m.
thumb jump Daumensprung m (range estimation).
thumb nut Drücker m (sight).
thumbscrew Flügelschraube f.
thumbtack Heftzwecke f, Reißnagel m.
thumb width Daumenbreite f (range estimation).
thunder Donner m.
thunderstorm Gewitter n.
theoretical time of flight schußtafelmäßige Flugzeit (Ballistics).
theory Lehre f, Theorie f.
theory of antiaircraft fire Flakschießlehre f.
theory of flight Fluglehre f.
theory of gunnery Schießlehre f; Flakschießlehre f (AA).
theory of tactics Gefechtslehre f.
thermal soaring Thermiksegeln n (glider).
thermite Thermit n.
thermite bomb Thermitbombe f.
thermite charge Thermitladung f (incendiary bomb).
thermite grenade Thermithandgranate f.
thermocouple meter Thermokreuzinstrument n.
thermograph Thermograph m.
thermo ice elimination Warmluftenteisung f (Avn).
thermometer Thermometer n.
thermos bottle Thermosflasche f.
thermostat Thermostat m.
thick dick, dicht.
thickness gage Fühlerlehre f.
thickness of armor Panzerstärke f (Tk).
thigh Schenkel m, Oberschenkel m.
thimble Kausche f (rigging, etc.).
thirsty durstig.
Thompson submachine gun Maschinenpistole Modell Thompson.
thread Gewinde n (Tech); Faden m (sewing).
threaded anvil Amboßschraube f (Am).
threaded breech hoop Spannschraube f (G).
threaded closing cap Verschlußschraube f (fuze).
threaded percussion primer Schlagzündschraube f (fuze).
threaded plug Verschraubung f.
threaded sleeve Muffe f (for pipe connections).
threat Drohung f, Bedrohung f.
three-axle vehicle Dreiachser m.
three-bank upright engine Dreireihenstandmotor m, W-Motor m.
three-blade controllable propeller Dreiblattverstellschraube f (Ap).
three-blade propeller Dreiflügelschraube f (Ap).
three-engine dreimotorig.
ticket Karte f, Schein m, Zettel m.
ticket office Fahrkartenausgabestelle f (office); Fahrkartenschalter m (window) (RR).
tide Gezeiten fpl.
tide station Gezeitenvermessungsstation f, Gezeitendienst m (CA).
tide table Gezeitentafel f.
tie n Schwelle f (RR); Bund m (lashing); Schlips m (Clo).
tie v binden, knüpfen; abbinden (Tp); anstechen (Engr).
tie plate Schienenunterlagplatte f (RR).
tie rod Lenkstange f, Spurstange f (MT); Kuppelstange f (split-trail carriage).
tighten zusammenziehen, verspannen.
tightening Verspannung f.
tilt n Schrägstellung f, Verkantung f.
tilt v verkanten, kippen.
timber raft Balkenfloß n (Bdg).
timber road Balkenbahn f (Engr).
timber road-block Balkensperre f (Engr).
time Zeit f.
time announcement Uhrzeitangabe f.
time blasting fuze Zeitzündschnur f (Engr).
time bomb Zeitbombe f, Bombe mit Verzugszeit.
time-delay relay Verzögerungsschütz m (Elec, Rad).
time difference Zeitunterschied m, Stoppzeit f (sound ranging).
time-difference method Zeitunterschiedverfahren n (sound ranging).
time distance Marschzeit f.
time fire Brennzünderschuß m (firing).
time fuze Zeitzünder m (Am); Zeitzündschnur f (blasting fuze); Brennzünder m (hand grenade, powder-train fuze).
time heading Zeitgruppe f (on Rad messages).
time interval Zeitabstand m, Zeitunterschied m (AA gunnery); Stoppzeit f (flash ranging).
time interval recorder Stoppuhr f.
time lag Stoppzeit f (flash ranging).
time length Vorbeimarschdauer f.
time of attack Angriffsbeginn m
time of departure Abfahrzeit f.
time of fall Fallzeit f, Bombenfallzeit f (bombing).
time of flight Flugzeit f; Flugzeitsekunden fpl (in seconds).
time-of-flight curve Flugzeitkurve f (Ballistics).
time of functioning Zünderlaufzeit f (fuze).
time of starting Abfahrzeit f.
time shell Granate mit Zeitzünder.
time signal Zeitzeichen n.
timetable Fahrplan m (RR); Zeiteinteilung f (Tac); Zeittafel f.
time train ring Satzstück n (time fuze).
timing Zündeinstellung f, Zündpunktverstellung f (ignition).
timing gear Steuerrad n (Mtr).
timing system Steuerung f (Mtr).
tin Zinn n.
tincture of iodine Jodtinktur f.
tin-plated verzinnt.
tinsmith Blechschmied m.
tip n Spitze f (point); Trinkgeld n (gratuity); Flügelende n (wing).
tip v kippen (tilt); umkippen (turn over).
tipping gradient Kippneigung f (MT).
tire n Reifen m, Radreifen m; Luftreifen m (pneumatic); Vollgummireifen m, Vollreifen m (solid).
tire v ermüden, ermatten.
tire casing Laufdecke f (MT).
tire flap Felgenband n, Schlauchschoner m (MT).
tire pressure gage Reifen-Luftdruckprüfer m.
tire tool Reifenheber m, Montierhebel m.
titanium tetrachloride Titantetrachlorid n (CWS).
TNT Sprengmunition 02 f, Füllpulver 02 n (abbr. Fp. 02).
tobacco Tabak m.
toe Zehe f.
toe-in Einschlag m, Vorspur f (MT).
toggle joint Kniegelenk n (pistol).
toggle switch Kippschalter m (Elec).
tolerance Toleranz f, gestattete Abweichung f (Tech).
tollgate Zollschranke f.
toll station Überweisungsamt n (Tp).
"tommy gun" Maschinenpistole f.
tompion Mündungskappe f, Mündungspfropfen m, Mundpfropfen m, Mittelpfropfen m (G).
ton Tonne f (metric ton of 1,000 kg).
ton capacity Tragfähigkeit f (MT).
tone Ton m; Tönung f (Photo).
tongs Zange f.
tongue Zunge f.
tonnage Schiffsraum m, Tonnengehalt m (Nav).
tonneau light Deckenlicht n (MT).
tool Werkzeug n.
tool bag Werkzeugtasche f.
tool box Werkzeugkasten m.
tool kit See **tool bag**.
tool steel Werkzeugstahl m.
tooth Zahn m.
toothache Zahnschmerzen mpl.
toothbrush Zahnbürste f.
toothpaste Zahnpaste f.
tooth powder Zahnpulver n.
top carriage Oberlafette f (G).
top chord Obergurt m (truss).
topographical crest Böschungskrone f.
topographical feature Geländeform f.
topographical map topographische Karte.
topographical point graphischer Punkt.
topographic survey Erdvermessung f.
topographic troops Karten- und Vermessungstruppen fpl.
topography Topographie f.
top sergeant Spieß m.
torch Fackel f.
torpedo n Torpedo n.
torpedo v torpedieren.
torpedo boat Schnellboot n.
torpedo bomber Torpedoflugzeug n, Torpedoflieger m.
torpedo-bomber pilot Torpedoflieger m.
torpedo-carrying flying boat Flugtorpedoboot n.
torpedo defense net Torpedoschutznetz n.
torpedoman Torpedo-Waffenleitvormann m (Nav).
torpedo plane Torpedoflugzeug n.
torpedo release Torpedoabwurf m, Torpedowurf m (Avn).
torpedo tube Torpedoausstoßrohr n, Torpedorohr n.
torque Drehmoment n (Mech, Mtr).
torque tube Verstellwelle f (Ap).
torsional vibration Drehschwingung f (Mtr).
torsional vibration damper Schwingungsdämpfer m (Mtr).
total elevation Gesamtrohrerhöhung f (G).
total loss Totalausfall m.
total mileage odometer Gesamtkilometerzähler m (speedometer).
total movement in elevation Höhenrichtfeld n (Ord).
total movement in traverse Schwenkbereich m, Seitenrichtbereich m, Seitenrichtfeld n (G, MG).
total traverse Gesamtseitenrichtung f (G).
total war totaler Krieg.
touch signal Berührungszeichen n (Tk).
tough zäh (tenacious); schwierig
tourniquet Aderpresse f.
tow v schleppen.
towed boat Schleppkahn m.
towed-sleeve target Schleppziel n, Schleppscheibe f, Luftsack m (AAA).
towel Handtuch n.
tower Turm m.
towing Abschleppen n.
towing equipment Abschleppgerät n.
towline Startseil n (glider).
town Stadt f, Ortschaft f.
town headquarters Stadtkommandantur f, Ortskommandantur f (Mil Govt).
tow rope Schlepptau n.
tow target Schleppscheibe f, gezogenes Ziel.
toxic giftig.
toxic agent Giftstoff m (CWS).
toxic smoke Giftnebel m (CWS).
toxic-smoke candle Giftrauchkerze f (CWS).
trace n Leuchtspur f (of tracer projectile); Geschirrtau n (harness).
trace v durchpausen (a map, etc.).
tracer Leuchtspurgeschoß n (projectile); Leuchtspursatz m (composition).
tracer ammunition Leuchtspurmunition f, Leuchtmunition f.
tracer bullet Leuchtspurgeschoß n.
tracer shell Leuchtspurgranate f (Am).
tracer thread Kennfaden m (field wire).
tracing paper Pauspapier n.
tracing tape Trassierband n (CWS, Engr).
track n Geleise n (RR); Schiene f (a rail); tatsächlich abgeflogener Kurs (Avn); Kette f (Tk); Spurweite f (MT); Rollbahn f (road).
track v festhalten (a target).
track block Kettenglied n (Tk, Trac).
track-connecting fixture Kettenspanner m (Tk, Trac).
tracked landing vehicle Kettenschwimmwagen m.
tracking dog Spürhund m.
track-laying vehicle Gleiskettenfahrzeug n, Kettenfahrzeug n, Raupenfahrzeug n.
track pin Kettenbolzen m (Tk, Trac).
tracks and suspensions Fahrwerk n (Tk).
track shield Kettenabdeckung f (Tk).
track shoe Kettenglied n (Tk, Trac).
track-supporting roller Stützrolle f (Tk).
traction Bodenhaftung f, Griffigkeit f (ground grip); Zugkraft f (tractional power).
traction aid Gleitschutzmittel n (MT).
traction device Greifervorrichtung f (MT).
tractional resistance Fahrwiderstand m (MT).
traction band Geländekette f (MT).
tractor Kraftschlepper m, Schlepper m, Trecker m; Planier-Raupenschlepper m (with angledozer).
tractor airplane Zugschrauber m.
tractor-drawn artillery Artillerie mit Kraftzug.
tractor propeller Zugschraube f (Ap).
trade test Berufsprüfung f.
trade wind Passatwind m.
traffic Verkehr m, Betrieb m.
traffic area Verkehrskreis m.
traffic block Verkehrsstoppung f.
traffic center Verkehrspunkt m.
traffic control Verkehrsregelung f.
traffic-control clearance Einfluggenehmigung f (Avn).
traffic control officer Straßenkommandant m.
traffic control post Verkehrsposten m (road); Ablaufposten m (Bdg).
traffic diagram Leitungsskizze f (Tp).
traffic element Verkehrsteilnehmer
traffic installations Verkehrsanlagen fpl.
traffic officer Bahnhofsoffizier m (RR).
traffic patrol Verkehrsstreife f.
traffic regulation Verkehrsregel f, Verkehrsbestimmung f; Vorfahrtregelung f (right-of-way procedure).
traffic sign Verkehrsschild n.
traffic supervision Verkehrsüberwachung f.
traffic symbol Verkehrszeichen n.
trail Lafettenschwanz m (G); Holm m (of split-trail); Hinterstütze f (MG tripod); Rücktrift f (bomb trajectory); Pfad m, Spur f, Piste f (path).
trail angle Rücktriftwinkel m (bomb trajectory).
trail assembly Lafettierung f (G).
trail box Lafettenkasten m (G).
trail bridge See **trail ferry**.
trailer Anhänger m (MT).
trailer load Anhängelast f (MT).
trailer mount Lafettenfahrzeug n (Arty).
trail ferry Gierfähre f (Engr).
trail-ferrying Gieren n (Engr).
trail float Schwanzblech n (G).
trail handspike Richtbaum m (G).
trailing edge Hinterkante f, Schleppkante f (Ap).
trailing-wire antenna Hängeantenne f, Schleppantenne f (Ap).
trail officer Schließender m (MT column).
trail rope Schlepptau n (Bln).
trail spade Erdsporn m, Lafettensporn m, Sporn m (G).
train Troß m, Kolonne f (supply vehicles, etc.); Zug m (RR).
train bombing Reihenabwurf m.
train commander Transportführer m, Zugkommandant m (RR).
trainee Rekrut m, Schüler m.
trainer Schulflugzeug n (Ap).
train guard Zugwache f, Zugbewachung f.
training Ausbildung f.
training agent Gasschutzübungsmittel n (CWS).
training airplane Schulflugzeug n, Übungsflugzeug n.
training aviation Schulflugwesen n, Lehrflugwesen n.
training center Ausbildungsstelle m.
training film Lehrfilm m.
training grenade Übungshandgranate f.
training installations Übungsanlagen fpl.
training instrument Ausbildungsgerät n.
training loss Ausbildungsausfall m.
training manual Ausbildungsvorschrift f.
training mask Übungsmaske f (CWS).
training munitions Übungsmunition f, Übungskriegsgerät n.
training of instructors Ausbildung von Ausbildern.
training of replacements Ersatzreserveausbildung f.
training order Ausbildungsanweisungen fpl.
training outlines Ausbildungsrichtlinien fpl.
training program Ausbildungsprogramm n.
training projectile Übungsgeschoß n.
training regulations Ausbildungsrichtlinien fpl.
training schedule Ausbildungsplan m.
training unit Übungseinheit f, Übungsverband m.
train of empties Leermaterial n (RR).
oscillations Schwingungszug m (Elec, Rad).
train release Reihenabwurf m, Reihenwurf m (Bombing).
train schedule Fahrplan m (RR).
train transportation officer Transportführer m.
train vehicle Troßfahrzeug n, Versorgungsfahrzeug n (march column).
traitor Verräter m.
trajectory Flugbahn f (Ballistics).
trajectory chart graphische Schußtafel f.
trajectory diagram Flugbahnaufriß m, Flugbahngrundriß m, Flugbahnbild n (Ballistics).
tramway Förderbahn f.
transceiver Senderempfänger m (Rad).
transconductance Steilheit f (Rad).
transcript Abschrift f; Fernspruch m (Tp).
transfer n Versetzung f (Pers); Verlegung f (installation, fire, etc.).
transfer v versetzen (Pers); verlegen (installation, fire, etc.).
transfer case Gruppengetriebe n, Zusatzgetriebe n.
transferred versetzt.
transformer Übertrager m, Umformer m, Transformator m (Elec).
transformer voltage Umformerspannung f.
transient target Augenblicksziel n.
transit Universalinstrument n (Surv).
transition Übergang m.
translate übersetzen; verdolmetschen (interpret).
translating lever Mitnehmer m (sighting mechanism).
translator Übersetzer m; Dolmetscher m (interpreter).
transloading point Umschlagstelle f.
transmission Wechselgetriebe n, Getriebe n (MT); Übermittlung f, Durchgabe f (of messages, etc.); Senden n, Tasten n (keying) (Rad).
transmission brake Getriebebremse f.
transmission case Getriebegehäuse n.
transmission grease Getriebefett n.
transmission in clear Klartextfunken n (Rad).
transmission main shaft Getriebehauptwelle f (MT).
transmission oil Getriebeöl n (MT).
transmission shaft Getriebewelle f (MT).
transmit funken, senden, geben (Rad, Tg); befördern, durchgeben (Sig C).
transmitter Sendegerät n, Funksender m (Rad); Geber m (AA director).
transmitter antenna Sendeantenne f (Rad).
transmitter tube Senderöhre f (Rad).
transom Querträger m, Unterzug m (Bdg).
transparent durchsichtig.
transparent reflector Reflexglas n (reflector sight).
transport Beförderung f, Transport m (transportation); Transporter m (Ap, Nav); Transportschiff n, Truppentransportschiff n (Nav); Transportflugzeug n (Ap). See also **motor transport**.
transportation Beförderungsmittel n, Transportmittel n (means); Beförderung f, Versand m, Verschickung f, Transport m; Eisenbahnbeförderung f (RR); Wassertransport m (by water); Kraftfahrtransport m (MT).
transportation company Transportkompanie f.
Transportation Corps Heerestransportkorps n (USA).
transportation headquarters Transportkommandantur f (RR).
transportation officer Transportführer m, Transportoffizier m (RR).
transportation of freight Frachtenbeförderung f.
transportation of the wounded Verwundetentransport m.
transportation of troops Truppenbeförderung f.
transportation order Transportbefehl m; Fahrbefehl m (MT).
transportation request Transportantrag m.
Transportation Service See **Transportation Corps**.
transportation system Transportwesen n.
transport aviation Transportluftfahrt f, Transportflugwesen n.
transport command Transportgeschwader n (Avn).
transport commander Transportkommandant m.
transport force Transportgeschwader n (Avn).
transport officer See **transportation officer**.
transposition cipher Kastenschlüssel m (Sig C).
transshipment Umladung f.
transshipment port Umschlagshafen
transverse beam Querträger m (Bdg).
transverse shutter Eisenbahnquerschnittblende f (Sig lamp).
transverse support Querträger m (Bdg).
trap n Falle f; Hinterhalt m (ambush).
trap v einkesseln (Tac).
trapezoid truss Trapez-Fachwerkträger m (Engr).
trap mine Schreckmine f, Schreckladung f, Sprengfalle f.
travel allowance Reisegeld n (money); Fahrkostenentschädigung f, Reisekostenvergütung f, Reisevergütung f (reimbursement).
traveling capacity Fahrleistung f (MT, Tk).
traveling distance Fahrbereich m (MT, Tk).
traveling position Fahrstellung f (Ord).
travel of target Vorauswanderungsstrecke f (during dead time) (AA gunnery).
travel order Marschbefehl m (official order); Fahrausweis m (traveling permit).
travel pay See **travel allowance**.
travel ration Reiseverpflegung f.
traverse Querdeckung f, Querwall m, Schulterwehr f (Ft); Streckenzug m (Surv).
traverse v schwenken (G); durchqueren (cross).
traverse method Streckenzugverfahren n.
traverse stop Seitenbegrenzer m, Begrenzungsstift m (G, MG).
traversing and searching fire Breiten- und Tiefenfeuer n (MG).
traversing arc Führungsstück n (MG).
traversing drive Seitenrichttrieb m (G, Mort).
traversing fire Breitenfeuer n (MG).
traversing handwheel Handrad zur Seitenrichtung, Seitenrichtrad n (G).
traversing lever Seitenhebel m.
traversing mechanism Seitenrichtmaschine f, Seitenrichtwerk n (G).
traversing rack Zahnkranz m (AA gun, Tk turret).
traversing screw Seitenrichtschraube f (G).
traversing slide Führungshülse f (MG).
traversing stop See **traverse stop**.
tread Tritt m (foot); Schützenauftritt m (firing step); Lauffläche f, Profil n (tire); Spurweite f (lateral distance between wheels) (MT).

treadway Spurtafel f.
treadway bridge Spurtafelbrücke f (duckboard), Kradschützensteg m (floating).
treason Landesverrat m, Kriegsverrat m.
treatment Behandlung f.
treaty Vertrag m.
tree Baum m.
tree stump Baumstumpf m.
tree-top height Baumhöhe f.
tree trunk Baumstamm m.
trellis mast Gittermast m.
trench Graben m, Schützengraben m.
trench board Holzrost m.
trench bottom Grabensohle f (Ft).
trench excavator Grabenbagger m.
trench mortar Granatwerfer m, Handwerfer m. See also mortar.
trench mouth Mundschleimhautentzündung f; Stomatitis f (Vincent's infection).
trench periscope Beobachtungsrohr n, Schützengrabenspiegel m, Deckungsspiegel m.
trench profile Grabenprofil n (Ft).
trench pump Grabenpumpe f (Ft).
trench shelter Deckungsgraben m, Splittergraben m.
trench system Grabensystem n.
trench timber Schurzholz n (Ft).
trench warfare Grabenkrieg m.
trestle Bock m, Joch n (Bdg).
trestle bridge Bockbrücke f; Bockschnellsteg m (hasty Bdg).
trestle carrier Bockwagen m (MT).
trestle leg Bockbein n (Bdg).
trestle setting Bocksetzen n (Bdg).
trial n Probe f (test); Versuch m (experiment); Prozeß m (law).
trial adj versuchsweise, Versuchs-.
trial balloon Pilotballon m.
trial fire Einschießen n (Gunnery).
trial run Versuchslauf m (Mtr).
triangle Dreieck n.
triangle exercise Dreieckzielen n (R practice).
triangle of error Fehlerdreieck n (Surv).
triangle of velocities Geschwindigkeitsdreieck n (Avn).
triangular dreieckig, dreigegliedert, dreigliedrig.
triangular division dreigliedrige Division.
triangular road junction Wegedreieck n.
triangular timber obstacle Dreieckbalkensperre f.
triangulation Triangulation f, Dreiecksaufnahme f (Surv).
triangulation point trigonometrischer Punkt (Surv).
trick List f.
tricycle landing gear Dreiradfahrgestell n, Bugradfahrgestell n (Ap).
trigger Abzug m (R); Dauerabzug m (for full-automatic fire) (MG).
trigger bar Abzugsschiene f (AA gun).
trigger cam Drucknase f (R).
trigger frequency Kippschwingung f (Rad).
trigger guard Abzugsbügel m (R).
trigger-guard screw Kreuzschraube f (R).
trigger lever Abzugshebel m (MG).
trigger mechanism Abzugsvorrichtung f (R).
trigger piece Abzugsstück n (on G breech mechanism).
trigger pin Abzugsstift m (R); Hahnbolzen m (MG).
trigger pull Abzugsgewicht n (Small Arms).
trigger sear Abzugsstollen m (R).
trigger-sear fork Abzugsgabel f (R).
trigger squeeze Abkrümmen n, Durchkrümmen n (R).
trigonometric function Kreisfunktion f.
trigonometry Trigonometrie f.
trimming Lastigkeitsregelung f (Ap).
trim tab Trimmklappe f, Trimmruder n, Ausgleichfläche f (Ap).
trinitrophenol Pikrinsäure f, Trinitrophenol n.
trinitrotoluol Trinitrotoluol n, Tolit n, Tolita n, Trilit n, Trotyl n, Tutol n; Sprengmunition 02, Fp. 02 (Ger).
triode grid-leak detector Audion n.
triode tube Dreielektrodenröhre f, Dreipolröhre f, Triode f (Rad).
trip n Reise f (journey); Spannfalle f (of firing pin, G); Auslösung f (Mech).
trip v stolpern (stumble); auslösen (release).
triplane Dreidecker m.
triple mixture Dreiergemisch n (gasoline 50%, benzol 40%, alcohol 10%).
triple rank Linie zu 3 Gliedern.
triplicate eine dritte Kopie.
in triplicate in dreifacher Ausführung.
trip mileage odometer Tageskilometerzähler m (speedometer).
tripod Dreibein n, Dreifuß m.
tripod cable support Dreibock m (Engr).
tripod extension piece Dreifußaufsatzstück n, Lafettenaufsatzstück n (MG).
tripod mast Dreibeinmast m (Nav).
tripod mount Dreibeinlafette f.
trip wire Stolperdraht m; Drahtschlinge f (snare).
trip-wire entanglement Stolperdrahthindernis n.
trip-wire mine Stolperdrahtmine f.
troop Schwadron f (Cav).
troop carrier Truppentransporter m (Ap).
troop-carrying glider Lastensegler m, Lastensegelflugzeug n.
troop commander Schwadronschef m, Schwadronführer m (Cav).
troop concentration Truppenmasse f.
trooper Reiter m.
troop headquarters detail Schwadronstrupp m (Cav).
troop movement Truppenbewegung f.
troops Truppe f (collective); Truppen fpl (plural).
troop school Truppensonderlehrgang
troopship Truppentransporter m, Truppentransportschiff n.
troops of occupation Besatzungstruppen fpl.
troop train Truppentransportzug m.
troop training camp Truppenübungslager n.
troop training grounds Truppenübungsplatz m.
troop transport Truppentransporter m (Ap, Nav). See also troopship.
troop unit Truppeneinheit f (usually has uniform type of weapons, as distinguished from Truppenverband, combined-arms unit); Truppenteil m.
tropical tropisch, Tropen-.
tropical air tropische Warmluft (Met).
troposphere Troposphäre f (Avn, Met).
trouble shooter Störungssucher m (Tp).
trouble truck Abschleppwagen m.
trough Trog m, Wanne f.
trousers Hosen fpl.
truce Waffenruhe f, örtlicher Waffenstillstand.
truck Lastkraftwagen m (MT); Drehgestell n (RR car).
truck driver Lastkraftfahrer m, Kraftfahrer m.
truckhead Ausladespitze f, Umschlagstelle einer Kraftwagenkolonne (MT).
truck-tractor Lastwagenschlepper m.
truck trailer Lastanhänger m (MT).
true azimuth rechtweisende Kompaßzahl f, rechtweisender Kurswinkel m.
true copy beglaubigte Abschrift.
true course rechtweisender Kurs (Air Navigation).
true declination Ortsmißweisung f.
true heading rechtweisender Windkurs (Air Navigation).
true north Geographisch-Nord m (Surv).
trumpet Trompete f (bugle); Lautsprechertrichter m (Rad).
trunk Rumpf m (anatomy); Koffer m (travel).
trunk cable Fernkabel n (Tp).
trunk circuit Hauptleitung f, Hauptkabel n, Stammleitung f (Sig).
trunk line Stammleitung f (Tp).
trunk-line construction Stammleitungsbau m (Tp).
trunk station Hauptanschluß m, Hauptstelle f (Tp).
trunnion Tragzapfen m, Zapfen m; Lagerzapfen m (aiming circle); Schildzapfen m (G).
trunnion bearing Pivotlager n, Schildzapfenlager n (G).
trunnion cap Schildzapfenlagerdeckel m (G).
trunnion socket Schildzapfenpfanne f (G).
truss Fachwerkträger m (Bdg).
truss bridge Fachwerkbrücke f.
try square Anschlagwinkel m.
tube Rohr n, Röhre f, Schlauch m; Kernrohr n, Seelenrohr n (G); Elektrodenröhre f (Rad); Luftschlauch m (inner tube) (MT).
tube base Röhrensockel m (Rad).
tube length Seelenlänge f (Ord).
tube-testing apparatus Röhrenprüfgerät n (Rad).
tubular chassis frame Rohrrahmen m
tubular handle Griffrohr n (trail spade).
tubular mast Röhrenmast m (Nav).
tubular mount Röhrenlafette f (MG).
tubular spirit level Röhrenlibelle f.
tubular trail Röhrenlafette f (G).
tug n Schlepper m (Nav).
tugboat Schlepper m; Hafenschlepper m (harbor); Hochseeschlepper m (ocean-going).
tumble sich überschlagen (projectile).
tune abstimmen (Rad).
tune in einstellen (Rad).
tungsten Wolfram n.
tuning coil Abstimmspule f (Rad).
tuning condenser Abstimmkondensator m (Rad).
tuning control Frequenzeinstellung f (Rad).
tuning knob Abstimmkondensatorgriff m (Rad).
tuning out Sperren n (Rad).
tuning scale Abstimmskala f (Rad).
tunnel Stollen m, Tunnel m (Engr).
turbine Turbine f.
turbo supercharger Zwischengebläse n (Ap engine).
turbulence Böigkeit f (Met).
turbulence chamber Wirbelkammer f (Diesel engine).
turn n Kehrkurve f, Kurve f, Kehrtwendung f, Wendung f (Avn); Krümmung f, Biegung f (road).
turn v drehen, wenden; schwenken (to wheel right or left); umgehen (to flank).
turn and bank indicator See bank and turn indicator.
turnback Verbindungsriemen m (harness).
turnbuckle Spannschloß n.
turn indicator Wendezeiger m (Ap).
turning combat Kurvenkampf m (Avn).
turning movement Umgehung f (Tac).
turntable Drehscheibe f (RR); Drehkranz m (seaplane catapult).
turntable gun carriage Drehscheibenlafette f.
turret Kanzel f (Ap); Turm m (Tk, Ft, Nav).
turret basket Kampfabteil m (Tk).
turret gun Turmgeschütz n.
turret gun mount Turmlafette f (Tk).
turret hatch Turmluk n, Turmluke f, Dachluke f, Turmklappe f (Tk).
turret hatch cover Turmlukendeckel m (Tk).
turret locking clamp Turmzurrung f (Ap, Tk).
turret mount Turmlafette f.
turret traversing mechanism Turmschwenkwerk n (Ap, Tk).
twenty-five percent rectangle 25%ige Trefferfläche (Ballistics).
twin barrels Zwillingsläufe mpl (MG).
twin-engine zweimotorig.
twin-float seaplane Zweischwimmer-Seeflugzeug n.
twin machine gun MG.-Zwilling m.
twin mount Zwillingslafette f (Ord).
twin rudders Doppelseitensteuer n (Ap).
twin-screw elevating mechanism Doppelschraubenrichtmaschine f (G).
twin tail Gabelschwanz m (Ap).
twist Drall m, Windung f (Ord).
twist drill Spiralbohrer m.
twist effect of slipstream Drallwirkung f (Avn).
two-axle vehicle Zweiachser m.
two-barreled mount Doppellafette f (Ord).
two-blade propeller Zweiflügel-Luftschraube f (Ap).
two-conductor firing wire Doppelsprengkabel n (Demolitions).
two-cycle engine Zweitaktmotor m.
two-man shelter tent Zweierzelt n.
two-place airplane Zweisitzer m.
two-point landing Radlandung f (Avn).
two-point resection Zweipunktverfahren n (Surv).
two-ship element Rotte f, Zweierverband m (Avn).
two-stage zweistufig.
two-stage supercharger Stufenlader m (Ap).
two-stage transmitter zweistufiger Sender (Rad).
two-station net Funklinie f (Rad).
two-station spotting Doppelanschnitt m.
two-stranded zweiadrig (Elec).
two-way break-in communication Gegensprechen n (Rad).
two-way communication Doppelverkehr m (Rad, Tp).
two-way radiophone communication Funkwechselsprechen n.
two-way radio traffic Funkwechselverkehr m (alternate); Funkdoppelverkehr m (simultaneous).
two-way telegraphy wechselseitige Telegraphie.
two-way telephone circuit gegenseitige Sprechverbindung.
two-way traffic Doppelverkehr m (simultaneous), Wechselverkehr m (alternate) (Rad).
type Art f, Baumuster n, Muster n, Typ m.
typewrite maschineschreiben, tippen.
typewriter Schreibmaschine f.
typhoid fever Typhus m, Unterleibstyphus m.
typhus Fleckfieber n, Flecktyphus m.
typist Maschinenschreiber m, Maschinenschreiberin f.

U

U-boat U-Boot n, Unterseeboot n.
U-frame U-Rahmen m (tubular chassis) (MT).
uhf See ultrahigh frequency.
ultimatum Ultimatum n.
ultrahigh frequency Ultrakurzwelle f.
ultrahigh frequency receiver Ultrakurzwellenempfänger m.
ultrahigh frequency transmitter Ultrakurzwellensender m.
umbrella antenna Schirmantenne f.
umpire n Schiedsrichter m; Stabsschiedsrichter m (at Hq).
unanchored contact mine Treibmine f.
unarmed unbewaffnet, waffenlos; unscharf (fuze, etc.).
unauthorized eigenmächtig, ohne Erlaubnis, unvorschriftsmäßig.
uncase entrollen (flag).
uncock entspannen (Ord).
unconditional surrender bedingungslose Unterwerfung, bedingungslose Übergabe.
unconscious ohnmächtig, bewußtlos (a physical state); unbewußt (unaware).
uncontrolled mosaic Bildskizze f (aerial Photo).
uncouple abprotzen (Arty).
uncover die Kopfbedeckung abnehmen (remove hat, etc.); entblößen (Tac).
undamped oscillations ungedämpfte Schwingungen (Rad).
undamped waves ungedämpfte Wellen (Rad).
under arms unter Waffen, bewaffnet.
underbrush Unterholz n, Gestrüpp n, Gesträuch n.
underdrive Geländegang m (MT).
underground cable Erdkabel n, unterirdisches Fernkabel (Tg, Tp).
underground movement illegale Bewegung (political).
underground water Grundwasser n.
undermine unterminieren.
underpass Bahnunterführung f (RR).
undershirt Unterhemd m.
underwater ranging battery Unterwassermeßbatterie f (CA).
underwear Unterwäsche f.
undesired frequency Störfrequenz f, fremde Wellen (Rad).
unescorted ohne Begleitung, ohne Geleit, ohne Deckung, ohne Schutz.
unescorted by fighters ohne Jägerschutz (Avn).
unevacuable nicht evakuierbar.
unevenness of ground Bodenunebenheit f.
unexploded bomb nicht explodierte Bombe.
unfavorable ungünstig, unvorteilhaft.
unfavorable weather ungünstige Wetterlage.
unfit untauglich, ungeeignet.
"Unfix, bayonets!" "Seitengewehr, an Ort!"
unfurl entrollen (flag).
unharness ausschirren.
uniform n Uniform f, Anzug m (Clo).
uniform adj einheitlich, gleichförmig, vorschriftsmäßig.
uniform allowance Einkleidungsbeihilfe f (for Clo).
uniform slope stetige Böschung (Top).
uniform twist gleichbleibender Drall, gleichförmiger Drall (Ord).
unilateral einseitig.
unimproved road Fahrweg, nicht jederzeit brauchbar.
Union Jack Lotsenflagge f (Nav).
unit Einheit f, Verband m, Truppenteil m (Tac).
unit assemblage Geräteeinheit f (of equipment, etc.).
unit commander Kommandeur eines Truppenteils.
United States Army Das Berufsheer der Vereinigten Staaten einschließlich der Nationalgarde und der organisierten Reserven. Compare Army of the United States.
United States Coast Guard Küstenwachkorps der Vereinigten Staaten.
United States Marine Corps Marinekorps der Vereinigten Staaten.
United States Navy Kriegsmarine der Vereinigten Staaten.
United States of America Die Vereinigten Staaten von Amerika.
unit engineer Pionierführer m.
unit fund Kasse eines Truppenteils.
unit of equipment Gerätsatz m.
unit of fire Munition für einen Tag.
unit of measurement Maßeinheit f.
universal joint Kreuzgelenk n.
universal-joint housing Gelenkgehäuse n (MT).
unlimber abprotzen (Arty).
unlimbered feuerbereit, abgeprotzt (Arty).
unload entladen, abladen, ausladen; löschen (a ship); entladen (a gun, etc.).
unloading party Abladekommando n.
unloading unit Ausladeeinheit f.
unmask enthüllen, verraten (position of a gun by opening fire); freigeben (field of fire for friendly troops).
unmilitary unsoldatisch, unmilitärisch.
unobserved fire Schießen ohne Beobachtung (Gunnery).
unqualified nicht qualifiziert, ungeeignet.
unsaddle absatteln.
unserviceable unbrauchbar, unbenutzbar.
"Unsling arms!" "Gewehr abnehmen!"
unsynchronized fire nicht synchronisiertes Feuer (Ap gun).
updraft carburetor Aufstromvergaser m (Mtr).
uphill bergauf, aufwärts.
upper band Oberring m (R).
upper-band spring Oberringfeder f
upper prism micrometer head Triebschraube f (panoramic sight).
upper sight Oberschild m (G).
upright engine Standmotor m.
upside-down flight Rückenflug m.
upstream oberstrom (Engr).
upstream anchor Stromanker m (Bdg).
up-sun approach Sturzflug aus der Sonne.
upwind adv windwärts.
urgent dringend; KR (in Rad procedure spoken Konrad Richard in accordance with German phonetic alphabet).
urgent call dringendes Gespräch, Ausnahmegespräch n (Tp).
urgent message dringende Meldung.
urgent radio message dringender Funkspruch.
urgent signal Dringlichkeitszeichen n (Sig Com).
urgent telephone call dringendes Ferngespräch.
urinate urinieren, Harn lassen, Wasser lassen.
urine Harn m, Urin m.
usable rate of fire praktische Feuergeschwindigkeit (Ord).
useful load Nutzlast f (vehicles); Zuladung f (Ap).
utilization of terrain Geländeausnutzung f.

V

vacancy freie Planstelle, Fehlstelle f (Adm).
vaccinate impfen.
vaccination Impfung f, Schutzimpfung f.
vaccination certificate Impfschein m.
vacuum Leere f, Luftleere f, Vakuum n; Luftsog m (resulting from explosion).
vacuum pump Vakuumpumpe f.
vacuum tank Unterdruckförderer m (MT).
vaccum tube Vakuumröhre f.
vacuum-tube amplifier Röhrenverstärker m (Rad).
vacuum-tube oscillator Röhrensummer m (Rad).
vacuum-tube voltmeter Röhrenspannungsmesser m.
valley Tal n.
valley dam Talsperre f.
valve Ventil n.
valve arrangement Ventilanordnung f (Mtr).
valve ball Ventilkegel m (MT).
valve chamber Ventilkammer f
valve cord Ventilleine f (Bln).
valve guide Ventilschaftführung f (Mtr).
valve head Ventilteller m (Mtr).
valve lifter Ventilstößel m, Stößel m, Rollenstößel m (roller type) (Mtr).
valve seat Ventilsitz m (Mtr).
valve spring Ventilfeder f (Mtr).
valve stem Ventilschaft m (Mtr).
valve-timing system Ventilsteuerung f (Mtr).
van See vanguard.
van Flügel m (Cml shell, bomb); Flügelkolben m (pump); Wetterfahne f (weather vane).
vapor Dampf m, Dunst m.
vapor detector kit Gasanzeiger m (CWS).
vapor particle Tröpfchen n (CWS).
vapor trail Kondensstreifen m (Avn).
variable condenser Drehkondensator
variable μ tube Regelröhre f (Rad).
variation Ortsmißweisung f (Air Navigation).
variometer Variometer n (Ap, Elec).
varnish Firnis m, Lack m.
veal Kalbfleisch n.
vector Vektor m.
veer wenden, umschwingen, nach der Seite abgelenkt werden.
vegetable(s) Gemüse n; Dörrgemüse n (dehydrated).
vegetation Bodenbewachsung f (Top).
vehicle Fahrzeug n.
vehicle assembly area Ablaufplatz m.
vehicle-borne verlastet.
vehicle park Kraftfahrpark m.
vehicle resistance Rollwiderstand m
vehicular station in ein Fahrzeug eingebautes Funkgerät (Rad).

velocity Geschwindigkeit *f.*
velocity error abweichende Anfangsgeschwindigkeit *(Ballistics).*
velocity of fall Fallgeschwindigkeit *f (Bombing, Ballistics).*
velocity of light Lichtgeschwindigkeit *f.*
velocity of sound Schallgeschwindigkeit *f.*
veneer Furnier *n.*
venereal disease Geschlechtskrankheit *f.*
V-engine Gabelmotor *m,* V-Motor *m.*
vent Düse *f (rocket);* Öffnung *f,* Austritt *m,* Loch *n.*
vent hole Zündkanal *m (obturator).*
ventilation Lüftung *f,* Belüftung *f;* Bewetterung *f (mines).*
ventilation system Belüftungsanlage *f;* Wetterführung *f (mines).*
ventilator Lüfter *m;* Aufbaulüfter *m (Tk hull).*
ventral gun mount Bodenlafette *f (Ap).*
ventral turret Bodenkanzel *f,* Wanne *f (Ap).*
verbal order mündlicher Befehl.
verdict Urteil *n,* Entscheidung *f;* Urteilsspruch *m (Law).*
verification Prüfung *f,* Nachprüfung
verification fire Prüfungsschießen *n.*
verify prüfen, nachprüfen; "Bitte prüfen" *(Rad procedure).*
vernier Nonius *m.*
vernier dial Feineinstellung *f (Rad).*
vertical senkrecht, lotrecht.
vertical aerial photograph Senkrechtbild *n,* Senkrechtluftbild *n* Senkrechtaufnahme *f,* Senkrechtluftaufnahme *f.*
vertical axis Hochachse *f (Ap).*
vertical axle displacement Kletterfähigkeit *f (MT).*
vertical deviation Höhenabweichung *f (Gunnery).*
vertical dive Kopfsturz *m (Avn).*
vertical frame Spant *m (Ap).*
vertical height Flughöhe *f (Ballistics).*
vertical interval senkrechter Abstand, Höhenabstand *m,* Höhenunterschied
vertical jump Abgangsfehlerwinkel *m (Ballistics).*
vertical lead Höhenwinkelvorhalt *m (AA Gunnery).*
vertical photograph Senkrechtaufnahme *f,* Senkrechtbild *n (aerial Photo).*
vertical plane Senkrechtebene *f.*
vertical projection Projektion auf die Senkrechtebene.
vertical ring Spant *m (Ap).*
vertical shot group Scheibentreffbild *n (Ballistics).*
vertical speed Senkrechtgeschwindigkeit *f (Avn).*
vertical spotting Beobachtung der Längenabweichung *(Gunnery).*
vertical stabilizer Seitenflosse *f (Ap).*
vertical target senkrechte Trefffläche *(Ballistics).*
vertical tracking telescope Höhenrichtfernrohr *n (height finder).*
vertical visual angle Höhenwinkel *m (AA Gunnery).*
Very light Leuchtkugel *f.*
Very light signal Leuchtsignal *n.*
Very pistol Leuchtpistole *f.*
Very signal cartridge Leuchtpatrone
Very signal light Leuchtkugel *f.*
vesicant *n* ätzender Kampfstoff, Hautgift *n,* blasenziehender Kampfstoff, Gelbkreuz *n (CWS).*
vesicant *adj* blasenziehend *(CWS).*
vessel Wasserfahrzeug *n (Nav).*
veteran Veteran *m,* ehemaliger Kriegsteilnehmer, ehemaliger Frontsoldat.
Veterans Administration Fürsorgeverwaltung für Kriegsteilnehmer *(USA).*
veterinarian Tierarzt *m,* Veterinär
veterinary aid man Veterinärgehilfe
veterinary aid station Pferdeverbandplatz *m.*
veterinary ambulance Pferdetransportwagen *m.*
veterinary blood-testing laboratory Tierblutuntersuchungsstelle *f.*
veterinary clearing station Pferdelazarett *n.*
veterinary collecting point Pferdekrankensammelpunkt *m.*
veterinary collecting station Pferdekrankensammelstelle *f,* Pferdekrankensammelplatz *m.*
veterinary company Veterinärkompanie *f.*
Veterinary Corps Veterinärkorps *n (USA).*
veterinary depot Veterinärpark *m.*
veterinary dispensary Pferdeverbandplatz *m.*
veterinary equipment Veterinärgerät
veterinary general hospital Heimat-Pferdelazarett *n (Z of I).*
veterinary hospital Pferdelazarett *n,* Krankenstall *m;* Heerespferdelazarett *n (GHQ).*
veterinary motor ambulance Pferdekrankenkraftwagen *m.*
veterinary officer Veterinäroffizier *m.*
veterinary personnel Veterinärpersonal *n.*
veterinary service Veterinärdienst
veterinary station hospital Standort-Pferdelazarett *n.*
V-formation Winkel *m,* Winkelform
viaduct Viadukt *m,* Überführung *f.*
vibration Schwingung *f (Mech).*
vibrator Wechselrichter *m,* Zerhacker *m (Rad).*
vice-admiral Admiral *m (Nav).*
victim Opfer *n.*
victor Sieger *m.*
victorious siegreich.
victory Sieg *m.*
Victory Medal Interalliierte Siegesmedaille *(USA, World War I).*
Victory ribbon Band der Interalliierten Siegesmedaille *(USA, World War I).*
view Blick *m,* Anblick *m,* Aussicht *f;* Ansicht *f (opinion).*
view finder Sucher *m.*
viewing slit Augenschlitz *m (telescopic sight).*
vigilance Wachsamkeit *f.*
village Dorf *n,* Ortschaft *f.*
vineyard Weingarten *m.*
violent heftig.
viscometer Dichtigkeitsmesser *m.*
vise Schraubstock *m (Tech).*
visible horizon sichtbarer Horizont, Kimm *m.*
visibility Sicht *f,* Sichtigkeit *f,* Sichtbarkeit *f;* Fernsicht *f (distant);* Sichtverhältnisse *npl (conditions).*
vision Sehkraft *f,* Sehvermögen *n,* Sehschärfe *f.*
vision slit Sehschlitz *m (Tk).*
visiting correspondent Sonderberichterstatter *m.*
visit of courtesy Höflichkeitsbesuch
visor Schirm *m (Clo).*
visual communication Zeichenverbindung *f.*
visual indicator Sichtanzeigegerät *n (Ap Inst).*
visual reconnaissance Augenaufklärung *f (Avn).*
visual signal Sichtzeichen *n.*
voice frequency band Sprachfrequenzband *n (Rad, Tp).*
voice radio Sprechfunk *m;* Telefon *(as marked on Rad set).*
voice-radio communication Funksprechen *n.*
voice transmission Sprachübertragung *f,* Sprechen *n (Rad, Tp);* Funksprechübermittlung *f,* Funksprechen *n (Rad).*
volatile chemical warfare agent Luftkampfstoff *m.*
volatility Flüchtigkeit *f (CWS).*
volley Gruppe *f (Arty);* Salve *f (Small Arms);* Ehrensalve *f (at burials).*
volley fire Gruppenfeuer *n,* Gruppenschießen *n (Arty).*
volt Volt *n.*
voltage Spannung *f (Elec).*
voltage across terminals Klemmenspannung *f (Elec).*
voltage divider Spannungsteiler *m (Rad).*
voltage drop Spannungsabfall *m.*
voltage regulator Spannungsregler *m.*
voltage variation Spannungsschwankung *f.*
voltmeter Spannungsmesser *m,* Voltmeter *n.*
volt-milliammeter Volt-Milliamperemeter *n.*
volume Lautstärke *f (Rad);* Rauminhalt *m (content).*
volume control Lautstärkenregler *m (Rad).*
volume of fire Feuerstärke *f.*
volume of reception Empfangslautstärke *f (Rad).*
volumetric mengenmäßig.
volumetric capacity Fassungsvermögen *n.*
volunteer *n* Freiwilliger *m.*
volunteer *adj* freiwillig.
volunteer *v* sich freiwillig melden.
volute spring Kegelfeder *f.*
voucher Beleg *m.*
V-turn Straßenknie *n,* Wegeknie *n (road).*
V-type belt Keilriemen *m (Mtr).*
V-type engine V-Motor *m.*
vulcanize vulkanisieren.
vulnerable verwundbar, verletzlich.

W

wad Pfropfen *m.*
wade waten.
wagon Wagen *m.*
waist Gürtellinie *f.*
waist gun Seiten-MG. *n (Ap).*
wait *v* warten.
waiver Erlaß *m,* Verzichtleistung *f,* Verzicht *m.*
wake Kielwasser *n (of a ship).*
walkie-talkie Feldfunksprecher *m,* tragbares Kleinfunksprechgerät.
walking wounded marschfähige Verwundete.
wall Wall *m (Ft);* Mauer *f (masonry);* Wand *f (interior);* Trachte *f (hoof).*
wallet Brieftasche *f.*
war Krieg *m.*
war chest Kriegskasse *f.*
war chevron Kriegsteilnehmerabzeichen für Überseedienst *(USA).*
war college Kriegsakademie *f.*
war correspondent Kriegsberichter *m.*
ward *n* Krankenstube *f,* Krankenabteilung *f (Med).*
ward attendant Krankenwärter *(Med).*
War Department Kriegsministerium *n,* Kriegsdepartement *n (USA).*
War Department General Staff Generalstab des Heeres.
war diary Kriegstagebuch *n*
ward master Krankenstubenaufseher *m,* Abteilungsaufseher *m (Med).*
ward officer leitender Arzt *(Med).*
war economy Wehrwirtschaft *f.*
war effort Kriegseinsatz *m.*
warehouse Lagerhaus *n,* Warenlager
warfare Krieg *m,* Kriegführung *f.*
war footing Kriegsfuß *m.*
war game Kriegsspiel *n (map maneuvers).*
war gas Kampfgas *n (CWS).*
warhead Gefechtskopf *m (of torpedo).*
warm front Aufgleitfront *f,* Warmluftfront *f (Met).*
warming-up shot Anwärmeschuß *m.*
warning Warnung *f.*
warning district Luftwarnbezirk *m.*
warning order Vorbefehl *m (Tac).*
warning signal Ankündigungssignal
war of attrition Abnutzungskrieg *m.*
war of movement Bewegungskrieg
war of position Stellungskrieg *m.*
warp *n* Beiende *n (on a rope).*
war photographer Bildberichter *m.*
war plant Rüstungswerk *n.*
warrant *n* Beförderungsurkunde *f.*
warrant officer Feldwebelleutnant *m (USA).*
war reserves Materialreserven *fpl.*
war service chevron *See* **war chevron.**
warship Kriegsschiff *n.*
war strength Kriegsstärke *f.*
war traitor Kriegsverräter *m.*
war treason Kriegsverrat *m.*
washer Abdichtungsring *m,* Dichtungsscheibe *f,* Unterlegscheibe *f,* Dichtungsring *m.*
washing soda Natriumkarbonat *n.*
waste *n* Abfall *m,* Altmaterial *n.*
waste of ammunition Munitionsvergeudung *f.*
watch *n* Wache *f (Nav);* Uhr *f (timepiece).*
watchtower Warte *f,* Wachtturm *m.*
watchword Kennwort *n,* Losungswort *n.*
water Wasser *n.*
water bag *See* **water-sterilizing bag.**
water chest Wasserbehälter *m.*
water circulation Wasserumlauf *m (Mtr).*
water-cooled wassergekühlt, mit Wasserkühlung.
water distributing point Wasserverteilungsstelle *f.*
watering Tränken *n (an animal).*
watering bridle Wassertrense *f (harness).*
water jacket Kühlmantel *m,* Wassermantel *m,* Kühlwassermantel *m.*
water level Wasserstand *m;* Wasserwaage *f (Instr).*
water-level gage Pegel *m (for rivers, lakes, etc.).*
waterline Wasserlinie *f.*
water obstacle Wassersperre *f.*
water pipe Wasserleitung *f.*
waterproof wasserdicht.
waterproof paper Guttaperchapapier *n (Engr).*
water pump Wasserpumpe *f.*
water-repellent wasserabstoßend.
water-sterilizing bag Wasserreinigungssack *m.*
water supply point Wasserversorgungsstelle *f.*
water temperature gage Fernthermometer *n (MT).*
watertight wasserdicht.
water tower Wasserturm *m.*
waterway Wasserstraße *f.*
waterworks Wasserwerk *n.*
watt Watt *n.*
wave *n* Welle *f (Rad, Tac, etc.).*
wave length Wellenlänge *f (Rad).*
wavemeter Wellenmesser *m (Rad).*
wave of tanks Treffen *n.*
wave propagation Wellenausbreitung *f (Rad).*
wave range Wellenbereich *m (Rad).*
wax Wachs *n.*
weapon Waffe *f.*
weapon carrier Waffenfahrzeug *n.*
weapons decontaminating agent Waffenentgiftungsmittel *n.*
weapons duel Feuerkampf *m.*
weapons platoon Maschinengewehr- und Granatwerferzug der Schützenkompanie *(USA).*
weapons troop Schwere Schwadron *(Cav).*
wear *n* Abnutzung *f.*
wear down zermürben *(Tac).*
wear-resistant abriebbeständig.
weather Wetter *n,* Witterung *f. See also* **meteorological, metro-.**
weather code Wetterschlüssel *m.*
weather conditions Wetterlage *f,* Wetterverhältnisse *npl.*
weather factors Witterungseinflüsse *mpl (Gunnery).*
weather factors and time difference Witterungseinflüsse und Zeitunterschied *(Sound Ranging).*
weather forecast Wettervoraussage *f,* Wettervorhersage *f.*
weather instruments Wetterdienstgeräte *npl.*
weather map Wetterkarte *f.*
weather message Wetterfunkmeldung *f,* Wetterfunkspruch *m (Rad).*
weather observation Wetterbeobachtung *f.*
weather reconnaissance Wettererkundung *f (Avn).*
weather region Wetterbezirk *m.*
weather report Wettermeldung *f.*
weather service Wetterdienst *m.*
weather side Luv *f (stream-crossing Opns).*
weather station Wetterstelle *f,* Wetterwarte *f.*
web Gurt *m,* Gewebe *n.*
web belt Stoffgurt *m.*
web girth Schnurrensattelgurt *m (saddle).*
wedge Keil *m;* Knagge *f (Engr).*
wedge formation Keil *m (Tac).*
wedge-type breechblock Keilverschluß *m;* Rundkeilverschluß *m (cylindrical).*
weighing anchor Ankerlichten *n.*
weigh off Ballast abwerfen *(Bln).*
weight Gewicht *n.*
weight of projectile Geschoßgewicht *n (Ballistics).*
weight per horsepower Leistungsgewicht *n.*
weir Wehr *n,* Stauwehr *n (Engr).*
weld *n* Schweißung *f,* Schweißnaht *f,* Schweißstelle *f.*
weld *v* schweißen.
welder Schweißer *m.*
welding rod Schweißelektrode *f.*
welding torch Schweißbrenner *m.*
well Brunnen *m,* Quelle *f.*
Western European time westeuropäische Zeit *(zero meridian time).*
Western Front Westfront *f.*
West Wall Westwall *m.*
wet naß.
wet-bulb thermometer feuchtes Thermometer *(Met).*
wharf Ladeplatz *m.*
Wheatstone bridge Meßbrücke *f (Elec).*
wheel *n* Rad *n.*
wheel *v* schwenken *(Tac).*
wheelbarrow Schubkarren *m.*
wheelbase Radstand *m (MT).*
wheel block Bremsklotz *m.*
wheel brake Fahrbremse *f (G carriage).*
wheel chocks Schießklötze *mpl (Mtz Arty).*
wheel control Radsteuerung *f (Ap).*
wheeled litter carrier Krankentragenfahrgerät *n (Med).*
wheeled tractor Radschlepper *m,* Radzugmaschine *f.*
wheeled vehicle Räderfahrzeug *n.*
wheel harness Hintersielengeschirr *n.*
wheel load Raddruck *m (MT).*
wheel spindle Achsschwingschenkel *m,* Schwingschenkel *m (G);* Achsschenkel *m (MT).*
wheel team Stangenpferde *npl.*
wheel-track car Räder-Raupen-Wagen *m.*
wheel-track drive Räder-Gleiskettenantrieb *m (MT).*
wheel-track vehicle Hilfskettenfahrzeug *n,* Räder-Raupen-Fahrzeug *n (MT).*
whetstone Wetzstein *m.*
whipstall "Männchen" *n (Avn).*
whisper *v* flüstern.
whistle *n* Pfeife *f (Inst);* Pfiff *m (sound).*
whistle signal Pfeifensignal *n,* Pfeifsignal *n.*
white weiß.
white dress uniform Sommeruniform
white line Furche *f (hoof).*
white phosphorus weißer Phosphor.
wick Docht *m.*
wide-angle photograph Weitwinkelaufnahme *f.*
wide gage Breitspur *f (RR).*
width Breite *f.*
in width flügelweise.
wigwag Winkzeichen mit einer einzigen Flagge oder Licht geben.
winch Spill *n,* Winde *f;* Windewagen *m (Trk).*
wind Wind *m.*
windage Einfluß des Querwinds, Ausschaltung des Querwindeinflusses.
wind arrow Windpfeil *m (Met).*
wind brace Windverband *m (Bdg).*
windbreak Windschutz *m.*
wind-component indicator Wetterspinne *f (Gunnery).*
wind cone Luftsack *m,* Windsack *m,* Windkegel *m.*
wind correction Ausschalten des Windes *(Gunnery);* Ausschalten der Windabtrift, Einrechnung des Luvwinkels, Einrechnung des Vorhaltewinkels *(Air Navigation).*
wind corrector and time scale Wezu-Gerät *n (Sound Ranging).*
wind deflection Ablenkung durch den Wind *(Gunnery).*
wind direction Windrichtung *f.*
wind-direction indicator Windrichtungsanzeiger *m (Avn);* Windpfeil *m (Met).*
wind drift Windabtrift *f.*
winded abgejagt *(worn out).*
wind factors Windverhältnisse *npl,* Windkomponenten *fpl (Ballistics).*
wind gage Windmesser *m,* Anemometer *n.*
wind indicator Windanzeiger *m.*
winding Wicklung *f (Elec, Rad).*
winding stem Aufziehachse *f (on blasting machine).*
windmill Windmühle *f.*
window Fenster *n.*
wind pressure Winddruck *m.*
wind reference number Windziffer *f (Gunnery).*
windshield Windschutzscheibe *f.*
windshield wiper Scheibenwischer *m.*
wind sock Windsack *m,* Luftsack *m.*
wind tee T-förmiger Windanzeiger.
wind test Windmessung *f (Met).*
wind tunnel Windkanal *m (Avn).*
wind vane Windfahne *f (Met).*
wind velocity Windstärke *f (Met).*
windward wirdwärts, windseitig.
wine Wein *m.*
wing Flügel *m (Ap, Tac);* Tragflügel *m,* Tragfläche *f (Ap);* Geschwader *n (Avn unit).*
wing area Flügelinhalt *m (Ap).*
wing assembly Tragwerk *n (Ap).*
wing attack Flügelangriff *m (Tac).*
wing bracing Flügelverspannung *f.*
wing center section Flügel-Mittelstück *n (Ap).*
wing chord Flügelsehne *f,* Profilsehne *f (Ap).*
wing column formation Geschwaderkolonne *f (Avn).*
wing commander Geschwaderkommodore *m,* Kommodore *m (Avn).*
wing cross section Flügelschnitt *m (Ap).*
wing dihedral V-Form der Tragflügel *(Ap).*
wing flap Landeklappe *f (Ap).*
wing float Stützschwimmer *m (flying boat).*
wing gun Flugzeug-Flügelkanone *f (G);* in Tragfläche eingebautes Maschinengewehr *(MG, Ap).*
wingheavy flügellastig *(Ap).*
wing loading Flächenbelastung *f (Ap).*
wing-mounted gun Flugzeug-Flügelkanone *f (G);* in Tragfläche eingebautes Maschinengewehr *(MG, Ap).*
wing net Geschwaderfunknetz *n (Avn).*
wing nut Flügelmutter *f.*
wing over *v* über den Flügel abkippen *(Avn).*
wing profile Flügelprofil *n (Ap).*
wing rail Flügelschiene *f (RR).*
wing rib Flügelrippe *f.*
wing root Flügelwurzel *f (Ap).*
"wings" Flugzeugführer-Abzeichen *n (insigne).*
wing setting Flügelanordnung *f.*
wing signal Flügelsignal *n.*
wing skin Flügelhaut *f.*
wing span Spannweite *f (Ap).*
wing spar Flügelholm *m.*
wing strut Flügelstrebe *f.*
wing strut system Flügelverstrebung
wing tip Flügelende *n,* Tragflügelende *n (Ap).*
wing-tip flare Flügelleuchtpatrone *f,* Landefackel *f (Ap).*
wing wedge formation Geschwaderkeil *m (Avn).*
winter cap Kopfschützer *m.*
winter equipment Winterausrüstung *f.*
winter warfare Winterkrieg *m.*
wire *n* Draht *m,* Kabel *n.*
wire brace Spanndraht *m.*
wire cable Drahtseil *n.*
wire-cable lashing Drahtbund *m (Engr).*
wire circuit Drahtverbindung *f (Tg, Tp).*
wire communication Drahtverbindung *f.*
wire cutters Drahtschere *f.*
wire-cutting party Hindernissprengtrupp *m (Engr).*
wire entanglement Drahthindernis *n;* Drahtverhau *m (with abatis).*
wire head Meldekopf *m (Sig Com).*

wire-laying team Feldfernkabeltrupp *m (Tp)*.
wire lead-in point Kabelaufführungspunkt *m (Elec, Tp)*.
wire line Drahtleitung *f*, Kabelleitung *f (Tp)*.
wire loop Drahtschleife *f (Elec)*.
wire mesh Maschendraht *m*.
wire mesh mat Drahtmatte *f (Engr)*.
wire mesh road Drahtstraße *f (Engr)*.
wire net Drahtnetz *n*; Fernsprechnetz *n (Tp)*; Telegraphennetz *n (Tg)*.
wire netting Drahtnetz *n*, Maschendraht *m*.
wire patrol Störungssuchtrupp *m (field Tp)*.
wire pike Drahtgabel *f (Tp)*.
wire roll Drahtrolle *f*.
wire-roll entanglement Drahtrolle *f*.
wire snare Drahtschlinge *f*.
wire splice Kabelverbindung *f (Tp)*.
wire system Drahtnachrichtennetz *n*.
wire telegraphy Drahttelegraphie *f*.
wire telephony Drahttelephonie *f*.
wire-testing instrument Kabelmeßgerät *n (Tp)*.
wire trench Kabelgraben *m (Tp)*.
wire turn Drahtschleife *f (Elec)*.
wire-wound gun barrel Drahtrohr *n*.
wiring diagram Leitungsplan *m*, Installationsplan *m*.
wiring system Leitungssystem *n (Elec)*; Bordnetz *n (Ap)*.
withdraw abziehen, ausweichen, absetzen, sich absetzen *(Tac)*.
withdrawal Abzug *m*, Entweichen *n*, Absetzbewegung *f*, Rückzug *m (Tac)*.
withdrawal from action Abbrechen des Gefechts.
withdrawal route Rückweg *m*, Rückzugstraße *f*, Rückzugslinie *f (Tac)*.
withers Widerrist *m (horse)*.
witness *n* Zeuge *m*.
woman auxiliary Stabshelferin *f*.
wood Holz *n*.
wood alcohol Holzgeist *m*.
wooded area Waldgelände *n*.
wooden baffle Holzgehäuse *n (Rad)*.
wooden grating Holzrost *m*.
wooden railing Holzgeländer *n*.
wood-gas engine Holzgasmotor *m*.
wood-gas generator Holzgasanlage *f*, Gasgenerator *m (MT)*.
wood-gas generator trailer Generatoranhänger *m (MT)*.
woodland Waldgelände *n*.
wood revetment Holzverkleidung *f*.
woods Wald *m*.
wood separator Holzzwischenlage *f (storage battery)*.
wool Wolle *f*.
woolen cap Kopfschützer *m*.
wording Wortlaut *m*.
work Arbeit *f (labor)*; Werk *n (Ft)*.
working blouse Arbeitsbluse *f*, Drillichrock *m*.
work order Werkstattauftrag *m*.
works Arbeiten *fpl*, Befestigungsarbeiten *fpl (Ft)*.
workshop Werkstatt *f*; Werft *f (Adrm)*.
work uniform Arbeitsanzug *m*, Drillichanzug *m*.
worm Schnecke *f (Mech)*.
worm and sector steering system Schneckenlenkung *f*, Segmentlenkung *f*, Zahnkranzlenkung *f (MT)*.
worm drive Schneckenantrieb *m*, Schneckentrieb *m (MT, Mech)*.
worm gear Schneckenrad *n (MG)*.
worm-gear housing Schneckengehäuse *n (panoramic telescope)*.
worm-gear rear-axle drive Schnecken-Hinterachsantrieb *m (MT)*.
worm shaft Schneckenwelle *f (Mech)*.
worn abgenutzt; abgetragen *(Clo)*.
wound *n* Wunde *f*.
wound *v* verwunden.
wound chevron Verwundetenabzeichen in Form eines Uniformwinkels *(USA)*.
woven wire Maschendraht *m*.
woven-wire fence Maschendrahtzaun *m*.
wrapped leggins Wickelgamaschen *fpl*.
wrapping Pakethülle *f*.
wrap puttees Wickelgamaschen *fpl*.
wreck *v* zertrümmern, zerstören; Schiffbruch erleiden *(be shipwrecked)*.
wrecker *See* **wrecking truck**.
wrecker platoon Abschleppzug *m (MT)*.
wrecking truck Abschleppkraftwagen *m*.
wrecking unit Abschleppkommando *n*.
wrench *n* Schraubenschlüssel *m*.
wrist Handgelenk *n*.
wrist pin *See* **piston pin**.
wrist watch Armbanduhr *f*.
write schreiben.
writing paper Briefpapier *n*.
written evidence Beweismaterial *n*.
written order schriftlicher Befehl.
wrought iron Schmiedeeisen *n*.

X

X-coordinate Abszisse *f (Math)*; Rechtswert *m (on coordinate scale)*.
X-line waagerechte Gitterlinie *(map grid)*.
X-ray *n* Röntgenaufnahme *f*, Röntgenphoto *n*.
X-ray *v* eine Röntgenaufnahme machen.
X-ray equipment Röntgeneinrichtung *f*.
X-rays Röntgenstrahlen *mpl*.
xylyl bromide Xylylbromid *n*, T-Stoff *m (CWS)*.

Y

yacht Jacht *f*.
yard Hof *m (courtyard)*; Rangierbahnhof *m (RR)*; Yard *n (0.914 m)*.
Y-azimuth Richtungswinkel *m*.
yaw *v* gieren *(Avn, Nav.)*
yawing Seitwärtsbewegung *f (Ap)*.
yawl Jolle *f (Nav)*.
yawmeter Gierungsmesser *m (Ap)*.
Y-connection Sternschaltung *f (Elec)*.
Y-coordinate Ordinate *f (Math)*; Hochwert *m (on coordinate scale in map reading)*.
yellow gelb.
yellow fever Gelbfieber *n*, gelbes Fieber.
yeoman Schreiber *m (Nav)*.
Y-gun Y-förmiger Wasserbombenwerfer *(Nav)*.
Y-line senkrechte Gitterlinie *(map grid)*.

Z

Zenith Zenit *m*, Scheitelpunkt *m*; Gipfel *m (summit)*.
zero *n* Null *f*.
zero *v* auf Null stellen *(a scale, etc.)*; Normalvisier stellen *(a gun sight)*.
zero beat Schwebungsnull *f*, Schwebungslücke *f (Rad)*.
zero hour X-Uhr *f*, Nullzeit *f*.
zero point Nullpunkt *m (Arty, Surv)*.
zigzag *v* zickzack fliegen *(Avn)*; Zickzackkurs fahren *(Nav)*.
zigzagging target kurvendes Ziel *(AAA)*.
zinc Zink *n*.
zinc container Zinkbecher *m (dry cell)*.
zipper Reißverschluß *m*.
zone *n* Zone *f*, Gebiet *n*, Fläche *f*, Bereich *m*, Streifen *m*, Raum *m*.
zone fire Flächenschießen *n*, Flächenfeuer *n*, Streuschießen *n (Gunnery)*.
zone map Kartenblatt *n*.
zone of action Gefechtsabschnitt *m*, Gefechtsstreifen *m (Tac)*; Angriffsabschnitt *m (in attack)*; Aktionsbereich *m (Ap, Tk, etc.)*.
zone of advance Vormarschstreifen *m*.
zone of defense Verteidigungszone *f*, Abwehrzone *f*.
zone of dispersion Streuungsbereich *m (Ballistics)*.
zone of fire Feuerbereich *m*, Feuerzone *f*.
zone of operations Operationsraum *m*, Operationsgebiet *n*.
zone of resistance Widerstandszone *f*; Tiefenzone *f (organized in depth)*.
zone of security Sicherungszone *f*.
zone of the interior Heimatgebiet *n*.
zoom Hochziehen *n (Ap)*.

II.1. German Equivalent Military and Party Ranks.

U.S. Army	German Military Ranks: Regular Army	Air Force	Navy	Waffen-SS **	German Political Ranks: SA (NSFK / NSKK‡)	Party Officials†
		Reichsmarshall				
No equivalent	Generalfeldmarschall	Generalfelfmarschall	Grossadmiral	Reichsführer-SS	- 0 -	- 0 -
General	berstgruppenführer	Generalloberst	Generaladmiral	Oberstgruppenführer	Stabchef der SA‡	Reichsleiter
Lieutenant General	General der (Branch)	General der (branch)	Admiral	Obergruppenführer	Obergruppenführer	Gauleiter
Major General	Generalleutnant	Generalleutnant	Vizeadmiral	Gruppenführer	Gruppenführer	Hauptbefehlsleiter
Brigadier General	Generalmajor	Generalmajor	Konteadmirtal	Brigadeführer	Brigadeführer	Hauptdienstleiter
No equivalent	- 0 -	- 0 -	Kommodore	Oberführer	Oberführer	Hauptbereichsleiter
Colonel	Oberst	Oberst	Kapitän zur See	Standartenführer	Standartenführer	Hauptabschnittsführer
Lieutenant Colonel	Oberstleutnant	Oberstleutnant	Fregattenkapitän	Obersturmbannführer	Obersturmbannführer	Hauptgemeinschaftleiter
Major	Major	Major	Korvettenkapitän	Sturmbannführer	Sturmbannführer	Gemeinschaftleiter
Capt ain	Hauptmann*	Hauptmann	Kapitän	Hauptsturmführer	Hauptsturmführer	Haupteinsatzleiter
1st Lieutenant	Oberleutnant	Oberleutnant	Oberleutnant zur See	Obersturmführer	Obersturmführer	Obereinsatzleiter
2d Lieutenant	Leutnant	Leutnant	Leutnant zur See	Untersturmführer	Sturmführer	Einsatzleiter
Warrant Officer	(Various offivials)	Wachtmeister*, etc.	Staboberfeldwebel			
Master Sergeant	Stabsfeldwebel	Stabsfeldwebel	Oberfeldwebel	Sturmscharführer	Haupttruppführer	Hauptbereitshaftsleiter
Technical Sergeant	Oberfeldwebel	Oberfeldwebel	Stabsfeldwebel	Hauptscharführer	Obertruppführer	Oberbereitshaftsleiter
Staff Sergeant	Feldwebel*	Feldwebel*	Feldwebel/Obermaat	Oberscharführer	Truppführer	Bereitschaftsleiter
Sergeant	Unterfeldwebel*	Unterfeldwebel*	Maat	Scharführer	Oberscharführer	- 0 -
Corporal	Unteroffizier	Stabs/Hauptgefreiter	Matrosenstabsgefreiter	Unterscharführer	SA-Scharführer	Hauptarbeitsleiter
Private First Class	Stabs/Obergefreiter*,	Obergefreiter*.	Matrosenhauptgefreiter	Stabsgefreiter	- 0 -	Oberarbeitsleiter
	Gefreiter*	Gefreiter*	Matrosenobergefreiter	Rottenführer	Rottenführer	Arbeitsleiter
Private	Obergrenadier		Matrosengefreiter	Sturmmann	Obersturmmann	Oberhelfer
No equivalent	Grenadier, Schütze	Flieger	Matrose	SS- Mann	Sturmmann	Helfer

* Various specific titles applied to some branches. For example the infantry in mountain, light, and parachute divisions were designated as Jäger. The sergeants in most of the mounted, artillery, and transport units were designated as Wachtmeister. The Captain in mounted units was designated as Rittmeister. The Air Force Flak (i.e. most of the German antiaircraft units) had a similar rank structure to Army artillery units.
** There were Waffen SS Police Divisions and Himmler was also Chief of the German Police. This included the main city and regional police, as well as the industrial (TN) and auxiliary police and fire departments. The rank structure varied widely but most of the officers carried same designation as in the Army, while the SS tended to use the two interchangeably. the Air Force had its own paramilitary Engineering Corps that performed technical or or engineering tasks. The latter were designated by the suffix "-ingeniur". Speer had the paramilitary Organization Todt (OT) which had its own rank structure and often supervised foreign laborers (Arbeiters).

‡ The SA was the predecessor of the SS and before mid 1934, the latter was part of the SA. The two had much similarity in their rank structure for this reason. After 1934 the NSKK, and NSFK were both separated from the SA although the latter maintained a strong affiliation. The top rank in the NSKK was Korpsführer (rather than Stabschef der SA) and Staffelführer replaced Sturmbannführer.
† This is just one of the many Party rank structures. For example, the Hitler Youth (HJ) had a unique rank structure, as did the Reich Labor Service (RAD),

II.2. German Equivalents to Common or Important Words.

Commands

English	German
Advance!	Vortreten!
Come forward!	" "
Careful!	Vorsicht!
Danger!	Gefahr!
Don't move!	Keine Bewegung!
Don't shoot!	Nicht schiessen!
Don't smoke!	Nicht rauchen!
Don't try any tricks!	Machen sie keine Geschichten!
Down!	Nieder!
Follow me/him!	Folgen sie mir/ihm!
Gas!	Gas!
Go ahead!	Vorwährts
Go slow!	Langsam geben!
Halt (or Stop)!	Halt!
Hurry!	Rasch!
Identify yourself!	Zeigen Sie mir Ihren Ausweis!
Lie down!	Hinlegen!
Line up! here/there	Antreten! hier/dort
Look out!	Aufpassen!
Move back!	Züruck!
Obey or I'll fire!	Wenn sie nicht gehorchen, schiesse ich!
Quickly!	Schnell!
Quiet!	Ruhe!
Raise your hands!	Hände hoch!
Right Away!	Sofort!
Surrender!	Ergeben Sie sich!
Take cover!	Deckung nehmen!
Throw down your arms!	Waffen niederlegen!
Turn around!	Rundrehen!
Wait here!	Warten Sie hier!
Who's there?	Wer da?

Communications

English	German
Antenna	Antenne
Batteries	Batterien
Electric Wire	Leitungsdraht
Message	Nachricht
Message Center	Nachrichtstelle
Panel	Tuchzeichen
Pigeon	Taube
Pigeon loft	Taubeschlag
Radio equipment or Radio set	Funkgerät
Radio station	Funkstelle
Reflector	Reflektor
Rockets	Raketen
Switchboard	Schaltisch
Telegraph set	Telegrafenapparat
Telephone	Fernsprecher
Telephone receiver	Telefonhörer
Teletypewriter	Fernschreiber

Equipment

English	German
Accelerator	Gashebel
Armor	Panzerung
Brakes	Bremsen
Bridel	Zügel
Carburetor	Vergaser
Caterpillar track	Gleiskette
Clutch	Kupplung
Controls	Leitwerk
Engine	Triebwerk
Fire extinguisher	Feuerlöscher
Fuel tank	Krafstoffbehälter, Benzintank
Fuselage	Rumpf
Horn	Hupe
Instruments	Instrumente
Light bulb	Glühbirne
Motor	Motor
Octane rating	Oktanzahl
Oil rating	Öl-Qualität
Oil viscosity	Öl-Zähigkeit
Pontoon	Schwimmer
Propeller	Luftschraube
Specification number	Fabriknummer
Spotlight	Scheinwerfer
Tail	Schwanz
Wings	Tragflachen

Geography & Terrain Features

English	German
Bridges	Brücken
Detours	Umleitung
flat	flach
Fords	Furten
Guideposts	Wegweiser
Guides	Führer
Glaciers	Gletscher
Hills	Hügel
impassable	unbegehbar
Lakes	Seen
mud puddles	Schlammlöcher
muddy	schlammig
Obstructions	Hindernisse
one-way stretches	Einbahnstrecken
potholes	Löcher
ruts	Wagenspuren
snowdrifts	Schneewehen
rocky	felsig
wet	feucht
Mountains	Berge
Passes	Passe
paths	Pfade
Rivers	Flüsse
roads	Wege
rocky	steinig
sandy	sandig
springs	Quellen
wells	Brunnen
Woods	Wald

Installations

English	German
Airfields	Flugplatze
Barracks	Unterkunst
Bivouacs	Biwaks
Booby Traps	Schreckladungen
Camp	Lager
Dumps	Materiallager
Fortified Towns	befestigte Ortschaften
Fox Hole	Schützenloch
Hangar	Halle, Scluppen
Message Centers	Nachrictenstellen
Messhall	Kantine
Mine Field	Minenfelder
Pillboxes	Bunker
Radio Stations	Funkstellen
Railheads	Ausladebahnhofe
Stable	Stall
Strong Points	Stützpunkte
Supply Depots	Nachshublager
Telephone centrals	Fernsprechvermittlungen
Telephone lines	Fernsprechleitungen
Trench / Trenches	Graben / Schützengräben

Miscellaneous

English	German
biplane / monoplane	Doppeldecker / Eindecker
Destroyer	Zerstörer
Dive bomber	Stuka
Mine sweeper	Minenräumer
Patrol	Patrouille
Reveille	das Wecken
Submarine	Unterseeboot, U-Boot
Taps	Zapentreich
Tank	Panzerkampfwagen
Warship	Kriegschiff

Radio

English	German
Acknowledge	Bitte Quittung / Bitte Bestätigung
Break	Trennung
Calling ____	____ kommen
Correction	Irrung
Do not answer	Keine Quittung
Groups ____	____ Gruppen
____, this is ____	____ von ____
Readability	Lautsärke
unreadable	eins
poor	zwei
fair	drei
good	vier
fully readable	fünf
Say again	Bitte wiederholen
That is all	Ende
Urgent	K.R.

Signs and Warnings

English	German
Bridge	Brücke
Caution	Vorsicht
Closed	Geschlossen
Crossroad	Kreuzung
Danger	Gefahr
Dangerous Corve	Kurve
Dead End	Sackgasse
Detour	Umleitung
Go slow	Langsam
Keep to the Right	Rechts fahren
Keep Out	Zutritt verboten
Men	Männer / Herren
No Smoking	Rauchen verboten or Nichtraucher
No Spitting	Nicht ausspucken
No Thoroughfare	Keine Durchfart
Offen	Open
One-way street	Einbahnstrasse
No Parking	Parken verboten
Railroad	Eisenbahn
Stop or Halt	Halt
Women	Frauen / Damen

Telephones & Switchboards

English	German
Are you through?	Wird noch gesprochen?
" " still on the line?	" "
Hang up your receiver.	Bitte trennen
Here is your party.	Teilnehmer kommt
I have a call for you	Ich habe einen Spruch fur Sie
I must interrupt, urgent call	Ich muss trennen dringendes Gesprach.
I shall disconnect.	Ich trenne.
I will give you the chief operator	Überwachung
I will ring again	Ich rufe wieder
Supervisor	Aufsicht
The line is busy	Besetzt
What central please?	Bitte, welche Vermittlung?
What number please? (Please repeat)	Bitte wiederholen Sie?

Vehicles & Transportation

English	German
airplane	ein Flugzeug
armored car	panzerauto
auto	Kraftwagen
bicycle	ein Fahrrad
boat	ein Boot
bus	ein Omnibus
car	einen Wagen
cargo ship	Frachtschiff
half-track vehicle	Halbketten-Fahrzeug
horse	ein Pferd
mule	ein Maultier
oxen	Ochsen
scout car	Spähwagen
sleigh	ein Sclitten
tanker	Tankschiff
train	ein Fuhrwerk
truck	Lastkraftwagen
wagon	ein sZug

Weapons

English	German
ammunition	Munition
antitank guns	Pakgeschutz
bayonet	Seitengewehr
bomb	Bombe
Canon	Kanone
carbine	Karabiner
cartridge	Patrone
fire (F) / safe (S)	Feuer (F) / Sicher (S)
gun	Geschutz
grenade, hand/rifle	Handgranate / Gewehrgranate
howitzer	Haubitze
machine gun	Machinegewehr
mine	Mine
Mortar	Granatwerfer
Pistol	Pistole
Rifle	Gewehr
Pistol	Pistole
Shell	Granate
Submachine gun	Maschinenpistole
Weapon	Waffe

Chapter III: Geographic Terms and Map Symbols

This chapter describes how symbols were used to represent military information, both on the ground and in maps. It consists of a description of : Symbols & Signals for Visual Communication; Map and Transportation Symbols; and Obstacles and Military Positions. The list of symbols may have a significance beyond the historical study of maps. How something was described (process) could be as vital as the substance of the action being described.

A. Visual Communication Symbols & Signals

Much communication on the modern battlefield took place beyond the range of words and most soldiers did not have personal access to radios. Semophore flags and various hand and arm signals accomplished in earlier wars. The advent of aviation and motor transport generally increased the recognition distance while reducing the available response time. Ground forces often had to promptly identify themselves at great distance, especially to aircraft.

This was accomplished with smoke, cloth panels, by the display of flags, recognition fans and a variety of auxiliary signals. German aircraft also identified themselves or communicate with ground forces by recognition lights, prearranged recognition very signals, by dropped smoke signals, and by dropped messages. These signals sometimes changed for reasons of security but the following were in general use.

☐ Distance Recognition

Symbol	Translation
Red Smoke or Very Signal (fired or dropped over target)	Enemy antitank defense such as antitank gun, antiaircraft gun, or tank obstacle.
Blue Smoke or Blue/Violet Very Signal	Numerous enemy tanks or armored cars
White Very Signal (also deep circling and tipping of wings)	Ground forces requested to identify themselves Orange smoke may confirm.
Green Very Signal (also deep circling and tipping of wings)	Observer desires to drop message. Ground to troops to indicate drop zone
Orange-colored Smoke Signal.	The principal signal used by ground force to say "We are here" /"Friendly troops"
White Very signals	May also be used for sabove.
Dropped messages (for aircraft) may be enclosed in tubes that emit light yellow smoke when dropped, or in red-and-white cloth containers	A number code is usually employed in the message and this may be supplemented by clear text as needed.
Recognition "Venetian Blinds" on Tanks (Erkennungsjalousien)	When closed these blinds blended with color of tanks (gray); when opened they display a solid white or red (in Winter)
Yellow Panels (When laid side by side these are easily recognizable from a medium altitude.	Used to indicate the most advanced line to exclusively mean "Here is our most advanced line."
White Panels (Red in Winter)	Used for same purpose as above by troops in rear areas or behind front line.
Swastika Flags	When yellow panels are not available these may be used by ground force to to say "We are here" /"Friendly troops" May be used with orange smoke.
Recognition Fans (Erkennungsfächer) are round fans of steel frames, covered with white cloth on one side and red cloth on the other side (for snow or sand). They are collapsible and are carried in a canvas bag attached to the belt	When recognition is requested by air, they are promptly opened and laid on the ground. Only used in the foremost lines.
Emergency Signals (waving of steel helmets, flags or handkerchiefs, etc..)	Are only used when no other means of identification are available.

☐ Ground Panels (Ground to Air)

These panels are employed by ground forces to communicate with aircraft. The usual length of these panels is about five yards and the color is white (red in snow or sandy soil).

Numerals:

Symbol			Symbol		
1	1	1	VI	6	6
Π	2	2	VII	7	7
Ⅲ OR ⊢⊣	3	3	X OR ΔI	8	8
4	4	4	IX OR IX	9	9
V OR V	5	5	OR X	0	0

Ground panel		
	eigene vordere Linie	Own front line (yellow panels)
+	Abwurfstelle für Meldungen und Versorgungsgut.	Dropping point for messages and provisons
V	Verstanden, ja	Understand, yes
Y	nicht verstanden	Do not understand
∇	nein	No
◇	Alles in Ordnung	Everything is in order (OK)
Z	Ziel (mit daneben ausgelegter Zahl)	Target (with number laid out beside it)

Ground panel		Translation
	Abteilung oder Bataillon	Battalion (battery, unit)
	Regiment	Regiment
	Division	Division
	Abwurfstelle für Abteilung	Dropping point for battalion
	Abwurfstelle für Regiment	Dropping point for regiment
	Abwurfstelle für Division	Dropping point for division
I	abgefeuert	Fired
II	Batterie feuerbereit	Battery (troop) ready
	Batterie nicht feuerbereit	Battery (troop) not ready
H	Batterie geht wieder zum geschützweisen Feuer über	Battery (troop) resumes fire by piece
	Batterie nimmt den angeforderten Zielwechsel vor	Battery (troop) commences fire at newly designated target
	Feuer beendet	Firing ceased
VV	Wirkungsschiessen	Fire for effect
T	feindlicher Widerstandsnest	Enemy resistance point (vertical line points toward enemy)
	feindliche Artillerie Stellungen	Enemy artillery positions
↑	Wir gehen vor	We are advancing
	Wir sind eingeschlossen	We are surrounded
	Feind bereitet Angriff vor	Enemy preparing to attack
A	Feind greift an	Enemy attacking
III	Feind in unsere Stellungen eingedrungen	Enemy penetrated our position
	Feind links von uns eingedrungen	Enemy penetrated to our left
	Feind rechts von uns eingedrungen	Enemy penetrated to our right
	feindl. Angriff abgeschlagen	Enemy attack repulsed
	Wir halten die Linie	We are holding the line
X X	Abwurfstelle für Vorräte	Dropping point for supplies
	Unterstützung nötig	Reinforcements needed
	Verpflegung nötig	Provisions needed
	Wasser nötig	Water needed
T	Betriebsstoff nötig	Motor fuel (POL) needed
	Munition nötig	Ammunition needed
	le. Granatwerfermunition nötig	Light mortar ammunition needed
	s. Granatwerfermunition nötig	Heavy mortar ammunition needed
	Artilleriemunition nötig	Artillery ammunition needed (75-mm)
	Nebelgranaten nötig	Smoke shells needed (105-mm)
	Pakmunition nötig	Antitank ammunition needed (37-mm)
	2 cm Munition nötig	20-mm ammunition needed
	Funkausrüstung nötig	Radio (WT) equipment needed
	medizinische Vorräte dringend nötig	Medical supplies urgently needed
	Landungsmöglichkeit	Landing possible here
	keine Landungsmöglichkeit	Landing impossible here
	feindlicher Widerstand	Enemy resistance
	höchste Gefahr	Extreme danger
	gebt an ob unser Artilleriefeuer wirksam ist	Indicate if our artillery fire effective
	gebt die Stellungen der von uns vorgeschobenen Einheiten an	Indicate positions of friendly units to our front
	feindl. Widerstand auf 100 m	Enemy resistance at 100 meters
	feindl. Widerstand auf 200 m	Enemy resistance at 200 meters
	feindl. Widerstand auf 300 m	Enemy resistance at 300 meters (additional horizontal lines increase meters up to [illegible])
ΛI	feindl. Widerstand auf 1000 m	Enemy resistance at 1,000 meters
	feindl. Widerstand auf 1100 m	Enemy resistance at 1,100 meters
	feindl. Widerstand auf 1200 m	Enemy resistance at 1,200 meters (additional horizontal lines increase meters up to 1,900)
ΛII	feindl. Widerstand auf 2000 m	Enemy resistance at 2,000 meters
ΛIII	feindl. Widerstand auf 3000 m	Enemy resistance at 3,000 [illegible] (additional vertical lines increase meters up [illegible])

höchste Gefahr auf 100 m	Extreme danger at 10[illegible] ... ner ...
höchste Gefahr auf 2200 m	Extreme danger [illegible]
Feindpanzer	Enemy ta[illegible]
Feindpanzer auf 1000 m	Enemy tank at 1,000 [illegible]
Feindpanzer auf 2100 m	[illegible] tank at 2,100 meters

☐ Road Signs

Road signs were among the most common visual symbols (III.1).

III.1. Signs Used to Mark Roads and Rail Lines.

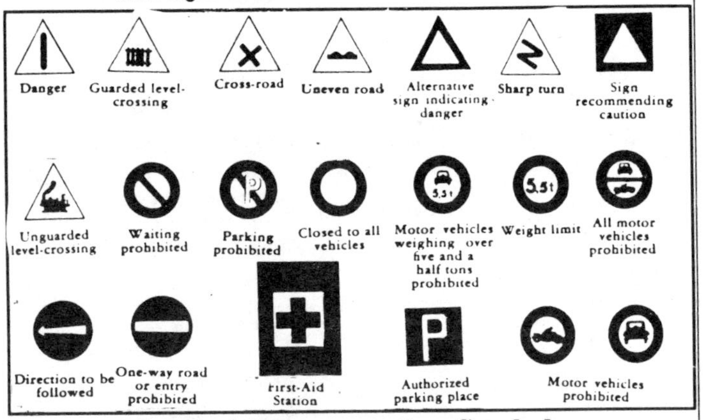

Map and Transportation Symbols

Most German military maps were at a scale of 1:100,000 or 1:25,000. The former scale did not permit as much detail to be recorded. If two symbols are shown then the one at the left pertains to the 1:100,000 scale but usually only the 1:25,000 is shown.

☐ Natural Terrain Features

1:25,000

Gebüsch	Bush, shrubs
Laubwald	Woods, deciduous
Nadelwald	Woods, evergreen
Mischwald	Woods, mixed
hervorragende Bäume	Prominent trees
Wiese	Meadow
nasse Wiese	Wet meadow
Sumpf und Moor	Marshland
Heide	Prairie
trockener Graben	Dry ditch
Steinriegel, Steinhaufen	Stone bar, stone pile
Sand oder Kies	Sand or gravel
Bruch mit Torfstich	Bog with peat trenches
unsicherer Boden	Unsafe ground
nasser Boden	Wet ground

☐ Roads and Highways

Reichsautobahn	National automobile highway
I A. Strasse etwa 5,5 m Mindestnutzbreite, mit gutem Unterbau, für Lastkraftwagen zu jeder Jahreszeit unbedingt brauchbar	I A. Highway of 5.5 meters (18 feet) minimum width, firm base, unlimited truck usability
I B. Strasse weniger fest, etwa 4,6 m Mindestnutzbreite, für Lastkraftwagen bedingt brauchbar	I B. Highway of 4.6 meters (15 feet) minimum width, less firm, limited truck usability
II A. Unterhaltener Fahrweg, für Personenkraftwagen jederzeit brauchbar	II A. Improved road, unlimited usability for passenger cars
II B. Unterhaltener Fahrweg, für Personenkraftwagen nicht jederzeit brauchbar	II B. Improved road, limited usability for passenger cars
III. Feld- und Waldweg	III. Dirt roads
IV. Fussweg (für Reiter brauchbar)	IV. Footpath (horse-path)
V. Schneise	V. Trail

☐ Railways

Eisenbahn, mehrgleisig	Railway with more than one track
Eisenbahn, eingleisig	Single-track railway
Schmalspurbahn	Narrow-gauge railway
Strassen-, Feld- und Wirtschaftsbahn	Street, field, and industrial railway
Seil- und Schwebebahn	Cable and suspension railway
Tunnel	Tunnel

☐ Bridges and Bridging Equipment

Stegbrücke	Foot bridge
Holzbrücke	Wooden bridge
Steinbrücke	Stone bridge
eiserne Brücke	Iron bridge
Schiffsbrücke	Ponton bridge
Schnellsteg oder Steg	Improvised bridge or footbridge
Brücke zu 2 t Tragkraft	2-ton bridge
Brücke zu 4 t Tragkraft	4-ton bridge
Brücke zu 8 t Tragkraft	8-ton bridge
Brücke zu 16 t Tragkraft	16-ton bridge
Brücke zu 30 t Tragkraft	30-ton bridge
Brücke zu 16 t Tragkraft im Bau	16-ton bridge under construction
Uferbalken	Sill (bridge)
Unterzug	Intermediate transom (bridge)
Bock	Trestle, pile
Halbponton	Half-size ponton
Ganzponton	Full-length ponton

☐ River Crossing and Ferry Operations

Fähre aus Halbponton	Ferry of half-size pontons
Fähre aus Ganzponton	Ferry of full-length pontons.
Doppelfähre aus Ganzponton	Double ferry of full-length pontons
Fähre aus Ganzponton mit 4 Aubo	Ferry of full-length pontons with 4 outboard motors
Fähre aus Halbponton mit 1 Aubo	Ferry of half-size pontons with 1 outboard motor
Fähre aus Halbponton mit 2 Aubo	Ferry of half-size pontons with 2 outboard motors
Doppelfähre aus Ganzponton mit 2 Aubo	Double ferry of full length pontons with 2 outboard motors
Fähre aus Halbponton geschleppt	Towed ferry of half-size pontons
Fährseil	Ferrying rope
Fähre am Fährseil aus Halbponton	Ferry of half-size pontons attached to ferrying rope
Doppelfähre am Fährseil und 1 Halbponton mit Aubo	Double ferry attached to ferrying rope and 1 half-size ponton with outboard motor
Windanker mit 2 Tauen	Downstream anchor with 2 ropes
Stromanker mit 1 Tau	Upstream anchor with 1 rope
Stromanker mit 2 Tauen	Upstream anchor with 2 ropes
Stromanker mit Kette und 2 Tauen	Upstream anchor with chain and 2 ropes
Furt	Ford
Schleuse	Sluice, lock
Übersatzstelle mit 3 grossen Flossäcken	Crossing point with three large pneumatic floats
Übersatzstelle mit 2 Fähren zu 4 t Tragkraft	Crossing point with two 4-ton ferries.
Übersatzstelle mit 1 Fähre zu 8 t Tragkraft	Crossing point with one 8-ton ferry
Übersatzstelle mit 1 Fähre zu 16 t Tragkraft	Crossing point with one 16-ton ferry
Übersatzstelle mit 1 Fähre zu 24 t Tragkraft	Crossing point with one 24-ton ferry

Obstacles and Military Positions

☐ Man-made Map and Terrain Features

Dorf	Village
Gehöft	Farm
Baumschule	Tree nursery
Weinberg	Vineyard
Hopfenpflanzung	Hop plantation
Hutung	Pasture
Park	Park
Zaun	Fence
Drahtzaun	Wire fence
Häuser aus Lehm oder Holz	Clay or frame houses
Häuser aus Stein	Stone houses
Kirche mit einem Turm	Church with 1 tower
Kirche mit Doppeltürmen	Church with 2 towers
Kirche mit einem Turm weit sichtbar	Church with 1 tower
Kirche mit Doppeltürmen weit sichtbar	Church with 2 towers
Damm, Deich	Dam, dike, embankment
Einschnitt	Cut
Ringwall	Rampart
Grube	Quarry
Steinbruch	Stone quarry
Mauer	Wall
Hecke	Hedge
Christen-Friedhof	Christian cemetery
Nichtchristen-Friedhof	Non-Christian cemetery
Einzelgrab	Single grave
Hünengräber	Prehistoric burial mounds
Turm	Tower
Schornstein	Smokestack
Schornstein weit sichtbar	Smokestack (landmark)
Windmühle	Windmill
Wassermühle	Watermill
Windmotor	Windpump
Denkmal	Monument
Höhenpunkt	Point of altitude (in meters)
Trigonometrischer Punkt	Triangulation point
Kilometerstein	Kilometer marker stone
Wegweiser	Road sign
Bake	Beacon
Leuchtbake	Light beacon
Ruine	Ruins
Försterei	(Forest) ranger station
Oberförsterei	Chief (forest) ranger station
Erratischer Block	Loose boulder
Bergwerk, im Betrieb	Mine, in operation
Bergwerk, verlassen	Mine, abandoned
Luftfahrtfeuer, freistehend	Aircraft beacon, detached
Luftfahrtfeuer auf Haus	Aircraft beacon on building
Nivellementspunkt	Precise benchmark
Stauanlage	Dam
Zusetzen eines Durchlasses oder einer Brückenöffnung für Stauzwecke	Blocking of a sluice or bridge arch for damming purposes
Anstauung oder Ansumpfung (Zeichnung in blauer Farbe)	Flooded area (colored blue)
Schlachtfeld	Battle field

☐ Man-made Obstacles

Drahtzaun (Flandernzaun)	Wire fence (double apron fence)
Flächendrahtsperre	Multiple wire entanglements
Maschendrahtsperre	Wire mesh obstacle
Stolperdraht	Trip wire
K- und S-Rollen	Concertina wire
Starkstromsperre	High voltage obstacle
zur Zerstörung vorbereitet	Prepared for demolition
zerstört	Demolished
leichte Baumsperre zur Zerstörung vorbereitet	Light abatis prepared for demolition
leichte Baumsperre zerstört	Light abatis demolished
schwere Baumsperre zur Zerstörung vorbereitet	Heavy abatis prepared for demolition
schwere Baumsperre zerstört	Heavy abatis demolished
Eisenbahnstrecke zur Zerstörung vorbereitet	Railway line prepared for demolition
Eisenbahnstrecke zerstört	Railway line demolished
Eisenbahngrenzsperre	Frontier railway barrier
zu sperrende Nachrichtenanlage	Signal installation to be blocked
gesperrte Nachrichtenanlage	Blocked signal installation
abzuschirmende Nachrichtenanlage	Signal installation to be screened off (in direction of arrow)
abgeschirmte Nachrichtenanlage	Signal installation screened off (in direction of arrow)
Baumverhau	Abatis
von Natur panzersicheres Gelände	Terrain impassable for tanks
Barrikade aus Wagen, Steinen, Erdwällen und Wirtschaftsgeräten	Barricade made of wagons, stones, earthworks, and agricultural implements
Barrikade mit Durchlass für eigenen Fahrzeugverkehr	Barricade with passage for own vehicular traffic
Drahtseilsperre	Wire cable obstacle
Sperre aus Stahlträgern oder Schienen	Obstacle of steel girders or rails
Pfahlsperre	Post obstacle
abgeholzter Wald	New ground, cleared forest
niedergelegtes Gehöft	Razed farm
durch Kampfstoffe vergiftete Zone (Zeichnung gelb schraffiert)	Gas-contaminated area (colored yellow)
einzelne Giftinseln (Zeichnung gelb schraffiert)	Isolated gas-contaminated areas (colored yellow)
durch Brand gesperrte Zone bei eingezeichnetem Einzelobjekt; Sperrung eines solchen durch Brand (Zeichnung in roter Farbe)	Area blocked by fire (individual objects fired marked) (colored red)
Kampfwagensperre (Höcker)	Tank obstacle (hurdles)
Kampfwagensperre (Pfähle)	Tank obstacle (posts)
Kampfwagensperre (Hemmkurve)	Tank obstacle (steel sloping-frames)
Kampfwagensperre (Eisenigel)	Tank obstacle (hedgehogs)
Panzerabwehrgraben	Tank trap

☐ Mines and Minefields

Tellermine (T-Mine)	…ine (antitank)
T-Mine gesprengt	T-mine, exploded
Schützenmine (S-Mine) oder Schreckladung	S-mine (antipersonnel) or booby trap
S-Mine oder Schreckladung gesprengt	S-mine or booby trap, exploded
T-Minen mit Brückenstangen	T-mines with connecting bars
T-Minenschnellsperre mit Druckschienen	Improvised road block of T-mines with pressure bars
Brettstückmine	Board mine
Brettstückmine gesprengt	Board mine, exploded
Schnelleingesetzte Schreckladung	Improvised booby trap
Behelfsmässige Schnellsperre	Improvised road block with mines
Brettstückminenfeld	Board mine field
S-Minenfeld	S-mine field
T-Minenfeld	T-mine field
Verminung mit Behelfsminen aller Art	Area mined with various types of improvised mines

T-Minenfeld offen verlegt mit bezeichneter Gasse	T-mine field, laid on surface, with marked lane
Brettstück-Minenfeld mit bezeichneter Gasse	Board mine field with marked lane
S-Minenfeld mit bezeichneter Gasse	S-mine field with marked lane
T-Minenfeld im Boden verlegt mit bezeichneter Gasse	T-mine field, buried, with marked lane
S-Minenfeld beseitigt	S-mine field, cleared
T-Minenfeld beseitigt	T-mine field, cleared

☐ Defensive Positions

Panzerwerk mit Maschinenanlage	Armored casemate with mechanical installation
Panzerwerk mit Maschinenanlage und Pak-Drehturm	Armored casemate with mechanical installation and revolving antitank turret
Panzerwerk mit Maschinenanlage und Artilleriedrehturm	Armored casemate with mechanical installation and revolving artillery turret
Panzerwerk ohne Maschinenanlage	Armored casemate without mechanical installation
Panzerwerk ohne Maschinenanlage mit Infanteriebeobachtungsturm	Armored casemate without mechanical installation, with infantry observation turret
Panzerwerk ohne Maschinenanlage mit Artilleriebeobachtungsturm	Armored casemate without mechanical installation, with artillery observation turret
Panzerwerk ohne Maschinenanlage mit Nachrichtenturm	Armored casemate without mechanical installation, with signal turret
M. G.- Schartenstand bzw. Kasematte	Embrasured machine-gun emplacement or casemate
M. G.- Doppelschartenstand	Double embrasured machine-gun emplacement for fire in 1 direction
Doppel M. G.- Kasematte	Double machine-gun casemate for fire in 2 different directions
Pak-Stand	Antitank gun emplacement
M. G.- und Pak-Stand	Machine-gun and antitank-gun emplacement
Pak-Unterstellraum	Antitank-gun pit
F. K. 16-Stand 7,5 cm	Emplacement for 75-mm field gun 16
Flak-Stand 8,8 cm	Emplacement for 88-mm antiaircraft gun
Stand mit l.H.T. (leichte Haubitze in Turm)	Emplacement with light howitzer in turret
Gefechtsstand oder Unterstand ohne Kampfraum	Command post or dugout without field of fire
Gefechtsstand oder Unterstand mit angehängtem Kampfraum	Command post or dugout with adjoining field of fire
Artillerie-Beobachtungsstand	Artillery observation post emplacement
Artillerie-Beobachtungsstand mit kleinem Artilleriebeobachtungsturm	Artillery observation post emplacement with small artillery observation turret
Gefechtsstand für Infanteriebeobachtung mit Kleinstglocke	Command post with cupola for infantry observation
Gefechtsstand für Infanteriebeobachtung mit Kleinstglocke und Kampfraum	Command post with cupola and field of fire for infantry observation
Blinkstand für Nachrichtenzwecke	Blinker light signaling emplacement
Unterstand für Nachrichtenzwecke (Grosschaltstelle)	Dugout for signal communications (main switching station)
Unterstand mit Funkanlage	Dugout with radio installation
Sammlerladestand	Emplacement for storage battery charging
Lichtmesstand für Artillerie	Artillery flash-ranging emplacement
Munitionsunterstand	Ammunition dugout
Sanitätsunterstand	Medical dugout
Hochstand für M.G.	Raised machine-gun position
Hochstand für Artilleriebeobachtung	Raised artillery observation post position
Geschützschartenstand	Embrasured light gun emplacement
Kanonenstand	Heavy gun emplacement
minierter Unterstand, stollenmässig oder nach Art der Hohlgänge	Dugout with tunneled or trench passages
Hohlgang	Communication trench
Fernsprecherdkabel	Underground telephone cable
Erdkabel (bombensicher verlegt)	Underground cable (buried below bomb-crater depth)
Erdkabel (weitsprechfähig)	Underground cable (long distance)
oberirdische Fernsprechlinie	Overhead telephone line
Schaltstelle (Kabelbrunnen)	Switching station (cable head)

☐ Miscellaneous Installations (Last 11 pertain to Navy)

geplante Anlage	Projected installation
im Bau befindliche Anlage	Installation under construction
fertige Anlage	Completed installation
Eisenbahnbrücke aus Stahl	Steel railway bridge
Eisenbahnbrücke aus Stein oder Beton	Stone or concrete railway bridge
Eisenbahnknotenpunkt	Railway junction
Bahnhof und Bahnhofsanlagen der Eisenbahn	Railway station and railway station installations
Tunnel	Tunnel
Kunstbauten an Wasserstrassen	Artificial structures on waterways
Staudamm	Dam
Werke für Flugzeugzellen-Herstellung	Aircraft frame manufacturing plant
Werke für Flugmotoren-Herstellung	Aircraft engine manufacturing plant
Werke für Motoren-Zubehör-Herstellung	Aircraft engine accessories manufacturing plant
Werke für Zellen u. Motorenherstellung	Aircraft frame and engine manufacturing plant
Werke für Bordwaffen-Herstellung	Aircraft weapons manufacturing
Waffenfabrik	Arsenal, munitions factory
Werke für Fahrzeug- einschl. Kampfwagen-Herstellung	Vehicle manufacturing plant, including combat vehicles
Munitionsfabrik	Ammunition plant
Hochöfen, Walzwerke, Stahlwerke u. Maschinenfabriken	Blast furnaces, rolling mills, steel mills, and machine plants
Betriebsstoff-Erzeugung, Veredlung, Grosstankanlagen	Gasoline production, refining, and bulk fuel storage plants
Pulver- u. Sprengstoffabrik	Powder and explosives factory
Chemische u. Kampfgasfabrik	Chemical and war gas factory
Kokereien	Coke plants
feinmechanische und optische Werke	Precision mechanics and optical plants
Gasschutzgerätefabrik	Gas defense equipment factory
Friedenswerft	Peacetime dry dock
Friedenshafenanlage	Peacetime port installations
Kriegswerften	Military dry docks
Kriegshafenanlage	Military port installation
Ballon-, Luftschiff-, Fallschirmfabrik	Balloon, lighter-than-air craft, and parachute manufacturing plant
elektr. Werk	Electric power plant
Gaswerk	Gas works
sonstige Fabrikanlagen	Other factory installations
Festungen	Fortifications
befestigte Brückenköpfe	Fortified bridgeheads
befestigte Räume	Fortified areas
kleinere Befestigungen	Minor fortifications
ständige Stellungen in feldmässiger Stärke	Existing positions suitable for military use
Grossgruppe	Large concentration of defensive installations
Hauptwerk	Principal defensive installation
Werk	Defensive installation
Zwischenwerk	Supporting defensive installation
Blockhaus, Unterstand, beton. Beob. Stand	Pillbox, dugout, concrete observation post
veraltete Werke	Obsolete defensive installations
Küstenbatterie unbekannter Art	Coastal battery of unknown type
Minen	Mines
Minensperre	Mine field
Minenverseuchtes Gebiet	Mined area
Netzsperre	Antisubmarine net
Netzsperre mit Minen	Mined antisubmarine net
Horchsperre	Hydrophone screen
Depot für Sperrwaffen	Net and boom defense depot
Balkensperre	Boom defenses
Gefecht	Engagement
ausser Gefecht gesetzt	Put out of action
Gesunken	Sunk

☐ Special Symbols on Situation Maps

Operational boundaries were applied with colors:

green	indicating German reconnaissance activity
blue	indicating German combat activities
red	indicating enemy activities.

Current	German	U. S.
	Heeresgruppengrenze	Army group boundary
	Armeegrenze	Army boundary
	Panzerarmeegrenze	Panzer army boundary
	Korpsgrenze	Corps boundary
	Divisionsgrenze	Division boundary
	Regimentsgrenze	Regimental boundary
	Bataillonsgrenze	Battalion boundary
	Kompaniegrenze	Company boundary
	Zielgrenze	Target boundary
	Aufklärungsgrenze	Limit of reconnaissance

Pertaining to Air Force

Grenze eines Luftflottenkommandos	Air Fleet boundary
Grenze eines Luftgaues	AF Administrative District boundary
Grenze eines Fliegerkorps bzw. Fliegerdivision	Boundary of an air corps or air division
Grenze eines Flughafenbereiches	Airfield area command boundary
Grenze eines Geschwader usw.	Boundary of an air wing or equivalent
Grenze eines Staffel usw.	Boundary of a squadron or equivalent
Aufklärerungsgrenze	Limit of reconnaissance
 Aufklärerungsraum	Reconnaissance sector
 Flugplatz stark belegt (über 20 Flugzeug erkannt)	Airfield occupied in force; over 20 aircraft observed (lack of circle would mean less than 20 aircraft)
 Flugplatz stark belegt, überwiegend Jagdflugzeug	Airfield occupied in force; mainly by fighter *aircraft
erkannt Flugplatzbelegung:	Observed occupation of aifield:
15(10-5-0) 10 einmotorige	10 single-engine
5 zweimotorige	5 twin-engine
0 mehrmotorige Flugzeug	0 multi-engine Aircraft

*Sometimes color coded (examples: green for fighters, red for bombers and blue for reconnaissance aircraft).

Service Installations were also shown in colors and should not be confused with above operational and tactical bounaries:

green	Administrative Services
blue	Ammunition
light red	Medical Services
carmine red	Veterinary Services
yellow	Army Postal services
brown	Supply Services
violet	Railway

Various colors were also used to indicate German allies.

☐ Signal Lines and Cables

In colored line diagrams **green** is used for infantry and **red** for artillery. **Brown** indicates division and **blue** is for corps. Army and army groups lines are shown in **black**. Some examples are:

German	U.S.
Feldkabeleinfachleitung	Field cable single-wire circuit
Feldkabeldoppelleitung	Field cable two-wire circuit
Feldfernkabel	Field trunk cable
Führungsfernkabel	Trunk cable of the Army High Command
Erdkabel	Underground cable
Erdkabel (bombensicher verlegt)	Underground cable (buried below bomb-crater depth)
Luftkabel	Overhead cable
Dezimeterverbindung	Decimeter wave circuit

☐ Map Abbreviations (Also see Chapter I for more detail)

Abbreviation	Meaning	Translation
A	Alp	Mountain pasture land, pasturage
Abl	Ablage	Depot, dump
adl	adlig	Noble, nobleman's
Anst	Anstalt	Depot, establishment, institution
B	Bach	Stream, brook
	Berg	Mountain
bäuerl	bäuerlich	Peasant (*adj.*)
Badeanst	Badeanstalt	Bathing place, public baths
Bew. M.	Bewässerungsmühle	Irrigation mill
Bf, Bhf.	Bahnhof	Railway station
Bge	Berge	Mountains
Bgr. Pl.	Begräbnisplatz für Nichtchristen	Burial place for non-Christians
Bgw	Bergwerk	Mine, mining
Blst	Blockstelle	Signal station, signal box
Br	Brunnen	Spring, well
Brn	Brennerei	Distillery
B.W.	Bahnwärter	Railway guard's station, linesman's hut
Ch. S., Ch. Hs.	Chausseehaus	Toll house, toll-gate
D. A.	Dampferanlegestelle	Dock for steamers
Denkm	Denkmal	Monument
Denkst	Denkstein	Memorial stone
D.F.	Dampfschiff-Fähre	Steamer ferry
D.M.	Dampfmühle	Steam mill
Dom	Domäne	Estate, demesne
D.W.	Dammwärter	Dike-watcher's hut
E.F.	Eisenbahnfähre	Train ferry
ehem.	ehemalig	Formerly
Ehr.Fdhf.	Ehrenfriedhof	Military cemetery
El.W.	Elektrizitätswerk	Power station
Entw.M.	Entwässerungsmühle	Drainage windmill
Erbbgr	Erbbegräbnis	Family burial ground
Err. Block	Erratischer Block	Loose boulder, erratic boulder, drift block
E. St.	Eisenbahnstation	Railway station
Exerz. Pl.	Exerzierplatz	Training ground
F	Fähre	Ferry
	Försterei	(Forest) ranger station, forester's house
Fbr	Fabrik	Factory
Fl	Fluss	River
F.P.	Festpunkt	Reference point
F.Sch.	Feuerschiff	Lightship
F.St.	Funkstelle	Radio (WT) station
F.T.	Funkturm (über 60 m)	Radio tower (WT mast) over 60 meters high
Ft	Furt	Ford
Gr	Graben	Ditch, water-ditch
	gross	Great
H	Hütte	Hut
Hbf	Hauptbahnhof	Main railway station
H.M.	Höhenmarke	Permanent important benchmark, spot height
H.O.	Hochofen	Blast furnace
Hp	Haltepunkt	Railway stop (halt)
Hr. Wk.	Hammerwerk	Foundry
Hs	Haus	House
Hst	Haltestelle	Railway station (halt)
Hügelgr	Hügelgrab	Prehistoric grave, cairn barrow, tumulus
Hünenst	Hünenstein	Prehistoric stone
Jg. Hb.	Jungendherberge	Youth hostel
J. Htt.	Jagdhütte	Huntsman's hut
K	Kirche	Church
(K)	Kirche (weithin sichtbar)	Church (landmark)
Kan	Kanal	Canal
Kap	Kapelle	Chapel
Kas	Kaserne	Barracks
K.D.	Kulturgeschichtliches Denkmal	Historical monument
K.F.	Kahnfähre	Boat ferry
Kgr	Kiesgrube	Gravel pit
Khf	Kirchhof	Churchyard
Klbf	Kleinbahnhof	Small railway station
Klst	Kloster	Monastery, convent
Klt	Kelter	Winepress
K.O.	Kalkofen	Limekiln
Kol	Kolonie	Colony
Kr	Krug	Inn
Lgr	Lehmgrube	Clay pit
L.M.	Lohmühle	Tanning mill
Lpl	Ladeplatz	Loading place, wharf
Lst	Ladestelle	Loading place, wharf
Luftf	Luftfahrtfeuer	Air navigation beacon
M	Mühle	Mill
(M)	Mühle (weithin sichtbar)	Mill (landmark)
Mag	Magazin	Magazine, depot
Mgr	Mergelgrube	Marl pit
M.H.	Meierhof	Farmhouse
Mlst	Meilenstein	Milestone
M.M.	Mahlmühle	Grinding mill
Molk	Molkerei	Dairy
Mus	Museum	Museum
Naph. Br.	Naphtabrunnen	Naphtha well, oil well
N.D.	Naturdenkmal	Monument (natural feature)
Ndr	Nieder	Lower, nether
N.P.	Nivellementspunkt	Precise benchmark, spot height
N. S. G.	Naturschutzgebiet	National park, nature sanctuary
Obr	Ober	Upper
O.F.	Oberförsterei	Forestry headquarters, head ranger's house
O.M.	Ölmühle	Oil mill
P	Pegel	Water gauge
Pap.M.	Papiermühle	Paper mill
Pav	Pavillon	Pavilion
P.F.	Personenfähre	Passenger ferry
Pl	Platz	Place, square, etc.
P.M.	Pulvermühle	Powder mill
Pr	Preussisch	Prussian
Pumpw	Pumpwerk	Pumping station
Pvhs	Pulverhaus	Powder magazine
Qu	Quelle	Spring
R	Ruine	Ruins
Rbf	Reichsbahnhof	State railway station
Res	Reservoir	Reservoir
Röm. Ndlg., R.N.	Römische Niederlassung	Roman ruins, remains
S	See	Lake
	Schornstein	Chimney
(S)	Schornstein (weithin sichtbar)	Chimney (landmark)
Sch	Scheune	Barn
Schäf	Schäferei	Sheep farm
Schiess-St.	Schiess-Stand	Rifle range
Schlf	Schloss	Castle
Schl. M.	Schleifmühle	Grinding mill
Schlse	Schleuse	Lock, sluice
Schp	Schuppen	Shed
S.F.	Seilfähre	Cable ferry
S.H.	Sennhütte	Alpine herdsman's hut, alpine chalet
S.M.	Sägemühle	Sawmill
Soldgr	Soldatengrab	Soldier's grave
S. P.	Schreibpegel	Recording water gauge
Sp.Pl.	Sportplatz	Sports ground, playing field
Spr.Sch., Spr.Hgl.	Sprungschanze,-hügel	Ski jump
St	Stall	Stable, outhouse
	Stollen	Gallery (mining)
staatl	staatlich	State (*adj.*)
St.Br.	Steinbruch	Quarry
Sgr	Steingrube	Quarry
Stk	Steinkohle	Coal
Stsbf	Staatsbahnhof	State railway station
S. W.	Sägewerk	Sawmill
T	Teich	Pond
	Turm	Tower
(T)	Turm (weithin sichtbar)	Tower (landmark)
Tgr	Tongrube	Clay pit
T.O.	Teerofen	Tar works
U	Umformer	Transformer
unt	unter	Lower, nether
Usps	Umspannerhaus	Transformer
W	Warte	Watchtower
Wasserw	Wasserwerk	Waterworks
Wbh	Wasserbehälter	Reservoir
W.F.	Wagenfähre	Vehicle ferry
Wf	Wasserfall	Waterfall
Whr	Weiher	Fish pond
Whs	Wirtshaus	Inn
Wltg	Wasserleitung	Aqueduct
W.T.	Wasserturm	Water tower
W.W.	Wildwärter	Game warden's (keeper's) house
Zgl	Ziegelei	Brickyard
Z.O.	[illegible]	Cement works
Zollhs	Zollhaus	Customhouse

III.2. British vs. U.S. Terminology for German Terms.

☐ British versus American Terminology

Accumulator	Storage battery
Advanced HQ	Command Post
anchor with cables	anchor with ropes
Ammunition reloading	Ammunition transloading
Armament factory	Arsenal munitions factory
Armour	armor
Armoury platoon	Ordnance Repair
Army clothing	Quatermaster clothing
Army GHQ, War Ministry	High Command of the Army
Asparagus bundles	hedgehogs
Battery	could also apply to units as large as battalion
Barricade of stakes	Post obstacle
Battle transport	Combat train
Buried Signal Cable	Underground telephone cable
Bridge arch	Bridge opening
buried cable	underground cable
Bushes	Bush, Shrubs
carts	wagons
cavalryman	mounted trooper
centre	center
Chimney	Smokestack
column of route	March column
cm (ex. 8.8-cm gun)	10-mm (ex. 88-mm gun)
Commandant's office, garrison HQ	Administrative Headquarters
concertina wire obstacle	multiple wire entanglements
Coniferous Wood	Evergreen Woods
Crawl trench	Communication trench
Cut	Cutting
Corps, Arabic # (ex. 8)	Corps, Roman # (ex. VIII)
cyclist	bicycle
Dyke	Dike
Earth aerial (signal)	Ground aerial
Earthworks	Rampart
Engineer building co.	Bridge-construction company
Erratic boulder	Loose Boulder
Ethylisation section	Gasoline blending detachment

Exchange	Switching station
felled trees	cleared forest
Flash spotting troop	Flash-ranging battery
Forester's House	(Forest) ranger station
Garrison Command, town major's office	Military HQ in occupied territory (battalion-level)
GHQ	Army-level
gun dugout	gun pit
harbour	harbor
heap	pile
Heath	Prairie
High tension wire	High voltage
Hop Field	Hop plantation
Horse transport squadron	Horse-drawn transport troop
In construction	Under Construction
in tow	attached to ferrying rope
Infantry Gun	Infantry Howitzer
inflatable rubber boats	pneumatic floats
Kilometre	Kilometer
Light signalling section	Blinker detachment
Liquid fuel (POL)	Motor fuel
Line-of-communications	rear area
Local defence	regional defense
Lone trees	prominent trees
Long-range intercept	Signal intelligence
Marshland	Swamp and marsh
Mechanized	Motorized
metre	meter
Mineral Oil	Crude Oil
motor transport repair	motor vehicle maintenance
mountain carrier	mountain pack
open-cast mining	open-pit mining
pack wireless telephone	portable radio
Planned	Projected
posts	stakes
Panzer Grenadier	Motorized
Petroleum testing sect.	Motor fuel testing detachment
phone	telephone
piquet	Picket

Pz Kw IV (II, V, etc.)	Tank, M4 (2, 5, etc.)
Radio Mast	Radio tower
responsible officer	officer in charge
Riflemen in weapon pit	Group of entrenched riflemen
scrambler line	Transposed air line
screened off	blocked
section	platoon (AA, SL, plotting, survey, meteoroligical units)
Signpost	Roadsign
smoke battery	projector battalion
Snow clearance party	Snow removal detachment
spare parts echelon	supply train for spare parts
Spot height	Precise benchmark
Static refuelling point	Stationary filling station
star working	directed radio net
subsection (printing)	detachment
supply echelon	supply train
tank squadron	tank company
tank ditch	tank trap
Tanker train (filled)	Railway filling station (full)
Tank proof ground	terrain impassable for tanks
teleprint	teletype
tow rope of ferry	ferrying rope
tractor	Gun-towing motor vehicle
tractor repair platoon	Prime mover maintenance
Tree plantation	Tree bursery
tree-trunk obstacle Large/small	Abatis, heavy / light
troop (artillery)	battery
Tumuli, barrows	Prehistoric burial grounds
Tyre echelon	Tire supply train
unloading	detrucking
Various	isolated
View point	Point of Altitude
Water meadow	Wet meadow
Waterways clearing	Waterway clearing
workshop company	repairshop company
Wireless Transmitter	Radio
Wood	Woods
Yugoslav	Jugoslav

☐ British Terminology and Place Names During World War 2

To reduce confusion in this chapter an the one that follows, table III.2 gives a short list of differences between British and U.S. terminology as used in translating German terms. (The original version of this dictionary had equivalent British terminology for item more than 90% of these were the same and reflected similar organization.) It includes a sample of organizational and spelling differences. The British more closely reflect European usage but are not necessarily more concise.

The language of place names is a related challenge to studies of World War 2. For example, in the Balkans alone there were some five major languages, before the Italians, English, and Germans came with their battle maps to further confuse future historians. The partial list that follows as Table III.3 augments the VALOR books on the subject as a small effort to clarify the geography. To unravel the geographic terminolgy used by the dozens of participants in the war there is no substitute for a good gazetteer.

A-B-C-D-E

Alba Julia	Karlsburg
Adria Meer	Adriatic Sea; Jadranske More
Agais Meer	Aegean Sea
Agram	Zagreb
Allenstein	Olsztyn
Alpenvorland	South Tyrol; 1944 Annexation
Altsohl	Zvolen
Amselfeld	Kossovo Polje
Angerapp	Ozersk
Antrea	Kamennogorsk (Finland)
Arnswalde	Choszcno
Arnheim	Arnhem
Arys	Orzysz
Athen	Athen; Athinai, Athens
Auschwitz	Oswiecim
Bad Reinerz	Duszinki Zdroj
Balaton Lake	Plattensee
Baltischport	Paldiski
Bartenstein	Bartoszyce
Bela Crkva	Weisskirchen
Belgard	Bialogard
Beograd	Belgrade
Berent	Koscierzyna
Bialogard	Belgard
Bielawa	Langenbielau
Bischofsburg	Biskupiec
Beuthen	Bytom
Bohnsack	Sobieszewo
Boleslawiec	Bunzlau
Bosnien,	Bosnia
Böhmischer Wald	Sumava
Brac	Brazza
Brasov	Kronstadt
Brdywald	Brdy

Brest-Litovsk	Brest; Brzesc-nad-Bugiem (Pol)
Breslau	Wroclaw
Brieg	Brzeg
Bromberg	Bydgoszcz
Brunn	Brno
Brüx	Most
Brzeg	Brieg
Bucharest	Bucuresti
Budweis	Ceske Budejovice
Bunzlau	Boleslawiec
Butow	Bytow
Burgstudl	Hradiste
Bydgoszcz	Bromberg
Bytom	Bethen
Bytow	Butow
Calarasi	Kalarash (Moldavia)
Carinthia	German Annexation of Slovenia
Ceske Budejovice	Budweis
Cēsis	Tsesis
Cilli	Celje
Chaklov	Orenburg
Chalkai	Calchi (It.)
Cheb	Efer (Czech)
Chelmno	Kulm
Chelmza	Kulmzee
Chemnitz	Karl-Marx-Stadt
Chernyakhovsk	Insterburg
Chisinau	Kishinev (Romania); Kischinew
Chojnice	Könitz
Chojnow	Haynau
Chorzow	Konigshutte; Krolewska Huta
Choszcno	Arnswalde
Cieszyn	Teschen; Cesky Tesin
Clerf	Clervaux
Cluj	Klausenburg; Kolosvar
Cosel	Kozle

Crossen	Krosno
Dabie	Altdamm
Dalmatian	Italian Annexation of Slovenia
Danzig	Gdansk
Daugavpils	Dvinsk
Darlowo	Rügenwalde
Debno	Neudamm
Decin	Tetschen
Demotikabeit	Greek/Turkish border zone
Deutsch Eylau	Ilawa
Deutsche Krone	Walcz
Dhodekani	Dodekanes; Dodecanese Islands
Dirschau	Tczew
Dnepr	Dnjepr; Dnieper (River)
Dnjestr	Dniestr; Nitrul
Donau	Danube, Dunav, Dunarea
Dorpat	Tartu
Drau	Drava
Drohobycz	Drogobych
Dubrovnik	Ragusa
Dünaberg	Daugavpils
Durres	Durazzo
Duszinki Zdroj	Bad Reinerz
Dzerzhinsk	Rastyapino
Dzialdowo	Soldau
Dzierzoniow	Reichenbach
Edineti	Yedintsy
Edirne	Adrianopel
Efer	Cheb
Eger	Ochre
Eisenstadt	Kismarton
Eisernes Tor	Orsova
Elblag	Elbing
Epirus	Bootien+Thessalien (W.Greece)
Ersekujavar	Nove Zamky

III.3. Selected Place Names During World War 2.

III.3. (cont.) Selected Place Names During World War 2.

Erzgebirge	Krusne Hory
Esseg	Osijek
Euboa	Evvoia (long island above Athens)
Eydtkau	Chernysshevskoye
Eylau	Ilawa

F-G-H-I

Falkenberg	Niemodlin
Fiume	Fiume; Rijeka
Flatow	Zlotow
Firenze	Florence
Fischausen	Primorsk
Frauenburg	Frombork; Saldus
Freiburg	Swiebodzice
Fünfkirchen	Pecs
Freiburg	Swiebodzice
Friedau	Ormoz
Gablonz	Jablonec
Gatchina	Krasnovardeisk
Gotenhafen	Gdynia; Gdingen
Genova	Genoa
Gerdauen	Zheleznodorozhny
Georgenberg	Miasteczko
Gevgeli	Djevdjelia
Gitchin	Jicin
Glatz	Klodzko
Gleiwitz	Gilwice
Glogau	Glogow
Glubczyce	Leobshütz
Gnesen	Gniezno
Goleniow	Gollnow
Gombin	GabinGorkiy; Nizhniy Novgorod
Gorkiy	Nizhniy Novgorod
Görlitz	Zgorzelec
Gorzow Wielkopolski	Landsberg
Gran	Esztergom
Grudziadz	Graudenz
Greffenberg	Gryfow Slaski
Gross Kanischa	Nagykanizsa
Grosswardein	Oradea
Grusbach	Hrusovay
Grünberg	Zielona Gora
Gumbinnen	Gusev
Haapsalu	Khaapsalu (Estonian)
Haynau	Chojnow
Heiligenbeil	Mamonovo
Heilsberg	Lidzbark
Hermannstadt	Sibiu
Herzegowina	Herzegovina; Occupied by Croatia
Hindenburg	Zabrze
Hirschberg	Jelenia Gora
Hohensalza	Inowroclaw
Hungerburg	Narva-Joesuu
Huszt	Khust; Chust
Ilawa	Eylau
Inowroclaw	Hohensalza
Insterburg	Chernyakhovsk
Istria	Kuestenland, 1944 Annexation

J-K-L

Jablonec	Gablonz
Jachymov	Joachimstal
Jastrow	Jastrowiec
Jääski	Kesogorskiy
Jassy	Iasi
Jauer	Jawor
Jelgava;	Yelgava
Jelenia Gora	Hirschberg
Jewe	Johvi
Jicin	Gitchin
Jonvi	Yykhvi
Kadiyevka	Sergo (Ukraine)
Kamienna Gora	Landeshut
Karlsbad	Karlovy Vary
Karpacz	Krummhubel
Kartuzy	Karthaus
Kaunas	Kovno; Kauen
Karlsburg	Alba Julia; Gyulafehervar (Hung)
Karpacz	Krummhubel
Karpfen	Krupina
Karthaus	Kartuzy
Kaschau	Kosice
Kattowitz	Katowice
Katzbach Gebirge	Kaczawa
Kephalonia	Cephalonia; Kefallinia
Kepno	Kempen
Kesogorskiy	Jääski
Ketrzyn	Rastenburg
Khaapsalu	Haapsalu (Estonian)
Khios	Chios
Kholodnaya	Novo-Voykovo
Khust	Chust, Huszt
Kirov	Vyatka
Kischinew	Chisinau; Kishnev
Kiviyli	Kiviloi
Klaipeda	Memel (Lithuania)
Klausenburg	Cluj; Kolozsvar (Hung.)
Klodzko	Glatz
Kluczborg	Kreuzberg
Köln	Cologne
Königsberg	Kaliningrad
Königshutte	Chorzow; Krolewska Huta
Könitz	Chojnice
Kohlfurt	Weglinec
Kosino	Kosa
Koslin	Koszalin
Kostrzyn	Küstrin
Koszalin	Köslin
Kolberg	Kolobrzeg
Kolomyja	Kolomyya
Kolosjoki	Nikel'
Komintern	Novoshakhtinsk
Komorn	Komarno
Konstantinigrad	Krasnograd
Korcula	Curzola
Korfu	Corfu; Kerkira
Korneva	Zinten
Korschen	Korsze
Kos (Island)	Coo (It.)
Koscierzyna	Berent
Kotor	Cattaro
Kotovsk	Birzula (Ukr)
Kowel (P)	Kove; (Ukr)
Kozle	Cosel
Krakau	Krakow
Krapnitz	Krapkowice
Krasnozagvardeisk	Gatchina
Krasnodon	Sorokino
Krasnograd	Konstantinigrad
Krasnoostovskiy	Byerskiy
Krasnoturinsk	Turinskiy
Krasnozavodsk	Zagorsky
Kremenets	Krzemieniec
Kremnitz	Kremnica
Kreta	Crete
Kreuzburg	Slavskoye
Kroatia	Croatia; Bosnien, Lika, Syrmien
Kronstadt	Brasov; Brasso (Hung.)
Krosno	Crossen
Kulm	Chelmno
Kreuzberg	Kluczborg
Küstrin	Kostrzyn
Küstenland	Istria; 1944 Annexation
Kulmzee	Chelmza
Kuybishev	Samara
Kwidzyn	Marienwerder
Labiau	Polessk
Laibach	Ljubljana
Landeshut	Kamienna Gora
Landsberg	Gorzow Wielkopolski
Langenbielau	Bielawa
Lauenburg	Lebork
Lautern	Lutry
Lebork	Lauenburg
Leghorn	Livorno
Lemberg	Lwow ; L'vov
Leningrad	St. Petersburg; Petrograd
Leobshutz	Glubczyce
Leslau	Wloclawek
Lessen	Lasin
Lesvos	Lesbos; Mytilini
Leszno	Lissa
Lesvos	Lesbos; Mytilini
Libau	Liepaya
Liberec	Reichenberg
Lidzbark	Heilsberg
Liegnitz	Legnica
Liepaya	Libau
Limnos	Lemnos
Lissa	Leszno
Ljubljana	Laibach
Loslau	WodizislawHermannstadt
Lothringen	Lorraine
Luettich	Liege
L'vov	Lemberg Lwow (P)
Lyck	Elk

M-N-O-P

Macedonia	SE Yugoslavia, inc. Kossovo Pole
Marienburg	Malbork
Marienwerder	Kwidzyn
Mariatheresiopel	Subotica
Mariupol	Zhdanov
Marburg	Maribor
Massow	Maszewo
Memel	Klaipeda
Meseritz	Miedzyrzecz
Messina	Milazzo
Mljet	Meleda
Meseritz	Miedzyrzecz; Mezhirichi
Mielau	Mlawa
Misslitz	Miroslav
Miedzyrzecz	Meseritz; Mitau
Mitau	Jelgava; Yelgava
Mittenwalde	Miedzylesie
Moldau	Vltava
Molodeszno	Molodechno
Morszyn	Morshin (Ukr.)
Moskau	Moscow; Moskva
Most	Brüx
München	Munich
Münsterburg	Ziebice
Mysliborz	Soldin
Nagykanizsa	Gross Kanischa
Neman	Ragnit
Nesterov	Stallupönen
Neubulgarien	Macedonia, SE Yugoslavia (included Kossowo Polje)
Neuhausel	Nove Samky
Neumarkt	Targu-Mures
Neusalz	Novisad
Neusohl	Banska Bystrica; Besztercebanya
Neustadt	Prudnik; Wejherowo
Neustettin	Szczecinek
Neutra	Nitra
Nikolai	Mikolow
Nis	Nisch
Nizhnegorskiy	Seytler
Novisad	Neusalz
Nowogrodek	Novogrudek
Novoshakhtinsk	Komintern
Oberglogau	Glogowek
Oder	Odra (River)
Oderburg	Bohumin
Oppeln	Opole
Oradea	Grosswardein
Oranienmaum	Lomonosov
Orenburg	Chaklov
Orsova	Orsova (Eisernes Tor)
Orstelburg	SzczytnoPalmnicken; Yantarny
Osijek	Esseg
Pancevo	Pantschova
Paldiski	Baltischport
Pecs	Funfkirchen
Perm	Molotov
Petasmo	Pechenga (Fin)
Pervomansk	TashinoPetasmo; Pechenga (Fin)
Petrograd	(Veliki) Betschkerek
Petroskoi	Petrozavodsk
Pila	Schneidemühl
Plzen	Pilsen
Plattensee	Balaton Lake
Plicksen	Plikiai
Pilzen	Pilsen
Ploehnen	Plonsk
Plovdiv	Philipopel
Polessk	Labiau
Pozarevac	Passarovitz
Posen	Poznan
Potok Zloty (P)	Zoloty Potok (Ukr.)
Pozarevac	Passarovitz
Poznan	Posen
Praust	Pruzcz
Preekuln	Priekule
Pressburg	Bratislava; Pozony (Hung.)
Primorsk	Fischausen
Prudnik	Neustadt
Pruth	Prutul
Putzinger Nehrung	Hel Peninsula

III.3. (cont.) German Place Names During World War 2.

Q-R-S

Raciborz	Ratibor
Ragnit	Neman
Rakvere	Wesenberg
Rastenburg	Ketrzyn
Ratibor	Raciborz
Reichenbach	Dzierzoniow
Reichenberg	Liberec
Riesengebirge	Krakonosze
Rhodos	Rhodes; Rodi (It.)
Rosenberg	Susz
Rosenow	Rasina
Rowne	Rovno
Rügenwalde	Darlowo
Rummelsburg	Miastko
Salla	Kuolayarvi
Salonika	Thessaloni; Salonici
Sardegna	Sardinia
Sassmacken	Valdemarpils
Sauer	Sure (River)
Schemnitz	Banska Stiavnica
Schieratz	Sieradz
Schivelbein	Swidwin
Schneidemuehl	Pila
Schoden	Skuodas
Schoeneck	Skarszewy
SchwarzesMeer	Black Sea
Semlin	Zemun
Seytler	Nizhnegorskiy
Shekesfehervar	Stuhlweissenburg
Sibiu	Hermannstadt
Sillein	Zsolna
Siebenbürgen	Transylvania; Erdely (Hung.)
Skoplje	Uskub;Skopje
Skotschau	Skoczow
Skutari	Shkoder; Shkoderi
Smederevo	Semendria
Soldau	Dzialdowo
Soldin	Soliborz
Split	Spalato; Spoleto
Sporaden	Sporades
Stallupönen	Nesterov
Sohrau	Zory
Sovetsk	Tilsit
Steinamanger	Szombathely
Stettin	Szczecin
Stolpmünde	Ustka
Strehlen	Strzelin
Stuhlweissenburg	Shekesfehervar
Stuhm	Sztum
Sulecin	Zielenzig
Susak	Rijeka
Svalyava	Szolyva (H); Svalava (C)
Swinoujscie	Swinemünde
Syrmien	Smyria
Szamotuly	Samter
Szczecin	Stettin
Szczecinek	Neustettin
Szczytno	Ortelsburg
Szombathely	Steinamanger

T-U-V

Tallinn	Revel; Reval
Tarnopol	Ternopol (Ukr)
Tbilisi	Tiflis
Tczew	Dirshau
Telsiai	Tel'shyay
Temeschburg	Timisoara
Teschen	Cieszyn; Cesky Tesin
Tetschen	Decin
Theben	Devin
Theiss	Tisza; Tisa (River)
Thessaloniki	Saloniki Salonici
Thorn	Torun
Tiflis	Tbilisi
Tilsit	Sovetsk
Timisoara	Temeschburg
Tisa	Theiss; Tisza
Torun	Thorn
Trachenberg	Zmigrod
Transylvanian Alps	Transilvanische Alpen; Carpathi meridienali
Trento area	Trient (1944 Annexation Zone)
Treptow	Trzebiatow
Treuburg	Olecko
Tsesis	Cēsis
Turgel	Türi; Tyu
Türi	Tyuri
Tver	Kalinin
Tyrnau	Trnava
Uhtua	Uktua
Ustka	Stolpmünde
Uzhgorod	Uzhorod (C); Ungvar (H)
Varsna	Vyartsilya
Vrsac	Werschetz
Valka	Valga; Varsna; Vyartsilya
Ventspils	Windau
Viipuri	Vyborg
Vil'nyus	Vilna; Wilno
Vis	Lissa
Vistula	Wisla
Viona	Valona; Vlore
Vöru	Vyru
Walbrzych	Waldenburg
Walcz	Deutsche Krone
Waldenburg	Walbrzych
Wansen	Wiazow
Warschau	Warszawa; Warsaw
Wartenburg	Barczewo
Warthenau	Zawiercje
Wehlau	Znamensk
Weglinec	Kohlfurt
Weisskirchen	Bela Crkva
Werschetz	Vrsac
Wesenberg	Rakvere
Wielbark	Willenberg
Weichsel	Wisla; Vistula River
Wielbark	Willenberg
Wien	Vienna; Becs (Hung.)
Wienerwald	Vienna Forest
Wejherowo	Neustadt
Willenberg	Wielbark
Wilno	Vil'nyus; Vilna
Windau	Ventspils
Wolkowysk	Volkovysk
Wolozyn	Volozhin
Wormditt	Orneta
Wroclaw	Breslau
Yantarny	Palmnicken
Yelgava	Mitau
Zabeln	Sabile
Zablotow	Zabolotov
Zabrze	Hindenberg
Zagan	Sagan
Zagreb	Agram
Zakinthos	Zante
Zary	Sorau
Zemun	Semlin
Zhdanov	Mariupol
Zheleznodorozhny	Gerdauen
Ziebice	Münsterburg
Zielenzig	Sulecin
Zielona Gora	Grünberg
Zinten	Korneva
Zlochow (P)	Zolochev (Ukr.)
Zmigrod	Trachenberg
Znamensk	Wehlau
Zydaczow (P)	Zhidachov (Ukr) ■

☐ Symbols for Transportation and Movement Control

The following provides symbols of some installations related to the general control of transport with some specific examples of railway transportation ss ymbols.

	German	U. S.
W.T.Ltg	Wehrmachttransportleitung	Armed Forces transportation control
W.V.D	Wehrmachtverkehrsdirektion	Armed Forces traffic supervision.
Gen d Trsp.w	General des Transportwesens bei einer H. Gru.	Commanding general of transportation service at an army group
Bv.T.O	Bevollmächtigter Transportoffizier bei einer H. Gru. oder A. O. K.	Officer in charge of transportation at an army group or army
BGO	Beauftragter Generalstabsoffizier	Specially assigned General Staff officer
T.O.	Transportoffizier	Transportation officer
T.V.St	Transportverbindungsstelle	Transportation intermediate station.
Trsp.Kdtr	Transportkommandantur	Transportation Hq
Ausl.K	Ausladekommissar	Detrucking (or detraining) officer
Bhf.Kdtr	Bahnhofskommandantur	Railway station command
H.F.O.	Hafenoffizier	Port officer
W.St.	Weiterleitungsstelle	Forwarding station

RAILWAY TRANSPORTATION

	Munitionszug	Ammunition train (railway)
	Betriebsstoffzug	Motor fuel train (railway).
	Verpflegungszug	Ration train (railway)
	Mehlzug	Flour train (railway)
	Haferzug	Oats train (railway)
	Viehzug	Cattle train (railway)
	Truppentransportzug (haltend)	Troop train (halted)
	Truppentransportzug (in Fahrt)	Troop train (moving)
	Leerzug (haltend)	Empty train (halted)
	Leerzug (in Fahrt)	Empty train (moving)
	Transportbewegung der 7. Inf. Div. nach Gegend Ulm mit 24 Zügen täglich	7th infantry division moving by rail toward Ulm with 24 trains daily
	In einem Raum abgestellte Vollzüge (72)	Area containing 72 loaded trains
S.Bhf	Sammelbahnhof	Railroad collecting station
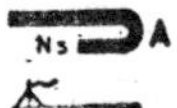	Ausladebahnhof für Nachschub der Armee	Army railhead
	Ausladehafen für Nachschub	Debarkation port for supplies
	Umschlaghafen	Transloading port
	Nachschubsammelhafen	Collecting port for supplies

Chapter IV: Basic Tactical Symbols in Situation Diagrams

Basic Symbols of Army Headquarters and Branches

☐ Introduction

Most of the German Armed Forces consisted of ground units. Even most of the Air Force, which was never more than a quarter of the Armed Forces, consisted mainly of ground troops in the form of Flak artillery and parachute combat divisions. The first part of this chapter depicts symbols used by the ground forces. Some of the Air Force and Navy headquarters symbols are shown in the second part of the chapter.

More specific unit descriptions related to the Army and Air Force will be found in VALOR Book #2, *Hitler's Dying Ground and Organizations* or #5 *Hitler's Elite Guard*. Some listing of school units and training symbols is provided in #4. German Replacement Army. This was separated because of context; here the dozen different symbols for an infantry company mean little but they become clear when put alongside the appropriate organization charts and descriptions.

The Navy symbols are included as a separate category in this chapter and the brevity of the section reflects a narrow mission. The German Navy was never more than 9% of the Armed Forces in size and the nature of its operations was based on the U-Boat fleet for most of the war. There was no independent aviation branch or the equivalent of a Marine amphibious assault force. As in the case of the Air Force some Navy information has been excluded to avoid duplication.

☐ Headquarters are Represented by Flag Symbols.

Specific types of units are based on adding a basic symbol for the respective branch of service. The following is a list of basic symbols for headquarters. It is followed by three examples of unit types.

Oberkommando des Heeres ---------- High Command of the Army
Heeresgruppenkommando ---------- Hq of an army group
Armeeoberkommando ---------- Hq of an army
General(Korps)kommando ---------- Corps Hq
Divisionskommando ---------- Division Hq
Brigadestab ---------- Brigade Hq
Regimentsstab ---------- Regimental Hq
Bataillonsstab ---------- Battalion Hq
Führer einer Kompanie ---------- Hq (or commander) of a company (or equivalent unit)

Examples:

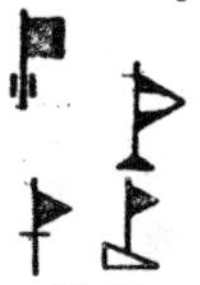

Stab eines Artillerieregiments ---------- Hq of an artillery regiment
Kommando einer Gebirgsdivision ---------- Hq of a mountain division
Stab einer Panzerjägerabteilung ---------- Hq of an antitank battalion

☐ Branches of Service

The following lists the basic symbols used to represent the various Arms and Services of the German Army.

Infanterie ---------- Infantry
Gebirgstruppe ---------- Mountain troops
Kradschützen ---------- Motorcycle riflemen
Panzer[1] ---------- Armored, tank
Panzerjäger ---------- Antitank
Radfahreinheiten ---------- Bicycle units
Artillerie ---------- Artillery
Fla- und Flak-Einheiten ---------- Antiaircraft
Vermessungstruppe ---------- Survey troops

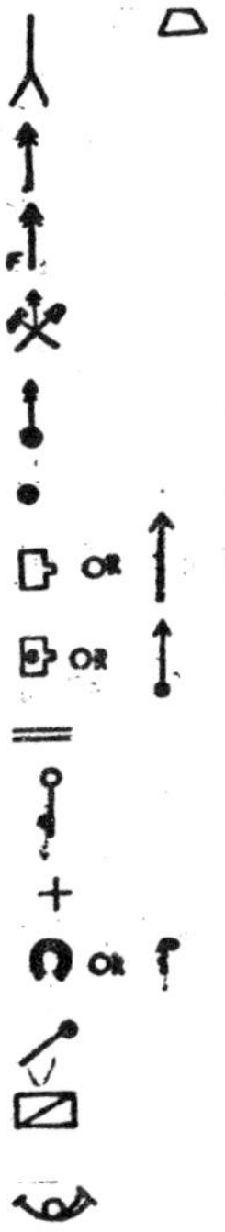

Nebeltruppe ---------- Chemical warfare (smoke) troops
Pioniere ---------- Engineers
Festungspioniere ---------- Fortress engineers
Baupioniere ---------- Construction engineers
Eisenbahnpioniere ---------- Railway engineers
Eisenbahnbetriebstruppe (*formerly* Feldeisenbahntruppe) ---------- Railway operating troops
Nachrichtentruppe ---------- Signal troops
Eisenbahnnachrichtentruppe ---------- Railway signal troops
Nachschubdienste ---------- Supply services
Fahrtruppe ---------- Transport troops
Sanitätsdienste ---------- Medical services
Veterinärdienste ---------- Veterinary services
Verkehrsregelungsdienste ---------- Traffic control services
Feldgendarmerie ---------- Military police
Feldpostdienste ---------- Army postal services

☐ Basic Symbols for Weapons and Equipment.

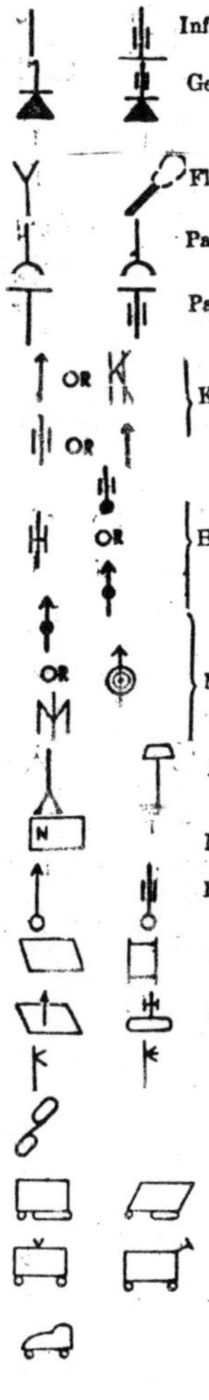

Infanteriegeschütz ---------- Infantry howitzer
Gebirgs-Infanteriegeschütz ---------- Mountain infantry howitzer
Flammenwerfer ---------- Flame thrower
Panzerbüchse ---------- Antitank rifle
Panzerjägerkanone ---------- Antitank gun
Kanone ---------- Gun
Haubitze ---------- Howitzer
Mörser ---------- Heavy high-angle howitzer
Nebelwerfer ---------- Projector
Nebelgeräte ---------- Chemical warfare (smoke) equipment
Fliegerabwehrkanone ---------- Antiaircraft gun
Panzerkampfwagen ---------- Tank
Sturmgeschütz ---------- Assault gun
Scheinwerfer ---------- Searchlight
Ballonsperre ---------- Balloon barrage
Schützenpanzerwagen ---------- Half-track personnel carrier
Volkswagen ---------- German version of U. S. ("Jeep") ¼-ton truck
Panzerspähwagen ---------- Scout car

[1] Component parts of panzer divisions are indicated by the following symbol: 

IV.1. Classification to Indicate Caliber of Weapons.

German classification:	Antitank rifles	Infantry howitzers (guns)	Mortars	Antitank guns	Smoke mortars/ rocket projectors	Guns	Howitzers	Heavy high-angle howitzers ("Mörser")	Antiaircraft guns
Light (*leicht*, or *l*, or *le*	Up to 7.9 mm	Up to 75 mm	Up to 79 mm	Up to 39 mm	Up to 109 mm	Up to 99 mm	Up to 129 mm	---------	Up to 36 mm
Medium (*mittel*, or *m*)	---------	---------	80 to 119 mm	40 to 59 mm	110 to 159 mm	---------	---------	---------	37 to 59 mm
Heavy (*schwer*, or *s*)	8 mm and larger	76 mm and larger	120 mm and larger	60 to 89 mm	160 to 219 mm	100 to 209 mm	130 to 209 mm	210 to 249 mm	60 to 159 mm
Superheavy (*schwerste* or *sw*)	---------	---------	---------	90 mm and larger	220 mm and larger	210 mm and larger	210 mm and larger	250 mm and larger	160 mm and larger

☐ Supplementary Symbols and Numbers.

Table III.1 outlines specific classifications used in indicating the caliber of weapons. This system was radically simplified in 1943 as noted below. Three symbols were often used to indicate the increased caliber of types of weapons. Basically additional symbols were added as the caliber increased.

1. For **guns** the symbol — indicated increases in caliber.

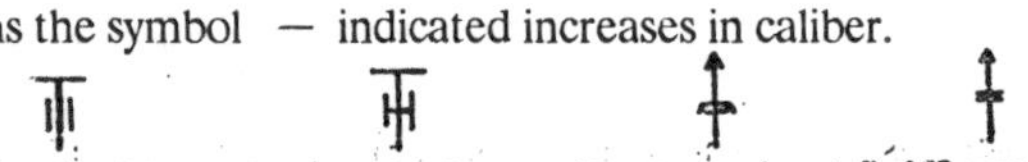

75-mm antitank gun 88-mm antitank gun 120-mm gun (coastal) 150-mm gun

2. For **small arms and guns** lighter than those above, the ∧ symbol indicated increases in caliber.

Machine gun (tripod)[1] (MMG) 37-mm antitank gun 50-mm antitank gun

3. For **howitzers** and heavy high-angle weapons, the o symbol ndicated increases in caliber.

150-mm howitzer 210-mm heavy high-angle howitzer 305-mm heavy high-angle howitzer

☐ Symbols to Indicate Methods of Transport

Most of the German Army relied on horse drawn transportation. If no addition is made to the basic unit symbol, then it could be assumed that it was either horse drawn or relied on foot mobility. Usually fortress or other "static" units, which lacked organic transport, were so indicated.

Fully motorized units were indicated by wheels, tracks, or a rhomboid for panzer units. Half-track units were indicated by a wheel and a track. Towed units had wheels on top of the symbol. Partly motorized units had one wheel. Sleds or sledges were indicate accordingly, and the letter "E" indicated rail transport. Specific examples follow.

1. **Panzer units** are indicated by a rhomboid shape or by a track symbol. Units with weapons on self-propelled mounts (*Sfl* or *Sf*) were indicated by the ▭ symbol placed below the unit. The latter were not necessarily armor protected on the top.

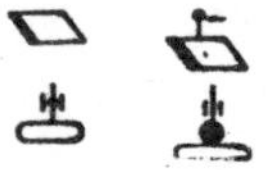

Panzerkompanie.................... Tank company
Haubitze auf Selbstfahrlafette........ Howitzer on self-propelled mount

2. **Half-Track** (Semi-tracked) units mounted on armored half-track vehicles (*gep*) were indicated by the symbol o▭ placed below the unit symbol:

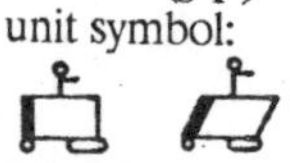

Panzergrenadierkompanie (gep)....... Armored (half-track) rifle company

3. **Fully Motorized** (mot) headquarters and units, except panzer units, were indicated by the symbols o o.

Kommando einer Panzergrenadier-division Hq of a motorized infantry division
Grenadierkompanie (mot)............ Motorized rifle company

4. **Partly Motorized** (*Tmot*) headquarters and units were indicated by the symbol o with the unit:

Stab einer Gebirgsdivisionsnach-richtenabteilung (tmot) Hq of a partly motorized signal battalion of a mountain division
Nachrichtenkompanie (tmot) einer Infanteriedivision Partly motorized signal company of an infantry division

5. **Towed (Tractor-Drawn)** units with towed weapons (*mot Z*) were indicated by the symbol o—o placed above the unit;

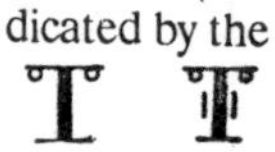

Infanteriegeschützkompanie (mot Z).. Infantry howitzer company towed weapons

6. **Ski** units and headquarters were indicatedby the symbol ⌣— below the unit symbol:

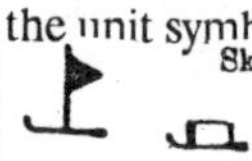

Skibataillon....................... Ski battalion
Skikompanie...................... Ski company

7. **Sled** (Sledge) units and units moving on sleds were indicated by the symbol ⌣= below the unit symbol. Vehicles with Sled (Sledge) trailers had the similar symbol Ah by the unit symbol.

Panzerjägerkompanie auf Schlitten.... Antitank company on sleds
Panzerkompanie mit Schlittenanhänger.. Tank company with sled trailers.

8. **Railway** and transportation by railway was indicated by the letter "E" to the right of the basic symbol:

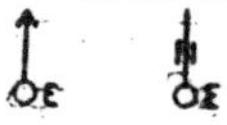

Eisenbahn-Fliegerabwehrkanone........ Railway antiaircraft gun

☐ Company and Platoon Symbols

The method of indicating battalions is covered below under "unit indications" and branches of service. The basic building block unit was the company and battery. These were indicated in two ways.

1. **Thickened Side** for the Basic Symbol for the Branch of Service or rectangle with thickened side around the Basic Branch Symbol:

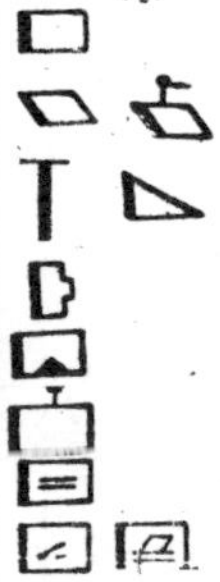

German	U. S.
Schützenkompanie	Rifle company
Panzerkompanie	Tank company
Panzerjägerkompanie	Antitank company
Nachrichtenkompanie	Signal company
Gebirgsjägerkompanie	Mountain rifle company
Pionierkompanie	Engineer company
Nachschubkompanie	Supply company
Granatwerferkompanie[1]	Mortar company medium mortar.

2. **Thickened Part** of Symbol for Weapon of Equipment. In the case of certain artillery batteries (Troops) there might also be an arabic number to indicate the number of weapons in the unit (see # below).

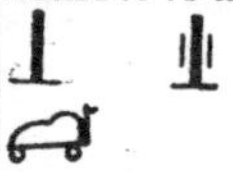

Infanteriegeschützkompanie.......... Infantry howitzer company
Panzerspähkompanie.............. Scout car company

3. **Platoons** and their equivalents were also indicated by the company symbols above, except without the thickened side.

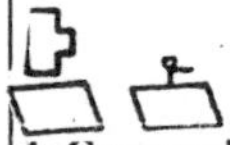

Nachrichtenzug.................. Signal platoon
Panzerzug....................... Tank platoon

4. **Composite Units**, especially in the case of headquarters and heavy (weapons) companies, consisted of several component units. In such cases the letter St (Stab) or S (Schwer) might be placed within the basic tactical symbol, but component units might also be listed.

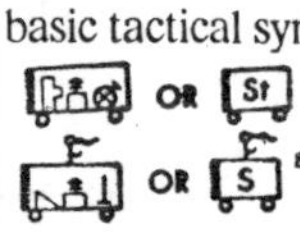

Stabskompanie (mot) eines Grenadier-regiments (mot) Motorized Hq company of a motorized infantry regiment
schwere Kompanie einer Panzeraufklärungsabteilung Heavy weapons company of a panzer reconnaissance squadron

☐ Revision of the System of Military Symbols

The system of German military symbols changed substantially during 1943 as the types of weapons proliferated. Many of the changes are listed on the pages that follow, mainly as they applied to weapons and equipment. In general, in this volume the symbol at the right indicates the older version. It should also be noted that were various semiofficial auxiliary symbols. especially at the company level. Also the older symbols contined to be used throughout the war by some units.

☐ Supplemtary Numbers in Describing Equipment

The load capacity of transport columns and the **carrying capacity** of ferries and bridges were indicated by placing the number in tons (the word "tons" or "t" not used) below the center of the symbols.

leichte Artilleriekolonne (mot) (48) — Artillery motorized light transport column of 48-ton capacity

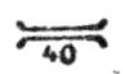

Brücke zu 40 t Tragefähigkeit — Bridge of 40-ton capacity

The **number of weapons or vehicles** in a unit could be indicated by Arabic numerals below the unit symbol or beneath that of the specific weapon or vehicle symbol. These were sometimes shown below added symbols if there were several types of weapons or vehicles. Here, and the examples below, show how the unit symbols became more simple.

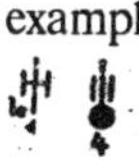

Batterie le. Feldhaubitzen zu 4 Geschützen — 4-gun battery of light field howitzers

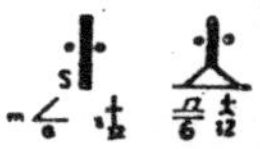

Maschinengewehrkompanie mit 12 schweren Maschinengewehren und 6 mittleren Granatwerfern — Machine-gun company with machine guns (tripod) and medium mortars

Tank types were often indicated by a Roman numeral within the basic tank symbol. A lightning symbol was used to denote **armored command vehicles.** The designation of le, m, and s were sometimes used to indicate tank units, but not to describe tanks.

Panzerkampfwagen IV — Tank, M4

Panzerbefehlswagen — Armored command vehicle
The M3 tank is represented by the old symbol.

leichte Panzerkompanie — Light tank company

As the use of **Antiaircraft Guns** became more extensive after 1942, they were were often integrated with other units. Those designated for home defense were indicated by the *"Hei"* (*Heimat-Flak*) on the right of the basic symbol. Emergency Antiaircraft Guns were indicated by an *"Al"* (*Alarm-Flak*) on the right of the basic symbol. The **gun length and caliber** were key concerns, so the caliber was often shown by placing numerals representing centimeters (unlike U.S. practice, the Germans designated guns above 20mm in centimeters) to the left of the basic symbol. It might also be indicated by letters *le* (*leicht*), *m* (*mittel*), *s* (*schwer*), and *sw* (*schwerste*) to the left of symbol, per table IV.1.

The country of origin of weapons might be indicated by placing supplementary lower case letters to the right of the basic symbol: for example *b* for *belgisch* (Belgian), *f* for *französisch* (French), etc.. This might indirectly indicate its physical characteristics. The letters *"k"* (*kurz*) and *"l"* (*lang*) were used to the right of the gun caliber number.

2 Granatwerfer, Kaliber 8 cm mit langem Rohr — Two 81-mm mortars with long barrels

mittlere Panzerkompanie zu 10 Pz. IV l. Rohr und 3 Pz. IV k. Rohr — Medium tank company of 10 M4 tanks with long-barreled guns and 3 M4 tanks with short-barrel

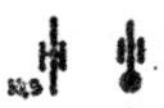

10,5 cm l.F.H. — 105-mm light field howitzer

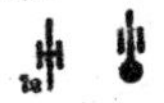

10,5 cm l.F.H.[1] — 105-mm light field howitzer

12 cm Granatwerfer — 120-mm mortar

Barrage Batteries (*Sperrfeuer-Battarien*) might be indicated by placing *"Sp"* to the left of the symbol below the caliber. The **weapon range** in kilometers was sometimes shown in arabic numerals above the basic symbol. The **number of weapons** was sometimes indicated by numerals placed below the symbol. When there were units of varying caliber within a unit, one basic symbol might have been used to indicate all the weapons, the numbers of each type given below it, commencing with the largest caliber to the left.

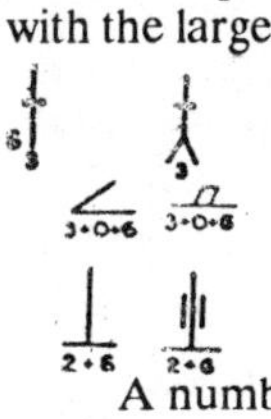

3 schwere Maschinengewehre — 3 machine guns (tripod)

3 s. und 6 le. Granatwerfer — 3 heavy and 6 light light mortars.

2 s. und 6 le. Infanteriegeschütze — 2 heavy and 6 light infantry howitzers

A number of symbols was used to indicate guns in position The symbol was used above the weapon symbol to indicate that a weapon was in position. This symbol was placed below the weapon if the position was considered fixed. The later was changed to if the positionwas being constructed from armor or concrete. This became a solid symbol 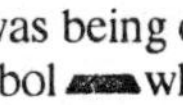 when construction was completed.

The three examples that follow illustrate the combination of these position designations, along with some of the above basic weapon and supplementary symbols. These show that the variety of supplementary numbers could be employed for **specific unit** characterization.

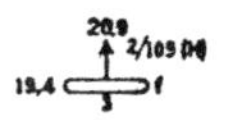

Army heavy self-propelled gun battery with French guns:
- Range — 20.9 km
- Caliber — 194 mm
- Number of guns — 3
- Unit — 2d Battery, 109th Artillery Regiment (Army)
- Origin — French

Naval coast artillery superheavy gun battery in fixed position under concrete:
- Range — 56 km
- Caliber — 405 mm
- Number of guns — 3
- Unit — 2d Battery, 256th Naval Coast Artillery Battalion

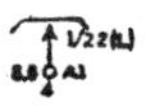

Air Force heavy "emergency" antiaircraft battery in position:
- Caliber — 88 mm
- Number of guns — 4
- Unit — 1st Battery, 22d Antiaircraft Regiment (Air Force)

Antitank gun in position

Gun in fixed position

Howitzer in fixed position under armor or concrete

☐ Numbers and Symbols for Higher Headquarters

Designations of headquarters, staffs, and units were placed on the right of the tactical symbols. The army group was named by a geographic designation or letter. Armies and division organizations were represented by **Arabic** numerals. **Roman numerals** were used to indicate corps.The following lists such headquarters at echelons above division.

Oberkommando des Heeres	High Command of the Army
Heeresgruppenkommando	Hq of an army group
Panzerarmeeoberkommando	Hq of a panzer army
Armeeoberkommando	Hq of an army
Generalkommando VIII. A. K.	Hq VIII Army Corps
Generalkommando (mot)	Hq of a motorized corps
Generalkommando eines Gebirgskorps	Hq of a mountain corps
Panzerkorpskommando	Hq of a panzer corps
Höheres Kommando	Military Hq in occupied territory (corps status)
Befehlshaber rückwärtiges Heeres-gebiet	Commander of an army group rear area
Kommando einer Infanteriedivision	Hq of an infantry division
Kommando einer leichten Infanterie-division (Jägerdivision)	Hq of a light infantry division
Kommando einer Sicherungsdivision	Hq of a line-of-communication (security) division
Kommando einer Landesschützen-division	Hq of a regional defense division
Kommando einer Panzergrenadier-division	Hq of a motorized infantry division
Kommando einer Gebirgsdivision	Hq of a mountain division
Kommando einer leichten Division (Jägerdivision) (mot)	Hq of a motorized light division
Kommando einer Panzerdivision	Hq of a panzer division
Kommando einer Kavalleriedivision	Hq of a cavalry division
Stab eines höheren Artilleriekommandeurs	Staff of a senior artillery commander at army group or army

Tactical Symbols for Combat Troop Headquarters.

This section and the one that follows provides an outline of the many types of **headquarters** that existed in the German Army. Specific examples of units are provided in VALOR books #2 and #5. Their inclusion in books about the German ground forces is appropriate because the military nature of various unit symbols often required descriptive information well beyond the definitions and scope of this dictionary. Some example of unit organization, including diagrammatic tables of organization, are provided to indicate how a unit might be read.

☐ Tactical Symbols for Division Staffs and Brigade Headquarters.

The following presents examples of several division and brigade level command organizations. Some of them were specialized staffs and, although consisting of several branches, might just as properly have been placed in the next section. The regiment, separate battalion, and company organizations were represented by **Arabic** numerals. **Roman numerals** were used to regimental battalions and platoons.

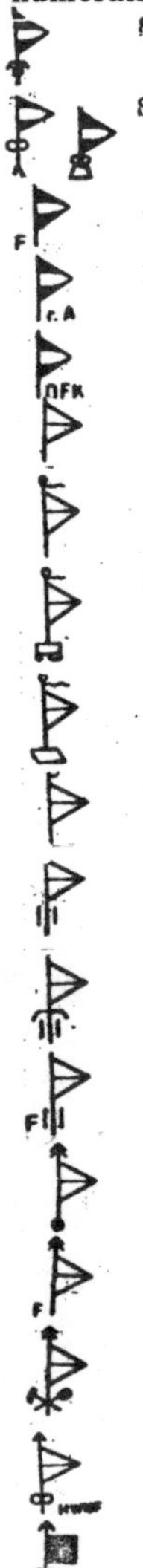

Stab eines höheren Küstenartillerie-kommandeurs	Staff of a senior coast artillery commander
Stab eines Kommandeurs der Nebeltruppe	Staff of a commander of chemical warfare (smoke) troops
Inspekteur der Befestigungen	Inspector of fortifications
Kommandant rückwärtiges Armeegebiet	Commander of an army rear area
Oberfeldkommandantur	Military Hq in occupied territory (division status)
Stab eines Infanterie-Brigadekommandeurs	Hq of an infantry brigade
Stab einer Panzergrenadierbrigade	Hq of an infantry brigade in a panzer division
Stab einer Panzergrenadierbrigade (gep)	Hq of an armored (half-track) infantry brigade
Stab einer Panzerbrigade	Hq of a tank brigade
Stab einer Reiterbrigade	Hq of a cavalry brigade
Stab eines Küstenartilleriekommandeurs	Hq of a coast artillery commander (brigade status)
Stab eines Festungsartilleriekommandeurs	Hq of a fortress artillery commander (brigade status)
Stab eines Artilleriekommandeurs	Hq of an artillery commander (brigade status)
Stab eines Befehlshabers der Eisenbahntruppen	Hq of a commander of railway troops
Stab eines Festungspionierkommandeurs	Hq of a fortress engineer commander
Stab eines höheren Pionierführers (*formerly* Oberbaustab)	Hq of a senior engineer commander (formerly construction staff of brigade status)
Stab eines höheren Wehrmachtnachrichtenführers	Hq of a senior officer responsible for the control of signal troops subordinate to the High Command of the Armed Forces
Kommandeur der Führungsnachrichtentruppen	Commander of the signal troops under control of the High Command of the Army

To simplify reference in this volume, many components of the German Armed Forces have been grouped together. In the case of Air Force units this may seem controversial but it should be noted that there were only about three thousand aircraft operational at any given time of the war and the unit structure was inflated to suit GÖRING's stature.

- Infantry (including motorized, armored, and mountain infantry)
- Tank, Antitank, and Cavalry
- Army Artillery, Smoke and Projector Units
- Combat Engineers and Technical Troops
- Construction and Railway Enginners
- Signal Troops
- Survey, Map Reproduction, and Trains of Combat Troop
- Supply and Transport Troops
- Other Army Services (Medical, Provost, Postal, etc.)
- Air Force Higher Headquarters, Signal Units, Supply, and Medical Units
- Air Force Aircraft and Antiaircraft Troops
- Air Force Parachute Units and Other Ground Assault Troops
- Navy Commands and Formations

As in the previous section, the following provides an outline of the many types of **headquarters** of various German Army units. The symbol used was often characteristic of weapons in that branch and most personnel were members of the branch indicated. There were hundreds of distinctive unit types and supplementary letters that appeared to the right of the tactical symbol denoted the character and subordination of the unit. If these letters, such as *"F, Gr, Ls, Sich, Str, T,* and *Wa"*, were on the left of the symbol they instead indicated special employment.

☐ Infantry (including motorized, armored, and mountain infantry)

The Infantry headquarters symbols are listed below. The term "armored" (*gep*) infantry originally denoted headquarters and units mounted on half-track personnel carriers but in December 1944 the infantry regiments in the motorized divisions were redesignated "Panzer Grenadier" Regiments and there was no longer a distinction between the two. It should be noted that in 1943, except in motorized or panzer divisions, cavalry and reconnaissance units were reclassified as infantry. The motorcycle (*Kradschützen*) battalions then became Panzer Reconnaissance battalions are therefore listed in the next section.

Grenadierregiment 18	18th Infantry Regiment.
Stab eines Grenadierregiments	Hq of an infantry regiment
Stab eines Sicherungsregiments	Hq of a line-of-communication (security) regiment
Stab eines Grenzschutzregiments	Hq of a frontier guard regiment
Stab eines Landesschützenregiments	Hq of a regional defense regiment
Stab eines Grenadierregiments (mot)	Hq of a motorized infantry regiment in a panzer division
Stab eines Panzergrenadierregiments	Hq of an armored (half-track) infantry regiment
Stab eines Gebirgsjägerregiments	Hq. of a mountain infantry regiment
Stab eines Grenadierbataillons	Hq of an infantry battalion
II. Bataillon G. R. 67	2d Battalion. 67th Infantry Regiment
Stab eines Radfahrbataillons (tmot)	Hq of a partly motorized bicycle battalion
Stab eines Sicherungsbataillons	Hq of a line-of-communication (security) battalion
Stab eines Grenzschutzbataillons	Hq of a frontier guard battalion
Stab eines Landesschützenbataillons	Hq of a regional defense battalion
Stab eines Wachbataillons	Hq of a guard battalion
Stab eines Panzergrenadierbataillons	Hq of a motorized infantry battalion
Stab eines Grenadierbataillons (mot)	Hq of a motorized infantry battalion in a panzer division
Stab eines Panzergrenadierbataillons (gep)	Hq of an armored (half-track) infantry battalion
Stab eines Maschinengewehrbataillons (mot)	Hq of a motorized machine-gun battalion
Stab eines Fliegerabwehrbataillons (mot Z)	Hq of an antiaircraft battalion with towed weapons
Stab eines Fliegerabwehrbataillons (Sf)	Hq of a self-propelled antiaircraft battalion
Stab eines Gebirgsjägerbataillons	Hq of a mountain infantry battalion
Stab eines Gebirgsradfahrbataillons (tmot)	Hq of a partly motorized mountain bicycle battalion
Führer einer Grenadierkompanie	Hq (or commander) of a rifle company
Führer einer Radfahrkompanie	Hq (or commander) of a bicycle company
Führer einer Grenadierkompanie (mot)	Hq (or commander) of a motorized rifle company
Führer einer Panzergrenadierkompanie	Hq (or commander) of a rifle company in a panzer division
Führer einer Panzergrenadierkompanie (gep)	Hq (or commander) of an armored (half-track) rifle company

Mounted Infantry. Part of a Cavalry and Reconnaissance arm prior to Spring 1943. Afterwards the non-armored units became part of the Infantry arm. Some units added mounted squadrons in mid-1944, but most infantry divisions used an augmented infantry battalion that was designated as a "*Füsilier*" unit.

Stab eines Reiterregiments	Hq of a cavalry regiment
Stab einer Reiterabteilung	Hq of a cavalry squadron
Stab einer Aufklärungsabteilung (tmot)	Hq of a partly motorized reconnaissance squadron
Stab einer Gebirgsaufklärungsabteilung (tmot)	Hq of a partly motorized mountain reconnaissance squadron
Stab einer Panzeraufklärungsabteilung	Hq of a panzer reconnaissance squadron
Führer einer Reiterschwadron	Hq (or commander) of a mounted troop
Führer einer schweren Schwadron (mot)	motorized heavy weapons troop
Führer einer Kavallerie-Maschinengewehrschwadron	Hq of a cavalry r) machine-gun troop
Führer einer Aufklärungsschwadron	Hq of a bicycle :r) reconnaissance troop

OR

☐ Tank, Antitank and Cavalry

Aside from some specialized security units, including a Cossack Division, the Army Cavalry units ceased to exist as a separate branch in 1943. Most of the combat units were converted into infanry reconnaissance squadrons or into the 24th Panzer Division which was allowed to retain the yellow Cavalry branch color but vehicles replaced horses. Besides the motorcycle companies, the ***Panzeraufklärungs* Battalion,** included companies mounted on halftracks (*gep*) and *Volkswagen* type vehicles and some units had halftrack motorcycles (*Kettenkrad*). After 1943, most assault gun units, previously part of the Artillery. were classified as part of the panzer troops. Both mounted and antitank units were also found in the infantry.

Stab eines Panzerregiments	Hq of a tank regiment
Stab einer Panzerabteilung	Hq of a tank battalion
Stab einer Panzer-Flammenwerfer-Abteilung	Hq of a flame-thrower tank battalion.
Führer einer Panzerkompanie	Hq (or commander) of a tank company
Führer einer Panzer-Flammenwerfer-Kompanie	Hq (or commander) of a flame-thrower tank company
Stab einer Panzerjägerabteilung	Hq of an antitank battalion.
Stab einer Panzerjägerabteilung in einer Panzerdivision	Hq of an antitank battalion in panzer division
Stab einer Panzerjägerabteilung (Sf) in einer Panzerdivision	Hq of a self-propelled antitank battalion in a panzer division
Führer einer Panzerjägerkompanie	Hq (or commander) of an antitank company
Führer einer Panzerjägerkompanie (Sf) in einer Panzerdivision	Hq (or commander) of a self-propelled antitank company in panzer division

☐ Army Artillery and Projector Units

The artillery included both coastal artillery ("⌐" in middle) and Army antiaircraft artillery (*Heeresflak*). These originally had symbols different from the Navy and Air Force counterparts; the infantry also had its own antiaircraft units (*Fla.*) The Chemical Warfare units were redesignated from *Nebelwerfer* to *Werfer* units in 1944 and include both smoke-mortar and rocket-projector units.

Stab eines reitenden Artillerieregiments	Hq of a horse-drawn artillery regiment
Stab eines Artillerieregiments	Hq of an artillery regiment
Stab eines Gebirgsartillerieregiments	Hq of a mountain artillery regiment.
Stab eines Artillerieregiments (mot)	Hq of a motorized artillery regiment.
Stab eines Panzerartillerieregiments	Hq of an artillery regiment of a panzer division
Stab eines Küstenartillerieregiments	Hq of a coast artillery regiment
Stab eines Leichtgeschützartillerieregiments	Hq of an artillery regiment with recoilless guns
Stab eines Werferregiments	Hq of a projector regimen
Stab einer leichten oder schweren Artillerieabteilung	Hq of a light or heavy artillery battalion
Stab einer leichten oder schweren Artillerieabteilung (mot)	Hq of a motorized light or heavy artillery battalion
Stab einer leichten oder schweren Panzerartillerieabteilung	Hq of a light or heavy artillery battalion of a panzer division
Stab einer reitenden Artillerieabteilung	Hq of a horse-drawn artillery battalion
Stab einer Gebirgsartillerieabteilung	Hq of a mountain artillery battalion.
Stab einer Beobachtungsabteilung (mot)	Hq of a motorized observation battalion
Stab einer Sturmgeschützabteilung	Hq of an assault-gun battalion
Stab einer Werferabteilung	Hq of a projector battalion
Stab einer Flakabteilung (mot)	Hq of a motorized antiaircraft battalion
Stab einer schweren Flakabteilung (mot Z)	Hq of a heavy antiaircraft with towed weapons
Führer einer Batterie	Hq (or commander) of a battery.

Bb

☐ Combat Engineers and Technical Troops

These include Pioneer Units, Field Waterway Troops, Fortress Engineers, and Technical Troops.

Stab eines Pionierregiments (mot)	Hq of a motorized engineer regimen
Festungspionierstab	Fortress engineer staff (regimental status)
Stab eines Kommandeurs der Technischen Truppen (mot)	Hq of a commander of motorized technical troops (regimental status)
Stab eines Pionierbataillons (tmot)	Hq of a partly motorized engineer battalion
Stab eines Pionierbataillons (mot)	Hq of a motorized engineer battalion
Stab eines Panzerpionierbataillons	Hq of a panzer engineer battalion
Stab eines Gebirgspionierbataillons (tmot)	Hq of a partly motorized mountain engineer battalion
Stab eines Brückenbaubataillons (tmot)	Hq of a partly motorized bridge-construction battalion
Stab einer Feldwasserstrassenräumabteilung	Hq of a field waterway clearing battalion
Festungspionierabschnittsgruppe	Hq of a fortress engineer sector group (battalion status)
Stab eines Technischen Bataillons (mot)	Hq of a motorized technical battalion.
Stab eines Technischen Bataillons "Mineralöl" (mot)	Hq of a motorized technical "crude oil" battalion
Stab eines Technischen Bataillons "Bergbau" (mot)	Hq of a motorized technical "mining" battalion
Stab einer Technischen Abteilung (mot)	Hq of a motorized technical battalion

☐ Construction Troops and Railway Engineers

These include Construction Engineers, Railway Engineers and Railway Operating Troops. The Construction troops (*Bautruppen*) were renamed *Baupionere.*, and Railway operating Troops (*Eisenbahntriebstruppe*) were formerly called Field Railway Troops

…nierregimentsstab z.b.V. (*formerly* Kommandeur der Bautruppen)	Engineer regimental staff for special employment (formerly commander of construction troops)
Stab eines Eisenbahnpionierregiments (mot)	Hq of a motorized railway engineer regiment
Stab eines Eisenbahnbetriebskommandos	Hq of a railway operating staff (regimental status)
Stab eines Baupionierbataillons	Hq of a construction engineer battalion

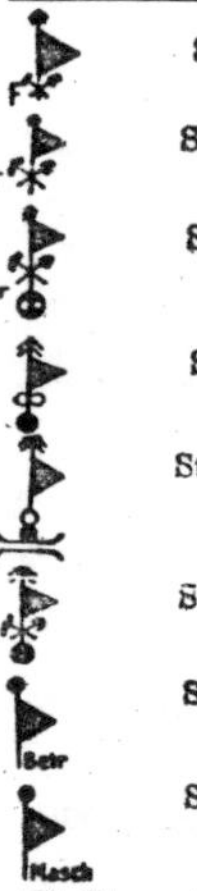

Stab Festungsbaubataillon	Hq of a fortress construction battalion
Stab eines (Strassen)baupionierbataillons	Hq of a (road) construction engineer battalion
Stab eines leichten Radfahr- (Strassen) baupionierbataillons	Hq of a light bicycle (road) construction engineer battalion
Stab eines Eisenbahnpionierbataillons (mot)	Hq of a motorized railway engineer battalion
Stab eines Eisenbahnbrückenbaubataillons (tmot)	Hq of a partly motorized railway bridge construction battalion
Stab eines Eisenbahnbaubataillons	Hq of a railway construction battalion
Stab einer Eisenbahnbetriebsabteilung	Hq of a railway operating battalion
Stab einer Eisenbahnbetriebsmaschinenabteilung	Hq of a railway operating machine-shop battalion

☐ Signal Troops

The Hq of motorized signal regiments *"Fü, H.Gr., A,* and *zbV"* existed as battalions (not shown). Also note how command signal staffs (four) are distinguished from the regiment or battalion; sometimes it was the same commander, but the latter was used to indicate a forward (combat) location. Most of the telephone and radio **station** symbols are shown here although they were no always military installations.

Stab eines Führungsnachrichtenregiments (mot)	Hq of a motorized signal regiment of the High Command of the Army
Stab eines Heeresgruppennachrichtenregiments (mot)	Hq of a motorized signal regiment of an army group
Stab eines Armeenachrichtenregiments (mot)	Hq of a motorized signal regiment of an army
Nachrichtenregimentsstab z.b.V. (mot)	Hq of a motorized signal regiment for special employment
Stab eines Panzerarmeenachrichtenregiments	Hq of a signal regiment of a panzer army
Stab eines Eisenbahnnachrichtenregiments (mot)	Hq of a motorized railway signal regiment
Stab eines Kommandeurs der Nachrichtenaufklärung (mot)	Hq of a commander of motorized signal intelligence troops
Stab eines Festungsnachrichtenkommandeurs	Hq of a fortress signal commander
Stab einer Führungsnachrichtenabteilung (mot)	Hq of a motorized signal battalion of Army High Command
Stab eines Heeresgruppennachrichtenführers	Hq of an army group signal commander
Stab eines Armeenachrichtenführers	Hq of an army signal commander
Stab eines höheren Nachrichtenführers	Hq of a senior signal commander (normally at corps)
Stab eines Panzerarmeenachrichtenführers	Hq of a panzer army signal commander
Stab einer Korpsnachrichtenabteilung (mot)	Hq of a motorized signal battalion of a corps
Stab einer Infanteriedivisionsnachrichtenabteilung (mot)	Hq of a motorized signal battalion of an infantry division
Stab einer Panzerdivisionsnachrichtenabteilung	Hq of a signal battalion of a panzer division
Stab einer Gebirgskorpsnachrichtenabteilung (tmot)	Hq of a partly motorized signal battalion of a mountain corps
Stab einer Gebirgsdivisionsnachrichtenabteilung (tmot)	Hq of a partly motorized signal battalion of a mountain division
Stab einer Eisenbahnnachrichtenabteilung (mot)	Hq of a motorized railway signal battalion
Stab einer Nachrichtenaufklärungsabteilung (mot)	Hq of a motorized signal intelligence battalion
Stab einer Feldschaltabteilung	Hq of a field switching battalion
Festungsnachrichtenstab	Hq of a fortress signal battalion
Führer einer Nachrichtenkompanie	Hq (or commander) of a signal company
Fernsprechstelle	Telephone station
Fernsprechvermittlung	Telephone exchange
Fernschreibstelle	Teletype station
Funkstelle	Radio station
feste Funkstelle (Deutsche Heeresfunkstelle)	Fixed radio station (German Army radio station)

☐ Trains of Combat Troops, Survey and Map Reproduction

The transport echelon of fighting troops were indicated by a cross in a rectangle "☒". Supplementary letters such as *"V, Gep, Gef"* indicate if it is ration, baggage, or combat train (*Verflegungstrosse, Gepäcktross*, or *Gefechtstross*). Ration Trains could be of two echelons (*I* and *II*). Wheel symbols ☒ show motorization. The basic symbol of the branch must be added if it is desired to show to which branch of service the train belongs (three examples shown). Two higher echelon map reproduction units are shown here, but smaller detachments were part of the division headquarters and accompanied the combat trains.

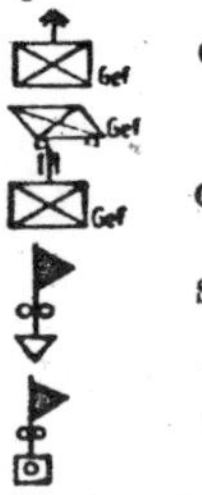

Gefechtstross eines Pionierbataillons	Combat train of an engineer battalion
Gefechtstross (mot) einer Panzerabteilung	Motorized combat train of a tank battalion
Gefechtstross einer Artillerieabteilung	Combat train of an artillery battalion
Stab Felddruckerei O.K.H. (mot)	Hq of motorized field printing press at the High Command of the Army
Stab einer Vermessungs- und Kartenabteilung (mot)	Hq of a motorized survey and map-reproduction battalion

☐ Supply and Transport Troops

Despite the apparent difference in the symbols of the Transport Troops (*Fahrruppen*), they are properly part of the Supply Branch (*Nachschubtruppen*). On the other hand, despite the similarity of symbols of motor maintenance/transport park troops (*Kraftfahrparktruppen*), in October 1942 these were formed into a separate branch to embrace all motor maintenance troops, repair services, etc. For purposes of this volume, however, units of this newer branch appear listed under the branch to which they originally belonged.

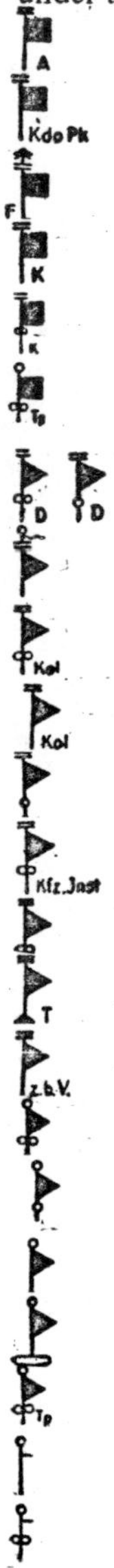

Stab eines Kommandeurs der Armeenachschubtruppen	Hq of a commander of service of supply of an army
Stab Kommando der Parke	Staff controlling equipment parks
Festungsnachschubstab	Hq of fortress service of supply
Stab eines Kommandeurs der Korpsnachschubtruppen	Hq of a commander of service of supply of a corps
Stab eines Kommandeurs der Korpsnachschubtruppen (mot)	Hq of a commander of motorized service of supply of a corps
Stab eines Kraftwagentransportregiments	Hq of a motor vehicle transport regiment (primarily troop-carrying)
Stab eines Kommandeurs der Divisionsnachschubtruppen (mot) (tmot)	Hq of a commander of motorized partly motorized service of supply of a division
Stab eines Kommandeurs der Panzerdivisionsnachschubtruppen	Hq of a commander of service of supply of a panzer division
Stab einer Nachschubkolonnenabteilung (mot)	Hq of a motorized supply column battalion
Stab einer Nachschubkolonnenabteilung	Hq of a supply column battalion
Stab eines Nachschubbataillons (tmot)	Hq of a partly motorized supply battalion
Stab einer Kraftfahrzeuginstandsetzungsabteilung (mot)	Hq of a motorized motor vehicle maintenance battalion
Stab eines Nachschubbataillons (mot)	Hq of a motorized supply battalion
Stab eines Gebirgsträgerbataillons	Hq of a mountain pack battalion
Nachschubstab z.b.V. (Ver- oder Entladestab)	Special supply staff (for loading or unloading)
Stab einer Kraftfahrabteilung	Hq of a motor transport battalion
Stab einer Fahrabteilung (tmot)	Hq of a partly motorized transport battalion
Stab einer Fahrabteilung	Hq of a horse-drawn transport battalion
Stab einer Kraftfahrabteilung (gep) (Sf)	Hq of an armored self-propelled motor transport battalion
Stab einer Kraftwagentransportabteilung	Hq of a motor vehicle transport battalion (primarily troop-carrying)
Führer einer Fahrschwadron	Hq (or commander) of a horse-drawn transport troop
Führer einer Kraftfahrkompanie	Hq (or commander) of a motor transport company

Note: On color charts or maps, most supply services were shown in brown, ammunition was depicted in blue, and rail transport was violet.

☐ Other Army Services (Medical, Provost, Postal, etc.)

Some units, as those of Administrative and Veterinary Troops, did not maintain separate headquarters outside the above supply staffs and many of them were combined under a Service Regiment in 1944. On colored maps or charts medical services were shown in light red, veterinary services were carmine red, administration was green and postal services were in yellow.

Feldkommandantur	Military Hq in occupied territory (brigade status)
Kreiskommandantur	Military Hq in occupied territory (regimental status)
Ortskommandantur	Military Hq in occupied territory (battalion status)
Kgf. Bezirkskommandantur	District Hq for prisoners of war.
Stab einer Feldgendarmerieabteilung (mot)	Hq of a motorized military police battalion
Stab eines Verkehrsregelungsbataillons (mot)	Hq of a motorized traffic control battalion
Stab einer Heeres(Armee)-Sanitätsabteilung (mot)	Hq of a motorized medical battalion of an army
Stab einer Kriegslazarettabteilung	Hq of a motorized hospital battalion
Stab eines Kriegslazaretts (R) (mot)	Hq of a motorized rear area hospital (reserve)
Stab einer Krankentransportabteilung (mot)	Hq of a motorized ambulance battalion
Stab Heeresfeldpostmeister	Hq of the Army postal service.
Stab Armeefeldpostmeister	Hq of the postal service of an army

☐ Air Force Higher Headquarters (Signal, Supply, Medical Units)

Some Air Force terms lacked equivalents and are therefore quoted in German. For example a *Luftgau* was Air Force Administrative District and also had characteristics of the Air Fleet (*Luftflotte*) Headquarters which was mainly deployed outside Germany. It controlled air and *flak* corps, divisions, or brigades. Supplementary roman numbers (on right) were for *luftgau*, corps, brigades, and battalions; arabic designated *luftflotte*, divisions, regiments, and companies.

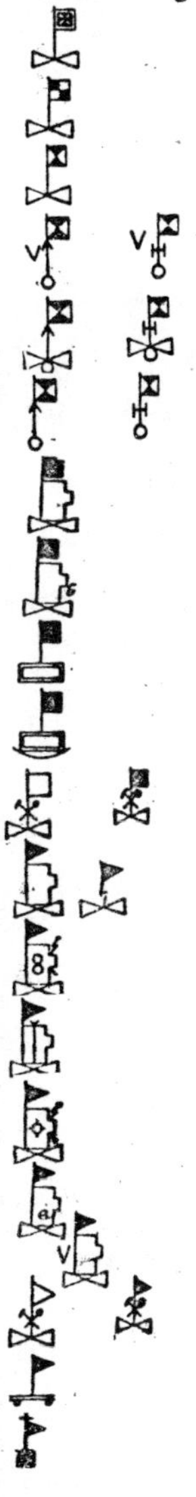

Oberbefehlshaber der Luftwaffe	Commander in Chief of the Air Force
Luftflottenkommando	Hq of a "Luftflotte"
Generalkommando eines Fliegerkorps	Hq of a "Fliegerkorps"
Kommando der Luftverteidigungszone	Hq of an air defense zone
Luftgaukommando	Hq of a "Luftgau"
Generalkommando eines Flakkorps	Hq of an antiaircraft corps
Stab eines Luftnachrichtenregiments	Hq of an Air Force signal regiment
Stab eines Luftgau-Nachrichtenregiments	Hq of a "Luftgau" signal regiment
Stab eines Kommandeurs der Luftzeuggruppe	Hq of a commander of the Air Force equipment group
Stab des Kommandeurs der Luftzeuggruppe (See)	Hq of the commander of the Air Force equipment group (sea)
Stab eines Luftwaffen-Bauregiments	Hq of an Air Force construction regiment
Stab einer Luftnachrichtenabteilung	Hq of an Air Force signal battalion
Stab einer Luftnachrichten-Flieger-abteilung	Hq of an Air Force signal battalion (flying)
Stab einer Luftnachrichten-Betriebsabteilung	Hq of an Air Force signal operating battalion
Stab einer Luftnachrichten-Bauabteilung	Hq of an Air Force signal construction battalion
Stab einer Luftnachrichten-Flugsicherungsabteilung	Hq of an Air Force signal flight control battalion
Stab einer Flugmeldeabteilung	Hq of an aircraft reporting battalion
Stab einer Luftverteidigungs-Nachrichtenabteilung	Hq of an air defense signal battalion
Stab eines Luftwaffen-Baubataillons	Hq of an Air Force construction battalion
Nachschubkolonnenabteilungsstab	Hq of a supply column battalion
Stab einer Luftgau-Sanitätsabteilung	Hq of a "Luftgau" medical battalion

☐ Air Force Aircraft and Antiaircraft Troops

The corps, divisions, or brigades served as administrative headquarters for *flak* regiments and groups (*gruppe*), or wings (*geschwader*), which controlled *flak untergruppe* or air *gruppe*; and under these were batteries or squadrons (*staffel*). Under the newer system the same basic symbol " " represented both headquarters and units of air troops (*Fliegertruppen*) except the flag is filled in for *geschwader* and *gruppe* and added as " " to show the headquarters of a *staffel*. The newer flak symbols were the same as used by the Army. Searchlights were classified as light for 60 cm and heavy for 150 cm.

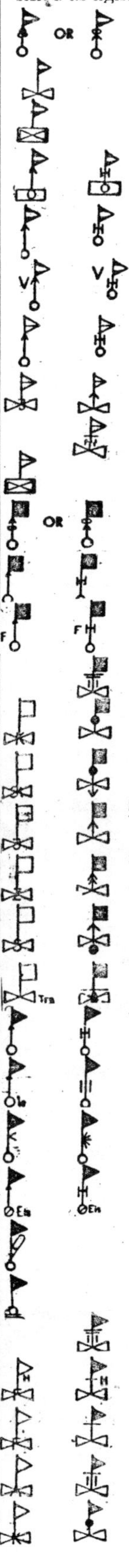

Stab einer Flak-Div. (mot)	Hq of a motorized antiaircraft division
Stab einer Fliegerdivision	Hq of a "Fliegerdivision"
Stab eines Höheren Flieger-Ausbildungskommandeurs	Hq of a senior flying-personnel training commander
Höherer Kommandeur der Flakartillerie-Schulen	Senior commander of the antiaircraft schools
Flakartillerie-Kommandeur eines Luftgaukommandos	Antiaircraft commander of a "Luftgau" Hq
Kommando eines Luftverteidigungsgebietes	Hq of an air defense territory
Stab einer Flakbrigade	Hq of an antiaircraft brigade
Stab eines Jagdfliegerführers bei einer Luftflotte	Hq of a commander of fighter aircraft at a "Luftflotte".
Stab eines Kommandeurs der Luftwaffe bei einem Armeeoberkommando	Hq of an Air Force commander at Hq of an army
Stab eines Flieger-Ausbildungskommandeurs	Hq of a flying-personnel training commander
Stab einer Flak-Regts. (mot)	Hq of a motorized antiaircraft regiment
Stab eines Flakregiments	Hq of an antiaircraft regiment
Stab eines Festungsflakregiments	Hq of a fortress antiaircraft regiment
Stab eines Aufklärungsgeschwaders	Hq of a reconnaissance "Geschwader"
Stab eines Kampfgeschwaders	Hq of a bomber "Geschwader"
Stab eines Sturzkampfgeschwaders	Hq of a dive-bomber "Geschwader"
Stab eines Jagdgeschwaders	Hq of a single-engine fighter "Geschwader"
Stab eines Zerstörergeschwaders	Hq of a twin-engine fighter "Geschwader"
Stab eines Schlachtgeschwaders	Hq of a ground-attack "Geschwader"
Stab eines Träger-Geschwaders	Hq of a carrier-based "Geschwader"
Stab einer Flakabteilung	Hq of an antiaircraft battalion.
Stab einer leichten Flakabteilung	Hq of a light antiaircraft battalion.
Stab einer Flak-Scheinwerferabteilung	Hq of an antiaircraft searchlight battalion
Stab einer Reserve-Eisenbahn-Flakabteilung	Hq of a "Reserve" railway antiaircraft battalion
Stab einer Luftsperrabteilung	Hq of a barrage balloon battalion.
Stab einer Flaktransportabteilung	Hq of an antiaircraft transport battalion
Stab einer gemischten Aufklärungsgruppe	Hq of a mixed reconnaissance "Gruppe"
Stab einer Aufklärungsgruppe (F) des Ob.d.H.	Hq of a long-range reconnaissance "Gruppe" of the Commander in Chief of the Army
Stab einer Aufklärungsgruppe (F) des Ob.d.L.	Hq of a long-range reconnaissance "Gruppe" of the Commander in Chief of the Air Force
Stab einer Aufklärungsgruppe (H)	Hq of an Army reconnaissance "Gruppe"
Stab einer Kampfgruppe	Hq of a bomber "Gruppe".

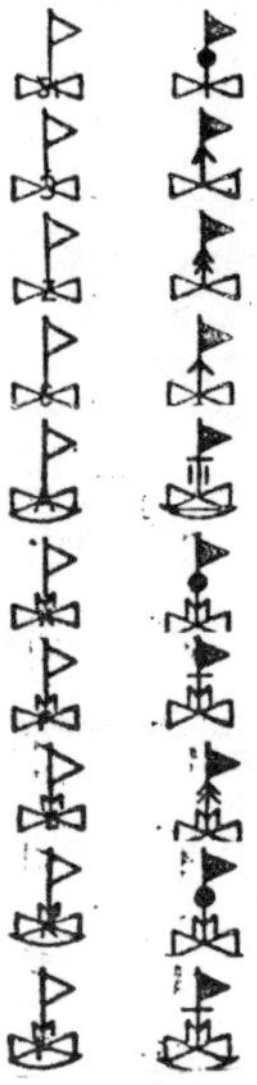

Stab einer Sturzkampfgruppe	Hq of a dive-bomber "Gruppe".
Stab einer Jagdgruppe	Hq of a single-engine fighter "Gruppe"
Stab einer Zerstörergruppe	Hq of a twin-engine fighter "Gruppe"
Stab einer Schlachtgruppe	Hq of a ground-attack "Gruppe"
Stab einer Bordfliegergruppe	Hq of a ship-based "Gruppe"
Stab einer Küstenfliegergruppe (M) mit Kampfflugzeugen (Ld)	Hq of a coastal aircraft "Gruppe" (Navy) with land-based bombers
Stab einer Küstenfliegergruppe (F) mit Landflugzeugen	Hq of a coastal long-range reconnaissance "Gruppe" with land-based aircraft
Stab einer Küstenfliegergruppe mit Zerstörerflugzeugen	Hq of a coastal "Gruppe" with twin-engine fighter aircraft
Stab einer Küstenfliegergruppe (M) mit Kampfflugzeugen (See)	Hq of a coastal "Gruppe" (Navy) with bombers (sea)
Stab einer Küstenfliegergruppe (F) mit Seeflugzeugen	Hq of a coastal long-range reconnaissance "Gruppe" with seaplanes

□ Air Force Parachute Units and Other Ground Assault Troops

Both the Air Force ground combat troops (*Luftwaffenverbände*) and Hermann Göring division used Army type tactical symbols except the letters "(L)" or "HG" were added to the units numbers. The distinctive parachute symbols are also shown but these units later also adopted Army symbols to avoid confusion in joint operations.

Stäbe der Fallschirmtruppen	Hq of parachute units
Stäbe der Luftlandetruppen	Hq of air-landing units
Stäbe der Luftlande-Sturmtruppen	Hq of air-landing assault units
Stab einer Fsch. Jäger-Division	Hq of a parachute infantry division
Stab einer L.L.-Division	Hq of an air-landing division
Stab eines Fsch. Jäger-Regiments	Hq of a parachute infantry regiment
Stab eines L.L.-Regiments	Hq of an air-landing regiment
Stab eines Luftlande-Sturmregiments	Hq of an air-landing assault regiment
Stab eines Luftlande-Bataillons	Hq of an air-landing battalion
Stab eines Luftlande Sturm-Btl.	Hq of an air-landing assault battalion
Stab eines Fsch. Pionierbataillons	Hq of a parachute engineer battalion
Stab eines Fsch. J.-Maschinengewehr-bataillons	Hq of a parachute infantry machine-gun battalion

mmands and Formations

Führer einer Fsch. Pionier-Kp.	Hq (or commander) of a parachute engineer company

□ Navy Commands and Formations

Oberbefehlshaber der Kriegsmarine	Commander in Chief of the Navy
Flottenchef, selbstständiger Seebefehlshaber	Commander in Chief of the fleet, task force commander
Befehlshaber der Schlachtschiffe	Commander of battleship divisions
Befehlshaber der Kreuzer (B.d.K.)	Commander of cruiser squadrons
Befehlshaber der U-Boote (B.d.U.)	Commander of submarine squadrons
Führer der Zerstörer (F.d.Z.)	Commander of destroyer squadrons
Führer der Torpedoboote (F.d.T.)	Commander of torpedoboat squadrons
Führer der Minensuchboote (F.d.M.)	Commander of minesweeper squadrons
Divisionschef einer Zerstörerdivision bzw. eines Verbandes von Flottillenführern, Flottillenchef, Führer einer Hilfskreuzergruppe	Commander of a destroyer division or of a formation of flotilla leaders, commander of a flotilla, commander of a group of cruisers
Gruppenführer von kleinen Fahrzeugen, Halbflottillenchef, Führer eines Verbandes von Hilfsschiffen usw.	Commander of a group of small vessels, commander of a half-flotilla, commander of a formation of auxiliary vessels, etc.
Festungskommandant, Festungskommandantur	Fortress commandant, fortress command
Standortsältester, Standortskommando	Garrison commandant, garrison command

Zerstörer, Flottillenführer	Destroyer, flotilla leader
leichter Kreuzer	Light cruiser.
schwerer Kreuzer	Heavy cruiser.
Grosskampfschiff, Schlachtschiff	Battleship.
Flugzeugträger	Aircraft carrier.
Flugzeugmutterschiff	Seaplane tender
Minenleger (unter 2,000 t)	Mine layer (under 2,000 tons)
Minenschiff (über 2,000 t)	Mine layer (over 2,000 tons).
kleiner Hilfskreuzer (unter 10,000 t)	Small armed merchant cruiser (under 10,000 tons)
grosser Hilfskreuzer (über 10,000 t)	Large armed merchant cruiser (over 10,000 tons)
Grosskampfschiff mit Flottenchef an Bord	Battleship flying flag of the Commander in Chief of the fleet
Kreuzer mit B.d.K. an Bord	Cruiser flying flag of the Commander in Chief of cruisers
Zerstörer mit Divisionschef an Bord	Destroyer flying flag of division commander
Gros	Battle fleet
Teilgros	Part of main battle fleet
Boot	Boat.
Rotte	Subdivision (2 or 3 ships)
Torpedoboot	Torpedo boat
Feuerschiff	Lightship
Unterseeboot	Submarine
Minen-U-Boot	Mine-laying submarine.
1. Unterseebootsflottille, bestehend aus 6 Booten	1st Submarine Flotilla, consisting of 6 boats
U-Bootsmutterschiff	Submarine tender
Schnellbootsdoppelrotte aus 3 Booten	PT boat double subdivision of 3 boats each
Minensuchboot	Minesweeper
Räumbootsdoppelrotte	Motor minesweeper double subdivision
Vorpostenbootsrotte	Patrol craft subdivision
1. Flottille von Torpedobooten, bestehend aus 4 Booten	1st Torpedo Boat Flotilla, consisting of 4 boats
1. Schnellbootsflottille, bestehend aus 10 Booten	1st PT Boat Flotilla, consisting of 10 boats
3. Minensuchflottille, bestehend aus 6 Booten	3rd Minesweeper Flotilla, consisting of 6 boats
1. Räumbootsflottille, bestehend aus 7 Booten	1st Motor Minesweeper Flotilla, consisting of 7 boats
B-Gruppe der 2. Vorpostenflottille, bestehend aus 4 Booten	Section B of the 2nd Patrol Craft Flotilla, consisting of 4 boats
Blockschiff	Block ship (for blocking channels, etc.)
Handelsschiff	Merchant vessel.
Kohlenschiff	Collier
Lazarettschiff	Hospital ship
Sperrbrecher	Mine-destructor vessel.
Tankschiff	Tanker
Transportschiff	Troop transport
Schnellbootsmutterschiff	PT boat tender
Räumbootsmutterschiff	Motor minesweeper tender
Werkstattschiff	Repair ship
Minenprahm	Mine barge
IV. Sperrbrechergruppe, bestehend aus 4 Schiffen	4th Mine Destructor Vessel Group, consisting of 4 ships
Geleitzug, bestehend aus 10 Schiffen	Convoy, consisting of 10 ships
Truppentransport, bestehend aus 4 Schiffen	Troop transport, consisting of 4 ships
Tross, bestehend aus 7 Schiffen	Supply group, consisting of 7 ships

Battalion Tactical Symbols

☐ Organization Diagrams and March Columns

The basic similarity among the tactical organizations may be noted among ten examples below (most use new symbols). The march column symbols are also basically alike..

Grenadierbataillon zu: Stab; 3 Grenadierkompanien mit je 12 l. M. G., 3 l. Gr. W., 3 Panzerbüchsen; Maschinengewehrkompanie mit 12 s. M. G., 6 m. Gr. W.	**Infantry battalion, consisting of:** Hq; 3 rifle companies, each with 12 machine guns (bipod), 3 light mortars, 3 antitank rifles; Machine-gun company with 12 machine guns (tripod), 6 medium mortars

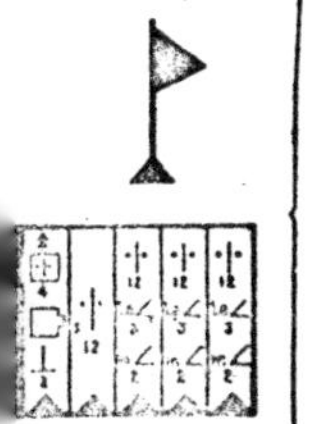

Gebirgsjägerbataillon zu: Stab; 3 Gebirgsjägerkompanien mit je 12 l.M.G., 3 l.Gr.W., 2 m.Gr.W.; Gebirgsjägermaschinengewehrkompanie mit 12 s.M.G.; Stabskompanie mit Pionierzug zu 4 l.M.G., Nachrichtenzug, Gebirgsinfanteriegeschützzug zu 2 l.I.G.	**Mountain infantry battalion, consisting of:** Hq; 3 mountain rifle companies, each with 12 machine guns (bipod), 3 light mortars, 2 medium mortars; Mountain infantry machine-gun company with 12 machine guns (tripod); Hq company, consisting of engineer platoon with 4 machine guns (bipod); signal platoon; mountain infantry howitzer platoon with 2 light howitzers

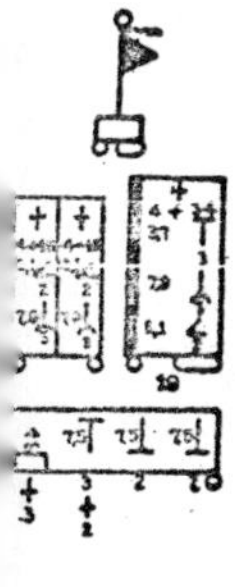

Panzergrenadierbataillon zu: Stab; Panzergrenadierkompanie (gep) mit 34 l.M.G., 4 s.M.G., 3–3,7 cm Pak, 3 Panzerbüchsen, 2 m.Gr.W.—auf 19 S.P.W; 2 Panzergrenadierkompanien mit je 18 l.M.G., 4 s.M.G., 3 Panzerbüchsen, 2 m.Gr.W.; schwere Kompanie (mot) mit 2 Infanteriegeschützzüge zu je 2 l.I.G.; Panzerjägerzug zu 2 l.M.G., 3–7,5 cm Pak; Pionierzug zu 3 l.M.G	**Motorized infantry battalion, consisting of:** Hq; Armored (half-track) rifle company with 34 machine guns (bipod), 4 machine guns (tripod), three 37-mm antitank guns, 3 antitank rifles, and 2 medium mortars—on 19 half-track personnel carriers; 2 motorized rifle companies, each with 18 machine guns (bipod), 4 machine guns (tripod), 3 antitank rifles, and 2 medium mortars; Motorized heavy weapons company with 2 infantry howitzer platoons, each with 2 light infantry howitzers; antitank platoon with 2 machine guns (bipod), three 75-mm antitank guns; engineer platoon with 3 machine guns (bipod)

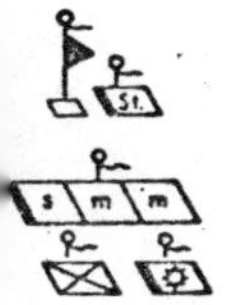

Panzerabteilung zu: Stab; Stabskompanie; 2 mittleren Panzerkompanien; 1 schwere Panzerkompanie; Werkstattkompanie; Staffel	**Tank battalion, consisting of:** Hq; Hq company; 2 medium tank companies; 1 heavy tank company; Repair-shop company; Supply train

Panzerjägerabteilung (Sf) in einer Panzerdivision zu: Stab mit Nachrichtenzug (mot); 3 Panzerjägerkompanien (Sf) mit je 9-7, 5 cm Panzerjägerkanonen, 6 l.M.G.	**Self-propelled antitank battalion in a panzer division, consisting of:** Hq with motorized signal platoon; 3 self-propelled antitank companies, each with nine 75-mm antitank guns, 6 machine guns (bipod)

Abteilung leichte Feldhaubitzen zu: Stab mit Nachrichtenzug, Artillerievermessungstrupp; 3 Batterien l.F.H. 18 mit je 4 Geschützen, 2 l.M.G.	**Battalion of light field howitzers, consisting of:** Hq with signal platoon and artillery survey detachment; 3 batteries of light field howitzers 18, each with 4 pieces and 2 machine guns (bipod)

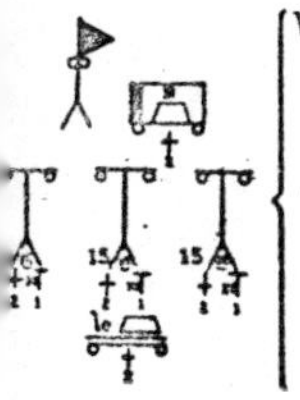

Werferabteilung zu: Stab mit Stabsbatterie mit 2 l. M. G.; 3 Batterien mit je 6-15 cm Nebelwerfer 1-3,7 cm Pak, 2 l.M.G.; le. Werferkolonne mit 2 l.M.G.....	**Projector battalion, consisting of:** Hq with Hq battery with 2 machine guns (bipod); 3 batteries, each with six 150-mm smoke projectors, one 37-mm antitank gun, 2 machine guns (bipod); Projector light transport column with 2 machine guns

Technisches Bataillon (mot) zu: Stab; 2 Technischen Kompanien "Elektrizität" (mot) mit je 3 l.M.G.; Technische Kompanie "Gas-Wasser" (mot) mit 3 l.M.G.	**Motorized technical battalion, consisting of:** Hq; 2 motorized technical "electricity" companies, each with 3 machine guns (bipod); Motorized technical "gas and water" company with 3 machine guns (bipod)

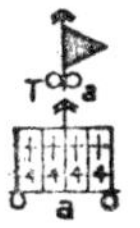

Technische Abteilung (mot) zu: Stab; 4 Technischen Kompanien mit je 4 l.M.G.	**Motorized technical battalion, consisting of:** Hq; 4 technical companies, each with 4 machine guns (bipod)

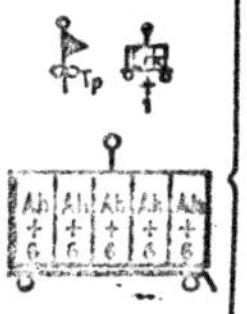

Kraftwagentransportabteilung zu: Stab mit Erkundungszug zu 1 l.M.G.; 5 Kraftwagentransportkompanien (Lastkraftwagen mit Anhänger) mit je 6 l.M.G.	**Motor vehicle transport battalion (primarily troop-carrying), consisting of:** Hq with terrain reconnoitering platoon with 1 machine gun (bipod); 5 motor vehicle transport companies (trucks with trailers) (primarily troop-carrying), each with 6 machine guns

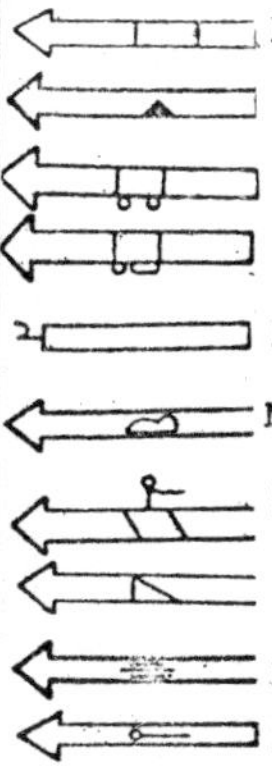

Marschkolonne von Infanterieeinheiten	Infantry units in march column
Gebirgsjägereinheiten	Mountain
Marschkolonne von Grenadiereinheiten (mot)	Motorized infantry units in march column
Marschkolonne von Panzergrenadiereinheiten (gep)	Armored (half-track) infantry units in march column
Marschkolonne von Kavallerie-Einheiten	Cavalry units in march column
Marschkolonne von Aufklärungseinheiten	Reconnaissance units in march column
Marschkolonne von Panzereinheiten	Tank units in march column
Marschkolonne von Panzerjägereinheiten	Antitank units in march column.
Marschkolonne von Artillerieeinheiten	Artillery units in march column.
Marschkolonne von Fahreinheiten	Transport units in march column

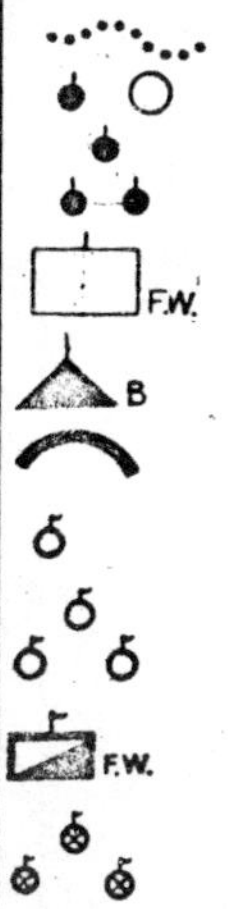

Schützen in Entwicklung	Deployed riflemen
einzelner Schütze	Rifleman.
Feldposten, Spähtrupp	Patrol
Feldwache	Picket
Beobachtungsstelle	Observation post.
Schützennest	Group of entrenched riflemen
Reiterposten	Mounted trooper
Reiterfeldposten, Reiterspähtrupp	Cavalry patrol
Reiterfeldwache	Cavalry picket
Radfahrfeldposten, Radfahrspähtrupp	Bicycle patrol.

☐ Weapon, Vehicle, and Equipment Symbols (2d half Semiofficial)

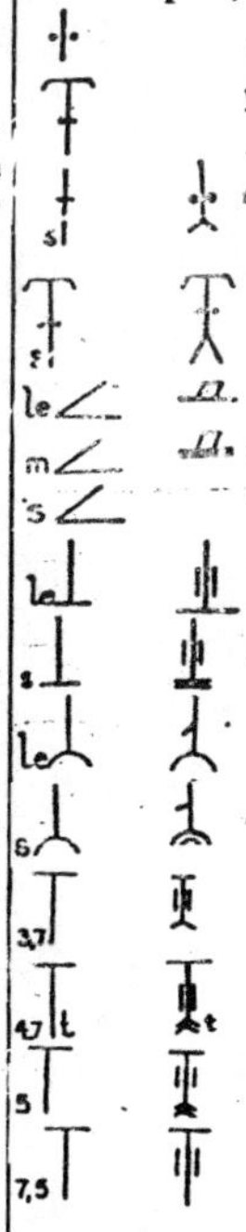

leichtes Maschinengewehr	Machine gun (bipod)
leichtes Maschinengewehr in Stellung	Machine gun (bipod) in position
schweres Maschinengewehr	Machine gun (tripod)
schweres Maschinengewehr in Stellung	Machine gun (tripod) in position
leichter Granatwerfer	Light mortar
mittlerer Granatwerfer[1]	Medium mortar
schwerer Granatwerfer	Heavy mortar
leichtes Infanteriegeschütz	Light infantry howitzer
schweres Infanteriegeschütz	Heavy infantry howitzer
Panzerbüchse	Antitank rifle.
schwere Panzerbüchse 41	Heavy antitank rifle 41
Panzerjägerkanone 3,7 cm	37-mm antitank gun
Panzerjägerkanone 4,7 cm (t)	47-mm antitank gun (Czech)
Panzerjägerkanone 5 cm	50-mm antitank gun
Panzerjägerkanone 7,5 cm	75-mm antitank gun.

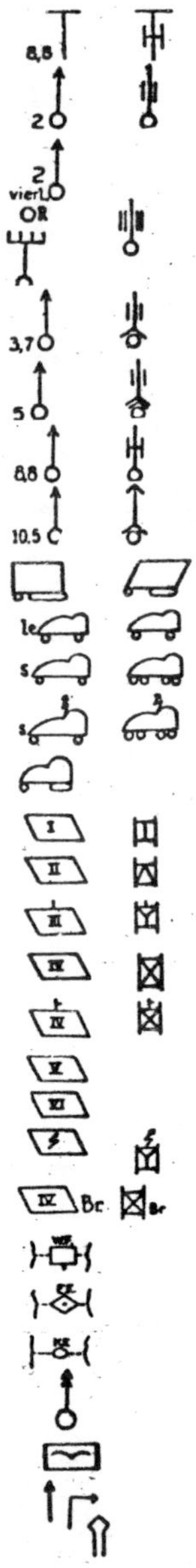

Panzerjägerkanone 8,8 cm	88-mm antitank gun
Fliegerabwehrgeschütz 2 cm	20-mm antiaircraft gun
Fliegerabwehrgeschütz 2 cm (Vierling)	20-mm antiaircraft gun (four-barreled)
Fliegerabwehrgeschütz 3,7 cm	37-mm antiaircraft gun
Fliegerabwehrgeschütz 5 cm	50-mm antiaircraft gun
Fliegerabwehrgeschütz 8,8 cm	88-mm antiaircraft gun
Fliegerabwehrgeschütz 10,5 cm	105-mm antiaircraft gun
Schützenpanzerwagen	Half-track personnel carrier
leichter Panzerspähwagen	Light scout car
schwerer Panzerspähwagen (8-Rad)	Heavy scout car (8 wheels)
schwerer Panzerspähwagen (8-Rad) (Funk)	Heavy scout car (8 wheels) (with radio)
Panzerspähwagen auf Halbketten	Scout car (half-track)
Panzerkampfwagen I	Tank, M1
Panzerkampfwagen II	Tank, M2
Panzerkampfwagen III (eines Zugführers)	Tank, M3 (of a platoon leader)
Panzerkampfwagen IV	Tank, M4
Panzerkampfwagen IV (eines Kompanieführers)	Tank, M4 (of a company commander)
Panzerkampfwagen V	Tank, M5 (Panther)
Panzerkampfwagen VI	Tank, M6 (Tiger)
Panzerbefehlswagen [1]	Armored command vehicle
Panzerkampfwagen-Brückenleger (eines Panzerpionierbataillons)	Bridge-laying tank (of a panzer engineer battalion)
Wagenfähre	Vehicle ferry
Eisenbahnfähre	Railway ferry
Kahnfähre	Ferry boat
M. Boot	Motor boat
Brieftaubenschlag	Carrier pigeon loft
Hochantenne	Overhead aerial
Bodenantenne	Ground aerial
Rahmenantenne	Frame aerial

☐ Semiofficial Auxiliary Symbols for Personnel and Equipment

There were a number of widely used symbols that originated independently and were widely used in various manuals. Sometimes two or three symbols are shown for the same subject and even this is not exhaustive. Only the most frequently encountered ones are shown.

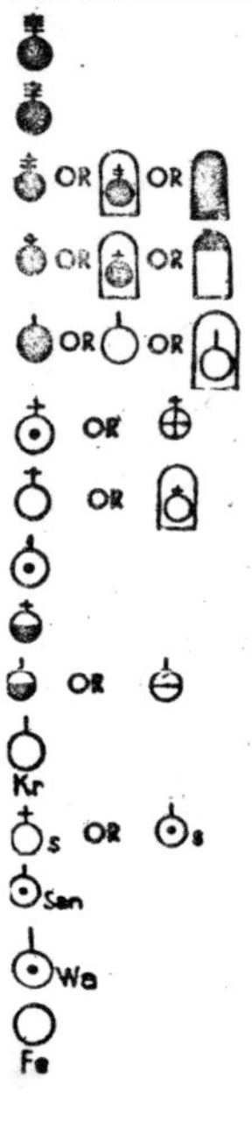

Regimentskommandeur	Regimental commander
Bataillonskommandeur	Battalion commander
Kompanieführer	Company commander
Zugführer	Platoon leader
Gruppenführer	Squad leader
Oberfeldwebel	"Oberfeldwebel" (technical sergeant)
Feldwebel	"Feldwebel" (staff sergeant)
Komp.-Truppführer	Leader of company Hq detachment
Zugtruppführer	Leader of platoon Hq detachment
Truppführer, stellv. Gruppenführer	Detachment leader, assistant squad leader
Kradstaffelführer	Leader of motorcycle detachment
Schirrmeister	Supply sergeant
Sanitätsfeldwebel	Medical sergeant
Waffenfeldwebel	Armorer
Fernsprecher	Telephone operator

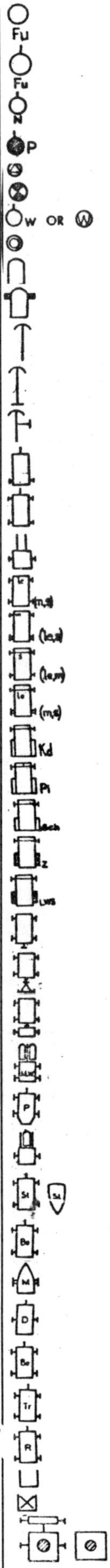

Funker	Radio operator
Funkmeister	Radio sergeant
Führer der Nachrichtenstaffel	Leader of signal detachment
Führer d. Pz.B. Trupp	Leader of antitank rifle detachment
Führer des Gefechtstrosses	Leader of combat train
Radfahrer	Bicyclist
Waffen- zugl. Gerät-Unteroffizier	Sergeant in charge of weapons and
Kompanie-Trupp	Company Hq detachment
Pferd	Horse
Tragtier	Pack animal
le. Krad	Light motorcycle
m. Krad	Medium motorcycle
s. Krad mit Beiwagen	Heavy motorcycle with sidecar
1-achs. Bespannfahrzeug	Horse-drawn vehicle (single axle)
2-achs. Bespannfahrzeug	Horse-drawn vehicle (double axle)
1-spanniger Gebirgskarre	Single animal-drawn mountain cart
Pkw. le, m, s	Passenger vehicle, light, medium, heavy
gl. Pkw., le, m, s	Cross-country passenger vehicle, light, medium, heavy
Lkw., le, m, s	Truck, light, medium, heavy
gl. Lkw., le, m, s	Cross-country truck, light, medium, heavy
Kommando-Panzerwagen	Half-track command vehicle
Pionier-Panzerwagen	Engineer half-track vehicle
Schützenpanzerwagen	Half-track personnel carrier
Zugkraftwagen	Prime mover
Land- u. Wasserschlepper	Special tractor for towing barges
Pkw. mit Zugvorrichtung	Passenger vehicle with towing device
Pkw. mit Pak	Passenger vehicle with towed antitank gun
Pkw. mit Muni-Anhänger	Passenger vehicle with ammunition trailer
Mun. Wagen	Ammunition wagon
Pontonwagen	Ponton wagon
Gefechtskarre	Combat cart
Sturmbootwagen	Assault-boat wagon
Sturmboot	Assault boat
Bockwagen	Bridge pile wagon
M. Bootanhänger	Trailer, carrying motorboat
Drucklufterzeuger	Air compressor wagon
Belagwagen	Bridge planking material wagon
Trägerwagen	Girder wagon
Rampenwagen	Bridge transom wagon
Halbponton	Half-size ponton
Ganzponton	Full-length ponton
Feldküche am Wagen	Field kitchen on truck
Feldküche	Field kitchen

Specific symbols for German units are available in the *German Armed Forces Order of Battle Series*, Valor Books numbers 2 to 8.

List of Books Available from Valor Publishing

Quantity	Description of Books Planned Or Available	Price, July 1992	Status (earliest print date)
Handbooks (51/2 x 81/2" format)			
	1 Polish 2d Corps & Italian Campaign	$14	
	2 Hitler's Dying Ground: German WW2 Disintegration	$16*	
	3 German Field Army & Officer Corps	$16*	Out (1993)
	4 German Replacement Army	$16*	
	5 Hitler's Elite Guards, Waffen SS & Parachutists, 4th ed.	$16*	this volume
	6 Axis Navies: German and Italy	new	1993
	7 Motorization Myth	$14	
	8 German War Machine	$14	
	9 Italian Army Order of Battle, 1940-44	$16*	
	10 Italian Army Handbook, 1940-44	$16	Out (1993)
	11 Southeast Axis Order of Battle	$14	Out (1993)
	12 Southeast Europe Axis Handbook	$14	
	13 Hitler's Axis Alliance	new	1993
	14 Russo-German War, Early Campaigns	Out	(50% Credit* on 26 to 29)
	15 Russo-German War, Operations Against Breakthroughs	$14*	
	16 Soviet Army Order of Battle (Gehlen Red Book) 1941-5	$14	Out (1993)
	17 Japanese Army Order of Battle, 1937-45 (Divisions)	$14	Out (1993)
	18 Japanese Army Order of Battle, 1937-45 (Services)	$16	Out (1993)
	19 Japanese Mobilization &Pacific Campaign	$16	
	20 US Army OB, Europe/Mediterranean	$14	
	21 US Army OB, Europe (Companies/Regiments)	$14	Out (1993)
	22 US Army OB, Pacific Divisions	$14	
	23 US Army OB, Pacific Command	$14	
	24 Russo-German War, Small Unit Actions	$14	
Texts (81/4 x 103/4" format)			
	25 German Dictionary of Mili. Terms, Symbols & Abbr.	$18	
	26 Russo-German War, Summer 1941	$18	
	27 " " Autumn 1941	$18	
	28 " " Winter-Spring 1942	$18	1993
	29 " " Summer-Autumn 1942	$18	1993
	30 " " Winter-Spring 1943	$18	1993
	31 " " Summer-Fall 1943	$18	
	32 " " Winter-Spring 1944	$18	
	33 " " Summer 1944	$18*	Out (1993) 50/50
	34 " " Autumn 1944-Jan.45	$18*	Out (1993) 50/50
	35 " " 25 Jan to May 1945	$18	
	36 " " Balkans Supplement, 1940-1944	$18*	
	37 " " Bibliography, (Free with #30)	new	1993
Valor Notes Supplement (100 page monograph)			
	38 Fascism Today, The legacy of World War 2	$14	1993
Map Supplements (8x10" pictures in full color)			
	Map Supplement #1 (4 maps Summer 1941)	$14	
	Map Supplement #13 (4 maps) 8 April & 22 June 1944	$14	
	Map Supplement 14A-D (4 Maps each) July-Aug 1944	$14	each (4 different sets)
	Map Supplement 15A-D (4 Maps each) Sept.-Dec. 1944	$14	each (4 different sets)
	Map Supplement 16A-B (4 Maps) January-March 1944	$14	each (2 different sets)
	Map Supplement 17 (4 Maps) 12 April & 4 May1945	$14	
	Photo Supplement 36 (B&W Photo + 2 color maps)	$14	1993

* Exchange Policy:

Like almanacs, as old editions of the books are phased out they are replaced with new ones. Our publishing company is unique in that it will accept old editions in 50% credit on new ones (up to 90 days from purchase date). Old volumes must be complete, regardless of bad condition. Offer is also good at participating dealers (2 for 1 basis).

United Valor is Stronger

We have been in business for over 8 years and are now seeking investors to help us carry on publishing new editions without interference or censorship. Venture capitalists should know that we are unwilling to release editorial control; potential co-publishers influenced by large corporations will not be considered; and most of the foreign controlled book publishing industrial-complex need not apply. Since we condemn corporations that are wealthier than countries, our appeal should be understandable.

The offer is based on a $3000 minimum investment with a 20% 1st year return. Please write to the Allentown office for information.